Statements on Auditing Standards (AICPA)—*Concluded*

SAS No.	Year Issued	AU Section	Original Pronouncement Title
74	1995	801	Compliance Auditing Considerations in Audits of Governmental Entities and Recipients of Governmental Financial Assistance
76	1995	634	Amendments to Statement on Auditing Standards No. 72, Letters for Underwriters and Certain Other Requesting Parties
77	1995	341, 544, 623	Amendments to Statements on Auditing Standards No. 22, Planning and Supervision, No. 59, The Auditor's Consideration of an Entity's Ability to Continue as a Going Concern, and No. 62, Special Reports
79	1995	508	Amendment to Statement on Auditing Standards No. 58, Reports on Audited Financial Statements
84	1997	315	Communications Between Predecessor and Successor Auditors
85	1997	333	Management Representations
86	1998	634	Amendment to Statement on Auditing Standards No. 72, Letters for Underwriters and Certain Other Requesting Parties
87	1998	532	Restricting the Use of an Auditor's Report
88	1999	324, 420	Service Organizations and Reporting on Consistency
89	1999	310, 333	Audit Adjustments
91	2000	411	Federal GAAP Hierarchy
92	2000	332	Auditing Derivative Instruments, Hedging Activities, and Investments in Securities
93	2000	315, 411, 508	Omnibus Statement on Auditing Standards-2000
95	2001	150	Generally Accepted Auditing Standards
97	2002	625	Amendment to Statement on Auditing Standards No. 50, Reports on the Application of Accounting Principles
98	2002	150, 161, 324, 508, 530, 550, 551, 558, 560, 561	Omnibus Statement on Auditing Standards-2002
99	2002	316	Consideration of Fraud in a Financial Statement Audit
100	2002	722	Interim Financial Information
101	2003	328	Auditing Fair Value Measurements and Disclosures
102	2005	120	Defining Professional Requirements in Statements on Auditing Standards
103	2005	339, 530	Audit Documentation
104	2006	230	Amendment to Statement on Auditing Standards No. 1, Codification of Auditing Standards and Procedures (*"Due Professional Care in the Performance of Work"*)
105	2006	150	Amendment to Statement on Auditing Standards No. 95, Generally Accepted Auditing Standards
106	2006	326	Audit Evidence
107	2006	312	Audit Risk and Materiality in Conducting an Audit
108	2006	311	Planning and Supervision
109	2006	314	Understanding the Entity and Its Environment and Assessing the Risks of Material Misstatement
110	2006	318	Performing Audit Procedures in Response to Assessed Risks and Evaluating the Audit Evidence Obtained
111	2006	350	Amendment to Statement on Auditing Standards No. 39, Audit Sampling
113	2006	Various	Omnibus 2006
114	2006	311, 380	The Auditor's Communication With Those Charged With Governance
115	2008	325	Communicating Internal Control Related Matters Identified in an Audit
116	2009	722	Interim Financial Information

Statements on Auditing Standards (AICPA) that have been superseded are omitted from this list. Visit the AICPA website *www.aicpa.org* for an updated list of the AU Sections and Related Interpretations. AU Section numbering is subject to change.

AUDITING & ASSURANCE SERVICES

A SYSTEMATIC APPROACH

Seventh Edition

William F. Messier, Jr.
University of Nevada, Las Vegas
Department of Accounting
and
Norwegian School of Economics
and Business Administration
Department of Accounting, Auditing and Law

Steven M. Glover
Brigham Young University
Marriott School of Management
School of Accountancy

Douglas F. Prawitt
Brigham Young University
Marriott School of Management
School of Accountancy

McGraw-Hill
Irwin

AUDITING AND ASSURANCE SERVICES: A SYSTEMATIC APPROACH

Published by McGraw-Hill/Irwin, a business unit of The McGraw-Hill Companies, Inc., 1221 Avenue of the Americas, New York, NY, 10020.

Some ancillaries, including electronic and print components, may not be available to customers outside the United States.

This book is printed on acid-free paper.

3 4 5 6 7 8 9 0 DOW/DOW 0

ISBN   978-0-07-352708-6
MHID   0-07-352708-4

Vice president and editor-in-chief: *Brent Gordon*
Editorial director: *Stewart Mattson*
Publisher: *Tim Vertovec*
Senior sponsoring editor: *Dana Woo*
Director of development: *Ann Torbert*
Development editor: *Katie Jones*
Vice president and director of marketing: *Robin J. Zwettler*
Marketing director: *Sankha Basu*
Vice president of editing, design and production: *Sesha Bolisetty*
Lead project manager: *Pat Frederickson*
Lead production supervisor: *Carol A. Bielski*
Designer: *Matt Diamond*
Senior media project manager: *Allison Souter*
Cover designer: *Laurie Entringer*
Typeface: *10/12 New Aster*
Compositor: *Macmillan Publishing Solutions*
Printer: *R. R. Donnelley*

Library of Congress Cataloging-in-Publication Data

Messier, William F.
    Auditing & assurance services : a systematic approach / William F. Messier, Jr.,
Steven M. Glover, Douglas F. Prawitt. —7th ed.
        p. cm.
    Includes index.
    ISBN-13: 978-0-07-352708-6 (alk. paper)
    ISBN-10: 0-07-352708-4 (alk. paper)
    1. Auditing. I. Glover, Steven M., 1963- II. Prawitt, Douglas F. III. Title.
IV. Title: Auditing and assurance services.
HF5667.M46 2010
657'.45—dc22
                                2009035671

www.mhhe.com

The authors dedicate this book to the following individuals:

Teddie, Stacy, Mark, Bob, Brandon, and Zachary
—William F. Messier, Jr.

Tina, Jessica, Andrew, Jennifer, Anna, Wayne, and Penny
—Steven M. Glover

Meryll, Nathan, Matthew, Natalie, Emily, AnnaLisa, Leah, George, and Diana
—Douglas F. Prawitt

Why a New Edition?

Dear Colleagues and Friends,

As you know, this decade has brought possibly the most far-reaching changes in the history of modern financial markets and the financial statement auditing environment. In the face of the challenges presented during this unprecedented period, we are committed to providing to you and your students the most complete and up-to-date materials possible.

Although the auditing environment has become even more complex and demanding, at the same time it is increasingly important that students gain a deep understanding and working knowledge of fundamental auditing concepts and how they are applied. From the beginning we have worked hard to make this book the most "student-friendly" introductory auditing book on the market. In this new edition we have focused on making the book even more clear and understandable and on encouraging your students (and ours) to think more clearly and deeply about what they are studying. This was accomplished primarily by:

(1) Introducing "stop and think" and "pause to test your intuition" phrases at key places throughout the chapters to encourage students to more fully internalize key concepts

(2) Clarifying explanations and adding easy-to-understand examples throughout the book

(3) Making several chapters more concise and enhancing the focus on key concepts by deleting noncentral detail

(4) Improving end-of-chapter and supplementary materials throughout the book and on the Web site by clarifying or replacing existing questions and problems.

This new edition also contains several important updates to reflect changes in auditing standards, such as the PCAOB's proposed Risk Assessment standards, the new AICPA Quality Control Standard, the new standard on communicating with those charged with governance, and the IIA's new *International Standards for the Practice of Internal Auditing*. Because of their increasing complexity and importance to the audit process, this new edition also includes discussions of auditing tax liability and auditing fair value measurements. Plus, the book has been updated for the FASB's new GAAP Codification. Finally, the authors took a hands-on role in improving this edition's test bank, online quizzes, instructor PowerPoint slides, and the instructor's manual.

While we are very much aware of the extra investment required when a book rolls to a new edition, we believe that we owe it to our colleagues and students to provide the most up-to-date materials possible so their hard work and energy in teaching and studying represents an investment in the latest, most current concepts. We are confident that the changes made in this edition will make it easier for you to teach effectively and for your students to learn more efficiently.

Thank you for your support of this text and the many compliments we have received regarding past editions. We are gratified by the enthusiastic response the text has received as we have done our best to create a clear, easy-reading, student-friendly auditing textbook. We welcome your suggestions and hope you will be impressed with the updates we have made in this new edition.

Warm regards,

William F. Messier, Jr.   *Steven M. Glover*   *Douglas F. Prawitt*

About the Authors

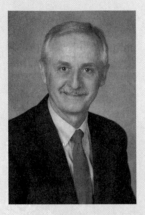

William F. Messier, Jr. holds the Kenneth and Tracy Knauss Endowed Chair in Accounting at the Department of Accounting, University of Nevada, Las Vegas. He is also the PricewaterhouseCoopers Professor II at the Department of Accounting, Auditing and Law at the Norwegian School of Economics and Business Administration. Professor Messier holds a B.B.A. from Siena College, an M.S. from Clarkson University, and an M.B.A. and D.B.A. from Indiana University. He is a CPA in Florida and has held faculty positions at the University of Florida (Price Waterhouse Professor) and Georgia State University (Deloitte & Touche Professor). Professor Messier was a visiting faculty member at SDA Bocconi in Milan and the University of Michigan. Professor Messier served as the Academic Member of the AICPA's Auditing Standards Board and as Chair of the AICPA's International Auditing Standards Subcommittee. He is a past editor of *Auditing: A Journal of Practice & Theory* and formerly President of the Auditing Section of the American Accounting Association. Professor Messier was the recipient of the AAA Auditing Section's Outstanding Educator Award (2009) and the Distinguished Service in Auditing Award (2008). He has also served as an expert witness in a number of audit litigation cases.

Professor Steven M. Glover is the Mary & Ellis Professor of Accounting at the Marriott School of Management, Brigham Young University. Professor Glover is a CPA in Utah and holds a PhD and BS from the University of Washington and an AA in Business from BYU – Idaho. He previously worked as an auditor for KPMG LLP and as a director in the national office of PricewaterhouseCoopers LLP. Professor Glover serves on the audit committee of a nonprofit organization and has served on the board of advisors for technology companies and he actively consults with public companies and public accounting firms. He has also served as an expert witness. Professor Glover is the President Elect of the Auditing Section of the American Accounting Association. He has been on auditing-related task forces of the AICPA. Professor Glover is on the editorial boards of *Auditing: A Journal of Practice & Theory, The Accounting Review,* and *Accounting Horizons.* He has authored or coauthored over 30 articles and books primarily focused in the areas of auditor decision making, audit education, and audit practice.

Professor Douglas F. Prawitt is the Glen Ardis Professor of Accountancy at the Marriott School of Management, Brigham Young University. Professor Prawitt is a CPA in Utah. He holds a PhD from the University of Arizona, and BS and MAcc degrees from Brigham Young University. Professor Prawitt was awarded the Marriott School's Teaching Excellence and Outstanding Researcher awards in 1998 and 2000. He received the Merrill J. Bateman Student Choice Teaching Award in 2002 and BYU's Wesley P. Lloyd Award for Distinction in Graduate Education in 2006. He consults actively with international, regional, and local public accounting firms. He worked extensively over a five-year period with the Committee of Sponsoring Organizations (COSO) on the COSO *Enterprise Risk Management Framework* and *Internal Control over Financial Reporting—Guidance for Smaller Public Companies* projects, and served a three-year appointment as a voting member of the AICPA Auditing Standards Board, from 2005–2008. Professor Prawitt has also served in several capacities with the American Accounting Association and is on the editorial boards of *Auditing: A Journal of Practice & Theory, Behavioral Research in Accounting,* and *Accounting Horizons.* He has authored or coauthored over 30 articles and books, primarily in the areas of auditor judgment and decision making, audit education, and audit practice.

Update your auditing classes!

Don't ask your students to invest their time studying obsolete material! The Messier, Glover, and Prawitt text and complete learning and teaching package provide the most up-to-date coverage available for you and your auditing students.

All chapters include the following important enhancements:

- "Stop and Think" and "Test your Intuition" phrases to encourage students to more fully internalize key concepts
- Improved end-of-chapter questions and problems
- User-focused, user-friendly improvements
  - Clarifying meaning of technical business and accounting jargon
  - Improved linkage between chapter content and end-of-chapter material
- References to accounting standards have been updated to reflect the new FASB GAAP Codification

Here is a sampling of the changes made in this edition to improve each chapter:

Chapter 1, *Introduction to Assurance and Financial Statement Auditing*

- Overall audit process model modified by deleting the "establish materiality and assess risks" step. This is now treated as part of the "planning the audit" component
- Decreased emphasis on a broader set of assurance services to sharpen focus on introduction to financial statement auditing

Chapter 2, *The Financial Statement Auditing Environment*

- Updated for key developments, e.g., brief discussion of move toward convergence of U.S. and international accounting standards
- Shortened and simplified to enhance focus on key concepts by eliminating or shortening discussion of noncentral detail

Chapter 3, *Risk Assessment and Materiality, and Chapter 4, Audit Evidence and Audit Documentation*

- Updated to include the PCAOB Risk Assessment Standards

Chapter 5, *Audit Planning and Types of Audit Tests*

- Updated for PCAOB Risk Assessment Standards
- Improved discussion on the use of a specialist

Chapter 6, *Internal Control in a Financial Statement Audit*

- Updated for PCAOB Risk Assessment Standards
- Substantially reorganized to present the auditing of internal control with enhanced clarity
- Updated for new SAS on Communication of Internal Control–Related Matters

Chapter 7, *Auditing Internal Control over Financial Reporting*

- Updated for PCAOB Risk Assessment Standards
- Substantially revised to present material more concisely

Chapter 8, *Audit Sampling: An Overview and Application to Tests of Controls*

- Updated for changes in the 2008 AICPA *Audit Sampling* Guide
- Added more guidance and a table on "small population sample sizes" for controls that occur infrequently (e.g., quarterly, monthly, weekly)

Chapter 9, *Audit Sampling: An Application to Substantive Tests of Account Balances*

- Updated for changes in the 2008 AICPA *Audit Sampling* Guide
- Simplified discussion and related computation for manually evaluating monetary unit sample results

Chapter 10, *Auditing the Revenue Process*

- Revised for enhanced clarity and brevity

Chapter 11, *Auditing the Purchasing Process*

- New Advanced Module: Auditing the Tax Provision and Related Balance Sheet Accounts

Chapter 12, *Auditing the Human Resource Management Process*

- Added coverage of auditing third-party providers of payroll and HR processes
- Updated discussion of scandals related to options backdating

Chapter 13, *Auditing the Inventory Management Process*

- Added discussion of inventory observation "cycle counts"
- New in-chapter practice problem on analytical procedures and inventory turnover

Chapter 14, *Auditing the Financing/Investing Process: Prepaid Expenses, Intangible Assets, and Plant, Property, and Equipment*

- New in-chapter practice problem relating to prepaid insurance
- Updated examples of recent large impairment losses

Chapter 15, *Auditing the Financing/Investing Process: Long-Term Liabilities, Stockholders' Equity, and Income Statement Accounts*

- Added discussion of AIG derivatives scandal and housing meltdown

Chapter 16, *Auditing the Financing/Investing Process: Cash and Investments*

- New Advanced Module on Auditing Fair Value Measurements, with related end-of-chapter questions/problems and instructor resource material
- Added discussion of the inherent risk associated with investments

Chapter 17, *Completing the Audit Engagement*

- Revised for greater conciseness and clarity, enhanced focus on key concepts
- Several enhanced explanations and examples to illustrate key concepts in chapter

Chapter 18, *Reports on Audited Financial Statements*

- Updated for recent developments (e.g., the updated chapter notes that the "Rule 203" exception has been essentially eliminated with the FASB's adoption of the new "GAAP Hierarchy")

Chapter 19, *Professional Conduct, Independence, and Quality Control*

- Chapter shortened and simplified to enhance focus on key professional ethics concepts by eliminating or shortening discussion of noncentral detail, e.g., discussion of the developmental stages of moral reasoning, detailed tables of rules, etc., thereby enhancing the chapter's focus on essential content
- Added discussion of quality control and peer review/inspection updated for recent developments, including Statement on Quality Control Standards No. 7

Chapter 20, *Legal Liability*

- Updated for important recent case law, e.g., *Stoneridge* and *Tellabs* cases
- Added discussion on availability of liability insurance for auditors
- Enhanced legal liability information on the book's Web site
  - Updated legal case descriptions for new cases
  - New summary diagrams for common and statutory law
  - Moved Phar-Mor Advanced Module to web site

Chapter 21, *Assurance, Attestation, and Internal Auditing Services*

- Updated standards relating to attestation engagements
- Updated internal auditing standards to reflect IIA's recent major revision

The recent implosion of financial markets has had a significant effect on the auditing profession. In this ever changing environment, it is crucial that students learn from the most up-to-date resources. Once again, the author team of *Auditing & Assurance Services: A Systematic Approach* is dedicated to providing the most current professional content and real-world application, as well as helping prepare students for the CPA exam.

In their 7th edition, authors Messier, Glover, and Prawitt continue to reinforce the fundamental values central to their past six editions:

Student Engagement. The authors believe students are best served by acquiring a strong understanding of the basic concepts that underlie the audit process and how to apply those concepts to various audit and assurance services. The primary purpose for an auditing text is not to serve as a reference manual but to facilitate student learning, and this text is written accordingly. The text is accessible to students through straightforward writing and the use of engaging, relevant real-world examples, illustrations, and analogies. The text explicitly encourages students to think through fundamental concepts and to avoid trying to learn auditing through rote memorization. New to this edition, students are prompted by the text to "stop and think," at important points in the text, in order to help them apply the principles covered. Consistent with this aim, the text's early chapters avoid immersing students in unnecessary detail, focusing instead on students' understanding of fundamental audit concepts. Additionally, the case involving EarthWear Clothiers, a mail-order retailer, has been updated and integrated throughout the book and the Online Learning Center and now also involves several useful hands-on mini-cases. Finally, the addition of "practice insights" throughout the book engages students and helps them understand the practical nature of auditing.

A Systematic Approach. The text continues to take a systematic approach to the audit process by first introducing the three underlying concepts: audit risk, materiality, and evidence. This is followed by a discussion of audit planning, the assessment of control risk, and a discussion of the nature, timing, and extent of evidence necessary to reach the appropriate level of detection risk. These concepts are then applied to each major business process and related account balances using a risk-based approach. The text has been revised to include the risk assessment process included in the standards adopted by the Auditing Standards Board and the International Auditing and Assurance Standards Board, as well as the PCAOB proposed Risk Assessment Standards.

Decision Making. In covering these important concepts and their applications, the book focuses on critical judgments and decision-making processes followed by auditors. Much of auditing practice involves the application of auditor judgment. If a student understands these basic concepts and how to apply them to an audit engagement, he or she will be more effective in today's dynamic audit environment.

for the accounting profession?

Real-World Integration and Hands-On Mini-Cases.

Mini EarthWear cases

New and improved "hands-on" mini-cases are integrated throughout the text and on the Web site (www.mhhe.com/messier7e), giving your students the opportunity to actually do some common auditing procedures.

HANDS-ON CASES

EarthWear Online

Control Environment and Internal Control Documentation
Complete remaining sections of the EarthWear control environment and internal control questionnaires.
Visit the book's Online Learning center at www.mhhe.com/messier7e to find a detailed description of the case and to download required materials.

Tests of Controls (Part A)
Complete controls testing on a sample of EarthWear voucher packets and judgmentally evaluate the results of the tests of controls. (In Part B of this mini-case you are asked to statistically quantify and evaluate the results of tests of controls. Part B is described in Chapter 8.).
Visit the book's Online Learning Center at www.mhhe.com/messier7e to find a detailed description of the case and to download required materials.

Practice Insight

Practice Insights in each chapter highlight important and interesting real-world trends and practices.

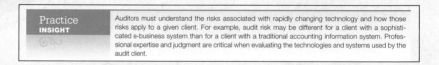

Practice INSIGHT

Auditors must understand the risks associated with rapidly changing technology and how those risks apply to a given client. For example, audit risk may be different for a client with a sophisticated e-business system than for a client with a traditional accounting information system. Professional expertise and judgment are critical when evaluating the technologies and systems used by the audit client.

Free ACL software

The educational version of ACL software is packaged for free with each new book. Once again, the authors wrote chapter-specific ACL assignments and created Roger Company ACL files, all of which are found on the text Web site at www.mhhe.com/messier7e. Exposing students to ACL allows them the opportunity to work with *real* professional audit software.

ACL

www.mhhe.com/ messier7e

Visit the book's Online Learning Center for problem material to be completed using the *ACL* software packaged with your new text.

CPA Exam Review.

Kaplan CPA Review Simulations

Created exclusively for McGraw-Hill textbooks, each CPA simulation demonstrates auditing concepts in a Web-based interface, *identical* to that used in the actual CPA Exam. In addition to providing essential practice, CPA simulations help students:

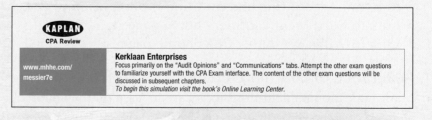

KAPLAN CPA Review

www.mhhe.com/ messier7e

Kerklaan Enterprises
Focus primarily on the "Audit Opinions" and "Communications" tabs. Attempt the other exam questions to familiarize yourself with the CPA Exam interface. The content of the other exam questions will be discussed in subsequent chapters.
To begin this simulation visit the book's Online Learning Center.

- prepare for the CPA Exam
- build professional skills
- stay current on best business practices

Approximately one simulation is available per chapter, identified with the Kaplan CPA logo where appropriate. Simulations are accessible via the text Web site (www.mhhe.com/messier7e).

7th edition teaching and learning package

For Instructors...

Instructor's Resource CD-ROM (ISBN 9780077243548, MHID 0077243544): Contains all essential course supplements:

- **Solutions Manual,** revised by William F. Messier, Jr., Steven M. Glover, and Douglas F. Prawitt
- **Instructor's Manual,** revised by Cassy Budd, Brigham Young University, and the text authors
- **Test Bank** with AACSB, AICPA, and Bloom's Taxonomy tags, revised by Cassy Budd and the text authors
- **EZ Test Computerized Test Bank**
- **PowerPoint Presentations,** revised by Cassy Budd and the text authors

Online Learning Center (OLC): mhhe.com/messier7e
The Instructor Edition of the Auditing & Assurance Services, 7e OLC is password-protected and another convenient place for instructors to access essential course supplements. Additional resources include: Links to Professional Resources, Sample Syllabi, Text Updates, and Solutions to ACL assignments.

For Students...

Online Learning Center (OLC): mhhe.com/messier7e
The Student Edition contains tools designed to enhance students' learning experience:

- EarthWear Mini-Cases, by Messier, Glover, and Prawitt
- ACL Assignments, by Messier, Glover, and Prawitt
- Roger Company ACL files for use with assignments
- Kaplan CPA Review Simulations
- Online multiple choice chapter quizzes, by Cassy Budd, Brigham Young University, and revised by the text authors
- PowerPoint Presentations, by Cassy Budd and revised by the text authors
- Chapter Learning Objectives
- Relevant Accounting and Auditing Pronouncements by chapter
- Link to EarthWear Clothiers home page
- Link to Willis & Adams, CPAs home page

Assurance of Learning Ready

Many educational institutions today are focused on the notion of *assurance of learning*, an important element of some accreditation standards. Messier's *Auditing and Assurance Services: A Systematic Approach* is designed specifically to support your assurance of learning initiatives with a simple, yet powerful, solution.

Each test bank question for *Auditing and Assurance Services: A Systematic Approach* maps to a specific chapter learning outcome/objective listed in the text. You can use our test bank software, EZ Test and EZ Test Online, to easily query for learning outcomes/objectives that directly relate to the learning objectives for your course. You can then use the reporting features of EZ Test to aggregate student results in similar fashion, making the collection and presentation of assurance of learning data simple and easy.

AACSB Statement

The McGraw-Hill Companies is a proud corporate member of AACSB International. Understanding the importance and value of AACSB accreditation, *Auditing and Assurance Services* 7e recognizes the curricula guidelines detailed in the AACSB standards for business accreditation by connecting selected questions in the test bank to the six general knowledge and skill guidelines in the AACSB standards.

The statements contained in *Auditing and Assurance Services* 7e are provided only as a guide for the users of this textbook. The AACSB leaves content coverage and assessment within the purview of individual schools, the mission of the school, and the faculty. While *Auditing and Assurance Services* 7e and the teaching package make no claim of any specific AACSB qualification or evaluation, we have within *Auditing and Assurance Services* 7e labeled selected questions according to the six general knowledge and skills areas.

Tegrity Campus is a service that makes class time available 24/7 by automatically capturing every lecture in a searchable format for students to review when they study and complete assignments. With a simple one-click start-and-stop process, you capture all computer screens and corresponding audio. Students can replay any part of any class with easy-to-use browser-based viewing on a PC or Mac.

Educators know that the more students can see, hear, and experience class resources, the better they learn. In fact, studies prove it. With Tegrity Campus, students quickly recall key moments by using Tegrity Campus's unique search feature. This search helps students efficiently find what they need, when they need it, across an entire semester of class recordings. Help turn all your students' study time into learning moments immediately supported by your lecture. To learn more about Tegrity, watch a 2-minute Flash demo at **http://tegritycampus.mhhe.com.**

McGraw-Hill Customer Care Contact Information

At McGraw-Hill, we understand that getting the most from new technology can be challenging. That's why our services don't stop after you purchase our products. You can e-mail our Product Specialists 24 hours a day to get product-training online. Or you can search our knowledge bank of Frequently Asked Questions on our support website. For Customer Support, call **800-331-5094,** e-mail **hmsupport@mcgraw-hill.com,** or visit **www.mhhe.com/support.** One of our Technical Support Analysts will be able to assist you in a timely fashion.

Acknowledgments

First and foremost, we thank our families for their continuous support. We would like to acknowledge the American Institute of Certified Public Accountants for permission to quote from auditing standards, the Code of Professional Conduct, the Uniform CPA Examination, and the *Journal of Accountancy*. We would also like to thank ACL Services, Ltd., for granting permission to distribute the educational version of ACL software with our textbook. We are grateful to Helen Roybark of Radford University for her careful accuracy check of the text manuscript, solutions manual, and supplements. Finally, we would like to extend our gratitude to Jace Garrett, Brant Christensen, Jonathan Liljegren, and Daniel Strange for their research assistance.

We received extensive feedback from users and nonusers of the 3rd, 4th, 5th, and 6th editions of the text via surveys and in-depth reviews. These comments helped us develop and enhance the 7th edition; thank you to the following colleagues for their invaluable advice:

Pervaiz Alam,
Kent State University

Jeffrey Archambault,
Marshall University

Deborah Archambeault,
University of Tennessee Chatanooga

Jeff Austin,
Southern Methodist University

David S. Baglia,
Grove City College

Katherine Barker,
*University of South Florida
    St. Petersburg*

Thomas Batina,
University of Minnesota

Duane M. Brandon,
Auburn University

Kevin F. Brown,
Wright State University

Linda Chase,
Baldwin Wallace College

Bob Cluskey,
University of West Georgia

Jeffrey Cohen,
Boston College

James Crockett,
University of Southern Mississippi

Mary Curtis,
University of North Texas

Frank Darcoa,
Loyola Marymount University

Laura DeLaune,
Louisiana State University

Todd DeZoort,
The University of Alabama

William Dilla,
Iowa State University

Timothy Dimond,
Northern Illinois University

Mary Doucet,
California State University Bakersfield

Robert Eskew,
Purdue University

William Felix,
University of Arizona

Ross D. Fuerman,
Suffolk University

David Gelb,
Seton Hall University

Tony Greig,
Purdue University

James D. Hansen,
Minnesota State University Moorhead

Julia Higgs,
Florida Atlantic University

Vicky Hoffman,
University of Pittsburgh

Charles Holley,
Virginia Commonwealth University

Carl Hollingsworth,
Clemson University

Venkat Iyer,
*University of North Carolina,
    Greensboro*

Mary Keim,
California State University, San Marcos

William Kerler III,
University of North Carolina Wilmington

Linda Larson,
*Central Washington University – Lynwood
    Center*

Pam Legner,
College of DuPage (IL)

Ralph Licastro,
*Pennsylvania State University,
University Park*

Robert McCabe,
California State University, Fullerton

Mark McLaren,
Washington University

Robert Minnear,
Emory University

Natalia Mintchik,
University of Missouri, St. Louis

Jennifer Mueller,
Auburn University

Albert Nagy,
John Carroll University

Vincent Owhoso,
Bentley College

Susan Parker,
Santa Clara University

Abe Qastin,
Lakeland College

John Rigsby,
Mississippi State University

Sandra Robertson,
Furman University

Pamela Roush,
University of Central Florida

Helen M. Roybark,
Radford University

Lydia Schleifer,
Clemson University

Brian Shapiro,
University of Minnesota, Minneapolis

Charles Stanley,
Baylor University

Jay Thibodeau,
Bentley College

Bill Thomas,
Baylor University

Don Tidrick,
Northern Illinois University

Rick Turpen,
University of Alabama at Birmingham

Scott Vandervelde,
University of Southern Carolina

Thomas Vermeer,
University of Delaware

Paul Walker,
University of Virginia

Glen Van Whye,
Pacific Lutheran University

George Young,
Florida Atlantic University

Brief Contents

Table of Contents

PART 2

BASIC AUDITING CONCEPTS: RISK ASSESSMENT, MATERIALITY, AND EVIDENCE   67

Chapter 3

Risk Assessment and Materiality   69

PART 4

STATISTICAL AND NONSTATISTICAL SAMPLING TOOLS FOR AUDITING   269

Chapter 8

Audit Sampling: An Overview and Application to Tests of Controls   271

PART 5
AUDITING BUSINESS PROCESSES   349

Chapter 10
Auditing the Revenue Process   351

Chapter 14

Auditing the Financing/Investing Process: Prepaid Expenses, Intangible Assets, and Property, Plant, and Equipment   497

Chapter 15

Auditing the Financing/Investing Process: Long-Term Liabilities, Stockholders' Equity, and Income Statement Accounts   521

Chapter 18
Reports on Audited Financial Statements   609

PART 7
PROFESSIONAL RESPONSIBILITIES   637

Chapter 19
Professional Conduct, Independence, and Quality Control   639

Chapter 20

Legal Liability 683

PART 8
ASSURANCE, ATTESTATION, AND INTERNAL AUDITING SERVICES 717

Chapter 21

Assurance, Attestation, and Internal Auditing Services 719

INTRODUCTION TO ASSURANCE AND FINANCIAL STATEMENT AUDITING

1

An Introduction to Assurance and Financial Statement Auditing

2

The Financial Statement Auditing Environment

CHAPTER 1

LEARNING OBJECTIVES

Upon completion of this chapter you will

[1] Understand why studying auditing can be valuable to you and why it is different from studying accounting.

[2] Be able to explain why there is a demand for auditing and assurance.

[3] Understand intuitively the demand for auditing and the desired characteristics of auditors and audit services through an analogy to a house inspector and a house inspection service.

[4] Understand the relationships among auditing, attestation, and assurance services.

[5] Know the basic definition and three fundamental concepts of a financial statement audit.

[6] Understand why on most audit engagements an auditor tests only a sample of transactions that occurred.

[7] Be able to describe the basic financial statement auditing process and the phases in which an audit is carried out.

[8] Know what an audit report is and the nature of an unqualified report.

[9] Understand why auditing demands logic, reasoning, and resourcefulness.

RELEVANT ACCOUNTING AND AUDITING PRONOUNCEMENTS

AU 110, Responsibilities and Functions of the Independent Auditor

AU 150, Generally Accepted Auditing Standards

AU 311, Planning and Supervision

AU 312, Audit Risk and Materiality in Conducting an Audit

AU 314, Understanding the Entity and Its Environment and Assessing the Risks of Material Misstatement

AU 315, Communications between Predecessor and Successor Auditors

AU 318, Performing Audit Procedures in Response to Assessed Risks and Evaluating the Audit Evidence Obtained

AU 326, Audit Evidence

AU 508, Reports on Audited Financial Statements

An Introduction to Assurance and Financial Statement Auditing

As you will learn in this chapter, auditing consists of a set of practical conceptual tools that help a person to find, organize, and evaluate evidence about the assertions of another party. The demand for capable accountants and auditors of high integrity has never been greater. Opportunities for auditors are plentiful and rewarding, and can lead to attractive career opportunities in other areas. Those who practice as auditors often later go into financial management, becoming controllers, chief financial officers (CFOs), and even chief executive officers (CEOs). But even those who do not plan to become an auditor can benefit greatly from an understanding of financial statement auditing and its underlying concepts. Learning these tools will be valuable to any business decision maker.

While opportunities in auditing are great, the last several years have been challenging for the auditing profession. In the early 2000s, a series of high-profile accounting frauds began to cause investors to doubt the integrity of the nation's financial reporting system, including the role of the external auditor. To restore investor confidence, Congress passed the *Sarbanes-Oxley Public Company Accounting Reform and Investor Protection Act* in July 2002—the most significant legislation related to financial statement audits of public companies since the Securities Acts of 1933 and 1934. The implications of the Sarbanes-Oxley Act are discussed throughout the text in appropriate places. While the scandals, public scrutiny, government reforms, and a new regulated process for establishing auditing standards for public companies have been painful for accountants and auditors, the events of the last several years have also been a powerful reminder of just how critical the roles of accounting and auditing are in our society.

We live in a time when the amount of information available for decision makers via electronic databases, the Internet, and other sources is rapidly expanding, and there is a great need for the information to be reliable, credible, relevant, and timely. High quality information is necessary if managers, investors, creditors, and regulatory agencies are to make informed decisions. Auditing and assurance services play an important role in ensuring the reliability, credibility, relevance, and timeliness of business information.

The following examples present situations where auditing enters into economic transactions and increases the reliability and credibility of an entity's financial statements:

Sara Thompson, a local community activist, has been operating a not-for-profit center that provides assistance to abused women and their children. She has financed most of her operations from private contributions. Ms. Thompson applied to the State Health and Human Services Department requesting a large grant to expand her two shelters to accommodate more women. In completing the grant application, Ms. Thompson discovered that the state's laws for government grants require that recipients be audited to ensure that existing funds are being used appropriately. Ms. Thompson hired a CPA to audit the center's financial statements. Based on the center's activities, the intended use of the funds, and the auditor's report, the grant was approved.

Conway Computer Company is a wholesaler of computer products. The company was started by George and Jimmy Steinbuker five years ago. Two years ago, a venture capital firm acquired 40 percent of the company and thus provided capital for expansion. Conway Computer's revenues and profits increased by 25 percent in each of the last two years, and the Steinbuker brothers and the venture capital firm decided to take the company public through a stock sale. However, they found that the company's financial statements needed to be audited by a reputable public accounting firm before a registration statement could be filed with the Securities and Exchange Commission. The company hired a major public accounting firm to perform its audits and the company successfully sold stock to the public.

These situations show the importance of auditing to both private and public enterprise. By adding an audit to each situation, the users of the financial statements have additional assurance that the financial statements do not contain material misstatements or omissions, and they will be more willing to rely on those statements. Auditors can also provide valuable assurance for operating information, information systems reliability and security, and the effectiveness of an entity's internal control. Consider the following example:

EarthWear Clothiers is a successful mail-order retailer of high-quality clothing for outdoor sports. Over the last few years the company has expanded sales through its Internet site. EarthWear's common stock is listed and traded on NASDAQ. Securities laws require company officials to certify that they have properly designed, implemented, and tested internal control over their accounting and reporting information systems. EarthWear's public accounting firm, Willis & Adams, examines on a yearly basis the design and documentation of EarthWear's internal control and conducts independent tests to verify that EarthWear's system is operating effectively. Willis & Adams issues a report to the public expressing its opinion on management's assertion that EarthWear's internal control is well designed and operating effectively. In this way, stockholders, creditors, and other stakeholders have increased confidence in the financial reports issued by EarthWear's management.

Most readers of an introductory auditing text initially have little understanding of what auditing and assurance services entail. Thus, we start by helping you understand in general terms why there is a demand for auditing and assurance services. We then compare auditing to other well-known forms of assurance to provide an intuitive understanding of the role auditing plays in economic transactions. Finally, we define auditing, attestation, and assurance services, and give you an overview of the financial statement auditing process. 🌐

The Study of Auditing

[LO 1] You will find that the study of auditing is different from any of the other accounting courses you have taken in college, and for good reason. Most accounting courses focus on learning the rules, techniques, and computations required to prepare and analyze financial information. Auditing focuses on learning the analytical and logical skills necessary to evaluate the relevance and reliability of the systems and processes responsible for recording and summarizing that information, as well as the information itself. As such, you will find the study of auditing to be much more conceptual in nature than your other accounting courses. This is simply due to the nature of auditing. Thus, we will periodically prompt you to "stop and think" about the concepts being discussed throughout the book. Seeking to thoroughly understand and apply principles as you read them will greatly improve your success in studying auditing.

Learning auditing essentially helps you understand how to gather and assess evidence so you can evaluate assertions (or claims) made by others. This text is filled with the tools and techniques used by financial statement auditors in practice. You'll find that the "tool kit" used by auditors consists of a coherent logical framework, together with tools and techniques useful for analyzing financial data and gathering evidence about others' assertions. Acquiring and learning to use this conceptual tool kit can be valuable in a variety of settings, including practicing as an auditor, running a small business, providing consulting services, and even making executive business decisions. An important implication is that learning this framework makes the study of auditing valuable to future accountants and business decision makers, whether or not they plan to become auditors.

While we are convinced the concepts and techniques covered in this book will be useful to you regardless of your career path, our experience is that students frequently fall into the trap of defining auditing in terms of memorized lists of rules, tools, and techniques. The study of auditing and the related rules, tools, and techniques will make a lot more sense if you can first build up your intuition of why audits are needed, what an auditor does, and the necessary characteristics of audits and auditors.

Reliable information is important for managers, investors, creditors, and regulatory agencies to make informed decisions. Auditing helps ensure that information is reliable, credible, relevant, and timely. You will find that the concepts behind financial statement auditing provide a useful tool kit that can improve the reliability of information for decision makers of all kinds.

The Demand for Auditing and Assurance[1]

[LO 2] Why would an entity decide to spend money on an audit? This is an important question in view of the fact that many of the largest companies spend millions of dollars each year for their annual audit. Some might answer that audits are required by law. While true in certain circumstances, this answer is far too simplistic. Audits are often utilized in situations where they are not required by law, and audits were in demand long before securities laws required them. In fact, evidence shows that some forms of accounting and auditing existed in Greece as early as 500 BC.[2] However, the development of the corporate form of business and the expanding world economy over the last 200 years have given rise to an explosion in the demand for the assurance provided by auditors. In 1926, several years prior to the Securities Acts of 1933 and 1934 requiring audits for publicly traded companies in the United States, 82 percent of the companies on the New York Stock Exchange were audited by independent auditors.[3]

Principals and Agents

The demand for auditing can be understood through the need for accountability when business owners hire others to manage their businesses, as is typical in modern corporations. Until the late 18th and early 19th centuries, most organizations were relatively small and were owned and operated as sole proprietorships or partnerships. Because businesses were generally run by their owners, there was limited accountability to outside parties. The birth of modern accounting and auditing occurred during the industrial revolution, when companies became

---

[1]See G. L. Sundem, R. E. Dukes, and J. A. Elliott, *The Value of Information and Audits* (New York: Coopers & Lybrand, 1996), for a more detailed discussion of the demand for accounting information and auditing.

[2]G. J. Costouros, "Auditing in the Athenian State of the Golden Age (500–300 BC)," *The Accounting Historian Journal* (Spring 1978), pp. 41–50.

[3]G. J. Benston, "The Value of the SEC's Accounting Disclosure Requirements," *The Accounting Review* (July 1969), pp. 515–32.

larger and needed to raise capital to finance expansion.[4] Over time, securities markets developed, enabling companies to raise the investment capital necessary to expand to new markets, to finance expensive research, and to fund the buildings, technology, and equipment needed to deliver a product to market. A capital market allows a public company to sell small pieces of ownership (i.e., stocks) or to borrow money in the form of thousands of small loans (i.e., bonds) so that vast amounts of capital can be raised from a wide variety of investors and creditors. A *public company* is a company that sells its stocks or bonds to the public, giving the public a valid interest in the proper use of, or stewardship over, the company's resources. Thus, the growth of the modern corporation led to diverse groups of owners who are not directly involved in running the business (stockholders) and the use of professional managers hired by the owners to run the corporation on a day-to-day basis. In this setting, the managers serve as *agents* for the owners (sometimes referred to as *principals*) and fulfill a *stewardship* function by managing the corporation's assets.

Accounting and auditing play important roles in this principal–agent relationship. We first explain the roles of accounting and auditing from a conceptual perspective. Then we'll use an analogy involving a house inspector to illustrate the concepts. It is important to understand that the relationship between an owner and manager often results in information asymmetry between the two parties. *Information asymmetry* means that the manager generally has more information about the "true" financial position and results of operations of the entity than does the absentee owner. Before continuing, stop and consider the following questions. What negative consequences could this information asymmetry have for the absentee owner? How do the perspectives and motives of the manager and absentee owner differ?

Because their goals may not coincide, there is a natural *conflict of interest* between the manager and the absentee owner. If both parties seek to maximize their self-interest, the manager may not always act in the best interest of the owner. For example, the risk exists that a manager may follow the example of Tyco Inc.'s former CEO Dennis Kozlowski, who spent Tyco funds on excessive personal benefits such as $6,000 shower curtains, or the example of Andrew Fastow, the former CFO of Enron, who pleaded guilty to manipulating the reported earnings of Enron in order to inflate the price of the company's stock so that he could earn larger bonuses and sell his stock holdings at artificially high prices. The owner can attempt to protect him or herself against the possibility of improper use of resources by reducing the manager's compensation by the amount of company resources that the owner expects the manager to consume. But rather than accept reduced compensation, the manager may agree to some type of monitoring provisions in his or her employment contract, providing assurance to the owner that he or she will not misuse resources. For example, the two parties may agree that the manager will periodically report on how well he or she has managed the owner's assets. Of course, a set of criteria is needed to govern the form and content of the manager's reports. In other words, reporting of this financial information to the owner must follow some set of agreed-upon accounting principles. As you can see, one primary role of accounting information is to hold the manager accountable to the owner—hence the word "accounting."

The Role of Auditing

Of course, reporting according to an agreed-upon set of accounting principles doesn't solve the problem by itself. Because the manager is responsible for

---

[4]Also see M. Chatfield, *A History of Accounting Thought* (Hinsdale, IL: Dryden Press, 1974), for a discussion of the historical development of accounting and auditing. See D. L. Flesher, G. J. Previts, and W. D. Samson, "Auditing in the United States: A Historical Perspective," *ABACUS* (2005), pp. 21–39, for a discussion of the development of auditing in the United States.

reporting on the results of his or her own actions, which the absentee owner cannot directly observe, the manager is in a position to manipulate the reports. Again, the owner adjusts for this possibility by assuming that the manager will manipulate the reports to his or her benefit and by reducing the manager's compensation accordingly. It is at this point that the demand for auditing arises. If the manager is honest, it may very well be in the manager's self-interest to hire an auditor to monitor his or her activities. The owner likely will be willing to invest more in the business and to pay the manager more if the manager can be held accountable for how he or she uses the owner's invested resources. Note that as the amount of capital involved and the number of potential owners increase, the potential impact of accountability also increases. The auditor's role is to determine whether the reports prepared by the manager conform to the contract's provisions, including the agreed-upon accounting principles. Thus, the auditor's verification of the financial information adds credibility to the report and reduces *information risk*, or the risk that information circulated by a company will be false or misleading. Reducing information risk potentially benefits both the owner and the manager. While other forms of monitoring might be possible, the extensive presence of auditing in such situations suggests that auditing is a cost-effective monitoring device. Figure 1–1 provides an overview of this agency relationship.

While the setting we've outlined is very simple, understanding the basics of the owner-manager relationship is helpful in understanding the concepts underlying the demand for auditing. The principal–agent model is a powerful conceptual tool that can be extrapolated to much more complex employment and other

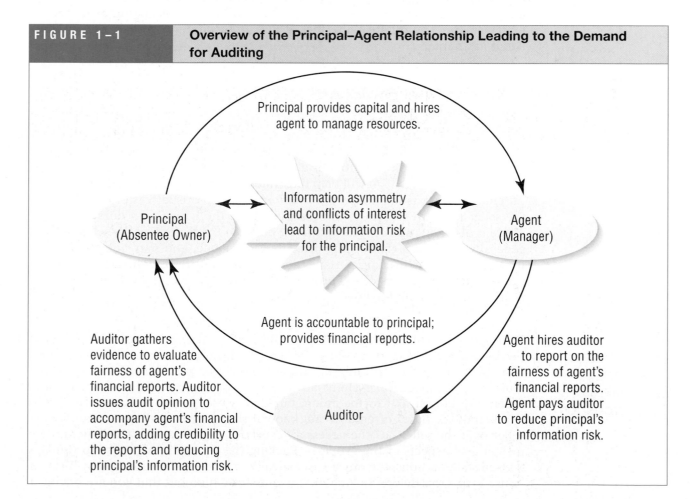

FIGURE 1–1   **Overview of the Principal–Agent Relationship Leading to the Demand for Auditing**

Principal provides capital and hires agent to manage resources.

Principal (Absentee Owner)

Information asymmetry and conflicts of interest lead to information risk for the principal.

Agent (Manager)

Agent is accountable to principal; provides financial reports.

Auditor

Auditor gathers evidence to evaluate fairness of agent's financial reports. Auditor issues audit opinion to accompany agent's financial reports, adding credibility to the reports and reducing principal's information risk.

Agent hires auditor to report on the fairness of agent's financial reports. Agent pays auditor to reduce principal's information risk.

contractual arrangements, and these same ideas apply to other relationships that involve the entity. For example, how can a lender prevent management from taking the borrowed funds and using them inappropriately? One way is to place restrictive covenants in the debt agreement that must be complied with by the entity and its management. Again, this arrangement gives rise to a demand for auditing of information produced by management.

While laws and regulations account for some of the demand for auditing, they do not account for all of it. Auditing is demanded because it plays a valuable role in monitoring the contractual relationships between the entity and its stockholders, managers, employees, and debt holders. Certified public accountants have been charged with providing audit services because of their traditional reputation of competence, independence, objectivity, and concern for the public interest. As a result, they are able to add credibility to information produced by management. The role of the Certified Public Accountant is discussed in more detail in Chapter 2.

An Assurance Analogy: The Case of the House Inspector

[LO 3] Before we discuss financial statement auditors further, let's consider a context that often involves an "auditor" or assurance provider as an analogy: buying an older home. This analogy will help illustrate the concepts we just covered. In the purchase of an existing house, *information asymmetry* usually is present because the seller typically has more information about the house than does the buyer. There is also a natural *conflict of interest* between the buyer and the seller. Sellers generally prefer a higher selling price to a lower one, and may be motivated to overstate the positive characteristics and to understate or remain silent about the negative characteristics of the property they have for sale. In other words, there is *information risk* to the buyer.

Seller Assertions, Information Asymmetry, and Inspector Characteristics

To support the asking price, sellers typically make *assertions* about their property. For instance, the seller of an older home might declare that the roof is watertight, that the foundation is sound, that there is no rot or pest damage, and that the plumbing and electrical systems are in good working order. Fortunately, many sellers are honest and forthcoming, but this is not always the case. The problem is that the buyer often does not know if she or he is dealing with an honest seller or if the seller has the necessary expertise to evaluate all the structural or mechanical aspects of the property. Lacking the necessary expertise to validate the seller's assertions, the buyer can logically reduce information risk by hiring a house inspector. Before moving on, imagine for a moment that you are buying a

TABLE 1–1	Important Characteristics of House Inspectors and Inspections

Desirable Characteristics of House *Inspectors*
- Competent—they possess the required training, expertise, and experience to evaluate the property for sale.
- Objective—they have no reason to side with the seller; they are independent of the seller's influence.
- Honest—they will conduct themselves with integrity, and they will share all of their findings with the buyer.
- Skeptical—they will not simply take the seller's assertions at face value; they will conduct their own analysis and testing.
- Responsible and/or liable—they should stand behind their assessment with a guarantee and/or be subject to litigation if they fail to act with due care.

Desirable Characteristics of a House Inspection *Service*
- Timely—the results of the service are reported in time to benefit the decision maker.
- Reasonably priced—the costs of the services must not exceed the benefits. For this to occur the service provider will likely need to focus attention on the most important and risky assertions and likely can't provide absolute assurance.
- Complete—the service addresses all of the most important and risky assertions made by the seller.
- Effective—the service provides some degree of certainty that it will uncover significant risks or problems.
- Systematic and reliable—the service is based on a systematic process, and the conclusions are based on reliable evidence. In other words, another comparable inspector would likely find similar things and come to similar conclusions.
- Informative—the service provides a sense for how likely mechanical or structural failure is in the near future and provides an estimate of the cost to repair known defects or failures.

house and are wisely considering hiring an inspector. Test your intuition—what characteristics would you like your inspector to possess? In Table 1–1 we have listed several characteristics we think would be desirable.

Desired Characteristics of the House Inspection Service

Now that you have identified some of the characteristics of a good inspector, consider the key characteristics of the service he or she will provide. Are some of the seller's assertions more important than others? For instance, you are probably not equally concerned with the assertion that there is no structural rot and the assertion that the lightbulbs in the bathroom are relatively new. Depending on what you are willing to pay, the inspection could theoretically range from the extremes of driving past the house to taking the home entirely apart, board by board. How thorough do you want the inspector to be? Do you want the inspector to issue a "pass-fail" grade or would you like more details, such as costs of necessary repairs? As you can see, there are many factors to take into account in deciding on the nature and extent of the assurance service you want to buy. In Table 1–1 we have also listed what we think are desirable characteristics of the service provided by a house inspector.

Table 1–1 contains concepts that are in fact fundamental to most forms of inspection (and all financial statement audits). Certainly home inspections and other assurance services must focus on the assertions that are most important, and they must be conducted in a timely and cost-effective manner. Some assertions are more important than others because of their potential risk or cost. For example, a house inspector should recognize the signs that indicate an increased risk for a leaky roof. If those signs are present, he or she should investigate further, because damage caused by a leaky roof can be very expensive to repair. At the same time, just because the seller asserts that he or she recently lubricated all the door and window hinges doesn't mean it would be wise to pay the inspector to validate this assertion. Before going on, stop and think for a moment about how the house inspection example might relate to a financial statement audit.

Relating the House Inspection Analogy to Financial Statement Auditing

Now that we have discussed some of the basic characteristics of inspectors and their services, let's consider how these relate to financial statement auditors. As noted previously, the demand for the assurance provided by a house inspector comes from information asymmetry and conflicts of interest between the buyer and the seller. One important difference between our house inspector example and financial statement auditing is that the buyer of a home typically hires the inspector. In other words, the buyer identifies and hires the inspector rather than using someone that the seller recommends—presumably because by hiring an inspector directly, they increase the likelihood that the inspector will be objective and independent.

However, as was discussed previously, there are some important differences in most statement audit settings that shift the model so that the companies selling stocks or bonds to the public typically hire and pay the auditor, rather than the other way around. To raise capital in the marketplace, companies often sell many small parcels of stocks and bonds to small investors. Suppose a financial statement audit of a given company would cost $500,000. Under such circumstances, it obviously doesn't make sense for each individual investor to pay for an audit. Instead, the company hires and pays for the auditor because a reputable independent auditor's opinion can provide assurance to thousands of potential investors. In addition, recall from our previous discussion that the initial demand for auditing comes not from the principal but from the agent. By purchasing the assurance provided by an audit, the company can sell its stocks and bonds to prospective owners and creditors at more favorable prices, significantly reducing the cost of capital. In fact, studies indicate that audits save companies billions of dollars in costs of obtaining capital.

Given that the seller of stocks and bonds typically hires the auditor, consider just how crucial a strong reputation is to an independent auditor. Four large, international accounting firms dominate the audits of large publicly traded companies, auditing over 95 percent of the revenue produced by all such companies in the United States. One reason these firms dominate the audits of large companies is because they have well-known names and strong reputations. Entities who buy assurance from these firms know that potential investors and creditors will recognize the auditing firm's name and reputation and feel assured that they therefore face reduced information risk.

The fact that the entity being audited typically hires the auditor also highlights just how important auditor objectivity and independence are to the investing public. In fact, Arthur Andersen, the once highly regarded member of the former "Big 5" international accounting firms, arguably failed in 2002 at least in part because the firm lost its reputation as a high-quality, objective auditor whose opinion could be relied upon by investors and creditors. Later in the book we will discuss some recent changes enacted to strengthen the independence of financial statement auditors, including prohibiting auditors from providing many kinds of consulting services to their public audit clients.

Management Assertions and Financial Statements

We've seen that home sellers make a number of different assertions about which a home buyer might want independent assurance. What assertions does a seller of stocks or bonds make? Some of the most important assertions entities make to investors are implicit in the entities' financial statements. Immediately after this chapter you will find a set of financial statements for EarthWear, a hypothetical seller of high-quality outdoor clothing. We'll use EarthWear examples and exercises throughout the book to illustrate important audit concepts and techniques. Let's consider what assertions EarthWear makes to potential investors when it publishes its financial statements. For example, EarthWear lists the asset account "Cash" on its balance sheet and indicates that the account's year-end balance was $48.9 million. Pause and consider for a moment what assertions the company is making about cash. An obvious answer is that EarthWear is asserting the cash really exists. EarthWear is also implicitly asserting that the cash amount is fairly and accurately recorded, that all cash is included, and that no other parties have valid claims to the cash. Because EarthWear is publicly traded, the company must report in accordance with generally accepted accounting principles (GAAP). Such assertions are implicit for each account in the financial statements.

Obviously, information asymmetry exists between the managers of Earth-Wear and potential investors. The interests of EarthWear managers and investors may also conflict. For example, if managers are overly optimistic or if they wish to inflate their bonus compensation, they may unintentionally or intentionally overstate the company's earnings and assets (e.g., by understating the allowance for doubtful accounts or by claiming to have more cash than they really have).

One of the main tasks of the auditor is to collect sufficient appropriate evidence that management's assertions regarding the financial statements are correct. If you were asked to audit EarthWear, how would you go about collecting evidence for the cash account? The process is logical and intuitive. First, you would carefully consider the most important assertions the company is making about the account, and then you would decide what evidence you would need to substantiate the truthfulness of each important assertion. For example, to ensure the cash exists, you might call the bank, examine bank statements, or send a letter to the bank requesting confirmation of the balance. To ensure the cash hasn't been pledged or restricted, you might review the minutes of key management meetings to look for discussions on this issue. Once you have finished auditing the important assertions relating to the accounts contained in the company's financial statements, you will need to report your findings to the company's shareholders and to the investing public because EarthWear is publicly traded.

Instead of EarthWear's auditor, imagine you are a prospective investor in EarthWear. As an investor, would the reputation of the company's auditor matter to you? What if the lead partner on the audit were related to EarthWear's president? Would you want to know that the audit firm used a well-recognized audit approach to gather sufficient, appropriate evidence? What form of report would you expect? These questions lead to characteristics of auditors and audit services that are quite similar to those relating to house inspectors and the house inspection service.

We hope the analogy of house inspectors and auditors as assurance providers has helped you understand the basic intuition behind the necessary characteristics of auditors and auditing and why auditing is in demand, even when it is not required by law. We will refer back to this analogy occasionally throughout the book to remind you of this basic intuition. Before you memorize lists of standards, techniques, or concepts, we encourage you to consider how the information relates to your basic understanding of important characteristics of "information inspectors" and the services they offer. Keep the big picture in mind!

Auditing, Attest, and Assurance Services Defined

[LO 4] The professional literature refers to three general types of services that provide assurance: auditing, attest, and assurance services. Many times these terms are used interchangeably because they are related, and, at a general level, they encompass the same process: *the evaluation of evidence to determine the correspondence of some information to a set of criteria, and the issuance of a report to indicate the degree of correspondence.*

Figure 1–2 shows the relationship among auditing, attest, and assurance services. Auditing services are a subset of attest services, which, in turn, are a subset of assurance services.

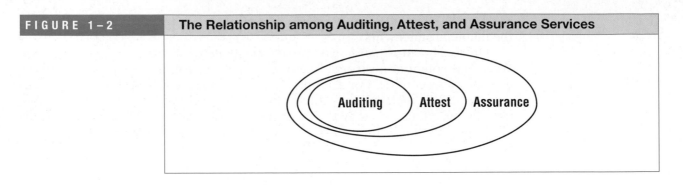

FIGURE 1–2   **The Relationship among Auditing, Attest, and Assurance Services**

Auditing

The Committee on Basic Auditing Concepts provided the following general definition of auditing:

> **Auditing** is a systematic process of objectively obtaining and evaluating evidence regarding assertions about economic actions and events to ascertain the degree of correspondence between those assertions and established criteria and communicating the results to interested users.[5]

A number of phrases in this definition deserve attention. The phrase "systematic process" implies that there should be a well-planned and thorough approach for conducting an audit. This plan involves "objectively obtaining and evaluating evidence." Two activities are involved here. The auditor must *objectively search for* and *evaluate* the relevance and validity of evidence. While the type, quantity, and reliability of evidence may vary between audits, the process of obtaining and evaluating evidence makes up most of the auditor's activities on an audit.

As our analogy between house inspection and auditing illustrates, the evidence gathered by the auditor must relate to "assertions about economic actions and events." The auditor compares the evidence gathered to assertions about economic activity in order to assess "the degree of correspondence between those assertions and established criteria." While numerous sets of "criteria" might be available in various settings, generally accepted accounting principles usually serve as the auditor's basis for assessing management's assertions in the context of a financial statement audit.

The last important phrase, "communicating the results to interested users," is concerned with the type of report the auditor provides to the intended users. The communication will vary depending on the type and purpose of the audit. In the case of financial statement audits, very specific types of reports are prescribed by auditing standards to communicate the auditor's findings. We briefly introduce audit reports later in this chapter.

Attestation

Auditors have a reputation for independence and objectivity. As a result, various users in the past requested that auditors attest to information beyond historical financial information, but traditional auditing standards did not provide for such services. The profession responded to this demand for services by establishing a separate set of attestation standards in the 1980s. Attestation standards provide the following definition for attest services:

> **Attest** services occur when a practitioner is engaged to issue . . . a report on subject matter, or an assertion about subject matter, that is the responsibility of another party.

This definition is broader than the one previously discussed for auditing because it is not limited to economic events or actions. The subject matter of attest

---

[5]American Accounting Association, Committee on Basic Auditing Concepts, "A Statement of Basic Auditing Concepts" (Sarasota, FL: AAA, 1973).

services can take many forms, including prospective information, analyses, systems and processes, and even the actions of specified parties. Note that financial statement auditing is a specialized form of an attest service.

Assurance

The accounting profession, through the work of the Special Committee on Assurance Services,[6] expanded the potential breadth of auditors' activities beyond auditing and attest services to include *assurance services*. Extending auditors' activities to assurance services allows the auditor to report not only on the reliability and credibility of information but also on the *relevance* and *timeliness* of that information. Assurance services are defined as follows:

> **Assurance services** are independent professional services that improve the quality of information, or its context, for decision makers.

This definition captures a number of important concepts. First, the definition focuses on decision making. Making good decisions requires quality information, which can be financial or nonfinancial. Second, it relates to improving the quality of information or its context. An assurance service engagement can improve quality through increasing confidence in the information's reliability and relevance. Context can be improved by clarifying the format and background with which the information is presented. Third, the definition includes independence, which relates to the objectivity of the service provider. Last, the definition includes the term *professional services*, which encompasses the application of professional judgment. To summarize, assurance services can capture information, improve its quality, and enhance its usefulness for decision makers.

This text focuses primarily on financial statement auditing because it represents the major assurance service offered by most public accounting firms. In addition, in many instances, the approach, concepts, methods, and techniques used for financial statement audits also apply to other attest and assurance service engagements. While this text focuses primarily on financial statement auditing, Chapters 2 and 21 describe various examples of audit, attest, and assurance services commonly offered by auditors, including *internal auditors* who are employed by the company they audit.

Fundamental Concepts in Conducting a Financial Statement Audit

✂ [LO 5]   Figure 1–3 presents a simplified overview of the process for a financial statement audit. The auditor gathers evidence about the business transactions that have occurred ("economic activity and events") and about management (the preparer of the financial statements). The auditor uses this evidence to compare the assertions contained in the financial statements to the criteria used by management in preparing them (i.e., GAAP). The auditor's report communicates to the user the degree of correspondence between the assertions and the criteria.

The conceptual and procedural details of a financial statement audit build on three fundamental concepts: audit risk, materiality, and evidence relating to management's financial statement assertions. The auditor's assessments of audit risk and materiality influence the nature, timing, and extent of the audit work to be performed (referred to as the *scope* of the audit). This briefly discusses the concepts of audit risk, materiality, and evidence. Chapters 2 through 4 cover these concepts in greater depth.

---

[6]See the *Report of the AICPA Special Committee on Assurance Services (Elliott Committee)*, New York, NY: AICPA, 1996.

FIGURE 1-3	An Overview of the Financial Statement Audit Process

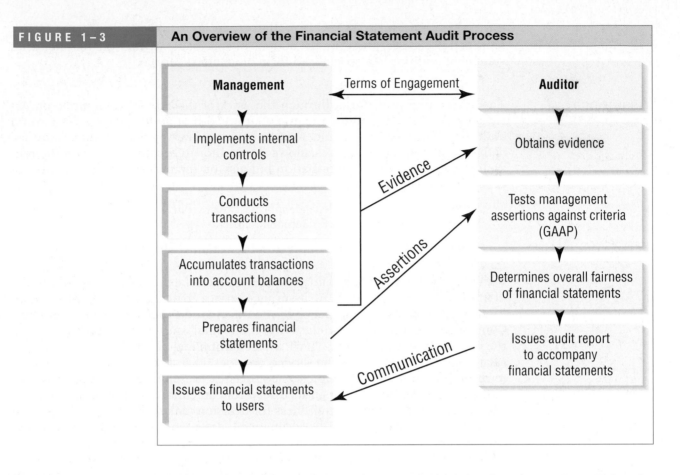

Audit Risk

The first major concept involved in auditing is *audit risk,* which is the risk that the auditor may unknowingly give a "clean" opinion on financial statements that are materially misstated.

> **Audit risk** is the risk that the auditor may unknowingly fail to appropriately modify his or her opinion on financial statements that are materially misstated.[7]

The auditor's standard report states that the audit provides only reasonable assurance that the financial statements do not contain material misstatements. The term *reasonable assurance* implies some risk that a material misstatement could be present in the financial statements and the auditor will fail to detect it. The auditor plans and conducts the audit to achieve an acceptably low level of audit risk. The auditor controls the level of audit risk by the effectiveness and extent of the audit work conducted. The more effective and extensive the audit work, the lower the risk that a misstatement will go undetected and that the auditor will issue an inappropriate report. However, the concept of reasonable assurance means that an auditor could conduct an audit in accordance with professional auditing standards and issue a clean opinion, and the financial statements might still contain material misstatements. A house inspector cannot absolutely guarantee the absence of problems without taking apart a house board by board, which of course is highly impractical. Similarly, due to cost considerations and the sheer impossibility of investigating every item reflected in an entity's financial statements, the risk that an auditor will mistakenly issue a clean opinion on financial statements that are in fact materially misstated cannot be driven to zero. Even careful and competent auditors can only offer reasonable, rather than absolute, assurance.

---

[7]AU 312, Audit Risk and Materiality in Conducting an Audit.

<table>
<tr><td>Practice
INSIGHT</td><td>Auditors must understand the risks associated with rapidly changing technology and how those risks apply to a given client. For example, audit risk may be different for a client with a sophisticated e-business system than for a client with a traditional accounting information system. Professional expertise and judgment are critical when evaluating the technologies and systems used by the audit client.</td></tr>
</table>

Materiality

The second major concept involved in auditing is materiality. The auditor's consideration of materiality is a matter of *professional judgment*. It reflects what the auditor perceives as the view of a reasonable person who is relying on the financial statements. The Financial Accounting Standards Board has provided the following definition of materiality:

> **Materiality** is the magnitude of an omission or misstatement of accounting information that, in the light of surrounding circumstances, makes it probable that the judgment of a reasonable person relying on the information would have been changed or influenced by the omission or misstatement.[8]

The focus of this definition is on the users of the financial statements. In planning the engagement, the auditor assesses the magnitude of a misstatement that may affect the users' decisions. This assessment helps the auditor determine the nature, timing, and extent of audit procedures. Relating the concept of materiality to our house inspector analogy is rather intuitive—a house inspector will not validate the remaining life on lightbulbs or thoroughly test every cabinet hinge or drawer glide. These items are not critical to the buyer's decision.

While other qualitative factors must be considered in determining materiality, a common rule of thumb is that total (aggregated) misstatements of more than about 3 to 5 percent of net income before tax would cause financial statements to be materially misstated. Suppose the auditor decides that the financial statements of a client will be materially misstated if total misstatements exceed $400,000. The auditor would design audit procedures to test accounts to a sufficient level of detail. When testing is complete for all accounts, the auditor will issue a clean audit opinion if the unadjusted misstatements in all the accounts in total add up to less than overall materiality of $400,000.

As we shall see later in this chapter, the wording of the auditor's standard audit report includes the phrase "the financial statements present fairly *in all material respects.*" This is the manner in which the auditor communicates the notion of materiality to the users of the auditor's report. Keep in mind, as we explained in connection with the concept of audit risk, there can be no guarantee that the auditor will uncover *all* material misstatements. The auditor can only provide *reasonable assurance* that all material misstatements are detected; in the context of financial statement auditing, reasonable assurance has been defined to mean a high but not absolute level of assurance. The auditor provides no assurance that immaterial misstatements will be detected.

Evidence Regarding Management Assertions

The third major concept involved in auditing is *evidence regarding management's assertions*. Most of the auditor's work in arriving at an opinion on the financial statements consists of obtaining and evaluating evidence. Chapter 2 contains more detail about the specific assertions relevant to financial statement auditing. Audit evidence consists of the underlying accounting data and any additional

---

[8]Financial Accounting Standards Board, Statement of Financial Accounting Concepts No. 2, "Qualitative Characteristics of Accounting Information" (CON2). This definition is also included in AU 312, Audit Risk and Materiality in the Conduct of an Audit.

information available to the auditor, whether originating from the client or externally.[9]

As illustrated earlier in our discussion about EarthWear, management's assertions are used as a framework to guide the collection of audit evidence. The assertions, in conjunction with the assessment of materiality and audit risk, are used by the auditor to determine the nature, timing, and extent of evidence to be gathered. Once the auditor has obtained sufficient appropriate evidence that the management assertions can be relied upon for each significant account and disclosure, reasonable assurance is provided that the financial statements are fairly presented.

In obtaining and evaluating the appropriateness of audit evidence, the auditor is concerned with the relevance and reliability of the evidence. *Relevance* refers to whether the evidence relates to the specific management assertion being tested. *Reliability* refers to the diagnosticity of the evidence. In other words, can a particular type of evidence be relied upon to signal the true state of the account balance or assertion being examined? Using the house inspection example, inspecting the foundation of a house would not give us relevant evidence about whether the roof leaks. Likewise, the seller's opinion of the home's roof would not be as reliable as that of the inspector, because the seller has an incentive to deceive the buyer.

The auditor seldom has the luxury of obtaining completely convincing evidence about the true state of a particular assertion. In most situations, the auditor is able to obtain only enough evidence to be persuaded that the assertion is fairly stated. Additionally, for many parts of an audit, the auditor examines only a sample of the transactions processed during the period.

Sampling: Inferences Based on Limited Observations

✕ [LO 6]   You might ask why the auditor relies on concepts such as audit risk and materiality in designing an audit. Why not test all transactions that occurred during the period so that audit risk can be driven to zero, even for immaterial misstatements? The main reason is the cost and feasibility of such an audit. In a small business, the auditor might be able to examine all transactions that occurred during the period and still issue the audit report in a reasonable amount of time. However, it is unlikely that the owner of the business could afford to pay for such an extensive audit. For a large organization, the sheer volume of transactions, which might well reach into the millions, prevents the auditor from examining every transaction. Thus, just as with a house inspector, there is a trade-off between the exactness or precision of the audit and its cost.

To deal with the problem of not being able to examine every transaction, the auditor uses (1) his or her knowledge about the transactions; and/or (2) a sampling approach to examine a subset of the transactions. Many times the auditor is aware of items in an account balance that are likely to contain misstatements based on previous audits, a solid understanding of the client's internal control system, or knowledge of the client's industry. For example, the auditor's prior knowledge may indicate that transactions with certain types of customers are relatively likely to contain misstatements. The auditor can use this knowledge to specifically select those transactions (e.g., specific accounts receivable) for examination. When the auditor has no special knowledge about which particular transactions or items may be misstated, he or she uses sampling procedures that increase the likelihood of obtaining a sample that is *representative* of the

---

[9]AU 326, Audit Evidence.

population of transactions or account items. In such cases, the auditor uses the laws of probability to make inferences about potential misstatements based on examining a sample of transactions or items.

The size of the auditor's sample is a function of materiality and desired level of assurance for the account or assertion being examined. There is an *inverse* relation between sample size and materiality and a direct relation between sample size and desired level of assurance. For example, if an auditor assesses materiality for an account to be a small amount, a larger sample will be needed than if materiality were a larger amount. This occurs because the auditor must gather more evidence (a larger sample) to have a reasonable likelihood of detecting smaller errors. You can think of materiality as the "fineness of the auditor's filter." A lower materiality amount requires the auditor to use a finer filter in order to detect smaller errors, and it takes more work to create a finer filter. Similarly, as the desired level of assurance increases for a given materiality amount, the sample size necessary to test an assertion becomes greater.

The Audit Process

[LO 7] This section provides an overview of how auditors go about the process of auditing financial statements and then presents the major phases that the auditor performs during a financial statement audit. Later chapters provide detailed coverage of the process and the phases of the audit.

Overview of the Financial Statement Auditing Process

Consider the auditor's task from a logical perspective. The end product of a financial statement auditor's work is an audit opinion indicating whether or not the client's financial statements are free of material misstatement. What might an auditor do to obtain the information needed to develop and support that opinion? The auditor must first obtain a thorough understanding of the client, its business, and its industry. The auditor must understand the risks the client faces, how it is dealing with those risks, and what remaining risks are most likely to result in a material misstatement in the financial statements. Armed with this understanding, the auditor plans procedures that will produce evidence helpful in developing and supporting an opinion on the financial statements.

To understand this process intuitively, consider what financial statements are made of. From your financial accounting courses, you know that accounting systems capture, record, and summarize individual transactions. Entities, of course, must design and implement controls to ensure that those transactions are initiated, captured, recorded, and summarized appropriately. These individual transactions are grouped and summarized into various account balances, and finally, financial statements are formed by organizing meaningful collections of those account balances. We have just identified three stages in the accounting process that take place in the preparation of financial statements: *internal controls* are implemented to ensure appropriate capturing and recording of *individual transactions*, which are then collected into ending *account balances*. This summary might seem like an oversimplification, but it will help you understand the stages of a client's accounting process on which auditors focus to collect evidence.

Keep in mind that the auditor's job ultimately is to express an opinion on *whether the financial statements are fairly stated*. It makes sense, then, that the auditor can design procedures to collect *direct* information about the ending account balances that make up the financial statements. For example, an auditor might confirm the ending balance of the cash account by contacting the client's bank, or the auditor might verify the ending balance of the inventory account by physically examining individual inventory items that make up the ending balance. But remember—account balances are made up of *individual transactions* that occurred over the past year (or beyond). If the auditor designs procedures to test whether the transactions were actually captured and handled properly, the auditor can obtain indirect information about whether the ending account balances are likely to be fairly stated. This information is clearly one step removed from the ending account balances themselves. But we can even back up one more step. If the auditor designs procedures to test whether the entity's *internal control* over financial transactions is effective, the auditor can obtain additional indirect information regarding whether the account balances are fairly stated. Take a moment to think through the logic in this last step: If controls are effective, then the transactions will probably be captured and summarized properly, which means in turn that the account balances are likely to be free of material misstatement. Thus, information about internal control is even more indirect than information about transactions, but it is useful information nonetheless! In fact, while it is indirect, evidence about internal control is usually a relatively cost-effective form of audit evidence.

In summary, the auditor can collect evidence in each of three different stages in a client's accounting system to help determine whether the financial statements are fairly stated: (1) the *internal control* put in place by the client to ensure proper handling of transactions (e.g., evaluate and test the controls); (2) the *transactions* that affect each account balance (e.g., examine a sample of the transactions that happened during the period); and (3) the ending *account balances* themselves (e.g., examine a sample of the items that make up an ending account balance at year-end). Evidence that relates directly to ending account balances is usually the highest quality, but also the costliest, evidence. Thus, an auditor will usually rely on a combination of evidence from all three stages in forming an audit opinion regarding the fairness of the financial statements. On which of these three areas it is best to focus depends on the circumstances, and this is generally left to the auditor's discretion. Chapter 4 addresses the types of procedures and types of evidence available to the auditor in more detail.

Major Phases of the Audit

The audit process can be broken down into a number of audit phases (see Figure 1–4). While the figure suggests that these phases are sequential, they are actually quite iterative and interrelated in nature. Phases often include audit procedures designed for one purpose that provide evidence for other purposes, and sometimes audit procedures accomplish purposes in more than one phase. Figure 1–4 shows the specific chapters where each of these phases is discussed in detail.

Client Acceptance/Continuance and Establishing an Understanding with the Client

Professional standards require that public accounting firms establish policies and procedures for deciding whether to accept new clients and to retain current clients. The purpose of such policies is to minimize the likelihood that an auditor will be associated with clients who lack integrity. If an auditor is associated with a client who lacks integrity, the risk increases that material misstatements may exist and not be detected by the auditor. This can lead to lawsuits brought by users of the financial statements. For a prospective new client, auditors are required to confer with the predecessor auditor and frequently conduct background checks on top management. The knowledge that the auditor gathers during the acceptance/continuance process provides valuable

FIGURE 1–4	Major Phases of an Audit

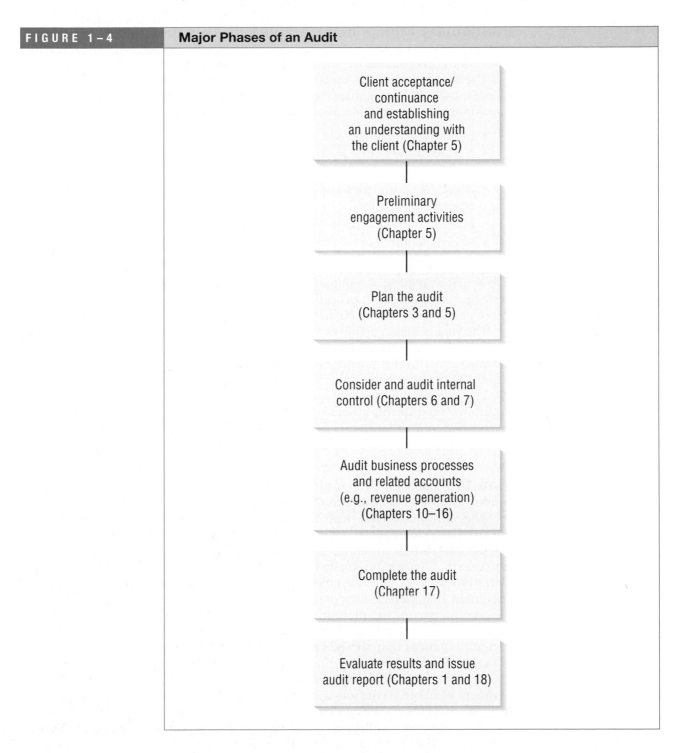

understanding of the entity and its environment, thus helping the auditor assess risk and plan the audit. Once the acceptance/continuance decision has been made, the auditor establishes an understanding with the client regarding the services to be performed and the terms of the engagement. Such terms would include, for example, the responsibilities of each party, the assistance to be provided by client personnel and internal auditors, the timing of the engagement, and the expected audit fees.

Preliminary Engagement Activities   There are generally two preliminary engagement activities: (1) determining the audit engagement team requirements; and (2) ensuring the independence of the audit team and audit firm.

The auditor starts by updating his or her understanding of the entity and its environment. The auditor's understanding of the entity and its environment should include information about each of the following categories:

- Industry, regulatory, and other external factors.
- Nature of the entity, including the entity's application of accounting policies.
- Objectives, strategies and related business risks, including the entity's risk assessment process.
- Measurement and review of the entity's financial performance.
- Internal control.

Because the understanding of the entity and its environment is used to assess the risk of material misstatement and to set the scope of the audit, the auditor should perform risk assessment procedures to support that understanding (e.g., inquiring of personnel, reading business plans and strategies).

The engagement partner or manager ensures that the audit team is composed of team members who have the appropriate audit and industry experience for the engagement. The partner or manager also determines whether the audit will require IT or other types of specialists (e.g., actuaries or appraisers).

The independence of the auditor from the client in terms of freedom from prohibited relationships that might threaten the auditor's objectivity must also be established up front. Chapter 5 addresses the preliminary engagement activities of the audit process in more detail.

Plan the Audit   Proper planning is important to ensure that the audit is conducted in an effective and efficient manner. In order to plan the audit properly, the audit team must make a preliminary assessment of the client's business risks and determine materiality. The audit team relies on these judgments to then assess risk relating to the likelihood of material misstatements in the financial statements. Chapter 3 discusses both of these concepts. In developing the audit plan, the auditor should be guided by (1) the procedures performed to gain and document an understanding of the entity and (2) the results of the risk assessment process. As part of the planning process, the auditor may conduct preliminary analytical procedures (such as ratio analysis) to identify specific transactions or account balances that should receive special attention due to an increased risk of material misstatement. Audit planning should take into account the auditor's understanding of the entity's internal control system (discussed next). This assessment of internal controls will be in greater depth if the client is a public company, because for public companies the auditor is required to report on both the company's internal control over financial reporting and the company's financial statements. The outcome of the auditor's planning process is a written audit plan that sets forth the nature, extent, and timing of the audit work. Chapters 3 and 5 cover the issues that are involved in this phase of the audit.

Consider and Audit Internal Control   Internal control is designed and effected by an entity's board of directors, management, and other personnel to provide reasonable assurance regarding the achievement of objectives in the following categories: (1) reliability of financial reporting, (2) effectiveness and efficiency of operations, and (3) compliance with applicable laws and regulations. When obtaining an understanding of the entity and its environment, the auditor should gain an understanding of internal control to help the auditor assess risk and identify areas where financial statements might be misstated. Chapter 6 covers the role of internal control in a financial statement audit, and Chapter 7 specifically addresses the audit of internal control for public companies. Later chapters apply the process of considering and auditing internal control in the context of various business processes.

Practice
INSIGHT

The audit of internal control over financial reporting is often referred to in practice as the "404 audit" in reference to Rule 404 of the Sarbanes-Oxley Act.

Audit Business Processes and Related Accounts   The auditor typically assesses the risk of material misstatement by examining the entity's business processes or accounting cycles (e.g., purchasing process or revenue process). The auditor then determines the audit procedures that are necessary to reduce the risk of material misstatement to a low level for the financial statement accounts affected by a particular business process. Individual audit procedures are directed toward specific assertions in the account balances that are likely to be misstated. For example, if the auditor is concerned about the possibility of obsolete inventory, the auditor could gather evidence to determine if the inventory on hand is properly valued at the lower of cost or market. On most engagements, actually conducting the planned audit tests comprises most of the time spent on a financial statement audit or an audit of internal control over financial reporting. For public company clients, the audit of internal control is done in an integrated way with the financial statement audit. This topic is addressed in Chapter 7 and throughout the book where appropriate.

Complete the Audit   After the auditor has finished gathering evidence relating to financial statement assertions, the sufficiency of the evidence gathered is evaluated. The auditor must obtain sufficient appropriate evidence in order to reach and justify a conclusion on the fairness of the financial statements. In this phase, the auditor also assesses the possibility of contingent liabilities, such as lawsuits, and searches for any events subsequent to the balance sheet date that may impact the financial statements. Chapter 17 covers each of these issues in detail.

[LO 8]   Evaluate Results and Issue Audit Report   The final phase in the audit process is to evaluate results and choose the appropriate audit report to issue. The auditor's report, also known as the audit opinion, is the main product or output of the audit. Just as the report of a house inspector communicates the inspector's findings to a prospective buyer, the audit report communicates the auditor's findings to the users of the financial statements.

At the completion of the audit work, the auditor determines if the preliminary assessments of risks were appropriate in light of the evidence collected and whether sufficient evidence was obtained. The auditor then aggregates the total uncorrected misstatements that were detected and determines if they cause the financial statements to be materially misstated. If the uncorrected misstatements are judged to be material, the auditor will request that the client correct the misstatements. If the client refuses, the auditor issues an opinion that explains that the financial statements are materially misstated. If the uncorrected misstatements do not cause the financial statements to be materially misstated, or if the client is willing to correct the misstatements, the auditor issues an unqualified (i.e., "clean") report.

The Unqualified Audit Report

The unqualified audit report is by far the most common type of report issued. In this context, *unqualified* means that because the financial statements are free of material misstatements, the auditor does not find it necessary to *qualify* his or her opinion about the fairness of the financial statements. While it is fairly common for the auditor to find misstatements needing correction, audit clients are almost always willing to make the necessary adjustments to receive a clean opinion. Exhibit 1–1 presents an audit report issued on EarthWear Clothier's financial statements. This report covers financial statements that include balance sheets for two years and statements of income, stockholders' equity, and cash flows for three years. The audit report presented in Exhibit 1–1 is the standard type of unqualified audit opinion issued for publicly traded companies.

EXHIBIT 1–1	The Auditor's Standard Unqualified Report—Comparative Financial Statements (with explanatory paragraph)
Title:	REPORT OF INDEPENDENT REGISTERED PUBLIC ACCOUNTING FIRM
Addressee:	*To the Stockholders of EarthWear Clothiers*
Introductory paragraph:	We have audited the consolidated balance sheets of EarthWear Clothiers as of December 31, 2009 and 2008, and the related consolidated statements of operations, stockholders' equity, and cash flows for each of the three years in the period ended December 31, 2009. These financial statements are the responsibility of the Company's management. Our responsibility is to express an opinion on these financial statements based on our audits.
Scope paragraph:	We conducted our audits in accordance with the standards of the Public Company Accounting Oversight Board (United States). Those standards require that we plan and perform the audit to obtain reasonable assurance about whether the financial statements are free of material misstatement. An audit includes examining, on a test basis, evidence supporting the amounts and disclosures in the financial statements. An audit also includes assessing the accounting principles used and significant estimates made by management, as well as evaluating the overall financial statement presentation. We believe that our audits provide a reasonable basis for our opinion.
Opinion paragraph:	In our opinion, the consolidated financial statements referred to above present fairly, in all material respects, the financial position of the Company as of December 31, 2009 and 2008, and the results of its operations and its cash flows for each of the three years in the period ended December 31, 2009, in conformity with U.S. generally accepted accounting principles.
Explanatory paragraph referring to the audit of internal control:	We also have audited, in accordance with the standards of the Public Company Accounting Oversight Board (United States), the effectiveness of EarthWear Clothiers' internal control over financial reporting as of December 31, 2009, based on criteria established in *Internal Control—Integrated Framework* issued by the Committee of Sponsoring Organizations of the Treadway Commission (COSO), and our report dated February 15, 2010, expressed an unqualified opinion that EarthWear Clothiers maintained, in all material respects, effective internal control over financial reporting.
Name of auditor:	*Willis & Adams* *Boise, Idaho*
Date of report:	*February 15, 2010*

Take a moment to read through the report. You will see that the title refers to the "Independent Registered Public Accounting Firm" issuing the audit report. The report is addressed to the individual or group that is the intended recipient of the report. The body of the report begins with an introductory paragraph indicating which financial statements are covered by the report, that the statements are the responsibility of management, and that the auditor has a responsibility to express an opinion.

The second, or scope, paragraph communicates to the users, in very general terms, what an audit entails. In addition to indicating that the audit was conducted in accordance with applicable auditing standards, it emphasizes the fact that the audit provides only reasonable assurance that the financial statements contain no material misstatements. The scope paragraph also discloses that an audit involves an examination of evidence on a test basis (i.e., using samples rather than examining entire populations), an assessment of accounting principles used and significant estimates, and an overall evaluation of financial statement presentation. Finally, the scope paragraph asserts the auditor's belief that the audits provide a reasonable basis for the opinion to be expressed in the report.

The third paragraph contains the auditor's opinion concerning the fairness of the financial statements based on the audit evidence. Note two important phrases contained in this paragraph. First, the phrase "present fairly . . . in conformity with U.S. generally accepted accounting principles," indicates the criteria against which the auditor assesses management assertions. Second, the opinion paragraph contains the phrase "in all material respects," emphasizing the concept of materiality. Note that the scope paragraph indicates *how the audit was conducted*—in accordance with the standards of the PCAOB because EarthWear is a publicly traded company. Audit reports for nonpublic companies refer instead to "generally accepted auditing standards." At the same time, the opinion paragraph indicates the auditor's opinion as to whether the financial statements are fairly presented in accordance with the *criteria against which they were audited*—GAAP.

The fourth paragraph contains explanatory language. As shown in Exhibit 1–1, when the auditor's opinion on a public company's financial statements is presented separately from the auditor's report on the client's internal control over financial reporting, as is the case here, the report must refer to the audit of internal control in an explanatory paragraph. You will learn more about the audit of internal control over financial reporting and the types of reports associated with that audit in Chapter 7.

The financial statement audit report concludes with the manual or printed signature of the CPA firm providing the audit and with the date of the report. The audit report date indicates the last day of the auditor's responsibility for the review of significant events that have occurred after the date of the financial statements.

Other Types of Audit Reports

For an audit report to be unqualified, the audit must be done in accordance with applicable standards, the auditor must be independent, there must be no significant limitations imposed on the auditor's procedures, and the client's financial statements must be free of material departures from GAAP. If any one of these conditions is not met, the auditor issues a report that appropriately conveys to the reader the nature of the report and the reasons why the report is not unqualified.

For example, suppose a client's financial statements contain a misstatement that the auditor considers material and the client refuses to correct the misstatement. The auditor will likely *qualify* the report, explaining that the financial statements are fairly stated *except for* the misstatement identified by the auditor. If the misstatement is considered so material that it pervasively affects the interpretation of the financial statements, the auditor will issue an *adverse* opinion, indicating that the financial statements are not fairly stated and should not be relied upon. Other types of reports are available to the auditor as well, depending on the circumstances. While it is important for you to be familiar with the basic components of the audit report as part of understanding an overview of the audit process, we cover the different types of financial statement audit reports in detail in Chapter 18. Our experience is that students find it more intuitive to learn the fundamental concepts of auditing and how an audit is conducted before being immersed in the details of audit reporting.

The audit report represents the culmination of the audit process and is the auditor's primary venue for communicating his or her opinion about a client's financial statements with outside parties. An example of an unqualified or clean audit report is included in this chapter to give you a basic idea of what the most common type of audit report looks like.

Conclusion

✂ **[LO 9]**   You can see from this chapter that a good financial statement auditor needs to understand not only accounting but also the concepts and techniques of gathering and evaluating evidence to assess management's financial statement assertions. In addition, an auditor needs a deep understanding of business in general as well as of the specific industries in which his or her clients operate. This is why professionals with auditing experience frequently have attractive opportunities to move into other areas of business and management. Chief executive officers, business owners, chief financial officers, consultants, and controllers are often former auditors.

This chapter is designed to help you develop an intuitive understanding of basic auditing concepts. As you study auditing, you will need to commit some details to memory. But you will understand and appreciate the details of the auditing process much more fully if you have a good grasp of the underlying concepts—why financial statement auditing is in demand, what it is, and the basic process by which it is carried out.

Keep in mind that auditing is a fundamentally logical process of thinking and reasoning—don't be hesitant to exercise your common sense and reasoning skills! You will benefit much more from your reading of this text if you study it with a reasoning, inquisitive approach, rather than merely attempting to memorize details. As you learn new auditing concepts, take some time to understand the underlying logic and how the concepts interrelate with other concepts. As you learn about auditing procedures, ask yourself how and why the procedure might yield relevant evidence, and try to think of other ways you might obtain useful evidence. Rote memorization alone is not a good way to study auditing!

Being a good auditor sometimes requires imagination and innovation. For example, a few years back an auditor was faced with figuring out how to verify a client's assertion regarding the existence of inventory. The problem was that the "inventory" consisted of thousands of head of cattle on a ranch covering dozens of square miles. There was no standard procedure manual for the auditor to refer to—he simply had to figure out an effective and efficient way to obtain persuasive evidence that the cattle existed in the numbers asserted by the ranch's management.

In the end, the auditor decided to charter a small airplane to fly over the ranch and take photos—one per fifty square acres. The auditor was able to obtain a count of the cattle from the photos. He also evaluated veterinary records to see if the number of required annual vaccinations approximated the number of cattle counted in the photos. Finally, he did some calculations based on average bovine birth and death rates, taking into account recorded purchases and sales of livestock during the year. Using this combination of procedures, the auditor was able to obtain persuasive evidence supporting management's assertion regarding inventory (and got an airplane ride in the process).

We hope this example helps illustrate why you will need to approach the study of auditing differently from that of most other accounting courses. As you learn the concepts and techniques of auditing, you are not only acquiring the tools to become an effective financial statement auditor but also a conceptual tool kit that can be useful to you in many different settings and contexts.

KEY TERMS

Assurance Services. Independent professional services that improve the quality of information, or its context, for decision makers. Encompasses attest services and financial statement audits.

Attest. A service when a practitioner is engaged to issue or does issue a report on subject matter, or an assertion about subject matter, that is the responsibility of another party. Encompasses financial statement audits.

Audit evidence. All the information used by the auditor in arriving at the conclusions on which the audit opinion is based; includes the information contained in the accounting records underlying the financial statements and other information.

Audit risk. The risk that the auditor may unknowingly fail to appropriately modify his or her opinion on financial statements that are materially misstated.

Auditing. A systematic process of (1) objectively obtaining and evaluating evidence regarding assertions about economic actions and events to ascertain the degree of correspondence between those assertions and established criteria and (2) communicating the results to interested users.

Financial statement assertions. Expressed or implied representations by management that are reflected in the financial statement components.

Information asymmetry. The concept that the manager generally has more information about the true financial position and results of operations of the entity than the absentee owner does.

Materiality. The magnitude of an omission or misstatement of accounting information that, in light of surrounding circumstances, makes it probable that the judgment of a reasonable person relying on the information would have been changed or influenced.

Misstatement. An instance where a financial statement assertion is not in accordance with the criteria against which it is audited (e.g., GAAP). Misstatements may be classified as fraud (intentional), other illegal acts such as noncompliance with laws and regulations (intentional or unintentional), and errors (unintentional).

Reasonable assurance. The concept that an audit done in accordance with auditing standards may fail to detect a material misstatement in a client's financial statements. In an auditing context this term has been defined to mean a high but not absolute level of assurance.

Reporting. The end product of the auditor's work, indicating the auditing standards followed, and expressing an opinion as to whether an entity's financial statements are fairly presented in accordance with agreed-upon criteria (e.g., GAAP).

Risk of material misstatement. The risk that the entity's financial statements will contain a material misstatement whether caused by error or fraud.

Unqualified audit report. A "clean" audit report, indicating the auditor's opinion that a client's financial statements are fairly presented in accordance with agreed-upon criteria (e.g., GAAP).

www.mhhe.com/
messier7e

Visit the book's Online Learning Center for a multiple-choice quiz that will allow you to assess your understanding of chapter concepts.

REVIEW QUESTIONS

[LO 1]   1-1   Why is studying auditing different from studying other accounting topics? How might understanding auditing concepts prove useful for consultants, business managers, and other business decision makers?

[2]   1-2   Discuss why there is a demand for auditing services in a free-market economy. What evidence suggests that auditing would be demanded even if it were not required by government regulation?

[2]   1-3   What is meant by the statement, "The agency relationship between absentee owners and managers produces a natural conflict of interest"?

[3]   1-4   Why is independence such an important requirement for auditors? How does independence relate to the agency relationship between owners and managers?

[4]   1-5   Define *auditing, attest,* and *assurance services.*

[4]   1-6   The Committee on Basic Auditing Concepts has provided a widely cited definition of auditing. What does the phrase "systematic process" mean in this definition?

[5]   1-7   Define *audit risk* and *materiality.* How are these concepts reflected in the auditor's report?

[6]   1-8   Briefly describe why on most audit engagements an auditor tests only a sample of transactions that occurred.

[7]   1-9   What are the major phases of an audit?

[7]   1-10   The auditor's understanding of the entity and its environment should include knowledge of which categories of information?

[8]   1-11   Identify the four paragraphs of the auditor's standard unqualified report for a public company client.

[9]   1-12   Briefly discuss why auditors must often exercise creativity and innovation in auditing financial statements. Give an example different from the one offered in the text.

MULTIPLE-CHOICE QUESTIONS

[LO 2,3,4]   1-13   An independent audit aids in the communication of economic data because the audit
   a. Confirms the exact accuracy of management's financial representations.
   b. Lends credibility to the financial statements.
   c. Guarantees that financial data are fairly presented.
   d. Assures the readers of financial statements that any fraudulent activity has been corrected.

[2,3,4]   1-14   Which of the following best describes the reason why an independent auditor is often retained to report on financial statements?
   a. Management fraud may exist, and it is more likely to be detected by independent auditors than by internal auditors.
   b. Different interests may exist between the entity preparing the statements and the persons using the statements, and thus outside assurance is needed to enhance the credibility of the statements.

     c. A misstatement of account balances may exist, and all misstatements are generally corrected as a result of the independent auditor's work.

     d. An entity may have a poorly designed internal control system.

[4]   1-15 Which of the following best describes relationships among auditing, attest, and assurance services?

     a. Attest is a type of auditing service.

     b. Auditing and attest services represent two distinctly different types of services.

     c. Auditing is a type of assurance service.

     d. Assurance is a type of attest service.

[4]   1-16 Which of the following statements relating to attest and assurance services is not correct?

     a. Independence is an important attribute of assurance service providers.

     b. Assurance services can be performed to improve the quality or context of information for decision makers.

     c. Financial statement auditing is a form of attest service but it is not an assurance service.

     d. In performing an attest service, the CPA determines the correspondence of the subject matter (or an assertion about the subject matter) against criteria that are suitable and available to users.

[5,7]   1-17 For what primary purpose does the auditor obtain an understanding of the entity and its environment?

     a. To determine the audit fee.

     b. To decide which facts about the entity to include in the audit report.

     c. To plan the audit and determine the scope of audit procedures to be performed.

     d. To limit audit risk to an appropriately high level.

[5]   1-18 Which of the following statements best describes the role of materiality in a financial statement audit?

     a. Materiality refers to the "material" from which audit evidence is developed.

     b. The higher the level at which the auditor assesses materiality, the greater the amount of evidence the auditor must gather.

     c. The lower the level at which the auditor assesses materiality, the greater the amount of evidence the auditor must gather.

     d. The level of materiality has no bearing on the amount of evidence the auditor must gather.

[7]   1-19 Which of the following is the most important reason for an auditor to gain an understanding of an audit client's system of internal control over financial reporting?

     a. Understanding a client's system of internal control can help the auditor assess risk and identify areas where financial statement misstatements might be more likely.

     b. Understanding a client's system of internal control can help the auditor make valuable recommendations to management at the end of the engagement.

     c. Understanding a client's system of internal control can help the auditor sell consulting services to the client.

     d. Understanding a client's system of internal control is not a required part of the audit process.

[7]   1-20 Preplanning the audit includes:

     a. Understanding the client and the client's industry.

     b. Determining audit engagement team requirements.

c. Ensuring the independence of the audit team and audit firm.

d. All of the above.

[8] 1-21 Which of the following statements best describes what is meant by an unqualified audit opinion?

a. Issuance of an unqualified auditor's report indicates that in the auditor's opinion the client's financial statements are not fairly enough presented in accordance with agreed-upon criteria to qualify for a clean opinion.

b. Issuance of an unqualified auditor's report indicates that the auditor is not qualified to express an opinion that the client's financial statements are fairly presented in accordance with agreed-upon criteria.

c. Issuance of an unqualified auditor's report indicates that the auditor is expressing different opinions on each of the basic financial statements regarding whether the client's financial statements are fairly presented in accordance with agreed-upon criteria.

d. Issuance of a standard unqualified auditor's report indicates that in the auditor's opinion the client's financial statements are fairly presented in accordance with agreed-upon criteria, with no need for the inclusion of qualifying phrases.

[8] 1-22 The auditing standards used to guide the conduct of the audit are

a. Implicitly referred to in the opening paragraph of the auditor's standard report.

b. Explicitly referred to in the opening paragraph of the auditor's standard report.

c. Implicitly referred to in the scope paragraph of the auditor's standard report.

d. Explicitly referred to in the scope paragraph of the auditor's standard report.

e. Implicitly referred to in the opinion paragraph of the auditor's standard report.

f. Explicitly referred to in the opinion paragraph of the auditor's standard report.

[8] 1-23 A client has used an inappropriate method of accounting for its pension liability on the balance sheet. The resulting misstatement is moderately material, but the auditor does not consider it to be pervasive. The auditor is unable to convince the client to alter its accounting treatment. The rest of the financial statements are fairly stated in the auditor's opinion. Which kind of audit report would an auditor most likely issue under these circumstances?

a. Standard unqualified opinion.

b. Qualified opinion due to departure from GAAP.

c. Adverse opinion.

d. No opinion at all

PROBLEMS

[1,2,3] 1-24 You recently attended your five-year college reunion. At the main reception, you encountered an old friend, Lee Beagle, who recently graduated from law school and is now practicing with a large law firm in town. When you told him that you were a CPA and employed by a regional CPA firm, he made the following statement: "You know, if the securities acts had not been passed by Congress in the 1930s, no one would be interested in having an audit performed. You auditors are just creatures of regulation."

Required:

Draft a memo that highlights your thoughts about Lee's statement that auditors are "creatures of regulation." Be sure to consider relevant evidence of a demand for auditing services outside of legal and regulatory requirements in your memo, and focus on the value that auditing provides.

[2,3] 1-25 Greenbloom Garden Centers is a small, privately held corporation that has two stores in Orlando, Florida. The Greenbloom family owns 100 percent of the company's stock, and family members manage the operations. Sales at the company's stores have been growing rapidly, and there appears to be a market for the company's sales concept—providing bulk garden equipment and supplies at low prices. The controller prepares the company's financial statements, which are not audited. The company has no debt but is considering expanding to other cities in Florida. Such expansion may require long-term borrowings and is likely to reduce the family's day-to-day control of the operations. The family does not intend to sell stock in the company.

Required:

Discuss the factors that may make an audit necessary and potentially valuable for the company. Be sure to consider the concept of information risk.

[3,5] 1-26 You were recently hired by the CPA firm of Honson & Hansen. Within two weeks, you were sent to the first-year staff training course. The instructor asks you to prepare answers for the following questions:

a. How is audit evidence defined?

b. How should audit evidence relate to assertions and to the audit report?

c. What characteristics of evidence should an auditor be concerned with when searching for and evaluating audit evidence?

[7] 1-27 John Josephs, an audit manager for Tip, Acanoe, & Tylerto, was asked to speak at a dinner meeting of the local Small Business Administration Association. The president of the association has suggested that he talk about the various phases of the audit process. John has asked you, his trusted assistant, to prepare an outline for his speech. He suggests that you answer the following:

a. List and describe the various phases of an audit.

b. Describe how audit procedures designed for one purpose might provide evidence for other purposes. Give an example.

c. One of the phases involves understanding an entity's internal control. Why might the members of the association be particularly interested in the work conducted by auditors in this phase of the audit?

[8] 1-28 Many companies post their financial statements and auditor's report on their home pages, generally under a heading labeled "investor relations." Use one of the Internet search engines to do the following:

a. Visit Intel's (www.intel.com) and Microsoft's (www.microsoft.com) home pages and review their financial statements, including their auditors' reports.

b. Search the Web for the home page of a non-U.S. company and review its financial statements, including its auditor's report. For example, BMW's home page (www.bmwgroup.com) allows a visitor to download the financial statements as a .pdf file. Identify the auditing standards followed by the company's auditors.

c. Compare the standard U.S. audit report with the audit report for the non-U.S. company (e.g., BMW). Note that in some cases, non-U.S.-based companies' reports use a U.S. audit report.

d. Visit the SEC's Web site (www.sec.gov), and find the link for EdgarScan. Find, download, and print the auditor's report for a U.S. company of your choice. Identify whether or not the audit report is an unqualified, or "clean," opinion.

[8]   1-29   Using the audit report included in Chapter 1, identify and record the phrases or words that indicate to the users that the financial statements are not an "exact" representation of the results of operations and financial position of a company.

DISCUSSION CASE

[1,3,5,8,9]   1-30   The Government Accountability Office (GAO) gave the following results in a report based on an examination of 39 failed banks:[10]

> The early warning system provided by bank call reports* is seriously flawed. The 39 failed banks' call reports did not provide the regulators with advance warning of the true magnitude of the deterioration in the banks' financial condition. As a result of the asset valuations FDIC prepared after these banks failed, loss reserves increased from $2.1 billion to $9.4 billion. A major portion of the $7.3 billion deterioration in asset values was not previously reported because deficiencies in GAAP allowed bank management to unduly delay the recognition of losses and mask the need for early regulatory intervention that could have minimized losses to the Bank Insurance Fund.
>
> The key to successful bank regulation is knowing what banks are really worth. The 39 bank failures are expected to cost the fund $8.9 billion. Large banks present a major threat to the solvency of the Bank Insurance Fund and need closer scrutiny.
>
> The corporate governance system upon which successful regulation depends is seriously flawed. Of the 39 banks, 33 had serious internal control problems that regulators cited as contributing significantly to their failure. Had these problems been corrected, the banks might not have failed or their failure could have been less expensive to the fund.
>
> Many of the 39 failed banks did not obtain an independent audit in their last year prior to failure. Without an audit, a troubled institution's management can more easily conceal its financial difficulties.
>
> Audits would enhance both the corporate governance and regulatory functions. In addition, the roles of both management and the auditors would be strengthened if they were required to assume responsibility for assessing and reporting on the condition of internal control, a significant cause of bank failures.

Required:
Describe in one or two concise, informative paragraphs how audits by external auditors could have prevented or limited the losses incurred by the Bank Insurance Fund.

---

[10]U.S. Government Accountability Office, *Failed Banks: Accounting and Auditing Reforms Urgently Needed* (GAO/AFMD-91-43) (April 1991).

*A call report is a Quarterly Consolidated Report of Condition and Income submitted by management to bank regulators. It consists of unaudited financial information that is required to be prepared in accordance with federal regulatory requirements, which are generally consistent with GAAP.

INTERNET ASSIGNMENTS

[1,9]   1-31   Using an Internet browser, identify five Internet sites that contain accounting or auditing resources. For each site identified, prepare a brief summary of the types of information that are available. For example, the PCAOB's home page (www.pcaob.org) contains extensive information on the organization's activities (you may use the PCAOB site as one of the five).

 HANDS-ON CASES

EarthWear Online	**EarthWear Introduction** Overview of EarthWear assignments and an introduction to the information contained on EarthWear Clothiers' and Willis and Adams' home pages. *Visit the book's Online Learning Center at www.mhhe.com/messier7e to find a detailed description of the case and to download required materials.*

ACL

www.mhhe.com/ messier7e	Visit the book's Online Learning Center for problem material to be completed using the *ACL* software packaged with your new text.

CHAPTER 2

LEARNING OBJECTIVES

Upon completion of this chapter you will

[1] Understand the significant changes that have taken place in the auditing profession over the past several years.

[2] Recognize that auditing takes place in a context that is shaped largely by the audit client's business, industry, and economic environment.

[3] Understand a high-level model of a business entity, including corporate governance, objectives, strategies, processes, controls, transactions, and financial statements.

[4] Be familiar with a five-component model of business processes (or cycles) that auditors often use in organizing the audit into manageable components.

[5] Recognize the sets of management assertions that are implicit in a business entity's financial statements.

[6] Understand that auditing standards are established by the AICPA's Auditing Standards Board (ASB) for private entities, and by the Public Company Accounting Oversight Board (PCAOB) for public companies.

[7] Be familiar with the 10 "generally accepted auditing standards" (GAAS).

[8] Understand the nature of the Statements on Auditing Standards (SAS) as interpretations of the 10 GAAS.

[9] Be aware that the PCAOB adopted the ASB's SAS on an interim basis and is now issuing its own Auditing Standards (AS) that apply to the audits of public companies.

[10] Understand that auditing is a profession that places a premium on ethical behavior and that is governed by a Code of Professional Conduct.

[11] Know that management is primarily responsible for the entity's financial statements and understand the auditor's responsibility for detecting errors, material fraud, and illegal acts.

[12] Understand the organization and composition of public accounting firms.

[13] Be familiar with the various services offered by assurance providers.

[14] Be familiar with the different types of auditors.

[15] Identify and be familiar with the major organizations that affect the public accounting profession's environment.

RELEVANT ACCOUNTING AND AUDITING PRONOUNCEMENTS

FASB Statement of Financial Accounting Concepts No. 2, Qualitative Characteristics of Accounting Information

AT 50, Attestation Standards

AU 110, Responsibilities and Functions of the Independent Auditor

AU 150, Generally Accepted Auditing Standards

AU 316, Consideration of Fraud in a Financial Statement Audit

AU 326, Audit Evidence

The Financial Statement Auditing Environment

This chapter covers the context or environment in which auditors function, starting with an overview of the far-reaching changes in the public accounting profession over the past several years. One of the most important and useful skills auditors develop is the ability to quickly understand and analyze various business models, strategies, and processes and to identify key risks relevant to a particular client. Further, these elements largely shape the context in which auditing is performed. Accordingly, the chapter introduces a high-level model of business and then offers a model of business processes that is useful for organizing an audit. The chapter then expands on the concept of management assertions introduced in Chapter 1 and introduces auditing standards, explaining how these standards are established in today's professional and regulatory environment. Ethical behavior and reputation play key roles in shaping the public accounting profession and its environment, and the chapter explains that the auditing profession is governed by a Code of Professional Conduct. Management's primary responsibility for the financial statements is then discussed, along with the auditor's responsibility to provide reasonable assurance. The chapter concludes by discussing public accounting firms and the major categories of services they offer, the various types of auditors other than financial statement auditors, and the major organizations that affect the public accounting profession and its environment.

A Time of Challenge and Change for Auditors

[LO 1]   The environment in which auditors work has been dramatically reshaped by events taking place in the business world during the past several years. This section briefly discusses the events that led up to the dramatic changes imposed on the profession through the Sarbanes-Oxley Act in 2002 and the establishment of the Public Company Accounting Oversight Board (PCAOB) as the standard setter and regulator for public company audits.

During the economic boom of the late 1990s and early 2000s, accounting firms aggressively sought opportunities to market a variety of high-margin non-audit services to their audit clients. Independence standards in force at the time allowed auditors to perform many such services, including information systems design and implementation and internal audit services, even for public company audit clients. The consulting revenue of the largest public accounting firms grew very rapidly, until in many instances consulting revenues from audit clients far exceeded the fee for the external audit. Exhibit 2–1 provides a sample of audit and nonaudit fees reported two years prior to the Sarbanes-Oxley Act.

A Series of Scandals

In October 2001, Enron, one of the largest public companies in the United States at the time, became the subject of an SEC investigation into its accounting practices. The investigation quickly uncovered massive financial deception that had been going on for several years. The company released an earnings restatement for previous years, disclosing billions of dollars in overstated earnings and previously undisclosed debt obligations. Arthur Andersen, the public accounting firm that audited Enron's financial statements, immediately became embroiled in the controversy, because the firm had failed to report the vast extent of Enron's improper accounting. Many argued that this failure came about at least in part because Andersen was paid tens of millions of dollars in separate fees for consulting and internal auditing services, which amounted to more than the fee for the external audit. In August 2002, Andersen stopped providing audits of public companies and began to dismantle its business. Andersen's collapse resulted from the firm's loss of reputation brought about by a string of audit failures and by the firm's indictment and subsequent conviction on federal charges of obstruction of justice. Though the conviction was overturned by the U.S. Supreme Court a few years later, the fatal damage had been done. Ironically, for most of Andersen's 89 years of existence it enjoyed a sterling reputation as one of the world's biggest and most respected accounting firms.

| EXHIBIT 2–1 | **Examples of Audit and Nonaudit Fees in the Pre-Sarbanes-Oxley Environment** | | | |

		Types of Fees (in millions)		
Company	*Auditor*	*Audit*	*IT*	*Other*
J. P. Morgan Chase	PricewaterhouseCoopers	21.3	11.1	73.1
General Electric	KPMG	23.9	11.5	68.2
Waste Management	Andersen	48.0	31.0	
Sprint	Ernst & Young	2.5	12.4	51.4
Delphi Auto Systems	Deloitte	6.6	41.3	9.5
AOL Time Warner	Ernst & Young	7.9	7.2	43.8

Source: J. Well and J. A. Tannenbaum, "Big Companies Pay Audit Firms More for Other Services," *The Wall Street Journal* (April 10, 2000), pp. C1–C2.

earthwear

2009 ANNUAL REPORT

Company History and Operations

EarthWear Clothiers was founded in Boise, Idaho, by James Williams and Calvin Rogers in 1973 to make high-quality clothing for outdoor sports, such as hiking, skiing, fly-fishing, and white-water kayaking. Over the years, the company's product lines have grown to include casual clothing, accessories, shoes, and soft luggage. EarthWear offers its products through three retailing options: catalogs, retail outlets, and its website.

The company strives to provide excellent, high-quality products at reasonable prices. EarthWear has a commitment to excellence in customer service and an unconditional guarantee. The Company is also conscious of its environmental responsibilities. All company facilities are insulated, recycle, and conserve power. The Company continuously monitors the environmental impact of its products. The Company believes that many of its customers share this concern for the environment.

The Company offers its products principally through regular mailings of its monthly catalogs in the United States, Europe, and Japan. EarthWear has 10 U.S. outlet stores, four in the U.K., two in Germany, and two in Japan. The Company also offers its products over the Internet (www.mhhe.com/earthwear). During 2009, the Company expanded its global presence by launching sites in France, Italy, Ireland, and several eastern European countries. Currently, revenue from catalog sales, retail outlets, and the website are 74 percent, 5 percent, and 21 percent, respectively. Management expects that Internet sales will grow significantly in the future, perhaps replacing catalogs as the major source of sales.

EarthWear was incorporated in Idaho in 1975 and became a Delaware corporation in 1986 when it went public.

COMPANY GROWTH STRATEGY EarthWear's growth strategy has three elements. First, the Company attempts to increase sales by expanding its customer base and by increasing sales to existing customers through improved product offerings. Second, the Company seeks to generate additional sales by targeted mailings of special issues of its catalogs and by offering its products through its web site. Third, the Company is pursuing additional opportunities to expand its merchandising skills internationally.

CATALOGS AND SALES OPERATIONS During 2009 the company mailed 12 issues of its regular monthly catalog with an average of 75 pages per issue from its U.S. operations. Worldwide, the company mailed approximately 160 million full-price catalogs. EarthWear views each catalog issue as a unique opportunity to communicate with its customers. Products are described in visual and editorial detail, and the Company uses such techniques as background stories and distinctive covers to stimulate the readers' interest.

Each issue of the regular catalog offers certain basic product lines for men and women. The regular catalog also offers seasonal merchandise. In addition, EarthWear mails two end-of-season clearance catalogs. The Company mails its catalogs to prospective customers who are identified based on lists of magazine subscribers and lists of households meeting certain demographic criteria. In addition, the company identifies prospective new customers through its national advertising campaign.

In 1991 the Company introduced its first business specialty catalog, which offered its products to groups and companies for corporate incentive programs. EarthWear's embroidery capabilities allow for the design and monogram of unique logos or emblems for groups and companies. In 2009 the company mailed five issues of its corporate sales catalogs.

The international business segment includes operations in Japan, Germany, and the United Kingdom, and various Internet sites. Catalogs mailed in those countries are written in the local languages and denominated in local currencies. In the spring of 2009, EarthWear launched local websites in each of these countries in their respective languages and currencies.

CUSTOMER DATABASE A principal factor in the Company's success has been the development of its own list of active customers. At the end of 2009 the Company's mailing list consisted of about 21.1 million persons, approximately 7 million of whom were viewed as customers because they had made at least one purchase from the Company within the last 24 months. The Company routinely updates and refines the database before mailing catalogs to monitor customer interest as reflected in criteria such as the recency, frequency, dollar amount, and product type of purchases.

EarthWear believes that its customer database has desirable demographic characteristics and is well suited to the products offered in "the company's" catalogs. A survey conducted by the Company in the United States during 2008 indicated that approximately 50 percent of its customers were in the 35–54 age group and had median incomes of $78,000.

The Company advertises nationally to build its reputation and to attract new customers. In 2009 an advertising campaign appeared in about 40 national magazines, as well as on five national cable television networks. In addition, the Company advertises in approximately 75 national, regional, and local publications in Canada, the United Kingdom, Germany, and Japan. EarthWear also advertises on a number of Internet search engines and websites.

PRODUCT DEVELOPMENT EarthWear concentrates on clothing and other products that are aimed at customers interested in outdoor activities. The Company products are styled and quality crafted to meet the changing tastes of the Company's customers rather than to mimic the changing fads of the fashion world. At the same time, the Company seeks to maintain customer interest by developing new products, improving existing core products, and reinforcing its value positioning.

The Company continues to incorporate innovations in fabric, construction, and detail that add value and excitement and differentiate EarthWear from the competition. In order to ensure that products are manufactured to the Company's quality standards at reasonable prices, product managers, designers, and quality assurance specialists develop the Company's own products.

EarthWear deals directly with its suppliers and seeks to avoid intermediaries. All goods are produced by independent manufacturers except for most of its soft luggage, which is assembled at the company's facilities. During 2009 the Company purchased merchandise from approximately 300 domestic and foreign manufacturers. One manufacturer and one intermediary accounted for about 14 and 29 percent of the Company's received merchandise, respectively, in 2009. In 2009 about 80 percent of the Company's merchandise was imported, mainly from Asia, Central America, Mexico, and Central America. The Company will continue to take advantage of worldwide sourcing without sacrificing customer service or quality standards.

Order Entry, Fulfillment, and Delivery

EarthWear has toll-free telephone numbers that customers can call 24 hours a day, seven days a week (except Christmas Day) to place orders or to request a catalog. Approximately 90 percent of catalog orders are placed by telephone. Telephone calls are answered by the company's well-trained sales representatives, who utilize online computer terminals to enter customer orders and to retrieve information about product characteristics and availability. The Company's three U.S. telephone centers are located in Boise, Idaho; Reston, Virginia; and Canton, Ohio. International telephone centers are located in London, England; Tokyo, Japan; and Mannheim, Germany.

The Company's order entry and fulfillment system permits shipment of in-stock orders on the following day, but orders requiring monogramming or inseaming typically require one or two extra days. The Company's" sales representatives enter orders into an online order entry and inventory control system. Customers using the Company's Internet site see color photos of the products, their availability, and prices. When ordering a product over the Internet, the customer completes a computer screen that requests information on product code, size, color, and so on. When the customer finishes shopping for products, he or she enters delivery and credit card information into a computer-based form. EarthWear provides assurance through CPA *WebTrust* SM that the website has been evaluated and tested to meet *WebTrust* SM principles and criteria. This assurance service is provided by the Company's independent auditors, Willis & Adams, LLP.

Orders are generally shipped by United Parcel Service (UPS) at various tiered rates that depend on the total dollar value of each customer's order. Other expedited delivery services are available at additional charge. Domestically, the Company utilizes two-day UPS service at standard rates, enhancing its customer service. Comparable services are offered in international markets.

MERCHANDISE LIQUIDATION Liquidations (sales of overstock and end-of-season merchandise at reduced prices) were approximately 12 percent, 11 percent, and 8 percent of net sales in 2009, 2008, and 2007, respectively. Most liquidation sales were made through catalogs and other print media. The balance was sold principally through the Company's outlet retail stores.

COMPETITION The Company's principal competitors are retail stores, including specialty shops, department stores, and other catalog companies. Direct competitors include Eddie Bauer, Land's End, L. L. Bean, Patagonia, and Timberland. The Company may also face increased competition from other retailers as the number of television shopping channels and the variety of merchandise offered over the Internet increase. The apparel retail business in general is intensely competitive. EarthWear competes principally on the basis of merchandise value (quality and price), its established customer list, and customer service, including fast order fulfillment and its unqualified guarantee.

TRADEMARKS The Company uses the trademarks of "EarthWear" and "EWC" on products and catalogs.

SEASONALITY OF BUSINESS The Company's business is highly seasonal. Historically, a disproportionate amount of the Company's net sales and most of its profits have been realized during the fourth quarter. If the Company's sales were materially different from seasonal norms during the fourth quarter, the Company's annual operating results could be materially affected. Accordingly, results for the individual quarters do not necessarily indicate results to be expected for the entire year. In 2009, 37 percent of the Company's total revenue came in the fourth quarter.

EMPLOYEES The Company believes that its skilled and dedicated workforce is one of its key resources. Employees are not covered by collective bargaining agreements, and the Company considers its employee relations to be excellent. As a result of the highly seasonal nature of the Company's business, the size of the company's workforce varies, ranging from approximately 3,500 to 5,300 individuals in 2009. During the peak winter season of 2009, approximately 2,700 of the Company's 5,300 employees were temporary employees.

EXECUTIVE OFFICERS OF THE COMPANY

James G. Williams, 65, is chairman of the board and former chief executive officer. Mr. Williams was one of the two original founders of EarthWear. He stepped down as chief executive officer in December 1999.

Calvin J. Rogers, 57, is president and chief executive officer of the Company. Mr. Rogers was one of the two original founders of the Company. He assumed his present position in December 1999.

Dominique DeSantiago, 56, is executive vice president and chief operating officer. Mr. DeSantiago joined the Company as chief operating officer in June 1991. He was promoted to vice president in October 1994. Mr. DeSantiago was previously employed by Eddie Bauer in various capacities.

Linda S. McDaniel, 45, is senior vice president of sales. She joined the Company in July 1996. Ms. McDaniel served as divisional vice president, merchandising, with Patagonia between 1986 and 1990. Ms. McDaniel was the president and chief executive officer for Mountain Goat Sports from 1990 until 1996. She has been serving as a director of the Company since November 1997.

James C. ("JC") Watts, 45, is senior vice president and chief financial officer. Mr. Watts joined the Company in May 1996, assuming his current position. He was previously employed by Federated Department Stores.

Mary Ellen Tornesello, 47, is senior vice president of operations. Ms. Tornesello joined the Company in 1994 as operations manager. She served as vice president of operations from 1995 until 1997, at which time she assumed her present position.

EarthWear

Market information The common stock of the Company is listed and traded on NASDAQ under the symbol EWCC. The high and low prices of the Company's common stock for 2009 were $52.50 and $21.75 per share. The closing price of the Company's stock on December 31, 2009, was $26.75 per share.

Shareholders As of December 31, 2009, the number of shareholders of record of common stock of the Company was 2,120. This number excludes shareholders whose stock is held in nominee or street name by brokers.

Independent Auditors The Company has been audited by Willis & Adams since incorporation in 1975.

EARTHWEAR CLOTHIERS

Consolidated Statements of Operations
(In thousands, except share data)

	For the period ended December 31		
	2009	2008	2007
Net Sales	$ 950,484	$ 857,885	$ 891,394
Cost of sales	546,393	472,739	490,530
Gross Profit	404,091	385,146	400,864
Selling, general, and administrative expenses	364,012	334,994	353,890
Nonrecurring charge (credit)	—	(1,153)	8,190
Income from operations	40,079	51,305	38,784
Other income (expense):			
Interest expense	(983)	(1,229)	(5,027)
Interest income	1,459	573	10
Other	(4,798)	(1,091)	(1,593)
Total other income (expense), net	(4,322)	(1,747)	6,609
Income before income taxes	35,757	49,559	32,175
Income tax provision	13,230	18,337	11,905
Net income	$ 22,527	$ 31,222	$ 20,270
Basic earnings per share	1.15	1.60	1.02
Diluted earnings per share	1.14	1.56	1.01
Basic weighted average shares outstanding	19,531	19,555	19,806
Diluted weighted average shares outstanding	19,774	20,055	19,996

EARTHWEAR CLOTHIERS

Consolidated Balance Sheets

(In thousands)

	December 31	
Assets	**2009**	2008
Current assets:		
Cash and cash equivalents	$ 48,978	$ 49,668
Receivables, net	12,875	11,539
Inventory	122,337	105,425
Prepaid advertising	11,458	10,772
Other prepaid expenses	6,315	3,780
Deferred income tax benefits	7,132	6,930
Total current assets	209,095	188,115
Property, plant, and equipment, at cost		
Land and buildings	70,918	66,804
Fixtures and equipment	67,513	66,876
Computer hardware and software	64,986	47,466
Leasehold improvements	3,010	2,894
Total property, plant, and equipment	206,426	184,040
Less accumulated depreciation and amortization	85,986	76,256
Property, plant, and equipment, net	120,440	107,784
Intangibles, net	423	628
Total assets	$ 329,959	$ 296,527

Liabilities and shareholders' investment		
Current liabilities:		
Lines of credit	$ 11,011	$ 7,621
Accounts payable	62,509	48,432
Reserve for returns	5,890	5,115
Accrued liabilities	26,738	28,440
Accrued profit sharing	1,532	1,794
Income taxes payable	8,588	6,666
Total current liabilities	116,268	98,067
Deferred income taxes	9,469	5,926
Shareholders' investment:		
Common stock, 26,121 shares issued	261	261
Donated capital	5,460	5,460
Additional paid-in capital	20,740	19,311
Deferred compensation	(79)	(153)
Accumulated other comprehensive income	3,883	1,739
Retained earnings	317,907	295,380
Treasury stock, 6,546 and 6,706 shares at cost	(143,950)	(129,462)
Total shareholders' investment	204,222	192,535
Total liabilities and shareholders' investment	$ 329,959	$ 296,527

EARTHWEAR CLOTHIERS

Consolidated Statements of Cash Flows

(*In thousands*)

	For the period ended December 31		
Cash flows from (used for) operating activities:	**2009**	2008	2007
Net income	**$ 22,527**	$ 31,222	$ 20,270
Adjustments to reconcile net income to net cash flows from operating activities:			
Nonrecurring charge (credit)		(1,153)	8,190
Depreciation and amortization	**15,231**	13,465	12,175
Deferred compensation expense	**75**	103	424
Deferred income taxes	**3,340**	5,376	(3,866)
Loss on disposal of fixed assets	**$284**	602	381
Changes in assets and liabilities excluding the effects of divestitures:			
Receivables, net	**(1,336)**	2,165	(3,666)
Inventory	**(16,912)**	37,370	13,954
Prepaid advertising	**(686)**	3,110	(1,849)
Other prepaid expenses	**(2,534)**	1,152	(1,628)
Accounts payable	**14,078**	(8,718)	2,716
Reserve for returns	**775**	439	692
Accrued liabilities	**(709)**	(4,982)	4,545
Accrued profit sharing	**(262)**	328	(1,320)
Income taxes payable	**1,923**	(2,810)	(3,834)
Tax benefit of stock options	**1,429**	1,765	349
Other	**2,144**	437	733
Net cash from (used for) operating activities	**39,367**	79,871	48,269
Cash flows from (used for) investing activities:			
Cash paid for capital additions	**(28,959)**	(18,208)	(30,388)
Net cash flows used for investing activities	**(28,959)**	(18,208)	(30,388)
Cash flows from (used for) financing activities:			
Proceeds from (payment of) short-term debt	**3,390**	(17,692)	4,228
Purchases of treasury stock	**(18,192)**	(2,935)	(23,112)
Issuance of treasury stock	**3,704**	4,317	1,199
Net cash flows used for financing activities	**(11,097)**	(16,310)	(17,685)
Net increase (decrease) in cash and cash equivalents	**(690)**	45,352	197
Beginning cash and cash equivalents	**49,668**	4,317	4,120
Ending cash and cash equivalents	**$ 48,978**	$ 49,668	$ 4,317
Supplemental cash flow disclosures:			
Interest paid	**$ 987**	$ 1,229	$ 5,000
Income taxes paid	**6,278**	13,701	18,107

EARTHWEAR CLOTHIERS

Consolidated Statements of Stockholders' Investment

(In thousands)

	Comprehensive Income	Common Stock	Donated Capital	Additional Paid-In Capital	Deferred Compensation	Accumulated Other Comprehensive Income	Retained Earnings	Treasury Stock	Total
Balance, December 31, 2006		$ 261	$ 5,460	$ 17,197	($ 681)	$ 569	$243,888	($108,931)	$ 157,763
Purchase of treasury stock								(23,112)	(23,112)
Issuance of treasury stock								1,199	1,199
Tax benefit of stock options exercised				349					349
Deferred compensation expense					424				424
Comprehensive income:									
Net income	$ 20,270						20,270		20,270
Foreign currency translation adjustments	733					733			733
Comprehensive income	$ 21,003								
Balance, December 31, 2007		$ 261	$ 5,460	$ 17,546	($ 257)	$ 1,302	$264,158	($130,844)	$ 157,626
Purchase of treasury stock								(2,935)	(2,935)
Issuance of treasury stock								4,317	4,317
Tax benefit of stock options exercised				1,765					1,765
Deferred compensation expense					103				103
Comprehensive income:									
Net income	$ 31,222						31,222		31,222
Foreign currency	60					60			60
translation adjustments	377					377			377
Comprehensive income	$ 31,659								
Balance, December 31, 2008		$ 261	$ 5,460	$ 19,311	($ 154)	$ 1,739	$295,380	($129,463)	$ 192,534
Purchase of treasury stock								(18,192)	(18,192)
Issuance of treasury stock								3,704	3,704
Tax benefit of stock options exercised				1,429					1,429
Deferred compensation expense					75				75
Comprehensive income:									
Net income	$ 22,527						22,527		22,527
Foreign currency translation adjustments	(1,151)					(1,151)			(1,151)
Unrealized gain on forward contracts	3,295					3,295			3,295
Comprehensive income	$ 24,671								
Balance, December 31, 2009		$ 261	$ 5,460	$ 20,740	($ 79)	$ 3,883	$ 317,907	($143,950)	$ 204,222

EARTHWEAR CLOTHIERS

Five-Year Consolidated Financial Summary (unaudited)
(In thousands, except per share data)

| | For the period ended December 31 | | | | |
	2009	2008	2007	2006	2005
Income statement data:					
Net Sales	**950,484**	857,885	891,394	821,359	503,434
Pretax Income	**35,757**	49,559	32,175	66,186	38,212
Percent of net sales	**3.8%**	5.8%	3.6%	8.1%	7.6%
Net income	**22,527**	31,222	20,270	41,698	22,929
Per share of common stock:					
Basic earnings per share	**1.15**	1.60	1.02	2.01	1.54
Diluted earnings per share	**1.14**	1.56	1.01	2.00	1.53
Common shares outstanding	**19,531**	19,555	19,806	20,703	14,599
Balance sheet data:					
Current assets	**209,095**	188,115	191,297	194,445	122,418
Current liabilities	**116,268**	98,067	133,434	118,308	65,505
PPE and intangibles	**120,863**	108,412	105,051	87,312	46,658
Total assets	**329,959**	296,527	296,347	281,757	170,121
Noncurrent liabilities	**9,469**	5,926	5,286	5,686	4,211
Shareholders' investment	**204,222**	192,535	157,627	157,763	100,405
Other data:					
Net working capital	**92,827**	90,048	57,863	76,136	56,913
Capital expenditures	**28,959**	18,208	30,388	31,348	8,316
Depreciation and amortization expense	**15,231**	13,465	12,175	9,833	6,101
Return on average shareholders' investment	**11%**	18%	13%	28%	24%
Return on average assets	**7%**	11%	7%	16%	15%

NET INCOME

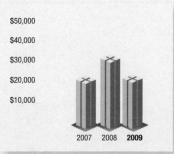

NET SALES

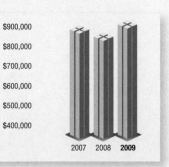

NET INCOME PER SHARE

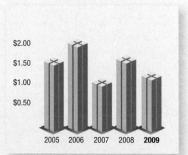

NOTE A: SUMMARY OF SIGNIFICANT ACCOUNTING POLICIES

NATURE OF BUSINESS EarthWear markets high quality clothing for outdoor sports, casual clothing, accessories, shoes, and soft luggage. The Company manages its business in three operating segments consisting of core, business-to-business, and international. The Company's primary market is the United States; other markets include Canada, Europe, and Japan.

PRINCIPLES OF CONSOLIDATION The consolidated statements include the accounts of the Company and its subsidiaries after elimination of intercompany accounts and transactions.

USE OF ESTIMATES The preparations of financial statements in conformity with generally accepted accounting principles requires management to make estimates and assumptions that affect the reported amounts of assets and liabilities and disclosure of contingent assets and liabilities at the date of the financial statements and the reported amounts of revenues and expenses during the reporting periods. Actual results may differ from these estimates.

REVENUE RECOGNITION The Company records revenue at the time of shipment for catalog and e-commerce sales and at the point of sale for stores. The Company provides a reserve for returns.

RESERVE FOR LOSSES ON CUSTOMER RETURNS At the time of sale, the Company provides a reserve equal to the gross profit on projected merchandise returns, based on prior returns experience.

INVENTORY Inventory is stated at the last-in, first-out (LIFO) cost, which is lower than market. If the first-in, first-out method of accounting for inventory had been used, inventory would have been approximately $10.8 million and $13.7 million higher than reported at December 31, 2009 and 2008, respectively.

ADVERTISING The Company expenses the costs of advertising for magazines, television, radio, and other media the first time the advertising takes place, except for direct-response advertising, which is capitalized and amortized over its expected period of future benefits. Direct-response advertising consists primarily of catalog production and mailing costs, which are generally amortized within three months from the date catalogs are mailed.

DEPRECIATION Depreciation expense is calculated using the straight-line method over the estimated useful lives of the assets, which are 20 to 30 years for buildings and land improvements and 5 to 10 years for leasehold improvements and furniture, fixtures, equipment, and software. The Company allocates one half year of depreciation to the year of addition or retirement.

INTANGIBLES Intangible assets consist primarily of goodwill, which is amortized over 15 years on a straight-line basis.

FINANCIAL INSTRUMENTS WITH OFF-BALANCE-SHEET RISK The Company uses import letters of credit to purchase foreign-sourced merchandise. The letters of credit are primarily U.S. dollar-denominated and are issued through third-party financial institutions to guarantee payment for such merchandise within the agreed-upon time periods. At December 31, 2009, the Company had outstanding letters of credit of approximately $23 million, all of which had expiration dates of less than one year.

FOREIGN CURRENCY TRANSLATIONS AND TRANSACTIONS Financial statements of the foreign subsidiaries are translated into U.S. dollars in accordance with Statement of Financial Accounting Standards No. 52. Translation adjustments are recorded in accumulated other comprehensive income, which is a component of stockholders' equity.

NOTE B: STOCKHOLDERS' EQUITY

COMMON STOCK The Company currently is authorized to issue 70 million shares of $0.01 par value common stock.

TREASURY STOCK The Company's board of directors has authorized the purchase of a total of 12.7 million shares of the Company's common stock. A total of 6.5 million and 6.7 million had been purchased as of December 31, 2009 and 2008, respectively.

STOCK AWARDS AND GRANTS The Company has a restricted stock award plan. Under the provisions of the plan, a committee of the Company's board may award shares of the Company's common stock to its officers and key employees. Such shares vest over a 10-year period on a straight-line basis.

The granting of these awards has been recorded as deferred compensation based on the fair market value of the shares at the date of the grant. Compensation expense under these plans is recorded as shares vest.

STOCK OPTIONS The Company has 3.5 million shares of common stock that may be issued pursuant to the exercise of options granted under the company's stock option plan. Options are granted at the discretion of a committee of the Company's board of directors to officers and key employees of the Company. No option may have an exercise price less than the fair market value per share of the common stock at the date of the grant.

NOTE C: LINES OF CREDIT

The Company has unsecured domestic lines of credit with various U.S. banks totaling $150 million. There were $23.4 million amounts outstanding at December 31, 2009 compared to $20.2 million outstanding at December 31, 2008. In addition, the company has unsecured lines of credit with foreign banks totaling the equivalent of $30 million for its wholly owned subsidiaries. At December 31, 2009, $11 million was outstanding at interest rates averaging 4.6 percent, compared with $7.6 million at December 31, 2008.

NOTE D: LONG-TERM DEBT

There was no long-term debt at December 31, 2009 and 2008.

NOTE E: LEASES

The Company leases store and office space and equipment under various lease arrangements. The leases are accounted for as operating leases.

NOTE F: RETIREMENT PLANS

The Company has a retirement plan that covers most regular employees and provides for annual contributions at the discretion of the board of directors. Included in the plan is a 401(k) feature that allows employees to make contributions.

MANAGEMENT'S DECISION AND ANALYSIS:

2009 was a year during which we've seen the results of our strategic initiatives of the last two years take hold. Sales momentum picked up toward the end of the third quarter and continued strongly through our all-important holiday season, and we reported a double-digit increase in both revenue and earnings for the fourth quarter. This success enabled us to complete the year with an annual 10.8 percent increase in total revenue, but a 27.8 percent decrease in earnings, mainly due to the weakness of the first nine months. Our strong finish for the year was gratifying in the face of a difficult economy.

MANAGEMENT'S DISCUSSION AND ANALYSIS: RESULTS OF OPERATIONS FOR 2009 COMPARED TO 2008

TOTAL REVENUE INCREASED BY 10.8 PERCENT

Total revenue for the year just ended was $950.5 million, compared with $857.9 million in the prior year, an increase of 10.8 percent. Seasonally strong sales resulted in a higher level of backorders during the fourth quarter and a first-time fulfillment rate of 85 percent for the year as a whole, slightly below the prior year's rate. Overall merchandise sales growth was primarily attributable to changes in circulation, which included adding back our post-Thanksgiving catalog and our January full-price catalog, shifting the timing of our fall/winter mailings, increasing page circulation and improving merchandise selection and creative presentations.

NET INCOME DECREASED Net income for 2009 was $22.5 million, down 27.8 percent from the $31.2 million earned in 2008. Diluted earnings per share for the year just ended were $1.14, compared with $1.56 per share for the prior year. The diluted weighted average number of common shares outstanding was 19.8 million for 2009 and 20.0 million for 2008.

GROSS PROFIT MARGIN Gross profit for the year just ended was $404 million, or 42.5 percent of total revenue, compared with $385 million, or 44.9 percent of total revenue, for the prior year. Liquidations were about 11 percent of net merchandise sales in 2009, compared with 12 percent in the prior year. In 2009, the cost of inventory purchases was down 2.0 percent, compared with deflation of 2.7 percent in 2008. This reduction was a result of improved sourcing. As a result, the LIFO inventory reserve was reduced by $2.8 million and $3.8 million in 2009 and 2008, respectively.

SELLING, GENERAL, AND ADMINISTRATIVE EXPENSES Selling, general, and administrative (SG&A) expenses increased 9.0 percent to $364 million in 2008, compared with $334 million in the prior year. As a percentage of sales, SG&A was 38.3 percent in 2009 and 38.9 percent in the prior year. The decrease in the SG&A ratio was primarily the result of lower catalog costs associated with increased page circulation, as well as lower information services expenses as we continued to invest in the Internet and upgrade systems capabilities. The cost of producing and mailing catalogs represented about 39 percent and 38 percent of total SG&A in 2009 and 2008, respectively.

CREDIT LINES AND CAPITAL EXPENDITURES Interest expense on lines of credit was down in 2009 due to lower average borrowing levels. Interest expense decreased to $1.0 million in 2009, compared to $1.2 million in 2008. We spent $29 million in cash on capital expenditures, which included $20 million for computer hardware and software. In addition, the company acquired a new airplane by exchanging two of its own aircraft in 2009. Also, we purchased about $18 million in treasury stock. No long-term debt was outstanding at year-end 2009. Depreciation and amortization expense was $15.2 million, up 13.1 percent from the prior year, mainly due to computer software. Rental expense was $10.4 million, up 3.4 percent from 2008, primarily due to additional computer

To the Stockholders

EarthWear Clothiers, Inc.

Management of EarthWear Clothiers, Inc. (the "Company") is responsible for the preparation, consistency, integrity, and fair presentation of the consolidated financial statements. The consolidated financial statements have been prepared in accordance with accounting principles generally accepted in the United States of America applied on a consistent basis and, in management's opinion, are fairly presented. The financial statements include amounts that are based on management's informed judgments and best estimates.

Management has established and maintains comprehensive systems of internal control that provide reasonable assurance as to the consistency, integrity, and reliability of the preparation and presentation of financial statements; the safeguarding of assets; the effectiveness and efficiency of operations; and compliance with applicable laws and regulations. The concept of reasonable assurance is based upon the recognition that the cost of the controls should not exceed the benefit derived. Management monitors the systems of internal control and maintains an independent internal auditing program that assesses the effectiveness of internal control. Management assessed the Company's internal control over financial reporting for financial presentations in conformity with accounting principles generally accepted in the United States of America. This assessment was based on criteria for effective internal control over financial reporting established in Internal Control—Integrated Framework issued by the Committee of Sponsoring Organizations of the Treadway Commission (the COSO report). Based on this assessment, management believes that the Company maintained effective internal control over financial reporting for financial presentations in conformity with accounting principles generally accepted in the United States of America as of December 31, 2009.

The Board of Directors exercises its oversight role with respect to the Company's systems of internal control primarily through its Audit Committee, which is comprised solely of outside directors. The Committee oversees the Company's systems of internal control and financial reporting to assess whether their quality, integrity, and objectivity are sufficient to protect shareholders' investments.

The Company's consolidated financial statements have been audited by Willis & Adams LLP ("Willis & Adams"), independent auditors. As part of its audit, Willis & Adams considers the Company's internal control to plan the audit and determine the nature, timing, and extent of auditing procedures considered necessary to render its opinion as to the fair presentation, in all material respects, of the consolidated financial statements, which is based on independent audits made accordance with the standards of the Public Company Accounting Oversight Board (United States). Management has made available to Willis & Adams all the Company's financial records and related data, and information concerning the Company's internal control over financial reporting, and believes that all representations made to Willis & Adams during its audits were valid and appropriate.

Calvin J. Rogers

President and Chief
Executive Officer

James C. Watts

Senior Vice President and
Chief Financial Officer

To the Stockholders

EarthWear Clothiers, Inc.

We have audited EarthWear Clothiers' internal control over financial reporting as of December 31, 2009, based on criteria established in Internal Control–Integrated Framework issued by the Committee of Sponsoring Organizations of the Treadway Commission (COSO). EarthWear Clothiers' management is responsible for maintaining effective internal control over financial reporting and for its assessment of the effectiveness of internal control over financial reporting, included in the accompanying Management Report on the Financial Statements and Internal Control. Our responsibility is to express an opinion on the effectiveness of the company's internal control over financial reporting based on our audit.

We conducted our audit in accordance with the standards of the Public Company Accounting Oversight Board (United States). Those standards require that we plan and perform the audit to obtain reasonable assurance about whether effective internal control over financial reporting was maintained in all material respects. Our audit of internal control over financial reporting included obtaining an understanding of internal control over financial reporting, assessing the risk that a material weakness exists, and testing and evaluating the design and operating effectiveness of internal control based on the assessed risk. Our audits also included performing such other procedures as we considered necessary in the circumstances. We believe that our audit provides a reasonable basis for our opinion.

A company's internal control over financial reporting is a process designed to provide reasonable assurance regarding the reliability of financial reporting and the preparation of financial statements for external purposes in accordance with generally accepted accounting principles. A company's internal control over financial reporting includes those policies and procedures that (1) pertain to the maintenance of records that, in reasonable detail, accurately and fairly reflect the transactions and dispositions of the assets of the company; (2) provide reasonable assurance that transactions are recorded as necessary to permit preparation of financial statements in accordance with generally accepted accounting principles, and that receipts and expenditures of the company are being made only in accordance with authorizations of management and directors of the company; and (3) provide reasonable assurance regarding prevention or timely detection of unauthorized acquisition, use, or disposition of the company's assets that could have a material effect on the financial statements.

Because of its inherent limitations, internal control over financial reporting may not prevent or detect misstatements. Also, projections of any evaluation of effectiveness to future periods are subject to the risk that controls may become inadequate because of changes in conditions, or that the degree of compliance with the policies or procedure may deteriorate.

In our opinion, EarthWear Clothiers maintained effective internal control over financial reporting as of December 31, 2009, in all material respects, based on criteria established in Internal Control–Integrated Framework issued by the Committee of Sponsoring Organizations of the Treadway Commission (COSO).

We have also audited, in accordance with the standards of the Public Company Accounting Oversight Board (United States), the consolidated financial of EarthWear Clothiers and our report dated February 15, 2010 expressed an unqualified opinion.

Willis & Adams

Willis & Adams, CPAs
Boise, Idaho
February 15, 2010

REPORT OF INDEPENDENT REGISTERED PUBLIC ACCOUNTING FIRM

To the Stockholders

EarthWear Clothiers, Inc.

We have audited the consolidated balance sheets of EarthWear Clothiers as of December 31, 2009 and 2008, and the related consolidated statements of operations, stockholders' equity, and cash flows for each of the three years in the period ended December 31, 2009. These financial statements are the responsibility of the Company's management. Our responsibility is to express an opinion on these financial statements based on our audits.

We conducted our audits in accordance with the standards of the Public Company Accounting Oversight Board (United States). Those standards require that we plan and perform the audit to obtain reasonable assurance about whether the financial statements are free of material misstatement. An audit includes examining, on a test basis, evidence supporting the amounts and disclosures in the financial statements. An audit also includes assessing the accounting principles used and significant estimates made by management, as well as evaluating the overall financial statement presentation. We believe that our audits provide a reasonable basis for our opinion.

In our opinion, the consolidated financial statements referred to above present fairly, in all material respects, the financial position of the Company as of December 31, 2009 and 2008, and the results of its operations and its cash flows for each of the three years in the period ended December 31, 2009, in conformity with U.S. generally accepted accounting principles.

We also have audited, in accordance with the standards of the Public Company Accounting Oversight Board (United States), the effectiveness of EarthWear Clothiers' internal control over financial reporting as of December 31, 2009, based on criteria established in Internal Control—Integrated Framework issued by the Committee of Sponsoring Organizations of the Treadway Commission (COSO) and our report dated February 15, 2010 expressed an unqualified opinion. EarthWear Clothiers maintained, in all material respects, effective internal control over financial reporting.

Willis & Adams

Willis & Adams, CPAs

Boise, Idaho
February 15, 2010

Shortly after the Enron scandal, numerous other scandals involving corporate giants (e.g., Tyco, WorldCom, Xerox, Adelphia, and Ahold), brokerage firms (e.g., Merrill Lynch), stock exchanges (e.g., the New York Stock Exchange), mutual fund managers (e.g., Piper Jaffray), and several of the large public accounting firms were uncovered. The Enron scandal alone weakened investor confidence in the stock market, but the subsequent series of scandals caused a crisis of confidence in the integrity of the entire system of public ownership and accountability in the United States.

Government Regulation

Under pressure to restore public confidence, Congress passed the *Sarbanes-Oxley Public Company Accounting Reform and Investor Protection Act* in July 2002. Similar to the impact of the Securities Acts of 1933 and 1934, the Sarbanes-Oxley Act (commonly known as SOX or Sarbox) started a process of broad reform in corporate governance practices that would affect the duties and practices of public companies, financial analysts, external auditors, and securities exchange markets.[1]

With respect to the accounting profession, the Sarbanes-Oxley Act effectively transferred authority to set and enforce auditing standards for public company audits to the Public Company Accounting Oversight Board (discussed in more detail below). In addition, the Act mandated that the SEC impose strict independence rules, prohibiting the provision of many types of nonaudit services to public company audit clients (see Chapter 19). The Act imposed several other important mandates, including that audit firms rotate audit partners off audit engagements every five years, and that public companies obtain an *integrated audit* (including audits of both financial statements and internal control over financial reporting). The Act is extremely important in its implications for boards and managements of public companies, for the accounting profession, and for the capital markets system in the United States. Chapter 20 provides further discussion of the Sarbanes-Oxley Act.

Back to Basics

It would be difficult to overemphasize the impact of the events of the late 1990s and early 2000s, culminating in the Sarbanes-Oxley Act of 2002 and the formation of the PCAOB. The public accounting profession has been through a revolutionary shift from self-regulation toward government regulation and oversight. Most of the large firms, prohibited from providing many nonaudit services for public company audit clients, sold their consulting divisions and began to refocus their efforts and attention once again on their core services: the financial statement audit and the newly required audit of internal control over financial reporting. While these changes caused pain and turmoil, they served to highlight

---

[1]See William R. Kinney, Jr., "Twenty-Five Years of Audit Deregulation and Re-Regulation: What Does it Mean for 2005 and Beyond?" *Auditing: A Journal of Practice & Theory*, vol. 24, supplement, 2005, for an excellent discussion of the developments that gave rise to government regulation over the auditing profession.

and reaffirm the essential importance of auditing in our economic system and the accounting profession was powerfully reminded of the importance of integrity and professionalism in protecting the public interest.

The Context of Financial Statement Auditing

❧ [LO 2]   The first chapter explained why assurance is in demand, defined what auditing is, and laid out the phases through which financial statement auditing is carried out. This chapter is designed to help you understand the forces of change in the auditing profession as well as the overall business and regulatory environment in which auditing takes place.

Business as the Primary Context of Auditing

In studying subsequent chapters, you will be building your auditing tool kit. How you apply auditing tools on any particular engagement will depend greatly on the nature of the client's business. For example, if you are auditing a computer hardware manufacturer, one of your concerns will be whether your client has inventories that are not selling quickly and are becoming obsolete due to industry innovation. Such inventory might not be properly valued on the client's financial records. If you are auditing a jeweler you will probably not be as worried about obsolescence, but you will still be interested in whether the diamonds and other gems in inventory are valued properly. You may need to hire a qualified gemologist to help you assess the valuation assertion, and you would certainly want to keep up on the dynamics of the international diamond and gem markets. The point is that the context provided by the client's business greatly impacts the auditor and the audit, and is thus a primary component of the environment in which financial statement auditing is conducted. While every business is different, business organizations can be conceptualized or modeled in common ways. The next section describes the essential characteristics of a business: governance, objectives, strategies, processes, risks, controls, and reporting.

Practice
INSIGHT

The nature of a client's business can have a dramatic effect on the nature of the auditor's work and work environment. For example, an auditor working at a meat-packing client will have very different experiences from an auditor working at a banking client. Further, many auditors eventually specialize in certain industries and acquire significant expertise in those industries. This expertise and specialization often leads to attractive employment opportunities as a member of management. Thus, in choosing which firm (or which office of a large firm) at which to seek a job, new auditors are well advised to carefully consider whether the firm (or office) has a significant presence in the industries in which the prospective auditor is most interested.

A Model of Business

❧ [LO 3]   Business organizations exist to create value for their stakeholders. To form a business enterprise, entrepreneurs decide on an appropriate organizational form (e.g., corporation or partnership) and hire managers to manage the resources that have been made available to the enterprise through investment or lending.

Corporate Governance

Due to the way resources are invested and managed in the modern business world, a system of *corporate governance* is necessary, through which managers are overseen and supervised. Simply defined, corporate governance consists of all the people, processes, and activities in place to help ensure proper stewardship over an entity's assets. Good corporate governance ensures that those managing an entity properly utilize their time, talents, and the entity's resources in the best interest of absentee owners, and that they faithfully report the economic condition and performance of the enterprise. The body primarily responsible for management oversight in U.S. corporations is the *board of directors*. The *audit committee*, consisting of members of the board, oversees the internal and external auditing work done for the organization. Through this link, and through the audit of financial statements, auditors play an important role in facilitating effective corporate governance.

Objectives, Strategies, Processes, Controls, Transactions, and Reports

Management, with guidance and direction from the board of directors, decides on a set of *objectives*, along with *strategies* designed to achieve those objectives. The organization then undertakes certain *processes* in order to implement its strategies. The organization must also assess and manage risks that may threaten the achievement of its objectives. While the processes implemented in business organizations are as varied as the different types of businesses themselves, most business enterprises establish processes that fit in five broad *process categories*, sometimes known as *cycles*. The five categories that characterize the processes of most businesses are the *revenue process*, the *purchasing process*, the *human resource management process*, the *inventory management process*, and the *financing process*. Each process involves a variety of important transactions.

The enterprise must design and implement *accounting information systems* to capture the details of those transactions. It must also design and implement a *system of internal control* to ensure that the transactions are handled and recorded appropriately and that its resources are protected. The accounting information system must be capable of producing financial reports, which summarize the effects of the organization's transactions on its account balances and which are used to establish management accountability to outside owners. The next section provides a brief overview of the five process categories listed above. Auditors often rely on this process model to divide the audit of a business's financial statements into manageable pieces. Chapters 10 through 16 go into considerable detail regarding how these processes typically function and how they are used to organize an audit.

Practice
INSIGHT

It has been said that no man can serve two masters. In some respects, this saying reflects the delicate balance that the external auditor must achieve—serving the client, while protecting the public. Prior to 2002, the external auditor often was engaged by and reported directly to the client's senior management, which was also responsible for the financial statements being audited. Section 301 of the Sarbanes-Oxley Act of 2002 mandates that the client's *audit committee* be directly responsible for the appointment, compensation, and oversight of the work of the auditor. In addition, the auditor now reports directly to the audit committee. Further, Section 303 makes it unlawful for an officer or director to take any action to fraudulently influence, coerce, or manipulate the work or conclusions of the auditor.

A Model of Business Processes: Five Components

[LO 4]   Figure 2–1 illustrates the five basic business processes into which auditors typically organize a financial statement audit in context with the overall business model presented in the previous section. Let's briefly discuss each of the five processes.

| FIGURE 2–1 | An Overview of Business |

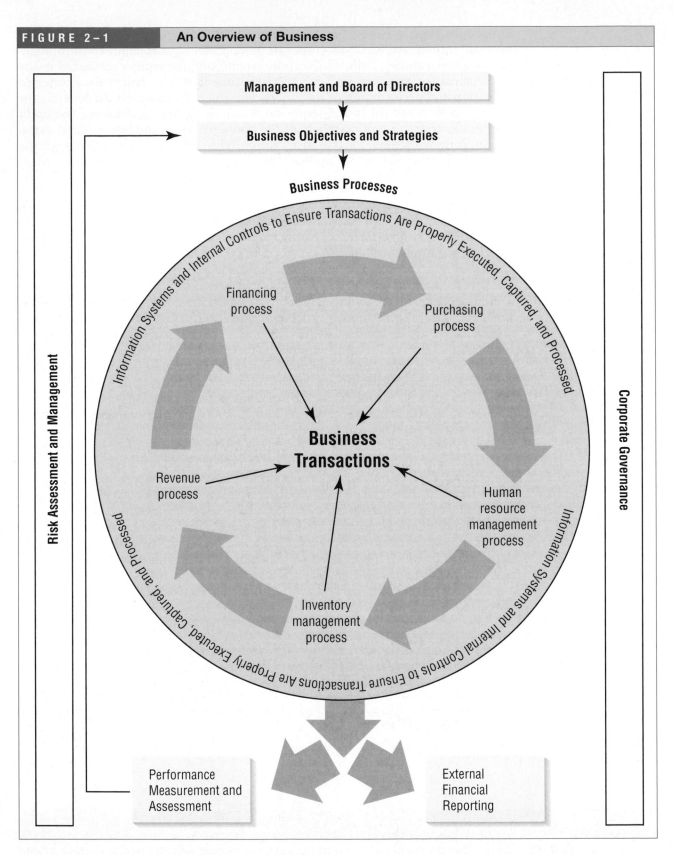

The Financing Process

Businesses obtain capital through borrowing or soliciting investments from owners and typically invest in assets such as land, buildings, and equipment in accordance with their strategies. As part of this process, businesses also need to repay lenders and provide a return on owner investments. These types of transactions are all part of the financing process. For example, EarthWear tends not to rely on long-term debt financing. Instead, it primarily uses capital provided by shareholders to invest in long-term assets, such as its headquarters building, retail stores, and various order and distribution centers across the United States and in Japan, Germany, and the United Kingdom.

The Purchasing Process

Businesses must acquire goods and services to support the sale of their own goods or services. For example, EarthWear must purchase inventory to sell to its customers. The company must also purchase office supplies, needed services, and many other items to support its activities.

The Human Resource Management Process

Business organizations hire personnel to perform various functions in accordance with the enterprise's mission and strategy. At EarthWear this process starts with the establishment of sound policies for hiring, training, evaluating, counseling, promoting, compensating, and terminating employees. The main transaction in this process that affects the financial statement accounts is a payroll transaction, which usually begins with an employee performing a job and ends with payment being made to the employee.

The Inventory Management Process

This process varies widely between different types of businesses. Service providers (such as auditors, lawyers, or advertising agencies) rarely have significant inventories to manage, since their primary resources typically consist of information, knowledge, and the time and effort of people. Manufacturers, wholesalers, and retailers, including EarthWear, all typically have significant, numerous, and often complex transactions belonging to the inventory management process. While the actual purchasing of finished goods or raw materials inventories is included in the purchasing process (see above), the inventory management process for a manufacturer includes the cost accounting transactions to accumulate and allocate costs to inventory.

The Revenue Process

Businesses generate revenue through sales of goods or services to customers, and collect the proceeds of those sales in cash, either immediately or through collections on receivables. For example, EarthWear Inc. retails high-quality clothing for outdoor activities. To create value for its customers, employees, and owners, EarthWear must successfully process orders for, and deliver its clothing to, customers. It must also collect cash on those sales, either at the point of sale or through later billing and collection of receivables. Management establishes controls to ensure that sales and collection transactions are appropriately handled and recorded.

Relating the Process Components to the Business Model

Pause for a moment and take another look at Figure 2-1. How might the components of our model differ for a client in automobile manufacturing versus banking, and how might those differences affect the auditor's work? How might differences in these components affect the risk of material misstatement in the financial statements? Management establishes processes in the five categories discussed above to implement the organization's strategies and achieve its objectives. Management then identifies risks, or possible threats to the achievement of established objectives (including compliance with applicable laws and regulations and reliable external reporting), and ensures that the organization's system of internal control mitigates those risks to acceptable levels. The organization's accounting information system must be capable of reliably measuring the performance of the business to assess whether objectives are being met and to comply with external reporting requirements. Financial statements, which are affected by all the different components of our business model, represent an important output of the entity's efforts to measure the organization's performance and an important form of external reporting and accountability.

Management Assertions

> **[LO 5]**   In Chapter 1, we introduced the concept that the financial statements issued by management contain both explicit and implicit assertions. Table 2–1 summarizes and explains management assertions. Take a few minutes to examine and understand these assertions—you will see over the next several chapters that this simple conceptual tool is actually quite powerful and underlies much of what auditors do.

The presentation of management assertions in Table 2–1 is consistent with international auditing standards and the "risk assessment suite" of standards issued by the AICPA Auditing Standards Board in early 2006. Though it is also conceptually consistent with the more basic list of five assertions sometimes used, this presentation explicitly recognizes that auditors evaluate management assertions as they are applied to three aspects of information reflected in the financial statements: transactions, account balances, and presentation and disclosure. For example, management asserts, among other things, that transactions relating to inventory actually *occurred*, that they are *complete* (i.e., no valid transactions were left out), that they are *classified* properly (e.g., as an asset rather than an expense), and that they are recorded *accurately* and in the correct period. Similarly, management asserts that the inventory represented

---

TABLE 2–1	**Summary of Management Assertions by Category**

Assertions about classes of transactions and events for the period under audit:
- **Occurrence**—transactions and events that have been recorded have occurred and pertain to the entity.
- **Completeness**—all transactions and events that should have been recorded have been recorded.
- **Authorization**—all transactions and events have been properly authorized.*
- **Accuracy**—amounts and other data relating to recorded transactions and events have been recorded appropriately.
- **Cutoff**—transactions and events have been recorded in the correct accounting period.
- **Classification**—transactions and events have been recorded in the proper accounts.

Assertions about account balances at the period end:
- **Existence**—assets, liabilities, and equity interests exist.
- **Rights and obligations**—the entity holds or controls the rights to assets, and liabilities are the obligations of the entity.
- **Completeness**—all assets, liabilities, and equity interests that should have been recorded have been recorded.
- **Valuation and allocation**—assets, liabilities, and equity interests are included in the financial statements at appropriate amounts and any resulting valuation or allocation adjustments are appropriately recorded.

Assertions about presentation and disclosure:
- **Occurrence and rights and obligations**—disclosed events, transactions, and other matters have occurred and pertain to the entity.
- **Completeness**—all disclosures that should have been included in the financial statements have been included.
- **Classification and understandability**—financial information is appropriately presented and described, and disclosures are clearly expressed.
- **Accuracy and valuation**—financial and other information are disclosed fairly and at appropriate amounts.

*International and AICPA auditing standards consider Authorization to be a subset of the Occurrence assertion and thus do not list it separately. We list Authorization as a separate assertion about classes of transactions and events for instructional clarity.

in the inventory account balance *exists,* that the entity *owns* the inventory, that the balance is *complete,* and that the inventory is properly *valued*. Finally, management asserts that the financial statements properly *classify* and *present* the inventory (e.g., inventory is appropriately listed as a current asset on the balance sheet) and that all required *disclosures* having to do with inventory (e.g., a footnote indicating that the company uses the FIFO inventory method) are *complete, accurate,* and *understandable*. Understanding the assertions in terms of transactions, account balances, and presentation and disclosure is helpful because the three categories help the auditor focus on the different types of audit procedures needed to test the assertions in the three different categories. Chapter 5 discusses the types of procedures available to the auditor in more detail.

Although all balance-related assertions apply to nearly every account, not every assertion is equally important for each account. Recognizing the assertions that deserve the most emphasis depends on an understanding of the business and of the particular type of account being audited. For example, auditors typically consider the completeness assertion to be the most important assertion for liability accounts for two reasons. First, when all obligations are not properly included in the liability account, the result is an understatement of liabilities and often an overstatement of net income. Second, management is more likely to have an incentive to understate a liability than to overstate it.

Pause and test your intuition: Why might auditors consider existence to be a crucial assertion for Accounts Receivable? Why would they normally consider existence to be more important than completeness for receivables?

Auditing Standards

✄ [LO 6,7]   *Auditing standards* serve as a guideline for and a measure of the quality of the auditor's performance. Auditing standards help ensure that financial statement audits are conducted in a thorough and systematic way that produces reliable conclusions.

The Roles of the ASB and the PCAOB

Until 2003, the Auditing Standards Board (ASB) was responsible for establishing auditing standards in the U.S. The ASB is sponsored by the American Institute of CPAs (AICPA), a private, nongovernmental professional association. However, when the U.S. Congress passed the Sarbanes-Oxley Act of 2002, it gave the Public Accounting Oversight Board (PCAOB) the authority to either set auditing standards for public company audits itself or to delegate that role to another party. The PCAOB chose to take on the standard-setting role in-house. The PCAOB is a quasi-governmental organization overseen by the Securities and Exchange Commission (SEC). The AICPA, the SEC, and the PCAOB are described in more detail below.

Public accounting firms that audit the financial statements of *public* companies are required to follow the auditing and related professional practice standards established by the PCAOB. Firms that audit the financial statements of *nonpublic* entities are required to comply with the auditing standards established by the AICPA's Auditing Standards Board.

As of the writing of this text, with the exception of the PCAOB requirement for an integrated audit of internal control and financial statements (see Chapter 7) and various improvements to the ASB's standards that are not yet reflected in PCAOB standards, the standards of the ASB and the PCAOB are still quite similar. This is because the PCAOB adopted the ASB's auditing standards that existed as of April 2003. Because the PCAOB's auditing standards are currently quite similar to those of the ASB, we describe auditing standards in terms of those promulgated by the ASB, while noting throughout the text where PCAOB standards differ in important ways (e.g., see Chapter 7). You can see the latest standards established by the PCAOB on its Web site (www.pcaob.org).

The 10 Generally Accepted Auditing Standards

The ASB first issued what are known as the 10 generally accepted auditing standards (GAAS) in 1947 and has periodically modified them to meet changes in the auditor's environment. The PCAOB adopted these standards and refers to them, together with its own standards, as "the standards of the PCAOB." The generally accepted auditing standards are composed of three categories of standards: general standards (three), standards of field work (three), and standards of reporting (four). Table 2–2 contains the 10 generally accepted auditing standards. The ASB recently modified the wording of the 10 GAAS but their substance was left essentially unchanged. Table 2–2 reflects the modified wording. As of the writing of this text, the ASB is working to overhaul and restructure the 10 GAAS under the label, "Principles Governing an Audit."

Three General Standards

The three general standards deal with the auditor's qualifications and the quality of his or her work. These standards will remind you of the characteristics of a reliable house inspector listed in Chapter 1. The first general standard recognizes that an auditor must have adequate training and proficiency. This is gained through formal education, continuing education programs, and experience. It should be recognized that this training is ongoing, with a requirement on the part of the auditor to stay up-to-date with current accounting and auditing pronouncements. Auditors should also stay current with developments in the business world that may affect their clients.

The second general standard requires that the auditor maintain an attitude of independence on an engagement. Independence precludes relationships that may impair the auditor's objectivity. A distinction is often made between *independence in fact* and *independence in appearance*. An auditor must not only be independent in fact (i.e., actually be objective) but also avoid actions or relationships that may *appear* to affect independence. If an auditor is perceived as lacking independence,

TABLE 2–2	Generally Accepted Auditing Standards

General Standards:
1. The auditor must have adequate technical training and proficiency to perform the audit.
2. The auditor must maintain independence in mental attitude in all matters relating to the audit.
3. The auditor must exercise due professional care in the performance of the audit and the preparation of the report.

Standards of Field Work:
1. The auditor must adequately plan the work and must properly supervise any assistants.
2. The auditor must obtain a sufficient understanding of the entity and its environment, including its internal control, to assess the risk of material misstatement of the financial statements whether due to error or fraud, and to design the nature, timing, and extent of further audit procedures.
3. The auditor must obtain sufficient appropriate audit evidence by performing audit procedures to afford a reasonable basis for an opinion regarding the financial statements under audit.

Standards of Reporting:
1. The auditor must state in the auditor's report whether the financial statements are presented in accordance with generally accepted accounting principles (GAAP).
2. The auditor must identify in the auditor's report those circumstances in which such principles have not been consistently observed in the current period in relation to the preceding period.
3. When the auditor determines that informative disclosures are not reasonably adequate, the auditor must so state in the auditor's report.
4. The auditor must either express an opinion regarding the financial statements, taken as a whole, or state that an opinion cannot be expressed, in the auditor's report. When the auditor cannot express an overall opinion, the auditor should state the reasons therefor in the auditor's report. In all cases where an auditor's name is associated with financial statements, the auditor should clearly indicate the character of the auditor's work, if any, and the degree of responsibility the auditor is taking, in the auditor's report.

users may lose confidence in the auditor's ability to report truthfully on financial statements. For example, an auditor might borrow a large sum of money from an audit client's CEO but still conduct the audit in an objective manner (i.e., be independent in fact). Third parties, however, cannot observe whether or not the auditor is acting objectively, and may question whether the auditor is really independent due to her or his financial relationship with the CEO. Thus, such financial relationships are strictly prohibited. The AICPA's Code of Professional Conduct and the SEC's independence regulations identify a number of relationships (such as having business interests in clients or providing certain types of consulting services) that are believed to impair the auditor's appearance of independence and that are thus prohibited.

Due professional care is the focus of the third general standard. In simple terms, due care means that the auditor plans and performs his or her duties with the skill and care that is commonly expected of accounting professionals.

Three Standards of Field Work

The standards of field work relate to the actual conduct of the audit. These three standards provide the conceptual background for the audit process (and will remind you of some of the desirable characteristics of a house inspection service). The first standard of field work deals with planning and supervision. Proper planning leads to a more effective audit that is more likely to detect a material misstatement and facilitates completing the engagement in a reasonable amount of time. This standard also requires that assistants on the engagement be properly supervised.

The second standard of field work requires that the auditor gain a sufficient understanding of the entity and its environment, including its internal control, to assess the risk of material misstatement of the financial statements, whether due to error or fraud, and to effectively plan the nature, timing, and extent of further audit procedures. The degree to which the auditor relies on the auditee's internal control directly affects the nature, timing, and extent of the work performed by the independent auditor. In this context, nature refers to what procedures are performed, timing refers to when the audit work is done (whether at interim or at period-end), and extent refers to how much work is done. In addition, if the auditor can identify areas of weakness in a client's internal control, this information can help the auditor focus on areas where misstatements may be more likely to occur.

Sufficient, appropriate evidence is the focus of the third field work standard. Most of the auditor's work involves the search for and of evidence regarding management's assertions in the financial statements. The auditor uses various audit procedures to gather this evidence. For example, if the balance sheet shows an amount for accounts receivable of $1.5 million, management asserts that this amount reflects valid claims from customers (existence). The auditor can send confirmations to customers and examine subsequent customer payments to gather sufficient appropriate evidence on whether the claimed amount of receivables exists as of the balance sheet date. You should be aware that auditing standards typically give general guidance; the point at which the evidence for a particular management assertion is sufficient and appropriate is generally a matter of professional judgment.

Four Standards of Reporting

The four standards of reporting require that the auditor consider each of the following issues before rendering an audit report: (1) whether the financial statements are presented in accordance with accepted accounting principles; (2) whether those principles are consistently applied; (3) whether all informative disclosures have been made; and (4) what degree of responsibility the auditor is taking, as well as the character of the auditor's work. An overview of the nature of the auditor's report was given in Chapter 1, and further detail is offered in Chapter 18.

Statements on Auditing Standards—Interpretations of GAAS

✄ [LO 8,9] Statements on Auditing Standards (SAS) are issued by the Auditing Standards Board and can be viewed as interpretations of GAAS. The GAAS and the SAS are considered to be *minimum standards* of performance for auditors. (The term "GAAS" generally refers to the 10 GAAS *and* the SAS.) As with the 10 GAAS, the PCAOB adopted the ASB's Statements on Auditing Standards as constituted as of April 2003. Standards issued by the PCAOB are simply called "Auditing Standards" (AS). The AS issued by the PCAOB will add to or modify the existing body of standards adopted by the PCAOB. We provide additional information on the PCAOB below and in Chapter 20.

Unlike financial accounting pronouncements, which usually provide very specific rules, the ASB's *Statements on Auditing Standards* and the PCAOB's *Auditing Standards* tend to be more general in nature. The auditor must apply due diligence and sound professional judgment given the particular circumstances of the engagement in conducting an audit. Keep in mind that the auditor *never* has sufficient evidence to "guarantee" that the financial statements do not contain material misstatements and must use judgment to determine when he or she has sufficient appropriate evidence to reach a justified conclusion.

ASB and PCAOB auditing standards include requirements that convey varying levels of auditor responsibility. The words "must," "shall," and "is required" indicate unconditional responsibilities with which the auditor must comply. The word "should" indicates a responsibility to comply unless the auditor decides on alternative actions that are sufficient to achieve the objectives of the requirement. Finally, the words "may," "might," and "could" describe actions and procedures that auditors have a responsibility to consider.

SAS are classified by two numbering categories: SAS and AU numbers ("AU" for Auditing Standards). The SAS numbering applies to the order in which the standards are issued by the ASB and are thus chronological. The SAS, many of which contain material that is relevant to more than one of the 10 GAAS, are then reorganized or "codified" by topical content, closely following the structure of the 10 GAAS. The summary below shows how the SAS are reorganized into the AU codification with the numbers in parentheses representing the AU sections:

Introduction (100s)

The General Standards (200s)

The Standards of Field Work (300s)

The First, Second, and Third Standards of Reporting (400s)

The Fourth Standard of Reporting (500s)

Other Types of Reports (600s)

Special Topics (700s)

Compliance Auditing (800s)

Special Reports of the Committee on Auditing Procedures (900s)

For example, SAS No. 39, "Audit Sampling," is found under AU 350 because the AU 300s relate to the standards of field work, which involves evidence collection and evaluation. Similarly, SAS No. 58, "Reports on Audited Financial Statements," is found in AU 508 because SAS No. 58 relates to the fourth standard of reporting. While both are commonly cited, the AU codification is used more frequently because some SAS affect several AU sections. For example, SAS No. 98, "Omnibus Statement on Auditing Standards," was reorganized into over nine AU sections. The PCAOB's AS are currently classified only by the order in which the standards are issued (i.e., AS No. 1, AS No. 2, etc.). While the PCAOB currently references AU sections in its public communications, it is not yet clear how the Board will organize the topics addressed in its various Auditing Standards as they are issued.

A major complication for auditors in the future will be the development of two different sets of auditing standards as the PCAOB standards diverge from those it adopted from the ASB and as the ASB improves and develops its own standards. It is possible that there will eventually be very different sets of standards for public company audits and for nonpublic entity audits, which we believe would greatly and unnecessarily complicate the auditing standards environment. The emergence of *International Auditing Standards,* to which the ASB is attempting to converge its standards, further complicates the environment for large public accounting firms that practice internationally.[2]

Ethics, Independence, and the Code of Professional Conduct

[LO 10] As indicated by the second general standard, ethical behavior and independence on the part of the auditor are vital to the audit function. The demand for auditing arose from the need for a competent, independent person to monitor the contractual arrangements between principal and agent. If an auditor is incompetent or lacks independence, the parties to the contract will place little or no value on the service provided.

Ethics refers to a system or code of conduct based on moral duties and obligations that indicate how we should behave. *Professionalism* refers to the conduct, aims, or qualities that characterize or mark a profession or professional person.[3] All professions (e.g., medicine, law, and accounting) operate under some type of code of ethics or code of conduct. The 10 GAAS and the AICPA's Code of Professional Conduct establish guidance for acceptable behavior for auditors. The Code of Professional Conduct contains principles, rules of conduct, and interpretations of the rules that clarify the intent of the 10 GAAS. A major portion of the Code identifies actions that may impair auditors' independence.

The AICPA's Code of Professional Conduct applies to all auditors, including those auditing public companies. Why? Because the SEC requires that the auditor signing an audit report for a public company be a CPA, and the courts have consistently held CPAs to the standards of conduct established by the Code. Further, the Code of Professional Conduct has been adopted into the laws of many of the individual states and was also adopted by the PCAOB in 2003. Thus, the Code is an important element of the environment in which auditors work.

Auditors are frequently faced with situations that may test their professionalism, ethical character, and independence. For example, auditors' independence is tested when clients engage in *opinion shopping*—that is, when clients seek the views of other CPAs, hoping to find an auditor who will agree with the client's desired accounting treatment. Chapter 19 contains an in-depth discussion of professional ethics and the Code of Professional Conduct.

---

[2]See S. Glover, D. Prawitt, and M. Taylor, "Audit Standard Setting and Inspection for U.S. Public Companies: A Critical Assessment and Recommendations for Fundamental Change," *Accounting Horizons*, vol. 23, no. 2, 2009.

[3]S. Mintz, *Cases in Accounting Ethics and Professionalism,* 3rd ed. (New York: McGraw-Hill, 1997).

Society's Expectations and the Auditor's Responsibilities

[LO 11]   Financial statement audits play an important role in the functioning of our economy, and thus our society expects auditors to exercise due care in their work. Due professional care requires that the auditor exercise *professional skepticism,* which is an attitude that includes a questioning mind and a critical assessment of audit evidence. If the auditor fails to exercise due professional care, he or she can be held liable for civil damages and even criminal penalties.

Many readers of financial statements believe that auditors are ultimately responsible for the financial statements or at least that they have a responsibility to detect *all* errors, fraud, and illegal acts. This is simply not true. While auditors must exercise due care in their work, the financial statements ultimately are the responsibility of management (note that the assertions are called *management assertions*). In fact, the Sarbanes-Oxley Act of 2002 requires that CEOs and CFOs of public companies take explicit responsibility for their company's financial statements by "certifying," among other things, that they are responsible for establishing and maintaining internal control, and that the financial statements fairly present the entity's financial conditions and operations. It is important to remember that while auditors have important responsibilities, *management* is primarily responsible for the fairness of the company's financial statements.

Auditing standards (AU 110.02) provide the following responsibility for auditors:

> The auditor has a responsibility to plan and perform the audit to obtain reasonable assurance about whether the financial statements are free of material misstatement, whether caused by error or fraud. Because of the nature of audit evidence and the characteristics of fraud, the auditor is able to obtain reasonable, but not absolute, assurance that material misstatements are detected. The auditor has no responsibility to plan and perform the audit to obtain reasonable assurance that misstatements, whether caused by errors or fraud, that are *not material* to the financial statements will be detected.

The auditor's responsibility to provide reasonable assurance with respect to errors, fraud, and illegal acts clearly shapes the auditor's environment. More information on the auditor's responsibility for errors, fraud, and illegal acts is contained in Chapters 3 and 5, and details on auditors' potential legal liability are provided in Chapter 20.

Public Accounting Firms

[LO 12]   Small organizations can be audited by a single auditor, operating as the sole owner of a public accounting firm. However, auditing larger businesses and other organizations requires significantly more resources than a single auditor can provide. Thus, public accounting firms range in size from a single proprietor to thousands of owners (or "partners") together with tens of thousands of professional and administrative staff employees. Public accounting firms typically offer a variety of professional services in addition to financial statement audits.

Organization and Composition

Public accounting firms are organized as proprietorships, general or limited liability partnerships, or corporations. Typically, local public accounting firms are organized as proprietorships, general partnerships, or corporations. Regional, national, and international accounting firms are normally structured as general or limited liability partnerships. Structuring public accounting firms as proprietorships and ordinary general partnerships does not provide limited liability for the owners or partners. In such cases, aggrieved parties can seek recourse not only against the CPA firm's assets but also against the personal assets of individual partners.

Because of the risk of litigation against CPAs, public accounting firms organize as corporations when possible. However, corporations are created and governed by individual states, and some states do not allow accounting firms to organize as corporations. Thus, because they span state boundaries, it is generally not possible for larger firms to structure themselves as corporations. However, the national and international firms have restructured themselves as limited liability partnerships (LLPs). An LLP is generally governed by the laws applicable to general partnerships. However, this organizational structure provides greater personal protection against lawsuits. Under an LLP, partners are not *personally* responsible for firm liabilities arising from *other* partners' and most employees' negligent acts.[4] However, the personal assets of the *responsible* partner(s) and the assets of the partnership itself are vulnerable to lawsuits resulting from partners' or employees' acts.

Public accounting firms are often categorized by size. For example, the largest firms are the "Big 4" public accounting firms: Deloitte, Ernst & Young, KPMG, and PricewaterhouseCoopers. These large international organizations have annual global revenues ranging from about $23 billion to over $28 billion. U.S. revenues for these firms range from over $6 billion to $11 billion. As a group, the Big 4 audit about 80 percent of all publicly traded companies in the United States and about 98 percent of public companies with annual sales greater than $1 million.[5]

Following the Big 4 in size are several national firms with international affiliations. These "mid-tier" firms include such firms as Grant Thornton, RSM McGladrey, and BDO Seidman. The annual U.S. revenues for these firms are in the range of about $650 million to $1.4 billion. Last, there are thousands of regional and local CPA firms that have one or a few offices. These CPA firms provide audit, tax, accounting, and other services, generally to smaller entities.

Audits are usually conducted by teams of auditors. The typical audit team is composed of, in order of authority, a partner, a manager, one or two seniors, and several staff members. Audit teams for large international entities are typically made up of several partners and managers and many seniors and staff. The lead engagement partner has the authority and decision-making responsibility for auditing matters, including the issuance of the audit report. Table 2–3 summarizes the duties performed by each member of the audit team.

---

[4]G. Simonetti, Jr. and A. R. Andrews, "Limiting Accountants' Personal Liability Won't Solve the Country's Liability Crisis!" *Journal of Accountancy* (April 1994), pp. 46–54, for an excellent discussion of organizational reform of CPA firm structure.

[5]U.S. Government Accountability Office Report to Congressional Addressees, "Continued Concentration in Audit Market for Large Public Companies Does Not Call for Immediate Action," January 2008.

TABLE 2-3	Selected Duties of Audit Team Members

Audit Team Member	Selected Duties
Partner	• Reaching agreement with the client on the scope of the service to be provided. • Ensuring that the audit is properly planned. • Ensuring that the audit team has the required skills and experience. • Supervising the audit team and reviewing the working papers. • Signing the audit report.
Manager	• Ensuring that the audit is properly planned, including scheduling of team members. • Supervising the preparation of and approving the audit program. • Reviewing the working papers, financial statements, and audit report. • Dealing with invoicing and ensuring collection of payment for services. • Informing the partner about any auditing or accounting problems encountered.
Senior/In-charge	• Assisting in the development of the audit plan. • Preparing budgets. • Assigning audit tasks to associates and directing the day-to-day performance of the audit. • Supervising and reviewing the work of associates. • Informing the manager about any auditing or accounting problems encountered.
Associate/Staff	• Performing the audit procedures assigned to them. • Preparing adequate and appropriate documentation of completed work. • Informing the senior about any auditing or accounting problems encountered.

Types of Other Audit, Attest, and Assurance Services

[LO 13]   Opportunities where auditors can provide auditing, attest, or assurance services arise from the need for management to be accountable to employees, shareholders, customers, and communities. In this section, examples of these types of services are briefly discussed.

Other Audit Services

In addition to the financial statement audit, there are four major types of audits: internal control audits, compliance audits, operational audits, and forensic audits. These audits can be performed by public accounting firms or by other types of auditors such as internal or governmental auditors, discussed below.

Internal Control Audits   Financial statement auditors have always had the option of testing controls to obtain indirect evidence about the fairness of the financial statements on which they have been engaged to express an opinion. However, until recently, auditors were generally neither required nor allowed to express an opinion on a client's system of internal control as part of a financial statement audit.[6] This changed when the Sarbanes-Oxley Act required (1) that managements of public companies assert to the effectiveness of their internal control systems; and (2) that auditors of public companies be hired to provide an opinion on the effectiveness of internal control. An audit of internal control is available but not required for private entities.

Because the objectives and work involved in performing an audit of internal control and an audit of financial statements are closely interrelated, auditing standards for public companies require an *integrated audit* of internal control and financial statements. More detailed information about the internal control audit for public companies is provided in Chapter 7.

---

[6]Exceptions include audits of government agencies and audits of large banks complying with the Federal Depository Institution Corporation Improvement Act (FDICIA) of 1991, which, similar to the Sarbanes-Oxley requirement for all public companies, required both a management assertion as to the bank's internal control and an auditor attestation regarding that assertion.

Compliance Audits A compliance audit determines the extent to which rules, policies, laws, covenants, or government regulations are followed by the entity being audited. For example, a university may ask auditors to determine whether applicable rules and policies are being followed with respect to admissions decisions or the granting of student loans. Another example is the examination of tax returns of individuals and companies by the Internal Revenue Service for compliance with the tax laws.

Operational Audits An operational audit involves a systematic review of part or all of an organization's activities to evaluate whether resources are being used effectively and efficiently. The purpose of an operational audit is to assess performance, identify areas for improvement, and develop recommendations. Sometimes this type of audit is referred to as a *performance audit* or *management audit*. Operational audits present different challenges than financial statement audits or compliance audits because operational audits often require the auditor to identify or create objective, measurable criteria against which to assess effectiveness and efficiency. Operational auditing has increased in importance in recent years, and this trend will likely continue. An example is when entities employ auditors to assess the efficiency and effectiveness of the entity's use of information technology resources.

Forensic Audits A forensic audit's purpose is the detection or deterrence of fraudulent activities. The use of auditors to conduct forensic audits has increased significantly in recent years. Some examples of where a forensic audit might be conducted include

- Business or employee fraud.
- Criminal investigations.
- Shareholder and partnership disputes.
- Business economic losses.
- Matrimonial disputes.

For example, in a business fraud engagement, an audit might involve tracing expenditures or identifying and recovering assets. Exhibit 2–2 describes a forensic audit conducted by a major accounting firm for the board of directors of Lernout & Hauspie Speech Products NV. Some public accounting firms specialize in forensic audit services.

Practice
INSIGHT

Occupational fraud is a widespread problem that affects practically every organization, regardless of size, location, or industry. Occupational fraud is defined as the use of one's occupation for personal gain through the deliberate misuse or misapplication of the employer's resources or assets. Occupational fraud can be committed by employees, managers, or executives. The *Uniform Occupational Fraud Classification System* puts occupational frauds into one of three major categories: asset misappropriations, corruption, and fraudulent financial statements. While auditors are concerned with all three types of potential fraud at audit clients, financial statement fraud typically represents the gravest concern for auditors because the amounts involved are often highly material.

Attest Services   Auditors can provide numerous types of attest services regarding almost any subject matter. One example is briefly discussed here; Chapter 21 presents more detailed information about attest services.

EXHIBIT 2–2	PricewaterhouseCoopers Issues Report on Fraudulent Activities at Lernout & Hauspie

Lernout & Hauspie Speech Products NV (L&H), headquartered in Leper, Belgium, was a leader in speech translation software. L&H went public in late 1995 on the NASDAQ stock exchange and at one time had a market captialization of nearly $6 billion. In 2000, the high-flying company came under an SEC probe for reported revenues in Asia. Subsequently, the company filed for bankruptcy in both Belgium and the United States.

At the request of the company's new management, PricewaterhouseCoopers (PwC) was hired to conduct a forensic audit of the accounting fraud. Its audit discovered that most of the fraud occurred in L&H's Korean unit. In an effort to obtain bonuses based on sales targets, the managers of the Korean unit went to great lengths to fool L&H's auditor, KPMG. The PwC auditors reported that the Korean unit used two types of schemes to perpetrate the fraud. One involved factoring of receivables with banks to obtain cash to disguise the fact that the receivables were not valid. L&H Korea gave the banks side letters that provided that the money would be given back if the banks could not collect them. These side letters were concealed from KPMG. The second scheme arose after KPMG questioned why L&H Korea was not collecting more of its outstanding receivables. L&H Korea had its customers transfer their contracts to third parties who then took out bank loans to pay L&H Korea. L&H Korea provided the collateral for the loans. PwC reported that nearly 70 percent of the $160 million in sales booked in the Korean unit of L&H were fictitious.

Source: M. Maremont, J. Elsinger, and J. Carreyrou, "How High-Tech Dream at Lernout & Houspie Crumbled in a Scandal," *The Wall Street Journal* (December 7, 2000), pp. A1, A18; J. Carreyrou and M. Maremont, "Lernout Unit Engaged in Massive Fraud to Fool Auditors, New inquiry Concludes," *The Wall Street Journal* (April 6, 2001), p. A3; and J. Carreyrou, "Lernout Unit Booked Fictitious Sales, Says Probe," *The Wall Street Journal* (April 9, 2001), p. B2.

Reporting on Internal Control   Though not required, private companies or other entities sometimes ask auditors to provide an attest report on management's assertions about the effectiveness of the organization's internal control. Until the Sarbanes-Oxley Act required an audit of internal control for all public companies, auditors provided this service as a separate attest service only when requested by a client (and for banks for which the service was required under federal banking regulations). When asked by a private entity to evaluate internal control, auditors still perform the service as a separate attest service rather than as part of an integrated audit.

Assurance Services

As we discussed in Chapter 1, auditing is a specialized form of assurance service. Here we offer two examples of services that are not audits or attestations but that do qualify as assurance services. Note that the Sarbanes-Oxley Act prohibited external auditors from providing many forms of nonaudit assurance and consulting work to a public company that is also a financial statement audit client (see Chapter 19). Assurance services provided by CPAs are governed by either the attest or consulting standards. Chapter 21 provides more detailed information.

Risk Assessment   Organizations that manage risk well are more likely to succeed in an environment marked by ever-changing technology and globalization. In fact, Enterprise Risk Management (ERM) is emerging as a major trend in today's business world. Auditors can provide assurance on an entity's profile of business risks and can evaluate whether the entity has appropriate systems in place to manage those risks effectively. Many companies use the *Enterprise Risk Management–Integrated Framework* produced by the Committee of Sponsoring Organizations (COSO) to organize their risk management efforts.

Performance Measurement   Many organizations ask their auditors to provide assistance in benchmarking their business processes and performance. While traditionally this service mainly involved financial measures, clients now often seek help with measuring leading indicators such as customer satisfaction, effectiveness of employee training, and product quality. Through performance measurement services, the accountant can assist a client to understand drivers of the business and to measure their performance. For example, accountants have helped many companies implement a balanced scorecard approach to performance measurement.

Other Nonaudit Services

In addition to the audit, attest, and assurance services discussed in this chapter, public accounting firms perform three other broad categories of services.

Tax Preparation and Planning Services   Many public accounting firms have tax departments that assist clients with preparing and filing tax returns, provide advice on tax and estate planning, and provide representation on tax issues before the Internal Revenue Service or tax courts.

Management Advisory Services   Management advisory services (MAS) are consulting activities that may involve providing advice and assistance concerning an entity's organization, personnel, finances, operations, systems, or other activities. Because of independence and other issues, a number of the major firms have sold their consulting practices. However, these firms' assurance practices continue to perform MAS, primarily for nonpublic or nonaudit clients. Figure 2–2 presents the practice mix of the major international firms. Due to the Sarbanes-Oxley Act, accounting and consulting firms have experienced significant growth in the area of internal control consulting for nonaudit clients.

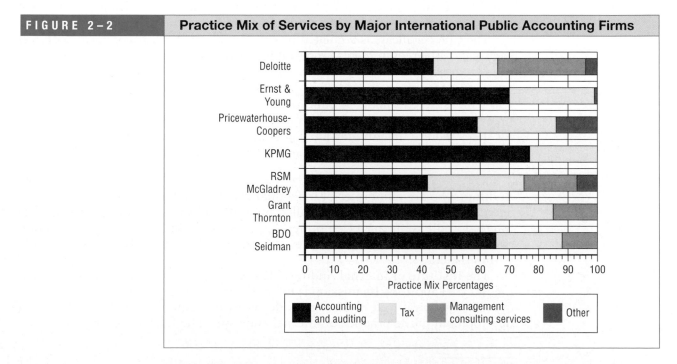

| FIGURE 2–2 | Practice Mix of Services by Major International Public Accounting Firms |

Source: Adapted from Public Accounting Report's Annual Survey of National Accounting Firms—2008 (Public Accounting Report, April 15, 2008). Copyright 2008 by Aspen Publishers, Inc., 1185 Avenue of the Americas, New York, NY 10036. 646-728-3048. Percentages based on U.S. net revenue by practice area; firms listed in order of total U.S. net revenue.

Accounting and Review Services   Public accounting firms perform a number of accounting services for their nonpublic or nonaudit clients. These services include bookkeeping, payroll processing, and preparing financial statements. When a public accounting firm provides nonaudit accounting services relating directly to the financial statements of companies, the services are known as compilations or reviews. These forms of services are less rigorous and provide less assurance than a financial statement audit. Accounting services are discussed in more detail in Chapter 21.

Types of Auditors

✎ [LO 14]   A number of different types of auditors can be identified; however, most can be classified under four headings: external auditors, internal auditors, government auditors, and forensic auditors. One important requirement for each type of auditor is independence in some form from the entity being audited. As described below, each different type of auditor usually specializes in a particular type of audit work. However, they each often provide more than one, or even all, of the types of audit and other services described in the previous section.

External Auditors

External auditors are often referred to as *independent auditors* or *certified public accountants* (CPAs). An external auditor may practice as a sole proprietor or as a member of a CPA firm, as discussed above. Such auditors are called "external" or "independent" because they are not employees of the entity being audited. In this book, the terms *external auditor, independent auditor,* and *CPA* are generally used interchangeably. External auditors audit financial statements for publicly traded and private companies, partnerships, municipalities, individuals, and other types of entities. They may also conduct compliance, operational, and forensic audits for such entities. However, as mentioned above, auditing standards restrict the other types of audit services that an external auditor can provide for financial statement audit clients that are public companies.

The CPA certificate is regulated by state law through licensing departments in each state.[7] The requirements for becoming a CPA vary among the states, with most states requiring at least a four-year college degree with selected courses in business and accounting. In addition, the District of Columbia and 46 states require 150 semester credit hours of education at an accredited college or university, and many states require professional experience before the CPA certificate is granted. All states require that an individual pass the Uniform CPA Examination, administered by the American Institute of Certified Public Accountants (see Exhibit 2–3).

Internal Auditors

Auditors who are employees of individual companies, partnerships, government agencies, and other entities are called internal auditors. In major corporations, internal audit staffs are often quite large, and the director of internal auditing (sometimes called the chief audit executive, or CAE) is usually a major job title within the entity.

The Institute of Internal Auditors (IIA) is the primary organization supporting internal auditors. Its mission is to be "the primary international professional association, organized on a worldwide basis, dedicated to the promotion and development of the practice of internal auditing." The IIA has developed a set of

---

[7]The National Association of State Boards of Accountancy (NASBA) maintains a listing of the CPA Licensure Requirements by state, as well as links to individual state boards of accountancy. See www.nasba.org.

EXHIBIT 2–3	The Computer-Based Uniform CPA Examination

The Uniform CPA Examination has a long and trusted history in the licensing of certified public accountants. The examination is delivered in a computer-based format at test centers across the United States.

Examination Content

The CPA examination has a total length of 14 hours and has four sections: Auditing and Attestation, Financial Accounting and Reporting, Regulation, and Business Environment and Concepts (BEC).

Each exam section contains five units called "testlets." A testlet is comprised of either a group of approximately 25 multiple-choice questions (MCQs) or one complete case study known as a simulation. Simulations provide a set of facts and require candidates to complete related tasks and access authoritative literature. Each exam section except BEC contains three MCQ testlets and two simulations. BEC contains three MCQ testlets only.

Sections
- Auditing and Attestation (4.5 hours). Covers knowledge of auditing procedures, generally accepted auditing standards, and other standards related to attest engagements and the skills needed to apply that knowledge in those engagements.
- Financial Accounting and Reporting (4 hours). Covers knowledge of generally accepted accounting principles for business enterprises, not-for-profit organizations, and governmental entities and the skills needed to apply that knowledge.
- Regulation (3 hours). Covers knowledge of federal taxation, ethics, professional and legal responsibilities, and business law and the skills needed to apply that knowledge.
- Business Environment and Concepts (2.5 hours). Covers knowledge of general business environment and business concepts that candidates need to know in order to understand the underlying business reasons for and accounting implications of business transactions and the skills needed to apply that knowledge.

This book includes links to Kaplan CPA exam simulations to help you prepare for the CPA exam. Look for the Kaplan logo at the end of each chapter.

Source: www.cpa-exam.org/.

standards to be followed by internal auditors and has established a certification program. An individual who meets the certification requirements established by the IIA, including passing a uniform written examination, can become a certified internal auditor (CIA).[8] Many internal auditors also have a CPA certificate.

The IIA defines internal auditing as "an independent, objective assurance and consulting activity designed to add value and improve an organization's operations. It helps an organization accomplish its objectives by bringing a systematic, disciplined approach to evaluate and improve the effectiveness of risk management, control, and governance processes."

Internal auditors often conduct financial, internal control, compliance, operational, and forensic audits within their organizations (see previous section). They in some cases may assist the external auditors with the annual financial statement audit. Internal auditors also often are involved in assurance and consulting engagements for their entities. Chapter 21 offers more detail on the IIA and the internal auditing profession.

Government Auditors

Government auditors are employed by federal, state, and local agencies. They generally can be considered a subset of the broader category of internal auditors. At the federal level, two agencies use auditors extensively: the

---

[8]See the IIA's home page (www.theiia.org) for more information on the IIA and the certified internal auditor program.

Government Accountability Office (GAO) and the Internal Revenue Service (IRS). The GAO is under the direction of the comptroller general of the United States and is responsible to Congress. GAO auditors conduct audits of activities, financial transactions, and accounts of the federal government. They also assist Congress by performing special audits, surveys, and investigations. The majority of the audits conducted by GAO auditors are compliance and operational audits.

The IRS is part of the U.S. Treasury Department. The main activity of IRS auditors is examining and auditing the books and records of organizations and individuals to determine their federal tax liability. IRS audits are compliance audits, ensuring that individuals and organizations are complying with federal tax laws.

Two other federal agencies that conduct audits are the Army Audit Agency and the Federal Bureau of Investigation (FBI). FBI auditors, for example, frequently audit for fraud in government agencies and organizations subject to federal laws. Last, most state and local governments have auditing agencies that perform functions similar to GAO and IRS auditors but at the state level.

Forensic Auditors

Forensic auditors are employed by corporations, government agencies, public accounting firms, and consulting and investigative services firms. They are trained in detecting, investigating, and deterring fraud and white-collar crime (see the discussion of forensic auditing earlier in this chapter). Some examples of situations where forensic auditors have been involved include

- Reconstructing incomplete or damaged accounting records to settle an insurance claim over inventory valuation.
- Probing money-laundering activities by reconstructing cash transactions.
- Investigating and documenting embezzlement and negotiating insurance settlements.

The Association of Certified Fraud Examiners (ACFE) is the primary organization supporting forensic auditors. The ACFE is a 40,000-member professional organization dedicated to educating certified fraud examiners (CFEs), who are trained in the specialized aspects of detecting, investigating, and deterring fraud and white-collar crime.

The ACFE offers a certification program for individuals wanting to become CFEs. Individuals interested in becoming a CFE must pass the Uniform CFE Examination.[9] CFEs come from various professional backgrounds, including auditors, accountants, fraud investigators, loss prevention specialists, attorneys, educators, and criminologists. CFEs gather evidence, take statements, write reports, and assist in investigating fraud in its varied forms.

Organizations That Affect the Public Accounting Profession

[LO 15]   A chapter on the environment of auditing wouldn't be complete without a discussion of the organizations that affect the practice of auditing by independent auditors. Figure 2–3 provides a representation of the relationship of these organizations to a financial statement audit. The following subsections discuss the activities of four of these organizations.

---

[9]See the Association of Certified Fraud Examiners' home page (www.acfe.org) for more information on the association and the CFE program.

FIGURE 2-3	Organizations Affecting the Financial Statement Audit

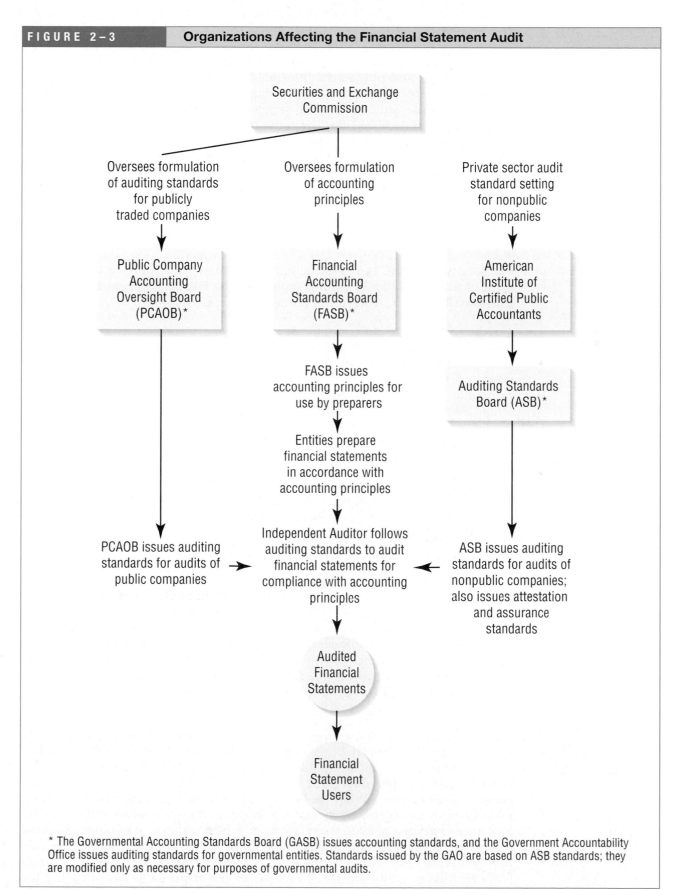

* The Governmental Accounting Standards Board (GASB) issues accounting standards, and the Government Accountability Office issues auditing standards for governmental entities. Standards issued by the GAO are based on ASB standards; they are modified only as necessary for purposes of governmental audits.

Securities and Exchange Commission (SEC)

The Securities and Exchange Commission (SEC) is a government agency that administers the Securities Act of 1933, the Securities Exchange Act of 1934, and the Sarbanes-Oxley Act of 2002, among others. The Securities Act of 1933 regulates disclosure of material information in a registration statement for an initial public offering of securities. *S forms,* which are used for issuing the securities, contain the audited financial statements of the registrant. The Securities Exchange Act of 1934 regulates ongoing reporting by companies whose securities are listed and traded on a stock exchange or that possess assets greater than $1 million and equity securities held by 500 or more persons. The most common documents encountered by auditors under the Securities Exchange Act of 1934 are the *10K, 10Q,* and *8K.* The 10K and 10Q are, respectively, annual and quarterly reports, which include the financial statements that are filed with the SEC by a publicly traded company. An 8K is filed whenever a significant event occurs that may be of interest to investors (such as sale of a division or a change of auditor).

Because the SEC has responsibility and authority to oversee the establishment of accounting and auditing standards, the FASB, ASB, and PCAOB work closely with the SEC when formulating such standards.

American Institute of Certified Public Accountants (AICPA)

The AICPA performs a number of functions that directly bear on the activities of member CPAs. The most important of these functions is the promulgation of rules and standards that guide audit and related services provided to nonpublic companies, governmental entities such as states, counties, municipalities and school districts, and other entities such as universities and charities.

In addition to the Auditing Standards Board, which we've already discussed in this chapter, the AICPA houses several standing committees that issue professional rules and standards relevant to assurance providers. We list the most important of them here but discuss them in other chapters:

- *The Code of Professional Conduct,* covered in detail in Chapter 19.
- *Quality control and peer review standards,* covered in Chapter 19.
- *Attestation standards,* covered in Chapter 21.
- *Compilation and review standards,* covered in Chapter 21.

In addition to its standard-setting role, the AICPA supports accounting and auditing research, produces a number of important publications, and provides a wide range of continuing education programs. For example, the AICPA publishes the *Journal of Accountancy, The Tax Advisor,* various Auditing Research Monographs, Auditing Practice Releases, and Industry Audit and Accounting Guides. The AICPA is responsible for preparing and grading the Uniform CPA Examination and plays an important role in administering the CPA certification in conjunction with the individual State Boards of Accountancy.

Public Company Accounting Oversight Board (PCAOB)

The Public Company Accounting Oversight Board describes itself as "a private-sector, nonprofit corporation, created by the Sarbanes-Oxley Act of 2002, to oversee the auditors of public companies in order to protect the interests of investors and further the public interest in the preparation of informative, fair, and independent audit reports." While the board is a private-sector, nonprofit corporation, it is in reality a quasi-governmental regulatory agency overseen by the SEC. The Sarbanes-Oxley Act of 2002 essentially transferred authority for standard setting, inspection, investigation, and enforcement for public company audits from the profession (as represented by the AICPA) to the PCAOB. All public accounting firms providing audits for public companies are required to register with, pay fees to, and follow the rules and standards of the PCAOB. As of April 2009 the board had approved the registration of nearly 2,000 public accounting firms.

The PCAOB conducts a program of regular inspections to assess the degree of compliance of registered public accounting firms with the Sarbanes-Oxley Act, PCAOB and SEC rules, and professional standards. The PCAOB also has broad investigative and disciplinary authority over public company audit firms. The PCAOB does not have authority to set standards relating to the audits of entities that are not publicly traded companies.

The PCAOB has authority to impose sanctions designed to deter a possible recurrence of rule violations and to enhance the quality and reliability of future audits. The sanctions can range from revoking a firm's registration or barring a particular individual from participating in audits of public companies to monetary penalties and requirements for remedial measures.

Financial Accounting Standards Board (FASB)

The Financial Accounting Standards Board (FASB) is a privately funded body whose mission is to establish standards for financial accounting and reporting. You should already be familiar with the operations of the FASB from your financial accounting classes. The FASB's Accounting Standards Codification (Codification or ASC) is recognized as the single source of U.S. GAAP by the SEC, the PCAOB, and the AICPA.

An important group within the FASB is the Emerging Issues Task Force (EITF). The EITF was established by the FASB to meet accountants' needs for timely guidance on accounting practices and methods and to limit the number of issues requiring formal pronouncements from the FASB. See the FASB's Web site (www.fasb.org) for more information on the FASB's activities. An aspect of accounting standard-setting that will be particularly important for you to follow is the effort to converge U.S. standards with those of the International Accounting Standards Board (IASB).

Conclusion

Chapter 1 introduced the concept of assurance and discussed the basics of financial statement auditing. This chapter explains the broader context in which financial statement auditing takes place. To fully understand auditing, you must be aware of the factors that shape the auditing environment, including the general economic and business environment, clients' particular businesses and industries, and the standards, social responsibilities, and codes of conduct that guide the financial statement auditor's work. You must also understand the nature of public accounting firms within which auditors organize themselves to conduct audits of organizations of various sizes, and you must be aware of the outside professional, regulatory, and standard-setting bodies that directly impact how auditing is done. This chapter provides an introduction to the complex and ever-changing environment in which financial statement auditing is performed.

KEY TERMS

Audit committee. A committee consisting of members of the board of directors, charged with overseeing the entity's system of internal control over financial reporting, internal and external auditors, and the financial reporting process. Members typically must be independent of management.

Board of directors. Persons elected by the stockholders of a corporation to oversee management and to direct the affairs of the corporation.

Business processes. Processes implemented by management to achieve entity objectives. Business processes are typically organized into the following categories: revenue, purchasing, human resource management, inventory management, and financing processes.

Corporate governance. The oversight mechanisms in place to help ensure the proper stewardship over an entity's assets. Management and the board of directors play primary roles, and the independent auditor plays a key facilitating role.

Ethics. A system or code of conduct based on moral duties and obligations that indicates how an individual should behave.

Financial Statement Assertions. Expressed or implied representations by management about information that is reflected in the financial statements. The three sets of assertions relate to ending account balances, transactions, and presentation and disclosure.

Generally accepted accounting principles (GAAP). Accounting principles that are generally accepted for the preparation of financial statements in the United States. GAAP standards are currently issued primarily by the FASB, with oversight and influence by the SEC.

Generally accepted auditing standards (GAAS). Ten broad statements guiding the conduct of financial statement auditing.

Illegal acts. Violations of laws or government regulations.

Independence. A state of objectivity in fact and in appearance, including the absence of any significant conflicts of interest.

Integrated audit. An audit of both financial statements and internal control over financial reporting, provided by the external auditor. Required for public companies.

Management advisory services. Consulting services that may provide advice and assistance concerning an entity's organization, personnel, finances, operations, systems, or other activities.

Public accounting firm. An organization created to provide professional accounting-related services, including auditing. Usually formed as a proprietorship or as a form of partnership.

Standards of the PCAOB. Standards regarding the conduct of financial statement auditing for public companies. Currently consist primarily of standards and statements established by the AICPA's Auditing Standards Board, as these statements and standards were adopted by the PCAOB in 2003 on an interim basis, though the PCAOB has added a few significant standards.

Statements on Auditing Standards (SAS). Statements issued by the AICPA's Auditing Standards Board, considered as interpretations of the 10 GAAS statements.

www.mhhe.com/messier7e	Visit the book's Online Learning Center for a multiple-choice quiz that will allow you to assess your understanding of chapter concepts.

REVIEW QUESTIONS

[LO 1] 2-1 Briefly discuss the key events that led up to the Sarbanes-Oxley Act of 2002 and the creation of the PCAOB.

[1] 2-2 Discuss how the events that have so dramatically affected auditors and the public accounting profession since the Enron scandal may in some senses be "healthy" for the profession.

[3] 2-3 Briefly discuss each of the components of the high-level model of business offered in the chapter (i.e., objectives, strategies, processes, etc.). Why might understanding the characteristics of a client's business in each of these areas be important for a financial statement auditor?

[3,4]   2-4   What roles do information systems and systems of internal control play in the high-level model of business discussed in the chapter, and why might it be important for an auditor to understand these roles?

[5]   2-5   How might the three categories of management assertions provide a powerful tool for the financial statement auditor?

[7]   2-6   List the three categories of GAAS. Discuss why the GAAS and the SAS are considered minimum standards of performance for auditors.

[10]   2-7   Why is independence such an important standard for auditors? How does auditor independence relate to the agency relationship between owners and managers discussed in Chapter 1?

[11]   2-8   Compare and contrast management's responsibility for the entity's financial statements with the auditor's responsibilities for detecting errors and fraud in the financial statements.

[13]   2-9   Give one example each of compliance, operational, and forensic audits.

[14]   2-10   List the various types of auditors.

[15]   2-11   The AICPA performs a number of functions that directly bear on independent auditors of nonpublic entities, including promulgation of rules and standards. List four types of standards issued by the AICPA.

[15]   2-12   What kind of organization is the PCAOB, why was it formed, and what does it do?

[15]   2-13   What role does the SEC play in the establishment of accounting and auditing standards for public companies?

[15]   2-14   What are some of the common documents encountered by auditors that are required by the Securities Exchange Act of 1934? What is the purpose of each of these documents?

MULTIPLE-CHOICE QUESTIONS

[1]   2-15   Which of the following best places the events of the last several years in proper sequence?
   a. Sarbanes-Oxley Act, increased consulting services to audit clients, Enron and other scandals, prohibition of most consulting work for audit clients, establishment of PCAOB.
   b. Increased consulting services to audit clients, Sarbanes-Oxley Act, Enron and other scandals, prohibition of most consulting work for audit clients, establishment of PCAOB.
   c. Enron and other scandals, Sarbanes-Oxley Act, increased consulting services to audit clients, prohibition of most consulting work for audit clients, establishment of PCAOB.
   d. Increased consulting services to audit clients, Enron and other scandals, Sarbanes-Oxley Act, prohibition of most consulting work for audit clients, establishment of PCAOB.

[3,4]   2-16   Which of the following best describes the relationship between business objectives, strategies, processes, controls, and transactions?
   a. To achieve its objectives, a business formulates strategies and implements processes, which are carried out through business transactions. The entity's information and internal control systems must be designed to ensure that the transactions are properly executed, captured, and processed.
   b. To achieve its strategies, a business formulates objectives and implements processes, which are carried out through the entity's information and internal control systems. Transactions are conducted to ensure that the processes are properly executed, captured, and processed.

c. To achieve its objectives, a business formulates strategies to implement its transactions, which are carried out through business processes. The entity's information and internal control systems must be designed to ensure that the processes are properly executed, captured, and processed.

d. To achieve its business processes, a business formulates objectives, which are carried out through the entity's strategies. The entity's information and internal control systems must be designed to ensure that the entity's strategies are properly executed, captured, and processed.

[6]   2-17   Which of the following is correct regarding the types of audits over which the AICPA's Auditing Standards Board and the PCAOB, respectively, have standard-setting authority?

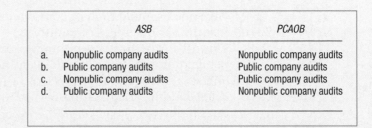

	ASB	PCAOB
a.	Nonpublic company audits	Nonpublic company audits
b.	Public company audits	Public company audits
c.	Nonpublic company audits	Public company audits
d.	Public company audits	Nonpublic company audits

[7]   2-18   Which of the following best describes the general character of the three generally accepted auditing standards classified as standards of field work?

a. The competence, independence, and professional care of persons performing the audit.

b. Criteria for the content of the auditor's report on financial statements and related footnote disclosures.

c. Criteria for audit planning and evidence gathering.

d. The need to maintain an independence of mental attitude in all matters relating to the audit.

[11]   2-19   Which of the following statements best describes management's and the external auditor's respective levels of responsibility for a public company's financial statements?

a. Management and the external auditor share equal responsibility for the fairness of the entity's financial statements in accordance with GAAP.

b. Neither management nor the external auditor has significant responsibility for the fairness of the entity's financial statements in accordance with GAAP.

c. Management has the primary responsibility to ensure that the company's financial statements are prepared in accordance with GAAP, and the auditor provides reasonable assurance that the statements are free of material misstatement.

d. Management has the primary responsibility to ensure that the company's financial statements are prepared in accordance with GAAP, and the auditor provides a guarantee that the statements are free of material misstatement.

[15]   2-20   The Public Company Accounting Oversight Board

a. Is a quasi-governmental organization that has legal authority to set auditing standards for audits of public companies.

b. Is a quasi-governmental organization that has legal authority to set accounting standards for public companies.

c. Is a quasi-governmental organization that has a policy to ignore public comment and input in the process of setting auditing standards.

d. Is a quasi-governmental organization that is independent of the SEC in setting auditing standards.

[14]   2-21   Which of the following is not a part of the role of internal auditors?

a. Assisting the external auditors.

b. Providing reports on the reliability of financial statements to investors and creditors.

c. Consulting activities.

d. Operational audits.

[13]   2-22   Operational auditing is oriented primarily toward

a. Future improvements to accomplish the goals of management.

b. The accuracy of data reflected in management's financial records.

c. Verification that an entity's financial statements are fairly presented.

d. Past protection provided by existing internal control.

[13]   2-23   Which of the following would be considered an assurance service engagement?

I. Expressing an opinion about the reliability of a client's financial statements.

II. Reviewing and commenting on a client-prepared business plan.

a. I only.

b. II only.

c. Both I and II.

d. Neither I nor II.

PROBLEMS

[7]   2-24   Dale Boucher, the owner of a small electronics firm, asked Sally Jones, CPA, to conduct an audit of the company's records. Boucher told Jones that the audit was to be completed in time to submit audited financial statements to a bank as part of a loan application. Jones immediately accepted the engagement and agreed to provide an auditor's report within one month. Boucher agreed to pay Jones her normal audit fee plus a percentage of the loan if it was granted.

Jones hired two recent accounting graduates to conduct the audit and spent several hours telling them exactly what to do. She told the new hires not to spend time reviewing the client's system of internal control but to concentrate on proving the mathematical accuracy of the general and subsidiary ledgers and summarizing the data in the accounting records that supported Boucher's financial statements. The new hires followed Jones's instructions and after two weeks gave Jones the financial statements excluding footnotes. Jones reviewed the statements and prepared an unqualified auditor's report. The report did not refer to generally accepted accounting principles, and no audit procedures were conducted to verify the year-to-year application of such principles.

Required:

Briefly describe each of the generally accepted auditing standards and indicate how the action(s) of Jones resulted in a failure to comply with *each* generally accepted auditing standard.

(AICPA, adapted)

[7]   2-25   Terri Harrison, CPA, has discussed various reporting considerations with three of her audit clients. The three clients presented the following situations and asked how they would affect the audit report.

a. A client has changed its depreciation method on its machinery from straight line to double declining balance. Both Harrison and the client agree that the new depreciation method better reflects the usage of the machinery in the manufacturing process. The client agrees with Harrison that the change is material but claims that it needs disclosure only in the "Summary of Significant Accounting Policies" footnote to the financial statements, not in Harrison's report.

b. A client has a loan agreement that restricts the amount of cash dividends that can be paid and requires the maintenance of a particular current ratio. The client is in compliance with the terms of the agreement, and it is not likely that there will be a violation in the foreseeable future. The client believes there is no need to mention the restriction in the financial statements because such mention might mislead the readers.

c. During the year, a client correctly accounted for the acquisition of a majority-owned domestic subsidiary but did not properly present the minority interest in retained earnings or net income of the subsidiary in the consolidated financial statements. The client agrees with Harrison that the minority interest presented in the consolidated financial statements is materially misstated but takes the position that the minority shareholders of the subsidiary should look to that subsidiary's financial statements for information concerning their interest therein.

Required:
Each of the situations presented relates to one of the four generally accepted auditing standards of reporting. Identify and describe the applicable generally accepted auditing standard of reporting in each situation, and discuss how the particular client situation relates to the standard.

(AICPA, adapted)

[13,14]   2-26   Audits can be categorized into five types: (1) financial statement audits, (2) audits of internal control, (3) compliance audits, (4) operational audits, and (5) forensic audits.

Required:
For each of the following descriptions, indicate which type of audit (financial statement audit, audit of internal control, compliance audit, operational audit, or forensic audit) best characterizes the nature of the audit being conducted. Also indicate which type of auditor (external auditor, internal auditor, government auditor, or forensic auditor) is likely to perform the audit engagement.

a. Evaluate the policies and procedures of the Food and Drug Administration in terms of bringing new drugs to market.

b. Determine the fair presentation of Ajax Chemical's balance sheet, income statement, and statement of cash flows.

c. Review the payment procedures of the accounts payable department for a large manufacturer.

d. Examine the financial records of a division of a corporation to determine if any accounting irregularities have occurred.

e. Evaluate the feasibility of forecasted rental income for a planned low-income public housing project.

f. Evaluate a company's computer services department in terms of the efficient and effective use of corporate resources.

g. Audit the partnership tax return of a real estate development company.

h. Investigate the possibility of payroll fraud in a labor union pension fund.

DISCUSSION CASE

[2,7,13]   2-27   Part I: Merry-Go-Round (MGR), a clothing retailer located primarily in shopping malls, was founded in 1968.[10] By the early 1990s, the company had gone public and had expanded to approximately 1,500 stores, 15,000 employees, and $1 billion in annual sales. The company's locations in malls targeted the youth and teen market. The company was listed by *Forbes* magazine as one of the top 25 companies in the late 1980s. However, in the early 1990s, the company faced many challenges. One of its cofounders died, and the other left to pursue unrelated business interests. The company faced stiff competition from other retailers (e.g., The Gap and Banana Republic), fashion trends changed, and mall traffic declined. Sales fell, and experts speculated that MGR failed to anticipate key industry trends and lost sight of its customer market. To try to regain its strong position, the company acquired Chess King, Inc., a struggling chain of men's clothing stores located in malls, in 1993.

The company's sales continued to fall, and later in 1993, it brought back one of its cofounders to manage the company and wrote down a significant amount of inventory. However, this inventory write-down caused the company to violate loan covenants. Facing bankruptcy, the company, based on the advice of its newly hired law firm Swidler and Berlin, hired turnaround specialists from Ernst and Young (E&Y) to help overcome the financial crisis and develop a long-term business plan. However, the company's decline continued, and it filed for Chapter 11 reorganization in 1994. In 1996, the remaining assets were sold for pennies on the dollar.

Subsequently, a group of 9,000 creditors (including former employees and stockholders) began litigation against parties it deemed responsible for their losses. These parties included E&Y, which the creditors sued for $4 billion in punitive and compensatory damages (E&Y's fees from MGR totaled $4.5 million).

The lawsuit alleged that E&Y's incompetence was the main cause of MGR's decline and demise. The lawsuit alleged in part that

- The turnaround team did not act fast enough.
- The leader of the team took an eight-day vacation at a critical point during the engagement.
- The cost-cutting strategy called for only $11 million in annual savings, despite the fact that the company was projected to lose up to $200 million in 1994.
- While store closings were key to MGR's survival, by 1995 only 230 of 1,434 stores had been closed and MGR still operated two stores in some malls.

---

[10]The following articles were sources for the information in the case: E. MacDonald, "Ernst & Young Will Pay $185 Million to Settle Claims of Merry-Go-Round," *The Wall Street Journal*, April 29, 1999, and E. McDonald and S. J. Paltrow, "Merry-Go-Round: Ernst & Young Advised the Client, but Not about Everything—It Didn't Reveal Business Ties Alleged to Pose Conflict with Its Consulting Job—Settlement for $185 Million," *The Wall Street Journal*, August 8, 1999, p. A1.

- The turnaround team included inexperienced personnel—a retired consultant, a partner with little experience in the United States and with retail firms, and two recent college graduates.
- E&Y charged exorbitant hourly rates and charged unreasonable expenses (e.g., charges included reimbursement for a dinner for three of the consultants totaling in excess of $200).
- E&Y denied any wrongdoing but in April 1999 agreed to pay $185 million to settle with the injured parties.

Required:
a. Although this was not an audit engagement for E&Y, some of the allegations against the firm can be framed in terms of the 10 generally accepted auditing standards. Which of the 10 GAAS was E&Y alleged to have violated?
b. Should there be specific professional standards for CPAs who consult? Given that non-CPAs who consult do not have formal professional standards, describe the advantages and disadvantages that result from such standards.

[10] 2-28 Part II: Merry-Go-Round. Additional charges made against E&Y included the following (recall that MGR hired Ernst and Young for turnaround consulting services):

- E&Y had a close relationship with Rouse Co., one of MGR's primary landlords (E&Y was soliciting business from Rouse and provided significant tax services).
- Swidler (the law firm that recommended E&Y to MGR) and E&Y had participated in at least 12 different business arrangements, some of which resulted in Swidler receiving significant fees from E&Y.
- E&Y did not disclose either of these relationships to MGR.

Required:
a. Do you think that E&Y acted unethically given that it had these relationships?
b. How could these relationships have affected E&Y's advice to MGR? In other words, refer to the charges above and speculate as to whether any of the charges against E&Y may have stemmed from the relationships described above.

To assist you in answering this question, consider the articles about MGR in footnote 10.

INTERNET ASSIGNMENTS

[15] 2-29 a. Go to the AICPA's Web site (www.aicpa.org). Find the AICPA's mission statement (currently under the link "About the AICPA"). Read and briefly summarize the AICPA's mission as described in its mission statement.
b. Go to the Security and Exchange Commission's Web site (www.sec.gov). Find the SEC's description of its mission (currently under the "What We Do" link under the heading "About the SEC"). Read the material under the link "Introduction," describing the SEC's primary mission and purpose. Write a paragraph summarizing the SEC's mission and purpose.

c. Go to the SEC's Web site (www.sec.gov). Read the material under the link "Creation of the SEC," describing the SEC's creation in the 1930s. Write a paragraph summarizing when and why the SEC was formed. What were the triggering events leading up to the SEC's formation?

d. Go to the Public Company Accounting Oversight Board's Web site (www.pcaob.com). Find and briefly summarize the PCAOB's description of its standard-setting process (currently under the "Standards" link along the top of the page, then select "Standards-Setting" from the drop down menu). Identify the section of the Sarbanes-Oxley Act of 2002 that empowers the PCAOB to set auditing standards for the audits of public companies.

[13,14,15]   2-30   Visit the GAO's home page (www.gao.gov) and search for a recently completed audit. Prepare a summary of the GAO audit that includes background on the issue and the GAO's findings and recommendations.

 HANDS-ON CASES

ACL

www.mhhe.com/ messier7e	Visit the book's Online Learning Center for problem material to be completed using the *ACL* software packaged with your new text.

KAPLAN
CPA Review

www.mhhe.com/ messier7e	**Kerklaan Enterprises** Focus primarily on the "Audit Opinions" and "Communications" tabs. Attempt the other exam questions to familiarize yourself with the CPA Exam interface. The content of the other exam questions will be discussed in subsequent chapters. *To begin this simulation visit the book's Online Learning Center.*

BASIC AUDITING CONCEPTS: RISK ASSESSMENT, MATERIALITY, AND EVIDENCE

CHAPTER 3

LEARNING OBJECTIVES

Upon completion of this chapter you will

[1] Understand the concept of audit risk.

[2] Learn the form and components of the audit risk model.

[3] Understand how to use the audit risk model.

[4] Learn the limitations of the audit risk model.

[5] Understand the auditor's risk assessment process.

[6] Know the factors that determine the auditor's assessment of the risk of material misstatement.

[7] Learn how to respond to the results of the risk assessments.

[8] Learn how to evaluate the results of the audit tests.

[9] Understand the documentation requirements for risk assessments and responses.

[10] Learn the auditor's communication requirements to management, the audit committee, and others.

[11] Understand the concept of materiality.

[12] Know the steps to applying materiality in an audit.

[13] Apply the materiality steps to an example (EarthWear).

RELEVANT ACCOUNTING AND AUDITING PRONOUNCEMENTS

FASB Statement of Financial Accounting Concepts No. 2, Qualitative Characteristics of Accounting Information

AICPA, *Audit Sampling* (Audit Guide) (New York: AICPA, 2008)

AICPA, *Assessing and Responding to Audit Risk in a Financial Statement Audit* (Audit Guide) (New York: AICPA, 2006)

AU 311, Planning and Supervision

AU 312, Audit Risk and Materiality in Conducting an Audit

AU 314, Understanding the Entity and Its Environment and Assessing the Risks of Material Misstatement

AU 316, Consideration of Fraud in a Financial Statement Audit

AU 317, Illegal Acts by Clients

AU 318, Performing Audit Procedures in Response to Assessed Risks and Evaluating the Audit Evidence Obtained

AU 326, Audit Evidence

AU 332, Auditing Accounting Estimates

AU 333, Management Representations

AU 339, Audit Documentation

AU 350, Audit Sampling

AU 380, The Auditor's Communication with Those Charged with Governance

PCAOB Auditing Standard No. 3, Audit Documentation (AS3)

PCAOB Proposed Auditing Standards Related to the Auditor's Assessment of and Response to Risk, PCAOB Release No. 2008-006 (October 21, 2008)

SEC Staff Accounting Bulletin No. 99, Materiality

SEC Staff Accounting Bulletin No. 108, Considering the Effects of Prior Year Misstatements when Quantifying Misstatements in Current Year Financial Statements

Risk Assessment and Materiality

In Chapter 1 the three fundamental concepts that underlie the conduct of a financial statement audit were briefly discussed. This chapter provides detailed coverage of two of those concepts: *audit risk* and *materiality*. Audit risk and materiality significantly impact the auditor's evidence decisions. The auditor considers both concepts in planning the nature, timing, and extent of audit procedures and in evaluating the results of those procedures.

The audit risk model serves as a framework for assessing audit risk. The auditor follows a risk assessment process to identify the risk of material misstatement in the financial statement accounts. The risk of material misstatement is composed of two components of the audit risk model: inherent risk and control risk. The risk of material misstatement is used to determine the acceptable level of detection risk and to plan the auditing procedures to be performed. The auditor restricts audit risk at the account balance level in such a way that, at the end of the engagement, he or she can express an opinion on the financial statements, taken as a whole, at an acceptably low level of audit risk.

The auditor considers materiality from a reasonable user perspective and follows a three-step process in applying materiality on an audit. The auditor must recognize that there is an inverse relationship between audit risk and materiality, and between the desired level of audit risk and the amount of audit evidence the auditor must collect.

Audit Risk

[LO 1]   *Audit risk* is the first fundamental concept that underlies the audit process. Because of the nature of audit evidence and the characteristics of management fraud, an auditor can only provide reasonable assurance, as opposed to absolute assurance, that the financial statements are free of material misstatement. The term "reasonable assurance" is used in the scope paragraph of the auditor's report to inform the reader that there is some level of risk that the audit did not detect *all* material misstatements. Audit risk is defined as follows:

> **Audit risk** is the risk that the auditor may unknowingly fail to appropriately modify the opinion on financial statements that are materially misstated.

In simple terms, audit risk is the risk that an auditor will issue unqualified opinion on materially misstated financial statements. The auditor should perform the audit to reduce audit risk to a sufficiently low level for expressing an opinion on the overall financial statements.

While the auditor is ultimately concerned with audit risk at the financial statement level, as a practical matter audit risk must be considered at more detailed levels through the course of the audit, including the account balance, class of transaction, or disclosure level. For ease of presentation, we will use the term *assertion* to refer to consideration of audit risk at these lower levels. In other words, consideration of audit risk at the assertion level means that the auditor must consider the risk that he or she will conclude that an assertion for a particular account balance (e.g., existence of accounts receivable), a particular class of transactions (e.g., classification of capital lease transactions), or a particular disclosure (e.g., valuation of amounts disclosed in a footnote dealing with stock compensation) is fairly stated, when in fact it is materially misstated.

Thus, at the assertion level, audit risk consists of:

1. The risk that the relevant assertions related to balances, classes of transactions, or disclosures contain misstatements that could be material to the financial statements when aggregated with misstatements in other balances, classes, or disclosures (inherent risk and control risk).
2. The risk that the auditor will not detect such misstatements (detection risk).

In other words, audit risk is the combination of these two elements—that the client's financial statements will contain material misstatements and that the auditor will fail to detect any such misstatements.

In addition to audit risk, an auditor is subject to *engagement risk*. Engagement risk is the risk that the auditor is exposed to financial loss or damage to his or her professional reputation from litigation, adverse publicity, or other events arising in connection with financial statements audited and reported on. For example, an auditor may conduct an audit in accordance with auditing standards and still be sued by the client or a third party. Although the auditor has complied with professional standards and may ultimately win the lawsuit, his or her professional reputation may be damaged in the process by the negative publicity.

Engagement risk cannot be directly controlled by the auditor, although some control can be exercised through the careful acceptance and continuance of clients. Achieved audit risk, on the other hand, can be directly controlled by manipulating detection risk. The auditor manipulates detection risk by changing the scope (see Practice Insight on the next page) of the auditor's test procedures. As the next section demonstrates, the *audit risk model* provides a framework for auditors to follow in planning audit procedures and evaluating audit results.

Practice INSIGHT	When auditors use the term "scope" they are referring to the *nature, timing,* and *extent* of audit procedures, where nature refers to the type of evidence; timing refers to when the evidence will be examined; and extent refers to how much of the type of evidence will be gathered.

The Audit Risk Model

✂ **[LO 2]**

The auditor considers audit risk at the relevant assertion level because this directly assists the auditor to plan the appropriate audit procedures for the accounts, transactions, or disclosures. The risk that the relevant assertions are misstated consists of two components:

- *Inherent risk* (IR) is the susceptibility of a relevant assertion to misstatements that could be material, either individually or when aggregated with other misstatements, assuming there are no related controls. In other words, IR is the likelihood that a material misstatement exists in the financial statements without the consideration of internal control.
- *Control risk* (CR) is the risk that a material misstatement that could occur in a relevant assertion will not be prevented, or detected and corrected on a timely basis by the entity's internal control. CR is a function of the effectiveness of the design and operation of internal control in achieving the entity's objectives relevant to preparation of the entity's financial statements. CR will always exist because of the inherent limitations of internal control.

Inherent risk and control risk exist independently of the audit. In other words, the levels of inherent risk and control risk are functions of the entity and its environment. The auditor has little or no control over these risks. Auditing standards refer to the combination of IR and CR as the *risk of material misstatement* (RMM). Some auditors refer to this combination as "client risk" because it stems from decisions made by the client (e.g., what kinds of business transactions to engage in, how much to invest in internal controls, etc.). To properly assess CR, the auditor must understand the client's controls and perform audit procedures to determine if the controls are operating effectively. You will learn about controls and tests of controls in Chapters 6 and 7.

Detection risk (DR) is the risk that the auditor will not detect a misstatement that exists in a relevant assertion that could be material either individually or when aggregated with other misstatements. Detection risk is determined by the effectiveness of the audit procedure and how well the procedure is applied by the auditor. Thus, detection risk cannot be reduced to zero because the auditor seldom examines 100 percent of the account balance or class of transactions (sampling risk). In addition, the auditor's work is subject to *nonsampling risk*. **Nonsampling risk** is the risk that the auditor might select an inappropriate audit procedure, misapply the appropriate audit procedure, or misinterpret the audit results. Nonsampling risk can be reduced through adequate planning, proper assignment of audit staff to the engagement team, the application of professional skepticism, supervision and review of the audit work performed, and supervision and conduct of a firm's audit practice in accordance with appropriate quality control standards.[1]

Detection risk has an inverse relationship to inherent risk and control risk. For example, if an auditor judges a client's inherent risk and control risk to be high, the auditor would accept a lower level of detection risk in order to achieve the planned level of audit risk. Conversely, if inherent risk and control risk are low, the auditor can accept higher detection risk.

---

[1]See T. B. Bell, M. E. Peecher, and I. Solomon, *The 21st Century Public Company Audit: Conceptual Elements of KPMG's Global Audit Methodology* (KPMG 2005) for a detailed discussion of the importance of recognizing the potential for non-sampling risk when conducting an audit.

The audit risk model can be specified as

$$AR = RMM \times DR$$

This model expresses the general relationship of audit risk and the risks associated with the auditor's assessments of risk of material misstatement (inherent risk and control risk) and the risks that substantive tests will fail to detect a material misstatement in a relevant assertion (detection risk).

The determination of audit risk and the use of the audit risk model involve considerable judgment on the part of the auditor. The audit risk model assists the auditor in determining the scope of auditing procedures for a relevant assertion in an account balance, class of transactions, or disclosure. Auditing standards do not provide specific guidance on what is an acceptable level of audit risk.

The auditor's assessment of audit risk and its component risks (*RMM* and *DR*) is a matter of professional judgment. At the completion of the audit, the *actual* or *achieved* level of audit risk is *not* known with certainty by the auditor. If the auditor assesses the *achieved* audit risk as being less than or equal to the *planned* level of audit risk, an unqualified report can be issued. If the assessment of the achieved level of audit risk is greater than the planned level, the auditor should either conduct additional audit work or qualify the audit report. In either case, the judgments involved are often highly subjective.

Use of the Audit Risk Model

✂ **[LO 3]**

The audit risk model is not intended to be a precise formula that includes all factors influencing the assessment of audit risk. However, auditors find the logic that underlies the model useful when planning risk levels (and thus making scoping decisions) for audit procedures. The discussion that follows concerning the audit risk model is limited to its use as an audit planning tool. Three steps are involved in the auditor's use of the audit risk model at the assertion level:

1. Setting a planned level of audit risk.
2. Assessing the risk of material misstatement.
3. Solving the audit risk equation for the appropriate level of detection risk.

Practice INSIGHT ᘉᕫ   Auditing standards allow the auditor to directly assess the RMM, or to separately assess the two components of RMM—IR and CR. This choice is typically built into each audit firm's methodology.

In applying the audit risk model in this manner, the auditor determines or assesses each component of the model using either quantitative or qualitative terms. In step 1, the auditor sets audit risk for each account balance, class of transaction, or disclosure in such a way that, at the completion of the engagement, an opinion can be issued on the financial statements with an acceptably low level of audit risk. Step 2 requires that the auditor assess the risk of material misstatement (see Practice Insight above). To assess the risk of material misstatement, the auditor evaluates the entity's business risks and how those business risks could lead to material misstatements. Figure 3–1 shows the relationship of the assessment of the entity's business risks and risk of material misstatement to the audit risk model. The assessment of business risks is described in detail in the next two sections of the chapter. In step 3, the auditor determines the appropriate level of detection risk by solving the audit risk model as follows:

$$AR = RMM \times DR$$
$$DR = AR/RMM$$

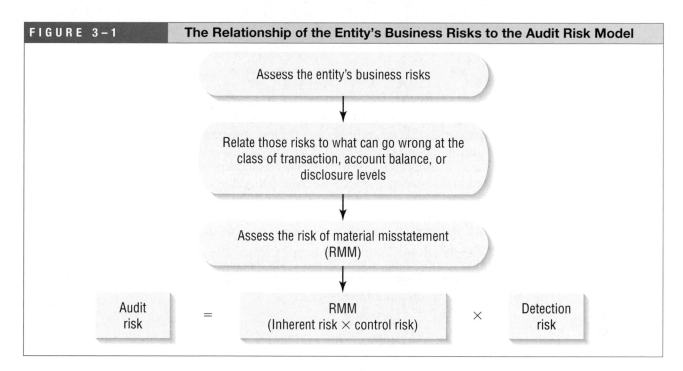

FIGURE 3-1 **The Relationship of the Entity's Business Risks to the Audit Risk Model**

The auditor uses the planned level of detection risk to design the audit procedures that will reduce audit risk to an acceptably low level. However, even if the risk of material misstatement is judged to be very low, the auditor must still perform some substantive procedures before concluding that an account balance is not materially misstated. Auditing standards include this caveat because of the imprecision that may occur in assessing the risk of material misstatement.

Consider the following numerical example:

> Suppose that the auditor has determined that the planned audit risk for the accounts receivable balance should be set at .05 based on the significance of the account to the financial statements. By establishing a relatively low level of audit risk, the auditor is minimizing the possibility that the account may contain a material misstatement. Assume further that the auditor assesses the risk of material misstatement for accounts receivable to be .60. Substituting the values for *AR* and *RMM* into the equation indicates that the auditor should set *DR* at approximately .08 (*DR* = .05/.60) for testing the accounts receivable balance. Thus, the auditor establishes the scope of the audit for accounts receivable so that there is only an 8 percent chance that a material misstatement, if present, is not detected.

Due to the subjectivity involved in judging the audit risk model's components, many public accounting firms find it more appropriate to use qualitative terms, rather than percentages, in the model. For example, planned audit risk might be classified into two categories, very low and low. Auditing standards state that audit risk must be reduced to at least a low level. Likewise, the risk of material misstatement and detection risk might be classified into three categories (e.g., *low, moderate,* or *high*). The logic behind the audit risk model is the same whether the auditor uses percentages or qualitative terms. When using qualitative terms, audit risk is set using one of the category choices. Similarly, the auditor selects the category for the risk of material misstatement that is most appropriate under the circumstances. The specified combination of audit risk and risk of material misstatement is then used to determine the appropriate level of detection risk. Following are three examples of the use of a qualitative approach to the audit risk model.

Example	AR	RMM	DR
1	Very low	High	Low
2	Low	Moderate	Moderate
3	Very low	Low	High

In Example 1, the auditor has determined that a very low level of audit risk is appropriate for this account because of its importance to the financial statement. The auditor has assessed the risk of material misstatement as high, indicating that there is a high risk of a material misstatement that was not prevented, or detected and corrected, by the internal control system. Given a very low level of audit risk and a high level of risk of material misstatement, the auditor would set detection risk as low. A low assessment for detection risk implies that the auditor will conduct a more detailed investigation of this account than if the assessment of detection risk were high. Before you continue, think about the other two examples in the chart above. What does the implied DR level mean about how much evidence must be gathered during the audit? Would a lower DR lead you to gather more or less audit evidence?

Limitations of the Audit Risk Model

✂ [LO 4]

Standard setters developed the audit risk model as a *planning* tool. However, the model has a number of limitations that must be considered by auditors and their firms when the model is used to *revise* an audit plan or to *evaluate* audit results.[2] In those instances, the *actual* or *achieved* level of audit risk may be smaller or greater than the audit risk indicated by the formula. This can occur because the auditor *assesses* the risk of material misstatement and such an assessment may be higher or lower than the *actual* risk of material misstatement that exists for the client. Inaccurate assessments are likely to result in a flawed determination of detection risk. Thus, the desired level of audit risk may not actually be achieved. In addition, the audit risk model also does not specifically consider nonsampling risk. While the audit risk model has limitations, it serves as an important tool that auditors can use for planning an audit engagement.

The Auditor's Risk Assessment Process

✂ [LO 5]

To properly assess the risks of material misstatement and engagement risk, the auditor performs risk assessment procedures. The auditor should obtain an understanding of management's objectives and strategies and the related business risks that may result in material misstatement of the financial statements. The following sections discuss management's strategies, objectives, and business risks. We then discuss the auditor's risk assessment process.

Management's Strategies, Objectives, and Business Risks

Strategies are the operational approaches used by management to achieve objectives. To achieve their business objectives, managers pursue strategies, such as being the low-cost or high-quality provider of a product. Typical business objectives include growth in market share, first-rate reputation, and excellent service. Business risks are threats to management's ability to achieve its objectives. Business risks are risks that result from significant conditions, events, circumstances,

---

[2]See B. E. Cushing and J. K. Loebbecke, "Analytical Approaches to Audit Risk: A Survey and Analysis," *Auditing: A Journal of Practice and Theory* (Fall 1983), pp. 23–41; W. R. Kinney, Jr., "A Note on Compounding Probabilities in Auditing," *Auditing: A Journal of Practice and Theory* (Spring 1983), pp. 13–22; and W. R. Kinney, Jr., "Achieved Audit Risk and the Audit Outcome Space," *Auditing: A Journal of Practice and Theory* (Supplement 1989), pp. 67–84, for more detailed discussions of the limitations of the audit risk model.

and actions or inactions that could adversely affect management's ability to execute its strategies and to achieve its objectives, or through the setting of inappropriate objectives or strategies. Business activities, strategies, objectives, and the business environment are ever-changing, and the dynamic and complex nature of business causes business risks. For example, risks arise from the development of a new product because the product may fail or because flaws in the product may result in lawsuits or damage to the company's reputation. Management is responsible for identifying such risks and responding to them. Usually, management develops approaches to address business risks by implementing a risk assessment process.

Business Risk and the Risk of Material Misstatement

Business risk is a broader concept than the risk of material misstatement. However, most business risks have the potential to affect the financial statements either immediately or in the long run. Auditors need to identify business risks and understand the potential misstatements that may result. Before you continue, pause and consider how a specific business risk could lead to misstatements in the financial statements. For example, consider a client who sells goods to a declining customer base. What risks does this client face? How will these risks impact the audit? This client faces pressure to maintain historical profit margins, which increases the risk of misstatement associated with the valuation of assets such as receivables. However, the same risk may also have longer-term implications to the company's overall health if the economy remains depressed. In such a case, the auditor should consider the likelihood that the client will not remain financially viable and whether the going concern assumption is still appropriate.

Understanding the Entity and Its Environment

Figure 1–3 presented an overview of the audit process. This process starts by obtaining an understanding of the entity and its environment. Obtaining an understanding of the entity and its environment is a continuous, dynamic process of gathering, updating, and analyzing information throughout the audit. The goal of this step is to assess the business risks faced by the entity. Based on the auditor's understanding of the entity's business risks and how those risks are controlled or not controlled by the entity, the auditor assesses the risk of material misstatement at the assertion level. Figure 3–2 provides an overview of the auditor's assessments of business risks and the risk of material misstatement (i.e., the auditor's risk assessment process). Unless otherwise stated in the text, the risk of material misstatement refers to misstatements caused by *errors* or *fraud*.

The auditor's understanding of the entity and its environment includes knowledge about the following categories:

- Nature of the entity.
- Industry, regulatory, and other external factors.
- Objectives and strategies and related business risks.
- Entity performance measures.
- Internal control.

In obtaining knowledge about each of these categories, the auditor should be particularly alert for the following conditions and events that may indicate the existence of business risks:

- Significant changes in the entity such as large acquisitions, reorganizations, or other unusual events.
- Significant changes in the industry in which the entity operates.
- Significant new products or services or significant new lines of business.
- New locations.

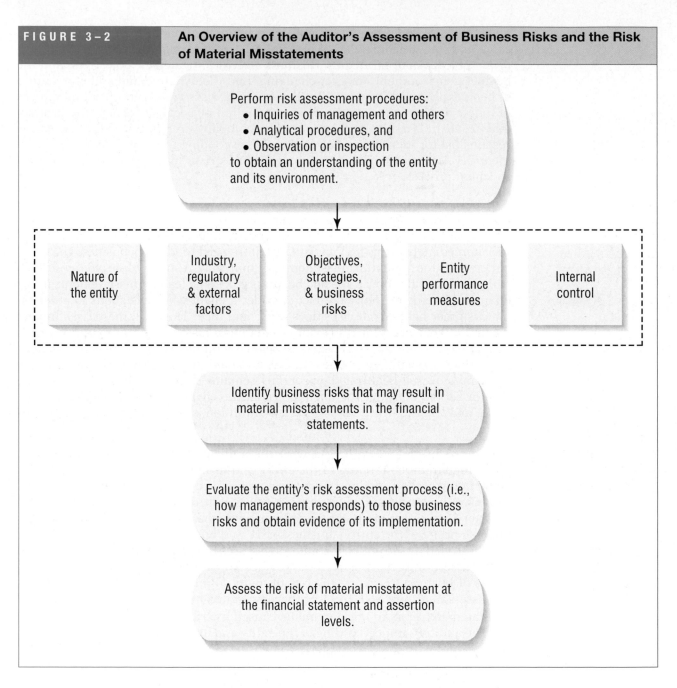

FIGURE 3–2 An Overview of the Auditor's Assessment of Business Risks and the Risk of Material Misstatements

- Significant changes in the IT environment.
- Operations in areas with unstable economies.
- High degree of complex regulation.

Nature of the Entity   Obtaining an understanding of the nature of the entity includes obtaining an understanding of the following:

- The entity's organizational structure and management personnel.
- The sources of funding of the entity's operations and investment activities, including the entity's capital structure, noncapital funding, and other debt instruments.
- The entity's investments.
- The entity's operating characteristics, including its size and complexity.

- The sources of the entity's earnings, including the relative profitability of key products and services.
- Key supplier and customer relationships.

An understanding of the nature of an entity gives the auditor a better idea of what potential misstatements might be found in the financial statements. Take a moment and think about how an entity with a complex structure may give rise to a risk of material misstatement as a result of the accounting for investments in joint ventures, subsidiaries, equity investments, or variable interest entities.

For public entities, the PCAOB states that the auditor should consider performing the following additional procedures as part of understanding the entity:

- Reading public information about the company relevant to the evaluation of the likelihood of material financial statement misstatements and the effectiveness of the company's internal control over financial reporting.
- Observing or reading transcripts of earnings calls.
- Obtaining information about significant unusual developments regarding trading activity in the company's securities.
- Obtaining an understanding of compensation arrangements with senior management, including incentive compensation arrangements, changes or adjustments to those arrangements, and special bonuses.

Industry, Regulatory, and Other External Factors

Industry, regulatory, and other external factors are relevant to the auditor's understanding of the entity. Obtaining an understanding of these factors aids the auditor in identifying risks of material misstatements. Some industries are subject to risks of material misstatement as a result of unique accounting estimates. For example, a property and casualty insurance company needs to establish loss reserves based on historical data that may be subject to misstatement. Table 3–1 presents examples of industry, regulatory, and other external factors that should be considered by the auditor.

Objectives, Strategies, and Related Business Risks

As discussed previously the auditor must identify and understand the entity's objectives and strategies used to achieve its objectives and the business risks associated with those

TABLE 3–1	Industry, Regulatory, and Other External Factors

Industry conditions:
- The market and competition, including demand, capacity, and price competition
- Cyclical or seasonal activity
- Product technology relating to the entity's products
- Supply availability and cost

Regulatory environment:
- Accounting principles and industry specific practices
- Regulatory framework for a regulated industry
- Legislation and regulation that significantly affect the entity's operations
- Taxation (corporate and other)
- Government policies currently affecting the conduct of the entity's business
- Environmental requirements affecting the industry and the entity's business

Other external factors:
- General level of economic activity (e.g., recession, growth)
- Interest rates and availability of financing
- Inflation and currency revaluation

TABLE 3-2	Examples of Business Risks That the Auditor Considers When Developing an Understanding of the Entity's Objectives and Strategies

- Industry developments
- New products and services
- Expansion of the business
- New accounting requirements
- Regulatory requirements
- Current and prospective financing requirements
- Use of IT
- Effects of implementing a strategy, particularly any effects that will lead to new accounting requirements

objectives and strategies. Table 3–2 provides examples of business risks the auditor considers when developing an understanding of the entity's objectives and strategies.

Entity Performance Measures   Internally generated information used by management to measure and review the entity's financial performance may include key performance indicators (KPIs), both financial and nonfinancial; budgets; variance analysis; subsidiary information and divisional, departmental, or other level performance reports; and comparisons of an entity's performance with that of competitors. External parties (e.g., analysts and credit rating agencies) may also measure and review the entity's financial performance. Internal measures provide management with information about progress toward meeting the entity's objectives. Thus, a deviation in the entity's performance measures may indicate a risk of misstatement in the related financial statement information. When the auditor intends to make use of the entity's performance measures for the purpose of the audit, the auditor should consider whether the information provided is reliable and trustworthy and whether it is sufficiently detailed or precise. Both internal and external information is useful to the auditor's understanding of the entity and its environment.

Internal Control   Internal control is the label given to the entity's policies and procedures designed to provide reasonable assurance about the achievement of the entity's objectives. Internal control is implemented by the client's board of directors, management, and other personnel. Because of the significance of internal control to the financial statement audit, we cover it in great detail in Chapter 6. To provide you with an introduction to the concept of internal control, here are several examples of policies and procedures that may be a part of an entity's internal control:

- Active and qualified board of directors and audit committee (see Chapter 5 for a detailed discussion of the audit committee) with members independent from the company.
- Effective risk assessment process.
- Competent and objective internal audit personnel.
- Proper authorization of transactions (e.g., a supervisor must approve all purchases over $5,000).
- Procedures to ensure assets exist (e.g., inventory counts).
- Monitoring of controls (e.g., supervisor observes the procedures at the loading dock to ensure control procedures are properly followed).

The auditor should understand and assess the effectiveness of internal control. The auditor uses the understanding of internal control to identify types of potential misstatements; consider factors that affect the risks of material misstatement; and design appropriate audit procedures.

Auditor's Risk Assessment Procedures

The auditor obtains an understanding of the entity and its environment by performing the following risk assessment procedures: inquiries of management, other entity personnel, and others outside the entity; analytical procedures; and observation and inspection.

Inquiries of Management, Other Entity Personnel, and Others Outside the Entity
The auditor obtains information about the entity and its environment through inquiry of management, individuals responsible for financial reporting, and other personnel within the entity. Making inquiries of others *within* the entity may be useful in providing the auditor with a perspective different from that of management and those responsible for financial reporting. The auditor might make inquiries of:

- Those charged with governance (e.g., board of directors or audit committee).
- Internal audit personnel.
- Employees involved in initiating, authorizing, processing, or recording complex or unusual transactions.
- In-house legal counsel.
- Production, marketing, sales, and other personnel.

For example, inquiries directed to internal audit personnel might relate to their activities concerning the design and operating effectiveness of the entity's internal controls. The auditor might also inquire of the in-house legal counsel about issues such as litigation, compliance with laws and regulations, and the meaning of contract terms.

The auditor might inquire of others *outside* the entity. For example, the auditor may consider it is appropriate to make inquiries of customers, suppliers, or valuation specialists. Such discussions may provide information that will assist the auditor in uncovering fraud. For example, customers may report that they received large quantities of unordered products from the audit client just before year-end. This would be an indicator of overstated revenues.

Analytical Procedures
Analytical procedures are evaluations of financial information made by a study of plausible relationships among both financial and nonfinancial data. Auditing standards require that the auditor conduct analytical procedures in planning the audit. Such preliminary analytical procedures assist the auditor in understanding the entity and its environment and in identifying areas that may represent specific risks relevant to the audit. Analytical procedures can be helpful in identifying the existence of unusual transactions or events and amounts, ratios, and trends that might have implications for audit planning. In performing such analytical procedures, the auditor should develop expectations about plausible relationships that are expected to exist, based on the understanding of the entity and its environment. However, the results of such high-level analytical procedures provide only a broad initial indication about whether a material misstatement may exist. Analytical procedures are discussed in more detail in Chapter 5.

Observation and Inspection
Observation and inspection include audit procedures such as:

- Observation of entity activities and operations.
- Inspection of documents (e.g., business plans and strategies), records, and internal control manuals.

TABLE 3–3	Sources of Information for Understanding the Entity and Its Environment

- Cumulative knowledge and experience obtained from prior audits.
- Procedures performed in client acceptance and continuance process.
- Knowledge obtained from performing interim procedures.
- Consulting, tax, or other engagements performed for the entity.
- Communications with predecessor auditors including review of predecessor auditor working papers.
- Published annual reports and interim reports to shareholders, if applicable.
- Discussions with management.
- Minutes of board of directors and/or audit committee meetings.
- Entity's business/strategic plans, budgets, or other documentation.
- Reports prepared by analysts, banks, underwriters, rating agencies, and the like.
- Individuals knowledgeable about the industry, such as the engagement team members for clients in a similar business/industry.
- Audit firm-generated industry guidance, databases, and practice aids, where applicable.
- Government statistics.
- Economic and financial journals.
- Industry or trade journals.
- Client press releases, publications, and brochures.
- Internal audit reports.

- Reading reports prepared by management, those charged with governance, and internal audit.
- Visits to the entity's premises and plant facilities.
- Tracing transactions through the information system relevant to financial reporting, which may be performed as part of a walkthrough.

The auditor may also read about industry developments and trends, read the current year's interim financial statements, and review regulatory or financial publications. Table 3–3 presents sources where the auditor can obtain information for developing an understanding of the entity and its environment.

Evaluate the Entity's Risk Assessment Process

Management has a responsibility to identify, control, and mitigate business risks that may affect the entity's ability to achieve its objectives. The auditor should obtain information on the entity's risk assessment process and whether it is operating effectively. If the entity's response to the identified risk is adequate, the risk of material misstatement may be reduced. However, if the entity's response to the identified risk is inadequate, the auditor's assessment of the risk of material misstatement may increase. If the entity does not respond adequately to business risks, the auditor will have to develop tests to determine if any misstatements are present in the related account balances or class of transactions. Chapter 6 provides detailed coverage of the entity's risk assessment management process.

Assessing the Risk of Material Misstatement Due to Error or Fraud[3]

[LO 6]   Based on knowledge of the entity and its environment, the auditor should assess the risk of material misstatement at the assertion level and determine the audit procedures that are necessary based on that risk assessment (see Figure 3–2). At this point in the risk assessment process, the auditor has identified the entity's business risks. To assess the risk of material misstatement, the auditor must then consider how the identified risks could result in a material misstatement in the

---

[3]See recent surveys by KPMG (*KPMG Forensic: Integrity Survey 2005–2006*, KPMG LLP, New York: 2005) and PwC (*Fourth Biennial Global Economic Crime Survey 2007*, PwC, New York: 2007) for information on the incidence of fraud.

financial statements. This includes considering whether the magnitude and likelihood of the risk could result in a material misstatement. For example, the entity's risk assessment process may have identified product obsolescence as a business risk that could result in a material misstatement to the inventory and cost-of-goods accounts. However, the entity's risk assessment process has determined that there is a low likelihood that such a misstatement could occur because the entity has installed strong controls that track inventory levels and market pricing.

This section will first review the types and causes of misstatements, and then focuses primarily on assessing the risk of material misstatement due to fraud, sometimes referred to as the *fraud risk assessment.*

Types and Causes of Misstatements[4]

Misstatements can result from errors or fraud. The term *errors* refers to *unintentional* misstatements of amounts or disclosures in financial statements. The term *fraud* refers to an *intentional* act by one or more among management, those charged with governance, employees, or third parties, involving the use of deception to obtain an unjust or illegal advantage. Thus, the primary distinction between errors and fraud is whether the misstatement was intentional or unintentional. Unfortunately, it is often difficult to determine intent. For example, the auditor detects a misstatement in an account that requires an estimate, such as bad debt expense; it may be difficult to determine whether the misstatement was intentional.

Some examples of misstatements due to errors or fraud include:

- An inaccuracy in gathering or processing data from which financial statements are prepared.
- A difference between the amount of a reported financial statement account and the amount that would have been reported under GAAP.
- The omission of a financial statement element, account, or item.
- An incorrect accounting estimate arising from an oversight or misinterpretation of facts.

Fraud can be classified into two types: (1) misstatements arising from fraudulent financial reporting; and (2) misstatements arising from misappropriation of assets. The previous list of misstatements deals with fraudulent financial reporting. Misstatements arising from misappropriation of assets (sometimes referred to as *defalcation*) involve the theft of an entity's assets where the theft causes the financial statements to be misstated. Examples of misappropriation include:

- Embezzling cash received.
- Stealing assets.
- Causing the entity to pay for goods or services not received.

Practice INSIGHT

In a study conducted by the Association of Certified Fraud Examiners (2008), fraudulent financial statements accounted for some 10 percent of fraud cases but they had the highest median loss, at $2 million. The CFE Study found that financial statement fraud generally involves the intentional misstatement or omission of material information from the organization's financial reports. Financial statement fraud cases often involve the reporting of fictitious revenues or the concealment of expenses or liabilities in order to make an organization appear more profitable than it really is.

Misstatements may be of two types: *known* and *likely.*

---

[4]See A. Eilifsen and W. F. Messier, Jr., "Auditor Detection of Misstatements: A Review and Integration of Empirical Research," *Journal of Accounting Literature* 2000 (19), pp. 1–43, for a detailed review of research studies that have examined auditor-detected misstatements.

Known Misstatements   Known misstatements are misstatements about which there is no uncertainty. For example, an auditor may test a sales invoice and determine that the prices applied to the products ordered are incorrect. Once the products are correctly priced, the amount of misstatement is known. In such cases, the auditor knows the exact amount of the misstatement.

Likely Misstatements   These are misstatements that:

- Arise from differences between management's and the auditor's judgments concerning accounting estimates that the auditor considers unreasonable or inappropriate.
- The auditor considers likely to exist based on an extrapolation from audit evidence. For example, the amount obtained by projecting known misstatements identified in an audit sample to the entire population.

The Fraud Risk Identification Process

The auditor performs the following steps to identify the risks of material misstatement due to fraud:

- Discussion among the audit team members regarding the risks of material misstatement due to fraud.
- Inquire of management and others about their views on the risks of fraud and how it is addressed.
- Consider any unusual or unexpected relationships that have been identified in performing analytical procedures in planning the audit.
- Understand the client's period-end closing process and investigate unexpected period-end adjustments.

The following two sections address the first two bulleted items.

Discussion among the Audit Team   Auditing standards require that the audit team have discussions about the entity's financial statements susceptibility to material misstatements. In planning the audit, the engagement partner or manager should communicate with members of the audit team regarding the potential for material misstatement due to fraud. This brainstorming session can be held separately, or concurrently, with the discussion required as part of understanding the entity and its environment (AU 318.14). The engagement partner or manager should determine which audit team members should be included in the communication, how it should occur, and the extent of the communication. The objectives of the brainstorming meeting are to

- Share insights about the entity and its environment and the entity's business risks.
- Provide an opportunity for the team members to discuss how and where the entity might be susceptible to fraud.
- Emphasize the importance of maintaining *professional skepticism* throughout the audit regarding the potential for material misstatement due to fraud.

Engagement team members should be encouraged to communicate and share information obtained throughout the audit that may affect the assessment of risks of material misstatement or the auditor's responses to those risks.

The auditor should conduct the engagement assuming there is a possibility that a material misstatement due to fraud could be present, regardless of any prior beliefs or past experience with the entity and regardless of the auditor's belief about management's honesty and integrity. Pretend for a moment that you are a member of the audit team assigned to the EarthWear audit participating in the fraud brainstorming session. What are one or two of the external/internal influences that might create pressure for EarthWear to commit fraud? (See Table 3–4 below.)

Inquiries of Management and Others

The auditor should inquire about management's knowledge of fraud within the entity. The auditor should also understand the programs and controls that management has established to mitigate specific risk factors and how well management monitors those programs and controls. Some of the inquiry would take place when the auditor obtains an understanding of the entity and its environment.

The entity's audit committee should assume an active role in oversight of the assessment of the risk of fraud. The auditor should obtain an understanding of how the audit committee exercises its oversight activities, including direct inquiry of audit committee members. The auditor also should inquire of internal audit personnel about their assessment of the risk of fraud, including whether management has satisfactorily responded to internal audit findings during the year.

The auditor should also consider inquiries from others within the entity and third parties. For example, the auditor also may consider making inquiries of third parties, such as vendors, customers, or regulators. It can be uncomfortable to inquire about potentially fraudulent activities; however, it is much more uncomfortable to fail to detect a material fraud.

Conditions Indicative of Fraud and Fraud Risk Factors

Three conditions are generally present when material misstatements due to fraud occur:

1. Management or other employees have an *incentive* or are under *pressure* that provides a reason to commit fraud.
2. Circumstances exist that provide an *opportunity* for a fraud to be carried out.
3. Those involved are able to *rationalize* committing a fraudulent act. Some individuals possess an *attitude*, character, or set of ethical values that allow them to knowingly and intentionally commit a dishonest act.

Even honest individuals can commit fraud in an environment where sufficient pressure is being exerted on them. The greater the incentive or pressure, the more likely an individual will be able to rationalize the acceptability of committing fraud. Withholding evidence or misrepresenting information through falsified documentation, including forgery, may conceal fraud. Fraud also may be concealed through collusion among management, employees, or third parties.

Management has the ability to perpetrate fraud because it is in a position to directly or indirectly manipulate the accounting records and prepare fraudulent financial reports. In most cases, fraudulent financial reporting also involves some management override of controls.

Because of the characteristics of fraud, particularly those involving concealment through collusion; withheld, misrepresented, or falsified documentation; and the ability of management to override or instruct others to override controls, an auditor may unknowingly rely on audit evidence that appears to be valid, but in fact is false and fraudulent. Thus, fraud risk factors related to fraudulent financial reporting and misappropriation of assets can be classified among the three conditions generally present when fraud exists:

- An *incentive/pressure* to perpetrate fraud.
- An *opportunity* to carry out the fraud.
- An *attitude/rationalization* to justify the fraudulent action.

These three conditions are sometimes referred to as the fraud risk triangle.

Fraudulent Financial Reporting Tables 3–4 to 3–6 present the risk factors related to each category of conditions for the potential for fraudulent financial reporting. Table 3–4 contains numerous risk factors that, if present, may suggest that management and others have incentives to manipulate financial reporting. For example, the entity may be facing increased competition that results in declining profit margins. Similarly, in the high-technology sector, rapid changes in technology can affect the profitability and the fair market value of products. Entities that have recurring operating losses and negative cash flow from operations may face bankruptcy, foreclosure, or takeover. In each of these situations, management may have incentives to manipulate reported earnings. Management (or the board of directors) may also be facing pressures to maintain the entity's reported earnings to meet analysts' forecasts because bonuses or personal wealth is tied to the entity's stock price (see Exhibit 3–1).

TABLE 3–4	Risk Factors Relating to Incentives/Pressures to Report Fraudulently

- Financial stability or profitability is threatened by economic, industry, or entity operating conditions, such as
  - High degree of competition or market saturation, accompanied by declining margins.
  - High vulnerability to rapid changes, such as changes in technology, product obsolescence, or interest rates.
  - Significant declines in customer demand and increasing business failures in either the industry or overall economy.
  - Operating losses making the threat of bankruptcy, foreclosure, or hostile takeover imminent.
  - Rapid growth or unusual profitability, especially compared with that of other companies in the same industry.
  - New accounting, statutory, or regulatory requirements.
- Excessive pressure exists for management to meet requirements or expectations of third parties due to
  - Profitability or trend level expectations of investment analysts, institutional investors, significant creditors, or other external parties.
  - Need to obtain additional debt or equity financing to stay competitive.
  - Adverse effects of reporting poor financial results on significant pending transactions.
- Management or the board of directors' personal financial situations are threatened by the entity's financial performance.

TABLE 3–5	Risk Factors Relating to Opportunities to Report Fraudulently

- The nature of the industry or the entity's operations provide opportunities to engage in fraudulent financial reporting due to
  - Significant related-party transactions.
  - Assets, liabilities, revenues, or expenses based on significant estimates that involve subjective judgments or uncertainties that are difficult to corroborate.
  - Significant, unusual, or highly complex transactions.
- There is ineffective monitoring of management.
- There is a complex or unstable organizational structure.
- Internal control components are deficient.

TABLE 3–6	Risk Factors Relating to Attitudes/Rationalizations to Report Fraudulently

- Ineffective communication implementation, support, and enforcement of the entity's values or ethical standards by management, or the communication of inappropriate values or ethical standards.
- Nonfinancial management's excessive participation in, or preoccupation with, the selection of accounting principles or the determination of significant estimates.
- Known history of violations of securities laws or other laws and regulations, or claims against the entity, its senior management, or board members alleging fraud or violations of laws and regulations.
- Excessive interest by management in maintaining or increasing the entity's stock price or earnings trend.
- A practice by management of committing to analysts, creditors, and other third parties to achieve aggressive or unrealistic forecasts.
- Recurring attempts by management to justify marginal or inappropriate accounting on the basis of materiality.

EXHIBIT 3-1	Satyam Computer Services Ltd. — India's Enron!

On January 7, 2009, B. Ramalinga Raju, Chairman and Founder of Satyam, sent a letter to Satyam's board of directors informing them that he had carried out a massive financial statement fraud. In his letter, Raju stated that the fraud "attained unmanageable proportions as the size of the company operations grew." Satyam was India's fourth largest technology company. Its stock traded on the NYSE and it was audited by Price Waterhouse, a separate legal entity within the PricewaterhouseCoopers global business network. Some of the companies for which Satyam does outsourcing work include Citicorp, Caterpillar, and Coca-Cola. Ironically, Satyam means "truth" in Sanskrit.

For the year ended March 31, 2008, Satyam reported sales of $2.1 billion and profits of $427.6 million. However, Mr. Raju's letter indicated that in the quarter ended September 30, 2008, Satyam reported $555 million in sales instead of the true figure of $434 million. The company reported $136 million in profit, but the real amount was $12.5 million. Accounts receivable were reported at $545.6 million but Mr Raju indicated in reality they totaled only $444.8 million. Most importantly, Satyam reported $1.1 billion in available cash, but had only $66 million on hand. More than $1 billion of Satyam's cash was either missing or never existed!

The Indian government ousted the Board of Directors and Price Waterhouse was removed as the company's auditors. KPMG and Deloitte were hired as the new auditors.

Investigators determined that Satyam's account-balance statements and letters of confirmation of account balances at HSBC Holdings PLC of the United Kingdom, Citigroup Inc. of the United States, and HDFC Bank and ICICI Bank Ltd. of India were forgeries.

Selected Sources: B. R. Raju, Letter to Satyam's Board of Directors" (January 7, 2009); N. Sheth, J. Range, and G. Anand, "Corporate Scandal Shakes India," *The Wall Street Journal* (January 8, 2009), pp. A1 and A9; J. Range and S. Patterson, "Pricewaterhouse Defends Its Audit Procedures," *The Wall Street Journal* (January 9, 2009), p. B5; G. Anand and R. Guha, "Satyam Bank Documents at Issue," *The Wall Street Journal* (January 20, 2009), p. B3; and E. Bellman and N. Sheth, "Satyam Founder Accused of Falsely Inflating Size of Staff," *The Wall Street Journal* (January 23, 2009), p. B1.

Management must also have the opportunity to commit the fraud. Table 3–5 lists the opportunities that may be available to management or the board of directors to perpetuate fraudulent financial reporting. For example, assets, liabilities, revenues, or expenses may be based on subjective estimates that may be difficult for the auditor to corroborate. Two examples of such situations are the recognition of income on long-term contracts when the percentage of completion method is used and establishing the amount of loan loss reserves for a financial institution. Another opportunity for fraudulent financial reporting is when a single person or small group dominates management. Dominance by one individual may lead to processing accounting transactions that are not consistent with the entity's controls.

Risk factors reflective of attitudes/rationalizations by board members, management, or employees may allow them to engage in and/or justify fraudulent financial reporting. Table 3–6 lists a number of attitudes or rationalizations that may be used to justify fraudulent financial reporting. For example, the entity may have weak ethical standards for management behavior or poor communication channels for reporting such behavior. Management may fail to correct weaknesses in internal control or use inappropriate accounting. Last, management may have strained relationships with its predecessor and current auditors.

Misappropriation of Assets   Risk factors that relate to misstatements arising from misappropriation of assets also are classified along the three conditions generally present when fraud exists. Some of the risk factors related to misstatements arising from fraudulent financial reporting also may be present when misstatements arising from misappropriation of assets exist (see Exhibit 3–2). Table 3–7 presents risk factors related to each category of conditions for the potential of misappropriation of assets. For example, an employee may have financial problems that create an incentive to misappropriate the cash.

EXHIBIT 3–2 | **Madoff's $50 Billion Ponzi Scheme**

In early December 2008, Bernie Madoff told his two sons that his investment advisory business, Bernard Madoff Investment Securities (BMIS), was basically a giant Ponzi scheme. Madoff had falsely represented to investors that returns were being earned on their accounts at BMIS and that he was investing their money in securities. In fact, Madoff paid earlier investors with funds raised from later investors. Authorities believe that the fraud may date back at least three decades. Madoff estimated the losses from the fraud at as much as $50 billion. Madoff's investors included many famous individuals and charities, some of whom lost their entire savings.

While Madoff told prosecutors that he had acted alone, one of the major issues is how much others may have been involved. Others include the value of any remaining assets in BMIS, whether Madoff hid some of the assets, and how much of his personal assets can be used to pay off investors.

Selected Sources: Securities and Exchange Commission Complaint, United States District Court, Southern District of New York (December 11, 2008); A. Efrati and C. Bray, "U.S.: Madoff had $173 Million in Checks," *The Wall Street Journal* (January 9, 2009), p. C5; T. Lauricella and A. Lucchetti, "Madoff Brother, at Arm's Length?," *The Wall Street Journal* (January 10–11, 2009), pp. B1 and B6; T. Lauricella and A. Lucchetti, "Sons' Roles in Spotlight," *The Wall Street Journal* (January 24–25, 2009), p. B1 and B6;

TABLE 3–7 | **Risk Factors Relating to the Misappropriation of Assets**

Incentives/pressures:
- Personal financial obligations may create pressure for management or employees with access to cash or other assets susceptible to theft to misappropriate those assets.
- Adverse relationships between the entity and employees with access to cash or other assets susceptible to theft may motivate those employees to misappropriate those assets.

Opportunities:
- Certain characteristics or circumstances may increase the susceptibility of assets to misappropriation (for example, large amounts of cash on hand or processed).
- Inadequate internal control over assets may increase the susceptibility of misappropriation of those assets. For example, misappropriation of assets may exist because there is inadequate management oversight of employees responsible for assets (for example, inadequate supervision or monitoring of remote locations).

Attitudes/rationalizations:
- Disregard for the need for monitoring or reducing risks related to misappropriations of assets.
- Disregard for internal control over misappropriation of assets by overriding existing controls or by failing to correct known internal control deficiencies.
- Changes in behavior or lifestyle that may indicate assets have been misappropriated.

Similarly, in order for the employee who has financial problems to misappropriate cash, he or she must have access to the cash. This is likely to occur only when there is inadequate segregation of duties or poor oversight by personnel responsible for the asset. Finally, an employee who has access to assets susceptible to misappropriation may have a change in behavior or lifestyle that may indicate he or she has misappropriated assets.

The Auditor's Response to the Results of the Risk Assessments

[LO 7]   Figure 3–3 provides an overview of how the auditor responds to the results of the risk assessments. Once the risks of material misstatement have been identified, the auditor determines whether they relate more pervasively to the overall financial statements and potentially affect many relevant assertions or whether the identified risks relate to specific relevant assertions related to classes of transactions, account balances, and disclosures.

| FIGURE 3-3 | Relating the Assessment of the Risk of Material Misstatement to the Design and Performance of Audit Procedures |

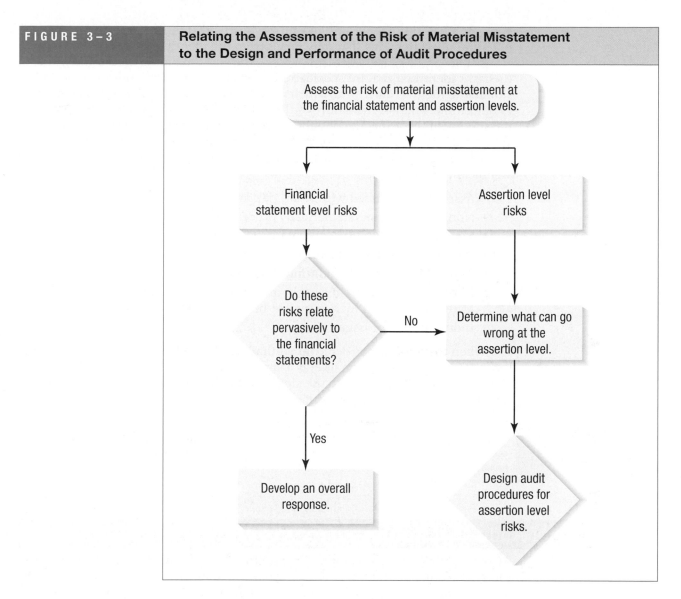

To respond appropriately to financial statement level risks, the auditor may choose to reconsider the overall audit approach. The response to such pervasive risks may include:

- Emphasizing to the audit team the need to maintain professional skepticism in gathering and evaluating audit evidence.
- Assigning more experienced staff or those with specialized skills or using specialists.
- Providing more supervision.
- Incorporating additional elements of unpredictability in the selection of audit procedures to be performed.

When the risks relate to a single assertion or set of assertions for the same business process or account, the auditor should consider the entity's internal controls. As discussed in Chapter 6, the auditor needs to consider the design and operation of controls within a business process to determine if they prevent, or detect and correct, misstatements. If the controls are properly designed, and the auditor intends to rely on those controls, the auditor will test the operating effectiveness of the controls. Depending on the operating effectiveness of the entity's controls, the auditor will design and perform substantive tests directed at the potential misstatements that may result from the identified risks.

As part of the risk assessment process, the auditor should determine which of the risks identified require special audit consideration. The auditor uses professional judgment to determine which risks are significant, and uses that judgment to determine whether the nature of the risk, the likely magnitude of the potential misstatement including the possibility that the risk may give rise to multiple misstatements, and the likelihood of the risk occurring are such that they require special audit consideration. Examples of the types of items that may result in significant risks include:

- Assertions identified with fraud risk factors.
- Nonroutine or unsystematically processed transactions.
- Significant accounting estimates and judgments.
- Highly complex transactions.
- Application of new accounting standards.
- Revenue recognition in certain industries or for certain types of transactions (see Practice Insight below).
- Industry specific issues.

When the auditor has determined that an assessed risk of material misstatement at a relevant assertion level is a significant risk, the auditor should perform tests of controls that mitigate the significant risk or substantive procedures that directly respond to the significant risk.

Practice **INSIGHT**	Auditing standards state that the auditor should presume that there is a fraud risk involving improper revenue recognition on every audit engagement. The auditor must evaluate the types of revenue or revenue transactions that are subject to such a risk.

Evaluation of Audit Test Results

⚙ [LO 8]   At the completion of the audit, the auditor should consider whether the accumulated results of audit procedures cause the financial statements to be materially misstated. If the auditor concludes that the total misstatements cause the financial statements to be materially misstated, the auditor should request that management eliminate the material misstatement. If management does not eliminate the material misstatement, the auditor should issue a qualified or adverse opinion. On the other hand, if the uncorrected total misstatements do not cause the financial statements to be materially misstated, the auditor should issue an unqualified opinion.

The *Advanced Module* provides a detailed overview of the audit risk model and the relationships of its components. If the auditor has determined that the misstatement is or may be the result of fraud, and either has determined that the effect could be material to the financial statements or has been unable to evaluate whether the effect is material, the auditor should

- Attempt to obtain audit evidence to determine whether, in fact, material fraud has occurred and, if so, its effect.
- Consider the implications for other aspects of the audit.
- Discuss the matter and the approach to further investigation with an appropriate level of management that is at least one level above those involved in committing the fraud and with senior management.
- If appropriate, suggest that the client consult with legal counsel.

If the results of the audit tests indicate a significant risk of fraud, the auditor should consider withdrawing from the engagement and communicating the reasons for withdrawal to the audit committee or others with equivalent authority and responsibility.

Documentation of the Auditor's Risk Assessment and Response

✎ [LO 9]   The auditor has extensive documentation requirements for risk assessment (including fraud risk assessment) and audit responses to identified risks. For example, the auditor should document the risk of material misstatement for all material accounts and classes of transactions in terms of the related assertions. The level of risk may be described quantitatively or qualitatively (high, medium, or low). Exhibit 3–3 shows the use of a questionnaire to document the nature of the entity. Briefly review this exhibit. After considering the responses listed on the document, how would this information guide the planning of your audit? Other areas that require documentation include the following:

- The nature and results of the communication among engagement personnel that occurred in planning the audit regarding the risks of material misstatement.
- The steps performed in obtaining knowledge about the entity's business and its environment. The documentation should include:
  — The risks identified.
  — An evaluation of management's response to such risks.
  — The auditor's assessment of the risk of error or fraud after considering the entity's response.
- The nature, timing, and extent of the procedures performed in response to the risks of material misstatement due to fraud and the results of that work.
- Fraud risks or other conditions that caused the auditor to believe that additional audit procedures or other responses were required to address such risks or other conditions.
- The nature of the communications about or error fraud made to management, the audit committee, and others.

Communications about Fraud to Management, the Audit Committee, and Others

✎ [LO 10]   Whenever the auditor has found evidence that a fraud may exist, that matter should be brought to the attention of an appropriate level of management. Fraud involving senior management and fraud that causes a material misstatement of the financial statements should be reported directly to the audit committee of the board of directors. In addition, the auditor should reach an understanding with the audit committee regarding the expected nature and extent of communications about misappropriations perpetrated by lower-level employees.

The disclosure of fraud to parties other than the client's senior management and its audit committee ordinarily is not part of the auditor's responsibility and ordinarily would be precluded by the auditor's ethical or legal obligations of

EXHIBIT 3-3	A Partial Questionnaire for Documenting the Understanding of EarthWear Clothiers and Its Environment

CLIENT NAME: EARTHWEAR CLOTHIERS
Entity and Environment Category: Nature of the Entity
Year ended: December 31, 2009

Completed by: _____
Reviewed by: _____

Risk Factors	Description/Response	Any Remaining Risk
What are the entity's major sources of revenue, including the nature of its products and/or services?	EarthWear Clothiers generates revenue mainly through the sale of high-quality clothing for outdoor sports, such as hiking, skiing, fly-fishing, and white-water kayaking. The company's product lines also include casual clothes, accessories, shoes, and soft luggage. These sales are made mainly through the company's toll-free number and over its Internet Web sites. In 2009, Internet sales accounted for 21 percent of total revenue.	No. The company uses conservative methods to record revenue and provides an adequate reserve for returned merchandise.
Who are the entity's key customers?	The company's key customers are the 21.5 million persons on its mailing list, approximately 7 million of whom are viewed as "current customers" because they have purchased from the company in the last 24 months. Market research as of January 2008 indicates that approximately 50 percent of customers are in the 35–54 age group and had a median income of $62,000. Almost two-thirds are in professional or managerial positions.	No.
Who are the entity's key suppliers?	During 2009, the company had purchase orders for merchandise from about 300 domestic and foreign manufacturers, including intermediaries (agents). One manufacturer and one intermediary accounted for about 14 and 29 percent of the company's received merchandise dollars, respectively, in 2009. In 2009, about 80 percent of the merchandise was imported, mainly from Asia, Central America, Mexico, South America, and Europe. The remaining 20 percent was made in the United States. The company will continue to take advantage of worldwide sourcing without sacrificing customer service or quality standards.	Yes. The company would be subject to some risk in finding alternative sourcing if this manufacturer and/or intermediary experiences prolonged work stoppages or economic problems. The availability and cost of certain foreign products may be affected by United States and other countries' trade policies, economic events, and the value of the U.S. dollar relative to foreign currencies.
What is the entity's organizational structure?	The company has a well-developed organizational structure with clear lines of authority among the various operating departments and staff functions. The organizational structure is appropriate for EarthWear's activities.	No.
Where are its major locations?	Boise, Idaho, is the main corporate location. EarthWear also has phone and distribution centers in the United Kingdom, Germany, and Japan. During 2009, EarthWear expanded its global Internet presence by launching sites in France, Italy, Ireland, and several eastern European countries.	Yes. France and Italy have restrictive trade laws where local companies get a certain degree of protection from the government when their markets are threatened. Political instability in the eastern European countries could affect EarthWear's sales activities in these countries.
What are the entity's major assets?	The major assets of the company are inventory; property, plant, and equipment; and its customer mailing list.	No.
What are the entity's major liabilities?	The company has no long-term debt. However, it maintains a line of credit for financing purchases during the peak purchasing season.	No. The company has adequate cash flow to meet its current obligations.
What are the entity's financial characteristics including financing sources and current and prospective financial condition?	The company uses its line of credit to meet its normal financing activities. Overall the company's financial condition is good.	No.
Are there any potential related parties?	No.	No.
Are there any individually significant events and transactions such as acquisitions or disposals of subsidiaries, businesses, or product lines during the year?	The expansion of the company's Internet presence to France, Italy, Ireland, and several eastern European countries.	Yes. Restrictive trade laws and the potential for political instability in the eastern European countries.
Does the entity have any major uncertainties or contingencies?	No.	No.

confidentiality. The auditor should recognize, however, that in the following circumstances a duty to disclose outside the entity may exist:

- To comply with certain legal and regulatory requirements.
- To a successor auditor when the successor makes inquiries in accordance with AU 315, Communications between Predecessor and Successor Auditors.
- In response to a subpoena.
- To a funding agency or other specified agency in accordance with requirements for the audits of entities that receive governmental financial assistance.

Materiality[5]

[LO 11] The auditor's consideration of materiality on an audit is a matter of *professional judgment.* Materiality is assessed in terms of the potential effect of a misstatement on decisions made by a reasonable user of the financial statements. This focus arises from the FASB's Statement of Financial Accounting Concepts No. 2, "Qualitative Characteristics of Accounting Information," which provides the following definition:

> **Materiality** is the magnitude of an omission or misstatement of accounting information that, in the light of surrounding circumstances, makes it probable that the judgment of a reasonable person relying on the information would have been changed or influenced by the omission or misstatement.

This definition in the accounting literature is equivalent to the courts' determination of materiality in interpreting the federal securities laws. For example, the U.S. Supreme Court stated that a fact is material if there is "a substantial likelihood that the . . . fact would have been viewed by the reasonable investor as having significantly altered the 'total mix' of information made available."[6] Both of these perspectives require that the auditor assess the amount of misstatement that could affect a reasonable user's decisions. The auditing standard on materiality provides guidance to auditors in assessing the effects of a misstatement on the economic decisions of users. Users are assumed to:

- Have an appropriate knowledge of business and economic activities and accounting and a willingness to study the information in the financial statements with an appropriate diligence.
- Understand that financial statements are prepared and audited to levels of materiality.
- Recognize the uncertainties inherent in the measurement of amounts based on the use of estimates, judgment, and the consideration of future events.
- Make appropriate economic decisions on the basis of the information in the financial statements (AU 312.06).

The determination of materiality, therefore, takes into account how users with such characteristics could reasonably be expected to be influenced in making economic decisions. It is important to note that the opinion paragraph of the auditor's report states that the financial statements present fairly, "in all material respects." This phrase

---

[5]See W. F. Messier, Jr., N. Martinov, and A. Eilifsen, "A Review and Integration of Empirical Research on Materiality: Two Decades Later," *Auditing: A Journal of Practice & Theory* (November 2005), pp. 153–87, for a discussion of materiality research.

[6]*TSC Industries v. Northway, Inc.,* 426 U.S. 438, 449 (1976).

TABLE 3-8	Qualitative Factors That May Affect Establishing and Evaluating Materiality: Steps 1 and 3

Establishing the preliminary judgment about materiality (Step 1):
- Material misstatements in prior years.
- Potential for fraud or illegal acts.
- Small amounts may violate covenants in a loan agreement.
- Small amounts may affect the trend in earnings.
- Small amounts may cause entity to miss forecasted revenue or earnings.

Evaluating the materiality of unadjusted misstatements (Step 3):
- Whether the misstatement masks a change in earnings or trends.
- Whether the misstatement hides a failure to meet analysts' consensus expectations.
- Whether the misstatement changes a loss into income or vice versa.
- Whether the misstatement concerns a segment or other portion of the business that has been portrayed as playing a significant role in the operations or profitability of the entity.
- Whether the misstatement affects compliance with regulatory requirements.
- Whether the misstatement affects compliance with loan covenants or other contractual requirements.
- Whether the misstatement increases management's compensation.
- Whether the misstatement involves the concealment of an unlawful transaction.
- Whether the misstatement may result in a significant positive or negative market reaction.
- Whether small intentional misstatements are part of actions to "manage" earnings.

communicates to third parties that the audit report is limited to material information. Financial statements are materially misstated if they contain errors or fraud that causes them not to present fairly in conformity with GAAP.

The following sections present an approach to assessing materiality. The presentation is based on the general approach provided by auditing standards and to some extent on the more specific policies and procedures suggested by the AICPA.[7] While the policies and procedures of individual CPA firms may differ in some respects, the approach presented here provides the reader with a basic framework for understanding the consideration of materiality in an audit.

In establishing materiality for an audit, the auditor should consider both quantitative and qualitative aspects of the engagement. Although materiality may be planned and implemented using a quantitative approach, the qualitative aspects of misstatements of small amounts may also materially affect the users of financial statements. Table 3–8 presents a list of qualitative factors that may be considered in establishing and evaluating materiality. For example, a client may illegally pay a commissioned agent to secure a sales contract. While the amount of the illegal payment may be immaterial to the financial statements, the disclosure of the illegal act may result in loss of the contract and substantial penalties that may be material. Consider for a moment the impact of a one cent misstatement on earnings per share. In what situations would this one cent misstatement be material? What if that one cent meant the company just met analysts' earnings expectations? The next section presents an approach to applying materiality, which is then followed by an example.

Steps in Applying Materiality

✎ [LO 12]

Figure 3–4 presents the three major steps in the application of materiality to an audit. Steps 1 and 2 are normally performed early in the engagement as part of planning the audit (see Figure 1–4 in Chapter 1). Step 3 is performed usually just prior to, or when the auditor evaluates the evidence at the completion of the audit to determine if it supports the fair presentation of the financial statements (again, refer to Figure 1–4).

Step 1: Determine a Materiality Level for the Overall Financial Statements

The auditor should establish a materiality level for the financial statements taken as a whole. We will refer to this level of materiality as *planning* materiality. Planning materiality is the maximum amount by which the auditor

---

[7]American Institute of Certified Public Accountants, Audit Guide, *Audit Sampling* (New York: AICPA, 2008).

FIGURE 3-4	Steps in Applying Materiality on an Audit

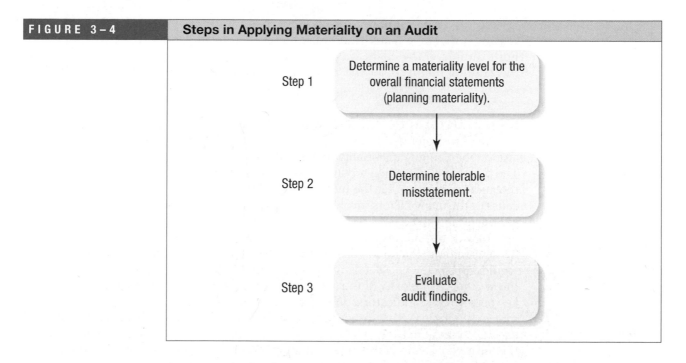

believes the financial statements could be misstated and still *not* affect the decisions of users. Materiality, however, is a relative, not an absolute, concept. For example, $5,000 might be considered highly material for a small sole proprietorship, but this amount would clearly be immaterial for a large multinational corporation. Thus, the relative size of the company being audited affects planning materiality.

Examples of benchmarks that might be appropriate for determining planning materiality include total revenues, gross profit, and other categories of reported income (e.g., profit before tax from continuing operations, net income from continuing operations, or net income before taxes). Net income from continuing operations might be a suitable benchmark for a profit-oriented entity with stable earnings. For a not-for-profit entity, total revenues or total expenses might be more appropriate benchmarks. Lastly, asset-based entities (e.g., investment funds) might use net assets as a benchmark.

A common rule of thumb in practice is to use 5 percent of pretax net income for profit-oriented entities. However, if current year pretax income is not stable, predictable, or representative of an entity's size, auditors might use an average of the previous year's income or another base. Difficulties also arise in using net income as a base when the entity is close to breaking even or experiencing a loss. For example, suppose that an entity has net income before taxes of $3,000,000 one year and the auditor decides that 5 percent of that amount, $150,000, would be material. The scope of the audit in that year would be based on a planning materiality of $150,000. Suppose, in the following year, the entity's net income before taxes falls to $250,000 due to a temporary decrease in sales prices for its products. If the auditor uses the 5 percent factor, the planning materiality would be $12,500 ($250,000 × .05), and a much more extensive audit would be required. Thus, with fluctuating net income, using an average of the prior three years' net income or another base such as total assets or total revenues may provide a more stable benchmark from year to year.

Some examples of percentages applied to benchmarks that might be considered include the following:

- For a profit-oriented entity, 3 to 5 percent of profit before tax from continuing operations, or .5 percent of total revenues.
- For a not-for-profit entity, .5 percent of total expenses or total revenues.
- For an entity in the mutual fund industry, .5 percent of net asset value.

The resulting computation of planning materiality may also be adjusted down for any qualitative factors that may be relevant to the entity (refer to Table 3–8). For example, if the client was close to violating a covenant in a loan agreement, the auditor might lower the planning materiality to respond to this qualitative factor.

Step 2: Determine Tolerable Misstatement[8]

Step 2 involves determining tolerable misstatement based on planning materiality. Tolerable misstatement is the amount of planning materiality that is allocated to an account or class of transactions. The purpose of allocating a portion of planning materiality is to establish a scope for the audit procedures for the individual account balance or class of transactions. Because of the many factors involved, there is no required or optimal method for allocating materiality to an account balance or class of transactions.

As with overall materiality, there are qualitative factors that must be considered in determining tolerable misstatement. Examples of qualitative factors auditors would consider when determining tolerable misstatement for an account include the size and complexity of the account, the importance of changes in the account to key performance indicators, debt covenants, and meeting published forecasts or estimates (see Table 3–8). In practice, auditors commonly set tolerable misstatement for each account at between 50 and 75 percent of planning materiality. Qualitative factors also play a role in this determination. Obviously, these approaches result in an allocation of combined tolerable misstatement that is greater than materiality. Some firms cap the size of combined or aggregated tolerable misstatement to a multiple of materiality. For example, combined tolerable misstatement allocated to accounts can be up to a multiple of four times planning materiality. There are a number of reasons why allocating combined tolerable misstatement greater than materiality makes sense from an audit planning perspective:

- Not all accounts will be misstated by the full amount of their tolerable misstatement allocation.
- Audits of the individual accounts are conducted simultaneously (typically by different members of the audit team). If accounts were audited sequentially, unadjusted misstatements observed during testing would count against materiality and theoretically the auditor could carry the unused portion of materiality to the next account and so forth.
- Materiality as a percentage of large accounts, such as inventory; accounts receivable; revenues; or plant, property, and equipment, is often a very small fraction of the account (less than 2 percent), and the scope of planned auditor procedures will be sufficiently precise to identify significant misstatements.
- When errors are identified, the auditors typically perform additional procedures in that, and related, accounts
- Overall financial statement materiality serves as a "safety net." If individual unadjusted misstatements are less than tolerable misstatement, but aggregate to an amount greater than materiality, then (1) the audit client will need to make adjustments to decrease the unadjusted misstatements below materiality; (2) the auditor will need to perform more testing; and/ or (3) the auditor will issue a qualified or adverse opinion.

---

[8]The term "performance materiality" is now used in the international auditing standards and in the ASB's redraft of Materiality in Planning and Performing an Audit (AU 312). The auditor is required by the proposed standard to determine performance materiality. Performance materiality is a concept similar to tolerable misstatement. Performance materiality is determined in order to address the risk that the aggregate of individually immaterial misstatements may cause the financial statements to be materially misstated and provide a margin for possible undetected misstatements. Tolerable misstatement is the application of performance materiality to a particular sampling procedure. Tolerable misstatement may be the same amount or an amount lower than performance materiality.

Taken together, these points suggest that it would be inefficient for the auditor to simply subdivide materiality proportionally to each account. This would result in unnecessarily low tolerable misstatement levels. The lower the tolerable misstatement, the more extensive the required audit testing. In the extreme, if tolerable misstatement were very small or zero, the auditor would have to test every transaction making up an account. Imagine how a house inspector's investigation and related costs would differ if she or he were asked to identify all potential problems greater than $2 versus a "tolerable damage" threshold of $2,000. Similarly, auditing standards recognize that an auditor works within economic limits, and for the audit opinion to be economically useful it must be completed in a reasonable length of time at reasonable costs.

Step 3: Evaluate Audit Findings

Step 3 is completed near the end of the audit, when the auditor evaluates all the evidence that has been gathered. Based on the results of the audit procedures conducted, the auditor aggregates misstatements from each account or class of transactions. The aggregate amount includes known and likely misstatements (see definitions presented earlier in the chapter). In evaluating likely misstatements, the auditor should be very careful in considering the risk of material misstatement in accounts that are subject to estimation. Examples of such estimates include inventory obsolescence, loan loss reserves, uncollectible receivables, and warranty obligations. Seldom can accounting estimates be considered accurate with certainty. If, based on the best audit evidence, the auditor believes the estimated amount included in the financial statements is unreasonable, the difference between that estimate and the closest reasonable estimate should be treated as a likely misstatement. The *closest reasonable estimate* may be a range of acceptable amounts or a precisely determined point estimate, if that is a better estimate than any other amount (AU 312.57). For example, suppose that the auditor concludes based on the evidence that the allowance for doubtful accounts should be between $210,000 and $270,000. If management's recorded estimate falls within this range (say $250,000), the auditor may conclude that the recorded amount is reasonable and no difference would be aggregated. If the recorded estimate falls outside this range (say $190,000), the difference between the recorded amount and the amount at the closest end of the auditor's range ($20,000) would be aggregated as a likely misstatement.

In evaluating the aggregate misstatement, the auditor should consider the effect of misstatements not adjusted in the prior period because they were judged to be immaterial. The auditor compares this aggregate misstatement to the planning materiality. (Refer to Problem 3-33 for an example of the auditor's consideration of prior year misstatements in the evaluation of current year audit results.)

If the auditor's judgment about materiality at the planning stage (Step 1) was based on the same information available at the evaluation stage (Step 3), materiality for planning and evaluation would be the same. However, the auditor may identify factors or items during the course of the audit that cause a revision to the planning materiality. Thus, planning materiality may differ from the materiality used in evaluating the audit findings. When this occurs, the auditor should carefully document the reasons for using a different materiality level.

When the aggregated misstatements are less than the planning materiality, the auditor can conclude that the financial statements are fairly presented. Conversely, when the aggregated misstatements are greater than planning materiality, the auditor should request that the client adjust the financial statements. If the client refuses to adjust the financial statements for the likely misstatements, the auditor should issue a qualified or adverse opinion because the financial statements do not present fairly in conformity with GAAP.

An Example

❧ **[LO 13]**

In this example, the three steps for applying materiality are discussed using financial information for EarthWear Clothiers for the year ended December 31, 2009. This financial information is taken from the case illustration included in Chapter 1.

Step 1: Determine the Planning Materiality

EarthWear Clothiers' net income before taxes is $36 million (rounded). Assume that the auditors, Willis & Adams, have decided that 5 percent of this benchmark is appropriate for planning materiality. Thus, they determine planning materiality to be $1,800,000 ($36,000,000 × .05). To determine the final amount for materiality, the auditors should consider whether any qualitative factors are relevant for the engagement (see Table 3–8). In our example, assume that the auditors have determined that none of the qualitative factors are relevant and that the $1,800,000 will be used for planning materiality. This is the amount that is allocated to the specific accounts or classes of transactions in Step 2.

Step 2: Determine Tolerable Misstatement

Public accounting firms use a number of different approaches to accomplish this step. In our example, for simplicity of presentation, we assume that EarthWear's auditors allocate 50 percent of planning materiality to each account as tolerable misstatement. Therefore, tolerable misstatement is $900,000 ($1,800,000 × .50).

Step 3: Evaluate Audit Findings

Tolerable misstatement can be used for determining the fair presentation of the individual accounts after completion of the audit work. Auditing standards require that the auditor document the nature and effect of aggregated misstatements. Exhibit 3–4 presents an

EXHIBIT 3-4	Example Working Paper for Estimating Likely Misstatements

EARTHWEAR CLOTHIERS
Schedule of Proposed Adjusting Entries
12/31/09

Workpaper Ref.	Proposed Adjusting Entry	Assets	Liabilities	Equity	Revenues	Expenses
N10	Payroll expense					75,000
	Bonuses					140,000
	Accrued liabilities		215,000			
	To accrue payroll through 12/31 and recognize 2009 bonuses.					
F20	Cost of sales					312,500
	Inventory	(312,500)				
	To adjust ending inventory based on sample results.					
F22	Inventory	227,450				
	Accounts payable		227,450			
	To record inventory in transit at 12/31.					
R15	Accounts receivable	79,850				
	Sales				79,850	
	To record sales cutoff errors at 12/31.					
	Total	(5,200)	442,450		79,850	527,500

Tolerable Misstatement = $900,000 (50 percent of planning materiality).
Conclusion: Based on the above analysis, the account balances for EarthWear Clothiers are fairly stated in accordance with GAAP.

example of a working paper that can be used to aggregate the effects of misstatements identified during the audit. Assume that during the course of the audit the auditor identified four misstatements. The misstatements are compared to the tolerable misstatement allocated to each account. For example, the first misstatement indicates a known error in the accrual of payroll expense and bonuses. The total misstatement of accrued payroll is $215,000. The second entry is based on the results of a statistical sampling application for inventory. The statistical results indicated there is a likely misstatement of $312,500. In this example, no error is larger than the tolerable misstatement amount of $900,000, and the total of the misstatements is also less than overall financial statement materiality. Before making a final decision, the auditor should consider further possible misstatements that may be due to sampling and misstatements that carry forward from the prior year. The auditor should document his or her conclusion as to whether the aggregated misstatements cause the financial statements to be materially misstated (see Exhibit 3–4). If one of the entries were in excess of the tolerable misstatement for an account balance, or if the aggregated misstatements were greater than materiality, the client would have to adjust the financial statements or the auditor would have to issue a qualified or adverse opinion.

Advanced Module: The Relationships within the Audit Risk Model

The diagram below shows the relationships between risk factors, the components (planned and achieved) of the audit risk model, audit evidence, and the outcome of the audit process.

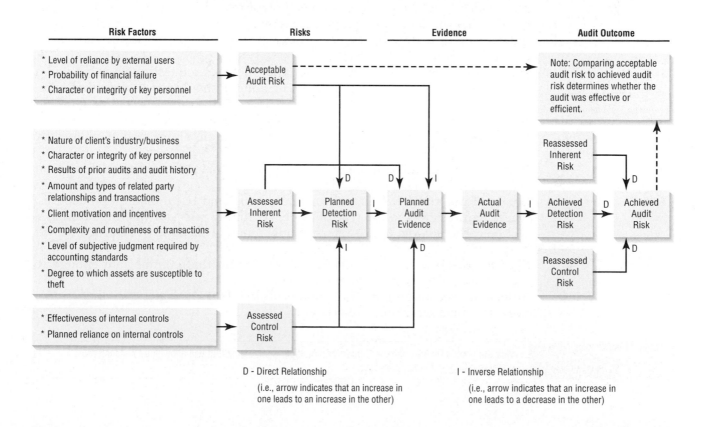

KEY TERMS

Analytical procedures. Evaluations of financial information made by a study of plausible relationships among both financial and nonfinancial data.

Audit procedures. Specific acts performed by the auditor in gathering evidence to determine if specific assertations are being met.

Audit risk. The risk that the auditor may unknowingly fail to appropriately modify the opinion on materially misstated financial statements.

Business risks. Risks resulting from significant conditions, events, circumstances, and actions or inactions that could adversely affect management's ability to execute its strategies and to achieve its objectives, or through the setting of inappropriate objectives or strategies.

Closest reasonable estimate. A range of acceptable amounts or a precisely determined point estimate for an estimate (e.g., uncollectible receivables), if that is a better estimate than any other amount.

Control risk. The risk that material misstatements that could occur will not be prevented, or detected and corrected, by internal controls.

Detection risk. The risk that the auditor will not detect a material misstatement that exists in the financial statements.

Engagement risk. The risk that the auditor is exposed to financial loss or damage to his or her professional reputation from litigation, adverse publicity, or other events arising in connection with financial statements audited and reported on.

Errors. Unintentional misstatements or omissions of amounts or disclosures.

Fraud. Intentional misstatements that can be classified as fraudulent financial reporting and/or misappropriation of assets.

Inherent risk. The susceptibility of an assertion to material misstatement, assuming no related controls.

Materiality. The magnitude of an omission or misstatement of accounting information that, in light of surrounding circumstances, makes it probable that the judgment of a reasonable person relying on the information would have been changed or influenced.

Professional skepticism. An attitude that includes a questioning mind and a critical assessment of audit evidence. The auditor should not assume that management is either honest or dishonest.

Risk assessment. The identification, analysis, and management of risks relevant to the preparation of financial statements that are fairly presented in conformity with GAAP.

Risk of material misstatement. The auditor's combined assessment of inherent risk and control risk.

Scope of the audit. Refers to the *nature, timing,* and *extent* of audit procedures, where nature refers to the type of evidence; timing refers to when the evidence will be gathered; and extent refers to how much of the type of evidence will be evaluated.

Significant risk. A risk of material misstatement that is important enough to require special audit consideration.

Tolerable misstatement. The amount of the planning materiality that is allocated to a financial statement account.

Visit the book's Online Learning Center for a multiple-choice quiz that will allow you to assess your understanding of chapter concepts.

REVIEW QUESTIONS

[LO 1] 3-1 Distinguish between audit risk and engagement risk.

[1,2] 3-2 How do inherent risk and control risk differ from detection risk?

[4] 3-3 What are some limitations of the audit risk model?

[2] 3-4 Distinguish between sampling and nonsampling risk.

[5,6] 3-5 In understanding the entity and its environment, the auditor gathers knowledge about which categories of information?

[5,6] 3-6 Give three examples of conditions and events that may indicate the existence of business risks.

[5,6] 3-7 Distinguish between errors and fraud. Give three examples of each.

[11,12] 3-8 Why is it important for CPA firms to develop policies and procedures for establishing materiality?

[12] 3-9 List and describe the three major steps in applying materiality to an audit.

[12] 3-10 While net income before taxes is frequently used for calculating planning materiality, discuss circumstances when total assets or revenues might be better bases for calculating planning materiality.

[11] 3-11 Give three examples of qualitative factors that might affect the planning materiality.

[11] 3-12 List four qualitative factors that the auditor should consider when evaluating the unadjusted misstatements detected during the audit.

MULTIPLE-CHOICE QUESTIONS

[1,11] 3-13 Which of the following concepts are pervasive in the application of generally accepted auditing standards, particularly the standards of fieldwork and reporting?
a. Internal control.
b. Expected misstatement.
c. Control risk.
d. Materiality and audit risk.

[1] 3-14 The existence of audit risk is recognized by the statement in the auditor's standard report that the auditor
a. Obtains reasonable assurance about whether the financial statements are free of material misstatement.
b. Assesses the accounting principles used and also evaluates the overall financial statement presentation.
c. Realizes that some matters, either individually or in the aggregate, are important while other matters are not important.
d. Is responsible for expressing an opinion on the financial statements, which are the responsibility of management.

[1,2] 3-15 Risk of material misstatement refers to a combination of which two "client" components of the audit risk model?
a. Audit risk and inherent risk.
b. Audit risk and control risk.
c. Inherent risk and control risk.
d. Control risk and detection risk.

[6,8] 3-16 Auditing standards require auditors to make certain inquiries of management regarding fraud. Which of the following inquiries is required?
a. Whether management has ever intentionally violated the securities laws.

b. Whether management has any knowledge of fraud that has been perpetrated on or within the entity.

c. Management's attitudes toward regulatory authorities.

d. Management's attitude about hiring ethical employees.

[5,6]   3-17   Which of the following characteristics most likely would heighten an auditor's concern about the risk of intentional manipulation of financial statements?

a. Turnover of senior accounting personnel is low.

b. Insiders recently purchased additional shares of the entity's stock.

c. Management places substantial emphasis on meeting earnings projections.

d. The rate of change in the entity's industry is slow.

[5,6]   3-18   Which of the following is a misappropriation of assets?

a. Classifying inventory held for resale as supplies.

b. Investing cash and earning a 3 percent rate of return as opposed to paying off a loan with an interest rate of 7 percent.

c. An employee of a consumer electronics store steals 12 CD players.

d. Management estimates bad debt expense as 2 percent of sales when it actually expects bad debts equal to 10 percent of sales.

[6,8]   3-19   Which of the following is an example of fraudulent financial reporting?

a. Company management falsifies inventory count tags, thereby overstating ending inventory and understating cost of sales.

b. An employee diverts customer payments to his personal use, concealing his actions by debiting an expense account, thus overstating expenses.

c. An employee steals inventory, and the shrinkage is recorded as a cost of goods sold.

d. An employee borrows small tools from the company and neglects to return them; the cost is reported as a miscellaneous operating expense.

[5,6]   3-20   When is a duty to disclose fraud to parties other than the client's senior management and its audit committee most likely to exist?

a. When the amount is material.

b. When the fraud results from misappropriation of assets rather than fraudulent financial reporting.

c. In response to inquiries from a successor auditor.

d. When a line manager rather than a lower-level employee commits the fraudulent act.

[12,13]   3-21   Tolerable misstatement is

a. The amount of misstatement that management is willing to tolerate in the financial statements.

b. Materiality for the balance sheet as a whole.

c. Materiality for the income statement as a whole.

d. Materiality allocated to a specific account.

[3,12]   3-22   As lower acceptable levels of both audit risk and materiality are established, the auditor should plan more work on individual accounts to

a. Find smaller errors.

b. Find larger errors.

c. Increase the tolerable misstatements in the accounts.

d. Decrease the risk of overreliance.

PROBLEMS

[1,2,3,11]   3-23   The auditor should consider audit risk and materiality when planning and performing an examination of financial statements in accordance with generally accepted auditing standards. Audit Risk and materiality should also be considered together in determining the nature, timing, and extent of auditing procedures and in evaluating the results of those procedures.

Required:

a. Define *audit risk* and *materiality*.

b. Describe the components of audit risk (e.g., inherent risk, control risk, and detection risk).

c. Explain how these components are interrelated.

d. Discuss the factors that affect the determination of planning materiality.

e. Describe the relationship between materiality for planning purposes and materiality for evaluation purposes.

(AICPA, adapted)

[1,2,3]   3-24   The CPA firm of Lumley & Lu uses a quantitative approach to implementing the audit risk model. Calculate detection risk for each of the following hypothetical clients.

Client No.	Audit Risk	Risk of Material Misstatement	Detection Risk
1	5%	20%	
2	5%	50%	
3	10%	15%	
4	10%	40%	

[1,2,3]   3-25   The CPA firm of Quigley & Associates uses a qualitative approach to implementing the audit risk model. Audit risk is categorized using two terms: very low and low. The risk of material misstatement and detection risk are categorized using three terms: low, moderate, and high. Calculate detection risk for each of the following hypothetical clients.

Client No.	Audit Risk	Risk of Material Misstatement	Detection Risk
1	Low	Moderate	
2	Very low	High	
3	Low	Low	
4	Very low	Moderate	

[1,2,3]   3-26   You are considering acceptable audit risk at the financial statement level. For each of the following independent scenarios, based only on the information provided, indicate the effect on acceptable audit risk compared to a typical private company audit client.

a. LVD is a pharmaceutical company that has three successful drugs. They have recently decided to make a public offering of their stock.

b. Budd Co., a private company, has approached your audit firm to bid on their annual audit. During discussions with the CFO, you learn that the company is filing for bankruptcy.

c. Stephens Inc., a private company, has recently installed a new accounting information system.

[1,2,3]   3-27   When planning a financial statement audit, a CPA must understand audit risk and its components. The firm of Pack & Peck evaluates the risk of material misstatement (RMM) by disaggregating RMM into its two components: inherent risk and control risk.

Required:

For each illustration, select the component of audit risk that is most directly illustrated. The components of audit risk may be used once, more than once, or not at all.

Components of Audit Risk:
a. Engagement risk
b. Control risk
c. Detection risk
d. Inherent risk

Illustration	Component of Audit Risk
1. A client fails to discover employee fraud on a timely basis because bank accounts are not reconciled monthly.	
2. Cash is more susceptible to theft than an inventory of coal.	
3. Confirmation of receivables by an auditor fails to detect a material misstatement.	
4. Disbursements have occurred without proper approval.	
5. There is inadequate segregation of duties.	
6. A necessary substantive audit procedure is omitted.	
7. Notes receivable are susceptible to material misstatement, assuming there are no related internal controls.	
8. Technological developments make a major product obsolete.	
9. An auditor complies with GAAS on an audit engagement, but the shareholders sue the auditor for issuing misleading financial statements.	
10. XYZ Company, a client, lacks sufficient working capital to continue operations.	

[3,5,6]   3-28   For each of the following situations, explain how risk of material misstatement should be assessed and what effect that assessment will have on detection risk.

a. Johnson, Inc., is a fast-growing trucking company operating in the wsoutheastern part of the United States. The company is publicly held, but Ivan Johnson and his sons control 55 percent of the stock. Ivan wJohnson is chairman of the board and CEO. He personally makes all major decisions with little consultation with the board of directors. Most of the directors, however, are either members of the Johnson family or long-standing friends. The board basically rubber-stamps Ivan Johnson's decisions.

b. MaxiWrite Corporation is one of several companies engaged in the manufacture of high-speed, high-capacity data storage devices. The industry is very competitive and subject to quick changes in technology. MaxiWrite's operating results would place the company in the second quartile in terms of profitability and financial position. The company has never been the leader in the industry, with its products typically slightly behind the industry leader's in terms of performance.

c. The First National Bank of Pond City has been your client for the past two years. During that period you have had numerous arguments with the president and the controller over a number of accounting issues. The major issue has related to the bank's reserve for loan losses and the value of collateral. Your prior audits have indicated that a significant adjustment is required each year to the loan loss reserves.

[5,6,9]   3-29   Management fraud (e.g., fraudulent financial reporting) is a relatively rare event. However, when it does occur, the frauds (e.g., Enron and WorldCom) can have a significant effect on shareholders, employees, and other parties. SAS No. 99 (AU 316) provides the relevant guidance for auditors.

Required:

a. What is the auditor's responsibility for detecting fraud?

b. Describe the three conditions that are generally present when fraud occurs?

c. What are the objectives of the "brainstorming" meeting that is held among the engagement team members?

d. What is the required documentation for identified risk factors?

[5,6,7,8]   3-30   Assume that your firm is considering accepting NewSkin Pharma as a new audit client. NewSkin is a start-up biotech firm that has publicly traded stock on NASDAQ. Your audit partner has asked you to perform some preliminary work for the firm's client acceptance process.

Required:

a. Prepare a list of business risks that NewSkin likely will face as a start-up biotech firm.

b. Choose two of these risks and consider how they might affect your decision to accept NewSkin as a client.

[12,13]   3-31   For each of the following scenarios, perform the three steps in the materiality process: (1) determine planning materiality; (2) determine tolerable misstatement; and (3) evaluate the audit findings.

Scenario 1:

Murphy & Johnson is a manufacturer of small motors for lawnmowers, tractors, and snowmobiles. The components of its financial statements are (1) net income before operations = $21 million; (2) total assets = $550 million; and (3) total revenues = $775 million.

a. Determine planning materiality, and determine tolerable misstatement. Justify your decisions.

   During the course of the audit, Murphy & Johnson's CPA firm detected two misstatements that aggregated to an overstatement of net income of $1.25 million.

b. Evaluate the audit findings. Justify your decisions.

Scenario 2:

Delta Investments provides a group of mutual funds for investors. The components of its financial statements are (1) net income before operations = $40 million; (2) total assets = $4.3 billion; and (3) total revenues = $900 million.

a. Determine planning materiality, and determine tolerable misstatement. Justify your decisions.

   During the course of the audit, Delta's CPA firm detected two misstatements that aggregated to an overstatement of net income of $5.75 million.

b. Evaluate the audit findings. Justify your decisions.

Scenario 3:

Swell Computers manufactures desktop and laptop computers. The components of the financial statements are: (1) net income = $500,000; (2) total assets = $2.2 billion; and (3) total revenues = $7 billion.

a. Determine planning materiality and tolerable misstatement. Justify your decisions. During the course of the audit, Swell's CPA firm detected one misstatement that resulted in an overstatement of net income by $1.5 million.

b. Evaluate the audit findings. Justify your decisions.

DISCUSSION CASES

[5,6]   3-32   **CarProof Corp. (CarProof).** CarProof is a public company founded in 2000 to manufacture and sell specialty auto products mainly relating to paint protection and rustproofing. By 2007, the CarProof board of directors felt that the company's products had fully matured and that it needed to diversify. CarProof aggressively sought out new products, and in March 2008 it acquired the formula and patent for a specialized motor lubricant (Run-Smooth) from SIM, LLC. In addition, the company purchased 15 percent of SIM's outstanding common stock. At the time of the stock purchase, Steve Matthews owned 100 percent of SIM; he retained ownership of 85 percent of SIM after CarProof's 15 percent purchase. In December 2008, the board of directors appointed Mr. Matthews to be president of CarProof.

Run-Smooth is unlike conventional motor lubricants. Its innovative molecular structure accounts for what management believes is its superior performance. Although it is more expensive to produce and has a higher selling price than its conventional competitors, management believes that it will reduce maintenance costs and extend the life of equipment in which it is used.

CarProof's main competitor is a very successful multinational conglomerate that has excellent customer recognition of its products and a large distribution network. To create a market niche for Run-Smooth, CarProof's management is targeting commercial businesses in western states that service vehicle fleets and industrial equipment.

CarProof's existing facilities were not adequate to produce Run-Smooth in commercial quantities. In June 2009 CarProof commenced construction of a new plant in Nevada. After lengthy negotiation, it received a $900,000 grant from the state government. The terms of the grant require CarProof to maintain certain employment levels in Nevada over the next three years or the grant must be repaid. The new facilities became operational on December 1, 2009. CarProof financed its recent expansion with a term bank loan. Management is considering issuing additional stock later in 2010 to address the company's cash flow problems.

CarProof's auditors resigned in February 2010, after which Steve Matthews contacted your firm. The previous auditors informed Mr. Matthews that they disagreed with CarProof's valuation of deferred development costs for Run-Smooth.

It is now April 20, 2010, and you and a partner in your firm have just met with Steve Matthews to discuss the services your firm can provide to CarProof for the year ending March 31, 2010. During your meeting, you collected the following information:

- CarProof incurred substantial losses during each of the past three fiscal years.
- There have been no significant orders of Run-Smooth received to date.
- CarProof has commenced a lawsuit against a major competitor for patent infringement and industrial espionage. Management has evidence that it believes will result in a successful action, and wishes to record

the estimated gain on settlement of $4 million. Although no court date has been set, legal correspondence shows that the competitor intends "to fight this action to the highest court in the land."

- Deferred development costs of $2 million represent material, labor, and subcontract costs incurred during 2008 and 2009 to evaluate the Run-Smooth product and prepare it for market. CarProof has not taken any amortization to date but thinks that a period of 20 years would be appropriate.
- Royalties of $0.25 per liter of Run-Smooth produced are to be paid annually to SIM.
- The $3.514 million term bank loan is secured by a floating charge over all corporate assets. The loan agreement requires CarProof to undergo an annual environmental assessment of its old and new blending facilities.

As you return to the office, the partner tells you that he is interested in having CarProof as an audit client. She wants a memo from you covering in detail the audit and business risks you foresee arising from this potential engagement.

Required:
Prepare the memo requested by the audit partner.

[11,12,13]   3-33   **Wyly Waste Management.** SEC Staff Accounting Bulletin No. 108, *Considering the Effects of Prior Year Misstatements When Quantifying Misstatements in Current Year Financial Statements* (SAB 108) was issued in 2006. The SEC stipulates that a registrant should quantify a current year misstatement using both the iron curtain approach and the rollover approach.

Iron Curtain Method—this approach quantifies the misstatement based on the amount required to correct the misstatement in the balance sheet at the period end, regardless of the misstatement's year of origination.

Rollover Method—this approach quantifies the misstatement based on the amount of the error that originates in the current year income statement. This approach ignores the effects of correcting the portion of the current year balance sheet misstatements that originated in prior years (i.e., it ignores the "carryover effects" of prior year misstatements).

If a misstatement is considered material to the financial statements, after all of the relevant quantitative and qualitative factors are considered, the registrant's financial statements would need to be adjusted.

Wyly Waste Management ("WWM") is an SEC registrant and your firm is its auditor. Planning materiality for the audit is $100,000. Shortly after the end of the year, WWM's CFO is meeting with your audit partner to review the preliminary results of the audit. Your partner presents a copy of the draft unadjusted error summary to the CFO, which contains one error.

During the year, WWM did not capitalize individual expenditures of less than $10,000, which is in accordance with its company policy. In the past, WWM's capital expenditures have been relatively constant each period and the expensing of the items has not caused any material errors. In the prior year two years, the expensed items totaled $7,500 and $5,000 respectively. However, in the current year, WWM undertook significant development of a new waste disposal plant. As a result, WWM incurred eight capital expenditures of less than $10,000 each that were not capitalized. These purchases totaled $75,000.

Required:
a. Should your partner require WWM to record an adjustment for the expensed items in the current year?
b. Suppose the facts were changed and the expensed items for the prior two years totaled $22,500 and $15,000, respectively. Should your partner require WWM to record an adjustment for the expensed items in the current year?
c. Given the facts as presented in b, above, how much of an adjustment should the auditor require before being willing to issue an unqualified audit opinion?

INTERNET ASSIGNMENTS

[5,6,7]   3-34   Auditors are required to obtain and support an understanding of the entity and its environment in order to identify business risks. Much of the information needed to identify the risks can be obtained from the company's annual report, 10K, and proxy materials. Many companies publish these documents on their Web site. Additionally, industry information on these companies can be obtained from Web sites such as Yahoo (yahoo. marketguide.com).
a. In groups of two or three members, complete the questionnaire for a real-world company assigned by your instructor. There may be some questions asked on the questionnaire that you will be unable to answer. If you cannot answer a question, respond "information not available."
b. The measurement and performance section asks for information on the entity's key performance indicators (KPIs). Identify what you think the KPIs are for the company assigned, and how the company compares to its industry averages and major competitors. Prepare tables for this data and a memo of your analyses.

Risk Response Table

Business Risks	Audit Area Affected	Assertion	Response

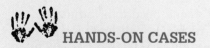

HANDS-ON CASES

	Materiality and Tolerable Misstatement Using Willis and Adams' guidelines and EarthWear's unaudited financial statements, determine materiality and allocate tolerable misstatement to accounts. *Visit the book's Online Learning Center at www.mhhe.com/messier7e to find a detailed description of the case and to download required materials.*
EarthWear Online	**Understanding the Entity and Its Environment** Complete the questionnaire for documenting the understanding of EarthWear Clothiers and its environment. *Visit the book's Online Learning Center at www.mhhe.com/messier7e to find a detailed description of the case and to download required materials.*

| www.mhhe.com/
messier7e | Visit the book's Online Learning Center for problem material to be completed using the ACL software packaged with your new text. |

KAPLAN
CPA Review

| www.mhhe.com/
messier7e | **Nivotny and Assoc. and Schmidt Ltd.**
This simulation will test your understanding of materiality, fraud risk, and the assertions about account balances at the period end. The research question on working papers is given in preparation for Chapter 4. *To begin this simulation, visit the book's Online Learning Center.* |

CHAPTER 4

LEARNING OBJECTIVES

Upon completion of this chapter you will

[1] Understand the relationship between audit evidence and the auditor's report.

[2] Know management assertions about classes of transactions and events for the period under audit, assertions about account balances at the period end, and assertions about presentation and disclosure.

[3] Know why audit procedures are performed.

[4] Learn the basic concepts of audit evidence.

[5] Know the audit procedures used for obtaining audit evidence.

[6] Understand the reliability of the types of evidence.

[7] Understand the objectives of audit documentation.

[8] Develop an understanding of the content, types, organization, and ownership of audit documentation.

RELEVANT ACCOUNTING AND AUDITING PRONOUNCEMENTS

FASB Statement of Financial Accounting Concepts No. 2, Qualitative Characteristics of Accounting Information

AICPA, *Assessing and Responding to Audit Risk in a Financial Statement Audit* (Audit Guide) (New York: AICPA, 2006)

AU 120, Defining Professional Requirements in Statements on Auditing Standards

AU 311, Planning and Supervision

AU 312, Audit Risk and Materiality in Conducting an Audit

AU 314, Understanding the Entity and Its Environment and Assessing the Risks of Material Misstatement

AU 316, Consideration of Fraud in a Financial Statement Audit

AU 318, Performing Audit Procedures in Response to Assessed Risks and Evaluating the Audit Evidence Obtained

AU 326, Audit Evidence

AU 329, Analytical Procedures

AU 330, The Confirmation Process

AU 339, Audit Documentation

AU 342, Auditing Accounting Estimates

PCAOB, Rule 3100: Compliance with Auditing and Related Professional Practice Standards

PCAOB Auditing Standard No. 3, Audit Documentation (AS3)

PCAOB, Proposed Auditing Standards Related to the Auditor's Assessment of and Response to Risk, PCAOB Release No. 2008-006 (October 21, 2008)

Audit Evidence and Audit Documentation

This chapter covers the third of the three fundamental audit concepts introduced in Chapter 1: *audit evidence.* Audit evidence is all the information used by the auditor in arriving at the conclusions on which the audit opinion is based, including the information contained in the accounting records underlying the financial statements and other information. In Chapter 1, we indicated that auditing is essentially a set of conceptual tools that guide an auditor in collecting and evaluating evidence regarding others' assertions, and we assured you that these conceptual tools are extremely useful in a variety of settings. We encourage you to keep this perspective in mind as you study Chapter 4. While this chapter does contain some lists you will likely want to commit to memory (e.g., management assertions and characteristics of audit evidence), remember that these are not just lists—they constitute powerful conceptual tools that can help you in almost any setting that requires you to collect and evaluate evidence. Understanding the nature and characteristics of evidence is fundamental to effective auditing and is a key part of the conceptual tool kit we hope to help you acquire as you go through this book.

On a typical audit most of the auditor's work involves obtaining and evaluating evidence using procedures such as inspection of records and confirmations to test the fair presentation of the financial statements. To perform this task effectively and efficiently, an auditor must thoroughly understand the important aspects of audit evidence. This includes understanding how audit evidence relates to financial statement assertions and the auditor's report, the sufficiency and competency of evidence, types of audit procedures, and the documentation of evidence in the working papers. Each of these topics is covered in this chapter. 🌐

The Relationship of Audit Evidence to the Audit Report

[LO 1] Auditing standards provide the basic framework for the auditor's understanding of audit evidence and its use in supporting his or her opinion on the financial statements. The auditor gathers evidence by conducting audit procedures to test management assertions. This evidence serves as the support for the auditor's opinion about whether the financial statements are fairly presented. Figure 4–1 presents an overview of the relationships among the financial statements, management assertions about components of the financial statements, audit procedures, and the audit report. More specifically, the financial statements reflect management's assertions about the various financial statement components. The auditor tests management's assertions by conducting audit procedures that provide evidence on whether each relevant management assertion is supported. When the evidence supports management's assertions, the auditor can issue an unqualified audit report.

Auditors typically divide financial statements into components or segments in order to manage the audit. A component can be a financial statement account or a business process. As indicated in Chapter 2, the basic processes of most businesses are the *revenue process,* the *purchasing process,* the *human resource management process,* the *inventory management process,* and the *financing/investing process.* Sometimes business processes are referred to as transaction cycles (e.g., the revenue cycle). Each process may involve a number of important transactions. Business processes support functions such as sales and services, materials acquisition, production and distribution, human resource management, and treasury management. This text focuses on business processes and their related transactions and financial statement accounts. Examining business processes and their related accounts allows the auditor to gather evidence by examining the processing of related transactions through the information system from their origin to their ultimate disposition in the accounting journals and ledgers. Later chapters in this text cover each of the major business processes that auditors typically encounter on an engagement.

FIGURE 4–1	An Overview of the Relationships among the Financial Statements, Management Assertions, Audit Procedures, and the Audit Report

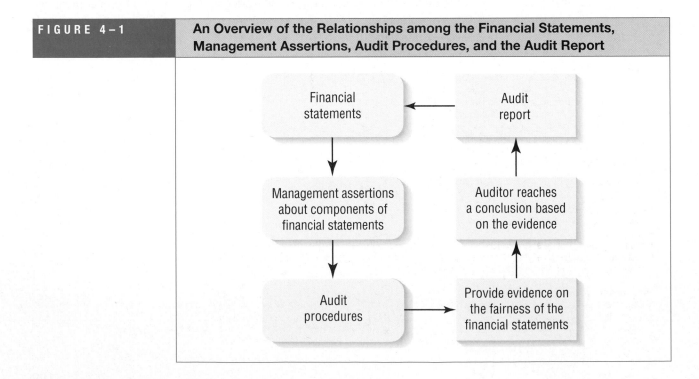

Management Assertions

[LO 2] Management is responsible for the fair presentation of the financial statements. *Assertions* are expressed or implied representations by management regarding the recognition, measurement, presentation, and disclosure of information in the financial statements and related disclosures (AU 326.14). For example, when the balance sheet contains a line item for accounts receivable of $5 million, management asserts that those receivables exist and have a net realizable value of $5 million. Management also asserts that the accounts receivable balance arose from selling goods or services on credit in the normal course of business. As another example, take a moment and consider what the relevant management assertions are when the financial statements show a net sales figure of $10 million. Here, management asserts that the sales exist (existence assertion), were all conducted within the current time frame (cutoff assertion), and have been recorded in their correct amounts (accuracy assertion).

Under current auditing standards, management assertions fall into the following categories:

* Assertions about classes of transactions and events for the period under audit.
* Assertions about account balances at the period end.
* Assertions about presentation and disclosure.

Practice INSIGHT

Auditing standards allow the auditor to use the categories of assertions as shown here or to express them differently. For example, the PCAOB standards do not separate the assertions into the three categories presented here. Instead they just list five assertions (existence/occurrence, completeness, valuation/allocation, rights and obligations, and presentation and disclosure). We use the three categories presented here (consistent with ASB and IAASB standards) because we believe that tests of assertions are more easily understood when considered separately in terms of transactions, account balances, and disclosures.

Table 4–1 presents the definitions of each assertion by category while Table 4–2 shows how the assertions are related across categories.

TABLE 4–1	Definitions of Management Assertions by Category

Assertions about classes of transactions and events for the period under audit:
* **Occurrence**—transactions and events that have been recorded have occurred and pertain to the entity (sometimes referred to as validity).
* **Completeness**—all transactions and events that should have been recorded have been recorded.
* **Authorization**—all transactions and events have been properly authorized.
* **Accuracy**—amounts and other data relating to recorded transactions and events have been recorded appropriately and properly accumulated from journals and ledgers.
* **Cutoff**—transactions and events have been recorded in the correct accounting period.
* **Classification**—transactions and events have been recorded in the proper accounts.

Assertions about account balances at the period end:
* **Existence**—assets, liabilities, and equity interests exist.
* **Rights and obligations**—the entity holds or controls the rights to assets, and liabilities are the obligations of the entity.
* **Completeness**—all assets, liabilities and equity interests that should have been recorded have been recorded.
* **Valuation and allocation**—assets, liabilities, and equity interests are included in the financial statements at appropriate amounts, and any resulting valuation or allocation adjustments are appropriately recorded.

Assertions about presentation and disclosure:
* **Occurrence and rights and obligations**—disclosed events, transactions, and other matters have occurred and pertain to the entity.
* **Completeness**—all disclosures that should have been included in the financial statements have been included.
* **Classification and understandability**—financial information is appropriately presented and described, and disclosures are clearly expressed.
* **Accuracy and valuation**—financial and other information are disclosed fairly and at appropriate amounts.

TABLE 4–2	Summary of Management Assertions by Category		
	Categories of Assertions		
	Classes of Transactions and Events during the Period	*Account Balances at the End of the Period*	*Presentation and Disclosure*
Occurrence/Existence	Transactions and events that have been recorded have occurred and pertain to the entity.	Assets, liabilities, and equity interests exist.	Disclosed events and transactions have occurred and pertain to the entity.
Rights and Obligations	—	The entity holds or controls the rights to assets, and liabilities are the obligations of the entity.	—
Completeness	All transactions and events that should have been recorded have been recorded.	All assets, liabilities, and equity interests that should have been recorded have been recorded.	All disclosures that should have been included in the financial statements have been included.
Authorization	All transactions and events that should have been recorded have been authorized.	—	—
Accuracy/Valuation and Allocation	Amounts and other data relating to recorded transactions and events have been recorded appropriately and properly accumulated from journals and ledgers.	Assets, liabilities, and equity interests are included in the financial statements at appropriate amounts and any resulting valuation or allocation adjustments are recorded appropriately.	Financial and other information is disclosed fairly and at appropriate amounts.
Cutoff	Transactions and events have been recorded in the correct accounting period.	—	—
Classification and Understandability	Transactions and events have been recorded in the proper accounts.	—	Financial information is appropriately presented and described, and disclosures are expressed clearly.

Pay close attention to the wording of the assertions as defined and described below. The way auditors use certain words as they relate to assertions may differ somewhat from your everyday usage of the terms, and part of mastering auditing is learning the language of auditors.

Assertions about Classes of Transactions and Events during the Period

Assertions about classes of transactions and events relate to the transactions that flow through a particular business process and accumulate in one or more financial statement accounts. Auditors perform audit procedures to gather evidence about relevant assertions related to those transactions. Transaction-related assertions help the auditor conceptualize, plan, and perform those audit procedures.

Occurrence   The occurrence assertion relates to whether all recorded transactions and events have occurred and pertain to the entity. For example, management asserts that all revenue transactions recorded during the period were valid transactions. Take a minute and consider this assertion further. For which accounts would an auditor worry that the client might record transactions that did not occur? The occurrence assertion is relevant for revenue transactions because the client might have incentives to record fictitious transactions. Occurrence is sometimes also referred to as validity.

Completeness   The completeness assertion relates to whether all transactions and events that occurred during the period have been recorded. For example, if a client fails to record a valid revenue transaction, the revenue account will be understated. Note that the auditor's concern with the completeness assertion is opposite the concern for occurrence. Failure to meet the completeness assertion results in an understatement in the related account, while failure to meet the occurrence assertion results in an overstatement in the account.

Authorization   The authorization assertion relates to whether all transactions have been properly authorized. For example, the purchase of a significant new manufacturing facility should be approved by the board of directors. Auditing standards use the word "accuracy" to reflect that transactions and events have been both recorded accurately and properly authorized. Since an unauthorized transaction could be accurately recorded, we have found that it is easier to think of proper authorization and accurate recording as separate assertions.

Accuracy   The accuracy assertion addresses whether amounts and other data relating to recorded transactions and events have been recorded appropriately and properly accumulated from journals and ledgers. Generally accepted accounting principles establish the appropriate method for recording a transaction or event. For example, the amount recorded for the cost of a new machine includes its purchase price plus all reasonable costs to install it. As another example, a sale to a customer that is recorded at an incorrect amount due to omission of an applicable discount would be considered a valid but inaccurate sales transaction.

Cutoff   The cutoff assertion relates to whether transactions and events have been recorded in the correct accounting period. The auditor's procedures must ensure that transactions occurring near year-end are recorded in the financial statements in the proper period. For example, the auditor may want to test proper cutoff of revenue transactions at December 31, 2009. The auditor can examine a sample of shipping documents and sales invoices for a few days before and after year-end to test whether the sales transactions are recorded in the proper period. The objective is to determine that all 2009 sales and no 2010 sales have been recorded in 2009. Thus, the auditor examines the shipping documents to ensure that no 2010 sales have been recorded in 2009 and that no 2009 sales are recorded in 2010.

Classification   The classification assertion is concerned with whether transactions and events have been recorded in the proper accounts. For example, management asserts that all direct cost transactions related to inventory have been properly classified in either inventory or as part of cost of sales. As another example, purchases are properly recorded as either assets or expenses, as appropriate.

Assertions about Account Balances at the Period End

Assertions about account balances relate directly to the ending balances of the accounts included in the financial statements. Auditors perform audit procedures to gather evidence relating to assertions relevant to those account balances. Balance-related assertions help the auditor conceptualize, plan, and perform such audit procedures.

Existence   The assertion about existence addresses whether ending balances of assets, liabilities, and equity interests included in the financial statements actually exist at the date of the financial statements. For example, management asserts that inventory shown on the balance sheet exists and is available for sale.

Rights and Obligations   The assertions about rights and obligations address whether the entity holds or controls the rights to assets included on the financial statements, and that liabilities are the obligations of the entity. For example, management asserts that the entity has legal title or rights of ownership to the inventory shown on the balance sheet. Similarly, amounts capitalized for leases reflect assertions that the entity has rights to leased property and that the corresponding lease liability represents an obligation of the entity.

Completeness   The assertion about completeness addresses whether all assets, liabilities, and equity interests that should have been included as ending balances on the financial statements have been included. For example, management implicitly asserts that the ending balance shown for accounts payable on the balance sheet includes all such liabilities as of the balance sheet date.

Valuation and Allocation   Assertions about valuation or allocation address whether assets, liabilities, and equity interests included in the financial statements are at appropriate amounts and any resulting valuation or allocation adjustments are appropriately recorded. For example, management asserts that inventory is carried at the lower of cost or market value on the balance sheet. Similarly, management asserts that the cost of property, plant, and equipment is systematically allocated to appropriate accounting periods by recognizing depreciation expense.

Assertions about
Presentation and
Disclosure

This category of assertions relates to presentation of information in the financial statements and disclosures in the footnotes that are directly related to a specific transaction or account balance (e.g., disclosures related to property and equipment) and those that apply to the financial statements in general (e.g., the footnote for the summary of significant accounting policies). Auditors perform audit procedures to gather evidence relating to assertions relevant to presentation and disclosure.

Occurrence and Rights and Obligations   The assertions about occurrence and rights and obligations address whether disclosed events, transactions, and other matters have occurred and pertain to the entity. For example, when management presents capitalized lease transactions on the balance sheet as leased assets, the related liabilities as long-term debt, and the related footnote, it is asserting that a lease transaction occurred, it has a right to the leased asset, and it owes the related lease obligation to the lessor. In addition, there is a footnote disclosure that provides additional information on the lease such as future payments.

Completeness   The completeness assertion in this category relates to whether all disclosures that should have been included in the financial statements have been included. Therefore, management asserts that no material disclosures have been omitted from the footnotes and other disclosures accompanying the financial statements.

Classification and Understandability   The assertions related to classification and understandability address whether the financial information is appropriately presented and described, and disclosures are clearly expressed. For example, management asserts that the portion of long-term debt shown as a current liability will mature in the current year. Similarly, management asserts that all major restrictions on the entity resulting from debt covenants are disclosed in footnotes and are able to be understood by the users of the financial statements.

TABLE 4–3	Management Assertions, Possible Misstatements, and Illustrative Audit Procedures	
Management Assertions about the Accounts Receivable Component of the Financial Statements	Possible Misstatement	Example Audit Procedures for Accounts Receivable
Existence	Fictitious customer.	Confirm accounts receivable.
Rights and obligations	Receivables have been sold or factored.	Inquire of management whether receivables have been sold.
Completeness	Customer accounts are not recorded.	Agree total of accounts receivable subsidiary ledger to accounts receivable control account.
Valuation or allocation	Delinquent customer carried at full amount.	Test the adequacy of the allowance for doubtful accounts.

Accuracy and Valuation   The accuracy and valuation assertions address whether financial and other information is disclosed fairly and at appropriate amounts. For example, when management discloses the fair value of stock or bond investments, it is asserting that these financial instruments are properly valued in accordance with GAAP. In addition, management may disclose in a footnote other information related to financial instruments.

Before we discuss important characteristics of evidence available to the auditor, pause for a moment to consider the usefulness of the sets of management assertions we have just discussed. The assertions collectively provide a road map for the auditor in determining what evidence to collect regarding various transactions, account balances, and required financial statement disclosures. The auditor determines the type of evidence to gather by considering what possible misstatements could occur. Table 4–3 shows the management assertions for the accounts receivable balance. It also shows some of the misstatements that might occur if management's assertions are not correct. For example, the existence assertion might not be met if the accounts receivable balance includes fictitious customers. Management assertions also guide the auditor in designing audit procedures to collect the needed evidence, as well as assisting the auditor in evaluating the appropriateness and sufficiency of the evidence. For example, once the auditor is comfortable that he or she has gathered sufficient appropriate evidence relating to each balance-related assertion for the accounts payable account, the auditor can rest assured that no important aspect of that account has been neglected. The management assertions help the auditor focus his or her attention on all the various aspects of transactions, account balances, and required disclosures that need to be considered—they help the auditor ensure that "all the bases are covered." As such, the three sets of management assertions constitute a powerful conceptual tool in the auditor's toolbox.

Audit Procedures

[LO 3] Audit procedures are specific acts performed by the auditor to gather evidence about whether specific assertions are being met. Audit procedures are performed to

- Obtain an understanding of the entity and its environment, including its internal control, to assess the risks of material misstatement at the financial statement and relevant assertion levels. Such audit procedures are referred to as *risk assessment procedures*. These procedures were discussed in Chapter 3.

- Test the operating effectiveness of controls in preventing or detecting material misstatements at the relevant assertion level. Audit procedures performed for this purpose are referred to as *tests of controls*. Tests of controls are discussed in Chapters 5 and 6.
- Detect material misstatements at the relevant assertion level. Such audit procedures are referred to as *substantive procedures*. Substantive procedures include tests of details of classes of transactions, account balances and disclosures, and substantive analytical procedures. Substantive procedures are discussed in detail in Chapter 5 and in each business process chapter.

A set of audit procedures prepared to test assertions for a component of the financial statements is usually referred to as an *audit program*. Table 4–3 illustrates an audit procedure for each assertion related to the audit of accounts receivable. The reader should note that there is not a one-to-one relationship between assertions and audit procedures. In some instances more than one audit procedure is required to test an assertion. Conversely, in some cases an audit procedure provides evidence for more than one assertion. Note that the assertions do not change whether information is processed manually or electronically. However, the methods of applying audit procedures may be influenced by the method of information processing. Examples of audit procedures used to test various account balances will be presented in later chapters.

The Concepts of Audit Evidence

✎ [LO 4]   Audit evidence is all the information used by the auditor in arriving at the conclusions on which the audit opinion is based, and includes the information contained in the accounting records underlying the financial statements and other information. A solid understanding of the characteristics of evidence is obviously an important conceptual tool for auditors as well as for professionals in a variety of other settings. The following concepts of audit evidence are important to understanding the conduct of the audit:

- The nature of audit evidence.
- The sufficiency and appropriateness of audit evidence.
- The evaluation of audit evidence.

The Nature of Audit Evidence

Evidence is the information gathered or used by the auditor to support his or her opinion. The *nature* of the evidence refers to the form or type of information, which include accounting records and other available information. *Accounting records* include the records of initial entries and supporting records, such as checks and records of electronic fund transfers; invoices; contracts; the general and subsidiary ledgers, journal entries, and other adjustments to the financial statements that are not reflected in formal journal entries; and records such as work sheets and spreadsheets supporting cost allocations, computations, reconciliations, and disclosures. Many times the entries in the accounting records are initiated, recorded, processed, and reported in electronic form. *Other information* that the auditor may use as audit evidence includes minutes of meetings; confirmations from third parties; industry analysts' reports; comparable data about competitors (benchmarking); controls manuals; information obtained by the auditor from such audit procedures as inquiry, observation, and inspection; and other information developed by, or available to, the auditor that permits the auditor to reach conclusions through valid reasoning (AU 326.05).

For some entities, accounting records and other information may be available only in electronic form.[1] Thus, source documents such as purchase orders, bills of lading, invoices, and checks are replaced with electronic messages or electronic images. Two common examples are electronic data interchange (EDI) and image-processing systems.[2] A client that uses EDI may process sales or purchase transactions electronically. For example, the client's EDI system can contact a vendor electronically when supplies of a part run low. The vendor will then ship the goods to the client and send an invoice electronically. The client can authorize its bank to make an electronic payment directly to the vendor's bank account. In an image-processing system, documents are scanned and converted to electronic images to facilitate storage and reference, and the source documents may not be retained after conversion. In such systems, electronic evidence may exist at only a certain point in time and may not be retrievable later. This may require the auditor to select sample items several times during the year rather than at year-end.

The Sufficiency and Appropriateness of Audit Evidence

Sufficiency is the measure of the *quantity* of audit evidence. *Appropriateness* is a measure of the *quality* of audit evidence. Sufficiency and appropriateness of audit evidence are interrelated. The auditor must consider both concepts when assessing risks and designing audit procedures.

The quantity of audit evidence needed is affected by the risk of misstatement and by the quality of the audit evidence gathered. Thus, the greater the risk of misstatement, the more audit evidence is likely to be required to meet the audit test. And the higher the quality of the evidence, the less evidence that may be required to meet the audit test. Accordingly, there is an inverse relationship between the sufficiency and appropriateness of audit evidence.

In most instances, the auditor relies on evidence that is *persuasive* rather than *convincing* in forming an opinion on a set of financial statements. This occurs for two reasons. First, because an audit must be completed in a reasonable amount of time and at a reasonable cost, the auditor examines only a sample of the transactions that compose the account balance or class of transactions. Thus, the auditor reaches a conclusion about the account or class based on a subset of the available evidence.

Second, due to the nature of evidence, auditors must often rely on evidence that is not perfectly reliable. As discussed in the next section, the types of audit evidence have different degrees of reliability, and even highly reliable evidence has weaknesses. For example, an auditor can physically examine inventory, but such evidence will not ensure that obsolescence is not a problem. Therefore, the nature of the evidence obtained by the auditor seldom provides absolute assurance about an assertion.

Evidence is considered appropriate when it provides information that is both relevant and reliable.

Relevance   The relevance of audit evidence refers to its relationship to the assertion or to the objective of the control being tested. If the auditor relies on evidence that is unrelated to the assertion, he or she may reach an incorrect conclusion about the assertion. For example, suppose the auditor wants to check the

---

[1]The AICPA's Audit Practice Release, *The Information Technology Age: Evidential Matter in the Electronic Environment* (AICPA 1997), provides nonauthoritative implementation guidance about electronic evidence and its impact on the audit. See also A. L. Williamson, "The Implications of Electronic Evidence," *Journal of Accountancy* (February 1997), pp. 69–71.

[2]The AICPA's Audit Practice Release, *Audit Implications of Electronic Document Management* (AICPA 1997), discusses the issues faced by auditors when a client uses electronic document management that includes image-processing systems. Discussion of such issues is beyond the scope of this text.

completeness assertion for recording sales transactions; that is, all goods shipped to customers are recorded in the sales journal. A normal audit procedure for testing this assertion is to trace a sample of shipping documents (such as bills of lading) to the related sales invoices and entries in the sales journal. If the auditor samples the population of sales invoices issued during the period, the evidence would not relate to the completeness assertion (that is, the auditor would not detect shipments made that are not billed or recorded). The auditor should check the log or record of prenumbered bills of lading, after ascertaining that such documents were issued for all customer shipments. Any conclusion based on the population of sales invoices would not be based on evidence relevant to testing the completeness assertion.

Reliability   The reliability or validity of evidence refers to whether a particular type of evidence can be relied upon to signal the true state of an assertion. Because of varied circumstances on audit engagements, it is difficult to generalize about the reliability of various types of evidence. However, the reliability of evidence is influenced by its source and by its nature and is dependent on the individual circumstances under which it is obtained.

- *Knowledgeable independent source of the evidence.* Evidence obtained directly by the auditor from a knowledgeable independent source outside the entity is usually viewed as more reliable than evidence obtained solely from within the entity. Thus, a confirmation of the client's bank balance received directly by the auditor would be viewed as more reliable than examination of the cash receipts journal and cash balance as recorded in the general ledger. Additionally, evidence that is obtained from the client, but that has been subjected to verification by a knowledgeable independent source, is viewed as more reliable than evidence obtained solely from within the entity. For example, a canceled check held by the client would be more reliable than a duplicate copy of the check because the canceled check would be endorsed by the payee and cleared through the bank—in other words, it has been verified by an independent source.

- *Effectiveness of internal control.* A major objective of a client's internal control is to generate reliable information to assist management decision making. As part of the audit, the effectiveness of the client's internal control is assessed. When the auditor assesses the client's internal control as effective (that is, low control risk), evidence generated by that accounting system is viewed as reliable. Conversely, if internal control is assessed as ineffective (that is, high control risk), the evidence from the accounting system would not be considered reliable. Thus, the more effective the client's internal control, the more assurance it provides about the reliability of audit evidence.

- *Auditor's direct personal knowledge.* Evidence obtained directly by the auditor (e.g., observation of the performance of a control) is generally considered to be more reliable than evidence obtained indirectly or by inference (e.g., inquiry about the performance of a control). For example, an auditor's physical inspection of a client's inventory is considered to be relatively reliable because the auditor has direct personal knowledge regarding the inventory. There are, of course, exceptions to this general rule. For example, if an auditor examined an inventory composed of diamonds or specialty computer chips, the auditor may lack the expertise to appropriately assess the validity and valuation of such inventory items. In such cases, the auditor may need the skill and knowledge of a specialist to assist with the inventory audit.

- *Documentary evidence.* Audit evidence is more reliable when it exists in documentary form, whether paper, electronic, or other medium. Thus, a written record of a board of directors meeting is more reliable than a subsequent oral representation of the matters discussed.
- *Original documents.* Audit evidence provided by original documents is more reliable than audit evidence provided by photocopies or facsimiles. An auditor's examination of an original, signed copy of a lease agreement is more reliable than a photocopy.

Determining the sufficiency and appropriateness of evidence are two of the more critical decisions the auditor faces on an engagement. Before continuing, take a moment and consider which of the following sources of evidence are more reliable:

- Inquiry of an accounts receivable clerk regarding the accounts receivable balance *or* accounts receivable confirmations sent to a sample of customers.
- Physical examination of lumber inventory performed by the external auditor *or* physical examination of inventory performed by internal auditors.

The Evaluation of Audit Evidence

The ability to evaluate evidence appropriately is another important skill an auditor must develop. Proper evaluation of evidence requires that the auditor understand the types of evidence that are available and their relative reliability or diagnosticity. The auditor must be capable of assessing when a sufficient amount of appropriate evidence has been obtained in order to determine the fairness of management's assertions.

In evaluating evidence, an auditor should be *thorough* in searching for evidence and *unbiased* in its evaluation. For example, suppose an auditor decides to mail accounts receivable confirmations to 50 of the largest customers of a client that has a total of 5,000 customer accounts receivable. Even if some of the 50 customers do not respond directly to the auditor, the auditor must gather sufficient evidence on each of the 50 accounts, which could include searching for subsequent cash receipts, shipping documents, invoices, and so forth. In evaluating evidence, the auditor must remain objective and must not allow the evaluation of the evidence to be biased by other considerations. To illustrate, in evaluating a client's response to an audit inquiry, the auditor must not allow any personal factors (e.g., the client is likeable and friendly) to influence the evaluation of the client's response.

Audit Procedures for Obtaining Audit Evidence

[LO 5] In conducting audit procedures, the auditor examines various types of audit evidence. Evidence is commonly categorized into the following types:

- Inspection of records or documents
- Inspection of tangible assets
- Observation
- Inquiry
- Confirmation
- Recalculation
- Reperformance
- Analytical procedures
- Scanning

Inspection of
Records or
Documents

Inspection consists of examining internal or external records or documents that are in paper form, electronic form, or other media. On most audit engagements, inspection of records or documents makes up the bulk of the evidence gathered by the auditor. Two issues are important in discussing inspection of records or documents: the reliability of such evidence and its relationship to specific assertions.

Reliability of Records or Documents   A previous section noted the independence of the source of evidence as a factor that affected the reliability of audit evidence. In particular, evidence obtained from a knowledgeable source outside the entity is generally considered more reliable than evidence obtained solely from within the entity. Typically a distinction is made between internal and external documents. *Internal* documents are generated and maintained within the entity; that is, these documents have not been seen by any party outside the client's organization. Examples include duplicate copies of sales invoices and shipping documents, materials requisition forms, and work sheets for overhead cost allocation. *External* documents are of two forms: documents originating within the entity but circulated to independent sources outside the entity and documents generated outside the entity but included in the client's accounting records. Examples of the first include remittance advices returned with cash receipts from customers and payroll checks, while examples of the second include bank statements and vendors' invoices.

In general, external documentary evidence is viewed as more reliable than internal evidence because a third party either initiated or reviewed it. However, the difference in reliability between internal and external documents depends on a number of factors, including the reliability of controls over preparation and storage of internal documents, and various factors affecting the reliability of external documents.

Documentary Evidence Related to Assertions   The second issue concerning records or documents relates directly to the occurrence and completeness assertions and to the *direction of testing* taken when documentary evidence is examined. Figure 4–2 presents an overview of this relationship.

The *direction of testing* between the accounting records and source documents (such as sales invoices or shipping documents) is important when testing the occurrence and completeness assertions. *Vouching* refers to selecting an item for testing from the accounting journals or ledgers and then examining the underlying source document. Thus, the direction of testing is from the journals or ledgers back to the source documents. This approach provides evidence that items included in the accounting records have *occurred* (or are valid transactions). For example, an auditor may want to examine a sample of sales transactions from the sales journal to ensure that sales are not fictitious. If adequate source documents exist for each sales transaction selected from the sales journal,

FIGURE 4–2	Direction of Testing for Validity and Completeness

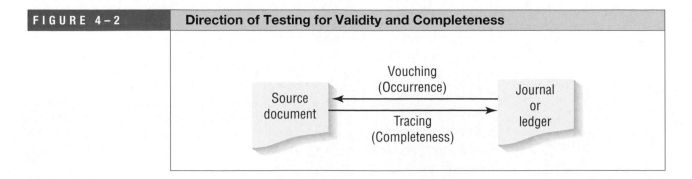

the auditor can conclude that each sale was valid. *Tracing* refers to first selecting a source document and then following it into the journal or ledger. The direction of testing in this case is from the source documents to the journals or ledgers. Testing in this direction ensures that transactions that occurred are recorded (*completeness*) in the accounting records. For example, if the auditor selects a sample of shipping documents and traces them to the related sales invoices and then to the sales journal, he or she would have evidence on the completeness of sales. Take a few moments to be sure you understand how the direction of testing relates to the completeness and occurrence assertions. This is an important concept for auditors to understand (and one that is heavily tested on the CPA exam and in other settings!). To help you better understand this concept, review each of the following examples and determine (1) if you are vouching or tracing and (2) how that relates to either the occurrence or completeness assertion:

- Selecting a sample of transactions in the purchases journal and ensuring that they are supported by receiving documents.
- Selecting a sample of inventory tags used during the observation of the entity's physical inventory count and ensuring that they agree with the inventory ledger.

Inspection of Tangible Assets

Inspection of tangible assets consists of physical examination of the assets. Inspection is a relatively reliable type of evidence that involves the auditor inspecting or counting a tangible asset. An audit engagement includes many situations in which the auditor physically examines an entity's assets. Some examples might be counting cash on hand, examining inventory or marketable securities, and examining tangible fixed assets. This type of evidence primarily provides assurance that the asset exists. In some instances, such as examining inventory, physical examination may provide evidence on valuation by identifying items that are obsolete or slow-moving. However, physical examination provides little or no assurance for the rights and obligations assertion.

Observation

Observation consists of looking at a process or procedure being performed by others. The actions being observed typically do not leave an audit trail that can be tested by examining records or documents. Examples include observation of the counting of inventories by the entity's personnel and observation of the performance of control activities. Observation provides audit evidence about the performance of a process or procedure but is limited to the point in time at which the observation takes place. It is also limited by the fact that the client personnel may act differently when the auditor is not observing them. Observation is useful in helping auditors understand client processes, but is generally not considered very reliable and thus generally requires additional corroboration by the auditor. Corroborating evidence includes data or documents from the accounting records and other documentary information (e.g., contracts and written confirmations).

Students often confuse the technical auditing definition of the term *observation* with the common usage of the word. As a result, students will use the term *observation* to describe such audit procedures as inspection of tangible assets or documents and records. However, as we discussed above, "observation" in the auditing sense consists of looking at *a process or procedure being performed by others*. Technical terms or jargon serve an important role in efficient professional communication, and you will want to develop the proper vocabulary. Just as technical accounting terms such as *revenue* and *income* are not used interchangeably by professional accountants, professional auditors do not use *observation* and *inspection* interchangeably.

TABLE 4–4	Techniques for Conducting and Evaluating Inquiries
	In conducting inquiry, the auditor should • Consider the knowledge, objectivity, experience, responsibility, and qualifications of the individual to be questioned. • Ask clear, concise, and relevant questions. • Use open or closed questions appropriately. • Listen actively and effectively. • Consider the reactions and responses and ask follow-up questions. • Evaluate the response.

Inquiry

Inquiry consists of seeking information of knowledgeable persons (both financial and nonfinancial) throughout the entity or outside the entity. Inquiry is an important audit procedure that is used extensively throughout the audit and often is complementary to performing other audit procedures. For example, much of the audit work conducted to understand the entity and its environment including internal control involves inquiry.

Inquiries may range from formal written inquiries to informal oral inquiries. Evaluating responses to inquiries is an integral part of the inquiry process. Table 4–4 provides guidance for conducting and evaluating inquiries.

Responses to inquiries may provide the auditor with information not previously possessed or with corroborative audit evidence. Alternatively, responses might provide information that differs significantly from other information that the auditor has obtained, for example, information regarding the possibility of management override of controls. The reliability of audit evidence obtained from responses to inquiries is also affected by the training, knowledge, and experience of the auditor performing the inquiry, because the auditor analyzes and assesses responses while performing the inquiry and refines subsequent inquiries according to the circumstances. In some cases, the nature of the response may be so significant that the auditor requests a written representation from the source.

Inquiry alone ordinarily does not provide sufficient audit evidence, and the auditor will gather additional corroborative evidence to support the response.

Confirmation[3]

Confirmation is the process of obtaining a representation of information or of an existing condition directly from a third party. Confirmations also are used to obtain audit evidence about the absence of certain conditions, for example, the absence of a "side agreement" that may influence revenue recognition. Auditors usually use the term *inquiry* to refer to unwritten questions asked of the client or of a third party, and the term *confirmation* to refer to written requests for a written response from a third party.

The reliability of evidence obtained through confirmations is directly affected by factors such as

- The form of the confirmation.
- Prior experience with the entity.
- The nature of the information being confirmed.
- The intended respondent.

Confirmations are used extensively on audits; they generally provide reliable evidence for the existence assertion and, in testing certain financial statement components (such as accounts payable), can provide evidence about the completeness assertion. Evidence about other assertions can also be obtained through

---

[3]See Professional Issues Task Force, Practice Alert 03-1, Confirmations (June 2007) and AU 9330, Use of Electronic Confirmations, for recent guidance on the use of various types of confirmations (www.aicpa.org).

TABLE 4–5	**Amounts and Information Frequently Confirmed by Auditors**

Amounts or Information Confirmed	Source of Confirmation
Cash balance	Bank
Accounts receivable	Individual customers
Inventory on consignment	Consignee
Accounts payable	Individual vendors
Bonds payable	Bondholders/trustee
Common stock outstanding	Registrar/transfer agent
Insurance coverage	Insurance company
Collateral for loan	Creditor

the use of confirmations. For example, an auditor can send a confirmation to a consignee to verify that a client's inventory has been consigned. The returned confirmation provides evidence that the client owns the inventory (rights and obligations assertion). Table 4–5 lists selected amounts and information confirmed by auditors. Accounts receivable, accounts payable, and bank confirmations are discussed in more detail in later chapters.

Recalculation

Recalculation consists of checking the mathematical accuracy of documents or records. Recalculation can be performed through the use of information technology (e.g., by obtaining an electronic file from the entity and using computer-assisted audit techniques, or CAATs, to check the accuracy of the summarization of the file). Specific examples of this type of procedure include recalculation of depreciation expense on fixed assets and recalculation of accrued interest. Recalculation also includes footing, crossfooting, reconciling subsidiary ledgers to account balances, and testing postings from journals to ledgers. Because the auditor creates this type of evidence, it is normally viewed as highly reliable.

Reperformance

Reperformance involves the independent execution by the auditor of procedures or controls that were originally performed by company personnel. For example, the auditor may reperform the aging of accounts receivable. Again, because the auditor creates this type of evidence, it is normally viewed as highly reliable.

Analytical Procedures

Analytical procedures are an important type of evidence on an audit. They consist of evaluations of financial information made by a study of plausible relationships among both financial and nonfinancial data (AU 329). For example, the current-year accounts receivable balance can be compared to the prior-years' balances after adjusting for any increase or decrease in sales and other economic factors. Similarly, the auditor might compare the current-year gross margin percentage to the gross margin percentage for the previous five years. The auditor makes such comparisons either to identify accounts that may contain material misstatements and require more investigation or as a reasonableness test of the account balance. Analytical procedures are an effective and efficient form of evidence.

The reliability of analytical procedures is a function of (1) the availability and reliability of the data used in the calculations, (2) the plausibility and predictability of the relationship being tested, and (3) the precision of the expectation and the rigor of the investigation. Because of the importance of this type of evidence in auditing, analytical procedures are covered in greater detail in Chapter 5.

Scanning

Scanning is the review of accounting data to identify significant or unusual items. This includes the identification of anomalous individual items within account balances or other client data through the scanning or analysis of entries in transaction listings, subsidiary ledgers, general ledger control accounts, adjusting entries, suspense accounts, reconciliations, and other detailed reports. Scanning includes searching for large and unusual items in the accounting records (e.g., nonstandard journal entries), as well as reviewing transaction data (e.g., expense accounts, adjusting journal entries) for indications of errors that have occurred. It might be used in conjunction with analytical procedures but also as a stand-alone procedure. Scanning can be performed either manually or through the use of CAATs.

Reliability of the Types of Evidence

[LO 6]   Table 4–6 presents a hierarchy of the reliability of the types of evidence. Inspection of tangible assets, reperformance, and recalculation are generally considered of high reliability because the auditor has direct knowledge about them. Inspection of records and documents, scanning, confirmation, and analytical procedures are generally considered to be of medium reliability. The reliability of inspection of records and documents depends primarily on whether a document is internal or external, and the reliability of confirmation is affected by the four factors listed previously. The reliability of analytical procedures may be affected by the availability and reliability of the data. Finally, observation and inquiry are generally low-reliability types of evidence because both require further corroboration by the auditor.

The reader should understand, however, that the levels of reliability shown in Table 4–6 are general guidelines. The reliability of the types of evidence may vary considerably across entities, and it may be subject to a number of exceptions. For example, in some circumstances, confirmations may be viewed as a highly reliable source of evidence. This may be true when a confirmation is sent to an independent third party who is highly qualified to respond to the auditor's request for information. Inquiries of client personnel or management provide another example.

Practice INSIGHT	If audit evidence obtained from one source is inconsistent with that obtained from another, or if the auditor has doubts about the reliability of information to be used as audit evidence, the auditor should perform the audit procedures necessary to resolve the matter and should assess the effect, if any, on other aspects of the audit.

TABLE 4–6	**General Guidelines for the Reliability Hierarchy by Evidence Type**

General Reliability Relationship*	*Types of Evidence*
Higher	Inspection of tangible assets, reperformance, recalculation
↕	Inspection of records and documents, confirmation, analytical procedures, scanning
Lower	Observation, inquiry

*This figure illustrates general hierarchical guidelines. The reliability of the evidence will depend on the facts and circumstances. For example, confirmations may be highly reliable in some circumstances.

Audit Documentation

Objectives of Audit Documentation

✂ [LO 7]

Audit documentation consists of the record of audit procedures performed, relevant audit evidence obtained, and conclusions the auditor reached (AU 339.05). Audit documentation also facilitates the planning, performance, and supervision of the engagement and provides the basis for the review of the quality of the work by providing the reviewer with written documentation of the evidence supporting the auditor's significant conclusions (AS 3 and AU 339).

You can think of audit documentation as the "story" of the audit. It should allow the reader to easily understand the issues and risks, the assertions tested, the audit procedures performed to gather evidence, the findings, and the conclusion. The basic characteristics of good audit documentation are similar to good documentation in other fields (e.g., medical and legal research).

Audit documentation is also referred to as *working papers* or the *audit file*. Auditing standards (AS 3 and AU 339) stipulate that working papers have two functions: (1) to provide principal support for the representation in the auditor's report that the audit was conducted in accordance with GAAS (AU 339.03) and (2) to aid in the planning, performance, and supervision of the audit (AS 3 ¶2). The form and content of the working papers are a function of the circumstances of the specific engagement.

While some working papers may be prepared in hard-copy format, audit software is normally used to prepare and store them.

Practice INSIGHT

Most firms use standard templates (e.g., for sampling applications) to record the results of their audit procedures, thus providing consistency in the manner in which evidence is recorded in the working papers.

Support for the Audit Report   When the engagement is complete, the auditor must decide on the appropriate type of report to issue. The basis for this decision rests in the audit evidence gathered and the conclusions reached and documented in the working papers. The working papers also document that the scope of the audit was adequate for the report issued. Information on the correspondence of the financial statements with GAAP is also included in the working papers.

Planning, Performance, and Supervision of the Audit   The working papers document the auditor's compliance with auditing standards. In particular, working papers document the auditor's compliance with the standards of fieldwork. The planning of the engagement, along with the execution of the audit plan, is contained in the working papers. The working papers are also the focal point for reviewing the work of subordinates and quality control reviewers.

Content of Audit Documentation

✂ [LO 8]

Audit documentation is the principal record of auditing procedures applied, evidence obtained, and conclusions reached by the auditor in the engagement. Because audit documentation provides the principal support for the representations in the auditor's report, it should

- Demonstrate how the audit complied with auditing and related professional practice standards.

- Support the basis for the auditor's conclusions concerning each material financial statement assertion.
- Demonstrate that the underlying accounting records agreed or reconciled with the financial statements.

Audit documentation should include a written audit program (or set of audit programs) for the engagement. The audit program should set forth in reasonable detail the auditing procedures that the auditor believed necessary to accomplish the objectives of the audit. Audit documentation should be sufficient to show that standards of fieldwork have been followed.

Audit documentation should enable a reviewer with relevant knowledge and experience to

- Understand the nature, timing, extent, and results of the procedures performed, evidence obtained, and conclusions reached.
- Determine who performed the work and the date such work was completed, as well as the person who reviewed the work and the date of such review.

The auditor should consider the following factors when determining the form and extent of the documentation for a particular audit area or auditing procedure:

- The auditing procedures to be performed and the nature of the evidence to be obtained.
- Risk of material misstatement associated with the assertion, account, or class of transactions.
- Extent of judgment involved in performing the work and evaluating the results.
- Significance of the evidence obtained to the assertion being tested.
- Any exceptions identified with a discussion of the underlying cause, potential implications, auditor evaluation, and the client's response.
- The need to document a conclusion or the basis for a conclusion not readily determinable from the documentation of the work performed (AU 339.12).

AS 3 contains specific documentation requirements for audits of public companies for significant findings or issues, actions taken to address them (including additional evidence obtained), and the basis for the conclusions reached. Examples of significant findings or issues are shown in Table 4–7. Additionally, the

TABLE 4–7	**Examples of Significant Findings or Issues That Require Documentation under PCAOB Auditing Standard No. 3**

- Significant matters involving the selection, application, and consistency of accounting principles, including related disclosures (e.g., accounting for complex or unusual transactions, accounting estimates, and uncertainties as well as related management assumptions).
- Results of auditing procedures that indicate a need for significant modification of planned auditing procedures or the existence of material misstatements or omissions in the financial statements or the existence of significant deficiencies in internal control over financial reporting.
- Audit adjustments and the ultimate resolution of these items.
- Disagreements among members of the engagement team or with others consulted on the engagement about conclusions reached on significant accounting or auditing matters.
- Significant findings or issues identified during the review of quarterly financial information.
- Circumstances that cause significant difficulty in applying auditing procedures.
- Significant changes in the assessed level of audit risk for particular audit areas and the auditor's response to those changes.
- Any other matters that could result in modification of the auditor's report.

TABLE 4–8	Documentation Requirements for Items Tested

The identification of the items tested may be satisfied by indicating the source from which the items were selected and the specific selection criteria:

- If an audit sample is selected from a population of documents, the documentation should include identifying characteristics (e.g., the specific check numbers of the items included in the sample).
- If all items over a specific dollar amount are selected from a population of documents, the documentation need describe only the scope and the identification of the population (e.g., all checks over $10,000 from the July cash disbursements journal).
- If a systematic sample is selected from a population of documents, the documentation need only provide an identification of the source of the documents and an indication of the starting point and the sampling interval (e.g., a systematic sample of sales invoices was selected from the sales journal for the period from January 1 to October 1, starting with invoice number 375 and selecting every 50th invoice).

TABLE 4–9	Examples of Information Included in Permanent and Current Files

Permanent File:
Copies of, or excerpts from, the corporate charter.
Chart of accounts.
Organizational chart.
Accounting manual.
Copies of important contracts (pension contracts, union contracts, leases, etc.).
Documentation of internal control (e.g., flowcharts).
Terms of stock and bond issues.
Prior years' analytical procedure results.

Current File:
Copy of financial statements and auditor's report.
Audit plan and audit programs.
Copies of, or excerpts from, minutes of important committee meetings.
Working trial balance.
Adjusting and reclassification journal entries.
Working papers supporting financial statement accounts.

auditor must identify all significant findings or issues in an engagement completion memorandum. This memorandum should be specific enough for a reviewer to gain a thorough understanding of the significant findings or issues.

When documenting the quantity of evidence gathered through inspection of documents or confirmation of balances, the auditor should identify the items tested. Where appropriate, the audit files should contain abstracts or copies of documents such as significant contracts or agreements. Table 4–8 presents the documentation requirements for items tested by the auditor.

Most public accounting firms maintain audit documentation in two types of files: permanent and current. Permanent files contain historical data about the client that are of continuing relevance to the audit. Current files, on the other hand, include information and data related specifically to the current year's engagement. Table 4–9 contains examples of the types of information included in each type of file.

Examples of Audit Documentation

[LO 8]

Audit documentation comes in a variety of types. The more common audit documentation includes the audit plan and programs, working trial balance, account analysis and listings, audit memoranda, and adjusting and reclassification entries.

Audit Plan and Programs The audit plan contains the strategy to be followed by the auditor in conducting the audit. This document outlines the auditor's understanding of the client and the potential audit risks. It contains the basic framework for how the audit resources (budgeted audit hours) are to be allocated

EXHIBIT 4–1	An Example of a Partial Working Trial Balance

EARTHWEAR CLOTHIERS
Partial Working Trial Balance
December 31, 2009

Account Description	W/P Ref.	Balance 12/31/08	Balance 12/31/09	Adjustments		Adjusted T/B	Reclassification		Financial Statements
				DR	CR		DR	CR	
Cash and cash equivalents	C lead	$ 49,668	$ 48,978						
Receivables	E lead	11,539	12,875						
Inventory	F lead	105,425	122,337						
Prepaid advertising	G lead	10,772	11,458						

to various parts of the engagement. The audit programs contain the audit procedures that will be conducted by the auditor. Generally, each business process and account balance has a separate audit program.

Working Trial Balance   The working trial balance links the amounts in the financial statements to the audit working papers. Exhibit 4–1 illustrates a partial working trial balance for EarthWear Clothiers. In addition to a column for account name, the trial balance contains columns for working paper references, the prior-year balances, the unadjusted current-year balances, and columns for adjusting and reclassification entries. The last column would agree to the amounts contained in the financial statements after combining common account balances. A lead schedule is then used to show the detailed general ledger accounts that make up a financial statement category (cash, accounts receivable, and so on). For example, the trial balance would contain only one line for "cash and cash equivalents" and the "C lead" schedule would list all general ledger cash accounts. This approach is described in more detail later in the chapter.

Account Analysis and Listings   Account analysis working papers generally include the activity in a particular account for the period. For example, Exhibit 4–2 shows the analysis of legal and audit expense for EarthWear Clothiers for the year ended December 31, 2009. Listings represent a schedule of items remaining in the ending balance of an account and are often called trial balances. For example, the auditor may obtain a listing of all amounts owed to vendors that make up the accounts payable balance as of the end of the year. This listing would represent a trial balance of unpaid vendors' invoices.

Audit Memoranda   Much of the auditor's work is documented in written memoranda. These include discussions of items such as internal controls, inventory observation, errors identified, and problems encountered during the audit.

Adjusting and Reclassification Entries   The audit documentation should also include the adjusting and reclassification entries identified by the auditor or client. Adjusting entries are made to correct misstatements in the client's records. For example, if the auditor discovered that certain inventory items were improperly valued, an adjusting entry would be proposed to correct the dollar misstatement. Adjusting entries are posted in both the client's records and the working trial balance.

EXHIBIT 4–2	Example of an Account Analysis Working Paper

T20
GMP
2/4/10

EARTHWEAR CLOTHIERS
Analysis of Legal and Audit Expense
12/31/09

Date	Payee	Amount	Explanation
Feb. 1	Katz & Fritz	$ 28,500.00V	For services related to a patent infringement suit by Gough Mfg. Co. Lawsuit was dismissed.
April 10	Willis & Adams	950,000.00V	Annual audit fee.
Oct. 1	Katz & Fritz	26,200.00V	Legal fee for patent infringement suit against Weshant, Inc.
Oct. 20	Smoothe, Sylk, Fiels, Goode & Associates	2,100.00V	Legal services for a purchase contract with McDonald Merchandise, Inc.
		1,006,800.00	
		F T/B	

Tick Mark Legend
   V = Examined payees' bills for amount and description.
   F = Footed.
   T/B = Agreed to trial balance.
Conclusion: Based on the audit work performed, EarthWear's legal and audit expense account is not materially misstated.

Reclassification entries are made to properly present information on the financial statements. A reclassification entry affects income statement accounts or balance sheet accounts, but not both. For example, a reclassification entry might be necessary to present as a current liability the current portion of long-term debt.

Format of Audit Documentation

✄ [LO 8]

Audit documentation may be prepared in both hard copy and electronically. Most auditors now use personal computers and have electronic documentation programs. Whether the documentation is prepared manually or electronically, the manner in which it is formatted usually contains three general characteristics.

Heading   All audit documentation should have a proper heading. The heading should include the name of the client, the title of the working paper, and the client's year-end date. Exhibit 4–2 shows a working paper with a proper heading.

Indexing and Cross-Referencing   The audit documents must be organized so that members of the audit team or firm can find relevant audit evidence. Some firms use a lettering system; other firms use some type of numbering system. For example, the general working papers may be labeled "A," internal control systems working papers "B," cash working papers "C," and so on. When the auditor performs audit work on one working paper and supporting information is obtained from another working paper, the auditor cross-references (it can be "linked" in audit software) the information on each working paper. This process of indexing and cross-referencing provides a trail from the financial statements to the individual audit documents that a reviewer can easily follow. Indexing and cross-referencing are discussed further in the next section.

Tick Marks   Auditors use *tick marks* to document work performed. Tick marks are simply notations that are made by the auditor near, or next to, an item or amount on an audit document. The tick mark symbol is typically explained or defined at the bottom of the audit document, although many firms use a standard set of tick marks. Exhibit 4–2 shows some examples of tick marks. In this example of documentation, the tick mark "V" indicates that the auditor examined the bills sent to the client by the payee for proper amount and description.

Many public accounting firms document their conclusions about individual accounts or components of the financial statements. Exhibit 4–2 shows an example of how an auditor might document a conclusion about an individual account.

Organization of Audit Documentation

✂ [LO 8]

The audit documentation needs to be organized so that any member of the audit team (and others) can find the audit evidence that supports each financial statement account. While auditing standards do not dictate how this should be accomplished, the following discussion presents a general approach that is commonly used.

The financial statements contain the accounts and amounts covered by the auditor's report. These accounts come from the working trial balance, which summarizes the general ledger accounts contained on each lead schedule. Each lead schedule includes the general ledger accounts that make up the financial statement account. Different types of audit documentation (account analysis, listings, confirmations, and so on) are then used to support each of the general ledger accounts. Each of these audit documents is indexed, and all important amounts are cross-referenced between audit documents.

Figure 4–3 presents an example of how audit documents could be organized to support the cash account. Note that the $15,000 shown on the balance sheet agrees to the working trial balance. The "A lead" schedule in turn contains the three general ledger accounts that are included in the $15,000 balance. Audit documents then support each of the general ledger accounts. For example, the audit documents indexed "A2" provide the audit evidence supporting the general cash balance of $12,000. Also note that each important amount is cross-referenced. For example, the balance per bank of $14,000 on "A2" is referenced to "A2.1" and the cash balance on "A2.1" is referenced back to "A2."

Practice INSIGHT	Whether hard copy or electronic, never leave an unanswered question in the working papers. Consider the third general auditing standard, due professional care: could the auditor claim that due care was exercised if the auditor had a question, but did not exercise sufficient due diligence to answer the question? Probably not, so it's important to answer all questions and document all conclusions.

Ownership of Audit Documentation

✂ [LO 8]

Audit documentation is the property of the auditor. This includes not only audit documents prepared by the auditor but also documents prepared by the client at the request of the auditor. The auditor should retain audit documents for a reasonable period of time in order to meet the needs of his or her practice and legal record retention requirements.

Although the auditor owns the audit documents, they cannot be shown, except under certain circumstances, to outside parties without the client's consent. Chapter 19 discusses the confidentiality of audit documentation.

FIGURE 4–3	An Example of the Organization of Audit Documents

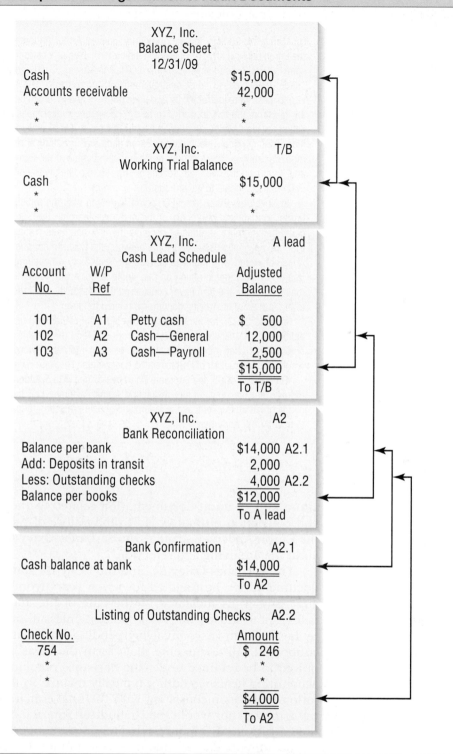

Audit Document Archiving and Retention

Legal and auditing standards have long required auditors to retain their audit files for a number of years after an audit report is filed. However, the events leading up to the Sarbanes-Oxley Act focused the spotlight on the practice of archiving and retaining audit documentation. Exhibit 4–3 describes Arthur Andersen's federal indictment and conviction on obstruction of justice charges for deletions and

EXHIBIT 4–3	The Wholesale Destruction of Documents and the Indictment of Arthur Andersen

On March 14, 2002, a federal grand jury indicted Arthur Andersen, initiating the first criminal charge in the Enron bankruptcy. The one-count indictment, alleging obstruction of justice, read that for a one-month span in October and early November 2001, "Andersen . . . did knowingly, intentionally, and corruptly persuade" employees to "alter, destroy, mutilate, and conceal." The indictment charged that Arthur Andersen employees "were instructed by Andersen partners and others to destroy immediately documentation relating to Enron and told to work overtime if necessary to accomplish the destruction." The indictment also called the destruction an "unparalleled initiative to shred physical documentation and delete computer files. Tons of paper relating to the Enron audit was promptly shredded as part of the orchestrated document destruction. The shredder at the Andersen office at the Enron building was used virtually constantly and, to handle the overload, dozens of large trunks filled with Enron documents were sent to Andersen's main Houston office to be shredded."

In November 2001, the SEC served Andersen with the anticipated subpoena relating to its work for Enron. In response, members of the Andersen team on the Enron audit were alerted finally that there could be "no more shredding" because the firm had been "officially served" for documents. During the trial, the only major issue of dispute between the government and defense was whether anyone at Arthur Andersen acted with intent to impede the regulatory proceeding prior to being "officially served." The fate of Arthur Andersen hung on this single issue. Arthur Andersen's specialists on securities regulation maintained that the firm never considered the possibility of a federal inquiry in fall 2001 at a time others in the firm were destroying documents related to Enron.

In June 2002, the federal jury convicted Arthur Andersen of obstruction of justice after 10 days of deliberation. Ironically, in interviews, jurors said that they reached their decision because an Arthur Andersen lawyer had ordered critical deletions to an internal memorandum, rather than because of the firm's wholesale destruction of Enron-related documents (*The New York Times,* June 15, 2002).

On May 31, 2005, the Supreme Court overturned Arthur Andersen's conviction. The court ruled unanimously that the Houston jury that found Arthur Andersen LLP guilty of obstruction of justice was given overly broad instructions by the federal judge who presided at the trial. However, this ruling came too late to save Arthur Andersen.

alterations of audit documentation related to the Enron audit. The indictment and conviction ultimately led to the failure of Arthur Andersen. In the wake of the Enron-Andersen scandal, the Sarbanes-Oxley Act imposed new guidelines for audit file archiving and retention.

The Sarbanes-Oxley Act and the PCAOB's standard (AS 3) require that audit documentation be retained for seven years from the date of completion of the engagement, as indicated by the date of the auditor's report (or the date that fieldwork is substantially completed), unless a longer period of time is required by law (e.g., in cases involving pending or threatened lawsuit, investigation, or subpoena). All documents that "form the basis of the audit or review" are required to be retained under the Sarbanes regulations. Prior to Sarbanes, public accounting firms would not typically include in their working papers documentation that was inconsistent with the final conclusion of the audit team regarding a matter, nor would they include all internal correspondence leading up to a final decision. AS 3 requires that any document created, sent, or received, including documents that are inconsistent with a final conclusion, be included in the audit files for all significant matters. This includes any correspondence between engagement teams and national technical accounting or auditing experts in a public accounting firm's national office. All current auditing standards (AS 3 and AU 339) require such document retention to facilitate any subsequent investigations, proceedings, and litigation.

Some states (e.g., New York and California) have adopted similar archiving and retention policies for all audits, including audits of nonpublic companies.

KEY TERMS

Accounting records. The records of initial entries and supporting records, such as checks and records of electronic fund transfers; invoices; contracts; the general and subsidiary ledgers, journal entries, and other adjustments to the financial statements that are not reflected in formal journal entries; and records such as work sheets and spreadsheets supporting cost allocations, computations, reconciliations, and disclosures.

Analytical procedures. Evaluations of financial information made by a study of plausible relationships among both financial and nonfinancial data.

Assertions. Expressed or implied representations by management regarding the recognition, measurement, presentation, and disclosure of information in the financial statements and related disclosures.

Audit documentation (working papers). The auditor's principal record of the work performed and the basis for the conclusions in the auditor's report. It also facilitates the planning, performance, and supervision of the engagement and provides the basis for the review of the quality of the work by providing the reviewer with written documentation of the evidence supporting the auditor's significant conclusions.

Audit evidence. All the information used by the auditor in arriving at the conclusions on which the audit opinion is based, and includes the information contained in the accounting records underlying the financial statements and other information such as minutes of meetings; confirmations from third parties; industry analysts' reports; controls manuals; information obtained by the auditor through audit procedures such as inquiry, observation, and inspection.

Audit procedures. Specific acts performed by the auditor in gathering evidence to determine if specific assertions are being met.

Confirmation. The process of obtaining and evaluating a direct communication from a third party in response to a request for information about a particular item affecting financial statement assertions.

Inquiry. Seeking information of knowledgeable persons, both financial and nonfinancial, throughout the entity or outside the entity.

Inspection of records and documents. Examination of internal or external records or documents that are in paper form, electronic form, or other media.

Inspection of tangible assets. Physical examination of the tangible assets.

Observation. Process of watching a process or procedure being performed by others.

Other information. Audit evidence that includes minutes of meetings; confirmations from third parties; industry analysts' reports; comparable data about competitors (benchmarking); controls manuals; information obtained by the auditor from such audit procedures as inquiry, observation, and inspection; and other information developed by, or available to, the auditor that permits the auditor to reach conclusions through valid reasoning.

Recalculation. Determination of the mathematical accuracy of documents or records.

Relevance of evidence. The relevance of audit evidence refers to its relationship to the assertion or to the objective of the control being tested.

Reliability of evidence. The diagnosticity of evidence; that is, whether the type of evidence can be relied on to signal the true state of the assertion.

Reperformance. The auditor's independent execution of procedures or controls that were originally performed as part of the entity's internal control, either manually or through the use of computer-assisted audit techniques.

Scanning. Reviewing accounting data to identify significant or unusual items; including the identification of anomalous individual items within account balances or other client data through the scanning or analysis of entries in transaction listings, subsidiary ledgers, general ledger control accounts, adjusting entries, suspense accounts, reconciliations, and other detailed reports.

www.mhhe.com/ messier7e	Visit the book's Online Learning Center for a multiple-choice quiz that will allow you to assess your understanding of chapter concepts.

REVIEW QUESTIONS

[LO 1]   4-1   Explain why the auditor divides the financial statements into components or segments in order to test management's assertions.

[1]   4-2   How do management assertions relate to the financial statements?

[2]   4-3   List and define the assertions about classes of transactions and events for the period under audit.

[2]   4-4   List and define the assertions about account balances at the period end.

[4]   4-5   Define audit evidence. Provide an example of evidence from accounting records and other information.

[4]   4-6   Explain why in most instances audit evidence is persuasive rather than convincing.

[5]   4-7   List and define the audit procedures for obtaining audit evidence.

[5,6]   4-8   In a situation that uses inspection of records and documents as a type of evidence, distinguish between vouching and tracing in terms of the direction of testing and the assertions being tested.

[5,6]   4-9   Why is it necessary to obtain corroborating evidence for inquiry and for observation?

[6]   4-10   Discuss the relative reliability of the different types of audit procedures.

[8]   4-11   Why are indexing and cross-referencing important to the documentation of audit working papers?

MULTIPLE-CHOICE QUESTIONS

[2,3]   4-12   Which of the following procedures would an auditor most likely rely on to verify management's assertion of completeness?
a. Reviewing standard bank confirmations for indications of cash manipulations.
b. Comparing a sample of shipping documents to related sales invoices.
c Observing the client's distribution of payroll checks.
d. Confirming a sample of recorded receivables by direct communication with the debtors.

[2,5,6]   4-13   In testing the existence assertion for an asset, an auditor ordinarily works from the
a. Financial statements to the potentially unrecorded items.
b. Potentially unrecorded items to the financial statements.
c. Accounting records to the supporting documents.
d. Supporting documents to the accounting records.

[4,5]   4-14   Which of the following statements concerning audit evidence is correct?
a. To be appropriate, audit evidence should be either persuasive or relevant but need not be both.

b. The measure of the reliability of audit evidence lies in the auditor's judgment.

c. The difficulty and expense of obtaining audit evidence concerning an account balance is a valid basis for omitting the test.

d. A client's general ledger may be sufficient audit evidence to support the financial statements.

[5,6]   4-15   Which of the following procedures would provide the most reliable audit evidence?

a. Inquiries of the client's internal accounting staff.

b. Inspection of prenumbered client purchase orders filed in the vouchers payable department.

c. Observation of procedures performed by the client's personnel on the entity's trial balance.

d. Inspection of bank statements obtained directly from the client's financial institution.

[5,6]   4-16   Which of the following types of audit evidence is the least reliable?

a. Prenumbered purchase order forms prepared by the client.

b. Bank statements obtained from the client.

c. Test counts of inventory performed by the auditor.

d. Correspondence from the client's attorney about litigation.

[5,6]   4-17   Audit evidence can come in different forms with different degrees of reliability. Which of the following is the most persuasive type of evidence?

a. Bank statements obtained from the client.

b. Computations made by the auditor.

c. Prenumbered client sales invoices.

d. Vendors' invoices included in the client's files.

[5,6]   4-18   An auditor would be least likely to use confirmations in connection with the examination of

a. Inventory held in a third-party warehouse.

b. Refundable income taxes.

c. Long-term debt.

d. Stockholders' equity.

[8]   4-19   The current file of the auditor's working papers should generally include

a. A flowchart of the accounting system.

b. Organization charts.

c. A copy of the financial statements.

d. Copies of bond and note indentures.

[8]   4-20   The permanent file section of the working papers that is kept for each audit client most likely contains

a. Review notes pertaining to questions and comments regarding the audit work performed.

b. A schedule of time spent on the engagement by each individual auditor.

c. Correspondence with the client's legal counsel concerning pending litigation.

d. Narrative descriptions of the client's accounting system and control procedures.

[8]   4-21   An audit document that reflects the major components of an amount reported in the financial statements is referred to as a(n)

a. Lead schedule.

b. Supporting schedule.

c. Audit control account.

d. Working trial balance.

PROBLEMS

[2]   **4-22**   Management makes assertions about components of the financial statements. Match the management assertions shown in the left-hand column with the proper description of the assertion shown in the right-hand column.

Management Assertion	Description
a. Existence or occurrence b. Rights and obligations c. Completeness d. Valuation or allocation	1. The accounts and transactions that should be included are included; thus, the financial statements are complete. 2. Assets, liabilities, equity revenues, and expenses are appropriately valued and are allocated to the proper accounting period. 3. The assets are the rights of the entity, and the liabilities are its obligations. 4. The assets and liabilities exist, and the recorded transactions have occurred.

[2]   **4-23**   Management assertions about classes of transactions are:
   a. Occurrence.
   b. Completeness.
   c. Authorization.
   d. Accuracy.
   e. Cutoff.
   f. Classification.
   For each management assertion, indicate an example of a misstatement that could occur for revenue transactions.

[5]   **4-24**   For each of the following specific audit procedures, indicate the type of audit procedure it represents: (1) inspection of records or documents, (2) inspection of tangible assets, (3) observation, (4) inquiry, (5) confirmation, (6) recalculation, (7) reperformance, (8) analytical procedures, and (9) scanning.
   a. Sending a written request to the client's customers requesting that they report the amount owed to the client.
   b. Examining large sales invoices for a period of two days before and after year-end to determine if sales are recorded in the proper period.
   c. Agreeing the total of the accounts receivable subsidiary ledger to the accounts receivable general ledger account.
   d. Discussing the adequacy of the allowance for doubtful accounts with the credit manager.
   e. Comparing the current-year gross profit percentage with the gross profit percentage for the last four years.
   f. Examining a new plastic extrusion machine to ensure that this major acquisition was received.
   g. Watching the client's warehouse personnel count the raw materials inventory.
   h. Performing test counts of the warehouse personnel's count of the raw material.
   i. Obtaining a letter from the client's attorney indicating that there were no lawsuits in progress against the client.
   j. Tracing the prices used by the client's billing program for pricing sales invoices to the client's approved price list.
   k. Reviewing the general ledger for unusual adjusting entries.

[2,5]   **4-25**   For each of the audit procedures listed in Problem 4-24, identify the category (assertions about classes of transactions and events or assertions about account balances) and the primary assertion being tested.

[1,4,5,7] 4-26 a. The first generally accepted auditing standard of fieldwork requires, in part, that "the work is to be adequately planned." An effective tool that aids the auditor in adequately planning the work is an audit program.

Required:
Describe an audit program and the purposes it serves.

b. Auditors frequently refer to "standards" and "procedures." Standards are measures of the quality of the auditor's performance. Standards specifically refer to the 10 generally accepted auditing standards. Procedures relate to acts that the auditor performs while trying to gather evidence. Procedures specifically refer to the methods or techniques the auditor uses in conducting the examination.

Required:
List at least eight different types of procedures an auditor would use in examining financial statements. For example, a type of procedure an auditor would use frequently is the observation of activities and conditions. Do not discuss specific accounts.

(AICPA, adapted)

[5,6] 4-27 Evidence comes in various types and has different degrees of reliability. Following are some statements that compare various types of evidence.
a. A bank confirmation versus observation of the segregation of duties between cash receipts and recording payment in the accounts receivable subsidiary ledger.
b. An auditor's recalculation of depreciation versus examination of raw material requisitions.
c. A bank statement included in the client's records versus shipping documents.
d. Physical inspection of common stock certificates held for investment versus physical examination of inventory components for a personal computer.

Required:
For each situation, indicate whether the first or second type of evidence is more reliable. Provide a rationale for your choice.

[5,6] 4-28 Inspection of records and documents relates to the auditor's examination of client accounting records and other information. One issue that affects the reliability of documentary evidence is whether the documents are internal or external. Following are examples of documentary evidence:
1. Duplicate copies of sales invoices.
2. Purchase orders.
3. Bank statements.
4. Remittance advices.
5. Vendors' invoices.
6. Materials requisition forms.
7. Overhead cost allocation sheets.
8. Shipping documents.
9. Payroll checks.
10. Long-term debt agreements.

Required:
a. Classify each document as internal or external evidence.
b. Classify each document as to its reliability (high, moderate, or low).

[5,6]   4-29   The confirmation process is defined as the process of obtaining and evaluating a direct communication from a third party in response to a request for information about a particular item affecting financial statement assertions.

Required:
a. List the factors that affect the reliability of confirmations.
b. One of the allegations in the Satyam Computer Services Ltd. fraud (see Exhibit 3–1) was that confirmations of account balances to various banks were determined to be forgeries. Auditing standards state that "an audit rarely involves the authentication of documentation, nor is the auditor trained as or expected to be an expert in such authentication." What steps could Satyam's auditors have taken to ensure that bank confirmations were reliable?
c. Refer back to EarthWear Clothiers' financial statements included after Chapter 1. Identify any information on EarthWear's financial statements that might be verified through the use of confirmations.

[7,8]   4-30   Audit documentation is the auditor's record of work performed and conclusions reached on an audit engagement.

Required:
a. What are the purposes of audit documentation?
b. List and describe the various types of audit documents.
c. What factors affect the auditor's judgment about the form and extent of audit documentation for a particular engagement?

DISCUSSION CASES

[4,5,6]   4-31   Part I. Lernout & Hauspie (L&H) was the world's leading provider of speech and language technology products, solutions, and services to businesses and individuals worldwide. Both Microsoft and Intel invested millions in L&H. However, accounting scandals and fraud allegations sent the company's stock crashing, and forced the firm to seek bankruptcy protection in Belgium and the United States. The following selected information pertains to L&H's sales and accounts receivable:
- Consolidated revenue increased 184 percent from the 1997 fiscal year to the 1998 fiscal year.
- Revenue in South Korea, which has a reputation as a difficult market for foreign companies to enter, increased from $97,000 in the first quarter of 1999 to approximately $59 million in the first quarter of 2000.
- In the second quarter of 2000, sales grew by 104 percent but accounts receivable grew by 128 percent.
- Average days outstanding increased from 138 days in 1998 to 160 days for the six-month period ended June 30, 2000.

Required:
a. Based on the above information, which assertion(s) for sales should the auditor be most concerned with? Why?

b. Based on the above information, which assertion(s) for accounts receivable should the auditor be most concerned with? Why?

c. What audit evidence should the auditor gather to verify the assertion(s) for sales and accounts receivable? Be specific as to how each type of evidence relates to the assertions you mentioned in parts (a) and (b) of this question.

Part II. L&H's auditor did not confirm accounts receivable from customers in South Korea. However, *The Wall Street Journal* contacted 18 of L&H's South Korean customers and learned the following:

• Three out of 18 customers listed by L&H stated that they were not L&H customers.

• Three others indicated that their purchases from L&H were smaller than those reported by L&H.

Required:

a. If L&H's auditor had confirmed these receivables and received such responses, what additional evidence could he or she have gathered to try to obtain an accurate figure for sales to and accounts receivable from customers in South Korea?

b. If you were L&H's auditor and you had received such responses from South Korean customers, how likely would you be to use inquiry of the client as an audit procedure? Why?

Sources: M. Maremont, J. Eisinger, and J. Carreyrou, "How High-Tech Dream at Lernout & Hauspie Crumbled in a Scandal," *The Wall Street Journal* (December 7, 2000), pp. A1, A18; J. Carreyrou and M. Maremont, "Lernout Unit Engaged in Massive Fraud to Fool Auditors, New Inquiry Concludes," *The Wall Street Journal* (April 6, 2001), p. A3; and J. Carreyrou, "Lernout Unit Booked Fictitious Sales, Says Probe," *The Wall Street Journal* (April 9, 2001), p. B2.

[4,5,6]   4-32   Bentley Bros. Book Company publishes more than 250 fiction and nonfiction titles. Most of the company's books are written by southern authors and typically focus on subjects popular in the region. The company sells most of its books to major retail stores such as Waldenbooks and B. Dalton.

Your firm was just selected as the new auditors for Bentley Bros., and you have been appointed as the audit manager for the engagement based on your prior industry experience. The prior auditors were removed because the client felt that it was not receiving adequate service. The prior auditors have indicated to you that the change in auditors did not result from any disagreements over accounting or auditing issues.

Your preliminary review of the company's financial statements indicates that the allowance for return of unsold books represents an important account (that is, high risk) because it may contain material misstatements. Consistent with industry practice, retailers are allowed to return unsold books for full credit. You know from your prior experience with other book publishers that the return rate for individual book titles can range from 30 to 50 percent. The client develops its allowance for return of unsold books based on internally generated records; that is, it maintains detailed records of all book returns by title.

Required:

a. Discuss how you would assess the reliability of the client's records for developing the allowance for return of unsold books.

b. Discuss how you would determine the return rate for relatively new titles.

c. Consider whether any external evidence can be obtained that would provide additional evidence on the reasonableness of the account.

INTERNET ASSIGNMENTS

[4,5,6]   4-33   Use an Internet browser to search for the following terms:
- Electronic data interchange (EDI)
- Image-processing systems

Prepare a memo describing EDI and image-processing systems. Discuss the implications of each for the auditor's consideration of audit evidence.

HANDS-ON CASES

EarthWear Online	**Evaluation of Audit Evidence** Evaluate a portion of the evidence that Willis and Adams gathered during an inventory observation for accuracy, completeness and existence. *Visit the book's Online Learning Center at www.mhhe.com/messier7e to find a detailed description of the case and to download required materials.*

ACL

www.mhhe.com/ messier7e	Visit the book's Online Learning Center for problem material to be completed using the ACL software packaged with your new text.

KAPLAN
CPA Review

www.mhhe.com/ messier7e	**Tomaszeski** This simulation will test your understanding of audit evidence, the confirmation process, and the types of audit reports. The content of the other exam questions will be discussed in subsequent chapters. *To begin this simulation, visit the book's Online Learning Center.*

Part **3**

PLANNING THE AUDIT, AND UNDERSTANDING AND AUDITING INTERNAL CONTROL

CHAPTER 5

LEARNING OBJECTIVES

Upon completion of this chapter you will

[1] Understand the auditor's requirements for client acceptance and continuance.

[2] Know what is required to establish an understanding with the client.

[3] Know the types of information that are included in an engagement letter.

[4] Understand how the work of the internal auditors can assist in the performance of the audit.

[5] Know the responsibilities of the audit committee and how it relates to the external auditors.

[6] Understand the steps that are involved in the preliminary engagement activities.

[7] Know the steps that are performed in planning an audit engagement.

[8] Know the types of audit tests.

[9] Learn the purposes and types of analytical procedures.

[10] Understand the audit testing hierarchy.

[11] Be familiar with financial ratios that are useful as analytical procedures.

RELEVANT ACCOUNTING AND AUDITING PRONOUNCEMENTS

FASB ASC Topic 850, Related Party Disclosures

AICPA, *Assessing and Responding to Audit Risk in a Financial Statement Audit* (Audit Guide) (New York: AICPA, 2006)

AU 311, Planning and Supervision

AU 312, Audit Risk and Materiality in Conducting an Audit

AU 314, Understanding the Entity and Its Environment and Assessing the Risks of Material Misstatement

AU 315, Communications between Predecessor and Successor Auditors

AU 316, Consideration of Fraud in a Financial Statement Audit

AU 317, Illegal Acts by Clients

AU 318, Performing Audit Procedures in Response to Assessed Risks and Evaluating the Audit Evidence Obtained

AU 322, The Auditor's Consideration of the Internal Audit Function in an Audit of Financial Statements

AU 329, Analytical Procedures

AU 334, Related Parties

AU 336, Using the Work of a Specialist

AU 339, Audit Documentation

AU 342, Auditing Accounting Estimates

AU 350, Audit Sampling

AU 380, The Auditor's Communication with Those Charged with Governance

PCAOB Auditing Standard No. 3, Auditing Documentation

PCAOB, Proposed Auditing Standards Related to the Auditor's Assessment of and Response to Risk, PCAOB Release No. 2008-006 (October 21, 2008) (AS3)

QC 10, A Firm's System of Quality Control

Audit Planning and Types of Audit Tests

Major Phases of an Audit

Client acceptance/
continuance and establishing
an understanding with the client
(Chapter 5)

Preliminary engagement
activities
(Chapter 5)

Plan the audit
(Chapters 3 and 5)

Consider and audit
internal control
(Chapters 6 and 7)

Audit business processes
and related accounts
(e.g., revenue generation)
(Chapters 10–16)

Complete the audit
(Chapter 17)

Evaluate results and
issue audit report
(Chapters 1 and 18)

The first standard of fieldwork requires that the audit be properly planned. Planning an audit includes establishing the overall audit strategy for the engagement and developing an audit plan, which includes risk assessment procedures and planned audit responses to the risks of material misstatement. If the audit is not properly planned, the auditor may issue an incorrect audit report or conduct an inefficient audit. The audit starts with the initial appointment or reappointment of the auditor by the client or audit committee. Next, the auditor performs a number of activities that go into developing an overall audit strategy.

This chapter covers the following phases of the audit identified in Chapter 1, Figure 1–4:

- Client acceptance and continuance, and establishing an understanding with the client.
- Preliminary engagement activities.
- Planning the audit.

It then reviews the major types of audit tests and covers analytical procedures. Analytical procedures are required to be performed as part of the planning of the audit and as part of wrapping up the audit. They are also often useful for providing substantive audit evidence during the conduct of the audit of business processes and related accounts. The *Advanced Module* presents ratios that are useful for analytical procedures.

Client Acceptance and Continuance

✎ [LO 1]   The first phase of the audit process that relates to audit planning is client acceptance and continuance (see Figure 5–1). The extent of effort that goes into evaluating a new client is normally much greater than the decision to continue with an existing client. With a continuing client the auditor possesses extensive knowledge about the entity and its environment.

Prospective
Client
Acceptance

Public accounting firms should investigate a prospective client prior to accepting an engagement. Table 5–1 lists procedures that a firm might conduct to evaluate a prospective client. Performance of such procedures would normally be documented in a memo or by completion of a client acceptance questionnaire or checklist.

When the prospective client has previously been audited, auditing standards (AU 315) require that the successor auditor make certain inquiries of the predecessor auditor before accepting the engagement. The successor auditor should

FIGURE 5–1	The Phases of an Audit That Relate to Audit Planning

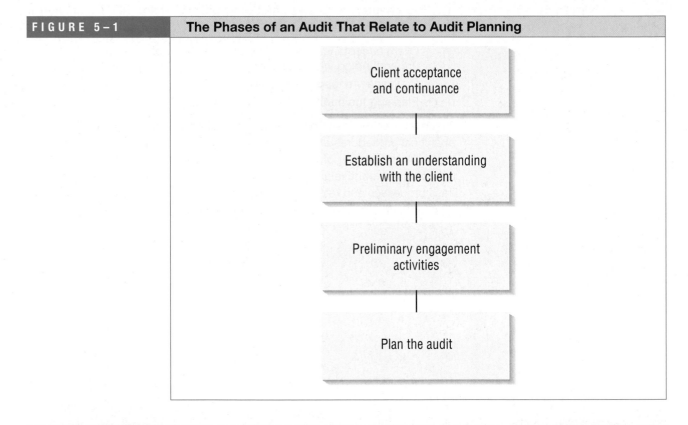

TABLE 5–1	Procedures for Evaluating a Prospective Client

1. Obtain and review available financial information (annual reports, interim financial statements, income tax returns, etc.).
2. Inquire of third parties about any information concerning the integrity of the prospective client and its management. (Such inquiries should be directed to the prospective client's bankers and attorneys, credit agencies, and other members of the business community who may have such knowledge.)
3. Communicate with the predecessor auditor as required by auditing standards about whether there were any disagreements about accounting principles, audit procedures, or similar significant matters.
4. Consider whether the prospective client has any circumstances that will require special attention or that may represent unusual business or audit risks, such as litigation or going-concern problems.
5. Determine if the firm is independent of the client and able to provide the desired service.
6. Determine if the firm has the necessary technical skills and knowledge of the industry to complete the engagement.
7. Determine if acceptance of the client would violate any applicable regulatory agency requirements or the Code of Professional Conduct.

request permission of the prospective client before contacting the predecessor auditor. Because the Code of Professional Conduct does not allow an auditor to disclose confidential client information without the client's consent, the prospective client must authorize the predecessor auditor to respond to the successor's requests for information. The successor auditor's communications with the predecessor auditor should include questions related to the integrity of management; disagreements with management over accounting and auditing issues; communications with the audit committee (or those charged with governance) regarding fraud, illegal acts, and internal control weaknesses; and the predecessor's understanding of the reason for the change in auditors. Such inquiries of the predecessor auditor may help the successor auditor determine whether to accept the engagement. The predecessor auditor should respond fully to the successor's requests unless an unusual circumstance (such as a lawsuit) exists. If the predecessor's response is limited, the successor auditor must be informed that the response is limited.

In the unusual case where the prospective client refuses to permit the predecessor to respond, the successor auditor should have reservations about accepting the client. Such a situation should raise serious questions about management's motivations and integrity. In addition, if the client has unusual business risks such as possible going concern issues, the auditor is not likely to accept the prospective client because the engagement risk may be too high.

After accepting the engagement, the successor auditor may need information on beginning balances and consistent application of GAAP in order to issue an unqualified report. The successor auditor should request that the client authorize the predecessor auditor to permit a review of his or her working papers. In most instances, the predecessor auditor will allow the successor auditor to make copies of any working papers of continuing interest (for example, details of selected balance sheet accounts).

If the client has not previously been audited, the public accounting firm should complete all the procedures listed in Table 5–1, except for the communication with the predecessor auditor. The auditor should review the prospective client's financial information and carefully assess management integrity by communicating with the entity's bankers and attorneys, as well as other members of the business community. Many public accounting firms have full time staff that complete background checks and monitor news of public clients.

Continuing Client Retention

Public accounting firms should evaluate periodically whether to retain their current clients. This evaluation may take place at or near the completion of an audit or when some significant event occurs. Conflicts over accounting and auditing issues or disputes over fees may lead a public accounting firm to disassociate itself from a client.

Establishing an Understanding with the Client

[LO 2] The auditor should establish an understanding with the client about the terms of the engagement. This understanding reduces the risk that either party may misinterpret what is expected or required of the other party. The terms of the engagement, which are documented in the engagement letter, should include the objectives of the engagement, management's responsibilities, the auditor's responsibilities, and the limitations of the engagement. In establishing an understanding with the client, three topics should be discussed: (1) the engagement letter, (2) the internal auditors; and (3) the audit committee.

The Engagement Letter

✂ [LO 3]

Auditing standards state that the auditor should document the understanding through a written communication with the client. An *engagement letter* is used to formalize the arrangements reached between the auditor and the client. This letter serves as a contract, outlining the responsibilities of both parties and preventing misunderstandings between the two parties. Exhibit 5–1 shows a sample engagement letter for EarthWear.

In addition to the items mentioned in the sample engagement letter in Exhibit 5–1, the engagement letter may include

- Arrangements involving the use of specialists or internal auditors.
- Any limitation of the liability of the auditor or client, such as indemnification to the auditor for liability arising from knowing misrepresentations to the auditor by management or alternative dispute resolution procedures. (Note that regulatory bodies, such as the SEC, may restrict or prohibit such liability-limiting arrangements.) See Practice Insight below.
- Additional services to be provided relating to regulatory requirements.
- Arrangements regarding other services (e.g., assurance, tax, or consulting services).

Internal Auditors

✂ [LO 4]

When the client has internal auditors, the auditor may request their assistance in conducting the audit. The auditor first needs to obtain an understanding of the internal audit function, including information about the activities that it performs. The auditor next must determine whether any of these activities are relevant to the audit of the financial statements.[1] A major issue for the independent auditor is accessing the competence and objectivity of the internal auditors and the effect of their work on the audit. Table 5–2 presents factors that the auditor should consider when assessing the competence and objectivity of the internal auditors. In Chapter 7 we discuss the effect the Sarbanes-Oxley Act has had on the use and assessment of internal auditors for the audit of internal control over financial reporting.

The internal auditors' work may affect the nature, timing, and extent of the audit procedures performed by the independent auditor. For example, as part of their regular work, internal auditors may review, assess, and monitor the entity's controls that are included in the accounting system. Similarly, part of their work may include confirming receivables or observing certain physical inventories. If the internal auditors are competent and objective, the independent auditor may use the internal auditors' work in these areas to reduce the scope of audit work. The materiality of the account balance or class of transactions and its related audit risk may also determine how much the independent auditor can rely on the internal auditors' work. When internal auditors provide direct assistance, the auditor should supervise, review, evaluate, and test their work.

---

[1] In Chapter 7, we discuss the auditor's consideration of the internal audit function in an audit of internal control over financial reporting.

EXHIBIT 5-1	A Sample Engagement Letter—EarthWear Clothiers

Willis & Adams, P.C.
Boise, Idaho

April 1, 2009

Mr. Calvin J. Rogers
EarthWear Clothiers
P.O. Box 787
Boise, Idaho 83845

Dear Mr. Rogers:

The purpose of this letter is to confirm our understanding of the terms of our engagement as independent accountants of EarthWear Clothiers (the "Company").

Services and Related Report

We will audit the financial statements of the Company at December 31, 2009, and for the year then ending. We will also audit the effectiveness of internal control over financial reporting at December 31, 2009. Upon completion of our audits, we will provide you with our audit report on the financial statements and internal control. If, for any reasons caused by you or relating to the affairs of the Company, we are unable to complete the audits, we may decline to issue a report as a result of this engagement.

In conjunction with the annual audit, we will perform reviews of the Company's unaudited quarterly financial statements and related data for each of the first three quarters in the year ending December 31, 2009, before the Form 10-Q is filed. These reviews will be conducted in accordance with standards established by the Public Company Accounting Oversight Board (United States), and are substantially less in scope than audits. Accordingly, a review may not reveal material modifications necessary to make the quarterly financial information conform with generally accepted accounting principles. We will communicate to you for your consideration any matters that come to our attention as a result of the review that we believe may require material modifications to the quarterly financial information to make it conform with generally accepted accounting principles.

Our Responsibilities and Limitations

The objective of the audits is the expression of opinions on the financial statements and internal controls. We will be responsible for performing the audit in accordance with standards established by the Public Company Accounting Oversight Board (United States). These standards require that we plan and perform the audit to obtain reasonable assurance about whether the financial statements are free of material misstatement. The audit will include examining, on a test basis, evidence supporting the amounts and disclosures in the financial statements, assessing accounting principles used and significant estimates made by management, and evaluating the overall financial statement presentation.

The objective of our audit of internal control over financial reporting is to express an opinion on the effectiveness of the company's internal control over financial reporting based on our audit. We will be responsible for performing the audit of internal control over financial reporting in accordance with the standards of the Public Company Accounting Oversight Board (United States). Those standards require that we plan and perform the audit to obtain reasonable assurance about whether effective internal control over financial reporting was maintained in all material respects. Our audit includes obtaining an understanding of internal control over financial reporting, testing and evaluating the design and operating effectiveness of internal control, and performing such other procedures as we consider necessary in the circumstances.

We will design our audit to obtain reasonable, but not absolute, assurance of detecting errors or fraud that would have a material effect on the financial statements as well as other illegal acts having a direct and material effect on financial statement amounts. Our audit will not include a detailed audit of transactions, such as would be necessary to disclose errors or fraud that did not cause a material misstatement of the financial statements. It is important to recognize that there are inherent limitations in the auditing process. Audits are based on the concept of selective testing of the data underlying the financial statements, which involves judgment regarding the areas to be tested, and the nature, timing, extent, and results of the tests to be performed. Audits are, therefore, subject to the limitation that material errors or fraud or other illegal acts having a direct and material financial statement impact, if they exist, may not be detected. Because of the characteristics of fraud, particularly those involving concealment through collusion and falsified documentation (including forgery), an audit designed and executed in accordance with standards established by the Public Company Accounting Oversight Board (United States) may not detect a material fraud. Further, while effective internal control reduces the likelihood that errors, fraud, or other illegal acts will occur and remain undetected, it does not eliminate that possibility. For these reasons we cannot ensure that errors, fraud, or other illegal acts, if present, will be detected. However, we will communicate to you, as appropriate, any illegal act, material errors, or evidence of fraud identified during our audit.

Management's Responsibilities

The financial statements are the responsibility of the management of the Company. In this regard, management is responsible for properly recording transactions in the accounting records and for establishing and maintaining internal control sufficient to permit the preparation of financial statements in conformity with generally accepted accounting principles. Management is responsible for adjusting the financial

(continued)

EXHIBIT 5-1	A Sample Engagement Letter—EarthWear Clothiers (continued)

statements to correct material misstatements and for affirming to us that the effects of any uncorrected misstatements aggregated by us during the current engagement and pertaining to the year ending December 31, 2009, are immaterial, both individually and in the aggregate, to the financial statements taken as a whole. Management also is responsible for identifying and ensuring that the Company complies with the laws and regulations applicable to its activities.

Management is also responsible for maintaining effective internal control over financial reporting and for its assessment of the effectiveness of internal control over financial reporting. Management must accept responsibility for the effectiveness of the entity's internal control over financial reporting; evaluate the effectiveness of the entity's internal control over financial reporting using suitable control criteria; support its evaluation with sufficient evidence, including documentation; and present a written assessment of the effectiveness of the entity's internal control over financial reporting as of the end of the entity's most recent fiscal year.

Management is responsible for making available to us, on a timely basis, all of the Company's original accounting records and related information and company personnel to whom we may direct inquiries. As required by standards established by the Public Company Accounting Oversight Board (United States), we will make specific inquiries of management and others about the representations embodied in the financial statements and the effectiveness of internal control over financial reporting. Standards established by the Public Company Accounting Oversight Board (United States) also require that we obtain written representations covering audited financial statements from certain members of management. The results of our audit tests, the responses to our inquiries, and the written representations, comprise the evidential matter we intend to rely upon in forming our opinion on the financial statements.

Other Documents

Standards established by the Public Company Accounting Oversight Board (United States) require that we read any annual report that contains our audit report. The purpose of this procedure is to consider whether other information in the annual report, including the manner of its presentation, is materially inconsistent with information appearing in the financial statements. We assume no obligation to perform procedures to corroborate such other information as part of our audit.

With regard to electronic filings, such as in connection with the SEC's Electronic Data Gathering, Analysis, and Retrieval ("EDGAR") system, you agree that, before filing any document in electronic format with the SEC with which we are associated, you will advise us of the proposed filing on a timely basis. We will provide you with a signed copy of our report(s) and consent(s). These manually signed documents will serve to authorize the use of our name prior to any electronic transmission by you. For our files, you will provide us with a complete copy of the document as accepted by EDGAR.

The Company may wish to include our report on these financial statements in a registration statement to be filed under the Securities Act of 1933 or in some other securities offering. You agree that the aforementioned audit report, or reference to our Firm, will not be included in any such offering without our prior permission or consent. Any agreement to perform work in connection with an offering, including an agreement to provide permission or consent, will be a separate engagement.

Timing and Fees

Completion of our work is subject to, among other things, (1) appropriate cooperation from the Company's personnel, including timely preparation of necessary schedules; (2) timely responses to our inquiries; and (3) timely communication of all significant accounting and financial reporting matters. When and if for any reason the Company is unable to provide such schedules, information, and assistance, Willis & Adams and the Company will mutually revise the fee to reflect additional services, if any, required of us to complete the audit.

Our fee estimates are based on the time required by the individuals assigned to the engagement. Individual hourly rates vary according to the degree of responsibility involved and experience and skill required. We estimate our fees for this integrated audit of internal control and financial statements will be $950,000, exclusive of out-of-pocket expenses. This estimate takes into account the agreed-upon level of preparation and assistance from company personnel; we will advise management should this not be provided or should any other circumstances arise which may cause actual time to exceed that estimate. Invoices rendered are due and payable upon receipt.

This engagement letter reflects the entire agreement between us relating to the services covered by this letter. It replaces and supersedes any previous proposals, correspondence, and understandings, whether written or oral. The agreements of the Company and Willis & Adams contained in this engagement letter shall survive the completion or termination of this engagement.

If you have any questions, please contact us. If the services outlined herein are in accordance with your requirements and if the above terms are acceptable to you, please have one copy of this letter signed in the space provided below and return it to us.

Very truly yours,

Willis & Adams

M. J. Willis

M. J. Willis, Partner

APPROVED:

By *Calvin J. Rogers*

Chief Executive Officer

Date April 3, 2009

TABLE 5–2	Factors for Assessing the Competence and Objectivity of Internal Auditors

Competence
- Educational level and professional experience.
- Professional certification and continuing education.
- Audit policies, procedures, and checklists.
- Practices regarding their assignments.
- The supervision and review of their audit activities.
- The quality of their working paper documentation, reports, and recommendations.
- Evaluation of their performance.

Objectivity
- The organizational status of the internal auditors responsible for the internal audit function (for example, the internal auditor reports to an officer of sufficient status to ensure that the audit coverage is broad and the internal auditor has access to the board of directors or the audit committee).
- Policies to maintain internal auditors' objectivity about the areas audited (for example, internal auditors are prohibited from auditing areas to which they have recently been assigned or are to work upon completion of responsibilities in the internal audit function).

The Audit Committee

[LO 5]

An audit committee is a subcommittee of the board of directors that is responsible for the financial reporting and disclosure process.[2] Under Section 301 of the Sarbanes-Oxley Act, the audit committee of a public company has the following requirements:

- Each member of the audit committee must be a member of the board of directors and shall be independent. "Independent" is defined as not receiving, other than for service on the audit committee, any consulting, advisory, or other compensatory fee and not being affiliated with the company.
- The audit committee is directly responsible for the appointment, compensation, and oversight of the work of any registered public accounting firm employed by the company.
- The audit committee must preapprove all audit and nonaudit services provided by its auditor.
- The audit committee must establish procedures for the receipt, retention, and treatment of complaints received by the company regarding accounting, internal control, and auditing.
- Each audit committee member must have the authority to engage independent counsel or other advisors, as it determines necessary to carry out its duties.

The audit committee should also interact with the internal audit function. An ideal arrangement for establishing the independence of the internal audit function is for the head of internal auditing to report either directly or indirectly to the audit committee.

The audit committee should meet with the external auditor before the engagement starts to discuss the auditor's responsibilities and significant accounting policies. It may also provide limited input into the scope of the auditor's work, such as requesting that the external auditor visit certain locations. The audit committee may also engage the external or internal auditors to conduct special investigations. The external auditor is required to make a number of important communications to the audit committee during or at the end of the engagement. Most of the required communications are made at the completion of the engagement. Chapter 17 covers them in detail.

---

[2]Some privately held companies may not have an audit committee. In those circumstances the auditor should communicate with *those charged with governance*. Those charged with governance are persons with the responsibility for overseeing the strategic direction of the entity and obligations related to the accountability of the entity (AU 380).

Preliminary Engagement Activities

⚹ [LO 6]   There are generally two preliminary engagement activities: (1) determining the audit engagement team requirements; and (2) ensuring that the audit team and audit firm are in compliance with ethical requirements, including independence.

Determine
the Audit
Engagement
Team
Requirements

Public accounting firms need to ensure that their engagements are completed by auditors having the proper degree of technical training and proficiency given the circumstances of the clients. Factors that should be considered in determining staffing requirements include engagement size and complexity, level of risk, any special expertise, personnel availability, and timing of the work to be performed. For example, if the engagement involves a high level of risk, the firm should staff the engagement with more experienced auditors. Similarly, if the audit involves a specialized industry (banking, insurance, and so on) or if the client uses sophisticated IT processing or holds financial instruments, the firm must ensure that members of the audit team possess the requisite expertise. Generally, a time budget for planned work is prepared in order to assist with the staffing requirements and to schedule the fieldwork.

Assess
Compliance
with Ethical
Requirements,
including
Independence

The second general standard requires that the auditor be independent of the client in order to issue an opinion. According to the Statements on Quality Control Standards, a public accounting firm should establish policies and procedures to ensure that persons at all organizational levels within the firm meet the profession's ethical requirements, including maintaining independence in accordance with Rule 101 of the Code of Professional Conduct (see Chapter 19). A firm should document compliance with this policy by having all personnel complete an annual independence questionnaire or report. This questionnaire requests information about the auditor's financial or business relationships with the firm's clients. Under certain circumstances, family members' financial or business relationships are attributable to the auditor. For example, if the spouse of an auditor participating in an engagement was an accounting supervisor for the client, independence would be considered impaired.

At the engagement level, the partner-in-charge should ensure that all individuals assigned to the engagement are independent of the client. This can be accomplished by reviewing the annual independence reports for each member of the audit team or through the firm's independent database.

Another area of concern related to independence is unpaid client fees. If an account receivable from a client takes on the characteristics of a loan, the auditor's independence may be impaired. Many public accounting firms adopt a policy of not completing the current audit until all of the prior year's fees have been paid.

Finally, the CPA firm must be concerned when it also provides consulting services for an audit client. While the performance of consulting services does not, in and of itself, impair independence, the audit team must remain objective when evaluating client activities that were developed by its firm's consultants. For companies currently subject to the Sarbanes-Oxley Act, the auditor is not permitted to provide certain types of consulting services for audit clients. See Chapter 19 for a list of these services.

In the rare instance where the auditor is not independent of the client, the type of audit opinion should be discussed during the planning stage. As discussed in Chapters 1 and 18, a disclaimer of opinion must be issued when the auditor is not independent.

Planning the Audit

➤ [LO 7]   Engagement planning involves all the issues the auditor should consider in developing an *audit strategy* for conducting the audit. In determining the audit strategy, the auditor should determine the scope of the engagement, ascertain the reporting objectives to plan the timing of the audit, consider the factors that will determine the focus of the audit team's efforts (determination of appropriate materiality levels, areas of high risk of material misstatement, etc.). Developing the audit strategy helps the auditor determine what resources are needed to perform the engagement.

Once the overall audit strategy has been established, the auditor develops an *audit plan*. The audit plan is more detailed than the audit strategy. In the audit plan, the auditor documents a description of (1) the nature, timing, and extent of the planned risk assessment procedures to be used, (2) the nature, timing, and extent of planned further audit procedures at the assertion level for each class of transactions, account balance, and disclosure, and (3) a description of other audit procedures to be performed in order to comply with auditing standards. Basically, the audit plan should consider how to conduct the audit in an effective and efficient manner.

When preparing the audit plan, the auditor should be guided by the results of the risk assessment procedures performed to gain the understanding of the entity. Additional steps that should be performed include

- Assess business risks and establish materiality.
- Assess the need for specialists.
- Assess the possibility of illegal acts.
- Identify related parties.
- Conduct preliminary analytical procedures.
- Consider additional value-added services.

Assess Business Risks and Establish Materiality

Chapter 3 provided a detailed discussion of the process used to assess the client's business risks and to establish materiality. The auditor restricts audit risk at the account balance level in such a way that, at the end of the engagement, he or she can express an opinion on the financial statements, taken as a whole, at an acceptably low level of audit risk. The audit risk model serves as a framework for this process. The auditor obtains an understanding of the entity and its environment. Based on this understanding, the auditor identifies those business risks that may result in material misstatements. The auditor evaluates the client's response to those business risks and ensures that those responses have been adequately implemented. Based on this information, the auditor assesses the level of risk of material misstatement of assertions in relation to financial statement accounts. The risk of material misstatement is used to determine the acceptable level of detection risk and to plan the auditing procedures to be performed. The auditor considers materiality from a reasonable user perspective and follows a three-step process in applying materiality on an audit. You should consider returning to Chapter 3 to review the important issues related to these concepts.

Assess the Need for Specialists

A major consideration in planning the audit is the need for specialists (AU 336). Auditing standards define a *specialist* as a person or firm possessing special skill or knowledge in a field other than accounting or auditing. This would include specialists in finance, tax, valuation, pension, and information technology (IT). Such specialists may assist the auditor with the valuation of financial instruments, determining physical quantities, determining amounts derived from specialized techniques, or interpretations of regulations or agreements. The use of an IT specialist is a significant aspect of most audit engagements. If deciding whether an IT specialist is to be used, a primary concern is the extent to which IT is used in processing accounting information. The presence of complex information technology may require the use of an IT specialist. Chapter 6 covers these issues in more detail. Chapter 7 addresses the requirements for the audit of internal controls for public companies.

The auditor is still ultimately responsible for work performed by the specialist. In relying on the specialist, the auditor should evaluate the competence and objectivity of the specialist, audit the inputs used by the specialist (e.g., census data for actuaries) and reconcile the output (e.g., an estimate should be found in the financial statements or disclosures), and review the specialist's work for reasonableness, including the reasonableness of assumptions.

Assess the Possibility of Illegal Acts

The term *illegal acts* refers to violations of laws or governmental regulations. In some instances, fraud may also consist of illegal acts (see Chapter 3). Auditing standards (AU 317) distinguish between illegal acts that have *direct and material* effects on the financial statements and those that have *material but indirect* effects. The auditor should consider laws and regulations that are generally recognized as having a direct and material effect on the determination of financial statement amounts. For example, tax laws and laws and regulations that may affect the amount of revenue recognized under a government contract fall into this category. Auditing standards state that the auditor's responsibility for detecting illegal acts having a direct and material effect on the financial statements is the same as that for errors or fraud.

Other illegal acts, such as violations of the securities acts or occupational safety and health, Food and Drug Administration, environmental protection, equal employment regulations, and price-fixing or other antitrust violations, may materially but indirectly affect the financial statements. The auditor should be aware that such illegal acts may have occurred. If specific information comes to the auditor's attention that provides evidence concerning the existence of such material but indirect illegal acts, the auditor should apply audit procedures specifically directed at determining whether illegal acts have occurred. However, an audit conducted in accordance with auditing standards provides no assurance that illegal acts will be detected or that any contingent liability that may result will be disclosed.

Table 5–3 presents some examples of specific information or circumstances that indicate the possibility of an illegal act. For example, the business world has seen a number of instances where payments of sales commissions or agent's fees were really bribes to secure contracts. When the auditor becomes aware of such a possible illegal act, he or she should obtain an understanding of the nature of

TABLE 5-3	Information or Circumstances That May Indicate an Illegal Act

Unauthorized transactions, improperly recorded transactions, or transactions not recorded in a complete or timely manner.
An investigation by a government agency, an enforcement proceeding, or payment of unusual fines or penalties.
Violations of laws or regulations cited in reports of examinations by regulatory agencies.
Large payments for unspecified services to consultants, affiliates, or employees.
Sales commissions or agents' fees that appear excessive.
Large payments in cash or bank cashiers' checks.
Unexplained payments to government officials.
Failure to file tax returns or pay government duties.

the act, the circumstances in which it occurred, and sufficient other information to evaluate its effects on the financial statements. The auditor should then discuss the matter with the appropriate level of management. If management does not provide satisfactory information, the auditor should consult with the client's legal counsel and apply additional audit procedures, if necessary.

If an illegal act has occurred or is likely to have occurred, the auditor should consider its implications for other aspects of the audit, particularly the reliability of management representations. The auditor should ensure that the audit committee or those charged with governance are adequately informed about significant illegal acts. The auditor should also recognize that, under the circumstances noted previously, he or she may have a duty to notify parties outside the client.

Identify Related Parties[3]

FASB ASC Topic 850, "Related Party Disclosures," defines *related parties* as

> Affiliates of the enterprise; entities for which investments are accounted for by the equity method by the enterprise; trusts for the benefits of the employees, such as pension and profit-sharing trusts that are managed by or under the trusteeship of management; principal owners of the enterprise; its management; members of the immediate families of the principal owners of the enterprise and its management; and other parties with which the enterprise may deal if one party controls or can significantly influence the management or operating policies of the other to the extent that one of the transacting parties might be prevented from fully pursuing its own separate interests. Another party also is a related party if it can significantly influence the management or operating policies of the transacting parties or if it has an ownership interest in one of the transacting parties and can significantly influence the other to an extent that one or more of the transacting parties might be prevented from fully pursuing its own separate interests.

Practice
INSIGHT

The Baptist Foundation of Arizona (BFA) was organized as a nonprofit organization for the purpose of providing financial support to various Southern Baptist initiatives. Starting in 1991, BFA failed to disclose related-party transactions. In its 1997 memorandum, Arthur Andersen noted that its 1996 audit recommendations regarding related-parties had not been implemented. Like its 1996 opinion, the firm issued an unqualified opinion on BFA's 1997 financial statements, without requiring adequate disclosures concerning the concentration of credit risk among the organization's related parties. BFA's management perpetrated a fraudulent scheme, which resulted in the largest bankruptcy of a religious nonprofit in U.S. history, ultimately costing some 13,000 investors more than $590 million.

Auditors should attempt to identify all related parties during the planning phase of the audit. AU 334, "Related Parties," provides guidance on searching for and reporting on related parties. It is important to identify related party transactions because the transaction may not be "at arm's length." For example, the client may lease property from an entity owned by the chief executive officer at lease rates in excess of prevailing market rates. The auditor can identify related parties by evaluating the client's procedures for identifying related parties, requesting a list of related parties from management, and reviewing filings with the Securities and Exchange Commission and other regulatory agencies. Once related parties have been identified, audit personnel should be provided with

---

[3]See E. A. Gordon, E. Henry, T. J. Louwers, and B. J. Reed, "Auditing Related Party Transactions: A Literature Overview and Research Synthesis," *Accounting Horizons* (March 2007), pp. 81–102 for a review of research on related parties.

the names so that transactions with such parties are identified and investigated. Here are some additional audit procedures that may identify transactions with related parties:

- Review the minutes of the board of directors and executive or operating committees for information about material transactions authorized or discussed at their meetings.
- Review conflict-of-interest statements obtained by the company from management.
- Review the extent and nature of business transacted with major customers, suppliers, borrowers, and lenders for indications of previously undisclosed relationships.
- Review accounting records for large, unusual, or nonrecurring transactions or balances, paying particular attention to transactions recognized at or near the end of the reporting period.
- Review confirmations of loans receivable and payable for indications of guarantees. If guarantees are identified, determine their nature and the relationships of the guarantor to the entity.

Conduct Preliminary Analytical Procedures

Analytical procedures are defined as consisting of evaluations of financial information made by a study of plausible relationships among both financial and nonfinancial data (AU 329). Auditing standards require that the auditor apply analytical procedures at the planning phase for all audits. The main objectives of preliminary analytical procedures conducted at planning are (1) to understand the client's business and transactions and (2) to identify financial statement accounts that are likely to contain errors. By identifying where errors are likely, the auditor can allocate more resources to investigate those accounts. Suppose, for example, that an auditor computes a client's inventory turnover ratio for the last five years as follows:

$$\text{Inventory turnover} = \frac{\text{Cost of goods sold}}{\text{Inventory}}$$

The results of this analysis show the following trend, which is compared to industry data:

	2005	2006	2007	2008	2009
Client	8.9	8.8	8.5	8.0	7.9
Industry	8.8	8.7	8.8	8.6	8.6

The client's inventory turnover ratio in this case has declined steadily over the five-year period, while the industry turnover ratio shows only a minor decline over the same period. The auditor might suspect that the client's inventory contains slow-moving or obsolete inventory. The auditor would then plan additional testing for selected assertions such as valuation, completeness, and existence.

Consider Additional Value-Added Services

As part of the planning process, the auditor should look for opportunities to recommend additional value-added services. Traditionally, value-added services have included tax planning, system design and integration, and internal reporting processes. With auditors taking a more global view of the entity and its environment, there are new opportunities to provide valuable services for the client. For example, the assurance services (introduced in Chapter 2 and discussed in more detail in Chapter 21) include risk assessment, business performance measurement (benchmarking), and electronic commerce. The auditor also can provide recommendations based on the assessment of the entity's business risks. With the knowledge gathered through assessing business risks, the auditor can provide important feedback to management and the board of directors on the strengths and weaknesses of business processes, strategic planning, and emerging trends. Proper consideration of value-added services during the planning process should alert the audit team to proactively identify opportunities to improve client service. Of course, auditors who audit public companies are limited in the types of consulting services they can offer their audit clients (see Chapter 19).

Document the Overall Audit Strategy, Audit Plan, and Prepare Audit Programs

The auditor should document the audit strategy and audit plan. This involves documenting the decisions about the nature, timing, and extent of audit tests. At this stage, the auditor compiles his or her knowledge about the client's business objectives, strategies, and related business and audit risks. The auditor records how the client is managing its risks (i.e., through internal control processes) and then documents the effect of the risks and controls on the planned audit procedures. Auditors ensure they have addressed the risks they identified in their understanding of the risk assessment process by documenting the linkage from the client's business objectives and strategy to audit plans. The form of documentation varies from firm to firm, but a simple illustration using EarthWear might look as follows:

Business Objectives and Strategy	Business Risks	Account(s)/ (Assertions)	Audit Risks	Controls	Effect on Audit Plan
Increase market share through sales at new international locations (e.g., during the current year Web sites were developed for France, Italy, Ireland, and several eastern European countries).	Restrictive trade laws may affect sales tactics. Strong consumer protection laws in European countries. Political instability in less developed countries (LDCs).	Revenue: accuracy and valuation. Reserve for returns: completeness.	Overstated due to pricing issues. Understated due to failure to properly track returns in new locations.	EwC has installed a special group to track compliance with local and international laws. EwC has placed more frequent review of returns in new locations.	Observe and test group's policies and procedures (see workpaper R-11). Extend audit work on EwC's return tracking with emphasis on new locations (see workpaper R-15).
	Foreign currency risks.	Gains/losses from currency hedging: valuation and accuracy.	Gains/losses not properly calculated or accrued on hedging activity.	EwC has strong controls in the Treasury Department to account for hedging activities.	Increase the number of hedging contracts tested with particular emphasis on contracts in currencies from LDCs (see work-paper S-14).

The audit strategy and audit plan are documented in a written plan (AS3 and AU 339). Audit programs containing specific audit procedures are also prepared. Exhibit 5–2 presents a partial audit program for substantive tests of accounts receivable. The types of audit tests are discussed in the next section.

Types of Audit Tests

✂ [LO 8]   There are three general types of audit tests:

- Risk assessment procedures.
- Tests of controls.
- Substantive procedures.

EXHIBIT 5–2	A Partial Audit Program for Substantive Procedures Testing of Accounts Receivable			
	Audit Procedures	W/P Ref.	Completed by	Date

1. Obtain the December 31, 2009, aged accounts receivable trial balance and
   a. Foot the trial balance and agree total to accounts receivable control account.
   b. Randomly select thirty accounts from the aged trial balance; agree the information per the aged trial balance to the original sales invoice and determine if the invoice was included in the appropriate aging category.
2. Confirm accounts receivable using a monetary-unit sampling plan. Set the desired confidence level = 90%, tolerable misstatement = $50,000, and expected misstatement = $20,000.
   a. For all responses with exceptions, follow up on the cause of the error.
   b. For all nonresponses, examine subsequent cash receipts and/or supporting documents.
   c. Summarize the sampling test results.
   d. Summarize the confirmation results.
3. Test sales cutoff by identifying the last shipping advice for the year and examining five large sales for three days before and after year-end.
4. Test the reasonableness of the allowance for doubtful accounts by the following:
   a. Test the reasonableness using past percentages on bad debts.
   b. For any large account in the aged trial balance greater than 90 days old, test for subsequent cash receipts.
   c. For the following financial ratios, compare the current year to the trend of the prior three years' results and internal budgets:
      • Number of days outstanding in receivables.
      • Aging of receivables.
      • Write-offs as a percentage of sales.
      • Bad debt expense as a percentage of sales.
5. Prepare a memo summarizing the tests, results, and conclusions.

Risk Assessment Procedures

Auditor risk assessment procedures are used to obtain an understanding of the entity and its environment, including its internal control. Risk assessment procedures include inquiries of management and others, analytical procedures, and observation and inspection. Such procedures are used to assess the risks of material misstatement at the financial statement and assertion levels. Risk assessment procedures were covered in depth in Chapter 3.

Tests of Controls

Tests of controls are audit procedures performed to test the operating effectiveness of controls in preventing, or detecting and correcting, material misstatements at the relevant assertion level. The following audit procedures are examples of tests of controls:

- Inquiries of appropriate management, supervisory, and staff personnel.
- Inspection of documents, reports, and electronic files.
- Observation of the application of specific controls.

TABLE 5-4	Examples of Internal Controls and Tests of Controls
Internal Controls	*Test of Controls*
Create a separation of duties between the shipping function and the order entry and billing functions.	Observe and evaluate whether shipping personnel have access to the order entry or billing activities.
Credit Department personnel initial sales orders, indicating credit approval.	Inspect a sample of sales orders for presence of initials of Credit Department personnel.
Billing Department personnel account for the numerical sequence of sales invoices.	Inquire of Billing Department personnel about missing sales invoice numbers.
Agree sales invoices to shipping document and customer order for product types, price, and quantity.	Recompute the information on a sample of sales invoices.

- Walkthroughs, which involve tracing a transaction from its origination to its inclusion in the financial statements through a combination of audit procedures including inquiry, observation, and inspection.
- Reperformance of the application of the control by the auditor.

For example, in evaluating the design of an automated IT application control and determining whether it has been implemented, the auditor may make inquiries of entity personnel and inspect relevant systems documentation, reports, or other documents. Table 5–4 provides additional examples of controls that are normally present in the processing of revenue transactions and tests of controls that the auditor might use to test the operating effectiveness of the controls. While always an option, tests of controls are necessary in two circumstances for nonpublic clients. When the auditor's risk assessment includes an expectation of the operating effectiveness of controls, the auditor is required to test those controls to support the risk assessment. In addition, when substantive procedures alone do not provide sufficient appropriate audit evidence, the auditor is required to perform tests of controls to obtain audit evidence about their operating effectiveness. Tests of controls will be discussed further in Chapter 6. For public clients, tests of controls are required for selected controls as part of the integrated audit of internal control and of financial statements. We discuss these requirements for public company audits in Chapter 7.

Substantive Procedures

Substantive procedures detect material misstatements (that is, monetary errors) in a transaction class, account balance, and disclosure component of the financial statements. There are two categories of substantive procedures: (1) tests of details of classes of transactions, account balances, and disclosures and (2) substantive analytical procedures.

Tests of Details of Classes of Transactions, Account Balances, and Disclosures

Tests of details are usually categorized into two types: (1) substantive tests of transactions and (2) tests of details of account balances and disclosures. *Substantive tests of transactions* test for errors or fraud in individual transactions. For example, an auditor may examine a large purchase of inventory by testing that the cost of the goods included on the vendor's invoice is properly recorded in the inventory and accounts payable accounts. This gives the auditor evidence about the occurrence, completeness, and accuracy assertions.

Tests of details of account balances and disclosures focus on the items that are contained in the financial statement account balances and disclosures. These important tests establish whether any material misstatements are included in the accounts or disclosures in the financial statements. For example, the auditor may want to test accounts receivable. To detail-test the balance of accounts receivable, the auditor will likely send confirmations to a sample of customers in order to gather evidence about the existence assertion. Such tests also provide evidence regarding the transaction assertions of accuracy and cutoff.

Substantive Analytical Procedures   Because of the importance of substantive analytical procedures, they are discussed in more detail in the next section.

Dual-Purpose Tests

Tests of controls check the operating effectiveness of controls, while substantive tests of transactions are concerned with monetary misstatements. However, it often makes more sense to design audit procedures to conduct both test of controls or a substantive test of transactions simultaneously on the same document. For example, in Table 5–4, the last control procedure shown is agreement of sales invoices to shipping documents and customer orders for product type, price, and quantity. The test of controls shown is to recompute the information on a sample of sales invoices. While this test primarily checks the effectiveness of the control, it also provides evidence on whether the sales invoice contains the wrong quantity, product type, or price. Dual-purpose tests can also improve the efficiency of the audit (AU 327.33).

This text discusses tests of controls within each business process. Substantive tests of transactions are discussed along with the other substantive tests when the financial statement accounts affected by the business process are discussed. You should remember, however, that in most audit situations substantive tests of transactions are conducted at the same time as tests of controls.

Substantive Analytical Procedures

Analytical Procedures

✂ **[LO 9]**

Auditing standards (AU 329) define analytical procedures as consisting of evaluations of financial information made by a study of plausible relationships among both financial and nonfinancial data. An important aspect of the definition of analytical procedures is that they involve a comparison of recorded values with *expectations* developed by the auditor. Analytical procedures can facilitate an effective audit by helping the auditor understand the client's business, directing attention to high-risk areas, identifying audit issues that might not be otherwise apparent, providing audit evidence, and assisting in the evaluation of audit results.

Purposes of Analytical Procedures

Analytical procedures are used for three purposes:

1. *Preliminary analytical procedures* are used to assist the auditor to better understand the business and to plan the nature, timing, and extent of audit procedures.
2. *Substantive analytical procedures* are used as a substantive procedure to obtain evidential matter about particular assertions related to account balances or classes of transactions.
3. *Final analytical procedures* are used as an overall review of the financial information in the final review stage of the audit.

Auditing standards require the use of analytical procedures for the first and third purposes. However, analytical procedures are also commonly used to gather substantive evidence because they are effective at detecting misstatements.[4] Analytical procedures are also relatively inexpensive tests to perform.

---

[4]A. Eilifsen and W. F. Messier, Jr., "Auditor Detection of Misstatements: A Review and Integration of Empirical Research," *Journal of Accounting Literature* 2000 (19), pp. 1–43, reviews the audit research on this issue.

The purpose of the analytical procedures and the facts and circumstances will dictate the type of analytical procedure used to form an expectation and the techniques involved in investigating a significant difference. Analytical procedures may range from the use of simple trend analysis to the use of complex regression models. The discussion of analytical procedures in this chapter is limited to the following three types of analytical procedure:

1. Trend analysis—the examination of changes in an account over time.
2. Ratio analysis—the comparison, across time or to a benchmark, of relationships between financial statement accounts or between an account and nonfinancial data.
3. Reasonableness analysis—development of a model to form an expectation using financial data, nonfinancial data, or both, to test account balances or changes in account balances between accounting periods.

The use of regression analysis as an analytical procedure is covered in auditing texts devoted to statistical auditing methods.[5]

Preliminary analytical procedures were discussed earlier in this chapter.

Substantive Analytical Procedures

Figure 5–2 presents an overview of the auditor's decision process when using substantive analytical procedures to collect audit evidence. While the overall process is similar for the other two purposes of analytical procedures (i.e., preliminary and final analytical procedures), we will identify important differences as we discuss each step in the process.

Develop an Expectation

The first step in the decision process is to develop an expectation for the amount or account balance. This is the most important step in performing analytical procedures. Auditing standards require the auditor to have an expectation whenever analytical procedures are used. An expectation can be developed using any of the types of analytical procedures discussed previously using information available from a variety of sources, such as

- Financial and operating data
- Budgets and forecasts
- Industry publications
- Competitor information
- Management's analyses
- Analysts' reports

Precision of the Expectation.   The quality of an expectation is referred to as the *precision* of the expectation. Precision is a measure of the potential effectiveness of an analytical procedure; it represents the degree of reliance that can be placed on the procedure. Precision is a measure of how closely the expectation approximates the "correct" but unknown amount. The degree of desired precision will differ with the specific purpose of the analytical procedure. The precision of the expectation is a function of the materiality and required detection risk for the assertion being tested. If the assertion being tested requires a low level of detection risk, the expectation needs to be very precise. However, the more precise the expectation, the more extensive and expensive the audit procedures used to develop the expectation, which results in a cost-benefit trade-off.

---

[5]See A. D. Bailey, Jr., *Statistical Auditing: Review, Concepts, and Problems* (New York: Harcourt Brace Jovanovich, 1981), Chapter 10, for a detailed discussion of regression analysis applied to auditing.

FIGURE 5–2	Overview of the Auditor's Decision Process for Substantive Analytical Procedures

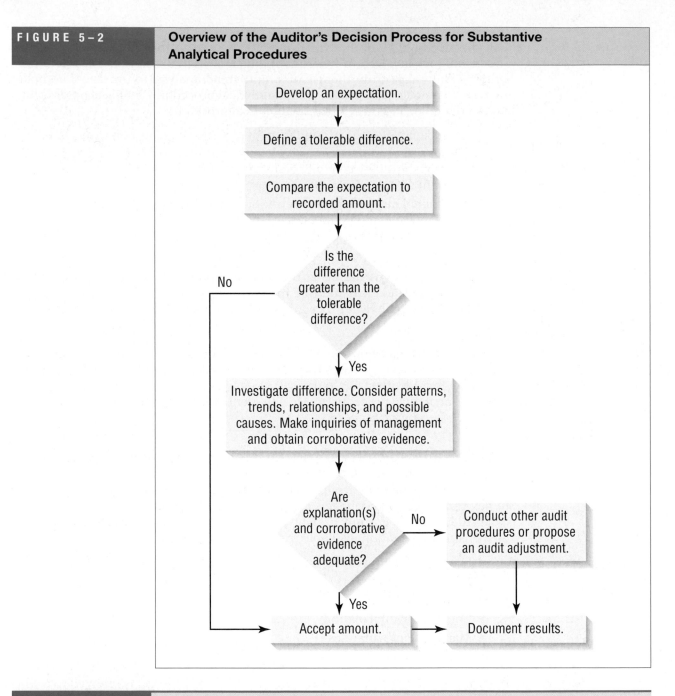

The PCAOB inspection teams have identified audit deficiencies, many of which had to do with analytical procedures. In one audit, the firm failed to develop expectations that were precise enough to identify material misstatements, whether individually or in the aggregate. In another audit, the firm developed its expectation using the same data from which the actual account balance was formed. The firm failed to test this data before using it to create its expectation (PCAOB Release 104-2009-064, 104-2008-069, and 104-2008-146).

The following four factors affect the precision of analytical procedures.

Disaggregation

The more detailed the level at which an expectation is formed, the greater the precision. For example, expectations formed using monthly data will be more precise than expectations formed using annual data. Similarly, expectations formed at an individual product level will be more precise than expectations formed for all products combined.

Preliminary and final analytical procedures are often conducted at relatively high levels of aggregation. However, analytical procedures conducted to provide substantive evidence normally cannot be performed at aggregated levels (e.g., annual data, total revenues). Misstatements are difficult to detect when analyzing data at aggregate levels, due to offsetting trends or activities that can mask risks and misstatements. Examples later in the chapter illustrate this concept.

The Plausibility and Predictability of the Relationship Being Studied

As indicated previously, analytical procedures involve the study of plausible relationships among financial and nonfinancial data. The primary concern with plausibility is simply whether the relationship used to test the assertion makes sense. For example, it is usually plausible to expect that an increase in sales should lead to an increase in accounts receivable. Many factors, including changes in the business or industry, influence the predictability of relationships among financial and nonfinancial data. Income statement items tend to be more predictable than balance sheet items because income statement accounts involve transactions over a period of time, whereas balance sheet accounts represent amounts at a specific point in time. The more plausible and predictable the relationship, the more precise the expectation.

Data Reliability

The ability to develop precise expectations is influenced by the reliability of the available data. The reliability of data for developing expectations depends on the three factors discussed in Chapter 4 under the appropriateness of audit evidence (e.g., the independence of the source of the evidence, the effectiveness of internal controls, and the auditor's direct personal knowledge). In addition, data for analytical procedures are more reliable when the data are subjected to audit in the current or prior periods and when the expectation is developed from multiple sources of data.

Type of Analytical Procedure Used to Form an Expectation

The three types of analytical procedures discussed earlier (trend, ratio, and reasonableness analysis) represent different ways to form an expectation. In general, trend analysis is the least precise method used and reasonableness analysis is the most precise. All three types are used for substantive analytical procedures, but reasonableness analysis is not commonly used for preliminary or final analytical procedures. Table 5–5 provides the definitions of the types of analytical procedures; and then we present several examples.

Examples of Expectations Formed by Analytical Procedures

Proper application of analytical procedures requires that the auditor have knowledge of the client's business and industry. Without such knowledge, the auditor may be unable to develop appropriate expectations or properly evaluate the results of the procedures. The auditor can use a number of different analytical procedures to form expectations. Some common examples include the following:

Comparison of Current-Year Financial Information with Comparable Prior Period(s) after Consideration of Known Changes. This is perhaps the most commonly used analytical procedure. The comparison of financial statement amounts can be done using absolute amounts (i.e., trend analysis) or by converting the financial statement amounts to "common-size" financial statements (ratio analysis). Exhibit 5–3 presents an example of a common-size income statement for EarthWear for 2009–2007. An auditor may compare the amounts shown for the three years and investigate those amounts that are out of line by some

TABLE 5–5	Definitions of the Types of Analytical Procedures Used to Form Expectations*

Trend analysis is the analysis of changes in an account over time. Simple trend analyses compare last year's account balance (the "expectation") with the current balance. Trend analysis can also encompass multiple time periods and includes comparing recorded trends with budget amounts and with competitor and industry information. The number of time periods used is a function of predictability and desired precision. The more stable the operations over time, the more predictable the relationship and the more appropriate the use of multiple periods. Generally, the more time periods used and the more disaggregated the data, the more precise the expectation. Because trend analysis relies on a single predictor (i.e., prior period information for an account balance), it does not normally yield as precise an expectation as the other two types.

Ratio analysis is the comparison, across time or to a benchmark, of relationships between financial statement accounts (e.g., return on equity) or between an account and nonfinancial data (e.g., cost per square foot or sales per item). Ratio analysis also includes "common-size" analysis, which is the conversion of financial statement amounts to percentages. Industry or competitor ratios are often used to benchmark the client's performance. The *Advanced Module* in this chapter illustrates selected financial ratios useful in analytical procedures. Ratio analysis is often more effective at identifying risks and potential misstatements than trend analysis because comparisons of relationships between accounts and operating data are more likely to identify unusual patterns than is an analysis only focused on an individual account. As with trend analysis, to gather substantive evidence effectively, ratio analysis should be performed on disaggregated data (e.g., by product, location, or month) over multiple periods where applicable.

Reasonableness analysis involves forming an expectation using a model. In many cases, a simple model may be sufficient. For example, ticket revenue can be modeled by taking average attendance by average ticket price. Similarly, depreciation expense can be modeled by taking book value divided by average useful life for a class of assets. Because it forms an explicit expectation, reasonableness analysis typically forms a more precise expectation than trend or ratio analysis. Of course, the precision of an expectation formed with a reasonableness test depends on the other factors influencing precision (i.e., disaggregation, predictability, and reliability).

*Regression analysis is another type of analytical procedure. Because it involves relatively complex statistical modeling in audit settings, we do not discuss it in this text. See footnote 5 for further information.

EXHIBIT 5–3	Common-Size Income Statement for EarthWear Clothiers (in thousands)

	December 31					
	2009		**2008**		**2007**	
Net Sales	$950,484	100.00%	$857,885	100.00%	$891,394	100.00%
Cost of sales	546,393	57.49%	472,739	55.11%	490,530	55.03%
Gross Profit	404,091	42.51%	385,146	44.89%	400,864	44.97%
Selling, general, and administrative expenses	364,012	38.30%	334,994	39.05%	353,890	39.70%
Nonrecurring charge (credit)	—		(1,153)	−0.13%	8,190	0.92%
Income from operations	40,079	4.21%	51,305	5.97%	38,784	4.35%
Other income (expense):						
Interest expense	(983)	−0.10%	(1,229)	−0.14%	(5,027)	−0.56%
Interest income	1,459	0.15%	573	0.07%	10	0.00%
Other	(4,798)	−0.50%	(1,091)	−0.13%	(1,593)	−0.18%
Total other income (expense), net	(4,322)	−0.45%	(1,747)	−0.20%	(6,609)	−0.74%
Income before income taxes	35,757	3.76%	49,558	5.77%	32,175	3.61%
Income tax provision	13,230	1.39%	18,337	2.14%	11,905	1.34%
Net income	$22,527	2.37%	$31,222	3.61%	20,270	2.27%
Basic earnings per share	1.15		1.60		1.02	
Diluted earnings per share	1.14		1.56		1.01	
Basic weighted average shares outstanding	19,531		19,555		19,806	
Diluted weighted average shares outstanding	19,774		20,055		19,996	

predetermined cutoff percentage or absolute amount. Before continuing, pause for a moment and consider the financial data presented in Exhibit 5–3. Using your developing skills as an auditor, consider one or two trends or ratios that would cause you as an auditor to pause and want to investigate further.

For example, the auditor can compare the current-year gross profit balance with the prior year's balance. Referring to Exhibit 5–3, we see that gross profit has increased in absolute amounts from $385.1 million to $404.1 million but decreased in percentage terms from 44.89 to 42.51 percent. Because this type of analytical procedure is typically performed on the aggregated companywide financial statements, the expectation that the current-year gross profit percentage will be the same as the prior year is relatively imprecise. Thus, it is typically used for planning and final review purposes, but is not considered particularly useful for providing substantive evidence about a particular account balance or class of transactions. At planning, the auditor would investigate this increase in cost of sales which resulted in the decline in gross profit and adjust the planned audit procedures to address risks associated with the increase. To illustrate the effect of conducting analytical procedures at aggregated companywide levels, consider what effect this decline in gross profit percentage has on income from operations. Recall from Chapter 3 that planning materiality for EarthWear was set at $1,800,000 and tolerable misstatement was set at $900,000. Income from operations declined from $51.3 million to $40.1 million. The 2.38 percentage point (44.89 to 42.51) decrease in gross profit resulted in income from operations being approximately $22.67 million lower than expected (sales = $950.4 × .0238). However, this analysis does not provide appropriate evidence to explain the increase in cost of sales. The auditor would have to perform additional procedures to corroborate the increase in cost of sales. This simple example highlights that it is difficult to obtain useful audit evidence from high-level companywide analytical procedures because the expectations are typically not sufficiently precise. In other words, whether or not the auditor observes a significant difference using a year-to-year comparison may be useful for planning purposes, but it would provide little or no audit evidence because of the imprecision of the expectation.

Comparison of Current-Year Financial Information with Budgets, Projections, and Forecasts.   This technique is usually performed using trend analysis and is similar to the previous example except that the current-year budget, projection, or forecast represents the expectation (rather than the expectation being provided by prior-year data). For example, the auditor can test the fairness of advertising expense by comparing the current-year amount to the client's budget and investigating differences.

Relationships among Elements of Financial Information within the Current Period.   There are many examples of one element in the financial statements directly relating to another element. This is particularly true for the association between certain balance sheet accounts and their related income or expense accounts. In these situations, reasonableness analysis is typically used to model the association. Taking this information into account, consider some of the relationships between income statement and balance sheet accounts you would expect to see in a growing company. Ask yourself what the relationship would normally be between sales and accounts receivable? What about the relationship between PP&E and depreciation expense? For example, there should be a relationship between the balance for long-term debt and interest expense. The auditor can model interest expense by multiplying the average long-term debt for the period by the period's average interest rate. This estimate of interest expense can be compared to the balance of interest expense shown on the trial balance. Later in the chapter we present a comprehensive example of an interest expense reasonableness test for EarthWear Clothiers.

Comparison of the Client's Financial Information with Industry Data.   The auditor can compare the client's financial ratios (receivable turnover, inventory turnover, and so on) to industry averages. The industry information can serve as a benchmark for assessing how well the client's financial position and performance compare with other companies in the industry. Robert Morris Associates, Dun & Bradstreet, and Standard & Poor's publish this type of industry data. Exhibit 5–4 contains an extract of industry data from *RMA eStatement Studies,*

EXHIBIT 5–4 | **An Example of Industry Data Available from Published Sources**

454113 - Mail-Order Houses
2008–09 Annual Statement Studies
National - All Regions

	% of Total Assets
Cash & Equivalents	16.1
Trade Receivables - (net)	11.1
Inventory	38
All Other Current Assets	4.8
Total Current Assets	**69.9**
Fixed Assets (net)	12.8
Intangibles (net)	9.5
All Other Non-Current Assets	7.8
Total Assets	**100**
Notes Payable-Short Term	11.6
Cur. Mat.-L/T/D	3.1
Trade Payables	22.5
Income Taxes Payable	0.3
All Other Current Liabilities	12.7
Total Current Liabilities	**50.2**
Long Term Debt	11.8
Deferred Taxes	0.6
All Other Non-Current Liabilities	6.9
Net Worth	30.6
Total Liabilities & Net Worth	**100**

	% of Net Sales
Net Sales	100
Gross Profit	43.1
Operating Expenses	39.5
Operating Profit	3.7
All Other Expenses (net)	0.8
Profit Before Taxes	2.9
Net Sales ($)	**$ 12,385,152,000**
Total Assets ($)	**$ 5,015,679,000**

	Quartile		
RATIOS	**Upper**	**Medium**	**Lower**
Solvency:			
Quick	1.2	0.4	0.1
Current	2.8	1.5	1.1
Fixed / Net Worth	0.1	0.3	2
Debt / Net Worth	0.7	1.7	19.5
Earnings before interest and taxes	15.9	3.9	1.4
Efficiency:			
Sales / Receivables	44.5	67.6	24.4
Sales / Net Working Capital	6.8	13.7	54
Cost of Sales / Inventory	9.3	4.7	3.1
Cost of Sales / Payables	19.9	10.6	5.8
Profitability:			
% Profit before Taxes / Tangible Net Worth	60.9	31.1	9.4
% Profit before Taxes / Total Assets	20.5	8.1	1.1
Sales / Net Fixed Assets	121.9	37.6	14.9
Sales / Total Assets	4.5	3.2	2.2

Source: RMA eStatement Studies

published by Robert Morris Associates. The *Advanced Module* in this chapter illustrates several ratios used in ratio analysis.

Relationships of Financial Information to Nonfinancial Information. The auditor may have relevant nonfinancial information available for comparison purposes or for developing estimates of the client's financial information. This might include such items as cost per employee, sales per square foot, utility expense per hour, and so on. For example, in a telecom company, the auditor can multiply the number of cell phone subscribers by the average billing rate to test a client's total revenue. Other examples include computing the average number of days a product is in inventory or developing an expectation for commission expense by multiplying commissioned sales by the average commission rate and comparing this estimate to the client's recorded commission expense.

Practice **INSIGHT**	Using nonfinancial information in analytical procedures can be an effective way to identify potential frauds because, while perpetrators of fraud can manage financial numbers, it is difficult or impossible to manage nonfinancial data (e.g., square feet, days in the calendar year, number of employees). For example, auditors could compare a client's actual square footage of warehouse space with the amount of square footage that would be required to store the inventory as listed on the books.

Plotting Trends over Multiple Periods. It can be very beneficial to plot or graph trends over several periods. Figure 5–3 provides a monthly plot of ending inventory for a three-year period. Suppose the auditor is auditing year-ending inventory for year 3 and that years 1 and 2 have been previously audited. The pattern of previously audited financial information suggests some inventory "spikes" every six months. These spikes may be due to inventory buildup around busy seasons (e.g., holidays). The star at the end of year 3 indicates the auditor's expectation based on the past trends. The auditor would investigate the cause of the large increase in ending inventory at the end of year 3. Note that the potentially problematic spikes would not have shown up at all if the auditor had just plotted

FIGURE 5–3	An Illustration of a Monthly Plot of Ending Inventory (in millions)

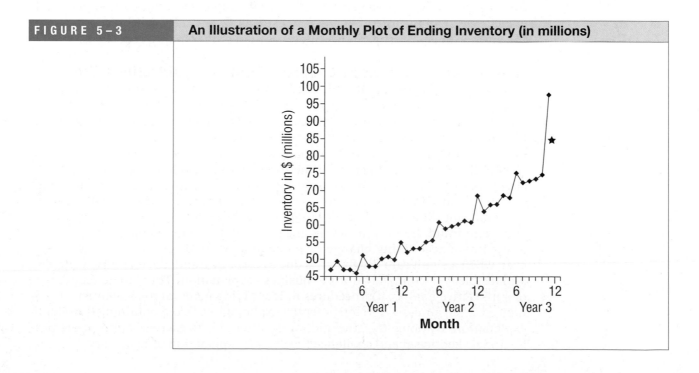

year-end inventory balances rather than monthly balances! Again, using detailed data is critical in enhancing precision.

The foregoing discussion and examples have all related to the first step in the analytical procedures decision process (see Figure 5–2). The first step is the most important step in performing effective substantive analytical procedures.

Define a Tolerable Difference   The second step in the analytical procedures decision process (see Figure 5–2) is to define a tolerable difference. Since the expectation developed by the auditor will rarely be identical to the client's recorded amount, the auditor must decide the amount of difference that would require further investigation. The size of the tolerable difference depends on the significance of the account, the desired degree of reliance on the substantive analytical procedure, the level of disaggregation in the amount being tested, and the precision of the expectation. The amount of difference that can be tolerated will always be lower than planning materiality, and when testing an entire account with a substantive analytical procedure, tolerable differences will usually be equal to the account's tolerable misstatement. Sometimes, to achieve the desired level of assurance with a substantive analytical procedure, the auditor will use a tolerable difference that is less than full tolerable misstatement for the account. In these instances, the auditor may use a rule of thumb such as, "tolerable difference is 5 percent of the client's recorded amount, but not to exceed tolerable misstatement."

Practice INSIGHT

In 2008, the PCAOB inspection team identified audit deficiencies that had to do with the tolerable difference used in analytical procedures. In one audit, the firm used analytical procedures as the primary substantive test of the existence of revenue, but the tolerable difference set by the firm allowed some differences to go uninvestigated even though they exceeded materiality as set by the firm during the planning stage (PCAOB Release 104-2009-064).

Compare the Expectation to the Recorded Amount   The next step in the analytical procedures decision process (Figure 5–2) is to determine if the amount of difference between the auditor's expectation and the recorded amount exceeds the auditor's predetermined "tolerable difference." If the observed difference is less than the tolerable difference, the auditor accepts the account. If not, the auditor must investigate the difference using other audit procedures.

Investigate Differences Greater Than the Tolerable Difference
The fourth step in the analytical procedures decision process (Figure 5–2) is the investigation of significant differences and the formation of conclusions. Differences identified by substantive analytical procedures indicate an increased likelihood of misstatements. The more precise the expectation, the greater the likelihood that the difference is actually a misstatement. Inquiry of the client is frequently an important aspect of the investigation of differences. Nevertheless, client inquiry should not be the sole support for an explanation without quantification and corroboration (discussed below). There are four possible causes of significant differences—accounting changes, economic conditions or events, error, and fraud. In most instances, the cause of an identified difference involves a legitimate accounting change or an economic condition or event. However, even when a significant difference is due to error or fraud, the client may provide a plausible, yet ultimately untrue, business explanation. Thus, the effectiveness of substantive analytical procedures in identifying material misstatements is enhanced when auditors develop potential explanations *before* obtaining the client's explanation. By doing this, the auditor is better able to exercise appropriate professional skepticism and challenge the client's explanation, if necessary.

The development of potential explanations need not be time-consuming. Auditors typically reexamine and understand the various relationships in the financial and nonfinancial data. Then, based on their previous experience with the client, other audit work performed, and discussions with other members of the audit team, they develop potential explanations for the observed difference. The independent consideration of potential explanations is more important for more significant accounts and when a higher degree of assurance is desired from substantive analytical procedures.

Explanations for significant differences observed for substantive analytical procedures must be followed up and resolved through quantification, corroboration, and evaluation.

Quantification.   It is usually not practicable to identify an explanation for the exact amount of a difference between an analytical procedure's expectation and the client's recorded amount. However, auditors should quantify the portion of the difference that can be explained. Quantification involves determining whether the explanation or error can explain the observed difference. This may require the recalculation of the expectation after considering the additional information. For example, a client may offer the explanation that the significant increase in inventory over the prior year is due to a 12-percent increase in raw materials prices. The auditor should compute the effects of the raw materials price increase and determine the extent to which the price increase explains (or does not explain) the increase in the overall inventory account.

Corroboration.   Auditors must corroborate explanations for unexpected differences by obtaining sufficient appropriate audit evidence linking the explanation to the difference and substantiating that the information supporting the explanation is reliable. This evidence should be of the same quality as the evidence obtained to support tests of details. Such evidence could vary from simply comparing the explanation to the auditor's knowledge from other areas, to employing other detailed tests to confirm or refute the explanation. Common corroborating procedures include examination of supporting evidence, inquiries of independent persons, and evaluating evidence obtained from other auditing procedures.

Practice
INSIGHT

During an inspection in 2007, the PCAOB inspection team identified audit deficiencies, one of which had to do with the lack of corroboration when investigating differences found through analytical procedures. In one audit, the firm failed to test almost half of the issuer's total revenue beyond confirming certain accounts receivable and performing analytical procedures. In some cases, the firm failed to corroborate management's explanations of significant differences observed by these analytical procedures (PCAOB Release 104-2008-069).

Evaluation.   The key mind-set behind effectively performing substantive analytical procedures is one of appropriate professional skepticism, combined with the desire to obtain sufficient appropriate audit evidence, similar to other auditing procedures. The auditor should evaluate the results of the substantive analytical procedures to conclude whether the desired level of assurance has been achieved. If the auditor obtains evidence that a misstatement exists and can be sufficiently quantified, the auditor makes note of his or her proposed adjustment to the client's financial statements. Toward the end of the audit, all such proposed adjustments are accumulated, summarized, and evaluated before being presented to the client (Chapter 17 provides further details).

If the auditor concludes that the substantive analytical procedure performed did not provide the desired level of assurance, additional substantive analytical procedures and/or tests of details should be performed to achieve the desired assurance.

The Investigation of Differences for Planning and Final Analytical Procedures   The way in which differences are investigated diverges in important ways for preliminary and final analytical procedures. At planning, the auditor is not required to obtain corroborative evidence because preliminary analytical procedures are not intended to provide substantive audit evidence regarding specific assertions. Rather, the auditor normally determines whether the planned audit procedures need to be revised in light of the results of preliminary analytical procedures. For example, to address the increased risk posed by the spike in inventory illustrated in Figure 5–3, the auditor may decide to expand the number of items tested during the observation of the year-end physical inventory count.

When conducting final analytical procedures, the auditor investigates unexpected differences by first going to the working papers to determine if sufficient appropriate evidence has already been gathered to explain the difference (rather than going to the client for an explanation). If the auditor cannot find sufficient evidence within the working papers, then the auditor would formulate possible explanations, conduct additional testing, and seek an explanation from the client.

Comprehensive EarthWear Example

Suppose we want to use substantive analytical procedures to test the reasonableness of interest expense reported by EarthWear Clothiers (i.e., a "reasonableness test"). Consider the following example:

> EarthWear's 2009 income statement shows $983,000 of interest expense. To conduct a substantive analytical procedure on this account, the auditor could develop an expectation using reasonableness analysis by building a model in the following manner. Obtain the ending monthly balance for the short-term line of credit from the monthly bank loan statement and calculate the average monthly ending balance. Trace the monthly loan balances to the general ledger. Determine the average interest rate for the year for the short-term line of credit based on the bank's published rate in the monthly bank loan statement. Multiply the average monthly balance previously calculated by the average interest rate, and compare the result to the recorded interest expense. Suppose that the auditor obtained the following information from EarthWear's general ledger:

Month	Balance in thousands)
January	$ 21,500
February	18,600
March	18,100
April	17,900
May	16,100
June	15,500
July	14,200
August	20,200
September	34,500
October	28,100
November	15,200
December	11,000
Total	$230,900
Average	$ 19,240

Further, assume that interest rates recorded on the loan statements have remained stable over the year, fluctuating between 5 and 5.5 percent. If the auditor uses 5.25 percent as the average interest rate, the expectation for interest expense is $1,010,000 ($19,240,000 × 0.0525).

As shown in Figure 5–2, once an expectation is developed, the next step is to determine the tolerable difference. Because interest expense is a predictable account, the information used to form the expectation is deemed reliable, and the substantive analytical procedure will be the primary substantive test, the auditor forms a fairly precise expectation and will define a more precise tolerable difference than full tolerable misstatement for the account. Accordingly, the tolerable difference is set at 5 percent of recorded interest expense or $49,150 (.05 × $983,000). The next step is to compare the expectation of $1,010,000 to the recorded value of $983,000 to determine if the difference is greater than can be tolerated. Because the difference between the auditor's expectation and the recorded amount, $27,000, is less than the tolerable difference, the auditor would accept the interest expense account as fairly stated. However, if the difference between the recorded amount and the expectation is greater than the tolerable difference, the auditor will need to investigate the difference. In the example above, the auditor would likely examine loan activity within each month to determine if there was significant variation in the balance that was not accounted for by the month-end model used to form the expectation. If the difference could still not be explained, the auditor would inquire of management about the cause of the difference. If the client provides a plausible explanation (e.g., interest expense reported in the financial statements also includes interest paid for other short-term loans that were only outstanding for a few days at a time), auditing standards require the auditor to obtain corroborating evidence. If the client's explanation and the corroborating evidence are not adequate, or if no corroborative evidence is available, the auditor will need to conduct additional audit procedures. If the explanation and evidence are adequate for resolving the difference, the auditor can accept the amount as being fairly presented.

As with other audit procedures, when analytical procedures are used to gather substantive evidence, the auditor's purpose is to evaluate one or more assertions. For example, in the interest expense example, the auditor is testing primarily the completeness and valuation assertions. The effectiveness and efficiency of substantive analytical procedures in identifying material misstatements depend on

- The plausibility and predictability of the relationship.
- The availability and reliability of the data used.
- The precision of the expectation.
- The rigor and sufficiency of the investigation of observed differences (if greater than tolerable difference).
- The nature of the assertion.

We have already discussed all but the last item on the above list.

The Nature of the Assertion   Substantive analytical procedures can be used to test all transactions and balance assertions except rights and obligations. However, they may be more effective at identifying certain types of misstatements than testing individual transactions. For example, they may be more effective at detecting omissions (completeness assertion) than providing detailed documentary evidence. The key points are that (1) some assertions are more amenable to examination through analytical procedures than others; and (2) the auditor must ensure that the analytical procedure performed is appropriate for the assertion being examined.

Documentation Requirements   When a substantive analytical procedure is used as the principal substantive procedure for a significant financial statement assertion, the auditor should document all of the following:

- The expectation and how it was developed.
- Results of the comparison of the expectation to the recorded amounts or ratios developed from recorded amounts.

- Any additional auditing procedures performed in response to significant unexpected differences arising from the analytical procedure and the results of such additional procedures.

Final Analytical Procedures

The objective of analytical procedures at the overall review stage of an audit is to assist the auditor in assessing the conclusions reached and evaluating the overall financial statement presentation. This requires reviewing the trial balance, financial statements, and footnotes in order to (1) judge the adequacy of the evidence gathered to support any unusual or unexpected balances investigated during the audit; and (2) determine if any other unusual balances or relationships have not been investigated.

In the first instance, appropriate evidence in the working papers should support any differences from the auditor's expectations. For example, the auditor can compare the audited balances from the current year with the audited balances from the prior year. If there is a material difference, the auditor's working papers should explain the difference. In the second instance, this comparison of audited values may reveal some unusual items that have not been investigated and explained. Assuming that the difference between the auditor's expectation and the recorded amount is material, the auditor will have to perform additional audit work before an audit report can be issued.

The Audit Testing Hierarchy

[LO 10] The risk-based audit approach we have discussed so far in the text is often referred to as a "top-down" approach where the auditor obtains an understanding of the client's business objectives and strategies, identifies business and audit risks, documents an understanding of internal control, and then gathers sufficient, appropriate audit; evidence using a combination of tests of controls, substantive analytical procedures, and tests of details to support the audit opinion (or audit opinions—remember that for public companies, the auditor performs an integrated audit and opines on both internal control and the financial statements).

Now that we have discussed evidence (Chapter 4) and introduced you to the types of audit tests (risk assessment procedures, tests of controls, substantive analytical procedures, and tests of details), you are ready to be introduced to the thought process auditors use in choosing audit tests and in what order. The overall decision approach used to gather evidence is depicted in Figure 5–4 and is referred to in later chapters as the *audit testing hierarchy*.

The audit testing hierarchy starts with tests of controls and substantive analytical procedures. Starting with tests of controls and substantive analytical procedures is generally both more effective and more efficient than starting with tests of details.

- *Applying the audit testing hierarchy is more effective.* The auditor's understanding and testing of controls will influence the nature, timing, and extent of substantive testing and will enhance the auditor's ability to home in on areas where misstatements are more likely to be found. If controls are highly effective, less extensive substantive procedures (i.e., substantive analytical procedures and tests of details) will need to be performed. Similarly, substantive analytical procedures can direct attention to higher-risk areas where the auditor can design and conduct focused tests of details.
- *Applying the audit testing hierarchy is more efficient.* Generally, tests of controls and substantive analytical procedures are less costly to perform than are tests of details. This is usually because tests of controls and substantive analytical procedures provide assurance on multiple

FIGURE 5–4	Audit Testing Hierarchy: An Evidence Decision Process for Testing Significant Balances or Classes of Transactions

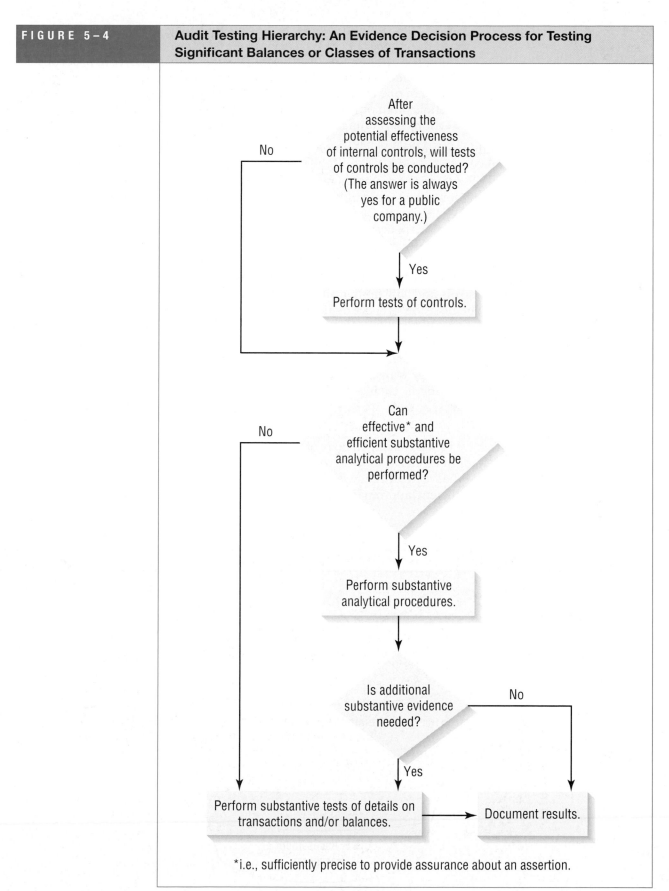

*i.e., sufficiently precise to provide assurance about an assertion.

transactions. In other words, by testing controls and related processes, the auditor generally gains a degree of assurance over thousands or even millions of transactions. Furthermore, substantive analytical procedures often provide evidence related to more than one assertion and often more than one balance or class of transactions. On the other hand, tests of details often only obtain assurance related to one or two specific assertions pertaining to the specific transaction(s) or balance tested.

Auditing standards require that auditors perform substantive procedures for significant account balances and classes of transactions regardless of the assessed risk of material misstatement. In other words, assurance obtained solely from testing controls is not sufficient for significant balances and classes of transactions. Substantive procedures include substantive analytical procedures and tests of details. For this reason, Figure 5–4 depicts that either substantive analytical procedures, tests of details, or both will always be conducted for significant accounts or classes of transactions. For high-risk areas or highly material accounts, the auditors will almost always perform some tests of details in addition to tests of controls and substantive analytical procedures.

The decision process depicted in Figure 5–4 recognizes that, for some assertions, tests of details may be the only form of testing used, because in some cases it is more efficient and effective to move directly to tests of details. Examples of situations where the auditor might move directly to tests of details include a low volume of large transactions (e.g., two large notes payable issued) and poor controls resulting in client data that are unreliable for use in substantive analytical procedures.

An "Assurance Bucket" Analogy

We have found that an analogy often helps students understand and visualize how an auditor decides on the proper mix of testing and evidence. Figure 5–5 illustrates what we call the "assurance bucket." The assurance bucket must be filled with sufficient appropriate evidence to obtain the level of assurance necessary

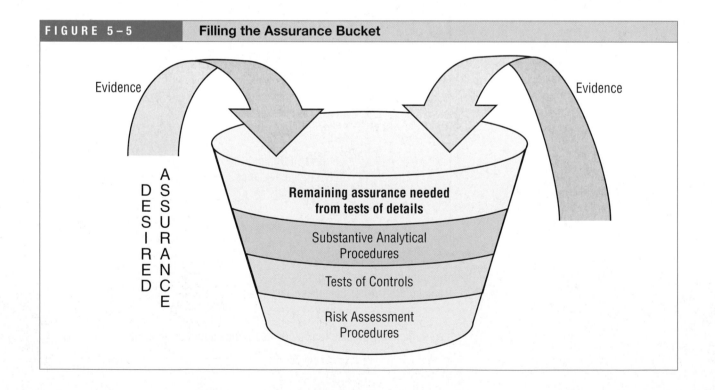

FIGURE 5–5   **Filling the Assurance Bucket**

Evidence

Evidence

DESIRED ASSURANCE

Remaining assurance needed
from tests of details

Substantive Analytical
Procedures

Tests of Controls

Risk Assessment
Procedures

to support the auditor's opinion. Following the top-down audit testing hierarchy means that auditors first begin to fill the bucket with evidence from the risk assessment procedures. In Figure 5–5, after completing risk assessment procedures, the auditor sees that the assurance bucket for a particular account and assertion is about 20-percent full. The auditor would next conduct control testing. In our example, control testing might add about another 30 percent to the bucket. How would the auditor know just how full the bucket is after testing controls? This is clearly a very subjective evaluation, and it is a matter of professional judgment.

The auditor next performs substantive analytical procedures and adds the assurance gained from these procedures to the bucket. In Figure 5–5 the bucket is now about 70-percent full. In this illustration, the auditor would need to top off the assurance bucket with evidence obtained through tests of details.

For lower-risk, well-controlled accounts, the assurance bucket may be entirely filled with tests of controls and substantive analytical procedures. For other accounts or assertions, the bucket may be filled primarily with tests of details.

The size of the assurance bucket can vary, depending on the auditor's risk assessment and the assertion being tested. Obviously, certain assertions will be more important or present bigger risks for some accounts than for others. For instance, existence (or validity) is typically more important for accounts receivable than it is for accounts payable. After the auditor has determined the risks associated with the assertions for an account balance, she or he can determine the size of the assurance buckets (i.e., how much assurance is needed) and then begin filling the buckets by applying the audit testing hierarchy. Figure 5–6 illustrates these concepts for accounts payable. Note that the largest bucket is for the completeness assertion, because with liability accounts the auditor is primarily concerned with potential understatement errors. The example in Figure 5-6 also illustrates that some assertions may be filled entirely with tests of details

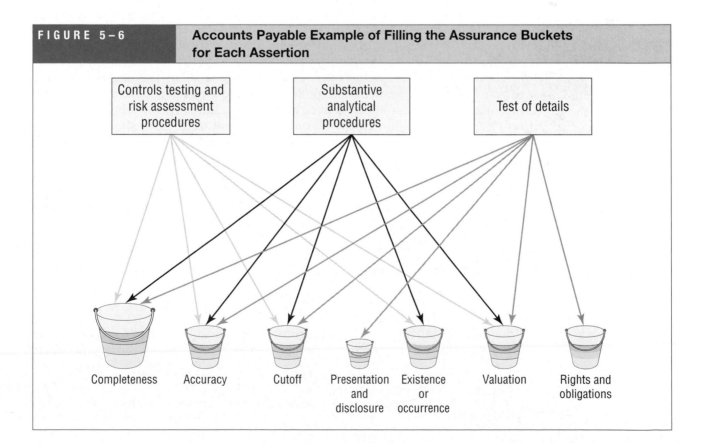

FIGURE 5–6   Accounts Payable Example of Filling the Assurance Buckets for Each Assertion

(e.g., rights and obligations) and that others may not require any tests of details (e.g., existence). Again, these are subjective matters that require considerable professional judgment.

Advanced Module: Selected Financial Ratios

Selected Financial Ratios Useful as Analytical Procedures

[LO 11]   A number of financial ratios are used by auditors as analytical procedures. These ratios are broken down into four categories: short-term liquidity, activity, profitability, and coverage ratios. Although the ratios discussed apply to most entities, auditors may also use other industry-specific ratios. As follows, each ratio is calculated for EarthWear Clothiers for the year ended December 31, 2009.

A few points are worth mentioning before the financial ratios are discussed. First, in many instances, the auditor may compare the client's ratios with industry averages (see Exhibit 5–4). While the industry averages serve as useful benchmarks, certain limitations should be recognized. Because the industry ratios are averages, they may not capture operating or geographical factors that may be specific to the client. The use of different accounting principles for valuing inventory or calculating depreciation may also result in differences from industry averages for certain ratios. Finally, the industry data may not be available in sufficient detail for a particular client. For example, if the auditor was looking for industry information on a company that solely operated in the wireless industry, such industry ratio data might be combined with other companies within the telecommunications industry.

Second, audit research has shown that material misstatements may not significantly affect certain ratios.[6] This is particularly true for activity ratios. Third, the auditor must be careful not to evaluate a financial ratio in isolation. In certain cases, a ratio may be favorable because its components are unfavorable. If related ratios are not examined, the auditor may draw an incorrect conclusion. For example, suppose that a client's days outstanding in accounts receivable is getting larger and the inventory turnover ratio is getting smaller. The negative trend in these ratios may indicate that accounts receivable are getting older and that some inventory may be obsolete. However, both of these factors positively affect the current ratio. If the auditor calculates only the current ratio, he or she may reach an incorrect conclusion about the entity's ability to meet current obligations.

Short-Term Liquidity Ratios

Short-term liquidity ratios indicate the entity's ability to meet its current obligations. Three ratios commonly used for this purpose are the current ratio, quick (or acid test) ratio, and the operating cash flow ratio.

Current Ratio   The current ratio is calculated as follows:

$$\text{Current ratio} = \frac{\text{Current assets}}{\text{Current liabilities}} = \frac{209,095}{116,268} = 1.80$$

It includes all current assets and current liabilities and is usually considered acceptable if it is 2 to 1 or better. Generally, a high current ratio indicates an entity's

---

[6]See W. R. Kinney, Jr., "Attention-Directing Analytical Review Using Accounting Ratios: A Case Study," *Auditing: A Journal of Practice and Theory* (Spring 1987), pp. 59–73, for a discussion of this limitation of analytical procedures.

ability to pay current obligations. However, if current assets include old accounts receivable or obsolete inventory, this ratio can be distorted.

Quick Ratio
The quick ratio includes only assets that are most readily convertible to cash and is calculated as follows:

$$\text{Quick ratio} = \frac{\text{Liquid assets}}{\text{Current liabilities}} = \frac{48{,}978 + 12{,}875}{116{,}268} = .53$$

Thus, inventories and prepaid items are not included in the numerator of the quick ratio. The quick ratio may provide a better picture of the entity's liquidity position if inventory contains obsolete or slow-moving items. A ratio greater than 1 generally indicates that the entity's liquid assets are sufficient to meet the cash requirements for paying current liabilities.

Operating Cash Flow Ratio
The operating cash flow ratio measures the entity's ability to cover its current liabilities with cash generated from operations and is calculated as follows:

$$\text{Operating cash flow ratio} = \frac{\text{Cash flow from operations}}{\text{Current liabilities}} = \frac{39{,}367}{116{,}268} = .34$$

The operating cash flow ratio uses the cash flows as opposed to assets to measure short-term liquidity. It provides a longer-term measure of the entity's ability to meet its current liabilities. If cash flow from operations is small or negative, the entity will likely need alternative sources of cash, such as additional borrowings or sales of assets, to meet its obligations.

Activity Ratios

Activity ratios indicate how effectively the entity's assets are managed. Only ratios related to accounts receivable and inventory are discussed here because for most wholesale, retail, or manufacturing companies these two accounts represent the assets that have high activity. Activity ratios may also be effective in helping the auditor determine if these accounts contain material misstatements.

Receivables Turnover and Days Outstanding in Accounts Receivable
These two ratios provide information on the activity and age of accounts receivable. The receivables turnover ratio and days outstanding in accounts receivable are calculated as follows:

$$\text{Receivables turnover} = \frac{\text{Credit sales}}{\text{Receivables}} = \frac{950{,}484}{12{,}875} = 73.8$$

$$\text{Days outstanding in accounts receivable} = \frac{365 \text{ days}}{\text{Receivables turnover}} = 4.94 \text{ days}$$

The receivables turnover ratio indicates how many times accounts receivable are turned over during a year. However, the days outstanding in accounts receivable may be easier to interpret because this ratio can be compared to the client's terms of trade. For example, if an entity's terms of trade are 2/10, net/30, the auditor would expect that if management were doing a good job of managing receivables, the value for this ratio would be 30 days or less. If the auditor calculates the days outstanding to be 43 days, he or she might suspect that the account contains a material amount of bad debts. Comparing the days outstanding to industry data may be helpful in detecting a slowdown in payments by customers that is affecting the entire industry. EarthWear's ratio is 4.94 days because most sales are paid by credit card.

Inventory Turnover and Days of Inventory on Hand   These activity ratios provide information on the inventory and are calculated as follows:

$$\text{Inventory turnover} = \frac{\text{Cost of goods sold}}{\text{Inventory}} = \frac{546{,}398}{122{,}337} = 4.47$$

$$\text{Days of inventory on hand} = \frac{365 \text{ days}}{\text{Inventory turnover}} = 81.7 \text{ days}$$

Inventory turnover indicates the frequency with which inventory is consumed in a year. The higher the ratio, the better the entity is at liquidating inventory. This ratio can be easily compared to industry standards. Suppose that the auditor calculates the inventory turnover to be 4.7 times a year. If the industry average is 8.2 times a year, the auditor might suspect that inventory contains obsolete or slow-moving goods. The days of inventory on hand measures how much inventory the entity has available for sale to customers.

Profitability Ratios

Profitability ratios indicate the entity's success or failure for a given period. A number of ratios measure the profitability of an entity, and each ratio should be interpreted by comparison to industry data.

Gross Profit Percentage   The gross margin percentage ratio is generally a good indicator of potential misstatements and is calculated as follows:

$$\text{Gross profit percentage} = \frac{\text{Gross profit}}{\text{Net sales}} = \frac{404{,}091}{950{,}484} = 42.5\%$$

If this ratio varies significantly from previous years or differs significantly from industry data, the entity's financial data may contain errors. Numerous errors can affect this ratio. For example, if the client has failed to record sales, the gross profit percentage will be less than in previous years. Similarly, any errors that affect the inventory account can distort this ratio. For example, if the client has omitted goods from the ending inventory, this ratio will be smaller than in previous years.

Profit Margin   The profit margin ratio is calculated as follows:

$$\text{Profit margin} = \frac{\text{Net income}}{\text{Net sales}} = \frac{22{,}527}{950{,}484} = 2.4\%$$

While the gross profit percentage ratio measures profitability after cost of goods sold is deducted, the profit margin ratio measures the entity's profitability after all expenses are considered. Significant fluctuations in this ratio may indicate that misstatements exist in the selling, general, or administrative expense accounts.

Return on Assets   This ratio is calculated as follows:

$$\text{Return on assets} = \frac{\text{Net income}}{\text{Total assets}} = \frac{22{,}527}{329{,}959} = 6.8\%$$

This ratio indicates the return earned on the resources invested by both the stockholders and the creditors.

Return on Equity   The return on equity ratio is calculated as follows:

$$\text{Return on equity} = \frac{\text{Net income}}{\text{Stockholders' equity}} = \frac{22{,}527}{204{,}222} = 11.0\%$$

This ratio is similar to the return on assets ratio except that it shows only the return on the resources contributed by the stockholders.

Coverage Ratios

Coverage ratios provide information on the long-term solvency of the entity. These ratios give the auditor important information on the ability of the entity to continue as a going concern.

Debt to Equity   This ratio is calculated as follows:

$$\text{Debt to equity} = \frac{\text{Short-term debt} + \text{Long-term debt}}{\text{Stockholders' equity}} = \frac{(116{,}668 + 0)}{204{,}222} = .569$$

This ratio indicates what portion of the entity's capital comes from debt. The lower the ratio, the less debt pressure on the entity. If the entity's debt to equity ratio is large relative to the industry's, it may indicate that the entity is too highly leveraged and may not be able to meet its debt obligations on a long-term basis.

Times Interest Earned   This ratio is calculated as follows:

$$\text{Times interest earned} = \frac{\text{Net income} + \text{Interest expense}}{\text{Interest expense}}$$

$$= \frac{(22{,}527 + 983)}{983} = 23.9$$

The times interest earned ratio indicates the ability of current operations to pay the interest that is due on the entity's debt obligations. The more times that interest is earned, the better the entity's ability to service the interest on long-term debt.

KEY TERMS

Analytical procedures. Evaluations of financial information made by a study of plausible relationships among both financial and nonfinancial data.

Audit committee. A subcommittee of the board of directors that is responsible for the financial reporting and disclosure process.

Audit procedures. Specific acts performed as the auditor gathers evidence to determine if specific audit objectives are being met.

Audit strategy. The auditor's plan for the expected conduct, organization, and staffing of the audit.

Dual-purpose tests. Tests of transactions that both evaluate the effectiveness of controls and detect monetary errors.

Engagement letter. A letter that formalizes the contract between the auditor and the client and outlines the responsibilities of both parties.

Illegal act. A violation of laws or government regulations.

Substantive procedures. Audit procedures performed to test material misstatements in an account balance, transaction class, or disclosure component of the financial statements.

Substantive tests of transactions. Tests to detect errors or fraud in individual transactions.

Tests of controls. Audit procedures performed to test the operating effectiveness of controls in preventing or detecting and correcting, material misstatements at the relevant assertion level.

Tests of details of account balances and disclosures. Substantive tests that concentrate on the details of items contained in the account balance and disclosure.

www.mhhe.com/ messier7e	Visit the book's Online Learning Center for a multiple-choice quiz that will allow you to assess your understanding of chapter concepts.

REVIEW QUESTIONS

[LO 1]   5-1   What types of inquiries about a prospective client should an auditor make to third parties?

[1]   5-2   Who is responsible for initiating the communication between the predecessor and successor auditors? What type of information should be requested from the predecessor auditor?

[2,3]   5-3   What is the purpose of an engagement letter? List the important information that the engagement letter should contain.

[4]   5-4   What factors should an external auditor use to assess the competence and objectivity of internal auditors?

[5]   5-5   What is an audit committee, and what are its responsibilities?

[6,7]   5-6   List the matters an auditor should consider when developing an audit plan.

[7]   5-7   Distinguish between illegal acts that are "direct and material" and those that are "material but indirect." List five circumstances that may indicate that an illegal act may have occurred.

[7]   5-8   List three audit procedures that may be used to identify transactions with related parties.

[8]   5-9   What are the three general types of audit tests? Define each type of audit test and give two examples.

[9]   5-10   What are the purposes for using preliminary analytical procedures?

[9]   5-11   When discussing the use of analytical procedures, what is meant by the "precision of the expectation"? In applying this notion to an analytical procedure, how might an auditor calculate a tolerable difference?

[9]   5-12   Significant differences between the auditor's expectation and the client's book value require explanation through quantification, corroboration, and evaluation. Explain each of these terms.

[10]   5-13   Why does the "audit testing hierarchy" begin with tests of controls and substantive analytical procedures?

[10]   5-14   Consider the "assurance bucket" analogy. Why are some of the buckets larger than others for particular assertions or accounts?

[11]   5-15   List and discuss the four categories of financial ratios that are presented in the chapter.

MULTIPLE-CHOICE QUESTIONS

[1]   5-16   Before accepting an audit engagement, a successor auditor should make specific inquiries of the predecessor auditor regarding the predecessor's
     a. Awareness of the consistency in the application of generally accepted accounting principles between periods.
     b. Evaluation of all matters of continuing accounting significance.
     c. Opinion of any subsequent events occurring since the predecessor's audit report was issued.
     d. Understanding as to the reasons for the change of auditors.

[3]   5-17   A written understanding between the auditor and the client concerning the auditor's responsibility for the discovery of illegal acts is usually set forth in a(n)
     a. Internal control letter.
     b. Letter of audit inquiry.

c. Management letter.

d. Engagement letter.

[4]   5-18   Miller Retailing, Inc., maintains a staff of three full-time internal auditors who report directly to the audit committee. In planning to use the internal auditors to help in performing the audit, the independent auditor most likely will

a. Place limited reliance on the work performed by the internal auditors.

b. Decrease the extent of the tests of controls needed to support the assessed level of detection risk.

c. Increase the extent of the procedures needed to reduce control risk to an acceptable level.

d. Avoid using the work performed by the internal auditors.

[6]   5-19   During the initial planning phase of an audit, a CPA most likely would

a. Identify specific internal control activities that are likely to prevent fraud.

b. Evaluate the reasonableness of the client's accounting estimates.

c. Discuss the timing of the audit procedures with the client's management.

d. Inquire of the client's attorney if it is probable that any unrecorded claims will be asserted.

[6,7]   5-20   When planning an audit, an auditor should

a. Consider whether the extent of substantive procedures may be reduced based on the results of the internal control questionnaire.

b. Determine planning materiality for audit purposes.

c. Conclude whether changes in compliance with prescribed internal controls justify reliance on them.

d. Prepare a preliminary draft of the management representation letter.

[5]   5-21   As generally conceived, the audit committee of a publicly held company should be made up of

a. Representatives of the major equity interests (preferred stock, common stock).

b. The audit partner, the chief financial officer, the legal counsel, and at least one outsider.

c. Representatives from the client's management, investors, suppliers, and customers.

d. Members of the board of directors who are not officers or employees.

[1,7]   5-22   An auditor who discovers that a client's employees paid small bribes to municipal officials most likely would withdraw from the engagement if

a. The payments violated the client's policies regarding the prevention of illegal acts.

b. The client receives financial assistance from a federal government agency.

c. Documentation that is necessary to prove that the bribes were paid does not exist.

d. Management fails to take the appropriate remedial action.

[7]   5-23   Which of these statements concerning illegal acts by clients is correct?

a. An auditor's responsibility to detect illegal acts that have a direct and material effect on the financial statements is the same as that for errors and fraud.

b. An audit in accordance with generally accepted auditing standards normally includes audit procedures specifically designed to detect illegal acts that have an indirect but material effect on the financial statements.

c. An auditor considers illegal acts from the perspective of the reliability of management's representations rather than their relation to audit objectives derived from financial statement assertions.

d. An auditor has no responsibility to detect illegal acts by clients that have an indirect effect on the financial statements.

[8,9]   5-24 To help plan the nature, timing, and extent of substantive procedures, preliminary analytical procedures should focus on
   a. Enhancing the auditor's understanding of the client's business and of events that have occurred since the last audit date.
   b. Developing plausible relationships that corroborate anticipated results with a measurable amount of precision.
   c. Applying ratio analysis to externally generated data such as published industry statistics or price indexes.
   d. Comparing recorded financial information to the results of other tests of transactions and balances.

[9]   5-25 The primary objective of final analytical procedures is to
   a. Obtain evidence from details tested to corroborate particular assertions.
   b. Identify areas that represent specific risks relevant to the audit.
   c. Assist the auditor in assessing the validity of the conclusions reached.
   d. Satisfy doubts when questions arise about a client's ability to continue in existence.

[9]   5-26 For all audits of financial statements made in accordance with generally accepted auditing standards, the use of analytical procedures is required to some extent

	In the Planning Stage?	As a Substantive Test?	In the Review Stage?
a.	Yes	No	Yes
b.	No	Yes	No
c.	No	Yes	Yes
d.	Yes	No	No

[10]   5-27 The substantive analytical procedure known as trend analysis is best described by
   a. The comparison, across time or to a benchmark, of relationships between financial statement accounts or between an account and nonfinancial data.
   b. Development of a model to form an expectation using financial data, nonfinancial data, or both to test account balances or changes in account balances between accounting periods.
   c. The examination of changes in an account over time.
   d. The comparison of common-size financial statements over time.

[10]   5-28 The assurance bucket is filled with all of the following types of evidence except
   a. Test of controls.
   b. The audit report.
   c. Substantive analytical procedures.
   d. Tests of details.

PROBLEMS

[1,3]   5-29 The audit committee of the board of directors of Rebel Corporation asked Tish & Field, CPAs, to audit Rebel's financial statements for the year ended December 31, 2009. Tish & Field explained the need to make an inquiry of the predecessor auditor and requested permission to do so. Rebel's management agreed and authorized the predecessor auditor to respond fully to Tish & Field's inquiries.

Required:
   a. What information should Tish & Field obtain during its inquiry of the predecessor auditor prior to accepting the engagement?
   b. What additional audit procedures should Tish & Field perform in evaluating Rebel as a potential client?

c. After a satisfactory communication with the predecessor auditor, Tish & Field drafted an engagement letter that was mailed to the audit committee of the board of directors of Rebel Corporation. The engagement letter clearly set forth the arrangements concerning the involvement of the predecessor auditor and other matters. What other matters would Tish & Field generally have included in the engagement letter?

(AICPA, adapted)

[2,6,7] 5-30 Parker is the in-charge auditor for the upcoming annual audit of FGH Company, a continuing audit client. Parker will supervise two assistants on the engagement and will visit the client before the fieldwork begins.

Parker has completed the engagement letter and established an understanding with the Chief Internal Auditor on the assistance to be provided by the internal audit function.

Required:
List the preliminary engagement and planning activities that Parker needs to complete.

(AICPA, adapted)

[2,3] 5-31 A CPA has been asked to audit the financial statements of a publicly held company for the first time. All preliminary verbal discussions and inquiries among the CPA, the company, the predecessor auditor, and all other necessary parties have been completed. The CPA is now preparing an engagement letter.

Required:
a. List the items that should be included in the typical engagement letter in these circumstances.
b. Describe the benefits derived from preparing an engagement letter.

(AICPA, adapted)

[5] 5-32 For many years the financial and accounting community has recognized the importance of the use of audit committees and has endorsed their formation. By now the use of audit committees has become widespread. Independent auditors have become increasingly involved with audit committees and consequently have become familiar with their nature and function.

Required:
a. Describe what an audit committee is.
b. Identify the reasons why audit committees have been formed and are currently in operation.
c. Describe the functions of an audit committee.

(AICPA, adapted)

[7,8] 5-33 Exhibit 5–2 contains a partial audit program for substantive tests of accounts receivable.

Required:
For audit procedures 1–4, identify the primary assertion being tested.

[9] 5-34 Analytical procedures consist of evaluations of financial information made by a study of plausible relationships among both financial and nonfinancial data. They range from simple comparisons to the use of complex models involving many relationships and elements of data. They compare recorded amounts, or ratios developed from recorded amounts, to expectations developed by the auditor.

Required:

a. Describe the purposes of analytical procedures.

b. Identify the sources of information from which an auditor develops expectations.

c. Describe the factors that influence an auditor's consideration of the reliability of data for the purpose of testing assertions.

(AICPA, adapted)

[9]   5-35   At December 31, 2009, EarthWear has $5,890,000 in a liability account labeled "Reserve for returns." The footnotes to the financial statements contain the following policy: "At the time of sale, the company provides a reserve equal to the gross profit on projected merchandise returns, based on prior returns experience." The client has indicated that returns for sales that are six months old are negligible, and gross profit percentage for the year is 42.5 percent. The client has also provided the following information on sales for the last six months of the year:

Month	Monthly Sales (000s)	Historical Return Rate
July	$ 73,300	.004
August	82,800	.006
September	93,500	.010
October	110,200	.015
November	158,200	.025
December	202,500	.032

Required:

a. Using the information given, develop an expectation for the reserve for returns account. Because the rate of return varies based on the time that has passed since the date of sale, do not use an average historical return rate.

b. Determine a tolerable difference for your analytical procedure.

c. Compare your expectation to the book value and determine if it is greater than tolerable difference.

d. Independent of your answer in part (c), what procedures should the auditor perform if the difference between the expectation and the book value is greater than tolerable misstatement?

[9,11]   5-36   Arthur, CPA, is auditing The Home Improvement Store as of December 31, 2010. As with all audit engagements, Arthur's initial procedures are to analyze the client's financial data by reviewing trends in significant ratios and comparing the company's performance with the industry so that he better understands the business and can determine where to concentrate his audit efforts. As part of Arthur's audit of The Home Improvement Store, he performed analytical procedures by calculating the following ratios and obtaining related industry data.

	The Home Improvement Store					Industry				
	2006	2007	2008	2009	2010	2006	2007	2008	2009	2010
Quick ratio	0.67	0.73	1.38	0.45	0.29	0.79	0.81	0.87	0.91	1.08
Days of inventory on hand	62.73	75.15	82.40	84.02	80.52	82.26	79.89	86.86	84.13	75.04
Inventory/current assets	53.48%	45.51%	48.42%	62.28%	80.81%	58.04%	56.44%	60.19%	60.92%	50.33%
Return on assets	16.10%	9.75%	5.70%	2.16%	6.05%	6.98%	8.87%	7.05%	5.06%	11.73%
Debt to equity	0.02	0.07	1.47	2.36	0.72	0.44	0.31	0.56	0.53	0.57

Required:
Compare The Home Improvement Store's ratios with those of its industry. You may want to reference the advanced module in this chapter for more information regarding the ratios used in the analytical procedure. For each ratio provided in the table above:
a. Indicate the potential risks the ratio and/or historical patterns may present.
b. Indicate one or two plausible explanations for why The Home Improvement Store's ratios or historical patterns differ from those of the industry.

DISCUSSION CASES

[7,8]   5-37   Forestcrest Woolen Mills is a closely held North Carolina company that has existed since 1920. The company manufactures high-quality woolen cloth for men's and women's outerwear. Your firm has audited Forestcrest for 15 years.

Five years ago, Forestcrest signed a consent decree with the North Carolina Environmental Protection Agency. The company had been convicted of dumping pollutants (such as bleaching and dyeing chemicals) into the local river. The consent decree provided that Forestcrest construct a water treatment facility within eight years.

You are conducting the current-year audit, and you notice that there has been virtually no activity in the water treatment facility construction account. Your discussion with the controller produces the following comment: "Because of increased competition and lower sales volume, our cash flow has decreased below normal levels. You had better talk to the president about the treatment facility."

The president (and majority shareholder) tells you the following: "Given the current cash flow levels, we had two choices: lay off people or stop work on the facility. This is a poor rural area of North Carolina with few other job opportunities for our people. I decided to stop work on the water treatment facility. I don't think that the state will fine us or close us down." When you ask the president if the company will be able to comply with the consent decree, he informs you that he is uncertain.

Required:
a. Discuss the implications of this situation for the audit and audit report.
b. Would your answer change if these events occurred in the seventh year after the signing of the consent decree?

[9]   5-38   The auditors for Weston University are conducting their audit for the fiscal year ended December 31, 2009. Specifically, the audit firm is now focusing on the audit of revenue from this season's home football games. While planning the audit of sales of football tickets, one of their newer staff people observed that, in prior years, many hours were spent auditing revenue. This staff associate pointed out that perhaps the firm could apply analytical procedures to evaluate whether it appears that the revenue account is properly stated.

The staff associate noted that information for a typical home game could be used to estimate revenues for the entire season. The home football season consisted of seven home games—one against a nationally ranked powerhouse, Bloomington University, and six games against conference opponents. One of these conference games is Weston's in-state archrival, Norwalk University. All of these games were day games except for the game against a conference opponent, Westport University.

The auditors will base their estimate on the game played against Kramer College, a conference opponent. This game is considered to be an average home game for Weston University. The following information concerning that game is available:

Total attendance   24,000 (stadium capacity is 40,000)

This attendance figure includes the 500 free seats described below, and the 24,000 figure should be used as a basis for all further calculations.

Ticket prices
Box seats $12 per ticket
End-zone seats   8 per ticket
Upper-deck seats   5 per ticket

At the game against Kramer College, total attendance was allocated among the different seats as follows:

Box seats   70%
End-zone seats   20%
Upper-deck seats   10%

Based on information obtained in prior year audits, the following assumptions are made to assist in estimating revenue for all other games:

- Attendance for the Bloomington University game was expected to be 30-percent higher than total attendance for an average game, with the mix of seats purchased expected to be the same as for a regular game; however, tickets are priced 20-percent higher than for a normal game.
- The game against Norwalk University was expected to draw 20 percent more fans than a normal game, with 75 percent of these extra fans buying box seats and the other 25 percent purchasing upper-deck seats.
- To make up for extra costs associated with the night game, ticket prices were increased by 10 percent each; however, attendance was also expected to be 5-percent lower than for a normal game, with each type of seating suffering a 5-percent decline.
- At every game, 500 box seats are given away free to players' family and friends. This number is expected to be the same for all home games.

Required:
1. Based on the information above, develop an expectation for ticket revenue for the seven home football games.
2. Reported ticket revenue was $2,200,000. Is the difference between your estimate and reported ticket revenue large enough to prompt further consideration? Why or why not? If further consideration is warranted, provide possible explanations for the difference between estimated and actual football ticket revenue. What evidence could you gather to verify each of your explanations?
3. Under what conditions are substantive analytical procedures likely to be effective in a situation such as that described in this problem?

INTERNET ASSIGNMENTS

[4]   5-39   Visit the Institute of Internal Auditors (IIA) home page (www.theiia.org) and familiarize yourself with the information contained there. Search the site for information about the IIA's requirements for the objectivity and independence of internal auditors.

2009

[7]   5-40   EarthWear Clothiers makes high-quality clothing for outdoor sports. It sells most of its products through mail order. Use the Internet to obtain information about the retail mail-order industry.

HANDS-ON CASES

EarthWear Online	**Client Acceptance** Using Willis and Adams' client acceptance/continuance forms, evaluate the continuance decision for EarthWear as an audit client. *Visit the book's Online Learning Center at www.mhhe.com/messier7e to find a detailed description of the case and to download required materials.* **Preliminary Analytical Procedures** Complete and evaluate Willis and Adams' preliminary analytical procedures on EarthWear's unaudited financial statements. Preliminary analytical procedures include trend, ratio, and common size analyses. *Visit the book's Online Learning Center at www.mhhe.com/messier7e to find a detailed description of the case and to download required materials.* **Planning Memo** Using information from the text as well as from EarthWear Clothiers' and Willis & Adams' home pages, prepare an audit planning memo. *Visit the book's Online Learning Center at www.mhhe.com/messier7e to find a detailed description of the case and to download required materials.*

www.mhhe.com/ messier7e	Visit the book's Online Learning Center for problem material to be completed using the ACL software packaged with your new text.

KAPLAN
CPA Review

www.mhhe.com/ messier7e	**Woodson Flavors International** This simulation will test elements of engagement planning covered in this chapter including engagement letters, analytical procedures, and financial ratios. *To begin this simulation visit the book's Online Learning Center.*

CHAPTER 6

LEARNING OBJECTIVES

Upon completion of this chapter you will

[1] Understand the importance of internal control to management and auditors.

[2] Know the definition of internal control.

[3] Know what controls are relevant to the audit.

[4] Understand the effect of information technology on internal control.

[5] Be familiar with the components of internal control.

[6] Understand how to plan an audit strategy.

[7] Know how to develop an understanding of an entity's internal control.

[8] Be familiar with the tools available for documenting the understanding of internal control.

[9] Know how to assess the level of control risk.

[10] Know the types of tests of controls.

[11] Understand audit strategies for the nature, timing, and extent of substantive procedures based on different levels of detection risk.

[12] Understand the considerations for the timing of audit procedures.

[13] Be familiar with how to assess control risk when an entity's accounting transactions are processed by a service organization.

[14] Understand the auditor's communication of internal control-related matters.

[15] Be familiar with general and application controls.

[16] Understand how to flowchart a business process.

RELEVANT ACCOUNTING AND AUDITING PRONOUNCEMENTS

COSO, *Internal Control—Integrated Framework* (New York: AICPA, 1992)

COSO, *Enterprise Risk Management—Integrated Framework* (New York: AICPA, 2004)

COSO, *Internal Control over Financial Reporting—Guidance for Smaller Public Companies* (New York: AICPA, 2006)

COSO, *Guidance on Monitoring Internal Control Systems* (New York: AICPA, 2009)

AU 311, Planning and Supervision

AU 312, Audit Risk and Materiality in Conducting an Audit

AU 313, Substantive Tests Prior to the Balance-Sheet Date

AU 314, Understanding the Entity and Its Environment and Assessing the Risks of Material Misstatement

AU 316, Consideration of Fraud in a Financial Statement Audit

AU 318, Performing Audit Procedures in Response to Assessed Risks and Evaluating the Audit Evidence Obtained

AU 322, The Auditor's Consideration of the Internal Audit Function in an Audit of Financial Statements

AU 324, Service Organizations

AU 325, Communicating Internal Control–Related Matters Identified in an Audit

AU 326, Audit Evidence

AU 336, Using the Work of a Specialist

AU 339, Audit Documentation

AU 532, Restricting the Use of an Auditor's Report

PCAOB Auditing Standard No. 3, Audit Documentation (AS3)

PCAOB Auditing Standard No. 5, An Audit of Internal Control Over Financial Reporting That Is Integrated with An Audit of Financial Statements (AS5)

PCAOB Proposed Auditing Standards Related to the Auditor's Assessment of and Response to Risk, PCAOB Release No. 2008-006 (October 21, 2008)

Internal Control in a Financial Statement Audit

Major Phases of an Audit

Client acceptance/
continuance and establishing
an understanding with the client
(Chapter 5)

Preliminary engagement
activities
(Chapter 5)

Plan the audit
(Chapters 3 and 5)

Consider and audit
internal control
(Chapters 6 and 7)

Audit business processes
and related accounts
(e.g., revenue generation)
(Chapters 10–16)

Complete the audit
(Chapter 17)

Evaluate results and
issue audit report
(Chapters 1 and 18)

In Chapter 3, we noted that a major part of the auditor's understanding of the entity and its environment involves knowledge about the entity's internal control. In Chapter 5, we introduced you to the concepts of the assurance testing hierarchy and the "assurance bucket," which indicate that the auditor typically obtains assurance from tests of controls before performing substantive procedures. This chapter provides detailed coverage of the auditor's assessment of control risk. It addresses the importance of internal control and its components, as well as how evaluating internal control relates to substantive testing. This chapter covers the COSO framework, basic concepts that apply to auditing internal control, and how the auditor's consideration of a client's internal control impacts the financial statement audit. The approach and techniques discussed in this chapter are equally applicable for an audit of internal control over financial reporting as required by the Sarbanes-Oxley Act of 2002 and discussed in Chapter 7. This chapter also discusses the timing of audit procedures, service organizations, and the required communications of internal control–related matters.

Introduction

[LO 1] Internal control plays an important role in how management meets its steward-ship or agency responsibilities. Management has the responsibility to maintain controls that provide reasonable assurance that adequate control exists over the entity's assets and records. Strong internal controls ensure that assets and records are properly safeguarded. Management also needs a control system that generates reliable information for decision making. If the information system does not generate reliable information, management may be unable to make in-formed decisions about issues such as product pricing, cost of production, and profit information.

The auditor needs assurance about the reliability of the data generated by the information system in terms of how it affects the fairness of the financial statements and how well the assets and records of the entity are safeguarded. The auditor uses risk assessment procedures to obtain an understanding of the entity's internal control. The auditor uses this understanding of internal control to identify the types of potential misstatements, ascertain factors that affect the risk of material misstatement, and design tests of controls and substantive pro-cedures. As we discussed previously, there is an inverse relationship between the reliability of internal control and the amount of substantive evidence required of the auditor. In other words, when the auditor is filling the assurance bucket for an assertion (see Figure 5–6), obtaining more controls evidence means he or she needs to obtain less substantive evidence to top it off.

As we shall see in this chapter, the auditor's understanding of internal control is a major factor in determining the overall audit strategy. After providing an overview of internal control and the COSO framework, we discuss the auditor's responsibilities for internal control under two major topics: (1) obtaining an un-derstanding of internal control and (2) assessing control risk.

Internal Control—An Overview

Definition of Internal Control

[LO 2] According to COSO's Internal Control—Integrated Framework, internal control is designed and effected by an entity's board of directors, management, and other personnel to provide reasonable assurance about the achievement of the entity's objectives in the following categories: (1) reliability of financial reporting; (2) effectiveness and efficiency of operations; and (3) compliance with applicable laws and regulations.

Internal control over the safeguarding of assets against unauthorized acquisi-tion, use, or disposition is also important, and may include controls relating to financial reporting and operations objectives.

Controls Relevant to the Audit

[LO 3] While an entity's internal controls address objectives in each category, not all of these objectives and their related internal controls are relevant to a financial statement audit. Generally, internal controls pertaining to the preparation of fi-nancial statements for external purposes are relevant. Controls relating to opera-tions and compliance objectives may be relevant when they relate to data the auditor uses to apply auditing procedures. For example, the internal controls that relate to operating statistics may be important because such statistics may be utilized by the auditor as data for analytical procedures. On the other hand, some controls that relate to management's planning or operating decisions may not be relevant. In summary, the controls relevant to the audit are those that are likely to prevent, or detect and correct, material misstatements in the financial statement assertions.

TABLE 6–1	Potential Benefits and Risks to an Entity's Internal Control from IT

Benefits
- Consistent application of predefined business rules and performance of complex calculations in processing large volumes of transactions or data.
- Enhancement of the timeliness, availability, and accuracy of information.
- Facilitation of additional analysis of information.
- Enhancement of the ability to monitor the performance of the entity's activities and its policies and procedures.
- Reduction in the risk that controls will be circumvented.
- Enhancement of the ability to achieve effective segregation of duties by implementing security controls in applications, databases, and operating systems.

Risks
- Reliance on systems or programs that inaccurately process data, process inaccurate data, or both.
- Unauthorized access to data that may result in destruction of data or improper changes to data, including the recording of unauthorized or nonexistent transactions or inaccurate recording of transactions.
- Unauthorized changes to data in master files.
- Unauthorized changes to systems or programs.
- Failure to make necessary changes to systems or programs.
- Inappropriate manual intervention.
- Potential loss of data.

The Effect of Information Technology on Internal Control
✎ [LO 4]

The extent of an entity's use of information technology (IT) can affect internal control. The use of IT affects the way transactions are initiated, authorized, recorded, processed, and reported.

Controls in most information systems consist of a combination of manual controls and automated controls. In such systems, manual controls may be independent of, or dependent on, IT. Manual controls may also use information produced by IT, or they may be limited to monitoring the functioning of IT and automated controls and to handling exceptions. An entity's mix of manual and automated controls varies with the nature and complexity of the entity's use of IT.

Table 6–1 lists the benefits and risks of using IT for an entity's internal control. The risks to internal control vary depending on the nature and characteristics of the entity's information system. For example, where multiple users may access a common database, a lack of control at a single user entry point may compromise the security of the entire database. This may result in improper changes to or destruction of data. When IT personnel or users are given, or can gain access privileges beyond those necessary to perform their assigned duties, a breakdown in segregation of duties can occur. This may result in unauthorized transactions or changes to programs or data.

The COSO Framework

Components of Internal Control
✎ [LO 5]

Internal control as defined by the **COSO** framework consists of five components:

- The control environment.
- The entity's risk assessment process.
- The information system and related business processes relevant to financial reporting and communication.
- Control activities.
- Monitoring of controls.

Table 6–2 defines each of the components, while Figure 6–1 shows how the categories of objectives of internal control, including safeguarding of assets, relate to the five components. You can see that each of the five components impacts each of the objectives. However, as mentioned above, the auditor is mainly concerned with how the five components affect the financial reporting objective. In terms of

TABLE 6–2	Components of Internal Control

Control environment The control environment sets the tone of an organization, influencing the control consciousness of its people. It is the foundation for effective internal control, providing discipline and structure. The control environment includes the attitudes, awareness, policies, and actions of management and the board of directors concerning the entity's internal control and its importance in the entity.

The entity's risk assessment process The process for identifying and responding to business risks and the results thereof. For financial reporting purposes, the entity's risk assessment process includes how management identifies risks relevant to the preparation of financial statements that are fairly presented in conformity with generally accepted accounting principles, estimates their significance, assesses the likelihood of their occurrence, and decides upon actions to manage them.

The entity's information system and related business processes relevant to financial reporting, and communication The information system relevant to financial reporting objectives, which includes the accounting system, consists of the procedures, whether automated or manual, and records established to initiate, record, process, and report entity transactions and to maintain accountability for the related assets, liabilities, and equity. Communication involves providing an understanding of individual roles and responsibilities pertaining to internal control over financial reporting.

Control activities Control activities are the policies and procedures that help ensure that management directives are carried out, for example, that necessary actions are taken to address risks to achievement of the entity's objectives. Control activities, whether automated or manual, have various objectives and are applied at various organizational and functional levels.

Monitoring of controls A process to assess the quality of internal control performance over time. It involves assessing the design and operation of controls on a timely basis and taking necessary corrective actions.

FIGURE 6–1	The Relationship of the Objectives of Internal Control to the Five Components of Internal Control

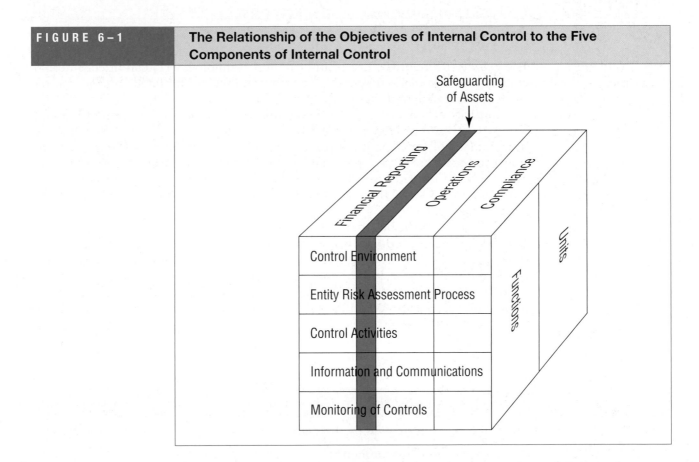

safeguarding assets, the auditor is generally concerned with controls that are relevant to the reliability of financial reporting. For example, access controls, such as passwords, that limit access to data and programs that process transactions may be relevant to the audit.

Control Environment

The control environment sets the tone of an organization, influencing the control consciousness of its people. It is the foundation for all other components of internal control, providing discipline and structure.

The importance of control to an entity is reflected in the overall attitude, awareness of, and actions of the board of directors, management, and owners

TABLE 6–3	Factors Affecting the Control Environment
	Communication and enforcement of integrity and ethical values.
	A commitment to competence.
	Participation of those charged with governance (i.e., board of directors or audit committee).
	Management's philosophy and operating style.
	Organizational structure.
	Assignment of authority and responsibility.
	Human resource policies and practices.

regarding control. The control environment can be thought of as an umbrella that covers the entire entity and establishes the framework for implementing the entity's accounting systems and internal controls. Factors that affect the control environment are shown in Table 6–3.

Communication and Enforcement of Integrity and Ethical Values

The effectiveness of an entity's internal controls is influenced by the integrity and ethical values of the individuals who create, administer, and monitor the controls. An entity needs to establish ethical and behavioral standards that are communicated to employees and are reinforced by day-to-day practice. For example, management should remove incentives or opportunities that might lead personnel to engage in dishonest, illegal, or unethical acts. Some examples of incentives that may lead to unethical behavior are pressures to meet unrealistic performance targets and performance-dependent rewards. Examples of opportunities include an ineffective board of directors, a weak internal audit function, and insignificant penalties for improper behavior. Management can best communicate integrity and ethical behavior within an entity by example and through the use of policy statements, codes of conduct, and training.

A Commitment to Competence

Competence is the knowledge and skills necessary to accomplish the tasks that define an individual's job. Management must specify the competence level for a particular job and translate it into the required level of knowledge and skills. For example, an entity should have a job description for each job. Management then must hire employees who have the appropriate competence for their jobs. Good human resource policies (discussed later in this section) help attract and retain competent and trustworthy employees.

Participation of Those Charged with Governance[1]

The board of directors and the audit committee significantly influence the control consciousness of the entity. The board of directors and the audit committee must take their fiduciary responsibilities seriously and actively oversee the entity's accounting and reporting policies and procedures. Factors that can impact the effectiveness of the board or audit committee include the following:

- Its independence from management.
- The experience and stature of its members.
- The extent of its involvement with and scrutiny of the entity's activities.
- The appropriateness of its actions.
- The information it receives.

---

[1] See PricewaterhouseCoopers, *2009 Current Developments For Directors* (New York: PricewaterhouseCoopers, 2009), for a discussion of audit committees and corporate governance. Also see information published by KPMG's Audit Committee Institute (www.kpmg.com/aci).

- The degree to which difficult questions are raised and pursued with management.
- Its interaction with the internal and external auditors.

Management's Philosophy and Operating Style   Establishing, maintaining, and monitoring the entity's internal controls are management's responsibility. Management's philosophy and operating style can significantly affect the quality of internal control. Characteristics that may signal important information to the auditor about management's philosophy and operating style include the following:

- Management's approach to taking and monitoring business risks.
- Management's attitudes and actions toward financial reporting (conservative or aggressive selection from available alternative accounting principles, and the conscientiousness and conservatism with which accounting estimates are developed).
- Management's attitudes toward information processing and accounting functions and personnel.

Organizational Structure   The organizational structure defines how authority and responsibility are delegated and monitored. It provides the framework within which an entity's activities for achieving entitywide objectives are planned, executed, controlled, and reviewed. An entity develops an organizational structure suited to its needs. Establishing a relevant organizational structure includes considering key areas of authority and responsibility and appropriate lines of reporting.

The appropriateness of an entity's organizational structure depends on its size and the nature of its activities. Factors such as the level of technology in the entity's industry and external influences such as regulation play a major role in the type of organizational structure used. For example, an entity in a high-tech industry may need an organizational structure that can respond quickly to technological changes in the marketplace. Similarly, an entity that operates in a highly regulated industry, such as banking, may be required to maintain a very tightly controlled organizational structure in order to comply with federal or state laws.

Assignment of Authority and Responsibility   This control environment factor includes how authority and responsibility for operating activities are assigned and how reporting relationships and authorization hierarchies are established. It includes policies regarding acceptable business practices, knowledge and experience of key personnel, and resources provided for carrying out duties. It also includes policies and communications directed at ensuring that all personnel understand the entity's objectives, know how their individual actions interrelate and contribute to those objectives, and recognize how and for what they will be held accountable.

An entity can use a number of controls to meet the requirements of this control environment factor. For example, the entity can have a well-specified organizational chart that indicates lines of authority and responsibility. Further, management and supervisory personnel should have job descriptions that include their control-related responsibilities.

Human Resource Policies and Procedures   The quality of internal control is directly related to the quality of the personnel operating the system. The entity should have sound personnel policies for hiring, orienting, training,

evaluating, counseling, promoting, compensating, and taking remedial action. For example, in hiring employees, standards that emphasize seeking the most qualified individuals, with emphasis on educational background, prior work experience, and evidence of integrity and ethical behavior, demonstrate an entity's commitment to employing competent and trustworthy people. Research into the causes of errors in accounting systems has shown personnel-related issues to be a major cause of error.[2]

The Entity's Risk Assessment Process

An entity's risk assessment process is its process for identifying and responding to business risks. This process includes how management identifies risks relevant to the preparation of financial statements, estimates their significance, assesses the likelihood of their occurrence, and decides on how to manage them. For example, the entity's risk assessment process may address how the entity identifies and analyzes significant estimates recorded in the financial statements.

This risk assessment process should consider external and internal events and circumstances that may arise and adversely affect the entity's ability to initiate, authorize, record, process, and report financial data consistent with the assertions of management in the financial statements. Once risks have been identified, management should consider their significance, the likelihood of their occurrence, and how they should be managed. Management should initiate plans, programs, or actions to address specific risks. In some instances, management may accept the consequences of a possible risk because of the costs to remediate or other considerations. Client business risks can arise or change due to the following circumstances:

- *Changes in the operating environment.* Changes in the regulatory or operating environment can alter competitive pressures and create significantly different risks.
- *New personnel.* New personnel may have a different focus on or understanding of internal control.
- *New or revamped information systems.* Significant and rapid changes in information systems can change the risk relating to internal control.
- *Rapid growth.* Significant and rapid expansion of operations can strain controls and increase the risk of a breakdown of controls.
- *New technology.* Incorporating new technologies into production processes or information systems may change the risk associated with internal control.
- *New business models, products, or activities.* Entering business areas or transactions with which an entity has little experience may introduce new risk associated with internal control.
- *Corporate restructurings.* Restructuring may be accompanied by staff reductions and changes in supervision and segregation of duties that may change the risk associated with internal control.
- *Expanded international operations.* The expansion or acquisition of international operations carries new and often unique risks that may impact internal control.

---

[2]A. Eilifsen and W. F. Messier, Jr., "Auditor Detection of Misstatements: A Review and Integration of Empirical Research," *Journal of Accounting Literature* 2000 (19), pp. 1–43, reviews research studies that have examined the causes of auditor-detected misstatements. For example, A. Wright and R. H. Ashton, "Identifying Audit Adjustments with Attention-Directing Procedures," *The Accounting Review* (October 1989), pp. 710–28, find that approximately 55 percent of the errors detected by auditors resulted from personnel problems, insufficient accounting knowledge, and judgment errors.

- **New accounting pronouncements.** Adopting new accounting principles or changing accounting principles may affect the risk involved in preparing financial statements.

Information System and Communication

An information system consists of infrastructure (physical and hardware components), software, people, procedures (manual and automated), and data. The information system relevant to the financial reporting objective includes the accounting system and consists of the procedures (whether automated or manual) and records established to initiate, authorize, record, process, and report an entity's transactions and to maintain accountability for the related assets and liabilities. An effective accounting system gives appropriate consideration to establishing methods and records that will

- Identify and record all valid transactions.
- Describe on a timely basis the transactions in sufficient detail to permit proper classification of transactions for financial reporting.
- Measure the value of transactions in a manner that permits recording their proper monetary value in the financial statements.
- Determine the time period in which transactions occurred to permit recording of transactions in the proper accounting period.
- Properly present the transactions and related disclosures in the financial statements.

Communication involves providing an understanding of individual roles and responsibilities pertaining to internal control over financial reporting. It includes the extent to which personnel understand how their activities in the financial reporting information system relate to the work of others and the means of reporting exceptions to an appropriate higher level within the entity. Policy manuals, accounting and reporting manuals, and memoranda communicate policies and procedures to the entity's personnel. Communications can also be made electronically, orally, or through the actions of management.

Control Activities

Control activities are the policies and procedures that help ensure that management's directives are carried out and are implemented to address risks identified in the risk assessment process. Control activities include a range of activities, including approvals, authorizations, verifications, reconciliations, reviews of operating performance, and segregation of duties. They occur throughout the organization, at all levels and in all functions. Control activities are commonly categorized into the following four types:

- Performance reviews.
- Information processing controls, including authorization and document-based controls.
- Physical controls.
- Segregation of duties.

Performance Reviews   A strong accounting system should have controls that independently check the performance of the individuals or processes in the system. For example, senior management should review actual performance versus budgets, forecasts, prior periods, and competitors. Similarly, managers running functions or activities should review performance reports. For example, a manager responsible for a bank's consumer loans should review loan reports by type, checking summarizations and identifying trends, and relating results to economic statistics and targets. Lastly, persons within the entity should review and analyze the relationships among both financial and non-financial data [e.g., key performance indicators (KPIs)], investigate any unusual items, and take corrective actions when necessary.

Information Processing Controls   These controls are performed to check accuracy, completeness, and authorization of transactions. Data entered are subject to on-line edit checks or matching to approved control files. For example, a customer's order is accepted only after reference to an approved customer file and credit limit. In addition, development of new systems and changes to existing ones are controlled, as is access to data, files, and programs. The two broad categories of information systems controls are general controls and application controls. *General controls* relate to the overall information processing environment and include controls over data center and network operations; system software acquisition, change, and maintenance; access security; and application system acquisition, development, and maintenance. For example, an entity's controls for developing new programs for existing accounting systems should include adequate documentation and testing before implementation. *Application controls* apply to the processing of individual applications and help ensure the occurrence (validity), completeness, and accuracy of transaction processing. General and application controls are covered in more detail in *Advanced Module 1* at the end of this chapter.

Physical Controls   These controls include the physical security of assets (e.g., equipment, inventories, securities, cash, and other assets) and the periodic counting and comparison with amounts shown in control records.

Segregation of Duties   It is important for an entity to segregate the authorization of transactions, recording of transactions, and custody of the related assets. Independent performance of each of these functions reduces the opportunity for any one person to be in a position to both perpetrate and conceal errors or fraud in the normal course of his or her duties. For example, if an employee receives payment from customers on account and has access to the accounts receivable subsidiary ledger, it is possible for that employee to misappropriate the cash and cover the shortage in the accounting records. Pause for a moment and consider: Why is it important that different individuals perform the duties of authorization, recording, and custody? What could happen, for example, if an individual were responsible for both the receipt of customer payments and their recording in the accounts receivable ledger?

Monitoring of
Controls

This monitoring component has received increased attention in recent years. In 2009, COSO issued *Guidance on Monitoring Internal Control Systems*, an integral part of its framework. Monitoring of controls is a process that assesses the quality of internal control performance over time. To provide reasonable assurance that an entity's objectives will be achieved, management should monitor controls to determine whether they are operating effectively. Since risks change over time, management needs to monitor whether controls need to be redesigned when risks change. Figure 6–2 shows how monitoring applies to the other four components of internal control.

Effective monitoring involves (1) establishing a baseline for control effectiveness; (2) designing and executing monitoring procedures that are based on the significance of business risks relative to the entity's objectives; and (3) assessing and reporting results, including follow-up on corrective actions.

Monitoring can be done through ongoing activities or separate evaluations. Ongoing monitoring procedures are built into the normal, recurring activities of the entity and include regular management and supervisory activities. Management can use internal auditors or personnel performing similar functions to monitor the

---

FIGURE 6–2   **How Monitoring Applies to the Components of Internal Control**

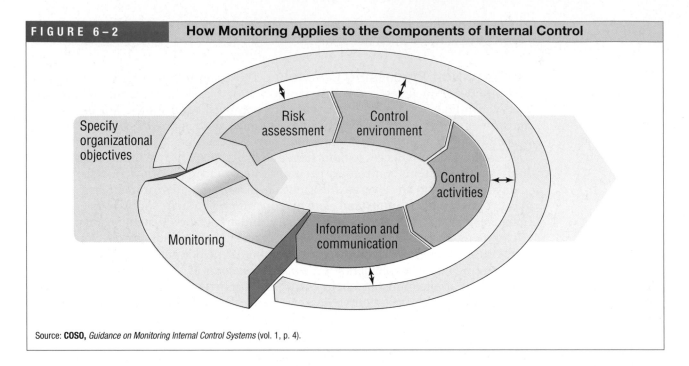

Source: **COSO,** *Guidance on Monitoring Internal Control Systems* (vol. 1, p. 4).

---

operating effectiveness of internal control. For example, management might review whether bank reconciliations are being prepared on a timely basis and reviewed by the internal auditors. In many entities, the information system produces much of the information used in monitoring. If management assumes that data used for monitoring are accurate, errors may exist in the information, potentially leading management to incorrect conclusions. Take a moment and think about other examples of monitoring controls.

Planning an Audit Strategy

✂ [LO 6]   The audit risk model states that $AR = RMM \times DR$ where $RMM = IR \times CR$. In this definition, the auditor's assessment of RMM must consider the level of CR in applying the audit risk model. How the auditor determines the appropriate level of CR is described in the remainder of this chapter. Figure 6–3 presents a flowchart of the auditor's decision process when considering internal control. As we discussed in Chapter 3, the auditor must assess the risk of material misstatement (refer to Figure 3–1). The information gathered by performing risk assessment procedures is used to evaluate the *design* of controls and to determine whether the controls have been *implemented*. This is the first step in Figure 6–3. The auditor then documents this understanding of the internal controls. With a recurring engagement, the auditor is likely to possess substantial knowledge about the client's internal controls and may be able to choose an audit strategy after only updating the understanding of the entity's internal control. For a new client, the auditor may delay making a judgment about an audit strategy until a more detailed understanding of internal control is obtained.

Practice
INSIGHT

Another common challenge that increases control risk is the fact that many clients have a large variety of technological platforms, software, and hardware. Companies that have grown through merger and acquisition frequently band the legacy systems together rather than replace one or both systems. The resulting montage of servers, computers, off-the-shelf and custom-programmed software, and so on creates a complex and potentially risk-prone IT environment.

FIGURE 6-3   **Flowchart of the Auditor's Consideration of Internal Control and Its Relation to Substantive Procedures**

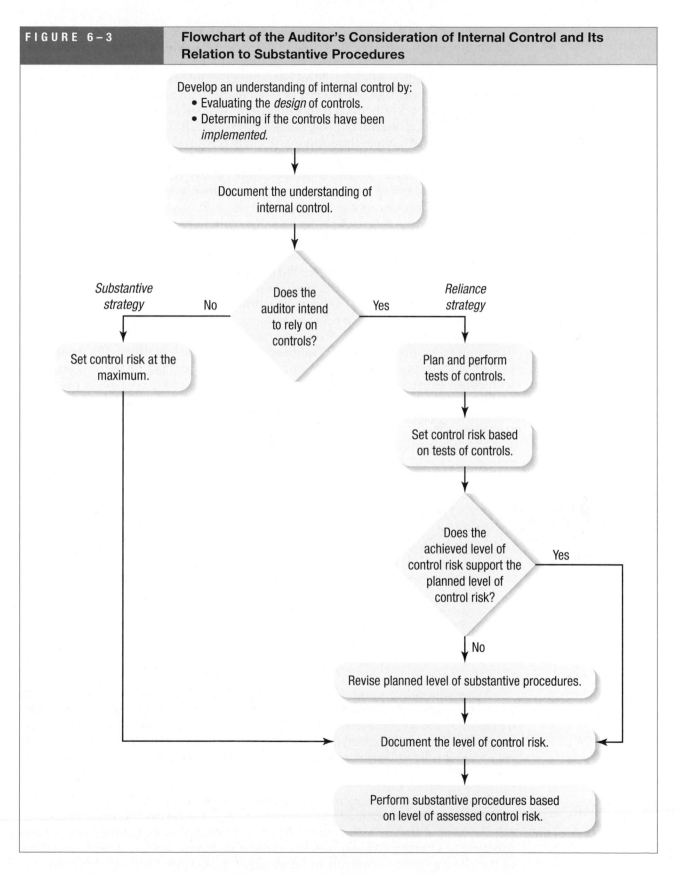

The next step for the auditor is whether or not to rely on the controls. When the auditor's risk assessment procedures indicate that the controls are not properly designed or not implemented, the auditor will not rely on the controls. In this instance, the auditor will set control risk at maximum and use substantive procedures to reduce the risk of material misstatement to an acceptably low level (i.e., the assurance bucket is filled almost entirely with substantive evidence). When the auditor's risk assessment procedures suggest that the controls are properly designed and implemented, the auditor will likely rely on the controls. If the auditor intends to rely on the controls, tests of controls are required to be performed to obtain audit evidence that the controls are operating effectively. The auditor will make an assessment of control risk based on the results of the tests of controls.

To assist your comprehension of how the auditor uses the understanding and assessment of internal control to determine the nature, timing, and extent of audit procedures, we describe only two audit strategies: a substantive strategy and a reliance strategy. However, keep in mind that there is no single strategy for the entire audit; rather the auditor establishes a strategy for individual business processes (such as revenue or purchasing) or by specific assertion (occurrence, completeness, and so on) within a business process. Furthermore, even when auditors follow a reliance strategy, the amount of assurance obtained by controls testing will vary from assertion to assertion. In other words, a reliance strategy just means the auditor intends to begin filling the assurance bucket with tests of controls evidence, but the percentage of the bucket filled with controls evidence will differ between assertions and across accounts in the various business processes. Finally, it is important to understand that auditing standards require some substantive evidence for all significant accounts and assertions. Thus, a reliance strategy reduces but does not eliminate the need to gather substantive evidence.

Practice **INSIGHT**	In some situations the auditor may find it necessary to rely on evidence stored by the client in electronic form. In such situations, a reliance strategy may be required due to the importance of controls in maintaining the integrity of the electronic evidence. Examples include the following: • An entity that initiates orders using electronic data interchange (EDI) for goods based on predetermined decision rules and pays the related payables based on system-generated information regarding receipt of goods. No other documentation is produced or maintained. • An entity that provides electronic services to customers, such as an Internet service provider or a telephone company, and uses IT to log services provided to users, initiate bills for the services, process the billing transactions, and automatically record such amounts in electronic accounting records.

As we discuss in more detail in the next chapter, the Sarbanes-Oxley Act of 2002 as implemented by AS5 requires public company auditors to test and report on the *design* and *effectiveness* of public company internal controls over financial reporting. Thus, it is expected that every public company audit will follow a reliance strategy for at least some account balances or assertions.

Substantive Strategy

A substantive audit strategy means that the auditor has decided not to rely on the entity's controls and instead use substantive procedures as the main source of evidence about the assertions in the financial statements. As Figure 6–3 shows, a substantive strategy still requires the auditor to have a sufficient understanding of the client's internal controls to know whether they are properly designed and implemented. This knowledge includes an understanding of the five components of internal control (discussed later).

The auditor may decide to follow a substantive strategy for some or all assertions because of one or all of the following factors:

- The implemented controls do not pertain to the assertion the auditor is considering.
- The implemented controls are assessed as ineffective.
- Testing the operating effectiveness of the controls would be inefficient.

The auditor next documents the level of control risk at the maximum. Finally, substantive procedures are designed and performed based on the assessment of a maximum level of control risk. Therefore, when the auditor follows a substantive strategy, the assurance bucket (refer to Figure 5–5) is filled with some evidence from the risk assessment procedures and an extensive amount of evidence from substantive procedures (i.e., substantive analytical procedures and tests of details).

Auditing standards point out that the auditor needs to be satisfied that performing only substantive procedures would be effective in restricting detection risk to an acceptable level. For example, the auditor may determine that performing only substantive procedures would be effective and more efficient than performing tests of controls for an entity that has a limited number of long-term debt transactions because corroborating evidence can be obtained by examining the loan agreements and confirming relevant information.

Reliance Strategy

A reliance strategy means that the auditor intends to rely on the entity's controls. If a reliance strategy is followed, the auditor may need a more detailed understanding of internal control to develop a preliminary or "planned" assessment of control risk. The auditor will then plan and perform tests of controls. The auditor uses the test results to assess the "achieved" level of control risk. If the test results indicate that achieved control risk is higher than planned, the auditor will normally increase the planned substantive procedures and document the revised control risk assessment. If the planned level of control risk is supported, no revisions of the planned substantive procedures are required. The level of control risk is documented, and substantive procedures are then performed. Keep in mind that there may be different degrees of control reliance for different business processes or assertions within a process.

From a practical standpoint, the level of control risk is normally set in terms of the assertions about classes of transactions and events for the period under audit. Table 6–4 presents the assertions related to transactions and events that were discussed in Chapter 4 and control activities that are normally in place for each assertion to protect against material misstatements. For example, the use and tracking of prenumbered documents is a control procedure typically found in each business process to ensure occurrence and completeness. In a revenue process, accounting for prenumbered shipping documents provides reasonable assurance that all revenue is recorded (completeness). Similarly, reconciliation of the accounts receivable subledger to the general ledger accounts receivable account provides a control to help ensure that the occurrence assertion is met. Later chapters show these control activities for each business process.

Obtain an Understanding of Internal Control

Overview

[LO 7]

Auditing standards require the auditor to obtain an understanding of each of the five components of internal control in order to plan the audit. This understanding includes knowledge about the design of relevant controls and whether they

TABLE 6–4	Assertions about Classes of Transactions and Events and Related Control Procedures

Assertion	Control Activities
Occurrence	• Segregation of duties. • Prenumbered documents that are accounted for. • Daily or monthly reconciliation of subsidiary records with independent review.
Completeness	• Prenumbered documents that are accounted for. • Segregation of duties. • Daily or monthly reconciliation of subsidiary records with independent review.
Accuracy	• Internal verification of amounts and calculations. • Monthly reconciliation of subsidiary records by an independent person.
Authorization	• General and specific authorization of transactions at important control points.
Cutoff	• Procedures for prompt recording of transactions. • Internal review and verification.
Classification	• Chart of accounts. • Internal review and verification.

have been placed in operation by the entity. The auditor uses this knowledge to

- Identify the types of potential misstatement.
- Pinpoint the factors that affect the risk of material misstatement.
- Design tests of controls and substantive procedures.

In deciding on the nature and extent of the understanding of internal control needed for the audit, the auditor should consider the complexity and sophistication of the entity's operations and systems, including the extent to which the entity relies on manual controls or on automated controls. The auditor may determine that the engagement team needs an IT specialist. In determining whether an IT specialist is needed, the following factors should be considered:

- The complexity of the entity's IT systems and controls and the manner in which they are used in conducting the entity's business.
- The significance of changes made to existing systems, or the implementation of new systems.
- The extent to which data are shared among systems.
- The extent of the entity's participation in electronic commerce.
- The entity's use of emerging technologies.
- The significance of audit evidence that is available only in electronic form.

The IT specialist can be used to assist the engagement team in a number of ways. For example, the IT specialist can inquire of the entity's IT personnel about how data and transactions are initiated, authorized, recorded, processed, and reported, and how IT controls are designed; inspect the system's documentation; observe the operation of IT controls; and plan and perform tests of IT controls. The auditor should have sufficient IT-related knowledge to communicate the assertions to the IT specialist, to evaluate whether the specified procedures meet the auditor's objectives, and to evaluate the results of the audit procedures completed by the IT specialist.

To properly understand a client's internal control, an auditor must understand the five components of internal control. The auditor may use the following audit procedures to obtain an understanding of a client's internal control:

- Inquiry of appropriate management, supervisory, and staff personnel.
- Inspection of entity documents and reports.
- Observation of entity activities and operations.

Understanding
the Control
Environment

The auditor should gain sufficient knowledge about the control environment to understand management's and the board of directors' attitudes, awareness, and actions concerning the control environment, considering both the substance of controls and their collective effect. This includes knowledge of the factors contained in Table 6–3. Exhibit 6–1 presents a questionnaire that includes the type of information the auditor would document about EarthWear's control environment (see the EarthWear Online Case at the end of this chapter for additional information).[3]

Pause for a moment and review Exhibit 6–1. Do any possible control risks jump out at you from this questionnaire? Do you believe that any of the responses merit further inquiry? How would an auditor obtain this information?

Understanding
the Entity's Risk
Assessment
Process

The auditor should obtain sufficient information about the entity's risk assessment process to understand how management considers risks relevant to financial reporting objectives and decides on appropriate actions to address those risks. For example, suppose a client operates in the oil industry, where there is always some risk of environmental damage. The auditor should obtain sufficient knowledge about how the client manages its environmental risks, because environmental accidents can result in costly litigation against the entity.

Understanding
the Information
System and
Communications

The auditor should obtain sufficient knowledge of the information system to understand the following:

- The classes of transactions in the entity's operations that are significant to the financial statements.
- The procedures, both automated and manual, by which transactions are initiated, authorized, recorded, processed, and reported, from their occurrence to their inclusion in the financial statements.
- The related accounting records, whether electronic or manual, supporting information, and specific accounts in the financial statements that are involved in initiating, recording, processing, and reporting transactions.
- How the information system captures other events and conditions that are significant to the financial statements.
- The financial reporting process used to prepare the entity's financial statements, including significant accounting estimates and disclosures.

The auditor must learn about each business process that affects significant account balances in the financial statements. This includes understanding how transactions are initiated and authorized, how documents and records are generated, and how the documents and records flow to the general ledger and financial statements. Understanding the information system also requires knowing how IT is involved in data processing.

The auditor should understand the automated and manual procedures used by the entity to prepare financial statements and related disclosures. Such procedures include

- The procedures used to enter transaction totals into the general ledger.
- The procedures used to initiate, authorize, record, and process journal entries in the general ledger.
- Other procedures used to record recurring and nonrecurring adjustments to the financial statements.

---

[3]Exhibit 6–1 shows how the understanding of internal control can be developed and documented using a separate internal control questionnaire. Some or all of the information on the components of the entity's internal control may be captured as part of the auditor's understanding of the entity and its environment (see Chapter 3).

EXHIBIT 6-1   **An Excerpt from Questionnaire for Documenting the Auditor's Understanding of the Control Environment**

CONTROL ENVIRONMENT QUESTIONNAIRE

Client: EarthWear Clothiers		Balance Sheet Date: 12/31/2009
Completed by: SAA Date: 9/30/09		Reviewed by: DRM Date: 10/15/09

COMMUNICATION AND ENFORCEMENT OF INTEGRITY AND ETHICAL VALUES

The effectiveness of controls cannot rise above the integrity and ethical values of the people who create, administer, and monitor them. Integrity and ethical values are essential elements of the control environment, affecting the design, administration, and monitoring of other components. Integrity and ethical behavior are the product of the entity's ethical and behavioral standards, how they are communicated, and how they are reinforced in practice.

	Yes, No, N/A	Comments
Have appropriate entity policies regarding matters such as acceptable business practices, conflicts of interest, and codes of conduct been established, and are they adequately communicated?	Yes	*The permanent work papers contain a copy of EarthWear's conflict-of-interest policy.*
Does management demonstrate the appropriate "tone at the top," including explicit moral guidance about what is right or wrong?	Yes	*EarthWear's management maintains high moral and ethical standards and expects employees to act accordingly.*
Are everyday dealings with customers, suppliers, employees, and other parties based on honesty and fairness?	Yes	*EarthWear's management maintains a high degree of integrity in dealing with customers, suppliers, employees, and other parties; it requires employees and agents to act accordingly.*
Does management document or investigate deviations from established controls?	Yes	*To our knowledge, management has not attempted to override controls. Employees are encouraged to report attempts to bypass controls to appropriate individuals within the organization.*

COMMITMENT TO COMPETENCE

Competence is the knowledge and skills necessary to accomplish tasks that define the individual's job. Commitment to competence includes management's consideration of the competence levels for particular jobs and how those levels translate into requisite skills and knowledge.

Does the company maintain formal or informal job descriptions or other means of defining tasks that comprise particular jobs?	Yes	*EarthWear has formal written job descriptions for all supervisory personnel, and job duties for nonsupervisory personnel are clearly communicated.*
Does management determine to an adequate extent the knowledge and skills needed to perform particular jobs?	Yes	*The job descriptions specify the knowledge and skills needed. The Human Resources Department uses this information in hiring, training, and promotion decisions.*
Does evidence exist that employees have the requisite knowledge and skills to perform their job?	Yes	*Our prior experiences with EarthWear personnel indicate that they have the necessary knowledge and skills.*

Understanding
Control
Activities

As the auditor learns about the other components of internal control, he or she is also likely to obtain information about control activities. For example, in examining the information system that pertains to accounts receivable, the auditor is likely to see how the entity grants credit to customers. The extent of the auditor's understanding of control activities is a function of the audit strategy adopted. When the auditor decides to follow a substantive strategy approach, little work is done on understanding specific control activities. When a reliance strategy is followed, the auditor has to understand the control activities that relate to assertions for which a lower level of control risk is expected. Auditors normally use walkthroughs to develop an understanding of control activities.

Understanding
Monitoring of
Controls

The auditor should obtain an understanding of the major types of activities that the entity uses to monitor internal control, including the sources of the information related to those activities, and how those activities are used to initiate corrective actions to its controls.

Documenting the
Understanding of
Internal Control

✄ **[LO 8]**

Auditing standards require that the auditor document his or her understanding of the entity's internal control components. A number of tools are available to the auditor for documenting the understanding of internal control. These include

- The entity's procedures manuals and organizational charts.
- Narrative description.
- Internal control questionnaires.
- Flowcharts.

Procedures Manuals and Organizational Charts   Many organizations prepare procedures manuals that document the entity's policies and procedures. Portions of such manuals may include documentation of the accounting systems and related control activities. The entity's organizational chart presents the designated lines of authority and responsibility. Copies of both of these documents can help the auditor document his or her understanding of the internal control system.

Narrative Description   The understanding of internal control may be documented in a memorandum. This documentation approach is most appropriate when the entity has a simple internal control system.

Internal Control Questionnaires   Internal control questionnaires are one of many types of questionnaires used by auditors. Questionnaires provide a systematic means for the auditor to investigate various areas such as internal control. An internal control questionnaire is generally used for entities with a relatively complex internal control structure. It contains questions about the important factors or characteristics of the five internal control components. Exhibit 6–1 provides an example of the use of such questionnaires. The auditor's responses to the questions included in the internal control questionnaire provide the documentation for his or her understanding.

Flowcharts   Flowcharts provide a diagrammatic representation, or "picture," of the entity's accounting system. The flowchart outlines the configuration of the system in terms of functions, documents, processes, and reports. This documentation facilitates an auditor's analysis of the system's strengths and weaknesses. Figure 6–4 presents a simple example of a flowchart for the order entry portion

---

FIGURE 6–4

FIGURE 6–4   **An Example of a Flowchart for the Order Entry Portion of the Revenue Process**

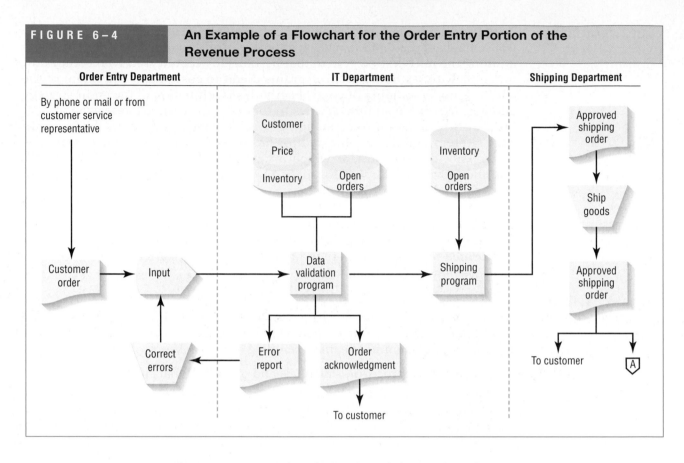

---

of a revenue process. *Advanced Module 2* to this chapter provides detailed coverage of flowcharting techniques. Flowcharts are used extensively in this book to represent accounting systems.

On many engagements, auditors combine these tools to document their understanding of the components of internal control. The combination depends on the complexity of the entity's internal control system. For example, in a complex information system where a large volume of transactions occur electronically, the auditor may document the control environment, the entity's risk assessment process, and monitoring activities using a memorandum and internal control questionnaire. Documentation of the information system and communication component, as well as control activities, may be accomplished through the use of an internal control questionnaire and a flowchart. For a small entity with a simple information system, documentation using a memorandum may be sufficient.

The Effect of Entity Size on Internal Control

The size of an entity may affect how the various components of internal control are implemented. While large entities may be able to implement the components in the fashion just described, small to midsize entities sometimes use alternative approaches and still achieve effective internal control. For example, a large entity may have a written code of conduct, while a small or midsize entity may not. However, a small entity may achieve a similar objective by developing a culture that emphasizes integrity and ethical behavior through oral communication and the example of the owner-manager.

While the basic concepts of the five components should be present in all entities, they are likely to be less formal in a small or midsize entity than in a large entity. For example, in a small entity, the owner-manager's involvement in day-to-day activities can provide a highly effective control that identifies and monitors risks that may affect the entity. A small entity can also have effective communication channels due to its size, the fact that there are fewer levels in the organizational hierarchy, and management's greater visibility. The monitoring component can also be effective in a small to midsize entity as a result of management's close involvement in operations. For example, the owner may review all daily cash disbursements to ensure that only authorized payments are made to vendors. By being involved in day-to-day operations, management may be better able to identify variances from expectations and inaccuracies in financial data.

The Limitations of an Entity's Internal Control	An internal control system should be designed and operated to provide reasonable assurance that an entity's objectives are being achieved. The concept of reasonable assurance recognizes that the cost of an entity's internal control system should not exceed the benefits that are expected to be derived. Balancing the cost of controls with the related benefits requires considerable estimation and judgment on the part of management. The effectiveness of any internal control system is subject to certain inherent limitations, including management override of internal control, personnel errors or mistakes, and collusion. For example, in a recent survey by PwC (see Figure 6–5), "insufficient controls" and "able to use authority to override control" were two of the major corporate causes cited for why fraud occurred.

Management Override of Internal Control   In some cases, an entity's controls may be overridden by management. For example, a senior-level manager can require a lower-level employee to record entries in the accounting records that are not consistent with the substance of the transactions and that violate the entity's controls. The lower-level employee may record the transaction, even

FIGURE 6–5   **Reasons Cited by Companies for Why Fraud Occurred**

Individual reasons (incentives and means for rationalization):
- Financial incentives (greed): 57
- Low temptation threshold: 44
- Lack of awareness of wrongdoing: 40
- Expensive lifestyle: 36
- Denial of financial consequences: 26
- Career disappointment: 12
- Potential redundancy: 8

Corporate causes (controls and cultural issues):
- Low commitment to brand: 34
- Insufficient controls: 34
- Able to use authority to override control: 19
- Too great staff anonymity: 17
- High company targets: 13
- Corporate ethics unclear: 14

% companies

Source: PricewaterhouseCoopers, *Economic Crime: People, Culture And Controls*. The Fourth Biennial Global Economic Crime Survey, 2007.

though he or she knows that it violates the entity's controls, out of fear of losing his or her job. In another example, management may enter into side agreements with customers that alter the terms and conditions of the entity's standard sales contract in ways that should preclude revenue recognition.

The auditor is particularly concerned when senior management is involved in such activities because it raises serious questions about management's integrity. Violations of control activities by senior management, however, are often particularly difficult to detect with normal audit procedures.

Human Errors or Mistakes   The internal control system is only as effective as the personnel who implement and perform the controls. Breakdowns in internal control can occur because of human failures such as simple errors or mistakes. For example, errors may occur in designing, maintaining, or monitoring automated controls. If IT personnel do not completely understand how a revenue system processes sales transactions, they may erroneously design changes to the system to process sales for a new line of products.

Collusion   The effectiveness of segregation of duties lies in individuals' performing only their assigned tasks or in the performance of one person being checked by another. There is always a risk that collusion between individuals will destroy the effectiveness of segregation of duties. For example, an individual who receives cash receipts from customers can collude with the one who records those receipts in the customers' records to steal cash from the entity.

Assessing Control Risk

[LO 9]   Assessing control risk is the process of evaluating the effectiveness of an entity's internal control in preventing, or detecting and correcting, material misstatements in the financial statements. As discussed earlier, the auditor can set control risk at the maximum (a substantive strategy) or at a lower level (a reliance strategy). As shown in Figure 6–3, when the auditor sets control risk at the maximum, he or she documents control risk assessment and performs substantive procedures. The discussion in this section focuses on the situation where the auditor plans to set control risk below the maximum (i.e., a reliance strategy). To set control risk below the maximum, the auditor must:

- Identify specific controls that will be relied upon.
- Perform tests of controls.
- Conclude on the achieved level of control risk.

Identifying Specific Controls That Will Be Relied Upon

The auditor's understanding of internal control is used to identify the controls that are likely to prevent, or detect and correct, material misstatement in specific assertions. In identifying controls to be relied upon, the auditor should consider that the controls could have a pervasive effect on many assertions. For example, the conclusion that an entity's control environment is highly effective may influence the auditor's decision about the number of an entity's locations at which auditing procedures are to be performed. Alternatively, some controls only affect an individual assertion contained in a financial statement account, such as, for example, a credit check performed on a customer's order specifically related to the valuation assertion for the accounts receivable balance.

Advanced Module 1 at the end of the chapter provides a discussion of the types of general and application controls that should be considered by the auditor. General controls are pervasive to all information systems, while application controls relate to a specific business process such as sales or purchasing. It is important to note that the reliability of application controls, especially those that are automated, is affected by the reliability of the general controls. For example, if there were no general controls over program changes, it would be possible for a programmer to make inappropriate changes to circumvent particular application controls in an information system.

Performing Tests of Controls

✂ [LO 10]

Tests of controls are audit procedures performed to test the effectiveness of controls in preventing, or detecting and correcting, material misstatements at the relevant assertion level. Tests of controls are performed in order to provide evidence to support the lower level of control risk. Tests of controls directed toward the effectiveness of the design of a control are concerned with evaluating whether that control is suitably designed to prevent, or detect and correct, material misstatements. Tests of controls directed toward operating effectiveness are concerned with assessing how the control was applied, the consistency with which it was applied during the audit period, and by whom it was applied. Procedures that are used for tests of controls are listed below with examples of how the auditor might apply each:

Types of Tests of Controls	Examples
Inquiry of appropriate entity personnel.	Inquiry of credit manager about the policies for writing off uncollectible accounts.
Inspection of documents, reports, or electronic files indicating the performance of the control.	Inspect bank reconciliations prepared by the internal auditors.
Observation of the application of the control.	Observe how controls are applied to the handling of cash to ensure that there is proper segregation of duties.
Reperformance of the application of the control by the auditor.	Reperform the authorization control used for granting credit.

A combination of these procedures may be necessary to evaluate the effectiveness of the design or operation of a control. For example, auditors perform walkthroughs of a client's business process (i.e., revenue) where they "walk" a sales transaction from its origination (customer order) to its inclusion in the financial statements. While performing the walkthrough, the auditor will inquire of, and observe, client personnel and inspect relevant documents.

The operating effectiveness of the control can be affected by whether the control is performed manually or is automated. If the control is performed manually, it may be subject to human errors or mistakes in its application. If properly designed, automated controls should operate more consistently, and the auditor usually does not need to test as many instances of an automated control's operation because automated application controls should function consistently unless the program is changed. To test automated controls, the auditor may need to use techniques that are different from those used to test manual controls. For example, computer-assisted audit techniques may be used to test automated controls. The *Advanced Module* in Chapter 7 discusses computer-assisted audit techniques.

Concluding on the Achieved Level of Control Risk

After the tests of controls have been completed, the auditor should reach a conclusion on the *achieved level of control risk.* The auditor uses the achieved level of control risk and the assessed level of inherent risk to assess the risk of material misstatement and to then determine the level of detection risk needed to bring audit risk to an acceptably low level. The level of detection risk is used to determine the nature, timing, and extent of substantive tests.

Figure 6–3 shows the decision process followed by the auditor upon completing the planned tests of controls. If the tests of controls are consistent with the auditor's planned assessment of control risk, no revision in the nature, timing, or extent of substantive procedures is necessary. On the other hand, if the tests of controls indicate that the controls are not operating as preliminarily assessed, this means that the achieved level of control risk is higher than the planned level, and the nature, timing, and extent of planned substantive procedures will have to be modified.

Documenting the Achieved Level of Control Risk

The auditor should document the achieved level of control risk for the controls evaluated. The auditor's assessment of the level of control risk can be documented using a structured working paper, an internal control questionnaire, or a memorandum.

An Example

Table 6–5 presents two account balances from EarthWear Clothiers' financial statements that differ in terms of their nature, size, and complexity. The differences in these characteristics result in different levels of understanding of internal control and different control risk assessments. Before reading further, review Table 6–5 and its information. Why would an auditor decide to follow a substantive strategy for the Prepaid Advertising account but a reliance strategy for the Inventory account?

In this example, inventory is a material account balance that is composed of numerous products. This account also contains significant inherent risk, and the data for this account are generated by a complex computer system. For inventory, the auditor must understand the control environment factors, risk assessment factors, monitoring activities, significant classes of transactions, inventory pricing policies, the flow of transactions, and what control activities will be relied upon. The auditor will use the audit procedures discussed earlier in the chapter to obtain an understanding of internal control for inventory. In contrast, while prepaid advertising is a significant account, it contains few transactions. There is little or no inherent risk and the accounting records are simple, so the

TABLE 6–5	**An Example of How Account Characteristics Affect the Auditor's Understanding of Internal Control, Control Risk Assessment, and Planned Substantive Procedures**			
EarthWear Account Balance	*Account Characteristics*	*Extent of Understanding Needed to Plan the Audit*	*Control Risk Assessment*	*Planned Substantive Procedures*
Inventory ($122,337,000)	• Material balance. • Numerous transactions from a large product base. • Significant inherent risk related to overstock and out-of-style products. • Complex computer processing.	• Entity control environment factors. • Risk assessment factors. • Monitoring activities. • Significant classes of transactions. • Inventory pricing policies. • Initiation, processing, and recording of transactions. • Control procedures to be relied upon.	• Control risk is assessed to be *low* because tests of controls conducted on relevant controls in the purchasing and inventory cycles were consistent with the planned assessment of control risk.	Substantive procedures will include • Physical examination of inventory. • Information technology–assisted audit techniques to audit the inventory compilation.
Prepaid advertising ($11,458,000)	• Significant balance. • Few transactions. • Little or no inherent risk. • Simple accounting procedures.	• Entity control environment factors. • Nature of the account balance. • Monitoring activities.	• Control risk is assessed at the maximum because there are few transactions and the procedures for amortizing advertising expenditures are simple, a substantive strategy is selected.	• Substantive procedures will recalculate the amortization of the advertising expenditures.

knowledge needed about the client's risk assessment, information system and communication, and monitoring regarding this account is minimal. In this instance, the auditor needs only to understand the control environment factors, the nature of the account balance, and the client's monitoring activities. Limited knowledge of the client's control activities is necessary for this account. Audit procedures for the prepaid advertising account would likely be limited to recalculation of amortization of advertising.

Substantive Procedures

[LO 11] The last step in the decision process under either strategy is performing substantive procedures. As discussed in Chapter 5, substantive procedures include substantive analytical procedures and tests of details.

Table 6–6 presents two examples of how the nature, timing, and extent of substantive procedures may vary as a function of the detection risk level for the purchasing process and inventory account. Assume that audit risk is set low for both clients but that client 1 has a high level of risk of material misstatement (inherent risk and control risk), while client 2 has a low level of risk of material misstatement. The use of the audit risk model results in setting detection risk at low for client 1 and high for client 2. For client 1, to achieve a low detection risk the auditor must (1) obtain more reliable types of evidence, such as confirmation and reperformance; (2) conduct most of the audit work at year-end (as such tests are usually considered to be stronger than tests done at an interim date); and (3) make the tests more extensive (larger sample size). This is because the auditor must fill the assurance bucket almost entirely with substantive evidence. In contrast, client 2 has a high detection risk, which means that (1) less reliable types of evidence, such as analytical procedures, can be obtained; (2) most of the audit work can be conducted at an interim date; and (3) tests of the inventory account would involve a smaller sample size. Another major difference between the two strategies involves the physical examination of the inventory on hand. For the low-detection-risk strategy, physical inventory would be examined at year-end because the control risk was assessed to be high. For the high-detection-risk strategy, the auditor can examine the physical inventory at an interim date because the control risk assessment indicates little risk of material misstatement.

TABLE 6–6	Audit Strategies for the Nature, Timing, and Extent of Substantive Procedures Based on Different Levels of Detection Risk for Inventory
Low-Detection-Risk Strategy—Client 1	
Nature	Audit tests for all significant audit assertions using the following types of audit procedures: • Physical examination (conducted at year-end). • Review of external documents. • Confirmation. • Reperformance.
Timing	All significant work completed at year-end.
Extent	Extensive testing of significant accounts or transactions.
High-Detection-Risk Strategy—Client 2	
Nature	Corroborative audit tests using the following types of audit tests: • Physical examination (conducted at an interim date). • Analytical procedures. • Substantive tests of transactions and balances.
Timing	Interim and year-end.
Extent	Limited testing of accounts or transactions.

Timing of Audit Procedures

✎ [LO 12]   Audit procedures may be conducted at an interim date or at year-end. Figure 6–6 presents a timeline for planning and performing a midsize to large audit for an entity such as EarthWear Clothiers with a 12/31/09 year-end. In this example, the audit is planned and preliminary analytical procedures are conducted around 5/31/09. The interim tests of controls are conducted sometime during the time frame 7/31/09 to 11/30/09. Substantive procedures are planned for the time frame 11/30/09 to 2/15/10, when the audit report is to be issued. The auditor's considerations of conducting tests of controls and substantive tests at an interim date are discussed in turn.

Interim Tests of Controls

An auditor might test controls at an interim date because the assertion being tested may not be significant, the control has been effective in prior audits, or it may be more efficient to conduct the tests at that time. A reason why it may be more efficient to conduct interim tests of controls is that staff accountants may be less busy at the time, and it may minimize the amount of overtime needed at year-end. Additionally, if the controls are found not to be operating effectively, testing them at an interim date gives the auditor more time to reassess the control risk and modify the audit plan. It also gives the auditor time to inform management so that likely misstatements can be located and corrected before the rest of the audit is performed.

An important question the auditor must address is the need for additional audit work in the period following the interim testing period. For example, suppose the auditor examines controls over a sample of sales transactions for the period 1/1/09 to 8/31/09. What testing, if any, should the auditor conduct for the period 9/1/09 to 12/31/09? In making this decision, the auditor should consider factors such as the significance of the assertion, the evaluation of the design and operation of the relevant controls, the results of tests of controls, the length of the remaining period, and the planned substantive procedures in determining the nature and extent of audit work for the remaining period. At a minimum, the auditor would inquire about the nature and extent of changes in policies, procedures, or personnel that occurred subsequent to the interim period. If significant changes have occurred, or if the results of tests of controls are unfavorable, the auditor may need to conduct additional audit procedures for the remaining period.

Interim Substantive Procedures

Conducting substantive procedures only at an interim date may increase the risk that material misstatements are present in the financial statements. The auditor can control for this potential problem by considering when it is appropriate to examine an account at an interim date and by performing selected audit procedures for the period between the interim date and year-end.

FIGURE 6–6	A Timeline for Planning and Performing the Audit of EarthWear Clothiers

Beginning of the year — 1/1/09

Plan audit and conduct preliminary analytical procedures — 5/31/09

Conduct interim tests of controls — 7/31/09 to 11/30/09

Financial statement date — 12/31/09

Issue audit report — 2/15/10

Conduct substantive tests

The auditor should consider the following factors when substantive procedures are to be completed at an interim date:

- The control environment and other relevant controls.
- The availability of information at a later date that is necessary for the auditor's procedures (e.g., information stored electronically for a limited period of time).
- The objective of the substantive procedure.
- The assessed risk of material misstatement.
- The nature of the class of transactions or account balance and relevant assertions.
- The ability of the auditor to reduce the risk that misstatements existing at the period's end are not detected by performing appropriate substantive procedures or substantive procedures combined with tests of controls to cover the remaining period.

For example, if the entity's accounting system has control weaknesses that result in a high level of assessed control risk, it is unlikely that the auditor would conduct substantive procedures at an interim date. In this instance, the auditor has little assurance that the accounting system will generate accurate information during the remaining period.

When the auditor conducts substantive procedures of an account at an interim date, some additional substantive procedures are ordinarily conducted in the remaining period. Generally, this would include comparing the year-end account balance with the interim account balance. It might also involve conducting analytical procedures or reviewing related journals and ledgers for large or unusual transactions. If misstatements are detected during interim testing, the auditor will have to revise the planned substantive procedures for the remaining period or perform some additional substantive procedures at year-end.

Auditing Accounting Applications Processed by Service Organizations

[LO 13] In some instances, a client may have some or all of its accounting transactions processed by an outside service organization. Examples of such service organizations include mortgage bankers that service mortgages for others and trust departments that invest or hold assets for employee benefit plans. More frequently, however, service organizations are IT service centers that process transactions such as payroll and the related accounting reports. Auditing standards provide guidance to the auditor when a client uses a service organization to process certain transactions.

When a client obtains services from a service organization, those services must be considered as part of an entity's information system if they affect any of the following:

- How the client's transactions are initiated.
- The accounting records, supporting information, and specific accounts in the financial statements involved in the processing and reporting of the client's transactions.
- The accounting processing involved from the initiation of the transactions to their inclusion in the financial statements, including electronic means used to transmit, process, maintain, and access information.
- The financial reporting process used to prepare the client's financial statements, including significant accounting estimates and disclosures.

The significance of the controls of the service organization to those of the client depends primarily on the nature and materiality of the transactions it processes for the client and the degree of interaction between its activities and those of the client. For example, if the client initiates transactions and the service organization executes and does the accounting processing of those transactions, there is a high degree of interaction.

Because the client's transactions are subjected to the controls of the service organization, one of the auditor's concerns is the internal control system in place at the service organization. The auditor's understanding of the client's internal control components may include controls placed in operation by the client and the service organization.

After obtaining an understanding of internal control, the auditor identifies controls that are applied by the client or the service organization that will allow an assessment of reduced control risk. The auditor may obtain evidence to support the lower assessment of control risk by testing the client's controls over the activities performed by the service organization or by tests of controls at the service organization.

Because service organizations process data for many customers, it is not uncommon for them to have an auditor issue a report on their operations. Such reports can be distributed to the auditors of a service organization's customers. A service organization's auditor can issue one of two types of reports. One type of report is a description of the service organization's controls and an assessment of whether they are suitably designed to achieve specified internal control objectives. The other type of report goes further by testing whether the controls are operating effectively and thus that they provide reasonable assurance that the related control objectives were achieved during the period. An auditor may reduce control risk below the maximum only on the basis of a service auditor's report that includes tests of the controls.

Practice **INSIGHT**	During an inspection of one of the Big 4 firms conducted in 2008, the PCAOB inspection team identified matters that it considered to be audit deficiencies, one of which had to do with using information provided by a service organization to estimate a significant contingency. In this audit, the firm failed to test the completeness of information provided by a service organization used to calculate this liability. The firm also failed to test controls regarding this information and thus failed to obtain sufficient evidence to support the firm's opinion on the issuer's internal control over financial reporting.

Communication of Internal Control–Related Matters

[LO 14] Standards for reporting internal control deficiencies differ for public versus private entities (referred to as "nonissuers"). Under the Sarbanes-Oxley Act of 2002, management of public companies must prepare an assertion on internal control effectiveness and its registered auditors must issue an opinion on the effectiveness of internal control. These requirements are covered in Chapter 7.

Although a financial statement audit for private companies does not include an audit of the client's system of internal control, the auditor may discover deficiencies in the client's internal controls during the audit. A *control deficiency* in internal control exists when the design or operation of a control does not allow management or employees, in the normal course of performing their assigned functions, to prevent, or detect and correct, misstatements on a timely basis. A *material weakness* is a deficiency, or combination of deficiencies, in internal control, such that there is a reasonable possibility that a material misstatement of the entity's financial statements will not be prevented, or detected and corrected, on a timely basis. A *significant deficiency* is a deficiency, or a combination of deficiencies, in internal control that is less severe than a material weakness, yet important enough to merit attention by those charged with governance. Significant

TABLE 6-7	Examples of Circumstances That May Be Control Deficiencies, Significant Deficiencies, or Material Weaknesses

Deficiencies in the Design of Controls
- Inadequate design of internal control over the preparation of the financial statements being audited.
- Inadequate design of internal control over a significant account or process.
- Inadequate documentation of the components of internal control.
- Insufficient control consciousness within the organization, for example, the tone at the top and the control environment.
- Absent or inadequate segregation of duties within a significant account or process.
- Absent or inadequate controls over the safeguarding of assets.
- Inadequate design of information technology (IT) general and application controls.
- Employees or management who lack the qualifications and training to fulfill their assigned functions.
- Inadequate design of monitoring controls.
- The absence of an internal process to report deficiencies in internal control to management on a timely basis.

Failures in the Operation of Internal Control
- Failure in the operation of effectively designed controls over a significant account or process.
- Failure of the information and communication component of internal control to provide complete and accurate output because of deficiencies in timeliness, completeness, or accuracy.
- Failure of controls designed to safeguard assets from loss, damage, or misappropriation.
- Failure to perform reconciliations of significant accounts.
- Undue bias or lack of objectivity by those responsible for accounting decisions.
- Misrepresentation by client personnel to the auditor (an indicator of fraud).
- Management override of controls.
- Failure of an application control caused by a deficiency in the design or operation of an IT general control.
- An observed deviation rate that exceeds the number of deviations expected by the auditor in a test of operating effectiveness of a control.

Source: AU 235, Appendix.

deficiencies and material weaknesses may be identified as part of the auditor's consideration of the five components of internal control or through substantive procedures. Table 6–7 presents examples of circumstances that might indicate a control deficiency, significant deficiency, or material weakness.

The auditor must communicate, in writing, any discovered significant deficiencies and material weaknesses to management and those charged with governance.

Advanced Module 1: Types of Controls in an IT Environment

✎ **[LO 15]** There are two broad categories of information systems control activities: general controls and application controls. *General controls* relate to the overall information processing environment and have a pervasive effect on the entity's computer operations. General controls are sometimes referred to as supervisory, management, or information technology controls. *Application controls* apply to the processing of specific computer applications and are part of the computer programs used in the accounting system (for example, revenues or purchasing).

General Controls

General controls include controls over:

- Data center and network operations.
- System software acquisition, change, and maintenance.
- Access security.
- Application system acquisition, development, and maintenance.

Data Center and Network Operations Controls   Data center and network operations controls include controls over computer and network operations, data preparation, work flow control, and library functions. Important controls over computer and network operations should prevent unauthorized access to the network programs, files, and systems documentation by computer operators. In IT systems, traditional controls such as rotation of operator duties and mandatory vacations should be implemented. The operating systems log, which documents all program and operator activities, should be regularly reviewed to ensure that operators have not performed any unauthorized activities.

Controls over data preparation include proper entry of data into an application system and proper oversight of error correction. Controls over work flow include scheduling of application programs, proper setup for programs, and use of the correct files. The library function needs controls to ensure that (1) the correct files are provided for specific applications; (2) files are properly maintained; and (3) backup and recovery procedures exist.

Systems Software Acquisition, Change, and Maintenance Controls

Systems software are computer programs that control the computer functions and allow the application programs to run. These programs include operating systems, library and security packages, and database management systems. For example, the operating system controls the operations of the computer and allocates computer resources among the application programs. The operating system also detects and corrects processing errors. The entity should have strong controls that ensure proper approval for purchases of new system software and adequate controls over changes and maintenance of existing systems software. Generally, an approval process similar to the one described below for application systems can accomplish this.

Access and Security Controls

These general controls are concerned with (1) physical protection of computer equipment, software, and data; and (2) loss of assets and information through theft or unauthorized use. Security controls include locating the computer facilities in a separate building or in a secure part of a building. They also include limiting access to the computer facilities through the use of locked doors with authorized personnel being admitted through use of a conventional key, an authorization card, or physical recognition. Control must also be enforced within the computer facility. For example, programmers must not be allowed access to the computer room; this restriction will prevent them from making unauthorized modifications to systems and application programs.

There must also be adequate protection against events such as fire and water damage, electrical problems, and sabotage. Proper construction of computer facilities can minimize the damage from such events. In order to ensure that the entity's operations are not interrupted by such events, the entity should have an operational disaster recovery plan, which may include an off-site backup location for processing critical applications.

Unauthorized access to programs or data can cause loss of assets and information. Physical control over programs and data can be maintained by a separate library function that controls access and use of files. In IT systems with online, real-time database systems and telecommunications technologies, programs and data can be accessed from outside the computer facility. Access controls in IT systems should thus include physical security over remote terminals, authorization controls that limit access only to authorized information, firewalls, user identification controls such as passwords, and data communication controls such as encryption of data. Without such controls, an unauthorized user could access the system, with a resulting loss of assets or a decrease in the reliability of data.

Application Systems Acquisition, Development, and Maintenance Controls

These controls are critical for ensuring the reliability of information processing. The ability to audit accounting systems is greatly improved if (1) the entity follows common policies and procedures for systems acquisition or development; (2) the internal and/or external auditors are involved in the acquisition or development process; and (3) proper user, system operator, and program documentation is provided for each application.[4] For example, having internal or external auditors involved early in the design of the system can ensure that proper controls are built into the system.

The entity should establish written policies and procedures for planning, acquiring or developing, and implementing new systems. Normally, a request for a new system is submitted by the user department to the IT department or an information services committee. A feasibility study may be conducted that includes cost-benefit analysis, hardware and software needs, and the system's impact on current applications and operations. Next, the system is acquired or designed, programmed, tested, and implemented. Last, the entity should prepare good documentation, including flowcharts, file layouts, source code listings, and operator instructions. This level of documentation is necessary for the auditors to understand the accounting systems, including application controls, so that tests of controls and substantive testing can be properly planned and conducted.

The entity must also have strong controls to ensure that once programs are placed into operation, all authorized changes are made and unauthorized changes are prevented. Although not as detailed, the controls for program changes are similar to those followed for new systems development. From the auditor's perspective, the important issue here is whether changes to programs are properly authorized, tested, and implemented.

Application Controls

Application controls apply to the processing of individual accounting applications, such as sales or payroll, and help ensure the completeness and accuracy of transaction processing, authorization, and validity. Although application controls are typically discussed under the categories of input, processing, and output controls, changes in technology have blurred the distinctions among input, processing, and output. For example, many of the data validation checks that were once performed as part of production programs are now accomplished with sophisticated editing routines and intelligent data-entry equipment. As a result, application controls are discussed under the following categories:

- Data capture controls.
- Data validation controls.
- Processing controls.
- Output controls.
- Error controls.

Data Capture Controls

Data capture controls must ensure that (1) all transactions are recorded in the application system; (2) transactions are recorded only once; and (3) rejected transactions are identified, controlled, corrected, and reentered into the system. Thus, data capture controls are concerned primarily with *occurrence, completeness,* and *accuracy assertions.* For example, checking that all transactions are recorded in the system relates to the completeness objective.

There are three ways of capturing data in an information system: (1) source documentation, (2) direct data entry, or (3) a combination of the two. When source documents are present, batch processing is an effective way of controlling

---

[4]Note that external auditor involvement in the information systems acquisition and development process is severely limited when the client is a public company. See Chapter 19 for further details.

data capture. Batching is simply the process of grouping similar transactions for data entry. It is important that each batch be well controlled. This can be accomplished by assigning each batch a unique number and recording it in a batch register or log. A cover sheet should also be attached to each batch with spaces for recording the batch number, the date, the signatures of various persons who processed the batch, and information on errors detected. To ensure complete processing of all transactions in a batch, some type of batch total should be used.

Direct data entry, on the other hand, involves online processing of the data with no source documents. The combination method may involve entry of the data from source documents directly through online processing. If direct data entry or a combination of source documents and direct data entry is used, the system should create a transaction log. The log should contain a detailed record of each transaction, including date and time of entry, terminal and operator identification, and a unique number (such as customer order number).

Data Validation Controls   These controls can be applied at various stages, depending on the entity's IT capabilities, and are mainly concerned with the accuracy assertion. When source documents are batch-processed, the data are taken from source documents and transcribed to tape or disk. The data are then validated by an edit program or by routines that are part of the production programs. When the data are entered directly into off-line storage through an intelligent terminal or directly into a validation program with subsequent (delayed or real-time) processing into the application system, each individual transaction should be subjected to a number of programmed edit checks. Table 6–8 lists common validation tests. For example, a payroll application program may have a limit test that subjects any employee payroll transaction involving more than 80 hours worked to review before processing.

Some entities use turnaround documents to improve data accuracy. *Turnaround documents* are output documents from the application that are used as source documents in later processing. For example, a monthly statement sent to a customer may contain two parts; one part of the monthly statement is kept by the customer, while the other part is returned with the payment. The latter part of the statement contains encoded information that can be processed using various input devices. By using a turnaround document, the entity does not have to reenter the data, thus avoiding data capture and data validation errors.

With direct data (online) entry, accuracy can be improved by special validation routines that may be programmed to *prompt* the data entry personnel. Here the system requests the desired input data and then waits for an acceptable response before requesting the next piece of input data. In many cases, the screen displays

TABLE 6–8	**Common Data Validation Controls**
Data Validation Control	*Description*
Limit test	A test to ensure that a numerical value does not exceed some predetermined value.
Range test	A check to ensure that the value in a field falls within an allowable range of values.
Sequence check	A check to determine if input data are in proper numerical or alphabetical sequence.
Existence (validity) test	A test of an ID number or code by comparison to a file or table containing valid ID numbers or codes.
Field test	A check on a field to ensure that it contains either all numeric or all alphabetic characters.
Sign test	A check to ensure that the data in a field have the proper arithmetic sign.
Check-digit verification	A numeric value computed to provide assurance that the original value was not altered.

the document format with blanks that are completed by data entry personnel. The validation routine should include a completeness test to ensure that all data items are completed before processing. Airline reservation systems and catalog retailers (like EarthWear) that take phone orders use this type of entry system. Entering data over an entity's Web site can be controlled in a similar manner.

Processing Controls   These are controls that ensure proper processing of transactions. In some information systems, many of the controls discussed under data validation may be performed as part of data processing. General controls play an important role in providing assurance about the quality of processing controls. If the entity has strong general controls (such as application systems acquisition, development, and maintenance controls; library controls; personnel practices; and separation of duties), it is likely that programs will be properly written and tested, correct files will be used for processing, and unauthorized access to the system will be limited.

Output Controls   Output includes reports, checks, documents, and other printed or displayed (on terminal screens) information. Controls over output from computer systems are important application controls. The main concern here is that computer output may be distributed or displayed to unauthorized users. A number of controls should be present to minimize the unauthorized use of output. A report distribution log should contain a schedule of when reports are prepared, the names of individuals who are to receive the report, and the date of distribution. Some type of transmittal sheet indicating the intended recipients' names and addresses should be attached to each copy of the output. A release form may be part of the transmittal sheet and should be signed by the individual acknowledging receipt of the report.

The data control group should be responsible for reviewing the output for reasonableness and reconciling the control or batch totals to the output. The user departments should also review the output for completeness and accuracy because they may be the only ones with sufficient knowledge to recognize certain types of errors.

Error Controls   Errors can be identified at any point in the system. While most transaction errors should be identified by data capture and data validation controls, some errors may be identified by processing or output controls. After identification, errors must be corrected and resubmitted to the application system at the correct point in processing. Error controls help ensure that errors are handled appropriately. For example, if a transaction is entered with an incorrect customer number, it should be rejected by a validity test. After the customer number is corrected, it should be resubmitted into the system. Errors that result from processing transactions (such as data entry errors) should be corrected and resubmitted by the data center control group. Errors that occur outside the IT department (like omitted or invalid data) should be corrected by the appropriate user department and resubmitted. This segregation of duties prevents the data center control group from processing invalid transactions.

Advanced Module 2: Flowcharting Techniques

[LO 16]   From the auditor's perspective, a flowchart is a diagrammatic representation of the entity's accounting system. The information systems literature typically discusses three types of flowcharts: document flowcharts, systems flowcharts, and program flowcharts. A *document flowchart* (or data flow diagramming) represents the flow

FIGURE 6-7	Flowcharting Symbols	
Input/Output Symbols	**Processing Symbols**	**Data Flow and Storage Symbols**
Magnetic tape	Processing function	Annotation
Magnetic disk	Manual operation	Off-page connector
Diskette	Auxiliary operation	On-page connector
Online storage	Keying operation	Off-line storage
Input through online device	Decision operation	Communication link
Display		Flow arrow
Punched tape		
Transmittal tape		
Document		

of documents among departments in the entity. A *systems flowchart* extends this approach by including the processing steps, including computer processing, in the flowchart. A *program flowchart* illustrates the operations performed by the computer in executing a program. Flowcharts that are typically used by public accounting firms combine document and systems flowcharting techniques. Such flowcharts show the path from the origination of the transactions to their recording in the accounting journals and ledgers. While there are some general guidelines on preparing flowcharts for documenting accounting systems, the reader should understand that public accounting firms often modify these techniques to correspond with their firm's audit approaches and technologies.

Following are a number of common guidelines that are used in preparing flowcharts.

Symbols

A standard set of symbols is used to represent documents and processes. Figure 6–7 presents examples of the more commonly used symbols. Note that the symbols are divided into three groups: input/output symbols, processing symbols, and data flow and storage symbols.

Organization and Flow

A well-designed flowchart should start in the upper left part of the page and proceed to the lower right part of the page. When it is necessary to show the movement of a document or report back to a previous function, an on-page connector should be used. When the flowchart continues to a subsequent page, the movement of documents or reports can be handled by using an off-page connector. Flow arrows show the movement of documents, records, or information. When processes or activities cannot be fully represented by flowchart symbols, the auditor should supplement the flowchart with written comments. This can be accomplished by using the annotation symbol or just writing the comment directly on the flowchart.

A flowchart is typically designed along the lines of the entity's departments or functions. It is thus important to indicate the delineation of activities between the departments or functions. As shown in Figure 6–4, this can be accomplished by using a vertical dashed line.

KEY TERMS

Application controls. Controls that apply to the processing of specific computer applications and are part of the computer programs used in the accounting system.

Computer-assisted audit techniques (CAATs). Computer programs that allow auditors to test computer files and databases.

Control activities. The policies and procedures that help ensure that management's directives are carried out.

Control deficiency. A deficiency in internal control exists when the design or operation of a control does not allow management or employees, in the normal course of performing their assigned functions, to prevent, or detect and correct misstatements on a timely basis.

Control environment. The tone of an organization, which reflects the overall attitude, awareness, and actions of the board of directors, management, and owners influencing the control consciousness of its people.

Control risk. The risk that material misstatements that could occur will not be prevented, or detected and corrected, by internal controls.

Electronic (Internet) commerce. Business transactions between individuals and organizations that occur without paper documents, using computers and telecommunication networks.

Electronic data interchange. The transmission of business transactions over telecommunications networks.

General controls. Controls that relate to the overall information processing environment and have a pervasive effect on the entity's computer operations.

Internal control. The method by which an entity's board of directors, management, and other personnel provide reasonable assurance about the achievement of objectives in the following categories: (1) reliability of financial reporting, (2) effectiveness and efficiency of operations, and (3) compliance with applicable laws and regulations.

Material weakness. A deficiency, or combination of deficiencies, in internal control, such that there is a reasonable possibility that a material misstatement of the entity's financial statements will not be prevented, or detected and corrected, on a timely basis.

Monitoring of controls. A process that assesses the quality of internal control performance over time.

Reliance strategy. The auditor's decision to rely on the entity's controls, test those controls, and reduce the direct tests of the financial statement accounts.

Significant deficiency. A deficiency, or a combination of deficiencies, in internal control that is less severe than a material weakness, yet important enough to merit attention by those charged with governance.

Substantive strategy. The auditor's decision not to rely on the entity's controls and to audit the related financial statement accounts by relying more on substantive procedures.

www.mhhe.com/ messier7e	Visit the book's Online Learning Center for a multiple-choice quiz that will allow you to assess your understanding of chapter concepts.

REVIEW QUESTIONS

[LO 1]   6-1   What are management's incentives for establishing and maintaining strong internal control? What are the auditor's main concerns with internal control?

[4]   6-2   What are the potential benefits and risks to an entity's internal control from information technology?

[5]   6-3   Describe the five components of internal control.

[5]   6-4   What are the factors that affect the control environment?

[6]   6-5   What are the major differences between a substantive strategy and a reliance strategy when the auditor considers internal control in planning an audit?

[7]   6-6   Why must the auditor obtain an understanding of internal control?

[7]   6-7   What is meant by the concept of reasonable assurance in terms of internal control? What are the inherent limitations of internal control?

[8]   6-8   List the tools that can document the understanding of internal control.

[8,9]   6-9   What are the requirements under auditing standards for documenting the assessed level of control risk?

[11,12]   6-10   What factors should the auditor consider when substantive procedures are to be completed at an interim date? If the auditor conducts substantive procedures at an interim date, what audit procedures would normally be completed for the remaining period?

[14]   6-11   What is the auditor's responsibility for communicating control deficiencies that are severe enough to be considered significant deficiencies or material weaknesses?

MULTIPLE-CHOICE QUESTIONS

[1]   6-12   An auditor's primary consideration regarding an entity's internal controls is whether they
a. Prevent management override.
b. Relate to the control environment.
c. Reflect management's philosophy and operating style.
d. Affect the financial statement assertions.

[1,7]   6-13   Which of the following statements about internal control is correct?
a. A properly maintained internal control system reasonably ensures that collusion among employees cannot occur.
b. The establishment and maintenance of internal control is an important responsibility of the internal auditor.
c. An exceptionally strong internal control system is enough for the auditor to eliminate substantive procedures on a significant account balance.
d. The cost-benefit relationship is a primary criterion that should be considered in designing an internal control system.

[5]   6-14   Which of the following is not a component of an entity's internal control system?
a. Control risk.
b. The entity's risk assessment process.
c. Control activities.
d. Control environment.

[4] 6-15 In which of the following situations would an auditor most likely use a reliance strategy?
a. The client has been slow to update its IT system to reflect changes in billing practices.
b. The auditor hired an IT specialist whose report to the auditor reveals that the specialist did not perform sufficient procedures to allow the auditor to properly assess the effect of the IT system on control risk.
c. A client receives sales orders, bills customers, and receives payment based only on information generated from its IT system—no paper trail is generated.
d. The auditor has been unable to ascertain whether all changes to a client's IT system were properly authorized.

[7] 6-16 After obtaining an understanding of an entity's internal control system, an auditor may set control risk at the maximum level for some assertions because he or she
a. Believes the internal controls are unlikely to be effective.
b. Determines that the pertinent internal control components are not well documented.
c. Performs tests of controls to restrict detection risk to an acceptable level.
d. Identifies internal controls that are likely to prevent material misstatements.

[6,10] 6-17 Regardless of the assessed level of control risk, an auditor would perform some
a. Tests of controls to determine the effectiveness of internal controls.
b. Analytical procedures to verify the design of internal controls.
c. Substantive procedures to restrict detection risk for significant transaction classes.
d. Dual-purpose tests to evaluate both the risk of monetary misstatement and preliminary control risk.

[9] 6-18 Assessing control risk below maximum involves all of the following except
a. Identifying specific controls to rely on.
b. Concluding that controls are ineffective.
c. Performing tests of controls.
d. Analyzing the achieved level of control risk after performing tests of controls.

[10] 6-19 Which of the following audit techniques would most likely provide an auditor with the most assurance about the effectiveness of the operation of a control?
a. Inquiry of client personnel.
b. Reperformance of the control by the auditor.
c. Observation of client personnel.
d. Walkthrough.

[10] 6-20 Audit evidence concerning proper segregation of duties ordinarily is best obtained by
a. Inspection of documents prepared by a third party, but which contain the initials of those applying client controls.
b. Observation by the auditor of the employee performing control activities.
c. Preparation of a flowchart of duties performed and available personnel.
d. Making inquiries of co-workers about the employee who applies control activities.

[13]   6-21   Reports by the service organization's auditor typically
a. Provide reasonable assurance that their financial statements are free of material misstatements.
b. Ensure that the client will not have any misstatements in areas related to the service organization's activities.
c. Ensure that the client is billed correctly.
d. Assess whether the service organization's controls are suitably designed and operating effectively.

[14]   6-22   Significant deficiencies are matters that come to an auditor's attention that should be communicated to an entity's audit committee because they represent
a. Disclosures of information that significantly contradict the auditor's going concern assumption.
b. Material fraud or illegal acts perpetrated by high-level management.
c. Significant deficiencies in the design or operation of the internal control.
d. Manipulation or falsification of accounting records or documents from which financial statements are prepared.

[16]   6-23   An auditor's flowchart of a client's accounting system is a diagrammatic representation that depicts the auditor's
a. Program for tests of controls.
b. Understanding of the system.
c. Understanding of the types of fraud that are probable, given the present system.
d. Documentation of the study and evaluation of the system.

[3,6]   6-24   An auditor anticipates assessing control risk at a low level in an IT environment. Under these circumstances, on which of the following controls would the auditor initially focus?
a. Data capture controls.
b. Application controls.
c. Output controls.
d. General controls.

PROBLEMS

[2,5,6,9]   6-25   An auditor is required to obtain sufficient understanding of each component of an entity's internal control system to plan the audit of the entity's financial statements and to assess control risk for the assertions embodied in the account balance, transaction class, and disclosure components of the financial statements.

Required:
a. Define internal control.
b. For what purpose should an auditor's understanding of the internal control components be used in planning an audit?
c. What are an auditor's documentation requirements concerning an entity's internal control system and the assessed level of control risk?

[5,6]   6-26   Johnson, CPA, has been engaged to audit the financial statements of Rose, Inc., a publicly held retailing company. Before assessing control risk, Johnson is required to obtain an understanding of Rose's control environment.

Required:
a. Identify additional control environment factors (excluding the factors illustrated in the following example) that set the tone of an organization, influencing the control consciousness of its people.

b. For each control environment factor identified in part (a), describe the components and why each component would be of interest to the auditor. Use the following format:

Integrity and Ethical Values

The effectiveness of controls cannot rise above the integrity and ethical values of the people who create, administer, and monitor them. Integrity and ethical values are essential elements of the control environment, affecting the design, administration, and monitoring of other components. Integrity and ethical behavior are the products of the entity's ethical and behavioral standards, how they are communicated, and how they are reinforced in practice.

[4] 6-27 Assume that you are an audit senior in charge of planning the audit of a client that your firm has audited for the previous four years. During the audit planning meeting with the manager and partner in charge of the engagement, the partner noted that the client recently adopted an IT-based accounting system to replace its manual system. The manager and partner have limited experience with IT-based accounting systems and are relying on you to help them understand the audit implications of the client's change. Consequently, they have asked you to respond to a few concerns regarding automated accounting systems.

Required:
a. In previous years, the audit firm has relied heavily on substantive procedures as a source of audit evidence for this client. Given that the client now has changed its accounting system, what are some of the factors that you should consider when deciding whether to move to a reliance strategy?
b. Under what conditions should the audit firm consider engaging an IT specialist to assist in the evaluation? If the firm hires an IT specialist, what information should the auditors ask the specialist to provide?
c. How are the five components of the client's internal control affected by the client's change to an IT-based accounting system?

[8] 6-28 Auditors use various tools to document their understanding of an entity's internal control system, including narrative descriptions, internal control questionnaires, and flowcharts.

Required:
a. Identify the relative strengths of each tool.
b. Briefly describe how the complexity of an entity's internal control system affects the use of the various tools.

[11,12] 6-29 Cook, CPA, has been engaged to audit the financial statements of General Department Stores, Inc., a continuing audit client, which is a chain of medium-sized retail stores. General's fiscal year will end on June 30, 2009, and General's management has asked Cook to issue the auditor's report by August 1, 2009. Cook will not have sufficient time to perform all of the necessary fieldwork in July 2009 but will have time to perform most of the fieldwork as of an interim date, April 30, 2009.

After the accounts are tested at the interim date, Cook will also perform substantive procedures covering the transactions of the final two months of the year. This will be necessary to extend Cook's conclusions to the balance sheet date.

Required:

a. Describe the factors Cook should consider before applying substantive procedures to General's balance sheet accounts at April 30, 2009.
b. For accounts tested at April 30, 2009, describe how Cook should design the substantive procedures covering the balances as of June 30, 2009, and the transactions of the final two months of the year.

(AICPA, adapted)

[14]   6-30   Ken Smith, the partner in charge of the audit of Houghton Enterprises, identified the following significant deficiencies during the audit of the December 31, 2009, financial statements:
1. Controls for granting credit to new customers were not adequate. In particular, the credit department did not adequately check the creditworthiness of customers with an outside credit agency.
2. There were inadequate physical safeguards over the company's inventory. No safeguards prevented employees from stealing high-value inventory parts.

Required:

a. Draft the required communications to the management of Houghton Enterprises, assuming that both items are significant deficiencies.
b. Assume that Smith determined that the second item was a material weakness. How would the required communication change?

DISCUSSION CASE

[5,6]   6-31   Preview Company, a diversified manufacturer, has five divisions that operate throughout the United States and Mexico. Preview has historically allowed its divisions to operate autonomously. Corporate intervention occurred only when planned results were not obtained. Corporate management has high integrity, but the board of directors and audit committee are not very active. Preview has a policy of hiring competent people. The company has a code of conduct, but there is little monitoring of compliance by employees. Management is fairly conservative in terms of accounting principles and practices, but employee compensation packages depend highly on performance. Preview Company does not have an internal audit department, and it relies on your firm to review the controls in each division.

Chip Harris is the general manager of the Fabricator Division. The Fabricator Division produces a variety of standardized parts for small appliances. Harris has been the general manager for the last seven years, and each year he has been able to improve the profitability of the division. He is compensated based largely on the division's profitability. Much of the improvement in profitability has come through aggressive cost cutting, including a substantial reduction in control activities over inventory.

During the last year a new competitor has entered Fabricator's markets and has offered substantial price reductions in order to grab market share. Harris has responded to the competitor's actions by matching the price cuts in the hope of maintaining market share. Harris is very concerned because he cannot see any other areas where costs can be reduced so that the division's growth and profitability can be maintained. If profitability is not maintained, his salary and bonus will be reduced.

Harris has decided that one way to make the division more profitable is to manipulate inventory because it represents a large amount of the division's balance sheet. He also knows that controls over inventory are weak. He views this inventory manipulation as a short-run solution to the profit decline due to the competitor's price cutting. Harris is certain that once the competitor stops cutting prices or goes bankrupt, the misstatements in inventory can be corrected with little impact on the bottom line.

Required:

a. Evaluate the strengths and weaknesses of Preview Company's control environment.

b. What factors in Preview Company's control environment have led to and facilitated Harris's manipulation of inventory?

(Used with permission of the PricewaterhouseCoopers LLP Foundation.)

 HANDS-ON CASES

EarthWear Online	**Control Environment and Internal Control Documentation** Complete remaining sections of the EarthWear control environment and internal control questionnaires. *Visit the book's Online Learning center at www.mhhe.com/messier7e to find a detailed description of the case and to download required materials.* **Tests of Controls (Part A)** Complete controls testing on a sample of EarthWear voucher packets and judgmentally evaluate the results of the tests of controls. (In Part B of this mini-case you are asked to statistically quantify and evaluate the results of tests of controls. Part B is described in Chapter 8.). *Visit the book's Online Learning Center at www.mhhe.com/messier7e to find a detailed description of the case and to download required materials.*

ACL

www.mhhe.com/ messier7e	Visit the book's Online Learning Center for problem material to be completed using the ACL software packaged with your new text.

KAPLAN
CPA Review

www.mhhe.com/ messier7e	**Hardi Risk and Independence** This simulation will test your understanding of types of controls in an IT environment, audit risk, auditor independence, and audit reports. The "Communication" question regarding sampling will be discussed in detail in Chapter 8. *To begin this simulation, visit the book's Online Learning Center.*

CHAPTER 7

LEARNING OBJECTIVES

Upon completion of this chapter you will

[1] Understand management's responsibilities for reporting on internal control under Section 404 of the Sarbanes-Oxley Act.

[2] Understand the auditor's responsibilities for reporting on internal control under Section 404 of the Sarbanes-Oxley Act.

[3] Know the definition of internal control over financial reporting (ICFR).

[4] Be able to explain the differences between a control deficiency, a significant deficiency, and a material weakness.

[5] Understand management's assessment process.

[6] Know how auditors conduct an audit of ICFR.

[7] Understand how the auditor plans the audit of ICFR.

[8] Be able to describe the top-down, risk-based approach that auditors use for an audit of ICFR.

[9] Understand how to test the design and operating effectiveness of controls.

[10] Understand how to evaluate identified control deficiencies.

[11] Understand how remediation affects audit reporting.

[12] Know the written representations that the auditor must obtain from management.

[13] Be familiar with the auditor's documentation requirements.

[14] Understand auditor reporting for the audit of ICFR.

[15] Know the auditor's communication responsibilities on an audit of ICFR.

[16] Understand how to obtain assurance on controls at a service organization that processes transactions for the entity.

[17] Know management's and the auditor's responsibilities for controls that provide reasonable assurance for safeguarding company assets.

[18] Be familiar with computer-assisted audit techniques.

RELEVANT ACCOUNTING AND AUDITING PRONOUNCEMENTS

FASB ASC Topic 450, Contingencies

AU 314, Understanding the Entity and Its Environment and Assessing the Risks of Material Misstatement

AU 316, Consideration of Fraud in a Financial Statement Audit

AU 322, The Auditor's Consideration of the Internal Audit Function in an Audit of Financial Statements

AU 324, Service Organizations

COSO, *Internal Control—Integrated Framework* (New York: AICPA, 1992)

COSO, *Enterprise Risk Management—Integrated Framework* (New York: AICPA, 2004)

COSO, *Guidance on Monitoring Internal Control Systems* (New York: AICPA, 2009)

PCAOB Auditing Standard No. 3, Audit Documentation (AS3)

PCAOB Auditing Standard No. 4, Reporting on Whether a Previously Reported Material Weakness Continues to Exist (AS4)

PCAOB Auditing Standard No. 5, An Audit of Internal Control Over Financial Reporting That Is Integrated with An Audit of Financial Statements (AS5)

PCAOB Proposed Auditing Standards Related to the Auditor's Assessment of and Response to Risk, PCAOB Release No. 2008-006 (October 21, 2008)

Securities and Exchange Commission, Commission Guidance Regarding Management's Report on Internal Control Over Financial Reporting Under Section 13(a) or 15(d) of the Securities Exchange Act of 1934. (SEC 2007)

Auditing Internal Control over Financial Reporting

Major Phases of an Audit

Client acceptance/
continuance and establishing
an understanding with the client
(Chapter 5)

Preliminary engagement
activities
(Chapter 5)

Plan the audit
(Chapters 3 and 5)

Consider and audit
internal control
(Chapters 6 and 7)

Audit business processes
and related accounts
(e.g., revenue generation)
(Chapters 10–16)

Complete the audit
(Chapter 17)

Evaluate results and
issue audit report
(Chapters 1 and 18)

The Sarbanes-Oxley Act of 2002 was passed in response to a series of business scandals (e.g., Enron and WorldCom). A common question being asked at the time was, "Why did these companies' systems of internal control fail to prevent these frauds?" Failure of internal control over financial reporting was one of the major concerns addressed by Congress in the Sarbanes-Oxley Act, which imposes unprecedented requirements on both management and auditors of public companies. Section 404 of the Act requires that management report on the effectiveness of its internal control over financial reporting (ICFR) and that its auditor also provide an attestation on the effectiveness of ICFR based on standards issued by the Public Company Accounting Oversight Board (PCAOB).

In 2004, the PCAOB issued Auditing Standard No. 2, An Audit of Internal Control over Financial Reporting Performed in Conjunction with an Audit of Financial Statements (AS2), to provide guidance for the audit engagements referred to in Section 404. After the issuance of AS2, the SEC and the PCAOB monitored the implementation of its requirements. Based on this monitoring, the SEC issued guidance for management and the PCAOB issued AS5, which superseded AS2, for auditors. These documents require that management and their auditors follow a top-down, risk-based approach to evaluating ICFR. While the cost of compliance has been high, evidence exists that the audit of ICFR has produced significant benefits. This includes a reemphasis on corporate governance and controls, and higher-quality financial reporting.

This chapter covers what management must do in order to issue a report that the entity's ICFR is effective and how the entity's auditor performs an audit regarding the effectiveness of ICFR. The material covered in this chapter applies to companies subject to the reporting requirements of Section 404 of the Sarbanes-Oxley Act of 2002 (i.e., most public companies). 🌐

Management Responsibilities under Section 404

✥ [LO 1]   Section 404 of the Sarbanes-Oxley Act requires management of a publicly traded company to issue a report that accepts responsibility for establishing and maintaining adequate internal control over financial reporting (ICFR) and also assert whether ICFR is effective as of the end of the fiscal year. Note that the Act provides no guidance on what constitutes adequate internal control. Thus, the SEC and PCAOB were left to address the issue of adequacy. Further, the assessment is to be made as of a specific point in time—that is, "as of" the end of the fiscal year. Therefore, management's assessment does not cover the entire year. This has implications for the timing of both management's and the auditor's work and the handling of any control deficiencies discovered during the year. Most importantly, the "as-of" nature of the assessment in many cases allows management to remediate deficiencies discovered prior to year-end and still receive an unqualified opinion on ICFR. It also has implications for the use of the auditor's internal control work for financial statement audit purposes.

Management must comply with the following requirements in order for its registered public accounting firm (external auditor) to complete an audit of ICFR:

- Accept responsibility for the effectiveness of the entity's ICFR.
- Evaluate the effectiveness of the entity's ICFR using suitable control criteria.
- Support the evaluation with sufficient evidence, including documentation.
- Present a written assessment regarding the effectiveness of the entity's ICFR as of the end of the entity's most recent fiscal year.

Each of these steps is discussed below. Recognize, however, that the second and third bullets require a substantial investment of time, energy, and money on the part of the entity.

Auditor Responsibilities under Section 404 and AS5

✥ [LO 2]   Section 404 requires the entity's auditor to audit management's assertion about the effectiveness of ICFR. AS5 states that the auditor must conduct the audits of financial statements and ICFR in an integrated way because each audit provides the auditor with information relevant to the evaluation of the results of the other. AS5 makes it clear that while the two audits are to be integrated, they have different objectives. The auditor's objective in an audit of ICFR is "to express an opinion on the effectiveness of the company's internal control over financial reporting" (AS5, ¶3), while the objective in a financial statement audit is to express an opinion on whether the financial statements are fairly stated in accordance with generally accepted accounting principles (GAAP).

To form a basis for expressing an opinion on the effectiveness of ICFR, the auditor must plan and perform the audit to obtain *reasonable assurance* about whether the entity maintained, in all material respects, effective internal control as of the date specified in management's assessment. Reasonable assurance in this context recognizes that no system of internal control is perfect and that there is a remote likelihood that material misstatements will not be prevented, or detected on a timely basis, even if controls are, in fact, effective (AS5, ¶3). While reasonable assurance is not absolute assurance, in this context it indicates a high level of assurance.

Later in the chapter we discuss how the auditor applies the concepts of likelihood and materiality in an audit of ICFR.

Practice INSIGHT	Before deciding whether a significant deficiency or material weakness exists, AS5 requires the auditor to evaluate the effectiveness of compensating controls. To have a mitigating effect, the compensating control should operate at a level of precision that would prevent or detect a misstatement that could be material (AS5, ¶68).

Management's Assessment Process

[LO 5] In order to issue a report on the effectiveness of internal control, management needs to first design and implement an effective system of ICFR and then develop an ongoing assessment process. To assist management, the SEC issued guidance for evaluating and assessing ICFR. We do not provide detailed coverage of the SEC's guidance since this chapter focuses primarily on the external auditor's responsibilities. The reader should refer to the SEC's guidance for more detail.

The SEC's guidance provides a top-down, risk-based approach for management to follow in evaluating and assessing ICFR. The purpose of management's evaluation of ICFR is to provide management with a reasonable basis for its assessment as to whether any material weaknesses in ICFR exist as of the end of the period. The evaluation process has three steps:

1. Identify financial reporting risks and related controls.
2. Evaluate evidence about the operating effectiveness of ICFR.
3. Consider which locations to include in the evaluation.

Once the evaluation process is complete, management must address its reporting responsibilities.

Framework Used by Management to Conduct Its Assessment

Management is required to base its assessment of the effectiveness of the entity's ICFR on a suitable, recognized control framework established by a body of experts that follows due-process procedures. In the United States, most entities use the framework developed by COSO in the early 1990s (COSO, *Internal Control—Integrated Framework*). Some may use the new COSO, Enterprise Risk Management framework (*Enterprise Risk Management—Integrated Framework*), which subsumes and builds on the COSO internal control framework. Other suitable frameworks have been published in other countries. Review Chapter 6 for a discussion of the COSO framework.

Identify Financial Reporting Risks and Related Controls

Management must first identify and assess *financial reporting risks;* that is, the risk that a misstatement could result in a material misstatement of the financial statements. How management identifies financial reporting risks will vary based on the characteristics of the entity. Such characteristics include the size, complexity, and organizational structure of the entity and its processes and financial reporting environment.

Management then identifies controls that are in place to address the financial reporting risks. In addition to specific controls that address financial reporting risks, management also evaluates whether there are controls in place to address entity-level and other pervasive elements of ICFR. Entity-level controls can have a pervasive effect on the entity's ability to meet the COSO control criteria. Table 7–1 presents examples of entity-level controls.

TABLE 7–1	Examples of Entity-Level Controls

- Controls within the control environment (e.g., tone at the top, assignment of authority and responsibility, consistent policies and procedures, and companywide programs, such as codes of conduct and fraud prevention, that apply to all locations and business units);
- Controls over management override;
- The entity's risk assessment process;
- Centralized processing and controls, including shared service environments;
- Controls to monitor results of operations;
- Controls to monitor other controls, including activities of the internal audit function, the audit committee, and self-assessment programs;
- Controls over period-end financial reporting process; and
- Policies that address significant business control and risk management practices.

Source: AS5, ¶24.

TABLE 7–2	Controls Typically Included for Testing

- Controls over initiating, authorizing, recording, processing, and reporting significant accounts and disclosures and related assertions embodied in the financial statements.
- Controls over the selection and application of accounting policies that are in conformity with GAAP.
- Antifraud programs and controls.
- Controls, including IT general controls, on which other controls are dependent.
- Controls over significant nonroutine and nonsystematic transactions, such as accounts involving judgments and estimates.
- Entity-level controls (see Table 7–1).

Management should then consider the effect of information technology (IT) general controls that are necessary for proper and consistent operation of other technology-based controls designed to address financial reporting risks. Lastly, management must obtain and document reasonable evidential support for its assessment.

Evaluate Evidence About the Operating Effectiveness of ICFR

The evaluation of the operating effectiveness of a control considers whether the control is operating as designed and whether the person performing the control possesses the necessary authority and competence to perform the control effectively. Management should focus its evaluation on areas that pose the highest risk to ICFR. As the risk of control failure increases, management will need more evidence to support its conclusion about the operating effectiveness of the control. Table 7–2 shows controls that are typically included for testing.

Evidence on the operating effectiveness of a control may be obtained from direct testing of the control, ongoing monitoring, or both. Direct tests of controls are usually performed on a periodic basis by individuals with a high degree of objectivity (e.g., internal auditors) with respect to the control being tested. Ongoing monitoring includes self-assessment procedures and procedures to analyze performance measures (Key Performance Indicators) designed to track the performance of the control.

Management's assessment must be supported by evidence that provides reasonable support for its assessment. The nature and extent of this evidence will vary based on the assessed level of ICFR risk for controls over each of its financial reporting elements.

Consider Which Locations to Include in the Evaluation

Management should generally include all of its locations and business units when considering financial reporting risks. However, the approach followed by management in choosing which locations to include in its assessment of internal control is a function of the presence of entity-level controls and the financial reporting risk at the individual locations or business units. If financial reporting risks are adequately addressed by entity-level controls, then the evaluation approach for the locations and business units would focus on those entity-level controls. When controls that are necessary to address financial reporting risks operate at more than one location or business unit, management needs to evaluate evidence of the operation of the controls at the individual locations or business units.

If management determines that financial reporting risks for the controls that operate at individual locations or business units are low, management may rely on self-assessment processes in conjunction with entity-level controls for their assessment. When management determines that the financial reporting risks for the controls at an individual location are high, management will normally need to directly test the operation of the controls at that location. Take a moment and think about how a large multinational corporation would accomplish such a task.

Reporting Considerations

In determining its reporting responsibilities, management first evaluates the severity of the control deficiencies identified. Similar to the approach taken by the auditor, management considers the likelihood of and degree to which the financial statements could be misstated by the control failure. If management determines that no material weaknesses exist, they can conclude that the company's ICFR was effective. Exhibit 7–1 provides an example management report.

EXHIBIT 7–1

An Example of Management's Report on Internal Control over Financial Reporting

Management is responsible for establishing and maintaining adequate internal control over financial reporting of the company. Internal control over financial reporting is a process designed to provide reasonable assurance regarding the reliability of financial reporting and the preparation of financial statements for external purposes in accordance with accounting principles generally accepted in the United States of America.

The company's internal control over financial reporting includes those policies and procedures that (i) pertain to the maintenance of records that, in reasonable detail, accurately and fairly reflect the transactions and dispositions of the assets of the company; (ii) provide reasonable assurance that transactions are recorded as necessary to permit preparation of financial statements in accordance with accounting principles generally accepted in the United States of America, and that receipts and expenditures of the company are being made only in accordance with authorizations of management and directors of the company; and (iii) provide reasonable assurance regarding prevention or timely detection of unauthorized acquisition, use, or disposition of the company's assets that could have a material effect on the financial statements.

Because of its inherent limitations, internal control over financial reporting may not prevent or detect misstatements. Also, projections of any evaluation of effectiveness to future periods are subject to the risk that controls may become inadequate because of changes in conditions, or that the degree of compliance with the policies or procedures may deteriorate.

Management conducted an evaluation of the effectiveness of internal control over financial reporting based on the framework in Internal Control—Integrated Framework issued by the Committee of Sponsoring Organizations of the Treadway Commission (COSO). Based on this evaluation, management concluded that the company's internal control over financial reporting was effective as of December 31, 2008.

Samuel J. Palmisano
Chairman of the Board,
President and Chief Executive Officer
February 24, 2009

Mark Loughridge
Senior Vice President,
Chief Financial Officer
February 24, 2009

Source: IBM's Form 10K

EXHIBIT 7–2	An Example of the Disclosure of an Material Weakness by AIG's Management

As of December 31, 2007, controls over the AIGFP super senior credit default swap portfolio valuation process and oversight thereof were not effective. AIG had insufficient resources to design and carry out effective controls to prevent or detect errors and to determine appropriate disclosures on a timely basis with respect to the processes and models introduced in the fourth quarter of 2007. As a result, AIG had not fully developed its controls to assess, on a timely basis, the relevance to its valuation of all third party information. Also, controls to permit the appropriate oversight and monitoring of the AIGFP super senior credit default swap portfolio valuation process, including timely sharing of information at the appropriate levels of the organization, did not operate effectively. As a result, controls over the AIGFP super senior credit default swap portfolio valuation process and oversight thereof were not adequate to prevent or detect misstatements in the accuracy of management's fair value estimates and disclosures on a timely basis, resulting in adjustments for purposes of AIG's December 31, 2007, consolidated financial statements. In addition, this deficiency could result in a misstatement in management's fair value estimates or disclosures that could be material to AIG's annual or interim consolidated financial statements that would not be prevented or detected on a timely basis.

   Solely as a result of the material weakness in internal control over the fair value valuation of the AIGFP super senior credit default swap portfolio described above, AIG management has concluded that, as of December 31, 2007, AIG's internal control over financial reporting was not effective based on the criteria in *Internal Control — Integrated Framework* issued by the COSO.

Source: AIG's Form 10K

If a control deficiency is determined to be a material weakness, management must disclose the material weakness in its assessment of the effectiveness of ICFR on an annual basis. The disclosure about the material weakness(es) should include the following:

- The nature of the material weakness(es).
- Its impact on the company's financial reporting and its ICFR.
- Management's current plans, if any, for remediating the material weakness.

Exhibit 7–2 presents an example of management's disclosure of a material weakness. Any control deficiency that is considered a significant deficiency or material weakness should be reported to the audit committee and the external auditor.

Management's assessment process involves special consideration of two topics. These topics must also be considered by the auditor during the audit of ICFR. The two topics are

- Service organizations.
- Safeguarding assets.

Advanced Module 1 at the end of the chapter discusses each of these topics in detail.

Management's Documentation

The SEC's guidance allows considerable flexibility to management in how it documents reasonable support for its assessment. However, reasonable support would include the basis for management's assessment and conclusion. Such documentation would include the design of the controls management has placed in operation to adequately address identified financial reporting risks, including the entity-level and other pervasive elements necessary for effective ICFR. The guidance does not require management to identify and document every control in a process or to document the business processes impacting ICFR. Instead, documentation should focus on those controls management concludes are adequate to address the entity's financial reporting risks.

Documentation of ICFR may take many forms, such as paper, electronic files, or other media. It also includes a variety of information, such as policy manuals, process models, flowcharts, job descriptions, documents, and forms.

Performing an Audit of ICFR

[LO 6]   While the audit of ICFR and the audit of financial statements have different objectives, the auditor must plan and perform the audit work to achieve the objectives of both audits as an integrated audit. In planning the integrated audit, the auditor should design tests of controls to accomplish the objectives of both audits simultaneously. The purpose of tests of controls in an audit of ICFR is to provide evidence on the effectiveness of the entity's controls over financial reporting as of the end of the reporting period. The purpose of tests of controls in an audit of financial statements is to assist the auditor in assessing control risk, which in turn affects the nature, timing, and extent of the auditor's substantive tests.

The auditor should incorporate the results of tests of controls in the audit of ICFR into the tests of controls for the audit of the financial statements and should use those results for determining the nature, timing, and extent of substantive procedures. Similarly, the auditor should consider the results of substantive procedures on the conclusions about the effectiveness of ICFR. For example, if a misstatement is detected by substantive procedures, the auditor should consider how and why the controls failed to detect the misstatement and whether the control deficiency might affect the opinion on the audit of ICFR.

Figure 7–2 shows the steps involved in performing an audit of ICFR. While Figure 7–2 suggests a sequential process, the audit of ICFR involves an iterative process of gathering, updating, and analyzing information.

FIGURE 7–2	Steps in the Audit of ICFR

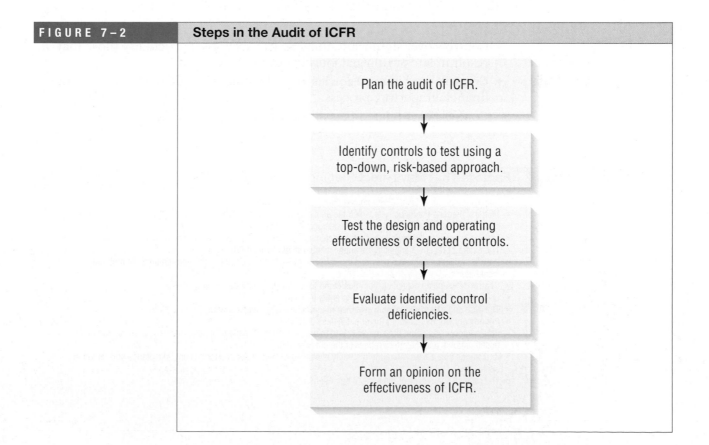

Plan the audit of ICFR.

Identify controls to test using a top-down, risk-based approach.

Test the design and operating effectiveness of selected controls.

Evaluate identified control deficiencies.

Form an opinion on the effectiveness of ICFR.

Planning the Audit of ICFR

✎ [LO 7]   The process for planning an audit of ICFR should be integrated with the planning of the financial statement audit. Table 7–3 contains some of the factors that may affect the planning of an audit of ICFR. A number of these factors are similar to those discussed in Chapter 5.

In planning an audit of ICFR, the auditor considers the following activities:

- The role of risk assessment and the risk of fraud.
- Scaling the audit.
- Using the work of others.
- Materiality.

The Role of Risk Assessment and the Risk of Fraud

A major premise of AS5 is that risk assessment underlies the entire audit of ICFR. In other words, there should be a direct relationship between the risk that a material weakness could exist in a particular area of the internal controls of the entity and the amount of audit work that is devoted to that area. Thus, the auditor should devote more attention to areas that have a high risk of a material weakness. This process is very similar to the risk assessment process followed by the auditor in the audit of financial statements (refer to Chapter 3).

A major part of risk assessment is assessing the risk of fraud. In considering the risk of fraud for the ICFR portion of the integrated audit, the auditor should refer to the work done as part of the audit of financial statements to comply with SAS No. 99, Consideration of Fraud in a Financial Statement Audit (AU 316). The auditor should evaluate the risk of material misstatement due to fraud and the risk of management override of controls. AS5 (¶14) points out that the following controls might address the risk of fraud and management override:

- Controls over significant, unusual transactions, particularly those that result in late or unusual journal entries.
- Controls over journal entries and adjustments made in the period-end financial reporting process.
- Controls over related-party transactions.

TABLE 7–3	Factors That May Affect Planning an Audit of ICFR

- Knowledge of the entity's ICFR obtained during other engagements.
- Matters affecting the industry in which the entity operates, such as financial reporting practices, economic conditions, laws and regulations, and technological changes.
- Matters relating to the entity's business, including its organization, operating characteristics, and capital structure.
- The extent of recent changes in the entity, its operations, or its ICFR.
- Preliminary judgments about materiality, risk, and other factors relating to the determination of material weaknesses.
- Control deficiencies previously communicated to the audit committee or management.
- Legal or regulatory matters of which the entity is aware.
- The type and extent of available evidence related to the effectiveness of the entity's ICFR.
- Preliminary judgments about the effectiveness of ICFR.
- Public information about the entity relevant to the evaluation of the likelihood of material financial statement misstatements and the effectiveness of the entity's ICFR.
- Knowledge about risks related to the entity evaluated as part of the auditor's client acceptance and retention evaluation.
- The relative complexity of the entity's operations.

Source: AS5, ¶9.

- Controls related to significant management estimates.
- Controls that mitigate incentives for, and pressures on, management to falsify or inappropriately manage financial results.

Scaling the Audit

AS5 (¶13) specifies that the "size and complexity of the company, its business processes, and business units, may affect the way in which the company achieves many of its control objectives." Allowing the concepts behind achieving effective internal control to be appropriately scaled to companies of different size and complexity is an extension of the risk-based approach required by AS5. AS5 explicitly recognizes and allows for the idea that a small, less-complex entity might achieve its control objectives differently from a large, complex entity.

Using the Work of Others

AS5 allows the auditor to use the work performed by, or receive direct assistance from, internal auditors, company personnel, and third parties working for management or the audit committee.

If the work of others is to be used, the auditor should assess the competence and objectivity of the persons whose work will be used. AS5 refers to AU 322, The Auditor's Consideration of the Internal Audit Function in an Audit of Financial Statements, for relevant guidance in assessing competence and objectivity. We previously discussed this standard in Chapter 5. Table 5–2 provides the factors for assessing competence and objectivity.

The risk associated with the control being tested also plays a role in using the work of others. As the risk associated with the control increases, the auditor should perform more of the work. For example, the auditor will rely less on the work of others for a control relating to transactions that involve subjective judgments or that are highly susceptible to manipulation than for a control that relates to routine, objective transactions.

Materiality

In planning the audit of ICFR and determining the magnitude of a control deficiency, the auditor should use the same materiality considerations that were used for planning the audit of financial statements. These considerations were covered in Chapter 3.

Using a Top-Down Approach

[LO 8]

The auditor should use a top-down approach to the audit of ICFR. As outlined in Figure 7–3, the auditor first identifies the entity-level controls. Next the auditor identifies the significant accounts and disclosures, and understands where the likely sources of misstatements occur. Based on this information, the auditor selects which controls to test.

Identify Entity-Level Controls

Table 7–1 contains a list of entity-level controls. Entity-level controls can have a pervasive effect on the entity's ability to meet the COSO control criteria, and thus the auditor must test their effectiveness. The auditor's evaluation of the entity-level controls can affect the extent of testing performed on other controls. AS5 (¶23) points out that entity-level controls vary in nature and precision.

Two categories of entity-level controls require evaluation by the auditor: (1) the control environment; and (2) the period-end financial reporting process.

FIGURE 7–3	Top-Down, Risk-Based Approach to the Audit of ICFR

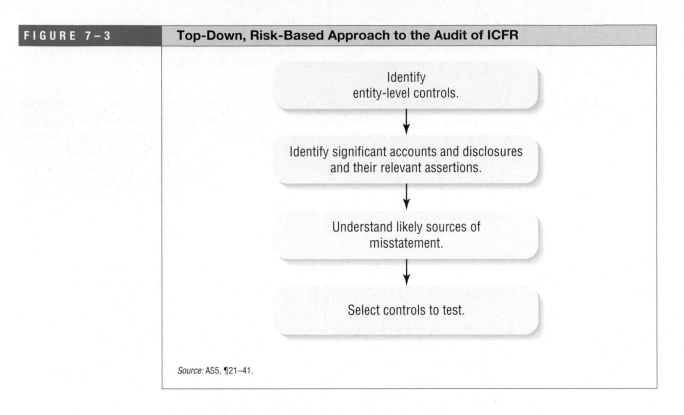

Source: AS5, ¶21–41.

Control Environment

Control Environment   Because of its importance to effective ICFR, the auditor must evaluate the control environment. In particular, the auditor should assess whether

- Management's philosophy and operating style promote effective ICFR.
- Sound integrity and ethical values, particularly of top management, are developed and understood.
- The Board or audit committee understands and exercises oversight responsibility over financial reporting and internal control.

Period-End Financial Reporting Process   The period-end financial reporting process is important to the auditor's opinion on ICFR and to financial statement reporting. The period-end financial reporting process controls include procedures used to enter transaction totals into the general ledger; select and apply accounting policies; initiate, authorize, record, and process period-end journal entries in the general ledger; record recurring and nonrecurring adjustments to the annual and quarterly financial statements; and prepare annual and quarterly financial statements and related disclosures. Even though these controls operate after the "as of" year-end reporting date, they are used to support the auditor's "as of" date opinion.

The auditor's evaluation of the period-end financial reporting process includes the inputs, procedures performed, and outputs of the processes the company uses to produce its annual and quarterly financial statements. The auditor should also consider the extent of IT involvement in each period-end financial reporting process, who participates from management, the number of locations involved, types of adjusting and consolidating entries, and the nature and extent of the oversight of the process by management, the board of directors, and the audit committee. The auditor's understanding of the entity's period-end financial reporting process and how it interrelates with the entity's other significant processes helps the auditor identify and test controls that are most relevant to financial statement risks. For example, it is common for entities to manually compile summary information for financial reporting purposes based on detailed financial information taken from accounting information systems. In some cases, entities use hundreds or even thousands of computer spreadsheets to summarize massive amounts of detailed data into financial statement accounts.

Due to the nature of spreadsheets and the operating environment in a typical organization, there is a heightened risk that controls over spreadsheets will not be effective. The external auditor must evaluate management's IT spreadsheet policy to determine the risks associated with its spreadsheet information. Because the data in spreadsheets can be easily changed, they are subject to increased inherent risk (input errors, logic errors, interface errors, etc.). The level of control over a spreadsheet should be relative to its use, complexity, and required reliability of the information. Ideally, the IT department should manage spreadsheets, so that there is central control, but this is often not the case.

Identifying Significant Accounts and Disclosures and Their Relevant Assertions

The auditor should identify significant accounts and disclosures and their relevant assertions. Relevant assertions are financial statement assertions (see Chapter 4) that have a reasonable possibility of containing a misstatement that would cause the financial statements to be materially misstated. To identify significant accounts and disclosures and their relevant assertions, the auditor uses the following risk factors:

- Size and composition of the account;
- Susceptibility to misstatement due to errors or fraud;
- Volume of activity, complexity, and homogeneity of the individual transactions processed through the account or reflected in the disclosure;
- Nature of the account or disclosure;
- Accounting and reporting complexities associated with the account or disclosure;
- Exposure to losses in the account;
- Possibility of significant contingent liabilities arising from the activities reflected in the account or disclosure;
- Existence of related-party transactions in the account; and
- Changes from the prior period in account or disclosure characteristics (AS5, ¶29).

The risk factors that the auditor evaluates for an audit of ICFR are essentially the same as those used in the audit of financial statements.

Understanding Likely Sources of Misstatements

In order to understand the likely sources of potential misstatements, the auditor needs to do the following:

- Understand the flow of transactions related to the relevant assertions, including how these transactions are initiated, authorized, processed, and recorded;
- Identify the points within the entity's processes at which a misstatement—including a misstatement due to fraud—could arise that, individually or in combination with other misstatements, would be material;

- Identify the controls that management has implemented to address these potential misstatements; and
- Identify the controls that management has implemented over the prevention or timely detection of unauthorized acquisition, use, or disposition of the company's assets that could result in a material misstatement of the financial statements (AS5, ¶34).

Performing walkthroughs is often the best way to identify sources of misstatements. To perform a walkthrough, the auditor traces a transaction from origination through the entity's processes and information system until it is reflected in the entity's financial reports. It should encompass the entire information flow through the subprocesses of initiating, authorizing, recording, processing, and reporting individual transactions for each of the significant processes identified. Walkthroughs help the auditor in confirming his or her understanding of control design and transaction process flow, as well as in determining whether all points at which misstatements could occur have been identified, evaluating the effectiveness of the design of controls, and confirming whether controls have been placed in operation.

In performing the walkthrough, the auditor should make inquiries of relevant personnel involved in significant aspects of the process or controls. The auditor should use probing questions to determine client personnel's understanding of what is required by the controls and determine whether the processing procedures are performed as understood and on a timely basis. These questions typically include inquiries on how exceptions are handled, how "hand-offs" are properly accomplished between previous and succeeding processes, and who performs the control when an employee is sick or absent. These questions help corroborate the client's design and transaction flow documentation. Walkthrough inquiries should include questions designed to identify abuse of controls (i.e., inappropriate management override) or indicators of fraud.

Select Controls to Test

The auditor does not need to test all controls—only those controls that are important to the auditor's conclusion about whether the entity's controls sufficiently address the assessed risk of misstatement to each relevant assertion, often referred to as key controls. Identifying the controls to be tested is a subjective task that requires professional judgment. Table 7–4 provides a list of factors that the auditor should consider in deciding which controls to test. The auditor should evaluate whether to test preventive controls, detective controls, or a combination of both. For example, a monthly reconciliation (a detective control) might detect an out-of-balance situation resulting from an unauthorized transaction being initiated

TABLE 7–4	Factors Commonly Considered When Identifying Controls to Test

- Points at which errors or fraud could occur.
- The nature of the controls implemented by management.
- The significance of each control in achieving the objectives of the control criteria and whether more than one control achieves a particular objective or whether more than one control is necessary to achieve a particular objective.
- The risk that the controls might not be operating effectively. Factors that affect whether the control might not be operating effectively include the following:
  — Whether there have been changes in the volume or nature of transactions that might adversely affect control design or operating effectiveness;
  — Whether there have been changes in the design of controls;
  — The degree to which the control relies on the effectiveness of other controls (e.g., the control environment or IT general controls);
  — Whether there have been changes in key personnel who perform the control or monitor its performance;
  — Whether the control relies on performance by an individual or is automated; and
  — The complexity of the control.

due to an ineffective authorization procedure (a preventive control). When determining whether the detective control is effective, the auditor should evaluate whether the detective control is sufficient to achieve the control objective to which the preventive control relates.

In selecting the controls to test, the auditor must make decisions similar to management in deciding which locations or business units to include for testing. Thus, the choice of which locations to include in the assessment of internal control is based on the presence of entity-level controls and the financial reporting risk at an individual location or business unit.

Test the Design and Operating Effectiveness of Controls

Evaluating Design Effectiveness of Controls

[LO 9]

Controls are effectively designed when they prevent or detect errors or fraud that could result in material misstatements in the financial statements. Once key controls are identified, the auditor evaluates design effectiveness through inquiry, observation, walkthroughs, inspection of relevant documentation, and subjective evaluations of whether the controls are likely to prevent or detect errors or fraud that could result in misstatements assuming they are operated as prescribed by qualified persons. The procedures performed by the auditor to test and evaluate design effectiveness might in some cases also provide some evidence about operating effectiveness.

Testing and Evaluating Operating Effectiveness of Controls

An auditor evaluates the operating effectiveness of a control by determining whether the control is operating as designed and whether the person performing the control possesses the necessary authority and competence to perform the control effectively. In testing the operating effectiveness of controls, the auditor needs to consider the scope (nature, timing, and extent) of testing. For each control selected for testing, the evidence necessary to persuade the auditor that the control is effective depends on the risk that a material weakness would result. As the risk associated with the control being tested increases, the quality and/or quantity of the evidence that the auditor should obtain also increases. Table 7–5 presents the factors that affect the risk associated with a control.

Nature of Testing Tests of controls for operating effectiveness include such procedures as inquiry of appropriate personnel, inspection of relevant documentation, observation of the entity's operations, and reperformance of the application of the control. In many instances, a combination of these procedures is necessary to ensure that a control is operating effectively.

TABLE 7–5	Factors That Affect the Risk Associated with a Control
	• The nature and materiality of misstatements that the control is intended to prevent or detect; • The inherent risk associated with the related account(s) and assertion(s); • Whether there have been changes in the volume or nature of transactions that might adversely affect control design or operating effectiveness; • Whether the account has a history of errors; • The effectiveness of entity-level controls, especially controls that monitor other controls; • The nature of the control and the frequency with which it operates; • The degree to which the control relies on the effectiveness of other controls; • The competence of the personnel who perform the control or monitor its performance and whether there have been changes in key personnel who perform the control or monitor its performance; • Whether the control relies on performance by an individual or is automated; and • The complexity of the control and the significance of the judgments that must be made in connection with its operation.

Inquiry is used extensively throughout the audit of internal control. Because inquiry alone does not provide sufficient evidence to support the operating effectiveness of a control, the auditor should perform additional tests of controls. For example, suppose an entity implements a control whereby its sales manager reviews and investigates a report listing invoices with unusually high or low gross margins. Inquiry of the sales manager as to whether he or she investigates discrepancies would not be sufficient evidence to ensure that the control is working effectively. The auditor should corroborate the sales manager's responses by performing other procedures, such as inspecting reports generated by the performance of the control and evaluating whether appropriate actions were taken.

The type of control often affects the nature of control testing the auditor can perform. For example, an entity may have a control that requires a signature (digital or otherwise) on a voucher package to indicate that the signer approved it. However, the presence of a signature does not necessarily mean that the person carefully reviewed the package before signing. As a result, the quality of the evidence regarding the effective operation of the control might not be sufficiently persuasive. In order to gain more persuasive evidence, the auditor could re-perform the control by checking the voucher package for accuracy and completeness, essentially repeating the steps taken to initially perform the control. The auditor might also inquire of the person responsible for approving voucher packages regarding what he or she looks for when approving packages and ask to see documentation of the errors that have been found and rectified in the recent past.

Timing of Tests of Controls   The auditor must perform tests of controls over a period of time that is adequate to determine whether the significant controls are operating effectively as of the date indicated in management's report. The period of time over which the auditor performs tests of controls will vary with the nature of the controls and the frequency with which they are applied. Some controls operate continuously (e.g., controls over the processing of routine sales transactions), while other controls operate only occasionally (e.g., monthly bank reconciliations). Routine transactions typically involve routine processing controls, such as verification of data entry, edit checks and validation controls, completeness controls, and so forth. For nonroutine transactions, especially those involving estimation, review and approval controls are usually considered more critical. In some cases, controls may operate after the "as of" date specified in management's report. For example, controls over a December 31 period-end financial reporting process normally operate in January of the following year.

In many instances, the auditor obtains evidence about the operating effectiveness of controls at an interim date for reporting on internal control even though the auditor's report on the effectiveness of internal control is for an "as of" date. For example, the auditor might test controls over the revenue process for the first nine months of the year. The auditor will then need to determine what additional evidence is needed concerning the operating effectiveness of the controls for the remaining three-month period. In deciding what additional evidence is needed, the auditor considers the specific controls tested prior to the "as of" date and the results of those tests, the sufficiency of the evidence of effectiveness obtained, the length of the remaining period, and the possibility that there have been significant changes in internal control subsequent to the interim date (AS5, ¶56). For controls over significant nonroutine transactions, controls over accounts or processes with a high degree of subjectivity or judgment in measurement, or controls over the recording of period-end adjustments, the auditor should perform tests closer to the as of date.

If management implements changes to the entity's controls to make them more effective or efficient prior to the date specified in management's report, the auditor might not need to evaluate the superseded controls.

Extent of Tests of Controls AS5 does not provide any detailed guidance on what constitutes a sufficient sample for testing the operating effectiveness of the control. This is left to the auditor as a matter of professional judgment.

The auditor should consider the following factors when deciding on the extent of testing:

- *Nature of the control.* Manual controls should be subjected to more extensive testing than automated controls in view of the greater variability inherent in controls involving people.
- *Frequency of operation.* Generally, the more frequently a manual control operates, the greater the number of operations of the control the auditor should test.
- *Importance of the control.* The more important the control, the more extensively it should be tested.

Most public accounting firms have developed firm-wide guidance for the sample sizes used to test for various types of controls. Chapter 8 provides guidance on using statistical and nonstatistical sampling for tests of controls.

AS5 provides guidance on incorporating knowledge obtained from prior years' audits into the decision-making process for determining the nature, timing, and extent of testing for the current year audit. Factors that may affect the risk associated with a control in the current year include:

- The nature, timing, and extent of procedures performed in previous audits;
- The results of the previous years' testing of the control; and
- Whether there have been changes in the control or the process in which it operates since the previous audit (AS5, ¶58).

For example, if the results for testing a particular control were favorable in the prior year, and no changes were made to the control, the auditor might assess the risk for the control lower and reduce the extent of testing in the current year. If the controls are automated, the auditor might consider using a benchmarking strategy.[1] A benchmarking strategy is an approach that allows the auditor to conclude that a previously tested automated control continues to be effective based on indicators of whether there has been any change in the operation of the control rather than on repeating the full extent of the prior detail-testing work.

Advanced Module 2 offers a brief discussion of computer-assisted audit techniques available to the auditor in testing the operating effectiveness of controls.

Evaluating Identified Control Deficiencies

[LO 10] The auditor is required to evaluate the severity of each control deficiency (AS5, ¶62). The assessment of the significance of a control deficiency depends on the *potential* for a misstatement, not on whether a misstatement actually has occurred. As discussed earlier, the severity of a control deficiency depends on two factors:

- Whether there is a reasonable possibility that the company's controls will fail to prevent or detect a misstatement of an account balance or disclosure (Likelihood).
- The magnitude of the potential misstatement resulting from the deficiency or deficiencies (Magnitude).

---

[1]For a discussion of how the auditor might use a benchmarking strategy, refer to AS5, ¶B28–B33.

TABLE 7–6	Risk Factors That Affect Whether There Is a Reasonable Possibility That a Control Deficiency (or a Combination of Control Deficiencies) Will Result in a Misstatement of an Account Balance or Disclosure

- The nature of the financial statement accounts, disclosures, and assertions involved;
- The susceptibility of the related asset or liability to loss or fraud;
- The subjectivity, complexity, or extent of judgment required to determine the amount involved;
- The interaction or relationship of the control with other controls, including whether they are interdependent or redundant;
- The interaction of the deficiencies; and
- The possible future consequences of the deficiency.

Source: AS5, ¶65.

TABLE 7–7	Indicators of Material Weaknesses

- Identification of fraud, whether or not material, committed by senior management;
- Restatement of previously issued financial statements to reflect the correction of a material misstatement;
- Identification by the auditor of a material misstatement of financial statements in the current period in circumstances that indicate that the misstatement would not have been detected by the company's ICFR; and
- Ineffective oversight of the company's external financial reporting and ICFR by the company's audit committee.

Source: AS5, ¶69.

Table 7–6 presents the risk factors that affect whether there is a reasonable possibility that a control deficiency, or a combination of control deficiencies, will result in a misstatement of an account balance or disclosure.

Factors that affect whether the magnitude of the misstatement might result in a material weakness include:

- The financial statement amounts or total of transactions exposed to the deficiency; and
- The volume of activity in the account balance or class of transactions exposed to the deficiency that has occurred in the current period or that is expected in future periods.

Table 7–7 presents indicators of material weaknesses in ICFR. AS5 provides the following guidance on assessing the severity of a control deficiency:

> When evaluating the severity of a deficiency, or combination of deficiencies, the auditor also should determine the level of detail and degree of assurance that would satisfy prudent officials in the conduct of their own affairs that they have reasonable assurance that transactions are recorded as necessary to permit the preparation of financial statements in conformity with generally accepted accounting principles. If the auditor determines that a deficiency, or combination of deficiencies, might prevent prudent officials in the conduct of their own affairs from concluding that they have reasonable assurance that transactions are recorded as necessary to permit the preparation of financial statements in conformity with generally accepted accounting principles, then the auditor should treat the deficiency, or combination of deficiencies, as an indicator of a material weakness (AS5, ¶70).

You will note that applying this guidance requires a good deal of judgment on the part of the auditor.

An Example

Exhibit 7–3 presents a detailed example of an auditor's test of the design and operating effectiveness for a daily IT-dependent manual control.

Following are examples of control deficiencies that may represent significant deficiencies or material weaknesses. For each control deficiency, indicate

EXHIBIT 7–3	An Example of an Auditor's Tests of a Daily Information Technology–Dependent Manual Control

Bill Boyd is manager for Emets & Shinn, the independent registered public accounting firm for Petheridge Packing Company (PPC). Based on discussions with PPC personnel and review of company documentation, the auditor learns that PPC had the following procedures in place over the entire period to account for cash received in the bank lockbox:

- The company receives from the bank an electronic file listing cash received from customers.
- The IT system applies cash received in the lockbox to individual customer accounts.
- Any cash received in the lockbox and not applied to a customer's account is listed on an exception report called the "unapplied cash exception report."

The application of cash to a customer's account is a *programmed application* control, while the review and follow-up of unapplied cash from the exception report is a *manual* control.

Boyd wants to determine whether misstatements in cash (primarily relating to the existence assertion) and accounts receivable (existence, valuation, and completeness) would be prevented or detected on a timely basis. In order to test these objectives, Boyd decides to test the manual control.

Nature, Timing, and Extent of Procedures

Objective of Test To determine whether there is a listing of nonmatching cash items on the exception report.

Boyd decides to perform the following tests of controls to ensure the *operating effectiveness* of the control for the review and follow-up on the daily unapplied cash exception report.

1. Inquired of company personnel about the procedures in place to ensure that all unapplied items are resolved, the time frame in which such resolution takes place, and whether unapplied items are handled properly within the system.

   Findings: Boyd discussed these matters with the employee responsible for reviewing and resolving the daily unapplied cash exception reports. Boyd learned that items appearing on the daily unapplied cash exception report must be manually entered into the system. The employee typically performs the resolution procedures the next business day. In most cases, items that appear on the daily unapplied cash exception report relate to payments made by a customer who failed to reference an invoice number or purchase order number, or to underpayments of an invoice due to quantity or pricing discrepancies.

2. Reperformed the control.

   Findings: Boyd selected 25 daily unapplied cash exception reports from the period January to September and reperformed the follow-up procedures that the employee performed. Boyd inspected the documents and sources of information used in the follow-up and determined that the transaction was properly corrected in the system. He also scanned other daily unapplied cash exception reports to determine that the control was performed throughout the period of intended reliance.

3. Follow-up tests: Because the tests were performed at an interim date, Boyd asked entity personnel about the procedures in place at year-end. The procedures had not changed from the interim period; therefore, Boyd observed that the controls were still in place by scanning daily unapplied cash exception reports to determine the control was performed on a timely basis during the period from September to year-end. No exceptions were noted.

Based on the audit procedures, Boyd concluded that the employee was clearing exceptions in a timely manner and that the control was operating effectively as of year-end.

whether it is a significant deficiency or material weakness. Justify your decision.[2] After you have tried on your own to assess the situation, look at the solution to see how well you did!

Scenario 1 Murray Company processes a significant number of routine intercompany transactions on a monthly basis. Individual intercompany transactions are not material, and primarily relate to balance sheet activity, for example, cash transfers between business units to finance normal operations.

A formal management policy requires monthly reconciliation of intercompany accounts and confirmation of balances between business units. However, there is no process in place to ensure performance of these procedures. As a

[2]See the Willis & Adams Policy Statement on Evaluating Control Deficiencies (www.mhhe.com/messier7e) for more detailed guidance on evaluating deficiencies.

result, detailed reconciliations of intercompany accounts are not performed on a timely basis. Management does perform monthly procedures to investigate selected large-dollar intercompany account differences. In addition, management prepares a detailed monthly variance analysis of operating expenses to assess their reasonableness.

Scenario 2   Ragunandan Company processes a significant number of inter-company transactions on a monthly basis. Intercompany transactions relate to a wide range of activities, including transfers of inventory with intercompany profit between business units, allocation of research and development costs to business units, and corporate charges. Individual intercompany transactions are frequently material.

A formal management policy requires monthly reconciliation of intercompany accounts and confirmation of balances between business units. However, there is no process in place to ensure that these procedures are performed on a consistent basis. As a result, reconciliations of intercompany accounts are not performed on a timely basis, and differences in intercompany accounts are frequent and significant. Management does not perform any alternative controls to investigate significant intercompany account differences.

Solution: Scenario 1   Based only on these facts, the auditor should determine that this control deficiency represents a significant deficiency for the following reasons: The magnitude of a financial statement misstatement resulting from this deficiency would reasonably be expected to not be material but significant because individual intercompany transactions are not material, and the compensating controls operating monthly should detect a material misstatement. Furthermore, the transactions are primarily restricted to balance sheet accounts. However, the compensating detective controls are designed only to detect material misstatements. The controls do not address the detection of misstatements that are significant but not material. Therefore, the likelihood that a misstatement could occur is reasonably possible.

Solution: Scenario 2   Based only on these facts, the auditor should determine that this deficiency represents a material weakness for the following reasons: The magnitude of a financial statement misstatement resulting from this deficiency would reasonably be expected to be material, because individual intercompany transactions are frequently material and relate to a wide range of activities. Additionally, actual unreconciled differences in intercompany accounts have been, and are, material. The likelihood of such a misstatement is reasonably possible because such misstatements have frequently occurred and compensating controls are not effective, either because they are not properly designed or are not operating effectively. Taken together, the magnitude and likelihood of misstatement of the financial statements resulting from this internal control deficiency meet the definition of a material weakness.

Remediation of a Material Weakness

[LO 11]   When an entity determines that it has a material weakness, it should take steps to correct it. This is referred to as *remediation*. If the material weakness cannot be corrected and/or properly tested before the "as of" date, management and the auditor would issue reports that the ICFR is not operating effectively. If management corrects a material weakness before the "as of" date, there must be sufficient time for both management and the auditor to adequately test the operating effectiveness of the control. If there is not sufficient time, then neither management nor the auditor can conclude that ICFR is effective. If there is sufficient time to remediate the material weakness and the testing shows that the new control is operating effectively, management and the auditor can issue a report that ICFR is operating effectively. Management would make the following disclosure in its FORM 10-K:

> The Company has been actively engaged in the implementation of remediation efforts to address the material weakness in controls over income tax accounting that was in existence at December 31, 2008. These remediation efforts are specifically designed to address the material weakness identified by management. As a result of its assessment of the effectiveness of internal control over financial reporting, management determined that as of December 31, 2009, the material weakness relating to the controls over income tax accounting no longer existed.

Written Representations

[LO 12] In addition to the management representations obtained as part of a financial statement audit (see Chapter 17), the auditor obtains written representations from management related to the audit of ICFR. Table 7–8 presents a typical set of management representations made to the auditor related to the audit of internal control. Failure to obtain written representations from management, including management's refusal to furnish them, constitutes a limitation on the scope of the audit sufficient to preclude an unqualified opinion. While the required representations are typically drafted by the auditor, they are addressed to the auditor and are signed (and worded as if written) by the CEO and CFO.

Auditor Documentation Requirements

[LO 13] The auditor should document the processes, procedures, judgments, and results relating to the audit of internal control. The auditor's documentation must include the auditor's understanding and evaluation of the design of each of the components of the entity's ICFR. The auditor also documents the process used to determine the points at which misstatements could occur within significant accounts and disclosures. The auditor must document the extent to which he or she relied upon work performed by others. Finally, the auditor must describe the evaluation of any deficiencies discovered, as well as any other findings, that could result in a modification to the auditor's report.

TABLE 7–8	**Written Representations Made by Management to the Auditor**
	• Management is responsible for establishing and maintaining effective ICFR. • Management has performed an evaluation and made an assessment of the effectiveness of the company's ICFR and specifying the control criteria. • Management did not rely on work performed by the auditor in forming its assessment of the effectiveness of ICFR. • Management's conclusion about the effectiveness of the entity's ICFR based on the control criteria as of a specified date. • Management has disclosed to the auditor all deficiencies in the design or operation of ICFR identified as part of management's evaluation and has identified all such deficiencies that it believes to be significant deficiencies or material weaknesses. • Descriptions of any material fraud and any other fraud that, although not material, involves senior management or management or other employees who have a significant role in the company's ICFR. • Control deficiencies identified and communicated to the audit committee during previous engagements have (or have not) been resolved (and specifically identifying any that have not). • Descriptions of any changes in ICFR or other factors that might significantly affect ICFR, including any corrective actions taken by management with regard to significant deficiencies and material weaknesses. *Source:* AS5, ¶75.

Auditor Reporting on ICFR

[LO 14]   After auditing the effectiveness of a client's internal control, an auditor issues an unqualified opinion if the client's internal control is designed and operating effectively in all material respects. Significant deficiencies do not require a departure from an unqualified opinion because they relate to possible financial statement misstatements that are less than material. If the scope of the auditor's work is limited, a disclaimer of opinion is issued on the effectiveness of ICFR. If a material weakness is identified, the auditor issues an adverse opinion. Figure 7–4 gives an overview of the types of audit reports relating to the effectiveness of ICFR.

Elements of the Auditor's Report

The auditor's report on the effectiveness of internal control has a number of required elements. The report identifies management's conclusion about the effectiveness of the company's ICFR and states that the assessment on which management's conclusion is based is the responsibility of management. The report defines ICFR and indicates that the standards of the PCAOB require that the auditor plan and perform the audit to obtain reasonable assurance about whether effective ICFR was maintained in all material respects. The report goes on to explain in general terms what an audit of ICFR entails and explicitly addresses the fact that even effective internal control cannot guarantee that misstatements will be prevented, or detected and corrected. Finally, the report concludes with the auditor's opinion on whether the company maintained, in all material respects, effective ICFR as of the end of the period.

The auditor may choose to issue separate reports on the company's financial statements and ICFR or may issue a combined report. Under either approach, the date of the two reports should be the same. The following sections explain the unqualified report, the adverse report for material weaknesses, and the disclaimer of opinion for scope limitations.

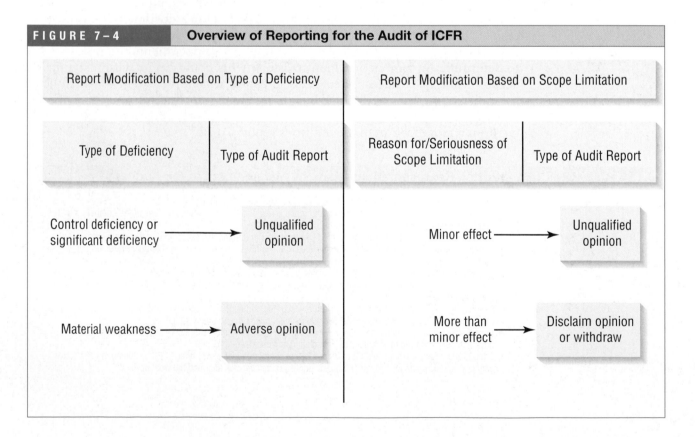

| FIGURE 7–4 | Overview of Reporting for the Audit of ICFR |

Unqualified
Report

An unqualified opinion regarding the effectiveness of the client's ICFR provides reasonable assurance that the client's controls are designed and operating effectively in all material respects as of the balance sheet date. The phrase "all material respects" means that the client's ICFR is free of any material weakness. An unqualified opinion can be issued even in the presence of significant deficiencies. Exhibit 7–4 presents an example of an auditor's unqualified report that is presented separately from the auditor's report on the financial statements. Note that the report includes an explanatory paragraph referring to the financial statement audit report. Exhibit 1–1 in Chapter 1 presents a separate report on the

---

EXHIBIT 7–4   **An Example of a Separate Report Giving an Unqualified Opinion on the Effectiveness of ICFR**

Report of Independent Registered Public Accounting Firm
[Introductory Paragraph]

We have audited EarthWear Clothiers' internal control over financial reporting as of December 31, 2009, based on criteria established in *Internal Control—Integrated Framework,* issued by the Committee of Sponsoring Organizations of the Treadway Commission (COSO). EarthWear Clothiers' management is responsible for maintaining effective internal control over financial reporting and for its assessment of the effectiveness of internal control over financial reporting. Our responsibility is to express an opinion on the company's internal control over financial reporting based on our audit.

[Scope Paragraph]

We conducted our audit in accordance with the standards of the Public Company Accounting Oversight Board (United States). Those standards require that we plan and perform the audit to obtain reasonable assurance about whether effective internal control over financial reporting was maintained in all material respects. Our audit included obtaining an understanding of internal control over financial reporting, testing and evaluating the design and operating effectiveness of internal control, and performing such other procedures as we considered necessary in the circumstances. We believe that our audit provides a reasonable basis for our opinion.

[Definition Paragraph]

A company's internal control over financial reporting is a process designed to provide reasonable assurance regarding the reliability of financial reporting and the preparation of financial statements for external purposes in accordance with generally accepted accounting principles. A company's internal control over financial reporting includes those policies and procedures that (1) pertain to the maintenance of records that, in reasonable detail, accurately and fairly reflect the transactions and dispositions of the assets of the company; (2) provide reasonable assurance that transactions are recorded as necessary to permit preparation of financial statements in accordance with generally accepted accounting principles, and that receipts and expenditures of the company are being made only in accordance with authorizations of management and directors of the company; and (3) provide reasonable assurance regarding prevention or timely detection of unauthorized acquisition, use, or disposition of the company's assets that could have a material effect on the financial statements.

[Inherent Limitations Paragraph]

Because of its inherent limitations, internal control over financial reporting may not prevent or detect misstatements. Also, projections of any evaluation of effectiveness to future periods are subject to the risk that controls may become inadequate because of changes in conditions or that the degree of compliance with the policies or procedures may deteriorate.

[Opinion Paragraph]

In our opinion, EarthWear Clothiers maintained, in all material respects, effective internal control over financial reporting as of December 31, 2009, based on criteria established in *Internal Control—Integrated Framework,* issued by the Committee of Sponsoring Organizations of the Treadway Commission (COSO).

[Explanatory Paragraph]

We have also audited, in accordance with the standards of the Public Company Accounting Oversight Board (United States), the consolidated financial statements of EarthWear Clothiers, and our report dated February 15, 2010, expressed an unqualified opinion.

Willis & Adams
Boise, Idaho
February 15, 2010

EXHIBIT 7–5	An Example of a Combined Report Expressing an Unqualified Opinion on Financial Statements and an Unqualified Opinion on the Effectiveness of ICFR

Report of Independent Registered Public Accounting Firm

[*Introductory paragraph*]

We have audited the accompanying balance sheets of EarthWear Clothiers as of December 31, 2009 and 2008, and the related statements of income, stockholders' equity and comprehensive income, and cash flows for each of the years in the three-year period ended December 31, 2009. We also have audited EarthWear Clothiers' internal control over financial reporting as of December 31, 2009, based on criteria established in *Internal Control—Integrated Framework* issued by the Committee of Sponsoring Organizations of the Treadway Commission (COSO). EarthWear Clothiers' management is responsible for these financial statements, for maintaining effective internal control over financial reporting, and for its assessment of the effectiveness of internal control over financial reporting, included in the accompanying Management Report on the Financial Statements and Internal Control. Our responsibility is to express an opinion on these financial statements and an opinion on the effectiveness of the company's internal control over financial reporting based on our audits.

[*Scope paragraph*]

We conducted our audits in accordance with the standards of the Public Company Accounting Oversight Board (United States). Those standards require that we plan and perform the audits to obtain reasonable assurance about whether the financial statements are free of material misstatement and whether effective internal control over financial reporting was maintained in all material respects. Our audit of financial statements included examining, on a test basis, evidence supporting the amounts and disclosures in the financial statements, assessing the accounting principles used and significant estimates made by management, and evaluating the overall financial statement presentation. Our audit of internal control over financial reporting included obtaining an understanding of internal control over financial reporting, testing and evaluating the design and operating effectiveness of internal control, and performing such other procedures as we considered necessary in the circumstances. We believe that our audits provide a reasonable basis for our opinions.

[*Definition paragraph*]

A company's internal control over financial reporting is a process designed to provide reasonable assurance regarding the reliability of financial reporting and the preparation of financial statements for external purposes in accordance with generally accepted accounting principles. A company's internal control over financial reporting includes those policies and procedures that (1) pertain to the maintenance of records that, in reasonable detail, accurately and fairly reflect the transactions and dispositions of the assets of the company; (2) provide reasonable assurance that transactions are recorded as necessary to permit preparation of financial statements in accordance with generally accepted accounting principles, and that receipts and expenditures of the company are being made only in accordance with authorizations of management and directors of the company; and (3) provide reasonable assurance regarding prevention or timely detection of unauthorized acquisition, use, or disposition of the company's assets that could have a material effect on the financial statements.

[*Inherent limitations paragraph*]

Because of its inherent limitations, internal control over financial reporting may not prevent or detect misstatements. Also, projections of any evaluation of effectiveness to future periods are subject to the risk that controls may become inadequate because of changes in conditions, or that the degree of compliance with the policies or procedures may deteriorate.

[*Opinion paragraph*]

In our opinion, the financial statements referred to above present fairly, in all material respects, the financial position of EarthWear Clothiers as of December 31, 2009 and 2008, and the results of its operations and its cash flows for each of the years in the three-year period ended December 31, 2009, in conformity with accounting principles generally accepted in the United States of America. Also, in our opinion, EarthWear Clothiers maintained, in all material respects, effective internal control over financial reporting as of December 31, 2009, based on criteria established in *Internal Control—Integrated Framework* issued by the Committee of Sponsoring Organizations of the Treadway Commission (COSO).

Willis & Adams
Boise, Idaho
February 15, 2010

financial statement audit. Note that the last paragraph of that report refers to the audit of ICFR and indicates that an unqualified opinion was issued with respect to the effectiveness of internal control.

Exhibit 7–5 presents an example of a *combined report* for EarthWear Clothiers that gives an unqualified opinion on both the financial statement audit and the audit

EXHIBIT 7–6	An Example of an Adverse Opinion on the Effectiveness of ICFR Because of the Existence of a Material Weakness

Report of Independent Registered Public Accounting Firm
[Standard Wording for the Introductory, Scope, Definition, and Inherent Limitations Paragraphs]
[Explanatory Paragraph]

A material weakness is a deficiency, or a combination of deficiencies, in internal control over financial reporting, such that there is a reasonable possibility that a material misstatement of the company's annual or interim financial statements will not be prevented or detected on a timely basis. The following material weakness has been identified and included in management's assessment. Treadron had an inadequate system for recording cash receipts, which could have prevented the Company from recording cash receipts on accounts receivable completely and properly. Therefore, cash received could have been diverted for unauthorized use, lost, or otherwise not properly recorded to accounts receivable. This material weakness was considered in determining the nature, timing, and extent of audit tests applied in our audit of the 2009 financial statements, and this report does not affect our report dated February 15, 2010, on those financial statements.

[Opinion Paragraph]

In our opinion, because of the effect of the material weakness described above on the achievement of the objectives of the control criteria, Treadron Company has not maintained effective internal control over financial reporting as of December 31, 2009, based on criteria established in *Internal Control—Integrated Framework,* issued by the Committee of Sponsoring Organizations of the Treadway Commission (COSO).

Mortensen & Mortensen
Houston, Texas
March 15, 2010

of ICFR. When the auditor elects to issue a combined report, the report may address multiple reporting periods for the financial statements presented but will address only the end of the most recent fiscal year for the effectiveness of internal control.

Adverse Report for a Material Weakness

The presence of a material weakness at the end of the period necessitates an adverse assessment by management and an adverse opinion by the auditor. An adverse report includes a definition of a material weakness and a description of the particular material weakness identified in the client's system of internal control, along with the auditor's opinion that the client has not maintained effective ICFR as of the report date. See Exhibit 7–6 for an example of an adverse report.

Practice INSIGHT	In 2004, the first year of compliance with Rule 404 of the Sarbanes-Oxley Act, about 15.9 percent of all auditor reports were adverse with respect to the effectiveness of internal control over financial reporting. In year 2005, the rate of adverse reports had fallen to slightly less than 10 percent. Keep in mind, though, that the smallest public companies were granted a delay in the effective date of Rule 404. The results of their 404 audits won't be known for some time, but it is expected that the rate of adverse reports for these smaller public companies might be significantly higher than for the larger companies that have already been through the process.

It is possible for the auditor to issue an adverse opinion on internal control while at the same time issuing an unqualified opinion on the financial statement audit. Such a conclusion is reached when a client's internal control is not effective at preventing or detecting material errors, but the auditor concludes (based on substantive procedures) that the client's financial statements do not contain material misstatements. Such circumstances can arise when an identified material weakness does not actually result in a misstatement in the financial statements or when a material weakness does result in a material misstatement but the client corrects the misstatement prior to issuing the financial statements.

Whether or not the auditor's opinion on the financial statements is affected by the adverse opinion on the effectiveness of ICFR, the report on ICFR (or the combined report) should indicate that the weakness was considered in determining the nature, timing, and extent of financial statement audit tests in the paragraph that describes the material weakness. Such disclosure is important to ensure that users of the auditor's report on the financial statements understand why the auditor issued an unqualified opinion on those statements.

Practice **INSIGHT**	In the first two years of Sarbanes-Oxley compliance, approximately 75 percent of the material weaknesses reported were identified when the auditor discovered a material misstatement while conducting substantive audit procedures. When a material misstatement is discovered, the auditor does a "root cause analysis" to find out why the client's internal control over financial reporting failed to prevent or detect the misstatement. Such an analysis usually leads to the identification of a material weakness.

Disclosure is also important when the auditor's opinion on the financial statements *is* affected by the adverse opinion on the effectiveness of internal control. In such a circumstance, the report on ICFR (or the combined report) should similarly indicate that the material weakness was considered in determining the nature, timing, and extent of procedures performed as part of the financial statement audit.

Disclaimer for Scope Limitation

The auditor can express an unqualified opinion on the effectiveness of ICFR only if the auditor has been able to apply all the procedures necessary in the circumstances. If the scope of the auditor's work is limited because of circumstances beyond the control of management or the auditor, the auditor should disclaim an opinion or withdraw from the engagement. The auditor's decision depends on an assessment of the importance of the omitted procedure(s) to his or her ability to form an opinion.

Other Reporting Issues

Management's Report Incomplete or Improperly Presented

If the auditor determines that elements of management's annual report on ICFR are incomplete or improperly presented, the auditor should modify his or her report to include an explanatory paragraph describing the reasons for this determination.

The Auditor Decides to Refer to the Report of Other Auditors

As discussed in Chapter 18 in connection with the financial statement audit, on some engagements, parts of the audit may be completed by another public accounting firm. In such circumstances, the auditor must decide whether to refer to work performed by the other auditor. The decision is based on factors similar to those considered by the auditor who uses the work and reports of other independent auditors when reporting on a company's financial statements. If the auditor decides to make reference to the report of the other auditor as a basis, in part, for his or her opinion, the auditor should refer to the report of the other auditor in describing the scope of the audit and in expressing the opinion (AS5, ¶C8–C14).

Subsequent Events

The auditor has a responsibility to report on any changes in internal control that might affect financial reporting between the end of the reporting period and the date of the auditor's report. Chapter 17 describes the types of procedures the auditor undertakes to search for subsequent events affecting a client's financial statements and affecting the client's ICFR. As noted in Chapter 17, the auditor's treatment of a subsequent event depends on whether the event reveals information about a material weakness that existed as of the end of the reporting period or whether the event creates or reveals information about a new condition that did not exist as of the end of the reporting period.

Management's Report Contains Additional Information

Management may include additional information in its report on ICFR. For example, management may include disclosures about corrective actions taken by the company after the date of management's assessment, the company's plans to implement new controls, or a statement that management believes the cost of correcting a material weakness would exceed the benefits to be derived from implementing new controls. The auditor should disclaim an opinion on such information and include the following language as the last paragraph of the report:

> We do not express an opinion or any other form of assurance on management's statement referring to the costs and related benefits of implementing new controls.

If the auditor believes that the additional information contains a material misstatement of fact, he or she should discuss the matter with management. If the auditor concludes that a material misstatement of fact remains after discussing it with management, he or she should notify the audit committee in writing. The auditor also should consider consulting the auditor's legal counsel about further actions to be taken, including the auditor's responsibility under the Securities Exchange Act of 1934 (AS5, ¶C14).

Reporting on a Remediated Material Weakness at an Interim Date

PCAOB Auditing Standard No. 4 provides direction for auditors in reporting on whether a material weakness continues to exist at an interim date. As a result of this standard, rather than making a client wait twelve months to receive a clean opinion regarding its ICFR in the next year-end report, the auditor can provide an interim opinion once management has remediated the material weakness. This standard allows auditors to attest on a timely basis as to whether a client has eliminated the cause of a previously issued adverse opinion regarding its ICFR.

Additional Required Communications in an Audit of ICFR

✎ [LO 15] The auditor has a number of communication responsibilities under AS5. The auditor must communicate in writing to management and the audit committee all significant deficiencies and material weaknesses identified during the audit. The written communication should be made prior to the issuance of the auditor's report on ICFR. The auditor's communication should distinguish clearly between those matters considered to be significant deficiencies and those considered to be material weaknesses. If a significant deficiency or material weakness exists because the oversight by the company's audit committee is ineffective, the auditor must communicate that specific significant deficiency or material weakness in writing to the board of directors.

In addition, the auditor should communicate to management, in writing, all control deficiencies (deficiencies in internal control that are not material or significant—(see Figure 7–1) identified during the audit and inform the audit committee when such a communication has been made. Keep in mind that the auditor's role is to identify material weaknesses. The auditor is not required to perform procedures to identify control deficiencies that do not rise to the level of a material weakness.

The auditor's written communication about control deficiencies states that the communication is intended solely for the information and use of the board of directors, audit committee, management, and others within the organization. When governmental authorities require the entity to furnish such a report, a specific reference to such regulatory agencies may be made in the report. These written communications also include the definitions of control deficiencies, significant deficiencies, and material weaknesses, and clearly identify the types of deficiencies being communicated. The auditor's communication may indicate that no material weaknesses were identified if none were found. However, because the auditor's procedures were geared toward detecting material weaknesses, the auditor may not represent that no significant deficiencies were noted during an audit of internal control.

When auditing ICFR, the auditor may become aware of fraud or other possible illegal acts. If the matter involves fraud, it must be brought to the attention of the appropriate level of management. If the fraud involves senior management, the auditor must communicate the matter directly to the audit committee. If the matter involves other possible illegal acts, the auditor must be assured that the audit committee is adequately informed, unless the matter is clearly inconsequential. When timely communication is important, the auditor communicates such matters during the course of the audit rather than at the end of the engagement.

Advanced Module 1: Special Considerations for an Audit of Internal Control

The PCAOB specifies two areas that require special consideration by management and the auditor during an audit of ICFR:

- Service organizations.
- Safeguarding assets.

Use of Service Organizations

[LO 16]

Many companies use service organizations to process transactions. If the service organization's services make up part of a company's information system, then they are considered part of the information and communication component of the company's ICFR. Thus, both management and the auditor must consider the activities of the service organization.

Management and the auditor should perform the following procedures with respect to the activities performed by the service organization: (1) obtain an understanding of the controls at the service organization that are relevant to the entity's internal control and the controls at the user organization over the activities of the service organization; and (2) obtain evidence that the controls that are relevant to management's assessment and the auditor's opinion are operating effectively.

Evidence about the operating effectiveness of controls that are relevant to management's assessment and the auditor's opinion may be obtained by performing tests of the user organization's controls over the activities of the service organization, performing tests of controls at the service organization, or obtaining a service auditor's report on the design and operating effectiveness of controls placed in operation at the service organization (often referred to as a "SAS No. 70 report"). If a service auditor's report on controls placed in operation and tests of operating effectiveness is available, management and the auditor separately evaluate whether this report provides sufficient evidence to support the assessment and opinion. Important factors that management and the auditor should consider include the scope of the examination, the controls tested, the results of those tests of controls, and the service auditor's opinion on the operating effectiveness of the controls. Management and the auditor should also make inquiries concerning the service auditor's reputation, competence, and independence.

When a significant period of time has elapsed between the time period covered by the tests of controls in the service auditor's report and the date of management's assessment, additional procedures should be performed.

If the auditor concludes that additional evidence about the operating effectiveness of controls at the service organization is required, the auditor should perform additional procedures. For example, the auditor might investigate whether management has taken actions to monitor or evaluate the quality of the service provider and evaluate the results of such actions. The auditor might also contact the service organization to obtain specific information, or request that a service auditor be engaged to perform procedures that will supply the necessary information. Finally, the auditor might even visit the service organization and perform such procedures firsthand. Based on the evidence obtained, management and the auditor should determine whether they have obtained sufficient evidence to obtain the reasonable assurance necessary for their assessment and opinion, respectively.

Safeguarding of Assets

✄ **[LO 17]**

Safeguarding of assets is defined in AS5 as policies and procedures that "provide reasonable assurance regarding prevention or timely detection of unauthorized acquisition, use or disposition of the company's assets that could have a material effect on the financial statements." This definition is consistent with the definition in the COSO framework. For example, a company could have safeguarding controls over inventory tags (preventive controls) and also perform timely periodic physical inventory counts (detective control) for its quarterly and annual financial reporting dates. Given that the definitions of material weakness and significant deficiency relate to the likelihood of misstatement of the financial statements, the failure of the inventory tag control will not result in a significant deficiency or material weakness if the physical inventory count prevents a misstatement of the financial statements. Therefore, the COSO definition indicates that although losses might occur, controls over financial reporting are effective if they provide reasonable assurance that those losses are properly reflected in the financial statements.

Advanced Module 2: Computer-Assisted Audit Techniques

✄ **[LO 18]**

Most major accounting firms have groups of auditors specializing in information technology. They often use computer-assisted audit techniques (CAATs) to assist the auditor in testing transactions, account balances, and application controls. Many of these controls are embedded into the client's computer programs and can thus be tested via CAATs. Additionally, the auditor may also gain great efficiencies by using CAATs to execute substantive procedures when the information is maintained in machine-readable form. The following types of CAATs are discussed:

- Generalized audit software
- Custom audit software
- Test data

Other techniques (parallel simulation, integrated test facility, and concurrent auditing techniques) are discussed in advanced IT auditing books.[3]

Generalized Audit Software

Generalized audit software (GAS) includes programs that allow the auditor to perform tests on computer files and databases. ACL, which is packaged with this text, is an example of a GAS program that is widely used in practice. GAS was

---

[3]For example, see J. D. Warren, Jr., L. W. Edelson, X. L. Parker, and R. M. Thurun, *Handbook of IT Auditing* (Boston, MA: RIA Group/WG&L, 1998).

TABLE 7-9	Functions Performed by Generalized Audit Software	
Function	**Description**	
File or database access	Reads and extracts data from a client's computer files or databases for further audit testing.	
Selection operators	Select from files or databases transactions that meet certain criteria.	
Arithmetic functions	Perform a variety of arithmetic calculations (addition, subtraction, and so on) on transactions, files, and databases.	
Statistical analyses	Provide functions supporting various types of audit sampling.	
Report generation	Prepares various types of documents and reports.	

developed so that auditors would be able to conduct similar computer-assisted audit techniques in different IT environments. For example, GAS permits an auditor to select and prepare accounts receivable confirmations from a variety of computer systems. This type of software provides a high-level computer language that allows the auditor to easily perform various functions on a client's computer files and databases. A sample of functions that can be performed by GAS is shown in Table 7–9.

GAS offers several advantages: (1) it is easy to use; (2) limited IT expertise or programming skills are required; (3) the time required to develop the application is usually short; and (4) an entire population can be examined, eliminating the need for sampling in some instances. Among the disadvantages of GAS are that (1) it involves auditing *after* the client has processed the data rather than while the data are being processed; (2) it provides a limited ability to verify programming logic because its application is usually directed to testing client files or databases; and (3) it is limited to audit procedures that can be conducted on data available in electronic form. Your instructor may assign you to use ACL to work some problems during your study of this text. Becoming familiar with ACL is a great opportunity to get a head start on others entering the profession because it is a widely used and very useful tool.

Custom Audit Software

Custom audit software is generally written by auditors for specific audit tasks. Such programs are necessary when the entity's computer system is not compatible with the auditor's GAS or when the auditor wants to conduct some testing that may not be possible with the GAS. It may also be more efficient to prepare custom programs if they will be used in future audits of the entity or if they may be used on similar engagements. The major disadvantages of custom software are that (1) it is expensive to develop; (2) it may require a long development time; and (3) it may require extensive modification if the client changes its accounting application programs.

Practice INSIGHT	When using ACL or any other auditing tool, remember to examine the underlying source documents. According to the PCAOB, one firm used a computer-assisted auditing procedure to identify potentially fraudulent journal entries, but the firm failed to examine the underlying documentation to determine whether any of the journal entries were in fact fraudulent (PCAOB Release 104-2005-120).

Inventory observation and testing provide a good example of where such a program might be useful. Suppose a client maintains computerized perpetual inventory records that are updated by the sales and purchasing systems. Further assume that the client conducts a physical inventory count once a year, at which time the perpetual records are corrected. At the time of the physical inventory count, the client's employees record the physical counts on special computer forms that are optically scanned to create a physical inventory file. The quantities on hand are priced using an approved price file. What results from this analysis is the inventory balance used for updating the perpetual records and the financial statements.

The auditors who observe the client's physical inventory count record the results on special computer forms that are optically scanned and used as input to the custom program. The custom program performs the following audit procedures: (1) traces the test counts into the client's perpetual inventory file and prints out any exceptions; (2) performs a complete mathematical test, including extensions, footings, crossfootings, and use of approved prices; (3) summarizes the inventory by type; and (4) prints out items in excess of a predetermined amount for review.

Test Data

The auditor uses test data for testing the application controls in the client's computer programs. In using this method, the auditor first creates a set of simulated data (that is, test data) for processing. The data should include both valid and invalid data. After calculating the expected results of processing the test data, the auditor uses the client's computer and application programs to process the data. The valid data should be properly processed, while the invalid data should be identified as errors. The results of this processing are compared to the auditor's predetermined results. This technique can be used to check

- Data validation controls and error detection routines.
- Processing-logic controls.
- Arithmetic calculations.
- The inclusion of transactions in records, files, and reports.

The objective of using the test data method is to ensure the accuracy of the computer processing of transactions.

The main advantage of the test data method is that it provides direct evidence on the effectiveness of the controls included in the client's application programs. However, the test data method has a number of potential disadvantages. First, it can be very time-consuming to create the test data. Second, the auditor may not be certain that all relevant conditions or controls are tested. The use of special computer programs called *test data generators* may help alleviate these potential disadvantages. Third, the auditor must be certain that the test data are processed using the client's regular production programs. This concern can be alleviated if the client's general controls for program changes, access, and library functions are reliable. Last, the auditor must be sure to remove the valid test data from the client's files.

KEY TERMS

Control deficiency. A weakness in the design or operation of a control such that management or employees, in the normal course of performing their assigned functions, fail to prevent or detect misstatements on a timely basis.

Control objective. An objective for ICFR generally relates to a relevant financial statement assertion and states a criterion for evaluating whether the company's control procedures in a specific area provide reasonable assurance that a misstatement or omission in that relevant assertion is prevented or detected by controls on a timely basis.

Entity-level controls. Controls that have a pervasive effect on the entity's system of internal control such as controls related to the control environment (for example, management's philosophy and operating style, integrity and ethical values; board or audit committee oversight; and assignment of authority and responsibility); controls over management override; the company's risk assessment process; centralized processing and controls, including shared service environments; controls to monitor results of operations; controls to monitor other controls, including activities of the internal audit function, the audit committee, and self-assessment programs; controls over the period-end financial reporting process; and policies that address significant business control and risk management practices.

Internal control over financial reporting. A process designed by, or under the supervision of, the company's principal executive and principal financial officers, or persons performing similar functions, and effected by the company's board of directors, management, and other personnel, to provide reasonable assurance regarding the reliability of financial reporting and the preparation of financial statements for external purposes in accordance with GAAP.

Material weakness. A deficiency, or a combination of deficiencies, in ICFR, such that there is a reasonable possibility that a material misstatement of the company's annual or interim financial statements will not be prevented or detected on a timely basis.

Relevant assertion. A financial statement assertion that has a reasonable possibility of containing a misstatement or misstatements that would cause the financial statements to be materially misstated.

Remediation. The process of correcting a material weakness as part of management's assessment of the effectiveness of ICFR.

Safeguarding of assets. Those policies and procedures that provide reasonable assurance regarding prevention or timely detection of unauthorized acquisition, use, or disposition of the company's assets that could have a material effect on the financial statements.

Significant account or disclosure. An account or disclosure is significant if there is a reasonable possibility that the account or disclosure could contain a misstatement that, individually or when aggregated with others, has a material effect on the financial statements, considering the risks of both overstatement and understatement.

Significant deficiency. A deficiency, or a combination of deficiencies, in ICFR that is less severe than a material weakness, yet important enough to merit attention by those responsible for oversight of the company's financial reporting.

Walkthrough. A transaction being traced by an auditor from origination through the entity's information system until it is reflected in the entity's financial reports. It encompasses the entire process of initiating, authorizing, recording, processing, and reporting individual transactions and controls for each of the significant processes identified.

www.mhhe.com/ messier7e | Visit the book's Online Learning Center for a multiple-choice quiz that will allow you to assess your understanding of chapter concepts.

REVIEW QUESTIONS

[LO1,2]   7-1   Briefly summarize management's and the auditor's basic responsibilities under Section 404 of the Sarbanes-Oxley Act of 2002.

[4]   7-2   Discuss how the terms *likelihood* and *magnitude* play a role in evaluating the significance of a control deficiency.

[5]   7-3   The first element in management's process for assessing the effectiveness of internal control is determining which controls should be tested. Identify the controls that would typically be tested by management.

[5,8]   7-4   Describe how management and the auditor decide on which locations or business units to test.

[5]   7-5   Management must document its assessment of internal control. What would such documentation include?

[6]   7-6   List the steps in the auditor's process for an audit of ICFR.

[7]   7-7   How does the auditor evaluate the competence and objectivity of others who perform work for management?

[7, 8]   7-8   Describe the steps in obtaining an understanding of ICFR using a top-down, risk-based approach.

[8]   7-9   The period-end financial reporting process controls are always important. What are those controls and what should the auditor's evaluation of those controls include?

[8]   7-10   A walkthrough involves tracing a transaction through the information system. What types of evidence does a walkthrough provide to the auditor?

[10]   7-11   AS5 indicates that certain circumstances are indicators of a material weakness. What are these circumstances, and why do you think the PCAOB assessed them as being of such importance?

[11]   7-12   Describe what is meant when management remediates a material weakness. If a material weakness is remediated and sufficiently tested before the "as of" date, what can management assert about ICFR?

[13]   7-13   What are the auditor's documentation requirements for an audit of ICFR?

[14]   7-14   What are the types of reports that an auditor can issue for an audit of ICFR? Briefly identify the circumstances justifying each type of report.

[14]   7-15   Under what circumstances would an auditor give an adverse opinion on the effectiveness of a client's ICFR?

[14]   7-16   Under what circumstances would an auditor disclaim an opinion on the effectiveness of a client's ICFR?

[16]   7-17   What should the auditor do when a significant period of time has elapsed between the service organization auditor's report and the date of management's assessment?

[18]   7-18   Distinguish between generalized and custom audit software. List the functions that can be performed by generalized audit software.

MULTIPLE-CHOICE QUESTIONS

[1,2]   7-19   The Sarbanes-Oxley Act of 2002 requires management to include a report on the effectiveness of ICFR in the entity's annual report. It also requires auditors to report on the effectiveness of ICFR. Which of the following statements concerning these requirements is false?
a. The auditor should evaluate whether internal controls are effective in accurately and fairly reflecting the firm's transactions.
b. Management's report should state its responsibility for establishing and maintaining an adequate internal control system.
c. Management should identify material weaknesses in its report.
d. The auditor should provide recommendations for improving internal control in the audit report.

[4,10]   7-20   A control deviation caused by an employee performing a control procedure that he or she is not authorized to perform is always considered a
a. Deficiency in design.
b. Deficiency in operation.
c. Significant deficiency.
d. Material weakness.

[4,10]   7-21   Which of the following is not a factor that might affect the likelihood that a control deficiency could result in a misstatement in an account balance?
a. The susceptibility of the related assets or liability to loss or fraud.
b. The interaction or relationship of the control with other controls.
c. The financial statement amounts exposed to the deficiency.
d. The nature of the financial statement accounts, disclosures, and assertions involved.

[6,8]   7-22   Entity-level controls can have a pervasive effect on the entity's ability to meet the control criteria. Which one of the following is not an entity-level control?
a. Controls to monitor results of operations.
b. Management's risk assessment process.
c. Controls to monitor the inventory taking process.
d. The period-end financial reporting process.

[8,9]   7-23   Which of the following controls would most likely be tested during an interim period?
a. Controls over nonroutine transactions.
b. Controls over the period-end financial reporting process.
c. Controls that operate on a continuous basis.
d. Controls over transactions that involve a high degree of subjectivity.

[8,9]   7-24   If the financial reporting risks for a location are *low* and the entity has good entity-level controls, management may rely on which of the following for their assessment.
a. Documentation and test controls over specific risks.
b. Self-assessment processes in conjunction with entity-level controls.
c. Documentation and test entity-level controls over the entire entity.
d. Selective control test at that location.

[8,9]   7-25   Auditing Standard 5 requires an auditor to perform a walkthrough as part of the internal control audit. A walkthrough requires an auditor to
a. Tour the organization's facilities and locations before beginning any audit work.
b. Trace a transaction from every class of transactions from origination through the company's information system.
c. Trace a transaction from each major class of transactions from origination through the company's information system.
d. Trace a transaction from each major class of transactions from origination through the company's information system until it is reflected in the company's financial reports.

[9]   7-26   When auditors report on the effectiveness of internal control "as of" a specific date and obtain evidence about the operating effectiveness of controls at an interim date, which of the following items would be the least helpful in evaluating the additional evidence to gather for the remaining period?
a. Any significant changes that occurred in internal control subsequent to the interim date.
b. The length of the remaining period.
c. The specific controls tested prior to the "as of" date and the results of those tests.
d. The walkthrough of the control system conducted at interim.

[14]   7-27   AnnaLisa, an auditor for N. M. Neal & Associates, is prevented by the management of Lileah Company from auditing controls over inventory. Lileah is a public company. Management explains that controls over inventory were recently implemented by a highly regarded public accounting firm that the company hired as a consultant and insists that it is a waste of time for AnnaLisa to evaluate these controls. Inventory is a material account, but procedures performed as part of the financial statement audit indicate the account is fairly stated. AnnaLisa found no material weaknesses in any other area of the client's internal control relating to financial reporting. What kind of report should AnnaLisa issue on the effectiveness of Lileah's internal control?

a. An unqualified report.

b. An adverse report.

c. A disclaimer of opinion.

d. An exculpatory opinion.

[14]   7-28   In auditing a public company client, Natalie, an auditor for N. M. Neal & Associates, identifies four deficiencies in ICFR. Three of the deficiencies are unlikely to result in financial misstatements that are material. One of the deficiencies is reasonably likely to result in misstatements that are not material but significant. What type of audit report should Natalie issue?

a. An unqualified report.

b. An adverse report.

c. A disclaimer of opinion.

d. An exculpatory opinion.

[14]   7-29   In auditing ICFR for a public company client, Emily finds that the company has a significant subsidiary located in a foreign country. Emily's accounting firm has no offices in that country, and the company has thus engaged another reputable firm to conduct the audit of internal control for that subsidiary. The other auditor's report indicates that there are no material weaknesses in the foreign subsidiary's ICFR. What should Emily do?

a. Disclaim an opinion because she cannot rely on the opinion of another auditor in dealing with a significant subsidiary.

b. Accept the other auditor's opinion and express an unqualified opinion, making no reference to the other auditor's report in her audit opinion.

c. Accept the other auditor's opinion after evaluating the auditor's work, and make reference to the other auditor's report in her audit opinion.

d. Qualify the opinion because she is unable to conduct the testing herself, and this constitutes a significant scope limitation.

[15]   7-30   Which of the following statements concerning control deficiencies is true?

a. The auditor should communicate to management, in writing, all control deficiencies in internal control identified during the audit.

b. All significant deficiencies are material weaknesses.

c. All control deficiencies are significant deficiencies.

d. An auditor must immediately report material weaknesses and significant deficiencies discovered during an audit to the PCAOB.

[15]   7-31   Significant deficiencies and material weaknesses must be communicated to an entity's audit committee because they represent

a. Material fraud or illegal acts perpetrated by high-level management.

b. Disclosures of information that significantly contradict the auditor's going concern assumption.

c. Significant deficiencies in the design or operation of internal control.

d. Potential manipulation or falsification of accounting records.

[18]   7-32   Which of the following most likely represents a weakness in internal control of an IT system?
a. The systems analyst reviews output and controls the distribution of output from the IT department.
b. The accounts payable clerk prepares data for computer processing and enters the data into the computer.
c. The systems programmer designs the operating and control functions of programs and participates in testing operating systems.
d. The control clerk establishes control over data received by the IT department and reconciles control totals after processing.

[18]   7-33   A primary advantage of using generalized audit software packages to audit the financial statements of a client that uses an IT system is that the auditor may
a. Consider increasing the use of substantive tests of transactions in place of analytical procedures.
b. Substantiate the accuracy of data through self-checking digits and hash totals.
c. Reduce the level of required tests of controls to a relatively small amount.
d. Access information stored on computer files while having a limited understanding of the client's hardware and software features.

PROBLEMS

[6,7,8]   7-34   Following are three examples of controls for accounts that you have determined are significant for the audit of ICFR. For each control, determine the nature, timing, and extent of testing of the design and operating effectiveness. Refer to Exhibit 7–3 for a way to format your answer.

Control 1. Monthly Manual Reconciliation: Through discussions with company personnel and review of company documentation, you find that company personnel reconcile the accounts receivable subsidiary ledger to the general ledger on a monthly basis. To determine whether misstatements in accounts receivable (existence, valuation, and completeness) would be detected on a timely basis, you decide to test the control provided by the monthly reconciliation process.

Control 2. Daily Manual Preventive Control: Through discussions with company personnel, you learn that company personnel make a cash disbursement only after they have matched the vendor invoice to the receiver and purchase order. To determine whether misstatements in cash (existence) and accounts payable (existence, valuation, and completeness) would be prevented on a timely basis, you decide to test the control over making a cash disbursement only after matching the invoice with the receiver and purchase.

Control 3. Programmed Preventive Control and Weekly Information Technology–Dependent Manual Detective Control: Through discussions with company personnel, you learn that the company's computer system performs a three-way match of the receiving report, purchase order, and invoice. If there are any exceptions, the system produces a list of unmatched items that employees review and follow up on weekly. The computer match is a programmed application control, and the review and follow-up of the unmatched items report is a manual detective control. To determine whether misstatements in cash (existence) and accounts payable–inventory (existence, valuation, and completeness) would be prevented or detected on a timely basis, you decide to test the programmed application control of matching the receiver, purchase order, and invoice, as well as the review and follow-up control over unmatched items.

Note:
In answering Problems 7–35 and 7–36, you may want to refer to Willis & Adams' Policy Statement on Evaluating Control Deficiencies. A copy of the policy can be downloaded from the firm's web site at (www.mhhe.com/messier7e).

[4,6,10] 7-35 Following are examples of control deficiencies that may represent significant deficiencies or material weaknesses. For each control deficiency, indicate whether it is a significant deficiency or material weakness. Justify your decision.

a. The company uses a standard sales contract for most transactions. Individual sales transactions are not material to the entity. Sales personnel are allowed to modify sales contract terms. The company's accounting function reviews significant or unusual modifications to the sales contract terms, but does not review changes in the standard shipping terms. The changes in the standard shipping terms could require a delay in the timing of revenue recognition. Management reviews gross margins on a monthly basis and investigates any significant or unusual relationships. In addition, management reviews the reasonableness of inventory levels at the end of each accounting period. The entity has experienced limited situations in which revenue has been inappropriately recorded in advance of shipment, but amounts have not been material.

b. The company has a standard sales contract, but sales personnel frequently modify the terms of the contract. The nature of the modifications can affect the timing and amount of revenue recognized. Individual sales transactions are frequently material to the entity, and the gross margin can vary significantly for each transaction. The company does not have procedures in place for the accounting function to regularly review modifications to sales contract terms. Although management reviews gross margins on a monthly basis, the significant differences in gross margins on individual transactions make it difficult for management to identify potential misstatements. Improper revenue recognition has occurred, and the amounts have been material.

c. The company has a standard sales contract, but sales personnel frequently modify the terms of the contract. Sales personnel frequently grant unauthorized and unrecorded sales discounts to customers without the knowledge of the accounting department. These amounts are deducted by customers in paying their invoices and are recorded as outstanding balances on the accounts receivable–aging. Although these amounts are individually insignificant, when added up they are material and have occurred regularly over the past few years.

[4,6,10] 7-36 Following are examples of control deficiencies that may represent significant deficiencies or material weaknesses. For each of the following scenarios, indicate whether the deficiency is a significant deficiency or material weakness. Justify your decision.

a. During its assessment of ICFR, the management of Lorenz Corporation and its auditors identified the following control deficiencies that individually represent significant deficiencies:

- Inadequate segregation of duties over certain information system access controls.

- Several instances of transactions that were not properly recorded in subsidiary ledgers. While the transactions that weren't recorded properly were not material, the gross amount of the transactions of that type totaled up to an amount several times materiality.
- A lack of timely reconciliations of the account balances affected by the improperly recorded transactions.

b. During its assessment of ICFR, management of First Coast BankCorp and its auditors identified the following deficiencies that individually represent significant deficiencies: the design of controls over the estimation of credit losses (a critical accounting estimate); the operating effectiveness of controls for initiating, processing, and reviewing adjustments to the allowance for credit losses; and the operating effectiveness of controls designed to prevent and detect the improper recognition of interest income. In addition, during the past year, First Coast experienced a significant level of growth in the loan balances that were subjected to the controls governing credit loss estimation and revenue recognition, and further growth is expected in the upcoming year.

[4,10,14] **7-37** For each of the following independent situations, indicate the type of report on ICFR you would issue. Justify your report choice.
  a. Johnson Company's management does not have an adequate antifraud program or controls.
  b. Tap, Tap, & Associates completed the integrated audit of Maxim Corporation. It did not identify any control deficiencies during its audit.
  c. During the audit of Fritz, Inc., Boyd & Company discovered a material misstatement that was not discovered by Fritz's internal control system.
  d. Scoles Manufacturing Company does not have adequate controls over nonroutine sales transactions.
  e. Lee, Leis, & Monk (LL&M) performs the audit of Freedom Insurance Company. LL&M has determined that Freedom has an ineffective regulatory compliance function.

[4,10,14] **7-38** For each of the following independent situations, indicate the type of report on ICFR you would issue. Justify your report choice.
  a. Hansen, Inc., has restated previously issued financial statements to reflect the correction of a misstatement.
  b. Shu & Han Engineering does not have effective oversight of the company's external financial reporting.
  c. Kim Semiconductor has an ineffective audit committee.
  d. The internal audit function at Smith Components, a very large manufacturing company, was ineffective. The company's auditor has determined that the internal audit function needed to be effective in order for the company to have an effective monitoring component.
  e. The auditors of Benron identified significant financial statement fraud by the company's chief financial officer.
  f. Conroy Trucking Company has an ineffective control environment.
  g. Edwards & Eddins, CPAs, communicated significant deficiencies to Waste Disposal's management and the audit committee for the last two years. At the end of the current year, these significant deficiencies remain uncorrected.

[10,14] **7-39** For each of the following independent situations relating to the audit of ICFR, indicate the reason for and the type of audit report you would issue.
  a. During the audit of Wood Pharmaceuticals, you are surprised to find several control deficiencies in the company's internal control. You determine

that there is a reasonable possibility that any one of them could result in a misstatement that is significant. Although the odds are extremely low that the deficiencies, singly or taken together, will result in a material misstatement of the company's financial statements, the large number of problems causes you concern. Management's written assessment concludes that the company's ICFR was effective as of the report date.

b. You agreed to perform an audit for Rodriguez & Co., after the client's year-end. Due to time constraints, your audit firm could not complete a full audit of ICFR. However, the evidence you did collect suggests that the company has exceptionally strong ICFR. You seriously doubt that a material weakness would have been found if time had permitted a more thorough audit. Management's written assessment concludes that the company's ICFR was effective as of the report date.

c. George & Diana Company's internal audit function identified a material weakness in the company's ICFR. The client corrected this weakness about four months prior to the end of the annual reporting period. Management reassessed controls in the area and found them effective. After reevaluating and retesting the relevant controls, you believe the controls to have been effective for a sufficient period of time to provide adequate evidence that they were designed and operating effectively as of the end of the client's reporting period. Management's written assessment concludes that the company's internal control was effective as of the report date.

d. Reynolds' Distilleries identified what you agree is a material weakness and made an adverse assessment in its report on ICFR. The company had not corrected the material weakness as of the end of the reporting period.

e. Cindy & David Company's management identified a material weakness in the company's ICFR during its assessment process. The client corrected this weakness about a month prior to the end of the annual reporting period. Management reassessed controls in the area, and believes they were effective as of the end of the reporting period. After reevaluating and retesting the relevant controls, you agree that the new controls are well designed, but since the controls over this particular area are applied only once at the end of each month (i.e., the controls have only operated two times since being corrected), you do not believe you have sufficient audit evidence to assess their operating effectiveness. Management's written assessment concludes that the company's internal control was effective as of the report date.

f. During the audit of ICFR for Big Al & Larry Industries, you discover several control deficiencies. You determine that there is more than a reasonable possibility that any one of them could result in a financial statement misstatement. Although you do not believe that any of the deficiencies taken individually will result in a material misstatement, you believe there is a moderately low likelihood that, taken together, the deficiencies could produce a material misstatement. Management's written assessment concludes that the company's internal control was effective as of the report date.

[10,14] 7-40 For each of the following independent situations, indicate the type of report on ICFR you would issue. Justify your report choice.

a. The management's report on ICFR issued by Graham Granary, Inc., includes disclosures about corrective actions taken by the company after the date of management's assessment and the company's plans to implement new controls.

b. Meryll Company's management identified a material weakness prior to the "as of" date and implemented controls to correct it. Management believes that the new controls have been operating for a sufficient period of time to determine that they are designed and operating effectively. However, Meryll's auditor disagrees with the sufficiency of the time period for testing the operating effectiveness of the controls.

[10,14]   7-41   Assume that scenario *a* in Problem 7-36 is a material weakness. Prepare a draft of the auditor's report for an audit of ICFR. Assume that Lorenz's auditor is issuing a separate report on internal control.

[10,14]   7-42   Assume that scenario *b* in Problem 7-36 is a material weakness. Prepare a draft of the auditor's report for an audit of ICFR. Assume that First Coast's auditor is issuing a combined report for the financial statement audit and audit of internal control.

[10,14]   7-43   The following audit report was drafted by a junior staff accountant of Lipske & Griffin, CPAs, at the completion of the audit of Douglas Company's ICFR. The report was submitted to the engagement partner, who reviewed matters thoroughly and properly concluded that there was a material weakness in the client's ICFR. Douglas's management agreed and wrote an assessment indicating that the company's ICFR was not effective as of the end of the reporting period. Sufficient, competent evidence was obtained during the financial statement audit to provide reasonable assurance that the overall financial statements present fairly in accordance with GAAP.

Required:

Identify the errors and omissions contained in the auditor's report as drafted by the staff accountant. Group the errors and omissions by paragraph, where applicable. Do not redraft the report.

Report of Independent Registered Public Accounting Firm

[Introductory paragraph]

We have audited management's assessment, included in the accompanying Management Report on the Financial Statements and Internal Control, that Douglas did not maintain effective internal control over financial reporting as of December 31, 2009, based on criteria established in Enterprise Risk Management—Integrated Framework issued by the Committee of Sponsoring Organizations of the Treadway Commission (COSO). Douglas's management is responsible for maintaining effective internal control over financial reporting and for its assessment of the effectiveness of internal control over financial reporting. Our responsibility is to express an opinion on management's assessment and an opinion on the effectiveness of the company's internal control over financial reporting based on our audit.

[Scope paragraph]

We conducted our audit in accordance with generally accepted auditing standards (United States). Those standards require that we plan and perform the audit to obtain assurance about whether effective internal control was maintained. Our audit included obtaining an understanding of internal control over financial reporting, evaluating management's assessment, testing and evaluating the operating effectiveness of internal control, and performing such other procedures as we considered necessary in the circumstances. We believe that our audit provides a reasonable basis for our opinion.

[Definition paragraph]

A company's internal control over financial reporting is a process designed to provide assurance regarding the reliability of financial reporting and the preparation of financial statements for external purposes in accordance with generally accepted auditing principles. A company's internal control over financial reporting includes those policies and procedures that (1) pertain to the maintenance of records that, in reasonable detail, accurately and fairly reflect the transactions and dispositions of the assets of the company; (2) provide assurance that transactions are recorded as necessary to permit preparation of financial statements in accordance with generally accepted auditing principles, and that receipts and expenditures of the company are being made only in accordance with authorizations of management and directors of the company; and (3) provide assurance regarding prevention or timely detection of unauthorized acquisition, use, or disposition of the company's assets that could have an inconsequential effect on the financial statements.

[Inherent limitations paragraph]

Because of its inherent limitations, internal control over financial reporting will prevent or detect misstatements. Also, projections of any evaluation of effectiveness to future periods are subject to the risk that controls may become inadequate because of changes in conditions, or that the degree of compliance with the policies or procedures may deteriorate.

[Opinion paragraph]

In our opinion, management's assessment that Douglas maintained ineffective internal control over financial reporting as of December 31, 2009, is fairly stated, in all material respects, based on criteria established in Enterprise Risk Management—Integrated Framework issued by the Committee of Sponsoring Organizations of the Treadway Commission (COSO). We therefore express an adverse opinion on management's assessment. Also in our opinion, Douglas maintained, in all material respects, effective internal control over financial reporting as of December 31, 2009, based on criteria established in Enterprise Risk Management—Integrated Framework issued by the Committee of Sponsoring Organizations of the Treadway Commission (COSO), except for one material weakness, which results in our issuing a qualified opinion on Douglas's internal control over financial reporting.

[Explanatory paragraph]

We have also audited, in accordance with generally accepted accounting standards (United States), the consolidated financial statements of Douglas, and our report dated February 15, 2009, expressed a qualified opinion.

Lipske & Griffin, CPAs
Mapleton, Arizona
March 11, 2010

[18] 7-44 Auditors use various audit techniques to gather evidence when a client's accounting information is processed using IT. Select the audit procedure from the following list and enter it in the appropriate place on the grid.

Audit procedure:
1. Test data method
2. Custom audit software
3. Auditing around the computer
4. Generalized audit software

Description of Audit Technique	Audit Technique
a. Program written by the auditor to perform a specific task for a particular client	
b. The auditor's auditing of the inputs and outputs of the system without verification of the processing of the data	
c. Processing fictitious and real data separately through the client's IT system	

[18] 7-45 Brown, CPA, is auditing the financial statements of Big Z Wholesaling, Inc., a continuing audit client, for the year ended January 31, 2009. On January 5, 2009, Brown observed the tagging and counting of Big Z's physical inventory and made appropriate test counts. These test counts have been recorded on a computer file. As in prior years, Big Z gave Brown two computer files. One file represents the perpetual inventory (first-in, first-out) records for the year ended January 31, 2009. The other file represents the January 5 physical inventory count.

Assume:

1. Brown issued an unqualified opinion on the prior year's financial statements.
2. All inventory is purchased for resale and located in a single warehouse.
3. Brown has appropriate computerized audit software.
4. The perpetual inventory file contains the following information in item number sequence:
   a. Beginning balances at February 1, 2008: item number, item description, total quantity, and price.
   b. For each item purchased during the year: date received, receiving report number, vendor item number, item description, quantity, and total dollar amount.
   c. For each item sold during the year: date shipped, invoice number, item number, item description, quantity, and dollar amount.
   d. For each item adjusted for physical inventory count differences: date, item number, item description, quantity, and dollar amount.
5. The physical inventory file contains the following information in item number sequence: tag number, item number, item description, and count quantity.

Required:

Describe the substantive auditing procedures Brown may consider performing with computerized audit software using Big Z's two computer files and Brown's computer file of test counts. The substantive auditing procedures described may indicate the reports to be printed out for Brown's follow-up by subsequent application of manual procedures. Do not describe subsequent manual auditing procedures.

Group the procedures by those using (a) the perpetual inventory file; and (b) the physical inventory and test count files.

INTERNET ASSIGNMENTS

[4,10,14]   7-46   Search the Internet (e.g., a company's Web site or sec.gov), and find an audit report for a company's audit of internal control over financial reporting. Determine whether the company used the combined or separate format.

[4,14]   7-47   Search the Internet (e.g., a company's Web site or sec.gov), and find an audit report for a company's audit of internal control over financial reporting that expresses an adverse opinion with respect to the effectiveness of internal control.

HANDS-ON CASES

ACL

STATISTICAL AND NONSTATISTICAL SAMPLING TOOLS FOR AUDITING

CHAPTER 8

LEARNING OBJECTIVES

Upon completion of this chapter you will

[1] Learn the definition of audit sampling and why auditors use sampling to gather evidence.

[2] Understand basic sampling terminology.

[3] Learn the types of audit procedures that do and do not involve sampling.

[4] Learn the types of audit sampling.

[5] Learn the sampling requirements in auditing standards.

[6] Learn how to apply attribute sampling to tests of controls.

[7] Work through an example of attribute sampling.

[8] Learn how to apply nonstatistical sampling to tests of controls.

RELEVANT ACCOUNTING AND AUDITING PRONOUNCEMENTS

AICPA, *Audit Sampling* (Audit Guide) (New York: AICPA, 2008)

AU 311, Planning and Supervision

AU 312, Audit Risk and Materiality in Conducting an Audit

AU 314, Understanding the Entity and Its Environment and Assessing the Risks of Material Misstatement

AU 316, Consideration of Fraud in a Financial Statement Audit

AU 318, Performing Audit Procedures in Response to Assessed Risks and Evaluating the Audit Evidence Obtained

AU 326, Audit Evidence

AU 339, Audit Documentation

AU 350, Audit Sampling

PCAOB Auditing Standard No. 3, Audit Documentation (AS3)

PCAOB Auditing Standard No. 5, An Audit of Internal Control Over Financial Reporting That Is Integrated with An Audit of Financial Statements (AS5)

PCAOB Proposed Auditing Standards Related to the Auditor's Assessment of and Response to Risk, PCAOB Release No. 2008-006 (October 21, 2008).

Audit Sampling: An Overview and Application to Tests of Controls

Major Phases of an Audit

Client acceptance/
continuance and establishing
an understanding with the client
(Chapter 5)

Preliminary engagement
activities
(Chapter 5)

Plan the audit
(Chapters 3 and 5)

Consider and audit
internal control
(Chapters 6 and 7)

Audit business processes
and related accounts
(e.g., revenue generation)
(Chapters 10–16)

Complete the audit
(Chapter 17)

Evaluate results and issue audit
report (Chapters 1 and 18)

In the next two chapters we examine how auditors apply sampling theory to gather evidence to confirm or disconfirm management's assertions. Sampling and statistics in general are topics that make many people feel uncomfortable. Before getting into technical audit sampling and statistical terms, we have found that it is useful for students to consider some of the basic concepts of sampling in a nontechnical context.

What If You Were an Apple Inspector?

Please imagine that you have just taken a job as an apple inspector for Best Apples, Inc.—a large apple grower. You are replacing a previous inspector who was recently fired for lack of due care, and your new employer has made it clear that you must meet high performance standards to make it through your probationary period. Best Apples owns and operates many apple orchards and sells its apples to major fruit processors (hereafter "buyers") whose products include fresh apples, apple sauce, and apple juice. Best Apple makes large shipments of apples to buyers on a daily basis during harvest season; each shipment contains approximately 1,500 bushels from various orchards. Each bushel contains 100 to 150 apples. The bushel indicates which orchard the apples come from. Your job is to manually inspect the quality of apples just prior to shipment. Obviously, there is neither the time nor need to inspect every apple, so you will examine a sample of apples.

Imagine it is your first day on the job; consider for a moment what information about the apples, your employer, or the buyer you would like to know before you begin your inspections. Among other things, it would be useful to know the answers to the following questions:

- For what purpose will the current shipment be used (e.g., fresh apples, sauce, or juice)?
- The definition of a defect—what constitutes a bad apple?
- Tolerable defect percentage—what percentage of defective apples will the buyers accept in a shipment?
- What has Best Apple's historical defect percentage been?
- Have growing conditions (e.g., weather, pests) been normal this year?
- What happens if we send a shipment that contains an unacceptably high percentage of defects?
- Level of assurance or confidence—how confident do I need to be in my testing results?
- What quality controls and processes does Best Apples have in place?
- Are the defect percentages the same for all orchards?

Suppose you receive satisfactory answers to these questions and you begin your testing. The primary purpose of sampling is to draw inferences about the whole population based on the results of testing only a subset of the population. You draw a sample of 20 apples and find 1 defective apple. Projecting your sample defect rate to the total population suggests a shipment defect rate of 5 percent (1/20). While 5 percent is your best estimate based on your sample results, will you be positive that you have determined the correct defect rate for the entire shipment? The obvious answer is no, because there is a chance the shipment defect rate could be higher or lower than your sample rate of 5 percent. The uncertainty associated with sampling is known as *sampling risk*. Whenever inspectors or auditors test less than the entire population, there is a risk that the sample results will not be similar to what the results would be if the inspector were to test the entire population. In other words, sampling risk is the risk that the results of a sample are not representative of the population.

Sampling theory allows us to measure the risk associated with sampling. For example, if we knew a buyer would accept up to 10 percent defective apples in a shipment, we can compute the risk that the actual shipment defect rate is higher than 10 percent (you will learn how to make such evaluations in this chapter). For a sample of 20 apples with 1 defective apple there is approximately a 40 percent chance that the actual shipment defect rate exceeds the buyer's tolerable defect rate of 10 percent. Inspectors and auditors can reduce sampling risk by taking larger samples. In the extreme, if you tested 100 percent of the apples in the shipment, then there would be no sampling risk because you would know with certainty the true shipment defect rate. While it would not be economical for you to inspect every apple, you could increase your sample size to reduce the risk that the shipment will contain an unacceptably high rate of defects. If you examine a sample of 100 apples and find 5 defects, sampling theory indicates that you would only face approximately a 6 percent chance that the true shipment defect rate exceeds the buyer's tolerable rate of 10 percent. So an important concept in audit sampling is that by increasing sample size, you can reduce uncertainty and risk.

The converse of sampling risk is *confidence level*. In other words, while both samples discussed above yielded a defect rate of 5 percent (1/20 and 5/100), with the larger sample you can be approximately 94 percent confident (100 percent – 6 percent sampling risk) that the shipment is acceptable. The smaller sample only allows you to be 60 percent confident (100 percent – 40 percent sampling risk). We will continue to refer to this apple inspector example as we introduce sampling terms and concepts in this chapter.

This chapter has two overall objectives: (1) to provide an introduction and overview of audit sampling; and (2) to apply statistical attribute sampling and nonstatistical sampling techniques to tests of controls. The sampling techniques covered in this chapter are applicable for testing conducted for both an audit of internal controls over financial reporting and a financial statement audit. In Chapter 9 we cover statistical and nonstatistical sampling techniques for substantive tests of account balances. 🐾

Introduction

[LO 1]   In the early days of auditing, it was not unusual for the independent auditor to examine all of the records of the company being audited.[1] However, as companies grew in size and complexity, it became uneconomical to examine all the accounting records and supporting documents. Auditors found it necessary to draw conclusions about the fairness of a company's financial statements based on an examination of a subset of the records and transactions. As a result, the auditor provides reasonable, not absolute, assurance (refer to the third standard

[1]See the introduction to the American Institute of Certified Public Accountants *Audit Sampling* (AICPA Audit Guide) (New York: AICPA, 2008) for a discussion of the development of sampling in auditing.

of fieldwork) that the financial statements are fairly presented. The justification for accepting some uncertainty is the trade-off between the cost of examining all the data and the cost of making an incorrect decision based on a sample of the data. As noted in Chapter 1, this concept of reasonable assurance is addressed in the auditor's report.

Auditing standards recognize and permit both statistical and nonstatistical methods of audit sampling. Research suggests that nonstatistical methods are the most common in practice.[2] Later in the chapter we discuss some reasons why nonstatistical sampling has become more common in practice. Both nonstatistical and statistical methods are based on the same fundamental sampling theories. In fact, the steps and techniques used for these two sampling approaches are far more similar than they are different, and auditing standards indicate the sample sizes for the two approaches should be approximately the same size (AU 350.22). To properly apply a nonstatistical sampling approach, it is necessary to understand the underlying statistical principles; thus, we cover statistical sampling before we discuss nonstatistical sampling.

Occasionally, students will ask if recent advances in technology have, or will have, eliminated the need for audit sampling. Two advances have reduced the number of times auditors need to apply sampling techniques to gather audit evidence. First, many companies have developed well-controlled, automated accounting systems that can process routine transactions with no or very few errors. Rather than rely on audit sampling to test routine transactions processed by these automated information systems, auditors test the processing software control configurations and general computer controls (e.g., restricted access, program change management) associated with the automated controls. Second, the advent of powerful audit software such as ACL allows auditors, in some situations, to download and examine electronic client data rather than sample.

While technology has reduced the number of situations where audit sampling is necessary, technology will never eliminate the need for auditors to rely on sampling to some degree because (1) many control processes require human involvement to operate effectively (e.g., reconciliations, review, and resolution of a system's generated exception reports); (2) many testing procedures require the auditor to physically inspect an asset (e.g., inventory) or inspect characteristics of a transaction or balance (e.g., terms in a contract); and (3) in many cases auditors are required to obtain and evaluate evidence from third parties (e.g., letters confirming accounts receivable balances from client customers). These situations require the auditor's "hands-on" attention. When the number of items or transactions in these populations is large, it is not economical for auditors to test 100 percent of the population; instead they use sampling to gather sufficient audit evidence.

Definitions and Key Concepts

Audit Sampling   *Audit sampling* is defined as the application of audit procedures to less than 100 percent of the items in a population of audit relevance selected in such a way that the auditor expects the sample to be representative of the population and thus likely to provide a reasonable basis for conclusions about the population. The fact that an audit involves sampling is expressed to users of the financial statements by the phrase "An audit includes examining, *on a test basis*" contained in the scope paragraph of the auditor's report.

---

[2]See N. Hitzig, "Audit Sampling: A Survey of Current Practice," *The CPA Journal* (July 1995), pp. 54–57, and W. F. Messier, Jr., S. J. Kachelmeier, and K. Jensen, "An Experimental Assessment of Recent Professional Developments in Nonstatistical Sampling Guidance," *Auditing: A Journal of Practice & Theory* (March 2001), pp. 81–96.

Sampling Risk

✂ [LO 2]

When sampling is used by an auditor, an element of uncertainty enters into the auditor's conclusions. This element of uncertainty, referred to as *sampling risk,* was discussed briefly under detection risk in Chapter 3 and in the apple inspector example at the beginning of this chapter. Sampling risk refers to the possibility that the sample drawn is not representative of the population and that, as a result, the auditor will reach an incorrect conclusion about the account balance or class of transactions based on the sample. When using audit sampling techniques to obtain evidence, the auditor must always accept some sampling risk. Sampling risk is one reason why auditors must accept some detection and audit risk, as discussed in Chapter 3.

Due to sampling risk, the auditor faces the chance that sampling may lead to one of two possible types of decision errors: (1) deciding that the population tested is not acceptable when in reality it is; and (2) deciding that the population tested is acceptable when in reality it is not. In statistical terms, these errors are known as Type I and Type II errors, respectively. More formally, Type I and Type II errors are defined as follows:

- *Risk of incorrect rejection (Type I).* In testing an internal control, this is the risk that the sample supports a conclusion that the control is not operating effectively when, in truth, it is operating effectively. When an auditor is evaluating the level of reliance that can be placed on a control in the context of a financial statement audit, this risk is also commonly referred to as the *risk of underreliance* or the *risk of assessing control risk too high.*

  In substantive testing, this is the risk that the sample supports the conclusion that the recorded account balance is materially misstated when it is actually not materially misstated.

- *Risk of incorrect acceptance (Type II).* In testing a control, this is the risk that the sample supports a conclusion that the control is operating effectively when, in truth, it is not operating effectively. When an auditor is evaluating the level of reliance that can be placed on a control in the context of a financial statement audit, this risk is also commonly referred to as the *risk of overreliance* or the *risk of assessing control risk too low.*

  In substantive testing, this is the risk that the sample supports the conclusion that the recorded account balance is not materially misstated when it is actually materially misstated.

The risk of incorrect rejection (a Type I decision error) relates to the *efficiency* of the audit. This type of decision error can result in the auditor conducting more audit work than necessary in order to reach the correct conclusion. The risk of incorrect acceptance (a Type II decision error) relates to the *effectiveness* of the audit. This type of decision error can result in the auditor failing to detect a material misstatement in the financial statements. This can lead to litigation against the auditor by parties that rely on the financial statements. Because of the potentially severe consequences of a Type II decision error, auditors design their sampling applications to keep this risk to an acceptably low level. Auditors typically focus only on Type II decision errors in determining their sample sizes, because Type I decision errors affect efficiency and not effectiveness and because, by controlling for the risk of Type II errors, they also obtain relatively good coverage for the risk of Type I errors. For these reasons, in this chapter we do not address the potential implications on sampling applications of Type I errors.

Audit sampling can also involve *nonsampling* risk. Nonsampling risk is the risk of auditor error and arises from the possibility that the auditor may sample the wrong population to test an assertion, fail to detect a misstatement when applying an audit procedure, or misinterpret an audit result. When applying audit sampling to substantive tests of details, both sampling and nonsampling risk make up the auditor's detection risk (see Chapter 3). While statistical sampling allows the auditor to quantify and control sampling risk, no sampling method allows the auditor to measure nonsampling risk. The uncertainty related to nonsampling risk can be controlled by adequate training, proper planning, and effective supervision.

Three Important Factors   In the preface to the chapter, we asked you to imagine that you were an apple inspector and we asked you to consider what information you would like to have before you began testing apples. While you would want answers to all the questions listed in the preface, you will find that three of the factors listed there are the most important inputs to determine sample sizes for all types of audit sampling. These three inputs are (1) desired level of assurance in the results (or confidence level); (2) acceptable defect rate (or tolerable error); and (3) historical defect rate (or expected error).

Confidence Level

The first input, *confidence level*, is the complement of sampling risk. For example, as an apple inspector you have to accept some risk that the shipment defect percentage is higher than your sample defect percentage, and higher than the defect rate the buyer will tolerate. You would determine your acceptable level of sampling risk by considering the amount of reliance to be placed on your tests and the consequences of a decision error. The more the reliance placed on your inspection (versus other testing or quality control measures) and the more severe the consequences of a Type II decision error (e.g., the apple buyer will stop doing business with your company if you mistakenly accept and send a failed shipment), the less risk you will want to accept and the more confident you will want to be in your testing. Auditors, like inspectors, focus on both risk and confidence level. In statistical terminology, a confidence level represents the probability that a given interval includes the true but unknown measure of the characteristic of interest. For example, to place reliance on a control, an auditor may want to be 95-percent confident that the control operates effectively at least 97 percent of the time (or fails to operate no more than 3 percent of the time). Because risk is the complement of confidence level, auditors can set either confidence level or sampling risk. For example, the auditor may set sampling risk for a particular sampling application at 5 percent, which results in a confidence level of 95 percent. Confidence level and sampling risk are related to sample size: The larger the sample, the higher the confidence level and the lower the sampling risk.

Tolerable and Expected Error

Once the desired confidence level is established, the appropriate sample size is determined largely by how much *tolerable error* exceeds *expected error*. The smaller the difference between these two variables, the more precise the sampling results must be, and therefore the larger the sample size needed. For example, assume that during your interview for the apple inspector position you were told that the historical shipment defect rate has averaged 3 percent ±2 percent and the buyers typically can accept up to 10 percent defective apples. However, as you are planning your sample on the first day of work, you learn that poor weather this year has resulted in an expected defect rate of 7 percent ±3 percent. All else equal, the new information will require a larger sample size because now there is a smaller margin for error or smaller difference between tolerable and expected error. This is because there is less room to accommodate sampling risk in the interval between 7 and 10 percent than there is in the interval between 3 and 10 percent. Similarly, even assuming the historical rate stayed at 3 percent, if a customer reduced their acceptance defect level from 10 percent to 6 percent the margin for error would be smaller. It doesn't matter which of the two factors, tolerable or expected error, causes a change in the difference between them to be smaller; the critical factor is how large the difference is between the defect rate (or misstatement) that is expected and the defect rate (or misstatement) that can be tolerated.

In typical statistical sampling terminology, the term *precision* relates to how close a sample estimate is to the population characteristic being estimated, given a specified sampling risk. Thus, precision at the planning stage of an audit sampling application is the difference between the expected and the tolerable deviation rate or misstatement. Auditing standards use the term *allowance for sampling risk* to reflect the concept of precision in a sampling application. For example, if an auditor expected that a control would have a 2 percent deviation (failure) rate and he or she was willing to tolerate a deviation rate of 5 percent, the allowance for sampling risk would be 3 percent. Remember that in order to successfully apply audit sampling to gather audit evidence, auditors must be able to "tolerate" some deviations (for controls testing) or misstatement (for substantive testing) to provide an allowance for sampling risk. The only way to completely remove this risk is to test all the items in a population.

Audit Evidence Choices That Do and Do Not Involve Sampling

[LO 3]

In assessing the risk of material misstatement, or in auditing an account balance or a class of transactions, the auditor seldom relies on a single test. Generally, the auditor applies a number of audit procedures in order to reach a conclusion. Some audit procedures involve sampling as defined by auditing standards, while others do not involve sampling. Table 8–1 indicates the types of evidence that are commonly gathered using audit sampling as well as types where sampling is generally not used.

We have already covered the types of evidence in earlier chapters, but here are some examples of typical sampling applications.

- **Inspection of tangible assets.** An auditor typically attends a client's year-end inventory count. Because the number of inventory items can be very large, the auditor may use audit sampling to select inventory items to physically inspect and count.

- **Inspection of records or documents.** A control may require that before a check is written to a vendor, the payables clerk must match an approved purchase order to an approved receiving report and vendor invoice and indicate an acceptable match by initialing a copy of the check stapled to the other three documents. For large companies, this sort of control would be performed many times a day. The auditors can gather evidence on the effectiveness of the control by testing a sample of the documentation packages.

- **Reperformance.** As discussed in Chapter 7, to comply with rule 404 of the Sarbanes-Oxley Act of 2002, publicly traded clients must document and test controls over important assertions for significant accounts. In

TABLE 8–1	Relationship between Evidence Types and Audit Sampling
Type of Evidence	*Audit Sampling Commonly Used*
Inspection of tangible assets	Yes
Inspection of records or documents	Yes
Reperformance	Yes
Recalculation	Yes
Confirmation	Yes
Analytical procedures	No
Scanning	No
Inquiry	No
Observation	No

assessing the competence and objectivity of the client's work, the auditor may reperform a sample of the tests performed by the client.

- **Confirmation.** A common technique to gather evidence that accounts receivable balances exist and are accurately recorded is to send letters to customers asking them to confirm their balance. Rather than send a letter to all customers, the auditor can select a sample of customers.

Testing All Items with a Particular Characteristic   Table 8–1 indicates that sampling is commonly used to gather evidence of the first five types. It is also common for auditors to use other testing approaches instead of sampling or in combination with sampling to gather evidence. For example, when an account or class of transactions is made up of a few large items, the auditor may test all the items in the account or class of transactions. Because the entire class or balance is subjected to a 100-percent examination, such an audit procedure does not involve sampling. More common than testing 100 percent of the items in an account balance or class of transactions is a technique in which the auditor tests all items with a particular characteristic of interest based on risk or monetary value. For example, if the auditor is aware of certain transactions that look unusual or present greater risk, the auditor should test all these items rather than applying audit sampling.

Similarly, if a relatively small number of large transactions make up a relatively large percentage of an account or class of transactions, auditors will typically test all the transactions greater than a particular dollar amount. As an illustration, an auditor may decide to audit all 15 individual accounts receivable balances greater than $100,000, because these large customers make up 70 percent of the total account balance. For the remaining 30 percent of the total account balance consisting of individual customer account balances less than $100,000, the auditor could apply audit sampling. Alternatively, the auditor could decide to apply substantive analytical procedures to the part of the total receivables balance consisting of individual customer accounts under $100,000, or may even decide to apply no audit procedures to this part of the total account because he or she deems that an acceptably low risk of material misstatement exists in this group. In these latter two instances, the auditor is not using sampling.

Testing Only One or a Few Items   Automated information systems process transactions consistently unless the system or programs are changed. When testing automated IT controls, the auditor may decide to test one or a few of each type of transactions at a point in time. In conjunction with that test of the automated controls, the auditor may test general controls over changes to the system and program in order to provide evidence that the automated controls have been operating over the audit period. This type of test of automated IT control does not involve audit sampling.

Types of Audit Sampling

Nonstatistical versus Statistical Sampling

⚓ [LO 4]

There are two general approaches to audit sampling: *nonstatistical* and *statistical*. In nonstatistical sampling, the auditor does not use statistical techniques to determine the sample size, select the sample, and/or measure sampling risk when evaluating results. Statistical sampling, on the other hand, uses the laws of probability to compute sample size and evaluate the sample results, thereby permitting the auditor to use the most efficient sample size and to quantify the sampling risk for the purpose of reaching a statistical conclusion about the population. Both approaches require the use of the auditor's professional judgment to plan, perform, and evaluate the sample evidence. The major advantages of statistical sampling are that it helps the auditor (1) design an efficient sample; (2) measure the sufficiency of evidence obtained; and (3) quantify sampling risk. The disadvantages of statistical sampling include additional costs of (1) training auditors in the proper use of sampling techniques; (2) designing and conducting the sampling application; and (3) lack of consistent application across audit teams due to the complexity of the underlying concepts.

With a nonstatistical sampling application, the auditor must rely on his or her professional judgment, in combination with audit firm guidance and knowledge of the underlying statistical sampling theories, to reach a conclusion about the audit test. Therefore, to properly apply nonstatistical sampling, auditors' judgment and their firm's sampling guidance must be grounded in statistical sampling theory. In fact, auditing standards indicate that sample sizes from statistical and nonstatistical sampling plans should be approximately the same (AU 350.22). Thus, a disadvantage of nonstatistical sampling is that auditor judgment may diverge significantly from sampling theory, resulting in testing that is not as effective as statistical sampling. Most firms address this concern by providing their auditors with nonstatistical sampling guidance and procedures that are easy to use, encourage consistency in sampling applications across engagement teams, and are grounded in sampling theory. Nonstatistical audit sampling can be simpler to use and more consistently applied than statistical sampling because some of the more difficult statistical decisions can be made by experts. The experts' decisions are then built into the audit firm's guidance and decision aids.

This chapter and Chapter 9 provide detailed coverage of both statistical and nonstatistical sampling. Even though nonstatistical sampling is very common in practice, we cover statistical sampling first because statistical theory provides the foundation for both sampling approaches.

Practice **INSIGHT**	Whether nonstatistical or statistical sampling is used, the sample size must be sufficient to support reliance on the type of controls and assertions being tested. PCAOB inspection teams have found auditors using sample sizes which were smaller than required to support their conclusions regarding the effectiveness of controls tested (e.g., PCAOB Release No. 104-2005-120).

Types of Statistical Sampling Techniques

Auditors use three major types of statistical sampling techniques: *attribute sampling, monetary-unit sampling,* and *classical variables sampling.*

Attribute Sampling

Attribute sampling is used to estimate the proportion of a population that possesses a specified characteristic. The most common use of attribute sampling is for tests of controls. In this case, the auditor wants to determine the deviation rate for a control implemented within the client's accounting system. For example, the auditor may want to gather evidence that a credit check is performed on customer orders before shipment. Measurement of the deviation rate provides evidence about whether the control is operating effectively to process accounting transactions properly and therefore provides support for the auditor's set level of control risk. Attribute sampling may also be used with a substantive test of transactions when such a test is conducted with a test of controls as a dual-purpose test.

Monetary-Unit Sampling

Monetary-unit sampling uses attribute-sampling theory and techniques to estimate the monetary amount of misstatement for a class of transactions or an account balance. Variations of monetary-unit sampling are known as *probability-proportional-to-size sampling* and *cumulative monetary amount sampling.* Auditors use this sampling technique extensively because it has a number of advantages over classical variables sampling. Monetary-unit sampling builds upon attribute-sampling theory to express a conclusion in dollar amounts. You will learn about monetary-unit sampling in Chapter 9.

Classical Variables Sampling Classical variables sampling includes the sampling techniques typically taught in an undergraduate statistics class. While auditors sometimes use variables sampling to estimate the dollar value of a class of transactions or account balance, it is more frequently used to determine whether an account is materially misstated. Classical variables sampling is covered in the *Advanced Module* in Chapter 9.

Regardless of the approach or type of sampling, auditing standards contain requirements that auditors must follow when planning, selecting a sample for, and performing and evaluating the audit sampling applications. We will refer to these requirements as we discuss the different approaches and types of audit sampling.

The remainder of this chapter presents an application of statistical attribute sampling to tests of controls, followed by a discussion of nonstatistical sampling applied to tests of controls.

Attribute Sampling Applied to Tests of Controls

[LO 5,6,7] Attribute sampling is a statistical sampling method used to estimate the proportion of a characteristic in a population. In applying this technique to tests of controls, the auditor normally attempts to determine the operating effectiveness of a control in terms of deviations from a prescribed internal control.

In conducting a statistical sample for a test of controls, auditing standards (AU 350) require the auditor to properly plan, perform, and evaluate the sampling application and adequately document each phase of the sampling application in the working papers. The following sections discuss the steps that are included in the three phases of an attribute-sampling application. Table 8–2 lists the steps involved in the three phases of an attribute-sampling application.

Calabro Wireless, Inc., Illustration Audit tests for the audit of Calabro Wireless Services, Inc., will be used to demonstrate an attribute-sampling application. Calabro is a business services company that uses wireless communications

TABLE 8–2	**Steps in Attribute Sampling**

Planning
1. Determine the test objectives.
2. Define the population characteristics:
   - Define the sampling population.
   - Define the sampling unit.
   - Define the control deviation conditions.
3. Determine the sample size, using the following inputs:
   - The desired confidence level or risk of incorrect acceptance.
   - The tolerable deviation rate.
   - The expected population deviation rate.

Performance
4. Select sample items.
5. Perform the auditing procedures:
   - Understand and analyze any deviations observed.

Evaluation
6. Calculate the sample deviation rate and the computed upper deviation rate.
7. Draw final conclusions.

technology to develop solutions for businesses. The company emphasizes its systems, reliability, solution-oriented marketing, and high level of customer service. The company provides high-quality, low-cost service to the marketplace. In recent years the company has experienced annual subscriber growth of about 20 percent per year. Andrew Judd is the audit senior on the Calabro audit and his firm has audited Calabro for 10 years. The auditors have developed an understanding of Calabro's revenue process and have decided to rely on selected controls to reduce control risk below the maximum for the current year financial statement audit.

Practice INSIGHT

Given the integrated audit of internal control and the financial statements for public companies, the auditor may perform tests of controls that simultaneously satisfy the objectives of both audits (AS5).

Planning

Proper planning of an attribute-sampling application involves completing a number of important steps. Each of these steps, in turn, requires the use of professional judgment on the part of the auditor. The following subsections document Judd's sampling plan on the Calabro Wireless Services audit. Typically, a public accounting firm uses a formal working paper or template to document the steps in the sampling plan.

Step 1: Determine the Test Objectives

Auditing standards require that sampling applications be well planned and take into consideration the relationship of the sample to the objective(s) of the test. The objective of attribute sampling when used for tests of controls is to evaluate the operating effectiveness of the internal control for purposes of the internal control audit for public companies (see Chapter 7) or to determine the degree of reliance that can be placed on controls for a financial statement audit. Thus, the auditor assesses the deviation or error rate that exists for each control selected for testing. Audit sampling for tests of controls is generally appropriate when the completion of a control procedure leaves documentary evidence (e.g., initials of approval).

In the Calabro audit, the objective of the test is to determine if Calabro's revenue process is functioning as documented. Judd, the audit senior, wants to determine if the controls identified concerning credit authorization, contract approval, and proper pricing are operating effectively and thus allow control risk to be set below the maximum.

Calabro's revenue transactions arise in the following manner:

> Subscribers may lease a wireless device (an electronic pager or mobile phone) from the company or purchase a wireless device and pay only an access fee for the company's wireless communication system. Each subscriber enters into a service contract with the company, which provides for the payment of the access fee and the purchase or lease of one or more wireless devices. Contracts with customers with large numbers of devices are typically for three- to five-year terms, while contracts for smaller quantities are typically for one-year terms with renewal options at the end of the terms.

For this sampling application, Judd has decided to rely on three controls in Calabro's revenue process. The three control procedures and their definitions are as follows:

1. ***Sales and service contracts are properly authorized for credit approval.*** Calabro's credit department personnel check the creditworthiness of new customers and establish a credit limit based on that evaluation. For existing customers, the amount of the new sale or lease is added to the existing accounts receivable balance, and the total

is compared to the customer's credit limit. If the amount is less than the credit limit, the transaction is processed. If the total is more than the credit limit, the transaction is subjected to review by the credit manager before the sale is approved.

2. ***Sales are not recorded without an approved sales and lease contract.*** Calabro's revenue process contains a control that no revenue transactions are to be recorded unless an approved sales or lease contract is sent to the billing department.

3. ***Sales and lease contracts are properly priced.*** Calabro's revenue process also includes a control that requires billing department personnel to use an authorized price list for the sale of wireless devices. Access and lease fees are determined based on a fee structure that includes volume discounts for large-unit subscribers.

Step 2: Define the Population Characteristics　To achieve the test objectives, the auditor must carefully consider the characteristics of the sampling population.

Define the Sampling Population.　All or a subset of the items that constitute the class of transactions (or account balance when not testing controls) make up the sampling population. The auditor must determine that the population from which the sample is selected is appropriate for the specific assertion, because sample results can be projected only to the population from which the sample was selected. For example, suppose the auditor is interested in examining the effectiveness of a control designed to ensure that all shipments to customers are billed by testing whether all shipments were, in fact, billed. If the auditor uses the population of sales invoices as the sampling population, he or she is not likely to detect goods shipped but not billed, because the population of sales invoices includes only sales that were billed. In this example, the correct sampling population for testing the completeness assertion would be the population of all shipped goods as documented by shipping records such as bills of lading.

There is a natural tendency to designate an entire class of transactions (or all the items in an account balance) as the population. However, the sample population should be restricted to the transactions and time period under the same system of controls that are relevant to the assertions being tested. For example, if the testing will be conducted in October for a calendar year-end client, the sampling population can be defined as all transactions in the first nine months of the year. The results of the sampling application in this case would apply only to the nine-month period tested. However, the auditor must also consider whether to conduct additional tests in the remaining period under audit through year-end (see Chapters 5 and 7 for discussions of what auditors do to "roll forward" testing between an interim date and year end).

Once the population has been defined, the auditor must determine that the physical representation (referred to as the *frame*) of the population is complete. This determination is typically made by comparing the frame, for example an accounts receivable listing, to the general ledger or by examining and accounting for the numerical sequence of prenumbered sales invoice documents. Because the auditor selects the sample from the frame, any conclusions relate only to that physical representation of the population. If the frame and the population differ, the auditor might draw the wrong conclusion about the population. In the example above, if the frame and the population differ, the sales journal (the frame) would not include all sales transactions during the period of interest (the population).

For the audit of Calabro's revenue process, Judd has decided the population will include all sales and leases recorded in the entire year. The physical representation of the population is the numeric file of sales and lease contracts maintained in the sales department. Based on a review of the client's procedures for completeness, which includes accounting for prenumbered documents, Judd has determined that the frame is complete. The population of sales and lease transactions for the year contains 125,000 items that are numbered from 1 to 125,000.

Define the Sampling Unit.   The individual members of the sampling population are called the *sampling units*. In the apple inspector example, the sampling unit is an individual apple. In auditing, a sampling unit may be a document, an entry, or a line item. Each sampling unit makes up one item in the population. The sampling unit should be defined in relation to the control being tested.

The sampling unit for the test of controls in the Calabro audit is defined as the sales or lease contract. Judd can perform all tests for the controls selected by examining this set of documents.

Define Control Deviation Conditions.   For tests of controls, a deviation is a departure from adequate performance of the internal control. It is important for the auditor to define carefully what is considered a deviation. Thinking back to the apple inspector example, before you begin your inspection, you need to know what constitutes a "bad" apple: Does it take a minor blemish or significant damage to conclude that an apple is defective?

Judd has defined control deviations for each of the internal controls being assessed as follows:

1. ***Sales and service contracts are properly authorized for credit approval.*** A deviation in this test is defined as the failure of Calabro's credit department personnel to follow proper credit approval procedures for new and existing customers.
2. ***Sales are not recorded without an approved sales and lease contract.*** For this control, a deviation is defined as the absence of an approved sales or lease contract.
3. ***Sales and lease contracts are properly priced.*** A deviation in this case is the use of an unauthorized price for a wireless device or an incorrect access or lease fee.

Step 3: Determine the Sample Size   Considerable judgment is required in determining the appropriate values for the inputs that are used to compute sample size. The three key inputs to determining the sample are the same as those discussed earlier: the desired confidence level, tolerable deviation rate, and expected population deviation rate. Auditing standards require that auditors give adequate consideration to the appropriate value of these inputs. Because of the difficulty of making these input judgments, determining the sample size is typically the most difficult step of an audit sampling application.

Desired Confidence Level.   As discussed earlier in the chapter, the complement of the confidence level is the risk that the sample results will support a conclusion that the control is functioning effectively when in truth it is not (i.e., the risk of incorrect acceptance). In a financial statement audit, this can result in assessing control risk too low. This risk influences the effectiveness of the audit. If the auditor sets control risk too low and overrelies on the controls, the level of substantive procedures may be too low to detect material misstatements that may be present in the financial statement account. This is because when control risk inappropriately decreases, the auditor increases the acceptable level of detection risk associated with substantive testing to compensate (see discussion of the audit risk model in Chapter 3). Thus, if control risk is mistakenly set at a low level, detection risk will be set too high. This increases the risk that the auditor will fail to detect a material misstatement if one exists in the account.

In setting the desired confidence level and acceptable level of risk, the auditor considers the significance of the account and the importance of the assertion on which the control provides assurance, as well as the degree of reliance to be placed on the control. Generally, when the auditor has decided to rely on controls, the confidence level is set at 90 or 95 percent, meaning that the auditor is willing to accept a 10- or 5-percent risk of accepting the control as effective when in fact it is not. However, the auditor must remember that there is a direct relationship between the confidence level and sample size: The more confident the auditor would like to be (and the less risk he or she is willing to accept), the larger the sample size must be, all else equal. For example, in the illustration below the effect on the sample size is substantial (a 21-percent increase) when the desired confidence level increases from 90 to 95 percent.

Desired Confidence Level	Sample Size[3]
90%	77
95%	93

Thus, the auditor must balance effectiveness concerns with efficiency concerns when setting the desired confidence level and acceptable risk of incorrect acceptance.

Tolerable Deviation Rate.   The tolerable deviation rate is the maximum deviation rate from a prescribed control that the auditor is willing to accept and still consider the control effective (i.e., the control procedure would be relied on).

It can seem odd to students that auditors will actually "tolerate" any deviations in a control. There are two reasons auditors will tolerate deviations and still consider a control to be effective. The first reason is technical and relates to sampling risk. Remember that for an auditor (or an apple inspector) to use sampling to gather evidence there must be some margin for error, because there is a risk that the sample deviation rate differs from the population deviation rate. Even if there are no deviations in a sample, there must still be an allowance (or upper confidence limit) for sampling risk. Just as in the apple inspector example, the only way to know with certainty what the shipment defect rate actually is would be to inspect all the apples.

The second reason auditors are willing to tolerate some control deviations relates to the purpose and application of controls. To be effective, most controls do not need to operate 100 percent of the time so long as the times the control fails to operate are not predictable and the person(s) performing the control investigates processing exceptions observed during the proper application of the control. By way of analogy, suppose you have battery-operated smoke detectors in your apartment or house and one of the alarms starts to signal a low battery. The fact that a day or two passes between the removal of the old battery and installation of a new one doesn't render the system of controls ineffective for the entire period you have lived in the apartment or house. The risk of fire is pretty remote, even if there were no smoke detectors at all. Also, if one detector isn't working, you have other smoke detectors that will sound if smoke appears. Obviously, if all the smoke detectors are disabled for long periods of time, the system of fire detection is not effective and the risk of injury due to fire increases. Similarly, when a control fails to operate, it usually does not result in a monetary misstatement to the financial statements, because most transactions are properly input and processed (i.e., actual inherent risk is less than 100 percent) and there are other

---

[3]The sample sizes assume a tolerable deviation rate of 5 percent, an expected population deviation rate of 1 percent, and a large population.

TABLE 8–3	Examples of Tolerable Deviation Rates for Assessed Importance of a Control

Assessed Importance of a Control	Tolerable Deviation Rate
Highly important	3–5%
Moderately important	6–10%

compensating controls or processes that might detect a misstatement should one occur. Furthermore, if the operator of the control investigates processing exceptions that are discovered, he or she can research the cause and potential implications of the exception(s) and take corrective actions if necessary.

To be effective, a control does need to operate effectively a reasonably high percentage of the time. Table 8–3 provides some examples of the relationship between the assessed importance of a control and the tolerable deviation rate.

A low tolerable deviation rate (such as 3 to 5 percent) is used when the auditor plans to test the effectiveness of a highly important control. A higher tolerable deviation rate (6 to 10 percent) is used when the auditor plans to test the effectiveness of a moderately important control.

The tolerable deviation rate is *inversely* related to the sample size. The lower the tolerable deviation rate, the larger the sample size. Recall that in testing controls, the key determinant of sample size is the amount by which tolerable deviation rate exceeds the expected deviation rate. For example, assuming a desired confidence level of 95 percent, an expected population deviation rate of 0 percent, and a large population, the effect of tolerable deviation rate on sample size is:

Tolerable Deviation Rate	Sample Size
2%	149
6%	49
10%	29

Expected Population Deviation Rate.   The expected population deviation rate is the rate the auditor expects to exist in the population. Some level of deviation is commonly expected because the controls that auditors typically use sampling to test will be dependent on some human involvement (e.g., matching documents, credit approval, following up on system-generated exception reports), and humans are not perfect. The auditor can develop this expectation based on prior years' results or on a pilot sample. If the auditor believes that the expected population deviation rate exceeds the tolerable deviation rate, the statistical testing should not be performed, because in such a situation no amount of sampling can reduce the population deviation rate below the tolerable rate. Instead, the auditor should perform additional substantive procedures rather than relying on the control.

The expected population deviation rate has a direct relationship to sample size; the larger the expected population deviation rate, the larger the sample size, all else equal. For example, assuming a desired confidence level of 95 percent, a tolerable deviation rate of 5 percent, and a large population, the effect of the expected population deviation rate on sample size is:

Expected Population Deviation Rate	Sample Size
1%	93
1.5%	124
2%	181
3%	*

*Sample size is too large to be cost-effective for most audit applications.

The dramatic effect of expected population deviation rate on sample size highlights the importance of a good estimate of the expected deviation rate. It is perplexing to some that an estimate of the expected population deviation rate is required as an input to determine sample size—after all, isn't the whole purpose of testing a sample to estimate the deviation rate in the population? The reason an estimate is necessary relates back to the notion of precision, or by how much the tolerable deviation rate exceeds the estimated deviation rate, as discussed earlier in the chapter. Recall the apple inspector illustration where the buyer's tolerable defect rate was 10 percent and poor weather increased the expected defect rate from a historical rate of 3 percent ±2 percent to 7 percent ±3 percent. All else equal, the increase in expected defect rate will require a larger sample size, because there is now less room for sampling risk to be accommodated, and thus the sampling conclusion needs to be more precise. Just as the historical defect rate is an important input for apple inspection, a good estimate of the expected population deviation rate is very important for attribute sampling because the statistical sample size will be just large enough such that if the auditor observes the deviation rate she or he expects or lower, the sampling application will support a conclusion that the control is operating effectively. Similarly, if the auditor observes a higher deviation rate than the expected rate used in the sample size calculation, this usually means the sample results are unacceptable. As such, it is wise to be conservative when estimating the expected population deviation rate so that the sample size will be adequate even if the population deviation rate is slightly larger than the auditor initially thought it would be.

Table 8–4 shows Judd's decision for each of the parameters required to determine sample size. Judd decides to set the desired confidence level at 95 percent (i.e., the risk of incorrect acceptance is 5 percent), the tolerable deviation rate at 6 percent, and the expected population deviation rate at 1 percent for control 1. For control 1, Judd has planned a high confidence level (see Table 8–3). A similar strategy is followed for control 3. For control 2, Judd has planned a moderate confidence level because he plans to place less reliance on the control. In this sampling plan, the effect of the population size can be ignored because the population is very large. The effect of population size on attribute sampling is discussed below.

Tables 8–5 and 8–6 are used to determine the sample size for each of the controls. For control 1, Judd uses Table 8–5 to determine the sample size because the desired confidence level is 95 percent. Judd identifies the column for a 6-percent tolerable deviation rate and reads down that column until the row for a 1-percent expected population deviation rate is found. The sample size for control 1 is 78 items. For control 2, Judd uses Table 8–6 because the desired confidence level is 90 percent. Reading down the 8-percent tolerable deviation

| TABLE 8–4 | The Auditor's Decisions for Sample Size in Calabro Wireless Example |

CWS

| | Control* | | |
Parameters	1	2	3
Desired confidence level	95%	90%	95%
Tolerable deviation rate	6%	8%	5%
Expected population deviation rate	1%	2%	1%
Sample size from table	78	48	93

*Control 1: Sales or lease contracts are properly authorized for credit approval.
Control 2: Sales are not recorded without an approved sales and lease contract.
Control 3: Sales and lease contracts are properly priced.

| TABLE 8-5 | | | Statistical Sample Sizes for Attribute Sampling—95-Percent Desired Confidence Level (i.e., 5-Percent Risk of Incorrect Acceptance) | | | | | | | | |

Expected Population Deviation Rate	Tolerable Deviation Rate										
	2%	3%	4%	5%	6%	7%	8%	9%	10%	15%	20%
0.00%	149(0)	99(0)	74(0)	59(0)	49(0)	42(0)	36(0)	32(0)	29(0)	19(0)	14(0)
.25	236(1)	157(1)	117(1)	93(1)	78(1)	66(1)	58(1)	51(1)	46(1)	30(1)	22(1)
.50	*	157(1)	117(1)	93(1)	78(1)	66(1)	58(1)	51(1)	46(1)	30(1)	22(1)
.75	*	208(2)	117(1)	93(1)	78(1)	66(1)	58(1)	51(1)	46(1)	30(1)	22(1)
1.00	*	*	156(2)	93(1)	78(1)	66(1)	58(1)	51(1)	46(1)	30(1)	22(1)
1.25	*	*	156(2)	124(2)	78(1)	66(1)	58(1)	51(1)	46(1)	30(1)	22(1)
1.50	*	*	192(3)	124(2)	103(2)	66(1)	58(1)	51(1)	46(1)	30(1)	22(1)
1.75	*	*	227(4)	153(3)	103(2)	88(2)	77(2)	51(1)	46(1)	30(1)	22(1)
2.00	*	*	*	181(4)	127(3)	88(2)	77(2)	68(2)	46(1)	30(1)	22(1)
2.25	*	*	*	208(5)	127(3)	88(2)	77(2)	68(2)	61(2)	30(1)	22(1)
2.50	*	*	*	*	150(4)	109(3)	77(2)	68(2)	61(2)	30(1)	22(1)
2.75	*	*	*	*	173(5)	109(3)	95(3)	68(2)	61(2)	30(1)	22(1)
3.00	*	*	*	*	195(6)	129(4)	95(3)	84(3)	61(2)	30(1)	22(1)
3.25	*	*	*	*	*	148(5)	112(4)	84(3)	61(2)	30(1)	22(1)
3.50	*	*	*	*	*	167(6)	112(4)	84(3)	76(3)	40(2)	22(1)
3.75	*	*	*	*	*	185(7)	129(5)	100(4)	76(3)	40(2)	22(1)
4.00	*	*	*	*	*	*	146(6)	100(4)	89(4)	40(2)	22(1)
5.00	*	*	*	*	*	*	*	158(8)	116(6)	40(2)	30(2)
6.00	*	*	*	*	*	*	*	*	179(11)	50(3)	30(2)
7.00	*	*	*	*	*	*	*	*	*	68(5)	37(3)

*Sample size is too large to be cost-effective for most audit applications. The number in parentheses represents the maximum number of deviations in a sample of that size that allows the auditor to conclude that the tolerable deviation rate is not exceeded.

| TABLE 8-6 | | | Statistical Sample Sizes for Attribute Sampling—90-Percent Desired Confidence Level (i.e., 10-Percent Risk of Incorrect Acceptance) | | | | | | | | |

Expected Population Deviation Rate	Tolerable Deviation Rate										
	2%	3%	4%	5%	6%	7%	8%	9%	10%	15%	20%
0.00%	144(0)	76(0)	57(0)	45(0)	38(0)	32(0)	28(0)	25(0)	22(0)	15(0)	11(0)
.25	194(1)	129(1)	96(1)	77(1)	64(1)	55(1)	48(1)	42(1)	38(1)	25(1)	18(1)
.50	194(1)	129(1)	96(1)	77(1)	64(1)	55(1)	48(1)	42(1)	38(1)	25(1)	18(1)
.75	265(2)	129(1)	96(1)	77(1)	64(1)	55(1)	48(1)	42(1)	38(1)	25(1)	18(1)
1.00	*	176(2)	96(1)	77(1)	64(1)	55(1)	48(1)	42(1)	38(1)	25(1)	18(1)
1.25	*	221(3)	132(2)	77(1)	64(1)	55(1)	48(1)	42(1)	38(1)	25(1)	18(1)
1.50	*	*	132(2)	105(2)	64(1)	55(1)	48(1)	42(1)	38(1)	25(1)	18(1)
1.75	*	*	166(3)	105(2)	88(2)	55(1)	48(1)	42(1)	38(1)	25(1)	18(1)
2.00	*	*	198(4)	132(3)	88(2)	75(2)	48(1)	42(1)	38(1)	25(1)	18(1)
2.25	*	*	*	132(3)	88(2)	75(2)	65(2)	42(1)	38(1)	25(1)	18(1)
2.50	*	*	*	158(4)	110(3)	75(2)	65(2)	58(2)	38(1)	25(1)	18(1)
2.75	*	*	*	209(6)	132(4)	94(3)	65(2)	58(2)	52(2)	25(1)	18(1)
3.00	*	*	*	*	132(4)	94(3)	65(2)	58(2)	52(2)	25(1)	18(1)
3.25	*	*	*	*	153(5)	113(4)	82(3)	58(2)	52(2)	25(1)	18(1)
3.50	*	*	*	*	194(7)	113(4)	82(3)	73(3)	52(2)	25(1)	18(1)
3.75	*	*	*	*	*	131(5)	98(4)	73(3)	52(2)	25(1)	18(1)
4.00	*	*	*	*	*	149(6)	98(4)	73(3)	65(3)	25(1)	18(1)
5.00	*	*	*	*	*	*	160(8)	115(6)	78(4)	34(2)	18(1)
6.00	*	*	*	*	*	*	*	182(11)	116(7)	43(3)	25(2)
7.00	*	*	*	*	*	*	*	*	199(14)	52(4)	25(2)

*Sample size is too large to be cost-effective for most audit applications. The number in parentheses represents the maximum number of deviations in a sample of that size that allows the auditor to conclude that the tolerable deviation rate is not exceeded.

rate column until the 2-percent expected population deviation rate is found, Judd determines that the sample size is 48. Finally, the sample size for control 3 is 93. This is found by using Table 8–5 and reading down the 5-percent toler-able deviation rate column until the 1-percent expected deviation rate row is reached.

Significant areas of Tables 8–5 and 8–6 are covered by asterisks. The correspond-ing note at the bottom of the tables states, "Sample size is too large to be cost-effective for most audit applications." Another way to explain the cause of the asterisks is in-sufficient precision. Recall that to apply sampling there must be sufficient margin for error. When tolerable and estimated deviation rates are too close together, sample sizes will become too large to be practical or are simply not computable because there is insufficient allowance for sampling risk. Furthermore, in some instances where an asterisk appears in the tables, the expected population deviation rate is greater than the tolerable deviation rate; audit sampling obviously is not appropriate in such situations because there is no allowance for sampling risk.

Auditors often establish one sample size for all controls tested within a busi-ness process. This is particularly true when all the tests of controls are to be conducted on the same sampling units. The auditor would use the largest sample size. Therefore, in this example, the auditor may decide to use a sample size of 93 to test the three controls. However, we will assume that the auditor in the Calabro example used the sample sizes shown in Table 8–4.

Computing Sample Size with ACL Software

Exhibit 8–1 shows the screen display from ACL™ for Windows software for de-termining the sample size for control 3.[4] The auditor opens a client workbook, chooses the "Sampling" button on the menu and selects "Calculate Sample Size." The size window is then displayed and the auditor enters the relevant data. Since this is attribute sampling, the auditor selects "Record" for type of sampling. The auditor enters "95" for "Confidence," "125000" for "Population" size (you do not include commas when entering values in ACL), and the "Upper Error Limit" of 5 percent (i.e., tolerable deviation rate) and "Expected Error Rate" of 1 percent (i.e., expected population deviation rate). This produces a sample size of 95 that is slightly larger than the amount determined using the tables.

Population Size.   Students and auditors are often surprised that the size of the population is not an important factor in determining sample size for attribute sampling. The population size has little or no effect on the sample size, unless the population is relatively small, say less than 500 items. In fact, so long as the population is made up of similar items under the same system of controls, it doesn't matter if the population is 100,000 items, 1 million items, 100 million items, or more; the sample size is the same. Popular audit sampling programs, like ACL, completely ignore the effects of population size when computing sam-ple size for attribute sampling. If you use the ACL software that accompanies the book, you can verify that ACL ignores population size when computing the sample size for attributes sampling. For example, what happens to the sample size if you enter a population size less than 95 along with the other inputs illus-trated in the example illustrated in Exhibit 8–1 (make sure you select "record" for the type of sampling)? Because most of the populations that auditors test are larger than a few hundred items, and because assuming large population

---

[4]This material is used with the permission of ACL Services Ltd. The authors are grateful to the company for allowing the use of this material.

EXHIBIT 8-1	Sample Screens from ACL™ Software

sample size does not reduce the effectiveness of the sampling application, we ignore the effects of population size in this chapter. However, in the *Advanced Module* in this chapter, we include a brief discussion of how sample sizes can be adjusted for smaller populations and we provide a small population sample size table developed by the profession for testing controls that operate infrequently (i.e., quarterly, monthly, weekly).

Table 8–7 summarizes the effects of the four factors on the size of the sample to be selected.

TABLE 8-7	The Effect of Sample Selection Factors on Sample Size

Factor	Relationship to Sample Size	Examples Change in Factor	Effect on Sample
Desired confidence level	Direct	Lower	Decrease
		Higher	Increase
Tolerable deviation rate	Inverse	Lower	Increase
		Higher	Decrease
Expected population deviation rate	Direct	Lower	Decrease
		Higher	Increase
Population size	Decreases sample size only when population size is small (e.g., 500 or fewer items). Therefore, population size generally has no effect on sample size.		

Performance

After the sampling application has been planned, an auditor performs each of the following steps.

Sample Selection

Step 4: Select Sample Items   Auditing standards require that the sample items be selected in such a way that the sample can be expected to represent the population. Thus, all items must have an equal opportunity to be selected. The following two selection methods are acceptable for attributes sampling.

Random-Number Selection.   The auditor may select a random sample using random numbers generated by a spreadsheet application or audit sampling software. Using this method of selection, every item in the population (such as a document or customer account) has the same probability of being selected as every other sampling unit in the population. Statistical sampling requires that the auditor be able to measure the probability of selecting the sampling units selected. Thus, random-number selection is used in many statistical sampling applications. Auditors typically use unrestricted random sampling without replacement for sampling applications. This means that once an item is selected, it is removed from the frame and cannot be selected a second time. Given the auditor's objectives, it seems sensible for an auditor to include an item only once in the sample. Random numbers can be obtained from random number tables or software such as MS Excel or ACL. For the Calabro audit, Judd used MS Excel to generate 93 (the sample size determined by using the tables) random numbers between 1 and 125,000 and collected sales and lease contracts corresponding to those random numbers for testing.

Obtaining Random Numbers from ACL Software

Exhibit 8–2 shows an example of the output from the random-number generator in ACL. The auditor chooses the "Tools" button on the menu and selects "Generate Random Numbers." The random window is then displayed and the auditor enters the relevant data. The sample size of 95 is entered for "Number." The "Seed" is used to start the random-number process. If no value is entered into ACL, then ACL automatically creates a random seed. The auditor then enters the range of the invoice number sequence (1 to 125,001).[5] The "Unique" and "Sorted" items should be checked so that each random number is unique and the output is produced in sequence. Rather than using random numbers, if the population data is available in electronic format, ACL or spreadsheet programs like MS Excel can randomly select the sample records directly from the population.[6]

Systematic Selection.   When using a systematic selection approach to select a sample, the auditor determines a sampling interval by dividing the sampling population by the sample size. A starting number is selected in the first interval, and then every *n*th item is selected. When a random starting point is used, systematic selection provides a sample where every sampling unit has an equal chance of being selected. For example, suppose the auditor wishes to select 100 items from a population of 15,000 items numbered 1 to 15,000. The sampling interval in this case is 150 (15,000 ÷ 100). The auditor chooses a random number in the first interval (i.e., between 1 and 150), say 125, and that item is selected for testing. The second item is 275 (125 + 150), the third item is 425, and so on. To avoid

---

[5]Each random number generated by ACL will be greater than or equal to the minimum value and less than the maximum value you specify. No random number will be equal to the maximum value. For this reason the maximum is input as 125,001.

[6]An example of sampling population data in an electronic format is provided in the ACL end-of-chapter problems for Chapter 9 available from the book's online learning center.

| EXHIBIT 8-2 | An Example of a Random Sample Drawn from ACL™ |

the possibility that a systematic sample will miss systematic deviations in the population (e.g., control deviations occurring every 300th unit or every Friday afternoon), the auditor can use several random starting points. In our example, after selecting 10 items, the auditor could use a new random start between the 10th and 11th interval to select the 11th item.

Step 5: Perform the Audit Procedures After the sample items have been selected, the auditor conducts the planned audit procedures. In conducting the audit procedures for tests of controls, the auditor may encounter the following situations:

- ***Voided documents.*** The auditor may occasionally select a voided document in a sample. If the transaction has been properly voided, it does not represent a deviation. The item should be replaced with a new sample item.

- ***Unused or inapplicable documents.*** Sometimes a selected item is not appropriate for the definition of the control. For example, the auditor may define a deviation for a purchase transaction as a vendor's bill not supported by a receiving report. If the auditor selects a telephone or utility bill, there will not be a receiving report to examine. In such a case, the absence of the receiving report would not be a deviation. The auditor would simply replace the item with another purchase transaction.

- ***Inability to examine a sample item.*** Auditing standards require that the auditor consider the effect of not being able to apply a planned audit procedure to a sample item. For most tests of controls, the auditor examines documents for evidence of the performance of the control. If the auditor is unable to examine a document or to use an alternative procedure to test whether the control was adequately performed, the sample item is a deviation for purposes of evaluating the sample results.

- ***Stopping the test before completion.*** If a large number of deviations are detected early in the tests of controls, the auditor should consider stopping the test as soon as it is clear that the results of the test will not support the planned assessed level of control risk. If such a case occurred in the context of an audit of internal controls for a public company, the client would be informed, and the exceptions would be considered a control deficiency unless remediation and retesting are successful or there are other controls that adequately address the increased risk of misstatement. In the context of a financial statement audit, the auditor would rely on other internal controls or set control risk at the maximum for the audit assertion affected, and appropriately enhance the related substantive tests.

Whenever a deviation is observed in controls, the auditor should investigate the nature, cause, and consequence of the exception.

Understand and Analyze Deviations Observed. The auditor should evaluate the qualitative aspects of the deviations identified. This involves two considerations. First, the nature of each deviation and its cause and consequences should be considered. For example, the auditor should determine if a deviation represents an unintentional error or a fraud and whether the deviation actually resulted in a monetary misstatement to the financial statements. The auditor should also attempt to determine whether a deviation resulted from a cause such as misunderstanding of instructions or carelessness. Understanding the nature and cause of a deviation helps the auditor better assess control risk and evaluate whether the deviation(s) represent control deficiencies. As noted in Chapter 7, AS5 lists specific deficiencies that are indicative of material weaknesses (e.g., deviations indicate management fraud, deviation(s) that resulted in monetary misstatements that are significant). Second, the auditor should consider how the deviations may impact the other phases of the audit. For example, suppose that deviations found in a test of the revenue process resulted from improper granting of credit. As a result, the risk that the valuation assertion was not met for accounts receivable would increase, and the auditor would therefore increase substantive procedures for the allowance for uncollectible accounts.

In the Calabro example, Judd examines each of the sample items for the presence of a deviation. Thus, for control 1, Judd tests the 78 sales and lease contracts (sample size from the table) for proper credit authorization procedures by credit department personnel. The results of the audit procedures can be documented in a working paper similar to the example shown in Exhibit 8–3. As noted earlier, when multiple controls are tested on one sampling unit, auditors often decide to test all controls for the full sample when such testing can be efficiently conducted. The choice of whether to test all controls for the full sample is a matter of risk management. The argument supporting this approach is that since the auditor is physically inspecting the documentation in the full sample, the auditor may want to reduce the risk that deficiencies go undetected in the documents examined for the full sample. The concern is that at some future date a litigation event may identify deviations in sample items 79 to 93 for control 1, and those deviations seem readily apparent to the courts based only on a cursory review of the documents. In legal terms, if the auditor failed to detect a deviation that a jury believes a professional auditor should have detected, then the risk that the auditor could

---

EXHIBIT 8–3	A Sample Working Paper for Recording the Results of Tests of Controls

CWS

B20
DLJ
2/3/10

CALABRO WIRELESS SERVICES
Controls Tested—Revenue Process
12/31/09

Sample Item	Sales and Lease Transaction Number	Control Procedure 1	Control Procedure 2	Control Procedure 3
1	35381	✓	✓	✓
2	82765	E	✓	✓
⋮		⋮	⋮	⋮
48	1347	✓	✓	✓
49	1283	E		✓
⋮		⋮		⋮
77	52140	✓		✓
78	88878	✓		✓
⋮				⋮
91	107409			✓
92	17080			✓
93	122891			✓

	1	2	3
Number of deviations	2	0	0
Sample size from tables	78	48	93
Sample deviation rate	2.6%	0%	0%
Desired confidence level	95%	90%	95%
Computed upper deviation rate from tables	8.2%	5.0%	3.3%
Tolerable deviation rate	6%	8%	5%
Auditor's decision	Does not support reliance	Supports reliance	Supports reliance

Tick Mark Legend
✓ = Sales or lease contract examined for proper performance of control procedure. No exception.
E = Control *not* performed properly.

be successfully sued for negligence increases. Chapter 20 covers auditor legal liability and the definitions of negligence.

Before calculating the sample results and drawing final conclusions on the sampling plan, Judd investigates the nature and cause of the exceptions. Judd also considers whether the deviations may impact the other phases of the audit. In the current example, two deviations were detected for control 1, which relates to proper authorization of credit. Judd's investigation indicates that both deviations had occurred when sales in excess of credit limits were made to existing customers. Further investigation disclosed that the sales manager instead of the credit manager had approved the sale. Judd now knows the nature and cause of the errors. The effect of the control deviations is likely to be an increase in the amount of audit work conducted on the allowance for uncollectible accounts.

After the audit procedures have been completed, the auditor proceeds with his or her evaluation of the sample results.

Step 6: Calculate the Sample Deviation and Computed Upper Deviation Rates
After completing the audit procedures, the auditor summarizes the deviations for each control tested and evaluates the results. Determining the sample results for an attribute-sampling application can be accomplished by the use of a computer program or attribute-sampling tables. The auditor calculates the sample deviation rate and the computed upper deviation rate. The sample deviation rate is simply the number of deviations found in the sample divided by the number of items in the sample. This calculation projects the sample results to the population and is required by auditing standards. For example, if 2 deviations were found in a sample of 50, the sample deviation rate would be 4 percent (2 ÷ 50). In attribute sampling, the sample deviation rate represents the auditor's best estimate of the population deviation rate. However, because this result is based on a sample, the auditor does not know the true population deviation rate and must consider an allowance for sampling risk.

In evaluating the results of testing a control, the auditor is normally concerned only with whether the true deviation rate exceeds the tolerable deviation rate. Because the auditor does not know the true deviation rate, he or she calculates a *computed upper deviation rate*. The computed upper deviation rate is the sum of the sample deviation rate and an appropriate allowance for sampling risk. This sum represents an upper limit on how high the population deviation rate might actually be, at a controlled level of sampling risk (e.g., 5 or 10 percent). In other words, at the 95-percent confidence level, there is only a 5-percent chance that the true population deviation rate exceeds the computed upper deviation rate. This is sometimes referred to as the *upper-limit approach*.

Exhibit 8–3 shows the results of the tests of the three controls for the Calabro audit. Judd calculates the sample deviation rate and the computed upper deviation rate for each control tested. To determine the computed upper deviation rate, Judd uses either Table 8–8 or Table 8–9, depending on the desired confidence level for the test. A 95-percent confidence level is desired for control 1, thus Judd uses Table 8–8 in the following way: The column for the actual number of deviations found (2 deviations) is read down until the appropriate row for sample size is found. If the exact sample size is not found, the closest smaller sample size is used. This approach provides a conservative (larger) computed upper deviation rate. For control 1, the row for a sample size of 75 is used. The computed upper deviation rate for control 1 is 8.2 percent. Thus, for control 1, the sample deviation rate is 2.6 percent and the allowance for sampling risk is 5.6 percent (8.2 − 2.6). For control 2, Table 8–9 is used because the desired confidence level is 90 percent. In this case, no deviations were found, so the sample deviation rate is 0 percent and the upper computed deviation rate is 5 percent (rounding the

| TABLE 8–8 | **Statistical Sample Results Evaluation Table (Computed Upper Deviation Rates) for Attribute Sampling—95-Percent Desired Confidence Level** |

	Actual Number of Deviations Found										
Sample Size	*0*	*1*	*2*	*3*	*4*	*5*	*6*	*7*	*8*	*9*	*10*
25	11.3	17.6	*	*	*	*	*	*	*	*	*
30	9.5	14.9	19.6	*	*	*	*	*	*	*	*
35	8.3	12.9	17.0	*	*	*	*	*	*	*	*
40	7.3	11.4	15.0	18.3	*	*	*	*	*	*	*
45	6.5	10.2	13.4	16.4	19.2	*	*	*	*	*	*
50	5.9	9.2	12.1	14.8	17.4	19.9	*	*	*	*	*
55	5.4	8.4	11.1	13.5	15.9	18.2	*	*	*	*	*
60	4.9	7.7	10.2	12.5	14.7	16.8	18.8	*	*	*	*
65	4.6	7.1	9.4	11.5	13.6	15.5	17.4	19.3	*	*	*
70	4.2	6.6	8.8	10.8	12.6	14.5	16.3	18.0	19.7	*	*
75	4.0	6.2	8.2	10.1	11.8	13.6	15.2	16.9	18.5	20.0	*
80	3.7	5.8	7.7	9.5	11.1	12.7	14.3	15.9	17.4	18.9	*
90	3.3	5.2	6.9	8.4	9.9	11.4	12.8	14.2	15.5	16.8	18.2
100	3.0	4.7	6.2	7.6	9.0	10.3	11.5	12.8	14.0	15.2	16.4
125	2.4	3.8	5.0	6.1	7.2	8.3	9.3	10.3	11.3	12.3	13.2
150	2.0	3.2	4.2	5.1	6.0	6.9	7.8	8.6	9.5	10.3	11.1
200	1.5	2.4	3.2	3.9	4.6	5.2	5.9	6.5	7.2	7.8	8.4

*Over 20 percent.

| TABLE 8–9 | **Statistical Sample Results Evaluation Table (Computed Upper Deviation Rates) for Attribute Sampling—90-Percent Desired Confidence Level** |

	Actual Number of Deviations Found										
Sample Size	*0*	*1*	*2*	*3*	*4*	*5*	*6*	*7*	*8*	*9*	*10*
20	10.9	18.1	*	*	*	*	*	*	*	*	*
25	8.8	14.7	19.9	*	*	*	*	*	*	*	*
30	7.4	12.4	16.8	*	*	*	*	*	*	*	*
35	6.4	10.7	14.5	18.1	*	*	*	*	*	*	*
40	5.6	9.4	12.8	16.0	19.0	*	*	*	*	*	*
45	5.0	8.4	11.4	14.3	17.0	19.7	*	*	*	*	*
50	4.6	7.6	10.3	12.9	15.4	17.8	*	*	*	*	*
55	4.1	6.9	9.4	11.8	14.1	16.3	18.4	*	*	*	*
60	3.8	6.4	8.7	10.8	12.9	15.0	16.9	18.9	*	*	*
70	3.3	5.5	7.5	9.3	11.1	12.9	14.6	16.3	17.9	19.6	*
80	2.9	4.8	6.6	8.2	9.8	11.3	12.8	14.3	15.8	17.2	18.6
90	2.6	4.3	5.9	7.3	8.7	10.1	11.5	12.8	14.1	15.4	16.6
100	2.3	3.9	5.3	6.6	7.9	9.1	10.3	11.5	12.7	13.9	15.0
120	2.0	3.3	4.4	5.5	6.6	7.6	8.7	9.7	10.7	11.6	12.6
160	1.5	2.5	3.3	4.2	5.0	5.8	6.5	7.3	8.0	8.8	9.5
200	1.2	2.0	2.7	3.4	4.0	4.6	5.3	5.9	6.5	7.1	7.6

*Over 20 percent.

sample size down to 45). No control deviations were found for control 3; therefore, the sample deviation rate is 0 percent. Table 8–9 shows a computed upper deviation rate of 3.3 percent (rounding the sample size down to 90). In other words, even though the auditor's best estimate based on the results of the testing is that the population contains no deviations, the allowance for sampling risk associated with the sample tested is 3.3 percent.

The upper limit represents the upper one-sided confidence limit for the population deviation rate based on the sample size, the number of deviations, and the planned level of confidence. In evaluating the results of testing a control, the auditor is normally concerned only with whether the true deviation rate exceeds the tolerable deviation rate. Therefore, the auditor is generally concerned only with how *high* the population deviation rate might be; it doesn't matter how *low* the population deviation rate might be.

Computing Upper Deviation Rate with ACL Software

Exhibit 8–4 shows the output from ACL for control 3. The auditor chooses the "Sampling" button on the menu bar and selects "Evaluate Error." The evaluate

---

EXHIBIT 8–4   **Evaluation Results from ACL™**

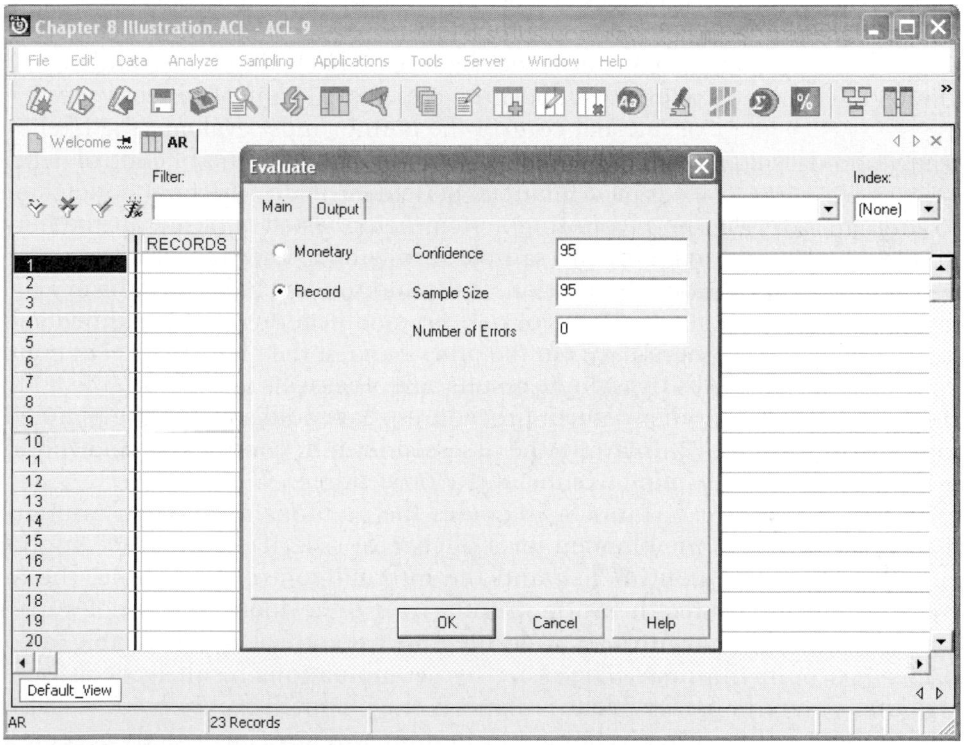

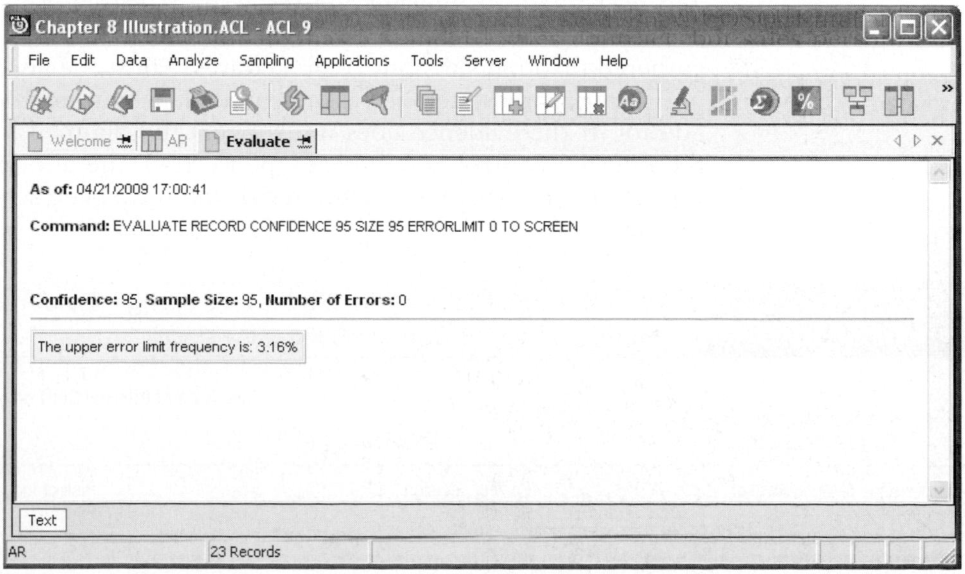

window is then displayed, and the auditor enters the relevant data for control 3: "Confidence" is 95 percent, "Sample Size" is 95 (based on ACL sample size computation), and 0 "Number of Errors." The estimated upper limit error frequency (i.e., computed upper deviation rate) is 3.16 percent.

Step 7: Draw Final Conclusions

In drawing a conclusion about the statistical sampling application for tests of controls, the auditor compares the tolerable deviation rate to the computed upper deviation rate. If the computed upper deviation rate is less than the tolerable deviation rate, the auditor can conclude that the control tested can be relied upon. If the computed upper deviation rate exceeds the tolerable deviation rate, the auditor will normally conclude that the control is not operating at an acceptable level. For an audit of internal control over financial reporting, the ineffective control would be considered a control deficiency unless the client remediates the control and both the client and the auditor retest to support the remediated control's effectiveness. For purposes of an audit of internal control the auditor must evaluate the likelihood and magnitude of a potential misstatement arising as a result of control deficiencies (see Chapter 7).

For a financial statement audit, the final conclusion about control risk for the accounting system being tested is based on the auditor's professional judgment of the sample results and other relevant tests of controls such as inquiry and observation. If the auditor concludes that the evidence supports the planned level of control risk, no modifications of the planned substantive procedures are necessary. On the other hand, if the planned level of control risk is not supported by the sample results and other tests of controls, the auditor should either (1) test other control procedures that could support the planned level of control risk; or (2) increase the assessed level of control risk and modify the nature, extent, or timing of substantive procedures.

Table 8–10 shows the auditor's risks when evaluating sample evidence on the planned level of control risk. If the evidence supports the planned level of control risk and the internal control is reliable, the auditor has made a correct decision. Similarly, if the evidence does not support the planned level of control risk and the internal control is not reliable, a correct decision has been made. The other two combinations result in decision errors by the auditor. If the evidence supports the planned level of control risk and the internal control is not reliable, the auditor will have incorrectly accepted the control as effective and overrelied on internal control (Type II error). This results in the auditor establishing detection risk too high and leads to a lower level of evidence being gathered through substantive procedures. Thus, the auditor's risk of not detecting material misstatement is increased. This can lead to a lawsuit against the auditor. If the evidence does not support the planned level of control risk and the internal control is reliable (Type I error), the auditor will have incorrectly rejected the control and detection risk will have been set too low. Thus, a higher

TABLE 8–10	The Auditor's Risks When Evaluating Sample Evidence on the Planned Level of Control Risk	
Auditor's Decision Based on Sample Evidence	**True State of Internal Control**	
	Reliable	*Not Reliable*
Supports the planned level of control risk	Correct decision	Risk of incorrect acceptance (Type II)
Does not support the planned level of control risk	Risk of incorrect rejection (Type I)	Correct decision

level of evidence will be gathered by substantive procedures, leading to over-auditing and an inefficient audit.

For the Calabro audit, Exhibit 8–3 shows that the sample evidence does not support the operating effectiveness of control 1 (credit authorization) because the computed upper deviation rate (8.2 percent) exceeds the tolerable deviation rate (6 percent). For control 1, the sample deviation rate was 2.6 percent and the allowance for sampling risk was 5.6 percent. In this example, there appear to be no other controls or other evidence to support the operating effectiveness of control 1. Thus, Judd increases both the assessed level of control risk and the substantive procedures related to the valuation assertion.

Judd's sample evidence supports the reliability of controls 2 and 3 because the computed upper deviation rates are less than the tolerable deviation rates. If Judd were performing tests of controls for the audit of internal control over financial reporting for a public company, he would conclude that controls 2 and 3 operate effectively and that the exceptions in control 1 represent a control deficiency. Judd would then need to evaluate the likelihood and magnitude of a potential misstatement arising as a result of the valuation-related control deficiency.

Nonstatistical Sampling for Tests of Controls

[LO 8]   When conducting a nonstatistical sampling application for tests of controls, the auditor considers each of the steps shown in Table 8–2. The differences between nonstatistical and statistical sampling occur in any or all of the following steps:

- Determining the sample size.
- Selecting the sample items.
- Calculating the computed upper deviation rate.

Determining the Sample Size

When a nonstatistical sampling application is used in determining sample size, the auditor should consider the desired confidence, the tolerable deviation rate, and the expected population deviation rate. While the auditor is not required to use a statistical formula or table to determine sample size, professional standards indicate that sample sizes for nonstatistical and statistical applications should be comparable. In other words, "nonstatistical" does not justify an auditor in using sample sizes that are too small to provide sufficient evidence. Nonstatistical sample sizes are determined by applying professional judgment and guidance in audit firm policy.

Practice INSIGHT   Remember that when control deficiencies are observed, the auditor should also evaluate the adequacy of any redundant, complementary, or compensating controls.

A number of public accounting firms establish guidelines for nonstatistical sample sizes for tests of controls. Typically, accounting firms' nonstatistical guidelines are consistent with sampling theory and are designed to provide two primary benefits: (1) to simplify the judgments required by field auditors by having experts at firm headquarters make firmwide judgments and (2) to improve consistency in sampling applications within and across engagement teams. For example, a firm might establish guidelines as follows:

Desired Level of Controls Reliance	Sample Size
Low	15–20
Moderate	25–35
High	40–60

In developing nonstatistical sampling guidelines like those above, the firm's experts have decided what confidence levels achieve low, moderate, and high assurance (say, 70–75, 80–85, and 90–95-percent confidence, respectively). The experts have decided reasonable levels of tolerable deviation rates (say, 5 to 10 percent), and they have decided to base an initial sample on zero expected deviations. Following this guidance, if one or more deviations are found in the sample, the auditor needs to expand the sample or increase the assessed level of control risk.

Selecting the Sample Items

While random-sample or systematic-sample (with a random start) selection is required for statistical sampling, nonstatistical sampling allows the use of those selection methods as well as other selection methods such as *haphazard sampling*. When a haphazard selection approach is used, sampling units are selected without any conscious bias—that is, without a special reason for including or omitting items from the sample. This does not imply that the items are selected in a careless manner; rather, the sampling units are selected to represent the population. Haphazard selection may be useful for nonstatistical sampling, but it should not be used for statistical sampling because the auditor cannot measure the probability of an item being selected. When using audit sampling, the auditor should avoid distorting the sample by selecting only items that are unusual or large or items that are the first or last items in the frame, because the auditor needs a sample that represents the population in order to draw inferences about the population from the sample. This is not to say that selection of unusual, large, or risky events, transactions, or balances should be avoided in other audit procedures that do not involve audit sampling. To the contrary, the auditor should focus specific audit procedures on all such items and not turn the selection of these items over to chance (i.e., random or haphazard selection), which is required for audit sampling.

Calculating the Computed Upper Deviation Rate

With a nonstatistical sample, the auditor can calculate the sample deviation rate but cannot quantify the computed upper deviation rate and the sampling risk associated with the test. The AICPA Audit Guide *Audit Sampling* provides the following advice for considering sampling risk in a nonstatistical test of controls:

> An auditor using nonstatistical sampling uses judgment to consider the allowance for sampling risk. For example, when the rate of deviation from the prescribed control exceeds the expected rate used to plan the sample, the auditor usually concludes that there is unacceptably high sampling risk and he or she typically would increase the assessed level of control risk or consider further whether to rely at all on the control.[7]

Suppose an auditor planned a nonstatistical sampling application by setting the desired confidence level at "high" (i.e., 90 to 95 percent), the expected population deviation rate at 1.5 percent, and the tolerable deviation rate at 8 percent. Assume the auditor judgmentally determines to select a sample size of 50 items and makes the selections haphazardly. If the auditor detects no control deviations, the sample deviation rate is 0 percent. In this instance, the sample deviation rate, 0 percent, is less than the expected population deviation rate, 1.5 percent, and there is an acceptable risk that the true population deviation rate exceeds the tolerable deviation rate.

---

[7]Adapted from American Institute of Certified Public Accountants, *Audit Sampling* (Audit Guide) (New York: AICPA, 2008).

Assume that one control deviation had been detected. The sample deviation rate is 2 percent, which is greater than the expected population deviation rate (1.5 percent). Now there is an unacceptably high risk that the true population deviation rate exceeds the tolerable deviation rate. Referring to the statistical evaluation table illustrates why the results of the nonstatistical sample are not likely to support the effectiveness of the control. Table 8–8 shows that if one deviation is found in a sample of 50 items, the computed upper deviation rate is 9.2 percent. This exceeds the tolerable deviation rate of 8 percent.

Students and auditors are sometimes confused by what causes a sampling approach to be "nonstatistical." An approach is nonstatistical if (1) judgment is used to determine the sample size; (2) a haphazard sample selection technique is used; and/or (3) the sample results are evaluated judgmentally. A nonstatistical approach can involve random selection and a judgmental evaluation. While haphazardly selected samples cannot be statistically evaluated, any randomly drawn sample can be statistically evaluated—even if the auditor labels the approach "nonstatistical" and even if the sample size was not statistically derived. This is an important point because it highlights the need for auditors to understand the key concepts of sampling theory even if they are using a nonstatistical approach. Remember, if an auditor randomly selects a sample and then evaluates the results judgmentally, the quality of his or her judgment can be evaluated against statistical theory by outside experts.

Conclusion

The use of sampling is common in auditing because of the need to gather evidence over large populations of client data in a cost-effective manner. In this chapter we discussed the basic concepts that are relevant to all forms of audit sampling, such as sampling risk. Whenever auditors use sampling techniques, they face the risk that their sample is not representative of the population, which could lead them to draw the wrong conclusions. Statistical theory allows auditors to measure this risk and manage it by taking the appropriate sample size. In this chapter we focused primarily on statistical attributes sampling for tests of controls and we provided a step-by-step approach to planning a sample, executing the sample testing, and evaluating the results from the sample. The steps were illustrated using both statistical tables and the audit software ACL. Nonstatistical sampling is commonly used in practice, but it is important to remember nonstatistical approaches must be founded in statistical theory.

In Chapter 9, you will learn about statistical and nonstatistical sampling techniques auditors use to gather substantive evidence.

Advanced Module: Considering the Effect of the Population Sizes

The population size generally has little or no effect on the sample size. If the population contains more than 500 units, the effect on the sample size is negligible.

The attribute-sampling tables presented earlier in this chapter assume a large population. When the population size is smaller than 500, the sample size taken from the tables can be adjusted by using the finite population correction factor as follows:

$$\text{Finite population correction factor} = \sqrt{1 - (n/N)}$$

where

n = the sample size from the tables.

N = the number of units in the population

For example, the sample size for a desired confidence of 90 percent, a tolerable deviation rate of 10 percent, and an expected population deviation rate of 1 percent is 39 when population size is 1,000. If the population size was 100, the sample size of 39 could be adjusted as follows:

$$\text{Sample size} = n\sqrt{1 - (n/N)}$$

$$= 39\sqrt{1 - (39/100)} = 31$$

Some controls may operate only weekly, monthly or quarterly. For infrequent controls some auditors use sample sizes provided in the following table:

Small Population Sample Size Table[8]

Control Frequency and Population Size	Sample Size
Quarterly (4)	2
Monthly (12)	2–4
Semimonthly (24)	3–8
Weekly (52)	5–9

[8]This is Table 3.5 from the American Institute of Certified Public Accountants, *Audit sampling* (Audit Guide) (New York: AICPA, 2008).

KEY TERMS

Allowance for sampling risk. The uncertainty that results from sampling; the difference between the expected mean of the population and the tolerable deviation or misstatement.

Attribute sampling. Sampling used to estimate the proportion of a population that possesses a specified characteristic.

Audit sampling. The application of audit procedures to less than 100 percent of the items in a population of audit relevance selected in such a way that the auditor expects the sample to be representative of the population and thus likely to provide a reasonable basis for conclusions about the population.

Classical variables sampling. The use of normal distribution theory to estimate the dollar amount of misstatement for a class of transactions or an account balance.

Desired confidence level. The probability that the true but unknown measure of the characteristic of interest is within specified limits.

Expected population deviation rate. The deviation rate that the auditor expects to exist in the population.

Monetary-unit sampling. Attribute-sampling techniques used to estimate the dollar amount of misstatement for a class of transactions or an account balance.

Nonsampling risk. The possibility that the auditor may use inappropriate audit procedures, fail to detect a misstatement when applying an audit procedure, or misinterpret an audit result.

Nonstatistical sampling. Audit sampling that relies on the auditor's judgment to determine sample size (typically of comparable size to a statistically based sampling approach), select the sample, and/or evaluate the results for the purpose of reaching a conclusion about the population.

Risk of incorrect acceptance. The risk that the sample supports the conclusion that the control is operating effectively when it is not or that the recorded account balance is not materially misstated when it is materially misstated.

Risk of incorrect rejection. The risk that the sample supports the conclusion that the control is not operating effectively when it actually is or that the recorded account balance is materially misstated when it is not materially misstated.

Sampling risk. The possibility that the sample drawn is not representative of the population and that, as a result, the auditor reaches an incorrect conclusion about the reliability of the control, the account balance, or class of transactions based on the sample.

Sampling unit. The individual member of the population being sampled.

Statistical sampling. Sampling that uses the laws of probability to select and evaluate the results of an audit sample, thereby permitting the auditor to quantify the sampling risk for the purpose of reaching a conclusion about the population.

Tolerable deviation rate. The maximum deviation rate from a prescribed control that the auditor is willing to accept without altering the planned assessed level of control risk.

www.mhhe.com/ messier7e	Visit the book's Online Learning Center for a multiple-choice quiz that will allow you to assess your understanding of chapter concepts.

REVIEW QUESTIONS

[LO 1] 8-1 Define audit sampling. Why do auditors sample instead of examining every transaction?

[2] 8-2 Distinguish between Type I and Type II errors. What terms are used to describe these errors when the auditor is conducting tests of controls and substantive tests? What costs are potentially incurred by auditors when such decision errors occur?

[3] 8-3 List audit evidence types that do not involve sampling and provide an example of a situation where an auditor would not use audit sampling.

[4] 8-4 Distinguish between nonstatistical and statistical sampling. What are the advantages and disadvantages of using statistical sampling?

[6,7] 8-5 Define attribute sampling. Why is this sampling technique appropriate for tests of controls?

[6,7,8] 8-6 How does the timing of controls testing affect the population definition?

[7] 8-7 List the four factors that enter into the sample size decision. What is the relationship between sample size and each of these factors?

[6,7,8] 8-8 In performing certain audit procedures, the auditor may encounter voided documents, inapplicable documents, or missing documents, or the auditor may stop testing before examining all the items selected for the sample. How should each of these situations be handled within the attribute-sampling application?

[6,7,8] 8-9 The auditor should evaluate the qualitative aspects of deviations found in a sampling application. What are the purposes of evaluating the qualitative aspects of deviations?

[8] 8-10 How should the results of a nonstatistical test of controls sample be evaluated in terms of considering sampling risk?

MULTIPLE-CHOICE QUESTIONS

[4]   8-11   An advantage of statistical sampling over nonstatistical sampling is that statistical sampling helps an auditor to
   a. Eliminate the risk of nonsampling errors.
   b. Reduce audit risk and materiality to a relatively low level.
   c. Measure the sufficiency of the evidential matter obtained.
   d. Minimize the failure to detect errors and fraud.

[4,6]   8-12   Samples to test internal controls are intended to provide a basis for an auditor to conclude whether
   a. The controls are operating effectively.
   b. The financial statements are materially misstated.
   c. The risk of incorrect acceptance is too high.
   d. Materiality for planning purposes is at a sufficiently low level.

[6,7]   8-13   When assessing the tolerable deviation rate, the auditor should consider that, while deviations from control procedures increase the risk of material misstatements, such deviations do not necessarily result in misstatements. This explains why
   a. A recorded disbursement that does not show evidence of required approval may nevertheless be a transaction that is properly authorized and recorded.
   b. Deviations would result in errors in the accounting records only if the deviations and the misstatements occurred on different transactions.
   c. Deviations from pertinent control procedures at a given rate ordinarily would be expected to result in misstatements at a higher rate.
   d. A recorded disbursement that is properly authorized may nevertheless be a transaction that contains a material misstatement.

[6,7]   8-14   Which of the following combinations results in the greatest decrease in sample size in an attribute sample for a test of controls?

	Desired Confidence Level	Tolerable Deviation Rate	Expected Population Deviation Rate
a.	Decrease	Decrease	Increase
b.	Increase	Increase	Decrease
c.	Decrease	Increase	Decrease
d.	Decrease	Increase	Increase

Questions 8-15 and 8-16 are based on the following information:
   An auditor desired to test credit approval on 10,000 sales invoices processed during the year. The auditor designed a statistical sample that would provide 1-percent risk of assessing control risk too low for the assertion that not more than 7 percent of the sales invoices lacked approval. The auditor estimated from previous experience that about 2½ percent of the sales invoices lacked approval. A sample of 200 invoices was examined, and 7 of them were lacking approval. The auditor then determined the computed upper deviation rate to be 8 percent.

[6,7]   8-15   In the evaluation of this sample, the auditor decided to increase the level of the preliminary assessment of control risk because the
   a. Tolerable deviation rate (7 percent) was less than the computed upper deviation rate (8 percent).
   b. Expected population deviation rate (7 percent) was more than the percentage of errors in the sample (3½ percent).

    c. Computed upper deviation rate (8 percent) was more than the percentage of errors in the sample (3½ percent).

    d. Expected population deviation rate (2½ percent) was less than the tolerable deviation rate (7 percent).

[6,7]   8-16 Based on the information above, the planned allowance for sampling risk was

    a. 5½ percent.

    b. 4½ percent.

    c. 3½ percent.

    d. 1 percent.

[2,6]   8-17 The following table depicts the auditor's estimated computed upper deviation rate compared with the tolerable deviation rate, and it also depicts the true population deviation rate compared with the tolerable deviation rate.

	True State of Population	
Auditor's Estimate Based on Sample Results	Deviation Rate Is Less Than Tolerable Deviation Rate	Deviation Rate Exceeds Tolerable Deviation Rate
Computed upper deviation rate is less than tolerable deviation rate.	1	3
Computed upper deviation rate exceeds tolerable deviation rate.	2	4

    As a result of tests of controls, the auditor assesses control risk higher than necessary and thereby increases substantive testing. This is illustrated by situation

    a. 1

    b. 2

    c. 3

    d. 4

[6]   8-18 Which of the following statements is correct concerning statistical sampling in tests of controls?

    a. Deviations from controls at a given rate usually result in misstatements at a higher rate.

    b. As the population size doubles, the sample size should also double.

    c. The qualitative aspects of deviations are not considered by the auditor.

    d. There is an inverse relationship between the sample size and the tolerable deviation rate.

[2,6]   8-19 What is an auditor's evaluation of a statistical sample for attributes when a test of 50 documents results in three deviations if the tolerable deviation rate is 7 percent, the expected population deviation rate is 5 percent, and the allowance for sampling risk is 2 percent?

    a. The planned assessed level of control risk should be modified because the tolerable deviation rate plus the allowance for sampling risk exceeds the expected population deviation rate.

    b. The sample results should be accepted as support for the planned assessed level of control risk because the sample deviation rate plus the allowance for sampling risk exceeds the tolerable deviation rate.

c. The sample results should be accepted as support for the planned assessed level of control risk because the tolerable deviation rate less the allowance for sampling risk equals the expected population deviation rate.

d. The planned assessed level of control risk should be modified because the sample deviation rate plus the allowance for sampling risk exceeds the tolerable deviation rate.

[2,6]   8-20   As a result of sampling procedures applied as tests of controls, an auditor incorrectly assesses control risk lower than appropriate. The most likely explanation for this situation is that

a. The deviation rates of both the auditor's sample and the population exceed the tolerable deviation rate.

b. The deviation rates of both the auditor's sample and the population are less than the tolerable deviation rate.

c. The deviation rate in the auditor's sample is less than the tolerable deviation rate, but the deviation rate in the population exceeds the tolerable deviation rate.

d. The deviation rate in the auditor's sample exceeds the tolerable deviation rate, but the deviation rate in the population is less than the tolerable deviation rate.

PROBLEMS

[1,2]   8-21   Audit sampling involves applying an audit procedure to less than 100 percent of the population for the purpose of evaluating some characteristic of the population. The fact that an audit involves sampling is noted in the scope paragraph of the auditor's report, which contains the phrase "An audit includes examining, on a test basis." When an auditor uses sampling, an element of uncertainty enters into the auditor's conclusions.

Required:

a. Explain the auditor's justification for accepting the uncertainties that are inherent in the sampling process.

b. Discuss the uncertainties that collectively embody the concept of audit risk.

c. Discuss the nature of sampling risk and nonsampling risk. Include the effect of sampling risk on tests of controls.

[2,3,4]   8-22   Match the term to the definition.

a.	Attribute sampling	1. The possibility that the sample drawn is not representative of the population and leads to an incorrect conclusion
b.	Desired confidence level	2. Relies on the auditor's judgment to determine sample size and evaluate the results
c.	Allowance for sampling risk	3. The maximum deviation rate from a prescribed control that an auditor is willing to accept
d.	Sampling risk	4. All or a subset of the items that constitute the class of transactions
e.	Sampling population	5. The probability that the true but unknown measure of the characteristic of interest is within specified limits
f.	Nonstatistical sampling	6. Used to estimate the proportion of a population that possesses a certain characteristic
g.	Tolerable deviation rate	7. The difference between the expected and the tolerable deviation rate

[6,7]   8-23   Following is a set of situations that may or may not involve sampling.
1. An auditor is examining loan receivables at a local bank. The population of loans contains two strata. One stratum is composed of 25 loans that are each greater than $1 million. The second stratum contains 450 loans that are less than $1 million. The auditor has decided to test all loans greater than $1 million and 15 loans less than $1 million.
2. Assume the same facts as number 1 except that the auditor decides to apply analytical procedures to the second strata of loans.
3. An auditor has haphazardly selected 30 sales invoices to be examined for proper pricing of the goods purchased by the customer.
4. The prepaid insurance account is made up of four policies that total $45,000. The auditor has decided that this account is immaterial and decides that no policies will be examined.

Required:
Indicate which situations involve audit sampling (statistical or nonstatistical) and why.

[6,7]   8-24   Jenny Jacobs, CPA, is planning to use attribute sampling in order to determine the degree of reliance to be placed on an audit client's system of internal control over sales. Jacobs has begun to develop an outline of the main steps in the sampling plan as follows:
1. State the test objectives (for example, to test the reliability of internal controls over sales).
2. Define the population (the period covered by the test, the sampling unit, the completeness of the population).
3. Define the sampling unit (for example, client copies of sales invoices).

Required:
a. What are the remaining steps in the outline that Jacobs should include in the statistical test of sales invoices?
b. What are the advantages of using statistical audit sampling?

(AICPA, adapted)

[6]   8-25   Determine the sample size for each of the control procedures shown in the following table (assuming a large population):

	Control Procedure			
Parameters	*1*	*2*	*3*	*4*
Risk of incorrect acceptance	5%	5%	10%	10%
Tolerable deviation rate	4%	5%	7%	8%
Expected population deviation rate	1%	2%	3%	4%
Sample size				

[6]   8-26   Using the sample sizes determined in Problem 8-25 and the number of deviations shown here, determine the sample deviation rate, the computed upper deviation rate, and the auditor's conclusion (i.e., testing results do or do not support operating effectiveness of the control) for each control procedure.

Results	Control Procedure			
	1	2	3	4
Number of deviations	0	5	4	3
Sample size				
Sample deviation rate				
Computed upper deviation rate				
Auditor's conclusion				

[6]   8-27   Determine the sample size for each of the control procedures shown in the following table:

Parameters	Control Procedure			
	1	2	3	4
Risk of incorrect acceptance	5%	5%	10%	10%
Tolerable deviation rate	6%	7%	4%	3%
Expected population deviation rate	2%	2%	1%	0%
Sample size				

[6]   8-28   Using the sample sizes determined in Problem 8-27 and the number of deviations shown here, determine the sample deviation rate, computed upper deviation rate, and the auditor's conclusion (i.e., testing results do or do not support operating effectiveness of the control) for each control procedure.

Results	Control Procedure			
	1	2	3	4
Number of deviations	4	2	2	0
Sample size				
Sample deviation rate				
Computed upper deviation rate				
Auditor's conclusion				

[8]   8-29   Calgari Clothing Company manufactures high-quality silk ties that are marketed under a number of trademarked names. Joe & Vandervelte have been the company's auditors for five years. Lisa Austen, the senior-in-charge of the audit, has reviewed Calgari's controls over purchasing and inventory, and she determined that a number of controls can be relied upon to reduce control risk. Austen has decided to test two control procedures over purchases and inventory: (1) purchase orders are agreed to receiving reports and vendor's invoices for product, quantity, and price; and (2) inventory is transferred to raw material stores using an approved, prenumbered receiving report.

Austen decided to use a nonstatistical sampling approach based on the following judgments for each control procedure and has judgmentally decided to use a sample size of 75 purchase orders for control 1 and 30 receiving reports for control 2.

Parameters	Control Procedure	
	1	2
Desired confidence	95%	90%
Tolerable deviation rate	7%	9%
Expected population deviation rate	2%	2.5%

After completing the examination of the sample items, Austen noted one deviation for each control procedure.

Required:
What conclusion should Austen reach about each control procedure? Justify your answer.

[8]   8-30   Nathan Matthews conducted a test of controls where the tolerable deviation rate was set at 6 percent and the expected population deviation rate was 3 percent. Using a sample size of 150, Matthews performed the planned test of controls. He found six deviations in the sample, and he calculated the computed upper deviation rate to be 7.8 percent.

Required:
a. Based on the sample results, what allowance for sampling risk is included in the computed upper deviation rate of 7.8?
b. Assume that Matthews preliminarily assessed control risk as "low." Given the results above, the auditor could decide to do one of three things: (1) increase the sample size; (2) increase the preliminary assessment of control risk; or (3) not adjust the preliminary assessment of control risk. Describe how Matthews could justify each of those three actions.

[8]   8-31   Doug Iceberge, senior-in-charge of the audit of Fisher Industries, has decided to test the following two controls for Fisher's revenue process.
1. All sales invoices are supported by proper documentation, that is, a sales order and a shipping document.
2. All sales invoices are mathematically correct.
   Iceberge has decided to use a nonstatistical sampling approach based on the following judgments for each control and has judgmentally decided to use a sample size of 50 sales invoice packets.

Parameters	Control Procedure	
	1	2
Desired confidence level	95%	90%
Risk of assessing control risk too low	5%	10%
Tolerable deviation rate	6%	8%
Expected population deviation rate	3%	3%

After completing the examination of the 50 sample items, Iceberge noted one deviation for control 1 and two deviations for control 2.

Required:
What should Iceberge conclude about each control? Justify your answer.

DISCUSSION CASE

[2,5,6]   8-32   Baker, CPA, was engaged to audit Mill Company's financial statements for the year ended September 30. After studying Mill's internal control, Baker decided to obtain evidence about the effectiveness of both the design and the operation of the controls that may support a low assessed level of control risk concerning Mill's shipping and billing functions. During the prior years' audits, Baker had used nonstatistical sampling, but for the current year Baker used a statistical sample in the tests of controls to eliminate the need for judgment.

Baker wanted to assess control risk at a low level, so a tolerable deviation rate of 20 percent was established. To estimate the population deviation rate and the computed upper deviation rate, Baker decided to apply an attribute sampling technique that would use an expected population deviation rate of 3 percent for the 8,000 shipping documents and to defer consideration of the allowable risk of assessing control risk too low until the sample results were evaluated. Baker used the tolerable deviation rate, the population size, and the expected population deviation rate to determine that a sample size of 80 would be sufficient. When it was subsequently determined that the actual population was about 10,000 shipping documents, Baker increased the sample size to 100.

Baker's objective was to ascertain whether Mill's shipments had been properly billed. Baker took a sample of 100 invoices by selecting the first 25 invoices from the first month of each quarter. Baker then compared the invoices to the corresponding prenumbered shipping documents.

When Baker tested the sample, eight deviations were discovered. Additionally, one shipment that should have been billed at $10,443 was actually billed at $10,434. Baker considered this $9 to be immaterial and did not count it as an error.

In evaluating the sample results, Baker made the initial determination that a 5-percent risk of assessing control risk too low was desired and, using the appropriate statistical sampling table, determined that for eight observed deviations from a sample size of 100, the computed upper deviation rate was 14 percent. Baker then calculated the allowance for sampling risk to be 5 percent, the difference between the actual sample deviation rate (8 percent) and the expected error rate (3 percent). Baker reasoned that the actual sample deviation rate (8 percent) plus the allowance for sampling risk (5 percent) was less than the computed upper deviation rate (14 percent); therefore, the sample supported a low level of control risk.

Required:
Describe each incorrect assumption, statement, and inappropriate application of attribute sampling in Baker's procedures.

(AICPA, adapted)

HANDS-ON CASES

EarthWear Online	**Tests of Controls (Part B)** Statistically quantify and evaluate the results of tests of controls from Part A (see Part A mini case description in Chapter 6). *Visit the book's Online Learning Center at www.mhhe.com/messier7e to find a detailed description of the case and to download required materials.*

| www.mhhe.com/ messier7e | Visit the book's Online Learning Center for problem material to be completed using the ACL software packaged with your new text. |

KAPLAN
CPA Review

| www.mhhe.com/ messier7e | **Ridge and Associates**
This simulation will test your understanding of audit sampling terminology and the impact of certain situations on audit risk.
To begin this simulation, visit the book's Online Learning Center. |

CHAPTER 9

LEARNING OBJECTIVES

Upon completion of this chapter you will

[1] Understand the similarities and differences between audit sampling for tests of controls and substantive tests of details of account balances.

[2] Learn to apply monetary-unit sampling.

[3] Work through an extended example of monetary-unit sampling.

[4] Learn to apply nonstatistical sampling techniques.

[5] Learn to apply classical variables sampling.

[6] Work through an example of classical variables difference estimation.

RELEVANT ACCOUNTING AND AUDITING PRONOUNCEMENTS

AICPA, *Audit Sampling* (Audit Guide) (New York: AICPA, 2008)

AU 311, Planning and Supervision

AU 312, Audit Risk and Materiality in Conducting an Audit

AU 314, Understanding the Entity and Its Environment and Assessing the Risks of Material Misstatement

AU 316, Consideration of Fraud in a Financial Statement Audit

AU 326, Audit Evidence

AU 339, Audit Documentation

AU 350, Audit Sampling

PCAOB Auditing Standard No. 3, Audit Documentation (AS3)

PCAOB Proposed Auditing Standards Related to the Auditor's Assessment of and Response to Risk, PCAOB Release No. 2008-006 (October 21, 2008).

Audit Sampling: An Application to Substantive Tests of Account Balances

Major Phases of an Audit

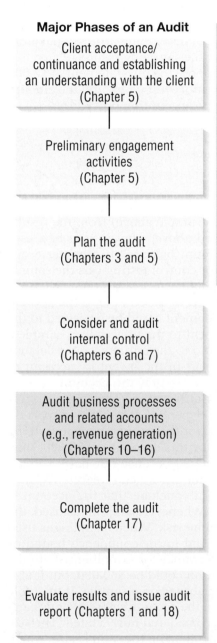

Client acceptance/
continuance and establishing
an understanding with the client
(Chapter 5)

Preliminary engagement
activities
(Chapter 5)

Plan the audit
(Chapters 3 and 5)

Consider and audit
internal control
(Chapters 6 and 7)

Audit business processes
and related accounts
(e.g., revenue generation)
(Chapters 10–16)

Complete the audit
(Chapter 17)

Evaluate results and issue audit
report (Chapters 1 and 18)

This chapter demonstrates the application of audit sampling to substantive tests of details of account balances. In Chapter 8, attribute sampling was used to determine whether controls were operating effectively and could therefore be relied on by the auditor to generate accurate accounting information. Thus, the objective of attribute sampling was to determine the reliability of the client's controls. In this chapter, the purpose of the sampling application is to determine if a financial statement account is fairly stated.

Two statistical sampling techniques, *monetary-unit sampling* and *classical variables sampling,* and nonstatistical sampling are demonstrated in this chapter. While both statistical sampling methods can provide sufficient, appropriate evidence, a monetary-unit sample may be more practical for most audit applications. The chapter starts with an introduction of monetary-unit sampling and an extended example. Nonstatistical sampling is then covered. The *Advanced Module* contains a discussion and example of classical variables sampling.

Sampling for Substantive Tests of Details of Account Balances

✂ [LO 1]   The basic statistical concepts discussed in Chapter 8 are also applicable for sampling approaches used to test account balances. Three important determinants of sample size are desired confidence level, tolerable misstatement, and estimated misstatement. Misstatements discovered in the audit sample must be projected to the population, and there must be an allowance for sampling risk.

In the preface to Chapter 8, we asked you to imagine that you were an apple inspector. We did this to illustrate some of the basic concepts of audit sampling before covering the technical details. Before we get into the details of audit sampling for substantive tests, we want you to use your developing professional judgment and understanding of sampling to evaluate the sampling results related to a test of the inventory balance provided below. Suppose the misstatement of $2,000 represents differences between the auditor's inventory test count and the amount in the client's records based on the client's inventory counting procedures:

Book value of the inventory account balance	$3,000,000
Book value of items sampled	$ 100,000
Audited value of items sampled	$ 98,000
Total amount of misstatement observed in audit sample	$ 2,000

The purpose of audit sampling is to draw inferences about the entire population (the reported inventory account balance in the example above) from the results of a sample. Using just the information provided above, what is your best estimate of the misstatement in the inventory account balance? In Chapter 8 our best estimate of the population deviation rate for control testing was the sample deviation rate. Similarly, when using audit sampling to test account balances, we will want to project the misstatement observed in the sample to the population. In the example above, the observed misstatement could be projected to the population by computing the ratio of misstatement to the total dollars sampled: 2 percent ($2,000 ÷ $100,000). Applying this ratio to the entire account balance produces a *best estimate* or *projected misstatement* in the inventory account of $60,000 (2% × $3,000,000). If your best estimate is that the account is overstated by $60,000, do you believe the account is fairly stated? The answer to this question, like many questions in auditing, is "it depends." It depends in part on the amount of misstatement that can be tolerated for the inventory account. If the amount of misstatement that can be tolerated for this account is $50,000, then we cannot conclude that the account is fairly stated because our best estimate (or projected misstatement) is higher than the amount we can tolerate. What if tolerable misstatement was $110,000; would you conclude that the account is fairly stated? The answer is again, "it depends." Whenever sampling is used, the evaluation must include an allowance for sampling risk. When sampling is used to estimate monetary misstatement, an upper and lower confidence bound or misstatement limit must be established as an allowance for sampling risk. In the above example, the misstatement in the population could be $60,000, but it also might be higher or lower because the estimate is based on a sample. If tolerable misstatement is $110,000, and the upper limit on the account's possible misstatement is less than $110,000, then the account is considered fairly stated. The size of the upper limit on misstatement is largely dependent on the sample size, which is also directly related to the desired confidence level.

You may remember from your statistics courses using concepts such as "standard deviation" and a "normal distribution" (i.e., Z scores or confidence coefficients) to compute *confidence limits* and *intervals*. This traditional statistical approach is used for classical variables sampling, which is covered in the *Advanced*

Module. Before personal computers were commonly available, the mathematical complexity of classical variable sampling was problematic for auditors. In response, auditors developed an audit sampling approach for testing balances called monetary-unit sampling. Monetary-unit sampling is based on attribute-sampling concepts. While the computations involved in classical variables sampling can now easily be performed with a personal computer or handheld calculator, auditors have found that monetary-unit sampling provides other important advantages. For this reason, popular audit software, such as ACL, include monetary-unit sampling but not classical variables sampling. However, monetary-unit sampling is not the best approach for all substantive tests of details; therefore, in this chapter we also cover nonstatistical sampling and classical variables sampling.

Monetary-Unit Sampling

[LO 2] Monetary-unit sampling (MUS) uses attribute-sampling theory to express a conclusion in dollar amounts rather than as a rate of occurrence. MUS was developed by auditors to overcome the computational complexity of other statistical sampling techniques and because most accounting populations contain relatively little misstatement. The statistical estimators of potential misstatement involved in classical variables sampling (see the *Advanced Module*) are not very effective in populations with little misstatement. MUS is commonly used by auditors to test accounts such as accounts receivable, loans receivable, investment securities, and inventory. While MUS is based on attribute-sampling theory, the fact that MUS is designed to test monetary amounts (e.g., dollars, yen, pesos) rather than internal control effectiveness causes important differences in these techniques. The differences are driven by the characteristics of control deviations and monetary misstatements. In attribute sampling, the control either works or it does not. Thus, all items sampled are either correct or a deviation. Attributes sampling provides an estimate and upper limit on the percentage of the time that a control is failing. With MUS, the sampling item tested may be valid and posted to the correct account in the correct period, but the dollar amount may not be accurately recorded. For instance, an invoice for $2,565 might be entered into the accounting system as $2,655. In this case there is a misstatement, but the misstatement is only about 3.5 percent of the transaction. A direct application of attribute sampling to monetary items would treat all misstatements as deviations, or 100 percent misstatements. However, doing so would not result in a useful estimate of the monetary misstatement in the population. MUS begins with attribute-sampling concepts as a foundation but takes into consideration misstatement amounts observed in each sampling unit when computing the best estimate of the population misstatement and formulating the confidence limits around this estimated misstatement. Over the years academics, audit firms, and software programmers (e.g., ACL) have developed slightly different MUS approaches and enhancements. However, the underlying concepts in all MUS approaches are similar to those discussed in this chapter.

To summarize, the basic underlying concepts of MUS are straightforward. MUS uses attribute-sampling theory to estimate the *percentage* of monetary units in a population that might be misstated and then multiplies this percentage by an estimate of *how much* the dollars are misstated. Keep these basic concepts in mind as you study MUS in this chapter.

MUS is designed primarily to test for *overstatement* errors. However, it can accommodate understatement errors if special considerations are made during the evaluation of the sample results. MUS is most appropriate for low-error-rate populations because it provides as effective a test as classical variables sampling does but has a more efficient sample size. Following are some advantages and disadvantages of MUS.

Advantages

- When the auditor expects little to no misstatements, MUS usually results in a smaller sample size than classical variables sampling.
- The calculation of the sample size and the evaluation of the sample results are *not* based on the variation (or standard deviation) in the population. The standard deviation is required to compute the sample size for a classical variables sampling application because it relies on the central limit theorem.
- When applied using a probability-proportional-to-size sample selection procedure as outlined in this text, MUS automatically results in a stratified sample because sampled items are selected in proportion to their dollar amounts. Thus, larger dollar items have a higher probability of being selected. With classical variables sampling, the population must be stratified in order to focus on larger items.

Disadvantages

- The selection of zero or negative balances generally requires special design consideration. For example, if examining zero balances is important (searching for unrecorded liabilities in accounts payable), the auditor must test those items separately because such items will not be selected using a probability-proportional-to-size selection method. Alternatively, if an account such as accounts receivable contains credit balances, the auditor should segregate those items and test them separately.
- The general approach to MUS assumes that the audited amount of the sample item is not in error by more than 100 percent. If the auditor detects items that are in error by more than 100 percent, special adjustments will be necessary when calculating sample results. For example, suppose an accounts receivable account contains a *debit* balance book value of $1,500. If the auditor determines that the correct value for the account should be a *credit* balance of $3,000, the account will be in error by 300 percent. Such an item would require special consideration when the auditor projects the amount of misstatement.
- When more than one or two misstatements are detected using an MUS approach, the sample results calculations as shown in the textbook may overstate the allowance for sampling risk. This occurs because the methods used to determine the amount of misstatement are conservative. Thus, an auditor is more likely to reject an acceptable recorded book value and overaudit.[1]

Applying Monetary-Unit Sampling

In Chapter 8 the general considerations when using sampling for substantive tests were discussed along with the steps in a sampling application. In conducting MUS for substantive tests of details of account balances, the auditor follows the same basic steps outlined in Chapter 8 for attribute sampling. Table 9–1 lists each step by the three phases in the sampling application. Again, the auditor is required to use substantial judgment and should adequately document the sampling application in the audit working papers.

Planning

Step 1: Determine the Test Objectives   Sampling may be used for substantive testing to (1) test the reasonableness of assertions about a financial statement amount (e.g., accuracy, existence); or (2) develop an estimate of

---

[1]There are alternative methods that overcome this disadvantage. However, these methods are more complex. See D. A. Leslie, A. D. Teitlebaum, and R. J. Anderson, *Dollar Unit Sampling: A Practical Guide for Auditors* (Toronto: Copp, Clark and Pitman, 1979), and W. L. Felix, Jr., R. A. Grimlund, F. J. Koster, and R. S. Roussey, "Arthur Andersen's New Monetary-Unit Sampling Approach," *Auditing: A Journal of Practice & Theory* (Fall 1990), pp. 1–16, for a discussion of alternative approaches.

TABLE 9-1	Steps in a Monetary-Unit Sampling Application

Planning
1. Determine the test objectives.
2. Define the population characteristics:
   - Define the population.
   - Define the sampling unit.
   - Define a misstatement.
3. Determine the sample size, using the following inputs:
   - The desired confidence level or risk of incorrect acceptance.
   - The tolerable misstatement.
   - The expected population misstatement.
   - Population size.

Performance
4. Select sample items.
5. Perform the auditing procedures:
   - Understand and analyze any misstatements observed.

Evaluation
6. Calculate the projected misstatement and the upper limit on misstatement.
7. Draw final conclusions.

some amount. The first use, which is the most frequent application of sampling as a substantive procedure in a financial statement audit, tests the assertion or hypothesis that a financial statement account is fairly stated. The second is less frequent but is occasionally used to develop an estimate of an amount as part of a consulting engagement or in some cases to provide evidence on a client estimate (e.g., sales returns for a new product). The discussion in this chapter is limited to using audit sampling to test the assertion that an account or monetary population is fairly stated. The objective of MUS for substantive tests of details is to test the assertion that no material misstatements exist in an account balance, a class of transactions, or a disclosure component of the financial statements.

Step 2: Define the Population Characteristics   To achieve the test objectives, the auditor must carefully consider the characteristics of the sampling population.

Define the Population.   The auditor must define the population so that the selected sample is appropriate for the assertions being tested, because sample results can be projected only to the population from which the sample was selected. For example, if the auditor is concerned about goods shipped but not billed, the population of shipping documents rather than sales invoices is the appropriate population for drawing the sample.

For MUS, the population is defined as the monetary value of an account balance, such as accounts receivable, investment securities, or inventory. As with attribute sampling, once the population has been defined, the auditor must determine that the physical representation, or *frame*, of the population is complete. For example, if the auditor is testing the accounts receivable account, he or she would foot the accounts receivable subsidiary ledger and agree the total to the general ledger account to verify the completeness of the frame. Because the auditor selects the sample from the frame, any conclusions about the population relate only to that frame, which is the physical representation of the population. If the frame and the intended sampling population differ, the auditor might very well draw an incorrect conclusion about the population.

Define the Sampling Unit.   With MUS, an *individual dollar* represents the sampling unit. In fact, this is where monetary-unit (or dollar-unit) sampling gets its name. For example, if the population to be sampled is the accounts receivable balance of $2.5 million, then there are 2.5 million sampling units in the population. However, because the accounts receivable balance is organized by customer or transaction (e.g., customer account or invoice number) and not individual dollars, the auditor does not audit the individual dollar but the customer account or transaction that contains the selected dollar. In other words, while the sampling unit is an individual dollar in a customer account (or invoice), the auditor can't very well audit a single dollar; instead, the auditor will audit the entire customer account (or transaction) that contains the selected dollar. The customer account or transaction that contains the selected dollar is called the *logical unit*. In essence, by selecting a dollar contained in a customer account (or transaction), the auditor by extension selects the logical unit that contains the selected monetary unit to audit.

Define a Misstatement.   For MUS, a misstatement is defined as the difference between monetary amounts in the client's records and amounts supported by audit evidence. A clear misstatement definition is important because definitions that are too narrow or too broad may result in inefficient or ineffective testing. For example, if an accounts receivable confirmation letter from a customer reports a difference between the customer records and the client's records, it would not be considered a misstatement if the difference is explainable and supportable by the circumstances, such as timing differences (e.g., the customer mistakenly confirms a balance as of January 31 when the confirmation letter requests the customer's balance as of the December 31 year-end) and other documentation supports the client's recorded value.

Step 3: Determine the Sample Size   Considerable judgment is required in determining the appropriate values for the inputs used to compute an MUS sample size. The following four factors must be considered.

Desired Confidence Level or Acceptable Risk of Incorrect Acceptance.   There is a *direct* relationship between the confidence level and sample size. The basic idea is fairly simple: To increase confidence, more work is required, which is reflected in a larger sample size. Confidence level and the risk of incorrect acceptance are complements. If the auditor wants to be 95-percent confident in the sampling conclusion, then he or she must be willing to accept a 5-percent risk of incorrect acceptance. The risk of incorrect acceptance is the risk that the sample supports the conclusion that the recorded account balance is fairly stated when in fact it is not (a Type II error). This risk relates to the effectiveness of the audit. In determining an acceptable risk of incorrect acceptance, the auditor should consider the components of the audit risk model: the acceptable level of audit risk and risk of material misstatement. For practical purposes, the acceptable risk of incorrect acceptance is the same as *detection risk (DR)* after considering the assessed level of detection risk based on other substantive procedures such as substantive analytical procedures. If the auditor incorrectly accepts an account balance as being fairly stated when it is actually materially misstated, he or she will allow the issuance of financial statements that are not fairly presented. The users of those financial statements may then sue the auditor for damages that result from relying on those financial statements. There is an *inverse* relationship between the risk of incorrect acceptance and sample size. The lower the acceptable risk of incorrect acceptance, the larger the sample size must be.

Tolerable Misstatement.   Tolerable misstatement is the maximum amount by which the account can be misstated and still be acceptable to the auditor as being fairly presented. It will always be less than planning materiality. In Chapter 3 we illustrated how planning materiality and tolerable misstatement are determined. Remember from Chapter 3 that for an audit to be economically feasible, the auditor and users of the financial statements must tolerate some margin for misstatement (i.e., the auditor provides reasonable assurance that the financial statements are fair, not absolute assurance that the financial statements are error-free).

Audit sampling techniques designed to test the assertion that an account is fairly stated cannot be performed unless tolerable misstatement exceeds expected misstatement by a sufficient amount, because there must always be room for an allowance for sampling risk between the two measures. Tolerable misstatement is also inversely related to sample size—the lower the amount of tolerable misstatement, the more precise the test the auditor needs, and the larger the sample size must be.

Expected Misstatement.   The expected misstatement is the dollar amount of misstatement that the auditor believes exists in the population. The auditor can develop this expectation based on the assessment of inherent risk, prior years' results, a pilot sample, the results of related substantive procedures, or the results of tests of controls. As the expected misstatement approaches the tolerable misstatement, the auditor needs more precise information from the sample. Therefore, there is a direct relationship to sample size: The larger the expected misstatement, the larger the sample size must be.

Population Size.   Population size is directly related to sample size. Because MUS populations are made up of individual dollars, populations tested with MUS are usually large. As such, some MUS approaches, like the one we demonstrate below using the attributes tables in Chapter 8, do not use population size directly as an input for sample size determination, but population size is used in the conversion of tolerable and expected misstatements to percentages. However, for approaches like the one used in ACL, population size is a direct input to determine sample size.

Table 9–2 summarizes the effects of the four factors on sample size.

Computing Sample Sizes Using the Attribute-Sampling Tables

A monetary-unit sample size can be determined by using the attribute sample size tables shown in Chapter 8. The auditor first determines the desired confidence level and then converts the tolerable misstatement and the expected misstatement to percentages of the book value of the balance tested. For example, suppose the auditor has established a tolerable misstatement of $125,000 and an expected misstatement of $25,000 for an accounts receivable account with a book value of $2,500,000. The tolerable misstatement would be 5 percent ($125,000 ÷ $2,500,000), and the expected misstatement would be 1 percent ($25,000 ÷ $2,500,000). If the desired confidence level is 95 percent (or a risk of

TABLE 9–2 | **The Effect of Sample Selection Factors on Sample Size**

		Examples	
Factor	*Relationship to Sample Size*	*Change in Factor*	*Effect on Sample*
Desired confidence level	Direct	Lower	Decrease
		Higher	Increase
Tolerable misstatement	Inverse	Lower	Increase
		Higher	Decrease
Expected misstatement	Direct	Lower	Decrease
		Higher	Increase
Population size	Direct	Lower	Decrease
		Higher	Increase

EXHIBIT 9–1 | **Sample Size Calculation Using ACL™ Software**

incorrect acceptance of 5 percent), the auditor would use Table 8–5 in Chapter 8. In this example, the sample size is 93. Be sure you can identify how the sample size was determined using Table 8–5 before moving on.

Computing Sample Sizes Using ACL

Software programs like ACL can also be used to determine sample size. Exhibit 9–1 shows the computation of sample size for the previous example using ACL software. To compute sample size, you open a workbook file (for sample size calculations, it can be any workbook file) and then select "Calculate Sample Size" from the "Sampling" menu. In the sample size dialogue box, select "Monetary" for MUS.

Enter the desired "Confidence," which in our example is 95 percent (input into ACL as 95). Enter the "Population," $2,500,000 in our example (input in ACL as 2500000). Enter "Materiality" or tolerable misstatement of $125,000 (input as 125000), and finally "Expected Total Errors" or expected misstatement of $25,000 (input as 25000), and then hit the "Calculate" button. Note that with ACL the auditor enters tolerable and expected misstatement in dollars rather than in percentage terms, like we did with attribute sampling in Chapter 8. The result is a sample size of 92, which is slightly smaller than the size determined using the tables.[2]

While the underlying concepts and sample sizes produced by the attribute-sampling tables in Chapter 8 and ACL are similar, ACL uses a different approach to compute sample sizes. Rather than first solve for sample size and then compute the sampling interval (discussed in the next section), ACL first computes the sampling interval (i.e., the interval in Exhibit 9–1 is defined as every 27,083rd dollar) using factors based on the proportion of expected misstatement to tolerable misstatement and a statistical value associated with the desired confidence level. ACL then divides the population by the sampling interval to determine the sample size. Interested students may want to enter different population sizes into ACL while maintaining the same tolerable and estimated misstatements to see that the interval is not affected by population size but that the sample size is affected.

Performance

Step 4: Select Sample Items   In selecting the sample items, the auditor attempts to draw the sample in such a way that it accurately represents the population. The auditor selects a sample for MUS by using a systematic selection approach called *probability-proportional-to-size selection*, often with the help of a computer program such as ACL. Probability proportional-to-size sample selection uses an interval to select sample items. Keep in mind that MUS defines an individual dollar (or other monetary unit) as the sampling unit. The sampling interval can be determined by dividing the book value of the population by the sample size. Because the first sampling item is randomly selected within the first interval, each individual dollar in the population has an equal chance of being selected. Figure 9–1 provides an example of how probability-proportional-to-size selection is applied.

| FIGURE 9–1 | **An Example of Probability-Proportional-to-Size Selection** |

Customer Number and Name (Logical Unit)	Customer Balance	Cumulative Dollars	Sample Items (Random start $3,977, interval $26,882)	
1001 Ace Emergency Center	$ 2,350	$ 2,350		
1002 Admington Hospital	15,495	17,845	(1)	$ 3,977
1003 Jess Base, Inc	945	18,790		
1004 Good Hospital Corp.	21,893	40,683	(2)	30,859
1005 Jen Mara Corp.	3,968	44,651		
1006 Axa Corporation	32,549	77,200	(3)	57,741
1007 Green River Mtg	2,246	79,446		
1008 Bead Hospital Centers	11,860	91,306	(4)	84,623
•	•	•		•
•	•	•		•
•	•	•		•
1213 Andrew Call Medical	0	2,472,032		•
1214 Lilly Health, Inc.	26,945	2,498,977	(93)	$2,477,121
1215 Jayne Ann Corp.	1,023	$2,500,000		
Total Accounts Receivable	$2,500,000			

---

[2]ACL software uses a different underlying statistical distribution than the attribute sampling tables, which in this case resulted in a slightly smaller sample size (see footnote 4).

In Figure 9–1, the total book value of the client's accounts receivable balance is $2,500,000, and the auditor determined a sample size of 93. The sampling interval will be $26,882 ($2,500,000 ÷ 93). To select a probability-proportional-to-size sample, the auditor arranges the client's accounts receivable records in some order (e.g., by customer number or alphabetically) and then creates a column of cumulative dollars. In Figure 9–1, the customer records are arranged by customer number. The auditor obtains a random number between 1 and the size of the sampling interval ($26,882) by using computer software such as ACL or MS Excel. The random number becomes the first sample item selected, and then the sampling interval is added to determine the second sampling item and so on for every 26,882th dollar in the population. In the example illustrated in Figure 9–1, the random start is $3,977, and the customer account that contains the 3,977th dollar is selected for testing. In this case, Admington Hospital, with a balance of $15,495, is selected for testing. The auditor then adds the sampling interval, either manually or with the aid of a computer program, through the population and selects each logical unit that contains the computed amount.[3] Following this process, the second customer account selected would be Good Hospital Corp., which contains the 30,859th dollar ($3,977 + 26,882) and has a balance of $21,893. The third account would be Axa Corporation, which contains the 57,741th dollar ($30,859 + 26,882), and so on until the entire population has been subjected to sampling and 93 units have been selected.

The advantage of using this approach to select the sample is that while each dollar in the population has an equal chance of being selected, *logical units* containing more dollars have a higher chance of being selected; hence the name, "probability-proportional-to-size" sample selection. Note that all logical units with a book value larger than the sampling interval (such as Axa Corporation and Lilly Health, Inc.) are certain to be selected using this method. From an audit perspective, this approach guarantees that all individually significant accounts are examined and that, in general, the sample will be made up of larger accounts. This approach is particularly appropriate when the auditor is primarily concerned about overstatements and larger overstatements are expected to be found in larger logical units (such as with accounts receivable). If the auditor is primarily concerned about understatements or unrecorded amounts, other selection techniques (e.g., random or specific identification) should be used. Let's check your understanding. In the example in Figure 9–1, what is the probability that customer 1213, Andrew Call Medical (with a zero balance), will be selected? The probability is zero, because the customer's balance is zero.

When the logical unit, a customer account in this example, exceeds the sampling interval, more than one sampling unit may be selected from the same logical unit. If this happens, the logical unit is included only once when the sample results are evaluated. Thus, the number of logical units examined may be less than the computed sample size, which is another advantage of this selection technique. In fact, once the auditor has used the computed sample size to determine an interval, the computed sample size is not used again in an MUS application. As you will see later, rather than use the computed sample size in the evaluation of results, the auditor uses the sampling interval.

---

[3]The "Sample Records" command in ACL's sampling menu can also be used to select a probability-proportional-to-size sample.

Step 5: Perform the Audit Procedures   After the sample items have been selected, the auditor conducts the planned audit procedures on the logical units containing the selected sampling units. In some instances, the auditor may not be able to conduct the planned procedures on a particular logical unit (e.g., customer account). This may occur, for example, because a supporting document is missing. Unless other evidence is available, such items should be considered misstatements. The auditor must also be careful to conduct the audit procedures so as to avoid nonsampling errors caused by carelessness, poor supervision, or mistaken judgment. After all the audit procedures have been completed, the auditor evaluates the sample results.

Evaluation

The evaluation phase of the sampling application includes the following steps.

Step 6: Calculate the Projected Misstatement and the Upper Limit on Misstatement   The misstatements detected in the sample must be projected to the population. As mentioned earlier, an MUS application is designed primarily to test for overstatement errors. The projection of the errors to the population is referred to as the *projected misstatement* (ACL refers to this as the *most likely error*); it is comparable to the sample deviation rate or best estimate in Chapter 8. The auditor calculates an allowance for sampling risk and adds it to the projected misstatement. The total of the projected misstatement and the allowance for sampling risk is referred to as the *upper misstatement limit* (ACL refers to this as the *upper error limit*). These computations are somewhat involved, so rather than talk about them in abstract terms, we explain them using an example.

✎ **[LO 3]**   **An Extended Example**   An example is used to demonstrate the computation and evaluation of projected and upper misstatement limit (UML) of a monetary-unit sampling application. The following information relates to the audit of a client's accounts receivable balance:

Example Information

- Book value = $2,500,000
- Tolerable misstatement = $125,000
- Sample size = 93
- Desired confidence level = 95%
- Expected amount of misstatement = $25,000
- Sampling interval = $26,882

The calculations of sample size and sampling interval using the attributes sampling tables were shown previously. Assume further that, based on the auditor's understanding of the business and previous experience auditing this account, the auditor is primarily concerned with overstatements.

Basic Precision   As you learned in Chapter 8 with attributes sampling, even when the auditor observes no control deviations, the allowance for sampling risk still results in a computed upper deviation limit. The same is true for MUS; if no misstatements are found in the sample, the projection or best estimate of the population misstatement would be zero dollars. However, even with zero projected misstatements, an allowance for sampling risk must be computed, which will result in an upper misstatement limit that is greater than zero. This allowance for sampling risk when no misstatements are observed is referred to as the *basic precision*. If the appropriate sample size was computed and used to derive the sampling interval and no misstatements were

TABLE 9-3	Monetary Unit Sampling Misstatement Factors for Sample Evaluation[4]				
	90% Desired Confidence Level			**95% Desired Confidence Level**	
Number of Misstatements	Misstatement Factor	Incremental Increase		Misstatement Factor	Incremental Increase
0	2.3	0.0		3.0	0.0
1	3.9	1.6		4.7	1.7
2	5.3	1.4		6.2	1.5
3	6.6	1.3		7.6	1.4
4	7.9	1.3		9.0	1.4
5	9.1	1.2		10.3	1.3
6	10.3	1.2		11.5	1.2

found in the logical units tested, then the auditor would be guaranteed that the upper misstatement limit would be less than or equal to the tolerable misstatement used to compute the sample size.

In evaluating MUS results, the sampling interval and the desired level of confidence are two of the important factors, along with the MUS misstatement factors in Table 9–3. In the example, the sampling interval is $26,882 and the desired level of confidence is 95 percent. For basic precision, use the factor associated with zero misstatements in Table 9–3. The misstatement factor is 3.0. The upper misstatement limit (and basic precision) is thus $80,646 (3.0 × $26,882). The basic precision essentially assumes any undetected misstatements in the population are misstated by 100 percent. This is a very conservative, but justifiable assumption given the high potential cost of underestimating the amount of misstatement in a client's financial statements.

In practice, auditors use firm-specific MUS guidance or software programs like ACL to determine MUS sample sizes and to evaluate MUS results. Although firms and software developers use different algorithms and assumptions in computing MUS misstatement limits, the underlying theory and ultimate conclusions are similar. Before demonstrating how to evaluate MUS results with ACL, we demonstrate how to manually complete the calculations. Demonstrating the manual calculation will help you better understand output from packages like ACL.

Misstatements Detected   Assume that the auditor sent confirmations to the customers selected from the client's accounts receivable account using a sampling interval of $26,882 as illustrated in Figure 9–1 and that all but four customers returned confirmations indicating the client's records are correct. Based on document inspection and inquiry of the client, the four detected misstatements appear to be unintentional processing errors. For example, discounts granted were not recorded or in the case of Learn Heart Centers the merchandise was

---

[4]The misstatement factors in Table 9–3 are based on computed upper deviation rate factors used in attribute sampling (binomial distribution). In MUS, the sampling interval and the tainting factor are used in the evaluation and not the original computed sample size. When the population is large and misstatement rate low (both common for MUS applications using accounting data) the limiting form of the binomial distribution is the Poisson distribution, which only requires the level of confidence to determine the appropriate misstatement factor to compute the upper misstatement limit (see Leslie et al., *Dollar Unit Sampling*). The Poisson distribution factors are nearly identical to the misstatement factors in Table 9–3. ACL uses the Poisson factors, which explains the slight differences in sample sizes and upper limits compared to the manual approach using the attribute sampling tables. Note that in evaluating MUS results, ACL does not require sample or population size because the interval, tainting factor, and desired confidence provide all the necessary information for evaluation (see Exhibit 9–2).

returned prior to year end, but the credit was not processed until the subsequent period. The following table lists the misstatements detected:

Customer	Book Value	Audit Value	Difference	Tainting Factor (column 4 ÷ column 2)
Good Hospital Corp.	$21,893	$18,609	$ 3,284	.15
Marva Medical Supply	6,705	4,023	2,682	.40
Learn Heart Centers	15,000	0	15,000	1.00
Axa Corp.	32,549	30,049	2,500	Not applicable*

*Book value is greater than sampling interval.

Overstatement Misstatements Detected   If misstatements are found in the sample, the auditor needs to calculate a projected misstatement and an allowance for sampling risk. Because in an MUS sample each selected dollar "represents" a group of dollars in the population, the percentage of misstatement in the logical unit represents the percentage of misstatement in the sampling interval from which the dollar was selected. Three types of situations can occur with detected misstatements.

1. ***The logical unit is equal to or greater than the sampling interval.*** In this situation, the projected misstatement is equal to the actual misstatement detected in the logical unit. For example, the Axa Corporation account in Figure 9–1 contained a balance of $32,549, which is larger than the sampling interval of $26,882. In the example, the projected misstatement associated with this account would be $2,500, and no sampling risk is added. No allowance for sampling risk is necessary for these large accounts because all accounts larger than the sampling interval will automatically be selected by an MUS sampling approach using probability-proportional-to-size selection. Since all the dollars in the large accounts are audited, there is no risk of additional potential misstatement associated with large accounts (logical units).

2. ***The logical unit's book value is less than the sampling interval, and it is misstated by less than 100 percent.*** This is the most common situation. The percentage of misstatement in the logical unit is referred to as the *tainting* factor. The tainting factor is calculated using the following formula:

$$\text{Tainting factor} = \frac{\text{Book value} - \text{Audit value}}{\text{Book value}}$$

   For example, the Good Hospital Corp. account is overstated by $3,284. Thus, the tainting factor for the account would be .15 [(21,893 − 18,609) ÷ 21,893]. The projected misstatement for the interval containing this logical unit would be $4,032 (.15 × $26,882). The tainting factor associated with the interval containing the Marva Medical Supply account is .40 ($2,682 ÷ $6,705), and the projected misstatement for the interval is $10,753 (.40 × $26,882). An allowance for sampling risk would be added to these projected misstatements as illustrated below.

3. ***The book value of the logical unit is less than the sampling interval, and it is 100-percent misstated.*** Because the logical unit represents the group of dollars in the sampling interval, the sampling interval is assumed to be 100 percent in error. In the above example, the audited value for Learn Heart Centers is $0. The projected error for the interval containing this logical unit is $26,882, which is determined by multiplying the percentage misstated (100 percent) by the size of the sampling interval ($26,882). An allowance for sampling risk would be added to this amount as illustrated below.

Computing Upper Misstatement Limit Manually

To compute the upper misstatement limit (UML), the auditor first computes basic precision and then ranks the detected misstatements based on the size of the tainting factor from the largest tainting factor to the smallest. Projected and upper misstatement limits are computed using the computed tainting factor and the appropriate misstatement factor from Table 9–3. Finally, misstatements detected in logical units greater than the sampling interval are added.

Customer Name	Tainting Factor	Sampling Interval	Projected Misstatement (columns 2 × 3)	95% Misstatement Factor or Increment (from Table 9–3)	Upper Misstatement Limit (columns 2 × 3 × 5)
Basic Precision	1.0	$26,882	NA	3.0	$ 80,646
Learn Heart Centers	1.0	26,882	26,882	1.7 (4.7 − 3.0)	45,700
Marva Medical	.40	26,882	10,753	1.5 (6.2 − 4.7)	16,130
Good Hospital	.15	26,882	4,032	1.4 (7.6 − 6.2)	5,645
Add misstatements detected in logical units greater than the sampling interval:					
Axa Corp.	NA	26,882	2,500	NA	2,500
			Upper Misstatement Limit		$150,621

NA = not applicable

The UML in this case is $150,621, and is calculated as follows. First, basic precision, $80,646, is computed by multiplying the sampling interval by the misstatement factor from Table 9–3, ($26,882 × 3.0). The $80,646 represents the sampling risk that exists even if no misstatements are observed in the sample. Remember, because we are basing our conclusions on a sample, we cannot be sure there are no misstatements in the population even if we find none in the sample.

Second, logical units smaller than the interval where misstatements are detected, Learn Heart Centers, Marva Medical, and Good Hospital, are ranked according to the size of their tainting factor from largest to smallest.

Third, the projected misstatements for Learn Heart Centers, Marva Medical, and Good Hospital are calculated. Projected misstatement is computed by multiplying the sampling interval by the tainting factor (column 2 × column 3). This calculation is based on the assumption that the dollar selected for testing represents the sampling interval. In turn, it is assumed that the extent of misstatement in the logical unit that contains the sampled dollar represents the amount of misstatement in the sampling interval.

Next, for the intervals containing the Learn Heart Centers, Marva Medical and Good Hospital accounts, an allowance for sampling risk is added to the projected misstatement by multiplying the projected misstatement by the incremental change in the misstatement factor for the desired confidence level. In this example, the desired confidence is 95 percent, so the misstatement factors are taken from the appropriate column in Table 9–3. For basic precision, the factor, 3.0, is taken from the "Misstatement Factor" column of Table 9–3 (95-percent confidence) because it is the first "layer" of the UML calculation.

For the first misstatement observed, Learn Heart Centers, the misstatement factor from Table 9–3 (95-percent confidence) is 4.7. However, the misstatement factors in Table 9–3 are cumulative. In other words, the factor for 1 misstatement, 4.7, includes the sampling risk associated with zero misstatements (i.e., it includes the misstatement factor 3.0). Since basic precision already includes the factor for zero misstatements, only the increase or *increment* is used for the first misstatement, and likewise for subsequent misstatements. The incremental change is calculated by simply subtracting the misstatement factor for the current number of misstatements from the factor for the previous number of misstatements (i.e., 4.7 − 3.0 = 1.7). Thus, for Good Hospital, the projected misstatement is $4,032, and the UML is $5,645 (1.7 × $4,032) as illustrated in the table above. The difference between the projected misstatement and the UML is the allowance for sampling risk. Thus, the allowance for sampling risk for Good Hospital is $1,613 ($5,645 − $4,032).

Ranking the logical units by their tainting factors leads to a UML that is conservative because the largest tainting factor is multiplied by the largest incremental change in the misstatement factor. This conservative approach means there is a higher risk that an acceptable account balance will be rejected by the auditor.

Finally, misstatements detected in logical units that are greater than the sampling interval are added to the upper limit. As noted earlier, the reason misstatements from logical units greater than the sampling interval do not require projection or the consideration of sampling risk is because all accounts larger than the sampling interval will automatically be selected by a probability-proportional-to-size sampling approach. Since all the dollars in the large accounts are audited, there is no sampling risk associated with large accounts (logical units). Thus, in the example above, the misstatement detected in Axa Corp.'s balance, $2,500 ($32,549 − $30,049), is simply added to the upper misstatement.

Step 7: Draw Final Conclusions   For this example, the final decision on whether the accounts receivable balance is materially misstated is made by comparing the tolerable misstatement to the UML. If the UML is less than or equal to the tolerable misstatement, the evidence supports the conclusion that the account balance is not materially misstated. In this case the UML of $150,621 is more than the tolerable misstatement of $125,000. Because the UML exceeds the tolerable misstatement of $125,000, the auditor has evidence that there is an unacceptably high risk that accounts receivable is materially misstated.

The auditor now has four options. First, the sample size can be increased. While this approach is possible in theory, it is not practical in many audit settings. Second, other substantive procedures can be performed. This approach might be followed if the auditor's qualitative analysis of the detected misstatements indicates that there is a systematic problem with the population. For example, the auditor might determine that three of the misstatements occurred in the pricing of one particular product line sold by the client. In this instance, he or she might design a substantive procedure that examines the pricing of all sales in that product line. Third, the auditor can request that the client adjust the accounts receivable balance. In our example, the minimum adjustment would be $25,621 ($150,621 − $125,000). If the client adjusts the account by $25,621, the UML will be equal to or less than the tolerable misstatement at a 5-percent risk of incorrect acceptance. Finally, if the client refuses to adjust the account, the auditor would issue a qualified or adverse opinion (this situation would be extremely rare).

Table 9–4 illustrates the risks auditors face when evaluating an account balance based on sample evidence. If the evidence supports the fairness of the account balance based on the sample evidence and the account is not materially misstated, the auditor has made a correct decision. If the evidence does not support the fairness of the account based on the sample evidence and the account is materially misstated, a correct decision has also been made. The other two combinations result in decision errors by the auditor. If the evidence does not support the fairness of the account when it is in reality not materially misstated (Type I error), the auditor will have incorrectly rejected the account. This

TABLE 9–4	The Auditor's Risks When Evaluating a Financial Statement Account Based on Sample Evidence	
	True State of Financial Statement Account	
Auditor's Decision Based on Sample Evidence	*Not Materially Misstated*	*Materially Misstated*
Supports the fairness of the account balance	Correct decision	Risk of incorrect acceptance (Type II)
Does not support the fairness of the account balance	Risk of incorrect rejection (Type I)	Correct decision

can lead to over-auditing and an inefficient audit. If the evidence supports the account as fairly stated when the account actually contains a material misstatement, the auditor will have incorrectly accepted the account (Type II error). Keep in mind, however, that the auditor almost never finds out the "true" account balance unless later events, such as lawsuits against the auditor for issuing a report on misleading financial statements, require an examination of the entire population.

Computing Projected Misstatement and Upper Misstatement Limit Using ACL

Exhibit 9–2 shows the evaluation of the sample results using ACL software. The UML is calculated to be $152,744. To use ACL to evaluate sample results, open a workbook file (for sample evaluation calculations, it can be any workbook file) and then select "Evaluate Error" from the "Sampling" menu. In the sample size dialogue box, select "Monetary" for MUS. Enter the desired confidence level, which in our example is 95 percent. Enter the sampling interval, in our example $26,882 (input into ACL as 26882). Enter book values followed by misstatement amount in the "Errors" box. When using ACL, the order in which misstatements are input does not affect the results. In comparing the manually computed UML, $150,621 (illustrated earlier), to ACL's UML, we see that the upper limit on basic precision is identical, as are projected misstatements in the manual calculation to the "Most Likely Error" in ACL. Similarly, the addition of misstatements from logical units greater than the sampling interval is the same for both methods. However, ACL uses a different underlying statistical distribution to estimate the UML than does the manual approach we illustrated.

You should also be aware that alternative methods of calculating the upper limit on misstatement are available and used by some public accounting firms. These alternative methods will produce UMLs that are somewhat different from those shown here. For example, some of these methods correct for the overstatement of sampling risk.

Practice
INSIGHT

Audit firms typically develop standardized documentation templates for audit sampling applications to ensure all steps in the process are completed and documented in a consistent manner.

The Effect of Understatement Misstatements   The methodology used earlier for computing the UML is based on the auditor's assumption, at the time of planning the sampling application, that all errors in the population are overstatements. Recall that MUS is not particularly effective at detecting understatements because under an MUS approach the probability of selecting

| EXHIBIT 9–2 | Sample Results with Overstatement Misstatements Using ACL™ Software |

Chapter 9 Illustration.ACL - ACL 9

File Edit Data Analyze Sampling Applications Tools Server Window Help

Welcome   AR

Filter: Index:
                                                                               (None)

Evaluate

Main | Output

○ Monetary   Confidence   95

○ Record   Interval   26882

                Item amount, Error

Errors   21893, 3284
                6705, 2682
                15000, 15000
                32549, 2500

        OK   Cancel   Help

RECORDS
1
2
3
4
5
6
7
8
9
10
11
12
13
14
15
16
17
18
19
20

Default_View

AR   23 Records

Chapter 9 Illustration.ACL - ACL 9

File Edit Data Analyze Sampling Applications Tools Server Window Help

Welcome   AR   Evaluate

As of: 04/21/2009 17:03:30

Command: EVALUATE MONETARY CONFIDENCE 95 ERRORLIMIT 21893, 3284,6705, 2682,15000, 15000,32549, 2500 INTERVAL 26882 TO SCREEN

Confidence: 95, Interval: 26882

	Item	Error	Most Likely Error	Upper Error Limit
Basic Precision				80,646.00
	15,000.00	15,000.00	26,882.00	47,043.50
	6,705.00	2,682.00	10,752.80	16,666.84
	21,893.00	3,284.00	4,032.36	5,887.25
	32,549.00	2,500.00	2,500.00	2,500.00
Totals			44,167.16	152,743.59

Text

AR   23 Records

a smaller account is proportionately lower than the probability of selecting a larger account. Thus, an understated account is, by definition, less likely to be selected than an overstated account. In the extreme, an account could be missing or it could be 100-percent understated and recorded at a value of $0; in either case the probability of the account being selected for audit will be zero. When understatement errors are detected, different approaches can be used. When understatements are entered into ACL, ACL adjusts the total "most likely error" downward, but does not adjust the "upper-error limit." To demonstrate this approach, assume that the auditor detected the four overstatement misstatements shown in the previous example and that the following understatement misstatement was also detected.

Customer	Book Value	Audit Value	Difference	Tainting Factor (column 4 ÷ column 2)
Wayne County Medical	$2,000	$2,200	−200	−.10

Exhibit 9–3 shows the evaluation of the sample results, including the understatement misstatement, using ACL software. Note that the UML is still $152,744, but that "most likely error" is now reduced by the projected understatement $2,688 (.10 × $26,882).

Some auditors also adjust down the UML by the projected understatement to obtain a *net* upper misstatement limit.[5] This approach is followed when the auditor believes that the overall misstatement in the population is in the direction of overstatement. The understatements identified are used to adjust the UML.

Using the UML computed in Exhibit 9–3, the adjusted or net UML is $150,056 ($152,744 − $2,688). Using the previous decision rule, the auditor would still conclude that the account was materially misstated because the net UML of $150,056 is more than the tolerable misstatement of $125,000.

Nonstatistical Sampling for Tests of Account Balances[6]

❧ [LO 4]   When conducting a nonstatistical sampling application for testing an account balance, the auditor considers each of the steps shown in Table 9–1. The sampling unit for nonstatistical sampling is normally a customer account, an individual transaction, or a line item on a transaction. When a nonstatistical sampling application is used, the following items need further explanation:

- Identifying individually significant items.
- Determining the sample size.
- Selecting sample items.
- Calculating the sample results.

Identifying Individually Significant Items

In many nonstatistical sampling applications, the auditor determines which items should be tested individually and which items should be subjected to sampling. The items that will be tested individually are items that may contain potential misstatements that individually exceed the tolerable misstatement. These items are tested 100 percent because the auditor is not willing to accept any sampling risk. For example, an auditor using nonstatistical sampling may be examining a client's accounts receivable balance in which 10 customer account balances are greater than tolerable misstatement. The auditor would

---

[5]See Leslie et al., *Dollar Unit Sampling*. Alternative approaches are also used in practice. For example, if the direction of the errors in the population is unknown, a two-sided confidence interval can be constructed by separating the understatements and calculating a lower limit on misstatements. See A. D. Bailey, Jr., *Statistical Auditing: Review, Concepts, and Problems* (New York: Harcourt Brace Jovanovich, 1981), for a discussion of this approach.

[6]The approach presented here for nonstatistical sampling is based on the American Institute of Certified Public Accountants, *Audit Sampling* (Audit Guide) (New York: AICPA, 2008).

EXHIBIT 9-3	Sample Results with Under- and Overstatements Using ACL™ Software

Chapter 9 Illustration.ACL - ACL 9

File   Edit   Data   Analyze   Sampling   Applications   Tools   Server   Window   Help

Welcome   AR

Filter: Index: (None)

Evaluate

Main | Output

- Monetary   Confidence   95
- Record   Interval   26882

Item amount, Error

Errors
```
21893, 3284
6705, 2682
15000, 15000
32549, 2500
2000, -200
```

OK   Cancel   Help

RECORDS
1
2
3
4
5
6
7
8
9
10
11
12
13
14
15
16
17
18
19
20

Default_View

AR   23 Records

Chapter 9 Illustration.ACL - ACL 9

File   Edit   Data   Analyze   Sampling   Applications   Tools   Server   Window   Help

Welcome   AR   Evaluate

As of: 04/21/2009 17:04:53

Command: EVALUATE MONETARY CONFIDENCE 95 ERRORLIMIT 21893, 3284,6705, 2682,15000, 15000,32549, 2500,2000, -200 INTERVAL 26882 TO SCREEN

Confidence: 95, Interval: 26882

	Item	Error	Most Likely Error	Upper Error Limit
Basic Precision				80,646.00
	15,000.00	15,000.00	26,882.00	47,043.50
	6,705.00	2,682.00	10,752.80	16,666.84
	21,893.00	3,284.00	4,032.36	5,887.25
	32,549.00	2,500.00	2,500.00	2,500.00
	2,000.00	-200.00	-2,688.20	0.00
Totals			41,478.96	152,743.59

Text

AR   23 Records

test all 10 large accounts, and supposing that those 10 made up 40 percent of the total account balance, the auditor would apply nonstatistical audit sampling to the remaining customer accounts making up the other 60 percent of the total balance. Testing all individually significant items produces an emphasis on large items similar to probability-proportional-to-size selection. Recall that probability-proportional-to-size selection guarantees that all items greater than the sampling interval will be included in the sample.

Determining the Sample Size

When determining the sample size, the auditor should consider the level of desired confidence, the risk of material misstatement, the tolerable and expected misstatements, and the population size. While an auditor may determine a nonstatistical sample size by using professional judgment, auditing standards indicate that the sample sizes for statistical and nonstatistical sampling should be similar (AU 350.22). Thus, it is common for firms to develop guidance for nonstatistical sampling based on statistical theory such as the formula provided below, which was adapted from the AICPA Audit Guide *Audit Sampling:*[7]

$$\text{Sample size} = \left(\frac{\text{Sampling population book value}}{\text{Tolerable} - \text{Expected misstatement}} \right) \times \text{Confidence factor}$$

The "sampling population book value" excludes the amount of items to be individually audited. The confidence factor is identified by determining the level of desired confidence (largely driven by the amount of other relevant audit evidence in the "assurance bucket"; see Chapter 5) and the risk of material misstatement (i.e., inherent and control risk). Table 9–5 contains the confidence factors for various combinations of desired confidence and risk assessment.

Selecting Sample Items

When any form of audit sampling is used to gather evidence, auditing standards require that the sample items be selected in such a way that the sample can be expected to represent the population. While some form of random sample or systematic selection (e.g., probability proportional to size) is required for statistical sampling, auditing standards allow the use of these selection methods, as well as other selection methods including haphazard sampling when using nonstatistical sampling. As discussed in Chapter 8, haphazard selection allows the auditor to "randomly" select items judgmentally (i.e., with no conscious biases or reasons for including or omitting items from the sample). This does not imply that the items are selected in a careless manner; rather, the sampling units are selected such that they will be representative of the population. The reason haphazard selection is not appropriate for statistical sampling is because people are not very good at being truly random, no matter how hard we may try. For example, the first item on a report or computer screen may never be selected by the auditor

TABLE 9–5	Confidence Factors for Nonstatistical Sampling		
		Desired Level of Confidence	
Assessment of Risk of Material Misstatement	*High*	*Moderate*	*Low*
High	3.0	2.3	2.0
Moderate	2.3	1.6	1.2
Low	2.0	1.2	1.0

---

[7]This formula is based on the statistical theory underlying monetary-unit sampling. This approach will yield lower confidence levels as expected misstatement becomes larger relative to tolerable misstatement.

because it doesn't feel "random" to the auditor to select the very first item. Such biases mean that each item in the population did not have an equal chance of being selected.

Calculating the Sample Results

Auditing standards require that the auditor project the amount of misstatement found in the sample to the population. The AICPA Guide *Audit Sampling* describes two acceptable methods of projecting the amount of misstatement found in a nonstatistical sample.

The first method of projecting the sample results to the population is to apply the misstatement ratio observed in the sample to the population. For example, if the auditor finds misstatements of $1,500 in a sample totaling $15,000, the misstatement ratio in the sample is 10 percent (1,500 ÷ 15,000), and that ratio is applied to the population. If the total population is $200,000, then projected misstatement using the ratio approach will be $20,000 (10% × $200,000). This method of projection is often referred to as *ratio projection*, and it is used with both nonstatistical sampling and classical variables statistical sampling (see the *Advanced Module* in this chapter). Ratio projection is used when the dollar amount of misstatement is expected to relate to the dollar amount of items tested.

The second method, referred to as *difference projection*, projects the average misstatement of each item in the sample to all items in the population and is used when the misstatement is expected to be relatively constant for all items in the population regardless of their dollar size. *Difference estimation* is the name of a sampling technique that uses information about misstatements to determine sample size, projected misstatement, and confidence bounds. Difference estimation is illustrated in the *Advanced Module*.

In evaluating the results of a nonstatistical sample, the auditor uses professional judgment and experience to draw a conclusion. If the sample is drawn haphazardly (versus randomly), the allowance for sampling risk cannot be statistically quantified within a specified level of confidence. The *Audit Sampling* guide provides the following direction:

> If the total projected misstatement is less than the tolerable misstatement for the account balance or class of transactions, the auditor then should consider the risk that such a result might be obtained even though the true monetary misstatement for the population exceeds tolerable misstatement. In other words, the auditor should consider the risk (for instance, sampling risk) that there might be other, undetected misstatements remaining in the population examined that might indicate a material misstatement exists. Alternatively, the auditor may compare the projected misstatement to the expected misstatement used in determining the sample size. When projected misstatement exceeds the expected misstatement, the sample may not have achieved an adequate allowance for sampling risk.

As noted in Chapter 8, students and auditors are sometimes unclear as to the factors that cause a sampling approach to be "nonstatistical." An approach is nonstatistical if (1) judgment is used to determine the sample size; (2) a haphazard sample selection technique is used; and/or (3) because the sample results are evaluated judgmentally. A nonstatistical approach can involve random selection and a judgmental evaluation. While haphazardly selected samples cannot be statistically evaluated, any randomly drawn sample can be statistically evaluated— even if the auditor labels the approach "nonstatistical" and even if the sample size was not statistically derived. This is an important point because it highlights the need for auditors to understand the key concepts of sampling theory *even if they are using a nonstatistical approach*. If an auditor randomly selects a sample and evaluates the results judgmentally, the quality of his or her judgment can be compared to statistical theory by an outside expert.

An Example of Nonstatistical Sampling

This example extends the example shown in Chapter 8 for the tests of controls of the revenue process for Calabro Wireless Services, Inc. The audit senior, Andrew Judd, has decided to design a *nonstatistical* sampling application to examine the accounts receivable balance of Calabro Wireless Services at December 31, 2009. As of December 31, there were 11,800 accounts receivable accounts with a balance of $3,717,900, and the population is composed of the following strata:

Number and Size of Accounts	Book Value of Stratum
15 accounts > $25,000	$ 550,000
250 accounts > $3,000	850,500
11,535 accounts < $3,000	2,317,400

Judd has made the following decisions:

- Based on the results of the tests of controls, the risk of material misstatement is assessed as low.
- The tolerable misstatement allocated to accounts receivable is $55,000, and the expected misstatement is $15,000.
- The desired level of confidence is moderate based on the other audit evidence already gathered.
- All customer account balances greater than $25,000 will be audited.

Based on these decisions, the sample size is determined as follows: First, individually significant items are deducted from the account balance, leaving a balance of $3,167,900 ($3,717,900 − $550,000) to be sampled. Second, the sample size for the remaining balance is determined using the nonstatistical sample size formula:

$$\text{Sample size} = \left(\frac{\$3,167,900}{\$55,000 - \$15,000} \right) \times 1.2 = 95$$

The confidence factor of 1.2 is determined by using Table 9–5 and a "Low" assessment for risk of material misstatement and "Moderate" level of desired confidence. The 95 sample items are divided between the two strata based on the recorded amount for each stratum. Accordingly, 26 [($850,500 ÷ $3,167,900) × 95] of the 95 are allocated to the stratum of accounts greater than $3,000 and 69 to the stratum of accounts less than $3,000. The total number of items tested is 110, composed of 15 individually significant accounts tested 100 percent and a sample of 95 items.

Judd mailed positive confirmations to each of the 110 accounts selected for testing. Either the confirmations were returned to Judd, or he was able to use alternative procedures to determine that the receivables were valid. Four customers indicated that their accounts were overstated, and Judd determined that the misstatements had resulted from unintentional errors by client personnel. The results of the sample are summarized as follows.

Stratum	Book Value of Stratum	Book Value of Sample	Audit Value of Sample	Amount of Overstatement
>$25,000	$ 550,000	$550,000	$549,500	$ 500
>$ 3,000	850,500	425,000	423,000	2,000
<$ 3,000	2,317,400	92,000	91,750	250

Based on analysis of the misstatements found, Judd concluded that the amount of misstatement in the population was likely to correlate to the total dollar amount of the items in the population and not to the number of items in the population. Thus, he decided to use ratio projection (applying the ratio of misstatement in the sampling strata) to compute the projected misstatement. His projection of the misstatements follows:

Stratum	Amount of Misstatement	Ratio of Misstatements in Stratum Tested	Projected Misstatement
>$25,000	$ 500	Not Applicable—100% Tested	$ 500
>$ 3,000	2,000	($2,000 ÷ 425,000) × $850,500	4,002
<$ 3,000	250	($250 ÷ 92,000) × $2,317,400	6,298
Total projected misstatement			$10,800

The total projected misstatement is $10,800. Judd should conclude that there is an acceptably low risk that the true misstatement exceeds the tolerable misstatement because the projected misstatement of $10,800 is less than the expected misstatement of $15,000.

Before reaching a final conclusion on the fair presentation of Calabro's accounts receivable balance, Judd would consider the qualitative characteristics of the misstatements detected and the results of other auditing procedures. If these steps are successfully completed, Judd can conclude that the accounts receivable balance is fairly presented in conformity with GAAP.

The Rise and Fall of Statistical Audit Sampling

Nonstatistical audit sampling is very common in practice. In the 1970s–1980s, statistical sampling was more common than it is today. In fact, many accounting firms developed proprietary statistical audit sampling software packages. Why did statistical sampling fall out of favor? We believe there were two primary reasons.

First, firms found that some auditors were overrelying on statistical sampling techniques to the exclusion of good judgment. As we discussed earlier, if the auditor can use knowledge and expertise to identify high-risk transactions or balances (e.g., large unusual items, transactions near period end, transactions in an area where material misstatements have been discovered in the past), then it is better to target those risky items and test 100 percent of them rather than to turn the selection procedure over to chance as is required by audit sampling.

The second reason relates to poor linkage between the applied audit setting and traditional statistical sampling applications. In most scientific statistical applications, a high degree of confidence, say 95 to 99 percent, is required. However, in an audit context, sampling is often used to just top off the "assurance bucket" (see Chapter 5), which already contains evidence from risk assessment procedures, tests of controls, substantive analytical procedures, and other audit testing. Thus, in some instances, the auditors only need a low or moderate level of confidence or assurance (e.g., 70 to 80 percent). Experienced auditors understood this intuitively but did not always have the knowledge to appropriately apply statistical sampling in an audit context. Thus, some of the audit firms simply moved to nonstatistical sampling with guidance based on judgment. With the increased scrutiny on audit firms in the last few years, the large firms have updated their nonstatistical sampling approaches to be more consistent with statistical theory.

Advanced Module: Classical Variables Sampling

[LO 5]   Classical variables sampling uses normal distribution theory to evaluate the characteristics of a population based on sample data. This approach to audit sampling is similar to the techniques taught in college introductory statistics courses. While this is not a statistics book, we do want to discuss briefly how distribution theory is helpful for audit sampling. In Figure 9–2 you will see two normally distributed, bell-shaped curves that depict sampling distributions. The mean or average of the distributions is $10,000. Auditors most commonly use classical variables sampling to estimate the size of misstatement, so in our example let's say the $10,000 represents the size of the total misstatement in an account or population. The flatter, wider distribution in Figure 9–2 is based on a sample size of 50, and the taller, thinner distribution is based on a sample of size 200. Both sampling distributions are taken from the same underlying population.

The sampling distributions are formed by plotting the projected misstatements yielded by an infinite number of audit samples of the same size taken from the same underlying population. For example, the height of the flatter distribution at $9,000 represents the number (or percent) of times a sample of size 50 would return a projected misstatement of $9,000.

Rather than actually take an infinite number of samples of the same size to form a picture of the distribution, the distribution is modeled using the mathematical properties of the normal distribution. Thus, a sampling distribution is really a theoretical distribution that models how the means of an infinite number of hypothetical samples of a given sample size would be distributed. A sampling distribution is useful because it allows us to estimate the probability of observing *any single* sample result. Two important features of sampling distributions are very useful for auditors:

- The mean of the sampling distribution will be equal to the true mean of the underlying population. Thus, Figure 9–2 tells us that the true misstatement in the population is $10,000.
- The area under the curve can be used to quantify likelihoods. For example, the standard error for the flatter curve is $1,000. If we look

FIGURE 9–2	Normally Distributed Sampling Distributions

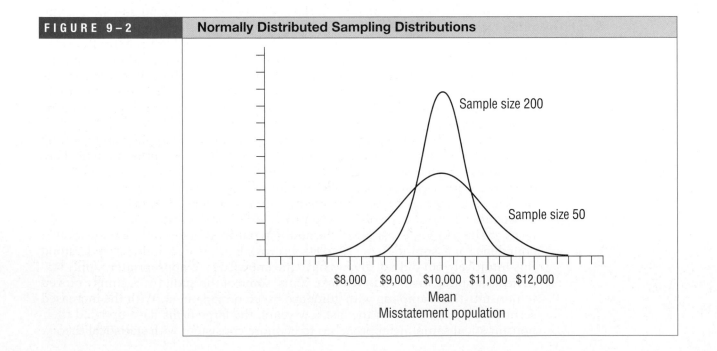

at the area covered by 2 standard errors above and 2 standard errors below the mean (i.e., the area under the curve between $8,000 and $12,000), we know that the area captures about 95 percent of all observed sample results. This is simply a mathematical property of a bell-shaped distribution.

Considering the first feature listed above, if auditors did actually take an infinite or even a very large number of samples of, say, size 50, they could determine with near certainty the amount of misstatement in an account. That seems easy enough— except that taking an infinite number or even 500 samples of size 50 is not economically practical. Instead, the auditor will only take one sample of size 50 and will use the results of that single sample to estimate the actual misstatement in the population. Given this audit approach, what information does distribution theory provide to an auditor that only takes one sample? Distribution theory can be very useful even when the auditor is only drawing one sample because the theory allows for an uncertain, but informed, prediction to be made about the underlying population.

Referring to the flatter distribution in Figure 9–2, which sampling outcome is more likely, a projected sample misstatement result of $10,000 or $12,000? The height of the curve in the middle indicates values around the mean of the distribution will be more commonly observed than values in the tails of the distribution. Because the most likely projected misstatement is one that is near the true misstatement, the auditor considers the observed projected sample misstatement as the best estimate of the true misstatement in the population. While the sample projection is the best estimate, the auditor understands there is uncertainty or sampling risk. Referring again to Figure 9–2, the most likely sample result is a projected misstatement at or near $10,000, but is it possible the auditor could draw a random sample of 50 that yields a projected misstatement of $8,000? Yes, due to sampling risk, it is possible to draw a nonrepresentative sample. However, observing a projected misstatement of $8,000 from a sample of 50 is not very likely given that the "true" population misstatement is $10,000. Now, consider the same question but with a sample size of 200 instead of 50. Could a sample of 200 produce a projected misstatement of $8,000? Again it is possible, but because the distribution for a sample of 200 is taller and tighter than the distribution for a sample of 50, it is much less likely that the auditor will get a projected misstatement result of $8,000 from a sample size of 200. The basic idea is simple: As the sample size increases, the results from the sample are increasingly likely to approximate the true population mean. In the extreme, if the sample size equaled the size of the population, the sample mean would exactly equal the true population mean.

Distribution theory allows auditors to quantify sampling risk through the use of *confidence bounds*, which are used to form what is commonly called a *confidence interval*. Referring to the flatter distribution in Figure 9–2, if the auditor wants to be 95-percent confident that his or her sample results include the true population misstatement, he or she would add and subtract 2 standard errors to and from the sample projected misstatement. For example, if the auditor takes a sample of 50 and computes a projected misstatement of $11,250, the auditor can be 95-percent confident that the interval between $9,250 and $13,250 ($11,250 ± $2,000) contains the true population misstatement. Thus, even though auditors do not know for sure which part of the actual sampling distribution their sample results come from (because they do not actually take an infinite number of samples to form the distribution), they use normal distribution theory to compute an interval of values that is likely to contain the true population value. The computational complexity of calculating classical variables sampling results, in particular computing the standard deviation, made it a difficult technique for auditors to use before electronic calculators and personal computers were common on audit engagements. This complexity was one of the factors that led to the development of MUS. Another important reason MUS was developed is that most accounting populations contain relatively little misstatement, and the estimators used to compute sample size and potential misstatement for some classical variables sampling techniques (e.g., difference estimation) are not effective in populations with little or no misstatement. Therefore, MUS is used in practice because of the advantages discussed earlier in the chapter.

Classical variables sampling can easily handle both overstatement and understatement errors. It is most appropriate for populations that contain a moderate-to-high rate of misstatement. Some applications of this sampling approach include auditing accounts receivable in which unapplied credits exist or a relatively large amount of misstatement is expected, and inventory in which significant audit differences are expected between test counts and pricing tests. Following are some of the advantages and disadvantages of classical variables sampling.

Advantages

- When the auditor expects a relatively large number of differences between book and audited values, classical variables sampling will normally result in a smaller sample size than monetary-unit sampling.
- Classical variables sampling techniques are effective for both overstatements and understatements. No special evaluation considerations are necessary if the sample data include both types of misstatements.
- The selection of zero balances generally does not require special sample design considerations because the sampling unit will not be an individual dollar but rather a customer account, a transaction, or a line item.

Disadvantages

- When using the approach to evaluate likely misstatement in an account or population, some classical variables sampling techniques (e.g., difference estimation) do not work well when little to no misstatement is expected.
- In order to determine the sample size for the technique illustrated in this text, the auditor must estimate the standard deviation of the audit differences. Since this value is unknown, auditors often use a surrogate such as the standard deviation of the recorded values in the population. However, this approach tends to overstate the standard deviation of the differences because recorded values tend to be more variable than audit differences in most accounting populations.
- If few misstatements are detected in the sample data, the true variance tends to be underestimated, and the resulting projection of the misstatements and the related confidence limits are not likely to be reliable.

A number of classical variables sampling techniques are available to the auditor for projecting the sample results to the population. These include mean per unit, difference, ratio, and regression techniques. These techniques differ basically on the assumed relationship between the book value and the audit value. We demonstrated ratio projection in the prior section on nonstatistical sampling. In this section we illustrate how the classical variables sampling technique known as difference estimation is used to determine sample size, project misstatement, and compute confidence bounds.[8]

Applying Classical Variables Sampling

The discussion in this section focuses on the special features that apply to classical variables sampling. A detailed example is included to demonstrate the application of classical variables sampling.

---

[8]See D. M. Roberts, *Statistical Auditing* (New York: AICPA, 1978), or see A. D. Bailey, Jr., *Statistical Auditing: Review, Concepts, and Problems* (New York: Harcourt Brace Jovanovich, 1981), for a discussion of the other classical variables sampling techniques.

[LO 6] **Defining the Sampling Unit** When an auditor uses classical variables sampling techniques, the sampling unit can be a customer account, an individual transaction, or a line item. For example, in auditing accounts receivable, the auditor can define the sampling unit to be a customer's account balance or an individual sales invoice included in the account balance.

Determining the Sample Size The following formula can be used to determine the sample size for a classical variables sample:

$$\text{Sample size} = \left[\frac{\text{Population size (\textit{in sampling units})} \times \text{CC} \times \text{SD}}{\text{Tolerable misstatement} - \text{Estimated misstatement}}\right]^2$$

where

CC = Confidence coefficient
SD = Estimated standard deviation of audit differences

Table 9–6 shows the confidence coefficient values for various levels of desired confidence. The risk of incorrect acceptance is the risk that the auditor will mistakenly accept a population as fairly stated when the true population misstatement is greater than tolerable misstatement, and is the complement of the level of confidence. For example, at a confidence level of 95 percent, the risk of incorrect acceptance is 5 percent (1 − .95).[9]

The following example demonstrates how to determine sample size using this formula. Assume that the auditor has decided to apply classical variables sampling to a client's accounts receivable account. Based on the results of testing internal controls over the revenue process, the auditor expects to find a moderate level of misstatement in accounts receivable due mainly to improper pricing of products on sales invoices. The year-end balance for accounts receivable contains 5,500 customer accounts and has a book value of $5,500,000. The tolerable misstatement for accounts receivable has been established at $50,000, and the expected misstatement has been estimated at $20,000. The auditor would like a high level of assurance from the test and has set the desired confidence level at 95 percent (risk of incorrect rejection of 5 percent). Based on the results of last year's audit work, the standard deviation of audit differences is set at $31. Using these parameters, a sample size of 125 is calculated (rounding up):

$$\text{Sample size} = \left[\frac{5,500 \times 1.96 \times \$31}{\$50,000 - \$20,000}\right]^2 = 125$$

In calculating the sample size, the confidence coefficient value (CC) for the desired level of confidence is taken from Table 9–6. The CC for a 95-percent confidence level is 1.96.

---

[9]Because an account can only be over- or understated, but not both, the risk of incorrect acceptance is commonly referred to in the technical literature as a *one-tailed test*. However, when an auditor uses a sample to evaluate the fairness of an account, she or he does not know with certainty the size or direction of the actual misstatement; therefore it is appropriate to use the traditional two-tailed values of the confidence coefficient as shown in the Table 9–6. The confidence coefficient associated with the risk of incorrect rejection can also be included in the sample size computation. If this risk is included in the formula, the sample size will be larger. In practice, the risk of incorrect rejection is typically not considered because it deals with efficiency and not effectiveness. When an account is incorrectly rejected due to a nonrepresentative sample, the auditor typically performs more work, which will provide evidence that the account is fairly stated. Auditors have determined that it is more costly to increase all sample sizes to control for the risk of incorrect rejection than it is to simply perform additional procedures when they believe an account is rejected incorrectly.

TABLE 9-6	Confidence Coefficient Values	

Desired Level of Confidence	Confidence Coefficient
95%	1.96
90%	1.64
80%	1.28
70%	1.04

Selecting the Sample   Sample selection for classical variables sampling normally relies on random-selection techniques. If the sampling unit is defined to be a customer account, the accounts to be examined can be selected randomly from the aged trial balance of accounts receivable. In this example, a random sample of 125 customer accounts is selected.

Calculating the Sample Results   *Difference projection* computes the sample projected misstatement by projecting the average misstatement of each item in the sample to all items in the population. Continuing with the prior example, assume that the auditor has confirmed 125 individual customer accounts receivable, and that confirmation evidence and alternative procedures, performed for customers who did not reply, results in the determination that 30 customer accounts contain misstatements. Table 9–7 presents the details of the 30 misstatements and the data necessary for calculating the sample results. The difference between the book value and the audited value is shown in the fifth column. The sixth column contains the square of each difference. The sum of these squared differences is needed to calculate the standard deviation.

TABLE 9-7	Summary of Misstatements Detected				
Sample Item Number	Account Number	Book Value	Audit Value	Audit Difference	(Audit Difference)^2
1	3892	$ 1,221.92	$ 1,216.40	$ 5.52	$ 30.47
4	1982	2,219.25	2,201.34	17.91	320.77
8	893	1,212.00	1,204.34	7.66	58.68
9	25	5,201.51	5,190.21	17.11	292.75
13	1703	7,205.40	7,188.29	−11.00	121.00
19	4258	3,685.62	3,725.62	−40.00	1,600.00
22	765	58.30	50.64	7.66	58.65
34	1256	17,895.15	17,840.30	54.85	3,008.52
36	3241	542.95	525.98	16.97	287.98
45	895	895.24	823.70	71.54	5,117.97
47	187	10,478.60	10,526.40	−47.80	2,284.84
55	4316	95.00	90.00	5.00	25.00
57	2278	1,903.51	1,875.00	28.51	812.82
59	1843	185.23	200.25	−15.02	225.60
61	64	4,759.65	4,725.32	34.33	1,178.55
69	2371	2,549.61	2,540.26	9.35	87.42
70	1982	12,716.50	12,684.23	32.27	1,041.35
72	2350	361.45	375.50	14.05	197.40
75	349	11,279.40	11,250.40	29.00	841.00
87	2451	74.23	95.40	−21.17	448.17
88	3179	871.58	837.96	33.62	1,130.30
91	1839	571.13	590.00	−18.87	356.08
93	4080	9,467.24	9,504.50	−37.26	1,388.31
97	13	45.20	40.75	4.45	19.80
100	1162	524.90	515.15	9.75	95.06
101	985	7,429.09	7,356.21	72.88	5,311.49
108	304	12,119.60	12,043.60	76.00	5,776.00
110	1977	25.89	26.89	−1.00	1.00
115	1947	1,982.71	2,025.87	−43.16	1,862.79
118	1842	6,429.35	6,384.20	45.15	2,038.52
Total		$123,995.91	$123,665.71	$330.20	$36,018.32

The first calculation is that of the mean misstatement in an individual account, which is calculated as follows:

$$\text{Mean misstatement per sampling item} = \frac{\text{Total audit difference}}{\text{Sample size}}$$

$$\$2.65 = \frac{\$330.20}{125}$$

Thus, the average misstatement in a customer account based on the sample data is an overstatement of $2.65.

The mean misstatement must then be projected to the population. The projected mean misstatement for the population is an overstatement of $14,575, which is determined as follows:

$$\begin{array}{ccccc}
\text{Projected population} & = & \text{Population size} & \times & \text{Mean misstatement} \\
\text{misstatement} & & (\textit{in sampling units}) & & \text{per sampling item} \\
\$14,575 & = & 5,500 & \times & \$2.65
\end{array}$$

The projected population misstatement is the auditor's "best estimate" of the misstatement present in the account. However, the auditor is relying on a sample, and the resulting uncertainty must be recognized by calculating an allowance for sampling risk. The allowance for sampling risk is represented by the confidence bound. To calculate the confidence bound, the auditor first calculates the standard deviation of audit differences (SD), by using the following formula:

$$SD = \sqrt{\frac{\text{Total squared audit differences} - (\text{Sample size} \times \text{Mean difference per sampling item}^2)}{\text{Sample size} - 1}}$$

$$SD = \frac{\$36,018.32 - (125 \times 2.65^2)}{125 - 1} = \$16.83$$

In our example, the standard deviation is $16.83. The confidence bound is then calculated using the following formula:

$$\begin{array}{cc}
\text{Confidence bound} = \text{Population size} \times CC \times & \dfrac{SD}{\sqrt{(\textit{Sample size})}} \\
(\textit{in sampling units}) &
\end{array}$$

$$\$16,228 = 5,500 \times (1.96) \times \frac{\$16.83}{\sqrt{125}}$$

In calculating the confidence bound, the auditor uses the confidence coefficient (CC) value for the desired level of confidence.[10] In our example, the confidence bound is $16,228. The auditor then calculates a confidence interval as follows:

$$\text{Confidence interval} = \text{Projected population misstatement} \pm \text{Confidence bound}$$
$$\text{Confidence interval} = \$14,575 \pm \$16,228$$

where $30,803 is the upper limit and –$1,653 is the lower limit. The auditor can be 95-percent confident that the actual misstatement in the population is between the upper and lower limits. Since the auditor can tolerate $50,000 misstatement (either under- or overstatement), the auditor can accept the population as fairly stated.

The auditor decides that the evidence supports or does not support the account balance by determining whether the upper and lower limits are within tolerable misstatement. If both limits are within the bounds of tolerable misstatement, the evidence supports the conclusion that the account is not materially misstated. If either limit is outside the bounds of tolerable misstatement, the evidence does not support the conclusion that the account is materially correct. In

---

[10]Note that the CC value simply represents the number of standard errors the auditor would like to use in establishing the confidence bounds around the sample result. The sample mean ±1 standard error results in about a 65-percent confidence interval, ±2 standard errors results in about a 95-percent confidence interval, and ±3 standard errors results in about a 99-percent confidence interval.

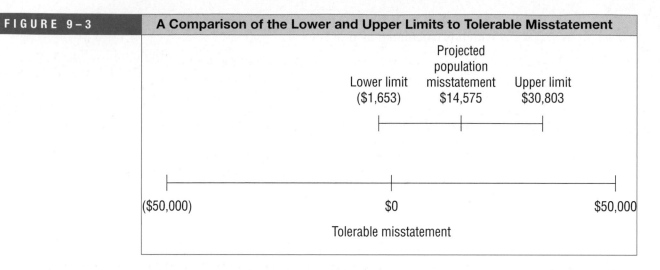

FIGURE 9–3 | **A Comparison of the Lower and Upper Limits to Tolerable Misstatement**

our example, the upper and lower limits are within the bounds of tolerable misstatement and the auditor can conclude the account is fairly stated. Figure 9–3 displays this result.

When the evidence indicates that the account may be materially misstated, the auditor must consider the same four options discussed under monetary-unit sampling: (1) increase sample size; (2) perform additional substantive procedures; (3) adjust the account; or (4) issue a qualified or adverse opinion.

KEY TERMS

Allowance for sampling risk. The uncertainty that results from sampling; the difference between the expected mean of the population and the tolerable deviation or misstatement.

Audit sampling. The application of an audit procedure to less than 100 percent of the items in a population of audit relevance selected in such a way that the auditor expects the sample to be representative of the population and thus likely to provide a reasonable basis for conclusions about the population.

Classical variables sampling. The use of normal distribution theory to estimate the dollar amount of misstatement for a class of transactions or an account balance.

Confidence bound. A measure of sampling risk added and subtracted to the projected misstatement to form a confidence interval.

Expected misstatement. The amount of misstatement that the auditor believes exists in the population.

Monetary-unit sampling (MUS). Attribute-sampling techniques used to estimate the dollar amount of misstatement for a class of transactions or an account balance.

Nonsampling risk. The possibility that the auditor may use inappropriate audit procedures, fail to detect a misstatement when applying an audit procedure, or misinterpret an audit result.

Nonstatistical sampling. Audit sampling that relies on the auditor's judgment to determine the sample size, select the sample, and/or evaluate the results for the purpose of reaching a conclusion about the population.

Projected misstatement. The extrapolation of sample results to the population. The projected misstatement represents the auditor's "best estimate" of the misstatement in the sampling population.

Risk of incorrect acceptance. The risk that the sample supports the conclusion that the recorded account balance is not materially misstated when it is materially misstated.

Risk of incorrect rejection. The risk that the sample supports the conclusion that the recorded account balance is materially misstated when it is not materially misstated.

Sampling risk. The possibility that the sample drawn is not representative of the population and that, as a result, the auditor reaches an incorrect conclusion about the account balance or class of transactions based on the sample.

Sampling unit. The individual member of the population being sampled.

Statistical sampling. Sampling that uses the laws of probability to select and evaluate the results of an audit sample, thereby permitting the auditor to quantify the sampling risk for the purpose of reaching a conclusion about the population.

Tolerable misstatement. The amount of planning materiality that is allocated to a financial statement account.

Upper misstatement limit. The total of the projected misstatement plus the allowance for sampling risk.

www.mhhe.com/ **messier7e**	Visit the book's Online Learning Center for a multiple-choice quiz that will allow you to assess your understanding of chapter concepts

REVIEW QUESTIONS

[LO 1] 9-1 List the steps in a statistical sampling application for substantive testing.

[1] 9-2 How is the sampling unit defined when monetary-unit sampling is used for statistical sampling? How is the sampling unit defined when classical variables sampling is used?

[1] 9-3 How are the desired confidence level, the tolerable misstatement, and the expected misstatement related to sample size?

[2] 9-4 Identify the advantages and disadvantages of monetary-unit sampling.

[2,3] 9-5 How does the use of probability-proportional-to-size selection provide an increased chance of sampling larger items?

[2,3] 9-6 What is the decision rule for determining the acceptability of sample results when monetary-unit sampling is used?

[1,4] 9-7 How do the desired confidence level, risk of material misstatement, and tolerable and expected misstatements affect the sample size in a nonstatistical sampling application?

[4] 9-8 Describe the two methods suggested for projecting a nonstatistical sample result. How does an auditor determine which method should be used?

[5] 9-9 What are the advantages and disadvantages of classical variables sampling?

[5,6] 9-10 What is the decision rule for determining the acceptability of sample results when classical variables sampling is used?

MULTIPLE-CHOICE QUESTIONS

[1,5] 9-11 Which of the following sampling methods would be used to estimate a numeric measurement of a population, such as a dollar value?
a. Random sampling.
b. Numeric sampling.
c. Attribute sampling.
d. Variable sampling.

[1]   9-12   A number of factors influence the sample size for a substantive test of details of an account balance. All other factors being equal, which of the following would lead to a larger sample size?
a. Greater reliance on internal controls.
b. Greater reliance on analytical procedures.
c. Smaller expected frequency of misstatements.
d. Smaller amount of tolerable misstatement.

[1,2,4,5]   9-13   Which of the following sample planning factors would influence the sample size for a substantive test of details for a specific account?

	Expected Misstatement	Tolerable Misstatement
a.	No	No
b.	Yes	Yes
c.	No	Yes
d.	Yes	No

[1]   9-14   The risk of incorrect acceptance relates to the
a. Effectiveness of the audit.
b. Efficiency of the audit.
c. Planning materiality.
d. Allowable risk of tolerable misstatement.

[2,3]   9-15   Which of the following statements concerning monetary-unit sampling is correct?
a. The sampling distribution should approximate the normal distribution.
b. Overstated units have a lower probability of sample selection than units that are understated.
c. The auditor controls the risk of incorrect acceptance by specifying the desired confidence level for the sampling plan.
d. The sampling interval is calculated by dividing the number of physical units in the population by the sample size.

[2,3]   9-16   How would increases in tolerable misstatement and assessed level of control risk affect the sample size in a substantive test of details?

	Increase in Tolerable Misstatement	Increase in Assessed Level of Control Risk
a.	Decrease sample size	Decrease sample size
b.	Decrease sample size	Increase sample size
c.	Increase sample size	Decrease sample size
d.	Increase sample size	Increase sample size

[2,5]   9-17   An auditor is performing substantive procedures of pricing and extensions of perpetual inventory balances consisting of a large number of items. Past experience indicates that there may be numerous pricing and extension errors. Which of the following statistical sampling approaches is most appropriate?
a. Classical variables sampling.
b. Monetary-unit sampling.
c. Stop-n-go sampling.
d. Attribute sampling.

[1,2,5]   9-18   Which of the following statements concerning the auditor's use of statistical sampling is correct?
a. An auditor needs to estimate the dollar amount of the standard deviation of the population in order to use classical variables sampling.
b. An assumption of monetary-unit sampling is that the underlying accounting population is normally distributed.

c. A classical variables sample needs to be designed with special considerations to include negative balances in the sample.

d. The selection of zero balances usually does not require special sample design considerations when using monetary-unit sampling.

[1,5]   9-19   In classical variables sampling, which of the following must be known in order to estimate the appropriate sample size required to meet the auditor's needs in a given situation?

a. The qualitative aspects of misstatements.

b. The total dollar amount of the population.

c. The acceptable level of risk.

d. The estimated percentage of deviations in the population.

[2,5]   9-20   Which of the following would most likely be an advantage in using classical variables sampling rather than monetary-unit sampling?

a. An estimate of the standard deviation of the population's recorded amounts is not required.

b. The auditor rarely needs the assistance of a computer program to design an efficient sample.

c. Inclusion of zero and negative balances generally does not require special design considerations.

d. Any amount that is individually significant is automatically identified and selected.

PROBLEMS

[1,2,5]   9-21   Edwards has decided to use monetary-unit sampling in the audit of a client's accounts receivable balance. Few, if any, misstatements of account balance overstatement are expected.

Required:

a. Identify the advantages of using monetary-unit sampling over classical variables sampling.

b. Calculate the sample size and the sampling interval Edwards should use for the following information:

Tolerable misstatement	$ 15,000
Expected misstatement	$ 6,000
Desired confidence level	95%
Recorded amount of accounts receivable	$300,000

c. Calculate the UML assuming that the following three misstatements were discovered in an MUS sample.

Misstatement Number	Book Value	Audit Value
1	$ 400	$ 320
2	500	0
3	3,000	2,500

(AICPA, adapted)

[2,3]   9-22   The firm of Le and Lysius was conducting the audit of Coomes Molding Corporation for the fiscal year ended October 31. Michelle Le, the partner in charge of the audit, decides that MUS is the appropriate sampling technique to use in order to audit Coomes's inventory account. The balance in the inventory at October 31 was $4,250,000. Michelle has established the following: risk of incorrect acceptance = 5% (i.e., the desired confidence level of 95%), tolerable misstatement = $212,500, and expected misstatement = $63,750.

Required:
a. Calculate the sample size and sampling interval.
b. Hon Zhu, staff accountant, performed the audit procedures listed in the inventory audit program for each sample item. Calculate the upper limit on misstatement based on the following misstatements. What should Hon conclude about Coomes's inventory account?

Error Number	Book Value	Audit Value
1	$ 6,000	$ 2,000
2	24,000	20,000
3	140,000	65,000

[2,3]   9-23   McMullen and Mulligan, CPAs, were conducting the audit of Cusick Machine Tool Company for the year ended December 31. Jim Sigmund, senior-in-charge of the audit, plans to use MUS to audit Cusick's inventory account. The balance at December 31 was $9,000,000.

Required:
a. Based on the following information, compute the required MUS sample size:
Tolerable misstatement = $360,000
Expected misstatement = $90,000
Risk of incorrect acceptance = 5%
b. Nancy Van Pelt, staff accountant, used the sample items selected in part (a) and performed the audit procedures listed in the inventory audit program. She notes the following misstatements:

Misstatement Number	Book Value	Audit Value
1	$10,000	$7,500
2	9,000	6,000
3	60,000	0
4	800	640

Using this information, calculate the upper misstatement limit. What conclusion should Van Pelt make concerning the inventory?

c. Assume that, in addition to the four misstatements identified in part (b), Van Pelt had identified the following two understatements:

Misstatement Number	Book Value	Audit Value
5	$6,000	$6,500
6	750	800

Calculate the net projected population misstatement.

[4]   9-24   The accounting firm of Johnson and Johnson has decided to design a nonstatistical sample to examine the accounts receivable balance of Francisco Fragrances, Inc., at October 31. As of October 31, there were 1,500 accounts receivable accounts with a balance of $5.5 million. The accounts receivable population can be segregated into the following strata:

Number and Size of Accounts	Book Value of Stratum
10 accounts > $50,000	$ 750,000
440 accounts > $5,000	3,000,000
1,050 accounts < $5,000	1,750,000

Jonathan L. Gren, senior-in-charge of the audit, has made the following decisions:
- Based on the results of the tests of controls and risk assessment procedures, a low assessment is made for the risk of material misstatement.
- The desired confidence level is moderate.
- The tolerable misstatement allocated to accounts receivable is $155,000, and the expected misstatement is $55,000.
- All the balances greater than $50,000 will be audited.

Required:
a. Using the nonstatistical sampling formula included in the textbook, compute the suggested sample size for this test.
b. Gren confirmed the accounts receivable accounts selected and noted the following results:

Stratum	Book Value of Stratum	Book Value of Sample	Audit Value of Sample	Amount of Overstatement
>$50,000	$ 750,000	$750,000	$746,500	$ 3,500
>$ 5,000	3,000,000	910,000	894,750	15,250
<$ 5,000	1,750,000	70,000	68,450	1,550

Using ratio projection, what is the total projected misstatement? What conclusion should Gren make concerning the accounts receivable balance?

[5,6]   9-25   World-famous mining mogul Steve Wilsey hired the public accounting firm of Joe Wang Associates, PC, to conduct an audit of his new acquisition, Cougar Goldust, Inc. The gold inventory was scheduled to be taken on November 30. The perpetual records show only the weight of the gold in various inventory bins. Wang has decided to use a variables sampling approach (difference estimation) to determine the correct weight of the gold on hand. (Note that the pricing of the inventory is straightforward because the market value on November 30 determines the price for balance sheet purposes.) There are 4,000 bins in the Cougar warehouse. The bins will serve as the sampling units. Wang's desired level of confidence is 90 percent. The tolerable misstatement is set at 35,000 ounces, and the expected misstatement is 10,000 ounces. The perpetual record shows 700,000 ounces on hand.

Required:
[Note: Parts (a) and (b) are independent of each other.]
a. Compute the preliminary sample size. The estimated standard deviation is 25 ounces.
b. Assume that Wang examined a sample of 100 bins. The following information summarizes the results of the sample data gathered by Wang:

Difference Number	Recorded Weight	Audited Weight	Audit Difference	(Audit Difference)^2
1	445	440	5	25
2	174	170	4	16
•	•	•	•	•
•	•	•	•	•
•	•	•	•	•
29	217	215	2	4
30	96	97	(1)	1
Total	24,000	23,600	400	17,856

Compute the sample results and indicate what conclusion Wang should make concerning the inventory balance.

[5,6]   9-26   You are in charge of the audit of Hipp Supply Company for the year ended December 31. In prior years, your firm observed the inventory and tested compilation and pricing. Various misstatements were always found. About 10 percent of the dollar value of the inventory is usually tested.

This year you have established the tolerable misstatement to be $5,000. The client's book value is $97,500. The client has 960 inventory items, the number of which has been determined by examining inventory codes. Each item will be tagged with a prenumbered inventory tag numbered from 1 to 960. You plan to evaluate the results using classical variables sampling (difference estimation).

Assume you have selected a sample of 100 items randomly. For each sample item, audit tests are performed to make sure that the physical count is correct, the pricing is accurate, and the extensions of unit price and quantity are correct. The results are summarized as follows:

Inventory Tag Number	Book Value	Audit Value	Audit Difference	(Audit Difference)^2
6	$ 100	$ 100	$ 0	$ 0
42	85	85	0	0
46	120	120	0	0
51	420	450	30	900
55	18	18	0	0
56	10	10	0	0
•	•	•	•	•
•	•	•	•	•
•	•	•	•	•
851	25	25	0	0
854	152	150	2	4
857	85	85	0	0
862	76	86	10	100
Total	$10,147	$9,666	$481	$8,895

There were 50 differences, making up the net difference of $481. The recorded total of the client's inventory sheets is $97,500.

Required:
Determine the results of the audit tests using a desired confidence level of 90 percent. Indicate whether the evidence supports the fair presentation of the inventory account.

DISCUSSION CASES

[1,2,5]   9-27   Mead, CPA, was engaged to audit Jiffy Company's financial statements for the year ended August 31. Mead is applying sampling procedures.

During the prior years' audits Mead used classical variables sampling in performing tests of controls on Jiffy's accounts receivable. For the current year Mead decided to use monetary-unit sampling in confirming accounts receivable because MUS uses each account in the population as a separate sampling unit. Mead expected to discover many overstatements but presumed that the MUS sample would still be smaller than the corresponding size for classical variables sampling.

Mead reasoned that the MUS sample would automatically result in a stratified sample because each account would have an equal chance of being selected for confirmation. Additionally, the selection of negative (credit) balances would be facilitated without special considerations.

Mead computed the sample size using the risk of incorrect acceptance, the total recorded book amount of the receivables, and the number of misstated accounts allowed. Mead divided the total recorded book amount of the receivables by the sample size to determine the sampling interval. Mead then calculated the standard deviation of the dollar amounts of the accounts selected for evaluation of the receivables.

Mead's calculated sample size was 60, and the sampling interval was determined to be $10,000. However, only 58 different accounts were selected because two accounts were so large that the sampling interval caused each of them to be selected twice. Mead proceeded to send confirmation requests to 55 of the 58 customers. Three selected accounts each had insignificant recorded balances under $20. Mead ignored these three small accounts and substituted the three largest accounts that had not been selected in the sample. Each of these accounts had a balance in excess of $7,000, so Mead sent confirmation requests to those customers.

The confirmation process revealed two differences. One account with an audited amount of $3,000 had been recorded at $4,000. Mead projected this to be a $1,000 misstatement. Another account with an audited amount of $2,000 had been recorded at $1,900. Mead did not count the $100 difference because the purpose of the test was to detect overstatements.

In evaluating the sample results, Mead determined that the accounts receivable balance was not overstated because the projected misstatement was less than the allowance for sampling risk.

Required:
Describe each incorrect assumption, statement, and inappropriate application of sampling in Mead's procedures.

(AICPA, adapted)

[LO 1,4]   9-28   Doug Stevens, CPA, is interested in testing the fairness of the ending inventory balance at an audit client, Morris Co. Doug has relatively little experience using statistical sampling methods and, quite frankly, doesn't like to turn anything over to random chance—especially the selection of items to test. Doug used a judgmental method of selecting items for testing. The method involves testing the inventory-item balances that he deems most risky or most likely to be misstated. Doug identified items to test based on size of balance, findings from prior years, age of inventory, description, and professional judgment.

He selected 26 items with a total book value of $720,000. In his "sample," he found a combined $80,000 in overstatement errors. The book value of inventory on the client's records is $1,090,000. Overall materiality for the engagement is $500,000. Doug's policy is to use 50 percent or less of overall materiality as tolerable misstatement for any one account.

Required:
a. What is your opinion of Doug's method of selecting his "sample"?
b. Evaluate Doug's results. Does he have sufficient evidence to conclude the balance is fairly stated?

 HANDS-ON CASES

www.mhhe.com/ messier7e	Visit the book's Online Learning Center for problem material to be completed using the ACL software packaged with your new text.

CPA Review

www.mhhe.com/ messier7e	**Fitzgerald, Inc.** This simulation contains questions regarding attribute and variable sampling, audit assertions, sampling risks and techniques, and audit evidence. The essay question will test your understanding of the advantages of probability-proportional-to-size (PPS) sampling (i.e., monetary unit sampling) and classical variables sampling. The "Research" question regarding specialists will be discussed further in Chapters 13 and 14. *To begin this simulation, visit the book's Online Learning Center.*

AUDITING BUSINESS PROCESSES

CHAPTER 10

LEARNING OBJECTIVES

Upon completion of this chapter you will

[1] Understand why knowledge of an entity's revenue recognition policies is important to the audit.

[2] Understand the revenue process.

[3] Know the types of transactions in the revenue process and the financial statement accounts affected.

[4] Be familiar with the types of documents and records used in the revenue process.

[5] Understand the functions in the revenue process.

[6] Know the appropriate segregation of duties for the revenue process.

[7] Understand the inherent risks relevant to the revenue process and related accounts.

[8] Know how to assess control risk for a revenue process.

[9] Know the key internal controls and develop relevant tests of controls for revenue, cash receipts, and sales returns transactions.

[10] Relate the assessment of control risk to substantive testing.

[11] Know the substantive analytical procedures used to audit accounts receivable and revenue-related accounts.

[12] Know the substantive tests of transactions used to audit accounts receivable and revenue-related accounts.

[13] Know the tests of details of account balances and disclosures used to audit accounts receivable and revenue-related accounts.

[14] Understand the confirmation process and how confirmations are used to obtain evidence about accounts receivable.

[15] Understand how to audit other types of receivables.

[16] Understand how to evaluate the audit findings and reach a final conclusion on accounts receivable and revenue-related accounts.

RELEVANT ACCOUNTING AND AUDITING PRONOUNCEMENTS

AICPA, Audit Guide, *Auditing Revenue in Certain Industries* (New York: AICPA, 2008)

FASB Statement of Financial Accounting Concepts No. 5, Recognition and Measurement in Financial Statements of Business Enterprises

FASB Statement of Financial Accounting Concepts No. 6, Elements of Financial Statements

FASB ASC Topic 850, Related Party Disclosures

SEC Staff Accounting Bulletin No. 101, Revenue Recognition in Financial Statements (SAB No. 101)

COSO, Internal Control—Integrated Framework (New York: AICPA, 1992)

COSO, *Enterprise Risk Management—Integrated Framework* (New York: AICPA, 2004)

COSO, *Internal Control over Financial Reporting—Guidance for Smaller Public Companies* (New York: AICPA, 2006)

COSO, *Guidance on Monitoring Internal Control Systems* (New York: AICPA, 2009)

AU 312, Audit Risk and Materiality in Conducting an Audit

AU 314, Understanding the Entity and Its Environment and Assessing the Risks of Material Misstatement

AU 316, Consideration of Fraud in a Financial Statement Audit

AU 318, Performing Audit Procedures in Response to Assessed Risks and Evaluating the Audit Evidence Obtained

AU 322, The Auditor's Consideration of the Internal Audit Function in an Audit of Financial Statements

AU 326, Audit Evidence

AU 329, Analytical Procedures

AU 330, The Confirmation Process

AU 339, Audit Documentation

AU 342, Auditing Accounting Estimates

PCAOB Auditing Standard No. 3, Audit Documentation (AS3)

PCAOB Auditing Standard No. 5, An Audit of Internal Control Over Financial Reporting That Is Integrated with An Audit of Financial Statements (AS5)

PCAOB Proposed Auditing Standards Related to the Auditor's Assessment of and Response to Risk, PCAOB Release No. 2008-006 (October 21, 2008)

Auditing the Revenue Process

Major Phases of an Audit

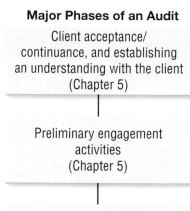

Client acceptance/
continuance, and establishing
an understanding with the client
(Chapter 5)

Preliminary engagement
activities
(Chapter 5)

Plan the audit
(Chapters 3 and 5)

Consider and audit
internal control
(Chapters 6 and 7)

Audit business processes
and related accounts
(e.g., revenue generation)
(Chapters 10–16)

Complete the audit
(Chapter 17)

Evaluate results and issue audit
report (Chapters 1 and 18)

Auditors generally divide an entity's information system into business processes or transaction cycles. Using this approach, the auditor is able to gather evidence by examining the processing of related transactions from their origin to their ultimate disposition in accounting journals and ledgers. We first introduced the concept of viewing a business from a process perspective in Chapter 2. Figure 10–1 summarizes a model of business centering on business processes or transaction cycles. As the figure shows, the five basic processes are (1) the revenue process; (2) the purchasing process; (3) the human resource management process; (4) the inventory management process; and (5) the financing process. Auditors divide the financial statement components into business processes or cycles in order to manage the audit better.

In this chapter, the concepts and techniques learned in the previous chapters are applied to determine the risk of material misstatement (i.e., setting the level of inherent risk and control risk) for the revenue process and related accounts. The revenue process focuses on the sale of goods and services to customers. For virtually all entities, the revenue and purchasing processes represent the two major business processes that affect the financial statements.

The chapter starts by reviewing the basic concepts related to revenue recognition. An overview of the revenue process is then presented as an aid in providing you with an understanding of the process. This is followed by a discussion of the specific factors that affect the assessment of inherent risk for the revenue process and the auditor's assessment of control risk. While the main focus of this chapter is auditing the revenue process for a financial statement audit, the concepts covered for setting control risk are applicable to an audit of internal control over financial reporting for public companies under the Sarbanes-Oxley Act of 2002. The remainder of the chapter discusses the substantive procedures the auditor conducts to reach the appropriate level of detection risk for the accounts affected by the revenue process. While the main emphasis is on accounts receivable, the discussion also covers the allowance for uncollectible accounts, bad-debt expense, and sales returns and allowances. Because the cash account is affected by other business processes, it is covered separately in Chapter 16.

FIGURE 10-1   **An Overview of Business**

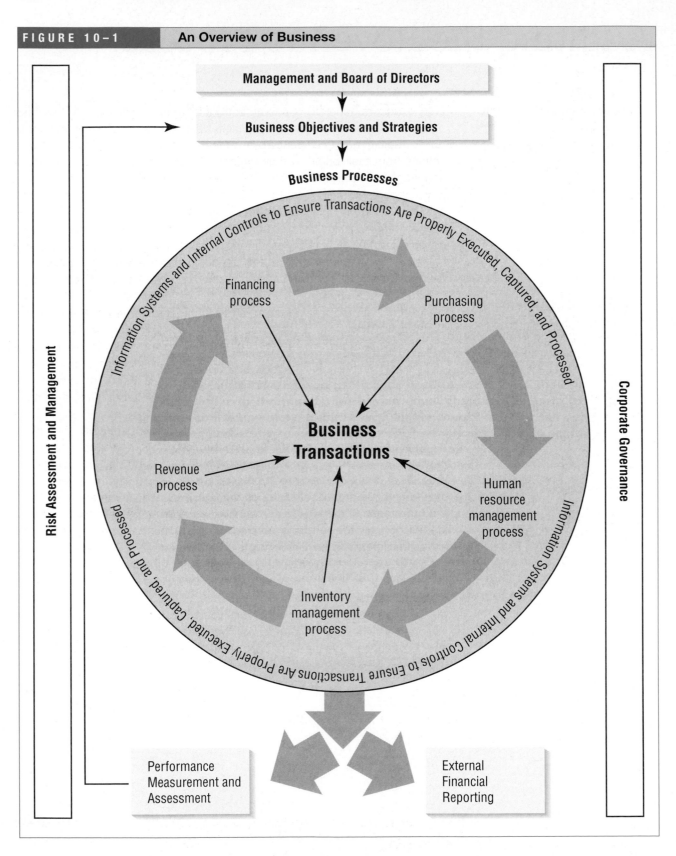

Management and Board of Directors

Business Objectives and Strategies

Business Processes

Information Systems and Internal Controls to Ensure Transactions Are Properly Executed, Captured, and Processed

Financing process

Purchasing process

Business Transactions

Revenue process

Human resource management process

Inventory management process

Risk Assessment and Management

Corporate Governance

Performance Measurement and Assessment

External Financial Reporting

Revenue Recognition

⚞ [LO 1]   Revenue recognition is reviewed at the beginning of this chapter because knowledge of this underlying concept is fundamental to auditing the revenue process. Additionally, revenue must be recognized in conformity with GAAP in order for an auditor to issue an unqualified opinion. FASB Statement of Financial Accounting Concepts No. 6, "Elements of Financial Statements," defines revenues as

> inflows or other enhancements of assets of an entity or settlements of its liabilities (or a combination of both) from delivery or producing goods, rendering services, or other activities that constitute the entity's major or central operations (¶78).

Revenues are measured by the exchange value of the goods and services provided. In general, the entity receives cash or claims to cash for the goods or services provided. Claims to cash are usually referred to as trade accounts receivable. FASB Statement of Financial Accounting Concepts No. 5, "Recognition and Measurement in Financial Statements of Business Enterprises" (¶83), requires that before revenue is recognized (recorded), it must be (1) *realized* or *realizable;* and (2) *earned.* Revenue is realized when a product or service is exchanged for cash, a promise to pay cash, or other assets that can be converted into cash. Revenue is earned when an entity has substantially completed the earning process, which generally means a product has been delivered or a service has been provided.

The SEC in SAB No. 101 provides the following criteria for revenue recognition:

- Persuasive evidence of an arrangement exists.
- Delivery has occurred or services have been rendered.
- The seller's price to the buyer is fixed or determinable.
- Collectibility is reasonably assured.

Revenue recognition continues to pose a significant audit risk to auditors and has resulted in questions about the integrity of the financial reporting process. In fact, the auditing standard on fraud states that the auditor should presume that there is a risk of material misstatement due to fraud relating to revenue recognition (AU 316.41).

Practice INSIGHT

According to the Association of Certified Fraud Examiners, there are eight common methods for committing financial statement fraud. These include:

1. early revenue recognition;
2. holding the books open past the accounting period;
3. fictitious sales;
4. failure to record returns;
5. fraud in the percentage of completion method;
6. related-party transactions;
7. overstating receivables and inventory; and
8. liability and expense omissions.

The auditor should be alert for the following activities that are fraud risks related to revenue recognition:

- Side agreements are arrangements that are used to alter the terms and conditions of recorded sales in order to entice customers to accept delivery of goods and services.

| EXHIBIT 10–1 | Channel Stuffing at Bristol-Myers Squibb Company |

In 2004, the Securities and Exchange Commission settled a civil fraud action against Bristol-Myers Squibb. The SEC charged that from the first quarter of 2000 through the fourth quarter of 2001, Bristol-Myers engaged in a fraudulent scheme to overstate its sales and earnings in order to create the false appearance that the company had met or exceeded financial projections set by the company and earnings estimates established by securities analysts. Bristol-Myers inflated its results primarily by (1) stuffing its distribution channels with excess inventory near the end of every quarter in amounts sufficient to meet sales and earnings targets set by officers and; (2) improperly recognizing about $1.5 billion in revenue from consignment-like sales associated with the channel stuffing in violation of GAAP. When the company did not meet the analysts' earnings estimates, the company used improper accounting, including "cookie jar" reserves, to further inflate its earnings.

Bristol-Myers consented, without admitting or denying the allegations in the SEC's complaint, to the following:

- A permanent injunction against future violations of certain antifraud, reporting, books and records and internal controls provisions of the federal securities laws.
- Monetary remedies for the benefit of shareholders, including a civil penalty of $100 million plus a $50 million shareholder fund.
- Various remedial undertakings, including the appointment of an independent advisor to review Bristol-Myers' accounting practices and internal control systems and to periodically assess the status of remedial actions undertaken or planned by the company in those and other areas, such as financial reporting.

Source: Accounting and Auditing Enforcement Release No. 2075, August 4, 2004; *Securities and Exchange Commission v. Bristol-Myers Squibb Company*, 04-3680 DNJ (2004). Downloadable at www.sec.gov.

- Channel stuffing (also known as *trade loading*) is a marketing practice that suppliers sometimes use to boost sales by inducing distributors to buy substantially more inventory than they can promptly resell (see Exhibit 10–1).
- Related-party transactions require special consideration because related parties may be difficult to identify. Related-party transactions also may pose significant "substance over form" issues.
- Bill and hold sales (also called parked inventory schemes) are sales where the customer agrees to purchase the goods but the seller retains physical possession until the customer requests shipments. Unless certain conditions are met, such an arrangement does not qualify as a sale because delivery has not occurred.

For most entities, the revenue recognition process occurs over a short period of time (days, weeks, or months), but in certain industries, such as construction or defense, the revenue recognition process may extend over a period of years.

An entity's revenue recognition policies affect how transactions are processed and how they are accounted for in the financial statements. Thus, an auditor must understand an entity's revenue recognition policies in order to audit the revenue process.

Overview of the Revenue Process

[LO 2]

In this section, we present an overview of the revenue process for Earth-Wear Clothiers, Inc., beginning with an order from a customer, proceeding to the exchange of goods or services for a promise to pay, and ending with the receipt of cash. Exhibit 10–2 describes EarthWear's revenue process. Before proceeding, take a moment and review this exhibit. Do any risks seem especially apparent? If so, how might these risks impact the nature, timing, and extent of your audit procedures?

EXHIBIT 10–2	Description of EarthWear's Revenue Process

EarthWear provides 24-hour toll-free telephone numbers that may be called seven days a week (except Christmas Day) to place orders. Telephone calls are answered by the company's sales representatives, who use online computer terminals to enter customer orders and to retrieve information about product characteristics and availability. The company's sales representatives enter orders into an online order entry and inventory control system. Customers using the company's Internet site complete a computer screen that requests information on product code, size, color, and so forth. When the customer finishes shopping for products, he or she enters delivery and credit card information into a computer-based form. EarthWear provides assurance through CPA *WebTrust* that the Web site has been evaluated and tested to meet *WebTrust* Principles and Criteria.

Computer order processing is performed each night on a batch basis, at which time shipping tickets are printed with bar codes for optical scanning. Inventory is picked based on the location of individual products rather than orders, followed by computerized sorting and transporting of goods to multiple packing stations and shipping zones. The computerized inventory control system also handles items that customers return. Orders are generally shipped by United Parcel Service (UPS) at various tiered rates, depending upon the total dollar value of each customer's order. Other expedited delivery services are available for additional charges.

With the exception of sales to groups and companies for corporate incentive programs, customers pay in cash (in stores) or with credit cards. EarthWear's major bank is reimbursed directly by credit card companies, usually within three days. Group and corporate accounts are granted credit by the credit department. When group or corporate orders are received from new customers, the credit department performs a credit check following corporate policies. A credit authorization form is completed with the credit limit entered into the customer database. When a group or corporate order is received from an existing customer, the order is entered, and the data validation program performs a credit check by comparing the sum of the existing order and the customer's balance to the customer's credit limit.

Figure 10–2 presents the flowchart of EarthWear's revenue process (excluding sales from Company stores), which will provide a framework for discussing controls and tests of controls in more detail. The discussion of the revenue process in this chapter can be applied equally well to manufacturing, wholesale, and service organizations. It should be kept in mind, however, that an accounting system must be tailored to meet the specific needs of an entity. Therefore, the reader should concentrate on understanding the basic concepts presented so that they can be applied to specific revenue systems.

The reader should also notice that the revenue process shown in Figure 10–2 interacts with the inventory management process. Many accounting systems integrate the revenue, purchasing, human resources, and inventory processes. The flowcharts used in this text to represent those processes show the points where the processes interact with one another. As entities use more IT, it is becoming easier to integrate the information flow among the various accounting processes.

We now discuss the following topics related to the revenue process:

- Types of transactions and financial statement accounts affected.
- Types of documents and records.
- The major functions.
- The key segregation of duties.

Types of Transactions and Financial Statement Accounts Affected

Three types of transactions are typically processed through the revenue process:

- The sale of goods or rendering of a service for cash or credit.
- The receipt of cash from the customer in payment for the goods or services.
- The return of goods by the customer for credit or cash.

[LO 3] The key controls involved in each of these transactions are discussed later in the chapter. For some entities, other types of transactions that may occur as part of the revenue process include scrap sales, intercompany sales, and related-party sales. The auditor should be aware of how these transactions are processed and their related controls when they represent material amounts in the financial statements.

The revenue process affects numerous accounts in the financial statements. The most significant accounts affected by each type of transaction are as follows:

Type of Transaction	Account Affected
Sales transactions	Trade accounts receivable
	Sales
	Allowance for uncollectible accounts
	Bad-debt expense
Cash receipts transactions	Cash
	Trade accounts receivable
	Cash discounts
Sales return and allowance transactions	Sales returns
	Sales allowances
	Trade accounts receivable

FIGURE 10–2   **Flowchart of the Revenue Process—EarthWear Clothiers, Inc.**

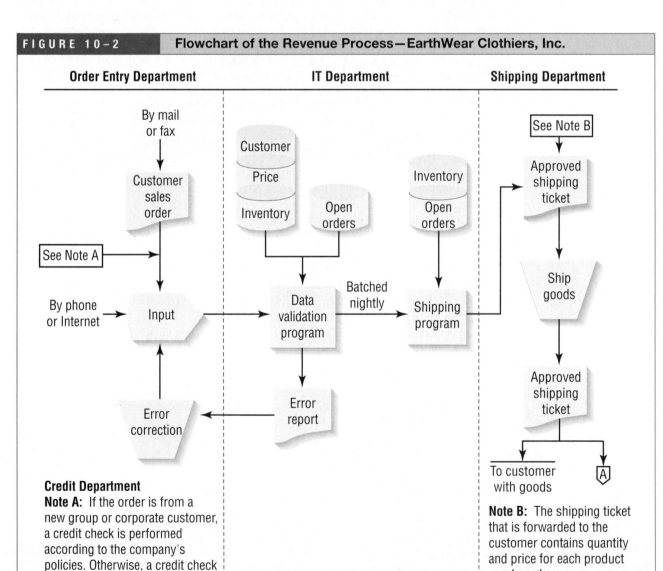

Credit Department

Note A: If the order is from a new group or corporate customer, a credit check is performed according to the company's policies. Otherwise, a credit check is performed by the data validation program.

Note B: The shipping ticket that is forwarded to the customer contains quantity and price for each product purchased.

FIGURE 10–2	Flowchart of the Revenue Process—EarthWear Clothiers, Inc. (*continued*)

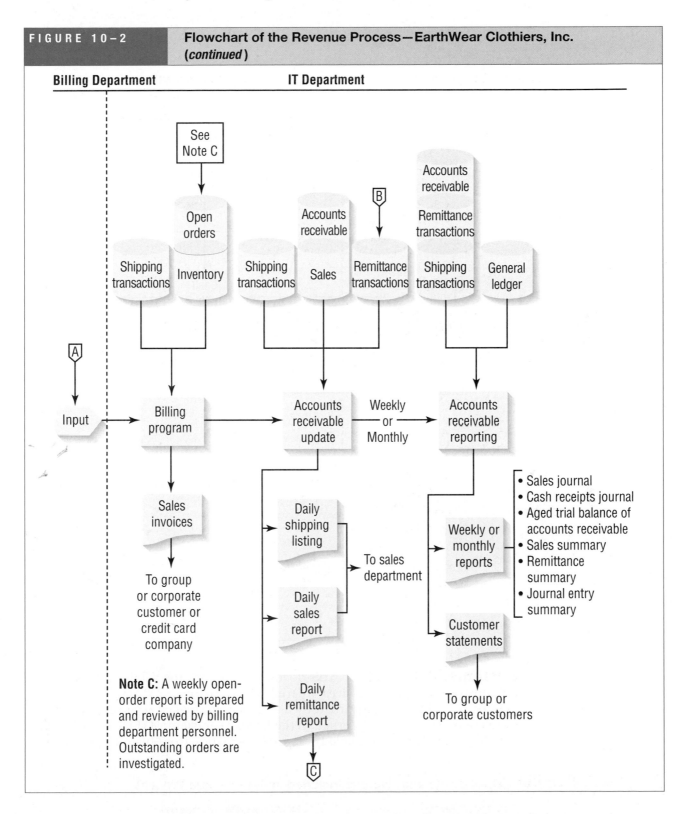

Billing Department

IT Department

See Note C

Open orders

Shipping transactions

Inventory

Accounts receivable

Shipping transactions

Sales

B

Remittance transactions

Accounts receivable

Remittance transactions

Shipping transactions

General ledger

A

Input

Billing program

Accounts receivable update

Weekly or Monthly

Accounts receivable reporting

Sales invoices

To group or corporate customer or credit card company

Daily shipping listing

Daily sales report

To sales department

Daily remittance report

C

Weekly or monthly reports

Customer statements

- Sales journal
- Cash receipts journal
- Aged trial balance of accounts receivable
- Sales summary
- Remittance summary
- Journal entry summary

To group or corporate customers

Note C: A weekly open-order report is prepared and reviewed by billing department personnel. Outstanding orders are investigated.

Types of Documents and Records

✄ **[LO 4]**

Table 10–1 lists the more important documents and records that are normally contained in the revenue process. Each of these items is discussed briefly in the order that they normally occur in the process. The reader should keep in mind that in some IT systems these documents and records may exist for only a short period of time or may be maintained only in machine-readable form.

FIGURE 10-2	Flowchart of the Revenue Process—EarthWear Clothiers, Inc. (*continued*)

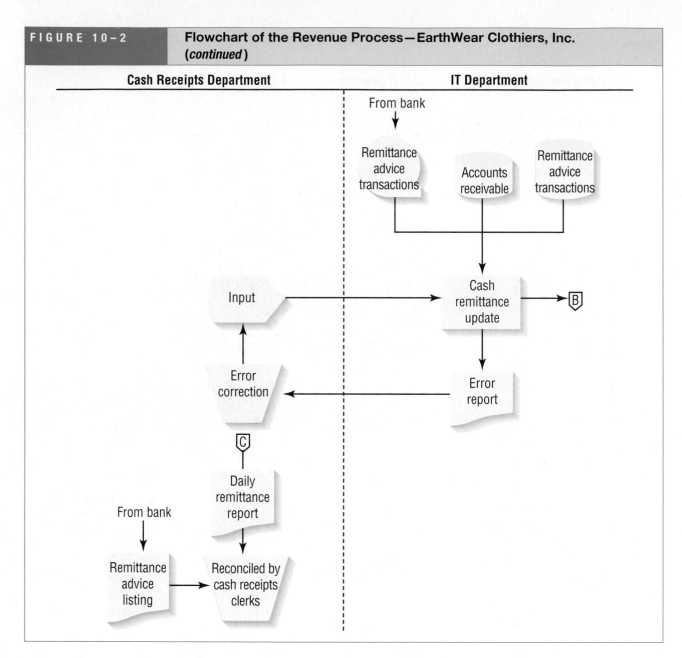

Customer Sales Order   This document contains the details of the type and quantity of products or services ordered by the customer. Customer sales orders may be prepared and forwarded by a salesperson, mailed or faxed, or received by telephone or over the Internet. In the EarthWear example (Figure 10–2), order entry personnel enter the mailed or faxed information from customer sales orders

TABLE 10-1	Documents and Records Included in the Revenue Process

Customer sales order	Accounts receivable subsidiary ledger
Credit approval form	Aged trial balance of accounts receivable
Open-order report	Remittance advice
Shipping document	Cash receipts journal
Sales invoice	Credit memorandum
Sales journal	Write-off authorization
Customer statement	

into the revenue system. Phone or Internet sales are entered directly into the data validation program.

Credit Approval Form   When a customer purchases products on credit from the client for the first time, the client should have a formal procedure for investigating the creditworthiness of the customer. The result of this procedure should be documented on some type of credit approval form. When the customer plans to purchase additional products in the future, this procedure should be used to establish the customer's credit limit. The amount of the credit limit should be documented on the approval form. When credit limits are included in the client's customer files, the approval forms represent the source documents authorizing the amounts contained in the information system. EarthWear follows such a policy for its group and corporate customers (see Exhibit 10–2).

Open-Order Report   This is a report of all customer orders for which processing has not been completed. In the typical revenue process, once a customer's order has been accepted, the order is entered into the system. After the goods have been shipped and billed, the order should be noted as filled. This report should be reviewed daily or weekly, and old orders should be investigated to determine if any goods have been shipped but not billed or to determine why orders have not been filled. Figure 10–2 shows that EarthWear has an open-order file. Note C indicates that an open-order report is prepared weekly and reviewed by billing department personnel for long overdue orders.

Shipping Document   A shipping document must be prepared any time goods are shipped to a customer. This document generally serves as a *bill of lading* and contains information on the type of product shipped, the quantity shipped, and other relevant information. In some revenue systems, the shipping document and bill of lading are separate documents. A copy of the shipping document is sent to the customer, while another copy of the shipping document is used to initiate the billing process. Figure 10–2 shows that EarthWear follows a similar process using a shipping ticket.

Sales Invoice   This document is used to bill the customer. The sales invoice contains information on the type of product or service, the quantity, the price, and the terms of trade. The original sales invoice is usually forwarded to the customer, and copies are distributed to other departments within the organization. The sales invoice is typically the source document that signals the recognition of revenue. The majority of EarthWear's sales are made to customers using credit cards, and they do not receive a bill directly from the company. However, the shipping ticket that accompanies the goods contains the quantity and prices for products purchased. That amount shows up on the customer's credit card statement.

Sales Journal   Once a sales invoice has been issued, the sale needs to be recorded in the accounting records. The sales journal is used to record the necessary information for each sales transaction. Depending on the complexity of the entity's operation, the sales journal may contain information classified by type of sale (for example, product line, intercompany sales, related parties). The sales journal contains columns for debiting accounts receivable and crediting the various sales accounts. EarthWear maintains such a journal.

Customer Statement   This document is usually mailed to a customer monthly. It contains the details of all sales, cash receipts, and credit memorandum transactions processed through the customer's account for the period. EarthWear prepares monthly statements only for group or corporate customers who have accounts receivable with the company.

Accounts Receivable Subsidiary Ledger   The accounts receivable subsidiary ledger contains an account and the details of transactions with each customer. A transaction recorded in the sales journal and cash receipts journal is posted to the appropriate customer's account in the accounts receivable subsidiary ledger. For IT systems such as EarthWear's, this information is maintained in the accounts receivable file (see Figure 10–2).

Aged Trial Balance of Accounts Receivable   This report, which is normally prepared weekly or monthly, summarizes all the customer balances in the accounts receivable subsidiary ledger. Customers' balances are reported in aging categories (such as 30 days or less, 31–60 days, 61–90 days, more than 90 days old) based on the time expired since the date of the sales invoice. The aged trial balance of accounts receivable is used to monitor the collection of receivables and to ensure that the details of the accounts receivable subsidiary ledger agree with the general ledger control account. The auditor uses this report for conducting much of the substantive audit work in accounts receivable. EarthWear prepares an aged trial balance of accounts receivable for group and corporate customers.

Remittance Advice   This document is usually mailed with the customer's bill and returned with the customer's payment for goods or services. A remittance advice contains information regarding which invoices are being paid by the customer. Many entities use turnaround documents, where a portion of the sales invoice serves as a remittance advice that is returned with the customer's payment. EarthWear receives remittance advices from group and corporate customers after the payment has been processed by the company's bank. Payments from credit card companies are also made directly to the bank, and a remittance advice listing is forwarded to EarthWear.

Cash Receipts Journal   This journal is used to record the entity's cash receipts. The cash receipts journal contains columns for debiting cash, crediting accounts receivable, and crediting other accounts such as scrap sales or interest income. EarthWear maintains such a journal.

Credit Memorandum   This document is used to record credits for the return of goods in a customer's account or to record allowances that will be issued to the customer. Its form is generally similar to that of a sales invoice, and it may be processed through the system in the same way as a sales invoice. Exhibit 10–3 describes how EarthWear handles goods returned from customers. The process of customer returns is not shown in the revenue flowchart (Figure 10–2).

EXHIBIT 10–3	Description of EarthWear Clothiers' Process for Handling Customer Returns

In order to receive credit for returned goods, customers must mail the goods to EarthWear's receiving department. There the goods are inspected, and a receiving document, which also serves as a credit memorandum, is prepared. Credit memoranda are entered into the revenue process along with the normal batching of customer orders. The customer receives either a replacement product, a cash refund, or a credit to his or her credit card.

The returned goods are placed back into inventory if they are not defective or damaged. If the goods are defective or damaged they are listed as "seconds" and sold at reduced prices. The inventory records are updated to reflect either the original cost or the reduced price.

TABLE 10–2	Functions in the Revenue Process
Order entry	Acceptance of customer orders for goods and services into the system in accordance with management criteria.
Credit authorization	Appropriate approval of customer orders for creditworthiness.
Shipping	Shipping of goods that has been authorized.
Billing	Issuance of sales invoices to customers for goods shipped or services provided; also, processing of billing adjustments for allowances, discounts, and returns.
Cash receipts	Processing of the receipt of cash from customers.
Accounts receivable	Recording of all sales invoices, collections, and credit memoranda in individual customer accounts.
General ledger	Proper accumulation, classification, and summarization of revenues, collections, and receivables in the financial statement accounts.

Write-Off Authorization This document authorizes the write-off of an uncollectible account. It is normally initiated in the credit department, with final approval for the write-off coming from the treasurer. Depending on the entity's accounting system, this type of transaction may be processed separately or as part of the normal stream of sales transactions. EarthWear has negligible bad debts because most sales are made by credit card. Any bad debts related to group or corporate sales are written off by the credit department after approval by the treasurer.

The Major Functions

❧ [LO 5]

The principal objective of the revenue process is selling the entity's goods or services at prices and terms that are consistent with management's policies. Table 10–2 summarizes the functions that normally take place in a typical revenue process.

Order Entry The initial function in the revenue process is the entry of new sales orders into the system. It is important that sales or services be consistent with management's authorization criteria before entry into the revenue process. In most entities, there is a separate order entry department (see Figure 10–2).

Credit Authorization The credit authorization function must determine that the customer is able to pay for the goods or services. Failure to perform this function properly may result in bad-debt losses. In many entities, customers have preset credit limits. The credit authorization function must ensure that the credit limit is not exceeded without additional authorization. Where credit limits are programmed into the information system, a sale that causes a customer's balance to exceed the authorized credit limit should not be processed. The system should also generate an exception report or review by the credit function prior to further processing. Periodically, each customer's credit limit should be reviewed to ensure that the amount is consistent with the customer's ability to pay.

The credit authorization function also has responsibility for monitoring customer payments. An aged trial balance of accounts receivable should be prepared and reviewed by the credit function. Payment should be requested from customers who are delinquent in paying for goods or services. The credit function is usually responsible for preparing a report of customer accounts that may require write-off as bad debts. However, the final approval for writing off an account should come from an officer of the company who is not responsible for credit or collections. If the authorization for bad-debt write-off is part of the credit function, it is possible for credit personnel who have access to cash receipts to conceal misappropriation of cash by writing off customers' balances. In many organizations, the treasurer approves the write-off of customer accounts because this individual is responsible for cash management activities and the treasurer's department is usually separate from the credit function. In some entities, the accounts written off are turned over to a collection agency for continuing collection efforts. By following this procedure, an entity discourages the use of fictitious bad-debt write-offs to conceal the misappropriation of cash. Most entities have a separate credit department.

Shipping   Goods should not be shipped, nor should services be provided, without proper authorization. The main control that authorizes shipment of goods or performance of services is payment or proper credit approval for the transaction. The shipping function must also ensure that customer orders are filled with the correct product and quantities. To ensure timely billing of customers, completed orders must be promptly forwarded to the billing function. The shipping function is normally completed within a separate shipping department.

Billing   The main responsibility of the billing function is to ensure that all goods shipped and all services provided are billed at authorized prices and terms. The entity's controls should prevent goods from being shipped to customers who are not being billed. In an IT system, an open-order report should be prepared and reviewed for orders that have not been filled on a timely basis. In other systems, all prenumbered shipping documents should be accounted for and matched to their related sales invoices. Any open or unmatched transactions should be investigated by billing department or sales department personnel.

The billing function is also responsible for handling goods returned for credit. The key control here is that a credit memorandum should not be issued unless the goods have been returned. A receiving document should first be issued by the receiving department to acknowledge receipt of the returned goods.

Cash Receipts   The collection function must ensure that all cash collections are properly identified and promptly deposited intact at the bank. Many companies use a lockbox system, in which customers' payments are sent directly to the entity's bank. The bank then forwards a file of cash receipts transactions and remittance advices to the entity. In situations where payments are sent directly to the entity, the checks should be restrictively endorsed and a "prelisting" or control listing prepared. All checks should be deposited daily.

Accounts Receivable   The accounts receivable function is responsible for ensuring that all billings, adjustments, and cash collections are properly recorded in customers' accounts receivable records. Any entries in customers' accounts should be made from authorized source documents such as sales invoices, remittance advices, and credit memoranda. In an IT system, the entries to the customers' accounts receivable records may be made directly as part of the normal processing of these transactions. The use of control totals and daily activity reports provides the control for ensuring that all transactions are properly recorded. The accounts receivable function is normally performed within the billing department or a separate accounts receivable department.

General Ledger   The main objective of the general ledger function in terms of a revenue process is to ensure that all revenues, collections, and receivables are properly accumulated, classified, and summarized in the accounts. In an IT system, the use of control or summary totals ensures that this function is performed correctly. One important function is the reconciliation of the accounts receivable subsidiary ledger to the general ledger control account. The general ledger function is also normally responsible for mailing the monthly customer account statements.

Key Segregation of Duties

[LO 6]

One of the most important controls in any accounting system is proper segregation of duties. This is particularly important in the revenue process because of the potential for theft and fraud. Therefore, individuals involved in the order entry, credit, shipping, or billing functions should not have access to the accounts receivable records, the general ledger, or any cash receipts activities. If IT is used extensively in the revenue process, there should be proper segregation of duties in the IT department. Table 10–3 contains some of the key segregation of duties for the revenue process, as well as examples of possible errors or fraud that can result from conflicts in duties.

Table 10–4 shows the proper segregation of duties for individual revenue functions across the various departments that process revenue transactions. Using this table, briefly analyze EarthWear's flowchart as shown in Figure 10–2. Evaluate whether EarthWear has sufficient segregation of duties. If not, what could happen as a result?

TABLE 10–3	Key Segregation of Duties in the Revenue Process and Possible Errors or Fraud
Segregation of Duties	*Possible Errors or Fraud Resulting from Conflicts of Duties*
The credit function should be segregated from the billing function.	If one individual has the ability to grant credit to a customer and also has responsibility for billing that customer, it is possible for sales to be made to customers who are not creditworthy. This can result in bad debts.
The shipping function should be segregated from the billing function.	If one individual who is responsible for shipping goods is also involved in the billing function, it is possible for unauthorized shipments to be made and for the usual billing procedures to be circumvented. This can result in unrecorded sales transactions and theft of goods.
The accounts receivable function should be segregated from the general ledger function.	If one individual is responsible for the accounts receivable records and also for the general ledger, it is possible for that individual to conceal unauthorized shipments. This can result in unrecorded sales transactions and theft of goods.
The cash receipts function should be segregated from the accounts receivable function.	If one individual has access to both the cash receipts and the accounts receivable records, it is possible for cash to be diverted and the shortage of cash in the accounting records to be covered. This can result in theft of the entity's cash.

| TABLE 10–4 | Segregation of Duties for Revenue and Accounts Receivable Functions by Department |

Revenue and Accounts Receivable Functions	Order Entry	Credit	Shipping	Accounts Receivable	Cash Receipts	IT	Treasurer
Receiving and preparing customer order	X						
Approving credit		X					
Shipping goods to customer and completing shipping document			X				
Preparing customer invoice				X		X	
Updating accounts receivable records for sales				X		X	
Receiving customer's remittance					X		
Updating accounts receivable for remittances				X		X	
Preparing accounts receivable aged trial balance				X		X	
Authorization of accounts receivable write-off							X

Inherent Risk Assessment

[LO 7]   In examining the revenue process, the auditor should consider the inherent risk factors that may affect both the revenue and cash receipts transactions and the financial statement accounts affected by those transactions. Most business risks are viewed as inherent risks. The assessment of the potential effects of inherent risk factors is one of the inputs for the risk of material misstatement. Chapter 3 pointed out the three conditions (incentive/pressure, opportunity, and attitude) that are generally present when fraud occurs. Four specific inherent risk factors that may affect the revenue process are the following:

- Industry-related factors.
- The complexity and contentiousness of revenue recognition issues.
- The difficulty of auditing transactions and account balances.
- Misstatements detected in prior audits.

Industry-Related Factors

Factors such as the profitability and health of the industry in which an entity operates, the level of competition within the industry, and the industry's rate of technological change affect the potential for misstatements in the revenue process. For example, if the industry is experiencing a lack of demand for its products, the entity may be faced with a declining sales volume, which can lead to operating losses and poor cash flow. Similarly, competition within the industry can affect the entity's pricing policies, credit terms, and product warranties. If such industry-related factors are present, management may engage in activities that can result in misstatements.

The level of government regulation within the industry may also affect sales activity. While all industries are regulated by legislation restricting unfair trade practices such as price fixing, a number of industries are more highly regulated. For example, banks and insurance companies are subject to both state and federal laws that may limit an entity's operations. The products developed and sold by pharmaceutical companies are regulated by the Food and Drug Administration. Finally, most states have consumer protection legislation that may affect product warranties, returns, financing, and product liability. Industry-related factors directly impact the auditor's assessment of inherent risk for assertions such as authorization and accuracy.

The Complexity and Contentiousness of Revenue Recognition Issues

For most entities the recognition of revenue is not a major problem because revenue is recognized when a product is shipped or a service is provided. However, for some entities the recognition of revenue may involve complex calculations.[1] Examples include recognition of revenue on long-term construction contracts, long-term service contracts, lease contracts, and installment sales. Briefly consider EarthWear and its revenue process. Does EarthWear's typical sales process indicate a higher or lower risk of material misstatement due to improper revenue recognition? In some cases, there may be disputes between the auditor and management over when revenue, expenses, and related profits should be recognized. In such circumstances, the auditor should assess the risk of material misstatement to be high. Revenue recognition may also have a significant impact on the cutoff and accuracy assertions.

---

[1]See American Institute of Certified Public Accountants, *Auditing Revenue in Certain Industries*, Audit Guide (New York: AICPA, 2008), for an overall discussion of the complexities of revenue recognition and, in particular, of the software and high-technology industries.

The Difficulty of Auditing Transactions and Account Balances

Accounts that are difficult to audit can pose inherent risk problems for the auditor. For example, management's estimate for the allowance for uncollectible accounts and sales returns can be difficult to audit because of the subjectivity that may be involved in determining proper value. The risk of a material misstatement for these estimates is a function of factors such as the complexity of the customer base and the reliability of the data available to test the accounts. For example, the only evidence available to determine the collectibility of a customer's account may be past payment history or a credit agency report. Such evidence is not as reliable as payments by the customer.

Misstatements Detected in Prior Audits

As discussed in earlier chapters, the presence of misstatements in previous audits is a good indicator that misstatements are likely to be present during the current audit. With a continuing engagement, the auditor has the results of prior years' audits to help in assessing the potential for misstatements in the revenue process.

Control Risk Assessment

✎ [LO 8]   The concepts involved in control risk assessment were discussed in Chapter 6. The following sections apply the approach outlined there to the revenue process. For discussion purposes, it is assumed that the auditor has decided to follow a reliance strategy for the revenue process. Figure 10–3 summarizes the three steps for setting control risk when a reliance strategy is being followed. Each of these steps is briefly reviewed within the context of the revenue process.

Understand and Document Internal Control

In order to assess the control risk for the revenue process, the auditor must understand the five components of internal control.

Control Environment   Table 6–3 in Chapter 6 listed the factors that are important in understanding the control environment (e.g. integrity and ethical

FIGURE 10–3	Major Steps in Setting Control Risk for the Revenue Process

Understand and document the revenue process based on a reliance approach.

↓

Plan and perform tests of controls on revenue transactions.

↓

Set and document the control risk for the revenue process.

values, commitment to competence, etc.). Because these factors have a pervasive effect on all accounting applications, understanding the control environment is generally completed on an overall entity basis. The auditor should, however, consider how the various control environment factors may affect the individual accounting applications. In the remaining discussion of the revenue process, it is assumed that the control environment factors, including general IT controls, are reliable.

The Entity's Risk Assessment Process

The auditor must understand how management considers risks that are relevant to the revenue process, estimates their significance, assesses the likelihood of their occurrence, and decides what actions to take to address those risks. Some of these risks include competition, rapid growth, and new technology. Each of these factors can represent a serious risk to an entity's internal controls over the revenue process.

Control Activities

When a reliance strategy is adopted for the revenue process, the auditor needs to understand the controls that exist to ensure that management's objectives are being met. More specifically, the auditor identifies what controls ensure that the assertions for transactions and events are being met. The auditor's understanding of the revenue process can be documented using procedures manuals, narrative descriptions, internal control questionnaires, and flowcharts.

Information Systems and Communication

For each major class of transactions in the revenue process, the auditor needs to obtain the following knowledge:

- The process by which sales, cash receipts, and sales returns and allowances transactions are initiated.
- The accounting records, supporting documents, and accounts that are involved in processing sales, cash receipts, and sales returns and allowances transactions.
- The flow of each type of transaction from initiation to inclusion in the financial statements, including computer processing of the data.
- The process used to prepare estimates for accounts such as the allowance for uncollectible accounts and sales returns.

The auditor can develop an understanding of an accounting (information) system such as the revenue process by conducting a walkthrough. This involves the auditor's "walking" a transaction through the accounting system and documenting the various functions that process it. In the case of a continuing audit, the auditor has the prior years' systems documentation to assist in the walkthrough, although the possibility of changes in the system must be considered. If the system has been changed substantially, or the audit is for a new client, the auditor should prepare new documentation of the system.

Monitoring of Controls

The auditor needs to understand the client's monitoring of controls in the revenue process. This includes understanding how management assesses the design and operation of controls in the revenue process. It also involves understanding how supervisory personnel within the system review the personnel who perform the controls and evaluate the performance of the entity's IT function, as well as the effectiveness of controls.

Plan and Perform Tests of Controls

The auditor should systematically examine the client's revenue process to identify relevant controls that help to prevent, or detect and correct, material misstatements. Because these controls are relied upon in order to set control risk below the maximum, the auditor conducts tests of controls to ensure that the controls in the revenue process operate effectively. Audit procedures used to test controls in the revenue process include inquiry of client personnel, inspection of documents and records, observation of the operation of the control, walkthroughs, and reperformance by the auditor of the control activities.

Subsequent sections examine tests of controls for each major type of transaction in the revenue process more specifically. Chapter 8 presented sampling approaches to conducting tests of controls.

Set and Document Control Risk

Once the tests of controls in the revenue process have been completed, the auditor sets the *achieved* level of control risk. If the results of the tests of controls support the planned level of control risk, the auditor conducts the planned level of substantive procedures for the related account balances. If the results of the tests of controls do not support the planned level of control risk, the auditor sets control risk at a level higher than planned. Additional substantive procedures in the accounts affected by the revenue process must then be conducted.

The auditor should document the achieved level of control risk. The level of control risk for the revenue process can be set using either quantitative amounts or qualitative terms such as "low," "medium," and "high." The documentation of the achieved level of control risk for the revenue process would include documentation of the accounting system such as the flowchart included in Figure 10–2, the results of the tests of controls, and a memorandum indicating the overall conclusions about control risk.

Control Activities and Tests of Controls—Revenue Transactions

[LO 9] Table 10–5 presents the assertions about transactions and events that were discussed in Chapters 2, 4, and 6. Table 10–6 summarizes the assertions for revenue transactions along with some examples of possible misstatements. For each of these misstatements we have included one or two possible control activities that management could implement to mitigate the risk as well as some

TABLE 10–5	Assertions about Classes of Transactions and Events for the Period under Audit

Occurrence. All revenue and cash receipt transactions and events that have been recorded have occurred and pertain to the entity.
Completeness. All revenue and cash receipt transactions and events that should have been recorded have been recorded.
Authorization. All revenue and cash receipt transactions and events are properly authorized.
Accuracy. Amounts and other data relating to recorded revenue and cash receipt transactions and events have been recorded appropriately and properly accumulated from journals and ledgers.
Cutoff. All revenue and cash receipt transactions and events have been recorded in the correct accounting period.
Classification. All revenue and cash receipt transactions and events have been recorded in the proper accounts.

TABLE 10–6	Summary of Assertions, Possible Misstatements, Example Control Activities, and Example Tests of Controls for Revenue Transactions		
Assertion	*Possible Misstatement*	*Example Control Activity*	*Example Test of Controls*
Occurrence	Fictitious revenue	Segregation of duties	Observation and evaluation of proper segregation of duties.
	Revenue recorded, goods not shipped, or services not performed	Sales recorded only with approved customer order and shipping document	Testing of a sample of sales invoices for the presence of authorized customer order and shipping document; if IT application, examination of application controls.
		Accounting for numerical sequences of sales invoices	Review and testing of client procedures for accounting for numerical sequence of sales invoices; if IT application, examination of application controls.
		Monthly customer statements; complaints handled independently	Review and testing of client procedures for mailing and handling complaints about monthly statements.
Completeness	Goods shipped or services performed, revenue not recorded	Accounting for numerical sequences of shipping documents and sales invoices	Review and testing of client's procedures for accounting for numerical sequence of shipping documents and sales invoices; if IT application, examination of application controls.
		Shipping documents matched to sales invoices	Tracing of a sample of shipping documents to their respective sales invoices and to the sales journal.
		Sales invoices reconciled to daily sales report	Testing of a sample of daily reconciliations.
		An open-order file that is maintained currently and reviewed periodically	Examination of the open-order file for unfilled orders.
Authorization	Goods shipped or services performed for a customer who is a bad credit risk	Proper procedures for authorizing credit and shipment of goods	Review of client's procedures for granting credit. Examination of sales orders for evidence of proper credit approval; if IT application, examination of application controls for credit limits.
	Shipments made or services performed at unauthorized prices or on unauthorized terms	Authorized price list and specified terms of trade	Comparison of prices and terms on sales invoices to authorized price list and terms of trade; if IT application, examination of application controls for authorized prices and terms.
Accuracy	Revenue transaction recorded at an incorrect dollar amount	Authorized price list and specified terms of trade	Same as above.
		Each sales invoice agreed to shipping document and customer order for product type and quantity; mathematical accuracy of sales invoice verified	Examination of sales invoice for evidence that client personnel verified mathematical accuracy. Recomputation of the information on a sample of sales invoices; if IT application, examination of application controls and consideration of use of computer-assisted audit techniques.
	Revenue transactions not posted correctly to the sales journal or customers' accounts in accounts receivable subsidiary ledger	Sales invoices reconciled to daily sales report	Examination of reconciliation of sales invoices to daily sales report.
		Daily postings to sales journal reconciled with posting to subsidiary ledger	Examination of reconciliation of entries to sales journal with entries to subsidiary ledger.
	Amounts from sales journal not posted correctly to general journal	Subsidiary ledger reconciled to general ledger control account	Review of reconciliation of subsidiary ledger to general ledger control account.
		Monthly customer statements with independent review of complaints	Review and testing of client procedures for mailing and handling complaints related to monthly statements.
Cutoff	Revenue transactions recorded in the wrong period	All shipping documents forwarded to the billing function daily	Comparison of the dates on sales invoices with the dates of the relevant shipping documents.
		Daily billing of goods shipped	Comparison of the dates on sales invoices with the dates they were recorded in the sales journal.
Classification	Revenue transaction not properly classified	Chart of accounts	Review of sales journal and general ledger for proper classification.
		Proper codes for different types of products or services	Examination of sales invoices for proper classification; if IT application, testing of application controls for proper codes.

example tests of controls that the auditor could use to test those controls. This table (and similar tables in later chapters) is not an exhaustive list of misstatements, control activities, or tests of controls for revenue transactions; rather it provides some specific examples by assertion to help you understand the underlying concepts. Most of these controls exist within EarthWear's revenue process (Figure 10–2).

The auditor's decision process for planning and performing tests of controls involves considering the assertions and the possible misstatements that can occur if internal control does not operate effectively. The auditor evaluates the client's accounting system to determine the controls that will prevent, or detect and correct, such misstatements. When controls are present and the auditor decides to rely on them, they must be tested to evaluate their effectiveness. For example, suppose the auditor's evaluation of the entity's revenue process indicates that monthly statements are mailed to customers by the accounts receivable department with complaints being handled by the billing department. This control is intended to prevent the recording of fictitious sales transactions. The auditor can review and test the client's procedures for mailing customer statements and handling complaints. If no exceptions or an immaterial number are noted, the auditor has evidence that the control is operating effectively.

Each of the assertions shown in Table 10–6 for revenue transactions is discussed mainly in terms of control activities and tests of controls. The column for test of controls includes both manual tests and computer-assisted audit techniques (CAATS). The choice of which type of test of controls is appropriate for a particular assertion will be a function of the following:

- The volume of transactions or data.
- The nature and complexity of the systems by which the entity processes and controls information.
- The nature of the available evidence, including audit evidence in electronic form.

The following sections also include a discussion of control activities and tests of controls that are relevant for EarthWear's revenue process.

Occurrence of Revenue Transactions

Auditors are concerned about the occurrence assertion for revenue transactions because clients are more likely to overstate sales than to understate them. The auditor is concerned about two major types of material misstatements: sales to fictitious customers and recording of revenue when goods have not been shipped or services have not been performed. In other words, the auditor needs assurance that all recorded revenue transactions are valid. The controls shown in Table 10–6 are designed to reduce the risk that revenue is recorded before goods are shipped or services are performed. The major control for preventing fictitious sales is proper segregation of duties between the shipping function and the order entry and billing functions. If these functions are not properly segregated, unauthorized shipments can be made to fictitious customers by circumventing normal billing control activities. Requiring an approved customer sales order and shipping document before revenue is recognized also minimizes the recording of fictitious sales in a client's records. Accounting for the numerical sequence of sales invoices can be accomplished manually or by computer. The use of monthly customer statements also reduces the risk of revenue being recorded before goods are shipped or services are performed because customers are unlikely to recognize an obligation to pay in such a circumstance. Figure 10–2 shows that EarthWear's revenue process includes these control activities where applicable.

For each of the controls shown, a corresponding test of control is indicated. For example, the auditor can observe and evaluate the segregation of duties. The auditor can also examine a sample of sales invoices for the presence of an authorized customer order and shipping document for each one. In an IT environment, such as EarthWear's revenue process, the auditor can test the application controls to ensure that revenue is recorded only after an approved customer order has been entered and the goods shipped.

Completeness of Revenue Transactions

The major misstatement that concerns both management and the auditor is that goods are shipped or services are performed and no revenue is recognized. Failure to recognize revenue means that the customer may not be billed for goods or services and the client does not receive payment. Control activities that ensure that the completeness assertion is being met include accounting for the numerical sequence of shipping documents and sales invoices, matching shipping documents with sales invoices, reconciling the sales invoices to the daily sales report, and maintaining and reviewing the open-order file. For example, EarthWear (Figure 10–2) reconciles the batch totals of orders entered and provides a reconciliation of the daily shipping listing and the daily sales report. Additionally, the open-order file is reviewed periodically with follow-up on any order older than some predetermined date.

Tests of controls for these control activities are listed in Table 10–6. For example, to test the control that shipping documents are matched to sales invoices, the auditor could select a sample of bills of lading and trace each one to its respective sales invoice and to the sales journal. If all bills of lading in the sample were matched to sales invoices and included in the sales journal, the auditor would have evidence that all goods shipped are being billed. The auditor could also use a generalized audit software package to print the items in the open-order file that are older than the client's predetermined time frame for completing a transaction. These transactions would then be investigated to determine why the sales were not completed.

Authorization of Revenue Transactions

Possible misstatements due to improper authorization include shipping goods to or performing services for customers who are bad credit risks and making sales at unauthorized prices or terms. As discussed earlier in this chapter, management should establish procedures for authorizing credit, prices, and terms. Additionally, no goods should be shipped without a properly authorized sales order. Table 10–6 lists a number of tests of controls for this assertion. In an IT revenue process such as EarthWear's, the auditor may need to review the application controls and use CAATs to test the proper authorization of revenue transactions.

Accuracy of Revenue Transactions

Accuracy is an important assertion because revenue transactions that are not processed accurately result in misstatements that directly affect the amounts reported in the financial statements. Again, the presence of an authorized price list and terms of trade reduces the risk of inaccuracies. There should also be controls that ensure proper verification of the information contained on the sales invoice, including type of goods and quantities shipped, prices, and terms. The sales invoice should also be verified for mathematical accuracy before being sent to the customer. If the controls are manual, the sales invoice may contain the initials of the client personnel who verified the mathematical accuracy. In an IT application such as EarthWear's, most of these controls would be programmed. For example, the price list is maintained in a master file. However, the client still needs controls to ensure that the authorized price list is updated promptly and that only authorized changes are made to the master file. The auditor can verify the application controls by using CAATs.

The accuracy assertion also includes the possibility that transactions are not properly summarized from source documents or posted properly from journals to the subsidiary and general ledgers. In the revenue process, control totals should be utilized to reconcile sales invoices to the daily sales report, and the daily recordings in the sales journal should be reconciled with the posting to the accounts receivable subsidiary ledger. The accounts receivable subsidiary ledger should periodically be reconciled to the general ledger control account. In a properly designed revenue system, such controls are programmed and reconciled by the control groups in the IT department and the user departments. The auditor can examine and test the application controls and various reconciliations. The use of monthly customer statements may also identify posting errors.

Cutoff of Revenue Transactions	If the client does not have adequate controls to ensure that revenue transactions are recorded on a timely basis, sales may be recorded in the wrong accounting period. The client should require that all shipping documents be forwarded to the billing function daily. The auditor can test this control by comparing the date on a bill of lading with the date on the respective sales invoice and the date the sales invoice was recorded in the sales journal. In EarthWear's revenue process, the shipping department forwards the approved shipping order to the billing department for entry into the billing program. In such a system, sales should be billed and recorded within one or two days of shipment.
Classification of Revenue Transactions	The use of a chart of accounts and proper codes for recording transactions should provide adequate assurance about this assertion. The auditor can review the sales journal and general ledger for proper classification, and can test sales invoices for proper classification by examining programmed controls to ensure that sales invoices are coded by type of product or service.

Control Activities and Tests of Controls—Cash Receipts Transactions

[LO 9] Table 10–7 summarizes the assertions for cash receipts transactions along with some examples of possible misstatements. For each of these misstatements we have included one or two possible control activities that management could implement to mitigate the risk as well as some example tests of controls that the auditor could use to test those controls. This table is not an exhaustive list of misstatements, control activities, or tests of controls for cash receipts transactions; rather it provides some specific examples by assertion to help you understand the underlying concepts. In assessing the control risk for cash receipts transactions, the auditor follows the same decision process as described for revenue transactions. Each of the assertions shown in Table 10–7 is discussed with an emphasis on the control activities and tests of controls. The substantive audit procedures for cash are covered in Chapter 16.

Practice	The risk of misappropriation of funds may be greatly reduced by implementing a central lockbox at a bank to receive payments instead of receiving customer payments directly at the organization's location.
INSIGHT	

TABLE 10-7	Summary of Assertions, Possible Misstatements, Example Control Activities, and Example Tests of Controls for Cash Receipts Transactions

Assertion	Possible Misstatement	Example Control Activity	Example Test of Controls
Occurrence	Cash receipts recorded but not received or deposited	Segregation of duties	Observation and evaluation of proper segregation of duties.
		Use of lockbox system	Inquiry of management about lockbox policy.
		Monthly bank reconciliations prepared and independently reviewed	Review of monthly bank reconciliation for indication of independent review.
Completeness	Cash receipts stolen or lost before recording	Same control procedures as above	Same tests of controls as above.
		Checks restrictively endorsed when received and daily cash list prepared	Observation of the endorsement of checks.
		Daily cash receipts reconciled with posting to accounts receivable subsidiary ledger	Testing of the reconciliation of daily cash receipts with posting to accounts receivable subsidiary ledger.
		Customer statements prepared on a regular basis; complaints handled independently	Inquiry of client personnel about handling of monthly statements and examination of resolution of complaints.
Authorization	Cash discounts not properly taken	Procedures specifying policies for cash discounts	Testing of a sample of cash receipts transactions for proper cash discounts.
Accuracy	Cash receipts recorded at incorrect amount	Daily remittance report reconciled to control listing of remittance advices	Review and testing of reconciliation.
		Monthly bank statement reconciled and independently reviewed	Examination of monthly bank reconciliation for independent review.
Cutoff	Cash receipts recorded in wrong period	Use of a lockbox system or a control procedure to deposit cash receipts daily	Examination of cash receipts for daily deposit.
Classification	Cash receipts posted to wrong customer account	Daily remittance report reconciled daily with postings to cash receipts journal and accounts receivable subsidiary ledger	Review and testing of reconciliation; if IT application, testing of application controls for posting.
		Monthly customer statements with independent review of complaints	Review and testing of client procedures for mailing statements and handling complaints from customers.
	Cash receipts not properly posted to general ledger accounts	Monthly cash receipts journal agreed to general ledger posting	Review of posting from cash receipts journal to the general ledger.
		Accounts receivable subsidiary ledger reconciled to general ledger control account	Examination of reconciliation of accounts receivable subsidiary ledger to general ledger control account.
	Cash receipts recorded in wrong financial statement account	Chart of accounts	Tracing of cash receipts from listing to cash receipts journal for proper classification.
			Review of cash receipts journal for unusual items.

Occurrence of Cash Receipt Transactions

The possible misstatement that concerns the auditor when considering the occurrence assertion is that cash receipts are recorded but not deposited in the client's bank account. In order to commit such a fraud, an employee needs access to both the cash receipts and the accounts receivable records; segregation of duties normally prevents this type of defalcation. Thus, proper segregation of duties between the cash receipts function and the accounts receivable function is one control procedure that can prevent such misstatements. Another very strong control that prevents such misstatements is the use of a lockbox system, such as the system used by EarthWear (Figure 10–2). With a lockbox system, the customers' cash receipts are mailed directly to the client's bank, thereby preventing the client's employees from having access to cash. The cash is deposited in the client's account, and the bank forwards the remittance advices and a file of the cash receipts transactions to the client for processing. Finally, preparation of monthly bank reconciliations that are independently reviewed reduces the possibility that cash receipts will be recorded but not deposited. Table 10–7 lists the tests of controls the auditor could conduct to assess the effectiveness of the client's controls over the occurrence assertion.

Completeness of Cash Receipts Transactions

A major misstatement related to the completeness assertion is that cash or checks are stolen or lost before being recorded in the cash receipts records. Proper segregation of duties and a lockbox system are strong controls for ensuring that this assertion is met. When a lockbox system is not used, checks should be restrictively endorsed when received, and a daily cash listing should be prepared. An additional control is reconciliation of the daily cash receipts with the amounts posted to customers' accounts in the accounts receivable subsidiary ledger. An example of this control is shown in EarthWear's system, where the total of the remittance advices is reconciled with the daily remittance report by the cash receipts department.

In terms of tests of controls, the controls conducted for the occurrence assertion also provide some evidence about completeness. In addition, the auditor can observe the client's personnel endorsing the checks and preparing the cash listing. The reconciliation of the daily cash receipts with the postings to the accounts receivable subsidiary ledger can be tested by the auditor on a sample basis.

When the client does not have adequate segregation of duties or if collusion is suspected, the possibility of defalcation is increased. An employee who has access to both the cash receipts and the accounts receivable records has the ability to steal cash and manipulate the accounting records to hide the misstatement. This is sometimes referred to as *lapping*. When lapping is used, the perpetrator covers the cash shortage by applying cash from one customer's account against another customer's account. For example, suppose customer 1 has a balance of $5,000 and mails a check for $3,000 as payment on the account. A client's employee who has access to both the cash receipts and the accounts receivable records can convert the $3,000 payment to his or her personal use. The theft of the cash can be covered in the following way: The $3,000 payment is not reflected in the customer's account. When a payment is subsequently received from customer 2, the payment is deposited in the client's cash account but applied to customer 1's accounts receivable account. Now the shortage of cash is reflected in customer 2's accounts receivable account. The client employee who stole the cash keeps hiding the theft by shifting the $3,000 difference from one customer's accounts receivable account to another's. If cash is stolen *before* it is recorded as just described, the fraud is difficult and time-consuming for the auditor to detect. If the auditor suspects that this has occurred, the individual cash receipts have to be traced to the customers' accounts receivable accounts to ensure that each cash receipt has been posted to the correct account. If a cash receipt is posted to a different account, this may indicate that someone is applying cash to different accounts to cover a cash shortage. However, if duties are not properly segregated, that person may also be able to hide the theft through use of a credit memorandum, bad-debt write-off, or no recognition of the revenue transaction. For example, the employee could issue a credit memorandum for $3,000 against the customer's accounts receivable account to cover the $3,000 difference.

Authorization of Cash Discounts

Terms of trade generally include discounts for payment within a specified period as a way of encouraging customers to pay on time. Controls in the accounting system should ensure that management's policies concerning cash discounts are followed. For example, the client may establish terms of trade of 2/10, net/30 days. Customers paying within 10 days are then entitled to a 2-percent discount. When the cash is received, client personnel should check to be sure that the customer is complying with the payment terms. The auditor can test this control by examining a sample of cash receipts transactions to determine if the client's cash discount policies are being followed.

Accuracy of Cash Transactions

There are several reasons why cash receipts might be recorded at an incorrect amount. For example, the wrong amount could be recorded from the remittance advice, or the receipt could be incorrectly processed during data entry. The controls listed in Table 10–7 provide reasonable assurance that such errors would be detected and corrected. The corresponding tests of controls involve examining and testing the various reconciliations that take place in this part of the revenue process.

The other major misstatements that can occur for the accuracy assertion are cash receipts being posted to the wrong customer account or the wrong general ledger account. This last misstatement should not be confused with the misstatement discussed under the classification assertion. For the classification assertion, the misstatement results from the wrong financial statement accounts being credited in the cash receipts journal. The misstatement related to the accuracy assertion involves accurately posting to the accounts receivable subsidiary ledger or from the totals in the cash receipts journal to the general ledger accounts.

The use of monthly customer statements provides a check on posting to the correct customer account because a customer who has made a payment and whose monthly statement does not reflect it will complain to the client. The other controls mainly involve the use of various reconciliations that ensure that cash receipts transactions are properly summarized and posted to the general ledger. Tests of controls that may be used by the auditor are presented for each control activity shown in Table 10–7.

Cutoff of Cash Receipts Transactions

If the client uses a lockbox system or if cash is deposited daily in the client's bank, there is a small possibility of cash being recorded in the wrong period. Generally, the auditor has little concern with this type of misstatement because most entities use such control activities.

Classification of Cash Receipts

The auditor seldom has major concerns about cash receipts being recorded in the wrong financial statement account. The major control for preventing cash from being recorded in the wrong account is a chart of accounts. The auditor's concern is with applying appropriate account codes to the individual cash receipts, especially cash receipts from unusual sources such as scrap sales, notes receivable, and proceeds from sales of equipment. The auditor can trace a sample of remittance advices to the cash receipts journal to ensure proper classification. The cash receipts journal can also be reviewed for unusual items.

Control Activities and Tests of Controls—Sales Returns and Allowances Transactions

[LO 9]   For most entities, sales returns and allowances transactions are few and do not represent a material amount in the financial statements. As a result, this text does not cover them in as much detail as revenue or cash receipts transactions.

However, credit memoranda that are used to process sales returns and allowances transactions can also be used to cover an unauthorized shipment of goods or conceal a misappropriation of cash.

Two important controls should be present regarding the processing of credit memoranda. First, each credit memorandum should be approved by someone other than the individual who initiated it. This provides proper segregation of duties between access to the customer's record and authorization for issuing a credit memorandum. Second, a credit for returned goods should be supported by a receiving document indicating that the goods have been returned. The auditor can perform tests of controls on credit memoranda by examining a sample of credit memoranda for proper approval and the presence of the respective receiving documents. For a credit memorandum issued for a reason other than a return of goods, approval by an appropriate individual is the critical control. See Exhibit 10–3 for a discussion of the control activities used by EarthWear to control sales returns.

For entities with few or immaterial sales returns and allowances transactions, the auditor may decide only to gain an understanding of how such transactions are processed and not to conduct tests of controls. Substantive analytical procedures (discussed later in this chapter) can then be used to provide sufficient evidence on the fairness of the sales returns and allowances account.

Relating the Assessed Level of Control Risk to Substantive Procedures

✂ [LO 10] The results of the auditor's testing of internal control for the revenue process directly impact detection risk and therefore the level of substantive procedures that will be required for the accounts affected by this process. This includes balance sheet accounts such as accounts receivable, allowance for uncollectible accounts, and cash, as well as income statement accounts such as sales, bad-debt expense, and sales returns and allowances.

When the results of testing controls support the planned level of control risk, the auditor can conduct substantive procedures of these accounts at the planned level. If the results of testing controls indicate that the control risk can be further reduced, the auditor can increase the detection risk. This might lead to a reduction in the amount or the mix of the substantive procedures. For example, if the tests of controls indicate that control risk is lower than planned, the auditor might plan to perform more substantive analytical procedures and fewer tests of details of account balances. However, if the results of the tests of controls do not support the planned level of control risk, the detection risk will have to be set lower. This normally leads to an increase in the amount of substantive procedures. For example, if controls for the occurrence assertion are weaker than planned for revenue transactions, the auditor might increase the number of accounts receivable confirmations mailed to customers.

Auditing Accounts Receivable and Related Accounts

The auditor uses substantive procedures to detect material misstatements in accounts receivable and related accounts.

As discussed in Chapter 5, there are two categories of substantive procedures: (1) substantive analytical procedures and; (2) tests of details of classes of transactions, account balances, and disclosures. Substantive analytical procedures are used to examine plausible relationships among accounts receivable

TABLE 10-8	Management Assertions about Account Balances and Disclosures for Accounts Receivable and Related Accounts

Assertions about account balances at the period end:
- **Existence.** Recorded accounts receivable and related accounts exist.
- **Rights and obligations.** The entity holds or controls the rights to accounts receivable and related accounts, and any liabilities related to those accounts are the obligations of the entity.
- **Completeness.** All accounts receivable and related accounts that should have been recorded have been recorded.
- **Valuation and allocation.** Accounts receivable and related accounts are included in the financial statements at appropriate amounts, and any resulting valuation or allocation adjustments are appropriately recorded.

Assertions about presentation and disclosure:
- **Occurrence and rights and obligations.** All disclosed events, transactions, and other matters relating to accounts receivable and related accounts have occurred and pertain to the entity.
- **Completeness.** All disclosures relating to accounts receivable and related accounts that should have been included in the financial statements have been included.
- **Classification and understandability.** Financial information relating to accounts receivable and related accounts is appropriately presented and described, and disclosures are clearly expressed.
- **Accuracy and valuation.** Financial and other information relating to accounts receivable and related accounts are disclosed fairly and at appropriate amounts.

and related accounts. This should include disaggregated analytical procedures for revenue (AU 316.29). Tests of details focus on transactions, account balances, or disclosures. In the revenue process, tests of details of transactions (also called *substantive tests of transactions*) focus mainly on the sales and cash receipts transactions. Tests of details of account balances concentrate on the detailed amounts or estimates that make up the ending balance for accounts receivable and related accounts. Tests of details of disclosures are concerned with the presentation and disclosures related to accounts receivable and related accounts.

Table 10–5 presented the assertions for revenue and cash receipt transactions and events. Table 10–8 lists the assertions for account balances and disclosures as they apply to accounts receivable and related accounts. The reader should note that the auditor may test assertions related to transactions (substantive tests of transactions) in conjunction with testing internal controls. If the tests of controls indicate that the controls are not operating effectively, the auditor may need to test transactions closer to year-end or the balance sheet date.

We discuss substantive analytical procedures first because, after control testing, the assurance "bucket" is usually filled with evidence from substantive analytical procedures before tests of details.

Substantive Analytical Procedures

[LO 11]   Substantive analytical procedures are useful audit tests for examining the fairness of accounts such as sales, accounts receivable, allowance for uncollectible accounts, bad-debt expense, and sales returns and allowances because such tests provide sufficient evidence at low cost. Table 10–9 lists examples of substantive analytical procedures that are useful in auditing accounts receivable and related accounts. Many of the analytical procedures listed in Table 10–9 could also be used for preliminary analytical procedures at the planning stage or as a final analytical procedure at the completion of the audit. Table 10–9 is not an exhaustive list of substantive analytical procedures for accounts receivable and related accounts; rather it provides some specific examples by account to help you understand the underlying concepts.

For example, what evidence might be provided by comparing this year's gross profit percentage with that of previous years? Further, what might it mean if this

TABLE 10–9	Examples of Substantive Analytical Procedures Used in Testing Accounts Receivable and Related Accounts

Example Substantive Analytical Procedure	Possible Misstatement Detected
Revenue	
Comparison of gross profit percentage by product line with previous years' and industry data.*	Unrecorded (understated) revenue.
Comparison of reported revenue to budgeted revenue.	Fictitious (overstated) revenue.
Analysis of the ratio of sales in the last month or week to total sales for the quarter or year.*	Changes in pricing policies.
Comparison of revenues recorded daily for periods shortly before and after the end of the audit period for unusual fluctuations such as an increase just before and a decrease just after the end of the period.*	Product-pricing problems.
Comparison of details of units shipped with revenues and production records and consideration of whether revenues are reasonable compared to levels of production and average sales price.*	
Comparison of the number of weeks of inventory in distribution channels with prior periods for unusual increases that may indicate channel stuffing.*	
Comparison of percentages and trends of sales into the distributor channel with industry and competitors' sales trends, if known.*	
Accounts Receivable, Allowance for Uncollectible Accounts, and Bad-Debt Expense	
Comparison of receivables turnover and days outstanding in accounts receivable to previous years' and/or industry data.	Under- or overstatement of allowance for uncollectible accounts and bad-debt expense.
Comparison of aging categories on aged trial balance of accounts receivable to previous years.*	
Comparison of bad-debt expense as a percentage of revenue to previous years' and/or industry data.	
Comparison of the allowance for uncollectible accounts as a percentage of accounts receivable or credit sales to previous years' and/or industry data.	
Examination of large customer accounts individually and comparison to previous year.	
Sales Returns and Allowances and Sales Commissions	
Comparison of sales returns as a percentage of revenue to previous years' or industry data.	Under- or overstatement of sales returns.
Comparison of sales discounts as a percentage of revenue to previous years' and/or industry data.	Under- or overstatement of sales discounts.
Estimation of sales commission expense by multiplying net revenue by average commission rate and comparison of recorded sales commission expense.	Under- or overstatement of sales commission expense and related accrual.

*Analytical procedures suggested in the AICPA's *Auditing Revenue in Certain Industries,* Audit Guide (New York: AICPA, 2001).

year's percentage is significantly *less* than last year's? What if it is significantly *more* than last year's? This comparison of gross profit percentage to previous years' or industry data may provide valuable evidence on unrecorded revenue (an understatement) or fictitious revenue (an overstatement) and related accounts receivable when this ratio is significantly higher or lower than previous years' or industry data. This ratio may also provide information on changes in pricing policies.

The five ratios shown under the "Accounts Receivable" subheading in Table 10–9 provide evidence on whether accounts receivable properly reflect net realizable value. Each ratio aids the auditor in assessing the fairness of the allowance for uncollectible accounts, which in turn affects the fairness of accounts receivable and bad-debt expense. The days outstanding in accounts receivable ratio for EarthWear provides a good example of a substantive analytical procedure that provides strong audit evidence support for the accurate valuation of accounts receivable. The days outstanding in accounts receivable ratio is 4.91 and 4.94 days for 2008 and 2009, suggesting that EarthWear collects its accounts receivable quickly. This result is consistent with the majority of the company's sales being made with credit cards. EarthWear is reimbursed in three to five days by its credit card providers. Given the relative size of accounts receivable and this result indicating that receivables are collected so quickly, EarthWear's auditors may do no further audit work on accounts receivable and instead rely on evidence gathered regarding cash receipts and the ending cash balance. Pretend for a moment that 2009's days outstanding in accounts receivable ratio increased substantially. How might this impact the nature, timing, and extent of your audit procedures? What types of EarthWear's customers would be the source of the bad debt problems?

Last, comparing the ratio of sales returns or sales discounts to revenue with previous years' and industry data provides the auditor with evidence on whether all sales returns or sales discounts have been recorded. The auditor can also estimate sales commission expense by multiplying the average commission rate by net sales and comparing that amount with recorded commission expense. In many situations, the auditor may be able to accept the sales returns, sales discounts, and sales commission expense as fairly presented without conducting any additional substantive tests if such substantive analytical procedures produce results that are consistent with the auditor's expectations.

Tests of Details of Classes of Transactions, Account Balances, and Disclosures

[LO 12]   Table 10–10 presents the assertions for accounts receivable, allowance for uncollectible accounts, and bad-debt expense along with related tests of transactions, account balances, and disclosures. This table should not be construed as an exhaustive list of substantive audit procedures for accounts receivable and related accounts.

Tests of details of transactions (substantive tests of transactions) are tests conducted to detect monetary misstatements in the individual transactions processed through all accounting applications. Often the auditor conducts substantive tests of transactions at the same time as tests of controls. Thus, it is often difficult to distinguish a substantive test of transactions from a test of controls because the specific audit procedure may both test the operation of a control procedure and test for monetary misstatement. If the controls are not operating effectively or if the auditor did not rely on those controls, substantive tests of transactions may be necessary for the auditor to reach an appropriate level of evidence. The cutoff assertion is the one that is most often conducted as a substantive procedure.

[LO 13]   Table 10–10 also presents the assertions for account balances and disclosures. For each assertion, one or more tests of details are presented. In the following subsection, we discuss how the auditor approaches the audit of each important assertion for accounts receivable and related accounts. We begin with the completeness assertion for the accounts receivable balance because the auditor must establish that the detailed records that support the account to be audited agree with the general ledger account. Note that we do not cover each assertion listed in Table 10–10 because they are not applicable to EarthWear or they would have been conducted as tests of controls.

Completeness and Accuracy

The auditor's concern with completeness is whether all accounts receivable have been included in the accounts receivable subsidiary ledger and the general ledger accounts receivable account. The reconciliation of the aged trial balance to the general ledger account should detect an omission of a receivable from *either* the accounts receivable subsidiary ledger or the general ledger account. If the client's accounting system contains proper control totals and reconciliations, such errors should be detected and corrected by the relevant control activities for accuracy and completeness. For example, in EarthWear's revenue process (Figure 10–2),

TABLE 10–10	Summary of Assertions and Related Tests of Transactions, Account Balances and Disclosures—Accounts Receivable, Allowance for Uncollectible Accounts, and Bad-Debt Expense

Assertions about Classes of Transactions	Substantive Tests of Transactions*
Occurrence	For a sample of sales transactions recorded in the sales journal, tracing of the sales invoices back to customer orders and shipping documents.
Completeness	Tracing of a sample of shipping documents to the details of the sales invoices and to the sales journal and customers' accounts receivable subsidiary ledger.
Authorization & Accuracy	Comparison of prices and terms on a sample of sales invoices with authorized price list and terms of trade.
Cutoff	Comparison of the dates on a sample of sales invoices with the dates of shipment and with the dates they were recorded in the sales journal.
Classification	Examine a sample of sales invoices for proper classification into revenue accounts.

Assertions about Account Balances	Tests of Details of Account Balances
Existence	Confirmation of selected accounts receivable.
	Performance of alternative procedures for accounts receivable confirmation exceptions and nonresponses.
Rights and obligations	Review of bank confirmations for any liens on receivables.
	Inquiry of management, review of any loan agreements, and review of board of directors' minutes for any indication that the accounts receivable have been sold.
Completeness	Obtaining of aged trial balance of accounts receivable and agreeing total to general ledger control accounts.
	Review results of testing the completeness assertion for assessing control risk; tracing of shipping documents into sales journal and to accounts receivable subsidiary ledger if such testing was not performed as a test of controls.
Valuation and allocation	Examination of the results of confirmations of selected accounts receivable.
	Examination of the adequacy of the allowance for uncollectible accounts.

Assertions about Presentation and Disclosure	Tests of Details of Disclosures
Occurrence, and rights and obligations	Determine whether any receivables have been pledged, assigned, or discounted. Determine if such items require disclosure.
Completeness	Complete financial reporting checklist to ensure that all financial statement disclosures related to accounts receivable and related accounts have been disclosed.
Classification and understandability	Review of aged trial balance for material credits, long-term receivables, and nontrade receivables. Determine whether such items require separate disclosure on the balance sheet.
	Read footnotes to ensure that required disclosures are understandable.
Accuracy and valuation	Read footnotes and other information to ensure that the information is accurate and properly presented at the appropriate amounts.

*Each of these substantive tests of transactions could be conducted as a test of controls or a dual-purpose test. Of these six assertions, the cutoff assertion is the one that is most often conducted as a substantive procedure.

control totals exist for daily shipping and billing. Personnel in the billing department would be responsible for reconciling the two totals. If such control activities do not exist in a client's accounting system, or if they are not operating effectively, the auditor will have to trace a sample of shipping documents to sales invoices, the sales journal, and the accounts receivable subsidiary ledger to ensure that the transactions were included in the accounting records.

The process followed by the auditor is to agree the accounts receivable subsidiary ledger of customer accounts to the general ledger accounts receivable (control) account. This is typically accomplished by obtaining a copy of the aged trial balance of accounts receivable and comparing the total balance with the general ledger accounts receivable account balance. Exhibit 10–4 presents an aged trial balance of accounts receivable working paper for a wireless services company: Calabro Wireless Services. An aged trial balance of the subsidiary ledger is used because the auditor will need this type of data to examine the allowance for uncollectible accounts.

EXHIBIT 10-4	Example of an Aged Trial Balance of Accounts Receivable Working Paper

CW5

CALABRO WIRELESS SERVICES
Aged Trial Balance—Accounts Receivable
12/31/09

E10
DLJ
2/15/2010

Customer Name	Total	≤30 Days	31–60 Days	61–90 Days	>90 Days
Abbott Construction	$ 10,945¥	$ 9,542	$ 1,403		
Acton Labs	9,705		5,205	$ 4,500	
•	•	•	•	•	•
•	•	•	•	•	•
•	•	•	•	•	•
Wright Industries	29,875¥	18,875	11,000		
Zorcon, Inc.	4,340				$ 4,340
Total	$3,717,900	$2,044,895	$1,301,215	$260,253	$111,537
	F T/B	F	F	F	F

F = Footed.
T/B = Agreed to trial balance.
¥ = Customer account traced to subsidiary ledger; agreed to total and proper aging tested.

The auditor must also have assurance that the detail making up the aged trial balance is accurate. This can be accomplished in a number of ways. One approach involves mainly manual audit procedures. First, the aged trial balance is footed and crossfooted. *Footing* and *crossfooting* mean that each column of the trial balance is added, and the column totals are then added to ensure that they agree with the total balance for the account. Then a sample of customer accounts included in the aged trial balance is selected for testing. For each selected customer account, the auditor traces the customer's balance back to the subsidiary ledger detail and verifies the total amount and the amounts included in each column for proper aging. A second approach involves the use of CAATs. If the general controls over IT are adequate, the auditor can use a generalized audit software package to examine the accuracy of the aged trial balance generated by the client's accounting system.

Cutoff

The cutoff assertion attempts to determine whether all revenue transactions and related accounts receivable are recorded in the proper period. While the auditor can obtain assurance about the cutoff assertion for sales by conducting tests of controls, in most cases, cutoff tests are conducted as substantive tests of transactions or as a dual-purpose test. Additionally, sales cutoff is usually coordinated with inventory cutoff because the shipment of goods normally indicates that the earnings process is complete. The auditor wants assurance that if goods have been shipped in the current period, the resulting sale has been recorded, and also that if the sales have been recorded, the corresponding inventory has been removed from the accounting records. In addition, the auditor needs to determine if there is proper cutoff for sales returns.

If there is not a proper cutoff of revenue transactions, both the revenue and accounts receivable accounts will be misstated for the current and following years. In most instances, errors related to sales cutoff are unintentional and are due to delays in recognizing the shipment of goods or the recognition of the sale. In other instances, the client may intentionally fail to recognize revenue transactions in the current period or may recognize sales from the next period in

EXHIBIT 10–5	Sunbeam Corporation Restates Financial Results

Sunbeam Corporation restated its financial results for 1996, 1997, and the first quarter of 1998 based on an extensive audit by its audit committee and two public accounting firms. The special audit found that the previously issued financial statements overstated the loss for 1996, overstated profits for 1997, and understated the loss for the first quarter of 1998. Sunbeam reported that, for certain periods, revenue was incorrectly recognized in the wrong period, partly because of the company's "bill and hold" practice of billing customers in the current period for products that were delivered in a later period. The company also booked a significant amount of sales that were made to customers under such liberal terms that they did not constitute valid sales at all, but rather appeared to be consignments or guaranteed sales. In 1997 revenue was restated from $1,186 million to $1,073 million, and earnings were reduced from $123.1 million to $52.3 million. The reporting of these financial irregularities led to the resignation of Sunbeam's CEO, Al Dunlap.

In 2001, the SEC sued five ex-executives of Sunbeam and Arthur Andersen. Andersen agreed to pay $110 million to settle an accounting-fraud lawsuit over its audit work for Sunbeam.

Sources: J. R. Liang, "Dangerous Games: Did "Chainsaw Al" Dunlap Manufacture Sunbeam's Earnings Last Year?" *Barron's* (June 8, 1998), pp. 17–19; M. Brannigan, "Sunbeam Audit to Repudiate '97 Turnaround," *The Wall Street Journal* (October 20, 1998), p. A3; "Sunbeam to Restate Financial Results; Discloses Adjustments for 1996, 1997, and First Quarter 1998," *The PointCast Network* (October 20, 1998); N. Harris, "Andersen to Pay $110 Million to Settle Sunbeam Account-Fraud Lawsuit," *The Wall Street Journal* (May 2, 2001), p. A3; and J. Weil, "Five Sunbeam Ex-Executives Sued by SEC," *The Wall Street Journal* (May 16, 2001), p. A3.

the current period (see Exhibit 10–5 and Problem 10–30). The first situation can occur by the revenue transactions not being recorded in the sales journal until the next period. For example, sales that take place on the last two days of the current year are recorded as sales in the next year by delaying entry until the current-year sales journal is closed. The second situation is generally accomplished by leaving the sales journal "open" and recognizing sales from the first few days of the next period as current-period sales.

The client's accounting system should have controls that ensure timely recording of revenue transactions. The results of tests of controls, if performed, should provide evidence of the cutoff assertion. Additionally, the client should have end-of-period control activities for ensuring a proper sales cutoff between accounting periods.

The test of sales cutoff is straightforward. The auditor first identifies the number of the last shipping document issued in the current period. Then a sample of sales invoices and their related shipping documents is selected for a few days just prior to, and subsequent to, the end of the period. Assuming that sales are recorded at the time of shipment (FOB–shipping point), sales invoices representing goods shipped prior to year-end should be recorded in the current period, and invoices for goods shipped subsequent to year-end should be recorded as sales in the next period. Any transaction recorded in the wrong period should be corrected by the client. For example, suppose the last shipping document issued in the current period was numbered 10,540. None of the recorded revenue transactions sampled from a few days prior to year-end should have related shipping document numbers higher than 10,540, and none of the sampled revenue transactions recorded in the first few days of the subsequent period should have related shipping document numbers lower than 10,540. In an IT system such tests are still necessary because a delay in entering data may occur, or management may manipulate the recognition of the transactions.

The processing of sales returns may differ across entities. When sales returns are not material, or if they occur irregularly, the entity may recognize a sales return at the time the goods are returned. However, for entities like EarthWear, sales returns may represent a material amount or may occur regularly. In this instance, the client may estimate an allowance for sales returns. When sales returns represent a material amount, the auditor needs to test for proper cutoff.

Substantive analytical procedures also may be used to test cutoff for sales returns. The ratio of sales returns to sales may indicate to the auditor that sales returns are consistent with expectations and therefore that the sales returns cutoff is adequate. If the auditor decides to conduct more detailed tests, the receiving documents used to acknowledge receipt of the returned goods must be examined. Using procedures similar to those for testing sales cutoff, the auditor selects a sample of receiving documents for a few days prior to and subsequent to the end of the period. The receiving documents are traced to the related credit memoranda. Sales returns recorded in the wrong period should be corrected, if material.

Existence

The existence of accounts receivable is one of the more important assertions because the auditor wants assurance that this account balance is not overstated through the inclusion of fictitious customer accounts or amounts. The major audit procedures for testing the existence assertion for accounts receivable are confirmation of customers' account balances and examination of subsequent cash receipts. If a customer does not respond to the auditor's confirmation request, additional audit procedures may be necessary. The confirmation process is discussed later in this chapter.

Rights and Obligations

The auditor must determine whether the accounts receivable are owned by the entity because accounts receivable that have been sold should not be included in the entity's financial statements. For most audit engagements, this does not represent a problem because the client owns all the receivables. However, in some instances a client may sell its accounts receivable. The auditor can detect such an action by reviewing bank confirmations, cash receipts for payments from organizations that factor accounts receivable, or corporate minutes for authorization of the sale or assignment of receivables.

Valuation and Allocation

The major valuation issue related to accounts receivable is concerned with the net realizable value of accounts receivable. The auditor is concerned with determining that the allowance for uncollectible accounts, and thus bad-debt expense, is fairly stated. The allowance for uncollectible accounts is affected by internal factors such as the client's credit-granting and cash collection policies and external factors such as the state of the economy, conditions in the client's industry, and the financial strength of the client's customers.

In verifying the adequacy of the allowance for uncollectible accounts, the auditor starts by assessing the client's policies for granting credit and collecting cash. If the client establishes strict standards for granting credit, the likelihood of a large number of bad debts is reduced. Generally, the auditor assesses the adequacy of the allowance account by first examining the aged trial balance for amounts that have been outstanding for a long time. The probability of collecting these accounts can be assessed by discussing them with the credit manager, examining the customers' financial statements, obtaining credit reports (such as from Dun & Bradstreet), or reviewing the customers' communications with the client related to payment.

The second step in assessing the adequacy of the allowance account involves examining the client's prior experience with bad debts. The problem with examining only delinquent accounts is that no consideration is given to accounts that are current but that may result in bad debts. By maintaining good statistics on bad debts, the client can determine what percentage of each aging category will become uncollectible. The auditor can test these percentages for reasonableness. Following is an example of how this approach would work.

Suppose Calabro Wireless Services developed the following historical data on bad debts:

Aging Category	Percentage as Bad Debts
<30 days	.001
31–60 days	.025
61–90 days	.14
>90 days	.55

The allowance for uncollectible accounts can be determined in the following manner, using the data from Exhibit 10–4:

<30 days	31–60 days	61–90 days	>90 days	Total
$2,044,895	$1,301,215	$260,253	$111,537	$3,717,900
× .001	× .025	× .14	× .55	
$ 2,045	$ 32,530	$ 36,435	$ 61,345	$ 132,355

Suppose that the balance in the allowance for doubtful accounts on Calabro's general ledger is $135,300. This general ledger balance appears reasonable, given the auditor's calculation of $132,355. If the percentage for bad debts in the 31–60 days column was 5 percent instead of 2.5 percent, would your conclusion change? What if it was 7.5 percent? While determining the proper amount for the allowance for uncollectible accounts may seem relatively straightforward, considerable judgment on the part of the auditor is involved. As mentioned, the auditor must evaluate the collectibility of individual problem accounts and consider whether the historically derived percentages are reasonable, given the current economic and industry conditions.

Classification and Understandability

The major issues related to the presentation and disclosure assertion about classification are (1) identifying and reclassifying any material credits contained in accounts receivable; (2) segregating short-term and long-term receivables; and (3) ensuring that different types of receivables are properly classified. In many entities, when a customer pays in advance or a credit is issued, the amount is credited to the customer's accounts receivable account. The auditor should determine the amount of such credits and, if material, reclassify them as either a deposit or another type of liability. The second issue requires that the auditor identify and separate short-term receivables from long-term receivables. Long-term receivables should not be included with trade accounts receivable. The auditor must also ensure that nontrade receivables are properly separated from trade accounts receivable. For example, receivables from officers, employees, or related parties should not be included with trade accounts receivable because users might be misled if such receivables are combined.

Other Presentation and Disclosure Assertions

Disclosure is important for accounts receivable and related accounts. While management is responsible for the financial statements, the auditor must ensure that all necessary disclosures are made. Most public accounting firms use some type of financial statement reporting checklist to ensure that all necessary disclosures are made for each account (completeness). Table 10–11 presents examples of disclosure items for the revenue process and related financial statement accounts. Exhibit 10–6 presents two examples of common disclosures for revenue-related accounts. The first disclosure relates to the basis for recognizing revenue. This disclosure is normally included in a footnote that describes significant accounting policies. The second example presents disclosure of related-party transactions. Disclosures about related-party transactions normally discuss the nature of the transactions, the amounts, and whether the transactions were similar in terms to those for unrelated parties.

TABLE 10–11	Examples of Disclosure Items for the Revenue Process and Related Accounts

Revenue recognition basis.
Revenues recognized under the percentage-of-completion method.
Long-term sales contracts.
Revenues by reportable segment of the business.
Revenues and receivables from related parties.
Receivables by type (trade, officer, employee, affiliate, and so on).
Short- and long-term receivables.
Pledged or discounted receivables.

EXHIBIT 10–6	Sample Disclosures for Revenue Recognition and Related-Party Transactions

Revenue Recognition

Sales are recognized when the company's products are shipped. Sales to customers with whom the company has reciprocal purchase agreements are accounted for in the same manner as intercompany transactions and are eliminated in the financial statements.

Related-Party Transactions

The company's chairman of the board is also chairman of the board of Dayco Industries. Net sales to Dayco were $990,000 and $1,244,000 for the two years ended 2009 and 2008. Accounts receivable from Dayco were $243,000 and $489,000 at December 31, 2009 and 2008, respectively. The company believes that the terms of sale were substantially the same as those available to unrelated parties for similar products.

The Confirmation Process—Accounts Receivable[2]

[LO 14]   Confirmation is the process of obtaining and evaluating a direct communication provided by a third party in response to an auditor's request for information about a particular item affecting financial statement assertions (AU 330). Confirmation of accounts receivable is considered a generally accepted auditing procedure (AU 330.34), and therefore auditors normally request confirmation of accounts receivable during an audit. However, auditing standards allow the auditor to omit confirming accounts receivable in the following circumstances:

- The accounts receivable are immaterial to the financial statements.
- The use of confirmations would not be effective as an audit procedure. (This might occur if, based on prior experience, the auditor determines that the response rate might be low or the responses might not be reliable.)
- The auditor's assessment of inherent risk and control risk is low, and evidence gathered from other substantive tests is sufficient to reduce audit risk to an acceptably low level.

Because of the importance of accounts receivable confirmations, the auditor should document completely the decision not to gather such evidence.

Practice **INSIGHT**	Audit deficiencies identified in PCAOB inspections include auditors not documenting how they overcame the presumption that the auditor will request the confirmation of accounts receivable and documenting reasons that are not among the acceptable conditions for not requesting confirmations.

---

[2]See Professional Issues Task Force, Practice Alert 03-1, Confirmations (June 2007) and Interpretation of AU ¶350 No. 1—Use of Electronic Confirmations (March 2007) for recent guidance on the accounts receivable confirmations (www.aicpa.org).

Confirmations can address more than one assertion. However, confirmations normally provide different levels of assurance for different assertions. Accounts receivable confirmations are generally a good source of evidence for testing the existence assertion. If the customer confirms the amount owed to the client, the auditor has appropriate evidence that the account receivable is valid.[3] Accounts receivable confirmations may also provide evidence on the cutoff, completeness, and valuation and allocation assertions. For example, a customer's confirmation of the dollar amount owed provides some evidence on the valuation assertion.

A number of factors affect the reliability of accounts receivable confirmations. The auditor should consider each of the following factors when using confirmations to test accounts receivable:

- The type of confirmation request.
- Prior experience with the client or similar engagements.
- The intended respondent.

The types of confirmations are discussed in the next section. The auditor should consider prior experience with the client in terms of confirmation response rates, misstatements identified, and the accuracy of returned confirmations when assessing the reliability of accounts receivable confirmations. For example, if response rates were low in prior audits, the auditor might consider obtaining evidence using alternative procedures. The intended respondents to accounts receivable confirmations may vary from individuals with little accounting knowledge to large corporations with highly qualified accounting personnel. The auditor should consider each respondent's competence, knowledge, ability, and objectivity when assessing the reliability of confirmation requests. For example, if an auditor is confirming accounts receivable for a small retail organization, it is possible that the respondents may not have the knowledge or ability to respond appropriately to the confirmation request. On the other hand, if confirmations are sent to medium-size or large corporations with well-controlled accounts payable systems, the information received in response to such confirmation requests is likely to be reliable. However, some large organizations and government agencies do not respond to confirmations because it may be difficult to accumulate the necessary data since they are on a voucher system. Such nonresponses must be tested using procedures discussed later in the chapter.

Types of Confirmations

There are two types of confirmations: *positive* and *negative*. A positive accounts receivable confirmation requests that customers indicate whether they agree with the amount due to the client stated in the confirmation. Thus, a response is required regardless of whether the customer believes the amount is correct or incorrect. Sometimes an auditor will use a "blank" form of positive confirmation, in which the request requires the customer to provide the amount owed to the client. Positive confirmations are generally used when an account's individual balances are large or if errors are anticipated because the risk of material misstatements has been judged to be high. Exhibit 10–7 presents an example of a positive confirmation request.

A negative confirmation requests that customers respond only when they disagree with the amount due to the client. An example of a negative confirmation request is shown in Exhibit 10–8. Negative confirmation requests are used when there are many accounts with small balances, control risk is assessed to be low,

[3]Research has shown that accounts receivable confirmations are not always a reliable source of evidence. See P. Caster, R. J. Elder, and D. J. Janvrin, "A Summary of Research and Enforcement Release Evidence on Confirmation Use and Effectiveness," *Auditing: A Journal of Practice & Theory* (November 2008), pp. 253–280, for a discussion of these findings.

EXHIBIT 10-7	Example of a Positive Confirmation Request

CALABRO WIRELESS SERVICES

CWS

Wright Industries
8440 S.W. 97 Boulevard
Starke, FL 32690

Dear Customers:

Please examine the accompanying statement carefully and either confirm its correctness or report any differences to our auditors

Abbott & Johnson, LLP
P.O. Box 669
Tampa, FL 32691

who are auditing our financial statements.
　　Your prompt attention to this request will be appreciated. An envelope is enclosed for your reply. Please do not send your payments to the auditors.

Sincerely,
Jan Rodriguez
Controller, Calabro Wireless Services

_____

Confirmation:

The balance receivable from us for $29,875 as of December 31, 2009, is correct except as noted below:

_____

_____

_____

Wright Industries

Date_____ By _____

EXHIBIT 10-8	Example of a Negative Confirmation Request

CALABRO WIRELESS SERVICES

CWS

Zorcon, Inc.
P.O. Box 1429
Melrose, FL 32692-1429

Dear Customers:

Please examine the accompanying statement carefully. If it does NOT agree with your records, please report any differences directly to our auditors

Abbott & Johnson, LLP
P.O. Box 669
Tampa, FL 32691

who are auditing our financial statements.
　　Your prompt attention to this request will be appreciated. An envelope is enclosed for your reply. Please do not send your payments to the auditors.

Sincerely,
Jan Rodriguez
Controller, Calabro Wireless Services

and the auditor believes that the customers will devote adequate attention to the confirmation. On some audit engagements, a combination of positive and negative confirmations is used to test accounts receivable because of materiality considerations and a mix of customers. For example, positive confirmations may be sent to selected large-dollar customer accounts and negative confirmations sent to a sample of small-dollar customer accounts.

Because positive accounts receivable confirmations require that customers respond to the auditor, any amounts for which responses are not received must be verified by the auditor using alternative procedures. Negative accounts receivable confirmations require a response only when the information about the customer's balance is incorrect. Therefore, a nonresponse to a negative confirmation request is generally assumed to represent a valid account receivable. This can be a major drawback to the use of negative confirmations.

The accuracy of the accounts receivable confirmation request can generally be improved if a copy of the customer's monthly statement is enclosed with the confirmation request.

Timing

Accounts receivable may be confirmed at an interim date or at year-end. Such considerations were discussed in Chapter 6. The confirmation request should be sent soon after the end of the accounting period in order to maximize the response rate. Sending the confirmations at the end of the accounting period reduces the chance of timing differences arising due to processing of purchases and cash disbursements by the customers.

Confirmation Procedures

The auditor must maintain control over the accounts receivable confirmations so as to minimize the possibility that direct communication between the customers and the auditor is biased by interception or alteration of the receivable confirmation by the client. For control purposes, the auditor should mail the confirmations outside the client's facilities. Direct mailing from the public accounting firm's office generally provides the best control. To ensure that any confirmations that are undeliverable by the post office are returned to the auditors and not the client, the confirmations should be mailed in envelopes with the public accounting firm's address listed as the return address. The envelope used by customers for returning the confirmation response should also be addressed to the public accounting firm.[4] The fact that undeliverable confirmations are returned directly to the auditor also provides some assurance that fictitious customers are identified.

The auditor should maintain a record of the confirmations mailed and those returned. When positive confirmations are used, the auditor generally follows up with second, and possibly third, requests to customers who do not reply, in an attempt to increase the response rate to the confirmation requests. In some cases, a customer may respond using electronic media (such as e-mail or fax) or orally. In such situations the auditor should verify the source and contents of the communication. For example, a fax response may be verified by a telephone call to the respondent, and an oral response can be verified by requesting a written communication from the respondent.

Each confirmation exception (that is, difference between the recorded balance and the balance confirmed by the customer) should be carefully examined by the auditor to determine the reason for the difference. In many cases, exceptions result from what are referred to as *timing differences*. Such differences occur because of delays in recording transactions in either the client's or the customer's

---

[4]R. H. Ashton and R. E. Hylas, "The Return of 'Problem' Confirmation Requests by the U.S. Postal Service," *The Accounting Review* (October 1980), pp. 275–85, shows that the U.S. Postal Service does an excellent job of returning undeliverable confirmations to the return address.

TABLE 10–12	Examples of Exceptions to Confirmation Requests

Type of Difference	Potential Cause
Goods not received by customer	Timing difference. Goods delivered to wrong customer. Invoice sent to wrong customer. Fictitious sale.
Payment not recorded in client's records	Timing difference. Payment applied to wrong customer account. Cash misappropriated.
Goods returned for credit by customer	Timing difference.
Processing error	Incorrect quantity or price. Recording error.
Amount in dispute	Price of goods in dispute. Goods do not meet specifications. Goods damaged in transit.

records. For example, the client may ship goods to a customer on the last day of the period and record it as a current-period sale. The customer will probably receive and record the goods as a purchase in the next period. Such situations are not errors and result only because of a delay in recording the transaction. Payment for goods by a customer at the end of the period can result in a timing difference if the customer prepares and records the check in the current period but the client receives and records the check in the following period. Again, the difference in the confirmed amount results from a timing difference. Table 10–12 presents some examples of exceptions and their potential causes.

The need to maintain control over accounts receivable confirmations and responses does not preclude the use of internal auditors in the confirmation process. For example, internal auditors may confirm accounts receivable as part of their normal duties, or they may directly assist the auditor in performing accounts receivable confirmations as part of the annual audit (AU 322). If internal auditors are used in this capacity, their work should be supervised, reviewed, evaluated, and tested by the independent auditor.

Practice
INSIGHT

According to Interpretation No. 1 of AU Section 330, *The Confirmation Process*, properly controlled electronic confirmations may be considered to be reliable audit evidence. If the auditor is satisfied that the electronic confirmation process is secure and properly controlled and the confirmation is directly from a third party who is a bona fide authorized respondent, electronic confirmations may be considered as an appropriate, valid confirmation response. Various means might be used to validate the sender of electronic information and the respondent's authorization to confirm the requested information. For example, the use of encryption and electronic digital signatures may improve the security of the electronic confirmation process. Capital Confirmation Inc. has created CONFIRM™, a secure electronic audit confirmation clearinghouse (see http://www.capitalconfirmation.com). With this service auditors can send and receive confirmations in as little as 24 hours with a very high response rate!

Alternative Procedures

When the auditor does not receive responses to positive confirmations, he or she must apply alternative procedures to determine the existence and valuation of the accounts receivable. Auditors normally send second and third requests; and if necessary, they also perform the following alternative audit procedures:

- Examination of subsequent cash receipts.
- Examination of customer orders, shipping documents, and duplicate sales invoices.
- Examination of other client documentation.

Examination of subsequent cash receipts involves checking the accounts receivable subsidiary ledger for payments of the specific sales invoices included in the customers' accounts receivable balances that were outstanding at the date of the confirmation. If the auditor has obtained evidence that the client's controls are strong for recording cash receipts and the amount collected is a significant portion of the accounts receivable balance, the auditor may stop at this point. If the client's controls are weak, the auditor may extend the testing by tracing the payment in the subsidiary ledger to the cash receipts journal and to the bank statement. If the customer has paid for the goods, the auditor has strong evidence concerning the existence and valuation of the accounts receivable.

If a customer has not paid the accounts receivable, the auditor can examine the underlying documentation that supports the revenue transaction. This documentation includes the original customer order, shipping document, and duplicate sales invoice. If this documentation indicates that the customer ordered the goods and the goods were shipped, then the auditor would have evidence supporting the validity of the accounts receivable. Last, the auditor may need to examine other correspondence between the client and the customer to obtain adequate evidence on the validity and valuation of the accounts receivable.

Practice **INSIGHT**	During a 2008 inspection, the PCAOB inspection team found that a regional accounting firm sent accounts receivable confirmations to selected accounts to test existence. For unreturned confirmations, the firm tested for subsequent cash receipts. However, many of those accounts had not received payment and the firm performed no additional procedures. (PCAOB Release 104-2009-053).

Auditing Other Receivables

[LO 15] Up to this point the discussion has concentrated on trade accounts receivable. Most entities, however, have other types of receivables that are reported on the balance sheet. Some examples include

- Receivables from officers and employees.
- Receivables from related parties.
- Notes receivable.

The auditor's concern with satisfying the assertions for these receivables is similar to that for trade accounts receivable. Typically, each of these types of receivables is confirmed and evaluated for collectibility. The transactions that result in receivables from related parties are examined to determine if they were at "arm's length." Notes receivable would also be confirmed and examined for repayment terms and whether interest income has been properly recognized.

Evaluating the Audit Findings—Accounts Receivable and Related Accounts

[LO 16] When the auditor has completed the planned substantive procedures, the aggregate misstatement for accounts receivable is determined and would include a projection or likely misstatement amount if either statistical or nonstatistical sampling techniques were used. The aggregate misstatement is then compared to the tolerable misstatement. If the aggregate misstatement is less than the tolerable misstatement, the auditor may accept the account as fairly presented. Conversely, if the aggregate misstatement exceeds the tolerable misstatement, the auditor may conclude that the account is not fairly presented. For example, in

Chapter 3, a tolerable misstatement for EarthWear was $900,000. Suppose that, after completing the substantive procedures, EarthWear's auditor determines that the aggregate misstatement is $250,000. In this case, the auditor may conclude that EarthWear's accounts receivable are not materially misstated. However, if the aggregate misstatement is $975,000, the auditor's conclusion will be that the account is materially misstated.

The auditor should also analyze the misstatements discovered through substantive procedures. In some instances, these misstatements may provide additional evidence on control risk. By identifying the causes of the misstatements, the auditor may determine that the original assessment of control risk was too low. For example, the auditor may lower his or her evaluation of the effectiveness of the control for granting credit (that is, may increase control risk) based on a large number of misstatements detected during tests of the allowance for uncollectible accounts. This may impact the auditor's assessment of audit risk.

If the auditor concludes that audit risk is unacceptably high, additional audit procedures should be performed, the client should adjust the related financial statement accounts to an acceptable level, or a qualified report should be issued. In the previous example, in which EarthWear's auditor determined that the aggregate misstatement was $975,000, additional audit procedures might be required. Such audit procedures would typically be directed at the *systematic* errors detected by the substantive procedures. For example, if the substantive tests of transactions indicated that sales invoices were priced incorrectly, the auditor's additional audit procedures would focus on determining the extent of pricing misstatements. Alternatively, the auditor could conclude that accounts receivable are fairly presented if EarthWear's management adjusts the financial statements by $75,000 or more ($975,000 − $900,000). While clients will typically make the full adjustment, an adjustment of at least $75,000 would result in the aggregate misstatement being equal to or less than the tolerable misstatement of $900,000.

In summary, the final decision about accounts receivable and the related accounts is based on whether sufficient appropriate evidence has been obtained from the substantive tests conducted.

KEY TERMS

Analytical procedures. Evaluations of financial information made by a study of plausible relationships among both financial and nonfinancial data.

Application controls. Controls that apply to the processing of specific computer applications and are part of the computer programs used in the accounting system.

Assertions. Expressed or implied representations by management that are reflected in the financial statement components.

Confirmation. The process of obtaining and evaluating direct communication from a third party in response to a request for information about a particular item affecting financial statement assertions.

General controls. Controls that relate to the overall information processing environment and have a pervasive effect on the entity's computer operations.

Lapping. The process of covering a cash shortage by applying cash from one customer's accounts receivable against another customer's accounts receivable.

Negative confirmation. A confirmation request to which the recipient responds only if the amount or information stated is incorrect.

Positive confirmation. A confirmation request to which the recipient responds whether or not he or she agrees with the amount or information stated.

Reliance strategy. The auditor's decision to rely on the entity's controls, test those controls, and reduce the direct tests of the financial statement accounts.
Substantive tests of transactions. Tests to detect errors or fraud in individual transactions.
Tests of controls. Audit procedures performed to test the operating effectiveness of controls in preventing or detecting material misstatements at the relevant assertion level.
Tests of details of account balances and disclosures. Tests that concentrate on the details of amounts contained in an account balance and in disclosures.

www.mhhe.com/ messier7e	Visit the book's Online Learning Center for a multiple-choice quiz that will allow you to assess your understanding of chapter concepts.

REVIEW QUESTIONS

[LO 1] 10-1 Accounting standards require that revenue must be *realized* or *realizable* and *earned* before it can be recognized. Discuss what is meant by the terms realized or realizable and earned.

[5] 10-2 Describe the credit function's duties for monitoring customer payments and handling bad debts.

[5,6] 10-3 When a client does not adequately segregate duties, the possibility of cash being stolen before it is recorded is increased. If the auditor suspects that this type of defalcation is possible, what type of audit procedures can he or she use to test this possibility?

[7] 10-4 The auditor needs to understand how selected inherent risk factors affect the transactions processed by the revenue process. Discuss the potential effect that industry-related factors and misstatements detected in prior periods have on the inherent risk assessment for the revenue process.

[8] 10-5 In understanding the accounting system in the revenue process, the auditor typically performs a walkthrough to gain knowledge of the system. What knowledge should the auditor try to obtain about the accounting system?

[9] 10-6 What are the two major controls for sales returns and allowances transactions?

[11] 10-7 List four analytical procedures that can be used to test revenue-related accounts. What potential misstatements are indicated by each of these analytical procedures?

[13] 10-8 Describe how the auditor verifies the accuracy of the aged trial balance.

[14] 10-9 List and discuss the three factors mentioned in the chapter that may affect the reliability of confirmations of accounts receivable.

[14] 10-10 Distinguish between positive and negative confirmations. Under what circumstances would positive confirmations be more appropriate than negative confirmations?

[15] 10-11 Identify three other types of receivables the auditor should examine. What audit procedures would typically be used to audit other receivables?

MULTIPLE-CHOICE QUESTIONS

[2,6] 10-12 For the control activities to be effective, employees maintaining the accounts receivable subsidiary ledger should not also approve
a. Employee overtime wages.
b. Credit granted to customers.

c. Write-offs of customer accounts.

d. Cash disbursements.

[2,8,9]   10-13   Which of the following controls is most likely to help ensure that all credit revenue transactions of an entity are recorded?

a. The billing department supervisor sends a copy of each approved sales order to the credit department for comparison to the customer's authorized credit limit and current account balance.

b. The accounting department supervisor independently reconciles the accounts receivable subsidiary ledger to the accounts receivable control account each month.

c. The accounting department supervisor controls the mailing of monthly statements to customers and investigates any differences reported by customers.

d. The billing department supervisor matches prenumbered shipping documents with entries in the sales journal.

[2,6,9]   10-14   Which of the following internal controls would be most likely to deter the lapping of collections from customers?

a. Independent internal verification of dates of entry in the cash receipts journal with dates of daily cash summaries.

b. Authorization of write-offs of uncollectible accounts by a supervisor independent of the credit approval function.

c. Segregation of duties between receiving cash and posting the accounts receivable ledger.

d. Supervisory comparison of the daily cash summary with the sum of the cash receipts journal entries.

[2,9]   10-15   Smith Corporation has numerous customers. A customer file is kept on disk. Each customer file contains a name, an address, a credit limit, and an account balance. The auditor wishes to test this file to determine whether credit limits are being exceeded. The best procedure for the auditor to follow would be to

a. Develop test data that would cause some account balances to exceed the credit limit and determine if the system properly detects such situations.

b. Develop a program to compare credit limits with account balances and print out the details of any account with a balance exceeding its credit limit.

c. Request a printout of all account balances so that they can be manually checked against the credit limits.

d. Request a printout of a sample of account balances so that they can be individually checked against the respective credit limits.

[2,9]   10-16   Cash receipts from sales on account have been misappropriated. Which of the following acts would conceal this defalcation and be least likely to be detected by an auditor?

a. Understating the sales journal.

b. Overstating the accounts receivable control account.

c. Overstating the accounts receivable subsidiary ledger.

d. Understating the cash receipts journal.

[10]   10-17   If accounts receivable turnover (credit sales/receivables) was 7.1 times in 2009 compared to only 5.6 times in 2010, it is possible that there were

a. Unrecorded credit sales in 2010.

b. Unrecorded cash receipts in 2009.

c. More thorough credit investigations made by the company late in 2009.

d. Fictitious sales in 2010.

[10] 10-18 If the number of days' sales in accounts receivable (365 days/receivables turnover) decreases significantly, which of the following assertions for accounts receivable most likely is violated?
a. Existence or occurrence.
b. Completeness.
c. Rights and obligations.
d. Classification.

[13] 10-19 Which of the following is most likely to be detected by an auditor's review of a client's sales cutoff?
a. Unrecorded sales for the year.
b. Lapping of year-end accounts receivable.
c. Excessive sales discounts.
d. Unauthorized goods returned for credit.

[13,14] 10-20 Negative confirmation of accounts receivable is less effective than positive confirmation of accounts receivable because
a. A majority of recipients usually lack the willingness to respond objectively.
b. Some recipients may report incorrect balances that require extensive follow-up.
c. The auditor cannot infer that all nonrespondents have verified their account information.
d. Negative confirmations do not produce evidence that is statistically quantifiable.

[13,14] 10-21 The negative request form of accounts receivable confirmation is useful particularly when

	The Assessed Level of Control Risk Relating to Receivables Is	The Number of Small Balances Is	Consideration by the Recipient Is
a.	Low	High	Likely
b.	Low	Low	Unlikely
c.	High	Low	Likely
d.	High	High	Likely

[13,14] 10-22 An auditor should perform alternative procedures to substantiate the existence of accounts receivable when
a. No reply to a positive confirmation request is received.
b. No reply to a negative confirmation request is received.
c. The collectibility of the receivables is in doubt.
d. Pledging of the receivables is probable.

[13,16] 10-23 In evaluating the adequacy of the allowance for doubtful accounts, an auditor most likely reviews the entity's aging of receivables to support management's financial statement assertion of
a. Existence.
b. Valuation and allocation.
c. Completeness.
d. Rights and obligations.

PROBLEMS

[1] 10-24 For each of the following situations based on SAB No. 101, indicate how and/or when the client should recognize the revenue. Justify your decision.
1. Your client, Thomson Telecom, maintains an inventory of telecommunications equipment. Bayone Telephone Company placed an order for 10 new transformers valued at $5 million, and Thomson delivered them just prior to December 31. Thomson's normal business practice for this

class of customer is to enter into a written sales agreement that requires the signatures of all the authorized representatives of Thomson and its customer before the contract is binding. However, Bayone has not signed the sales agreement because it is awaiting the requisite approval by the legal department. Bayone's purchasing department has orally agreed to the contract, and the purchasing manager has assured you that the contract will be approved the first week of next year.

2. Best Products is a retailer of appliances that offers "layaway" sales to its customers twice a year. Best retains the merchandise, sets it aside in its inventory, and collects a cash deposit from the customer. The customer signs an installment note at the time the initial deposit is received, but no payments are due until 30 days after delivery.

3. Dave's Discount Stores is a discount retailer who generates revenue from the sale of membership fees it charges customers to shop at its stores. The membership arrangement requires the customer to pay the entire membership fee (usually $48) at the beginning of the arrangement. However, the customer can unilaterally cancel the membership arrangement and receive a refund of the unused portion. Based on past experiences, Dave's estimates that 35 percent of the customers will cancel their memberships before the end of the contract.

[2,5,6,9]   **10-25**   The Art Appreciation Society operates a museum for the benefit and enjoyment of the community. During the hours the museum is open to the public, two clerks who are positioned at the entrance collect a five-dollar admission fee from each nonmember patron. Members of the Art Appreciation Society are permitted to enter free of charge upon presentation of their membership cards.

At the end of each day one of the clerks delivers the proceeds to the treasurer. The treasurer counts the cash in the presence of the clerk and places it in a safe. Each Friday afternoon the treasurer and one of the clerks deliver all cash held in the safe to the bank and receive an authenticated deposit slip, which provides the basis for the weekly entry in the cash receipts journal.

The board of directors of the Art Appreciation Society has identified a need to improve the internal control system over cash admission fees. The board has determined that the cost of installing turnstiles or sales booths or otherwise altering the physical layout of the museum would greatly exceed any benefits that might be derived. However, the board has agreed that the sale of admission tickets must be an integral part of its improvement efforts.

Smith has been asked by the board of directors of the Art Appreciation Society to review the internal control over cash admission fees and suggest improvements.

Required:
Indicate weaknesses in the existing internal control system over cash admission fees, which Smith should identify, and recommend one improvement for each of the weaknesses identified. Organize your answer as indicated in the following example:

Weakness	*Recommendation*
1. There is no basis for establishing the documentation of the number of paying patrons	1. Prenumbered admission tickets should be issued upon payment of the admission fee.

(AICPA, adapted)

[11,12,13,16] 10-26 Assertions are expressed or implied representations by management that are reflected in the financial statement components. The auditor performs audit procedures to gather evidence to test those assertions.

Required:
Your client is All's Fair Appliance Company, an appliance wholesaler. Select the most appropriate audit procedure from the following list and enter the number in the appropriate place on the grid. (An audit procedure may be selected once, more than once, or not at all.)

Audit Procedure:
1. Review of bank confirmations and loan agreements.
2. Review of drafts of the financial statements.
3. Selection of a sample of revenue transactions and determination that they have been included in the sales journal and accounts receivable subsidiary ledger.
4. Selection of a sample of shipping documents for a few days before and after year-end.
5. Confirmation of accounts receivable.
6. Review of aging of accounts receivable with the credit manager.

Assertion	Audit Procedure
a. Ensure that the entity has legal title to accounts receivable (rights and obligations).	
b. Confirm that recorded accounts receivable include all amounts owed to the client (completeness).	
c. Verify that all accounts receivable are recorded in the correct period (cutoff).	
d. Confirm that the allowance for uncollectible accounts is properly stated (valuation and allocation).	
e. Confirm that recorded accounts receivable are valid (existence).	

[13,14] 10-27 Adam Signoff-On, CPA, was auditing Defense Industries, Inc. Signoff-On sent positive accounts receivable confirmations to a number of Defense's government customers. He received a number of returned confirmations marked "We do not confirm balances because we are on a voucher system."

Required:
List three audit procedures that Signoff-On might use to ensure the validity of these accounts.

[13,14,16] 10-28 The "Accounts Receivable—Confirmation Statistics" working paper shown on the next page was prepared by an audit assistant for the 2009 audit of Lewis County Water Company, Inc., a continuing audit client. The engagement supervisor is reviewing the working papers.

Required:
Describe the deficiencies in the working paper that the engagement supervisor should discover. Assume that the accounts were selected for confirmation on the basis of a sample that was properly planned and documented on the working paper.

(AICPA, adapted)

[13,14,16] 10-29 During the year, Strang Corporation began to encounter cash-flow difficulties, and a cursory review by management revealed receivable collection

LEWIS COUNTY WATER CO., INC.
Accounts Receivable—Confirmation Statistics
12/31/09

	Accounts		Dollars	
	Number	*Percent*	*Amount*	*Percent*
Confirmation requests sent:				
Positives	54	2.7%	$ 260,000	13.0%
Negatives	140	7.0	20,000	10.0
Total sent	194	9.7	$ 280,000	23.0
Accounts selected/client asked us not to confirm	6	0.3		
Total selected for testing	200	10.0		
Total accounts receivable at 12/31/09, confirm date	2,000	100.0	$2,000,000✓✶	100.0
Results:				
Replies received through 2/25/10:				
Positives—no exception	44**C**	2.2	$ 180,000	9.0
Negatives—did not reply or replied "no exception"	120**C**	6.0	16,000	0.8
Total confirmed without exception	164	8.2	$ 196,000	9.8
Differences reported and resolved, no adjustment:				
Positives	6φ	0.3	$ 30,000	1.5
Negatives	12	0.6	2,000	0.1
Total	18‡	0.9	$ 32,000	1.6
Differences found to be potential adjustments:				
Positives	2**CX**	0.1	$ 10,000	0.5
Negatives	8**CX**	0.4	2,000	0.1
Total .6% adjustment, immaterial	10	0.5	$ 12,000	0.6
Accounts selected/client asked us not to confirm	6	0.3		

Tick Mark Legend
✓ = Agreed to accounts receivable subsidiary ledger.
✶ = Agreed to general ledger and lead schedule.
φ = Includes one related-party transaction.
C = Confirmed without exception, W/P B-4.
CX = Confirmed with exception, W/P B-5.

Conclusion: The potential adjustment of $12,000, or .6%, is below the materiality threshold; therefore, the accounts receivable balance is fairly stated.

Index	B-3

---

problems. Strang's management engaged Stanley, CPA, to perform a special investigation. Stanley studied the billing and collection process and noted the following:

- The accounting department employs one bookkeeper, who receives and opens all incoming mail. This bookkeeper is also responsible for depositing receipts, filing remittance advices on a daily basis, recording receipts in the cash receipts journal, and posting receipts in the individual customer accounts and the general ledger accounts. There are no cash sales. The bookkeeper prepares and controls the mailing of monthly statements to customers.
- The concentration of functions and the receivable collection problems caused Stanley to suspect that a systematic defalcation of customers' payments through a delayed posting of remittances (lapping of accounts receivable) is present. Stanley was surprised to find that no customers complained about receiving erroneous monthly statements.

Required:
Identify the procedures Stanley should perform to determine whether lapping exists. *Do not discuss deficiencies in the internal control system.*

(AICPA, adapted)

[13,16]   10-30   You are engaged to audit the Ferrick Corporation for the year ended December 31, 2009. Only merchandise shipped by the Ferrick Corporation to customers up to and including December 30, 2009, has been eliminated from inventory. The inventory as determined by physical inventory count has been recorded on the books by the company's controller. No perpetual inventory records are maintained. All sales are made on an FOB–shipping point basis. You are to assume that all purchase invoices have been correctly recorded.

The following lists of sales invoices are entered in the sales journal for the months of December 2009 and January 2010, respectively.

	Sales Invoice Amount	Sales Invoice Date	Cost of Merchandise Sold	Date Shipped
	December 2009			
a.	$ 3,000	Dec. 21	$2,000	Dec. 31
b.	2,000	Dec. 31	800	Dec. 13
c.	1,000	Dec. 29	600	Dec. 30
d.	4,000	Dec. 31	2,400	Jan. 9
e.	10,000	Dec. 30	5,600	Dec. 29*
	January 2010			
f.	$6,000	Dec. 31	$4,000	Dec. 30
g.	4,000	Jan. 2	2,300	Jan. 2
h.	8,000	Jan. 3	5,500	Dec. 31

*Shipped to consignee.

Required:
You are to ensure that there is proper cutoff of sales and inventory. If an item is not properly recorded, prepare the necessary adjusting entries.

DISCUSSION CASES

[1]   10-31   SEC Accounting and Auditing Enforcement Release (AAER) No. 108 specifies certain conditions or criteria that a bill and hold transaction of a public company should meet in order to qualify for revenue recognition. The AAER also specifies certain factors that should be considered in evaluating whether a bill and hold transaction meets the requirements for revenue recognition. AAER No. 108 states that a "bill and hold" transaction should meet the following conditions:
1. The risks of ownership must have passed to the buyer.
2. The customer must have made a fixed commitment to purchase the goods, preferably reflected in written documentation.
3. The buyer, not the seller, must request that the transaction be on a bill and hold basis. The buyer must have a substantial business purpose for ordering the goods on a bill and hold basis.
4. There must be a fixed schedule for delivery of the goods. The date for delivery must be reasonable and must be consistent with the buyer's business purpose (e.g., storage periods are customary in the industry).
5. The seller must not have retained any specific performance obligations such that the earning process is not complete.

6. The ordered goods must have been segregated from the seller's inventory and not be subject to being used to fill other orders.
7. The equipment must be complete and ready for shipment.

Required:

Identify and discuss the reliability of the types of evidence an auditor would need to determine whether each condition cited above was met for a bill and hold transaction.

[15,16]   10-32   Friendly Furniture, Inc., a manufacturer of fine hardwood furniture, is a publicly held SEC-registered company with a December 31 year-end. During May, Friendly had a flood due to heavy rains at its major manufacturing facility that damaged about $525,000 of furniture. Friendly is insured for the property loss at replacement value and carries business interruption insurance for lost production. The company anticipates that the total insurance proceeds will exceed the carrying value of the destroyed furniture and the cost of repairing the facility will be in the range of $700,000 to $1.75 million. The company believes that the insurance carrier will advance approximately 50 percent of the expected proceeds sometime during July. The company has resumed its operations to about one-half of normal capacity and expects to operate at full capacity by September. The company does not expect to file a formal insurance claim until then because it expects that the entire cost of the business interruption will not be known until September. Friendly expects to receive the proceeds of the settlement from the insurance carrier during its fourth quarter.

The company is in the process of making a stock offering and will file a registration statement with the SEC at the end of July, in which it will present stub period financial statements covering the six-month period through June 30. Based on the minimum amount of the expected proceeds, Friendly would like to recognize a receivable for the insurance proceeds and to report a gain in its financial statements for the period ended June 30. The company would also like to allocate a portion of the expected proceeds to cost of products sold.

Required:

a. How much of the expected proceeds from insurance coverage, if any, should Friendly include in its June 30 financial statements? Justify your answer with relevant accounting pronouncements.
b. Assuming that Friendly records a receivable from the insurance company at June 30 for the proceeds, what type of audit evidence would the auditor gather to support the amount recorded?

INTERNET ASSIGNMENTS

10-33   Visit the Web site of a catalog retailer similar to EarthWear Clothiers, and determine how it processes sales transactions, recognizes revenue, and reserves for returns.
10-34   Visit the SEC's Web site (www.sec.gov) and identify a company that has been recently cited for revenue recognition problems. Prepare a memo summarizing the revenue recognition issues for the company.

HANDS-ON CASES

EarthWear Online	**Tests of Details** Complete tests of details on a sample of accounts receivable confirmations from EarthWear's customers. Quantify and evaluate the results. *Visit the book's Online Learning Center at www.mhhe.com/messier7e to find a detailed description of the case and to download required materials.*

ACL

www.mhhe.com/ messier7e	Visit the book's Online Learning Center for problem material to be completed using the ACL software packaged with your new text.

KAPLAN
CPA Review

www.mhhe.com/ messier7e	**Abernathy and Chapman** This simulation addresses auditor independence, the confirmation process, sample size, and control weaknesses of the revenue cycle. The essay question will test your understanding of the confirmation process. *To begin this simulation, visit the book's Online Learning Center.*

CHAPTER 11

LEARNING OBJECTIVES

Upon completion of this chapter you will

[1] Understand why knowledge of an entity's expense and liability recognition policies is important to the audit.

[2] Understand the purchasing process.

[3] Know the types of transactions in the purchasing process and the financial statement accounts affected.

[4] Be familiar with the types of documents and records used in the purchasing process.

[5] Understand the functions in the purchasing process.

[6] Know the appropriate segregation of duties for the purchasing process.

[7] Understand the inherent risks relevant to the purchasing process and related accounts.

[8] Know how to assess control risk for a purchasing process.

[9] Know the key internal controls and develop relevant tests of controls for purchasing, cash disbursements, and purchase return transactions.

[10] Relate the assessment of control risk to substantive testing.

[11] Know the substantive analytical procedures used to audit accounts payable and accrued expenses.

[12] Know the tests of details of transactions used to audit accounts payable and accrued expenses.

[13] Know the tests of details of account balances and disclosures used to audit accounts payable and accrued expenses.

[14] Understand how confirmations are used to obtain evidence about accounts payable.

[15] Understand how to evaluate the audit findings and reach a final conclusion on accounts payable and accrued expenses.

[16] Understand how to audit the tax provision and related balance sheet accounts.

RELEVANT ACCOUNTING AND AUDITING PRONOUNCEMENTS

FASB Statement of Financial Accounting Concepts No. 5, Recognition and Measurement in Financial Statements of Business Enterprises

FASB Statement of Financial Accounting Concepts No. 6, Elements of Financial Statements

FASB ASC Topic 740, Income Taxes

FASB ASC Topic 850, Related Party Disclosures

COSO, *Internal Control—Integrated Framework* (New York: AICPA, 1992)

COSO, *Enterprise Risk Management—Integrated Framework* (New York: AICPA, 2004)

COSO, *Internal Control over Financial Reporting— Guidance for Smaller Public Companies* (New York: AICPA, 2006)

COSO, *Guidance on Monitoring Internal Control Systems* (New York: AICPA, 2009)

AU 312, Audit Risk and Materiality in Conducting an Audit

AU 314, Understanding the Entity and Its Environment and Assessing the Risks of Material Misstatement

AU 316, Consideration of Fraud in a Financial Statement Audit

AU 318, Performing Audit Procedures in Response to Assessed Risks and Evaluating the Audit Evidence Obtained

AU 322, The Auditor's Consideration of the Internal Audit Function in an Audit of Financial Statements

AU 326, Audit Evidence

AU 329, Analytical Procedures

AU 330, The Confirmation Process

AU 339, Audit Documentation

AU 342, Auditing Accounting Estimates

PCAOB Auditing Standard No. 3, Audit Documentation (AS3)

PCAOB Auditing Standard No. 5, An Audit of Internal Control Over Financial Reporting That Is Integrated with An Audit of Financial Statements (AS5)

PCAOB Proposed Auditing Standards Related to the Auditor's Assessment of and Response to Risk, PCAOB Release No. 2008-006 (October 21, 2008)

Auditing the Purchasing Process

The second major business process focuses on the purchase of and payment for goods and services from outside vendors. The acquisition of goods and services includes the purchase of raw materials, supplies, manufacturing equipment, furniture, and fixtures and payment for repairs and maintenance, utilities, and professional services. This process does not include hiring and paying employees or the internal allocation of costs within an entity. Chapter 12 covers the human resource management process.

This chapter begins by reviewing expense and liability recognition concepts with particular emphasis on the categories of expenses. The framework developed in Chapter 10 on the revenue process is used to present the auditor's consideration of internal control. This framework starts with an overview of the purchasing process, including the types of transactions, the documents and records involved, and the functions included in the process. Inherent risk factors that relate directly to the purchasing process are covered next. Assessment of control risk is then presented, followed by a discussion of control activities and tests of controls. The last sections of the chapter cover the audit of accounts payable and accrued expenses, the major liability accounts affected by the process. Auditing the expense accounts affected by the purchasing process is covered in Chapter 15. While the main focus of this chapter is auditing the purchasing process for a financial statement audit, the concepts covered for setting control risk are applicable to an audit of internal control over financial reporting for public companies under the Sarbanes-Oxley Act of 2002.

Practice **INSIGHT**	The WorldCom fraud exemplified how expenses may be improperly capitalized as assets to inflate net income. WorldCom inappropriately capitalized as assets costs associated with telephone line maintenance that should have been recorded as period expenses. Some common examples of fraudulent capitalization schemes include software development costs, research and development and start-up costs, interest and advertising costs, recording fictitious fixed assets, and depreciation and amortization schemes.

Expense and Liability Recognition

✀ [LO 1]   Many transactions processed through a typical purchasing process involve the recognition of an expense and its corresponding liability. As a result, the auditor should understand the basic underlying concepts of expense and liability recognition in order to audit the purchasing process. FASB Concept Statement No. 6, "Elements of Financial Statements," defines expenses and liabilities as follows:

> Expenses are outflows or other using up of assets or incurrences of liabilities (or a combination of both) from delivering or producing goods, rendering services, or carrying out other activities that constitute the entity's ongoing major or central operations. (¶85)
>
> Liabilities are probable future sacrifices of economic benefits arising from present obligations of a particular entity to transfer assets or provide services to other entities in the future as a result of past transactions or events. (¶35)

An entity's expense recognition policies and the type of expenses involved affect how the transactions are recorded and accounted for in the financial statements. FASB Statement of Financial Accounting Concepts No. 5, "Recognition and Measurement in Financial Statements of Business Enterprises," indicates that expenses can be classified into three categories.

1. Certain expenses can be matched directly with specific transactions or events and are recognized upon recognition of revenue. These types of expenses are referred to as *product costs* and include expenses such as cost of goods sold.
2. Many expenses are recognized during the period in which cash is spent or liabilities incurred for goods and services that are used up at that time or shortly thereafter. Such expenses cannot be directly related to specific transactions and are assumed to provide no future benefit. These expenses are referred to as *period costs*. Examples of such expenses include administrative salaries and rent expense.
3. Some expenses are allocated by systematic and rational procedures to the periods during which the related assets are expected to provide benefits. Depreciation of plant and equipment is an example of such an expense.

In general, the liabilities normally incurred as part of the purchasing process are trade accounts payable. Other incurred expenses are accrued as liabilities at the end of each accounting period. Most expenses recognized are product or period costs.

Overview of the Purchasing Process

✀ [LO 2]   A purchase transaction usually begins with a purchase requisition being generated by a department or support function. The purchasing department prepares a purchase order for the purchase of goods or services from a vendor. When

| **EXHIBIT 11–1** | **Description of EarthWear's Purchasing System** |

The major purchasing activity for EarthWear involves the purchase of clothing and other products that are styled and quality crafted by the company's design department. All goods are produced by independent manufacturers, except for most of EarthWear's soft luggage. The company purchases merchandise from more than 200 domestic and foreign manufacturers. For many major suppliers, goods are ordered and paid for through the company's electronic data interchange (EDI) system. The computerized inventory control system handles the receipt of shipments from manufacturers, permitting faster access to newly arrived merchandise.

Purchases of other goods and services are made in accordance with EarthWear's purchasing authorization policies. Company personnel complete a purchase requisition, which is forwarded to the purchasing department for processing. Purchasing agents obtain competitive bids and enter the information into the purchase order program. A copy of the purchase order is sent to the vendor. Goods are received at the receiving department, where the information is agreed to the purchase order (receiving report). The receiving report is forwarded to the accounts payable department, which matches the receiving report to the purchase order and vendor invoice. The accounts payable department prepares a voucher packet and enters the information into the accounts payable program.

When payment is due on a vendor invoice, the accounts payable program generates a cash disbursement report that is reviewed by the accounts payable department. Items approved for payment are entered into the cash disbursement program, and a check is printed. The checks are sent to the cashier's department for mailing. Final approval for electronic funds transfer for EDI transactions is made by the accounts payable department.

the goods are received or the services have been rendered, the entity records a liability to the vendor. Finally, the entity pays the vendor. Exhibit 11–1 describes EarthWear's purchasing system. Before proceeding, take a moment and review this exhibit. Do any risks seem especially apparent? If so, how might these risks impact the nature, timing, and extent of your audit procedures?

Figure 11–1 presents the flowchart for EarthWear's purchasing system, which serves as a framework for discussing control activities and tests of controls. As mentioned previously, accounting applications are tailored to meet the specific needs of the client. The reader should focus on the basic concepts so that they can be applied to the specific purchasing processes encountered. The following topics related to the purchasing process are covered:

- Types of transactions and financial statement accounts affected.
- Types of documents and records.
- The major functions.
- The key segregation of duties.

Types of Transactions and Financial Statement Accounts Affected
✎ [LO 3]

Three types of transactions are processed through the purchasing process:

- Purchase of goods and services for cash or credit.
- Payment of the liabilities arising from such purchases.
- Return of goods to suppliers for cash or credit.

The first type is a purchase transaction that includes acquiring goods and services. The second type is a cash disbursement transaction that involves paying the liabilities that result from purchasing goods and services. The final type is a purchase return transaction, in which goods previously purchased are returned to a supplier for cash or credit.

| FIGURE 11–1 | Flowchart of the Purchasing Process—EarthWear Clothiers, Inc. |

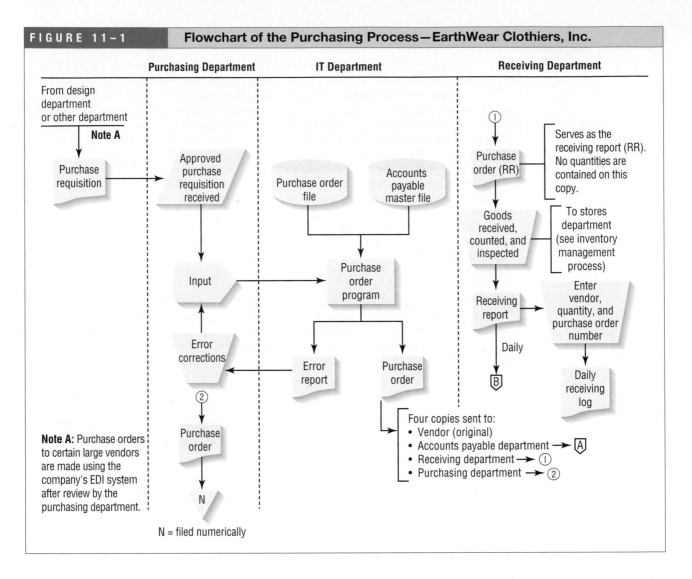

The purchasing process affects many accounts in the financial statements. The more common accounts affected by each type of transaction are

Type of Transaction	Account Affected
Purchase transaction	Accounts payable
	Inventory
	Purchases or cost of goods sold
	Various asset and expense accounts
Cash disbursement transaction	Cash
	Accounts payable
	Cash discounts
	Various asset and expense accounts
Purchase return transaction	Purchase returns
	Purchase allowances
	Accounts payable
	Various asset and expense accounts

Types of Documents and Records

Table 11–1 lists the important documents and records that are normally involved in the purchasing process. Each of these items is briefly discussed here. The use of an IT system may affect the form of the documents and the auditor's approach to testing the purchasing process.

FIGURE 11-1	Flowchart of the Purchasing Process—EarthWear Clothiers, Inc. (*continued*)

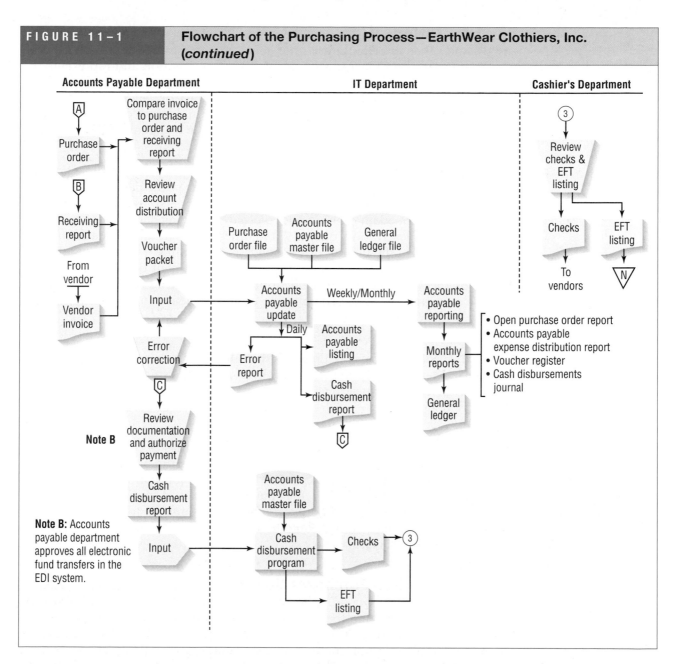

TABLE 11-1	Documents and Records Involved in the Purchasing Process

Purchase requisition.	Voucher register/purchases journal.
Purchase order.	Accounts payable subsidiary ledger.
Receiving report.	Vendor statement.
Vendor invoice.	Check/EFT.
Voucher.	Cash disbursements journal/check register.

✂ **[LO 4]** **Purchase Requisition** This document requests goods or services for an authorized individual or department within the entity. Examples of such requests include an order for supplies from an office supervisor and an order for newspaper advertising space from a marketing manager. In EarthWear's purchasing system, the design department would generate purchase requisitions to acquire goods for sale.

Purchase Order   This document includes the description, quality, and quantity of, and other information on, the goods or services being purchased. The purchase order also indicates who approved the acquisition and represents the authorization to purchase the goods or services. The purchase order may be mailed, faxed, or placed by telephone with the supplier or vendor. At EarthWear some purchase orders may be generated by the design department, reviewed by a purchasing agent, and then sent to a vendor using the company's EDI system.

Receiving Report   This document records the receipt of goods. Normally, the receiving report is a copy of the purchase order with the quantities omitted. This procedure encourages receiving department personnel to make an adequate, independent count of the goods received. Receiving department personnel record the date, description, quantity, and other information on this document. In some instances, the quality of the goods is determined by receiving department personnel. In other cases, an inspection department determines whether the goods meet the required specifications. The receiving report is important because receiving goods is generally the event that leads to recognition of the liability by the entity.

Vendor Invoice   This document is the bill from the vendor. The vendor invoice includes the description and quantity of the goods shipped or services provided, the price including freight, the terms of trade including cash discounts, and the date billed.

Voucher   This document is frequently used by entities to control payment for acquired goods and services. This document serves as the basis for recording a vendor's invoice in the voucher register or purchases journal. In many purchasing systems, such as EarthWear's, the voucher is attached to the purchase requisition, purchase order, receiving report, and vendor invoice to create a *voucher packet*. The voucher packet thus contains all the relevant documentation supporting a purchase transaction.

Voucher Register/Purchases Journal   A voucher register is used to record the vouchers for goods and services. The voucher register contains numerous columns for recording the account classifications for the goods or services, including a column for recording credits to accounts payable, and columns for recording debits to asset accounts such as inventory and expense accounts such as repairs and maintenance. The voucher register also contains columns for miscellaneous debits and credits. Some entities use a purchases journal instead of a voucher register. With a purchases journal, either vouchers or vendors' invoices may be used to record the liability. The major difference between a voucher register and a purchases journal is in the way individual vouchers or vendor invoices are summarized. When a voucher register is used, the details of accounts payable are normally represented by a list of unpaid vouchers. With a purchases journal, subsidiary records are normally maintained by the vendor in much the same manner as an accounts receivable subsidiary ledger. However, with computerization of accounts payable records, such distinctions are disappearing. By assigning a vendor number to each voucher, the voucher register can be sorted by vendor to produce a subsidiary ledger for accounts payable.

Accounts Payable Subsidiary Ledger   When a purchases journal is utilized, this subsidiary ledger records the transactions with, and the balance owed to, a vendor. When a voucher register system is used, the subsidiary ledger is a listing of the unpaid vouchers. The total in the subsidiary ledger should equal the balance in the general ledger accounts payable account.

Vendor Statement   This statement is sent monthly by the vendor to indicate the beginning balance, current-period purchases and payments, and the ending balance. The vendor's statement represents the purchase activity recorded on the vendor's records. It may differ from the client's records because of errors or, more often, timing differences due to delays in shipping goods or recording cash receipts. The client verifies the accuracy of its records by comparing vendor statements with the accounts payable records.

Check or Electronic Funds Transfer (EFT) Listing   These disbursements, signed by an authorized individual, pays for goods or services. Additionally, goods and services may be paid for through electronic transfer of funds.

Cash Disbursements Journal/Check Register   This journal records disbursements made by check. It is sometimes referred to as a *check register*. The cash disbursements journal contains columns for recording credits to cash and debits to accounts payable and cash discounts. Columns may also record miscellaneous debits and credits. Payments recorded in the cash disbursements journal are also recorded in the voucher register or in the accounts payable subsidiary ledger, depending on which system is used by the entity.

The Major
Functions

[LO 5]

The principal business objectives of the purchasing process are acquiring goods and services at the lowest cost consistent with quality and service requirements and effectively using cash resources to pay for those goods and services. Table 11–2 lists the functions that are normally part of the purchasing process.

Requisitioning   The initial function in the purchasing process is a request for goods or services by an authorized individual from any department or functional area within the entity (see Figure 11–1). The important issue is that the request meets the authorization procedures implemented by the entity. One frequent organizational control is the establishment of authorization dollar limits for different levels of employees and executives. For example, department supervisors may be authorized to acquire goods or services up to $1,000, department managers up to $5,000, and divisional heads up to $25,000, while any expenditure greater than $100,000 requires approval by the board of directors.

TABLE 11–2	Functions of the Purchasing Process	
	Requisitioning	Initiation and approval of requests for goods and services by authorized individuals consistent with management criteria.
	Purchasing	Approval of purchase orders and proper execution as to price, quantity, quality, and vendor.
	Receiving	Receipt of properly authorized goods or services.
	Invoice processing	Processing of vendor invoices for goods and services received; also, processing of adjustments for allowances, discounts, and returns.
	Disbursements	Processing of payment to vendors.
	Accounts payable	Recording of all vendor invoices, cash disbursements, and adjustments in individual vendor accounts.
	General ledger	Proper accumulation, classification, and summarization of purchases, cash disbursements, and payables in the general ledger.

Purchasing   The purchasing function executes properly authorized purchase orders. This function is normally performed by a purchasing department (see Figure 11–1), which is headed by a purchasing manager (or agent) and has one or more buyers responsible for specific goods or services. The purchasing function ensures that goods and services are acquired in appropriate quantities and at the lowest price consistent with quality standards and delivery schedules. Using multiple vendors and requiring competitive bidding are two ways the purchasing function can achieve its objectives.

Receiving   The receiving function is responsible for receiving, counting, and inspecting goods received from vendors. The personnel in the receiving department complete a receiving report that is forwarded to the accounts payable function.

Invoice Processing   The accounts payable department (see Figure 11–1) processes invoices to ensure that all goods and services received are recorded as assets or expenses and that the corresponding liability is recognized. This function involves matching purchase orders to receiving reports and vendor invoices as to terms, quantities, prices, and extensions. The invoice-processing function also compares the account distributions with established account classifications.

The invoice-processing function is also responsible for purchased goods returned to vendors. Appropriate records and control activities must document the return of the goods and initiate any charges back to the vendor.

Disbursements   The disbursement function is responsible for preparing and signing checks for paying vendors and authorizing electronic funds transfers. Adequate supporting documentation must verify that the disbursement is for a legitimate business purpose, that the transaction was properly authorized, and that the account distribution is appropriate. To reduce the possibility that the invoice will be paid twice, all documentation (such as purchase order, receiving report, and vendor invoice) should be marked "CANCELED" or "PAID" by the cashier's department. Finally, the checks should be mailed to the vendor by the cashier's department or treasurer.

If IT is used to prepare checks and EFTs, adequate user controls must ensure that only authorized transactions are submitted for payment. Adequate control totals should also be used to agree the amount of payables submitted with the amount of cash disbursed. Checks over a specified limit should be reviewed. For example, in EarthWear's system (see Figure 11–1), the accounts payable department matches the purchase order to the receiving report and the vendor's invoice. The voucher is then input into the accounts payable program. When the vouchers are due for payment, they are printed out on a cash disbursement report. Accounts payable personnel review the items to be paid and input them into the cash disbursement program. The checks are forwarded to the cashier's department for review and mailing to vendors. If a signature plate is used for signing checks, it must be properly controlled within the cashier's department or by the treasurer.

Practice INSIGHT	Fraudulent disbursements may include payments made to shell companies or ghost vendors, commission expense schemes, purchases made by employees for personal benefit, duplicate expense reimbursements, and other fictitious expenses.

Accounts Payable   The accounts payable department (see Figure 11–1) is also responsible for ensuring that all vendor invoices, cash disbursements, and adjustments are recorded in the accounts payable records. In IT systems, these entries may be made directly as part of the normal processing of purchase, cash disbursement, or returns and allowances transactions. Proper use of control totals and daily activity reports provides controls for proper recording.

General Ledger   The main objective of the general ledger function for the purchasing process is to ensure that all purchases, cash disbursements, and payables are properly accumulated, classified, and summarized in the accounts. In an IT system, such as at EarthWear, the use of control or summary totals ensures that this function is performed correctly. The accounting department is normally responsible for this function.

The Key
Segregation
of Duties

✁ **[LO 6]**

As discussed in previous chapters, proper segregation of duties is one of the most important control activities in any accounting system. Duties should be assigned so that no one individual can control all phases of processing a transaction in a way that permits errors or fraud to go undetected. Because of the potential for theft and fraud in the purchasing process, individuals responsible for requisitioning, purchasing, and receiving should be segregated from the invoice-processing, accounts payable, and general ledger functions. If IT is used in the purchasing application, there should be proper segregation of duties in the IT department. Table 11–3 shows the key segregation of duties for the purchasing process and examples of possible errors or fraud that can result from conflicts in duties.

Table 11–4 shows the proper segregation of duties for purchasing and accounts payable functions across the various departments that process purchase transactions. Using this table, briefly analyze EarthWear's flowchart as shown in Figure 11–1. Evaluate whether EarthWear has sufficient segregation of duties and if not, what errors or fraud could occur because of those conflicts of duties?

TABLE 11–3	Key Segregation of Duties in the Purchasing Process and Possible Errors or Fraud
Segregation of Duties	*Possible Errors or Fraud Resulting from Conflicts of Duties*
The purchasing function should be segregated from the requisitioning and receiving functions.	If one individual is responsible for the requisition, purchasing, and receiving functions, fictitious or unauthorized purchases can be made. This can result in the theft of goods and, possibly, payment for unauthorized purchases.
The invoice-processing function should be segregated from the accounts payable function.	If one individual is responsible for the invoice-processing and the accounts payable functions, purchase transactions can be processed at the wrong price or terms, or a cash disbursement can be processed for goods or services not received. This can result in overpayment for goods and services or the theft of cash.
The disbursement function should be segregated from the accounts payable function.	If one individual is responsible for the disbursement function and also has access to the accounts payable records, unauthorized checks supported by fictitious documents can be issued, and unauthorized transactions can be recorded. This can result in theft of the entity's cash.
The accounts payable function should be segregated from the general ledger function.	If one individual is responsible for the accounts payable records and also for the general ledger, that individual can conceal any defalcation that would normally be detected by reconciling subsidiary records with the general ledger control account.

TABLE 11–4	Segregation of Duties for Purchasing and Accounts Payable Functions by Department				
	Department				
Purchasing and Accounts Payable Function	*Purchasing*	*Receiving*	*Accounts Payable*	*Cashier*	*IT*
Preparation and approval of purchase order	X				
Receipt, counting, and inspection of purchased materials		X			
Receipt of vendor invoices and matching them with supporting documents			X		
Coding (or checking) of account distributions			X		
Updating of accounts payable records			X		X
Preparation of vendor checks					X
Signing and mailing of vendor checks				X	
Preparation of voucher register					X
Reconciliation of voucher register to general ledger			X		

Inherent Risk Assessment

✾ [LO 7]   At the beginning of the audit of the purchasing process and its related accounts, the auditor should consider the relevant inherent risk factors that may impact the transactions processed and the financial statement accounts. As mentioned previously, most business risks are viewed as inherent risks. The following factors taken from Chapter 3 should be considered by the auditor in assessing the inherent risk for the purchasing process.

Industry-Related Factors

When auditing the purchasing process, the auditor must consider two important industry-related factors in assessing inherent risk: whether the supply of raw materials is adequate and how volatile raw material prices are. If the entity deals with many vendors and prices tend to be relatively stable, there is less risk that the entity's operations will be affected by raw material shortages or that production costs will be difficult to control.

Some industries, however, are subject to such industry-related factors. For example, in the high-technology sector, there have been situations in which an entity has depended on a single vendor to supply a critical component, such as a specialized computer chip. When the vendor has been unable to provide the component, the entity has suffered production shortages and shipping delays that have significantly affected financial performance. Other industries that produce basic commodities such as oil, coal, and precious metals can find their financial results significantly affected by swings in the prices of their products. Additionally, industries that use commodities such as oil as raw materials may be subject to both shortages and price instability. The auditor needs to assess the effects of such industry-related inherent risk factors in terms of assertions such as valuation.

Misstatements Detected in Prior Audits

Generally, the purchasing process and its related accounts are not difficult to audit and do not result in contentious accounting issues. However, auditing research has shown that the purchasing process and its related accounts are likely to contain material misstatements.[1] The auditor's previous experience with the entity's purchasing process should be reviewed as a starting point for determining inherent risk.

---

[1]For example, see A. Eilifsen and W. F. Messier, Jr., "Auditor Detection of Misstatements: A Review and Integration of Empirical Research," *Journal of Accounting Literature* 2000 (19), pp. 1–43, for a detailed review of audit research studies that have examined sources of accounting errors.

Control Risk Assessment

[LO 8]   The discussion of control risk assessment follows the framework outlined in Chapter 6 on internal control and Chapter 10 on the revenue process. Again it is assumed that the auditor has decided to rely on controls (follow a reliance strategy). Figure 11–2 summarizes the major steps involved in setting control risk for the purchasing cycle.

Understand and Document Internal Control

In order to set control risk for the purchasing process, the auditor must understand the five components of internal control.

Control Environment   Table 6–3 in Chapter 6 lists factors that affect the control environment. Two factors are particularly important when the auditor considers the control environment and the purchasing process: the entity's organizational structure and its methods of assigning authority and responsibility. The entity's organizational structure for purchasing may impact the auditor's assessment of control risk because control activities are implemented within an organizational structure. Authority and responsibility for purchasing are usually granted via procedures that limit the amount of purchases that can be made by various levels of authority within the entity. The remaining discussions of the purchasing process assume that the control environment factors are reliable.

The Entity's Risk Assessment Process   The auditor must understand how management weighs the risks that are relevant to the purchasing process, estimates their significance, assesses the likelihood of their occurrence, and decides what actions to take to address those risks. Some of these risks include a new or revamped information system, rapid growth, and new technology. Each of these factors can represent a serious risk to an entity's internal control system over purchases.

Control Activities   When a reliance strategy is adopted for the purchasing process, the auditor needs to understand the controls that exist to ensure that management's objectives are being met. More specifically, the auditor identifies the controls that assure the auditor that the assertions are being met.

FIGURE 11–2   **Major Steps in Setting Control Risk for the Purchasing Process**

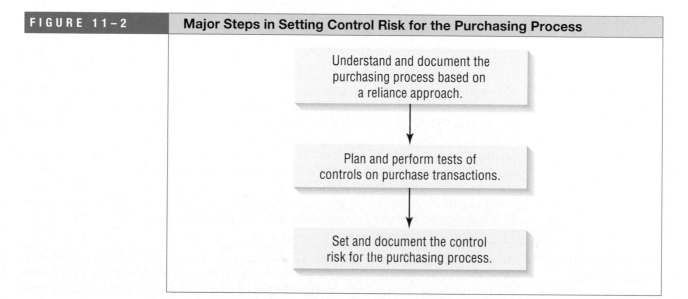

Understand and document the
purchasing process based on
a reliance approach.

↓

Plan and perform tests of
controls on purchase transactions.

↓

Set and document the control
risk for the purchasing process.

Information Systems and Communication   For each major class of transactions in the purchasing process, the auditor again needs to obtain the following information:

- How purchase, cash disbursements, and purchase return transactions are initiated.
- The accounting records, supporting documents, and accounts that are involved in processing purchases, cash disbursements, and purchase return transactions.
- The flow of each type of transaction from initiation to inclusion in the financial statements, including computer processing of the data.
- The process used to estimate accrued liabilities.

The auditor develops an understanding of the purchasing process by conducting a transaction walkthrough. In the case of a continuing audit, the auditor has the prior years' documentation of the process to assist in the walkthrough, although the possibility of changes in the system must be considered. If the system has been changed substantially or the audit is for a new client, the auditor should prepare new documentation of the system.

Monitoring of Controls   The auditor needs to understand the client's monitoring processes over the purchasing process, including how management assesses the design and operation of controls. It also involves understanding how supervisory personnel within the process review the personnel who perform the controls, and evaluating the performance of the entity's IT system.

The auditor can document the purchasing process using procedures manuals, narrative descriptions, internal control questionnaires, and flowcharts. For example, the following partial questionnaire could be used to record the auditor's documentation of the information about the controls in the purchasing process. A "Yes" response would indicate that the control was present.

Question	Yes	No
1. Are there written purchasing policies and procedures?		
2. Are purchase requisitions approved in accordance with management's authorization?		
3. Are purchases made from approved vendors?		
4. Are price quotations requested for purchases over an established amount?		
5. Do purchase orders include adequate descriptions, terms, and instructions?		
6. Are purchase orders approved by authorized personnel before issuance?		

Plan and Perform
Tests of Controls

The auditor systematically analyzes the purchasing process in order to identify controls that ensure that material misstatements are either prevented or detected and corrected. Such controls can be relied upon by the auditor to reduce the control risk. For example, the client may have formal procedures for authorizing the acquisition of goods and services. The auditor may decide to rely on these controls to reduce the control risk for the authorization assertion. Tests of controls would then be necessary to verify that this control is operating effectively. The auditor would examine a sample of purchase transactions to determine if the acquisition of the goods or services is consistent with the entity's authorization policy.

Set and Document
Control Risk

After the controls are tested, the auditor sets the achieved level of control risk. When tests of controls support the planned level of control risk, no modifications are normally necessary to the planned level of detection risk, and the auditor may proceed with the planned substantive procedures. When the tests of controls do not support the planned level of control risk, the auditor must set a higher level of control risk. This results in a lower level of detection risk and leads to more substantive procedures than originally planned.

As discussed earlier, the auditor should establish and document the achieved level of control risk. Documentation of the control risk for the purchasing process might include a flowchart, the results of tests of controls, and a memorandum indicating the auditor's overall conclusion about the control risk.

Control Activities and Tests of Controls—Purchase Transactions

[LO 9] Table 11–5 presents the assertions about transactions and events, while Table 11–6 summarizes the assertions for purchase transactions along with some examples of possible misstatements. For each of these misstatements we have included one or two possible control activities that management could implement to mitigate the risk as well as some example tests of controls that the auditor could use to test those controls. This table is not an exhaustive list of misstatements, control activities, or tests of controls for purchase transactions; rather it provides some specific examples by assertion to help you understand the underlying concepts. Most of these controls exist within EarthWear's purchasing process (see Figure 11–1). The following sections also discuss control activities and tests of controls that are relevant for EarthWear's purchasing process.

Occurrence of Purchase Transactions

The auditor's concern in testing the occurrence of purchase transactions is that fictitious or nonexistent purchases may have been recorded in the client's records. If fraudulent transactions are recorded, assets or expenses will be overstated. A liability will also be recorded and a resulting payment made, usually to the individual who initiated the fictitious purchase transactions. Proper segregation of duties is the major control for preventing fictitious purchases. The critical segregation of duties is the separation of the requisitioning and purchasing functions from the accounts payable and disbursement functions. If one individual can both process a purchase order and gain access to the accounting records, there is an increased risk that fictitious purchase transactions will be recorded.

The other control activities shown in Table 11–6 also reduce the risk of purchase transactions being recorded without the goods or services being received. Even with proper segregation of duties, no purchase transaction should be recorded without an approved purchase order and a receiving report. The presence of an approved purchase order ensures that the purchase was authorized, and the presence of a receiving report indicates that the goods were received. In an IT

TABLE 11–5	**Assertions about Classes of Transactions and Events for the Period under Audit**

- **Occurrence.** All purchase and cash disbursement transactions and events that have been recorded have occurred and pertain to the entity.
- **Completeness.** All purchase and cash disbursement transactions and events that should have been recorded have been recorded.
- **Authorization.** All purchase and cash disbursement transactions and events are properly authorized.
- **Accuracy.** Amounts and other data relating to recorded purchase and cash disbursement transactions and events have been recorded appropriately and properly accumulated from journals and ledgers.
- **Cutoff.** Purchase and cash disbursement transactions and events have been recorded in the correct accounting period.
- **Classification.** Purchase and cash disbursement transactions and events have been recorded in the proper accounts.

TABLE 11-6		Summary of Assertions, Possible Misstatements, Example Control Activities, and Example Tests of Controls for Purchase Transactions	
Assertion	*Possible Misstatement*	*Example Control Activity*	*Example Test of Controls*
Occurrence	Purchase recorded, goods or services not ordered or received	Segregation of duties	Observe and evaluate proper segregation of duties.
		Purchase not recorded without approved purchase order and receiving report	Test a sample of vouchers for the presence of an authorized purchase order and receiving report; if IT application, examine application controls.
		Accounting for numerical sequence of receiving reports and vouchers	Review and test client procedures for accounting for numerical sequence of receiving reports and vouchers; if IT application, examine application controls.
		Cancellation of documents	Examine paid vouchers and supporting documents for indication of cancellation.
Completeness	Purchases made but not recorded	Accounting for numerical sequence of purchase orders, receiving reports, and vouchers	Review client's procedures for accounting for numerical sequence of purchase orders, receiving reports, and vouchers; if IT application, examine application controls.
		Receiving reports matched to vendor invoices and entered in the purchases journal	Trace a sample of receiving reports to their respective vendor invoices and vouchers. Trace a sample of vouchers to the purchases journal.
Authorization	Purchase of goods or services not authorized	Approval of acquisitions consistent with the client's authorization dollar limits	Review client's dollar limits authorization for acquisitions.
		Approved purchase requisition and purchase order	Examine purchase requisitions or purchase orders for proper approval; if IT is used for automatic ordering, examine application controls.
	Purchase of goods or services at unauthorized prices or on unauthorized terms	Competitive bidding procedures followed	Review client's competitive bidding procedures.
Accuracy	Vendor invoice improperly priced or incorrectly calculated	Mathematical accuracy of vendor invoice verified	Recompute the mathematical accuracy of vendor invoice.
		Purchase order agreed to receiving report and vendor's invoice for product, quantity, and price	Agree the information on a sample of voucher packets for product, quantity, and price.
	Purchase transactions not posted to the purchases journal or the accounts payable subsidiary records	Vouchers reconciled to daily accounts payable listing	Examine reconciliation of vouchers to daily accounts payable report; if IT application, examine application controls.
	Amounts from purchases journal not posted correctly to the general ledger	Daily postings to purchases journal reconciled with postings to accounts payable subsidiary records	Examine reconciliation of entries in purchases journal with entries to accounts payable subsidiary records; if IT application, examine application controls.
		Voucher register or accounts payable subsidiary records reconciled to general ledger control account	Review reconciliation of subsidiary records to general ledger control account; if IT application, examine application controls.
		Vouchers reconciled to daily accounts payable listing	Test a sample of daily reconciliations.
Cutoff	Purchase transactions recorded in the wrong period	All receiving reports forwarded to the accounts payable department daily	Compare the dates on receiving reports with the dates on the relevant vouchers.
		Existence of procedures that require recording the purchases as soon as possible after goods or services are received	Compare the dates on vouchers with the dates they were recorded in the purchases journal.
Classification	Purchase transaction not properly classified	Chart of accounts	Review purchases journal and general ledger for reasonableness.
		Independent approval and review of accounts charged for acquisitions	Examine a sample of vouchers for proper classification.

Note: Receiving reports are used to acknowledge the receipt of tangible goods such as raw materials, office supplies, and equipment. For services such as utilities and advertising, receiving reports are not used.

environment, such as EarthWear's, the auditor can test the application controls to ensure that purchases are recorded only after an approved purchase order has been entered and the goods received. Accounting for the numerical sequence of receiving reports and vouchers can be accomplished either manually or by the computer. This control prevents the recording of fictitious purchase transactions through the use of receiving documents or vouchers that are numbered outside the sequence of properly authorized documents. Cancellation of all supporting documents ensures that a purchase transaction is not recorded and paid for a second time. You should keep in mind that there are some types of transactions that are processed through the purchasing process that will not be accompanied by a purchase requisition and receiving report. For example, services for utilities and advertising would not use a receiving report.

Completeness of Purchase Transactions

If the client fails to record a purchase that has been made, assets or expenses will be understated, and the corresponding accounts payable will also be understated. Controls that ensure that the completeness assertion is being met include accounting for the numerical sequences of purchase orders, receiving reports, and vouchers; matching receiving reports with vendor invoices; and reconciling vouchers to the daily accounts payable report. For example, EarthWear uses control totals to reconcile the daily number of vouchers processed with the daily accounts payable listing.

Tests of controls for these control activities are listed in Table 11–6. For example, the auditor can trace a sample of receiving reports to their corresponding vendor invoices and vouchers. The vouchers can then be traced to the voucher register to ensure that each voucher was recorded. Again, these tests can be performed either manually or with CAATs. If each receiving report is matched to a vendor invoice and voucher and the voucher was included in the voucher register, the auditor has a high level of assurance as to the completeness assertion.

The auditor's concern with the completeness assertion also arises when the accounts payable and accrued expenses accounts are audited at year-end. If the client has strong controls for the completeness assertion, the auditor can reduce the scope of the search for unrecorded liabilities at year-end. This issue is discussed in more detail later in this chapter.

Authorization of Purchase Transactions

Possible misstatements due to improper authorization include the purchase of unauthorized goods and services and the purchase of goods or services at unauthorized prices or terms. The primary control to prevent these misstatements is the use of an authorization schedule or table that stipulates the amount that different levels of employees are authorized to purchase. Tests of controls include examination of purchase requisitions and purchase orders for proper approval consistent with the authorization table. If the client uses a sophisticated production system that reorders goods automatically, the auditor should examine and test the programmed controls. Competitive bidding procedures should be followed to ensure that goods and services are acquired at competitive prices and on competitive terms.

Accuracy of Purchase Transactions

A possible misstatement for the accuracy assertion is that purchase transactions may be recorded at incorrect amounts due to improper pricing or erroneous calculations. The purchase order should contain the expected price for the goods or services being purchased, based on price quotes obtained by the purchasing agents or prices contained in catalogs or published price lists. If the goods or services are purchased under a contract, the price should be stipulated in the contract. For example, an accounts payable clerk should compare the purchase order with the receiving report and vendor invoice (see Figure 11–1) and investigate significant differences in quantities, prices, and freight charges. The accounts payable clerk also checks the mathematical accuracy of the vendor invoice. The auditor's test of controls for this assertion involves reperforming the accounts payable clerk's duties on a sample of voucher packets.

The accuracy assertion is also concerned with proper posting of information to the purchases journal, accounts payable subsidiary records, and general ledger. Control totals should be used to reconcile vouchers to the daily accounts payable listing, or else the daily postings to the purchases journal should be reconciled to the accounts payable subsidiary records. In addition, the voucher register or accounts payable subsidiary ledger should be reconciled to the general ledger control account. If these control activities are performed manually, the auditor can review and examine the reconciliations prepared by the client's personnel. In an IT application, such controls would be programmed and reconciled by the control groups in the IT and accounts payable departments. The auditor can examine the programmed controls and review the reconciliations.

Cutoff of Purchase Transactions

The client should have controls to ensure that purchase transactions are recorded promptly and in the proper period. For example, the client's procedures should require that all receiving reports be forwarded to the accounts payable department daily. There should also be a requirement in the accounts payable department that receiving reports be matched on a timely basis with the original purchase order and the related vendor invoice. In EarthWear's system, the receiving department forwards the receiving report to the accounts payable department daily. Within the accounts payable department, the vendor invoices are matched immediately with the original purchase orders and the receiving reports. The auditor can test these control activities by comparing the date on the receiving report with the date on the voucher. There should seldom be a long period between the two dates. The auditor also wants to ensure that the vouchers are recorded in the accounting records in the correct period. This can be tested by comparing the dates on vouchers with the dates the vouchers were recorded in the voucher register.

Classification of Purchase Transactions

Proper classification of purchase transactions is an important assertion for the purchasing process. If purchase transactions are not properly classified, asset and expense accounts will be misstated. Two main controls are used for ensuring that purchase transactions are properly classified. First, the client should use a chart of accounts. Second, there should be independent approval and review of the general ledger accounts charged for the acquisition. A typical procedure is for the department or function that orders the goods or services to indicate which general ledger account to charge. Accounts payable department personnel then review the account distribution for reasonableness (see Figure 11–1). A test of controls for this assertion involves examining a sample of voucher packets for proper classification.

Control Activities and Tests of Controls—Cash Disbursement Transactions

[LO 9]   Table 11–7 summarizes the assertions for cash disbursement transactions along with some examples of possible misstatements. For each of these misstatements we have included one or two possible control activities that management could implement to mitigate the risk as well as some example tests of controls that the auditor could use to test those controls. This table is not an exhaustive list of misstatements, control activities, or tests of controls for cash disbursement transactions; rather it provides some specific examples by assertion to help you understand the underlying concepts.

TABLE 11-7	Summary of Assertions, Possible Misstatements, Example Control Activities, and Example Tests of Controls for Cash Disbursement Transactions		
Assertion	**Possible Misstatement**	**Example Control Activity**	**Example Test of Controls**
Occurrence	Cash disbursement recorded but not made	Segregation of duties	Observe and evaluate proper segregation of duties.
		Vendor statements independently reviewed and reconciled to accounts payable records	Review client's procedures for reconciling vendor statements.
		Monthly bank reconciliations prepared and reviewed	Review monthly bank reconciliations for indication of independent review.
Completeness	Cash disbursement made but not recorded	Same as above	Same as above.
		Accounting for the numerical sequence of checks	Review and test client's procedures for numerical sequence of checks; if IT application, test application controls.
		Daily cash disbursements reconciled to postings to accounts payable subsidiary records	Review procedures for reconciling daily cash disbursements with postings to accounts payable subsidiary records; if IT application, test application controls.
Authorization	Cash disbursement not authorized	Segregation of duties	Evaluate segregation of duties.
		Checks prepared only after all source documents have been independently approved	Examine indication of approval on voucher packet.
Accuracy	Cash disbursement recorded at incorrect amount	Daily cash disbursements report reconciled to checks issued	Review reconciliation.
		Vendor statements reconciled to accounts payable records and independently reviewed	Review reconciliation.
		Monthly bank statements reconciled and independently reviewed	Review monthly bank reconciliations.
	Cash disbursement posted to the wrong vendor account	Vendor statements reconciled and independently reviewed	Review reconciliation.
	Cash disbursements journal not summarized properly or not properly posted to general ledger accounts	Monthly cash disbursements journal agreed to general ledger postings	Review postings from cash disbursements journal to the general ledger.
		Accounts payable subsidiary records reconciled to general ledger control account	Review reconciliation.
Cutoff	Cash disbursement recorded in wrong period	Daily reconciliation of checks issued with postings to the cash disbursements journal and accounts payable subsidiary records	Review daily reconciliations.
Classification	Cash disbursement charged to wrong account	Chart of accounts	Review cash disbursements journal for reasonableness of account distribution.
		Independent approval and review of general ledger account on voucher packet	Review general ledger account code on voucher packet for reasonableness.

Occurrence of Cash Disbursement Transactions

For the occurrence assertion, the auditor is concerned with a misstatement caused by a cash disbursement being recorded in the client's records when no payment has actually been made. A number of possibilities exist for the cause of this misstatement. For example, a check may be lost or stolen before it is mailed. The primary control activities used to prevent such misstatements include proper segregation of duties, independent reconciliation and review of vendor statements, and monthly bank reconciliations. In the purchasing system shown in Figure 11-1, checks are distributed by the cashier's department, which is independent of the accounts payable department (the department authorizing the payment).

Table 11–7 lists tests of controls that the auditor can use to verify the effectiveness of the client's controls. For example, the auditor can observe and evaluate the client's segregation of duties and review the client's procedures for reconciling vendor statements and monthly bank statements.

Completeness of Cash Disbursement Transactions

The major misstatement related to the completeness assertion is that a cash disbursement is made but not recorded in the client's records. In addition to the control activities used for the occurrence assertion, accounting for the numerical sequence of checks and reconciliation of the daily cash disbursements with postings to the accounts payable subsidiary records (see Figure 11–1) helps ensure that all issued checks are recorded. The auditor's tests of controls may include reviewing and testing the client's procedures for accounting for the sequence of checks and reviewing the client's reconciliation procedures.

Authorization of Cash Disbursement Transactions

Proper segregation of duties reduces the likelihood that unauthorized cash disbursements are made. It is important that an individual who approves a purchase not have direct access to the cash disbursement for it. Additionally, the individuals in the accounts payable department who initiate payment should not have access to the checks after they are prepared. In EarthWear's purchasing process, the purchasing department functions are segregated from those of the accounts payable and cashier's departments.

Checks are forwarded directly from the IT department to the cashier's department for mailing to the vendors. The other major control over unauthorized cash disbursements is that checks or EFTs are not prepared unless all source documents (purchase requisition, purchase order, receiving report, and vendor's invoice) are included in the voucher packet and approved. For EarthWear's purchasing process, a complete voucher packet must be present in order to record the liability and authorize payment.

Accuracy of Cash Disbursement Transactions

The potential misstatement related to the accuracy assertion is that the payment amount is recorded incorrectly. To detect such errors, the client's personnel should reconcile the total of the checks and EFTs issued on a particular day with the daily cash disbursements report. The client's control activities should require monthly reconciliation of vendor statements to the accounts payable records. Monthly bank reconciliations also provide controls for detecting misstatements caused by cash disbursements being made in incorrect amounts. Each of these reconciliations should be independently reviewed by the client's personnel. The auditor's test of controls involves reviewing the various reconciliations.

Two other possible misstatements are of concern with the accuracy assertion: (1) cash disbursements are posted to the wrong vendor accounts; and (2) the cash disbursements journal is not summarized properly or the wrong general ledger account is posted. The reconciliation of vendors' monthly statements is an effective control procedure for detecting payments posted to the wrong vendor accounts. Agreement of the monthly cash disbursements journal to general ledger postings and reconciliation of the accounts payable subsidiary records to the general ledger control account are effective control activities for preventing summarization and posting errors (see Figure 11–1). The auditor's tests of controls would include checking postings to the general ledger and reviewing the various reconciliations.

Cutoff of Cash Disbursement Transactions

The client should establish procedures to ensure that when a check is prepared, it is recorded on a timely basis in the cash disbursements journal and the accounts payable subsidiary records. As shown in Figure 11–1, when a check is prepared, it is simultaneously recorded in the accounting records by the application programs that control transaction processing. The auditor's tests of controls include reviewing the reconciliation of checks with postings to the cash disbursements journal and accounts payable subsidiary records. The auditor also tests cash disbursements before and after year-end to ensure transactions are recorded in the proper period.

Classification of Cash Disbursement Transactions

The auditor's concern with proper classification is that a cash disbursement may be charged to the wrong general ledger account. In most purchasing systems, purchases are usually recorded through the voucher register or purchases journal. Thus, the only entries into the cash disbursements journal are debits to accounts payable and credits to cash. If these procedures are followed, proper classification of cash disbursements is not a major concern.

Sometimes a client pays for goods and services directly from the cash disbursements journal without recording the purchase transaction in the purchases journal. If a client pays for goods and services directly from the cash disbursements journal, controls must be present to ensure proper classification. The use of a chart of accounts, as well as independent approval and review of the account code on the voucher packet, should provide an adequate control. The auditor can review the cash disbursements journal for reasonableness of account distribution as well as the account codes on a sample of voucher packets.

Control Activities and Tests of Controls—Purchase Return Transactions

[LO 9] The number and magnitude of purchase return transactions are not material for most entities. However, because of the possibility of manipulation the auditor should, at a minimum, inquire about how the client controls purchase return transactions. When goods are returned to a vendor, the client usually prepares a document (sometimes called a debit memo) that reduces the amount of the vendor's accounts payable. This document is processed through the purchasing process in a manner similar to the processing of a vendor invoice.

Because purchase returns are often few in number and not material, the auditor normally does not test controls of these transactions. Substantive analytical procedures are usually performed to test the reasonableness of purchase returns. For example, comparison of purchase returns as a percentage of revenue to prior years' and industry data may disclose any material misstatement in this account.

Relating the Assessed Level of Control Risk to Substantive Procedures

[LO 10] The decision process followed by the auditor is similar to that discussed in Chapter 10 for the revenue process. If the results of the tests of controls support the achieved level of control risk, the auditor conducts substantive procedures at the planned level. If the results indicate that control risk can be reduced further, the auditor can increase detection risk, which will reduce the nature, timing, and extent of substantive procedures needed. However, if the results of the tests of controls do not support the planned level of control risk, detection risk has to be set lower and substantive procedures increased.

The main accounts affected by the auditor's achieved control risk for the purchasing process include accounts payable, accrued expenses, and most of the expense accounts in the income statement. Additionally, the tests of controls over purchase transactions affect the assessment of detection risk for other business processes. For example, purchase transactions for the acquisition of inventory and property, plant, and equipment are subject to the controls included in the purchasing process. If those controls are reliable, the auditor may be able to increase the detection risk for the affected financial statement accounts and therefore reduce the number of substantive procedures needed.

Auditing Accounts Payable and Accrued Expenses

The assessment of the risk of material misstatement (inherent risk and control risk) for the purchasing process is used to determine the level of detection risk for conducting substantive procedures for accounts payable and accrued expenses. Accounts payable generally represent normal recurring trade obligations. Accrued expenses represent expenses that have been incurred during the period but that have not been billed or paid for as of the end of the period; these include accruals for taxes, interest, royalties, and professional fees. A number of accrued expenses are also related to payroll. Because there is little difference between accounts payable and accrued expenses, they are covered together in this section.

Substantive analytical procedures and tests of details of classes of transactions, account balances, and disclosures are used to test accounts payable and accrued expenses. Substantive analytical procedures are used to examine plausible relationships among accounts payable and accrued expenses. Tests of details focus on transactions, account balances, or disclosures. In the purchasing process, tests of details of transactions (also called *substantive tests of transactions*) focus mainly on the purchases and cash disbursement transactions. Tests of details of account balances concentrate on the detailed amounts or estimates that make up the ending balance for accounts payable and accrued expenses. Tests of details of disclosures are concerned with the presentation and disclosures related to accounts payable and accrued expenses.

Table 11–8 lists the assertions for account balances and disclosures as they apply to accounts payable and accrued expenses. The reader should note that the auditor may test assertions related to transactions (substantive tests of transactions) in conjunction with testing internal controls. If the tests of controls indicate that the controls are not operating effectively, the auditor may need to test transactions at the date the account balance is tested.

TABLE 11–8	Management Assertions about Account Balances, and Disclosures for Accounts Payable and Accrued Expenses

Assertions about Account Balances at the Period End:
- **Existence.** Accounts payable and accrued expenses are valid liabilities.
- **Rights and obligations.** Accounts payable and accrued expenses are the obligations of the entity.
- **Completeness.** All accounts payable and accrued expenses have been recorded.
- **Valuation and allocation.** Accounts payable and accrued expenses are included in the financial statements at appropriate amounts, and any resulting valuation or allocation adjustments are appropriately recorded.

Assertions about Presentation and Disclosure:
- **Occurrence and rights and obligations.** All disclosed events, transactions, and other matters relating to accounts payable and accrued expenses have occurred and pertain to the entity.
- **Completeness.** All disclosures relating to accounts payable and accrued expenses that should have been included in the financial statements have been included.
- **Classification and understandability.** Financial information relating to accounts payable and accrued expenses is appropriately presented and described, and disclosures are clearly expressed.
- **Accuracy and valuation.** Financial and other information relating to accounts payable and accrued expenses are disclosed fairly and at appropriate amounts.

TABLE 11-9	Examples of Substantive Analytical Procedures Used in Auditing Accounts Payable and Accrued Expenses

Example Substantive Analytical Procedure	*Possible Misstatement Detected*
Compare payables turnover and days outstanding in accounts payable to previous years' and industry data.	Under- or overstatement of liabilities and expenses.
Compare current-year balances in accounts payable and accruals with prior years' balances.	Under- or overstatement of liabilities and expenses.
Compare amounts owed to individual vendors in the current year's accounts payable listing to amounts owed in prior years.	Under- or overstatement of liabilities and expenses.
Compare purchase returns and allowances as a percentage of revenue or cost of sales to prior years' and industry data.	Under- or overstatement of purchase returns.

Substantive Analytical Procedures

✂ [LO 11]   Substantive analytical procedures can be useful substantive procedures for examining the reasonableness of accounts payable and accrued expenses. Substantive analytical procedures can effectively identify accounts payable and accrual accounts that are misstated, as well as provide evidence regarding the fairness of the recorded accounts. Table 11–9 contains some examples of substantive analytical procedures that can be used in the auditing of accounts payable and accrued expenses. Table 11–9 is not an exhaustive list; rather it provides some specific examples by account to help you understand the underlying concepts. Before moving on, calculate the days outstanding in accounts payable (365 days/payables turnover) using EarthWear's financial statements as presented earlier in the book. Do your findings provide evidence in support of the fair statement of accounts payable or suggest that additional audit work is necessary?

Tests of Details of Classes of Transactions, Account Balances, and Disclosures

✂ [LO 12,13]   Table 11–10 presents examples of tests of details of transactions, account balances, and disclosures for assertions related to accounts payable and accrued expenses. This table should not be construed as an exhaustive list of substantive audit procedures for accounts payable and accrued expenses. As discussed previously, tests of details of transactions (substantive tests of transactions) are tests conducted to detect monetary misstatements in the individual transactions processed through all accounting applications, are often conducted at the same time as tests of controls, and are often difficult to distinguish from a test of controls because the specific audit procedure may both test the operation of a control procedure and test for monetary misstatement. Table 11–10 presents a substantive test of transactions for each assertion for purchase transactions. Normally, most of these tests are conducted as tests of controls. However, if the controls are not operating effectively or if the auditor did not rely on those controls, substantive tests of transactions may be necessary for the auditor to reach an appropriate level of evidence. The cutoff assertion is the one that is most often conducted as a substantive procedure.

    The discussion that follows focuses on tests of details of account balances of accounts payable and accrued expenses. We begin with the completeness assertion for the accounts payable balance because the auditor must establish that the detailed records agree to the general ledger. Note that we do not cover all the assertions listed in Table 11–10 because they are not applicable to EarthWear Clothiers or they would have been conducted as tests of controls.

TABLE 11–10	Summary of Assertions and Related Tests of Transactions, Account Balances, and Disclosures—Accounts Payable and Accrued Expenses

Assertions about Classes of Transactions	Example Substantive Tests of Transactions*
Occurrence	Test a sample of vouchers for the presence of an authorized purchase order and receiving report.
Completeness	Tracing of a sample of vouchers to the purchases journal.
Authorization	Test a sample of purchase requisition for proper authorization.
Accuracy	Recompute the mathematical accuracy of a sample of vendors' invoices.
Cutoff	Compare dates on a sample of vouchers with the dates transactions were recorded in the purchases journal.
	Test transactions around year-end to determine if they are recorded in the proper period.
Classification	Verify classification of charges for a sample of purchases transactions.

Assertions about Account Balances	Example Tests of Details of Account Balances
Existence	Vouch selected amounts from the accounts payable listing and schedules for accruals to voucher packets or other supporting documentation.
	Obtain selected vendors' statements and reconcile to vendor accounts.
	Confirmation of selected accounts payable.†
Rights and obligations	Review voucher packets for presence of purchase requisition, purchase order, receiving report, and vendor invoice.
Completeness	Obtain listing of accounts payable and agree total to general ledger.†
	Search for unrecorded liabilities by inquiring of management and examining post-balance sheet transactions.
	Obtain selected vendors' statements and reconcile to vendor accounts.
	Confirmation of selected accounts payable.†
Valuation and allocation	Obtain listing of accounts payable and account analysis schedules for accruals; foot listing and schedules and agree totals to general ledger.†
	Trace selected items from the accounts payable listing to the subsidiary records† and voucher packets.
	Review results of confirmations of selected accounts payable.
	Obtain selected vendors' statements and reconcile to vendor accounts.

Assertions about Presentation and Disclosure	Example Tests of Details of Disclosures
Occurrence and rights and obligations	Inquire about accounts payable and accrued expenses to ensure that they are properly disclosed.
Completeness	Complete financial reporting checklist to ensure that all financial statement disclosures related to accounts payable and accrued expenses have been disclosed.
Classification and understandability	Review of listing of accounts payable for material debits, long-term payables, and nontrade payables. Determine whether such items require separate disclosure on the balance sheet.
	Read footnotes to ensure that required disclosures are understandable.
Accuracy and valuation	Read footnotes and other information to ensure that the information is accurate and properly presented at the appropriate amounts.

*These tests of details of transactions are commonly conducted as dual-purpose tests (i.e., in conjunction with tests of controls).
†These tests can be conducted manually or using CAATs.

Completeness and Accuracy

The completeness of accounts payable is first determined by obtaining a listing of accounts payable, footing the listing, and agreeing it to the general ledger control account. The items included on this listing are the unpaid individual vouchers (when a voucher system is used) or the balance in the individual vendor accounts in the subsidiary records (when a purchases journal is used). Exhibit 11–2 presents an example of the accounts payable listing for EarthWear in which the information is summarized by vendor from the accounts payable subsidiary ledger. Selected vouchers or vendor accounts are traced to the supporting documents or subsidiary accounts payable records to verify the accuracy of the details making up the listing. For example, the tick mark next to the balance for Aarhus Industries indicates that the auditor has verified the account by tracing the balance to the accounts payable subsidiary records.

For accrued expense accounts, the auditor obtains a detailed account analysis schedule. For example, Exhibit 11–3 shows an account analysis schedule for accrued real estate taxes. The credits to the accrual account represent the recognition of real estate taxes owed at the end of each month. This amount should

EXHIBIT 11–2	Example of an Accounts Payable Listing Working Paper

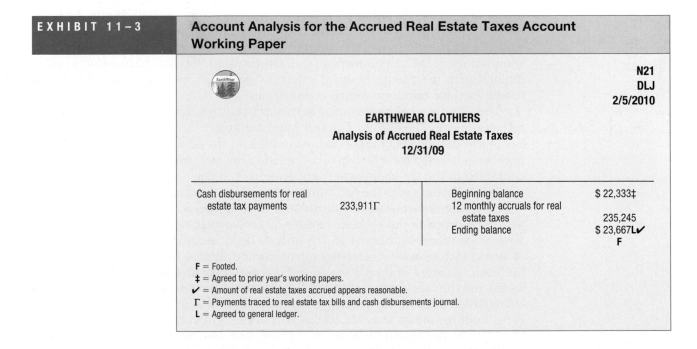

N10
DLJ
2/3/2010

EARTHWEAR CLOTHIERS
Accounts Payable Listing
12/31/09

Vendor Name	Amount Due
Aarhus Industries	$ 52,758†V
Anderson Clothes, Inc.	237,344V
.	
.	
.	
Washington Mfg., Inc.	122,465†V
Zantec Bros.	7,750
Total	$62,509,740
	F T/B

F = Footed.
† = Traced to accounts payable subsidiary records.
V = Voucher packets examined for transaction validity. No exceptions.
T/B = Agreed to trial balance.

EXHIBIT 11–3	Account Analysis for the Accrued Real Estate Taxes Account Working Paper

N21
DLJ
2/5/2010

EARTHWEAR CLOTHIERS
Analysis of Accrued Real Estate Taxes
12/31/09

Cash disbursements for real estate tax payments	233,911Γ		Beginning balance	$ 22,333‡
			12 monthly accruals for real estate taxes	235,245
			Ending balance	$ 23,667L✔
				F

F = Footed.
‡ = Agreed to prior year's working papers.
✔ = Amount of real estate taxes accrued appears reasonable.
Γ = Payments traced to real estate tax bills and cash disbursements journal.
L = Agreed to general ledger.

agree to the amount of real estate taxes expense shown in the income statement. The debits to the account are payments. This schedule is footed and agreed to the accrued real estate taxes account in the general ledger.

The second major test of the completeness assertion for accounts payable and accruals is concerned with unrecorded liabilities. Auditors frequently conduct extensive tests to ensure that all liabilities are recorded. Such tests are commonly referred to as a *search for unrecorded liabilities.* The following audit procedures may be used as part of the search for unrecorded liabilities:

1. Ask management about control activities used to identify unrecorded liabilities and accruals at the end of an accounting period.
2. Obtain copies of vendors' monthly statements and reconcile the amounts to the client's accounts payable records.
3. Confirm vendor accounts, including accounts with small or zero balances.
4. Vouch large-dollar items from the purchases journal and cash disbursements journal for a limited time after year-end; examine the date on each receiving report or vendor invoice to determine if the liability relates to the current audit period.
5. Examine the files of unmatched purchase orders, receiving reports, and vendor invoices for any unrecorded liabilities.

Existence

The auditor's major concern with the existence assertion is whether the recorded liabilities are valid obligations of the entity. To verify the validity of liabilities, the auditor can vouch a sample of the items included on the listing of accounts payable, or the accrued account analysis, to voucher packets or other supporting documents. If adequate source documents are present, the auditor has evidence that the amounts represent valid liabilities (see Exhibit 11–2). In some circumstances, the auditor may obtain copies of the monthly vendor statements or send confirmation requests to vendors to test the validity of the liabilities. Confirmation of accounts payable is discussed later in this chapter.

Cutoff

The cutoff assertion attempts to determine whether all purchase transactions and related accounts payable are recorded in the proper period. While the auditor can obtain assurance about the cutoff assertion for purchases by conducting tests of controls, in most cases cutoff tests are conducted as substantive tests of transactions or as a dual-purpose test. On most audits, purchase cutoff is coordinated with the client's physical inventory count. Proper cutoff should also be determined for purchase return transactions.

The client should have control activities to ensure that a proper purchase cutoff takes place. The auditor can test purchase cutoff by first obtaining the number of the last receiving report issued in the current period. A sample of voucher packets is selected for a few days before and after year end. The receiving reports contained in the voucher packets are examined to determine if the receipt of the goods is consistent with the recording of the liability. For example, suppose that the last receiving report issued by EarthWear in 2009 was number 15,755. A voucher packet recorded in the voucher register or accounts payable in 2009 should have a receiving report numbered 15,755 or less. If the auditor finds a voucher packet recorded in 2009 with a receiving report number higher than 15,755, the liability has been recorded in the wrong period. Accounts payable for 2009 should be adjusted and the amount included as a liability in the next period. For voucher packets recorded in 2010, the receiving reports should be numbered 15,756 or higher. If the auditor finds a voucher packet with a receiving report with a number less than 15,756, the liability belongs in the 2009 accounts payable.

Purchase returns seldom represent a material amount in the financial statements. If the client has adequate control activities for processing purchase return transactions, the auditor can use substantive analytical procedures to satisfy the cutoff assertion for purchase returns. For example, the prior-year and current-year amounts for purchase returns as a percentage of revenue or cost of sales can be compared. If the results of the substantive analytical procedures are consistent with the auditor's expectation, no further audit work may be necessary.

Rights and Obligations	Generally, there is little risk related to this assertion because clients seldom have an incentive to record liabilities that are not obligations of the entity. Review of the voucher packets for adequate supporting documents relating liabilities to the client provides sufficient evidence to support this assertion.

| Valuation | The valuation of individual accounts payable is generally not a difficult assertion to test. Accounts payable are recorded at either the gross amount of the invoice or the net of the cash discount if the entity normally takes a cash discount. The tests of details of account balances noted in Table 11–10 normally provide sufficient evidence as to the proper valuation of accounts payable. |

The valuation of accruals depends on the type and nature of the accrued expenses. Most accruals are relatively easy to value, and proper valuation can be tested by examining the underlying source documents. Real estate taxes and interest are examples of accruals that are generally easy to value. In the first case, real estate appraisals or bills usually serve as the basis for the accrual amount (see Exhibit 11–3). In the second case, the amount of interest accrued relates directly to the amount of debt and the interest rate stipulated in the loan agreement. Other accruals, however, may require the auditor to verify the client's estimates. Auditing standards (AU 342) provide the auditor with guidance in auditing client's estimates. Examples of such estimates include accruals for vacation pay, pension expense, warranty expense, and income taxes. The *Advanced Module* in this chapter provides a discussion of auditing the income tax provision and related balance sheet accounts.

| Classification and Understandability | The major issues related to the presentation and disclosure assertion about classification are (1) identifying and reclassifying any material debits contained in accounts payable; (2) segregating short-term and long-term payables; and (3) ensuring that different types of payables are properly classified. Proper classification can usually be verified by reviewing the accounts payable listing and the general ledger accounts payable account. If material debits are present, they should be reclassified as receivables or as deposits if the amount will be used for future purchases. Any long-term payables should be identified and reclassified to the long-term liability section of the balance sheet. Also, if payables to officers, employees, or related parties are material, they should not be included with the trade accounts payable. The auditor should also ensure that accrued expenses are properly classified. |

| Other Presentation Disclosure Assertions | Even though management is responsible for the financial statements, the auditor must ensure that all necessary financial statement disclosures are made for accounts payable and accrued expenses. Again, a reporting checklist is a useful tool. Table 11–11 presents examples of items that should be disclosed for accounts payable and accrued expenses. |

Two disclosures are particularly important. The auditor must ensure that all related-party purchase transactions have been identified. If material, such related-party purchase transactions should be disclosed. The other major disclosure issue

TABLE 11–11	**Examples of Disclosure Items for Purchasing Process and Related Accounts**

Payables by type (trade, officers, employees, affiliates, and so on).
Short- and long-term payables.
Long-term purchase contracts, including any unusual or adverse purchase commitments.
Purchases from and payables to related parties.
Dependence on a single vendor or a small number of vendors.
Costs by reportable segment of the business.

EXHIBIT 11–4	**A Sample Disclosure for Purchase Commitments**

> The company has various agreements that provide for the purchase at market prices of wood chips, bark, and other residual fiber from trees.
>
> The company also has an agreement to purchase at market prices through 2013 the entire production of an unbleached kraft paper–making machine at Johnson Forest Products Company. The capacity of this machine is estimated to be 30,000 tons a year.

is purchase commitments. When the client has entered into a formal long-term purchase contract, adequate disclosure of the terms of the contract should be provided in a footnote. Exhibit 11–4 provides a sample disclosure for a purchase commitment.

Accounts Payable Confirmations[2]

[LO 14]   Chapter 10 discussed the confirmation process in general and accounts receivable confirmations specifically. This section expands that discussion to include confirmation of accounts payable. Accounts payable confirmations are used less frequently by auditors than accounts receivable confirmations because the auditor can test accounts payable by examining vendor invoices, monthly vendor statements, and payments made by the client subsequent to year end. Because vendor invoices and statements originate from sources external to the client, this evidence is viewed as reliable. However, if the client has weak internal control, vendor statements may not be available to examine. In such a case, confirmations may be used as an important source of evidence.

While accounts payable confirmations provide evidence on a number of assertions, the assertion of primary interest with liabilities is the completeness assertion. If the client has strong control activities for ensuring that liabilities are recorded and the auditor has tested those controls, the auditor may be able to focus on confirmation of large-dollar accounts. However, because the possibility of unrecorded liabilities is usually considered an important concern, the auditor often also confirms balances with regular vendors that have small or zero balances. Small- and zero-balance accounts are confirmed because the client may owe such vendors for purchases but the amounts may not be recorded in the client's accounting records.

When confirming accounts payable, auditors generally use a form of positive confirmation referred to as a *blank* or *zero-balance* confirmation. This type of positive confirmation does not state the balance owed. Instead, the confirmation requests that the recipient fill in the amount or furnish other information. Exhibit 11–5 presents an example of an accounts payable confirmation request. Note that the confirmation requests the balance owed and a detailed statement of the account. The confirmation also requests additional information on notes payable and consigned inventory.

Generally, accounts payable confirmations are mailed at year-end rather than at an interim date because of the auditor's concerns about unrecorded liabilities. The selection and mailing of accounts payable confirmations should be controlled using the procedures outlined in Chapter 10. When accounts payable confirmations are received, the amounts provided by the vendors must be reconciled with the client's records. Differences are often due to the same types of timing differences noted in Chapter 10 for accounts receivable confirmations. The two major timing differences are due to inventory in transit to the client and cash paid by the client but not yet received by the vendor. Any inconsistencies not due to timing differences normally result in adjustments to the client's records.

---

[2]See Professional Issues Task Force, Practice Alert 03-1, Confirmations (June 2007) and Interpretation of AU ¶350 No. 1—Use of Electronic Confirmations (March 2007) for recent guidance on confirmations (www.aicpa.org).

EXHIBIT 11-5	Example of an Accounts Payable Confirmation Request

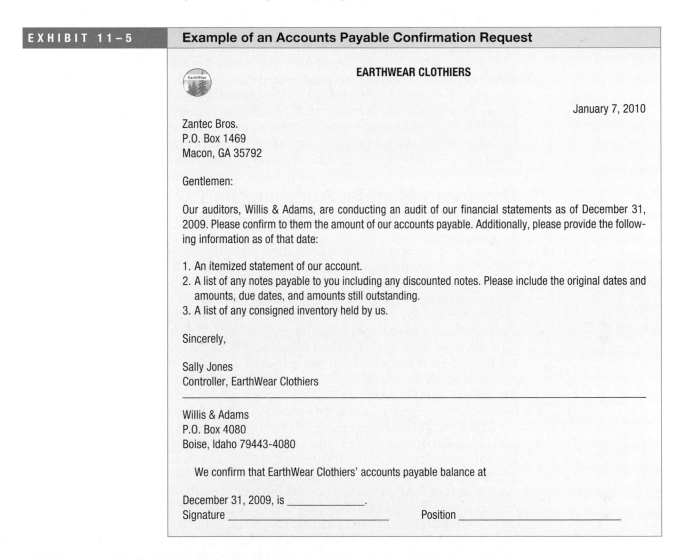

EARTHWEAR CLOTHIERS

January 7, 2010

Zantec Bros.
P.O. Box 1469
Macon, GA 35792

Gentlemen:

Our auditors, Willis & Adams, are conducting an audit of our financial statements as of December 31, 2009. Please confirm to them the amount of our accounts payable. Additionally, please provide the following information as of that date:

1. An itemized statement of our account.
2. A list of any notes payable to you including any discounted notes. Please include the original dates and amounts, due dates, and amounts still outstanding.
3. A list of any consigned inventory held by us.

Sincerely,

Sally Jones
Controller, EarthWear Clothiers

Willis & Adams
P.O. Box 4080
Boise, Idaho 79443-4080

We confirm that EarthWear Clothiers' accounts payable balance at

December 31, 2009, is _____.
Signature _____   Position _____

Evaluating the Audit Findings—Accounts Payable and Related

[LO 15] As discussed in previous chapters, when the auditor has completed the planned substantive procedures, all identified misstatements should be aggregated, including known misstatements detected by the auditor and projected misstatements plus an allowance for sampling risk. The aggregate misstatement is then compared to tolerable misstatement. If the aggregate misstatement is less than the tolerable misstatement, the auditor has evidence that the account is fairly presented. Conversely, if the aggregate misstatement exceeds the tolerable misstatement, the auditor should conclude that the account is not fairly presented.

For example, in Chapter 3, EarthWear's tolerable misstatement was $900,000. Exhibit 3–4 showed that Willis & Adams detected a misstatement in recording inventory that amounted to a $227,450 understatement of accounts payable. Because this misstatement ($227,450) is less than the tolerable misstatement of $900,000, Willis & Adams can conclude that the audit evidence supports fair presentation. However, if the misstatement was greater than the tolerable misstatement, the evidence would not support fair presentation. If the misstatement is greater than the tolerable misstatement, the auditor would have two choices: adjust the accounts to reduce the misstatement to an amount less than the tolerable misstatement, or qualify the audit report.

The auditor should again analyze the misstatements discovered through the application of substantive procedures because these misstatements may provide additional evidence as to the control risk. For example, if most misstatements identified indicate that accounts payable are not properly valued, the auditor may reassess the control activities used by the client for ensuring proper valuation. If the auditor concludes that the audit risk is unacceptably high, additional audit procedures should be performed, or the auditor must be satisfied that the client has adjusted the related financial statement accounts to an acceptable level. If the client does not adjust the accounts, the auditor should qualify the audit report.

Advanced Module: Auditing the Tax Provision and Related Balance Sheet Accounts

[LO 16]   The tax provision and related balance sheet accounts are usually material elements in the financial statements. The income tax provision (the amount that shows up on the income statement) is an estimate of the taxes that will ultimately be paid to the government on the current-year income reported in the financial statements. The income tax payable is the estimate of the taxes that the entity will actually pay the government based on the taxable income reported in the current-year tax return. Because there are significant differences between how revenue and expenses are treated for financial statements prepared according to GAAP and tax returns prepared according to IRS guidelines, there are significant differences between the current year tax provision and the current year income tax payable. These differences are categorized as either temporary or permanent.

Temporary differences are simply timing differences between the recognition of revenue or expense under GAAP and tax and are ultimately expected to reverse. Permanent differences are fundamental differences in what constitutes revenue or expense for GAAP and tax purposes. For example, interest on municipal bonds is income for GAAP purposes, but the interest is nontaxable income, so this represents a permanent difference between GAAP and tax. Deferred taxes recorded on the balance sheet are the estimate of the tax to be paid or recovered in future periods as a result of reversals of existing temporary book/tax differences.

Another important area in the accounting for income taxes is the consideration of uncertain tax positions that have been taken by the entity on its tax return. For example, an entity may choose to take a research and development credit on its tax return, but there is some uncertainty as to whether the project costs qualify for the credit. FASB ASC Topic 740, "Income Taxes," provides guidance on accounting for uncertain tax positions and requires that the company determine the likelihood that an aggressive tax position would be sustained by the Internal Revenue Service. If there is considerable doubt that the IRS will agree with the entity's position, the entity is not allowed to recognize the related tax benefit (lower income tax expense) in its financial statements. When it is determined that the benefit of an uncertain tax position should not be recognized, the entity records a FIN 48 liability for the amount of the tax benefit included in the tax return.

Properly accounting for the income tax provision and related balance sheet accounts is a complex area as evidenced by the large number of public companies reporting material weaknesses in internal control over financial reporting and financial statement restatements that occurred in the mid 2000s related to the accounting for income taxes.

A few specific examples of tax issues that might arise in a typical multinational corporation are provided below to highlight the complex nature of accounting for income taxes:

- The existence of foreign tax jurisdictions to which GAAP adjustments apply could result in the misstatement of foreign tax expense.

- The recording of and control over intercompany transactions could impact transfer pricing, effective tax rates, or other items in the tax accounts.
- The need to consider the specific tax attributes of transactions included in other areas (e.g., tax-exempt investments, capital transactions, etc.) which impact the tax provision computations.

In order to properly audit the tax provision and related balance sheet accounts, the auditor must be familiar with both the GAAP and tax accounting for revenue and expense items. Because of the technical complexities and ever-changing nature of the guidance in both accounting standards and the tax code, auditors are typically not capable of being expert in both areas simultaneously. In addition, auditors need to stay current in auditing methodology, auditing standards, and changes in information technology. Nonetheless, the auditor is ultimately responsible for opining on the fairness of the financial statements, including the tax provision.

For smaller entities with straightforward tax provisions, the auditor often can obtain sufficient appropriate evidence without the assistance of a tax specialist. However, for most large entities or for entities with complicated tax strategies, the auditor will seek the help of a tax specialist to gather sufficient appropriate audit evidence that the tax provision and related balance sheet accounts are fairly stated.

Examples of indicators suggesting the auditor should involve a tax specialist include:

- Multiple locations with significant foreign operations and related foreign tax credits/deductions.
- Business combinations and/or subsidiary dispositions.
- Material uncertain income tax positions with a governmental authority.
- Significant changes in ownership, business operations or tax status.

The involvement of tax specialists in the audit should take into consideration the complexity of the audit, the experience of both the audit and tax personnel, the size of the client, the sensitivity of historical and current tax issues, and the level of recurring tax involvement with the client. When the auditor determines that a tax specialist should be involved, the specialist will typically help gather evidence relating to the entity's controls and processes in the tax accounting area as well as evidence to support the tax accounts reported in the financial statements. The tax provision process is normally a significant process because of its complexity and importance to external financial reporting. The auditor and tax specialist need to understand the entity's tax provision process in order to identify and test controls that are most relevant to financial statement risks.

While the auditor will not possess as much tax accounting expertise as the tax specialist, the auditor must have enough knowledge of tax accounting and the client's specific tax issues to adequately supervise the work performed by the tax specialist. See additional discussion of the use of specialists in Chapter 5.

Some of the typical procedures that might be applied to the audit of the tax provision by the auditors and/or tax specialist include:

- Compare the size and trend in the tax provision and related balance sheet accounts over time.
- Perform walkthroughs and test the design and operating effectiveness of internal controls over the income tax provision (required for an integrated audit). Identify issues that should be given particular attention in substantive testing and evaluate the client's documentation.
- Document the testing performed to evaluate the design and operating effectiveness of internal controls over the income tax process (primarily integrated audits).

- Test the mathematical accuracy of the computations supporting the tax provision and related balance sheet accounts and vouch underlying data to supporting documentation.
- Identify and test significant permanent and temporary differences in the tax provision calculation.
- Review and evaluate management's position on significant uncertain tax positions for appropriate disclosure and accounting under FASB ASC Topic 740.
- Consider the realizability of net deferred tax assets.
- Test the reconciliation of income taxes payable, deferred income tax assets/liabilities (including any related valuation allowances), and tax liabilities to supporting documentation, including the general ledger, financial statements, and related footnote disclosure.
- Ensure proper documentation in the audit working papers to allow for reperformance of the audit procedures applied to the tax accounts.

KEY TERMS

Analytical procedures. Evaluations of financial information made by a study of plausible relationships among both financial and nonfinancial data.

Application controls. Controls that apply to the processing of specific computer applications and are part of the computer programs used in the accounting system.

Assertions. Expressed or implied representations by management that are reflected in the financial statement components.

Blank or zero-balance confirmation. A confirmation request on which the recipient fills in the amount or furnishes the information requested.

Confirmation. The process of obtaining and evaluating direct communication from a third party in response to a request for information about a particular item affecting financial statement assertions.

General controls. Controls that relate to the overall information-processing environment and have a pervasive effect on the entity's computer operations.

Positive confirmation. A confirmation request to which the recipient responds whether or not he or she agrees with the amount or information stated.

Reliance strategy. The auditor's decision to rely on the entity's controls, test those controls, and reduce the direct tests of the financial statement accounts.

Substantive tests of transactions. Tests to detect errors or fraud in individual transactions.

Tests of controls. Audit procedures performed to test the operating effectiveness of controls in preventing or detecting material misstatements at the relevant assertion level.

Tests of details of account balances and disclosures. Tests that concentrate on the details of amounts contained in an account balance and related footnotes.

www.mhhe.com/ messier7e	Visit the book's Online Learning Center for a multiple-choice quiz that will allow you to assess your understanding of chapter concepts.

REVIEW QUESTIONS

[LO 1]   11-1   Distinguish among the three categories of expenses. Provide an example of each type of expense.

[2,3]   11-2   What major types of transactions occur in the purchasing process? What financial statement accounts are affected by each type of transaction?

[4]   11-3   Briefly describe each of the following documents or records: purchase requisition, purchase order, receiving report, vendor invoice, and voucher. Why would an entity combine all documents related to a purchase transaction into a "voucher packet"?

[5,6]   11-4   List the key segregation of duties in the purchasing process. What errors or fraud can occur if such duties are not segregated?

[7]   11-5   List two inherent risk factors that directly affect the purchasing process. Why should auditors be concerned about issues such as the supply of raw materials and the volatility of prices?

[9]   11-6   What control activities typically ensure that the occurrence, authorization, and completeness assertions are met for a purchase transaction? What tests of controls are performed for each of these assertions?

[9]   11-7   Identify two tests of controls that could be performed using computer-assisted audit techniques (CAATs) for purchase transactions.

[11]   11-8   List two substantive analytical procedures that can test accounts payable. What potential errors or fraud can be identified by each analytical procedure?

[13]   11-9   List the procedures an auditor might use to search for unrecorded liabilities.

[13]   11-10   Identify four possible disclosure issues related to the purchasing process and related accounts.

[14]   11-11   What are the differences between accounts receivable and accounts payable confirmations?

[16]   11-12   What are some of the typical procedures that might be applied to the audit of the tax provision by an auditor and/or tax specialist?

MULTIPLE-CHOICE QUESTIONS

[2,4,9]   11-13   In a properly designed accounts payable system, a voucher is prepared after the invoice, purchase order, requisition, and receiving report are verified. The next step in the system is
    a. Cancellation of the supporting documents.
    b. Entry of the check amount in the check register.
    c. Entering of the voucher into the voucher register.
    d. Approval of the voucher for payment.

[2,4,9]   11-14   When goods are received, the receiving clerk should match the goods with
    a. The purchase order and the requisition form.
    b. The vendor invoice and the purchase order.
    c. The vendor shipping document and the purchase order.
    d. The vendor invoice and the vendor shipping document.

[2,4,9]   11-15   Internal control is strengthened when the quantity of merchandise ordered is omitted from the copy of the purchase order sent to the
    a. Department that initiated the requisition.
    b. Receiving department.
    c. Purchasing agent.
    d. Accounts payable department.

[5,6,9]   11-16   Which of the following control activities is *not* usually performed in the accounts payable department?
    a. Matching the vendor's invoice with the related receiving report.
    b. Approving vouchers for payment by having an authorized employee sign the vouchers.
    c. Indicating the asset and expense accounts to be debited.
    d. Accounting for unused prenumbered purchase orders and receiving reports.

[5,6,9]   11-17   In a properly designed purchasing process, the same employee most likely would match vendors' invoices with receiving reports and also
a. Post the detailed accounts payable records.
b. Recompute the calculations on vendors' invoices.
c. Reconcile the accounts payroll ledger.
d. Cancel vendors' invoices after payment.

[5,6,9]   11-18   For effective internal control purposes, which of the following individuals should be responsible for mailing signed checks?
a. Receptionist.
b. Treasurer.
c. Accounts payable clerk.
d. Payroll clerk.

[4,9,13]   11-19   To determine whether accounts payable are complete, an auditor performs a test to verify that all merchandise received is recorded. The population of documents for this test consists of all
a. Vendor invoices.
b. Purchase orders.
c. Receiving reports.
d. Canceled checks.

[9,13]   11-20   Which of the following audit procedures is best for identifying unrecorded trade accounts payable?
a. Examination of unusual relationships between monthly accounts payable balances and recorded cash payments.
b. Reconciliation of vendors' statements to the file of receiving reports to identify items received just prior to the balance sheet date.
c. Investigation of payables recorded just prior to and just subsequent to the balance sheet date to determine whether they are supported by receiving reports.
d. Review of cash disbursements recorded subsequent to the balance sheet date to determine whether the related payables apply to the prior period.

[9,13]   11-21   Purchase cutoff procedures should be designed to test whether all inventory
a. Purchased and received before the end of the year was paid for.
b. Ordered before the end of the year was received.
c. Purchased and received before the end of the year was recorded.
d. Owned by the company is in the possession of the company at the end of the year.

[13]   11-22   Which of the following procedures is *least* likely to be performed before the balance sheet date?
a. Test of internal control over cash.
b. Confirmation of receivables.
c. Search for unrecorded liabilities.
d. Observation of inventory.

[14]   11-23   When using confirmations to provide evidence about the completeness assertion for accounts payable, the appropriate population most likely would be
a. Vendors with whom the entity has previously done business.
b. Amounts recorded in the accounts payable subsidiary ledger.
c. Payees of checks drawn in the month after year-end.
d. Invoices filed in the entity's open invoice file.

PROBLEMS

[11]   11-24   You are the auditor for KPDZ Corporation. You gathered comparative information for inventory and accounts payable, and calculated the days purchases in accounts payable.

	2008	**2009**
Inventory	$34,270	$57,921
Accounts payable	$ 8,295	$10,628
Days purchases in accounts payable (365 days/payables turnover)	44.2 days	44.6 days

Required:

Prepare a list of possible concerns that you might have about potential misstatements in both accounts.

[2,4,5,6,9]   11-25   The flowchart shown below depicts the activities relating to the purchasing, receiving, and accounts payable departments of Model Company, Inc.

Required:

Based only on the flowchart, describe the control activities that most likely would provide reasonable assurance that specific assertions regarding purchases and accounts payable will be achieved. Do not describe weaknesses in internal control.

(AICPA, adapted)

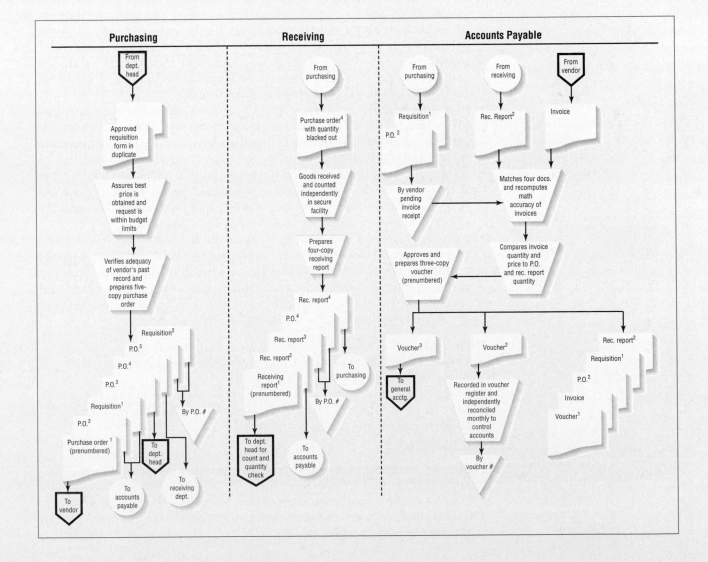

[2,5,6,9]   11-26   In 2007 Kida Company purchased more than $10 million worth of office equipment under its "special" ordering system, with individual orders ranging from $5,000 to $30,000. "Special" orders entail low-volume items that have been included in an authorized user's budget. Department heads include in their annual budget requests the types of equipment and their estimated cost. The budget, which limits the types and dollar amounts of office equipment a department head can requisition, is approved at the beginning of the year by the board of directors. Department heads prepare purchase requisition forms for equipment and forward them to the purchasing department. Kida's "special" ordering system functions as follows:

- *Purchasing:* Upon receiving a purchase requisition, one of five buyers verifies that the person requesting the equipment is a department head. The buyer selects the appropriate vendor by searching the various vendor catalogs on file. The buyer then phones the vendor, requests a price quotation, and gives the vendor a verbal order. A prenumbered purchase order is processed with the original sent to the vendor, a copy to the department head, a copy to receiving, a copy to accounts payable, and a copy filed in the open requisition file. When the buyer is orally informed by the receiving department that the item has been received, the buyer transfers the purchase order from the unfilled file to the filled file. Once a month the buyer reviews the unfilled file to follow up on and expedite open orders.
- *Receiving:* The receiving department receives a copy of the purchase order. When equipment is received, the receiving clerk stamps the purchase order with the date received and, if applicable, in red pen prints any differences between the quantity shown on the purchase order and the quantity received. The receiving clerk forwards the stamped purchase order and equipment to the requisitioning department head and orally notifies the purchasing department.
- *Accounts payable:* Upon receiving a purchase order, the accounts payable clerk files it in the open purchase order file. When a vendor invoice is received, the invoice is matched with the applicable purchase order, and a payable is set up by debiting the equipment account of the department requesting the items. Unpaid invoices are filed by due date, and at the due date a check is prepared. The invoice and purchase order are filed by purchase order number in a paid invoice file, and the check is then forwarded to the treasurer for signature.
- *Treasurer:* Checks received daily from the accounts payable department are sorted into two groups: those over $10,000 and those $10,000 and less. Checks for $10,000 and less are machine-signed. The cashier keeps the key and signature plate to the check-signing machine and records all use of the check-signing machine. All checks over $10,000 are signed by the treasurer or the controller.

Required:
a. Prepare a flowchart of Kida Company's purchasing and cash disbursements system.
b. Describe the internal control weaknesses relating to purchases of and payments for "special" orders of Kida Company for the purchasing, receiving, accounts payable, and treasurer functions.

(AICPA, adapted)

[11,12,13]   11-27   Following are audit procedures that are normally conducted in the purchasing process and related accounts.
1. Test a sample of purchase requisitions for proper authorization.
2. Test transactions around year-end to determine if they are recorded in the proper period.

3. Review results of confirmation of selected accounts payable.
4. Compare payables turnover to previous years' data.
5. Obtain selected vendors' statements and reconcile to vendor accounts.
6. Compare purchase returns and allowances as a percentage of revenue or cost of sales to industry data.

Required:
Identify whether the tests listed above are substantive analytical procedures, tests of details of transactions, or tests of details of account balances.

[11,12,13,14] 11-28 Coltrane, CPA, is auditing Jang Wholesaling Company's financial statements and is about to perform substantive audit procedures on Jang's trade accounts payable balances. After obtaining an understanding of Jang's internal control for accounts payable, Coltrane assessed control risk below the maximum. Coltrane requested and received from Jang a schedule of the trade accounts payable prepared using the trade accounts payable subsidiary ledger (voucher register).

Required:
Describe the substantive audit procedures Coltrane should apply to Jang's trade accounts payable balances. Do not include procedures that would be applied only in the audit of related-party payables, amounts withheld from employees, and accrued expenses such as pensions and interest.

(AICPA, adapted)

[13,14] 11-29 In obtaining evidence in support of financial statement assertions, the auditor develops specific audit procedures to access those assertions.

Required:
Your client is All's Fair Appliance Company, an appliance wholesaler. Select the most appropriate audit procedure from the list below and enter the number in the appropriate place on the grid. (An audit procedure may be selected once, more than once, or not at all.)

Audit Procedure:
1. Compare selected amounts from the accounts payable listing with the voucher and supporting documents.
2. Review drafts of the financial statements.
3. Search for unrecorded liabilities.
4. Select a sample of receiving documents for a few days before and after year-end.
5. Obtain a listing of the accounts payable and agree total to general ledger control account.

Specific Assertion	Audit Procedure
a. Verify that recorded accounts payable include all amounts owed to vendors. (completeness)	
b. Verify that all accounts payable are recorded in the correct period. (cutoff)	
c. Determine whether accounts payable have been properly accumulated from the journal to the general ledger. (accuracy)	
d. Determine whether recorded accounts payable are valid. (existence/occurrence)	

[12,13]   11-30   You are engaged to perform an audit of the Giordani Corporation for the year ended December 31, 2009. You have decided to perform the following cutoff test for payables and accruals: *Select all items greater than $25,000 for two business days before and after year-end from the purchases journal and ensure that all transactions are recorded in the proper period.*

During your firm's observation of Giordani's physical inventory you obtained the following cutoff information: the last receiving report number in 2009 was 49745. Your audit work identified the following items for further investigation:

Selection from the December 2009 Purchase Journal

	Date	RR#	Vendor Name	Amount	Explanation
a.	12/30	49742	Allen Chem.	$29,875	Chemicals purchased for manufacturing process.
b.	12/31	none	Khan Consulting	$45,000	Payment for consulting services for the three-month period beginning December 1, 2009. The $45,000 was charged to consulting expenses.
c.	12/31	49744	Goff Materials	$205,000	Raw materials used in the manufacturing process.

Selections from the January 2010 Purchase Journal

	Date	RR#	Vendor Name	Amount	Explanation
d.	1/02	49746	Temper Trucks	$75,985	Purchase of a new forklift.
e.	1/04	49743	Pack Products	$42,000	Paper products used in manufacturing process.
f.	1/04	none	Telecom Inc.	$32,450	December 2009 telephone bill.

Required:
For each of the six items provided in the table above, consider whether there is evidence of proper cutoff of payables and accruals (i.e., the transaction is recorded in the proper period). If the item is not properly recorded, prepare the necessary adjusting entries at December 31, 2009.

DISCUSSION CASE

[13,14]   11-31   Mincin, CPA, is the auditor of the Raleigh Corporation. Mincin is considering the audit work to be performed in the accounts payable area for the current year's engagement. The prior year's working papers show that confirmation requests were mailed to 100 of Raleigh's 1,000 suppliers. The selected suppliers were based on Mincin's sample, which was designed to select accounts with large-dollar balances. A substantial number of hours was spent by Raleigh and Mincin in resolving relatively minor differences between the confirmation replies and Raleigh's accounting records. Alternative audit procedures were used for suppliers who did not respond to the confirmation requests.

Required:
a. Discuss the accounts payable audit objectives that Mincin must consider in determining the audit procedures to be followed.
b. Discuss situations in which Mincin should use accounts payable confirmations, and discuss whether Mincin is required to use them.
c. Discuss why the use of large-dollar balances as the basis for selecting accounts payable for confirmation might not be the most efficient approach, and indicate what more efficient procedures could select accounts payable for confirmation.

(AICPA, adapted)

INTERNET ASSIGNMENTS

11-32   Visit the Web site of a catalog retailer similar to EarthWear Clothiers, and determine how it processes purchase transactions and recognizes expenses. Note that you may have to examine the entity's annual report and 10k.

11-33   Visit the SEC's Web site (www.sec.gov), and identify a company that has been recently cited for financial reporting problems related to the recognition of expenses. Prepare a memo summarizing the expense issues for the company.

 HANDS-ON CASES

ACL

| www.mhhe.com/ messier7e | Visit the book's Online Learning Center for problem material to be completed using the ACL software packaged with your new text. |

KAPLAN
CPA Review

| www.mhhe.com/ messier7e | **Earhart and King**
This simulation addresses auditing the purchasing process and also reviews certain elements of the revenue process. The essay and research questions discuss the relationship between a principal auditor and other auditors on consolidated financial statements.
To begin this simulation, visit the book's Online Learning Center. |

CHAPTER 12

LEARNING OBJECTIVES

Upon completion of this chapter you will

[1] Develop an understanding of the human resource management process.

[2] Be familiar with the types of transactions in the human resource management process and the financial statement accounts affected.

[3] Know and describe the types of documents and records used in the payroll process.

[4] Understand the functions in the human resource management process.

[5] Know the appropriate segregation of duties for the human resource management process.

[6] Know and evaluate inherent risks relevant to the human resource management process.

[7] Assess control risk for a human resource management process.

[8] Know key internal controls and develop relevant tests of controls for payroll transactions.

[9] Understand how to relate the assessment of control risk to substantive procedures.

[10] Be familiar with substantive analytical procedures used to audit payroll expense and payroll-related accrued expenses.

[11] Be familiar with tests of details of transactions used to audit payroll expense and payroll-related accrued expenses.

[12] Be familiar with tests of details of account balances and disclosures used to audit payroll expense and payroll-related accrued expenses.

[13] Understand how to evaluate the audit findings and reach a final conclusion on payroll expense and payroll-related accrued expenses.

RELEVANT ACCOUNTING AND AUDITING PRONOUNCEMENTS

FASB ASC Topic 715, Compensation—Retirement Benefits

FASB ASC Topic 718, Compensation—Stock Compensation

AU 312, Audit Risk and Materiality in Conducting an Audit

AU 314, Understanding the Entity and Its Environment and Assessing the Risks of Material Misstatement

AU 316, Consideration of Fraud in a Financial Statement Audit

AU 318, Performing Audit Procedures in Response to Assessed Risks and Evaluating the Audit Evidence Obtained

AU 324, Service Organizations

AU 326, Audit Evidence

AU 329, Analytical Procedures

AU 339, Audit Documentation

AU 342, Auditing Accounting Estimates

PCAOB Auditing Standard No. 3, Audit Documentation (AS3)

PCAOB Auditing Standard No. 5, An Audit of Internal Control Over Financial Reporting That Is Integrated with An Audit of Financial Statements (AS5)

PCAOB Proposed Auditing Standards Related to the Auditor's Assessment of and Response to Risk, PCAOB Release No. 2008-006 (October 21, 2008)

Auditing the Human Resource Management Process

Major Phases of an Audit

Client acceptance/
continuance and establishing
an understanding with the client
(Chapter 5)

Preliminary engagement
activities
(Chapter 5)

Plan the audit
(Chapters 3 and 5)

Consider and audit
internal control
(Chapters 6 and 7)

Audit business processes
and related accounts
(e.g., revenue generation)
(Chapters 10–16)

Complete the audit
(Chapter 17)

Evaluate results and issue audit
report (Chapters 1 and 18)

Compensation and related employee benefit costs represent major expenses for most entities. As a result, organizations tend to have strong control activities for processing payroll transactions. Additionally, because of the routine nature of these transactions, an entity's payroll is normally maintained on an IT system, or an outside service bureau is contracted to process the payroll.

This chapter starts with an overview of the human resource management process and then discusses the components of the audit risk model. Specifically, the inherent risks that affect the human resource management process are addressed followed by a discussion of the auditor's control risk assessment. While the main focus of this chapter is auditing the human resource management process for a financial statement audit, the concepts covered for setting control risk are applicable to an audit of internal control over financial reporting for public companies under the Sarbanes-Oxley Act of 2002. Last, the chapter covers substantive procedures for detection risk for payroll and related accounts. The *Advanced Module* contains a discussion of accounting for and auditing share-based compensation.

Overview of the Human Resource Management Process

[LO 1] The human resource process starts with the establishment of sound policies for hiring, training, evaluating, counseling, promoting, compensating, and taking remedial actions for employees. Once an individual has been hired as an employee, the main transaction that affects the financial statement accounts is a payroll (payment) transaction. A payroll transaction usually begins with an employee performing some job and recording the time spent on a time card or time sheet (often in electronic form). The time card or time sheet is approved by a supervisor before being forwarded to the payroll department. The data are then reviewed and sent to the IT department for processing. Finally, payment is made directly to the employee or deposited in the employee's bank account.

 Figure 12–1 presents a flowchart of EarthWear's payroll system that serves as a framework for discussing control activities and tests of controls. Although the description of EarthWear's payroll system is fairly typical, the reader should focus on the basic concepts so that they can be applied to the

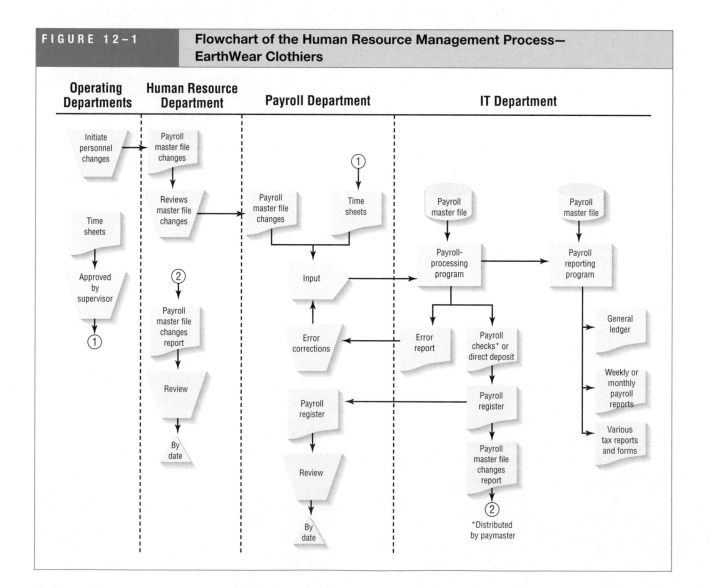

FIGURE 12–1   **Flowchart of the Human Resource Management Process—EarthWear Clothiers**

specific payroll systems encountered. The following topics related to the human resource management process are covered:

- Types of transactions and financial statement accounts affected.
- Types of documents and records.
- The major functions.
- The key segregation of duties.

Types of Transactions and Financial Statement Accounts Affected

✄ [LO 2]

Two main types of transactions are processed through the human resource management process:

- Payments to employees for services rendered.
- Accrual and payment of payroll-related liabilities arising from employees' services, including liabilities for Social Security and unemployment taxes.

The discussion of internal control focuses on payments to employees, including a description of how such transactions are processed and the key control activities that should be present to ensure that no material misstatements occur. The audit of payroll-related accruals is discussed later in the chapter.

The financial statement accounts that are generally affected by the two types of payroll-related transactions are

Type of Transaction	Account Affected
Payroll transaction	Cash Inventory Direct and indirect labor expense accounts Various payroll-related liability and expense accounts
Accrued payroll liability transactions	Cash Various accruals (such as payroll taxes and pension costs)

Types of Documents and Records

✄ [LO 3]

Table 12–1 lists the important documents and records that are normally involved in the payroll application. Each of these items is briefly discussed here. The use of IT systems may affect the form of the documents and the auditor's approach to testing the payroll application.

Personnel Records, Including Wage-Rate or Salary Authorizations
Personnel records contain information on each employee's work history, including hiring date, wage rate or salary, payroll deduction authorization forms, wage-rate and salary adjustment authorizations, performance evaluations, and termination notice, if applicable. Personnel records are normally maintained in the human resource department.

TABLE 12–1	Documents and Records Involved in the Payroll Application
	Personnel records, including wage-rate or salary authorizations W-4 and other deduction authorization forms Time card/time sheet Payroll check/direct deposit records Payroll register Payroll master file Payroll master file changes report Periodic payroll reports Various tax reports and forms

W-4 and Other Deduction Authorization Forms

The employee must authorize deductions from his or her pay. The organization should therefore use authorization forms to document such deductions. For example, the employee must complete a W-4 form to authorize the withholding of federal and state income tax. Similar forms should be used for deductions for medical insurance, retirement contributions, and other benefits.

Time Card/Time Sheet

Such documents record the hours worked by the employee, including the time the employee has started and stopped work. In some cases the employee fills in the time worked (typically in an electronic database); in other cases, the employee swipes an employee identification card, or enters an employee identification number into an electronic keypad, when they arrive and leave work and the time-tracking system records and accumulates the hours worked.

Payroll Check/Direct Deposit Records

These records indicate the amount paid to the employee for services rendered. The amount paid is the gross pay less any deductions. In many cases, the employee's pay is directly deposited into the individual's bank account, and the company produces a listing of employees' payments that were sent to their bank accounts.

Payroll Register

This document, which is also referred to as the *payroll journal*, summarizes all payroll payments issued to employees. A payroll register normally indicates employees' gross pay, deductions, and net pay. In an IT environment, the details for this document are maintained in the payroll master file.

Payroll Master File

This computer file maintains all the entity's records related to payroll, including information on each employee such as name, Social Security number, pay rate, and authorized deductions.

Payroll Master File Changes Report

This report contains a record of the changes made to the payroll master file. The human resource department reviews this report to ensure that all authorized changes have been properly made.

Periodic Payroll Reports

At the end of each week or month, a number of summary payroll reports may be prepared. The type of reports prepared depends on the type of organization. A manufacturing entity might have a payroll expense report that showed the allocation of direct labor to various products. EarthWear Clothiers reports a summary of payroll by various job classifications and departments. Department heads use this report to monitor payroll expense variances.

Various Tax Reports and Forms

Most companies are required to prepare various payroll tax reports for both the federal and state governments. Unemployment compensation forms must also be completed periodically. Additionally, an entity must provide each employee with a W-2 form at the end of the year. Compensation paid to a consultant or independent contractor must be reported on an IRS 1099 form.

The Major Functions

[LO 4]

The principal objectives of the human resource management process are to (1) record production and other types of payroll costs in the accounts; (2) ensure that payroll costs are for legitimate entity activities; and (3) accrue liabilities for salaries and wages, payroll taxes, and various employee benefit programs. Table 12–2 lists the functions that are normally part of the payroll application.

TABLE 12–2	Functions in the Payroll Application
Human Resources	Authorization of hiring, firing, wage-rate and salary adjustments, salaries, and payroll deductions.
Supervision	Review and approval of employees' attendance and time information; monitoring of employee scheduling, productivity, and payroll cost variances.
Timekeeping	Processing of employees' attendance and time information and coding of account distribution.
Payroll processing	Computation of gross pay, deductions, and net pay; recording and summarization of payments and verification of account distribution.
Disbursement	Payment of employees' compensation and benefits.
General ledger	Proper accumulation, classification, and summarization of payroll in the general ledger.

Human Resources   The Human Resources function is responsible for managing the personnel needs of the organization. This includes hiring and terminating employees, setting wage rates and salaries, and establishing and monitoring employee benefit programs. Most large organizations centralize these activities in a human resource department. However, in a small organization, these activities may be combined with the duties of selected operating and administrative personnel. In such organizations, control over human resource activities may not be as strong as when such activities are centralized. The human resource department maintains employees' personnel records. The human resource department may also be responsible for defining job requirements and descriptions, administering union contracts, and developing performance criteria and employee evaluation procedures.

Supervision   Supervisors within operating and supporting departments are responsible for reviewing and approving employees' attendance and time information. When time sheets or other documents are used to record an employee's time worked and job classification, the supervisor approves this information before processing by the payroll function. Additionally, supervisors should monitor labor productivity and labor cost variances. Standardized labor performance measures, such as standard productivity and wage rates, improve the monitoring of payroll costs. Labor cost variances should be investigated by supervisory personnel and communicated to upper-level management. When employees are not required to complete time cards/sheets or job classification documents, the entity needs to have control activities to notify the timekeeping or payroll-processing function about employees' absences and changes in employees' job classifications. This might be accomplished by having the supervisor submit a periodic attendance and job classification report.

Timekeeping   The timekeeping function prepares employees' time information for payroll processing. When payroll cost distribution is determined at the operating department level, the timekeeping function reviews this information before processing. Otherwise, the timekeeping function should be responsible for coding the payroll costs to appropriate accounts. In some organizations, a separate timekeeping department handles these functions. At EarthWear (see Figure 12–1), the operating and supporting departments are responsible for the timekeeping function.

Payroll Processing   The payroll-processing function is responsible for computing gross pay, deductions, and net pay. This function is also responsible for recording and summarizing payments and verifying account distribution. When IT is used to process payroll, as at EarthWear, the entity must have strong application controls to ensure proper payroll processing.

Some entities outsource their payroll processing to a third-party provider such as ADP™. These third-party providers can provide a range of services from basic payroll processing to full human resources services from employee hire to retire. When a client uses a third party to process payroll, the auditor will obtain evidence for important assertions associated with the data transferred to the service provider. The auditor must also consider the third-party services as part of the client's information system. Because the third-party provider provides services to many entities, the third-party provider will obtain a "SAS 70" audit report that the other entity's auditors can rely on (SAS No. 70 provides guidance on auditing service organizations). See Chapter 6 for a discussion of auditing accounting applications processed by service organizations.

Disbursement   The disbursement function is responsible for paying employees for services and benefits. In particular, this function oversees the preparation and distribution of payroll checks. Check preparation normally occurs in the IT department. Therefore, it is necessary to have control activities over access to blank checks and check signature plates. Checks are normally distributed by a paymaster, who is typically a member of the treasurer's department. When payments are directly deposited in employees' bank accounts, strong IT application controls are necessary. If payroll disbursements are handled by a third-party service provider, assurance over IT controls is provided in the SAS 70 report (see Chapter 6).

General Ledger   The general ledger function for the human resource management process is responsible for properly accumulating, classifying, and summarizing payroll and benefit transactions in the general ledger. When IT is used to process payroll transactions, control totals can help ensure that this function is performed properly. This function is normally performed by the general accounting department.

The Key
Segregation
of Duties

✂ [LO 5]

As discussed in prior chapters, proper segregation of duties is one of the most important control activities in any accounting system. Duties should be assigned to individuals in such a way that no one individual can control all phases of processing a transaction, thus permitting misstatements to go undetected. Before reading further, please look back at EarthWear's flowchart in Figure 12–1 in order to identify one or two duties that EarthWear segregates. What might happen if the duties you identified were not segregated?

Individuals responsible for supervision and timekeeping should be segregated from the personnel, payroll-processing, and general ledger functions. If IT is used extensively in the payroll application, duties should be properly segregated in the IT department. Table 12–3 contains some of the key segregation of duties for the human resource management process and examples of possible errors or fraud that can result from conflicts in duties.

Table 12–4 shows more detailed segregation of duties for individual payroll functions across the various departments that are involved in processing payroll transactions.

Returning to your analysis of EarthWear's flowchart (Figure 12–1), we see EarthWear has separated, for example, the supervising function performed by each operating department from the personnel records and the payroll-processing functions, which are performed by the Human Resources and IT departments respectively. For checks, EarthWear has also separated processing and preparation of the checks and distribution. However for direct deposit, IT both prepares and distributes the checks. Although not uncommon, the auditor would want to examine and test controls around the payroll preparation and direct deposit processes, particularly controls designed to ensure distributions are made only to valid employees.

TABLE 12–3	Key Segregation of Duties in the Human Resource Management Process and Possible Errors or Fraud
Segregation of Duties	*Possible Errors or Fraud Resulting from Conflicts of Duties*
The supervision function should be segregated from the personnel records and payroll-processing functions.	If one individual is responsible for the supervision, personnel records, and payroll-processing functions, fictitious employees can appear on the payroll records or unauthorized payments can be made. This can result in unauthorized payments to existing employees or payments to fictitious employees.
The disbursement function should be segregated from the personnel records, supervision, and payroll-processing functions.	If one individual is responsible for the disbursement function and also has the authority to hire and fire employees, approve time reports, or prepare payroll checks, unauthorized payroll checks can be issued.
The payroll-processing function should be segregated from the general ledger function.	If one individual is responsible for processing payroll transactions and also for the general ledger, that individual can conceal any defalcation that would normally be detected by independent review of accounting entries made to the general ledger.

TABLE 12–4	Segregation of Duties for Payroll Functions by Department					
	Department					
Payroll Function	*Operating or Supporting*	*Human Resource*	*Timekeeping*	*Payroll*	*IT*	*Treasurer*
Initiation of wage or salary changes	X					
Initiation of employee hiring and firing	X					
Approval of wage or salary changes		X				
Updating of personnel records		X				
Updating of payroll records		X				
Approval of time sheets and job classification	X					
Review of time data and payroll distribution			X			
Preparation of payroll				X	X	
Preparation and signing of payroll checks					X	
Distribution of payroll checks						X
Updating of general ledger for payroll activity					X	
Comparison of monthly departmental payroll expense to budget	X					
Calculation and recording of payroll taxes				X		

Inherent Risk Assessment

> **[LO 6]**   With the exception of executive and share-based compensation (see Exhibit 12–1 and the *Advanced Module*), few inherent risk factors directly affect the human resource management process and its related accounts for nonofficers. Some factors the auditor might consider are the effect of economic conditions on payroll costs and the supply of skilled workers. EarthWear is a seasonal business and experiences relatively high turnover in its seasonal employees with a workforce that fluctuates between 3,500 and 5,300 employees. How might seasonal employee turnover impact the inherent-risk assessment for payroll? High turnover will increase the inherent risk assessment due to the level of employee additions and terminations and the risk associated with processing. For example, there is a greater risk that pay will be inappropriately dispersed to terminated or fictitious employees. Additionally, the presence of labor contracts and legislation such as the Occupational Safety and Health Act may also affect the auditor's assessment of inherent risk. Because the payroll system and its related accounts generally contain few inherent risks, the auditor is normally able to set the inherent risk as low.

The inherent risk associated with executive compensation is frequently not set at low because, as illustrated in Exhibit 12–1, officers may have motive and

| EXHIBIT 12–1 | **Executive Compensation Abuses at Tyco** |

Tyco International Ltd.'s Dennis Kozlowski looms large as a rogue CEO for the ages. His $6,000 shower curtain and vodka-spewing, full-size ice replica of Michelangelo's David will not be soon forgotten. In essence, prosecutors accused Kozlowski and former Chief Financial Officer Mark Swartz of running a criminal enterprise within Tyco's executive suite. The two were hit with 38 felony counts for pilfering $170 million directly from the company and for pocketing an additional $430 million through tainted sales of stock. Ironically, both Kozlowski and Swartz were former auditors; Kozlowski has become the personification of the widespread irrational exuberance of the late 1990s. Kozlowski handpicked some of the members of the compensation committee, and the changes worked to his benefit as his total compensation rose from $8.8 million in 1997 to $67 million in 1998 to $170 million in 1999. But it appears that Kozlowski believed that he deserved more money than he was making. The more he was paid as a reward for Tyco's soaring stock price, the more he spent on luxuries—and the more he stole. During these years, Kozlowski was secretly selling lots of stock—$280 million worth, according to the Manhattan DA's indictment of Kozlowski.

Kozlowski also ran up a $242 million tab at Tyco under a loan program designed to finance the purchase of company stock. Rather than use the money to buy Tyco stock, he used it to purchase fine art and antiques, a yacht, and a Nantucket estate. The loans were forms of compensation, but characterizing the compensation as a loan provided significant tax and accounting benefits to the executive and the corporation. Tyco's board approved some, but not all, of the forms of compensation Kozlowski had tapped into.

When Congress learned of the level of abuse in corporate loans, it was shocked. In the Sarbanes-Oxley Act of 2002, Congress forbids public companies to make or even arrange new loans to executives or to modify or renew old ones. The penalties for a violation are up to 20 years in jail and fines reaching $5 million for executives and $25 million for companies.

In June 2005, Kozlowski and Swartz were each convicted on 22 criminal charges relating to their misdeeds at Tyco. Both were sentenced to serve up to 25 years in prison and pay fines and restitution totaling $240 million. In May of 2006 Kozlowski also agreed to pay $21.2 million dollars to New York State to settle tax-evasion charges that included millions in sales taxes, fines, and penalties related to his purchases of fine art.

Sources: Ashlea Ebeling, "The Lending Game," *Forbes* (May 10, 2004); Anthony Bianco, William Symonds, Nanette Byrnes, and David Polek, "The Rise and Fall of Dennis Kozlowski," *BusinessWeek* (December 12, 2002); Mark Maremont, "Tyco Figures Will Be Jailed at Least 7 Years," *The Wall Street Journal* (September 20, 2005); and Jennifer Levitz, "Former Tyco CEO to Settle Tax Case in New York State," *The Wall Street Journal* (May 13, 2006).

opportunity to take advantage of their high-ranking offices in the form of excessive compensation. Due to the complexity of accounting and disclosures associated with stock-based compensation (e.g., stock options, stock appreciation rights), combined with the degree of judgment and estimation involved in option-valuation models, there can also be substantial inherent risk associated with stock-based or share-based compensation. The *Advanced Module* in this chapter discusses share-based compensation.

| Practice **INSIGHT** | A relatively common payroll fraud involves an employee making false claims for compensation. Based on a study conducted by the Association of Certified Fraud Examiners (2008), nearly 10 percent of fraudulent disbursements are payroll schemes. |

Control Risk Assessment

[LO 7] The discussion of control risk assessment follows the framework outlined in previous chapters. However, the discussion is not as thorough as the discussion of the revenue or purchasing processes because it is assumed that the reader has now developed a reasonable understanding of the decision process followed by the

FIGURE 12-2	Major Steps in Setting Control Risk for the Human Resource Management Process

auditor when setting control risk. Figure 12–2 summarizes the three major steps involved in setting control risk for the human resource management process.

Understand and Document Internal Control

The level of understanding of the five internal control components should be similar to that obtained for the other processes. The auditor's understanding of the human resource management process is normally gained by conducting a walkthrough of the system to gather evidence about the various functions that are involved in processing the transactions through the system. For an ongoing audit, this process merely involves updating prior years' documentation of the payroll system by noting any changes that have occurred. For a new engagement, or if the system has undergone major changes, more time and effort are needed to document the understanding of internal control. The auditor's understanding of internal control for the payroll system should be documented in the working papers using flowcharts, internal control questionnaires, and memoranda.

Because the control environment pervasively affects all accounting applications, including the payroll system, two factors shown in Table 6–3 in Chapter 6 should be considered. First, the entity's organizational structure, its personnel practices, and its methods of assigning authority and responsibility must be examined. The proper organizational structure for processing payroll transactions was discussed in the previous section. Second, the entity should have sound policies for hiring, training, promoting, and compensating employees. These policies should include specific authority and responsibility for hiring and firing employees, for setting wage rates and making salary changes, and for establishing benefits.

Plan and Perform Tests of Controls

For audits of public companies subject to AS5 or when a reliance strategy is followed, the auditor must identify the control activities that ensure that material misstatements are either prevented or detected and corrected. For example, the client may have formal procedures for classifying payroll costs in appropriate accounts. The auditor may decide to rely on this control activity to reduce the control risk for the classification assertion. In this case, the client's procedures for classifying payroll transactions by types of payroll costs should be examined by the auditor.

Set and Document the Control Risk	After the tests of controls are completed, the auditor sets the level of control risk and documents that assessment. The documentation supporting the achieved level of control risk for the payroll system might include a flowchart, the results of tests of controls, and a memorandum indicating the overall conclusion about control risk. If control deficiencies are detected at a public company, the auditor would need to evaluate the likelihood and magnitude of the potential weakness (see Chapter 7).

Control Activities and Tests of Controls— Payroll Transactions

✽ [LO 8]	Table 12–5 summarizes the assertions and possible misstatements for payroll transactions. The table also includes examples of control activities for each assertion and examples of tests of controls that can test the effectiveness of the control activities. The discussion that follows focuses only on the most important assertions for the payroll system. EarthWear's payroll system contains all of the relevant control activities.
Occurrence of Payroll Transactions	The auditor wants assurance that payments for payroll-related services are being made to valid employees for time actually worked. Thus, the client needs control activities that prevent payments to fictitious employees and to valid employees who have not worked. Controls must also ensure that payroll payments stop once an employee is terminated. Using your developing auditor expertise, what controls would you expect to see at a company like EarthWear to ensure payments are not made to terminated or fictitious employees? Proper segregation of duties provides the main control against payments to fictitious employees. As noted in Table 12–4, proper segregation of duties among operating and supporting departments, the human resource department, and the payroll department minimizes the possibility of fictitious employees existing within the system. The maintenance of adequate personnel files should also prevent such misstatements. For example, a listing of terminated employees could be used to verify that no terminated employees are still listed in the active payroll master file.

The human resource department approves the termination of an employee and ensures that he or she is removed from the master payroll file. Required completion and approval of a time card/time sheet also prevent payments to terminated employees. Proper review and approval of time cards/sheets by supervisors should prevent valid employees from being paid for work not performed.

Practice **INSIGHT**	When an external payroll service provider is used to process the audit client's payroll, the controls of the provider must be understood and tested by the audit firm, or by the service provider's auditor in accordance with AU 324 (i.e., an "SAS 70" report), before the controls of the payroll service provider can be relied on.

Finally, when payroll transactions are processed by an IT system, a payroll check should not be prepared unless the employee transaction has a valid employee number. Review and observation are the main tests of controls the auditor uses to examine the control activities shown in Table 12–5.

Authorization of Payroll Transactions	As in the discussion of the authorization assertion for other accounting applications, there are key authorization points within the payroll system. The client should have authorization procedures for hiring and terminating employees, setting pay rates, making withholdings, awarding benefits, and issuing payroll checks. For example, the department supervisor should approve the amount of time reported

TABLE 12–5	Summary of Assertions, Possible Misstatements, Example Control Activities, and Example Tests of Controls for Payroll Transactions		
Assertion	*Possible Misstatement*	*Example Control Activity*	*Example Test of Controls*
Occurrence	Payments made to fictitious employees	Segregation of duties	Observe and evaluate proper segregation of duties.
	Payments made to terminated employees	Adequate personnel files	Review and test personnel files.
	Payments made to valid employees who have not worked	Initiation of changes in employment status, wages or salaries, and benefits made by operating departments reported to the office of human resources	Review and test client's procedures for changing employees' records; if IT application, test application controls.
		Time clocks used to record time	Observe employees' use of time clock.
		Time cards approved by supervisors	Inspect time cards presented for approval by supervisor.
		Only employees with valid employee numbers paid	Review and test client's procedures for entering and removing employee numbers from the payroll master file; if IT application, test application controls.
		Use of payroll budgets with review by department supervisors	Review client's budgeting procedures.
Completeness	Employee services provided but not recorded	Prenumbered time cards accounted for by client personnel	Check numerical sequence of time cards; if IT application, test application controls.
		Verification that all employees in the master payroll file submitted a time card for the pay period	Review and test client's verification procedures; if IT application, test application controls.
Authorization	Unauthorized payments made to employees	Authorization procedures for	Review and test authorization procedures for each point of authorization in the payroll cycle; if IT application, test application controls.
	Payments made to employees at a rate in excess of authorized amount or for unauthorized employee benefits	• Hiring and terminating employees • Time worked • Wage, salary, and commission rates • Withholdings • Benefits • Issuing payroll check	
Accuracy	Employee compensation and payroll deductions computed incorrectly	Verification of payroll amounts and benefit calculations	Review and test client's verification procedures; if IT application, test application controls.
		Review of payroll register for unusual amounts	If IT-prepared, use computer-assisted audit techniques to test computer program logic for calculating amounts.
		Use of payroll budgets with review by department supervisors	Review client's budgeting procedures.
	Payroll transactions not posted correctly to the payroll journal	Changes to master payroll file verified through "before and after" reports	Test reconciliation of "before and after" reports to payroll master file; if IT application, test application controls.
	Amounts from payroll journal not posted correctly to general ledger	Payroll master file (payroll register) reconciled to general ledger payroll accounts	Review reconciliation of payroll master file to general ledger payroll accounts; if IT application, test application controls.
Cutoff	Payroll transactions recorded in the wrong period	Notices of additions, terminations, and changes to salaries, wages, and deductions reported promptly to the payroll processing function, after which the changes are updated promptly on the master payroll file	Review and test client's procedures for changes to master payroll file; if IT application, test application controls.
		All time cards forwarded to the payroll department weekly	Review and test procedures for processing time cards.
		Procedures that require recording payroll liabilities as soon as possible after they are incurred	Review and test procedures for recording payroll liabilities.
Classification	Payroll transactions not properly classified	Chart of accounts	Review chart of accounts.
		Independent approval and review of accounts charged for payroll	Review and test procedures for classifying payroll costs.
		Use of payroll budgets with review by department supervisors	Review client's budgeting procedures.

by an employee on his or her time card/sheet. Similarly, hiring and termination of employees and changes in pay rates should be authorized by the human resource department consistent with union contracts or corporate policies. Last, a payroll check should not be issued unless an employee's time card/sheet has been approved and that employee has a valid employee number on the payroll master file.

Accuracy
of Payroll
Transactions

The main concern related to the accuracy assertion is that an employee's gross pay and payroll deductions may be incorrectly computed. For example, an employee may be paid at an improper rate or payroll deductions may be incorrectly computed. The client should maintain verification procedures to ensure correct payroll and benefit calculations. The auditor can review the client's verification procedures as a test of control. When IT is used to prepare the payroll, the auditor can use computer-assisted audit techniques (CAATs) to test the program logic for proper calculations. In a manual system, or if a service bureau is used, the auditor can recompute the payroll calculations for a sample of payroll transactions.

Classification
of Payroll
Transactions

Because classification is an important assertion for payroll transactions, control activities must ensure that the appropriate payroll accounts are charged. If payroll expense is charged to the wrong accounts, the financial statements may be misstated. For example, if payroll expense is not properly classified between direct and indirect labor, inventory and cost of goods sold may not be valued properly. The use of an adequate chart of accounts is one control activity that helps prevent misclassification. Additionally, the timekeeping function should review the payroll categories assigned by the operating departments. Budgets that compare actual payroll costs to budgeted payroll costs by each category of labor also provide a control over proper classification of payroll. The auditor can review and test the client's control activities for classifying payroll costs.

Relating the Assessed Level of Control Risk to Substantive Procedures

✄ [LO 9]   If the results of the tests of controls for the payroll system support the planned level of control risk, the auditor conducts substantive procedures of payroll-related accounts at the assessed level. EarthWear, for example, has a strong set of control procedures for processing payroll transactions. If the auditor's tests of Earth-Wear's controls indicate that the controls are operating effectively, then no adjustment of detection risk is necessary. However, if the results of the control tests do not support the planned level of control risk for EarthWear's payroll system, the detection risk will have to be set lower. This would require that the nature and extent of substantive testing of payroll-related accounts be increased.

Auditing Payroll-Related Accounts

Two categories of substantive procedures for auditing payroll expense and payroll-related liabilities are discussed here: (1) substantive analytical procedures; and (2) tests of details of classes of transactions, account balances, and disclosures. Table 12–6 presents the assertions for classes of transactions, events, account balances, and disclosures as they apply to payroll expense and payroll-related liabilities, which are often called *accrued payroll* expenses. You should note that the auditor may obtain assurance for assertions related to transactions (substantive tests of transactions) in conjunction with testing the internal controls. If the tests of controls indicate that the controls are not operating effectively, the auditor may need to test transactions at the date the account balance is tested.

TABLE 12-6	Assertions about Classes of Transactions, Events, Account Balances, and Disclosures for Payroll Expense and Payroll-Related Accruals

Assertions about Classes of Transactions and Events:
- **Occurrence.** Payroll transactions and events are valid.
- **Completeness.** All payroll transactions and events have been recorded.
- **Authorization.** All payroll transactions and events are properly authorized.
- **Accuracy.** Payroll transactions have been properly computed, and payroll expense has been properly accumulated from journals and ledgers.
- **Cutoff.** Payroll expense and related accruals are recorded in the correct accounting period.
- **Classification.** Payroll expense and related accruals have been recorded in the proper accounts.

Assertions about Account Balances at the Period End:
- **Existence.** Payroll expense is a valid expense and related accruals are valid liabilities.
- **Rights and obligations.** The payroll-related accruals are the obligations of the entity.
- **Completeness.** All payroll expense and related accruals have been recorded.
- **Valuation and allocation.** Payroll expense and related accruals are included in the financial statements at appropriate amounts, and any resulting valuation or allocation adjustments are appropriately recorded.

Assertions about Presentation and Disclosure:
- **Occurrence and rights and obligations.** All disclosed events, transactions, and other matters relating to payroll expense and related accruals have occurred and pertain to the entity.
- **Completeness.** All disclosures relating to payroll expense and related accruals that should have been included in the financial statements have been included.
- **Classification and understandability.** Financial information relating to payroll expense and related accruals is appropriately presented and described, and disclosures are clearly expressed.
- **Accuracy and valuation.** Financial and other information relating to payroll expense and related accruals are disclosed fairly and at appropriate amounts.

Substantive Analytical Procedures

⚓ [LO 10]   Substantive analytical procedures can be useful substantive tests for examining the reasonableness of payroll expenses and payroll-related accrual accounts. When utilized as part of planning, preliminary analytical procedures can effectively identify payroll expense accounts and accrual accounts that may be misstated. Take a break from reading and think about comparisons and reasonableness tests you could develop to obtain assurance that payroll expense appears reasonable and that wages payable at the end of the year is accurately stated.

Table 12–7 shows examples of substantive analytical procedures that can be used for auditing payroll. Two examples will help demonstrate their application in practice. First, the auditor can compare budgeted payroll costs with actual payroll costs. Variances due to quantity and wage differences should show up in the client's cost-accounting system (on weekly or monthly reports). If the variances are immaterial, the auditor has some evidence that payroll costs are reasonable.

TABLE 12-7	Example Substantive Analytical Procedures for Auditing Payroll Accounts and Payroll-Related Accruals

Example Substantive Analytical Procedures	Possible Misstatement Detected
Payroll Expense Accounts	
Compare current-year balances in the various payroll expense accounts with prior years' balances after adjustment for pay changes and number of employees.	Over- or understatement of payroll expense.
Compare payroll costs as a percentage of sales with prior years' and industry data.	Over- or understatement of payroll expense.
Compare labor utilization rates and statistics with industry data.	Over- or understatement of payroll expense.
Compare budgeted payroll expenses with actual payroll expenses.	Over- or understatement of payroll expense.
Estimate sales commissions by applying commission formulas to recorded sales totals.	Over- or understatement of sales commissions.
Payroll-Related Accrual Accounts	
Compare current-year balances in payroll-related accrual accounts with prior years' balances after adjusting for changes in conditions.	Over- or understatement of accrued liabilities.
Test reasonableness of accrual balances.	Over- or understatement of accrued liabilities.

If the variances are material, the auditor should investigate the potential causes of the differences. This substantive analytical procedure also helps the auditor determine the proper valuation of inventory when standard costs are used to value inventory. Second, the auditor can test the reasonableness of certain accrual balances. For example, if accrued wages represent payroll for two days, the auditor can multiply the total weekly payroll by 40 percent (2 days ÷ 5 days). If the auditor's calculation is close to the accrued amount, no further audit work may be required on the accrued wages account.

Tests of Details of Classes of Transactions, Account Balances, and Disclosures

[LO 11,12]   Table 12–6 presents the assertions for payroll expense and payroll-related liabilities. The intended purpose of tests of details of transactions is to detect monetary misstatements in the individual transactions processed through the payroll application. As previously mentioned, tests of details of transactions are often conducted in conjunction with tests of controls. Table 12–8 presents examples of tests of details of transactions, account balances, and disclosures for assertions

TABLE 12–8	Examples of Payroll Tests of Transactions, Account Balances, and Disclosures
Assertions about Classes of Transactions	**Example Substantive Tests of Transactions**
Occurrence	Trace a sample of payroll checks to the master employee list to verify validity.*
Completeness	Tracing of a sample of time cards/sheets to the payroll register.*
Authorization	Test a sample of payroll checks for the presence of an authorized time card/sheet.*
Accuracy	Recompute the mathematical accuracy of a sample of payroll checks: CAATS may be used to test the logic of the computer programs for proper calculation of gross pay, deductions, and net pay.
Cutoff	Trace a sample of time cards/sheets before and after period end to the appropriate weekly payroll report, and trace the weekly payroll report to the general ledger to verify payroll transactions are recorded in the proper period.*
Classification	Examine a sample of payroll checks for proper classification into expense accounts.*
Assertions about Account Balances at Period End	**Example Tests of Details of Account Balances**
Existence	Vouch selected amounts from the account analysis schedules for the accruals to supporting documentation (payroll tax returns, corporate benefit policies, etc.).
Rights and obligations	Review supporting documentation to determine that the entity is legally obligated to pay the liability. Test a sample of bank reconciliations for the payroll bank account (see Chapter 16).
Completeness	Search for unrecorded liabilities (see Chapter 11). Use CAATs to foot weekly payroll reports and reconcile the total to the general ledger (payroll expense and related accruals).
Valuation and allocation	Obtain an account analysis schedule for accrued payroll liabilities; foot schedules and agree total to general ledger. Compare amounts accrued to supporting documentation, such as payroll tax returns.
Assertions about Presentation and Disclosure	**Example Tests of Details of Disclosures**
Occurrence, and rights and obligations	Inquire about accruals to ensure that they are properly disclosed.
Completeness	Complete financial reporting checklist to ensure that all financial statement disclosures related to payroll expense and related accruals have been made.
Classification and understandability	Review accrued payroll liabilities for proper classification between short-term and long-term liabilities. Read footnotes to ensure that required disclosures are understandable.
Accuracy and valuation	Review benefit contracts for proper disclosure of pension and postretirement benefits. Read footnotes and other information to ensure that the information is accurate and properly presented at the appropriate amounts.

* These tests of details of transactions are commonly conducted as dual-purpose tests (i.e., in conjunction with tests of controls).

related to payroll. The discussion that follows focuses on tests of details of account balances of payroll expense and accrued payroll liabilities.

Payroll Expense Accounts

Payroll transactions affect many expense accounts, including direct and indirect manufacturing expense, general and administrative salaries, sales salaries, commissions, and payroll tax expenses. Some companies account for such expenses by product line or division. In addition, fringe benefits such as medical and life insurance may be paid at least partly by the organization. If the entity's internal control is reliable, the auditor generally does not need to conduct detailed tests of these payroll expense accounts. On such audits, sufficient evidence can be gathered through an understanding of internal control, tests of controls, tests of details of transactions, and substantive analytical procedures. Additional detail testing is necessary only when control weaknesses exist or when the other types of audit tests indicate that material misstatements may be present.

Several payroll expense accounts may still be examined even when control risk is low. For example, it is common to verify the compensation paid to officers of the company because information on executive salaries and bonuses is needed for the SEC form 10K, proxy statements, and the federal tax return. Limits may also be placed on officers' salaries and bonuses as part of lending agreements. If such limits are exceeded, the entity may be in default on the debt. Officers' compensation is also examined because, as noted earlier, officers are in a position to override the control activities and pay themselves more than they are authorized to receive (see Exhibit 12–2). Officers' compensation expense can be verified by comparing the amounts shown in the payroll records with the amounts authorized in either board of directors' minutes or employment contracts and by using CAATS to search for other cash payments made to the officer, his or her family, or related parties.

Accrued Payroll Liabilities

An entity incurs a number of payroll-related liabilities. In addition to these accrued expenses, the entity also withholds various amounts from an employee's pay. These withholdings include payroll taxes (federal and state income taxes and FICA), medical and life insurance premiums, pension, and other miscellaneous deductions. Some examples of accrued payroll liabilities include

- Accrued wages and salaries.
- Accrued payroll taxes.
- Accrued commissions.
- Accrued bonuses.
- Accrued benefits such as vacation and sick pay.

EXHIBIT 12–2	Questionable Salary Payments at Lincoln Savings and Loan

One of the most notorious cases noted during the savings-and-loan debacle was Lincoln Savings and Loan. In 1978 Charles Keating, Jr., founded American Continental Corporation (ACC), which acquired Lincoln six years later. In 1989 the Federal Home Loan Bank Board seized control of Lincoln Savings and Loan. The closing of Lincoln cost U.S. taxpayers approximately $2 billion. Exercising his ownership powers over Lincoln, Keating installed his son, Charles Keating III, as chairman of the board at an annual salary of $1 million. An examination report on ACC indicated that "funds sent by Lincoln to ACC were being used by ACC to fund treasury stock transactions [and] pay debt service, consulting fees, and exorbitant management salaries." The report estimated that $34 million had been expended on "Keating family benefits."

Source: The People v. Charles H. Keating, Jr. (31 Cal., App. 4th 1688, 1993).

EXHIBIT 12–3 | **Account Analysis for Accrued Payroll Taxes Account**

N25
DLJ
2/04/10

EARTHWEAR CLOTHIERS
Analysis of Accrued Payroll Taxes
12/31/09

Disbursements for payment of payroll taxes	$253,275£	Beginning balance		$9,450φ
		Weekly accruals for payroll tax expense		253,540✔
		Ending balance		$9,715λ L
				F

F = Footed.
φ = Traced to prior year's working papers.
L = Agreed to general ledger.
✔ = Traced three weeks' (2/19, 4/30, and 9/24) payroll expense accruals to weekly payroll records.
£ = Traced three payments of payroll taxes to the cash disbursements journal.
λ = Recomputed amount of unpaid payroll taxes for two weeks at the end of December 2009.

In auditing accrued payroll liabilities, the auditor is concerned mainly with five audit assertions: *existence, completeness, valuation, cutoff,* and presentation and disclosure assertion of *completeness*. When control risk is low or the amounts in the accounts are relatively small, the auditor can verify accrued payroll liabilities using substantive analytical procedures. For example, the auditor can compare the prior year's balance in each accrual with the current year's balance after considering changing conditions.

For accrued payroll liability accounts for which the control risk is high or whose amounts are material, the auditor can obtain a detailed account analysis schedule. For example, Exhibit 12–3 shows an account analysis schedule for EarthWear's accrued payroll taxes. The credits to the account represent the recognition of payroll tax expense at the end of each pay period. These amounts can be traced to the various payroll tax returns or other documentation filed by the entity and should agree with the amount of payroll tax expense included in the income statement. The debits to the account represent payments made to relevant government agencies. These payments can be verified by tracing the amounts to the cash disbursements journal.

An interesting aspect of this type of accrual account is that it periodically "clears out" the accrued amount. For example, if the client has to make payments for payroll taxes to the government on the 15th of each month, the accrued payroll taxes account will have a zero balance after the payment. Thus, at the end of any month, the accrued payroll taxes account should contain only an accrual for payroll taxes since the last payment (approximately two weeks). In many organizations, these costs are broken down into the various types of payroll taxes (employer's FICA and federal and state unemployment taxes).

Cutoff   The auditor also wants to determine whether all payroll-related liabilities are recorded in the proper period. An examination of supporting documentation for the accruals provides evidence on the proper period for recording the expense or liability. For example, an examination of the client's unemployment tax invoices should allow the auditor to determine if a proper accrual for unemployment tax has been made in the current period.

Existence and Valuation The existence and valuation assertions can generally be tested at the same time. The auditor's concerns are whether the recorded liabilities are valid obligations of the entity and whether they are included in the financial statements at the appropriate amount. To verify the existence and valuation of an accrued payroll liability, the auditor can generally trace the amounts included on the account analysis working paper to supporting documentation such as payroll tax reports. If adequate documentation is present, the auditor has evidence that the amount represents a valid liability. The auditor can usually verify the accuracy of the amounts by recalculating the figures.

Completeness The auditor wants to make sure that all payroll-related liabilities are recorded. The auditor should be aware of the normal payroll-related taxes that are paid by the entity and therefore should be able to determine if accruals have been made for payroll taxes such as Social Security taxes and unemployment insurance. In some instances, the auditor's search for unrecorded liabilities, which was discussed in Chapter 11, may provide evidence that all payroll-related liabilities are recorded.

Presentation and Disclosure: Completeness The auditor must ensure that all necessary financial statement disclosures for the human resource management process are made. Table 12–9 presents examples of items that should be disclosed.

Accounting standards require substantial disclosure. FASB ASC Topic 715 requires detailed disclosures of pension costs, postretirement benefits, and share-based compensation (see the *Advanced Module* in this chapter for a discussion of share-based compensation). Although a thorough discussion of the audit of these items is beyond the scope of this text, the reader should be aware that such disclosures are important to the fairness of the financial statements. Profit-sharing plans and deferred compensation arrangements also require disclosure in the footnotes.

TABLE 12-9	Sample Disclosure Items for the Human Resource Management Process
	Pension benefits
	Postretirement benefits
	Stock-based compensation
	Profit-sharing plans
	Deferred compensation arrangements

Practice INSIGHT

In early 2006 the SEC began a probe to detect possible stock-option abuses; particularly the impeccable timing of granting stock options to corporate executives. Analysis of stock price patterns and grant dates suggested that companies were backdating the grant date of stock-options to a low in the stock price so that executives and employees could benefit from sharp stock appreciation. One popular technology company involved in backdating was Apple Inc. In 2006, Apple disclosed that thousands of option grants between 1997 and 2002, including those to CEO Steve Jobs, were improperly dated. The SEC sued Apple's former CFO and general counsel alleging involvement in backdating; the law suits were settled out of court for $5.7 million. In a related shareholder lawsuit, Steve Jobs and other Apple executives agreed to settle claims about their alleged participation for $14 million. In July 2006, the SEC adopted new rules requiring detailed disclosure of stock-option grants. For a summary of the new disclosure requirements see www.sec.gov.

Sources: Charles Forelle and James Bandler, "Stock-Options Criminal Charge: Slush Fund and Fake Employees," *The Wall Street Journal* (August 10, 2006), and Nick Wingfield and Justin Scheck, "Jobs, Apple Executive Settle Suit," *The Wall Street Journal* (September 11, 2008).

Evaluating the Audit Findings— Payroll-Related Accounts

✂ [LO 13] When the auditor has completed the planned substantive procedures of the payroll-related accounts, all the identified misstatements should be aggregated. The likely misstatement is compared to the tolerable misstatement allocated to the payroll-related accounts. If the likely misstatement is less than the tolerable misstatement, the auditor may accept the accounts as fairly presented. Conversely, if the likely misstatement exceeds the tolerable misstatement, the auditor should conclude that the accounts are not fairly presented.

For example, in Chapter 3 the tolerable misstatement for EarthWear was set at $900,000. Exhibit 3–4 showed that Willis & Adams detected a misstatement in recording payroll expense and bonuses that amounted to a $215,000 understatement of accrued liabilities. Because this misstatement is less than the tolerable misstatement of $900,000, Willis & Adams can conclude that the audit evidence supports fair presentation. However, if the misstatement was greater than the tolerable misstatement, the evidence would not support fair presentation. In this case the auditor would have two choices: adjust the accounts to reduce the misstatement to an amount less than the tolerable misstatement or qualify the audit report.

The auditor should again analyze the misstatements discovered through the application of substantive procedures because these misstatements may provide additional evidence on the control risk for the payroll system. If the auditor concludes that the audit risk is unacceptably high, additional audit procedures should be performed, or the auditor must be satisfied that the client has adjusted the payroll-related financial statement accounts to an acceptable level. For example, suppose the auditor's substantive analytical procedures indicate that commissions expense is overstated. The auditor might perform detailed computations of commissions expense or request that the client adjust the account by the amount of the estimated misstatement.

Advanced Module: Share-Based Compensation

Accounting for stock options and similar compensation has been a controversial area for many years. In 1995 the FASB issued Statement No. 123, "Share-Based Compensation," which encouraged but did not mandate the use of the fair value method to determine compensation expense on the income statement. Initially, nearly all companies continued to use the intrinsic value method to report compensation expense, which typically resulted in zero compensation expense. After the accounting scandals of the early 2000s, some companies (e.g., Amazon, Coca-Cola) decided voluntarily to use the fair value method to determine share-based compensation expense as a way of signaling the high quality of their financial reporting to the capital markets. Within a few years, over 700 companies in the United States voluntarily applied the fair value method. The FASB revisited the issue of share-based compensation, and in December 2004 the FASB issued Statement No. 123R, "Share-Based Payment," requiring the expensing of the fair value of stock options granted and other share-based payments as compensation. Statement No. 123R (now found in FASB ASC Topic 718) became effective in 2006 for most public companies.

The determination of the fair value for share-based payments will require the use of an option-pricing model for most companies. The most common models are the Black-Scholes-Merton model and the binomial model. These models incorporate a variety of factors, including:

- The exercise price of the option.
- The term of the option.
- The current market price of the underlying stock.
- Expected volatility.

- Expected dividends.
- Expected risk-free rate.

Many of these factors are complex and involve forward-looking information. In addition to FASB ASC Topic 718, clients and auditors must also consider guidance found in FASB ASC Subtopic 505-50, "Equity Based Payments to Non-employees." As noted in the chapter, accounting for share-based payments often presents high inherent risk because of the complexity of the accounting rules and the degree of judgment and estimation that must go into the fair value determination. Audit firms develop extensive audit programs to help audit teams ensure that a client is appropriately accounting for stock-based compensation. While detailed coverage of auditing for share-based compensation is beyond the scope of this book, we provide a brief overview of issues and procedures.

Once the auditor has a general sense for the extent to which share-based compensation is used by the company, he or she would normally perform procedures such as:

- Read all applicable share-based plans and inquire of management whether other documents (e.g., employment agreements) contain relevant information.
- Understand policies, processes, and controls around share-based compensation.
- Test design and operating effectiveness of controls, including a determination that the transactions have been properly authorized.
- Obtain and verify the accuracy of schedules supporting the granting of share-based compensation awards.
- Review board of directors' minutes to ensure completeness of the supporting schedules and to identify modifications to the terms of outstanding awards or existing plans (e.g., exercise price or date).
- Perform analytical procedures to identify unusual fluctuations in compensation expense as well as related income/expense accounts.
- Determine if any awards were exercised for other than cash (e.g., loans) or if employees were offered the opportunity to replace an out-of-the-money award for another award.

In addition to these procedures the auditor would obtain evidence to support the fair value measurements or option pricing. With the movement in accounting standards toward more fair value accounting, auditors will need improved understanding of valuation issues. Because auditing fair value is further addressed in the *Advanced Module* in Chapter 16, "Auditing Fair Value Measurements," the discussion here will be brief. To obtain sufficient appropriate evidence on the fair value of options, the auditor is not required to become an option-pricing expert. If the client is using an approved model (e.g., Black-Scholes-Merton or binomial), the auditor would verify the mathematical accuracy of the client's calculations, tie the output of the model to the financial statements, and tie the known inputs (e.g., term, stock price) to relevant source documents. For forward-looking inputs (e.g., expected volatility, dividends, interest rate), the auditor would perform procedures to test the reasonableness of these inputs. The client should have a verifiable and consistent method to estimate these parameters.

Often the auditor will use the work of a valuation specialist to obtain evidence regarding fair value measurements. When specialists are used, the auditor is required to evaluate the specialist's qualifications and objectivity. The auditor also must determine if the valuation model used by the specialist is appropriate and consistent with GAAP, and the auditor must understand and agree with the reasonableness of the underlying assumptions.

KEY TERMS

Analytical procedures. Evaluations of financial information made by a study of plausible relationships among both financial and nonfinancial data.

Application controls. Controls that apply to the processing of specific computer applications and are part of the computer programs used in the accounting system.

Assertions. Expressed or implied representations by management that are reflected in the financial statement components.

General controls. Controls that relate to the overall information-processing environment and have a pervasive effect on the entity's computer operations.

Reliance strategy. The auditor's decision to rely on the entity's controls, test those controls, and reduce the direct tests of the financial statement accounts.

Substantive tests of transactions. Tests to detect errors or fraud in individual transactions.

Tests of controls. Audit procedures performed to test the operating effectiveness of controls in preventing or detecting and correcting material misstatements at the relevant assertion level.

Tests of details of account balances and disclosures. Substantive tests that concentrate on the details of items contained in the account balance and disclosures.

Tests of details of transactions. Tests to detect errors or fraud in individual transactions.

www.mhhe.com/ **messier7e**	Visit the book's Online Learning Center for a multiple-choice quiz that will allow you to assess your understanding of chapter concepts.

REVIEW QUESTIONS

[LO 1] 12-1 Why is the payroll system of most entities computerized?

[2] 12-2 What are the major types of transactions that occur in the payroll system? What financial statement accounts are affected by each of these types of transactions?

[3] 12-3 Briefly describe each of the following documents or records: payroll register, payroll master file, and payroll master file changes report.

[4] 12-4 What duties are performed within the human resource, timekeeping, and payroll-processing functions?

[5] 12-5 List the key segregation of duties in the human resource management process. What errors or fraud can occur if such duties are not segregated?

[7,8] 12-6 Discuss the two control environment factors that an auditor should consider when examining the human resource management process.

[8] 12-7 What are the key authorization points in a payroll system?

[8] 12-8 Why is it important for the client to establish control activities over the classification of payroll transactions?

[6] 12-9 List the inherent risk factors that affect the human resource management process.

[8,11] 12-10 What is an example of a test of control or test of details of transactions that can be performed using CAATs for payroll transactions?

[10] 12-11 List two substantive analytical procedures that can be used to provide audit evidence related to the payroll expense accounts and the payroll-related liabilities.

[12]   12-12   Discuss how an auditor would audit the accrued payroll taxes account.

[12]   12-13   Identify three possible disclosure issues for payroll expense and payroll-related liabilities.

MULTIPLE-CHOICE QUESTIONS

[3,8]   12-14   During the year being audited, the Matthews Corporation changed from a system of recording time worked on clock cards to an IT payroll system in which employees record time in and out with magnetic cards. The IT system automatically updates all payroll records. Because of this change

a. A generalized computer audit program must be used.

b. Without paper clock cards, part of the audit trail is altered.

c. The potential for payroll-related fraud is diminished.

d. Transactions must be processed in batches.

[3,5,8]   12-15   Which of the following procedures would most likely be considered a weakness in an entity's internal controls over payroll?

a. A voucher for the amount of the payroll is prepared in the general accounting department based on the payroll department's payroll summary.

b. Payroll checks are prepared by the payroll department and signed by the treasurer.

c. The employee who distributes payroll checks returns unclaimed payroll checks to the payroll department.

d. The personnel department sends employees' termination notices to the payroll department.

[4,5,8]   12-16   In meeting the control objective of safeguarding of assets, which department should be responsible for the following?

	Distribution of Paychecks	Custody of Unclaimed Paychecks
a	Treasurer	Treasurer
b	Payroll	Treasurer
c	Treasurer	Payroll
d	Payroll	Payroll

[5]   12-17   For an appropriate segregation of duties, journalizing and posting summary payroll transactions should be assigned to

a. The treasurer's department.

b. General accounting.

c. Payroll accounting.

d. The timekeeping department.

[5]   12-18   The purpose of segregating the duties of hiring personnel and distributing payroll checks is to separate the

a. Human resource function from the controllership function.

b. Administrative controls from the internal accounting controls.

c. Authorization of transactions from the custody-related assets.

d. Operational responsibility from the record-keeping responsibility.

[8]   12-19   An auditor who is testing IT controls in a payroll system would most likely use test data (discussed in *Advanced Module 1* in Chapter 6) that contain conditions such as

a. Deductions *not* authorized by employees.

b. Overtime *not* approved by supervisors.

c. Time cards with invalid job numbers.

d. Payroll checks with unauthorized signatures.

[8]   12-20   It would be appropriate for the payroll department to be responsible for which of the following functions?
a. Approval of employee time records.
b. Preparation of periodic governmental reports as to employees' earnings and withholding taxes.
c. Maintenance of records of employment, discharges, and pay increases.
d. Distribution of paychecks to employees.

[8]   12-21   Which of the following audit tests would most likely be used to test the occurrence assertion for payroll transactions?
a. Trace a sample of time sheets to the payroll register.
b. Recompute the mathematical accuracy of a sample of payroll checks.
c. Trace a sample of payroll checks to the approved time sheet summary and the master employee list to verify validity.
d. Test a sample of time sheets for the presence of authorization.

[8]   12-22   Effective control activities over the payroll function may include
a. Reconciliation of totals on job time cards with job reports by employees responsible for those specific jobs.
b. Verification of agreement of job time cards with employee clock card hours by a payroll department employee.
c. Preparation of payroll transaction journal entries by an employee who reports to the supervisor of the personnel department.
d. Custody of rate authorization records by the supervisor of the payroll department.

[9,10,12]   12-23   An auditor is most likely to perform substantive tests of details on payroll transactions and balances when
a. Cutoff tests indicate a substantial amount of accrued payroll expense.
b. The level of control risk relative to payroll transactions is set at low.
c. Substantive analytical procedures indicate unusual fluctuations in recurring payroll entries.
d. Accrued payroll expense consists primarily of unpaid commissions.

PROBLEMS

[4,5]   12-24   You have been hired by Morris & Son, Inc. to manage its Human Resource Department. As a first step, you want to determine personnel needs and assigned duties in order to prevent errors and fraud in the financial statements.

Required:
How many people would you utilize and what duties would you assign to each person hired to best help prevent errors and fraud in the financial statements? Be sure to explain your answer.

[4,5,7,8]   12-25   A CPA's audit documentation (working papers) contains a narrative description of a *segment* of the Croyden Factory, Inc., payroll system and an accompanying flowchart as follows.

Narrative
The internal control system with respect to the personnel department functions well and is not included in the accompanying flowchart.

At the beginning of each workweek, payroll clerk 1 reviews the payroll department files to determine the employment status of factory employees

Croyden Factory, Inc., Payroll System

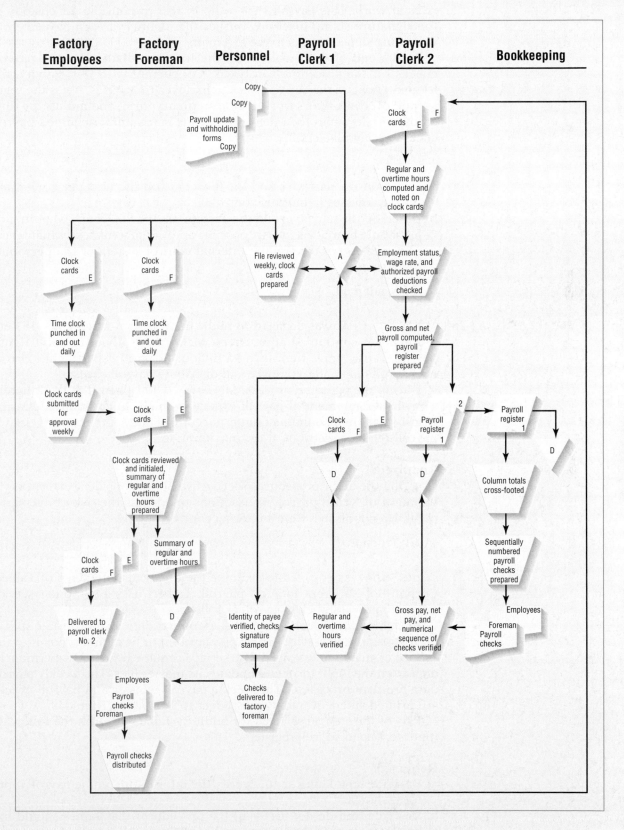

and then prepares time cards and distributes them as each individual arrives at work. This payroll clerk, who is also responsible for custody of the signature stamp machine, verifies the identity of each payee before delivering signed checks to the foreman.

At the end of each workweek, the foreman distributes the payroll checks for the preceding workweek. Concurrent with this activity, the foreman reviews the current week's employee time cards, notes the regular and overtime hours worked on a summary form, and initials the time cards. The foreman then delivers all time cards and unclaimed payroll checks to payroll clerk 2.

Required:
a. Based on the narrative and the flowchart on the next page, what are the weaknesses in internal control?
b. Based on the narrative and the accompanying flowchart, what inquiries should be made to clarify possible additional weaknesses in internal control? Do *not* discuss the internal control system of the personnel department.

(AICPA, adapted)

[10,11,12]   12-26   McCarthy, CPA, was engaged to audit the financial statements of Kent Company, a continuing audit client. McCarthy is about to audit Kent's payroll transactions. Kent uses an in-house payroll department to process payroll data and to prepare and distribute payroll checks.

During the planning process, McCarthy determined that the inherent risk of overstatement of payroll expense is high. In addition, McCarthy obtained an understanding of internal control and set the control risk for payroll-related assertions at the maximum level.

Required:
Describe the audit procedures McCarthy should consider performing in the audit of Kent's payroll transactions to address the risk of overstatement. Do not discuss Kent's internal control.

(AICPA, adapted)

[10,11,12]   12-27   James, who was engaged to examine the financial statements of Talbert Corporation, is about to audit payroll. Talbert uses a computer service center to process weekly payroll as follows.

Each Monday Talbert's payroll clerk inserts data in appropriate spaces on the preprinted service center-prepared input form and sends it to the service center via messenger. The service center extracts new permanent data from the input form and updates its master files. The weekly payroll data are then processed. The weekly payroll register and payroll checks are printed and delivered by messenger to Talbert on Thursday.

Part of the sample selected for audit by James includes the following input form and payroll register:

Required:
a. Describe how James should verify the information in the payroll input form shown.
b. Describe (but do not perform) the procedures that James should follow in examining the November 27, 2009, payroll register shown.

(AICPA, adapted)

TALBERT CORPORATION
Payroll Input
Week Ending Friday, November 27, 2009

Employee Data—Permanent File				**Current Week's Payroll Data**				
				Hours		**Special Deductions**		
Name	Social Security Number	W-4 Information	Hourly Rate	Regular	Overtime	Bonds	Union	Other
A. Bell	999-99-9991	M-1	$10.00	35	5	$18.75		
B. Carioso	999-99-9992	M-2	10.00	35	4			
C. Deng	999-99-9993	S-1	10.00	35	6	18.75	$4.00	
D. Ellis	999-99-9994	S-1	10.00	35	2		4.00	$50.00
E. Flaherty	999-99-9995	M-4	10.00	35	1		4.00	
F. Gillis	999-99-9996	M-4	10.00	35			4.00	
G. Hua	999-99-9997	M-1	7.00	35	2	18.75	4.00	
H. Jones	999-99-9998	M-2	7.00	35			4.00	25.00
I. King	999-99-9999	S-1	7.00	35	4		4.00	
New Employee:								
J. Smith	999-99-9990	M-3	7.00	35				

The Talbert payroll register is located on the next page.

DISCUSSION CASES

[7,8,9] 12-28 Service Corporation hired an independent computer programmer to develop a simplified payroll application for its newly purchased computer. The programmer developed an online database microcomputer system that minimized the level of knowledge required of the operator. It was based on typing answers to input cues that appeared on the terminal's viewing screen, examples of which follow:

A. Access routine:
  1. Operator access number to payroll file?
  2. Are there new employees?

B. New employee routine:
  1. Employee name?
  2. Employee number?
  3. Social Security number?
  4. Rate per hour?
  5. Single or married?
  6. Number of dependents?
  7. Account distribution?

C. Current payroll routine:
  1. Employee number?
  2. Regular hours worked?
  3. Overtime hours worked?
  4. Total employees this payroll period?

The independent auditor is attempting to verify that certain input validation (edit) checks exist to ensure that errors resulting from omissions, invalid entries, or other inaccuracies are detected during the typing of answers to the input cues.

Required:
a. Discuss the various types of input validation (edit) controls that the independent auditor would expect to find in the IT system.
b. Describe the assurances provided by each identified validation check.

(AICPA, adapted)

TALBERT CORPORATION
Payroll Register
November 27, 2009

Employee	Social Security Number	Hours Regular	Hours Overtime	Payroll Regular	Payroll Overtime	Gross Payroll	Taxes Withheld FICA	Taxes Withheld Federal	State	Other Withheld	Net Pay	Check Number
A. Bell	999-99-9991	35	5	$ 350.00	$ 75.00	$ 425.00	$ 26.05	$ 76.00	$ 27.40	$ 18.75	$ 276.80	1499
B. Carioso	999-99-9992	35	4	350.00	60.00	410.00	25.13	65.00	23.60		296.27	1500
C. Deng	999-99-9993	35	6	350.00	90.00	440.00	26.97	100.90	28.60	22.75	260.78	1501
D. Ellis	999-99-9994	35	2	350.00	30.00	380.00	23.29	80.50	21.70	54.00	200.51	1502
E. Flaherty	999-99-9995	35	1	350.00	15.00	365.00	22.37	43.50	15.90	4.00	279.23	1503
F. Gillis	999-99-9996	35		350.00		350.00	21.46	41.40	15.00	4.00	268.14	1504
G. Hua	999-99-9997	35	2	245.00	21.00	266.00	16.31	34.80	10.90	22.75	181.24	1505
H. Jones	999-99-9998	35		245.00		245.00	15.02	26.40	8.70	29.00	165.88	1506
I. King	999-99-9999	35	4	245.00	42.00	287.00	17.59	49.40	12.20	4.00	203.81	1507
J. Smith	999-99-9990	35		245.00		245.00	15.02	23.00	7.80		199.18	1508
Total		350	24	$3,080.00	$333.00	$3,413.00	$209.21	$540.90	$171.80	$159.25	$2,331.84	

[6,10,12]   12-29   Executive compensation ballooned in the 1990s, and as highlighted in Exhibit 12–1, there were notable compensation abuses. The most popular form of executive compensation in the 1990s was company stock (or options to purchase stock). Designers of these compensation plans argue that by compensating officers with stock, the officers will take actions in the best interest of the shareholders. Critics claim executive compensation is often too high in proportion to average salaries at companies and that the compensation levels motivate officers to take selfish actions.

Required:

a. Research executive compensation of some well-known companies. (You can find executive compensation in SEC filings on EDGAR at www.sec.gov or on a variety of Internet sites, such as eComp at www.ecomponline.com.) Use your best judgment to compute the proportion of executive compensation to average salary (i.e., are executives earning 5 times, or 10 times, or 100 times the average employee). In your opinion, are the executives worth it?

b. In your opinion, what are the costs and benefits associated with compensating executives with stock or options to purchase stock?

c. What do you believe are the most effective audit procedures to use to identify executive compensation abuse or fraud? Please explain why.

INTERNET ASSIGNMENTS

[11,12]   12-30   Using an Internet browser, search for information on labor costs in the retail catalog industry (e.g., labor costs as a percentage of sales).

HANDS-ON CASES

ACL

| www.mhhe.com/ messier7e | Visit the book's Online Learning Center for problem material to be completed using the ACL software packaged with your new text. |

CHAPTER 13

LEARNING OBJECTIVES

Upon completion of this chapter you will

[1] Develop an understanding of the inventory management process.

[2] Be able to identify and describe the types of documents and records used in the inventory management process.

[3] Understand the functions in the inventory management process.

[4] Know the appropriate segregation of duties for the inventory management process.

[5] Be able to identify and evaluate inherent risks relevant to the inventory management process.

[6] Know how to assess control risk for the inventory system.

[7] Know key internal controls and develop relevant tests of controls for inventory transactions.

[8] Understand how to relate the assessment of control risk to substantive procedures.

[9] Be familiar with substantive analytical procedures used to audit inventory and related accounts.

[10] Know how to audit standard costs.

[11] Know how to observe physical inventory.

[12] Be familiar with tests of details of transactions used to audit inventory and related accounts.

[13] Be familiar with tests of details of account balances used to audit inventory and related accounts.

[14] Understand how to evaluate the audit findings and reach a final conclusion on inventory and related accounts.

RELEVANT ACCOUNTING AND AUDITING PRONOUNCEMENTS

AU 312, Audit Risk and Materiality in Conducting an Audit

AU 314, Understanding the Entity and Its Environment and Assessing the Risks of Material Misstatement

AU 316, Consideration of Fraud in a Financial Statement Audit

AU 318, Performing Audit Procedures in Response to Assessed Risks and Evaluating the Audit Evidence Obtained

AU 326, Audit Evidence

AU 329, Analytical Procedures

AU 330, The Confirmation Process

AU 331, Inventories

AU 336, Using the Work of a Specialist

AU 339, Audit Documentation

AU 342, Auditing Accounting Estimates

PCAOB Auditing Standard No. 3, Audit Documentation (AS3)

PCAOB Auditing Standard No. 5, An Audit of Internal Control Over Financial Reporting That Is Integrated with An Audit of Financial Statements (AS5)

PCAOB Proposed Auditing Standards Related to the Auditor's Assessment of and Response to Risk, PCAOB Release No. 2008–006 (October 21, 2008)

Auditing the Inventory Management Process

Major Phases of an Audit

Client acceptance/
continuance and establishing
an understanding with the client
(Chapter 5)

Preliminary engagement
activities
(Chapter 5)

Plan the audit
(Chapters 3 and 5)

Consider and audit
internal control
(Chapters 6 and 7)

Audit business processes
and related accounts
(e.g., revenue generation)
(Chapters 10–16)

Complete the audit
(Chapter 17)

Evaluate results and issue audit
report (Chapters 1 and 18)

For most manufacturing, wholesale, and merchandising (retail) entities, inventory is a major component of the balance sheet. The complexity of auditing inventory may be affected by the degree of processing required to manufacture products. In a merchandising business, products are purchased directly from vendors with little or no additional processing by the entity before sale. In such cases, verifying inventory is relatively straightforward. On the other hand, determining a proper inventory value may be more difficult when the production process involves numerous steps. The presentation in this chapter mainly discusses inventory in terms of a merchandising company. However, the audit approach followed for merchandising entities is easily adapted to other types of inventory processes.

The coverage of the inventory management process follows the components of the audit risk model. An overview of the inventory management process is presented first, followed by discussion of the risk of material misstatement, specifically inherent risk factors and control risk assessment. While the main focus of this chapter is auditing the inventory management process for a financial statement audit, the concepts covered for setting control risk are applicable to an audit of internal control over financial reporting for public companies under the Sarbanes-Oxley Act of 2002. The last part of the chapter discusses the substantive procedures for inventory with particular emphasis on auditing standard costs and observing physical inventory.

Overview of the Inventory Management Process

≽ [LO 1]   The inventory management process is affected by the control activities previously discussed for the revenue, purchasing, and payroll processes. Figure 13–1 shows how each of these processes interacts with the inventory management process. The acquisition of and payment for inventory are controlled via the purchasing process. The cost of both direct and indirect labor assigned to inventory is controlled through the payroll process. Last, finished goods are sold and accounted for as part of the revenue process. Thus, the "cradle-to-grave" cycle for inventory begins when goods are purchased and stored and ends when the finished goods are shipped to customers.

Inventory can represent one of the most complex parts of the audit. For example, while determining the quantity of inventory on hand is usually an easy audit step to complete, assigning costs to value those quantities is more difficult. Additionally, there may be other troublesome valuation issues related to inventory such as obsolescence and lower-of-cost-or-market value.

Exhibit 13–1 describes EarthWear's inventory system, while Figure 13–2 flowcharts the system. This description and flowchart provide a framework

FIGURE 13–1	The Relationship of the Inventory Management Process to Other Accounting Processes

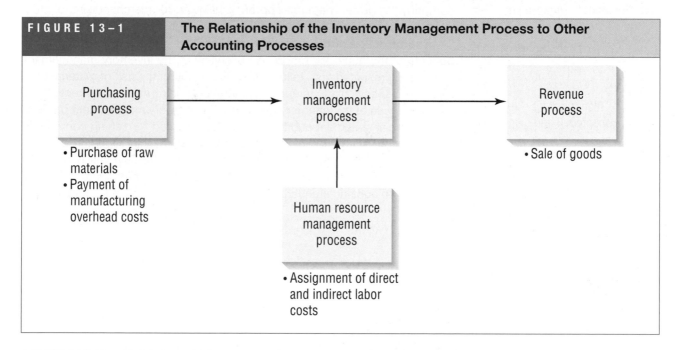

EXHIBIT 13–1	Description of EarthWear's Inventory System*

Clothing and other products sold by EarthWear are developed by the company's design department. All goods are produced by independent manufacturers, except for most of EarthWear's soft luggage. The company purchases merchandise from more than 200 domestic and foreign manufacturers. For many major suppliers, goods are ordered and paid for through the company's electronic data interchange (EDI) system. The computerized inventory control system handles the receipt of shipments from manufacturers. Goods are received at the receiving department, where the information is agreed to the purchase order (receiving report) and entered into the inventory control system.

The company's sales representatives enter orders into an online order entry and inventory control system; customers using the company's Internet site complete a computer screen that enters the orders. Computer processing of orders is performed each night on a batch basis, at which time shipping tickets are printed with bar codes for optical scanning. Inventory is picked based on the location of individual products rather than orders, followed by computerized sorting and transporting of goods to multiple packing stations and shipping zones.

*For simplicity of presentation, we have not included inventory processes at EarthWear's outlet stores.

for discussing the control activities and tests of controls for the inventory management process in more detail. However, because of differences in products and their subsequent processing, the inventory system usually differs from one entity to the next. The reader should concentrate on understanding the basic concepts of internal control. The following topics related to the inventory management process are discussed:

- Types of documents and records.
- The major functions.
- The key segregation of duties.

Types of Documents and Records

✂ [LO 2]

Table 13–1 lists the more important documents and records that are normally involved in the inventory system. Not all of these documents are presented in Figure 13–2. They are discussed here to give the reader information on documents and records that might exist in an inventory management process of a manufacturing company. The reader should keep in mind that in an IT system

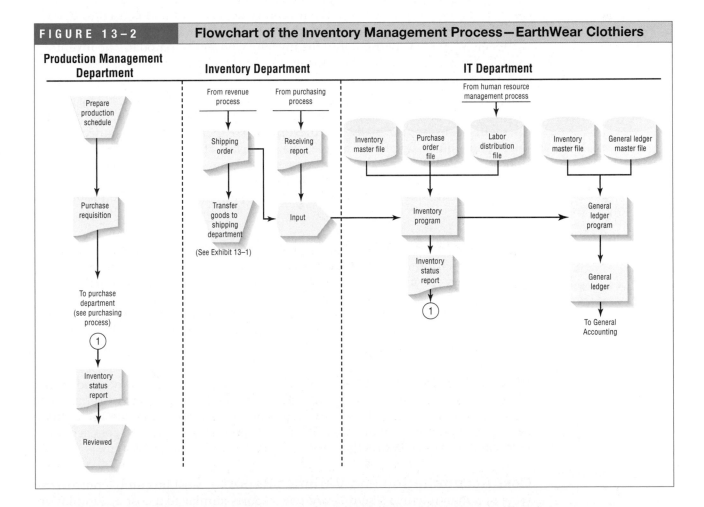

FIGURE 13–2   **Flowchart of the Inventory Management Process—EarthWear Clothiers**

TABLE 13–1	Documents and Records Included in the Inventory Management Process
Production schedule	Production data information
Receiving report	Cost accumulation and variance report
Materials requisition	Inventory status report
Inventory master file	Shipping order

some of these documents and records may exist for only a short time or only in digital form.

Production Schedule   A production schedule is normally prepared periodically based on the expected demand for the entity's products. The expected demand may be based on the current backlog of orders or on sales forecasts from the sales or marketing department. In EarthWear's system, this schedule is prepared by the design department. Production schedules determine the quantity of goods needed and the time at which they must be ready in order to meet the production scheduling. Many organizations use material requirements planning or just-in-time inventory programs to assist with production planning. Production schedules give the auditor information on the planned level of operating activity.

Receiving Report   The receiving report records the receipt of goods from vendors. This document was discussed as part of the purchasing process. It is reconsidered in the inventory management process because a copy of this document accompanies the goods to the inventory department and is used to update the client's perpetual inventory records. Note in Figure 13–2 that the data from the receiving report are input into the inventory program to update the inventory master file, which contains the information on the client's perpetual records.

Materials Requisition   Materials requisitions are normally used by manufacturing companies to track materials during the production process. Materials requisitions are normally prepared by department personnel as needed for production purposes. For example, the materials requisition is the document that authorizes the release of raw materials from the raw materials department. A copy of the materials requisition may be maintained in the raw materials department, and another copy may accompany the goods to the production departments.

Inventory Master File   The inventory master file contains all the important information related to the entity's inventory, including the perpetual inventory records. In sophisticated inventory systems such as EarthWear's, the inventory master file also contains information on the costs used to value inventory. In a manufacturing company, it would not be unusual for the inventory master file to contain the standard costs used to value the inventory at various stages of production.

Production Data Information   In a manufacturing company, production information about the transfer of goods and related cost accumulation at each stage of production should be reported. This information updates the entity's perpetual inventory system. It is also used as input to generate the cost accumulation and variance reports that are produced by the inventory system.

Cost Accumulation and Variance Report   Most inventory control systems in a manufacturing setting produce reports similar to a cost accumulation and variance report. Material, labor, and overhead costs are charged to inventory as part of the manufacturing process. The cost accumulation report summarizes the various costs charged to departments and products. The variance reports present the results of inventory processing in terms of actual costs versus standard or budgeted costs. The cost accounting and manufacturing departments review these reports for appropriate charges.

TABLE 13-2	Functions in the Inventory Management Process
Inventory management	Authorization of production activity and maintenance of inventory at appropriate levels; issuance of purchase requisitions to the purchasing department (see Chapter 11 on the purchasing process).
Raw materials stores	Custody of raw materials and issuance of raw materials to manufacturing departments.
Manufacturing	Production of goods.
Finished goods stores	Custody of finished goods and issuance of goods to the shipping department (see Chapter 10 on the revenue process).
Cost accounting	Maintenance of the costs of manufacturing and inventory in cost records.
General ledger	Proper accumulation, classification, and summarization of inventory and related costs in the general ledger.

Inventory Status Report   The inventory status report shows the type and amount of products on hand. Such a report is basically a summary of the perpetual inventory records. This report can also be used to determine the status of goods in process. In sophisticated inventory systems, this type of information can be accessed directly through computer terminals or PCs.

Shipping Order   This document was discussed as part of the revenue process. It is reconsidered here because a copy of this document is used to remove goods from the client's perpetual inventory records. Note in Figure 13–2 that the inventory master file is updated when a receiving report is processed or when a shipping order is generated.

The Major Functions

Table 13–2 summarizes the functions that normally take place in a typical inventory management process.

[LO 3]   Inventory Management   At EarthWear, the inventory management function is performed by the design department. This department is responsible for maintaining inventory at appropriate levels. It issues purchase requisitions to the purchasing department and thus represents the point at which the inventory management process integrates with the purchasing process. In a manufacturing company, a production management department would be responsible for managing inventory through planning and scheduling manufacturing activities.

Raw Materials Stores   In a manufacturing company, this function is responsible for the receipt, custody, and issuance of raw materials. When goods are received from vendors, they are transferred from the receiving department to the raw materials stores department. Once goods arrive in the raw materials storage area, they must be safeguarded against pilferage or unauthorized use. Finally, when goods are requested for production through the issuance of a materials requisition, this function issues the goods to the appropriate manufacturing department.

Manufacturing   The manufacturing function is responsible for producing the product. From an auditing perspective, there must be adequate control over the physical flow of the goods and proper accumulation of the costs attached to inventory. The manner in which costs are accumulated varies substantially from one entity to another. Entities may produce goods using a job order cost system, a process cost system, or some combination of both.

Finished Goods Stores   This function is responsible for the storage of and control over finished goods. When goods are completed by the manufacturing function, they are transferred to finished goods stores. Again, there must be adequate safeguards against pilferage or unauthorized use. When goods are ordered by a customer, a shipping order is produced by the revenue process and forwarded to the finished goods stores department. The goods are then transferred to the shipping department for shipment to the customer. Because EarthWear is a merchandising company, it maintains only finished goods (see Figure 13–2).

Cost Accounting   This function is responsible for ensuring that costs are properly attached to inventory as goods are processed through the manufacturing function. Cost accounting reviews the cost accumulation and variance reports after such data are processed into the accounting records.

General Ledger   The main objective of the general ledger function is to ensure that all inventory and costs of production are properly accumulated, classified, and summarized in the general ledger accounts. In an IT system, control or summary totals ensure that this function is performed correctly. One important control performed by the general ledger function is the reconciliation of the perpetual inventory records to the general ledger inventory accounts.

The Key
Segregation
of Duties

✂ [LO 4]

Segregation of duties is a particularly important control in the inventory management process because of the potential for theft and fraud. Therefore, individuals involved in the inventory management and inventory stores functions should not have access to the inventory records, the cost-accounting records, or the general ledger. When the inventory accounting records are maintained in an IT environment, there should be proper segregation of duties within the IT department. Table 13–3 shows the key segregation of duties for the inventory management process and examples of possible errors or fraud that can result from conflicts in duties. Table 13–4 shows the proper segregation of duties for individual inventory functions across the various departments that control inventory processing. Before reading further, please take a look at EarthWear's flowchart in Figure 13–2 and consider how EarthWear implements segregation of duties.

TABLE 13–3	**Key Segregation of Duties in the Inventory Management Process and Possible Errors or Fraud**
Segregation of Duties	*Possible Errors or Fraud Resulting from Conflicts of Duties*
The inventory management function should be segregated from the cost-accounting function.	If the individual responsible for inventory management also has access to the cost-accounting records, production and inventory costs can be manipulated. This may lead to an over- or understatement of inventory and net income.
The inventory stores function should be segregated from the cost-accounting function.	If one individual is responsible for both controlling and accounting for inventory, unauthorized shipments can be made or theft of goods can be covered up.
The cost-accounting function should be segregated from the general ledger function.	If one individual is responsible for the inventory records and also for the general ledger, it is possible for that individual to conceal unauthorized shipments. This can result in the theft of goods, leading to an overstatement of inventory.
The responsibility for supervising physical inventory should be separated from the inventory management and inventory stores functions.	If the individual responsible for production management or inventory stores function is also responsible for the physical inventory, it is possible that inventory shortages can be covered up through the adjustment of the inventory records to the physical inventory, resulting in an overstatement of inventory.

TABLE 13–4	Segregation of Duties for Inventory Functions by Department				
	Department				
Inventory Function	Inventory Management	Raw Materials Stores	Finished Goods Stores	Cost Accounting	IT
Preparation of production schedules	X				
Issuance of materials requisitions that accompany goods to the manufacturing department		X			
Updating of cost records with materials, labor, and overhead usage				X	X
Updating of inventory records				X	X
Release of goods to the shipping department			X		
Approval and issuance of purchase requisitions	X				

Inherent Risk Assessment

[LO 5] In examining the inventory management process, the auditor needs to consider the inherent risk factors that may affect the transactions processed by the system and the financial statement accounts affected by those transactions. The auditor should consider industry-related factors and operating and engagement characteristics (see Chapter 3) when assessing the possibility of a material misstatement.

Industry-Related Factors

A number of industry factors may indicate the presence of material misstatements in inventory. For example, if industry competition is intense, there may be problems with the proper valuation of inventory in terms of lower-of-cost-or-market values. Technology changes in certain industries may also promote material misstatement due to obsolescence (see Exhibit 13–2).

Engagement and Operating Characteristics

A number of engagement and operating characteristics are important to the assessment of inherent risk for inventory. First, the type of product sold by the client can increase the potential for defalcation. For example, products that are small and of high value, such as jewelry, are more susceptible to theft than large products are. Second, inventory is often difficult to audit, and its valuation may result in disagreements with the client. Finally, the auditor must be alert to possible related-party transactions for acquiring raw materials and selling the finished product. For example, the client may purchase raw materials from a company controlled by the chief executive officer at prices in excess of market value. In such a case, the value of inventory will be overstated, and cash will have been misappropriated from the entity.

EXHIBIT 13–2	Digital Cameras Sink Polaroid

Polaroid, the once high-flying company, filed for Chapter 11 bankruptcy in October 2001 after it was unable to meet payments on its heavy debt load. In August, the company's auditors, KPMG LLP, raised issue with the company's ability to continue as a going concern. The company, founded by Edward H. Land, was once one of the world's leading photography companies. Its main product was instant color film that developed when exposed to light. However, since 1995, Polaroid had faced stiff competition from one-hour photo shops and, more recently, from digital cameras. Polaroid was unable to restructure its debt or find a buyer for the company prior to seeking bankruptcy protection. In the years immediately before and after the bankruptcy, Polaroid recorded write-offs of tens of millions of dollars for obsolete inventory.

Sources: J. Bandler, "Polaroid Sustains Latest Setback as Auditor Questions Its Future," *The Wall Street Journal* (August 10, 2001), and J. Bandler and M. Pacelle, "Polaroid is Using Chapter 11 to Seek Buyer," *The Wall Street Journal* (October 15, 2001).

Audit research has also shown that there is a relatively high risk that inventory contains material misstatements.[1] In fact, some of the most notorious accounting frauds in history have involved inventory manipulations. For example, in the 1990s fraudsters at Phar-Mor, a discount store retail chain, recorded a debit to a fraudulent holding account rather than to cost of goods sold when inventory was sold. Then just before year-end, Phar-Mor accountants emptied the contents of the fraudulent holding account and allocated it to stores as fictitious inventory (see a detailed description of the Phar-Mor fraud and related trial on the book's web site www.mhhe.com/messier7e). Exhibit 13–3 describes the inventory fraud at Centennial Technologies, Inc.

EXHIBIT 13–3	Inventory Scams at Centennial Technologies

Background

Centennial Technologies designed, manufactured, and marketed an extensive line of PC cards: rugged, lightweight, credit card–sized devices inserted into a dedicated slot in a broad range of electronic equipment that contain microprocessors, such as portable computers, telecommunications equipment, and manufacturing equipment. The company's customer list included companies such as Digital Equipment Corporation, Philips Electronics, Sharp Electronics Corporation, and Xerox Corporation.

Emanuel Pinez was the CEO of technology highflier Centennial Technologies, Inc., in the mid-1990s. In 1996, Centennial's surging stock graduated to the New York Stock Exchange just two years after going public. It finished 1996 as the best-performing stock on the big board, up a stunning 451 percent. Just before the fraud was uncovered, analysts still had "strong buy" recommendations outstanding.

Pinez had an impressive resume, but it turns out much of it was false. After the scandal broke, investors and the auditors learned what Pinez's wife knew, that he was a "pathological liar." For example, as a young man he claimed to set a world record in an international swimming competition across the English Channel. The reports were published, and Pinez was hailed briefly as a national hero—until the truth came out that there was no such competition or record. Pinez constantly made aggressive estimates regarding Centennial's growth, and in 1996 he began telling investors that Centennial was negotiating an order worth more than $300 million with AT&T (no such deal ever took place or apparently even existed).

Card Scam

Centennial's growth attracted several sophisticated institutional investors, such as Oppenheimer Funds Inc. and Fidelity Investments. Some investors started to crave a firsthand look at Centennial's operations. One investor sent an analyst to meet with Pinez and tour the headquarters in Billerica, Massachusetts. Although the analyst noticed some computer equipment in the administrative offices, he was somewhat surprised that there was none in Pinez's office. During a tour of Centennial's manufacturing facilities, he saw "a room full of people banging on cards with rubber mallets. I had a bad feeling." He returned to his firm and "dumped the Centennial shares immediately."

In truth, Pinez had enlisted a handful of employees in the company's Billerica manufacturing plant to assemble fake memory cards by simply welding the casings together and leaving out a critical silicon computer chip. These fake cards made their way into inventory and sales.

Flash 98 Scam

In the fourth quarter of 1996 Centennial began shipping a new product called "Flash 1998." It was a miniature memory card for notebook computers. Sales for fiscal year 1996 amounted to about $2 million. The company told the auditors that it wanted to keep the details of the card relatively quiet for a few more months for competitive reasons. Pinez indicated that due to design advances developed by Centennial's research and development team, these new cards had an extremely low production cost, about 10 cents, with a sales price of a whopping $500. It turns out there was no such product. All sales were to one company, BBC. The company was run by a close personal friend of Pinez. To fool the auditors into thinking an actual sale took place, Pinez wired $1 million of his own personal funds to a third company, St. Jude Management Corp., which then paid Centennial on behalf of BBC for its Flash 98 purchases. After the fraud was uncovered, the auditors, Coopers & Lybrand, claimed that the Flash 98 scam was a "unique" fraud because it appeared that a product was going out and cash was coming in.

Aftermath

From his prison cell, Pinez denied any wrongdoing and indicated that his actions were undertaken to benefit the company. Pinez attributed his problems to the scrutiny that inevitably comes with success: "You get lightning when you're very high."

Sources: M. Beasley, F. Buckless, S. Glover, and D. Prawitt, "Auditing Cases: An Interactive Learning Approach," 4th ed., Prentice Hall, 2008, and J. Auerbach, "How Centennial Technologies, a Hot Stock, Cooled," *The Wall Street Journal* (April 11, 1997).

---

[1]A. Eilifsen and W. F. Messier, Jr., "Auditor Detection of Misstatements: A Review and Integration of Empirical Research," *Journal of Accounting Literature* 2000 (19), pp. 1–43.

Prior-year misstatements are good indicators of potential misstatements in the current year; thus, auditors should carefully consider if misstatements found in the prior years' audit may be present in the current inventory and plan the audit accordingly.

Control Risk Assessment

[LO 6]   The auditor may follow a substantive strategy when auditing inventory and cost of goods sold. When this is done, the auditor places no reliance on the control activities in the inventory management process and sets the level of control risk at the maximum. The auditor then relies on substantive procedures to determine the fairness of inventory. Such a strategy may be appropriate when internal control is not adequate.

In many cases, however, the auditor can rely on internal control for inventory. This normally occurs when the client has an integrated cost-accounting/inventory management system. For discussion purposes, it is assumed that the auditor has decided to follow a reliance strategy. Figure 13–3 summarizes the three steps for setting the control risk following this strategy. Each of these steps is only briefly reviewed within the context of the inventory management process because the reader should thoroughly understand the control risk setting process followed by auditors.

Understand and Document Internal Control

In order to set the control risk for the inventory management process, the auditor must understand the five internal control components. Two points should be mentioned. First, if the client uses IT for monitoring the flow of goods and accumulating costs, the auditor will need to evaluate both the general IT controls and the inventory application controls. Second, the auditor will need a thorough understanding of the process used by the client to value inventory.

Plan and Perform Tests of Controls

In performing this step, the auditor again must identify the relevant control activities within the client's inventory system that ensure that material misstatements are either prevented or detected and corrected. Audit procedures used to test the client's control activities in the inventory management process are discussed in subsequent sections.

FIGURE 13–3	**Major Steps in Setting the Control Risk in the Inventory Management Process**

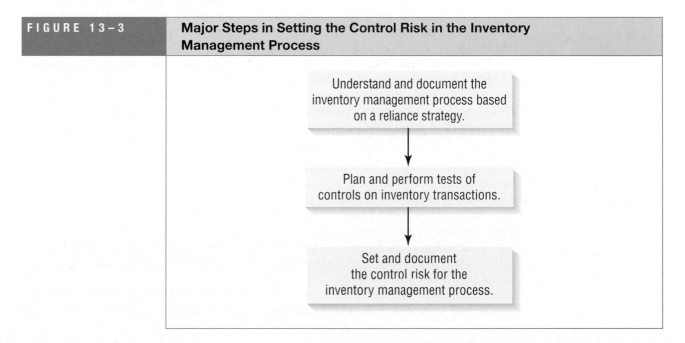

Understand and document the inventory management process based on a reliance strategy.

↓

Plan and perform tests of controls on inventory transactions.

↓

Set and document the control risk for the inventory management process.

Set and
Document the
Control Risk

Once the controls in the inventory system have been tested, the auditor sets the level of control risk. The auditor should document the achieved level of control risk using either quantitative amounts or qualitative terms. The documentation supporting the achieved level of control risk for the inventory management process might include a flowchart (such as the one shown in Figure 13–2), the results of the tests of controls, and a memorandum indicating the overall conclusions about control risk.

Control Activities and Tests of Controls— Inventory Transactions

> [LO 7]   Table 13–5 provides a summary of the possible misstatements, examples of control activities and examples of selected tests of controls for inventory transactions. The discussion includes control activities that are present in a manufacturing setting. Because EarthWear is a retailer, the controls over the production process are not relevant. A number of control activities in the revenue and purchasing processes provide assurance for selected assertions for inventory. The discussion that follows is limited to the more important assertions.

Occurrence
of Inventory
Transactions

The auditor's main concern is that all recorded inventory exists. The major control activity for preventing fictitious inventory transactions from being recorded is proper segregation of duties, in which the inventory management and inventory stores functions are separated from the departments responsible for inventory and cost-accounting records. This control prevents operating personnel from having access to both inventory and the perpetual inventory records. Additionally, prenumbered documents to handle the receipt, transfer, and withdrawal of inventory may prevent the recording of fictitious inventory in the accounting records.

The auditor should also be concerned that goods may be stolen. The auditor's concern about theft of goods varies, depending upon the type of product sold or manufactured by the client. Products that are large or cumbersome may be difficult to steal. However, products that are small and of high value, such as jewelry or computer memory chips, are more susceptible to theft. The client should maintain physical safeguards over inventory that are consistent with the susceptibility and value of the goods. What controls does EarthWear have in place to address the occurrence assertion? How would you gather audit evidence regarding the effectiveness of these controls?

Review and observation are the main tests of controls used by the auditor to test the control activities shown in Table 13–5. For example, the auditor can observe and evaluate the employees' segregation of duties. The auditor can also review and test the client's procedures for the transfer of raw materials from the receiving department and their issuance to the manufacturing departments.

Completeness
of Inventory
Transactions

The control activities for the completeness assertion relate to recording inventory that has been received. Typically, the control activities for this assertion are contained within the purchasing process. These control activities and the related tests of controls were presented in Table 11–6 in Chapter 11. For example, in some instances, additional control activities may be used in the raw materials stores department to ensure that the goods are recorded in the perpetual inventory records. This might include comparing a summary of the receiving reports to the inventory status report.

If goods are consigned, the client must have control activities to ensure that goods held on consignment by other parties are included in inventory and goods

TABLE 13–5	Summary of Assertions, Possible Misstatements, Example Control Activities, and Example Tests of Controls for Inventory Transactions		
Assertion	*Possible Misstatement*	*Example Control Activity*	*Example Test of Controls*
Occurrence	Fictitious inventory	Segregation of duties	Observe and evaluate proper segregation of duties
		Inventory transferred to inventory department using an approved, prenumbered receiving report	Review and test procedures for the transfer of inventory
		Inventory transferred to manufacturing using prenumbered materials requisitions	Review and test procedures for issuing materials to manufacturing departments
		Accounting for numerical sequence of materials requisitions	Review and test client procedures for accounting for numerical sequence of materials requisitions
	Inventory recorded but not on hand due to theft	Physical safeguards over inventory	Observe the physical safeguards over inventory
Completeness	Inventory received but not recorded	The same as the control activities for completeness in the purchasing process (see Table 11–6)	The same as the tests of controls performed on the control procedures in the purchasing process (see Table 11–6)
	Consigned goods not properly accounted for	Procedures to include goods out on consignment and exclude goods held on consignment	Review and test client's procedures for consignment goods
Authorization	Unauthorized production activity, resulting in excess levels of inventory	Preparation and review of authorized purchase or production schedules	Review authorized production schedules
	Inventory obsolescence	Use of material requirements planning and/or just-in-time inventory systems	Review and test procedures for developing inventory levels and procedures used to control them
		Review of inventory levels by design department	
Accuracy	Inventory quantities recorded incorrectly	Periodic or annual comparison of goods on hand with amounts shown in perpetual inventory records	Review and test procedures for taking physical inventory
	Inventory and cost of goods sold not properly costed	Standard costs that are reviewed by management	Review and test procedures used to develop standard costs
		Review of cost accumulation and variance reports	Review and test cost accumulation and variance reports
	Inventory obsolescence	Inventory management personnel review inventory for obsolete, slow-moving, or excess quantities	Review and test procedures for identifying obsolete, slow-moving, or excess quantities
	Inventory transactions not posted to the perpetual inventory records		
	Amounts for inventory from purchases journal not posted correctly to the general ledger inventory account	Perpetual inventory records reconciled to general ledger control account monthly	Review the reconciliation of perpetual inventory to general ledger control account
Cutoff	Inventory transactions recorded in the wrong period	All receiving reports processed daily by the IT department to record the receipt of inventory	Review and test procedures for processing inventory included on receiving reports into the perpetual records
		All shipping documents processed daily to record the shipment of finished goods	Review and test procedures for removing inventory from perpetual records based on shipment of goods
Classification	Inventory transactions not properly classified among raw materials, work in process, and finished goods	Materials requisitions and production data forms used to process goods through manufacturing	Review the procedures and forms used to classify inventory

held on consignment for others are excluded from inventory. The auditor can review the client's procedures for including or excluding consigned goods.

Authorization of Inventory Transactions

The control activities for the purchase of materials were discussed in Chapter 11 on the purchasing process. The auditor's concern with authorization in the inventory system is with unauthorized purchase or production activity that may lead to excess levels of certain types of finished goods. If such goods can quickly become obsolete, ending inventory may be overstated. The preparation and review of authorized purchase schedules by EarthWear's design department should prevent such misstatements. The use of some type of inventory-planning system, such as a material requirements planning system or a just-in-time inventory system, may also limit unauthorized production.

Accuracy of Inventory Transactions

Accuracy is an important assertion because inventory transactions that are not properly recorded result in misstatements that directly affect the amounts reported in the financial statements for cost of goods sold and inventory. The accurate processing of inventory purchase transactions involves applying the correct price to the actual quantity received. Similarly, when inventory is shipped, accurate processing requires that the actual number of items shipped be removed from inventory and that the proper cost be recorded to cost of goods sold. The use of a perpetual inventory system in conjunction with a periodic or annual physical inventory count should result in the proper quantities of inventory being shown in the client's perpetual inventory records. EarthWear maintains the purchase cost of its products in its master inventory file. Many manufacturing companies use standard cost systems to value their inventory. Standard costs should approximate actual costs, and the presence of large variances is one signal that the inventory may not be valued appropriately. Auditing the client's physical inventory and standard costs is discussed in more detail later in the chapter.

Management should also have controls in place to consider inventory obsolescence. Inventory management personnel should periodically review inventory on hand for obsolete, slow-moving, or excess inventory. Such inventory should be written down to its fair market value. The auditor can review the client's procedures for identifying obsolete, slow-moving, or excess inventory. EarthWear's design department closely monitors its products to identify any end-of-season merchandise or overstocks, which are then sold at liquidation prices through special catalog inserts.

Cutoff of Inventory Transactions

Inventory transactions recorded in the improper period could affect a number of accounts, as illustrated by this simple inventory computation:

Beginning inventory + Purchases − Cost of goods sold = Ending inventory

The cutoff risks, control activities, and tests of controls associated with inventory transactions were already addressed in Chapters 10 and 11, since the sale of inventory involves the revenue process and purchase of inventory involves the purchasing process. For sold (purchased) inventory, a common test of the client's controls to ensure transactions are recorded in a timely manner is to compare the date on the shipping document (receiving report) with the date in the sales journal (payment voucher). There should not be a long period between these two dates. As discussed later, auditors also often focus tests of details on transactions near year-end.

It is important to understand that failure to record inventory in the proper period can result in misstatements on both the balance sheet and income statement. For example, if items shipped FOB–destination point are recorded as sold before they are received by the customer, then revenue, costs of goods sold, and receivables will be overstated and inventory will be understated.

Classification of Inventory Transactions

Considering what you know about EarthWear's business, how important do you think the classification assertion is for EarthWear's inventory compared to inventory at a manufacturing company? Classification is not an important assertion for EarthWear because all goods are finished and ready for sale. However, in a manufacturing company, the client must have control activities to ensure that inventory is properly classified as raw materials, work in process, or finished goods. This can usually be accomplished by determining which departments in the manufacturing process are included in raw materials, work in process, and finished goods inventory. Thus, by knowing which manufacturing department holds the inventory, the client is able to classify it by type.

Relating the Assessed Level of Control Risk to Substantive Procedures

[LO 8] The same judgment process is followed in setting control risk in the inventory management process that was used with other processes. For example, EarthWear has strong controls over the processing of inventory transactions. The auditor can rely on those controls if tests of controls indicate that the controls are operating effectively. If the results of the tests of controls for the inventory system do not support the planned level of control risk, the auditor would set control risk higher and set detection risk lower. This would lead to increased substantive procedures.

Auditing Inventory

The discussion of the audit of inventory follows the process outlined in prior chapters. Two categories of substantive procedures are discussed: substantive analytical procedures and tests of details of classes of transactions, account balances, and disclosures. Table 13–6 presents the assertions for classes of transactions, events, account balances, and disclosures as they apply to inventory. You should note that

TABLE 13-6	Assertions about Classes of Transactions, Events, Account Balances, and Disclosures for Inventory

Assertions about Classes of Transactions and Events:
- **Occurrence.** Inventory transactions and events are valid.
- **Completeness.** All inventory transactions and events have been recorded.
- **Authorization.** All inventory transactions and events are properly authorized.
- **Accuracy.** Inventory transactions have been properly computed, and ending inventory and related revenue and cost of goods sold have been properly accumulated from journals and ledgers.
- **Cutoff.** Inventory receipts and shipments are recorded in the correct accounting period.
- **Classification.** Inventory is recorded in the proper accounts (e.g., raw materials, work in process, or finished goods).

Assertions about Account Balances at the Period End:
- **Existence.** Inventory recorded on the books and records actually exists.
- **Rights and obligations.** The entity has the legal right (i.e., ownership) to the recorded inventory.
- **Completeness.** All inventory is recorded.
- **Valuation and allocation.** Inventory is properly recorded in accordance with GAAP (e.g., lower of cost or market).

Assertions about Presentation and Disclosure:
- **Occurrence and rights and obligations.** All disclosed events, transactions, and other matters relating to inventory have occurred and pertain to the entity.
- **Completeness.** All disclosures relating to inventory that should have been included in the financial statements have been included.
- **Classification and understandability.** Financial information relating to inventory is appropriately presented and described, and disclosures are clearly expressed.
- **Accuracy and valuation.** Financial and other information relating to inventory are disclosed fairly and at appropriate amounts.

the auditor may gather evidence about assertions related to transactions (substantive tests of transactions) in conjunction with testing the internal controls. If the tests of controls indicate that the controls are not operating effectively, the auditor may need to test transactions at the date the account balance is tested.

Practice INSIGHT	Many companies rely on spreadsheets to support inventory transactions and balances that are recorded into the general ledger and financial statements. Such spreadsheets may include complex calculations with multiple-linked supporting spreadsheets. The importance of the integrity and reliability of the information generated by such spreadsheets increases as the complexity increases from low to high and as usage increases. The auditor should evaluate the controls over the inventory spreadsheets. Because spreadsheets can be generated by multiple users, easily changed, and may lack appropriate controls, the use of spreadsheets can increase inherent risk of misstatement.

Substantive Analytical Procedures

⚓ [LO 9]   Substantive analytical procedures are useful audit tests for examining the reasonableness of inventory and cost of goods sold. When performed as part of audit planning, preliminary analytical procedures can effectively identify whether the inventory and cost of goods sold accounts contain material misstatements. Final analytical procedures are useful as an overall review for inventory and related accounts to identify obsolete, slow-moving, and excess inventory. Substantive analytical procedures are useful for obtaining assurance on the valuation assertion for inventory. Such procedures can also identify problems with improper inclusion or exclusion of costs in overhead.

For example, inventory turnover (cost of goods sold ÷ inventory) can be compared over time or to the industry average. From an auditor's perspective, what questions, concerns or risks are suggested by the pattern of data in the table below?

	2007	2008	2009	Industry Average
Inventory	$14,800	$16,500	$26,250	
Inventory Turnover	13	12	9	18

The significant increase in inventory coupled with substantially slower inventory turnover may indicate the presence of slow-moving or obsolete inventory. The auditor would seek an explanation for the pattern from the client and the auditor may need to revise the audit plan for the physical inventory observation and detail testing over the inventory valuation assertion (inventory observation and detail testing are discussed later in the chapter). If inventory turnover is higher than the industry average it may indicate inefficient inventory policies.

Another common analytical procedure involves the gross profit percentages. The gross profit percentage can also be compared to previous years' or industry data and may provide valuable evidence on unrecorded inventory (an understatement) or fictitious inventory (an overstatement). This ratio may also provide information on the proper valuation of inventory. For example, a small or negative gross profit margin may indicate issues related to the lower-of-cost-or-market valuation of inventory. It is important that the auditor use sufficiently disaggregated analytical procedures in order to identify unusual patterns like the one illustrated in Figure 5–3, in Chapter 5. Table 13–7 lists examples of substantive analytical procedures that are useful in auditing inventory and related accounts at either the planning stage or as an overall review.

Prior to presenting the tests of account balances for inventory, this chapter discusses two significant audit procedures: auditing standard costs and observing physical inventory.

TABLE 13-7	Examples of Substantive Analytical Procedures Used in Testing Inventory and Related Accounts
Example Substantive Analytical Procedure	*Possible Misstatement Detected*
Compare raw material, finished goods, and total inventory turnover to previous years' and industry averages	Obsolete, slow-moving, or excess inventory
Compare days outstanding in inventory to previous years' and industry average	Obsolete, slow-moving, or excess inventory
Compare gross profit percentage by product line with previous years' and industry data	Unrecorded or fictitious inventory
Compare actual cost of goods sold to budgeted amounts	Over- or understated inventory
Compare current-year standard costs with prior years' after considering current conditions	Over- or understated inventory
Compare actual manufacturing overhead costs with budgeted or standard manufacturing overhead costs	Inclusion or exclusion of overhead costs

Auditing Standard Costs

[LO 10]   Many manufacturing entities use a standard cost system to measure performance and to value inventory. If a standard cost system is integrated with the general accounting records, cost accumulation and variance reports are direct outputs of the client's inventory-accounting system.

For accuracy and proper valuation, standard costs should approximate actual costs. To test the standard costs, the auditor should first review the client's policies and procedures for constructing standard costs. Once the policies and procedures are understood, the auditor normally tests the component cost buildup for a representative sample of standard product costs.

Three components make up the cost of producing a product: materials, labor, and overhead. For discussion purposes, suppose that Calabro Wireless Services (Calabro company background is provided in Chapter 8) assembles five types of wireless devices. Recall that Calabro is a business services company that uses wireless communications technology to develop solutions for businesses. Assume further that all parts used in the devices are purchased from outside vendors. The process followed in auditing the three components that make up the standard costs for a type of device follows. (Similar auditing techniques would be used for other clients with production processes.)

Materials

Determining the materials costs requires examining the quantity and type of materials included in the product and the price of the materials. The quantity and type of materials are tested by reviewing the engineering specifications for the product. For example, in the case of wireless devices, the auditor can obtain a set of engineering specifications that includes a blueprint and a list of materials needed to manufacture a particular device. The auditor can compare the list of materials with the standard cost documentation used to support the cost accumulation. The prices used on the standard cost documentation can be traced to vendors' invoices as a test of actual costs.

Labor

The determination of labor costs requires evidence about the type and amount of labor needed for production and the labor rate. Following our example, the amount of labor necessary to assemble a wireless device can be determined by reviewing engineering estimates, which may be based on time-and-motion studies or on historical information. The labor rates for each type of labor necessary to assemble a device can be tested by examining a schedule of authorized wages. Labor costs included in inventory are often tested in conjunction with payroll expense.

Overhead   The auditor gathers evidence regarding overhead costs by reviewing the client's method of overhead allocation for reasonableness, compliance with GAAP, and consistency. The auditor can examine the costs included in overhead to be sure that such costs can appropriately be assigned to the product. The inclusion or exclusion of such costs should be consistent from one period to the next. Using the wireless device example, the auditor would obtain a listing of expense accounts used to make up the overhead pool of costs. The auditor can compare the actual costs for the period to the budgeted costs. The auditor can also compare the costs included in the current year's listing with those in the prior year's listing.

Observing Physical Inventory

[LO 11]   The auditor's observation of inventory is a generally accepted auditing procedure (AU 331). However, the auditor is not required to observe all inventory, but only inventory that is material. Internal auditors may also observe physical inventory. The primary reason for observing the client's physical inventory is to establish the *existence* of the inventory. The observation of the physical inventory also provides evidence on the *accuracy, rights and obligations,* and *valuation* assertions. Based on the physical inventory count, the client compiles the physical inventory. While the form of compilation may differ among entities, it normally contains a list of the items by type and quantity, the assigned cost for each item, the inventory value for each item, and a total for the inventory.

Prior to the physical count of inventory, the auditor should be familiar with the inventory locations, the major items in inventory, and the client's inventory management processes and instructions for counting inventory. During the observation of the physical inventory count, the auditor should do the following:

- Ensure that no production is scheduled. If production is scheduled, ensure that proper controls are established for movement between departments in order to prevent double counting.
- Ensure that there is no movement of goods during the inventory count. If movement is necessary, the auditor and client personnel must ensure that the goods are not double counted and that all goods are counted.
- Make sure that the client's count teams are following the inventory count instructions. If the count teams are not following the instructions, the auditor should notify the client representative in charge of the area.
- Ensure that inventory tags are issued sequentially to individual departments. For many inventory counts, the goods are marked with multicopy inventory tags. The count teams record the type and quantity of inventory on each tag, and one copy of each tag is then used to compile the inventory. If the client uses another method of counting inventory, such as detailed inventory listings or handheld computers, the auditor should obtain copies of the listings or files prior to the start of the inventory count.
- Perform test counts and record a sample of counts in the working papers. This information will be used to evaluate the accuracy and completeness of the client's inventory compilation.
- Obtain tag control information for testing the client's inventory compilation. Tag control information includes documentation of the numerical sequence of all inventory tags and accounting for all used and unused inventory tags. If inventory listings are used by the client, copies of the listings will accomplish the objective of documenting the entire inventory count.
- Obtain cutoff information, including the number of the last shipping and receiving documents issued on the date of the physical inventory count.

- Observe the condition of the inventory for items that may be obsolete, slow-moving, or carried in excess quantities.
- Inquire about goods held on consignment for others or held on a "bill-and-hold" basis. Such items should not be included in the client's inventory. The auditor must also inquire about goods held on consignment for the client. These goods should be included in the inventory count.

If these audit procedures are followed, the auditor has reasonable assurance that a proper inventory count has been taken.

Some companies choose to count their inventory on a cyclical basis throughout the year instead of just once at the end of the year. They may choose to only count part of the warehouse each cycle, but ensure that the entire warehouse is counted at least once each year. If the auditor observes one or more of these interim cycle counts, the client must have a reliable perpetual inventory system so that the auditor can examine activity (on a test basis) between the count date(s) and year-end in order to obtain appropriate evidence about the year-end inventory balance.

Practice INSIGHT	One of the most effective ways for the auditor to evaluate the possibility of inventory fraud is to physically examine the client's inventory when an inventory count is being performed. But even physical examination procedures do not eliminate the risk of misstatement due to fraud since the client can perpetrate fraud such as:

- obtaining advance notice of the timing and location of the count, which can permit the client to conceal fictitious inventory at locations not visited;
- stacking empty containers at a warehouse where container contents are not checked during the count;
- falsifying shipping documents to show that inventory is in transit from one company location to another; and
- falsifying documents to show that inventory is located at a public warehouse or other location not controlled by the company.

If the auditor does not properly maintain control of a copy of the client's final count sheets to tie into final inventory records the client can also fraudulently overstate inventory by:

- following the auditor during the count and adding fictitious inventory to items not tested by the auditor; or
- entering additional quantities on manual and/or electronic inventory sheets that do not exist or adding a digit in front of the actual count.

Tests of Details of Classes of Transactions, Account Balances, and Disclosures

[LO 12] Table 13–6 presents the assertions for inventory. The intended purpose of tests of details of transactions is to detect monetary misstatements in the inventory account. The auditor may conduct tests of details of transactions specifically for inventory. However, because the inventory management process interacts with the revenue, purchasing, and human resource management processes, transactions involving the receipt of goods, shipment of goods, and assignment of labor costs are normally tested as part of those processes. For example, receiving department personnel prepare a receiving report that includes the quantity and type of goods received. The receiving report and vendor invoice are then used to record the accounts payable. If the auditor intends to obtain substantive evidence on the perpetual inventory records, the tests of receipt and shipment of goods can be extended by tracing the transactions into the perpetual inventory records. For example, the receiving report is generally used by the client to record the goods in the perpetual inventory records or inventory master file (see Figure 13–2). The auditor can perform a test of detail of transactions by tracing a sample of receiving reports into the perpetual inventory records. Labor costs can also be traced to individual inventory transactions and into the cost-accounting records.

✎ **[LO 13]**   As previously mentioned, tests of details of transactions are often conducted in conjunction with tests of controls. Table 13–8 presents examples of tests of details of transactions, account balances, and disclosures for assertions related to inventory. The discussion that follows focuses primarily on tests of details of account balances of inventory. Accuracy is the first assertion discussed because the auditor must establish that the detailed records that support the inventory account agree with the general ledger account.

TABLE 13–8	Examples of Inventory Tests of Transactions, Account Balances, and Disclosures
Assertions about Classes of Transactions	**Example Substantive Tests of Transaction***
Occurrence	Vouch a sample of inventory additions (i.e., purchases) to receiving reports and purchase requisitions.
Completeness	Trace a sample of receiving reports to the inventory records (i.e., master file, status report).
Authorization	Test a sample of inventory shipments to ensure there are approved shipping tickets and customer sales.
Accuracy	Recompute the mathematical accuracy of a sample of inventory transactions (i.e., price $\times$ quantity).
	Audit standard costs or other methods used to price inventory (see discussion in the chapter for the audit procedures used to audit standard costs).
	Trace costs used to price goods in the inventory compilation to standard costs or vendors' invoices.
Cutoff	Trace a sample of time cards before and after period end to the appropriate weekly inventory report, and trace the weekly inventory report to the general ledger to verify inventory transactions are recorded in the proper period.
Classification	Examine a sample of inventory checks for proper classification into expense accounts.
Assertions about Account Balances at Period End	**Example Tests of Details of Account Balances**
Existence	Observe count of physical inventory (see discussion in chapter for proper inventory observation procedures).
Rights and obligations	Verify that inventory held on consignment for others is not included in inventory.
	Verify that "bill-and-hold" goods are not included in inventory.
Completeness	Trace test counts and tag control information to the inventory compilation.
Valuation and allocation	Obtain a copy of the inventory compilation and agree totals to general ledger.
	Trace test counts and tag control information to the inventory compilation.
	Test mathematical accuracy of extensions and foot the inventory compilation.
	Inquire of management concerning obsolete, slow-moving, or excess inventory.
	Review book-to-physical adjustment for possible misstatements (see Table 13–9).
Assertions about Presentation and Disclosure	**Example Tests of Details of Disclosures**
Occurrence, and rights and obligations	Inquire of management and review any loan agreements and board of directors' minutes for any indication that inventory has been pledged or assigned.
	Inquire of management about issues related to warranty obligations.
Completeness	Complete financial reporting checklist to ensure that all financial statement disclosures related to inventory are made.
Classification and understandability	Review inventory compilation for proper classification among raw materials, work in process, and finished goods.
	Read footnotes to ensure that required disclosures are understandable.
Accuracy and valuation	Determine if the cost method is accurately disclosed (e.g., LIFO).
	Inquire of management about issues related to LIFO liquidations.
	Read footnotes and other information to ensure that the information is accurate and properly presented at the appropriate amounts.

*Many of these tests of details of transactions are commonly conducted as dual-purpose tests (i.e., in conjunction with tests of controls).

Accuracy

Gathering evidence on the accuracy of inventory requires obtaining a copy of the compilation of the physical inventory that shows inventory quantities and prices.

The inventory compilation is footed, and the mathematical extensions of quantity multiplied by price are verified. Additionally, test counts made by the auditor during the physical inventory and tag control information are traced into the compilation.

Many times the client has adjusted the general ledger inventory balance to agree to the physical inventory amounts (referred to as *book-to-physical adjustment*) before the auditor begins the substantive tests of account balances. If the client has made the book-to-physical adjustment, the totals from the compilation for inventory should agree with the general ledger.

When the client maintains a perpetual inventory system, the totals from the inventory compilation should also be agreed to these records. The auditor can use computer-assisted audit techniques to accomplish these audit steps. For example, the auditor can use a generalized or custom audit software package to trace costs used to price goods in the inventory compilation to standard cost files. The extensions and footing can also be tested at the same time.

Cutoff

In gathering evidence on the cutoff assertion for inventory, the auditor attempts to determine whether all sales of finished goods and purchases of raw materials are recorded in the proper period. For sales cutoff, the auditor can examine a sample of shipping documents for a few days before and after year-end for recording of inventory shipments in the proper period. For purchases cutoff, the auditor can examine a sample of receiving documents for a few days before and after year-end for recording of inventory purchases in the proper period. Chapters 10 and 11 discuss sales and purchases cutoff.

Existence

Existence is one of the more important assertions for the inventory account. The observation of the physical inventory is the primary audit step used to verify this assertion. The auditor obtains information regarding existence by observing inventory items in the client's warehouse, understanding and testing the client's count procedures addressing validity, and through the auditor's test counts. If the auditor is satisfied with the client's physical inventory count, the auditor has sufficient, appropriate evidence on the existence of recorded inventory.

Completeness

The auditor must determine whether all inventory has been included in the inventory compilation and the general ledger inventory account. The tests related to the observation of the physical inventory count provide assurance that all goods on hand are included in inventory. Observing that count teams have placed count tags on all inventory items provides evidence regarding completeness of the count. Tracing test counts and tag control information into the inventory compilation provide assurance that the inventory counted during the physical inventory observation is included in the compilation. In some cases, inventory is held on consignment by others or is stored in public warehouses (AU 331). The auditor normally confirms or physically observes such inventory.

Practice INSIGHT

Auditors should investigate significant differences between the physical count and detailed perpetual inventory records before the accounting and inventory records are adjusted to match the physical count. Understanding the nature of the significant difference may indicate problems with either the physical count, the perpetual system, or shrinkage (unaccounted reduction in inventory due to theft or damage).

Rights and
Obligations

The auditor must determine whether the recorded inventory is actually owned by the entity. Two issues related to ownership can arise. First, the auditor must be sure that the inventory on hand belongs to the client. If the client holds inventory on consignment, such inventory should not be included in the physical inventory. Second, in some industries, goods are sold on a "bill-and-hold" basis. In such cases, the goods are treated as a sale, but the client holds the goods until the customer needs them. Again, the auditor must be certain that such goods are segregated and not counted at the time of the physical inventory.

Valuation and
Allocation

A number of important valuation issues are related to inventory. The first issue relates to the costs used to value the inventory items included in the compilation. When the client, such as EarthWear, purchases inventory, valuation of the inventory can normally be accomplished by vouching the costs to vendors' invoices. When the client uses standard costs, the auditor audits the standard costs as discussed previously. The second valuation issue relates to the lower-of-cost-or-market tests for inventory. The auditor normally performs such tests on large-dollar items or on the client's various product lines. At EarthWear, the auditors would likely perform the lower-of-cost-or-market test on merchandise noted by management for liquidation. A third valuation issue relates to obsolete, slow-moving, or excess inventory. Inventory management personnel should periodically review inventory on hand for obsolete, slow-moving, or excess inventory. Such inventory should be written down to its fair market value. The auditor can review the client's procedures for identifying obsolete, slow-moving, or excess inventory. EarthWear's design department closely monitors its products to identify any end-of-season merchandise or overstocks, which are then sold at liquidation prices through special catalog inserts. The auditor should ask management about their procedures to identify obsolete, slow-moving, or excess inventory, and if it is determined that such inventory exists the auditor should determine whether the inventory has been properly written down. Finally, the auditor should investigate any large adjustments between the amount of inventory shown in the general ledger account and the amount determined from the physical inventory count (book-to-physical adjustments) for possible misstatements. Table 13–9 presents a list of items that may lead to book-to-physical differences.

Classification and
Understandability

The presentation and disclosure assertion of classification of inventory for EarthWear is not an issue because the company sells only finished products. However, in a manufacturing company, the auditor must determine that inventory is properly classified as raw materials, work in process, or finished goods. In most manufacturing companies, proper classification can be achieved by determining which manufacturing processing department has control of the inventory on the date of the physical count. For example, if inventory tags are used to count inventory and they are assigned numerically to departments, classification can be verified at the physical inventory. The auditor can ensure that each department is using the assigned tags. The tag control information by department can be compared to the information on the inventory compilation to ensure that it is properly classified among raw materials, work in process, and finished goods.

TABLE 13–9	Possible Causes of Book-to-Physical Differences
	Inventory cutoff errors
	Unreported scrap or spoilage
	Pilferage or theft

TABLE 13–10	Examples of Disclosure Items for Inventory and Related Accounts
	Cost method (FIFO, LIFO, retail method)
	Components of inventory
	Long-term purchase contracts
	Consigned inventory
	Purchases from related parties
	LIFO liquidations
	Pledged or assigned inventory
	Disclosure of unusual losses from write-downs of inventory or losses on long-term purchase commitments
	Warranty obligations

EXHIBIT 13–4	EarthWear's Financial Statement Disclosure for Inventory
	Inventory is stated at the last-in, first-out (LIFO) cost, which is lower than market. If the first-in, first-out method of accounting for inventory had been used, inventory would have been approximately $10.8 million and $13.6 million higher than reported at December 31, 2009 and 2008, respectively.

Other Presentation and Disclosure Assertions

Several important disclosure issues are related to inventory. Table 13–10 presents some examples of disclosure items for inventory and related accounts. For example, management must disclose the cost method, such as LIFO or FIFO, used to value inventory. Management must also disclose the components (raw materials, work in process, and finished goods) of inventory either on the face of the balance sheet or in the footnotes. Finally, if the entity uses LIFO to value inventory and there is a material LIFO liquidation, footnote disclosure is normally required.

Exhibit 13–4 presents EarthWear's financial statement disclosure for inventory. Note that the company uses LIFO to value inventory, and it discloses the approximate inventory value if FIFO had been used.

Practice INSIGHT

During an inspection of a Big 4 accounting firm, the PCAOB identified an audit deficiency in the work performed on inventory. The auditor failed to sufficiently test the valuation and existence assertions related to the issuer's inventory balance. The failure included failing to test key inputs used in calculating LIFO, failing to perform inventory price testing, and failing to test key assumptions used to calculate the inventory obsolescence reserve. (PCAOB Release 104-2006-205)

Evaluating the Audit Findings—Inventory

[LO 14] When the auditor has completed the planned substantive tests of the inventory account, all the identified misstatements should be aggregated. The likely misstatement is compared to the tolerable misstatement allocated to the inventory account. If the likely misstatement is less than the tolerable misstatement, the auditor may accept the inventory account as fairly presented. Conversely, if the likely misstatement exceeds the tolerable misstatement, the auditor should conclude that the inventory account is not fairly presented.

For example, in Chapter 3, tolerable misstatement was $900,000. Exhibit 3–4 showed that Willis & Adams detected two misstatements in inventory: one that resulted in an overstatement of inventory by $312,500 based on a projection of a sample and one misstatement that understated inventory by $227,450 due to inventory in transit. Because neither of these misstatements is greater than the tolerable misstatement, Willis & Adams can conclude that the audit evidence supports fair presentation. However, if these misstatements, either individually or in aggregate, had been greater than the tolerable misstatement, the evidence would not support fair presentation. In this case the auditor would have two choices: adjust the accounts to reduce the misstatement to an amount less than the tolerable misstatement or qualify the audit report.

The auditor should again analyze the misstatements discovered through the application of substantive procedures, because these misstatements may provide additional evidence on the control risk for the inventory management process. If the auditor concludes that the audit risk is unacceptably high, additional audit procedures should be performed, or the auditor must be satisfied that the client has adjusted the related financial statement accounts to an acceptable level.

KEY TERMS

Analytical procedures. Evaluations of financial information made by a study of plausible relationships among both financial and nonfinancial data.

Application controls. Controls that apply to the processing of specific computer applications and are part of the computer programs used in the accounting system.

Assertions. Expressed or implied representations by management that are reflected in the financial statement components.

Computer-assisted audit techniques (CAATs). Computer programs that allow auditors to test computer files and databases.

General controls. Controls that relate to the overall information-processing environment and have a pervasive effect on the entity's computer operations.

Reliance strategy. The auditor's decision to rely on the entity's controls, test those controls, and reduce the direct tests of the financial statement accounts.

Standard costs. Costs assigned to products based on expected costs, which may differ from actual costs.

Substantive tests of transactions. Tests to detect errors or fraud in individual transactions.

Tests of controls. Audit procedures performed to test the operating effectiveness of controls in preventing or detecting and correcting material misstatements at the relevant assertion level.

Tests of details of account balances and disclosures. Substantive tests that concentrate on the details of items contained in the account balance and disclosure.

www.mhhe.com/ messier7e	Visit the book's Online Learning Center for a multiple-choice quiz that will allow you to assess your understanding of chapter concepts.

REVIEW QUESTIONS

[LO 1] 13-1 Why does inventory represent one of the more complex parts of the audit?

[1] 13-2 How does the inventory management process relate to the revenue, purchasing, and payroll processes?

[2] 13-3 Briefly describe each of the following documents or records: production schedule, materials requisition, inventory master file, production data information, and cost accumulation and variance reports.

[3] 13-4 What duties are performed within the inventory management, stores, and cost-accounting functions?

[4] 13-5 List the key segregation of duties in the inventory management process. What errors or fraud can occur if such segregation of duties is not present?

[5] 13-6 List the inherent risk factors that affect the inventory management process.

[6]   13-7   List the major steps in setting control risk in the inventory management process.

[7]   13-8   What control activities can a client use to prevent unauthorized inventory production?

[9]   13-9   List three substantive analytical procedures that can test the fairness of inventory and related accounts.

[10]   13-10   Describe how an auditor audits standard costs.

[11]   13-11   List the procedures the auditor should perform during the count of the client's physical inventory.

[13]   13-12   What are some possible causes of book-to-physical inventory differences?

[13]   13-13   List five items for inventory and related accounts that may require disclosure.

MULTIPLE-CHOICE QUESTIONS

[1,3]   13-14   The objectives of internal control for an inventory management process are to provide assurance that transactions are properly authorized and recorded and that
  a. Independent internal verification of activity reports is established.
  b. Transfers to the finished goods department are documented by a completed production report and a quality control report.
  c. Production orders are prenumbered and signed by a supervisor.
  d. Custody of work in process and finished goods is properly maintained.

[2,7]   13-15   Which of the following control activities would be most likely to assist in reducing the control risk related to the occurrence of inventory transactions?
  a. Inventory manager does not have ability to record inventory transactions.
  b. Summary of the receiving reports is independently compared to the inventory status report.
  c. Inventory is periodically reviewed for slow-moving or obsolete items, which may require a write-down.
  d. Subsidiary ledgers are periodically reconciled with inventory control accounts.

[4,7]   13-16   Which of the following would most likely be an internal control activity designed to detect errors and fraud concerning the custody of inventory?
  a. Periodic reconciliation of work in process with job cost sheets.
  b. Segregation of functions between general accounting and cost accounting.
  c. Independent comparisons of finished goods records with counts of goods on hand.
  d. Approval of inventory journal entries by the storekeeper.

[4,7]   13-17   Independent internal verification of inventory (i.e., proper segregation of duties) occurs when employees who
  a. Issue raw materials obtain materials requisitions for each issue and prepare daily totals of materials issued.
  b. Compare records of goods on hand with physical quantities do not maintain the records or have custody of the inventory.
  c. Obtain receipts for the transfer of completed work to finished goods prepare a completed production report.
  d. Are independent of issuing production orders update records from completed job cost sheets and production cost reports on a timely basis.

[7]   13-18   An auditor's tests of controls over the issuance of raw materials to production would most likely include
  a. Reconciliation of raw materials and work-in-process perpetual inventory records to general ledger balances.
  b. Inquiry of the custodian about the procedures followed when defective materials are received from vendors.
  c. Observation that raw materials are stored in secure areas and that storeroom security is supervised by a responsible individual.
  d. Examination of materials requisitions and reperformance of client controls designed to process and record issuances.

[7]   13-19   Which of the following internal control activities is most likely to address the completeness assertion for inventory?
  a. The work-in-process account is periodically reconciled with subsidiary records.
  b. Employees responsible for custody of finished goods do *not* perform the receiving function.
  c. Receiving reports are prenumbered and periodically reconciled.
  d. There is a separation of duties between payroll department and inventory accounting personnel.

[8,11,13]   13-20   A client maintains perpetual inventory records in both quantities and dollars. If the level of control risk were set at high, an auditor would probably
  a. Insist that the client perform physical counts of inventory items several times during the year.
  b. Apply gross profit tests to ascertain the reasonableness of the physical counts.
  c. Increase the extent of tests of controls of the inventory system.
  d. Request that the client schedule the physical inventory count at the end of the year.

[11]   13-21   After accounting for a sequence of inventory tags, an auditor traces a sample of tags to the physical inventory listing to obtain evidence that all items
  a. Included in the listing have been counted.
  b. Represented by inventory tags are included in the listing.
  c. Included in the listing are represented by inventory tags.
  d. Represented by inventory tags are bona fide.

[11,13]   13-22   When auditing merchandise inventory at year-end, the auditor performs a purchase cutoff test to obtain evidence that
  a. All goods purchased before year-end are received before the physical inventory count.
  b. No goods held on consignment for customers are included in the inventory balance.
  c. Goods observed during the physical count are pledged or sold.
  d. All goods owned at year-end are included in the inventory balance.

[11,13]   13-23   Inquiries of warehouse personnel concerning possibly obsolete or slow-moving inventory items provide assurance about management's assertion of
  a. Completeness.
  b. Existence.
  c. Presentation.
  d. Valuation.

[11,13]   13-24   Periodic or cycle counts of selected inventory items are made at various times during the year rather than via a single inventory count at year-end. Which of the following is necessary if the auditor plans to observe inventory at interim dates?
  a. Complete recounts are performed by independent teams.
  b. Perpetual inventory records are maintained.

c. Unit cost records are integrated with production-accounting records.

d. Inventory balances are rarely at low levels.

[13]   13-25   An auditor would probably be least interested in which of the following fields in an electronic perpetual inventory file?

a. Economic re-order quantity.

b. Warehouse location.

c. Date of last purchase.

d. Quantity sold.

[13]   13-26   Which of the following audit procedures would probably provide the most reliable evidence concerning the entity's assertion of rights and obligations related to inventory?

a. Tracing of test counts noted during the entity's physical count to the entity's summarization of quantities.

b. Inquiry of management to determine whether there are significant purchase commitments that should be considered for disclosure.

c. Selection of the last few shipping advices used before the physical count and determination of whether the shipments were recorded as sales.

d. During physical observation of inventory verify that "bill-and-hold" inventory is segregated and not included in the ending inventory count.

PROBLEMS

[1,3,7]   13-27   Yardley, CPA, prepared the flowchart on the following page, which portrays the raw materials purchasing function of one of Yardley's clients, a medium-size manufacturing company, from the preparation of initial documents through the vouching of invoices for payment. The flowchart represents a portion of the work performed on the audit engagement to evaluate internal control.

Required:

Identify and explain the control weaknesses evident from the flowchart. Include the internal control weaknesses resulting from activities performed or not performed. All documents are prenumbered.

(AICPA, adapted)

[1,6,11,13]   13-28   Rasch is the partner-in-charge of the audit of Bonner Distributing Corporation, a wholesaler that owns one warehouse containing 80 percent of its inventory. Rasch is reviewing the working papers that were prepared to support the firm's opinion on Bonner's financial statements, and Rasch wants to be certain that essential audit tests are well documented.

Required:

a. What evidence should Rasch find in the working papers to support the fact that the audit was adequately planned and the assistants were properly supervised?

b. What substantive tests should Rasch expect to find in the working papers to document management's assertion about completeness as it relates to the inventory quantities at the end of the year?

(AICPA, adapted)

[11]   13-29   Abbott Corporation does not conduct a complete annual physical count of purchased parts and supplies in its principal warehouse but instead uses statistical sampling to estimate the year-end inventory. Abbott maintains a perpetual inventory record of parts and supplies and believes that statistical sampling is highly effective in determining inventory values and is sufficiently reliable to make a physical count of each item of inventory unnecessary.

Required:

a. Identify the audit procedures that should be used by the independent auditor that change, or are in addition to, normal required audit procedures when a client utilizes statistical sampling to determine inventory value and does not conduct a 100-percent annual physical count of inventory items.

b. List at least 10 normal audit procedures that should be performed to verify physical quantities whenever a client conducts a periodic physical count of all, or part, of its inventory.

(AICPA, adapted)

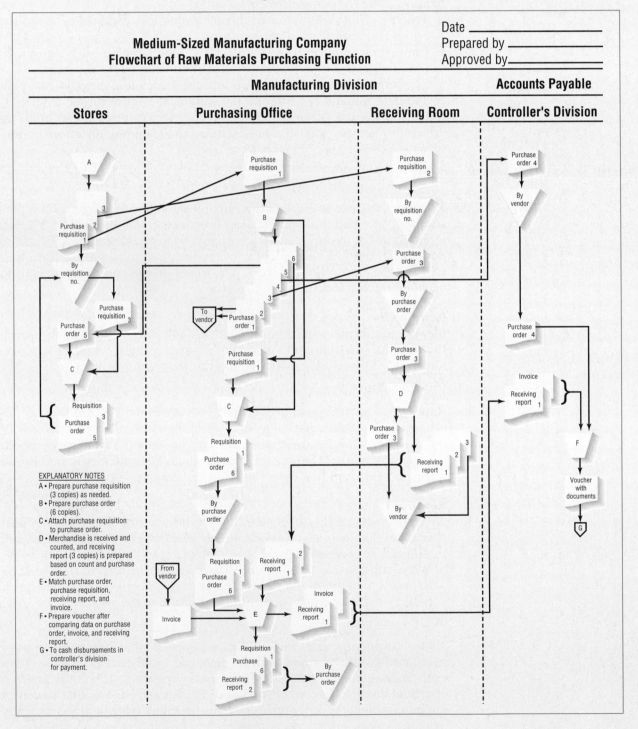

Medium-Sized Manufacturing Company
Flowchart of Raw Materials Purchasing Function

Date _____
Prepared by _____
Approved by _____

EXPLANATORY NOTES
A • Prepare purchase requisition (3 copies) as needed.
B • Prepare purchase order (6 copies).
C • Attach purchase requisition to purchase order.
D • Merchandise is received and counted, and receiving report (3 copies) is prepared based on count and purchase order.
E • Match purchase order, purchase requisition, receiving report, and invoice.
F • Prepare voucher after comparing data on purchase order, invoice, and receiving report.
G • To cash disbursements in controller's division for payment.

[11,13]   13-30   Kachelmeier, CPA, is auditing the financial statements of Big Z Wholesaling, Inc., a continuing audit client, for the year ended January 31, 2009. On January 5, 2009, Kachelmeier observed the tagging and counting of Big Z's physical inventory and made appropriate test counts. These test counts have been recorded on a computer file. As in prior years, Big Z gave Kachelmeier two computer files. One file represents the perpetual inventory (FIFO) records for the year ended January 31, 2009. The other file represents the January 5 physical inventory count.

Assume that:

1. Kachelmeier issued an unqualified opinion on the prior year's financial statements.
2. All inventory is purchased for resale and located in a single warehouse.
3. Kachelmeier has appropriate computerized audit software.
4. The perpetual inventory file contains the following information in item number sequence:
   - Beginning balances at February 1, 2008: item number, item description, total quantity, and price.
   - For each item purchased during the year: date received, receiving report number, vendor item number, item description, quantity, and total dollar amount.
   - For each item sold during the year: date shipped, invoice number, item number, item description, quantity, and dollar amount.
   - For each item adjusted for physical inventory count differences: date, item number, item description, quantity, and dollar amount.
5. The physical inventory file contains the following information in item number sequence: tag number, item number, item description, and quantity.

Required:
Describe the substantive auditing procedures Kachelmeier may consider performing with computerized audit software using Big Z's two computer files and Kachelmeier's computer file of test counts. The substantive auditing procedures described may indicate the reports to be printed out for Kachelmeier's follow-up by subsequent application of manual procedures. Group the procedures by those using (a) the perpetual inventory file; and (b) the physical inventory and test count files. Do *not* describe subsequent manual auditing procedures.

(AICPA, adapted)

[11,13]   13-31   An auditor is examining the financial statements of a wholesale cosmetics distributor with an inventory consisting of thousands of individual items. The distributor keeps its inventory in its own distribution center and in two public warehouses. An electronic inventory file is maintained on a computer disk, and at the end of each business day the file is updated. Each record of the inventory file contains the following data:

- Item number.
- Location of item.
- Description of item.
- Quantity on hand.
- Cost per item.
- Date of last purchase.
- Date of last sale.
- Quantity sold during year.

The auditor plans to observe the distributor's physical count of inventory as of a given date. The auditor will have available a computer tape of the data on the inventory file on the date of the physical count and a generalized audit software package.

Required:
The auditor is planning to perform basic inventory-auditing procedures. Identify the basic inventory-auditing procedures and describe how the use of the generalized audit software package and the tape of the inventory file data might help the auditor perform such auditing procedures. Organize your answer as follows:

Basic Inventory-Auditing Procedure	How a Generalized Audit Software Package and Tape of the Inventory File Data Might Be Helpful
1. Observation of the physical count, making and recording test counts where applicable	1. By determining which items are to be test counted by selecting a random sample of a representative number of items from the inventory file as of the date of the physical count?

(AICPA, adapted)

[13] 13-32 In obtaining evidential matter in support of financial statement assertions, the auditor develops specific audit procedures to address those assertions.

Required:
Your client is Hillmart, a retail department store that purchases all goods directly from wholesalers or manufacturers. Select the most appropriate audit procedure from the list below and enter the number in the appropriate place on the grid. (An audit procedure may be selected once, more than once, or not at all.)

Audit Procedure:
1. Examine current vendor price lists.
2. Review drafts of the financial statements.
3. Select a sample of items during the physical inventory count and determine that they have been included on count sheets.
4. Select a sample of recorded items and examine supporting vendor invoices and contracts.
5. Select a sample of recorded items on count sheets during the physical inventory count and determine that items are on hand.
6. Review loan agreements and minutes of board of directors' meetings.

Specific Assertion	Audit Procedure
a. Ensure that the entity has legal title to inventory (rights and obligations).	
b. Ensure that recorded inventory quantities include all products on hand (completeness).	
c. Verify that inventory has been reduced, when appropriate, to replacement cost or net realizable value (valuation).	
d. Verify that the cost of inventory has been properly determined (accuracy).	
e. Verify that the major categories of inventory and their bases of valuation are adequately reported in the financial statements (completeness and accuracy and valuation for presentation and disclosure).	

DISCUSSION CASE

[9,11,13,14]   13-33   The following discussion case extends Discussion Case 6-31 in Chapter 6.

Harris decided that the easiest way to make the Fabricator Division appear more profitable was through manipulating the inventory, which was the largest asset on the books. Harris found that by increasing inventory by 2 percent, income could be increased by 5 percent. With the weakness in inventory control, he felt it would be easy to overstate inventory. Employees count the goods using count sheets, and Harris was able to add two fictitious sheets during the physical inventory, even though the auditors were present and were observing the inventory. A significant amount of inventory was stored in racks that filled the warehouse. Because of their height and the difficulty of test-counting them, Harris was able to cover an overstatement of inventory in the upper racks.

After the count was completed, Harris added four additional count sheets that added $350,000, or 8.6 percent, to the stated inventory. Harris notified the auditors of the "omission" of the sheets and convinced them that they represented overlooked legitimate inventory.

The auditors traced the items on these additional sheets to purchase invoices to verify their existence and approved the addition of the $350,000 to the inventory. They did not notify management about the added sheets. In addition, Harris altered other count sheets before sending them to the auditors by changing unit designations (for example, six engine blocks became six "motors"), raising counts, and adding fictitious line items to completed count sheets. These other fictitious changes added an additional $175,000 to the inflated inventory. None of them was detected by the auditors.

Required:
a. What audit procedures did the auditors apparently not follow that should have detected Harris's fraudulent increase of inventory?
b. What implications would there be to an auditor of failure to detect material fraud as described here?
c. What responsibility did the auditors have to discuss their concerns with the client's audit committee?

Used with the permission of PricewaterhouseCoopers LLP Foundation.)

INTERNET ASSIGNMENTS

[9,13]   13-34   Using an Internet browser, search for information on inventory turnover and merchandise liquidations in the retail catalog industry.

[7,9,13,14]   13-35   Visit the SEC's Web site (www.sec.gov) and identify a company that has been recently cited for financial reporting problems related to inventory. Prepare a memo summarizing the inventory issues for the company.

HANDS-ON CASES

ACL

CHAPTER 14

LEARNING OBJECTIVES

Upon completion of this chapter you will

[1] Know the various types of prepaid expenses, deferred charges, and intangible assets.

[2] Understand the auditor's approach to auditing prepaid insurance and intangible assets.

[3] Develop an understanding of the property management process.

[4] Know the types of transactions in the property management process.

[5] Be familiar with the inherent risks for property, plant, and equipment.

[6] Assess control risk for property, plant, and equipment.

[7] Know the appropriate segregation of duties for property, plant, and equipment.

[8] Know the substantive analytical procedures used to audit property, plant, and equipment.

[9] Know the tests of details of account balances and disclosures used to audit property, plant, and equipment.

[10] Understand how to evaluate audit findings and reach a final conclusion on property, plant, and equipment.

RELEVANT ACCOUNTING AND AUDITING PRONOUNCEMENTS

FASB Statement of Financial Accounting Concepts No. 6, Elements of Financial Statements

FASB ASC Topic 350, Intangibles—Goodwill and Other

FASB ASC Topic 360, Property, Plant, and Equipment

FASB ASC Topic 835, Interest

FASB ASC Topic 840, Leases

FASB ASC Topic 985, Software

AU 312, Audit Risk and Materiality in Conducting an Audit

AU 314, Understanding the Entity and Its Environment and Assessing the Risks of Material Misstatement

AU 316, Consideration of Fraud in a Financial Statement Audit

AU 318, Performing Audit Procedures in Response to Assessed Risks and Evaluating the Audit Evidence Obtained

AU 326, Audit Evidence

AU 328, Auditing Fair Value Measurements and Disclosures

AU 329, Analytical Procedures

AU 336, Using the Work of a Specialist

AU 339, Audit Documentation

AU 342, Auditing Accounting Estimates

PCAOB Auditing Standard No. 3, Audit Documentation (AS3)

PCAOB Auditing Standard No. 5, An Audit of Internal Control Over Financial Reporting That Is Integrated with An Audit of Financial Statements (AS5)

PCAOB Proposed Auditing Standards Related to the Auditor's Assessment of and Response to Risk, PCAOB Release No. 2008-006 (October 21, 2008)

Auditing the Financing/Investing Process: Prepaid Expenses, Intangible Assets, and Property, Plant, and Equipment

Major Phases of an Audit

Client acceptance/
continuance and establishing
an understanding with the client
(Chapter 5)

Preliminary engagement
activities
(Chapter 5)

Plan the audit
(Chapters 3 and 5)

Consider and audit
internal control
(Chapters 6 and 7)

Audit business processes
and related accounts
(e.g., revenue generation)
(Chapters 10–16)

Complete the audit
(Chapter 17)

Evaluate results and issue audit
report (Chapters 1 and 18)

This chapter examines the audit of selected asset accounts. Three categories of asset accounts—prepaid expenses, intangibles, and property, plant, and equipment—are used as examples. While the audit approach taken for each category is similar, differences exist between these three categories of asset accounts. For example, while transactions for all three categories are subject to the control activities in the purchasing process, transactions involving intangible assets or property, plant, and equipment are likely to be subject to additional control activities because of their complexity or materiality. Additionally, prepaid expenses are normally classified as current assets, while intangibles and property, plant, and equipment are classified as noncurrent assets.

Auditing Prepaid Expenses

▶ [LO 1]   For many entities, accounts receivable and inventory represent the major current assets included in the financial statements. Also included in most financial statements are accounts that are referred to as *other assets*. When such assets provide economic benefit for less than a year, they are classified as current assets. A common type of other asset is a *prepaid expense*. Examples of prepaid expenses include

- Prepaid insurance.
- Prepaid rent.
- Prepaid interest.

One major difference between asset accounts such as accounts receivable or inventory and prepaid expenses is the materiality of the account balances. On many engagements, prepaid expenses, deferred charges, and intangible assets are not highly material. As a result, substantive analytical procedures are often used extensively to verify these account balances.

Inherent Risk Assessment—Prepaid Expenses

The inherent risk for prepaid expenses such as prepaid insurance would generally be assessed as low because these accounts do not involve any complex or contentious accounting issues. Moreover, misstatements that may have been detected in prior audits would generally be immaterial in amount.

Control Risk Assessment—Prepaid Expenses

Prepaid expenses are typically processed through the purchasing process. Common prepaid expenses include prepaid insurance, prepaid rent, prepaid maintenance or other service, and prepaid interest. The remaining discussion focuses on the prepaid insurance account as an illustration of auditing prepaid expenses because it is encountered on virtually all engagements. Prepaid insurance may relate to an insurance policy on a building or equipment. If, for example, the client borrowed money to purchase equipment, the creditor may have a *lien* on the equipment (i.e., the equipment is used as collateral for the loan). A lien gives the creditor the right to sell the equipment if the client fails to meet the obligations of a loan contract. When there is a lien on a client's building or equipment, the creditor typically requires the client to carry an insurance policy listing the creditor as the beneficiary (i.e., rightful recipient of insurance proceeds).

Part of the auditor's assessment of control risk for prepaid insurance transactions is based on the effectiveness of the control activities in the purchasing process. For example, the control activities in the purchasing process should ensure that new insurance policies are properly authorized and recorded.

Additional control activities may be used to control insurance transactions and information. For example, an *insurance register* may be maintained as a separate record of all insurance policies in force. The insurance register contains important information such as the coverage and expiration date of each policy. This register should be reviewed periodically by an independent person to verify that the entity has insurance coverage consistent with its needs.

The entity also needs to maintain controls over the systematic allocation of prepaid insurance to insurance expense. At the end of each month, client personnel should prepare a journal entry to recognize the expired portion of prepaid insurance. In some cases entities use estimated amounts when recording these journal entries during the year. At the end of the year, the prepaid insurance account is adjusted to reflect the actual amount of unexpired insurance.

Substantive Procedures—Prepaid Insurance

[LO 2]   On many audits the auditor can gather sufficient, appropriate evidence on prepaid insurance by performing substantive analytical procedures. Tests of details of transactions, if performed at all, are conducted as part of testing the purchasing process. Detailed tests of balances of the prepaid insurance balance are typically necessary only when misstatements are expected.

Substantive Analytical Procedures for Prepaid Insurance

Because there are generally few transactions in the prepaid insurance account and because the amount reported in the financial statements for prepaid insurance is usually immaterial, substantive analytical procedures are effective for verifying the account balance. The following substantive analytical procedures are commonly used to test prepaid insurance:

- Comparing the current-year balance in prepaid insurance and insurance expense with the prior years' balances, taking into account any changes in operations.
- Computing the ratio of insurance expense to assets or sales and comparing it with the prior years' ratios.
- Computing an estimate of the ending prepaid account balance(s) using the current premium and the amount of time remaining on the policy at the end of the period.

Using the third technique above, do the ending balances in Exhibit 14–1 appear reasonable? Looking at the Fire & Casualty policy, for example, the ending balance of $8,400 does appear reasonable ($8,400 = $33,600 × 3/12).

Tests of Details of the Prepaid Insurance

Tests of details of balances for prepaid insurance and insurance expense may be necessary when the auditor suspects misstatements based on prior years' audits or when substantive analytical procedures indicate that the account balance may be misstated. The auditor begins testing the prepaid insurance account balance by obtaining a schedule from the client that contains a detailed analysis of the policies included in the prepaid insurance account.

Exhibit 14–1 presents a prepaid insurance schedule for EarthWear Clothiers. The accuracy and completeness of this schedule is tested by footing it and tracing the ending balance to the prepaid insurance account in the general ledger. The auditor's work then focuses on testing the existence, completeness, rights and obligations, valuation, and disclosure-classification assertions. No footnote disclosures are generally necessary for prepaid insurance. These steps, along with other audit work, are documented in Exhibit 14–1.

Existence and Completeness

The auditor can test the existence and completeness of insurance policies included in the account analysis by sending a confirmation to the entity's insurance brokers, requesting information on each policy's number, coverage, expiration date, and premiums. This is an effective and efficient way of obtaining evidence on these two assertions. An alternative approach is examination of the underlying supporting documents such as the insurance bills and policies. This may be done on a test basis for the policies listed on the schedule. The auditor can also

EXHIBIT 14-1	Example of an Account Analysis Working Paper for Prepaid Insurance

G10
DLJ
2/15/10

EARTHWEAR CLOTHIERS
Analysis of Prepaid Insurance
12/31/09

Insurance Company	Policy Number	Coverage	Term	Premium	Beginning Balance 1/1/09	Additions	Expense	Ending Balance 12/31/09
Babcock, Inc.**C**	46-2074	Liability Umbrella Policy	1/15/09 1/15/10	$55,000	$ 2,100	$ 55,000V	$ 54,800	$ 2,300Ψ
Evans & Smith**C**	47801-X7	Fire & Casualty	3/30/09 3/30/10	33,600	7,500	33,600V	32,700	8,400Ψ
Nat'l Insurance**C**	8945-X7	Key Executive Term Life Insurance	9/30/09 9/30/10	15,000	11,250	15,000V	15,000	11,250Ψ
Total					$20,850¶	$103,600	$102,500L	$21,950LF
					F	F	F	F

F = Footed and crossfooted.
C = Information agreed to insurance company confirmation.
L = Agreed to general ledger.
¶ = Agreed to prior year's working papers.
V = Agreed to insurance company invoice.
Ψ = Amount recomputed by auditor.

Reconciliation of insurance expense accounts:
Merchandise overhead insurance expense $ 69,700L
General and administrative overhead insurance expense   32,800L
Total $102,500

obtain evidence regarding completeness by comparing the detailed policies in the current year's insurance register with the policies included in the prior year's insurance register.

Rights and Obligations

The beneficiary of the policy can be identified by requesting such information on the confirmations sent to the insurance brokers or by examining the insurance policies. If the beneficiary is someone other than the client, this could indicate an unrecorded liability or that another party has a claim against the insured assets.

Valuation

The auditor is concerned with whether the unexpired portion of prepaid insurance, and thus insurance expense, is properly valued. Evidence regarding proper valuation can be easily obtained by recomputing the unexpired portion of insurance after considering the premium paid and the term of the policy. By verifying the unexpired portion of prepaid insurance, the auditor also verifies the total amount of insurance expense. This is shown in Exhibit 14-1.

Classification

The auditor's concern with classification is that the different types of insurance are properly allocated to the various insurance expense accounts. Normally, an examination of the insurance policy's coverage indicates the nature of the insurance. For example, a fire insurance policy on the main manufacturing and administrative facilities should be charged both to the manufacturing overhead insurance expense account and to the general and administrative insurance expense account. Note in Exhibit 14-1 that the various insurance accounts included in the general ledger are reconciled to total insurance expense. One final procedure that the auditor should perform is to ask the client or its insurance broker about the adequacy of the entity's insurance coverage.

Auditing Intangible Assets

➤ [LO 1,2] *Intangible assets* are assets that provide economic benefit for longer than a year, but lack physical substance. The following list includes examples of five general categories of intangible assets:

1. *Marketing*—trademark, brand name, and Internet domain names.
2. *Customer*—customer lists, order backlogs, and customer relationships.
3. *Artistic*—items protected by copyright.
4. *Contract*—licenses, franchises and broadcast rights.
5. *Technology*—patented and unpatented technology.

Accounting standards do not allow companies to record internally generated intangibles as assets on the balance sheet. Rather, intangibles are recorded when the assets are acquired through a purchase or acquisition (FASB ASC Topic 350).[1] *Goodwill,* another common intangible asset, represents the difference between the acquisition price for a company and the fair values of the identifiable tangible and intangible assets.

Some intangible assets are amortized over time, while others like broadcast licenses, trademarks, and goodwill are considered to have indefinite lives and are not amortized. However, all intangibles must be tested for *impairment* at least annually, as well as on an interim basis if events or changes in circumstances indicate that the asset might be impaired.

Inherent Risk Assessment—Intangible Assets

The nature of the judgments involved in accounting for intangible assets raises serious inherent risk considerations. The accounting rules are complex and the transactions are difficult to audit. Pause and think for a moment. If Earthwear were to acquire another successful clothing company and record goodwill as part of the purchase, how would this change your audit plan and why? Judgment is required to initially value assets such as trademarks, customer relations, copyrights, customer order backlogs (i.e., backlogs represent expected future revenue), and goodwill when one company acquires another. Both the client and the auditor often use valuation specialists to assist in determining fair values. Considerable judgment is also required to determine useful lives for patents, copyrights, and order backlogs. Finally, asset impairment tests and determining the amount of impairment loss are complex procedures that involve estimation. Accounting standards require different asset impairment tests for different classes of intangible assets (FASB ASC Topic 350). With the judgment and complexity associated with valuation and estimation of intangible assets, the auditor is likely to assess the inherent risk as high.

Practice **INSIGHT**	FASB ASC Topic 350 requires the aggregate amount of goodwill impairment losses from continuing operations to be reported as a separate line item before income from continuing operations. Notice that in order to properly audit a client's impairment testing, the auditor needs expertise in both evidence evaluation and in financial reporting requirements.

---

[1]There are some notable exceptions to the general rule that internally generated intangibles are expensed. For example, once internally developed software has reached the technological feasibility stage, FASB ASC Topic 985 provides separate and specific accounting provisions that allow capitalization of further development costs. Also, legal and administrative fees associated with obtaining a trademark, copyright, or patent can be capitalized. Further discussion of these exceptions is beyond the scope of this book.

Control Risk Assessment—Intangible Assets

Management is responsible for making the fair value measurements and disclosures and therefore must es tablish an accounting and reporting process for determining the fair value measures, selecting the appropriate valuation methods, identifying and supporting significant assumptions used, and preparing the valuation and disclosures in accordance with GAAP.

Intangible asset transactions and initial valuation are typically processed through the client's business acquisition processes. To rely on controls in this process, the auditor needs to understand, document, and test the design and operating effectiveness of key controls. For public companies that are actively acquiring other companies or that engage in large-scale acquisitions, the business acquisition process would be considered a significant process for the audit of internal controls over financial reporting (see Chapter 7). For example, the control activities in the business acquisition process should ensure that all identifiable asset categories are separately valued and that any valuation specialists used are qualified and objective.

Additional control activities are required for impairment testing. For example, the client's policies and procedures should properly capture and evaluate potential events that may trigger impairment (e.g., significant change in market price or in the way the asset is being used), ensure that all intangible assets are tested for impairment at least annually, and verify that the impairment-testing policies and procedures are in compliance with GAAP.

In assessing control risk, the auditor considers factors such as:

- The expertise and experience of those determining the fair value of the asset.
- Controls over the process used to determine fair value measurements, including controls over data and segregation of duties between those committing the client to the purchase and those undertaking the valuation.
- The extent to which the entity engages or employs valuation specialists.
- The significant management assumptions used in determining fair value.
- The integrity of change controls and security procedures for valuation models and relevant information systems, including approval processes. (AU 328)

Substantive Procedures—Intangible Assets

Substantive Analytical Procedures for Intangible Assets

[LO 2]

While analytical procedures help direct the auditor's attention to situations needing additional investigation (e.g., potential asset impairment), unlike with prepaids, the principal substantive evidence regarding intangible assets is typically obtained via tests of details. Substantive analytical procedures generally are not useful in gathering sufficient, appropriate evidence regarding the assertions of primary interest for intangibles (valuation, existence, completeness, rights and obligations, and classification). As such, the discussion below is limited to substantive tests of details.

Tests of Details of Intangible Assets

Tests of details associated with valuation and impairment of intangible assets are often necessary because the complexity and degree of judgment increase the risk of material misstatement. Further, auditing standards require some substantive evidence for all significant accounts, and, as noted above, substantive analytical procedures are not likely to provide sufficient, appropriate evidence for significant transactions involving intangible assets.

Existence and Completeness   The auditor normally tests for the existence of intangible assets at the time they are acquired. For assets such as patents, copyrights, licenses, broadcast rights, and trademarks, the auditor would examine legal documentation supporting the validity of the asset. Similarly, customer backlogs can be validated by examining customer order information or by sending confirmations to customers requesting information on their order status.

The auditor's primary concern relative to the completeness assertion for intangible assets is to ensure that the client's impairment-testing procedures include all intangible assets. To test this assertion, the auditor would obtain a copy of the client's detail listing of intangible assets, which should agree with the total amount of intangible assets reported on the client's balance sheet. The auditor would also examine the client's impairment documentation to ensure that each asset is subject to the appropriate impairment testing in accordance with GAAP.

Valuation[2] It should be no surprise that valuation is the most important assertion associated with intangible assets. The initial valuation of assets typically involves an allocation of purchase price in proportion to fair values. Once an intangible asset is determined to be impaired, the current fair value must be determined to compute the impairment loss. When there is a market price for the intangible assets, the valuation issues are relatively straightforward. However, in the majority of the situations involving valuation of intangible assets, a readily determined market price is not available.

Accounting standards describe different acceptable valuation methods, but if a market price is not available, all remaining methods rely heavily on assumptions, likelihood assessments, and estimation. With the movement toward more fair value accounting, auditors need improved understanding of valuation issues. However, to obtain sufficient appropriate evidence on the valuation of intangible assets (either for initial valuation or after an impairment), the auditor is not required to become an expert in valuation. Rather, the auditor will typically rely on the help of a specialist. When specialists are used to obtain audit evidence, the auditor is required to evaluate the specialist's qualifications and objectivity. The auditor also must determine if the valuation model used by the specialist is appropriate and consistent with GAAP, and the auditor must understand and verify the reasonableness of the underlying data and assumptions.

In addition to initial valuation and impairment testing, the auditor would also test the reasonableness of the useful lives used for amortizing intangible assets that have definite lives. For example, even though a patent may have a legal life of 20 years, if the competitive advantages associated with the patent are expected to last only five years, the patent cost should be amortized over a shorter period.

Practice INSIGHT	During an inspection of one of the Big 4 firms the PCAOB identified deficiencies in the audit of intangible assets. There was no evidence that the audit firm evaluated whether goodwill should have been recorded. In this audit, the entity acquired another company and recorded substantial goodwill despite the fact that it discontinued the established business of the acquired company to start a new, unproven business. (PCAOB Release 104-2008-146)

Rights and Obligations Litigation regarding the rights associated with intangible assets such as trademarks, patents, copyrights, licenses, and Internet domains is relatively common. The auditor normally examines supporting legal and contractual documentation to verify the client's legal rights to these assets. The auditor also reads the minutes of board of directors meetings and communicates with the client's counsel to determine if there is pending litigation regarding legal rights (attorney's letters are discussed in Chapter 17). As mentioned above, the auditor needs to understand and test the client's business acquisition processes as well as the client's allocation of purchase price to various intangible assets.

---

[2]See American Institute of Certified Public Accountants, *Auditing Fair Value Measurements and Disclosures: A Toolkit for Auditors,* for detailed guidance on auditing fair value measurements required by FASB ASC Topic 350, 360.

Classification   The auditor's concern with classification is that the different types of intangible assets are properly identified and are accounted for separately. Before the FASB issued additional clarification on accounting for intangible assets in 2001, it was common for intangible assets to be lumped together into one "goodwill" account. As with the initial valuation, the identification of intangible assets is typically performed at the time a client acquires another business interest. Multiple intangible assets are typically acquired simultaneously in one purchase.

Auditing the Property Management Process

[LO 3]   For most entities, property, plant, and equipment represent a material amount in the financial statements. When the audit is an ongoing engagement, the auditor is able to focus his or her efforts on the current year's activity because the assets acquired in earlier years were subjected to audit procedures at the time of acquisition. However, on a new engagement the auditor has to verify the assets that make up the beginning balances in the client's property, plant, and equipment accounts.

The size of the entity may also affect the auditor's approach. If the client is relatively small with few asset purchases during the period, it is generally more cost-effective for the auditor to follow a substantive strategy. Following this strategy, the auditor conducts substantive analytical procedures and direct tests of the account balances. Large entities, on the other hand, are likely to have formal procedures for budgeting for and purchasing capital assets. While routine purchases might be processed through the purchasing process, as described in Chapter 11, acquisition or construction of specialized assets may be subject to different requisition and authorization procedures. When a private entity has a formal control system over the property management process, the auditor may choose to follow a reliance strategy and test controls. When the entity is a public company, the client should have a formal control system and the auditor will test the design and operating effectiveness of key controls as part of the integrated audit.

Types of Transactions

[LO 4]   Four types of propwerty, plant, and equipment transactions may occur:

- Acquisition of capital assets for cash or nonmonetary considerations.
- Disposition of capital assets through sale, exchange, retirement, or abandonment.
- Depreciation of capital assets over their useful economic life.
- Leasing of capital assets.

Overview of the Property Management Process

Larger entities generally use IT systems to process property, plant, and equipment transactions, maintain subsidiary records, and produce required reports. Figure 14–1 presents a flowchart of EarthWear's accounting system for the property management process. Transactions are periodically entered both from the purchasing process and through direct input into the system. The property, plant, and equipment master file is then updated, and a number of reports are produced. The periodic report for property, plant, and equipment transactions is reviewed for proper recording by the physical plant department. The property, plant, and equipment subsidiary ledger is a record of all capital assets owned by the entity. It contains information on the cost of the asset, the date acquired, the

FIGURE 14-1	Flowchart of the Property Management Process—EarthWear Clothiers

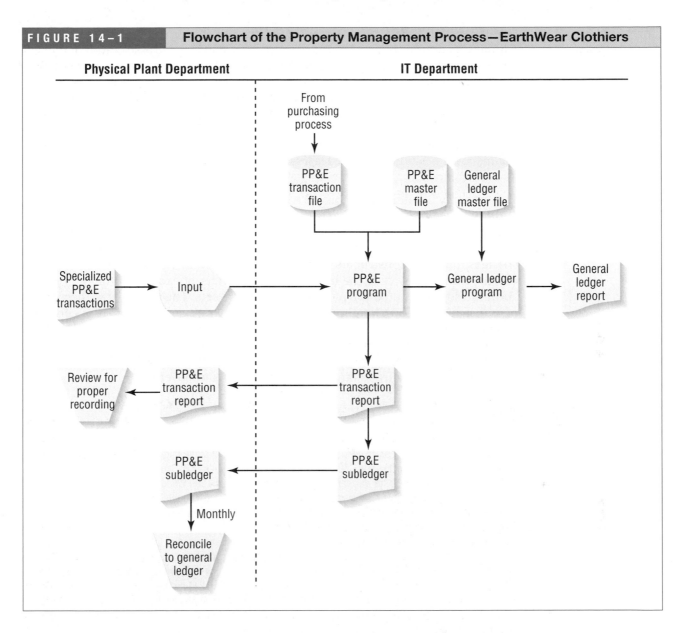

method of depreciation, and accumulated depreciation. The subsidiary ledger also includes the calculation of depreciation expense for both financial statement and income tax purposes. The general ledger is posted to reflect the new property, plant, and equipment transactions and depreciation expense. The subsidiary ledger is reconciled to the general ledger control account monthly.

Inherent Risk Assessment—Property Management Process

[LO 5] The assessment of inherent risk for the purchasing process provides a starting point for assessing inherent risk for property, plant, and equipment. The following three inherent risk factors classified as operating characteristics require consideration by the auditor:

- Complex accounting issues.
- Difficult-to-audit transactions.
- Misstatements detected in prior audits.

Complex Accounting Issues

A number of different types of property, plant, and equipment transactions involve complex accounting issues. Lease accounting, self-constructed assets, and capitalized interest are examples of such issues. For example, in the case of a lease transaction the auditor must evaluate the client's decision either to capitalize the lease or to treat it as an operating lease. Because of the complexity of the capitalization decision and the subjectivity involved in assessing the capitalization criteria, it is not uncommon for such transactions to be accounted for incorrectly by the client. For example, EarthWear leases store and office space accounted for as operating leases. Willis & Adams must be sure that these leases do not qualify as capital leases.

Easy and Difficult Transactions to Audit

The majority of additions to property, plant, and equipment are relatively easy to audit because they are purchased directly from vendors. For such purchases the auditor is able to obtain evidence for most assertions by examining the source documents. However, transactions involving donated assets, nonmonetary exchanges, and self-constructed assets are often difficult to audit. For example, it may be difficult to verify the trade-in value of an asset exchanged or to properly audit the cost accumulation of self-constructed assets. The presence of these types of transactions should lead to a higher inherent risk assessment. It is certainly worth noting that one of the largest accounting frauds in history, WorldCom, involved the improper capitalization of operating expenses as property, plant, and equipment to overstate income. See Exhibit 14–2 for a more detailed description of the company, the fraud, and how the fraud was uncovered.

EXHIBIT 14–2	**WorldCom Overstates PP&E and Net Income**

WorldCom started as a mom-and-pop long-distance company in 1983. But in the 1990s, it matured into a powerhouse. In 1997 it shocked the industry with an unsolicited bid to take over MCI, a company more than three times its size. In 1998 CFO Magazine named WorldCom's CFO, Scott Sullivan, one of the country's best CFOs. At age 37 he was earning $19.3 million a year. In 1999 WorldCom founder Bernie Ebbers moved the company to Clinton, Mississippi, his old college town, and everything changed. The stock price went through the roof. However, by early 2001, overexuberance for the telecom market had created a glut of companies like WorldCom, and earnings started to fall.

In March 2002, Cynthia Cooper, a WorldCom vice president and head of internal audit was informed by a worried executive in the wireless division that corporate accounting had taken $400 million out of his reserve account and used it to boost WorldCom's income. When Cooper went to WorldCom's external auditors, Arthur Andersen, to inquire about the maneuver, she was told matter-of-factly that it was not a problem. When she didn't relent, Sullivan angrily told Cooper that everything was fine and she should back off. He was furious at her, according to a person involved in the matter. Says Cooper, "When someone is hostile, my instinct is to find out why."

As the weeks went on, Cooper directed her team members to widen their net. Having watched the Enron implosion and Andersen's role in it, she was worried they could not necessarily rely on the accounting firm's audits. So the internal auditors decided to reaudit some areas. She and her team began working late into the night, keeping their project secret. In late May, Cooper and her group discovered a gaping hole in the books. In public reports, the company had classified billions of dollars as property, plant, and equipment in 2001, meaning the costs could be stretched out over a number of years into the future. However, these expenditures were for regular fees WorldCom paid to local telephone companies to complete calls and therefore were operating costs, which should be expensed in full each year. It was as if an ordinary person had paid his or her phone bills but written down the payments as if he or she were building a long-term asset, like a phone tower, in his or her backyard. The trick allowed WorldCom to turn a $662 million loss into a $2.4 billion profit in 2001.

Internal audit began looking for ways to somehow justify what it had found in the books. Finally, the internal auditors confronted WorldCom's controller, David Myers, who admitted the accounting could not be justified. Cooper told the audit committee that the company accountants had understated expenses and overstated income. Sullivan was provided the opportunity to present his side of the story, but he could not convince them regarding the propriety of the accounting. Within days, the company fired its famed chief financial officer, Scott Sullivan, and told the world that it had inflated its profits by $3.8 billion. After additional investigation, the number grew to over $9 billion, the largest accounting fraud ever up to that date.

Source: Amanda Ripley, "The Night Detective (Persons of the Year)," *Time* (December 30, 2002–January 6, 2003), p. 36.

Practice INSIGHT	One way to overstate the net carrying value of plant or equipment is to inappropriately extend the assets' depreciable life. Waste Management used such an approach to fraudulently boost profits. Management has considerable latitude in choosing a depreciation method. Changes to either the useful lives or depreciation methods should be scrutinized for both their purpose and financial effect.

Misstatements Detected in Prior Audits

If the auditor has detected misstatements in prior audits, the assessment of inherent risk should be set higher than if few or no misstatements had been found in the past.[3] For example, in prior years the auditor may have found numerous client misstatements in accumulating costs for valuing self-constructed capital assets. Unless the client has established new control activities over cost accumulation, the auditor should also expect to find misstatements during the current year's audit and therefore set inherent risk as high.

Control Risk Assessment—Property Management Process

✎ [LO 6]   Although auditors typically follow a substantive strategy when auditing the property management process, an understanding of internal control is still required on all audits, and obviously AS5 also requires design evaluation and testing of operating effectiveness of key controls for significant account balances and processes for public companies. The presentation that follows focuses on the major assertions, key control activities, and tests of controls that relate directly to the property management process. Other control activities related to the property management process were discussed as part of the purchasing process. Important examples of segregation of duties are also presented.

Occurrence and Authorization

The control activities for the occurrence and authorization assertions are normally part of the purchasing process. Purchase requisitions are initiated in relevant departments and authorized at the appropriate level within the entity. However, large capital asset transactions may be subject to control activities outside the purchasing process. For example, highly specialized technical equipment is likely to be purchased only after passing through a specific capital-budgeting process, which might require that purchase of equipment meet predefined internal rate-of-return criteria. The purchase of equipment may also require that highly skilled engineers approve the technical specifications for the equipment. For such transactions, the auditor may need to examine more than the vendor's invoice to test validity. A review of additional documentation, such as capital-budgeting documents and engineering specifications, may be needed.

Most entities have some type of authorization table based on the size of capital asset transactions. The client should have control activities to ensure that the authorization to purchase capital assets is consistent with the authorization table. For example, the control activities should specify dollar limits at each managerial level to ensure that larger projects are brought to the attention of higher levels of management for approval before commitments are made. Lease transactions should be subject to similar control activities. The entity also needs to have control activities for authorizing the sale or other disposition of capital assets. This should include a level of authorization above the department initiating the disposition. Control activities should also identify assets that are no longer used

---

[3]Research has shown that property, plant, and equipment accounts frequently contain misstatements. See A. Eilifsen and W. F. Messier, Jr., "Auditor Detection of Misstatements: A Review and Integration of Empirical Research," *Journal of Accounting Literature* 2000 (19), pp. 1–43, for a review of the audit research studies that have indicated that property, plant, and equipment accounts are likely to contain misstatements.

in operations because they may require different accounting treatment. Finally, all major maintenance or improvement transactions should be properly authorized by an appropriate level of management.

Completeness

Most entities use software to maintain detailed electronic property records (see Figure 14–1). The property, plant, and equipment subsidiary ledger usually includes the following information for each capital asset:

- Description, location, and ID number.
- Date of acquisition and installed cost.
- Depreciation methods for book and tax purposes, salvage value, and estimated useful life.

The control activities used in the purchasing process for ensuring completeness provide some assurance that all capital asset transactions are recorded in the property, plant, and equipment subsidiary ledger and general ledger. One procedure that helps to ensure that this assertion is met is periodic reconciliation of the property, plant, and equipment subsidiary ledger to the general ledger control accounts. Figure 14–1 shows this control activity as it is performed by Earth-Wear's physical plant department.

Another control activity that an entity may use to ensure that all capital assets are recorded is periodic comparison of the detailed records in the subsidiary ledger with the existing capital assets. This may be done in a number of ways. The client may make a complete physical examination of property, plant, and equipment on a periodic or rotating basis and compare the physical assets to the property, plant, and equipment subsidiary ledger. Alternatively, the physical examination may be limited to major capital assets or assets that are subject to loss. In both instances the entity's internal auditors may test the reliability of the subsidiary ledger. Larger entities sometimes employ outside specialists to physically examine property, plant, and equipment.

Segregation of Duties

✄ [LO 7]

The existence of adequate segregation of duties for the property management process depends on the volume and significance of the transactions processed. For example, if an entity purchases large quantities of machinery and equipment, or if it has large capital projects under construction, it will likely have a formal control process. On the other hand, if an entity has few capital asset purchases, it will generally not have a formal control system over such transactions. Table 14–1 shows the key segregation of duties for the property management process and examples of possible errors or fraud that can result from conflicts in duties.

TABLE 14–1	Key Segregation of Duties and Possible Errors or Fraud—Property Management Process
Segregation of Duties	*Possible Errors or Fraud Resulting from Conflicts of Duties*
The function of initiating a capital asset acquisition should be segregated from the final approval function.	If one individual is responsible for initiating a capital asset transaction and also has final approval, fictitious or unauthorized purchases of assets can occur. This can result in purchases of unnecessary assets, assets that do not meet the company's quality control standards, or illegal payments to suppliers or contractors.
The property, plant, and equipment records function should be segregated from the general ledger function.	If one individual is responsible for the property, plant, and equipment records and also for the general ledger functions, that individual can conceal any defalcation that would normally be detected by reconciling subsidiary records with the general ledger control account.
The property, plant, and equipment records function should be segregated from the custodial or safeguarding function.	If one individual is responsible for the property, plant, and equipment records and also has custodial responsibility for the related assets, tools and equipment can be stolen, and the theft can be concealed by adjustment of the accounting records.
If a periodic physical inventory of property, plant, and equipment is taken, the individual responsible for the inventory should be independent of the custodial and record-keeping functions.	If the individual who is responsible for the periodic physical inventory of property, plant, and equipment is also responsible for the custodial and record-keeping functions, theft of the entity's capital assets can be concealed.

Substantive Procedures—Property, Plant, and Equipment

As mentioned earlier, when the number of transactions is small, auditors often follow a substantive strategy when auditing property, plant, and equipment. Therefore, a detailed discussion of the substantive procedures for property, plant, and equipment is provided next. The discussion focuses on substantive analytical procedures and tests of details of transactions, account balances, and disclosures.

Substantive Analytical Procedures—Property, Plant, and Equipment
✂ [LO 8]

The following list provides examples of substantive analytical procedures that can be used in the audit of property, plant, and equipment:

- Compare prior-periods balances in property, plant, and equipment and depreciation expense with current-period balances, taking into account any changes in conditions or asset composition.
- Compute the ratio of depreciation expense to the related property, plant, and equipment accounts and compare to prior years' ratios.
- Compute the ratio of repairs and maintenance expense to the related property, plant, and equipment accounts and compare to prior years' ratios.
- Compute the ratio of insurance expense to the related property, plant, and equipment accounts and compare to prior years' ratios.
- Review capital budgets and compare the amounts spent with amounts budgeted.

For the first two procedures listed above, pause and consider what potential misstatements these procedures may help identify. If, for example, the ratio of depreciation expense to the related property, plant, and equipment accounts is less than prior years' and few assets have been disposed of, the auditor might be concerned that depreciation has not been taken on some assets included in the account and additional audit procedures would be performed.

Tests of Details of Transactions, Account Balances, and Disclosures—Property, Plant, and Equipment
✂ [LO 9]

Table 14–2 summarizes examples of substantive tests for the property, plant, and equipment accounts for each assertion relating to transactions and balances. The discussion that follows focuses on the major audit procedures conducted by the auditor. Completeness and accuracy are discussed first because the auditor must establish that the detailed property, plant, and equipment records are accurate and agree with the general ledger account.

TABLE 14–2	Examples of Tests of Transactions and Account Balances for Property, Plant, and Equipment (PP&E)
Assertions about Classes of Transactions	**Example Substantive Tests of Transactions***
Occurrence	Vouch significant additions and dispositions to vendor invoices or other supporting documentation. Review lease agreements to ensure that lease transactions are accounted for properly.
Completeness	Trace a sample of purchase requisitions to loading dock reports and to the PP&E records (i.e., transaction and master file).
Authorization	Vouch a sample of PP&E additions to documentation indicating proper authorization.
Accuracy	For assets written off, test amounts charged against income and accumulated depreciation.
Cutoff	Examine the purchases and sales of capital assets for a few days before and after year-end.
Classification	Vouch transactions included in repairs and maintenance for items that should be capitalized. Review lease transactions for proper classification between operating and capital leases.

(continued)

*These tests of details of transactions are commonly conducted as dual-purpose tests (i.e., in conjunction with tests of controls).

TABLE 14–2 (*continued*)	Examples of Tests of Transactions and Account Balances for Property, Plant, and Equipment (PP&E)
Assertions about Account Balances at Period End	**Example Tests of Details of Account Balances**
Existence	Verify the existence of major additions by physically inspecting the capital asset.
Rights and obligations	Examine or confirm deeds or title documents for proof of ownership.
Completeness	Obtain a lead schedule of property, plant, and equipment; foot schedule and agree totals to the general ledger.
	Obtain detailed schedules for additions and dispositions of property, plant, and equipment; foot schedule; agree amounts to totals shown on lead schedule.
	Physically examine a sample of capital assets and trace them into the property, plant, and equipment subsidiary ledger.
Valuation and allocation	Evaluate fixed assets for significant write-offs or impairments by performing procedures such as
	• Identify the event or change in circumstance indicating that the carrying value of the asset may not be recoverable.
	• Verify impairment loss by determining the sum of expected future cash flows and comparing that sum to the carrying value.
	• Examine client documentation supporting impairment of write-off.
	Test depreciation calculations for a sample of capital assets.

Completeness and Accuracy   The auditor verifies the accuracy of property, plant, and equipment by obtaining a lead schedule and detailed schedules for additions and dispositions of assets. The lead schedule is footed, and the individual accounts are agreed to the general ledger. The detailed schedules are also tested for accuracy. Exhibit 14–3 presents a lead schedule for EarthWear's property, plant, and equipment. Take a look at Exhibit 14–3 and ask yourself, "If I were EarthWear's auditor, where would I focus my tests of details?"

The auditor has some assurance about the completeness assertion from the control activities in the purchasing process and, if present, the additional control activities discussed previously in this chapter. If the auditor still has concerns about the completeness assertion, he or she can physically examine a sample of assets and trace them into the property, plant, and equipment subsidiary ledger. If the assets are included in the subsidiary ledger, the auditor has sufficient evidence supporting the completeness assertion.

A common cause of an understated property, plant, and equipment account is the incorrect classification of plant and equipment additions as repairs and maintenance (see the Classification assertion in Table 14–2).

Cutoff   On most engagements, cutoff is tested as part of the audit work in accounts payable and accrued expenses. By examining a sample of vendor invoices from a few days before and after year-end, the auditor can determine if capital asset transactions are recorded in the proper period. Inquiry of client personnel and a review of lease transactions for the same period can provide evidence on proper cutoff for leases.

Classification   First, the classification of a transaction into the correct property, plant, and equipment account is normally examined as part of the testing of the purchasing process. The auditor's tests of controls and substantive tests of transactions provide evidence as to the effectiveness of the control activities for this assertion.

Second, the auditor should examine selected expense accounts such as repairs and maintenance to determine if any capital assets have been incorrectly recorded in these accounts. An account analysis of transactions included in the repairs and maintenance account is obtained, and selected transactions are vouched to supporting documents. In examining the supporting documents, the auditor must

EXHIBIT 14–3	An Example of a Lead Schedule for Property, Plant, and Equipment

K Lead
JLJ
1/15/10

EARTHWEAR CLOTHIERS
Lead Sheet—Property, Plant, and Equipment
12/31/09

Account	W/P Ref.	Cost				Accumulated Depreciation			
		Beginning Balance	Additions	Deletions	Ending Balance	Beginning Balance	Additions	Deletions	Ending Balance
Land	K10	$ 6,593,000¶	$ 2,112,852	$ 1,786,852	$ 6,919,000L				
Buildings	K20	60,211,250¶	6,112,600	2,324,950	63,998,900L	$ 23,638,300¶	$ 3,411,493	$ 653,788	$26,396,005L
Fixtures, Computers, and Equipment	K30	114,342,050¶	19,791,763	1,634,988	132,498,825L	51,162,450¶	8,285,360	1,533,398	57,914,462L
Leasehold Improvements	K40	2,894,100¶	780,115	664,595	3,009,620L	1,455,500¶	413,952	194,019	1,675,433L
Totals		$184,040,400F	$28,797,330	$6,411,385	$ 206,426,345	$ 76,266,250F	$12,110,805	$2,381,155	$ 85,985,900
		F	F	F	F	F	F	F	F

F = Footed and crossfooted.
L = Agreed to general ledger.
¶ = Agreed to prior year's working papers.

determine if the transactions are truly expense items or whether it would be more appropriate to capitalize the costs. For example, the auditor may examine an invoice from a plumbing contractor that shows that the water pipe system for a building has been replaced during the current period. If the amount of this transaction was material and improved the building, it should not be expensed as a repair but rather should be capitalized as a building improvement.

Last, the auditor should examine each material lease agreement to verify that the lease is properly classified as an operating or capital lease.

Existence

Existence   Before continuing to read, use your developing audit knowledge to think of ways, beyond physical inspection, to obtain evidence on the existence of property, plant, and equipment.

To test existence, the auditor obtains a listing of all major additions and vouches them to supporting documents such as vendors' invoices. If the purchase was properly authorized and the asset has been received and placed in service, the transaction is valid. In addition, the auditor may want to verify that assets recorded as capital assets actually exist. For major acquisitions, the auditor may physically examine the capital asset.

Similarly, disposition of assets must be properly authorized, and the supporting documentation such as sales receipts should indicate how the disposal took place. Generally, the auditor obtains a schedule of all major dispositions and verifies that the asset was removed from the property, plant, and equipment records. If the disposition is the result of a sale or exchange, the auditor would verify the cash receipt for the sale of the asset or documentation that another asset was received in exchange.

The auditor must also ascertain the validity of lease transactions by examining the lease agreements entered into by the entity. If the lease agreement is properly authorized and the asset is placed in service, the evidence supports the validity of the recorded asset.

Rights and Obligations

Rights and Obligations   The auditor can test for rights or ownership by examining the vendor invoices or other supporting documents. In some instances, the auditor may examine or confirm property deeds or title documents for proof of ownership.

Valuation and Allocation

Valuation and Allocation   Capital assets are valued at acquisition cost plus any costs necessary to make the asset operational. The auditor tests the recorded cost of new assets by examining the vendor invoices and other supporting documents used by the client to establish the recorded value of the assets. If the client has material self-constructed assets, the auditor conducts detailed audit work on the construction-in-process account. This includes ensuring that interest is properly capitalized as a cost of the asset.

FASB ASC Topic 360, "Property, Plant, and Equipment," requires that long-lived assets be reviewed for impairment whenever events or changes in circumstances indicate that the assets' carrying amount may not be recoverable. In reviewing for recoverability, the entity should estimate future (undiscounted) cash flows from use and eventual disposition of the assets. If the sum of those future cash flows is less than the assets' carrying amount, the assets should be written down and a loss recognized. The standards provide guidance and illustrations on how to estimate future cash flows, but obviously this area requires substantial judgment and expertise. Typically, the auditor gathers evidence on the valuation of property, plant, and equipment through a variety of procedures (e.g., understanding of the business and industry and current events that may lead to impairment, tests of controls over the client's impairment evaluation, inquiry and observation regarding the condition and usefulness of long-lived assets, and tests of details of balances, such as those described in Table 14–2).

TABLE 14–3	Examples of Items Requiring Disclosure—Property, Plant, and Equipment
	Classes of capital assets and valuation bases Depreciation methods and useful lives for financial reporting and tax purposes Nonoperating assets Construction or purchase commitments Liens and mortgages Acquisition or disposal of major operating facilities Capitalized and other lease arrangements

EXHIBIT 14–4	Sample Disclosure of Nonoperating Property
	In March 2009 the company decided to temporarily idle the Southern Alabama Mill. The decision was made in response to adverse industry conditions, mainly reduced selling prices and increased raw material costs. In September 2009 it was further determined that because of continued deterioration of selling prices and the level of expenditures required to meet environmental restrictions, the Southern Alabama Mill would not resume operations. The assets of the mill cannot be sold for their historical cost, and in the third quarter the company recorded a $15.6 million loss on the mill.

The other valuation issue the auditor must address is the recognition of depreciation expense. If the client uses IT to process and account for capital assets, the auditor may be able to use computer-assisted audit techniques to verify the calculation of depreciation for various assets. Alternatively, the auditor may recompute the depreciation expense for a sample of capital assets. In making this calculation, the auditor considers the reasonableness of the estimated life of the asset, the depreciation methods used for book and tax purposes, and any expected salvage value.

Disclosure Issues   Table 14–3 shows a number of important items that may require disclosure as part of the audit of property, plant, and equipment. Some of these disclosures are made in the "summary of significant accounting policies" footnote, while other items may be disclosed in separate footnotes. Exhibit 14–4 is a sample disclosure for an entity's decision to discontinue operations at one of its operating facilities.

Evaluating the Audit Findings—Property, Plant, and Equipment

[LO 10]   The process for evaluating the audit findings for property, plant, and equipment is the same as was discussed in previous chapters. The auditor aggregates the likely misstatements and compares this amount to the tolerable misstatement. If the likely misstatement is less than the tolerable misstatement, the evidence indicates that the property, plant, and equipment accounts are not materially misstated. This is the case with EarthWear, as no misstatements were detected for property, plant, and equipment (see Exhibit 3–4).

KEY TERMS

Analytical procedures. Evaluations of financial information made by a study of plausible relationships among both financial and nonfinancial data.

Intangible asset. An asset that is not physical in nature. Corporate intellectual property (items such as patents, trademarks, copyrights), goodwill, and brand recognition are common intangible assets.

Lien. When a creditor or bank has the right to sell the mortgaged or collateral property of those who fail to meet the obligations of a loan contract.

Prepaid expense. A type of asset that arises on a balance sheet as a result of a business making payments for goods and services to be received in the near future. While prepaid expenses are initially recorded as assets, their value is expensed over time as the benefit is received.

Property, plant, and equipment (PP&E). An asset that is vital to business operations but cannot be easily liquidated (e.g., warehouse, manufacturing equipment).

Specialist. Experts engaged or employed by auditors to provide evidential matter. For example, a specialist may be an expert in determining fair values of intangible assets.

Substantive tests of transactions. Tests to detect errors or fraud in individual transactions.

Tests of controls. Audit procedures performed to test the operating effectiveness of controls in preventing or detecting and correcting material misstatements at the relevant assertion level.

Tests of details of account balances and disclosures. Substantive tests that concentrate on the details of items contained in the account balance and disclosure.

www.mhhe.com/ messier7e	Visit the book's Online Learning Center for a multiple-choice quiz that will allow you to assess your understanding of chapter concepts.

REVIEW QUESTIONS

[LO 1] 14-1 Distinguish between prepaid expenses and intangible assets. Give two examples of each.

[1,2] 14-2 Prepaid expenses are generally assessed to have a low inherent risk. Why would intangible assets present serious inherent risk consideration?

[2] 14-3 How does the purchasing process affect prepaid insurance and property, plant, and equipment transactions?

[2] 14-4 Identify two substantive analytical procedures that can be used to audit prepaid insurance.

[2] 14-5 Confirmation is a useful audit procedure for verifying information related to prepaid insurance. What type of information would be requested from an entity's insurance broker in such a confirmation?

[2,4] 14-6 List four categories of intangible assets and four types of property, plant, and equipment transactions.

[2,5] 14-7 Describe two or more factors that the auditor should consider in assessing the inherent risk for (a) intangible assets; and (b) the property management process.

[6] 14-8 What is a typical control over authorization of capital asset transactions?

[7] 14-9 What is one of the key segregation of duties for the property management process? What errors or fraud can occur if such segregation is not present?

[8] 14-10 Identify three substantive analytical procedures that can be used to audit property, plant, and equipment.

[9] 14-11 What procedures would an auditor use to verify the completeness, rights and obligations, and valuation assertions for property, plant, and equipment?

MULTIPLE-CHOICE QUESTIONS

[2] 14-12 When auditing prepaid insurance, an auditor discovers that the original insurance policy on a key piece of manufacturing equipment is not available for inspection. The policy's absence most likely indicates the possibility of a(n)
a. Insurance premium due but not recorded.

b. Fictitious piece of equipment.

c. Third-party lien holder with a secured interest in the equipment.

d. Understatement of insurance expense.

[3,6] 14-13 Which of the following internal controls is most likely to justify a reduction of control risk concerning plant and equipment acquisitions?

a. Periodic physical inspection and reconciliation of plant and equipment to the detailed accounting records by the internal audit staff.

b. Comparison of current-year plant and equipment account balances with prior-year actual balances.

c. Review of pre-numbered purchase orders to detect unrecorded trade-ins.

d. Approval of periodic depreciation entries by a supervisor independent of the accounting department.

[3,6] 14-14 To strengthen control over the custody of heavy mobile equipment, the client would most likely institute a policy requiring a periodic

a. Increase in insurance coverage.

b. Inspection of equipment and reconciliation with accounting records.

c. Verification of liens, pledges, and collateralizations.

d. Accounting for work orders.

[3,6] 14-15 Due to a weakness observed in a client's control over recording retirement of equipment, the auditor may decide to

a. Trace additions to the "other assets" account to search for equipment that is still on hand but no longer being used.

b. Select certain items of equipment from the accounting records and locate them in the plant.

c. Inspect certain items of equipment in the plant and trace those items to the accounting records.

d. Review the subsidiary ledger to ascertain whether depreciation was taken on each item of equipment during the year.

[3,6,7] 14-16 Which of the following procedures is most likely to prevent the improper disposition of equipment?

a. Separation of duties between those authorized to dispose of equipment and those authorized to approve removal work orders.

b. The use of serial numbers to identify equipment that could be sold.

c. Periodic comparison of removal work orders to authorizing documentation.

d. Periodic analysis of the scrap sales and the repairs and maintenance accounts.

[3,6,7] 14-17 Property acquisitions that are misclassified as maintenance expense would most likely be detected by an internal control system that provides for

a. Investigation of variances within a formal budgeting system.

b. Review and approval of the monthly depreciation entry by the plant supervisor.

c. Segregation of duties of employees in the accounts payable department.

d. Examination by the internal auditor of vendor invoices and canceled checks for property acquisitions.

[2] 14-18 Which of the following situations would not support the auditor's decision to reduce control risk below maximum for the audit of intangible assets?

a. The client employs a qualified specialist who reviews the value of the intangible assets on an annual basis for impairment.

b. The auditor documented, tested, and developed an understanding of the acquisition process and found the key controls to be effective.

c. The IT system that maintains the records for intangible assets has adequate controls to prevent unauthorized access.

      d. The company has made no acquisitions of other companies during the fiscal year under audit.

[3,6,9]   14-19   Which of the following control activities would most likely allow for a reduction in the scope of the auditor's tests of depreciation expense?

      a. Review and approval of the periodic equipment depreciation entry by a supervisor who does not actively participate in its preparation.

      b. Comparison of equipment account balances for the current year with the current-year budget and prior-year actual balances.

      c. Review of the miscellaneous income account for salvage credits and scrap sales of partially depreciated equipment.

      d. Authorization of payment of vendor's invoices by a designated employee who is independent of the equipment-receiving function.

[6,8,9]   14-20   When there are numerous property and equipment transactions during the year, an auditor who plans to set the control risk at a low level usually performs

      a. Substantive analytical procedures for property and equipment balances at the end of the year.

      b. Tests of controls and extensive tests of property and equipment balances at the end of the year.

      c. Substantive analytical procedures for current-year property and equipment transactions.

      d. Tests of controls and limited tests of current-year property and equipment transactions.

[9]   14-21   An auditor analyzes repairs and maintenance accounts primarily to obtain evidence in support of the assertion that all

      a. Noncapitalizable expenditures for repairs and maintenance have been properly charged to expense.

      b. Expenditures for property and equipment have not been charged to expense.

      c. Noncapitalizable expenditures for repairs and maintenance have been recorded in the proper period.

      d. Expenditures for property and equipment have been recorded in the proper period.

[9]   14-22   Which of the following combinations of procedures would an auditor be most likely to perform to obtain evidence about fixed-asset additions?

      a. Inspecting documents and physically examining assets.

      b. Recomputing calculations and obtaining written management representations.

      c. Observing operating activities and comparing balances to prior-period balances.

      d. Confirming ownership and corroborating transactions through inquiries of client personnel.

PROBLEMS

[1,2]   14-23   Natherson, CPA, is engaged to audit the financial statements of Lewis Lumber for the year ended December 31. Natherson obtained and documented an understanding of internal control relating to the purchasing process and set control risk at the maximum level. Natherson requested and obtained from Lewis a schedule analyzing prepaid insurance as of December 31 and sent confirmation requests to Lewis's insurance broker.

Required:

      a. Identify two substantive analytical procedures that Natherson could use to verify prepaid insurance.

b. What substantive audit procedures should Natherson conduct on the schedule of prepaid insurance?

[2] 14-24 Taylor, CPA, has been engaged to audit the financial statements of Palmer Company, a continuing audit client. Taylor is about to perform substantive audit procedures on Palmer's goodwill (excess of cost over fair value of net assets purchased) and trademark assets that were acquired in prior years' business combinations. An industry slowdown has occurred recently, and the operations purchased have not met profit expectations.

During the planning process, Taylor determined that there was a high risk that goodwill and the trademark are impaired and may be materially misstated. Taylor obtained an understanding of internal control and set the control risk at the maximum level for the assertions related to intangible assets.

Required:
a. Describe the substantive audit procedures Taylor should consider performing in auditing Palmer's goodwill and trademark assets. Do *not* discuss Palmer's internal controls.
b. If Taylor engages a valuation specialist, describe what the auditor's responsibility is if the work of the specialist will be used as audit evidence.

[6,7] 14-25 Nakamura, CPA, has accepted an engagement to audit the financial statements of Grant Manufacturing Company, a new client. Grant has an adequate control environment and a reasonable segregation of duties. Nakamura is about to set the control risk for the assertions related to Grant's property and equipment.

Required:
Describe the key internal controls related to Grant's property, equipment, and related transactions (additions, transfers, major maintenance and repairs, retirements, and dispositions) that Nakamura may consider in setting the control risk.

(AICPA, adapted)

[4,6,9,10] 14-26 Gonzales, CPA, is the auditor for a manufacturing company with a balance sheet that includes the entry "Property, plant, and equipment." Gonzales has been asked by the company's management if audit adjustments or reclassifications are required for the following material items that have been included in or excluded from "Property, plant, and equipment":
1. A tract of land was acquired during the year. The land is to be the future site of the client's new headquarters, which will be constructed next year. Commissions were paid to the real estate agent used to acquire the land, and expenditures were made to relocate the previous owner's equipment. These commissions and expenditures were expensed and are excluded from "Property, plant, and equipment."
2. Clearing costs were incurred to ready the land for construction. These costs were included in "Property, plant, and equipment."
3. During the land-clearing process, timber and gravel were recovered and sold. The proceeds from the sale were recorded as other income and are excluded from "Property, plant, and equipment."
4. A group of machines was purchased under a royalty agreement that provides royalty payments based on units of production from the machines. The costs of the machines, freight costs, unloading charges, and royalty payments were capitalized and are included in "Property, plant, and equipment."

Required:

a. Describe the general characteristics of assets, such as land, buildings, improvements, machinery, equipment, fixtures, and so on, that should normally be classified as "Property, plant, and equipment," and identify assertions in connection with the examination of "Property, plant, and equipment." Do not discuss specific audit procedures.

b. Indicate whether each of the items numbered 1 to 4 requires one or more audit adjustments or reclassifications, and explain why such adjustments or reclassifications are required or not required. Organize your answer as follows:

Item Number	Is Auditing Adjustment or Reclassification Required? (Yes or No)	Reasons Why Audit Adjustments or Reclassifications Are Required or Not Required

(AICPA, adapted)

[8,9]   14-27   To support financial statement assertions, an auditor develops specific substantive procedures to satisfy or address each assertion.

Required:

Items (a) through (c) represent assertions for the property and equipment accounts. Select the most appropriate audit procedure from the following list and enter the number in the appropriate place on the grid. (An audit procedure may be selected once or not at all.)

Audit Procedure

1. Trace opening balances in the summary schedules to the prior year's audit working papers.
2. Review the provision for depreciation expense and determine that depreciable lives and methods used in the current year are consistent with those used in the prior year.
3. Determine that the responsibility for maintaining the property and equipment records is segregated from the responsibility for custody of property and equipment.
4. Examine deeds and title insurance certificates.
5. Perform cutoff tests to verify that property and equipment additions are recorded in the proper period.
6. Determine that property and equipment are adequately insured.
7. Physically examine all major property and equipment additions.

Specific Assertion	Audit Procedure
a. Verify that the entity has the legal right to property and equipment acquired during the year (rights and obligations).	
b. Verify that recorded property and equipment represent assets that actually exist at the balance sheet date (existence).	
c. Verify that net property and equipment are properly valued at the balance sheet date (valuation and allocation).	

(AICPA, adapted)

[8,9]   14-28   Pierce, an independent auditor, was engaged to examine the financial statements of Wong Construction, Inc., for the year ended December 31. Wong's financial statements reflect a substantial amount of mobile construction equipment used in the firm's operations. The equipment is accounted for in a subsidiary ledger. Pierce developed an understanding of internal control and set the control risk at moderate.

Required:

Identify the substantive audit procedures Pierce should utilize in examining mobile construction equipment and related depreciation in Wong's financial statements.

(AICPA, adapted)

DISCUSSION CASE

[9,10]   14-29   On January 15, 2009, Leno, Inc., which has a March 31 year-end, entered into a transaction to sell the land and building that contained its manufacturing operations for a total selling price of $19,750,000. The book value of the land and the building was $3,420,000. The final closing was not expected to occur until sometime between July 2010 and March 2011.

On March 16, 2009, Leno, Inc., received an irrevocable letter of credit, issued by a major bank, for $5,000,000, which represented more than 25 percent of the sales price. Leno, Inc., would collect the $5,000,000 and would keep the money even if the buyer decided not to complete the transaction. The letter of credit had an option for an extension for up to one year for a total period of two years. At closing, the entire selling price was to be paid in cash.

Leno, Inc., was going to continue its manufacturing operations in the building and would continue to be responsible for all normal occupancy costs until final closing, when it would move to another location. After the sale, the building would be torn down and replaced by a large office building complex.

Required:

a. Based on relevant accounting pronouncements for the sale of real estate, how should Leno, Inc., account for the transaction at March 31, 2009?
b. What additional types of evidence should the auditor examine prior to recognizing any gain on the transaction?

INTERNET ASSIGNMENTS

[3,4,9]   14-30   Visit the Web site of another catalog retailer similar to EarthWear Clothiers, and determine what useful lives and depreciation methods are used for property, plant, and equipment. Compare those methods to EarthWear, and, if different, consider the implications for using competitor data for preliminary or substantive analytical procedures. Note that you may have to examine the entity's annual report and 10K.

[3,4,10]   14-31   Visit the SEC's Web site (www.sec.gov) and identify a company that has been recently cited for problems related to property, plant, and equipment or lease accounting (e.g., many retail companies had to recently restate earnings to comply with the SEC's clarification of lease accounting). Prepare a memo summarizing the property, plant, and equipment or lease accounting issues for the company.

HANDS-ON CASES

ACL

CHAPTER 15

LEARNING OBJECTIVES

Upon completion of this chapter you will

[1] Understand the types and features of long-term debt.

[2] Be familiar with assessing control risk for long-term debt.

[3] Be familiar with key control activities for long-term debt.

[4] Know how to conduct substantive audit procedures for long-term debt.

[5] Understand the types of stockholders' equity transactions.

[6] Be familiar with assessing control risk for stockholders' equity.

[7] Be familiar with key control activities for stockholders' equity.

[8] Know the appropriate segregation of duties for stockholders' equity.

[9] Know how to conduct substantive audit procedures for capital stock.

[10] Know how to conduct substantive audit procedures for dividends.

[11] Know how to conduct substantive audit procedures for retained earnings.

[12] Know how to assess control risk and conduct substantive audit procedures for income statement accounts.

RELEVANT ACCOUNTING AND AUDITING PRONOUNCEMENTS

FASB ASC Topic 480, Distinguishing Liabilities from Equity

FASB ASC Topic 505, Equity

FASB ASC Topic 815, Derivatives and Hedging

AU 312, Audit Risk and Materiality in Conducting an Audit

AU 314, Understanding the Entity and Its Environment and Assessing the Risks of Material Misstatement

AU 316, Consideration of Fraud in a Financial Statement Audit

AU 318, Performing Audit Procedures in Response to Assessed Risks and Evaluating the Audit Evidence Obtained

AU 326, Audit Evidence

AU 328, Auditing Fair Value Measurements and Disclosures

AU 329, Analytical Procedures

AU 330, The Confirmation Process

AU 339, Audit Documentation

AU 420, Consistency of Application of Generally Accepted Accounting Procedures

PCAOB Auditing Standard No. 3, Audit Documentation (AS3)

PCAOB Auditing Standard No. 5, An Audit of Internal Control Over Financial Reporting That Is Integrated with An Audit of Financial Statements (AS5)

PCAOB Proposed Auditing Standards Related to the Auditor's Assessment of and Response to Risk, PCAOB Release No. 2008-006 (October 21, 2008)

Auditing the Financing/Investing Process: Long-Term Liabilities, Stockholders' Equity, and Income Statement Accounts

Major Phases of an Audit

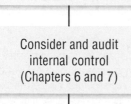

Client acceptance/
continuance and establishing
an understanding with the client
(Chapter 5)

Preliminary engagement
activities
(Chapter 5)

Plan the audit
(Chapters 3 and 5)

Consider and audit
internal control
(Chapters 6 and 7)

Audit business processes
and related accounts
(e.g., revenue generation)
(Chapters 10–16)

Complete the audit
(Chapter 17)

Evaluate results and issue audit
report (Chapters 1 and 18)

This chapter presents the audit of long-term liabilities, stockholders' equity, and income statement accounts. Long-term debt and equity are the major sources of financing for most entities. A substantive audit strategy is normally followed when long-term liabilities and stockholders' equity accounts are audited, because although the number of transactions is small, each transaction is often highly material. For public companies required to have an audit of internal controls over financial reporting, the auditor would also obtain evidence from tests of controls.

While the main focus of this chapter is auditing the long-term liabilities, stockholders' equity, and income statement accounts for a *financial statement audit,* the concepts covered for setting control risk are applicable to an audit of internal control over financial reporting. Last, the audit of selected income statement accounts is presented. The discussion of auditing the income statement focuses on how the auditor's work on internal control and substantive analytical procedures provide evidence on income statement accounts and how most income statement accounts are audited when their related balance sheet accounts are audited.

Auditing Long-Term Debt

[LO 1]   Common types of long-term debt financing include notes, bonds, and mortgages. More sophisticated types of debt financing include collateralized mortgage obligations, repurchase and reverse repurchase agreements, interest-rate swaps, financial futures, derivatives (see Exhibit 15–1), and myriad other financial instruments. Accounting for and auditing such sophisticated debt instruments and financial instruments with characteristics of both debt and equity can be complex and is beyond the scope of this text (see AU 328, FASB ASC Topic 480). Capitalized lease obligations also represent a form of long-term debt. While the concepts relating to the audit of most types of debt are similar, to simplify our discussion we focus on notes and bonds, including the audit of interest payable and interest expense.

Long-term debt may have a number of features that can affect the audit procedures used. For example, debt may be convertible into stock, or it may be combined with warrants, options, or rights that can be exchanged for equity. Debt may be callable under certain conditions, or it may require the establishment of a sinking fund, which is a pool of money set aside for repaying the debt or to repurchase a portion of the existing bonds every year. The sinking fund is often held by a bond trustee to ensure that the funds are only used for bond retirement. Last, debt may be either unsecured or secured by assets of the entity.

The auditor's consideration of long-term debt, however, is no different from that of any other financial statement account. The auditor must be assured that the amounts shown on the balance sheet for the various types of long-term debt are not materially misstated. This assurance extends to the proper recognition of interest expense in the financial statements.

EXHIBIT 15–1	**Derivatives Lead to Losses at AIG**

Derivatives are contracts that are written between two parties. The value of a derivative contract to one of the parties and the cost or obligation to the other is derived from the value of an underlying asset, such as currencies, equities, commodities, mortgages, interest rates, or from stock market or other indicators. While derivatives can be used wisely by management to hedge risk, they can also be used to create leverage and thereby greatly increase risk.

AIG identified a seemingly low-risk method of capitalizing on the housing boom in the mid-2000s. As the boom grew, fresh capital was needed to provide for the increased demand for home mortgages. A significant source of capital was obtained through the selling of pools of mortgages as bonds to investors (mortgages that are grouped and securitized are known as mortgage-backed securities or asset-backed securities). The mortgage holders selling the securitized bonds wanted a form of insurance that would cover their losses in case homeowners were to default on the underlying mortgages. This "insurance" was provided in the form of credit-default swaps (CDSs), which is a derivative contract, consisting basically of a promise to pay the value of the mortgage to the holder of the CDS in case of mortgage default. Many banks and institutions sold and purchased CDSs to hedge their exposure to potential losses on their investments in mortgage-backed securities. However, AIG only sold CDSs, which generated significant fee revenue at seemingly little risk . . . because everyone knows that housing prices always go up . . . well, not quite always, as AIG found out.

AIG's CDS strategy initially paid off handsomely because mortgage defaults are uncommon when home prices are rapidly appreciating. The problem was that the rapid appreciation in home prices actually represented a speculative "bubble." When the housing bubble burst and the subprime mortgage market collapsed, homeowners began defaulting on their mortgages in large numbers, and the value of the mortgage-backed securities plummeted. As the value of the bonds dropped, CDS holders demanded that AIG pay up in accordance with the contract. Because AIG had entered the CDS market in such an aggressive manner, the company's exposure to CDS claims was huge. In 2007 and 2008, AIG recognized $11.47 and $28.6 billion, respectively, in charges related to its CDS portfolio, and has survived to the date of this writing only as a result of a massive government bailout.

Source: AIG 2008 Form 10-K.

The approach to the audit of long-term debt varies depending on the frequency of the entity's financing activities. For entities that engage in frequent financing activities, the auditor may follow a reliance strategy under which internal control is formally evaluated and tests of controls are performed in order to set control risk. However, for the vast majority of entities, it is more efficient for the auditor to follow a substantive strategy and perform a detailed audit of long-term debt and the related interest accounts.

Inherent Risk Assessment—Long-Term Debt

Inherent risk for notes and bonds would normally be assessed as low to moderate because the volume of transactions is low, the accounting is usually not complex, and the client often receives third-party statements or amortization schedules. However, the amounts involved are usually large, and, as noted in the chapter introduction, the financial markets have developed very sophisticated instruments that can introduce an enormous amount of leverage and that can have characteristics of both debt and equity. The inherent risk associated with these sophisticated instruments is normally high. In this chapter we focus on notes and bonds.

Practice
INSIGHT

It's important for auditors to consider possible off-balance sheet financing. Enron had off-balance sheet financing through transactions with "Special Purpose Entities" (SPEs, now known as Variable Interest Entities). Enron did not consolidate these companies because the company claimed that the transactions with these SPEs were arm's-length and complied with the accounting standards.

The determination of whether an entity should be consolidated with its parent company should be evaluated and special attention should be given to these inherently complex classes of transactions. Off-balance sheet entities are often legitimate; however, they are also sometimes used to commit fraud. With an off-balance sheet entity, a parent company need only recognize net assets from the entity on its balance sheet. By doing so, the parent company avoids recording the debt of the entity on its balance sheet. Similarly, the parent only records net earnings or losses from the company on its balance sheet, which keeps the expenses of the entity from being disclosed on the parent's income statement. A fraud occurs when a company does not follow GAAP provisions for consolidation and purposefully excludes debt that should be reported in its financial statements.

Some of Enron's transactions involving SPEs were not arm's-length because Enron was the underlying guarantor of the SPE debt. In effect, by not consolidating the SPEs, Enron failed to report hundreds of millions in debt.

Control Risk Assessment—Long-Term Debt

[LO 2]   When a substantive strategy is followed, the auditor needs a sufficient understanding of the entity's internal control system over debt transactions to be able to anticipate the types of misstatements that may occur. The following discussion of control risk assessment for long-term debt focuses on the general types of control activities that should be present to minimize the likelihood of material misstatement. The assertions that are of primary concern to the auditor are *occurrence, authorization, completeness, valuation,* and *disclosure-classification.*

Assertions and
Related Control
Activities

Following are some of the more common controls that should be present for the important assertions for long-term debt.

[LO 3]   **Occurrence and Authorization**   The entity should have controls to ensure that any transactions involving long-term financing are properly initiated by authorized individuals. First, adequate documentation must be developed and kept to verify that a note or bond was properly authorized. The presence of adequate documentation, such as a properly signed lending agreement, allows the auditor to determine if the transaction was properly executed. Second, any significant debt commitments should be approved by the board of directors or by executives who have been delegated this authority. Entities that engage in recurring borrowing activities should have both general and specific controls. The board of directors should establish general controls to guide the entity's financing activities. The specific controls for borrowing and repayment may be delegated to an executive, such as the chief financial officer. When the chief financial officer or similar executive is responsible for both executing and accounting for long-term debt transactions, another executive body, such as the finance committee of the board of directors, should provide overall review and approval in the minutes. If the client has proper controls and documentation for debt transactions, it is generally easy for the auditor to obtain evidence on occurrence and authorization at the end of the period.

Completeness   The client should maintain detailed records of long-term debt transactions to ensure that all borrowings and repayments of principal and interest are recorded. One approach to handling detailed debt transactions is to maintain a subsidiary ledger that contains information about all the long-term debt owed by the client. The debt amount recorded in the subsidiary ledger should be reconciled to the general ledger control account regularly.

Valuation   Note and bond transactions are recorded in the accounting records at their face value plus or minus any premium or discount. Premiums or discounts should be amortized using the effective interest method to calculate interest expense. Sometimes an entity incurs "issuing costs" such as underwriter's fees, legal fees, and accounting fees. Such costs should be recorded as deferred charges and amortized over the life of the debt. Valuation issues for sophisticated financial instruments are far more complex. Although the client should have control activities to ensure that long-term debt is properly valued, the client may ask the auditor to assist with recording the debt properly.

Disclosure-Classification   Controls should ensure that the proper disclosures are provided for long-term debt. Common disclosures involve related party transactions, restrictive debt covenants, and revolving lines of credit. Controls should also ensure that notes and bonds are properly classified in the financial statements. The major issue is to properly classify as a short-term liability the portion of long-term debt that is due within the next year.

 One final issue related to control risk for long-term debt is that the client should have adequate custodial procedures for any unissued notes or bonds to safeguard against loss from theft. Procedures should provide for periodic inspections by an individual who is independent of both the custodial and accounting responsibilities for long-term debt.

Practice **INSIGHT**	Because the completeness assertion is more difficult to test, it is particularly important that the auditor use a top-down approach when obtaining evidence on the completeness assertion for liabilities. The auditor must evaluate the incentives, pressures, and tone at the top to assess the potential threat for omitted liabilities. Too much focus on transaction-level control activities, to the exclusion of assessing the bigger picture, increases the risk that the auditor will get an inflated sense of comfort and assurance regarding the completeness of the reported liabilities.

Substantive Procedures—Long-Term Debt

[LO 4]   A substantive strategy for auditing long-term debt involves examining any new debt agreements (debt agreements for bonds are called bond or trust indentures), determining the status of prior debt agreements, and confirming balances and other relevant information with outside parties.

Substantive analytical procedures are useful in auditing interest expense because of the direct relationship between long-term debt and interest expense. For example, the auditor could estimate interest expense by multiplying the 12 monthly balances for long-term debt by the average monthly interest rate. The reasonableness of interest expense could then be assessed by comparing this estimate to the interest expense amount recorded in the general ledger. If the two amounts are not materially different, the auditor can conclude that interest expense is fairly stated. If the estimated amount of interest expense is materially higher than the recorded amount, the auditor might conclude that the client has failed to record a portion of interest expense. On the other hand, if the recorded amount of interest expense is materially higher than the estimated amount, the client may have failed to record debt. Refer to Chapter 5 for an example of the use of a substantive analytical procedure to test the relationship between Earth-Wear's short-term line of credit and related interest expense.

Table 15–1 provides examples of tests of transactions and account balances for the key assertions of long-term debt. The following discussion will help you understand the general approach to auditing long-term debt accounts.

TABLE 15–1   Examples of Tests of Transactions and Account Balances for Long-Term Debt

Assertions about Classes of Transactions	Example Substantive Tests of Transactions*
Occurrence	Examine copies of new note or bond agreements. Examine board of directors' minutes for approval of new lending agreements.
Completeness	Trace large cash receipts and payments to source documents and general ledger (see Chapters 11 and 16). Review interest expense for payments to debt holders not listed on the debt analysis schedule. Review notes paid or renewed after the balance sheet date to determine if there are unrecorded liabilities at year-end. Evaluate lease contracts to determine if leases are properly accounted for as an operating or capital lease (i.e., if a lease should be a capital lease, it would likely require recognition of long-term debt).
Authorization	Examine board minutes for evidence of proper authorization of notes or bonds.
Accuracy	Test a sample of receipts and payments.
Cutoff	Review debt activity for a few days before and after year-end to determine if the transactions are included in the proper period.
Classification	Examine the due dates on notes or bonds for proper classification between current and long-term debt.

Assertions about Account Balances at Period End	Example Tests of Details of Account Balances
Existence	Confirm notes or bonds directly with creditors (in many instances, creditors are banks, insurance companies, or trustees representing the creditors).
Rights and obligations	Examine copies of note and bond agreements.
Completeness	Obtain an analysis of notes payable, bonds payable, and accrued interest payable; foot schedule and agree totals to the general ledger. Obtain a standard bank confirmation that requests specific information on notes from banks (see Chapter 16 for further discussion of bank confirmations). Confirm notes or bonds with creditors. Inquire of management regarding the existence of off-balance sheet activities. Review board meeting minutes for debt-related activity.
Valuation and allocation	Examine new debt agreements (e.g., bond indentures) to ensure that they were recorded at the proper value. Confirm the outstanding balance for notes or bonds and the last date on which interest has been paid. Recompute accrued interest payable. Verify computation of the amortization of premium or discount.

*These tests of details of transactions are commonly conducted as dual-purpose tests (i.e., in conjunction with tests of controls).

EXHIBIT 15–2 Analysis Schedule for Auditing Long-Term Debt and Accrued Interest Payable

P10
DLJ
1/2/10

CALABRO WIRELESS SERVICES
Schedule of Long-Term Debt and Accrued Interest Payable
12/31/09

Payee	Due Date	Face Amount	Security	Long-Term Debt				Accrued Interest Payable			
				Beginning Balance	Additions	Payments	Ending Balance	Beginning Balance	Expenses	Paid	Ending Balance
First National Bank—Line of credit	11/1/12	$ 7,000,000	All assets**C**	$ 200,000	$900,000	$300,000γ	$ 800,000	$ 1,875	$ 22,500λ	$ 22,815	$ 1,560
8.75% lease obligation Patriot Insurance Co.	12/15/11	$ 2,000,000	Communications equipment**C**	238,637		48,230γ	190,407	5,470	17,541λ	18,461	4,550
7% bonds payable—All American Insurance	6/30/14	$10,000,000	Land and buildings**C**	3,100,000		200,000γ	2,900,000	36,850	224,602λ	219,820	41,632
Total				$3,538,637	$900,000	$548,230	$3,890,407**L**	$44,195	$264,643**L**	$261,096	$47,742**L**
				F	**F**	**F**	**F**	**F**	**F**	**F**	**F**

Less current portion of long-term debt   424,061✓
$3,466,346

L = Agreed to general ledger.
γ = Traced payments to cash disbursements journal.
λ = Recomputed interest expense.
C = Agreed all information to confirmation.
F = Footed.
✓ = Tested amount of current portion of long-term debt.

EXHIBIT 15-3	**Sample Disclosure of Restrictive Loan Covenants**

The 7 percent bond agreement contains provisions (1) limiting funded debt, security interests, and other indebtedness; (2) requiring the maintenance of defined working capital and tangible net worth; and (3) imposing restrictions on the payment of cash dividends. The company was in compliance with, or received a waiver regarding, each of the agreements during the year ended 2009. Under the terms of these agreements, $825,000 of retained earnings was available for payment of cash dividends at December 31, 2009.

The auditor generally begins the audit of long-term debt by obtaining an analysis schedule for notes payable, bonds payable, and accrued interest payable. Exhibit 15–2 presents an example of such a schedule. Because EarthWear does not have long-term debt, the example in Exhibit 15–2 is based on Calabro Wireless Services. If there are numerous transactions during the year, this schedule may include only the debt outstanding at the end of the period. Note that this schedule includes a considerable amount of information on each debt transaction, including the payee, date due, interest rate, original amount, collateral, and paid and accrued interest.

Exhibit 15–2 also indicates the audit procedures performed on the details of the debt schedule. Take a break from reading for a moment and look at the tick mark descriptions in Exhibit 15–2 and see if you can identify the assertion each procedure is addressing. Evidence is gathered for the most important assertions as follows: Each debt instrument is confirmed with the debt holders and includes a request to verify the amount owed and last date on which interest has been paid.[1] Confirmation of the debt and accrued interest provides evidence on the existence, completeness, and valuation assertions. If the client's debt is guaranteed by another party, a confirmation should be sent to the guarantor to confirm the guarantee.

The auditor also examines the due dates for the debt to ensure proper classification between current and long-term liabilities. Last, the auditor examines the debt agreements for any restrictive covenants that require disclosure in the footnotes. Examples of such covenants include restrictions on the payment of dividends or the issuance of additional debt or equity, and the maintenance of certain financial ratios. Exhibit 15–3 is an example of the disclosure of restrictive covenants.

Auditing Stockholders' Equity

[LO 5] For most entities, stockholders' equity includes common stock, preferred stock, paid-in capital, and retained earnings. In recent years, numerous financial instruments have been developed that contain both debt and equity characteristics and affect the audit of stockholders' equity. A host of stock option and compensation plans also impact the audit of stockholders' equity. A discussion of these complex equity instruments and stock option plans is beyond the scope of this text (share-based compensation is discussed in the *Advanced Module* to Chapter 12).

---

[1]The debt instrument can also be confirmed with the bond trustee, which is a financial institution given fiduciary powers by the debt holder to enforce the terms of the debt instrument. The trustee ensures that interest payments are made on time.

Following are the three major types of transactions that occur in stockholders' equity:

- **Issuance of stock.** This includes transactions such as sale of stock for cash; the exchange of stock for assets, services, or convertible debt; and issuance of stock for stock splits.
- **Repurchase of stock.** This includes the reacquisition of stock (referred to as *treasury stock*) and the retirement of stock.
- **Payment of dividends.** This includes the payment of cash dividends or issuance of stock dividends.

Control Risk Assessment—Stockholders' Equity

✂ **[LO 6]**   A substantive strategy is most often used to audit stockholders' equity because the number of transactions is usually small. Although control risk can then be set at the maximum, the auditor must still understand the types of controls that are in place to prevent the misstatement of equity transactions. Further, the auditor must test the design and operating effectiveness of key controls over stockholders' equity if the client is a public company required to have an audit of internal controls over financial reporting.

Many large entities, such as publicly traded companies, use an independent *registrar, transfer agent*, and *dividend-disbursing agent* to process and record equity transactions. The registrar is responsible for ensuring that all stock issued complies with the corporate charter and for maintaining the control totals for total shares outstanding. The transfer agent is responsible for preparing stock certificates and maintaining adequate stockholders' records. The dividend-disbursing agent prepares and mails dividend checks to the stockholders of record. When an entity uses an independent registrar, transfer agent, and dividend-disbursing agent, the auditor may be able to obtain sufficient evidence by confirming the relevant information with those parties.

If an entity uses its own employees to perform the stock transfer and dividend disbursement functions, the auditor needs to perform more detailed testing of the stock-related records and transactions that occurred during the period. Next we'll discuss the assertions, control activities, and segregation of duties that are relevant when client personnel transfer stock and disburse dividends.

Assertions and Related Control Activities

Following are the major evidence-gathering procedures and assertions for stockholders' equity:

✂ **[LO 7]**
- Verify that stock and dividend transactions comply with the corporate charter (occurrence).
- Verify that all stock and dividend transactions have been properly posted and summarized in the accounting records (accuracy).
- Verify that stock and dividend transactions have been properly approved (authorization).
- Verify that stock and dividend transactions have been properly valued (valuation).

Occurrence   One of the entity's officers, such as the corporate secretary or legal counsel, should ensure that every stock or dividend transaction complies with the corporate charter or any regulatory requirement that affects the entity. This individual should also maintain the stockholders' ledger, which contains the name of each stockholder and the number of shares held by that shareholder.

Accuracy The control activities for this assertion include reconciliation of the stockholders' records with the number of shares outstanding and reconciliation of dividends paid with the total shares outstanding on the dividend record date.

Authorization For most entities, the board of directors or stockholders approve stock and dividend transactions. The authorization is normally documented in the minutes of the board of directors' meetings. The auditor can examine the board of directors' minutes for proper authorization.

Valuation Stock issuances, stock repurchases, and dividends should be recorded by the treasurer's department at an amount that conforms to GAAP. The auditor can recompute the recording of the stock and dividend transactions.

Segregation of Duties

[LO 8]

If the entity has enough personnel, the following segregation of duties should be maintained:

- The individuals responsible for issuing, transferring, and canceling stock certificates should not have any accounting responsibilities.
- The individual responsible for maintaining the detailed stockholders' records should be independent of the maintenance of the general ledger control accounts.
- The individual responsible for maintaining the detailed stockholders' records should not also process cash receipts or disbursements.
- Appropriate segregation of duties should be established among the preparation, recording, signing, and mailing of dividend checks.

Pause for a moment and consider what types of problems could occur if there were inadequate segregation of duties in each of the listed areas.

Auditing Capital-Stock Accounts

[LO 9] The capital-stock accounts include common stock, preferred stock, and paid-in capital. When auditing the capital-stock accounts, the auditor is normally concerned with the occurrence, completeness, valuation, and completeness of disclosures assertions. The auditor begins the audit of capital stock by obtaining a schedule of all activity in the accounts for the current period. The beginning balance is agreed to the prior year's working papers, and the ending balance is agreed to the general ledger. The majority of the auditor's work then focuses on the current-period activity in each account.

Occurrence and Completeness

All valid capital-stock transactions must be approved by the board of directors. Therefore, the auditor can obtain assurance on the occurrence of capital-stock transactions by tracing the transactions recorded in the current year to the board of directors' minutes. When an independent registrar and transfer agent are used by the entity, the auditor confirms the total number of shares outstanding at the end of the period. If the amount of shares listed as outstanding on the

TABLE 15–2	**Examples of Disclosure Items for Stockholders' Equity**
	Number of shares authorized, issued, and outstanding for each class of stock.
	Call privileges, prices, and dates for preferred stock.
	Preferred-stock sinking funds.
	Stock option or purchase plans.
	Restrictions on retained earnings and dividends.
	Any completed or pending transactions (such as stock dividends or splits) that may affect stockholders' equity.

confirmation reconciles to the general ledger capital-stock accounts, the auditor has evidence that the total number of shares outstanding at the end of the year is correct.

If the entity does not use outside agents, it will maintain a stock register and/or a stock certificate book. The auditor may perform the following procedures:

- Trace the transfers of shares between stockholders to the stock register and/or stock certificate book (accuracy and completeness).
- Foot the shares outstanding in the stock register and/or stock certificate book and agree them to total shares outstanding in the general ledger capital-stock accounts (completeness).
- Examine any canceled stock certificates (occurrence).
- Account for and inspect any unissued stock certificates in the stock certificate book (completeness).

Valuation

When capital stock is issued for cash, the assessment of proper valuation is straightforward. The par, or stated, value for the shares issued is assigned to the respective capital-stock account, while the difference between the price and par, or stated, value is allocated to paid-in capital. The auditor can recompute the values assigned to each transaction. The proceeds from the sale of stock are normally traced to the cash receipts records.

The valuation issue is more complex when capital stock is issued in exchange for assets or services, for a merger or acquisition, for convertible securities, or for a stock dividend. For example, when a stock dividend is declared and the number of shares issued is less than 20 percent of the shares outstanding, the dividend is recorded at fair market value. The fair market value of the stock dividend is charged to retained earnings and credited to common stock and paid-in capital. To obtain evidence on valuation, the auditor can recompute the stock dividend and trace the entries into the general ledger.

Completeness of Disclosures

A number of important disclosures are necessary for stockholders' equity. Table 15–2 contains examples of stockholders' equity disclosures. The normal sources of this information include the corporate charter, minutes of the board of directors' meetings, and contractual agreements.

Auditing Dividends

[LO 10]   Generally, all dividends that are declared and paid will be audited because of concerns with violations of corporate bylaws or debt covenants. When the entity uses an independent dividend-disbursing agent, the auditor can confirm the amount disbursed to the agent by the entity. This amount is agreed with the amount authorized by the board of directors. The auditor can recompute the dividend amount by multiplying the number of shares outstanding on the record date by the amount of the per-share dividend approved by the board of directors. This amount should agree to the amount disbursed to shareholders and accrued at year-end. If the auditor is concerned about the client's controls over dividend disbursements, he or she may compare the payee names and amounts on the individual canceled checks with the stock register or stock certificate book. The auditor also reviews the entity's compliance with any agreements that restrict the payments of dividends.

Auditing Retained Earnings

[LO 11] Under normal circumstances, retained earnings are affected by the current year's income or loss, as well as cash or stock dividends paid. However, certain accounting standards require that some transactions be made directly to retained earnings. Thus, additional audit procedures are sometimes required. Prior-period adjustments, correction of errors, stock retirements, valuation accounts for marketable securities and foreign currency translation, and changes in appropriations of retained earnings are examples of such transactions.

The auditor begins the audit of retained earnings by obtaining a schedule of the account activity for the period. The beginning balance is agreed to the prior year's working papers and financial statements. Net income or loss can be traced to the income statement. The amounts for any cash or stock dividends can be verified as described earlier. If there are any prior-period adjustments, the auditor must be certain that the transactions satisfy the requirements of the relevant accounting standards. Any new appropriations or changes in existing appropriations should be traced to the relevant contractual agreements. Last, the auditor must make sure that all necessary disclosures related to retained earnings are made in the footnotes. For example, many debt agreements restrict the amount of retained earnings that is available for payment as dividends (see Exhibit 15–3).

Practice INSIGHT	A substantive approach is appropriate when auditing the retained earnings account for a client not required to have an audit of internal control over financial reporting. Each transaction is often tested because there are relatively few transactions recorded in the account. Because retained earnings is a "residual" account, auditors typically do not allocate materiality or tolerable misstatement to retained earnings.

Auditing Income Statement Accounts

[LO 12] In auditing income statement accounts, the auditor must be satisfied that the revenue and expense accounts are not materially misstated and that they are accounted for in accordance with GAAP. The income statement is viewed as an important source of information by various users of the financial statements. For example, creditors or potential creditors look to an entity's profitability as one indicator of the entity's ability to repay debt. Potential investors look to the income statement when deciding whether to purchase the entity's stock. Finally, vendors may examine the entity's earnings potential in order to assess whether the entity will be able to pay for goods or services purchased on credit.

The audit of the revenue and expense accounts depends on the extent of work conducted by the auditor on the entity's control system and on the client's balance sheet accounts. For example, the likelihood of material misstatement in the various revenue and expense accounts is a function of the entity's controls. The level of control risk established for the different business processes directly affects the extent of testing that the auditor requires to audit the income statement accounts.

Auditing the income statement includes consideration of the results of audit work conducted in other parts of the audit and completion of additional substantive procedures on selected income statement accounts, including the following:

- The results of testing controls for the various business processes.
- The results of the detailed tests of balance sheet accounts and the related income statement accounts.
- Performance of substantive analytical procedures on income statement accounts.
- Detailed tests of selected income statement accounts.

Assessing Control Risk for Business Processes— Income Statement Accounts

In previous chapters, the auditor's approach to setting the control risk for various business processes was discussed. If the control risk is set at the maximum, the auditor does not rely on controls but conducts extensive substantive procedures. When a reliance strategy is followed, the auditor conducts tests of controls and substantive tests of transactions to determine if the client's controls are operating effectively. If the controls operate effectively, the auditor may reduce the control risk below the maximum.

To better understand the effect of a reduced control risk assessment on the audit of the revenue and expense accounts, consider the income statement accounts affected by the revenue and purchasing business processes. For example, a justifiably reduced control risk assessment for the revenue process provides evidence that the sales, accounts receivable, allowance for uncollectible accounts, and sales returns and allowances accounts are not materially misstated. Similarly, a reduced control risk assessment for the purchasing process provides evidence that financial statement accounts such as inventory; property, plant, and equipment; accounts payable; and most expense accounts are not materially misstated. The important point here is that the auditor already has reliable evidence on the accounts included in the income statement. The findings for the purchasing process are particularly relevant, since proper controls provide evidence on most of the expense accounts. This allows the auditor to do considerably fewer substantive procedures for these income statement accounts.

Substantive Procedures—Income Statement Accounts

Direct Tests of Balance Sheet Accounts

Income statement accounts are normally audited in the course of auditing the related balance sheet accounts. Table 15–3 lists balance sheet accounts and the related income statement accounts that are verified in this manner. For example, when the allowance for uncollectible accounts is audited, bad-debt expense is also tested. Similarly, when auditing notes receivable, the auditor can test interest income.

TABLE 15–3	Examples of Income Statement Accounts Audited in Conjunction with the Balance Sheet Account
Balance Sheet Account Audited	*Related Income Statement Account Audited*
Accounts receivable/allowance for uncollectible accounts	Bad-debt expense
Notes receivable/investments/accrued interest receivable	Interest income
Property, plant, and equipment/accumulated depreciation	Depreciation expense, gain/losses on sales or retirements of assets
Prepaid insurance	Insurance expense
Long-term debt/accrued interest payable	Interest expense

Substantive Analytical Procedures for Income Statement Accounts

Substantive analytical procedures can be used extensively to provide assurance on the revenue and expense accounts. The auditing standard on the consideration of fraud risk (AU 316) indicates that the auditor should ordinarily presume that there is a risk of material misstatement due to fraud relating to revenue recognition. Disaggregated analytical procedures are typically conducted on the revenue account to identify unusual or unexpected relationships that may be indicative of fraud.

One type of substantive analytical procedure involves comparing the current year's dollar amount for each revenue and expense account (e.g., by product, business segment, or geographic region) with the prior years' balances. Any account that deviates from the prior years' trend by more than a predetermined amount should be investigated. An alternative to this type of substantive analytical procedure involves calculating the ratio of individual expense accounts to net sales and comparing these percentages across years. The auditor can also compare these percentages to industry averages. Individual expense accounts that are judged by the auditor to be out of line are investigated further. While these types of substantive analytical procedures are common, it is important that substantive analytical procedures designed to provide evidence regarding the fairness of revenue or other income statement accounts be conducted at a sufficiently disaggregated (i.e., monthly or weekly data versus annual data, by business segment or product) level to detect potential misstatements. As noted in Chapter 5, even relatively small percentage misstatements in large income statement accounts are often material, thus the need for precise substantive analytical procedures.

Substantive analytical procedures can also be used to provide evidence of *specific* revenue or expense accounts. For example, the auditor can evaluate the reasonableness of sales commissions by using the client's commission schedule and multiplying commission rates by eligible sales. This estimate can be compared to the recorded commission expense. Other examples might include overall reasonableness tests for interest and depreciation expense.

Practice
INSIGHT

In a review of actual audit working papers, the Public Oversight Board found that auditors often over-rely on weak analytical procedures when a substantive analytical procedure is used as the primary substantive evidence for an income statement account. Research conducted to understand this finding suggests that auditors overestimate the quality and strength of evidence provided by a weak (i.e., highly aggregated) substantive analytical procedure if the procedure yields a "favorable" result (i.e., if it indicates that there is no material misstatement). However, keep in mind that the quality and strength of the evidence provided by a substantive analytical procedure can and should be measured before the procedure is performed. A weak analytical procedure is weak no matter the outcome of the test. See S. Glover, D. Prawitt, and J. Wilks, "Why do auditors over-rely on weak analytical procedures? The role of outcome and precision," *Auditing: A Journal of Practice & Theory,* vol. 25, 2005.

EXHIBIT 15–4	**Example of an Account Analysis Working Paper**

T20
SAA
2/4/10

EARTHWEAR CLOTHERS
Analysis of Legal and Audit Expense
12/31/09

Date	Payee	Amount	Explanation
Feb. 2	Katz & Fritz	$ 28,500.00V	For services related to a patent infringement suit by Gough Mfg. Co. Lawsuit was dismissed.
April 10	Willis & Adams	950,000.00V	Annual audit fee.
Oct. 1	Katz & Fritz	26,200.00V	Legal fee for patent infringement suit against Weshant, Inc.
Oct. 20	Smoothe, Sylk, Fiels, Goode & Associates	2,100.00V	Legal services for a purchase contract with McDonald Merchandise, Inc.
		$1,006,800.00	
		F T/B	

Tick Mark Legend
V = Examined payees' bills for amount and description.
F = Footed.
T/B = Agreed to trial balance.

Conclusion: Based on the audit work performed, EarthWear's legal and audit expense account is not materially misstated.

Tests of Selected Account Balances

Even though the auditor has gathered considerable evidence about revenue and expense accounts based on the audit procedures just discussed, the auditor may want to examine some accounts further. For these accounts, the auditor typically analyzes in detail the transactions included in each account. The auditor verifies the transactions by examining (vouching) the supporting documentation. Accounts examined in this manner are generally accounts that are not directly affected by a business process, accounts that may contain sensitive information or unusual transactions, or accounts for which detailed information is needed for the tax return or other schedules included with the financial statements. Some examples of such accounts include legal and audit expense, travel and entertainment, charity expense, other income and expenses, and any account containing related-party transactions. Exhibit 15–4 presents an account analysis for Earth-Wear's legal and audit expense. In auditing this account, the auditor vouches the transactions to the attorneys' invoices. The auditor should examine the invoice not only for the amount but also for information on potential uncertainties, such as lawsuits against the client.

KEY TERMS

Analytical procedures. Evaluations of financial information made by a study of plausible relationships among both financial and nonfinancial data.
Assertions. Expressed or implied representations by management that are reflected in the financial statement components.
Confirmation. The process of obtaining and evaluating direct communication from a third party in response to a request for information about a particular item affecting financial statement assertions.

Reliance strategy. The auditor's decision to rely on the entity's controls, test those controls, and reduce the direct tests of the financial statement accounts.

Substantive tests of transactions. Tests to detect errors or fraud in individual transactions.

Tests of controls. Audit procedures performed to test the operating effectiveness of controls in preventing or detecting and correcting material misstatements at the relevant assertion level.

Tests of details of account balances and disclosures. Substantive tests that concentrate on the details of items contained in the account balance and disclosure.

www.mhhe.com/ messier7e	Visit the book's Online Learning Center for a multiple-choice quiz that will allow you to assess your understanding of chapter concepts.

REVIEW QUESTIONS

[LO 1,4,5,9]   15-1   Why does the auditor generally follow a substantive strategy when auditing long-term debt and capital accounts? Under what conditions might the auditor follow a reliance strategy?

[2,3]   15-2   What are the most important assertions for long-term debt? What documents would normally contain the authorization to issue long-term debt?

[4]   15-3   Describe how substantive analytical procedures may be used to provide evidence on the reasonableness of interest expense.

[4]   15-4   Confirmations of long-term debt provide evidence about which assertions?

[5]   15-5   What are the functions of the registrar, the transfer agent, and the dividend-disbursing agent?

[8]   15-6   What is the major segregation of duties that should be maintained when the client does not use a registrar or transfer agent and sufficient personnel are available to perform the stock transactions?

[9]   15-7   List two common disclosures for stockholders' equity and why such disclosures are necessary.

[10,11]   15-8   Describe common audit procedures to audit dividends and retained earnings.

[12]   15-9   List three substantive analytical procedures that the auditor might use in auditing the income statement.

[12]   15-10   Why might the auditor do an account analysis and vouch selected transactions in income statement accounts such as legal expense, travel and entertainment, and other income/expenses?

MULTIPLE-CHOICE QUESTIONS

[3]   15-11   Which of the following questions would an auditor most likely include on a control questionnaire for notes payable?
a. Are assets that collateralize notes payable critically needed for the entity's continued existence?
b. Are two or more authorized signatures required on checks that repay notes payable?

    c. Are the proceeds from notes payable used to purchase noncurrent assets?

    d. Are direct borrowings on notes payable authorized by the board of directors?

[4] 15-12 An auditor's primary purpose in examining a letter received from the bank shortly after the balance sheet date that renews and extends a client's note payable is most likely to obtain evidence concerning management's assertions about

    a. Existence.

    b. Presentation and disclosure-classification.

    c. Accuracy.

    d. Valuation and allocation.

[4] 15-13 An audit program for long-term debt would most likely include steps that require

    a. Comparing the carrying amount of the debt to its year-end market value.

    b. Correlating the interest expense recorded for the period with the debt outstanding for the period.

    c. Verifying the existence of the holders of the debt by direct confirmation.

    d. Inspecting the accounts payable subsidiary ledger for unrecorded long-term debt.

[4] 15-14 A client has established a bond sinking fund to repurchase a portion of the outstanding bonds each year. The auditor can best verify the client's bond sinking fund transactions and year-end bond balance by

    a. Confirmation of retired bonds with individual holders.

    b. Confirmation with the bond trustee.

    c. Recomputation of interest expense, interest payable, and amortization of bond discount or premium.

    d. Examination and count of the bonds retired during the year.

[7,8,9] 15-15 When a client company does not maintain its own stock records, the auditor should obtain written confirmation from the transfer agent and registrar concerning

    a. Restrictions on the payment of dividends.

    b. The number of shares issued and outstanding.

    c. Guarantees of preferred stock liquidation value.

    d. The number of shares subject to agreements to repurchase.

[6,7,8] 15-16 The primary responsibility of a bank acting as a registrar of capital stock is to

    a. Ascertain that dividends declared do not exceed the statutory amount allowable in the state of incorporation.

    b. Account for stock certificates by comparing the total shares outstanding to the total in the shareholders' subsidiary ledger.

    c. Act as an independent third party between the board of directors and outside investors concerning mergers, acquisitions, and the sale of treasury stock.

    d. Verify that stock has been issued in accordance with the authorization of the board of directors and the articles of incorporation.

[9] 15-17 To obtain evidence on the authorization assertion, an auditor should trace corporate stock issuances and treasury stock transactions to the

    a. Numbered stock certificates.

    b. Articles of incorporation.

    c. Transfer agent's records.

    d. Minutes of the board of directors.

[9] 15-18 Although the quantity and content of audit working papers vary with each particular engagement, an auditor's permanent files most likely include
  a. Schedules that support the current year's adjusting entries.
  b. Prior years' accounts receivable confirmations that were classified as exceptions.
  c. Documentation indicating that the audit work was adequately planned and supervised.
  d. Information regarding the different classes of stock and the number of shares of each class that are authorized to be issued.

[12] 15-19 An auditor compares the current-year revenues and expenses with those of the prior year and investigates all changes exceeding 5 percent. By this procedure the auditor would be most likely to learn that
  a. Fourth-quarter payroll taxes in the current year were not paid.
  b. The client changed its capitalization policy for small tools in the current year.
  c. A current-year increase in property tax rates has not been recognized in the client's accrual.
  d. The current-year provision for uncollectible accounts is inadequate because of worsening economic conditions.

[12] 15-20 Which of the following comparisons would be most useful to an auditor in evaluating the overall financial results of an entity's operations?
  a. Prior-year accounts payable to current-year accounts payable.
  b. Prior-year payroll expense to budgeted current-year payroll expense.
  c. Current-year revenue to budgeted current-year revenue.
  d. Current-year warranty expense to current-year contingent liabilities.

PROBLEMS

[4] 15-21 Maslovskaya, CPA, has been engaged to examine the financial statements of Broadwall Corporation for the year ended December 31, 2009. During the year, Broadwall obtained a long-term loan from a local bank pursuant to a financing agreement that provided that
  1. The loan was to be secured by the company's inventory and accounts receivable.
  2. The company was not to pay dividends without permission from the bank.
  3. Monthly installment payments were to commence July 1, 2009. In addition, during the year, the company borrowed various short-term amounts from the president of the company, including substantial amounts just prior to year-end.

Required:
  a. For purposes of the audit of the financial statements of Broadwall Corporation, what procedures should Maslovskaya employ in examining the described loans?
  b. The loans from the president represent a related-party transaction. What financial statement disclosures do you believe would be appropriate for the loans from the president?

(AICPA, adapted)

[4] 15-22 Your audit client, The Brant Group, reported total interest expense for the year of $2,000. The table below provides the monthly balance of their long-term debt. Interest is paid monthly on the average daily balance during the month. The annual interest rate for the debt is 6%.

Balance of long-term debt @ Jan 31	100,000
Balance of long-term debt @ Feb 28	90,000
Balance of long-term debt @ Mar 31	80,000
Balance of long-term debt @ Apr 30	70,000
Balance of long-term debt @ May 31	90,000
Balance of long-term debt @ June 30	85,000
Balance of long-term debt @ July 31	80,000
Balance of long-term debt @ Aug 31	70,000
Balance of long-term debt @ Sept 30	60,000
Balance of long-term debt @ Oct 31	65,000
Balance of long-term debt @ Nov 30	75,000
Balance of long-term debt @ Dec 31	50,000

Required:
Based on the data provided, do you consider the reported interest expense fairly stated? Why or why not?

[4] 15-23 The long-term debt working paper on the next page was prepared by client personnel and audited by Andy Fogelman, an audit assistant, during the calendar year 2009 audit of American Widgets, Inc., a continuing audit client. The engagement supervisor is reviewing the working paper thoroughly.

Required:
There are a number of deficiencies in the working paper. For example, the subject of the working paper is not properly indicated in the title and there is also no indication that the unusually high average interest rate (20% = $281,333/$1,406,667) was noted or investigated. Identify at least five additional deficiencies that the engagement supervisor should discover.

(AICPA, adapted)

[8,9] 15-24 Lee, CPA, the continuing auditor of Wu, Inc., is beginning to audit the common stock and treasury stock accounts. Lee has decided to design substantive procedures without relying on the company's internal control system.

Wu has no par and no stated-value common stock, and it acts as its own registrar and transfer agent. During the past year Wu both issued and reacquired shares of its own common stock, some of which the company still owned at year-end. Additional common stock transactions occurred among the shareholders during the year.

Common stock transactions can be traced to individual shareholders' accounts in a subsidiary ledger and to a stock certificate book. The company has not paid any cash or stock dividends. There are no other classes of stock, stock rights, warrants, or option plans.

Required:
What substantive audit procedures should Lee apply in examining the common stock and treasury stock accounts?

(AICPA, adapted)

AMERICAN WIDGETS, INC.
Working Paper
December 31, 2009

	Initials	Date
Prepared By	AF	1/22/10
Approved By		

Lender	Interest Rate	Payment Terms	Collateral	Balance 12/01/08	2009 Borrowings	2009 Reductions	Balance 12/31/09	Interest Paid to	Accrued Interest Payable 12/31/09	Comments
First Commercial Bank φ	12%	Interest only on 25th of month, principal due in full 1/1/13; no prepayment penalty	Inventories	$ 50,000✓	$300,000A 1/31/09	$ 100,000☼ 6/30/09	$ 250,000CX	12/25/09	$2,500NR	Dividend of $30,000 paid 9/2/09 (W/P N-3) violates a provision of the debt agreement, which thereby permits lender to demand immediate payment; lender has refused to waive this violation.
Lender's Capital Corporation φ	Prime plus 1%	Interest only on last day of month, principal due in full 3/5/11	2nd mortgage on Park Street Building	100,000✓	50,000A 2/28/09	—	200,000C	12/31/09	—	Prime rate was 8% to 9% during the year.
Gigantic Building & Loan Association φ	12%	$5,000 principal plus Interest due on 5th of month, due in full 12/31/18	1st mortgage on Park Street Building	720,000✓	—	60,000θ	660,000C	12/5/09	5,642R	Reclassification entry for current portion proposed (see RJE-3).
J. Lott, majority stockholder φ	0%	Due in full 12/31/12	Unsecured	300,000✓	—	100,000N 12/31/09	200,000C	—	—	Borrowed additional $100,000 from J. Lott on 1/7/10
				$1,170,000✓ **F**	$350,000 **F**	$ 260,000 **F**	$1,310,000T/B **F**		$8,142T/B **F**	

Interest costs from long-term debt

Interest expense for year	$ 281,333T/B
Average loan balance outstanding	$ 1,406,667R

Five-year maturities (for disclosure purposes)

Year-end	12/31/10	$ 60,000
	12/31/11	260,000
	12/31/12	260,000
	12/31/13	310,000
	12/31/14	60,000
	Thereafter	360,000
		$1,310,000
		F

Tick Mark Legend

C = Confirmed without exception, W/P K-2.
F = Readded, foots correctly.
CX = Confirmed with exception, W/P K-3.
NR = Does not recompute correctly.
A = Agreed to loan agreement, validated bank deposit ticket, and board of directors' authorization, W/P W-7.
θ = Agreed to canceled checks and lender's monthly statements.
N = Agreed to cash disbursements journal and canceled check dated 12/31/09, clearing 1/8/10.
T/B = Traced to working trial balance.
✓ = Agreed to 12/31/08 working papers.
φ = Agreed interest rate, term, and collateral to copy of note and loan agreement.
☼ = Agreed to canceled check and board of directors' authorization, W/P W-7.

Conclusions: Long-term debt, accrued interest payable, and interest expense are correct and complete at 12/31/09.

DISCUSSION CASE

[4]   15-25   On September 10, Melinda Johnson was auditing the financial statements of a new audit client, Mother Earth Foods, a health-food chain that has a June 30 year-end. The company is privately held and has just gone through a leveraged buyout with long-term financing that includes various restrictive covenants.

In order to obtain debt financing, companies often have to agree to certain conditions, some of which may restrict the way in which they conduct their business. If the borrower fails to comply with the stated conditions, it may be considered in default, which would give the lender the right to accelerate the due date of the debt, add other restrictions, waive the default for a stated period, or revise the covenants. Usually there is a grace period during which the borrower can cure the default.

Johnson believes that it is possible that at August 31 Mother Earth was in violation of the debt covenant restrictions, which became effective on that date. The debt covenants require the company to maintain a certain receivable turnover rate. Johnson is not certain, however, because the accounting records, including period-end cutoffs for sales and purchases, have not been well maintained. Nevertheless, Mother Earth's executives assure Johnson that if they were in violation, the company will be able to obtain a waiver or modification of the covenant.

Required:
a. Discuss the audit procedures that Johnson would conduct to determine if Mother Earth violated the debt covenants. How would Johnson determine whether Mother Earth would be able to obtain a waiver, assuming that the company was in violation of the debt covenants?
b. Based on the case scenario and financial accounting pronouncements about the classification of obligations that are callable by the creditor, should Mother Earth continue to classify this debt as noncurrent? Justify your answer.

INTERNET ASSIGNMENT

[1,4]   15-26   Dynegy, Inc. is a large energy company based in Houston, Texas. In the spring of 2003, Dynegy restated four years of earnings, increasing the loss from 1999 through the third quarter of 2002 by $431 million to a total of $1.42 billion. On September 24, 2002, the SEC filed a settled enforcement action against Dynegy in connection with incorrect accounting practices in relation to a $300-million financing activity known as "Project Alpha."

Required:
Use the internet to obtain information about how Dynegy accounted for Project Alpha and what the results of the SEC's actions have been for Dynegy and its officers. Sources of information on this issue can be found at Web sites for Dynegy, Inc., the SEC, and various news providers (such as *The Wall Street Journal*). Write a brief memo describing what auditors could have done to discover this error. Also describe the judgments brought by the SEC and courts against the company and its officers.

HANDS-ON CASES

ACL

www.mhhe.com/ messier7e	Visit the book's Online Learning Center for problem material to be completed using the ACL software packaged with your new text.

KAPLAN
CPA Review

www.mhhe.com/ messier7e	**Amberly Tool & Die, Inc.** This simulation provides a comprehensive review of several business processes covered to this point, methods of obtaining evidence and completion of the collection of evidence. *To begin this simulation, visit the book's Online Learning Center.*

CHAPTER 16

LEARNING OBJECTIVES

Upon completion of this chapter you will

[1] Understand the relationship of the various business processes to cash.

[2] Know the different types of bank accounts.

[3] Know tests of details of transactions used to audit cash.

[4] Be able to explain tests of details of account balances used to audit cash.

[5] Know how to audit a bank reconciliation.

[6] Understand fraud-related audit procedures for cash.

[7] Understand why clients invest in securities of other entities.

[8] Be able to explain key controls for investments.

[9] Know the appropriate segregation of duties for investments.

[10] Know tests of details of account balances used to audit investments.

[11] Understand how to audit fair value measurements.

RELEVANT ACCOUNTING AND AUDITING PRONOUNCEMENTS

FASB ASC Topic 230, Statement of Cash Flows

FASB ASC Topic 320, Investments—Debt and Equity Securities

FASB ASC Topic 718, Compensation—Stock Compensation

FASB ASC Topic 820, Fair Value Measurements and Disclosures

AU 312, Audit Risk and Materiality in Conducting an Audit

AU 314, Understanding the Entity and Its Environment and Assessing the Risks of Material Misstatement

AU 316, Consideration of Fraud in a Financial Statement Audit

AU 318, Performing Audit Procedures in Response to Assessed Risks and Evaluating the Audit Evidence Obtained

AU 326, Audit Evidence

AU 328, Auditing Fair Value Measurements and Disclosures

AU 329, Analytical Procedures

AU 330, The Confirmation Process

AU 332, Auditing Derivative Instruments, Hedging Activities, and Investments in Securities

AU 339, Audit Documentation

PCAOB Auditing Standard No. 3, Audit Documentation (AS3)

PCAOB Auditing Standard No. 5, An Audit of Internal Control Over Financial Reporting That Is Integrated with An Audit of Financial Statements (AS5)

PCAOB Proposed Auditing Standards Related to the Auditor's Assessment of and Response to Risk, PCAOB Release No. 2008-006 (October 21, 2008)

Auditing the Financing/Investing Process: Cash and Investments

This chapter covers the audit of cash and investments. These are the last accounts studied in this text because each of the other business processes interacts with cash. Thus, the evidence gathered during the audit of other business processes affects the type and amount of evidence required to audit cash.

Proper management of cash and investments is essential to every entity. The principal goal of cash management is to ensure that sufficient cash is available to meet the entity's needs. Achieving this goal requires good forecasting of cash receipts and disbursements. By using sound cash-forecasting techniques, management can plan to (1) invest excess cash; and (2) borrow at favorable interest rates when cash is required. Because cash and investments are so liquid, they normally represent critical audit areas. The *Advanced Module* discusses auditing fair value measurements. 🌐

Auditing Cash

[LO 1] The line item "cash" reported in the financial statements represents currency on hand and cash on deposit in bank accounts, including certificates of deposit, time deposits, and savings accounts. Frequently, certain "cash equivalents" are combined with cash for presentation in the financial statements. FASB ASC Topic 230, "Statement of Cash Flows", defines *cash equivalents* as short-term, highly liquid investments that are readily convertible to cash or so near their maturity that there is little risk of change in their value (¶8). Examples of such financial instruments include Treasury bills, commercial paper, and money market funds.

Because virtually all accounting transactions pass through the cash account as part of their "cradle-to-grave" cycle, cash is affected in one way or another by all of the entity's business processes. Figure 16–1 shows the effect each major business process has on the cash account. Although the main source of cash receipts is the revenue process, other sources of cash include (1) the sale of property, plant, and equipment; and (2) the proceeds from issuing long-term debt or capital stock. The main sources of disbursements from cash are the purchasing and human resource management processes. Generally, large payments initiated in the purchasing process are for acquisitions of inventory and property, plant, and equipment. Payments on long-term debt and repurchase of stock are other types of cash disbursements.

Because of the close relationship of cash to the revenue and purchasing processes, issues relating to the inherent risk and control of cash were discussed in Chapters 10 and 11, respectively. Specifically regarding control risk, Table 10–7 summarized the assertions, possible misstatements, control activities, and tests of controls for cash receipt transactions. A similar summary was provided for cash disbursement transactions in Table 11–7. Therefore, we will not repeat the discussion of inherent or control risk for cash receipt and disbursement transactions in this chapter. However, the auditor's assessment of inherent risk and control risk for transactions processed through the revenue and purchasing processes strongly affects the nature and extent of testing for the ending cash balance. Before continuing, stop and think of the inherent and control risk assessments

FIGURE 16–1	**The Effects of Major Accounting Transactions/Business Processes on Cash**

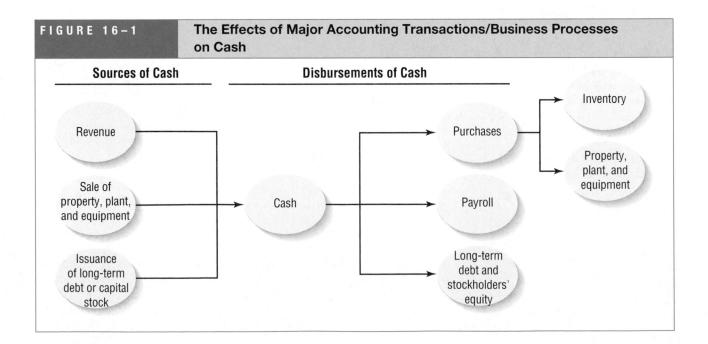

for cash receipts and disbursements. What characteristics of cash increase inherent risk and how would this impact the substantive procedures? What effect does the control risk assessment have on substantive testing for cash? If the control risk assessment is below the maximum for both cash receipts and disbursements, the auditor can reduce the extent of substantive evidence gathered for the cash balances. Be sure this concept makes sense to you before moving on.

Types of Bank Accounts

✂ [LO 2] Cash management is an important function in all organizations. In order to optimize its cash flow, an entity implements procedures for accelerating the collection of cash receipts and delaying the payment of cash disbursements, to the extent delay is appropriate. Such procedures allow the entity to earn interest on excess cash or to reduce the cost of cash borrowings.

Management must also be concerned with the control and safekeeping of cash. The use of different types of bank accounts aids in controlling the entity's cash. The following types of bank accounts are typically used:

- General cash account.
- Imprest cash accounts.
- Branch accounts.

It is important to understand each of the different types of bank accounts used. While the audit approach to each type of account is similar, the extent of testing varies from one account to the next. Each type of bank account is briefly discussed.

General Cash Account

The general cash account is the main cash account for most entities. The major source of cash receipts for this account is the revenue process, and the major sources of cash disbursements are the purchasing and human resource management processes. This cash account may also be used for receipts and disbursements from other bank accounts maintained by the entity. For many small entities, this is the only cash account maintained.

Imprest Cash Accounts

An imprest bank account contains a stipulated amount of money to be used for a specific purpose. For example, separate imprest accounts are frequently used for disbursing payroll and dividend checks. In the case of payroll, a separate bank account is established for disbursing payroll. Prior to the disbursement of payroll to employees through check or direct deposit, funds sufficient to cover payroll are transferred from the general cash account to the payroll imprest account. The payroll is then drawn on this imprest account, which reduces the imprest account balance back to a minimum required to keep the account open and active with the bank. Thus, the payroll account serves as a clearing account for payroll payments and facilitates the disbursement of cash while also helping to maintain adequate control over cash.

Use of imprest accounts also minimizes the time required to reconcile the general cash account.

Branch Accounts

Companies that operate branches in multiple locations may maintain separate accounts at local banks. This allows each branch to pay local expenses and to maintain a banking relationship in the local community. Branch cash accounts can be operated in a number of ways. In some cases, the branch accounts are nothing more than imprest accounts for branch payments in which a minimum

Management ordinarily uses a "sweep account" cash management strategy to transfer, on a nightly basis, any surplus cash in noninterest bearing commercial checking accounts to savings or money market accounts in order to earn higher returns on bank accounts.

balance is maintained. The branch submits periodic cash reports to headquarters, and the branch account receives a check or transfer from the general cash account. In other cases, the branch account functions as a general cash account by recording both cash receipts and cash disbursements.

For proper control, the branch should be required to submit periodic cash reports to headquarters, and the entity's management should carefully monitor the branch cash requests and account balances.

Control Risk Assessment—Cash

The reliability of the client's controls over cash receipts and cash disbursements affects the nature and extent of the auditor's tests of details. The preceding chapters discussed a number of important controls for both cash receipts and disbursements. For example, incoming checks are to be restrictively endorsed (stamped "For deposit only" to the company's bank account), and daily cash receipts from customers are to be reconciled with postings to the accounts receivable subsidiary ledger. The effective operation of these controls provides strong evidence that the completeness assertion is being met. Similarly, outgoing checks are to be signed only when all documents included in the voucher packet have been independently approved. The effective operation of this control activity provides the auditor with evidence on the authorization assertion.

A major control that directly affects the audit of cash is the completion of a monthly bank reconciliation by client personnel who are independent of the handling and recording of cash receipts and cash disbursements. Such bank reconciliations ensure that the client's books reflect the same balance as the bank's after reconciling items have been considered. Control can be improved further if an independent party such as the internal auditor reviews the bank reconciliation.

If the client has good bank reconciliation procedures that are promptly performed, the auditor may choose to test the client's reconciliation procedures as part of testing controls and thereby reduce the audit work on the ending cash balance.

Substantive Procedures—Cash

Substantive Analytical Procedures— Cash

[LO 3,4]

Because of its residual nature, cash does not have a predictable relationship with other financial statement accounts. As a result, the auditor's use of substantive analytical procedures for auditing cash is limited to comparisons with prior years' cash balances and to budgeted amounts. This limited applicability of substantive analytical procedures is normally offset by (1) extensive tests of controls and/or substantive tests of transactions for cash receipts and cash disbursements; or (2) extensive tests of the entity's bank reconciliations.

Substantive Tests of Details of Transactions and Balances— Cash

Table 16–1 contains examples of substantive tests of transactions for both cash receipts and cash disbursements. By testing both cash receipts and disbursements, the auditor obtains important evidence about the relevant assertions for the cash account. On most audits, the substantive tests of transactions for cash receipts and cash disbursements are conducted together with the tests of controls for the revenue and purchasing processes, respectively.

TABLE 16–1	Examples of Tests of Details of Transactions for Cash Receipts and Disbursements

	Example Substantive Tests of Transactions*	
Assertions about Classes of Transactions	*Cash Receipts*	*Cash Disbursements*
Occurrence	Vouch a sample of entries in the cash receipts journal to remittance advices, daily deposit slips, and bank statement	Vouch a sample of entries from the cash disbursements journal to canceled checks, voucher packet, and bank statement
Completeness	Trace a sample of remittance advices to cash receipts journal and, if necessary, to deposit slips	Trace a sample of canceled checks to the cash disbursements journal
Authorization	For a sample of days, examine the signature on the deposit slip and the check endorsements for proper authorization	Examine a sample of canceled checks for authorized signature and proper endorsement
Accuracy	For a sample of daily deposits, foot the remittance advices and entries on the deposit slip and agree to the cash receipts journal and bank statement	For a sample of voucher packets, agree amounts in purchase order, receiving report, invoice, canceled check, and disbursement journal
	For a sample of weeks, foot the cash receipts journal and agree posting to the general ledger	For a sample of weeks, foot the cash disbursements journal and agree posting to the general ledger
Cutoff	Compare the dates for recording a sample of cash receipts transactions in the cash receipts journal with the dates the cash was deposited in the bank (note any significant delays)	Compare the dates for a sample of checks with the dates the checks cleared the bank (note any significant delays)
	Observe cash on hand for the last day of the year, and trace deposits to cash receipts journal and cutoff bank statement	Record the last check issued on the last day of the year, and trace to cash disbursements journal
Classification	Examine a sample of remittance advices for proper account classification	Examine a sample of canceled checks for proper account classification

*These tests of details of transactions are commonly conducted as dual-purpose tests (i.e., in conjunction with tests of controls).

Balance-Related Assertions   Table 16–2 summarizes the assertions and tests of details of account balances for cash accounts. The rights and obligations assertion is not included in Table 16–2 because it is seldom important to the audit of the cash balance. The major audit procedures for each cash account involve tests of the bank reconciliation. The approach to auditing a bank reconciliation is basically the same regardless of the type of bank account being examined. However, the type and extent of the audit work are more detailed for the general cash account because it normally represents a material amount and because of the large amount of activity in the account.

TABLE 16–2	Examples of Tests of Details of Balances for Cash

Assertions about Account Balances at Period End	*Example Tests of Details Account Balances*
Existence Completeness Valuation and Allocation	Confirm bank account balance with financial institution Test bank reconciliation for each account: • Foot the reconciliation and the outstanding check listing. • Trace balances per book to the general ledger. • Obtain standard bank confirmation and trace balance per bank to the bank reconciliation. • Obtain cutoff bank statement. • Trace deposits in transit, outstanding checks, and other reconciling items to cutoff bank statement. If control risk is high or if fraud is suspected: • Perform extended bank reconciliation procedures. • Perform a proof of cash. • Test for kiting.

Auditing the General Cash Account

⚘ **[LO 5]**

Table 16–2 shows that the main source of evidence for the existence, completeness, and valuation assertions is the audit work completed on the bank reconciliation. To audit a cash account, the auditor should obtain the following documents:

- A copy of the bank reconciliation.
- A standard form to confirm account balance information with financial institutions (referred to as a *standard bank confirmation*).
- A cutoff bank statement.

Bank Reconciliation Working Paper   Exhibit 16–1 provides an example of a bank reconciliation working paper for EarthWear's general cash account. Note that the difference between the cash balance showed in Exhibit 16–1 and the balance in cash on the financial statements is represented by cash equivalents (Treasury bills and commercial paper). On most audits, the auditor obtains a copy of the bank reconciliation prepared by the client's personnel. The working paper reconciles the balance per the bank with the balance per the books. The major reconciling items are deposits in transit, outstanding checks, and other adjustments, such as bank service charges and any check returned because the customer did not have sufficient cash (i.e., an NSF check) in its account to cover payment of the check.

EXHIBIT 16–1	Example of a Bank Reconciliation Working Paper

		C10
		DLJ
		1/15/10

EARTHWEAR CLOTHIERS
Bank Reconciliation
12/31/09
General Cash Account

Balance per bank: **C11**		$ 1,854,890**C**
Add:		
Deposits in transit:		
12/30/09	$ 156,940✔	
12/31/09	340,875✔	497,815
Deduct:		
Outstanding checks:		
#1243	$ 121,843φ	
#1244	232,784φ	
#1247	30,431φ	
#1250	64,407φ	
#1251	123,250φ	(572,715)
Balance per books, unadjusted		1,779,990
Adjustments to books:		
Bank service charges	$ 250✔	
NSF check	7,400✔	(7,650)
Balance per books, adjusted		$ 1,772,340**L**
		F

F = Footed.
C = Traced balance to bank confirmation.
L = Agreed to cash lead schedule and general ledger.
✔ = Traced amount to cutoff bank statement.
φ = Examined canceled check for proper payee, amount, and endorsement.

Note: The controller has signed for the return of the cutoff bank statement.

Standard Bank Confirmation Form   The auditor generally confirms account balance information with every bank or financial institution that maintains an account for the client. The American Institute of Certified Public Accountants, American Bankers Association, and Bank Administration Institute have agreed on a standard format for confirming such information. Exhibit 16–2 contains a completed copy of the confirmation form, which is titled "Standard Form to Confirm Account Balance Information with Financial Institutions." This form is also used to obtain information about any loans the client may have with the bank.

Bank confirmations provide third party written evidence on bank account balances and other relevant information such as loans, lines of credit, security arrangements (e.g., account restrictions or guarantees), or complex relationships

EXHIBIT 16–2	Example of a Completed Standard Bank Confirmation Form

STANDARD FORM TO CONFIRM ACCOUNT BALANCE INFORMATION WITH FINANCIAL INSTITUTIONS

C11
DLJ
1/14/10

EarthWear Clothiers
CUSTOMER NAME

We have provided to our accountants the following information as of the close of business on _____ December 31, _____, 2009, regarding our deposit and loan balances. Please confirm the accuracy of the information, noting any exceptions to the information provided. If the balances have been left blank, please complete this form by furnishing the balance in the appropriate space below.° Although we do not request or expect you to conduct a comprehensive, detailed search of your records, if during the process of completing this confirmation additional information about other deposit and loan accounts we may have with you comes to your attention, please include such information below. Please use the enclosed envelope to return the form directly to our accountants.

Financial Institution's Name and Address   [First National Bank P.O. Box 1947 Boise, Idaho 79443]

1. At the close of business on the date listed above, our records indicated the following deposit balance(s):

ACCOUNT NAME	ACCOUNT NO.	INTEREST RATE	BALANCE°	
General Account	04-78925	None	$ 1,854,890.00	to C10
Payroll Account	01-04354	None	$ 5,000.00	to C20

2. We were directly liable to the financial institution for loans at the close of business on the date listed above as follows:

ACCOUNT NO./ DESCRIPTION	BALANCE°	DATE DUE	INTEREST RATE	DATE THROUGH WHICH INTEREST IS PAID	DESCRIPTION OF COLLATERAL

Sally Jones
(Customer's Authorized Signature)   12/31/09
                                             (Date)

The information presented above by the customer is in agreement with our records. Although we have not conducted a comprehensive, detailed search of our records, no other deposit or loan accounts have come to our attention except as noted below.

J J Hammer
(Financial Institution Authorized Signature)   1/5/10
                                                 (Date)

Branch Manager
(Title)

EXCEPTIONS AND/OR COMMENTS

Please return this form directly to our accountants:

Willis & Adams
P.O. Box 4080
Boise, Idaho 79443-4080

°Ordinarily, balances are intentionally left blank if they are not available at the time the form is prepared.

Approved 1990 by American Bankers Association, American Institute of Certified Public Accountants, and Bank Administration Institute. Additional forms available from AICPA — Order Department, P.O. Box 1003, NY, NY 10106-1003.

(e.g., derivative or commodity transactions). While alternative sources could be used to verify bank balances (e.g., bank statement or bank Web site), such procedures would not be effective at identifying the "other information." Note that, while it does request that bank personnel indicate any other deposits, loans, arrangements or transactions that come to their attention, the standard confirmation form does not require bank personnel to conduct a comprehensive, detailed search of the bank's records beyond the account information requested on the confirmation. As a result, this confirmation request cannot be relied upon to identify *all* information about a client's bank deposits or loans. If the auditor believes that additional information is needed about a client's arrangements with a financial institution, a separate confirmation letter signed by the client should be sent to the official at the financial institution responsible for the client's accounts. Details regarding lines of credit and compensating balances are examples of information that might be confirmed in this manner. This issue is discussed later in this chapter.

Bank confirmation requests should be sent and received under the auditor's control. The notorious and massive Parmalat fraud perpetuated through a fictitious $4.9 billion bank confirmation (and discussed in Exhibit 16–3) highlights the importance of auditors properly controlling the confirmation process and applying a healthy dose of professional skepticism when evaluating audit evidence, even for large and seemingly reputable clients.

Cutoff Bank Statement   A major step in auditing a bank reconciliation is verifying the propriety of the reconciling items such as deposits in transit and outstanding checks. The auditor obtains a *cutoff bank statement* to test the reconciling items included in the bank reconciliation. A cutoff bank statement normally covers the 7- to 10-day period after the date on which the bank account is reconciled. Any reconciling item should have cleared the client's bank account during the 7- to 10-day period. The auditor obtains this cutoff bank statement by having

EXHIBIT 16–3	**Parmalat's $4.9 Billion Fictitious Bank Confirmation**

In the early 1960s, after taking over his father's food distribution business, Calisto Tanzi founded a small milk pasteurization company near Parma, Italy. Later named Parmalat Finanziaria S.p.A., the company gained notoriety by acquiring a Swedish pasteurization technology called ultra-high temperature (UHT). This process created the long-life milk product for which the company is best known.

Over the next few decades, Parmalat expanded its operations through a number of acquisitions. By the end of the 1990s Parmalat was the fourth largest food company in Europe, employing over 36,000 people in 30 countries; however, to purchase these companies, Parmalat assumed a heavy debt burden.

Although Parmalat had a strong credit rating entering the 2000s, the business community began to question Parmalat's decision not to pay down acquisition debt with the large amount of cash it had on hand. Suspicions increased in December of 2003 when Parmalat was unable to make a £108 million bond payment. Parmalat officials claimed that the delay was caused by a temporary liquidity problem.

Shortly thereafter, Calisto Tanzi resigned as chairman and CEO. Following his resignation, allegations arose that Parmalat had forged a Bank of America confirmation for $4.9 billion and sent it to the company's auditors during the 2002 audit to corroborate the existence of cash. However, the cash did not exist. The forged confirmation was fuzzy and of poor quality because it is alleged that Parmalat officials ran the fake confirmation through the fax machine several times as part of its efforts to hide the fact that the document was a forgery.

Before the end of 2003, Parmalat filed for bankruptcy and investigations began uncovering what appeared to be a large and intricate accounting fraud, which in the end was hidden by the company's false cash deposits. Investors, creditors, and legal authorities immediately questioned the work performed by the auditors.

The Parmalat case is a high-profile and painful example of a failure in the audit of cash and how important it is to correctly verify cash balances. The Parmalat case demonstrates the importance of auditing standards regarding evidence and proper auditing procedures. You can find articles on the Parmalat fraud, as well as the SEC's Accounting and Auditing Enforcement Release No. 1936 charging Parmalat with fraud, on the Internet.

the client request that the bank send the statement, including canceled or substitute checks (see the *Check 21* Practice Insight below), directly to the auditor.

Tests of the Bank Reconciliation   The auditor typically uses the following audit procedures to test the bank reconciliation:

1. *Verify the mathematical accuracy of the bank reconciliation working paper and agree the balance per the books to the general ledger.* In Exhibit 16–1, the working paper has been footed and the balance per the books as shown on the reconciliation has been agreed to the general ledger.

2. *Agree the bank balance on the bank reconciliation with the balance shown on the standard bank confirmation.* The bank confirmation shown in Exhibit 16–2 has been prepared so that it corresponds to the bank reconciliation in Exhibit 16–1. The $1,854,890 shown on the bank reconciliation has been agreed to the $1,854,890 balance shown on the bank confirmation in Exhibit 16–2.

3. *Trace the deposits in transit on the bank reconciliation to the cutoff bank statement.* Any deposit in transit shown on the bank reconciliation should be listed as a deposit shortly after the end of the period. The tick mark next to the deposits in transit shown in Exhibit 16–1 indicates that the deposits were traced by the auditor to the cutoff bank statement.

4. *Compare the outstanding checks on the bank reconciliation working paper with the canceled (or substitute) checks contained in the cutoff bank statement for proper payee, amount, and endorsement.* The auditor should also ensure that no checks dated prior to December 31 are included with the cutoff bank statement that are not included as outstanding checks on the bank reconciliation. The tick mark next to the outstanding checks shown in Exhibit 16–1 indicates that the checks were traced by the auditor to the cutoff bank statement and that the canceled (or substitute) checks were examined for propriety.

5. *Agree any charges included on the bank statement to the bank reconciliation.* In some cases, these charges may result in an adjustment to the client's books. For example, the bank service charges of $250 and the NSF check for $7,400 received from a customer shown in Exhibit 16–1 require adjustment of the client's records.

6. *Agree the adjusted book balance to the cash account lead schedule.* The adjusted book balance would be part of the amount included in the financial statements for cash.

Fraud-Related Audit Procedures

✂ **[LO 6]**

If the client does not have adequate controls over cash or the auditor suspects that some type of fraud or defalcation involving cash has occurred, it may be necessary to extend the normal cash audit procedures. Although many types of fraud, such as forgery or collusion, are difficult to detect, auditing standards

(AU 316) indicate that the auditor has a responsibility to plan and perform the audit to obtain reasonable assurance about whether the financial statements are free of material misstatement, whether caused by error or fraud.

Three audit procedures that auditors typically use to detect fraudulent activities in the cash accounts are

- Extended bank reconciliation procedures.
- Proof of cash.
- Tests for kiting.

Extended Bank Reconciliation Procedures   In some instances, an unscrupulous client might use the year-end bank reconciliation to cover cash defalcations. This is usually accomplished by manipulating the reconciling items in the bank reconciliation. For example, suppose a client employee stole $5,000 from the client. The client's cash balance at the bank would then be $5,000 less than reported on the client's books. The employee could hide the $5,000 shortage in the bank reconciliation by including a fictitious deposit in transit. Thus, the typical approach to searching for possible fraud is to extend the bank reconciliation procedures to examine the disposition of the reconciling items included on the prior months' reconciliations and the reconciling items included in the current bank reconciliation.

For example, assume that the auditor suspected that some type of fraud had been committed. The auditor would examine the November and December bank reconciliations by ensuring that all reconciling items had been properly handled. For deposits in transit on the November bank reconciliation, the auditor would trace the deposits to the November cash receipts journal to verify that they were recorded. The deposits would also be traced to the December bank statement to verify that they were deposited in the bank. Checks listed as outstanding on the November bank reconciliation would be traced to the November cash disbursements journal, and the canceled or substitute checks returned with the December bank statement would be examined for propriety. Other reconciling items such as bank charges, NSF checks, and collections of notes by the bank similarly would be traced to the accounting records for proper treatment. The auditor would examine the reconciling items included on the December bank reconciliation in a similar fashion to ensure that such items were not being used to cover a cash defalcation. Further investigation would be required for any reconciling items not properly accounted for. The client's management should be informed if the auditor detects any fraudulent transactions.

While the audit of cash is typically uneventful, certainly it wasn't in the Parmalat audit (Exhibit 16–3) and it wasn't for a former auditor we know who arrived at the client's location a day early to audit cash. The surprised CFO, who had been stealing funds from the entity, stood up, turned around, and jumped out the window to his death.

Proof of Cash   A proof of cash is used to reconcile the cash receipts and disbursements recorded on the client's books with the cash deposited into and disbursed from the client's bank account for a specific time period. Exhibit 16–4 presents an example of a proof of cash for Calabro Wireless Services for one month, although on some audits a proof of cash is performed for the entire period under audit. Because the proof contains four columns, a proof of cash is commonly referred to as a *four-column proof* of cash. The four columns include

- A bank reconciliation for the beginning of the period.
- A reconciliation of the cash deposited in the bank with the cash receipts recorded in the cash receipts journal.

EXHIBIT 16–4	Example of a Proof of Cash

CW5

CALABRO WIRELESS SERVICES
Proof of Cash—General Cash
12/31/09

	11/30/09	December Receipts	December Disbursements	12/31/09
Balance per bank	$513,324	$457,822ϕ	$453,387ϕ	$517,759F
Deposits in transit:				
11/30/09	114,240	(114,240)		
12/31/09		116,437		116,437
Outstanding checks:				
12/30/09	(117,385)		(117,385)	
12/31/09			115,312	(115,312)
Bank charges			125	(125)ε
NSF checks		(5,250)		(5,250)ε
Balance per books	$510,179	$454,769γ	$451,439μ	$513,509FL
	F	F	F	F

F = Footed and crossfooted.
L = Agreed to general ledger.
ϕ = Traced to December bank statement.
γ = Agreed to December cash receipts journal.
μ = Agreed to December cash disbursements journal.
ε = Traced to the January 14, 2010 bank cutoff statement.

- A reconciliation of the cash disbursed through the bank account with the cash disbursements recorded in the cash disbursements journal.
- A bank reconciliation for the end of the period.

The primary purposes of the proof of cash are (1) to ensure that all cash receipts recorded in the client's cash receipts journal were deposited in the client's bank account; (2) to ensure that all cash disbursements recorded in the client's cash disbursements journal have cleared the client's bank account; and (3) to ensure that no bank transactions have been omitted from the client's accounting records. The reader should note that a proof of cash will *not* detect a theft of cash when the cash was stolen *before* it was recorded in the client's books. If the auditor suspects that cash was stolen without being recorded in the client's books, the audit procedures discussed under the completeness assertion for cash receipt transactions in Chapter 10 should be performed.

Practice INSIGHT	*Skimming* is the removal of cash from an organization prior to its entry in an accounting system. *Lapping* is one of the most common forms of concealing a skimming scheme. As discussed in Chapter 10, lapping occurs when the perpetrator covers the cash shortage by applying cash from one customer's account against another customer's account. The perpetrator then eliminates the shortage in the accounting records by recording credit memos or write-offs. Thus, to detect lapping, auditors would review the journal entries involving write-offs and credit memos as well as any irregular entries to the cash accounts.

| EXHIBIT 16-5 | | Example of an Interbank Transfer Schedule | | | | |

Transfer Number*	Amount	Disbursing Bank Account		Receiving Bank Account	
		Recorded in Client's Books	Paid by Bank	Recorded in Client's Books	Received by Bank
1	$15,000	12/28	12/30	12/28	12/29
2	7,500	12/30	1/2	12/30	12/31
3	8,400	12/31	1/2	12/31	1/2
4	10,000	1/2	1/2	12/30	12/31
5	3,000	1/3	1/3	1/3	12/30
6	17,300	1/2	1/4	1/2	1/2

*Explanation for each transfer in determining proper cash cutoff at 12/31:

1. The transfer was made on December 28 and recorded on the books as both a receipt and a disbursement on the same date. The check written was deposited on December 28 in the receiving bank account and credited on the bank statement the next day. The check cleared the disbursing bank account on December 30. All dates are in the same accounting period, so there are no questions as to the propriety of the cutoff.
2. This transfer is proper. However, the transfer check should appear as an *outstanding check* on the reconciliation of the disbursing bank account.
3. Transfer 3 is also proper. In this example, the transfer should appear as a *deposit in transit* on the reconciliation of the receiving bank account and as an outstanding check on the reconciliation of the disbursing bank account.
4. This transfer represents kiting because the receipt was recorded on the books in the period prior to that in which the corresponding disbursement was recorded. Cash is overstated by $10,000.
5. Transfer 5 is also improper. In this case a deposit was made in the receiving bank in one period without the receipt being made in the books until the subsequent period. Unless this matter is explained on the reconciliation for the receiving bank, the transfer was apparently made to temporarily cover a shortage in that account. While the shortage will become apparent in the accounts as soon as the transfer is recorded in the following period, it will be covered by an unrecorded deposit on the balance sheet date.
6. This transfer is proper.

Tests for Kiting   When cash has been stolen by an employee, sometimes the employee will attempt to cover the cash shortage by following a practice known as *kiting*. This involves an employee covering the cash shortage by transferring money from one bank account to another and recording the transactions improperly on the client's books. The employee does this by preparing a check on one account before year-end but not recording it as a cash disbursement in the account until the next period (paper checks are still commonly used, particularly by small businesses). The check is deposited and recorded as a cash receipt in a second account before year-end. The employee makes this deposit close enough to year-end so that the check will not clear the first bank account before the end of the year. While electronic wire transfers are recorded more rapidly than paper transactions, there is often still a one-day delay, which makes kiting possible even without the use of paper checks.

One approach that auditors commonly use to test for kiting is the preparation of an *interbank transfer schedule* such as the one shown in Exhibit 16–5. This exhibit provides six examples of the types of cash transfers an auditor might encounter. For example, transfer 2 is an example of a proper cash transfer. A check was drawn on the disbursing bank account and recorded as a cash disbursement on December 30. It was recorded as a cash receipt in the receiving bank account on December 30 and deposited in that account on December 31. The check cleared the disbursing account on January 2. The auditor would examine this transfer by tracing the check to the December cash disbursements and cash receipts journals and to the December 31 bank reconciliation. Because the check cleared the bank on January 2, it should be listed as an outstanding check on the December 31 bank reconciliation for the disbursing bank account. The reader will also notice that transfers 1, 3, and 6 are proper transfers.

Transfer 4 represents an example of kiting. A check was written on the disbursing bank account before year-end, but the disbursement was not recorded in the disbursements journal until after year-end (January 2). The check was deposited in the receiving bank account and recorded as a cash receipt before year-end. Thus, the cash shortage in the receiving bank account is covered by a cash

<table>
<tr><td>Practice
INSIGHT</td><td>According to the Association of Certified Fraud Examiners (2004), fraudulent cash disbursements can be divided into five distinct subcategories:</td></tr>
</table>

- *Billing Schemes*, in which an individual causes the organization to issue a payment by submitting invoices for fictitious goods or services, inflated invoices, or invoices for personal purchases;
- *Payroll Schemes*, in which an employee causes the organization to issue a payment by making false claims for compensation;
- *Expense Reimbursement Schemes*, in which an employee makes a claim for reimbursement of fictitious or inflated business expenses;
- *Check Tampering*, in which the perpetrator converts an organization's funds by forging or altering a check on one of the organization's bank accounts, or steals a check the organization has legitimately issued to another payee; and
- *Register Disbursement Schemes*, in which an employee makes false entries on a cash register to conceal the fraudulent removal of currency.

deposit from the disbursing bank account, and the net effect is that cash is overstated by $10,000. As noted in Exhibit 16–5, transfer 5 is also improper in that a deposit was made in the receiving bank in one period without the receipt being made in the books until the subsequent period. The matter should be included and explained on the reconciliation for the receiving bank.

In some instances an interbank transfer schedule is used even though control activities are adequate and no fraud is suspected. When a client maintains many cash accounts, cash transfers may be inadvertently mishandled. The use of an interbank transfer schedule provides the auditor with evidence on the proper cutoff for cash transactions.

Auditing a Payroll or Branch Imprest Account

The audit of any imprest cash account such as payroll or a branch account follows the same basic audit steps discussed under the audit of the general cash account. The auditor obtains a bank reconciliation, along with a standard bank confirmation and a cutoff bank statement. However, the audit testing is less extensive for two reasons. First, the imprest balance in the account is generally not material. For example, an imprest payroll or branch account may contain a minimum balance, of say $100, required by the bank to keep the account open and active except for the short time after a payroll deposit and before the related payroll disbursements have cleared. Second, the types of disbursements from the account are homogeneous. The checks are for similar types of transactions and for relatively small amounts. For example, there are often limits on the size of an individual payroll check.

Auditing a Petty Cash Fund

Most entities maintain a petty cash fund for paying certain types of expenses or transactions. Although the balance in the fund is not material (hence the word "petty"), there is a potential for defalcation because a client's employee may be able to process numerous fraudulent transactions through the fund over the course of a year. Auditors seldom perform substantive procedures on the petty cash fund, except when fraud is suspected. However, the auditor may document and perform limited testing of the controls over the petty cash fund, especially for smaller clients.

Control Activities—Petty Cash
A petty cash fund should be maintained on an imprest basis by an *independent* custodian. While it is preferable for the custodian not to be involved in any cash functions, this is not possible for many clients. When the petty cash custodian does have other cash-related functions to perform, another supervisory person such as the controller should review the petty cash activity.

Prenumbered petty cash vouchers should be used for withdrawing cash from the fund, and a limit should be placed on the size of reimbursements made from petty cash. Periodically, the petty cash fund is reimbursed from the general cash account for the amount of the vouchers in the fund. Accounts payable clerks should review the vouchers for propriety before replenishing the petty cash fund. Finally, someone independent of the cash function should conduct surprise counts of the petty cash fund.

Audit Tests–Petty Cash The first step is for the auditor to gain an understanding of the client's controls over petty cash. The adequacy of the client's controls determines the nature and extent of the auditor's work. The audit of petty cash focuses on both the transactions processed through the fund during the period and the balance in the fund. The auditor may select a sample of petty cash reimbursements and examine the propriety of the items paid for by the fund. This may be done as part of the auditor's tests of controls or tests of details of transactions for the cash disbursement functions. The auditor tests the balance in the petty cash fund by counting it. When the count is conducted, the total of cash in the fund plus the vouchers should equal the imprest balance. This count may be done at an interim date or at year-end.

EXHIBIT 16–6	Illustrative Letter for Confirmation of Compensating Balances

CWS

CALABRO WIRELESS SERVICES

December 31, 2009

Mr. John L. Gren
First National Bank
Tampa, FL 34201

Dear Mr. Gren:

In connection with an audit of the financial statements of Calabro Wireless Services as of December 31, 2009, and for the year then ended, we have advised our independent auditors that as of the close of business on December 31, 2009, there were compensating balance arrangements as described in our agreement dated June 30, 2005. Withdrawal by Calabro Wireless Services of the compensating balance was not legally restricted as of December 31, 2009. The terms of the compensating balance arrangements at December 31, 2009, were:

The company has been expected to maintain a compensating balance, as determined from your bank's ledger records without adjustment for estimated average uncollected funds, of 15% of its outstanding loans plus 10% of its unused line of credit.

The company was in compliance with, and there have been no changes in, the compensating balance arrangements during the year ended December 31, 2009, and subsequently through the date of this letter.

During the year ended December 31, 2009, and subsequently through the date of this letter, no compensating balances were maintained by the company at your bank on behalf of an affiliate, director, officer, or any other third party, and no third party maintained compensating balances at the bank on behalf of the company.

Please confirm whether the information about compensating balances presented above is correct by signing below and returning this letter directly to our independent auditors, Abbott & Johnson, LLP. P.O. Box 669, Tampa, FL 32691.

Sincerely,

Calabro Wireless Services

BY: _Jan Rodriguez_
    Jan Rodriguez, Controller

Dear Abbott & Johnson, LLP:

The above information regarding the compensating balance arrangement with this bank agrees with the records of this bank.

BY: _John L. Gren_   Date: _1/11/10_
    John L. Gren, Vice President

TABLE 16–3	Examples of Disclosure Items for Cash

Accounting policy for defining cash and cash equivalents
Any restrictions on cash such as a sinking fund requirement for funds allocated by the entity's board of directors
    for special purposes
Contractual obligations to maintain compensating balances
Cash balances restricted by foreign exchange controls
Letters of Credit

EXHIBIT 16–7	Sample Disclosure of Compensating Balances

Lines of Credit:

On December 31, 2005, the company established a line of credit with a bank that provides for unsecured borrowings of $7,000,000 at the bank's prime rate (7% at December 31, 2009). At December 31, 2008 and 2009, $200,000 and $800,000, respectively, had been borrowed under this arrangement. Under the credit arrangement, the company is expected to maintain compensating balances equal to 5 percent of the borrowings in excess of $500,000. This requirement is generally met through normal operating cash balances, which are not restricted as to withdrawal.

Disclosure Issues for Cash

The auditor must consider a number of important financial statement disclosures when auditing cash. Some of the more common disclosure issues are shown in Table 16–3. The auditor's review of the minutes of board of directors' meetings, line-of-credit arrangements, loan agreements, and similar documents is the primary source of the information for the financial statement disclosures. In addition, the auditor typically confirms items such as compensating balances required under a bank line of credit.

Exhibit 16–6 illustrates a letter for confirmation of compensating balances, while Exhibit 16–7 presents an example of footnote disclosures for compensating balances.

Auditing Investments

[LO 7] Entities frequently invest in securities of other entities. Such investments might include equity securities such as common and preferred stock, debt securities such as notes and bonds, and hybrid securities such as convertible bonds and stocks. The accounting for such instruments is affected by factors such as the percentage of the other entity owned, the degree of influence exercised over the entity, the classification of the investment as a current or noncurrent asset, fair-value considerations, and myriad other factors. For example, FASB ASC Topic 320, "Investments—Debt and Equity Securities", provides detailed guidance on how to account for investments in certain debt and equity securities. The *Advanced Module* at the end of this chapter discusses auditing fair value measurements.

On a general level, the auditor's consideration of investments is no different than for any other financial statement account. That is, the auditor must be assured that the amounts shown on the balance sheet for the various types of investments are not materially misstated. This includes the proper recognition of interest income, dividends, and changes in value that must be included in the financial statements.

The inherent risks associated with investments vary with the amount of activity, the complexity, and valuation considerations. For example, an investment in stock of a publicly traded company is relatively easy to account for and audit. However, more complex financial instruments, such as derivatives and asset-backed securities, have become increasingly common holdings in investment portfolios. These complex financial instruments often require substantial judgment by management in determining fair value measurements. Due to the judgment and complexity associated with these financial instruments, the auditor is likely to assess the inherent risk as high. For more information regarding the auditing of fair value measurements, see the *Advanced Module* at the end of this chapter.

For an entity that has a large investment portfolio, the auditor is likely to follow a reliance strategy in which internal control is formally evaluated and tests of controls are performed in order to set control risk below the maximum. However, for the vast majority of entities that do not require an audit of internal controls over financial reporting, it is more efficient for the auditor to follow a substantive strategy and perform a detailed audit of the investment securities at year-end.

Control Risk Assessment—Investments

✂ [LO 8] The discussion of investments that follows focuses on the general types of control activities that should be present to minimize the likelihood of a material misstatement. Even when a substantive strategy is followed, the auditor must reasonably understand control over investments in order to anticipate the types of misstatements that may occur and plan the substantive procedures. The main assertions that concern the auditor are occurrence, authorization, completeness, accuracy, and classification. Proper segregation of duties is important in ensuring the propriety of investments and will be discussed briefly.

Assertions and Related Control Activities

Following are some of the more common controls that should be present for each of the important assertions for investments.

Occurrence and Authorization

Controls must ensure that the purchase or sale of any investment is properly initiated by authorized individuals. First, the client should have adequate documents to verify that a particular purchase or sale of a security was properly initiated and approved. The presence of adequate documentation allows the auditor to determine the validity of the transaction. Second, the commitment of resources to investment activities should be approved by the board of directors or by an executive who has been delegated this authority. An entity engaging in recurring investment activities should have an entity-wide general investment policy as well as specific procedures and control activities around individual investment transactions. The board of directors should establish general policies to guide the entity's investment activities, while the specific procedures for the purchase and sale of securities may be delegated to an individual executive, investment committee, or outside investment advisers. If the client has proper controls for initiating and authorizing securities transactions, it is generally easy for the auditor to verify security transactions at the end of the period.

Completeness

The client should maintain adequate controls to ensure that all securities transactions are recorded, and the auditor should evaluate the design and operating effectiveness of the client's controls. One control for handling the detailed securities transactions is maintenance of a securities ledger that records all securities owned by the client. The client should reconcile the subsidiary ledger to the general ledger control account regularly. Personnel responsible for investment activities should periodically review the securities owned to ensure that all dividends and interest have been received and recorded in the entity's records.

Accuracy and Classification   Some important accuracy and classification issues are related to investment securities. As mentioned previously, ASC Topic 320, addresses accounting and reporting for investments in equity securities that have readily determinable fair values and for all investments in debt securities. The standard requires that those investments be classified in three categories and accounted for as follows:

- Debt securities that the entity has the positive intent and ability to hold to maturity are classified as *held-to-maturity securities* and reported at amortized cost.
- Debt and equity securities that are bought and held principally for the purpose of selling them in the near term are classified as *trading securities* and reported at fair value, with unrealized gains and losses included in earnings.
- Debt or equity securities not classified as either held-to-maturity or trading securities are classified as *available-for-sale securities* and are reported at fair value, with unrealized gains and losses excluded from earnings and reported in a separate component of shareholders' equity.

Practice INSIGHT	A company can manipulate financial statements by intentionally misclassifying securities or transferring securities to a different class of investment. For example, a company might transfer a security from held-to-maturity to either trading or available-for-sale, which would trigger the recognition of a gain or postpone the recognition of a loss.

The client's controls should ensure that securities are properly classified and that appropriate prices are used to accurately value investments for financial statement purposes.

One final issue related to the control risk for investments is that the client should have adequate custodial procedures to safeguard against theft. When securities are held by the client, they should be stored in a safe or safe-deposit box. Procedures should provide for periodic inspections by an individual independent of both the custodial and accounting responsibilities for securities. If an independent custodian such as a broker maintains securities, the client needs to establish procedures for authorizing the transfer of securities. For example, one approach would require dual authorization by appropriate management personnel.

Segregation
of Duties

✄ **[LO 9]**

Table 16–4 contains some key segregation of duties for investments and examples of possible errors or fraud that can result from conflicts in duties. However, only entities that engage in a significant number of investment activities are likely to have adequate segregation of duties for all investment activities. When some of the duties noted in Table 16-4 are not segregated, the client should have other compensating controls such as a regular review by a person in a higher level of management of the performance of the duty not segregated.

TABLE 16–4	**Key Segregation of Duties for Investments and Possible Errors or Fraud**
Segregation of Duties	*Possible Errors or Fraud Resulting from Conflicts of Duties*
The initiation function should be segregated from the final approval function.	If one individual is responsible for both the initiating and approving of securities transactions, fictitious transactions can be made or securities can be stolen.
The valuation-monitoring function should be segregated from the acquisition function.	If one individual is responsible for both acquiring and monitoring the valuation of securities, securities values can be improperly recorded or not reported to management.
Responsibility for maintaining the securities ledger should be separate from that of making entries in the general ledger.	If one individual is responsible for both the securities ledger and the general ledger entries, that individual can conceal any defalcation that would normally be detected by reconciliation of subsidiary records with general ledger control accounts.
Responsibility for custody of the securities should be separate from that of accounting for the securities.	If one individual has access both to securities and to the supporting accounting records, a theft of the securities can be concealed.

Substantive Procedures—Investments

[LO 10] As discussed earlier, it is generally more efficient to follow a substantive strategy for auditing investments. When the control risk is set at the maximum, the auditor conducts extensive substantive procedures to reach the planned level of detection risk. Additionally, because of the nature of the audit work, tests of details of transactions are seldom used as a source of evidence.

Substantive Analytical Procedures—Investments

Substantive analytical procedures such as the following can be used to evaluate the overall reasonableness of investments and related income statement accounts:

- Comparison of the balances in the current year's investment accounts with prior years' balances after consideration of the effects of current-year operating and financing activities on cash and investments.
- Comparison of current-year interest and dividend income with the reported income for prior years and with the expected return on investments.
- Recompute current-year interest income using the face amount of securities held, interest rate, and time period held.

Tests of Details—Investments

Auditing standards (AU 332) provide guidance concerning substantive auditing procedures the auditor can perform when gathering evidence related to assertions for investments. Table 16–5 summarizes the audit procedures performed on the investment account for balance and presentation and disclosure assertions. The discussion of the investment account audit procedures focuses on the more important assertions. The procedures shown for the other assertions should be familiar to the reader.

TABLE 16–5	Examples of Tests of Transactions and Account Balances and Disclosures—Investments
Assertions about Account Balances at Period End	**Example Test of Details of Account Balances**
Existence Rights and obligations Completeness	Inspect securities if maintained by client or obtain confirmation from independent custodian. Examine brokers' advices for a sample of securities purchased during the year. Search for purchases of securities by examining transactions for a few days after year-end. Confirm securities held by independent custodian. Review and test securities information to determine if all interest and dividend income has been recorded.
Valuation and allocation	Review brokers' invoices for cost basis of securities purchased. Determine basis for valuing investments by tracing values to published quotations for marketable securities. Determine whether there has been any permanent impairment in the value of the cost basis of an individual security. Examine sales of securities to ensure proper recognition of realized gains or losses. Obtain a listing of investments by category (held-to-maturity, trading, and available-for-sale); foot listing and agree totals to securities register and general ledger.
Assertions about Presentation and Disclosure	**Example Tests of Details of Disclosures**
Occurrence, and rights and obligations	Determine whether any securities have been pledged as collateral by (1) asking management; and (2) reviewing board of directors' minutes, loan agreements, and other documents.
Completeness	Determine that all disclosures required by ASC Topic 320 have been made for investments (both debt and equity securities). Complete financial reporting checklist to ensure all financial statement disclosures related to investments are made.
Classification and understandability	Review and inquire of management of proper classification of investments. Read footnotes to ensure that required disclosures are understandable.
Accuracy and valuation	Read footnotes and other information to ensure that the information is accurate and properly presented at the appropriate amounts.

Existence   Auditing standards state that the auditor should perform one or more of the following audit procedures when gathering evidence for existence:

- Physical examination.
- Confirmation with the issuer.
- Confirmation with the custodian.
- Confirmation of unsettled transactions with the broker-dealer.
- Confirmation with the counterparty.
- Reading executed partnership or similar agreements.

If the client maintains custody of the securities, the auditor normally examines the securities. During the physical count, the auditor should note the name, class and description, serial number, maturity date, registration in the name of the client, interest rates or dividend payment dates, and other relevant information about the various securities. The auditor should insist that a representative of the client be present during the physical inspection of securities in order to acknowledge that all securities inspected are returned. If the securities are held in a safe-deposit box and the auditor is unable to inspect and count the securities on the balance sheet date, the auditor should consider having the bank seal the safe deposit box until the auditor can count the securities at a later date. When the securities are held by an issuer or a custodian such as a broker or investment adviser, the auditor gathers sufficient, appropriate evidence for the existence assertion by confirming the existence of the securities. The information contained in the confirmation needs to be reconciled with the client's investment records.

Valuation and Allocation   When securities are initially purchased, they are recorded at their acquisition cost. The auditor can verify the purchase price of a security by examining a broker's invoice or similar document. Debt securities that are to be held to maturity should be valued at their amortized cost. The auditor should have verified the purchase price of the debt at the time of purchase, and the effective interest rate should be used to recognize the interest income, which the auditor can recompute. The fair value of most equity securities is available from securities exchanges registered with the Securities and Exchange Commission or on the over-the-counter market. The auditor can verify these values by tracing them to sources such as brokers, *The Wall Street Journal,* or other reliable financial publications.

The auditor must also determine if there has been any permanent decline in the value of an investment security. Auditing and accounting standards provide guidance for determining whether a decline in value below amortized cost is other than temporary. The following factors are indicators that the impairment of the investment may be other than temporary.

- Fair value is significantly below cost.
- The decline in fair value is attributable to specific adverse conditions affecting a particular investment.
- The decline in fair value is attributable to specific conditions, such as conditions in an industry or in a geographic area.
- Management does not possess both the intent and the ability to hold the investment long enough to allow for any anticipated recovery in fair value.
- The decline in fair value has existed for an extended period.
- A debt security has been downgraded by a rating agency.

- The financial condition of the issuer has deteriorated.
- Dividends have been reduced or eliminated, or scheduled interest payments on debt securities have not been made.

If the investment value is determined to be permanently impaired, the security should be written down and a new carrying amount established. Last, the auditor should examine the sale of any security to ensure that proper values were used to record the sale and any realized gain or loss.

Some investments do not have fair values that can be readily obtained from market data and thus require substantial judgment on the part of management. Auditing of fair value measurement is covered in the *Advanced Module* at the end of this chapter.

Disclosure Assertions   Two issues are important when the auditor examines the proper classification of investments. First, marketable securities need to be properly classified as held-to-maturity, trading, and available-for-sale because both the balance sheet and income statement are affected by misclassification. Second, the financial statement classification requires that all trading securities be reported as current assets. Held-to-maturity securities and individual available-for-sale securities should be classified as current or noncurrent assets based on whether management expects to convert them to cash within the next 12 months. If the security is expected to be converted to cash within 12 months, it should be classified as a current asset. The auditor should ask management about its plans to sell securities.

Auditing standards also guide auditors in evaluating both management's intent with regard to an investment and the entity's ability to hold a debt security to maturity. In evaluating management's intent, the auditor should consider whether investment activities corroborate or conflict with management's stated intent. The auditor should examine evidence such as written and approved records of investment strategies, records of investment activities, instructions to portfolio managers, and minutes of meetings of the board of directors or the investment committee. In evaluating an entity's ability to hold a debt security to maturity, the auditor should consider factors such as the entity's financial position, working capital needs, operating results, debt agreements, guarantees, and other relevant contractual obligations, as well as laws and regulations. The auditor should also consider operating and cash flow projections or forecasts when considering the entity's ability to hold the debt security to maturity.

ASC Topic 320 requires specific disclosures for securities. For example, the aggregate fair value and gross unrealized holding gains or losses on securities should be presented for securities classified as available-for-sale.

Most of the information necessary for such disclosures is developed as the other assertions are being tested. In addition, the amount of any securities pledged as collateral should be disclosed. To collect such information, the auditor might inquire of management, review the board of directors' minutes, and examine loan agreements and other relevant documents.

Advanced Module: Auditing Fair Value Measurements

❧ [LO 11]   FASB ASC Topic 820 establishes a framework for measuring fair value in accordance with GAAP. It defines *fair value* as the price that would be received to sell an asset or paid to transfer a liability in an orderly transaction between market participants at the measurement date. Because orderly transactions between market participants may or may not be observable at the measurement date, FASB ASC Topic 820 provides a hierarchy with three levels that distinguish the types of inputs used to value different types of assets and liabilities at their appropriate fair values:

- *Level 1:* Valuations are based on quoted prices in active markets for identical assets or liabilities. Sometimes called "marking to market," valuations in this category typically apply to assets such as publicly traded stocks, options, bonds, and mutual funds.

- *Level 2:* Valuations are based on directly or indirectly observable market data for similar or comparable assets or liabilities. Sometimes called "marking to matrix," Level 2 inputs include quoted prices for similar assets or liabilities in active markets or inputs other than quoted prices that are observable for the asset or liability (interest rates, standard deviation, default rates, etc.). Examples of assets in this category include infrequently traded bonds and some mortgage and asset-based securities.

- *Level 3:* Valuations are based on management's best judgment and involve management's assumptions about unobservable inputs and how the market would price the asset or liability. Unobservable inputs should be used to measure fair value in situations where there is little or no market activity for the asset or liability being valued. Sometimes called, "marking to model," valuation in this category may include assets such as long-term options, real estate, and private-equity investments.

An individual fair value measurement, such as an employee stock option, may contain inputs from one or all of the three levels, but the measurement in its entirety is categorized based on the lowest level of its significant inputs. For example, the Black Scholes option-pricing model requires the exercise price, stock price, length of time until option expires, stock price volatility, dividend yield, and risk-free rate as inputs. Some of these inputs, such as stock price, may be quoted in active markets and would be Level 1 inputs. However, other inputs, such as stock price volatility, are not likely Level 1 inputs as the volatility requires an estimate based on historical data over a period of time, which may or may not be expected to be representative of the future. Therefore, stock price volatility would likely be categorized as either a Level 2 or Level 3 input, depending on the availability of similar or comparable volatility data and estimates. Thus, the employee stock options as a whole would be categorized as either a Level 2 or Level 3 fair value measurement, consistent with the lowest level of input in categorizing the asset. Before continuing, stop and think about how these different levels might affect planned audit procedures. How would an audit plan for a client whose financial instruments are mostly Level 1 be different from that for a client whose financial instruments are mostly Level 2 or Level 3?

As preparers and auditors consider the implications of using the different fair value levels to value assets and liabilities, moving from Level 1's objective market-driven inputs to Level 2 or 3 inputs means objective measures are replaced with increasingly subjective inputs, some based on management's assumptions. Complicated financial instruments, such as credit default swaps, asset-backed securities, and collateralized debt obligations, among others, often are not traded on active markets, making accurate valuation of such instruments difficult. The valuation of assets and liabilities, and the related income statement effect of reductions in fair value, can have material implications for amounts reported in the financial statements. As a result, gathering sufficient, appropriate evidence to support the client's fair value measurements and related disclosures is an increasingly important—and risky—area of many audits.

As an example of how fair value measurements can materially impact an audit, let's return to our example of the Black Scholes option-pricing model. Assume the following information concerning the audit of a successful client in the computer and technology sector:

- Net income: $700 million.

- Planning materiality at 5 percent of net income before taxes: $35 million.

- Tolerable misstatement applied to stock compensation expense: $26.25 million.
- The company issued 7 million options throughout the year.

This client uses the Black Scholes option-pricing model to value its expense for employee stock options required under ASC Topic 718. For this model, the following values have been determined for the model's inputs:

- Stock price at valuation date: $130
- Exercise price: $140
- Dividend yield: 0.00 percent
- Time until expiration: 10 years
- Risk-free rate: 3.8 percent
- Volatility of stock price: between 36 and 40 percent

If management decides to calculate stock compensation expense based on the lower stock-price volatility, the model provides an expense equal to $471.1 million. However, if management were to use the higher range of volatility, the model provides an expense equal to $502.9 million. The difference between the two estimates is $31.8 million, which is greater than the tolerable misstatement applied to the account and almost as large as planning materiality for the entire engagement. This example demonstrates the significant impact that small changes in assumptions in fair value-measurement models can have on the financial statements.

In this module, we briefly cover four important areas in the auditing of fair value measurements from the more complete guidance provided in AU 328, *Auditing Fair Value Measurements and Disclosures*[1]:

- Obtaining an understanding of how management makes fair value measurements
- Considering whether specialized skills or knowledge are required
- Testing the entity's fair value measurements
- Evaluating the reasonableness of the fair value measurements

Understanding How Management Makes Fair Value Measurements

In order to plan the nature, timing, and extent of audit procedures associated with auditing fair value measurements, the auditor gains an understanding of the entity's process for determining fair value measurements and disclosures and of the relevant controls by considering factors such as:

- The types of accounts or transactions requiring fair value measurements
- The nature of the assumptions, including which of the assumptions are likely to be significant assumptions
- How management considered the nature of the asset or liability being valued, including how and why they selected a particular valuation method or model
- Whether the entity operates in a particular industry where specific models are commonly used for fair value measurement
- The extent to which the entity's process relies on a service organization to provide fair value measurements
- The nature and extent of documentation, if any, supporting management's assumptions
- The controls related to the review and approval of accounting estimates, (including the assumptions or inputs used in their development) by appropriate levels of management and, where appropriate, those charged with governance

---

[1]As of the writing of this text, the ASB was working on a revised SAS that would merge AU328 and AU342.

- The controls over how management determines the completeness, relevance, and accuracy of the data used to develop accounting estimates.

As the risk and complexity of the fair value measurements increase, so also does the extent of the audit procedures.

Considering Whether Specialized Skills or Knowledge Is Required

Auditors must have a good understanding of the accounting and auditing frameworks associated with fair value measurements, but it is not realistic to expect all auditors to be experts in the area of valuation. A valuation specialist is often engaged to help obtain audit evidence when the valuation model used by management is complex, the markets for the asset or liability are not currently active, or a high degree of estimation uncertainty exists. We discussed the use of specialists in Chapter 5, and auditing standards address the use of specialists in AU 336, *Using the Work of a Specialist*.

Testing the Entity's Fair Value Measurements

Based on the understanding of management's processes and the risk assessment, auditors plan the nature, timing, and extent of the testing. Substantive tests of fair value measurements for Level 1 assets or liabilities, such as publicly traded stocks and bonds, is relatively straightforward, as market pricing can be easily verified by the auditor by, for example, corroborating closing stock prices with prices published in *The Wall Street Journal*. Substantive audit procedures for Level 2 or Level 3 valuations, such as complicated derivatives, may include:

- Testing whether the assumptions appropriately reflect observable market assumptions
- Testing management's assumptions for bias
- Performing sensitivity analyses to determine the effects of changes in the assumptions on a fair value estimate
- Testing whether management's rationale for the method selected is reasonable
- Testing that the underlying data used in the valuation model is accurate, complete, and relevant
- Developing an independent point estimate or range for corroborative purposes
- Reviewing subsequent events and transactions

In testing the models used by management, it is important for auditors to understand the inherent weaknesses of valuation models. As opposed to active markets, valuation models do not take qualitative factors into account when creating a fair value. What do you think are some qualitative factors that would impact the valuation of an asset-backed security? Qualitative factors include an assessment of how active the market is and whether current exit prices should be used to value a security a client intends to hold. Models are tools used to capture and evaluate complex and uncertain inputs to derive estimated fair values, but they have limitations. Uncertainty arises for a variety of reasons including the length of forecast and the subjectivity and complexity associated with the factors in the model. Given the inherent uncertainty in the inputs, valuation models rarely provide the "correct" or exact value and should be viewed as providing a range of reasonable values, all of which should be considered in light of other industry and market information.

Further, auditors must test management's assumptions for bias, which can be difficult to detect at the account level. Such bias may be identified only by considering management's accounting estimates in aggregate or the accuracy of past estimates over a number of accounting periods. Although some form of management bias is inherent in subjective decisions, in making such judgments there may be no intention by management to mislead the users of financial statements. However, where the intent to mislead is present, management bias can be considered fraudulent in nature.[2]

Evidence obtained from audit procedures performed for other purposes also may provide evidence relevant to the measurement and disclosure of fair values. For example, inspection procedures to verify existence of an asset measured at fair value also may provide relevant evidence about its valuation, such as the physical condition of the asset.

Evaluating the Reasonableness of the Fair-Value Measurements

After obtaining sufficient appropriate evidence through substantive tests, the auditor then evaluates whether management's measurements and disclosures are in accordance with GAAP.

As capital markets continue to increase the complexity of financial instruments, it will be increasingly important for auditors to be proficient in understanding how fair value estimates are created and the impact they have on the overall audit plan.

Practice INSIGHT	During the inspections of two of the Big 4 firms, the PCAOB inspection team identified deficiencies having to do with auditing fair value. For example, one auditor failed to evaluate the reasonableness of some of the assumptions used to support the estimated fair values of certain illiquid securities. Another auditor failed to obtain an understanding of the methodologies used to develop the fair value measurement for securities that were not actively traded. (PCAOB Releases 104-2009-051 and 104-2009-038)

[2]See the proposed audit standard that will merge AU328 and AU342 at www.aicpa.org.

KEY TERMS

Analytical procedures. Evaluations of financial information made by a study of plausible relationships among both financial and nonfinancial data.

Assertions. Expressed or implied representations by management that are reflected in the financial statement components, and organized into three categories relating to transactions, balances, and disclosures.

Cash equivalents. Short-term, highly liquid investments that are readily convertible to cash or so near their maturity that there is little risk of change in their value (e.g., money market funds, Treasury bills).

Confirmation. The process of obtaining and evaluating direct communication from a third party in response to a request for information about a particular item affecting financial statement assertions.

Fair value. The price that would be received to sell an asset or paid to transfer a liability in an orderly transaction between market participants at the measurement date.

Imprest account. A bank account containing a stipulated amount of money used for limited purposes (e.g., imprest accounts are frequently used for disbursing payroll and dividend checks).

Proof of cash. A technique used to reconcile the cash receipts and disbursements recorded on the client's books with the cash deposited into and disbursed from the client's bank account for a specific time period.

Reliance strategy. The auditor's decision to rely on the entity's controls, test those controls, and reduce the direct tests of the financial statement accounts.

Substantive tests of transactions. Tests to detect errors or fraud in individual transactions.

Tests of controls. Audit procedures performed to test the operating effectiveness of controls in preventing or detecting and correcting material misstatements at the relevant assertion level.

Tests of details of account balance and disclosures. Substantive tests that concentrate on the details of items contained in the account balance and disclosure.

www.mhhe.com/ messier7e	Visit the book's Online Learning Center for a multiple-choice quiz that will allow you to assess your understanding of chapter concepts.

REVIEW QUESTIONS

[LO 1]   16-1   How do the client's controls over cash receipts and disbursements affect the nature and extent of the auditor's substantive tests of cash balances?

[2]   16-2   Briefly describe each type of bank account. How does an imprest account help to improve control over cash?

[3]   16-3   Why are analytical procedures of limited use in the audit of the cash balance?

[4,5]   16-4   Explain why the standard bank confirmation form does *not* identify all information about a client's bank accounts or loans.

[4,5]   16-5   Why does an auditor obtain a cutoff bank statement when auditing a bank account? What information is examined on the canceled or substitute checks returned with the cutoff bank statement?

[6]   16-6   List three fraud-related audit procedures for cash.

[6]   16-7   What approach is used by the auditor to test for kiting?

[8,9]   16-8   What are the main transaction-related assertions for investments? Identify the key segregation of investment-related duties and possible errors or fraud that can occur if this segregation is not present.

[10]   16-9   Briefly describe the classification and valuation issues related to investments in debt and equity securities.

[10]   16-10   What two presentation classification issues are important for the audit of investments?

[11]   16-11   How does the fair-value evidence the auditor is likely to gather differ between Level 1 and Level 3 assets?

MULTIPLE-CHOICE QUESTIONS

Questions 16-12 and 16-13 relate to the following bank transfer schedule.

MILES COMPANY
Bank Transfer Schedule
December 31

Check Number	Bank Account From	Bank Account To	Amount	Date Disbursed per Books	Date Disbursed per Bank	Date Deposited per Books	Date Deposited per Bank
2020	First National	Suburban	$32,000	12/31	1/5♦	12/31	1/3▲
2021	First National	Capital	21,000	12/31	1/4♦	12/31	1/3▲
3217	Second State	Suburban	6,700	1/3	1/5	1/3	1/6
0659	Midtown	Suburban	5,500	12/30	1/5♦	12/30	1/3▲

[4,6]   16-12   The tick mark ♦ most likely indicates that the amount was traced to the
a. December cash disbursements journal.
b. Outstanding check list of the applicable bank reconciliation.
c. January cash disbursements journal.
d. Year-end bank confirmations.

[4,6]   16-13   The tick mark ▲ most likely indicates that the amount was traced to the
a. Deposit in transit of the applicable bank reconciliation.
b. December cash receipts journal.
c. January cash receipts journal.
d. Year-end bank confirmations.

[5] 16-14 An auditor ordinarily sends a standard confirmation request to all banks with which the client has done business during the year under audit, regardless of the year-end balance. One purpose of this procedure is to
a. Provide the data necessary to prepare a proof of cash.
b. Request that a cutoff bank statement and related checks be sent to the auditor.
c. Detect kiting activities that may otherwise *not* be discovered.
d. Seek information about loans from the banks.

[5] 16-15 The primary evidence regarding year-end bank balances is documented in the
a. Standard bank confirmations.
b. Outstanding check listing.
c. Interbank transfer schedule.
d. Bank deposit lead schedule.

[5] 16-16 On receiving the cutoff bank statement, the auditor should vouch
a. Deposits in transit on the year-end bank reconciliation to deposits in the cash receipts journal.
b. Checks dated before year-end listed as outstanding on the year-end bank reconciliation to the cutoff statement.
c. Deposits listed on the cutoff statement to deposits in the cash receipts journal.
d. Checks dated after year-end to outstanding checks listed on the year-end bank reconciliation and to the cutoff statement.

[6] 16-17 Which of the following cash transfers results in a misstatement of cash at December 31?

Bank Transfer Schedule

	Disbursing Bank Account		Receiving Bank Account	
Transfer	Recorded in Client's Books	Paid by Bank	Recorded in Client's Books	Received by Bank
a.	12/31	1/4	12/31	12/31
b.	1/4	1/5	12/31	1/4
c.	12/31	1/5	12/31	1/4
d.	1/4	1/11	1/4	1/4

[8,9] 16-18 Which of the following controls would most effectively ensure that the proper custody of assets in the investing process is maintained?
a. Direct access to securities in the safe-deposit box is limited to one corporate officer.
b. Personnel who post investment transactions to the general ledger are *not* permitted to update the investment subsidiary ledger.
c. Purchase and sale of investments are executed on the specific authorization of the board of directors.
d. The recorded balances in the investment subsidiary ledger are periodically compared with the contents of the safe-deposit box by independent personnel.

[10] 16-19 An auditor testing long-term investments would ordinarily use substantive analytical procedures to ascertain the reasonableness of the
a. Existence of unrealized gains or losses in the portfolio.
b. Completeness of recorded investment income.
c. Classification between current and noncurrent portfolios.
d. Valuation of marketable equity securities.

[10] 16-20 To establish the existence and rights of a long-term investment in the common stock of a publicly traded company, an auditor ordinarily performs a security count or

a. Relies on the client's internal controls if the auditor has reasonable assurance that the control activities are being applied as prescribed.

b. Confirms the number of shares owned that are held by an independent custodian.

c. Determines the market price per share at the balance sheet date from published quotations.

d. Confirms the number of shares owned with the issuing company.

[10] 16-21 Which of the following is likely to be the most effective audit procedure for verifying dividends earned on investments in publicly traded equity securities?

a. Trace deposits of dividend checks to the cash receipts book.

b. Reconcile recorded earnings with the dividend earnings reported in the investment broker statement.

c. Compare the amounts received with prior-year dividends received.

d. Recompute selected extensions and footings of dividend schedules and compare totals to the general ledger.

[10] 16-22 An auditor would most likely verify the interest earned on bond investments by

a. Vouching the receipt and deposit of interest checks.

b. Confirming the bond interest rate with the issuer of the bonds.

c. Recomputing the interest earned on the basis of face amount, interest rate, and period held.

d. Testing the controls over cash receipts.

[11] 16-23 The audit firm's valuation specialist would likely be brought in to assist in the audit of fair value measurements at an entity when the following is present:

a. The entity is a new audit client.

b. Significant uncertainty exists in key inputs to the entity's valuation models.

c. The entity has a financial instrument with a Level 2 input.

d. The entity owns a large and diverse portfolio of publicly traded stock.

PROBLEMS

[7,8,9] 16-24 Cassandra Corporation, a manufacturing company, periodically invests large sums in investment (debt and equity) securities. The investment policy is established by the investment committee of the board of directors, and the treasurer is responsible for carrying out the investment committee's directives. All securities are stored in a bank safe-deposit vault.

The independent auditor's internal control questionnaire with respect to Cassandra's investments in debt and equity securities contains the following three questions:

- Is investment policy established by the investment committee of the board of directors?
- Is the treasurer solely responsible for carrying out the investment committee's directives?
- Are all securities stored in a bank safe-deposit vault?

Required:

In addition to these three questions, what questions should the auditor's internal control questionnaire include with respect to the company's investments in debt and equity securities?

(AICPA, adapted)

[4,6]   16-25   Sevcik Company's auditor received, directly from the banks, confirmations and cutoff statements with related checks and deposit tickets for Sevcik's three general-purpose bank accounts. The auditor determined that the controls over cash are satisfactory and can be relied upon. The proper cutoff of external cash receipts and disbursements was established. No bank accounts were opened or closed during the year.

Required:
Prepare the audit program of substantive procedures to verify Sevcik's bank balances. Ignore any other cash accounts.

[5]   16-26   The following client-prepared bank reconciliation is being examined by Zachary Kallick, CPA, during the examination of the financial statements of Simmons Company.

SIMMONS COMPANY
Bank Reconciliation
1st National Bank of U.S. Bank Account
September 30, 2009

				Procedure(s)
a. Select 2 procedures	Balance per bank		$28,375	
b. Select 5 procedures	Deposits in transit:			
	9/29/09	$4,500		
	9/30/09	1,525	6,025	
			$34,400	
c. Select 5 procedures	Outstanding checks:			
	988 8/31/09	2,200		
	1281 9/26/09	675		
	1285 9/28/09	850		
	1289 9/29/09	2,500		
	1292 9/30/09	7,225	(13,450)	
			$20,950	
d. Select 1 procedure	Error:			
	Check 1282, written on 9/25/09 for $270, was erroneously charged by bank as $720; bank was notified on 10/2/09.		450	
e. Select 1 procedure	Balance per books		$21,400	

Required:
Items (a) through (e) represent items an auditor would ordinarily find on a client-prepared bank reconciliation. The following list of audit procedures shows substantive auditing procedures. For each item, select one or more procedures, as indicated, that the auditor most likely would perform to gather evidence in support of that item. (The procedures on the list may be selected once, more than once, or not at all.)
Assume that
- The client prepared the bank reconciliation on 10/2/2009.
- The bank reconciliation is mathematically accurate.
- The auditor received a cutoff bank statement dated 10/7/2009 directly from the bank on 10/12/2009.
- The 9/30/2009 deposit in transit, outstanding checks 1281, 1285, 1289, and 1292, and the correction of the error regarding check 1282 appear on the cutoff bank statement.

- The auditor set control risk concerning the financial statement assertions related to cash at the maximum.

Audit Procedure:
1. Trace to cash receipts journal.
2. Trace to cash disbursements journal.
3. Compare to 9/30/2009 general ledger.
4. Directly confirm with bank.
5. Ascertain reason for unusual delay.
6. Inspect supporting documents for reconciling item not appearing on cutoff statement.
7. Vouch items on bank reconciliation to cutoff statement.
8. Vouch items on the cutoff statement to bank reconciliation.

(AICPA, adapted)

[7,8,10] 16-27 The schedule on the following page was prepared by the controller of World Manufacturing, Inc., for use by the independent auditors during their examination of World's year-end financial statements. All procedures performed by the audit assistant were noted in the "Legend" section; the schedule was properly initialed, dated, and indexed and then submitted to a senior member of the audit staff for review. Internal control was reviewed and is considered to be satisfactory.

Required:
a. What information that is essential to the audit of debt and equity securities is missing from this schedule?
b. What essential audit procedures were not noted as having been performed by the audit assistant?

(AICPA, adapted)

[10] 16-28 Phung, CPA, has been engaged to audit the financial statements of Vernon Distributors, Inc., a continuing audit client, for the year ended September 30. After obtaining an understanding of Vernon's internal control system, Phung set control risk at the maximum level for all financial statement assertions concerning investments. Phung determined that Vernon is unable to exercise significant influence over any investee and none are related parties. Phung obtained from Vernon detailed analyses of its investments in domestic securities showing

- The classification among held-to-maturity, trading, and available-for-sale securities.
- A description of each security, including the interest rate and maturity date of bonds and the par value and dividend rate of stocks.
- A notation of the location of each security, either in the treasurer's safe or held by an independent custodian.
- The number of shares of stock or face value of bonds held at the beginning and end of the year.
- The beginning and ending balances at cost and at market, and the unamortized premium or discount on bonds.
- Additions to and sales from the portfolios for the year, including date, number of shares, face value of bonds, cost, proceeds, and realized gain or loss.
- Valuation allowances at the beginning and end of the year and changes therein.
- Accrued investment income for each investment at the beginning and end of the year, and income earned and collected during the year.

WORLD MANUFACTURING, INC.
Marketable Securities
Year Ended December 31, 2009

Description of Security	%	Yr. Due	Serial No.	Face Value of Bonds	General Ledger 1/1	Purchased in 2009	Sold in 2009	Cost	General Ledger 12/31	12/31 Market	Dividends & Interest Pay Date(s)	Amt. Rec.	Accruals 12/31
Corp Bonds													
A	6	14	21-7	10,000	9,400a				9,400	9,100	1/15	300b,d	275
D	4	10	73-0	30,000	27,500a				27,500	26,220	7/15	300b,d	100
G	9	15	16-4	5,000	4,000a				4,000	5,080	12/1	1,200b,d	188
R	5	12	08-2	70,000	66,000a		57,000b,c	66,000			8/1	450b,d	
S	10	17	07-4	100,000		100,000c,e			100,000	101,250	7/1	5,000b,d	5,000
					106,900a	100,000	57,000	66,000	140,900	141,650		7,250	5,563
					a,f	**f**	**f**	**f**	**f,g**	**f**		**f**	**f**
Stocks													
P 1,000 shs. Common			1,044		7,500a				7,500	7,600	3/1	750b,d	
											6/1	750b,d	
											9/1	750b,d	
											12/1	750b,d	250
U 50 shs. Common			8,530		9,700a				9,700	9,800	2/1	800b,d	
											8/1	800b,d	667
					17,200				17,200	17,400		4,600	917
					a,f				**f,g**	**f**		**f**	**f**

Legends and comments relative to above schedule:

a = Beginning balances agreed to 2008 working papers.
b = Traced to cash receipts.
c = Board of directors' minutes examined—purchases and sales approved.
d = Agreed to 1099.
e = Confirmed by tracing to broker's advice.
f = Totals footed.
g = Agreed to general ledger.

Phung then prepared the following partial audit program of substantive audit procedures:

1. Foot and crossfoot the analyses.
2. Trace the September 30 balances to the general ledger and financial statements.
3. Trace the beginning balances to the prior year's working papers.
4. Obtain positive confirmation of the investments held by any independent custodian as of the balance sheet date.
5. Determine that income from investments has been properly recorded as accrued or collected by reference to published sources, by computation, and by tracing to recorded amounts.
6. For investments in nonpublic entities, compare carrying value to information in the most recently available audited financial statements.
7. Determine that all transfers among held-to-maturity, trading, and available-for-sale securities have been properly authorized and recorded.
8. Determine that any other-than-temporary decline in the price of an investment has been properly recorded.

Required:

a. For procedures 4 to 8, identify the primary financial statement assertion relative to investments that would be addressed by each procedure.
b. Describe three additional substantive auditing procedures Phung should consider in auditing Vernon's investments.

(AICPA, adapted)

[10] 16-29 To support financial statement assertions, an auditor develops specific audit procedures to satisfy or accomplish each assertion.

Required:

Items (a) through (c) represent assertions for investments. Select the most appropriate procedure from the following list and enter the number in the appropriate place on the grid. (An audit procedure may be selected once or not at all.)

Audit Procedure:

1. Vouch opening balances in the subsidiary ledgers to the prior year's audit working papers.
2. Determine that employees who are authorized to sell investments do not have access to cash.
3. Examine supporting documents for a sample of investment transactions to verify that prenumbered documents are used.
4. Determine that any impairments in the price of investments have been properly recorded.
5. Verify that transfers from the current to the noncurrent investment portfolio have been properly recorded.
6. Obtain positive confirmations as of the balance sheet date of investments held by independent custodians.
7. Trace investment transactions to minutes of board of directors' meetings to determine that transactions were properly authorized.

Specific Assertion	*Audit Procedure*
a. Verify that investments are properly described and classified in the financial statements (presentation and disclosure-classification).	
b. Verify that recorded investments represent investments actually owned at the balance sheet date (rights and obligations).	
c. Verify that investments are properly valued at the lower of cost or market at the balance sheet date (valuation and allocation).	

(AICPA, adapted)

[11]   16-30   Spencer, CPA, has been engaged to audit the fair value measurements of Christensen & Son, a high-tech company in the Midwest. During the audit, Spencer must obtain evidence that management of Christensen & Son has appropriately valued the following two accounts:

1. Available for Sale Stock Portfolio, containing investments in Fortune 100 company stocks.
2. Stock compensation expense related to stock options granted to Christensen's employees as valued by the Black Scholes option-pricing model. Christensen's stock is largely held by the owners and neither the company's stock nor the related stock options are actively traded.

Required:

For each account, complete the following:

a. Identify the fair value inputs to the value of each account.
b. Identify the valuation levels for each of the identified inputs as well as the account as a whole (i.e., Level 1, Level 2, or Level 3).
c. Create a summary audit plan, by account, for how Spencer can obtain assurance regarding the fair value of each of the inputs.

INTERNET ASSIGNMENT

[7,10]   16-31   Both Intel (www.intel.com) and Microsoft (www.microsoft.com) have large amounts of investment securities. Visit their home pages, and review their financial statements for information on how they account for investment securities and the amounts of those securities.

 **HANDS-ON CASES**

EarthWear Online	**Audit of Cash** Audit and evaluate evidence such as bank confirmations and bank reconciliations in the audit of Earth-Wear's cash balances. *Visit the book's Online Learning Center at www.mhhe.com/messier7e to find a detailed description of the case and to download required materials.*

ACL

www.mhhe.com/ messier7e	Visit the book's Online Learning Center for problem material to be completed using the ACL software packaged with your new text.

KAPLAN
CPA Review

www.mhhe.com/ messier7e	**Peters & Michael** This simulation provides a comprehensive assessment of your understanding of the audit procedures used in the audit of cash. *To begin this simulation, visit the book's Online Learning Center.*

Part **6**

COMPLETING THE AUDIT AND REPORTING RESPONSIBILITIES

CHAPTER 17

LEARNING OBJECTIVES

Upon completion of this chapter you will

[1] Be able to explain the audit issues related to contingent liabilities.

[2] Know the audit procedures used to identify contingent liabilities.

[3] Understand the audit issues related to a legal letter.

[4] Be able to explain why the auditor must be concerned with commitments.

[5] Know the types of subsequent events.

[6] Understand the effect of subsequent events on the dating of the audit report.

[7] Know the audit procedures used to identify subsequent events.

[8] Know the audit steps included in the auditor's final evidential evaluation process.

[9] Be able to explain how auditors identify and assess going concern problems.

[10] Understand the auditor's communication with management and those charged with governance and the matters that should be addressed.

[11] Know the auditor's responsibility for subsequent discovery of facts existing at the date of the auditor's report.

RELEVANT ACCOUNTING AND AUDITING PRONOUNCEMENTS

FASB ASC Topic 275, Risks and Uncertainties
FASB ASC Topic 450, Contingencies
FASB ASC Topic 855, Subsequent Events
AU 316, Consideration of Fraud in a Financial Statement Audit
AU 318, Performing Audit Procedures in Response to Assessed Risks and Evaluating the Audit Evidence Obtained
AU 329, Analytical Procedures
AU 330, The Confirmation Process
AU 333, Management Representations
AU 337, Inquiry of a Client's Lawyer Concerning Litigation, Claims, and Assessments
AU 341, The Auditor's Consideration of an Entity's Ability to Continue as a Going Concern

AU 342, Auditing Accounting Estimates
AU 380, The Auditor's Communication with Those Charged with Governance
AU 530, Dating of the Independent Auditor's Report
AU 560, Subsequent Events
AU 561, Subsequent Discovery of Facts Existing at the Date of the Auditor's Report
COSO, *Internal Control—Integrated Framework* (New York: AICPA, 1992)
PCAOB Auditing Standard No. 3, Audit Documentation (AS3)
PCAOB Auditing Standard No. 5, An Audit of Internal Control Over Financial Reporting That Is Integrated with An Audit of Financial Statements (AS5)

Completing the Audit Engagement

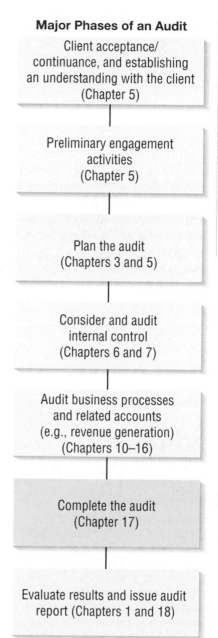

Major Phases of an Audit

Client acceptance/
continuance, and establishing
an understanding with the client
(Chapter 5)

Preliminary engagement
activities
(Chapter 5)

Plan the audit
(Chapters 3 and 5)

Consider and audit
internal control
(Chapters 6 and 7)

Audit business processes
and related accounts
(e.g., revenue generation)
(Chapters 10–16)

Complete the audit
(Chapter 17)

Evaluate results and issue audit
report (Chapters 1 and 18)

Once the various business processes, controls, and related financial statement accounts have been audited, the evidence is summarized and evaluated. Before determining the appropriate audit report, the auditor considers a number of additional issues that may impact the client's system of internal control over financial reporting and financial statements. This chapter discusses the following topics associated with completing the audit:

- Review for contingent liabilities.
- Commitments.
- Review for subsequent events.
- Final evidential evaluation processes.
- Communications with the audit committee and management.
- Subsequent discovery of facts existing at the date of the auditor's report.

Review for Contingent Liabilities

⚼ [LO 1]   A *contingent liability* is defined as an existing condition or set of circumstances involving uncertainty about a possible loss that will ultimately be resolved when some future event occurs or fails to occur. FASB ASC Topic 450, "Contingencies", states that when a contingent liability exists, the likelihood that the future event will result in a loss is to be assessed using three categories:

1. *Probable.* The future event is likely to occur.
2. *Reasonably possible.* The chance of the future event occurring is more than remote but less than likely.
3. *Remote.* The chance of the future event occurring is slight.

As you have learned in your financial accounting courses, if the event is probable and the amount of the loss can be reasonably estimated, the loss is accrued by a charge to income. When the outcome of the event is judged to be reasonably possible or the amount cannot be estimated, a disclosure of the contingency is made in the footnotes to the financial statements. Exhibit 17–1 presents an example of such disclosure taken from a recent annual report. In general, loss contingencies that are judged to be remote are neither accrued in the financial statements nor disclosed in the footnotes.[1] After you read Exhibit 17–1, pause and consider how much judgment is involved on the part of management and the auditor in making and assessing the reasonableness of this type of disclosure. This is just one example of how both accounting and auditing involve a great deal of subjectivity and professional judgment.

Examples of contingent liabilities include:

- Pending or threatened litigation.
- Actual or possible claims and assessments.
- Income tax disputes.
- Product warranties or defects.
- Guarantees of obligations to others.
- Agreements to repurchase receivables that have been sold.

EXHIBIT 17–1	**Example of Footnote Disclosure for a Contingency**

On October 31, 2007, a class action complaint was filed by a stockholder against the company and certain of its officers and directors in the United States District Court ("the court"). Shortly thereafter, other stockholders filed similar class action complaints. On February 1, 2008, a consolidated amended class action complaint against the company and certain of its officers and directors was filed in the court. In their consolidated complaint, the plaintiffs seek to represent a class consisting generally of persons who purchased or otherwise acquired the company's common stock in the period from March 5, 2007, through August 14, 2007. These actions claim damages related to alleged material misstatements and omissions of fact and manipulative and deceptive acts in violation of federal securities laws and common-law fraud. In December 2009 a motion filed by the plaintiffs to certify a class of purchasers of the company's common stock was approved with limited exceptions, and a class period for certain claims was established from March 5, 2007, to August 14, 2007. Also in December 2009, in response to a motion by the company and individual defendants, claims of common-law fraud, deceit, and negligence, misrepresentation, and certain of the violations of the federal securities laws against certain of the individual defendants were dismissed. At this time, it is not possible to predict the outcome of the pending lawsuit or the potential financial impact on the company of an adverse decision.

---

[1]As of the writing of this text, the FASB is deliberating a proposed amendment of FASB ASC Topic 450, "Contingencies." The amendment would increase GAAP reporting requirements for contingent liabilities, including requiring disclosure of contingencies regardless of the likelihood of loss under some circumstances.

Audit Procedures
for Identifying
Contingent
Liabilities

> **[LO 2]**

Examples of procedures that may help the auditor identify contingent liabilities
include:

1. Reading the minutes of meetings of the board of directors, committees of
    the board, and stockholders.
2. Reviewing contracts, loan agreements, leases, and correspondence from
    government agencies.
3. Reviewing tax returns, IRS reports, and schedules supporting the client's
    income tax liability.
4. Confirming or otherwise documenting guarantees and letters of credit
    obtained from financial institutions or other lending agencies.
5. Inspecting other documents for possible guarantees or other similar
    arrangements.

For example, the auditor usually reads the minutes of the board of directors'
meetings for identification of major events and approval of significant transactions.
Normally, the board of directors would discuss any material uncertainty that might
exist for the entity. Similarly, the auditor examines the entity's income tax expense
and accrued liability. The audit procedures for this account include determining
if the IRS has audited the entity's prior year's tax returns. If so, the auditor should
examine the IRS agents' report for any additional taxes assessed and determine
whether the entity will contest the additional assessment.

In addition, near the completion of the engagement the auditor conducts *specific*
audit procedures to identify contingent liabilities. Such procedures include

1. *Inquiry of and discussion with management about its policies and procedures
    for identifying, evaluating, and accounting for contingent liabilities.*
    Management has the responsibility for establishing policies and procedures
    to identify, evaluate, and account for contingencies. Large entities may
    implement such policies and procedures as part of their risk assessment
    process. Smaller private entities, however, sometimes rely on legal counsel
    or other parties to help them identify and account for contingencies.
2. *Examining documents in the entity's records such as correspondence and
    invoices from attorneys for pending or threatened lawsuits.* Even though
    the amount of the legal expense account may be immaterial, the auditor
    normally examines the transactions in the account (see Chapter 15). The
    purpose of this examination is to identify actual or potential litigation
    against the client. The account analysis can also be used to develop a list
    of attorneys who have been consulted by the entity.
3. *Obtaining a legal letter that describes and evaluates any litigation, claims,
    or assessments.* Legal letters are discussed in the next section.
4. *Obtaining written representation from management that all litigation,
    asserted and unasserted claims, and assessments have been disclosed in
    accordance with FASB ASC Topic 450.* This information is obtained in a
    representation letter furnished by the client. Representation letters are
    discussed later in this chapter.

Legal Letters

> **[LO 3]**

A letter of audit inquiry (referred to as a *legal letter*) sent to the client's attorneys
is the primary means of corroborating information provided by management to
the auditor about litigation, claims, and assessments. Auditors typically analyze
legal expense for the entire period and then ask management to send a legal letter to each attorney who has been consulted by management. Auditors should
be particularly vigilant with letters sent to the entity's general counsel and attorneys specializing in patent law or securities laws. General counsel will likely be
aware of any major litigation involving the client, and patent infringement and

TABLE 17-1	Examples of Types of Litigation

Breach of contract
Patent infringement
Product liability
Violations of government laws and regulation, including
    Securities laws
    Antidiscrimination statutes based on race, sex, age, and other characteristics
    Antitrust laws
    Income tax regulations
    Environmental protection laws
    Foreign Corrupt Practices Act
    Racketeer Influenced and Corrupt Organizations Act (RICO)

securities laws are major sources of litigation. Additionally, a legal letter should be obtained from the entity's general counsel. Table 17–1 provides examples of types of litigation that the auditor may encounter. Chapter 20 covers issues relating to auditor liability and litigation in detail.

The auditor should ask management to send a legal letter to the attorneys, requesting that they provide information about a number of items, including the following:

- A list of any pending or threatened litigation or any probable but as yet unasserted claims to which the attorney has devoted substantial attention or for which an unfavorable outcome is reasonably possible.
- A request that the attorney describe and evaluate each pending or threatened litigation; this should include the progress of the case, the action the entity plans to take, the likelihood of unfavorable outcome, and the amount or range of potential loss.
- A request that the attorney comment on unasserted claims where his or her views differ from management's evaluation.
- A request that the attorney indicate if his or her response is limited in any way and the reasons for such limitations.

Exhibit 17–2 presents an example of a legal letter for EarthWear. Attorneys are generally willing to provide evidence on actual or pending litigation. However, they are sometimes reluctant to provide information on unasserted claims or assessments. An unasserted claim or assessment is one in which the injured party or potential claimant has not yet notified the entity of a possible claim or assessment. For example, suppose there is a cave-in at one of a coal mining entity's mines and a number of miners are killed. Suppose further that a subsequent investigation shows that the client had failed to install proper safety equipment. The entity's fiscal year may end, and the financial statements for the period that includes the accident may be released. Although the families of the employees have not yet initiated or threatened litigation, an unasserted claim may very well exist at the financial statement date. In this case, the entity's attorneys may be reluctant to provide the auditor with information about the unasserted claims because of client-attorney privilege. The attorneys may also be concerned that disclosing the unasserted claim in the financial statements may actually encourage a lawsuit or make it more difficult for the entity to defend itself. This type of situation is generally resolved by having the attorneys corroborate management's understanding of their professional responsibility involving unasserted claims and assessments. Refer to the third paragraph in the legal letter shown in Exhibit 17–2 for the manner in which the client requests the attorneys to communicate to the auditor. In general, disclosing an unasserted claim is not required unless it is probable that the claim will be asserted and there is a reasonable possibility that the outcome will prove to be unfavorable.

EXHIBIT 17-2	Example of a Legal Letter

EARTHWEAR CLOTHIERS

January 15, 2010

Leon, Leon & Dalton
958 S.W. 77th Avenue
Boise, Idaho 79443

Gentlemen:

In connection with an audit of our financial statements for the year ended December 31, 2009, please furnish our auditors, Willis & Adams, P.O. Box 4080, Boise, Idaho 79443-4080, with the information requested below concerning contingencies involving matters with respect to which you have devoted substantial attention on behalf of the company in the form of legal consultation or representation. For the purposes of your response to this letter, we believe that as to each contingency an amount in excess of $25,000 would be material, and in the aggregate $150,000. However, determination of materiality with respect to the overall financial statements cannot be made until our auditors complete their examination. Your response should include matters that existed at December 31, 2009, and during the period from that date to the date of completion of their examination, which is anticipated to be on or about February 15, 2010.

Regarding pending or threatened litigations, claims, and assessments, please include in your response (1) the nature of each matter; (2) the progress of each matter to date; (3) how the company is responding or intends to respond (for example, to contest the case vigorously or seek an out-of-court settlement); and (4) an evaluation of the likelihood of an unfavorable outcome and an estimate, if one can be made, of the amount or range of potential loss. Please furnish to our auditors such explanation, if any, that you consider necessary to supplement the foregoing information, including an explanation of the matters as to which your views may differ from those stated.

We understand that in the course of performing legal services for us with respect to a matter recognized to involve an unasserted possible claim or assessment that may call for financial statement disclosure, if you have formed a professional conclusion that we should disclose or consider disclosure concerning such possible claim or assessment, as a matter of professional responsibility to us, you will so advise us and will consult with us concerning the question of such disclosure and the applicable requirements of FASB Accounting Standards Codification Topic 450, "Contingencies." Please specifically confirm to our auditors that our understanding is correct.

Please specifically identify the nature of and reasons for any limitation on your response.

Sincerely,

Calvin J. Rogers
Chief Executive Officer
EarthWear Clothiers

Attorneys may be unable to respond to the outcome of a matter because the factors in the case do not allow them to reasonably estimate the likelihood of the outcome or to estimate the possible loss. Refusal by a client's attorney to furnish information in a legal letter is a limitation on the scope of the audit sufficient to preclude an unqualified opinion.

Commitments

[LO 4] Companies often enter long-term commitments to purchase raw materials or to sell products at a fixed price. For example, an airline might commit to purchasing its jet fuel from a supplier at a predetermined price over a given time period. The main purpose of entering into such a purchase or sales contract is to obtain a favorable pricing arrangement or to secure the availability of raw materials. Pause for a moment and consider why an auditor might be concerned with commitments made by a client.

Long-term commitments are usually identified through inquiry of client personnel during the audit of the revenue and purchasing processes and through review of the minutes of board meetings. In most cases, such commitments are disclosed in a footnote to the financial statements. However, in certain instances the entity may have to recognize a loss on a long-term commitment even though there has been no exchange of goods.

For example, suppose a client produces woolen cloth for use in women's suits and that the company has a December 31 year-end. Suppose further that the client enters a noncancelable contract on September 30, 2009, to purchase 1 million pounds of wool at $1.00 per pound with delivery on March 31, 2010. At year-end (December 31, 2009), the auditor compares the current market price of wool with the contract price. If the current price of wool is $1.00 or greater, only footnote disclosure of the commitment is necessary if it is material. However, if the price of wool is less than $1.00, a loss would be recognized at December 31, 2009. For example, if the current market price of wool is $.75 per pound, the client would recognize a $250,000 loss (1,000,000 pounds × $.25 per pound) at year-end.

Review of Subsequent Events for Audit of Financial Statements

[LO 5]   Sometimes events or transactions that occur after the balance sheet date but before the issuance of the financial statements materially affect the financial statements. These events or transactions are referred to as *subsequent events* and require adjustment or disclosure in the financial statements. Management is required to disclose the date through which the entity has considered subsequent events (ASC 855). Auditors are responsible for evaluating the entity's handling of subsequent events in the financial statements (AU 560 and 561).

Two types of subsequent events require consideration by management and evaluation by the auditor:

1. **Type I:** Events that provide additional evidence about conditions that existed at the date of the balance sheet and affect the estimates that are part of the financial statement preparation process. Type I events require adjustment of the financial statements.

2. **Type II:** Events that provide evidence about conditions that did not exist at the date of the balance sheet but that arose subsequent to that date. Type II events usually require disclosure in the notes to the financial statements. In some instances where the effect of the event or transaction is very significant, pro forma financial statements may be required in order to prevent the financial statements from being misleading.

Examples of Type I events or conditions:

- An uncollectible account receivable resulting from continued deterioration of a customer's financial condition leading to bankruptcy after the balance sheet date.

- The settlement of a lawsuit after the balance sheet date for an amount different from the amount recorded in the year-end financial statements in accordance with FASB ASC Topic 450, "Contingencies."

Note that in both of these examples, additional evidence became available before the financial statements were issued that shed light on estimates previously made in the financial statements. Subsequent events affecting the realization of assets or the settlement of estimated liabilities normally require adjustment of the financial statements.

Examples of Type II events that result in disclosure include:

• Purchase or disposal of a business by the entity.
• Sale of a capital stock or bond issue by the entity.
• Loss of the entity's manufacturing facility or assets resulting from a casualty such as a fire or flood.
• Losses on receivables caused by conditions such as a business failure arising subsequent to the balance sheet date.

Pause for a moment to test your intuition. You'll recall that EarthWear has a December 31 year-end. Suppose the IRS notified EarthWear on January 5, 2010, that the company had made an error in its prior-year tax return, and as a result had underpaid its 2008 income taxes. If EarthWear settled the claim on February 27, 2010 (before issuing its 2010 financial statements), would the payment be classified as a Type I or Type II event? Now suppose that on February 20, 2010, EarthWear learned that a large wholesale customer, from whom EarthWear had a material receivable, had filed for bankruptcy. The customer's business had been destroyed by an earthquake on January 5, 2010. Would the bankruptcy constitute a Type I or Type II event? Once you've articulated your answers to your satisfaction, read on.

The IRS payment would be classified as a Type I event because it provides evidence about the underpayment of prior-year taxes, a condition that clearly existed prior to the balance sheet date. The bankruptcy would be a considered a Type II event because it resulted from the earthquake, which was not a condition that existed as of the balance sheet date. The loss of the receivable would be disclosed in the notes but would not require an adjustment to the 2009 financial statements.

Figure 17–1 presents a diagram of the subsequent-events period for EarthWear. The period from the date of the financial statements (December 31, 2009) to the date of the auditor's report (February 15, 2010) is sometimes referred to as the *formal* subsequent-events period. During this time frame, the auditor actively conducts audit procedures related to the current-year audit. The period from the date of the auditor's report to the issuance of the financial statements (March 5, 2010) is also part of the subsequent-events period, but the auditor is not responsible for making any inquiries or conducting any audit procedures after the date of the audit report. However, subsequent events may come to the auditor's attention during this period. If the subsequent event is Type I, the financial statements should be adjusted. Depending on the event and its circumstances, additional disclosure may be made in the footnotes. When the subsequent event is Type II, a footnote describing the event should be included with the financial statements.

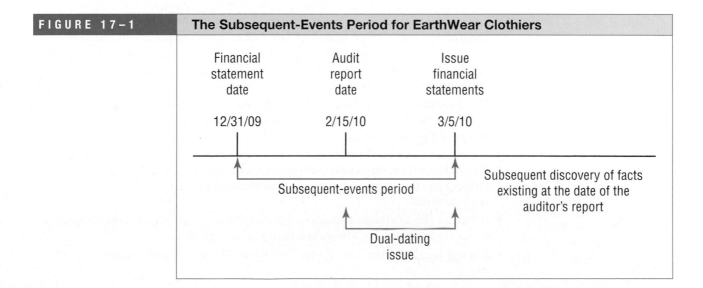

| FIGURE 17–1 | The Subsequent-Events Period for EarthWear Clothiers |

Figure 17–1 also refers to the possibility that the auditor will discover facts subsequent to the date of the auditor's report and the issuance of the financial statements to the public. We discuss this time period later in the chapter after covering the other steps the auditor takes to complete the audit.

Dual Dating
✺ [LO 6]

When a subsequent event is recorded or disclosed in the financial statements after the date on which the auditor has obtained sufficient appropriate audit evidence but before the issuance of the financial statements, the auditor must consider what date to put on the auditor's report. For example, suppose EarthWear notified Willis & Adams that the company had entered an agreement to purchase another catalog retailer on March 1, 2010. Such an event is not indicative of conditions that existed at the balance sheet date and therefore would require only disclosure in the footnotes to the December 31, 2009, financial statements. Two methods are available for dating the audit report: Willis & Adams may (1) "dual date" the report, using wording such as "February 15, 2010, except for Note 10, as to which the date is March 1, 2010" or (2) use the date of the subsequent event. Dual dating is intended to limit the auditor's responsibility for events occurring subsequent to the date on which the auditor has obtained sufficient appropriate audit evidence to the specific subsequent event referred to in the footnote. If the audit report is dated using only the March 1, 2010, date, the auditor's responsibility extends to that date. For this example, how do you think Willis & Adams would choose to date the audit report and why?

In this instance, due to the desire to not extend their responsibility for other events that might have occurred between February 15 and March 1 besides the one noted, Willis & Adams would most likely dual-date the report.

Audit Procedures for Subsequent Events
✺ [LO 7]

As you learned from previous chapters, some audit procedures for business processes and their related financial statement accounts are conducted before year-end, while others may be conducted during the subsequent-events period. Some of these audit procedures, such as testing proper sales and purchases cutoff, are applied to transactions *after* the balance sheet date. Such audit procedures may detect subsequent events. In addition, the auditor conducts audit procedures specifically to detect any subsequent events that might have occurred during the period between the balance sheet date and the date of the audit report. Examples of these audit procedures include:

- Asking management about the following matters: (a) whether there were or are any substantial contingent liabilities or commitments existing at the balance sheet date or at the date of inquiry; (b) whether there have been any significant changes in capital stock, long-term debt, or working capital; (c) the current status of any items in the financial statements that were accounted for based on preliminary or inconclusive data; and (d) whether any unusual adjustments have been made during the subsequent-events period.
- Reading any interim financial statements that are available for the period after year-end and comparing them to the prior-period statements; any unusual fluctuations are investigated.
- Examining the books of original entry (such as sales journal, purchases journal, cash receipts and cash disbursements journals, and general ledger) for the subsequent-events period and investigating any unusual transactions.
- Reading the available minutes of meetings of stockholders, directors, or other committees for the subsequent-events period.
- Asking legal counsel about any litigation, claims, or assessments against the company.

Review of Subsequent Events for the Audit of Internal Control over Financial Reporting

In addition to reporting subsequent events that have implications for the financial statement account balances, auditors of public companies are responsible for reporting any changes in internal control that might affect financial reporting between the end of the reporting period and the date of the auditor's report (AS5). The auditor's treatment of subsequent events relating to internal control is similar to the Type I and Type II treatments discussed above. In other words, the treatment depends on whether the change in control reveals information about a material weakness that existed as of the end of the reporting period or whether the event creates or reveals information about a new condition that did not exist as of the end of the reporting period.

If the event reveals information about a material weakness that existed as of the end of the reporting period, the auditor should issue an adverse opinion on the effectiveness of internal control over financial reporting (and add an explanatory paragraph to the auditor's report if management's report does not appropriately assess the effect of the subsequent event; see Chapter 7). If the auditor is unable to determine the effect of the subsequent event on the effectiveness of the company's internal control, the auditor should disclaim any opinion. If the event creates or reveals information about an internal control condition that did not exist as of the end of the reporting period and the information has a material effect on the company, the auditor includes an explanatory paragraph describing the event and its effects or directing the reader's attention to the event and its effects as disclosed in management's report.

Auditors of public companies are required to inquire of management whether there were any changes in internal control that might affect financial reporting between the end of the reporting period and the date of the auditor's report, and should obtain written representations regarding any such changes. The public company auditor should also inquire about and examine, for this subsequent period, the following:

- Relevant internal audit reports (or similar functions, such as loan review in a financial institution) issued during the subsequent period.
- Independent auditor reports (if other than the primary auditor's) of significant deficiencies or material weaknesses.
- Regulatory agency reports on the company's internal control over financial reporting, if any.
- Information about the effectiveness of the company's internal control over financial reporting obtained through other engagements (AS5).

Final Evidential Evaluation Processes

[LO 8] In addition to the search for unrecorded contingent liabilities and the review for subsequent events, the auditor conducts a number of audit steps before deciding on the appropriate audit report to issue for the entity. These include the following:

- Performance of final analytical procedures.
- Evaluation of the entity's ability to continue as a going concern.
- Obtaining a representation letter.
- Review of working papers.
- Final evaluation of audit results.
- Evaluation of financial statement presentation and disclosure.
- Obtaining an independent review of the engagement.

Final Analytical Procedures

Auditing standards (AU 329) require that the auditor perform analytical procedures both in planning and at the final review stage of the audit. The objective of conducting analytical procedures near the end of the engagement is to help the auditor assess the conclusions reached on the financial statement components and evaluate the overall financial statement presentation. These final analytical procedures may include recalculating some of the ratios discussed in the *Advanced Module* in Chapter 5 for planning the audit. However, more frequently, they involve reviewing the adequacy of the evidence gathered in response to unexpected fluctuations in the account balances identified during the planning of the audit and identifying any unusual or unexpected relationships not previously considered. These final analytical procedures may indicate that more evidence is needed for certain account balances.

The auditor performs final analytical procedures to consider the overall reasonableness of the financial statement amounts. In other words, final analytical procedures provide a sort of final, overall "smell test" by the auditor. In doing this analysis, the auditor reexamines the client's business risks (refer to Chapter 3). For example, the auditor considers the critical issues and significant industry business risks and whether such risks might impact the financial statements. The auditor also assesses the structure and profitability of the industry and how the client fits within the industry in terms of its profitability and solvency. In other words, the auditor considers whether the financial statement amounts make sense given the auditor's knowledge of the client's business risks.

Practice INSIGHT

Each year the PCAOB reviews the documentation for several audit engagements conducted during the prior year. The Board recently concluded that in several engagements it has reviewed, auditors appeared to take an unjustifiably uniform approach to their testing across processes, accounts, and assertions. Such an approach can result in auditors expending more effort than necessary in lower-risk areas and not enough effort in higher-risk areas.

Representation Letter

During the course of a financial statement or an integrated audit, management makes a number of representations to the auditor as part of the inquiries made to obtain sufficient competent evidence. Auditing standards require that the auditor obtain a *representation letter* from management. The purpose of this letter is to corroborate oral representations made to the auditor and to document the continued appropriateness of those representations. The representation letter also reduces the possibility of misunderstanding between management and the auditor.

For example, during the audit, the auditor may inquire about related parties and conduct specific audit procedures to identify related-party transactions. Even if the results of these audit procedures indicate that such transactions have been properly disclosed, the auditor obtains written representations indicating that management is not aware of any undisclosed related party transactions. In other instances, evidence may not be available to corroborate management's representations. For example, suppose that management indicates intent to refinance a short-term obligation in the next period and reclassifies it as a long-term liability in the current financial statements. The auditor would obtain written representation from management to confirm that the obligations will be refinanced in the next period. The auditor may also seek confirmation of such financing arrangements from the client's lender.

Exhibit 17–3 presents an example of a representation letter. Note the important types of information that management is asked to represent. The representation letter is addressed to the auditor and generally is given the same date as the

EXHIBIT 17–3	Example of a Representation Letter

EARTHWEAR CLOTHIERS

February 15, 2010

Willis & Adams
P.O. Box 4080
Boise, Idaho 79443-4080

Gentlemen:

We are providing this letter in connection with your audits of our assertion about the effectiveness of internal control over financial reporting at December 31, 2009, and of the consolidated financial statements of EarthWear Clothiers as of December 31, 2009 and 2008, for the years then ended. These audits were conducted for the purpose of expressing opinions on the effectiveness of EarthWear Clothiers' internal control over financial reporting, and whether our consolidated financial statements present fairly, in all material respects, the financial position, results of operations, and cash flows of EarthWear Clothiers in conformity with accounting principles accepted in the United States of America. We confirm that we are responsible for the fair presentation in the consolidated financial statements of financial position, results of operations, and cash flows in conformity with generally accepted accounting principles, for establishing and maintaining effective internal control over financial reporting, and for performing an assessment of the effectiveness of internal control over financial reporting.

    Certain representations in this letter are described as being limited to matters that are material. Items are considered material, regardless of size, if they involve an omission or misstatement of accounting information that, in the light of surrounding circumstances, makes it probable that the judgment of a reasonable person relying on the information would have been changed or influenced by the omission or misstatement.

    We confirm, to the best of our knowledge and belief, as of February 15, 2010, the following representations made to you during your audits.

1. The consolidated financial statements referred to above are fairly presented in conformity with accounting principles generally accepted in the United States of America, and include all disclosures necessary for such fair presentation and disclosures otherwise required to be included therein by laws and regulations to which the Company is subject.
2. We have made available to you all
   a. Financial records and related data.
   b. Minutes of the meetings of stockholders, directors, and committees of directors, or summaries of actions of recent meetings for which minutes have not yet been prepared.
3. There have been no communications from regulatory agencies concerning noncompliance with or deficiencies in financial reporting practices.
4. There are no material transactions, agreements, or accounts that have not been properly recorded in the accounting records underlying the financial statements.
5. The effects of the uncorrected financial statements misstatements summarized in the accompanying schedule are immaterial, both individually and in the aggregate, to the financial statements taken as a whole.
6. Receivables recorded in the financial statements represent valid claims against debtors for sales or other charges arising on or before the balance sheet date and have been appropriately reduced to their estimated net realizable value. Receivables classified as current do not include any material amounts which are collectible after one year.
7. Inventories recorded in the consolidated financial statements are stated at the lower of cost or market, cost being determined on the basis of LIFO, and due provision was made to reduce all slow-moving, obsolete, or unusable inventories to their estimated useful values. Inventory quantities at the balance sheet dates were determined from physical counts taken by competent employees at various times during the year. Liabilities for amounts unpaid are recorded for all items included in inventories at balance sheet dates and all quantities billed to customers at those dates are excluded from the inventory balances.
8. All liabilities of the Company of which we are aware are included in the financial statements at the balance sheet date. There are no other liabilities or gain or loss contingencies that are required to be accrued or disclosed by FASB ASC Topic 450, *Contingencies,* and no unasserted claims or assessments of which our legal counsel has advised us are probable of assertion and required to be disclosed in accordance with that Statement.
9. We acknowledge our responsibility for establishing and maintaining comprehensive systems of internal control that provide reasonable assurance as to the consistency, integrity, and reliability of the preparation and presentation of financial statements; the safeguarding of assets; the effectiveness and efficiency of operations; and compliance with applicable laws and regulations.
10. We monitor the systems of internal control and maintain an independent internal auditing program that assesses the effectiveness of internal control. We did not rely on the Willis & Adams's procedures performed during the audits of internal control over financial reporting or the financial statements as part of the basis for our assessment of the effectiveness of internal control over financial reporting.

(continued)

EXHIBIT 17-3 **Example of a Representation Letter (*continued*)**

11. We assessed the Company's internal control over financial reporting for financial presentations in conformity with accounting principles generally accepted in the United States of America. This assessment was based on criteria for effective internal control over financial reporting established in *Internal Control—Integrated Framework* issued by the Committee of Sponsoring Organizations of the Treadway Commission (the COSO Report). Based on this assessment, we believe that the Company maintained effective internal control over financial reporting for financial presentations in conformity with accounting principles generally accepted in the United States of America as of December 31, 2009.

12. There are no significant deficiencies, including material weaknesses, in the design or operation of internal controls that could adversely affect the Company's ability to record, process, summarize, and report financial data.

13. We acknowledge our responsibility for the design and implementation of programs and controls to prevent and detect fraud.

14. We have no knowledge of any fraud or suspected fraud affecting the entity involving:
    a. Management.
    b. Employees who have significant roles in internal control.
    c. Others that could have a material effect on the consolidated financial statements.

15. We have no knowledge of any allegations of fraud or suspected fraud affecting the entity received in communications from employees, former employees, analysts, regulators, short sellers, or others.

16. There have been no violations or possible violations of laws or regulations whose effects should be considered for disclosure in the consolidated financial statements or as a basis for recording a loss contingency.

17. The Company has no plans or intentions that may materially affect the carrying value or classification of assets and liabilities.

18. There have not been any changes, subsequent to the date being reported on, in internal control over financial reporting or other factors that might significantly affect internal control over financial reporting, including corrective actions with regard to significant deficiencies and material weaknesses.

19. All control deficiencies communicated to the audit committee during previous engagements have been resolved.

20. The following, if material, have been properly recorded or disclosed in the consolidated financial statements:
    a. Related-party transactions, including sales, purchases, loans, transfers, leasing arrangements, and guarantees, and amounts receivable from or payable to related parties (the term "related party" includes entities described in SAS No. 45, footnote 1).
    b. Guarantees, whether written or oral, under which the company is contingently liable.
    c. Significant estimates and material concentrations known to management that are required to be disclosed in accordance with the FASB ASC Topic 275, *Risks and Uncertainties.* (Significant estimates are estimates at the balance sheet date that could change materially within the next year. Concentrations refer to volumes of business, revenues, available sources of supply, or markets or geographic areas for which events could occur that would significantly disrupt normal finances within the next year.)

21. The Company has satisfactory title to all owned assets, and there are no liens or encumbrances on such assets, nor has any asset been pledged as collateral, except as disclosed in the consolidated financial statements.

22. The Company has complied with all aspects of contractual agreements that would have a material effect on the financial statements in the event of noncompliance.

23. The unaudited interim financial information has been prepared and presented in conformity with accounting principles generally accepted in the United States of America applicable to interim financial information and with Item 302(a) of Regulation S-K. The unaudited quarterly financial information for the year ended December 31, 2009, also has been prepared on a basis consistent with the corresponding interim periods in the year ended December 31, 2008, and, to the degree appropriate, with the consolidated financial statements for the years ended December 31, 2009, and December 31, 2008. The unaudited interim financial information for the three months ended December 31, 2009, and December 31, 2008, does not include any material amount of year-end adjustments that have not been disclosed or any material amounts that should have been included in earlier interim periods of the respective fiscal years.

24. Arrangements with financial institutions involving compensating balances or other arrangements involving restrictions on cash balances, line of credit, or similar arrangements have been properly disclosed.

25. We have fully disclosed to you all sales terms, including all rights of return of price adjustments and all warranty provisions.

26. The company has appropriately reconciled its books and records underlying the consolidated financial statements to their related supporting information. All related reconciling items considered to be material were identified and included on the reconciliations and were appropriately adjusted in the consolidated financial statements. There were no material unreconciled differences or material general ledger suspense account items. All intracompany and intercompany accounts have been eliminated or appropriately measured and considered for disclosure in the consolidated financial statements.

To the best of our knowledge and belief, no events have occurred subsequent to the balance sheet date and through the date of this letter that would require adjustment to or disclosure in the aforementioned financial statements.

Calvin J. Rogers
Chief Executive Officer

James C. Watts
Chief Financial Officer

auditor's report. Normally, the chief executive officer and chief financial officer sign the representation letter. Management's refusal to provide a representation letter results in a scope limitation that is sufficient to preclude an unqualified opinion and is ordinarily sufficient to cause an auditor to disclaim an opinion or withdraw from the engagement.

Practice **INSIGHT**	In practice, the management representation letter is typically drafted by the auditor and signed by management, though it is written as a letter addressed to the auditor from management. Practitioners often refer to a letter of representations as a "rep letter."

Working Paper Review

All audit work should be reviewed by an audit team member who is senior to the person preparing the working papers. Thus, the senior-in-charge should conduct a detailed review of the working papers prepared by staff auditors and follow up on any unresolved problems or issues. In turn, the manager should review all working papers. The engagement partner normally reviews working papers related to critical audit areas as well as working papers prepared by the manager. In reviewing the working papers, the reviewers must ensure that the working papers document that the audit was properly planned and supervised, that the evidence supports the assertions tested, and that the evidence is sufficient for the type of audit report issued.

Practice **INSIGHT**	Auditors must be careful not to leave "loose ends" in the working papers. Consider the third general auditing standard, relating to due professional care: will a regulator or a jury believe that the auditor exercised due care if a question is left unanswered or an audit step undocumented? There's a common saying in audit practice: "If you didn't document it, you didn't do it."

Final Evaluation of Audit Results

In conjunction with the review of the working papers, the auditor must evaluate the results of the audit tests. In Chapter 7 we discussed evaluating the results of the audit of internal control over financial reporting as well as evaluating the implications of the financial statement audit results in terms of the effectiveness of the client's internal control over financial reporting. The evaluation of the results of the financial statement audit is concerned with two issues: (1) the sufficiency of the audit evidence; and (2) the effects of detected misstatements in the financial statements. In evaluating the audit evidence, the auditor determines whether there is sufficient evidence to support each relevant assertion. This evaluation considers evidence obtained to support the assessment of the risk of material misstatement, as well as the evidence gathered to reach the planned level of detection risk (substantive procedures). If this evaluation indicates that the evidence is not sufficient to meet the planned level of audit risk, the auditor may need to gather additional evidence. For example, if the final analytical procedures indicate that inventory may still contain material misstatements, the auditor should gather additional audit evidence on the inventory account balance.

Any misstatements detected during the audit process must be considered in terms of their effects on the financial statements. This involves performing the third step in applying materiality (refer to Chapter 3). In particular, the auditor must estimate the likely misstatements and compare the amount arrived at to the amount of materiality allocated to the relevant component of the financial statement. The auditor should also consider the effects of unadjusted misstatements on aggregated components of the financial statements such as assets, liabilities, equity, revenues, and expenses.

EXHIBIT 17–4	Example Working Paper for Estimating Likely Misstatements

EARTHWEAR CLOTHIERS
Schedule of Proposed Adjusting Entries
12/31/09

Workpaper Ref.	Proposed Adjusting Entry	Assets	Liabilities	Equity	Revenues	Expenses
N10	Payroll expense					75,000
	Bonuses					140,000
	Accrued liabilities		215,000			
	To accrue payroll through 12/31 and recognize 2009 bonuses.					
F20	Cost of sales					312,500
	Inventory	(312,500)				
	To adjust ending inventory based on sample results.					
F20	Inventory	227,450				
	Accounts payable		227,450			
	To record inventory in transit at 12/31.					
R15	Accounts receivable	79,850				
	Sales				79,850	
	To record sales cutoff errors at 12/31.					
	Total	(5,200)	442,450		79,850	527,500

Tolerable Misstatement = $900,000 (50 percent of planning materiality)
Conclusion: Based on the above analysis, the account balances for EarthWear Clothiers are fairly stated in accordance with GAAP.

Exhibit 17–4 is the working paper that was first introduced in Exhibit 3–4. As noted in Chapter 3, none of the errors detected is material in terms of tolerable misstatement ($900,000). Additionally, the overall effect of the misstatements is not material in terms of aggregated components of the financial statements. Even though the misstatements shown in Exhibit 17–4 are not material, it is common practice for the auditor to communicate any such adjustments to the client to correct the books. It is normally expected that known misstatements will be corrected. However, the auditor would not necessarily require all proposed adjustments to be booked. For example, suppose the auditor identifies a misstatement in an account receivable for a particular customer in confirming a sample of accounts receivable. She or he will likely calculate an estimated or projected error in the population of accounts receivable based on the sample results (see Chapter 9). The auditor will normally expect the client to correct the specific customer account found to be in error, but may not require the client to book the full amount of the *projected* error in receivables if the amount is immaterial. If the likely misstatement for a particular account is greater than the tolerable misstatement, the account will require adjustment at least to the point at which the likely error remaining is less than tolerable misstatement.

Practice
INSIGHT

Determining whether an identified misstatement is material is not merely a quantitative exercise—qualitative factors can be more important than dollar amount. Auditors are particularly sensitive to misstatements that are *intentional* regardless of their size. If the auditor learns of an intentional misstatement, even when the misstatement is relatively small, he or she may be required to (1) reevaluate the degree of audit risk involved in the audit engagement; (2) determine whether to revise the nature, timing, and extent of audit procedures; and (3) consider whether to resign from the engagement.

Evaluating Financial Statement Presentation and Disclosure

The client normally drafts the financial statements, including footnotes. The auditor reviews the financial statements to ensure compliance with GAAP, proper presentation of accounts, and inclusion of all necessary disclosures. Most public accounting firms use some type of financial statement disclosure checklist to assist the auditor in ensuring that all required footnotes have been properly included.

Independent Engagement Quality Review

Most firms have a policy requiring an *engagement quality review* for publicly traded companies and for privately held companies whose financial statements are expected to be widely distributed.[2] The engagement quality reviewer is a partner who is not associated with the details of the engagement and is expected to provide an independent, objective review. The engagement quality reviewer should understand the audit approach, findings, and conclusions for critical audit areas and should review the audit report, financial statements, and footnotes for consistency.

Archiving and Retention

As discussed in Chapter 4, the events leading up to the Sarbanes-Oxley Act of 2002 focused a spotlight on the practice of archiving and retaining audit files (see Exhibit 4–3). The Sarbanes-Oxley Act of 2002 imposed new guidelines for audit file archiving and retention. The PCAOB's auditing standard, "Audit Documentation" (AS3), complies with the guidance under Sarbanes and requires that firms archive their public company audit files (working papers and other documentation) for retention within 45 days following the time the auditor grants permission to use the auditor's report in connection with the issuance of the company's financial statements. The Sarbanes-Oxley Act and the PCAOB's documentation standard require that audit documentation be retained for seven years from the date of completion of the engagement, as indicated by the date of the auditor's report, unless a longer period of time is required by law (e.g., pending or threatened lawsuit, investigation, or subpoena). Some states (e.g., New York and California) have adopted similar (or in some cases even more stringent) archiving and retention policies for all audits, including audits of nonpublic companies.

All documents that "form the basis of the audit or review" are required to be retained. The PCAOB documentation standard requires that any document created, sent, or received, including documents that are inconsistent with a final conclusion, be included in the audit files for all significant matters. This includes any correspondence between engagement teams and national technical accounting or auditing experts in a public accounting firm's national office. Also, when significant changes are made to the planned audit approach at any point during the audit, the final documentation should indicate the original plan, modifications to the plan, and the rationale for the change. Such document retention is intended to facilitate any subsequent investigations, proceedings, and litigation.

Going Concern Considerations

✂ [LO 9]

Auditing standards (AU 341) indicate that the auditor has a responsibility to evaluate whether there is substantial doubt about an entity's ability to continue as a *going concern* for a reasonable period of time. "Going concern" in this context means that the "concern" (i.e., entity) is likely to keep "going" (i.e., it is likely to be able to keep doing business). A reasonable period of time is considered to be no more than one year beyond the date of the financial statements being audited. While this assessment is made during the planning of the engagement, the auditor must also consider this issue near the end of the engagement.

---

[2]K. Epps and W. F. Messier, Jr., "Engagement Quality Reviews: A Comparison of Audit Firm Practices," *Auditing: A Journal of Practice & Theory,* November 2007, pp. 167–181.

Steps in the Going Concern Evaluation   The auditor follows three
overall steps in making the going concern evaluation:

1. Consider whether the results of audit procedures performed during the planning, performance, and completion of the audit indicate whether there is substantial doubt about the entity's ability to continue as a going concern for a reasonable period of time (one year).

2. If there is substantial doubt, obtain information about management's plans to mitigate the going concern problem and assess the likelihood that such plans can be successfully implemented.

3. Conclude, in light of management's plans, whether there is substantial doubt about the ability of the entity to continue as a going concern; if substantial doubt exists, consider the adequacy of the disclosures about the entity's ability to continue and include an explanatory paragraph in the audit report.

Let's discuss each of these steps in turn.

Identifying and Assessing Going Concern Problems. Ordinary audit procedures are normally sufficient to identify conditions and events that indicate going concern problems. Examples of audit procedures that are likely to identify these kinds of conditions and events include analytical procedures, review of subsequent events, tests for compliance with debt agreements, reading the minutes of board of directors' meetings, inquiry of legal counsel, and confirmations with lenders or investors regarding financial arrangements. Auditing standards identify four major categories of such conditions or events: *negative financial trends, other financial difficulties, internal problems,* and *external matters.*

Negative financial trends consist of poor results from operations and adverse financial ratios. Analytical procedures during the planning phase of the audit are often particularly helpful in identifying negative financial trends. Table 17–2 lists a number of important financial conditions and ratios that prior audit research has shown to be good indicators of financial distress that can lead to a going concern report. If the entity being evaluated meets a number of these financial conditions and also has adverse ratios, the auditor may conclude that the entity is not a going concern.

Conditions or events that may occur in the other three categories are shown in Table 17–3. Other financial difficulties are particularly important for the going concern assessment. For example, if an entity has violated certain debt covenants or is in default on its debt, the debt holders may call for immediate payment. In such circumstances, the entity may be unable to meet its cash requirements and may have to seek bankruptcy protection or liquidation. Similarly, internal

TABLE 17–2	**Financial Conditions and Ratios That Indicate Financial Distress**

Financial Conditions
  Recurring operating losses
  Current-year deficit
  Accumulated deficits
  Negative net worth
  Negative working capital
  Negative cash flow
  Negative income from operations
  Inability to meet interest payments

Ratios
  Net worth/total liabilities
  Working capital from operations/total liabilities
  Current assets/current liabilities
  Total long-term liabilities/total assets
  Total liabilities/total assets
  Net income before taxes/net sales

TABLE 17–3	Other Conditions and Events Indicating a Problem with the Going Concern Assumption

Other Financial Difficulties
Default on loans
Dividends in arrears
Restructuring of debt
Denial of trade credit by suppliers
No additional sources of financing

Internal Matters
Work stoppages
Uneconomic long-term commitments
Dependence on the success of one particular project

External Matters
Legal proceedings
Loss of a major customer or supplier
Loss of a key franchise, license, or patent

matters such as work stoppages may have severe consequences on the entity. In numerous recent instances strikes have caused entities to seek bankruptcy protection. Finally, external matters may cause an entity to be unable to continue as a going concern. For example, macroeconomic downturns or the loss of even one or two major customers have been known to cause companies to face severe financial difficulties.

Consideration of Management's Plans. Once conditions have been identified that indicate substantial doubt about the ability of the entity to continue, the auditor considers management's plans for dealing with the adverse effects of the conditions or events. Potential management responses include:

- Plans to dispose of assets.
- Plans to borrow money or restructure debt.
- Plans to reduce or delay expenditures.
- Plans to increase ownership equity.

For example, management may attempt to sell assets to pay off debt or dispose of operations that are losing money. Management may negotiate with creditors in order to restructure debt or seek additional financing. Frequently, management will develop plans to reduce wages or cut back the workforce. When evaluating management's plans, the auditor should obtain evidence about the elements of the plans and their likelihood of success. This requires examining the assumptions used by management in developing such plans. If the auditor concludes that there is substantial doubt about the entity's ability to continue as a going concern, the auditor will normally issue a modified audit report (i.e., an unqualified report with an explanatory paragraph describing the going concern issue) similar to the one shown in Chapter 18 (Exhibit 18–3).

Communications with Those Charged with Governance and Management

[LO 10] Auditing standards (AU 380) require that the auditor communicate certain matters related to the conduct of the audit to those individuals responsible for oversight of the entity's strategic direction and its financial reporting process, sometimes referred to as "those charged with governance." For publicly traded companies, "those charged with governance" would typically refer to the board of directors,

TABLE 17–4	**Items the Auditor Should Communicate to Those Charged with Governance**

The auditor's responsibilities under generally accepted auditing standards or under the standards of the PCAOB if the client is a public company
- The nature of the auditor's responsibility for forming and expressing an opinion about whether the financial statements are presented fairly, in all material respects, in conformity with generally accepted accounting principles.
- The fact that the audit of the financial statements does not relieve management or those charged with governance of their responsibilities with respect to the financial statements.

An overview of the planned scope and timing of the audit
- How the auditor proposes to address the significant risks of material misstatement, whether due to fraud or error.
- The auditor's approach to internal control relevant to the audit, including whether the auditor will express an opinion on the effectiveness of internal control over financial reporting.
- The concept of materiality in planning and executing the audit (but not specific thresholds or amounts).
- The extent to which the auditor will use the work of internal audit, and how the external and internal auditors can best work together.

Significant findings from the audit
- The auditor's views about qualitative aspects of the entity's significant accounting practices, including accounting policies, estimates, and financial statement disclosures.
- Significant difficulties, if any, encountered during the audit.
- Disagreements with management, if any.
- Other findings or issues arising from the audit that are, in the auditor's professional judgment, significant and relevant to those charged with governance.
- Uncorrected misstatements unless deemed by the auditor to be clearly trivial in nature.
- Corrected misstatements that were brought to management's attention by the auditor, including whether detected misstatements (whether or not material), may indicate a particular bias in the preparation of the financial statements.
- Representations the auditor is requesting from management.
- Management's consultations with other accountants.

(This list is not exhaustive; see AU 380.)

and the audit committee in particular. The intent of this communication is to encourage a healthy, two-way dialogue about financial reporting matters and to ensure that those charged with governance receive adequate information on significant audit-related issues. The items to be communicated are organized into three categories: the auditor's responsibilities under generally accepted auditing standards, an overview of the planned scope and timing of the audit, and significant findings from the audit. As shown in Table 17–4, there are several important topics in each of these categories that the auditor should discuss with the audit committee or other responsible body.

Communication regarding significant findings from the audit should be in writing when the auditor deems oral communication to be inadequate. Other parts of the communication may be oral or in writing.

Communications Regarding the Audit of Internal Control over Financial Reporting

The auditor also has a number of communication responsibilities with respect to the audit of internal control over financial reporting (AS5). The auditor must communicate in writing to management and the audit committee all significant deficiencies and material weaknesses identified during the audit. The written communication should be made prior to the issuance of the auditor's report on internal control over financial reporting. If a significant deficiency or material weakness exists because the oversight of external financial reporting and internal control over financial reporting by the company's audit committee is ineffective, the auditor must communicate that specific significant deficiency or material weakness in writing to the board of directors. The auditor also must communicate to management, in writing, all control deficiencies identified (including deficiencies in internal control that are of a lesser magnitude than significant deficiencies—see Chapter 7 for additional details regarding communication).[3]

---

[3]Auditing Standards also require the auditor to communicate fraud or illegal acts to the appropriate level of management, or the audit committee if senior management is involved.

<table>
<tr><td>Management
Letter</td><td>In addition to the communications discussed above, the auditor normally prepares a *management letter*. Be sure not to confuse the management letter with the management representation letter discussed previously in this chapter. The auditor uses the management letter to make recommendations to the client based on observations during the audit; the letter may include suggested improvements in various areas, such as organizational structure and efficiency issues.</td></tr>
</table>

Subsequent Discovery of Facts Existing at the Date of the Auditor's Report

✂ [LO 11] Earlier in this chapter we discussed procedures conducted as part of the audit to identify relevant events occurring after the date of the financial statements but *before* the statements and the accompanying audit report are *issued*. Although an auditor has no obligation to conduct any audit procedures after the financial statements and audit report have been issued, facts may come to the auditor's attention after issuance that might have affected the report had he or she known about them. In Figure 17–1, this would be events occurring after March 5, 2010. The most common situation is where the previously issued financial statements contain material misstatements due to either unintentional or intentional actions by management. For example, the auditor may learn that a material amount of inventory was not included in the financial statements because of a computer error. Alternatively, the auditor may learn that management inflated inventory quantities and prices in an effort to increase reported profits. A number of such situations have arisen in recent years (e.g., see Exhibit 17–5). Keep in mind that here we are discussing events occurring after the issuance of the financial statements that would have changed the statements or the auditor's opinion had the facts been known prior to issuance. Events that have no bearing on the prior period's financial statements will appropriately be recognized in the period in which they occur.

When facts are encountered that may affect the auditor's previously issued report, the auditor should consult with his or her attorney because legal implications may be involved and actions taken by the auditor may involve confidential client–auditor communications. The auditor should determine whether the facts are reliable and whether they existed at the date of the audit report. The auditor should discuss the matter with an appropriate level of management and request cooperation in investigating the potential misstatement.

EXHIBIT 17–5	**New Century Announces Financial Statements Should Not Be Relied Upon, Goes Bankrupt**
	New Century Financial Corporation was, at one point, the second largest originator of subprime loans in the United States. New Century's loan originations had risen from $14 billion in 2002 to about $60 billion in 2006. However, on February 7, 2007, New Century began to crumble as it restated its interim earnings for the first three quarters of 2006. A combination of allegedly shady accounting, insufficient loan loss reserves, and the collapse of the subprime mortgage market eventually led New Century to declare bankruptcy in 2007. In April 2007, KPMG, New Century's auditor, terminated its relationship with New Century. In May, New Century announced that that the December 2005 financial statements should no longer be relied upon. As of April 2009, litigation against KPMG by New Century's bankruptcy trustee is still pending.
	Sources: P. Brickley and A. Efrati, "KPMG Aided New Century Missteps, Report Says," *The Wall Street Journal,* March 27, 2008, p. A-12; D. Kardos, "KPMG is Sued Over New Century," *The Wall Street Journal,* April 2, 2009, p. C-3; New Century Chapter 11 Bankruptcy Report, Case No. 07-10416 (KJC), "Final Report of Michael J. Missal, Bankruptcy Court Examiner," United States Bankruptcy Court for the District of Delaware, February 20, 2008.

If the auditor determines that the previously issued financial statements are in error and the audit report is affected, he or she should request that the client issue an immediate revision to the financial statements. The reasons for the revisions should be described in the footnotes to the revised financial statements. If the effect on the financial statements cannot immediately be determined, the client should notify persons known to be relying on the financial statements and auditor's report. If the stock is publicly traded or subject to regulatory jurisdiction, the client should contact the SEC, stock exchanges, and other regulatory agencies as appropriate.

If the client refuses to cooperate and make the necessary disclosures, the auditor should notify the board of directors and take the following steps, if possible:

1. Notify the client that the auditor's report must no longer be associated with the financial statements.
2. Notify any regulatory agencies having jurisdiction over the client that the auditor's report can no longer be relied upon.
3. Notify each person known to the auditor to be relying on the financial statements. (Notifying a regulatory agency such as the SEC is often the only practical way of providing appropriate disclosure.)

The practical outcome of these procedures is that the auditor has withdrawn his or her report on the previously issued financial statements. In notifying the client, regulatory agencies, and other persons relying on the auditor's report, the auditor should disclose the effect the information would have had on the auditor's report had the information been known to the auditor prior to issuance of the report.

KEY TERMS

Analytical procedures. Evaluations of financial information made by a study of plausible relationships among both financial and nonfinancial data.

Contingent liability. An existing condition, situation, or set of circumstances involving uncertainty as to possible loss to an entity that will ultimately be resolved when some future event occurs or fails to occur.

Dual dating. The auditor's report is dual dated when a subsequent event occurs after the date on which the auditor has obtained sufficient appropriate audit evidence but before the financial statements are issued.

Engagement quality review. A review by a quality review partner of the financial statements and audit report to ensure the audit was properly conducted and an appropriate report issued.

Legal letter. An audit inquiry sent to the client's attorneys in order to obtain or corroborate information about litigation, claims, and assessments.

Management letter. A letter from the auditor to management making recommendations to the client based on observations during the audit; the letter may include topics relating to organizational structure and efficiency issues.

Representation letter. A letter that corroborates oral representations made to the auditor by management and documents the continued appropriateness of such representations.

Subsequent event. An event or transaction that occurs after the balance sheet date but prior to the issuance of the financial statements and the auditor's reports that may materially affect the financial statements.

Working papers. The auditor's record of the work performed and the conclusions reached on the audit.

www.mhhe.com/ messier7e	Visit the book's Online Learning Center for a multiple-choice quiz that will allow you to assess your understanding of chapter concepts.

REVIEW QUESTIONS

[LO, 1] 17-1 Define what is meant by *contingent liability*. What three categories are used to classify a contingent liability FASB ASC Topic 450, "Contingencies"? Give four examples of a contingent liability.

[3] 17-2 What information does the auditor ask the attorney to provide on pending or threatened litigation?

[4] 17-3 Provide two examples of commitments. Under what conditions do such commitments result in the recognition of a loss in the financial statements?

[5] 17-4 What are the types of subsequent events relevant to financial statement audits? Give one example of each type of subsequent event that might materially affect the financial statements.

[5,6] 17-5 Under what circumstances would the auditor dual date an audit report?

[8] 17-6 Are analytical procedures required as part of the final overall review of the financial statements? What is the purpose of such analytical procedures?

[8] 17-7 Why does the auditor obtain a representation letter from management?

[8] 17-8 Describe the purposes of an independent engagement quality review by a quality review partner.

[9] 17-9 List the three overall steps in the going concern evaluation process.

[9] 17-10 What four major categories of events or conditions may indicate going concern problems? Give two examples for each category.

[10] 17-11 What items should be included in the auditor's communication with those charged with governance, (i.e., the audit committee or similar group)?

[11] 17-12 What types of events would generally require restatement of the issued financial statements? What procedures should the auditor follow when the client refuses to cooperate and make the necessary disclosures?

MULTIPLE-CHOICE QUESTIONS

[1,2] 17-13 An auditor would be most likely to identify a contingent liability by obtaining a(n)
a. Accounts payable confirmation.
b. Bank confirmation of the client's cash balance.
c. Letter from the entity's general legal counsel.
d. List of subsequent cash receipts.

[3] 17-14 An auditor should request that an audit client send a letter of inquiry to those attorneys who have been consulted concerning litigation, claims, or assessments. The primary reason for this request is to provide
a. The opinion of a specialist as to whether loss contingencies are possible, probable, or remote.
b. A description of litigation, claims, and assessments that have a reasonable possibility of unfavorable outcome.
c. An objective appraisal of management's policies and procedures adopted for identifying and evaluating legal matters.
d. Corroboration of the information furnished by management concerning litigation, claims, and assessments.

[6] 17-15 An auditor issued an audit report that was dual dated for a subsequent event occurring after the date on which the auditor has obtained sufficient appropriate audit evidence but before issuance of the financial statements. The auditor's responsibility for events occurring subsequent to the date on which the auditor has obtained sufficient appropriate audit evidence was

a. Limited to the specific event referenced.

b. Extended to include all events occurring since the date on which the auditor has obtained sufficient appropriate audit evidence.

c. Extended to subsequent events occurring through the date of issuance of the report.

d. Limited to events occurring up to the date of the last subsequent event referenced.

[7]   17-16   Which of the following procedures would an auditor most likely perform to obtain evidence about the occurrence of any changes in internal control that might affect financial reporting between the end of the reporting period and the date of the auditor's report?

a. Review a fire insurance settlement during the subsequent period.

b. Examine relevant internal audit reports issued during the subsequent period.

c. Inquire of the entity's legal counsel concerning litigation, claims, and assessments arising after year-end.

d. Confirm bank accounts established after year-end.

[8]   17-17   Final analytical procedures are generally intended to

a. Provide the auditor with a final, overall evaluation of the relationships among financial statement balances.

b. Test transactions to corroborate management's financial statement assertions.

c. Gather evidence concerning account balances that have not yet been investigated.

d. Retest control activities that appeared to be ineffective during the assessment of control risk.

[9]   17-18   Which of the following audit procedures is most likely to assist an auditor in identifying conditions and events that may indicate substantial doubt about an entity's ability to continue as a going concern?

a. Review compliance with the terms of debt agreements.

b. Review management's plans to dispose of assets.

c. Evaluate management's plans to borrow money or restructure debt.

d. Consider management's plans to reduce or delay expenditures.

[10] 17-19   Auditing standards found in AU 380 primarily encourage which of the following conversations about financial reporting?

a. A conversation with those charged with governance to discuss matters pertaining to financial reporting.

b. A conversation with only management to discuss matters pertaining to financial reporting.

c. A conversation with the head of the client's internal audit department and those charged with governance to discuss matters pertaining to financial reporting.

d. A conversation in which those charged with governance report on management's views on matters pertaining to financial reporting.

[10] 17-20   Which of the following matters should an auditor communicate to those charged with governance?

	Significant Audit Adjustments	Management's Consultations with Other Accountants
a.	Yes	Yes
b.	Yes	No
c.	No	Yes
d.	No	No

[11]   17-21   Which of the following events occurring after the issuance of a set of financial statements and the accompanying auditor's report would be most likely to cause the auditor to make further inquiries about the financial statements?

a. A technological development in the industry that could affect the entity's future ability to continue as a going concern.

b. The entity's sale of a subsidiary that accounts for 30 percent of the entity's consolidated sales.

c. The discovery of information regarding a contingency that existed before the financial statements were issued.

d. The final resolution of a lawsuit explained in a separate paragraph of the auditor's report.

PROBLEMS

[1,2,3]   17-22   During an audit engagement, Harper, CPA, has satisfactorily completed an examination of accounts payable and other liabilities and now plans to determine whether there are any loss contingencies arising from litigation, claims, or assessments.

Required:

What audit procedures should Harper follow with respect to the existence of loss contingencies arising from litigation, claims, and assessments? Do not discuss reporting requirements.

(AICPA, adapted)

[3]   17-23   Cole & Cole, CPAs, are auditing the financial statements of Consolidated Industries Company for the year ended December 31, 2009. On April 2, 2010, an inquiry letter to J. J. Young, Consolidated's outside attorney, was drafted to corroborate the information furnished to Cole by management concerning pending and threatened litigation, claims, and assessments, as well as unasserted claims and assessments. On May 6, 2010, C. R. Cao, Consolidated's chief financial officer, gave Cole a draft of the inquiry letter below for Cole's review before mailing it to Young.

> May 6, 2010
>
> J. J. Young, Attorney at Law
> 123 Main Street
> Anytown, USA
>
> Dear J. J. Young:
>
> In connection with an audit of our financial statements at December 31, 2009, and for the year then ended, management of the company has prepared, and furnished to our auditors, Cole & Cole, CPAs, 456 Broadway, Anytown, USA, a description and evaluation of certain contingencies, including those set forth below involving matters with respect to which you have been engaged and to which you have devoted substantive attention on behalf of the company in the form of legal consultation or representation. Your response should include matters that existed at December 31, 2009. Because of the confidentiality of all these matters, your response may be limited.
>
> In November 2009 an action was brought against the company by an outside salesman alleging breach of contract for sales commissions and pleading a second cause of action for an accounting with respect to claims for fees and commissions. The salesman's action claims damages

of $300,000, but the company believes it has meritorious defenses to the claims. The possible exposure of the company to a successful judgment on behalf of the plaintiff is slight.

In July 2009 an action was brought against the company by Industrial Manufacturing Company ("Industrial") alleging patent infringement and seeking damages of $20 million. The action in U.S. District Court resulted in a decision on October 16, 2009, holding that the company had infringed seven Industrial patents and awarding damages of $14 million. The company vigorously denies these allegations and has filed an appeal with the U.S. Court of Appeals for the Federal Circuit. The appeal process is expected to take approximately two years, but there is some chance that Industrial may ultimately prevail.

Please furnish to our auditors such explanation, if any, that you consider necessary to supplement the foregoing information, including an explanation of those matters as to which your views may differ from those stated and an identification of the omission of any pending or threatened litigation, claims, and assessments or a statement that the list of such matters is complete. Your response may be quoted or referred to in the financial statements without further correspondence with you.

You also consulted on various other matters considered pending or threatened litigation. However, you may not comment on these matters because publicizing them may alert potential plaintiffs to the strengths of their cases. In addition, various other matters probable of assertion that have some chance of an unfavorable outcome, as of December 31, 2009, are unasserted claims and assessments.

C. R. Cao
Chief Financial Officer

Required:
Describe the omissions, ambiguities, and inappropriate statements and terminology in Cao's letter.

(AICPA, adapted)

[5,7]   17-24   Namiki, CPA, is auditing the financial statements of Taylor Corporation for the year ended December 31, 2009. Namiki plans to complete the fieldwork and sign the auditor's report about March 10, 2010. Namiki is concerned about events and transactions occurring after December 31, 2009, that may affect the 2009 financial statements.

Required:
a. What general types of subsequent events require Namiki's consideration and evaluation?
b. What auditing procedures should Namiki consider performing to gather evidence concerning subsequent events?

(AICPA, adapted)

[5,6,7]   17-25   For each of the following items, assume that Josh Feldstein, CPA, is expressing an opinion on Scornick Company's financial statements for the year ended December 31, 2009; that he completed fieldwork on January 21, 2010; and that he now is preparing his opinion to accompany the financial statements. In each item a subsequent event is described. This event was disclosed to the CPA either in connection with his review of subsequent events or after the date on which the auditor has obtained sufficient appropriate audit evidence. Describe the financial statement effects, if any, of each of the following subsequent events. Each of the five items is independent of the other four and is to be considered separately.

1. A large account receivable from Agronowitz Company (material to financial statement presentation) was considered fully collectible at December 31, 2009. Agronowitz suffered a plant explosion on January 25, 2010. Because Agronowitz was uninsured, it is unlikely that the account will be paid.

2. The tax court ruled in favor of the company on January 25, 2010. Litigation involved deductions claimed on the 2006 and 2007 tax returns. In accrued taxes payable, Scornick had provided for the full amount of the potential disallowances. The Internal Revenue Service will not appeal the tax court's ruling.

3. Scornick's Manufacturing Division, whose assets constituted 45 percent of Scornick's total assets at December 31, 2009, was sold on February 1, 2010. The new owner assumed the bonded indebtedness associated with this property.

4. On January 15, 2010, R. E. Fogler, a major investment adviser, issued a negative report on Scornick's long-term prospects. The market price of Scornick's common stock subsequently declined by 40 percent.

5. At its January 5, 2010, meeting, Scornick's board of directors voted to increase substantially the advertising budget for the coming year and authorized a change in advertising agencies.

[8] 17-26 Arenas, an assistant accountant with the firm of Gonzales & Ramirez, CPAs, is auditing the financial statements of Tech Consolidated Industries, Inc. The firm's audit program calls for the preparation of a written management representation letter.

Required:
a. In an audit of financial statements, in what circumstances is the auditor required to obtain a management representation letter? What are the purposes of obtaining the letter?
b. To whom should the representation letter be addressed, and when should it be dated? Who should sign the letter, and what would be the effect of his or her refusal to sign the letter?
c. In what respects may an auditor's other responsibilities be relieved by obtaining a management representation letter?

(AICPA, adapted)

[8] 17-27 During the examination of the annual financial statements of Amis Manufacturing, Inc., a nonpublic company, the company's president, R. Heinrich, and Luddy, the auditor, reviewed the matters that were to be included in a written representation letter. Upon receipt of the following client representation letter, Luddy contacted Heinrich to state that it was incomplete.

> To: E. K. Luddy, CPA
> In connection with your examination of the balance sheet of Amis Manufacturing, Inc., as of December 31, 2009, and the related statements of income, retained earnings, and cash flows for the year then ended, for the purpose of expressing an opinion as to whether the financial statements present fairly the financial position, results of operations, and cash flows of Amis Manufacturing, Inc., in conformity with generally accepted accounting principles, we confirm, to the best of our knowledge and belief,

the following representations made to you during your examination. There were no:

- Plans or intentions that may materially affect the carrying value or classification of assets and liabilities.
- Communications from regulatory agencies concerning noncompliance with, or deficiencies in, financial reporting practices.
- Agreements to repurchase assets previously sold.
- Violations or possible violations of laws or regulations whose effects should be considered for disclosure in the financial statements or as a basis for recording a loss contingency.
- Unasserted claims or assessments that our lawyer has advised are probable of assertion and must be disclosed in accordance with FASB ASC Topic 450, "Contingencies."
- Capital stock repurchase options or agreements or capital stock reserved for options, warrants, conversions, or other requirements.
- Compensating balance or other arrangements involving restrictions on cash balances.

R. Heinrich, President
Amis Manufacturing, Inc.
March 14, 2010

Required:
Identify the other matters that Heinrich's representation letter should specifically confirm.

(AICPA, adapted)

[2,3,7,8,10]   17-28   Items 1 through 16 represent a series of unrelated statements, questions, excerpts, and comments taken from various parts of an auditor's working paper file. Below is a list of the likely sources of the statements, questions, excerpts, and comments. Select, as the best answer for each item, the most likely source. Select only one source for each item. A source may be selected once, more than once, or not at all.

1. During our audit we discovered evidence of the company's failure to safeguard inventory from loss, damage, and misappropriation.
2. The company considers the decline in value of equity securities classified as available-for-sale to be temporary.
3. There have been no communications from regulatory agencies concerning noncompliance with or deficiencies in financial reporting practices.
4. It is our opinion that the possible liability to the company in this proceeding is nominal in amount.
5. As discussed in Note 4 to the financial statements, the company experienced a net loss for the year ended July 31, 2009, and is currently in default under substantially all of its debt agreements. In addition, on September 25, 2009, the company filed a pre-negotiated voluntary petition for relief under Chapter 11 of the U.S. Bankruptcy Code. These matters raise substantial doubt about the company's ability to continue as a going concern.
6. During the year under audit, we were advised that management consulted with Gonzales & Ramirez, CPAs. The purpose of this consultation was to obtain another CPA firm's opinion concerning the company's recognition of certain revenue that we believe should be deferred to future periods. Gonzales & Ramirez's opinion was consistent with our opinion, so management did not recognize the revenue in the current year.

7. The company believes that all material expenditures that have been deferred to future periods will be recoverable.
8. Our use of professional judgment and the assessment of audit risk and materiality for the purpose of our audit mean that matters may have existed that would have been assessed differently by you. We make no representation as to the sufficiency or appropriateness of the information in our working papers for your purposes.
9. Indicate in the space provided below whether this information agrees with your records. If there are exceptions, please provide any information that will assist the auditor in reconciling the difference.
10. Blank checks are maintained in an unlocked cabinet along with the check-signing machine. Blank checks and the check-signing machine should be locked in separate locations to prevent the embezzlement of funds.
11. The company has insufficient expertise and controls over the selection and application of accounting policies that are in conformity with GAAP.
12. The timetable set by management to complete our audit was unreasonable considering the failure of the company's personnel to complete schedules on a timely basis and delays in providing necessary information.
13. Several employees have disabled the antivirus detection software on their PCs because the software slows the processing of data and occasionally rings false alarms. The company should obtain antivirus software that runs continuously at all system entry points and that cannot be disabled by unauthorized personnel.
14. In connection with an audit of our financial statements, please furnish to our auditors a description and evaluation of any pending or probable litigation against our company of which you are aware.
15. The company has no plans or intentions that may materially affect the carrying value or classification of assets and liabilities.
16. In planning the sampling application, was appropriate consideration given to the relationship of the sample to the assertion and to planning materiality?

List of Sources:
A. Practitioner's report on management's assertion about an entity's compliance with specified requirements.
B. Auditor's communications on significant deficiencies and material weakness.
C. Audit inquiry letter to legal counsel.
D. Lawyer's response to audit inquiry letter.
E. Audit committee's communication to the auditor.
F. Auditor's communication to those charged with governance (other than with respect to significant deficiencies and material weakness).
G. Report on the application of accounting principles.
H. Auditor's engagement letter.
I. Letter for underwriters.
J. Accounts receivable confirmation request.
K. Request for bank cutoff statement.
L. Explanatory paragraph of an auditor's report on financial statements.
M. Partner's engagement review notes.
N. Management representation letter.
O. Successor auditor's communication with predecessor auditor.
P. Predecessor auditor's communication with successor auditor.

DISCUSSION CASES

[1,2,3]   17-29   In February 2010, Ceramic Crucibles of America was notified by the state of Colorado that the state was investigating the company's Durango facility to determine if there were any violations of federal or state environmental laws. In formulating your opinion on the 2009 financial statements, you determined that, based primarily on management's representations, the investigation did not pose a serious threat to the company's financial well-being.

The company subsequently retained a local law firm to represent it in dealing with the state commission. At the end of 2009, you concluded that the action did not represent a severe threat. However, you have just received the attorney's letter, which is a little unsettling. It states:

> On January 31, 2010, the U.S. Environmental Protection Agency (EPA) listed the Durango site in Durango, Colorado, on the National Priorities List under the Comprehensive Environmental Response, Compensation, and Liability Act (Superfund). The site includes property adjoining the western boundary of Ceramic Crucibles' plant in Durango and includes parts of Ceramic Crucibles' property. The EPA has listed Ceramic Crucibles as one of the three "potentially responsible parties" ("PRPs") that may be liable for the costs of investigating and cleaning up the site. The EPA has authorized $400,000 for a "Remedial Investigation and Feasibility Study" of the site, but that study will not begin until sometime later in 2010. Thus, we do not deem it possible or appropriate at this time to evaluate this matter with regard to potential liability or cost to the company.

You immediately set up a meeting with Dave Buff, Ceramic Crucibles' vice president; Ron Bonner, the company's attorney; and Margaret Osmond, an attorney who specializes in EPA-related issues. At the meeting you ascertain that

- Ceramic Crucibles bought the Durango facility from TW Industries in 1999.
- TW Industries had operated the facility as a manufacturer of ceramic tiles, and it had used lead extensively in incorporating color into the tile.
- The site has been placed on the National Priorities List ("the List") apparently because each state must have at least one site on the List. All sites on the List are rated on a composite score that reflects the relative extent of pollution. The Durango site has a rating of 8.3 compared to a rating of no less than 25 for the other sites on the List.
- The most severe lead pollution (based on toxicity) is in an area located on the other side of a levee behind Ceramic Crucibles' facilities. Although the area close to the building contains traces of lead pollution, the toxicity in this area is about 50 parts per million (ppm), compared to 19,000 ppm beyond the levee.
- Although Ceramic Crucibles used lead in coloring its crucibles until about 2001, the lead was locked into a ceramic glaze that met FDA requirements for appliances used in the preparation of food. Apparently, the acids used in determining the leaching properties of lead for EPA tests are stronger than that used by the FDA. Since 2001, Ceramic Crucibles has used lead-free mud in its crucibles.
- Affidavits taken from present and former employees of Ceramic Crucibles indicate that no wastewater has been discharged though the levee since Ceramic Crucibles acquired the property in 1999.
- The other PRPs and TW Industries are viable companies that should be in a position to meet their responsibilities resulting from any possible EPA action.

Materiality for purposes of evaluating a potential loss is $10 million to $13 million. This is based on the assumption that the loss would be deductible for income tax purposes. In that case, the loss would represent a reduction in stockholders' equity of 4.5 percent to 7.0 percent. Your best guess is that the company's exposure does not exceed that amount. Further, based on the financial strength of the company and its available lines of credit, you believe such an assessment would not result in financial distress to the company.

The creation of the Environmental Protection Agency (EPA) and that of the Comprehensive Environmental Response, Compensation, and Liability Act is a result of the increasing concern of Americans about pollution. An amendment to the act permits the EPA to perform the cleanup. The EPA has a national priorities list of several thousand sites thought to be severely damaged. The average cost of conducting remedial investigation and feasibility studies ranges from $750,000 to over $1 million, and such studies may take as long as three years. Cleanup costs can often exceed $10 million to $12 million. It is said that the current estimates of $100 billion to clean up nonfederal hazardous waste sites may be conservative.

The law requires the EPA to identify toxic waste sites and request records from PRPs. The PRPs are responsible for the cost of cleanup, but if they lack the funds, the EPA uses its funds for the cleanup. The EPA has spent $3.3 billion from its trust fund and collected only $65 million from polluters since the passage of the legislation.

Required:

a. How would this type of contingency be classified in the accounting literature, and how should it be accounted for?
b. Would the amount be material to the financial statements?
c. What additional evidence would you gather, and what kinds of representations should you require from the client?
d. Should the investigation affect your opinion on those financial statements?

[8]   17-30   Medical Products, Inc. (MPI), was created in 2007 and entered the optical equipment industry. Its made-to-order optical equipment requires large investments in research and development. To fund these needs, MPI made a public stock offering, which was completed in 2008. Although the offering was moderately successful, MPI's ambitious management is convinced that it must report a good profit this year (2009) to maintain the current market price of the stock. MPI's president recently stressed this point when he told his controller, Pam Adams, "If we don't make $1.25 million pretax this year, our stock will tank."

Adams was pleased that even after adjustments for accrued vacation pay, 2009 pretax profit was $1.35 million. However, MPI's auditors, Hammer & Bammer (HB), proposed an additional adjustment for inventory valuation that would reduce this profit to $900,000. HB's proposed adjustment had been discussed during the 2008 audit.

An additional issue discussed in 2008 was MPI's failure to accrue executive vacation pay. At that time HB did not insist on the adjustment because the amount ($20,000) was not material to the 2008 results and because MPI agreed to begin accruing vacation pay in future years. The cumulative accrued executive vacation pay amounts to $300,000 and has been accrued at the end of 2009.

The inventory issue arose in 2007 when MPI purchased $450,000 of specialized computer components to be used with its optical scanners for a special order. The order was subsequently canceled, and HB proposed to write down this inventory in 2008. MPI explained, however, that the components could easily be sold without a loss during 2009, and no adjustment was made. However, the equipment was not sold by the end of 2009, and prospects for future sales were considered nonexistent. HB proposed a write-off of the entire $450,000 in 2009.

The audit partner, Johanna Schmidt, insisted that Adams make the inventory adjustment. Adams tried to convince her that there were other alternatives, but Schmidt was adamant. Adams knew the inventory was worthless, but she reminded Schmidt of the importance of this year's reported income. Adams continued her argument, "You can't take both the write-down and the vacation accrual in one year; it doesn't fairly present our performance this year. If you insist on taking that write-down, I'm taking back the accrual. Actually, that's a good idea because the executives are such workaholics, they don't take their vacations anyway."

As Adams calmed down, she said, "Johanna, let's be reasonable; we like you—and we want to continue our good working relationship with your firm into the future. But we won't have a future unless we put off this accrual for another year."

Required:
a. Should the inventory adjustment be made in the 2009 financial statements?
b. Irrespective of your decision regarding the inventory adjustment, what is your reaction to Adams' suggestion to release the vacation accrual? Should the auditor insist on keeping the accrual of the executives' vacation pay?
c. Consider the conflict between Adams and Schmidt. Assuming that Schmidt believes the inventory adjustment and vacation pay accrual must be made and that she does not want to lose MPI as a client, what should she do?

INTERNET ASSIGNMENTS

[1]   17-31   A number of companies have pending lawsuits or other contingent liabilities reported in their financial statements.

Required:
a. Search the EDGAR database found at http://www.sec.gov/edgar/searchedgar/companysearch.html to find a company's 10-K that reports a contingent liability. Write a paragraph summarizing one of the liabilities found in the financial statements. Did the company disclose the liability in the footnotes only, or did it recognize the liability in the financial statements?
b. What procedures might the auditors use to search for the contingent liabilities listed in part a?

[5]   17-32   It is becoming increasingly common for an accounting firm to withdraw its opinion on a set of previously issued financial statements. Use an Internet search engine to find a recent example of a company that has had to restate its financials and whose public accounting firm has withdrawn its opinion.

HANDS-ON CASES

www.mhhe.com/ messier7e	Visit the book's Online Learning Center for problem material to be completed using the ACL software packaged with your new text.

KAPLAN
CPA Review

www.mhhe.com/ messier7e	**Lee Explorations** This simulation provides a comprehensive review of much of the material covered in this chapter, including representation letters, going-concern considerations, and communication with the audit committee. *To begin this simulation, visit the book's Online Learning Center.*

CHAPTER 18

LEARNING OBJECTIVES

Upon completion of this chapter you will

[1] Understand the various components of the standard unqualified financial statement audit report.

[2] Know the situations that result in the addition of explanatory language to the standard unqualified audit report.

[3] Be able to explain the conditions that lead to a departure from the standard unqualified audit report.

[4] Know the types of financial statement audit reports other than unqualified.

[5] Be able to explain the effect of materiality on the auditor's choice of audit reports.

[6] Understand the situations that may cause different types of reports on comparative financial statements.

[7] Know the auditor's responsibility for other information in documents containing audited financial statements.

[8] Understand the auditor's reporting responsibility for financial statements prepared on a comprehensive basis other than GAAP.

[9] Understand the auditor's responsibility for reporting on specified elements, accounts, or items of a financial statement.

[10] Understand the auditor's reporting responsibility for compliance with contractual agreements or regulatory requirements related to financial statements.

RELEVANT ACCOUNTING AND AUDITING PRONOUNCEMENTS

FASB ASC Topic 250, Accounting Changes and Error Corrections

FASB ASC Topic 450, Contingencies

AT 201, Agreed-Upon Procedures Engagements

AU 341, The Auditor's Consideration of an Entity's Ability to Continue as a Going Concern

AU 411, The Meaning of Present Fairly in Conformity with Generally Accepted Accounting Principles

AU 420, Consistency of Application of Generally Accepted Accounting Principles

AU 504, Association with Financial Statements

AU 508, Reports on Audited Financial Statements

AU 532, Restricting the Use of an Auditor's Report

AU 543, Part of Audit Performed by Other Independent Auditors

AU 550, Other Information in Documents Containing Audited Financial Statements

AU 623, Special Reports

Reports on Audited Financial Statements

Major Phases of an Audit

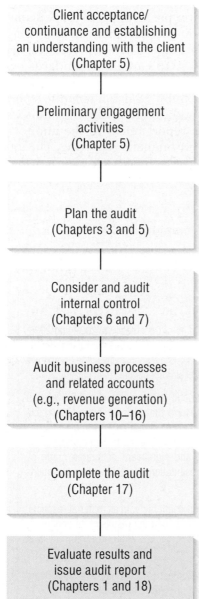

Client acceptance/
continuance and establishing
an understanding with the client
(Chapter 5)

Preliminary engagement
activities
(Chapter 5)

Plan the audit
(Chapters 3 and 5)

Consider and audit
internal control
(Chapters 6 and 7)

Audit business processes
and related accounts
(e.g., revenue generation)
(Chapters 10–16)

Complete the audit
(Chapter 17)

Evaluate results and
issue audit report
(Chapters 1 and 18)

This chapter discusses the auditor's report for audits of financial statements. The audit report is the most important "deliverable" on an audit engagement. In accordance with the fourth standard of reporting, whenever an auditor is associated with a client's financial statements, the auditor's report must contain an opinion regarding the financial statements taken as a whole or the reasons why an opinion cannot be issued. An auditor is associated with financial statements when he or she has consented to the use of his or her firm's name in a document such as an annual report.

The purpose of the fourth standard of reporting is to enable shareholders, bondholders, bankers, and other third parties who rely on the financial statements to understand the degree of responsibility taken by the auditor. To assist in accomplishing this goal, the auditing profession has adopted standardized wording for audit reports. As a result, you will notice that most audit reports look very much alike. This approach helps prevent misunderstandings in the message being communicated by the auditor to the users of the financial statements. At the same time, some argue that the "boilerplate" nature of the audit report prevents the auditor from conveying subjective information that could be useful to users of the financial statements. Regardless, it is important to keep in mind that the financial statements are the representations of management and that management is responsible for the fairness of the statements in conformity with GAAP.

In addition to reporting on financial statements, auditors must also perform and report on an audit of internal control over financial reporting for public company clients. Chapter 7 discusses the nature of the audit of internal control over financial reporting and presents the auditor's reporting requirements specific to the audit of internal control.

Reporting on the Financial Statement Audit: The Standard Unqualified Audit Report

[LO 1] Chapter 1 presented the auditor's standard unqualified financial statement audit report. This report is issued when the audit has been performed in accordance with GAAS, the auditor has gathered sufficient evidence, and the auditor believes that the financial statements conform to GAAP. Exhibit 18–1 shows the auditor's standard unqualified audit report for a public company client. This report contains eight elements: (1) the report title, (2) the addressee, (3) the introductory paragraph, (4) the scope paragraph, (5) the opinion paragraph, (6) an explanatory paragraph referring to the audit of internal control over financial reporting, (7) the name of the auditor, and (8) the audit report date. The EarthWear report refers to the audit of internal control and to the PCAOB's auditing standards because EarthWear is a publicly traded company and is subject to public company reporting requirements. The report presented in Exhibit 18–1 is a *separate report* on the financial statement audit, but as noted, in addition to giving the auditor's opinion on EarthWear's financial statements, the report refers to the auditor's opinion relating to the audit of internal control over financial reporting. The auditor's opinions on the financial statements and the effectiveness of internal control are often presented together, in a combined report format. However, when

EXHIBIT 18–1	The Auditor's Standard Unqualified Report—Comparative Financial Statements (with explanatory paragraph)
Title:	REPORT OF INDEPENDENT REGISTERED PUBLIC ACCOUNTING FIRM
Addressee:	*To the Stockholders of EarthWear Clothiers:*
Introductory paragraph:	We have audited the consolidated balance sheets of EarthWear Clothiers as of December 31, 2009 and 2008, and the related consolidated statements of operations, stockholders' equity, and cash flows for each of the three years in the period ended December 31, 2009. These financial statements are the responsibility of the Company's management. Our responsibility is to express an opinion on these financial statements based on our audits.
Scope paragraph:	We conducted our audits in accordance with the standards of the Public Company Accounting Oversight Board (United States). Those standards require that we plan and perform the audit to obtain reasonable assurance about whether the financial statements are free of material misstatement. An audit includes examining, on a test basis, evidence supporting the amounts and disclosures in the financial statements. An audit also includes assessing the accounting principles used and significant estimates made by management, as well as evaluating the overall financial statement presentation. We believe that our audits provide a reasonable basis for our opinion.
Opinion paragraph:	In our opinion, the consolidated financial statements referred to above present fairly, in all material respects, the financial position of the Company as of December 31, 2009 and 2008, and the results of its operations and its cash flows for each of the three years in the period ended December 31, 2009, in conformity with U.S. generally accepted accounting principles.
Explanatory paragraph referring to the audit of internal control:	We also have audited, in accordance with the standards of the Public Company Accounting Oversight Board (United States), the effectiveness of EarthWear Clothiers' internal control over financial reporting as of December 31, 2009, based on criteria established in Internal Control—Integrated Framework issued by the Committee of Sponsoring Organizations of the Treadway Commission (COSO), and our report dated February 15, 2010, expressed an unqualified opinion that EarthWear Clothiers maintained, in all material respects, effective internal control over financial reporting.
Name of auditor:	*Willis & Adams* *Boise, Idaho*
Date of report:	*February 15, 2010*

the two opinions are presented separately, as in Exhibit 18–1, the reports must have the same date and each must include an explanatory paragraph referring to the opinion expressed in the other report. Chapter 7 addresses reporting on the audit of internal control.

Explanatory Language Added to the Standard Unqualified Financial Statement Audit Report

❧ [LO 2] Under certain circumstances the auditor will modify the wording or add an explanatory paragraph to the standard unqualified audit report. In addition to the explanatory paragraph referring to the audit of internal control for public companies, there are four situations that may require the auditor to modify wording or add explanatory language to an unqualified report:

1. Opinion based in part on the report of another auditor.
2. Going concern.
3. Lack of consistency in the financial statements due to accounting changes.
4. Emphasis of a matter.

The first situation results in a modification of the wording for the introductory, scope, and opinion paragraphs included in the standard unqualified audit report. The other three situations lead to the addition of an explanatory paragraph following the opinion paragraph without any modification to the wording of the introductory, scope, or opinion paragraphs. The audit reports that are issued in these situations are still considered unqualified opinions and are discussed in this section.[1]

Opinion Based in Part on the Report of Another Auditor

On some audit engagements, parts of the audit may be completed by a separate, unaffiliated public accounting firm. For example, in reporting on consolidated financial statements, one of the client's subsidiaries might be located in a foreign country where the accounting firm does not have a strong presence, and thus may be audited by other auditors. In such cases, the auditor for the parent company must be satisfied that he or she is the *principal auditor*. This is normally determined by the portion of the consolidated financial statements audited by the parent-company auditor in relation to the portion of the consolidated financial statements audited by the other independent auditors.

The principal auditor at this point must decide whether to refer to the other auditors in the report. The principal auditor first assesses the *professional reputation* and *independence* of the other auditors. If the principal auditor is satisfied as to the professional reputation and independence of the other auditors and their audit work, an opinion may be expressed without referring to the work of the other auditors in the audit report. In so doing, the auditor accepts full responsibility for the work done and conclusions drawn by the other auditors.

However, in most situations where the subsidiary represents a material amount in the consolidated financial statements, the principal auditor refers to the other auditors. In referencing the other auditors, the principal auditor is sharing responsibility for the audit report.

---

[1]Until recently another condition existed that could result in the addition of explanatory language to an unqualified auditor's report. In certain circumstances (referred to as the "Rule 203 exception"), if the auditor agreed with the client that following GAAP would mislead financial statement users, the auditor could issue an unqualified opinion on financial statements that were not in accordance with GAAP, and add an explanatory paragraph to describe the situation. The exception was very rarely invoked, and was essentially eliminated with the FASB's adoption of the Accounting Standards Codification in September 2009.

EXHIBIT 18–2	Opinion Based in Part on the Report of Another Auditor

Independent Auditor's Report

To the Stockholders of
Collins Company:

We have audited the consolidated balance sheets of Collins Company as of December 31, 2009 and 2008, and the related consolidated statements of income, retained earnings, and cash flows for the years then ended. These financial statements are the responsibility of the Company's management. Our responsibility is to express an opinion on these financial statements based on our audits. *We did not audit the financial statements of Furillo Company, a wholly owned subsidiary, whose statements reflect total assets of $25,450,000 and $23,750,000 as of December 31, 2009 and 2008, respectively, and total revenues of $42,781,000 and $40,553,000 for the years then ended. Those statements were audited by other auditors whose report has been furnished to us, and our opinion, insofar as it relates to the amounts included for Furillo Company, is based solely on the report of the other auditors.*

We conducted our audit in accordance with auditing standards generally accepted in the United States of America. Those standards require that we plan and perform the audit to obtain reasonable assurance about whether the financial statements are free of material misstatement. An audit includes consideration of internal control over financial reporting as a basis for designing audit procedures that are appropriate in the circumstances, but not for the purpose of expressing an opinion on the effectiveness of the Company's internal control over financial reporting. Accordingly, we express no such opinion. An audit also includes examining, on a test basis, evidence supporting the amounts and disclosures in the financial statements, assessing the accounting principles used and significant estimates made by management, as well as evaluating the overall financial statement presentation. We believe that our audits and the report of other auditors provide a reasonable basis for our opinion.

In our opinion, *based on our audits and the report of the other auditors,* the consolidated financial statements referred to above present fairly, in all material respects, the financial position of Collins Company as of December 31, 2009 and 2008, and the results of its operations and its cash flows for the years then ended in conformity with accounting principles generally accepted in the United States of America.

Agassi, Connors, Evert & Co.
February 12, 2010

The portion of the consolidated financial statements audited by the other auditors is disclosed in the report. Exhibit 18–2 is an example of a report in which the principal auditor has referred to the other auditors. Generally, the other auditors are not referenced by name in the report. (For illustrative purposes only, the new wording is shown in italics.) Collins Company is a privately held company. Thus, the report indicates that the audit was conducted "in accordance with generally accepted auditing standards" and is titled "Independent Auditor's Report." If Collins were a public company, the report would be titled "Report of Independent Registered Public Accounting Firm" and would indicate that the audit was conducted "in accordance with the standards of the Public Company Accounting Oversight Board (United States)." Note also that this report expressly indicates that while internal control was considered for the purpose of designing financial statement audit procedures, no opinion is expressed on the effectiveness of internal control over financial reporting. Private companies can opt to have their audits done in accordance with PCAOB standards, in which case their audit reports must conform to PCAOB standards. The rest of the exhibits in the first part of this chapter represent audits of nonpublic companies. However, with the exceptions noted above, the wording is similar for audits of public companies.

If the other auditor's report is other than a standard unqualified audit report, the principal auditor needs to determine the nature of the departure and its significance in relation to the overall financial statements. If the departure is not material, the principal auditor need not refer to the departure in his or her report. If the principal auditor assesses that the departure is material, it may be necessary to refer to the matter underlying the other auditor's qualified opinion.

Going Concern

A basic assumption that underlies financial reporting is that an entity will continue as a going concern (i.e., that it will stay in business). As discussed in Chapter 17, auditing standards state that the auditor has a responsibility to evaluate whether

EXHIBIT 18–3	Unqualified Financial Statement Audit Report with an Explanatory Paragraph for Going-Concern Problems

Independent Auditor's Report

[*Standard introductory, scope, and opinion paragraphs*]

The accompanying financial statements have been prepared assuming that the Company will continue as a going concern. As discussed in Note 6 to the financial statements, the Company has suffered recurring losses from operations and has a net capital deficiency that raises substantial doubt about its ability to continue as a going concern. Management's plans in regard to these matters are also described in Note 6. The financial statements do not include any adjustments that might result from the outcome of this uncertainty.

there is substantial doubt about the entity's ability to continue as a going concern for a reasonable period of time, not to exceed one year beyond the date of the financial statements being audited.

When the auditor concludes that there is substantial doubt about an entity's ability to continue as a going concern, the auditor should consider the possible effects on the financial statements and the related disclosures. Additionally, the audit report should include an explanatory paragraph, such as the one shown in Exhibit 18–3. Alternatively, the auditor may disclaim an opinion on the entity. If the entity's disclosures with respect to its ability to continue as a going concern are inadequate, a departure from GAAP exists, resulting in a qualified or an adverse opinion (discussed later in this chapter). If a client received a going concern report in the prior period and the doubt regarding going concern is removed in the current period, the explanatory paragraph included with the prior year's audit report is not included with the auditor's report covering the comparative financial statements.

Lack of Consistency

A fundamental principle of accounting is that it should result in financial statements that are consistent and comparable across periods. The auditor's standard unqualified audit report implies that the comparability of the financial statements is not affected by changes in accounting principles or that any such change is immaterial. FASB ASC Topic 250, "Accounting Changes and Error Corrections," governs the accounting for changes in accounting principles. From the auditor's perspective, accounting changes can be categorized into changes that affect consistency and those that do not affect consistency.

Practice INSIGHT	FASB ASC Topic 250 requires "retrospective application" for accounting changes and corrections of errors. Retrospective application is the application of a different accounting principle to one or more previously issued financial statements, or to the statement of financial position at the beginning of the current period as if that principle had always been used, or a change to financial statements of prior accounting periods to present the financial statements of a new reporting entity as if it had existed in those prior years.

Changes Affecting Consistency   If a change in accounting principle or in the method of its application materially affects the comparability and the consistency of the financial statements, and the auditor concurs with the change, the auditor should discuss the change in an explanatory paragraph to highlight the lack of consistency. Auditing standards refer to the following accounting

EXHIBIT 18–4	**Unqualified Report with an Explanatory Paragraph for a Lack of Consistency**

Independent Auditor's Report

[*Standard wording for the introductory, scope, and opinion paragraphs*]

As discussed in Note 7 to the financial statements, the Company changed its method of computing depreciation in 2009.

changes as affecting comparability and consistency and requiring an explanatory paragraph:

1. *Change in accounting principle.* An example is a change from straight-line depreciation to an accelerated method for depreciating equipment.
2. *Change in reporting entity.* An example is the consolidation of a major subsidiary's financial statements with the parent company's financial statements in the previous year and accounting for the subsidiary on a cost or equity basis in the current year.
3. *Correction of an error in principle.* This refers to a situation in which a client has used an accounting principle that is not acceptable (for example, replacement cost for inventory) in prior years but changes to an acceptable accounting principle (such as FIFO) in the current year.

Exhibit 18–4 displays an example of an unqualified opinion with an explanatory paragraph for an accounting change that results in a lack of consistency. Note that adding an explanatory paragraph does not eliminate the auditor's responsibility to evaluate the adequacy of the required financial statement disclosures relating to accounting changes and corrections of errors.

Changes Not Affecting Consistency
Other changes may affect comparability but not consistency in the use of accounting principles. These include:

1. *Change in accounting estimate.* A change in the service life of a depreciable asset is an example of a change in estimate.
2. *Correction of an error that does not involve an accounting principle.* An example would be a mathematical mistake in a previously issued financial statement.
3. *Change in classification and reclassification.* If an item was included in operating expenses last year and in administrative expenses in the current year, this would be a change in classification but not in accounting principle.
4. *Change expected to have a material future effect.* This would be a change in accounting principle that has an immaterial effect in the current year but is expected to have a material effect in future years.

Changes that affect comparability but not consistency are normally disclosed in the notes to the financial statements. Such changes do not require an explanatory paragraph in the auditor's report.

Emphasis of
a Matter

Under certain circumstances an auditor may want to emphasize a specific matter regarding the financial statements even though he or she intends to express an unqualified opinion. Such information is presented in an explanatory paragraph. Two examples of situations that might cause the auditor to add an explanatory paragraph are significant related-party transactions that are appropriately disclosed by the client and important events occurring after the balance sheet date.

No explanatory paragraph is required in the auditor's report when a client has an FASB ASC Topic 450 contingency that is properly disclosed in the client's financial statements or footnotes.

Departures from an Unqualified Financial Statement Audit Report

While the vast majority of audit opinions issued to clients are unqualified, the auditor can assume differing degrees of responsibility on financial statements by issuing opinions that depart from the unqualified report. There are three such types of audit reports available to the auditor. We next discuss the conditions for issuing reports that depart from the unqualified report, and we then explain the nature of these reports.

Conditions for Departure

❧ [LO 3]

To this point we have been discussing the unqualified audit report, with or without additional explanatory language. Let's now take a look at the circumstances in which an audit report might depart from an unqualified or "clean" opinion. An auditor may be unable to express an unqualified opinion in three situations:

1. ***Scope limitation.*** A scope limitation results from an inability to collect sufficient competent evidence, such as when management or some set of circumstances prevents the auditor from conducting an audit procedure that the auditor considers necessary.

2. ***Departure from GAAP.*** A departure from GAAP exists when the financial statements are prepared or presented in a manner that conflicts with GAAP, whether due to error or fraud.

3. ***Lack of independence of the auditor.*** A lack of independence arises when the auditor and the client have any financial, business, or personal relationship prohibited by professional standards. The auditor must comply with the second general standard and Rule 101 of the *Code of Professional Conduct* in order to issue an unqualified opinion.

Practice
INSIGHT

Keep in mind that an unqualified opinion on the financial statement audit does not necessarily mean that the opinion on the audit of internal control will be unqualified. In fact, an auditor can issue an adverse opinion on the audit of internal control, and still issue an unqualified opinion on the financial statement audit if the audit evidence supports the conclusion that the financial statements are fairly presented.

Types of Financial Statement Audit Reports Other than Unqualified

❧ [LO 4]

The three types of reports available to the auditor other than unqualified are:

1. ***Qualified.*** The auditor qualifies his or her opinion when either a scope limitation or a specific departure from GAAP exists, but *overall* the financial statements present fairly in conformity with GAAP. If the auditor decides to qualify a report for a scope limitation, the report describes why the limitation arose, and indicates that the financial statements present fairly *except for* the possible effects of the limitation. If the auditor qualifies a report for a GAAP departure, the report describes the nature and impact of the faulty accounting, and indicates that the financial statements present fairly *except for* the effects of the departure. Note that a qualified report always uses the words "except for."

2. ***Disclaimer.*** The auditor disclaims an opinion on the financial statements either because there is insufficient appropriate evidence to form an opinion on the overall financial statements or because there is a lack of

FIGURE 18–1	An Overview of Financial Statement Audit Reporting

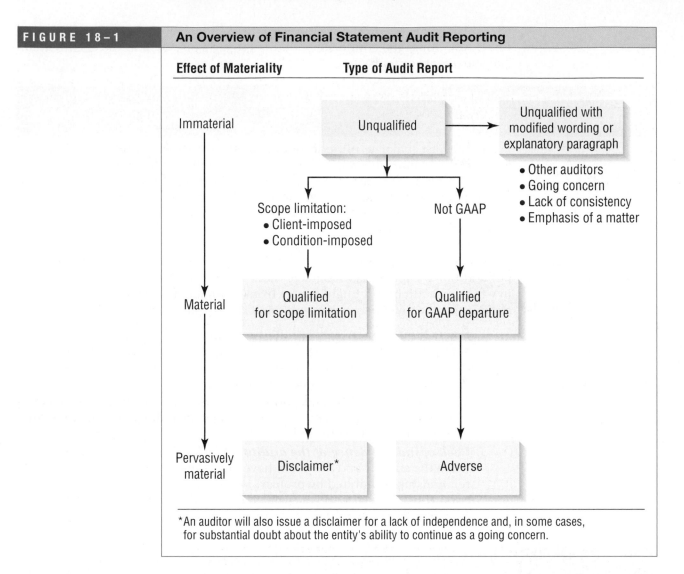

Effect of Materiality   Type of Audit Report

Immaterial → Unqualified → Unqualified with modified wording or explanatory paragraph
- Other auditors
- Going concern
- Lack of consistency
- Emphasis of a matter

Scope limitation:
- Client-imposed
- Condition-imposed

Not GAAP

Material → Qualified for scope limitation   Qualified for GAAP departure

Pervasively material → Disclaimer*   Adverse

*An auditor will also issue a disclaimer for a lack of independence and, in some cases, for substantial doubt about the entity's ability to continue as a going concern.

independence. In a disclaimer the auditor explains the reasons for withholding an opinion and explicitly indicates that no opinion is expressed.

3. ***Adverse.*** The auditor issues an adverse opinion when the financial statements do not present fairly due to a GAAP departure that materially affects the financial statements overall. In an adverse report the auditor explains the nature and size of the misstatement and states the opinion that the financial statements do not present fairly in accordance with GAAP.

The choice of audit report depends on both the nature and the materiality of the condition giving rise to the departure from the unqualified report. Figure 18–1 presents an overview of the auditor's reporting options, including the type of report to be issued under various conditions and the effect of materiality. We believe you will find Figure 18–1 to be one of the most helpful figures presented in this text—study it carefully!

The Effect of Materiality on Financial Statement Reporting

✂ [LO 5]

The concept of materiality plays a major role in the auditor's choice of audit reports. If the departure is judged by the auditor to be immaterial, a standard unqualified audit report can be issued. As the materiality of the condition increases, the auditor must judge the effect of the item on the overall financial statements.

When the auditor is faced with a *scope limitation*, the assessment of the omitted procedure(s) should include the nature and magnitude of the potential effects of the unexamined area and its significance to the overall financial statements. If the potential effects relate to many items in the financial statements or if the effect of the item is so significant that the financial statements are affected overall, the auditor is more likely to issue a disclaimer than a qualified report. In other words, the *pervasiveness* of the scope limitation's effect on the financial statements determines whether the auditor should issue a qualified opinion or disclaim an opinion. For example, suppose an auditor is unable to perform certain audit procedures considered necessary in determining the fairness of a client's inventory balance. Assume further that inventory represents approximately 10 percent of total assets. In such a situation, the auditor would probably consider the item material, but not to the extent that the financial statements are not presented fairly overall, and would most likely issue a qualified opinion. However, if inventory represented a larger percentage of total assets (such as 30 percent), the effect likely would be considered highly material and would thus lead the auditor to disclaim an opinion on the financial statements.

Judgments concerning the effects of a departure from GAAP are handled similarly. If the departure from GAAP is immaterial, the auditor issues an unqualified opinion. If the departure from GAAP is material but the financial statements still present fairly overall, the auditor issues a qualified opinion. If the departure is so pervasive that its effects are highly material, the auditor issues an adverse opinion. For example, suppose that a client accounts for leased assets as operating leases when proper accounting requires that the leases be capitalized. If a client has only one small piece of equipment that is accounted for inappropriately, the auditor will probably issue an unqualified opinion because the item is not material. However, if the client has many significant leased assets that are accounted for as operating leases instead of capitalized leases, the auditor will normally issue a qualified or adverse opinion, depending on the magnitude of the problem.

Materiality is not a factor in considering an auditor's independence. When according to the Code of Professional Conduct or other rules an auditor is not independent, the auditor must disclaim an opinion regardless of the significance of the condition that resulted in the lack of independence.

Discussion of Conditions Requiring Other Types of Financial Statement Audit Reports

Scope Limitation

A scope limitation results from an inability to obtain sufficient appropriate evidence about some component of the financial statements. This occurs because the auditor is unable to apply all the audit procedures considered necessary. Such restrictions on the scope of the audit may be imposed by the client or by the circumstances of the engagement. Auditors should be particularly cautious when a client limits the scope of the engagement because in such a situation the client may be trying to prevent the auditor from discovering material misstatements. Auditing standards suggest that when restrictions imposed by the client significantly limit the scope of the engagement, the auditor should consider disclaiming an opinion on the financial statements. However, some scope limitations arise due to reasons beyond the control of the client, such as a fire that destroys accounting records. If the auditor can overcome such a scope limitation by performing alternative procedures, a standard unqualified audit report can be issued.

A number of these types of situations can occur on audit engagements. For example, auditing standards require that the auditor observe the physical inventory count. However, circumstances may prevent the auditor from doing so. Suppose that the auditor is not engaged to conduct the audit until after the end of the period. In such a circumstance, the auditor may not be able to perform a number of audit procedures, including observing the year-end inventory count. If such

EXHIBIT 18-5	**Disclaimer of Financial Statement Audit Opinion—Scope Limitation**

Independent Auditor's Report

We were engaged to audit the accompanying balance sheet of Kosar Company as of December 31, 2009 and 2008, and the related statements of income, retained earnings, and cash flows for the years then ended. These financial statements are the responsibility of the Company's management.

[*Scope paragraph of standard report should be omitted*]

We were unable to observe the taking of physical inventories stated in the accompanying financial statements at $4,550,000 as of December 31, 2009, and at $4,275,000 as of December 31, 2008, since those dates were prior to the time we were engaged as auditors for the Company. The Company's records do not permit the application of other auditing procedures regarding the existence of inventories.

Since we did not observe physical inventories and we were not able to apply other auditing procedures to satisfy ourselves as to inventory quantities, the scope of our work was not sufficient to enable us to express, and we do not express, an opinion on these financial statements.

EXHIBIT 18-6	**Qualified Financial Statement Audit Report—Scope Limitation**

Independent Auditor's Report

[*Standard wording for the introductory paragraph*]

Except as discussed in the following paragraph, we conducted our audits in accordance with auditing standards generally accepted in the United States of America. Those standards require that . . . [*same wording as for the remainder of the standard scope paragraph*].

We were unable to obtain audited financial statements supporting the Company's investment in a foreign affiliate stated at $12,500,000 and $11,700,000 at December 31, 2009 and 2008, respectively, or its equity in earnings of that affiliate of $1,200,000 and $1,050,000, which is included in net income for the years then ended as described in Note 10 to the financial statements; nor were we able to satisfy ourselves as to the carrying value of the investment in the foreign affiliate or the equity in its earnings by other auditing procedures.

In our opinion, except for the effects of such adjustments, if any, as might have been determined to be necessary had we been able to examine evidence regarding the foreign affiliate and earnings, the financial statements referred to . . . [*same wording as for the remainder of the standard opinion paragraph*].

deficiencies in evidence cannot be overcome by other auditing procedures, the auditor will have to issue a qualified opinion or a disclaimer. Exhibit 18–5 is an example of a disclaimer of opinion due to this type of scope limitation.

Another example occurs when a client requests that the auditor not confirm accounts receivable because of concerns over customer relations. If the auditor is satisfied that the client's reasons for not confirming are legitimate and is unable to apply alternative audit procedures to determine fairness of the receivables, he or she would qualify the opinion or disclaim an opinion depending on the materiality of accounts receivable in the context of the financial statements. Exhibit 18–6 is an example of a qualified report for such a scope limitation.

Note that in all three examples the paragraph that explains the scope limitation is presented *before* the opinion or disclaimer paragraph.

Statements Not in Conformity with GAAP

If the financial statements are materially affected by a departure from GAAP, the auditor should express a qualified or adverse opinion. Examples of these types of departures include an accounting principle that is not acceptable, inadequate disclosure, or an unjustified change in accounting principle.

When the financial statements include an accounting principle that is not acceptable, the auditor should issue a qualified or adverse opinion, depending on materiality. When the auditor expresses a qualified opinion, a separate explanatory paragraph is added to the report *before* the opinion paragraph. The explanatory paragraph discloses the effects of the departure on the financial statements and the opinion paragraph will include the words "except for." Exhibit 18–7 is an example of a report that is qualified because of the use of an accounting principle that is not in accordance with GAAP.

If the departure's effect is so pervasive that the financial statements taken as a whole do not present the client's financial position, results of operations, and cash flows fairly in accordance with GAAP, the auditor should issue an adverse opinion. When an adverse opinion is issued, the auditor should add an explanatory paragraph that *precedes* the opinion paragraph. The explanatory paragraph should discuss the reasons for the adverse opinion and the effects of the departure on the financial statements. The opinion paragraph is modified to state that the financial statements *do not present fairly* in conformity with GAAP. Exhibit 18–8 is an example of an adverse report.

EXHIBIT 18-7	Qualified Financial Statement Audit Report—Not in Conformity with Generally Accepted Accounting Principles

Independent Auditor's Report

[Standard wording for the introductory and scope paragraphs]

The Company has excluded, from property and debt in the accompanying balance sheets, certain lease obligations that, in our opinion, should be capitalized in order to conform with generally accepted accounting principles. If these lease obligations were capitalized, property would be increased by $7,500,000 and $7,200,000, long-term debt by $6,900,000 and $6,600,000, and retained earnings by $1,420,000 and $1,290,000 as of December 31, 2009 and 2008, respectively. Additionally, net income would be increased by $250,000 and $220,000 and earnings per share would be increased by $.25 and $.22, respectively, for the years then ended.

In our opinion, except for the effects of not capitalizing certain lease obligations as discussed in the preceding paragraph, the financial statements referred to above present fairly, in all material respects, the financial position of the company as of December 31, 2009 and 2008, and the results of its operations and its cash flows for each of the three years in the period ended December 31, 2009, in conformity with the U.S. generally accepted accounting principles.

EXHIBIT 18-8	Adverse Financial Statement Audit Opinion—Not in Conformity with Generally Accepted Accounting Principles

Independent Auditor's Report

[Standard wording for the introductory and scope paragraphs]

As discussed in Note 6 to the financial statements, the Company carries its property, plant, and equipment accounts at appraisal values and determines depreciation on the basis of such values. Generally accepted accounting principles require that property, plant, and equipment be stated at an amount not in excess of cost, reduced by depreciation based on such amount. Because of the departures from generally accepted accounting principles identified above, as of December 31, 2009 and 2008, respectively, inventories have been increased $1,500,000 and $1,340,000 by inclusion in manufacturing overhead of depreciation in excess of that based on cost; property, plant, and equipment, less accumulated depreciation, is carried at $13,475,000 and $12,950,000 in excess of an amount based on the cost to the Company. For the years ended December 31, 2009 and 2008, cost of goods sold has been increased $4,200,000 and $3,600,000, respectively, because of the effects of the depreciation accounting referred to above, resulting in a decrease in net income of $2,520,000 and $2,160,000, respectively.

In our opinion, because of the effects of the matters discussed in the preceding paragraph, the financial statements referred to above do not present fairly, in conformity with accounting principles generally accepted in the United States of America, the financial position of Morton Company as of December 31, 2009 and 2008, or the results of its operation or its cash flows for the years then ended.

If a client fails to disclose information in the financial statements or footnotes as required by GAAP (e.g., significant related party transactions), the auditor should issue a qualified or adverse report, depending on the materiality of the omission. The auditor should provide the omitted information in the report, if practicable, unless the auditor is specifically not required by auditing standards to do so. For example, one situation in which the auditor would modify the opinion but would not have to provide the missing information is where the client has declined to include a statement of cash flows. Auditing standards do not require that the auditor prepare a statement when one has been omitted by the client. Exhibit 18–9 is a qualified report for inadequate disclosure. As a practical matter, qualified and adverse reports are quite rare because most clients are willing to make the financial statement adjustments needed in order to obtain a clean opinion.

Auditor Not Independent

Much of the value that users of financial statements place on the auditor's report is based on the assumption of an unbiased relationship between the auditor and the client (see Chapter 19). There are few situations in which an auditor would knowingly agree to audit a client's financial statements where independence between the two parties did not exist. However, it is possible that an auditor could be engaged by a client, believing that all members of the audit team were independent of the client. At the end of the engagement, it might come to the audit partner's attention that a member of the audit team had a prohibited financial interest in the client. This situation might jeopardize the audit firm's independence and result in the issuance of a report similar to the one shown in Exhibit 18–10.

EXHIBIT 18–9	**Qualified Financial Statement Audit Report—Inadequate Disclosure**

Independent Auditor's Report

We have audited the accompanying balance sheets of O'Dea Company as of December 31, 2009 and 2008, and the related statements of income and retained earnings for the years ended. These financial statements are the responsibility of the Company's management. Our responsibility is to express an opinion on these financial statements based on our audit.

[Standard wording for the scope paragraph]

The Company declined to present a statement of cash flows for the years ended December 31, 2009 and 2008. Presentation of such statement summarizing the Company's operating, investing, and financing activities is required by accounting principles generally accepted in the United States of America.

    In our opinion, except that the omission of a statement of cash flows results in an incomplete presentation as explained in the preceding paragraph, the financial statements referred to . . . *[same wording as for the remainder of the standard opinion paragraph]*.

EXHIBIT 18–10	**Disclaimer of Financial Statement Audit Opinion When the Auditor Is Not Independent**

Accountant's Report

We are not independent with respect to Jordan Company, Inc. Accordingly, we do not express an opinion on the accompanying balance sheet as of December 31, 2009, and the related statements of earnings, retained earnings, and cash flows for the year then ended.

If an auditor is not independent, a disclaimer of opinion must be issued. In the disclaimer, the auditor should *not* state the reasons for the lack of independence nor describe any audit procedures performed. This requirement is intended to prevent the auditor from attempting to minimize or explain away the circumstances. Note in Exhibit 18–10 that the title of the report does not contain the word "independent." A title is not required for the disclaimer.

Special Reporting Issues

In addition to the types of audit reports just discussed, auditors often encounter a number of special reporting issues that affect the financial statement audit report. Three topics are covered in the remainder of this section of the chapter:

- Reports on comparative financial statements.
- Other information in documents containing audited financial statements.
- Special reports.

Reports on Comparative Financial Statements

≫ [LO 6]   The fourth standard of reporting requires that the auditor either express an opinion on the financial statements taken as a whole or assert that an opinion cannot be expressed. When a client presents financial statements for the current period together with one or more prior periods, the auditor's report refers to the prior-period financial statements presented on a comparative basis. Exhibit 18–1 shows an unqualified standard audit report on EarthWcar's comparative financial statements that covers the balance sheets for two years and statements of income, stockholders' equity, and cash flows for three years. Normally, the date of the auditor's report on the comparative statements is the date of the most recently completed audit.

During the current-year audit, the auditor should be alert for events that may affect prior-period financial statements. Three relatively common situations are discussed.

Different Reports on Comparative Financial Statements   A number of situations may cause the auditor to express different reports on the comparative financial statements. One example is when the auditor expressed a standard unqualified opinion on prior years' financial statements but qualifies the current-year opinion. Exhibit 18–11 is an example of a report issued when a

EXHIBIT 18–11	Comparative Report—Unqualified in Prior Years but Qualified in Current Year for Not Being in Conformity with Generally Accepted Accounting Principles

Independent Auditor's Report

[Standard wording for the introductory and scope paragraphs]

The Company has excluded, from property and debt in the accompanying 2009 balance sheet, certain lease obligations that were entered into in 2009 which, in our opinion, should be capitalized in order to conform with accounting principles generally accepted in the United States of America. If these lease obligations were capitalized, property would be increased by $7,500,000, long-term debt by $6,900,000, and retained earnings by $1,420,000 as of December 31, 2009, net income would be increased by $250,000 and earnings per share would be increased by $.25, respectively, for the year then ended.

   In our opinion, except for the effects on the 2009 financial statements of not capitalizing certain lease obligations as discussed in the preceding paragraph, the financial statements referred to . . . *[same wording as for the remainder of the standard opinion paragraph]*.

EXHIBIT 18–12	Comparative Report When the Prior Year Was Disclaimed for a Scope Limitation and the Current Year Received an Unqualified Opinion

Independent Auditor's Report

[*Standard wording for the introductory paragraph*]

Except as explained in the following paragraph, we conducted our audits in accordance with auditing standards generally accepted in the United States of America . . . [*same wording as for the remainder of the standard scope paragraph*].

We did not observe the taking of the physical inventory as of December 31, 2007, since that date was prior to our appointment as auditors for the Company, and we were unable to satisfy ourselves regarding inventory quantities by means of other auditing procedures. Inventory amounts as of December 31, 2007, enter into the determination of net income and cash flows for the year ended December 31, 2008.

Because of the matter discussed in the preceding paragraph, the scope of our work was not sufficient to enable us to express, and we do not express, an opinion on the results of operations and cash flows for the year ended December 31, 2008.

In our opinion, the balance sheets of RUUD Rubber Company as of December 31, 2009 and 2008, and the related statements of income, retained earnings, and cash flows for the year ended December 31, 2009, present fairly, in all material respects, the financial position of RUUD Rubber Company as of December 31, 2009 and 2008, and the results of its operations and its cash flows for the year ended December 31, 2009, in conformity with accounting principles generally accepted in the United States of America.

company decided not to capitalize certain lease obligations in the current year. In prior years, the company did not have capitalized lease obligations, so the financial statements for those years conformed to GAAP.

Another situation occurs when the report on the current year is unqualified but prior-period financial statements were qualified or were disclaimed. Exhibit 18–12 is an example of a report issued when an auditor was hired subsequent to the observation of the physical inventory in the prior year, which resulted in a disclaimer of opinion for that period. In the current year, the auditor was able to conduct the audit without any scope limitation and thus issues an unqualified opinion.

A Change in Report on the Prior-Period Financial Statements

During the course of the current year's audit, the auditor may encounter circumstances or events that require updating the report issued on the prior-period financial statements. For example, the auditor may have issued a qualified or adverse opinion in the prior year because the client had not followed GAAP. If the client conforms to GAAP in the current year and appropriately restates the prior-period results, the auditor should express an unqualified opinion on the restated prior-period financial statements if they are presented along with the current period statements as comparatives. Exhibit 18–13 is an example of such a report. Note that the paragraph that precedes the opinion paragraph contains the date of the previous report, the type of opinion previously issued, the reasons for the previous report being issued, and mention of the fact that the current report differs from the previously issued report. In this example, after the client conformed to GAAP in accounting for property, plant, and equipment and for deferred taxes and restated the prior-period financial statements, the auditor issued an unqualified report for both the current and prior years. Since the paragraph included in Exhibit 18–13 contains all the information required, a separate explanatory paragraph is not necessary.

Report by a Predecessor Auditor

When an entity has changed auditors, the predecessor auditor can reissue, at the request of the client, his or her report on the financial statements of prior periods when those statements are presented on a comparative basis. In such a situation, the predecessor auditor must determine if the previously issued reports are still

EXHIBIT 18–13	Change in the Report on the Prior-Period Financial Statements

Independent Auditor's Report

[Standard wording for the introductory and scope paragraphs]

In our report dated March 1, 2009, we expressed an opinion that the 2008 financial statements did not fairly present financial position, results of operations, and cash flows in conformity with accounting principles generally accepted in the United States of America because of two departures from such principles: (1) the Company carried its property, plant, and equipment at appraisal values and provided for depreciation on the basis of such values; and (2) the Company did not provide for deferred income taxes with respect to differences between income for financial reporting purposes and taxable income. As described in Note 8, the Company has changed its method of accounting for these items and restated its 2008 financial statements to conform with accounting principles generally accepted in the United States of America. Accordingly, our present opinion on the 2008 financial statements, as presented herein, is different from that expressed in our previous report.

[Standard wording for the opinion paragraph]

appropriate, given the current circumstances. The predecessor auditor should do the following before reissuing the report:

1. Read the financial statements of the current period.
2. Compare the prior-period financial statements on which the predecessor previously reported with the current-year financial statements.
3. Obtain a letter of representations from the current-year, successor auditor.

The letter of representations from the successor auditor should indicate whether the successor auditor discovered any material items that might affect, or require disclosure in, the financial statements reported on by the predecessor auditor. If the predecessor auditor is satisfied that the financial statements previously reported on should not be revised, he or she reissues the audit report using the date of the previous report.

In the event that the predecessor auditor becomes aware of circumstances or events that may affect the previously issued financial statements, he or she should make inquiries and perform any procedures considered necessary. For example, the successor auditor may discover errors indicating that the prior year's financial statements were materially misstated. If the prior-period financial statements are restated, the predecessor auditor should revise the report as necessary and dual date the reissued report.

If the prior-period financial statements have been audited but the predecessor auditor's report will not be included, the successor auditor indicates in the report's introductory paragraph that the financial statements for the prior period were audited by other auditors and mentions the date and the type of report issued by the predecessor auditor. If the predecessor's report was not standard, the successor auditor should describe the nature of and reasons for the explanatory paragraph added to the predecessor's report.

Other Information in Documents Containing Audited Financial Statements

[LO 7] A client may publish documents, such as annual reports and registration statements, that contain other information in addition to the audited financial statements and the audit report. Auditing standards (AU 550) provide guidance for the auditor's consideration of other information contained in (1) annual reports of entities; and (2) other documents to which the auditor devotes attention at the client's request.

The auditor has no responsibility beyond the financial information contained in the report, and he or she has no obligation to perform any audit procedures to corroborate the other information. However, the auditor is required to read the other information and consider whether such information is consistent with the information contained in the audited financial statements. For example, the audited financial statements may show a 10-percent increase in sales and a 5-percent increase in net income. If the president's letter that is included in the annual report states that sales were up 15 percent and net income increased by 12 percent, a material inconsistency would exist. The auditor would then have to determine whether the financial statements or the president's letter required revision. If the financial statements were correct, the auditor would request that the president change the other information. If the other information were not revised, the auditor should include an explanatory paragraph in the audit report, withhold the report, or withdraw from the engagement depending on the severity of the circumstances.

Special Reports Relating to Financial Statements

The first standard of reporting requires the auditor to report on whether the financial statements conform to GAAP. Auditors, however, are sometimes engaged to report on financial statements that are not prepared on the basis of GAAP. Auditors may also be engaged to report on parts of the financial statements or on a client's compliance with contractual agreements or regulatory requirements. Auditing standards provide the auditor with specific guidance for such engagements and cover the auditor's reporting responsibilities for the following situations:

- Financial statements prepared on a comprehensive basis of accounting other than GAAP (e.g., the cash basis of accounting).
- Specified elements, accounts, or items of a financial statement.
- Compliance with aspects of contractual agreements or regulatory requirements related to audited financial statements.

Financial Statements Prepared on a Comprehensive Basis of Accounting Other Than GAAP

⚘ [LO 8]

A widely used type of special report is employed when an entity has prepared its financial statements on a comprehensive basis other than GAAP ("other comprehensive basis of accounting," or OCBOA). Auditing standards define OCBOA financial statements as including those prepared under the following bases:

- ***Regulatory basis.*** The basis used to comply with the requirements or financial reporting provisions of a governmental regulatory agency. An example would be when an insurance company reports in compliance with the rules of a state insurance commission.
- ***Tax basis.*** The basis the entity uses to file its income tax return. Real estate partnerships frequently use this basis for reporting to partners.
- ***Cash (or modified cash) basis.*** The entity reports on revenues when received and expenses when paid. The cash basis may be modified to record depreciation or to accrue income taxes.
- ***A definite set of criteria having substantial support.*** Financial statements prepared on a price level–adjusted basis are an example of such a set of criteria.

Exhibit 18–14 is an example of a report on a set of financial statements prepared on a tax basis. Note that the introductory paragraph identifies the financial statements on which a report is being issued. It is important that these financial statements be titled so that they are not confused with financial statements prepared on a GAAP basis. In this case, the report covers a *statement of assets, liabilities, and*

EXHIBIT 18-14	Financial Statements Prepared on the Entity's Income Tax Basis

Independent Auditor's Report

We have audited the accompanying statements of assets, liabilities, and capital–income tax basis of Patroon Partnership as of December 31, 2009 and 2008, and the related statements of revenue and expenses—income tax basis and of changes in partners' capital accounts–income tax basis for the years then ended. These financial statements are the responsibility of the Partnership's management. Our responsibility is to express an opinion on these financial statements based on our audits.

We conducted our audit in accordance with auditing standards generally accepted in the United States of America. Those standards require that we plan and perform the audit to obtain reasonable assurance about whether the financial statements are free of material misstatement. An audit includes consideration of internal control over financial reporting as a basis for designing audit procedures that are appropriate in the circumstances, but not for the purpose of expressing an opinion on the effectiveness of the Company's internal control over financial reporting. Accordingly, we express no such opinion. An audit also includes examining, on a test basis, evidence supporting the amounts and disclosures in the financial statements, assessing the accounting principles used and significant estimates made by management, as well as evaluating the overall financial statement presentation. We believe that our audit provides a reasonable basis for our opinion.

As described in Note 2, these financial statements were prepared on the basis of accounting the Partnership uses for income tax purposes, which is a comprehensive basis of accounting other than generally accepted accounting principles.

In our opinion, the financial statements referred to above present fairly, in all material respects, the assets, liabilities, and capital of Patroon Partnership as of December 31, 2009 and 2008, and its revenue and expenses and changes in partners' capital accounts for the years then ended, on the basis of accounting described in Note 2.

capital–income tax basis instead of a balance sheet, and a *statement of revenues and expenses–income tax basis* instead of a statement of income or operations.

The scope paragraph is identical to that included in the standard unqualified audit report. The third paragraph discloses the basis used to prepare the financial statements and refers to a note in the financial statements that describes the basis in more detail. The opinion paragraph is a positive statement about the fairness of presentation in conformity with the OCBOA.

If the financial statements are prepared on a regulatory basis, a paragraph such as the following is added to restrict the distribution of the report to those parties within the entity and those involved in filing with the regulatory agency:

> This report is intended solely for the information and use of the board of directors and management of Great Atlantic Insurance Company and for filing with the Excelsior State Insurance Agency and should not be used by anyone other than these specified parties.

Specified Elements, Accounts, or Items of a Financial Statement

✂ [LO 9]

In some situations an auditor may be engaged to audit only part of the financial statements. Examples include a report on rentals, royalties, or profit participation or on the provision for income taxes. The basis of accounting for the elements, accounts, or items may be GAAP, OCBOA, or a basis of accounting prescribed by a contract or agreement.

An engagement to express an opinion on one or more specified elements, accounts, or items of a financial statement may be performed as a separate engagement or as part of an audit of financial statements. The only exception is when the auditor is engaged to report on the entity's net income or stockholders' equity. In this case, the auditor must audit the entire set of financial statements.

Generally, an audit of an element, account, or item is more extensive than if the same information were considered as part of an audit of the overall financial statements. Thus, materiality needs to be set in relation to the individual element, account, or item and the auditor should consider how the item relates to other parts of the financial statements. For example, if the auditor is engaged to audit the entity's accounts receivable, other accounts such as sales and allowance for bad debts should also be considered.

Suppose an auditor is engaged to issue a special report on gross sales for a client whose rent payment is contingent on the total amount of sales for the period. The introductory paragraph states that this specific account was audited. Similar to the standard unqualified audit report, this paragraph states management's and the auditor's responsibilities. The scope paragraph differs from the standard report only in that it references the account being audited. The third paragraph expresses the auditor's opinion on the account. Finally, in the case when the specified element, account, or item is audited in compliance with the provisions of a contract or agreement, the auditor includes a paragraph limiting distribution of the report to the parties who are part of the contract.

Rather than auditing specified elements, accounts, or items, an auditor may be engaged to apply only *agreed-upon procedures*. Attestation standards (AT 201) provide the auditor with the necessary guidance for such engagements. An engagement to apply agreed-upon procedures is one in which the auditor is engaged by a client to issue a *report of findings* based on specific, agreed-upon procedures performed on the specific subject matter of specified elements, accounts, or items of a financial statement. The report does not express an opinion; it simply reports the results of the procedures that were conducted. On such engagements, the auditor does not take responsibility for the sufficiency of the agreed-upon procedures—instead, responsibility rests with the users.

Exhibit 18–15 is an example of an agreed-upon procedures report. The report (1) identifies the specified users; (2) references the specified elements, accounts, or items of a financial statement that were examined, and the nature of the engagement; (3) lists the procedures performed and related findings; (4) indicates that no opinion is expressed; and (5) states restrictions on the use of the report. Chapter 21 provides additional detail regarding agreed-upon procedures engagements.

EXHIBIT 18–15	**Agreed-Upon Procedures Report in Connection with Claims of Creditors**

Independent Auditor's Report on Applying Agreed-Upon Procedures

To the Trustee of Maxiscript Corporation:

We have performed the procedures described below, which were agreed to by the Trustee of Maxiscript Corporation, with respect to the claims of creditors to determine the validity of claims of Maxiscript Corporation as of May 31, 2009, as set forth in the accompanying Schedule A. Maxiscript Corporation is responsible for maintaining records of claims submitted by creditors of Maxiscript Corporation. This agreed-upon-procedures engagement was conducted in accordance with attestation standards established by the American Institute of Certified Public Accountants. The sufficiency of these procedures is solely the responsibility of the Trustee of Maxiscript Corporation. Consequently, we make no representation regarding the sufficiency of the procedures described below either for the purpose for which this report has been requested or for any other purpose.

The procedures and associated findings are as follows:

a. Compare the total of the trial balance of accounts payable at May 31, 2009, prepared by the company, to the balance in the Company's related general ledger account.

   The total of the accounts payable trial balance agreed with the balance in the related general ledger account.

b. Compare the amounts for claims received from creditors as shown in claims documents provided by Maxiscript Corporation to the respective amounts shown in the trial balance of accounts payable. Using the data included in the claims documents and in Maxiscript's accounts payable detail records, reconcile any differences to the accounts payable trial balance.

   All differences noted are presented in column 3 of Schedule A. Except for those amounts shown in column 4 of Schedule A, all such differences were reconciled.

c. Obtain the documentation submitted by the creditors in support of their claims and compare it to the following documentation in Maxiscript Corporation's files: invoices, receiving reports, and other evidence of receipt of goods or services.

   No exceptions were found as a result of these comparisons.

We were not engaged to, and did not, perform an audit, the objective of which would be the expression of an opinion on the claims of the creditors set forth in accompanying Schedule A. Accordingly, we do not express such an opinion. Had we performed additional procedures, other matters might have come to our attention that would have been reported to you.

This report is intended solely for the information and use of the Trustee of Maxiscript Corporation and is not intended to be and should not be used by anyone other than this specified party.

EXHIBIT 18–16	Report on Compliance with Contractual Provisions Given in a Separate Report

Independent Auditor's Report

We have audited, in accordance with auditing standards generally accepted in the United States of America, the balance sheet of Lynch Lumber Company as of December 31, 2009, and the related statement of income, retained earnings, and cash flows for the year then ended, and have issued our report thereon dated February 16, 2010.

In connection with our audit, nothing came to our attention that caused us to believe that the Company failed to comply with the terms, covenants, provisions, or conditions of sections 6.1 to 6.14, inclusive, of the indenture dated July 21, 2007, with First State Bank insofar as they relate to accounting matters. However, our audit was not directed primarily toward obtaining knowledge of such noncompliance.

This report is intended solely for the information and use of the board of directors and management of Lynch Lumber Company and First State Bank and is not intended to be and should not be used by anyone other than these specified parties.

Compliance Reports Related to Audited Financial Statements

✄ [LO 10]

An auditor may be asked to report on an entity's compliance with certain contractual agreements or regulatory requirements that are related to audited financial statements. For example, loan agreements may include covenants such as restrictions on dividends or maintenance of certain levels for selected financial ratios. Exhibit 18–16 is an example of a special report related to compliance with contractual provisions. Note that the auditor provides *negative assurance* as to the entity's compliance with the provisions of the loan agreement. Negative assurance consists of a statement that, in applying the specified procedures, nothing came to the auditor's attention that indicated that the provisions of the loan agreement had not been complied with. Note that in expressing negative assurance the auditor does not express an affirmative opinion about the client's compliance with the loan provisions.

KEY TERMS

Adverse opinion. The auditor's opinion that the financial statements do not present fairly in accordance with generally accepted accounting principles (or other comprehensive basis of accounting) due to a pervasively material misstatement.

Disclaimer of opinion. The auditor's indication that no opinion is expressed on the financial statements. The auditor will disclaim an opinion if a pervasive scope limitation arises or if it is determined that the auditor lacks independence.

Generally accepted auditing standards. Standards against which the quality of the auditor's performance is measured.

Materiality. The magnitude of an omission or misstatement of accounting information that, in light of surrounding circumstances, makes it probable that the judgment of a reasonable person relying on the information would have been changed or influenced.

Other comprehensive basis of accounting. Financial statements prepared under regulatory, tax, cash basis, or other definitive criteria having substantial support.

Qualified opinion. The auditor's opinion that the financial statements present fairly, in all material respects, in accordance with generally accepted accounting principles (or other comprehensive basis of accounting), *except for* a material misstatement that does not, however, pervasively affect users' ability to rely on the financial statements. Can also be issued for a scope limitation that is of limited significance.

Reasonable assurance. A term that implies some risk that a material misstatement could be present in the financial statements without the auditor detecting it, even when the auditor has exercised due care.

Representation letter. A letter that corroborates oral representations made to the auditor by management or by other auditors and documents the continued appropriateness of such representations.

Scope limitation. A lack of evidence that may preclude the auditor from issuing a clean opinion, usually resulting from an inability to conduct an audit procedure considered necessary.

Unqualified opinion. The auditor's opinion that the financial statements present fairly, in all material respects, the client's financial position, results of operations, and cash flows in accordance with generally accepted accounting principles (or other comprehensive basis of accounting)—i.e., a "clean" opinion.

www.mhhe.com/ messier7e	Visit the book's Online Learning Center for a multiple-choice quiz that will allow you to assess your understanding of chapter concepts.

REVIEW QUESTIONS

[INTRO] 18-1 Describe what is meant when an auditor is "associated with" a set of financial statements.

[LO 2] 18-2 Distinguish between accounting changes that affect consistency and changes that do not. How is it possible for an accounting change to affect comparability but not consistency?

[LO 3,5] 18-3 Give examples of a client-imposed and a condition-imposed scope limitation. Why is a client-imposed limitation generally considered more serious?

[5] 18-4 How does the materiality of a departure from GAAP affect the auditor's choice of financial statement audit reports?

[6] 18-5 In 2007 your firm issued an unqualified report on Tosi Corporation. During 2009 Tosi entered its first lease transaction, which you have determined is material but not pervasive and meets the criteria for a capitalized lease. Tosi Corporation's management chooses to treat the transaction as an operating lease. What types of reports would you issue on the corporation's comparative financial statements for 2008 and 2009?

[7] 18-6 What are the auditor's responsibilities for other information included in an entity's annual report?

[7] 18-7 If the auditor determines that other information contained with the audited financial statements is incorrect and the client refuses to correct the other information, what actions can the auditor take?

[8,9,10] 18-8 List three examples of special reports.

[8] 18-9 List four bases for OCBOA financial statements. Why is it important that the audit report clearly identify the basis of accounting used in the preparation of the financial statements?

MULTIPLE-CHOICE QUESTIONS

[1,2] 18-10 In which of the following situations would an auditor ordinarily issue an unqualified financial statement audit opinion with no explanatory paragraph?

a. The auditor wishes to emphasize that the entity had significant related-party transactions.

b. The auditor decides to refer to the report of another auditor as a basis, in part, for the auditor's opinion.

c. The entity issues financial statements that present financial position and results of operations but omits the statement of cash flows.

d. The auditor has substantial doubt about the entity's ability to continue as a going concern, but the circumstances are fully disclosed in the financial statements.

[1,2] 18-11 An entity changed from the straight-line method to the declining balance method of depreciation for all newly acquired assets. This change has no material effect on the current year's financial statements but is reasonably certain to have a substantial effect in later years. The client's financial statements contain no material misstatements and the auditor concurs with this change. If the change is disclosed in the notes to the financial statements, the auditor should issue a report with a(n)

a. "Except for" qualified opinion.

b. Explanatory paragraph.

c. Unqualified opinion.

d. Consistency modification.

[1,2] 18-12 An auditor includes a separate paragraph in an otherwise unmodified financial statement audit report to emphasize that the entity being reported upon had significant transactions with related parties. The inclusion of this separate paragraph

a. Is appropriate and would not negate the unqualified opinion.

b. Is considered an "except for" qualification of the opinion.

c. Violates generally accepted auditing standards if this information is already disclosed in footnotes to the financial statements.

d. Necessitates a revision of the opinion paragraph to include the phrase "with the foregoing explanation."

[2] 18-13 Eagle Company had a computer failure and lost part of its financial data. As a result, the auditor was unable to obtain sufficient audit evidence relating to Eagle's inventory account. Assuming the inventory account is at least material, the auditor would most likely choose either

a. A qualified opinion or a disclaimer of opinion.

b. A qualified opinion or an adverse opinion.

c. An unqualified opinion with no explanatory paragraph or an unqualified opinion with an explanatory paragraph.

d. A qualified opinion with no explanatory paragraph or a qualified opinion with an explanatory paragraph.

[3,4] 18-14 Tech Company has disclosed an uncertainty due to pending litigation. The auditor's decision to issue a qualified opinion on Tech's financial statements would most likely result from

a. Lack of sufficient evidence.

b. Inability to estimate the amount of loss.

c. Entity's lack of experience with such litigation.

d. Lack of insurance coverage for possible losses from such litigation.

[3,4,5] 18-15 In which of the following circumstances would an auditor usually choose between issuing a qualified opinion or an adverse opinion on a client's financial statements?

a. Departure from generally accepted accounting principles.

b. Inadequate disclosure of accounting policies.

c. Inability to obtain sufficient competent evidence.

d. Unreasonable justification for a change in accounting principle.

[3,4,5] 18-16 King, CPA, was engaged to audit the financial statements of Chang Company after its fiscal year had ended. King neither observed the inventory count nor confirmed the receivables by direct communication with debtors but was satisfied that both were fairly stated after applying appropriate alternative procedures. King's financial statement audit report most likely contained a(n)

a. Qualified opinion.

b. Disclaimer of opinion.

c. Unqualified opinion.

d. Unqualified opinion with an explanatory paragraph.

[6]   18-17   Comparative financial statements include the prior year's statements, which were audited by a predecessor auditor. The predecessor's report is not presented along with the comparative financial statements. If the predecessor's report was unqualified, the successor should

a. Express an opinion on the current year's statements alone and make no reference to the prior year's statements.

b. Indicate in the auditor's report that the predecessor auditor expressed an unqualified opinion.

c. Obtain a letter of representations from the predecessor concerning any matters that might affect the successor's opinion.

d. Request the predecessor auditor to reissue the prior year's report.

[6]   18-18   When reporting on comparative financial statements, which of the following circumstances should ordinarily cause the auditor to change the previously issued opinion on the prior year's financial statements?

a. The prior year's financial statements are restated following the purchase of another company in the current year.

b. A departure from generally accepted accounting principles caused an adverse opinion on the prior year's financial statements, and those statements have been properly restated.

c. A change in accounting principle causes the auditor to make a consistency modification in the current year's audit report.

d. A scope limitation caused a qualified opinion on the prior year's financial statements, but the current year's opinion is properly unqualified.

[7]   18-19   Which of the following best describes the auditor's responsibility for "other information" included in the annual report to stockholders that contains financial statements and the auditor's report?

a. The auditor has no obligation to read the "other information."

b. The auditor has no obligation to corroborate the "other information" but should read the "other information" to determine whether it is materially inconsistent with the financial statements.

c. The auditor should extend the examination to the extent necessary to verify the "other information."

d. The auditor must modify the auditor's report to state that the other information "is unaudited" or "is not covered by the auditor's report."

[8]   18-20   When reporting on financial statements prepared on the basis of accounting used for income tax purposes, the auditor should include in the report a paragraph that

a. Emphasizes that the financial statements have not been examined in accordance with generally accepted auditing standards.

b. Refers to the authoritative pronouncements that explain the income tax basis of accounting being used.

c. States that the income tax basis of accounting is a comprehensive basis of accounting other than generally accepted accounting principles.

d. Justifies the use of the income tax basis of accounting.

[9]   18-21   When an auditor is asked to express an opinion on an entity's rent and royalty revenues, he or she may

a. Not accept the engagement because to do so would be tantamount to agreeing to issue a piecemeal opinion.

b. Not accept the engagement unless also engaged to audit the full financial statements of the entity.

c. Accept the engagement provided the auditor's opinion is expressed in a special report.

d. Accept the engagement provided distribution of the auditor's report is limited to the entity's management.

PROBLEMS

[1,2,3,4,8]   18-22   For each of the following independent situations, indicate the type of financial statement audit report that you would issue and briefly explain your reasoning. Assume that each item is significant.

a. Barefield Corporation, a wholly owned subsidiary of Sandy, Inc., is audited by another CPA firm. As the auditor of Sandy, Inc., you have assured yourself of the other CPA firm's independence and professional reputation. However, you are unwilling to take complete responsibility for its audit work.

b. The management of Bonner Corporation has decided to exclude the statement of cash flows from its financial statements because it believes that its bankers do not find the statement to be very useful.

c. You are auditing Diverse Carbon, a manufacturer of nerve gas for the military, for the year ended September 30, 2009. On September 1, 2009, one of its manufacturing plants caught fire, releasing nerve gas into the surrounding area. Two thousand people were killed and numerous others paralyzed. The company's legal counsel indicates that the company is liable and that the amount of the liability can be reasonably estimated, but the company refuses to disclose this information in the financial statements.

d. During your audit of Cuccia Coal Company, the controller, Tracy Tricks, refuses to allow you to confirm accounts receivable because she is concerned about complaints from her customers. You are unable to satisfy yourself about accounts receivable by other audit procedures and you are concerned about Tracy's true motives.

e. On January 31, 2010, Asare Toy Manufacturing hired your firm to audit the company's financial statements for the year 2009. You were unable to observe the client's inventory on December 31, 2009. However, you were able to satisfy yourself about the inventory balance using other auditing procedures.

f. Gelato Bros., Inc., leases its manufacturing facility from a partnership controlled by the chief executive officer and major shareholder of Gelato. Your review of the lease indicates that the rental terms are in excess of rental terms for similar buildings in the area. The company refuses to disclose this related-party transaction in the footnotes.

g. Johnstone Manufacturing Company has used the double-declining balance method to depreciate its machinery. During the current year, management switched to the straight-line method because it felt that it better represented the utilization of the assets. You concur with its decision. All information is adequately disclosed in the financial statements.

[1,2,3,4,8]   18-23   For each of the following independent situations, indicate the reason for and the type of financial statement audit report that you would issue. Assume that each item is significant.

a. Thibodeau Mines, Inc., uses LIFO for valuing inventories held in the United States and a non-GAAP method for inventories produced and held in its foreign operations.

b. Walker Computers is suing your client, Super Software, for royalties over patent infringement. Super Software's outside legal counsel assures you that HiTech's case is completely without merit.

c. In previous years, your client, Merc International, has consolidated its Panamanian subsidiary. Because of restrictions on repatriation of earnings placed on all foreign-owned corporations in Panama, Merc International has decided to account for the subsidiary on the equity basis in the current year. You concur with the change.

d. In prior years Worcester Wool Mills has used current market prices to value its inventory of raw wool. During the current year Worcester changed to FIFO for valuing raw wool.

e. Upon review of the recent history of the lives of its specialized automobiles, Gas Leak Technology justifiably changed the service lives for depreciation purposes on its autos from five years to three years. This change resulted in a material amount of additional depreciation expense.

f. During the audit of Brannon Bakery Equipment, you found that a material amount of inventory had been excluded from the company's financial statements. After discussing this problem with management, you become convinced that it was an unintentional oversight. Management appropriately corrected the error prior to your finalization of field work.

g. Jay Rich, CPA, holds 10 percent of the stock in Rothenburg Construction Company. The board of directors of Rothenburg asks Rich to conduct its audit. Rich completes the audit and determines that the financial statements present fairly in accordance with generally accepted accounting principles.

h. Ramamoorthi Savings and Loan's financial condition has been deteriorating for the last five years. Most of its problems result from loans made to real estate developers in Saint Johns County. Your review of the loan portfolio indicates that there should be a major increase in the loan-loss reserve. Based on your calculations, the proposed write-down of the loans will put Ramamoorthi into violation of the state's capital requirements. The client refuses to make the adjustment or to disclose the possible going concern issue in the notes to the financial statements.

[2]   18-24   The CPA firm of May & Marty has audited the consolidated financial statements of BGI Corporation. May & Marty examined the parent company and all subsidiaries except for BGI-Western Corporation, which was audited by the CPA firm of Dey & Dee. BGI-Western constituted approximately 10 percent of the consolidated assets and 6 percent of the consolidated revenue.

Dey & Dee issued an unqualified opinion on the financial statements of BGI-Western. May & Marty will be issuing an unqualified opinion on the consolidated financial statements of BGI.

Required:

a. What procedures should May & Marty consider performing with respect to Dey & Dee's examination of BGI-Western's financial statements regardless of whether reference is to be made to the other auditors?

b. Describe the various circumstances under which May & Marty could take responsibility for the work of Dey & Dee and make no reference to Dey & Dee's examination of BGI-Western in its own report on the consolidated financial statements of BGI.

(AICPA, adapted)

[2,3,4,6]   18-25   Devon, Inc., engaged Rao to examine its financial statements for the year ended December 31, 2009. The financial statements of Devon, Inc., for the year ended December 31, 2008, were examined by Jones, whose March 31, 2009, auditor's report expressed an unqualified opinion. The report of Jones is not presented with the 2009–2008 comparative financial statements.

Rao's working papers contain the following information that does not appear in footnotes to the 2009 financial statements as prepared by Devon, Inc.:

- One director, appointed in 2009, was formerly a partner in Jones's accounting firm. Jones's firm provided financial consulting services to Devon during 2007 and 2006, for which Devon paid approximately $1,600 and $9,000, respectively.
- The company refused to capitalize certain lease obligations for equipment acquired in 2009. Capitalization of the leases in conformity with generally accepted accounting principles would have increased assets and liabilities by $312,000 and $387,000, respectively, decreased retained earnings as of December 31, 2009, by $75,000, and decreased net income and earnings per share by $75,000 and $.75, respectively, for the year then ended. Rao has concluded that the leases should have been capitalized.
- During the year, Devon changed its method of valuing inventory from the first-in, first-out method to the last-in, first-out method. This change was made because management believes LIFO more clearly reflects net income by providing a closer matching of current costs and current revenues. The change had the effect of reducing inventory at December 31, 2009, by $65,000 and net income and earnings per share by $38,000 and $.38, respectively, for the year then ended. The effect of the change on prior years was immaterial; accordingly, the change had no cumulative effect. Rao supports the company's position.

After completing the fieldwork on February 28, 2010, Rao concludes that the expression of an adverse opinion is not warranted.

Required:
Prepare the body of Rao's report, addressed to the board of directors, dated February 28, 2010, to accompany the 2009–2008 comparative financial statements. Devon is a public company. Rao has conducted an audit of Devon's internal controls over financial reporting based on the COSO framework. No material weaknesses were identified.

(AICPA, adapted)

[8]   18-26   On March 12, 2010, Kristen & Valentine, CPAs, completed the audit of the financial statements of Modern Museum, Inc., for the year ended December 31, 2009. Modern Museum presents comparative financial statements on a modified cash basis. Assets, liabilities, fund balances, support, revenues, and expenses are recognized when cash is received or disbursed, except that Modern includes a provision for depreciation of buildings and equipment. Kristen & Valentine believes that Modern's three financial statements, prepared in accordance with a comprehensive basis of accounting other than generally accepted accounting principles, are adequate for Modern's needs and wishes to issue a special report on the financial statements. Kristen & Valentine has gathered sufficient competent evidence to be satisfied that the financial statements are fairly presented according to the modified cash basis. Kristen & Valentine audited Modern's 2008 financial statements and issued an auditor's special report expressing an unqualified opinion.

Required:

Draft the audit report to accompany Modern's comparative financial statements. Modern is a privately held company.

(AICPA, adapted)

[1,3,4,6]   18-27   For the year ended December 31, 2008, Friday & Co., CPAs ("Friday"), audited the financial statements of Kim Company and expressed an unqualified opinion on the balance sheet only. Friday did not observe the taking of the physical inventory as of December 31, 2007, because that date was prior to its appointment as auditor. Friday was unable to satisfy itself regarding inventory by means of other auditing procedures, so it did not express an opinion on the other basic financial statements that year.

For the year ended December 31, 2009, Friday expressed an unqualified opinion on all the basic financial statements and satisfied itself as to the consistent application of generally accepted accounting principles. The fieldwork was completed on March 11, 2010; the partner-in-charge reviewed the working papers and signed the auditor's report on March 18, 2010. The report on the comparative financial statements for 2009 and 2008 was delivered to Kim on March 21, 2010.

Required:

Prepare Friday's audit report that was submitted to Kim's board of directors on the 2009 and 2008 comparative financial statements. Kim is a public company. Friday has conducted an audit of Kim's internal controls over financial reporting based on the COSO framework. No material weaknesses were identified.

(AICPA, adapted)

[1,8]   18-28   The following auditor's report was drafted by a staff accountant of Nathan and Matthew, CPAs, at the completion of the audit of the comparative financial statements of Monterey Partnership for the years ended December 31, 2009 and 2008. Monterey is a privately held company that prepares its financial statements on the income tax basis of accounting. The report was submitted to the engagement partner, who reviewed matters thoroughly and properly concluded that an unqualified opinion should be expressed. The draft of the report prepared by a staff account is as follows:

Auditor's Report

We have audited the accompanying statements of assets, liabilities, and capital—income tax basis of Monterey Partnership as of December 31, 2009 and 2008, and the related statements of revenue and expenses—income tax basis and changes in partners' capital accounts—income tax basis for the years then ended.

We conducted our audits in accordance with standards established by the American Institute of Certified Public Accountants. Those standards require that we plan and perform the audit to obtain reasonable assurance about whether the financial statements are free of material misstatement. An audit includes examining, on a test basis, evidence supporting the amounts and disclosures in the financial statements. An audit also includes assessing the accounting principles used as well as evaluating the overall financial statement presentation.

As described in Note A, these financial statements were prepared on the basis of accounting the Partnership uses for income tax purposes.

Accordingly, these financial statements are not designed for those who do not have access to the Partnership's tax returns.

In our opinion, the financial statements referred to above present fairly, in all material respects, the assets, liabilities, and capital of Monterey Partnership as of December 31, 2009 and 2008, and its revenue and expenses and changes in partners' capital accounts for the years then ended, in conformity with generally accepted accounting principles applied on a consistent basis.

Nathan and Matthew, CPAs
April 3, 2010

Required:
Identify the errors and omissions in the auditor's report as drafted by the staff accountant. Group the errors and omissions by paragraph, where applicable. Do not redraft the report.

(AICPA, adapted)

DISCUSSION CASE

[2]   18-29   You are auditing the financial statements for your new client, Paper Packaging Corporation, a manufacturer of paper containers, for the year ended March 31, 2010. Paper Packaging's previous auditors had issued a going concern opinion on the March 31, 2009, financial statements for the following reasons:
* Paper Packaging had defaulted on $10 million of unregistered debentures sold to three insurance companies, which were due in 2009, and the default constituted a possible violation of other debt agreements.
* The interest and principal payments due on the remainder of a 10-year credit agreement, which began in 2005, would exceed the cash flows generated from operations in recent years.
* The company had disposed of certain operating units. The proceeds from the sale were subject to possible adjustment through arbitration proceedings, the outcome of which was uncertain at year-end.
* Various lawsuits were pending against the company.
* The company was in the midst of tax proceedings as a result of an examination of the company's federal income tax returns for a period of 12 years.

You find that the status of the above matters is as follows at year-end, March 31, 2010:
* The company is still in default on $4.6 million of the debentures due in 2009 but is trying to negotiate a settlement with remaining bondholders. A large number of bondholders have settled their claims at significantly less than par.
* The company has renegotiated the 2005 credit agreement, which provides for a two-year moratorium on principal payments and interest at 8 percent. It also limits net losses ($2.25 million for 2010) and requires a certain level of defined cumulative quarterly operating income to be maintained.
* The arbitration proceedings were resolved in 2010.
* The legal actions were settled in 2010.
* Most of the tax issues have been resolved, and, according to the company's outside legal counsel, those remaining will result in a net cash inflow to the company.

At year-end Paper Packaging had a cash balance of $5.5 million and expects to generate a net cash flow of $3.2 million in the upcoming fiscal year.

The following information about Paper Packaging's plans for its operations for the fiscal year ending in 2011 may also be useful in arriving at a decision.

	Fiscal Year 2011 Budget	Fiscal Year 2010 Actual	Fiscal Year 2010 Budget
Net revenues	$66.2	$60.9	$79.8
Gross margin	34.7	33.6	45.6
Operating expenses	27.9	34.7	31.4
Interest—net	5.1	6.0	5.7
Other income (expenses)—net	(.8)	2.1	—
Earnings before income taxes and extraordinary items	1.5	(5.1)	(.2)
Cash flows:			
Receipts	69.9	79.7	
Disbursements	66.7	96.9	
Excess/deficit	3.2	(22.8)	

Required (for this question, you may wish to reference auditing standards—see AU 341):

a. What should you consider in deciding whether to discuss a going concern uncertainty in your report?

b. How much influence should the report on the March 31, 2009, financial statements have on your decision?

c. Should your report for the year ended March 31, 2010, include a discussion of a going concern uncertainty? Briefly explain why or why not.

 HANDS-ON CASES

www.mhhe.com/ messier7e	Visit the book's Online Learning Center for problem material to be completed using the ACL software packaged with your new text.

KAPLAN
CPA Review

www.mhhe.com/ messier7e	**Harrison Homes** This simulation covers items from previous chapters including audit committee communication, elements of fraud, types of assurance, and other audit procedures. The research question addresses the important considerations that should be made when using another auditor's report. *To begin this simulation, visit the book's Online Learning Center.*

Part 7

PROFESSIONAL RESPONSIBILITIES

19
Professional Conduct, Independence, and Quality Control

20
Legal Liability

CHAPTER 19

LEARNING OBJECTIVES

Upon completion of this chapter you will

[1] Know the definitions and general importance of ethics and professionalism.

[2] Be able to explain three basic theories of ethical behavior.

[3] Understand how to deal with ethical challenges through an example situation.

[4] Know how professional ethics standards for auditors have developed over time and the entities involved.

[5] Understand the framework for the Code of Professional Conduct.

[6] Know the principles of professional conduct.

[7] Understand the framework for the Rules of Conduct.

[8] Have a working knowledge of the rules of conduct that apply to independence, integrity, and objectivity.

[9] Know the basic differences between the SEC's independence rules for public company auditors and AICPA standards for audits of nonpublic entities.

[10] Know the rules of conduct that apply to general standards and accounting principles.

[11] Know the rules of conduct that apply to responsibilities to clients.

[12] Know the rules of conduct that apply to other responsibilities and practices.

[13] Be able to explain the definition of a system of quality control and the AICPA's peer review program.

[14] Be able to describe the elements of quality control and how a firm monitors its quality control system.

[15] Be familiar with the PCAOB inspection program for accounting firms that audit public companies.

RELEVANT ACCOUNTING AND AUDITING PRONOUNCEMENTS

AICPA, Code of Professional Conduct (ET 50-500)
AU 161, The Relationship of Generally Accepted Auditing Standards to Quality Control Standards
ISB 1, Independence Discussions with Audit Committees
ISB 3, Employment with Audit Clients
QC 20, System of Quality Control for a CPA Firm's Accounting and Auditing Practice
QC 30, Monitoring a CPA Firm's Accounting and Auditing Practice
PCAOB AS No. 1, References in Auditors' Reports to the Standards of the Public Company Accounting Oversight Board

PCAOB Rules on Auditor Ethics, Independence, and Tax Services, Rules No. 3520, 3521, 3522, 3523, and 3524
PR 100, Standards for Performing and Reporting on Quality Reviews
Securities and Exchange Commission Rule 2-01, Revision of the Commission's Auditor Independence Requirements
Statement on Quality Control Standards (SQCS) No. 7, "A Firm's System of Quality Control"

Professional Conduct, Independence, and Quality Control

In August 2008, the SEC required Deloitte, LLP to provide the names and titles of all personnel who had served a Deloitte audit client that had announced an acquisition of another public company in July 2007. As it turned out, former Deloitte vice chairman Thomas P. Flanagan had served as an advisory partner for that particular client and allegedly had purchased stock in the client's target approximately one week before the acquisition was publicly announced. This trade represented a serious violation of not only Deloitte's policies but also professional ethics rules. It would soon be alleged that this was far from the first case of improper trading performed by Flanagan contrary to the profession's Code of Professional Conduct.

Later that same month, the SEC asked about Deloitte's participation in the audits of several other companies during 2006 and 2007. A number of the companies were in fact Deloitte clients, and Flanagan was the advisory partner for a number of those clients. When confronted, Flanagan advised Deloitte that he was aware of the SEC's investigation, had spoken with regulators, and had retained legal counsel. On September 5, 2008, Flanagan resigned from Deloitte.

Between January 2005 and June 2008, Flanagan allegedly traded put and call options with respect to securities of at least twelve of Deloitte and Touche's audit clients, for seven of which Flanagan served as advisory partner. During that time, Flanagan reportedly misrepresented his investment activities and hid some of his brokerage accounts when filing annual independence representations required by Deloitte.

Deloitte sued Flanagan for compensation paid after breaching company policy, an act which "waived any right to amounts payable to him by Deloitte," and for losses suffered by Deloitte relating to the investigation of the case.[1] In a public statement, Deloitte "unequivocally condemns the actions of this individual, which are unprecedented in our experience. His personal trading activities were in blatant violation of Deloitte's strict and clearly stated policies for investments by partners and other professional personnel."[2]

Though the Flanagan case is still pending as of this writing, a federal court judge presiding over a 2004 case involving independence violations by Ernst & Young reiterated the importance of auditor independence:

> Auditors have been characterized as "gatekeepers" to the public securities markets that are crucial for capital formation. The independent public accountant performing this special

---

[1]For full details on the case and the source of the above quotes, see *Courthouse News Service,* October 30, 2008, www.courthousenews.com/2008/10/30/Deloitte.pdf.

[2]Ameet Sachdev (2008, November 7). "Insider trading alleged at Deloitte,"*Chicago Tribune,* www.chicagobusiness.com/cgi-bin/news.pl?id=31735&seenIt=1.

function owes ultimate allegiance to the corporation's creditors and stockholders, as well as to the investing public. This "public watchdog" function demands that the accountant maintain total independence from the client at all times and requires complete fidelity to the public trust.[3]

In this chapter, we discuss the importance of ethical and professional conduct by auditors. We begin by defining ethics and professionalism and offering a general framework within which ethical issues can be evaluated. We then provide an overview of the nature of the principles, rules, and regulations governing public accountants' conduct, followed by a discussion of the specific rules and regulations accountants, and auditors in particular, must follow. Independence, arguably the most complicated and controversial aspect of auditor professionalism, is prominently highlighted in this discussion. Finally, we discuss how public accounting firms are monitored and inspected to help ensure quality audits and compliance with professional standards, regulations, and codes of conduct. 🌐

Ethics and Professional Conduct

Ethics and Professionalism Defined
➤ [LO 1]

Ethical conduct is the bedrock of modern civilization—it underpins the successful functioning of nearly every aspect of society, from daily family life to law, medicine, business, and government. *Ethics* refers to a system or code of conduct based on moral duties and obligations that indicate how an individual should interact with others in society. A sense for ethics guides individuals to value more than their own self-interest and to recognize and respect the interests of others as well. Our society would fall into chaos if people were devoid of ethics and moral sentiments. Imagine what it would be like if everyone ignored rules of the road, moral standards, obligations, and the rights and interests of others! Life in such a society would be, as the philosopher Hobbes might say, "solitary, poor, nasty, brutish, and short."

Ethical conduct is also the bedrock of modern professionalism. *Professionalism*, broadly defined, refers to the conduct, aims, or qualities that characterize or mark a profession or professional person.[4] All professions establish rules or codes of conduct that define ethical (professional) behavior for members of the profession. These rules are established so that (1) users of the professional services know what to expect when they purchase such services; (2) members of the profession know what behavior is acceptable; and (3) the profession can use the rules to monitor the actions of its members and apply discipline where appropriate. Consider the medical profession. When you see a doctor for a potentially serious medical condition, you as a user of this professional service have a valid and vital interest in expecting competent and honest behavior that is free from conflicts of interest. You expect, for example, that the doctor will prescribe the best medication for your condition, rather than one for which the doctor earns a commission. To better meet these expectations, the medical profession requires particular training and certifications, and has a code of professional conduct, the earliest form of which arguably is the Hippocratic oath, written in about 400 BC. An essential distinguishing mark of a profession is that it recognizes its

---

[3]See *Initial Decision Release No. 249, Administrative Proceeding, File No. 3-10933, United States of America before the Securities and Exchange Commission in the Matter of Ernst & Young LLP*, www.sec.gov/litigation/aljdec/id249bpm.htm.

[4]S. M. Mintz, *Cases in Accounting Ethics and Professionalism*, 3rd ed. (New York: Irwin/McGraw-Hill, 1997), p. 4.

responsibility to place the interests of the public above its own when the two are in conflict.

Recall that in Chapter 1 we discussed the desired characteristics of a house inspector and concluded that competence, objectivity, and integrity are critical. We also discussed the role that auditors, as information inspectors, play in reducing information risk through *independent* verification of management assertions. To be a credible source of objective, independent assurance, the professional must have a solid reputation for competence and for unquestioned character and integrity. The concepts of ethical behavior and professional conduct are clearly central to the success of the accounting profession. In fact, those who enter the accounting profession and engage in unethical conduct will inevitably harm themselves, others, and the profession. The most important concept you will read in this chapter is that of personal responsibility and integrity. As an accountant, auditor, manager, or businessperson, you will face numerous difficult ethical issues, and you will experience pressures and temptations. Never forget that your most valuable assets as a professional are integrity and a solid reputation. We encourage you to continually evaluate your choices and behavior and commit to a high level of integrity and ethical behavior as a student, professional, and member of society.

Given the importance of reputation, ethical behavior, and professionalism, the accounting profession has developed a Code of Professional Conduct that guides the behavior of accounting professionals. The profession's Code of Professional Conduct, together with related rules and regulations, is discussed later in this chapter, after we discuss a framework for considering ethical issues.

Theories of Ethical Behavior

✄ [LO 2]

When individuals are confronted with situations that have moral and ethical implications, they do not always agree on the issues at hand, which individuals or groups will be affected and how, or what solutions or courses of actions are available or appropriate for dealing with the situation. Such differences may be caused by differences in the individuals' concepts of fairness and different opinions about the right action to take in a particular situation. Some ethical choices are difficult simply due to the temptation or pressure to pursue one's self-interest, which can cloud judgment regarding what is right or wrong. Other choices are complicated by the sheer difficulty of sorting out the issues and deciphering what might be appropriate or inappropriate actions to take.

S. M. Mintz has suggested that there are three overlapping methods or theories of ethical behavior that can guide the analysis of ethical issues in accounting.[5] These theories are (1) *utilitarianism*, (2) a *rights-based approach*, and (3) a *justice-based approach*. No single approach is necessarily better than another. In fact, elements of each theory may be appropriate for resolving ethical dilemmas in different circumstances.

Utilitarian theory recognizes that decision making involves trade-offs between the benefits and burdens of alternative actions, and it focuses on the consequences of a particular action on the individuals affected. The theory proposes that the interests of all parties affected, not just one's self-interest, should be considered. From this perspective, an action conforms to the principle of utility only if that action will produce more pleasure or happiness (or prevent more pain or unhappiness) than any other possible action. The value

---

[5]See S. M. Mintz, *Cases in Accounting Ethics and Professionalism*, 1997, for a more detailed discussion of each of these models.

of an action is determined solely by the consequences of the action on the welfare of individuals. This is why utilitarianism is sometimes also described as a "consequentialist" theory. One form of utilitarianism holds that rules have a central position in moral judgment due to the adverse consequences that would likely arise if everyone chose to break them. This approach has significance for auditors, who are expected to follow the Code of Professional Conduct in carrying out their responsibilities. One disadvantage in applying the utilitarian theory to ethical dilemmas is that it is often difficult to measure the potential costs and benefits of the actions to be taken. It may also be difficult to balance the interests of all parties involved when those interests conflict with one another.

The rights-based approach assumes that individuals have certain rights and other individuals have a duty to respect those rights. Thus, a decision maker who follows a theory of rights should undertake an action only if it does not violate the rights of any individual. An obvious disadvantage of the theory of rights is that it may be difficult or impossible to satisfy all rights of all affected parties, especially when those rights conflict. The theory of rights is important to auditors because of their public-interest responsibility. As the judge's ruling in this chapter's preface indicates, in conflicting situations, the right of the public to have objective and clear information from the auditor takes precedence over any right the auditor might have to enter into relationships with the client that might cloud the auditor's judgment. According to the concept known as the "moral point of view," auditors must be willing to put the interests of other stakeholders, such as investors and creditors, ahead of their own self-interests and those of the CPA firm. For example, if a difference of opinion with top management exists over an accounting or reporting issue, the auditor should emphasize the interests of the investors and creditors in deciding what action to take, even if it means losing the client.

The justice-based approach is concerned with issues such as equity, fairness, and impartiality. The theory of justice involves two basic principles.[6] The first principle posits that each person has a right to have the maximum degree of personal freedom that is still compatible with the liberty of others. The second principle asserts that social and economic actions should be to everyone's advantage and the benefits available to all. For example, someone in a position to accumulate wealth has a moral obligation to make sure that others are not treated unfairly as a result of his or her gains. Mintz argues that decisions made within this theory should fairly and equitably distribute resources among those individuals or groups affected. There may be difficulty in trying to apply this theory in practice because the rights of one or more individuals or groups may be affected when a better distribution of benefits is provided to others. Under this approach, the auditor considers what would be the most just decision in terms of allocation of resources among interested parties.

While none of these theories by itself can provide a perfect ethical framework, note that each emphasizes the need to consider more than one's self-interest, and each can be useful in helping an auditor to solve dilemmas by providing an ethical perspective.

Example—An Ethical Challenge   Consider how an auditor might reason through the following situation.

---

[6]*Theory of Justice* (The Belknap Press of Harvard University Press, 1971).

Sun City Savings and Loan Company

Pina, Johnson & Associates has recently been awarded the audit of Sun City Savings and Loan Company for the year just ended. Sun City Savings and Loan is now the largest client of the firm, and the fees from this engagement represent a significant portion of the firm's revenues. Upon accepting the Sun City engagement, the firm incurred additional costs by hiring several new employees and a new manager from a larger firm. In bidding on the engagement, Sam Johnson knew that the first-year fees would be just enough to cover the actual cost of the first year's audit, but he hoped that future audit fee increases might lead to a long-term, profitable engagement. Based on his discussions with the predecessor auditors, Johnson knew that there were possible problems with Sun City's loans because of the collateral used for security. Johnson was also concerned that there might be problems with loan-loss reserves due to the effects of the economic slowdown on the tourist industry in Sun City over the last two years. However, Johnson felt that these problems were manageable.

During the current year, the amount included in the loan-loss reserves account was $675,000, approximately the same as the figure for the prior year. The state's banking regulations require that an amount equal to 1.5 percent of the loans outstanding be included as a reserve against losses. The $675,000 was slightly above the statutory requirement. However, the audit staff identified two large loans, aggregating to $15 million, that appeared not to be collectible in full. The working papers disclosed that each loan had originated during the current year and that both had been in default for four months. Additionally, the collateral used to secure the loans was worth considerably less than the amount of the loans and was not in accordance with Sun City's loan policy procedures. Based on this information, the staff estimates that about 40 percent of the $15 million, or $6 million, will not be collected. The staff has also determined that these loans are to entities owned by Patricia Cabot, Sun City's CEO, and some of her business associates.

When Johnson met with Cabot to discuss the two delinquent loans, Cabot assured Johnson that the loans would be paid in full. She told Johnson that the loans had been properly made and that as soon as the economy picked up, payments would be made on the loans. She indicated that no additional reserves were needed and that if Johnson requires such adjustments, his firm might be replaced.

Johnson is concerned that if the loan-loss reserves are increased, Sun City Savings & Loan's owners and investors might be hurt financially. Further, if Johnson requires the adjustment, Pina, Johnson & Associates may lose Sun City as a client, his own career goals will be damaged, and the firm may have to lay off professional and staff employees. Johnson believes there could be serious consequences to several different parties whatever decision he makes.

⋊ [LO 3]   What ethical and professional concerns should Johnson consider in deciding on a course of action? How would Johnson's views differ if the dilemma were viewed with a utilitarian perspective? How about a rights-based or a justice-based approach?

In situations such as this one, an auditor is well advised to think about the ethical issues carefully and from several different perspectives. According to the utilitarian perspective, Johnson should consider the consequences of his actions on all affected parties and whether any rules exist that might require a particular action. He should think not only about the consequences of breaking any applicable rule in the current situation but also what the consequences would be if everyone else also broke the rule. Costs and benefits need to be assessed in terms of the public, Sun City's stockholders, Cabot's reputation, and the situation of the public accounting firm.

Using a rights-based approach, Johnson should consider the rights of the involved parties. If he does so, he will realize that the stockholders' right to fair and accurate information for decision-making purposes would clearly be violated if he does not require an increase in the loan-loss reserves. If Cabot has entered into inappropriate loans at the expense of the stockholders, they will not have received accurate information about Sun City's profitability, liquidity, and so on. Cabot, of course, has no defensible right to misappropriate funds or to report account balances incorrectly.

Finally, from a justice-based perspective, Johnson should think about whether his decision might yield advantages for some at the expense of others, focusing on the protection of those who may otherwise be at a disadvantage. Johnson should avoid favoring the interests of any individual or group and should not select an action that will confer unfair advantages on some (e.g., the management of the S&L) at the expense of others (e.g., the public). Integrity and objectivity require that Johnson not place his self-interest or that of the client ahead of the public interest. Instead, he must focus on Sun City's shareholders as members of the investing public.

If he does not allow his self-interest to cloud his judgment, Johnson will require the client to book the $6 million adjustment for the delinquent loans, regardless of the consequences to himself or to his firm. But, realistically, Johnson's professionalism is likely to be tested in this situation. While he realizes that the loan-loss reserves probably should be increased, he is also likely to be concerned about the possibility of losing this valuable client and the significant investment in new personnel that the firm has made. After all, he could easily rationalize that there is a good chance the economy will turn around and the loans will be repaid, as promised by Cabot. While it seems fairly clear what action should be taken, the question becomes—as it so often does—does the auditor have the courage to do the right thing?

Auditors *frequently* face ethical pressures, and the issues are often not quite as clear-cut as in the above example. It is important that auditors develop sound moral character so that they can respond appropriately in such situations. Mintz points out that auditors who possess certain "virtues" or traits of character are more capable of adhering to a moral point of view.[7] Examples of such virtues include honesty, integrity, impartiality, faithfulness, and trustworthiness. These characteristics are embodied in the profession's Principles of Professional Conduct discussed later in the chapter and are vital to the continued health of the profession.[8]

Practice
INSIGHT

In the final analysis, individual morality is the basis for effectively dealing with ethical challenges. Moral virtues, such as honesty and fairness, are essential characteristics for members of the accounting profession. Accountants who do not possess these foundational characteristics are likely to do great harm to themselves, the profession, and others.

An Overview of Ethics and Professionalism in Public Accounting

A Tale of Two Companies

A couple of true stories about two business organizations will help illustrate the importance of ethics and professionalism in accounting and auditing. The first Kmart store opened in Garden City, Michigan, in March 1962. Kmart Corp. filed for Chapter 11 bankruptcy protection in January 2002, representing the largest retail bankruptcy ever in the United States up to that time. In May 2002, Kmart announced that it was restating its earnings for the first three quarters of the preceding fiscal year to reflect an additional $554 million in losses for a 2001 loss of $2.4 billion. In January 2003, Kmart fired the last of 25 executives who pocketed a total of $28 million in loans that were forgiven before the company filed for bankruptcy. A month later, two former Kmart vice presidents, Enio Montini, Jr., and Joseph Hofmeister, were indicted for alleged crimes involving Kmart's

---

[7]S. M. Mintz, "Virtue, Ethics, and Accounting Education," *Issues in Accounting Education* (Fall 1995), pp. 24–31.

[8]J. E. Copeland, Jr., "Ethics as an Imperative," *Accounting Horizons* (March 2005), pp. 35–43.

accounting. In May 2003, Kmart emerged from bankruptcy and continued to operate independently for several years. The company now operates more than 1,300 stores as a wholly owned subsidiary of Sears Holding Company.

Arthur Andersen, originally founded in 1913 as Andersen, Delaney & Co., grew to become one of the five largest and most respected accounting firms in the world by the late 1990s, with about 85,000 employees. In fall 2001, it became clear that issues were arising in connection with the firm's audits of Enron Corp., and Andersen's Houston office undertook a massive shredding operation to destroy Enron-related documents in October and November 2001. The U.S. Justice Department indicted the firm in March 2002 on obstruction of justice charges relating to the shredding. Despite the fact that the Enron scandal was primarily centered in Texas, Andersen began to unravel quickly, losing over 400 of its publicly traded clients from all over the country by June 2002. The firm was convicted on a single count of obstruction of justice in June 2002, and the firm ceased to audit publicly held companies shortly thereafter. Ironically, the obstruction of justice charge was overturned by the U.S. Supreme Court in 2005, but this was a hollow victory for Andersen, as all of the firm's clients and audit staff had fled by that time to other firms.

Why was financially feeble Kmart able to continue its operations despite questionable accounting practices and federal indictments, while Arthur Andersen was not able to survive even though it was financially strong? The answer is that Kmart had physical assets and traded in physical goods, while Andersen's primary asset was its reputation for competence, professionalism, and integrity. That reputation was damaged prior to the Enron scandal by a string of questionable practices and audit failures (involving Sunbeam, Waste Management, the Baptist Foundation of Arizona, and others) and was finished off by the Enron scandal and indictment. The sudden death of one of the largest and formerly most respected public accounting firms was a serious wake-up call for the profession, and the collapse underscored the vital importance of ethical conduct and professionalism on the part of auditors.

Standards for Auditor Professionalism

✂ [LO 4]

This section provides an overview of the principles, rules, and regulations governing ethics and professionalism in public accounting. The topic is complicated by the fact that these rules and regulations were established over time by different professional and regulatory bodies and in some cases by legislation. Early in the history of the public accounting profession in the United States, nongovernmental associations took charge of setting standards and establishing codes of conduct for practicing accountants. In particular, the AICPA (and its predecessor, the American Association of Public Accountants) established auditing standards and a Code of Professional Conduct, mapping out the primary areas in which ethical conduct is expected of public accountants. The AICPA, being a private, nongovernmental association, only has the authority to require its members to comply with the Code. However, state and federal courts have consistently held that all practicing CPAs, whether in public or private practice and whether or not a member of the AICPA, must follow professional ethical standards as laid out in the Code of Professional Conduct. Further, most state boards of accountancy have adopted the Code, thus integrating it into state-level regulation of the practice of accountancy.

Practice
INSIGHT

It is important to understand that the U.S. capital markets system is based on public confidence. Public accountants play a central role in the public's ability to place confidence in companies' financial reports, and thus greatly influence how efficiently and effectively our capital markets work. Integrity and independence in fact and in appearance are cornerstones of the auditor's social responsibility and are critical to public confidence and to the proper functioning of our economic system.

The SEC has legal authority to oversee the public accounting profession. Through much of its history, the SEC has allowed private-sector entities such as the Financial Accounting Standards Board and the Auditing Standards Board (or ASB, a standing senior technical committee within the AICPA) to set accounting and auditing standards, respectively. However, the SEC exercises considerable influence in the standard-setting process and has established standards of its own from time to time, some of which differ from those established by private-sector bodies.

The PCAOB adopted the professional standards established by the AICPA on an interim basis in 2003, including the Code of Professional Conduct. However, the PCAOB and the SEC have additional, more stringent standards of professional conduct, mostly in the key area of auditor independence, which must be followed by auditors of public companies. Because the AICPA Code of Professional Conduct provides the broadest map of the areas in which professionalism is expected from auditors, the code serves as the organizing framework for the following discussion. However, we also highlight the more stringent independence requirements the SEC and PCAOB impose on public company auditors.

Figure 19–1 summarizes the auditor's responsibilities with respect to auditing standards and standards of professional conduct for the audits of private and public companies. As the figure illustrates, in auditing a *privately held* entity

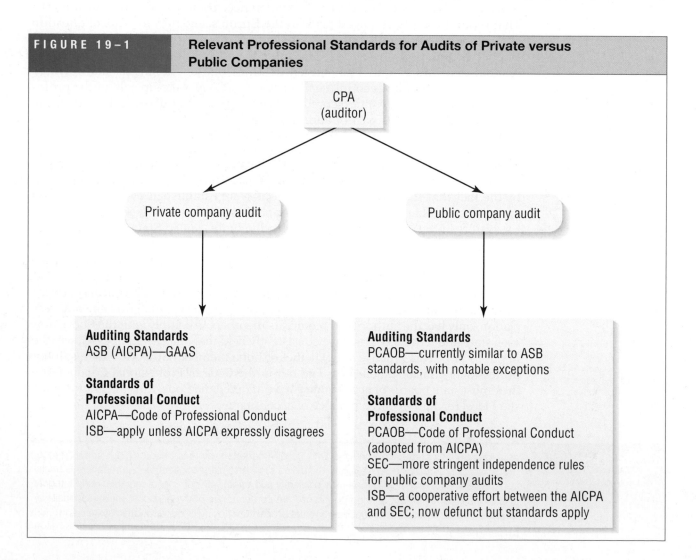

FIGURE 19-1   **Relevant Professional Standards for Audits of Private versus Public Companies**

CPA (auditor)

Private company audit

Public company audit

Auditing Standards
ASB (AICPA)—GAAS

Standards of Professional Conduct
AICPA—Code of Professional Conduct
ISB—apply unless AICPA expressly disagrees

Auditing Standards
PCAOB—currently similar to ASB standards, with notable exceptions

Standards of Professional Conduct
PCAOB—Code of Professional Conduct (adopted from AICPA)
SEC—more stringent independence rules for public company audits
ISB—a cooperative effort between the AICPA and SEC; now defunct but standards apply

a CPA must follow the auditing standards established by the ASB, and the independence and other standards of professional conduct established by the Code of Professional Conduct. In addition, the three standards and the three interpretations issued by the Independence Standards Board (ISB) during its short existence from 1997 to 2001 generally must be followed.[9]

In auditing a *publicly held* company, a CPA must follow the auditing standards of the PCAOB (currently similar to those of the AICPA with some notable exceptions), the Code of Professional Conduct, and also the more stringent independence requirements established by the SEC, ISB, and PCAOB.

The AICPA Code of Professional Conduct: A Comprehensive Framework for Auditors

[LO 5] The AICPA Code of Professional Conduct defines both ideal principles and a set of specific, mandatory rules describing minimum levels of conduct a CPA must maintain.

The AICPA Code of Professional Conduct consists of two sections:

- Principles of Professional Conduct (setting forth ideal attitudes and behaviors).
- Rules of Conduct (defining minimum standards).

The Principles of Professional Conduct provide the framework for the Rules of Conduct. Additional guidance for applying the Rules of Conduct is provided by:

- Interpretations of Rules of Conduct.
- Rulings by the Professional Ethics Executive Committee (PEEC).

The Interpretations of Rules of Conduct and Rulings are promulgated by the AICPA's PEEC to provide guidelines as to the scope and application of the Rules of Conduct. Unlike the Rules of Conduct, interpretations and ethics rulings are not specifically enforceable, but an auditor who departs from them has the burden of justifying such departures.

The guidance provided by the Code of Professional Conduct starts at a conceptual level with the principles and progressively moves to general rules and detailed interpretations and then to specific rulings on individual cases. Figure 19–2 illustrates the four parts of the Code of Professional Conduct.

Principles of Professional Conduct

[LO 6]

The framework for the Code of Professional Conduct is provided by six fundamental ethical principles. The preamble to the Principles of Professional Conduct states the following:

> They [the principles] guide members in the performance of their professional responsibilities and express the basic tenets of ethical and professional conduct. The principles call for an unswerving commitment to honorable behavior, even at the sacrifice of personal advantage. (ET 51.02)

Table 19–1 presents the definition of each of the six principles. Please take a moment to read these vital precepts. Why do you think the profession has adopted these high ideals for accountants and auditors?

---

[9]The committee within the AICPA that is charged with setting, deleting, or modifying rules and interpretations and delivering ethics rulings in response to specific questions is known as the Professional Ethics Executive Committee (PEEC).

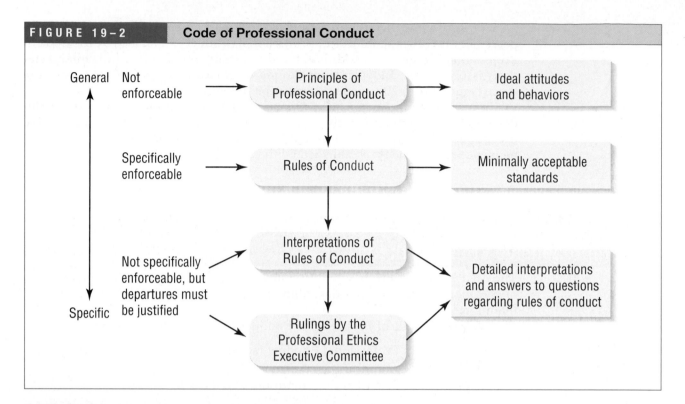

FIGURE 19–2   **Code of Professional Conduct**

General ── Not enforceable ──→ Principles of Professional Conduct ──→ Ideal attitudes and behaviors

Specifically enforceable ──→ Rules of Conduct ──→ Minimally acceptable standards

Not specifically enforceable, but departures must be justified ──→ Interpretations of Rules of Conduct ──→ Detailed interpretations and answers to questions regarding rules of conduct

Specific ──→ Rulings by the Professional Ethics Executive Committee

TABLE 19–1   **Principles of Professional Conduct**

Responsibilities: In carrying out their responsibilities as professionals, members should exercise sensitive professional and moral judgments in all their activities.

The public interest: Members should accept the obligation to act in a way that will serve the public interest, honor the public trust, and demonstrate commitment to professionalism.

Integrity: To maintain and broaden public confidence, members should perform all professional responsibilities with the highest sense of integrity.

Objectivity and independence: A member should maintain objectivity and be free of conflicts of interest in discharging professional responsibilities. A member in public practice should be independent in fact and appearance when providing auditing and other attestation services.

Due care: A member should observe the profession's technical and ethical standards, strive continually to improve competence and the quality of services, and discharge professional responsibility to the best of the member's ability.

Scope and nature of services: A member in public practice should observe the Principles of the Code of Professional Conduct in determining the scope and nature of services to be provided.

The first two principles address a CPA's responsibilities to exercise professional and moral judgment in a manner that serves the public interest. These principles reinforce the conviction that the CPA's role in society is to serve the public.

As indicated by the third and fourth principles, the public relies on a CPA's integrity, objectivity, and independence in providing high-quality services. Integrity requires that a CPA be honest and candid, and honor both the form and the spirit of ethical standards. Thus, a CPA should make judgments that are consistent with the theories of rights and justice. When faced with an ethical challenge, the CPA should ask, "What actions would an individual with integrity take, given these facts and circumstances?" Objectivity and independence are hallmarks of the public accounting profession. The principle of objectivity requires the CPA to be impartial and free of conflicts of interest. Independence requires that the CPA avoid relationships that would impair his or her objectivity. When a CPA provides auditing- or attestation-related services, independence in both fact and appearance must be maintained.

The fifth principle, due care, requires that the CPA perform his or her professional responsibilities with competence and diligence. While the performance of professional services must take into account the interests of the client, the public's interest must be considered more important when the two interests conflict. The last principle requires that the CPA determine that the services to be rendered are consistent with acceptable professional behavior for CPAs. This principle also requires that the CPA's firm maintain internal quality control activities to ensure that services are delivered competently and that no conflict of interest exists.

Rules of Conduct
✎ [LO 7]

The bylaws of the AICPA specifically require that members adhere to the Rules of Conduct of the Code of Professional Conduct. The PCAOB also requires auditors of public companies to adhere to the Rules of Conduct. Table 19–2 provides an overview of the existing Rules of Conduct. Take a few minutes to read through these rules. As you can see, the Rules of Conduct cover much of the same ground as the Principles of Professional Conduct, but are somewhat more specific. The rules are grouped and numbered in five categories:

- Independence, Integrity, and Objectivity (Section 100).
- General Standards and Accounting Principles (Section 200).
- Responsibilities to Clients (Section 300).
- Responsibilities to Colleagues (Section 400).[10]
- Other Responsibilities and Practices (Section 500).

Much of the original text of the rules is included in Table 19-2. The "nitty-gritty" details in implementing the rules are found in the *interpretations* of each rule. For example, while Rule 101 relating to independence is comprised of only one brief sentence, the 12 in-force interpretations of Rule 101 comprise over 25 pages of detail relating to financial or business interests that are, or are not, considered to compromise independence. In addition, there are dozens of ethics rulings related to independence. Interpretations of the other rules tend to be significantly shorter and less involved. This is because independence has become the most complex and controversial area of auditor ethics and professionalism—not only has the AICPA established multiple pages of interpretations and rulings regarding independence, but the SEC and the now defunct ISB also weighed in heavily on the independence issue.[11] Differences between AICPA independence standards and the SEC independence regulations, which apply only to the audits of public companies, are discussed in the context of the AICPA Code of Professional Conduct, which we'll now explore in more depth.

---

[10]Section 400 currently does not contain any rules because all the 400-series rules were repealed in the 1970s under pressure from the U.S. Justice Department and the Federal Trade Commission, which contended that the rules were anticompetitive. Prior to their repeal, these rules prohibited advertising, encroaching upon other CPAs' clients, and offering employment to other CPAs' employees.

[11]The ISB was created in 1997 as a joint effort of the AICPA and the SEC to address important issues relating to audits of public companies. The board was housed within the SEC Practice Section of the AICPA. In 2000 the SEC issued its own comprehensive rule on auditor independence for the audits of public companies, and the ISB was disbanded in July 2001, when the SEC concluded that "the board's mission had been substantially fulfilled." During its brief tenure, the ISB issued three standards and three interpretations. Although the ISB is now defunct, its standards are recognized by the SEC and the AICPA, and they currently remain in effect for public company audits. However, the most important aspects of the ISB's standards have been incorporated into the SEC's independence rules and the Code of Professional Conduct and are therefore not discussed separately in this chapter.

TABLE 19-2		Overview of AICPA Rules of Conduct
Rule No.	*Rule Title*	*Text of the Rule**
101	Independence	A member in public practice shall be independent in the performance of professional services as required by standards promulgated by bodies designated by Council.
102	Integrity and objectivity	In the performance of any professional service, a member shall maintain objectivity and integrity, shall be free of conflicts of interest, and shall not knowingly misrepresent facts or subordinate his or her judgment to others.
201	General standards	A member shall comply with the following standards and with any interpretations thereof by bodies designated by Council. A. Professional competence. B. Due professional care. C. Planning and supervision. D. Sufficient relevant data.
202	Compliance with standards	A member who performs auditing, review, compilation, management consulting, tax, or other professional services shall comply with standards promulgated by bodies designated by Council.
203	Accounting principles	A member shall not (1) express an opinion . . . that the financial statements or other financial data of any entity are presented in conformity with generally accepted accounting principles or (2) state that he or she is not aware of any material modifications that should be made . . . in order for them to be in conformity with generally accepted accounting principles, if such statements or data contain any departure from an accounting principle . . . that has a material effect. . . .
301	Confidential client information	A member in public practice shall not disclose any confidential client information without the specific consent of the client. . . . Members . . . shall not use to their own advantage or disclose any member's confidential client information that comes to their attention. . . .
302	Contingent fees	A member in public practice shall not (1) perform for a contingent fee any professional services for . . . a client for whom the member or the member's firm performs, an audit or review of a financial statement . . . or (2) prepare an original or amended tax return or claim for a tax refund for a contingent fee for any client.
501	Acts discreditable	A member shall not commit an act discreditable to the profession.
502	Advertising and other forms of solicitation	A member in public practice shall not seek to obtain clients by advertising or other forms of solicitation in a manner that is false, misleading, or deceptive. Solicitation by the use of coercion, overreaching, or harassing conduct is prohibited.
503	Commissions and referral fees	A member in public practice shall not for a commission recommend or refer to a client any product or service, or for a commission recommend or refer any product or service to be supplied by a client, or receive a commission, when the member or the member's firm also performs for that client an audit or review of a financial statement. . . . Any member who accepts a referral fee for recommending or referring any service of a CPA to any person or entity or who pays a referral fee to obtain a client shall disclose such acceptance or payment to the client.
505	Form of organization and name	A member may practice public accounting only in a form of organization permitted by law or regulation whose characteristics conform to resolutions of Council. A member shall not practice public accounting under a firm name that is misleading. Names of one or more past owners may be included in the firm name of a successor organization. A firm may not designate itself as "Members of the American Institute of Certified Public Accountants" unless all of its CPA owners are members of the Institute.

*Some of the longer rules have been excerpted or abridged. Refer to the full set of rules and interpretations at www.aicpa.org.

Independence, Integrity, and Objectivity

⚞ [LO 8]   Section 100 of the AICPA Rules of Conduct currently contains two rules related to independence, integrity, and objectivity. SEC and PCAOB rules and standards relating to auditor independence are also discussed in this section to the extent that they add to the AICPA's requirements. While we cover minimum guidelines required by the profession, it is important to note that firms often require their employees to comply with rules and guidelines that are even stricter than those imposed on them by outside bodies.

Independence   If an auditor is not perceived to be independent of his or her client, it is unlikely that a user of financial statements will place much reliance on the CPA's work. Rule 101 is a very general statement concerning auditor independence and relates only to attestation-related services, including audits.

Rule 101: A member in public practice shall be independent in the performance of professional services as required by standards promulgated by bodies designated by Council.

AICPA professional standards require a public accounting firm, including the firm's partners and professional employees, to be independent in accordance with AICPA Rule 101 whenever the firm performs an attest service for a client. Attest services include:

- Financial statement audits
- Financial statement reviews (See Chapter 21)
- Other attest services as defined in the Statements on Standards for Attestation Engagements (SSAEs).

Performing a compilation of a client's financial statements (see Chapter 21) does not require independence, but an accountant or firm that lacks independence must explicitly indicate this fact in the compilation report. Likewise, independence is not required to perform other nonattest services (e.g., tax preparation, financial planning, or consulting services) if those services are the only services provided to a particular client. Because of the difficulties that sometimes arise in defining independent relationships, numerous interpretations of Rule 101 have been issued.

Table 19–3 presents Interpretation 101-1, a major interpretation related to independence. In reading Interpretation 101-1 it is important to consider the definition of a "covered member." The AICPA uses an engagement team approach to determine independence. Under this approach, a covered member includes:

- An individual on the attest engagement team.
- An individual in a position to influence the attest engagement.
- A partner or manager who provides nonattest services to the attest client beginning once he or she provides 10 hours of nonattest services to the client within any fiscal year and ending on the later of the date (1) the firm signs the report on the financial statements for the fiscal year during which those services were provided; or (2) he or she no longer expects to provide 10 or more hours of nonattest services to the attest client on a recurring basis.
- A partner in the office in which the lead attest engagement partner primarily practices in connection with the attest engagement.
- The firm, including the firm's employee benefits plans.
- An entity whose operating, financial, or accounting policies can be controlled (as defined by generally accepted accounting principles for consolidation purposes) by any of the individuals or entities described above or by two or more such individuals or entities if they act together.

Note that the independence rules apply to more than just the partner on the attest engagement. Every individual on the engagement team and others who may be in a position to influence the engagement must be independent with respect to the attest client. Other partners or managers of the CPA firm who are not on the attest engagement team must also generally be independent of the client if they provide *nonattest* services to that client (such as tax or consulting services), or even if a partner simply works in the same office as the attest engagement's lead partner. Under the engagement team approach, a staff member of the CPA firm does not need to be independent of the attest client unless he or she performs work directly for the client or becomes a partner in the same office where the attest engagement's lead partner works.

TABLE 19–3	Interpretation 101-1 (Interpretation of Rule 101)*

Independence Shall Be Considered to Be Impaired If:

A. During the period of the professional engagement a covered member
    1. Had or was committed to acquire any direct or material indirect financial interest in the client.
    2. Was a trustee of any trust or executor or administrator of any estate if such trust or estate had or was committed to acquire any direct or material indirect financial interest in the client.
    3. Had a joint closely held investment that was material to the covered member.
    4. Except as specifically permitted in Interpretation 101-5, had any loan to or from the client, any officer or director of the client, or any individual owning 10 percent or more of the client's outstanding equity securities or other ownership interests.
B. During the period of the professional engagement, a partner or professional employee of the firm, his or her immediate family, or any group of such persons acting together owned more than 5 percent of a client's outstanding equity securities or other ownership interests.
C. During the period covered by the financial statements or during the period of the professional engagement, a firm, or partner or professional employee of the firm was simultaneously associated with the client as a(n)
    1. Director, officer, or employee, or in any capacity equivalent to that of a member of management;
    2. Promoter, underwriter, or voting trustee; or
    3. Trustee for any pension or profit-sharing trust of the client.

Application of the Independence Rules to Covered Members Formerly Employed by or Associated with a Client

An individual who was formerly employed by or associated with a client as a(n) officer, director, promoter, underwriter, voting trustee, or trustee for a pension or profit-sharing trust of the client would impair his or her firm's independence if the individual—
1. Participated on the attest engagement team or was an individual in a position to influence the attest engagement for the client when the attest engagement covers any period that includes his or her former employment or association with that client; or
2. Was otherwise a covered member with respect to the client unless the individual first dissociates from the client by—
    a. Terminating any relationships with the client described in Interpretation 101-1.C;
    b. Disposing of any direct or material indirect financial interest in the client;
    c. Collecting or repaying any loans to or from the client, except for loans specifically permitted or grandfathered under interpretation 101-5;
    d. Ceasing to participate in all employee benefit plans sponsored by the client, unless the client is legally required to allow the individual to participate in the plan (for example, COBRA) and the individual pays 100 percent of the cost of participation on a current basis; and
    e. Liquidating or transferring all vested benefits in the client's defined benefit plans, defined contribution plans, deferred compensation plans, and other similar arrangements at the earliest date permitted under the plan. However, liquidation or transfer is not required if a penalty significant to the benefits is imposed upon liquidation or transfer.

Application of the Independence Rules to a Covered Member's Immediate Family

Except as stated in the following paragraph, a covered member's immediate family is subject to Rule 101 [ET section 101.01], and its interpretations and rulings. The exceptions are that independence would not be considered to be impaired solely as a result of the following:
1. An individual in a covered member's immediate family was employed by the client in a position other than a key position.
2. In connection with his or her employment, an individual in the immediate family of one of the following covered members participated in a retirement, savings, compensation, or similar plan that is a client, is sponsored by a client, or that invests in a client (provided such plan is normally offered to all employees in similar positions):
    a. A partner or manager who provides ten or more hours of nonattest services to the client; or
    b. Any partner in the office in which the lead attest engagement partner primarily practices in connection with the attest engagement.
For purposes of determining materiality under Rule 101 the financial interests of the covered member and his or her immediate family should be aggregated.

Application of the Independence Rules to Close Relatives

Independence would be considered to be impaired if—
1. An individual participating on the attest engagement team has a close relative who had
    a. A key position with the client, or
    b. A financial interest in the client that
        (i) Was material to the close relative and of which the individual has knowledge; or
        (ii) Enabled the close relative to exercise significant influence over the client.
2. An individual in a position to influence the attest engagement or any partner in the office in which the lead attest engagement partner primarily practices in connection with the attest engagement has a close relative who had
    a. A key position with the client; or
    b. A financial interest in the client that
        (i) Was material to the close relative and of which the individual or partner has knowledge; and
        (ii) Enabled the close relative to exercise significant influence over the client.

Other Considerations

It is impossible to enumerate all circumstances in which the appearance of independence might be questioned. In the absence of an independence interpretation or ruling under Rule 101 [see ET section 101.01] that addresses a particular circumstance, members should evaluate whether that circumstance would lead a reasonable person aware of all the relevant facts to conclude that there is an unacceptable threat to the member's and the firm's independence. When making that evaluation, members should refer to the risk-based approach described in the Conceptual Framework for AICPA Independence Standards [see ET section 100.01]. If the threats to independence are not at an acceptable level, safeguards should be applied to eliminate the threats or reduce them to an acceptable level. In cases where threats to independence are not at an acceptable level, thereby requiring the application of safeguards, the threats identified and the safeguards applied to eliminate the threats or reduce them to an acceptable level should be documented.

*Interpretation 101-1 has been excerpted and abridged. Refer to the full set of rules and interpretations at www.aicpa.org.

The CPA firm itself must also be independent with respect to the client; for example, the CPA firm's benefit plan cannot invest in the firm's attest clients. Note that with few exceptions, the independence requirements under Rule 101 extend to the CPA's immediate family members (spouse, spousal equivalent, or dependents) and, in a few cases, to the CPA's close relatives (nondependent children, siblings, parents, etc.). The applicability of the independence requirements to family members and relatives is discussed later in this section.

Note the "Other Considerations" section at the end of Interpretation 101-1 (Table 19–3), which recognizes the impossibility of addressing all circumstances in which the appearance of independence might be questioned. In the absence of specific guidance, CPAs should evaluate whether a reasonable person would conclude that the member's and the firm's independence are unacceptably threatened. The AICPA has prepared a Conceptual Framework for AICPA Independence Standards for use in making such an evaluation. The conceptual framework, which became effective as of early 2006, describes the risk-based approach used by the PEEC when it develops independence standards. Under this approach, a CPA is required to identify and assess the extent to which a threat to independence exists. If such a threat does exist, the CPA considers whether the threat might reasonably be considered to compromise the member's professional judgment. If so, the CPA evaluates whether the threat can be effectively mitigated or eliminated. Depending on the evaluation, the CPA implements safeguards to eliminate or reduce the threats to an acceptable level or concludes that independence is impaired. However, the risk-based conceptual framework cannot be used to justify departures from specific independence standards.

While CPA firms are required to comply with Rule 101, most major CPA firms have their own firm-specific independence rules that are typically more stringent than the AICPA's standards. In addition, firms are required by AICPA and PCAOB standards to establish and maintain a system of quality control, a significant aspect of which is to ensure the firms' compliance with independence standards. Quality control requirements, the AICPA's peer review program, and the PCAOB's auditor inspection program are discussed later in this chapter.

Note that Interpretation 101-1 examines independence along two dimensions—*financial relationships* and *business relationships*—and also explicitly considers the effects of family relationships on independence. A number of other interpretations of Rule 101 provide further explanations on such relationships.

Practice INSIGHT

During the audit of a public company, a senior auditor at one of the Big 4 accounting firms purchased $5,000 of the company's stock. The auditor was sanctioned by the PCAOB, fired by the firm, and banned from association with a registered public accounting firm for one year. (PCAOB Release 105-2007-003.)

Financial Relationships   Interpretation 101-1 prohibits members from any financial relationship with a client that may impair or give the appearance of impairing independence. This includes any *direct* or *material indirect* financial interest in the client. Note that the materiality of the interest is only considered if the interest is indirect. A direct interest impairs independence even if it is so small as to be considered immaterial.

In 2005 the AICPA's PEEC adopted Interpretation 101-15, which defines financial interest, direct financial interest, and indirect financial interest as used in Interpretation 101-1 and provides guidance to members in determining whether financial interests should be considered direct or indirect financial interests. A *financial interest* is an ownership interest in an equity or a debt security issued by an entity, including rights and obligations to acquire such an interest.

A *direct financial interest* is a financial interest that is owned directly by an individual or entity, or is under the control of an individual or entity. A financial interest that is beneficially owned through an intermediary (e.g., an estate or trust) is also considered a direct financial interest when the beneficiary either controls the intermediary or has the authority to supervise or participate in the intermediary's investment decisions. A financial interest is beneficially owned when an individual or entity is not the recorded owner of the interest but has a right to some or all of the underlying benefits of ownership. With few exceptions (see below), direct financial interests by CPAs in attest clients impair independence.

An *indirect financial interest* arises when (a) an auditor or other covered member has a financial interest in an entity that is associated with an attest client; (b) the financial interest is beneficially owned through an investment vehicle, estate, trust, or other intermediary; and (c) the auditor *does not control* the intermediary or have authority to supervise or participate in the intermediary's investment decisions.

Indirect financial interests are generally permissible only if the amount involved is immaterial with respect to the covered member's income and wealth. For example, the ownership of shares in a mutual fund is considered to be a direct financial interest in the mutual fund. The securities that the mutual fund invests in are considered indirect financial interests to the covered member. Interpretation 101-15 indicates that if the mutual fund is diversified, and if the covered member owns 5 percent or less of the outstanding shares of the mutual fund, the investment would not be considered to constitute a material indirect financial interest in the underlying investments. However, if a covered member owns more than 5 percent of the outstanding shares of a diversified mutual fund, or if the mutual fund is not diversified, the covered member needs to evaluate the underlying investments of the mutual fund to determine whether the investment in the mutual fund constitutes a material indirect financial interest in any of the mutual fund's underlying investments.

Interpretation 101-15 offers the following example relating to investments in mutual funds: Assume that a nondiversified mutual fund owns shares in attest client Company A. Further assume that the mutual fund's net assets are $10,000,000; the covered member owns 1 percent of the outstanding shares of the mutual fund, having a value of $100,000; and the mutual fund has 10 percent of its assets invested in Company A. The indirect financial interest of the covered member in Company A is $10,000. This amount should be measured against the covered member's net worth (including the net worth of his or her immediate family) to determine if it is material.

You may have heard that in some circumstances, individuals can place their assets into a "blind trust" to avoid possible conflicts of interest. A blind trust is a trust in which the owner of the trust assets does not supervise or participate in the trust's investment decisions during the term of the trust. Interpretation 101-1 addresses the question of whether CPAs can avoid impairing their independence by placing financial interests in a client in a blind trust. Because the investments will ultimately revert to the owner and the owner usually retains the right to amend or revoke the trust, both the blind trust and the underlying investments are considered to be direct financial interests of the covered member.

Interpretation 101-15 clarifies other circumstances, such as ownership in retirement plans, partnerships, LLCs, and insurance policies of various types. For example, if a CPA owns an insurance policy issued by an attest client, independence is not considered to be impaired so long as the policy was purchased under the insurance company's normal terms and procedures and does not offer an investment option. Some insurance policies allow the policy owner to invest part of the cash value in a variety of underlying investments (stocks, bond, etc.). These underlying investments are considered to be a financial interest. Thus, in such circumstances the CPA must determine whether the underlying investments are direct or indirect financial interests.

| EXHIBIT 19–1 | **ESM Government Securities, Inc., Audit Partner Had "Loan" from Client** |

ESM Government Securities, Inc., was a Fort Lauderdale brokerage firm that specialized in buying and selling debt securities issued by the federal government and its various agencies. Its main customers were small to moderate-size banks and municipalities. The major type of transaction engaged in by ESM was known as a "repo," in which a securities dealer sells a customer a large block of federal securities and simultaneously agrees to repurchase the securities at a later date at an agreed-upon price. A massive fraud was conducted at ESM by Ronnie Ewton and Alan Novick, who hid trading losses and other misappropriations from ESM's auditor, Alexander Grant. The trading losses incurred by ESM were transferred to an affiliated company. When the thefts and trading losses were finally tallied, there was a net deficit of $300 million for ESM.

Sadly, the audit partner, Jose Gomez, was aware of the fraud. Gomez was admitted as a partner to Alexander Grant in 1979. His major client was ESM Securities. Shortly after making partner, Gomez was informed by Novick that the company's 1977 and 1978 financial statements had been misstated. Novick was able to convince Gomez not to withdraw Alexander Grant's audit report on the assumption that ESM would recoup its losses. Novick was aware that Gomez was experiencing financial problems in spite of his salary as a partner. Over the course of the fraud (1977–1984), Gomez received approximately $200,000 in payments from Novick to relieve his financial woes.

Generally a loan to or from a client is considered to impair the member's independence (see Exhibit 19–1). However, there are situations in which a CPA is permitted to obtain loans from a financial institution that is a client. Interpretation 101-5 permits the following types of personal loans from a client that operates as a financial institution:

- Automobile loans and leases collateralized by the automobile.
- Loans fully collateralized by the surrender value of an insurance policy.
- Loans fully collateralized by cash deposits at the same financial institution.
- Credit cards and cash advances where the aggregate outstanding balance is reduced to $10,000 or less by the payment due date.

Such loans must be made in accordance with the financial institution's *normal* lending procedures, terms, and requirements and must, at all times, be kept current as to all terms. *Normal lending procedures, terms, and requirements* are defined as lending procedures, terms, and requirements that are reasonably comparable to those relating to loans of a similar character given to other borrowers during the period in which the loan to the member is given.

A number of interesting issues arise when trying to apply the independence rules. Stop and think for a moment: could unpaid fees be considered an outstanding debt by the client to the auditor—a direct financial interest on the part of the auditor? In fact, the rulings and interpretations of Rule 101 specify that if fees pertaining to services provided more than one year prior to the date of the audit report remain unpaid, the auditor's independence is impaired with respect to that client. However, unpaid fees from a client that is in bankruptcy do not impair the auditor's independence.

Let's test your intuition. Think about the following situations to determine if the financial interest represented is a direct financial interest, an indirect financial interest, or neither. Also decide whether the financial interest would impair the auditor's independence: (1) The auditor owns a $100 investment in a mutual fund that spreads its holdings evenly across companies listed in the S&P 500. One of the auditor's clients is an S&P 500 company. (2) The managing audit partner of the office owns stock in one of the audit clients of the office, but the amount is immaterial and the managing partner is not involved in the audit.

The first situation represents an indirect financial interest in the audit client. The relationship would not impair independence because the fund is diversified and the auditor owns very little of the fund. The second scenario represents a direct financial interest by a covered member. Independence is considered impaired despite the fact that the amount of stock owned is immaterial.

Business Relationships   Rule 101 (including relevant interpretations) essentially indicates that the independence of a CPA is impaired if the CPA performs a managerial or other significant role for a client's organization during the time period covered by an attest engagement. Such situations often arise when a former employee of the client becomes employed by the CPA firm or, more commonly, when a CPA takes a job with a former audit client. Interpretations of this rule, however, provide for certain exceptions.

For example, a former employee of an attest client cannot become a member of the attest engagement team or be placed in a position to influence the engagement for that client unless the subject of the attest engagement does not include any period of his or her former employment or association with the client. In addition, if a client employee joins the CPA firm and becomes a covered member with respect to the client, the CPA firm is not independent unless the former client employee first dissociates from the client, essentially by terminating noncomplying managerial and financial relationships with the client (see Table 19–4 for details).

TABLE 19–4	Interpretation 101-2—Employment or Association with Attest Clients

A firm's independence will be considered to be impaired with respect to a client if a partner or professional employee leaves the firm and is subsequently employed by or associated with that client in a key position unless all the following conditions are met:

1. Amounts due to the former partner or professional employee for his or her previous interest in the firm and for unfunded, vested retirement benefits are not material to the firm, and the underlying formula used to calculate the payments remains fixed during the payout period. Retirement benefits may also be adjusted for inflation and interest may be paid on amounts due.
2. The former partner or professional employee is not in a position to influence the accounting firm's operations or financial policies.
3. The former partner or professional employee does not participate or appear to participate in, and is not associated with, the firm, whether or not compensated for such participation or association, once employment or association with the client begins. An appearance of participation or association results from such actions as:
   - The individual provides consultation to the firm.
   - The firm provides the individual with an office and related amenities (for example, secretarial and telephone services).
   - The individual's name is included in the firm's office directory.
   - The individual's name is included as a member of the firm in other membership lists of business, professional, or civic organizations, unless the individual is clearly designated as retired.
4. The ongoing attest engagement team considers the appropriateness or necessity of modifying the engagement procedures to adjust for the risk that, by virtue of the former partner or professional employee's prior knowledge of the audit plan, audit effectiveness could be reduced.
5. The firm assesses whether existing attest engagement team members have the appropriate experience and stature to effectively deal with the former partner or professional employee and his or her work, when that person will have significant interaction with the attest engagement team.
6. The subsequent attest engagement is reviewed to determine whether the engagement team members maintained the appropriate level of skepticism when evaluating the representations and work of the former partner or professional employee, when the person joins the client in a key position within one year of disassociating from the firm and has significant interaction with the attest engagement team. The review should be performed by a professional with appropriate stature, expertise, and objectivity and should be tailored based on the position that the person assumed at the client, the position he or she held at the firm, the nature of the services he or she provided to the client, and other relevant facts and circumstances. Appropriate actions, as deemed necessary, should be taken based on the results of the review.

Responsible members within the firm should implement procedures for compliance with the preceding conditions when firm professionals are employed or associated with attest clients.

With respect to conditions 4, 5, and 6, the procedures adopted will depend on several factors, including whether the former partner or professional employee served as a member of the engagement team, the positions he or she held at the firm and has accepted at the client, the length of time that has elapsed since the professional left the firm, and the circumstances of his or her departure.

Considering Employment or Association with the Client

When a member of the attest engagement team or an individual in a position to influence the attest engagement intends to seek or discuss potential employment or association with an attest client, or is in receipt of a specific offer of employment from an attest client, independence will be impaired with respect to the client unless the person promptly reports such consideration or offer to an appropriate person in the firm, and removes himself or herself from the engagement until the employment offer is rejected or employment is no longer being sought. When a covered member becomes aware that a member of the attest engagement team or an individual in a position to influence the attest engagement is considering employment or association with a client, the covered member should notify an appropriate person in the firm.

The appropriate person should consider what additional procedures may be necessary to provide reasonable assurance that any work performed for the client by that person was performed with objectivity and integrity as required under Rule 102 [ET section 102.01]. Additional procedures, such as reperformance of work already done, will depend on the nature of the engagement and the individual involved.

Next, consider the situation that arises when a CPA goes to work for a client of his or her former CPA firm. This has been a controversial area, because unfortunately several of the high-profile frauds of the last several years were facilitated by former auditors. Interpretation 101-2 indicates that a firm's independence is considered to be impaired with respect to a client if a partner or professional employee leaves the firm and is subsequently employed by or associated with that client in a *key position* unless a number of conditions are met (see the list of key terms at the end of the chapter for the definition of a key position). These conditions require that the CPA be completely disassociated from the CPA firm, and that the firm take steps to ensure that the engagement team exercises sufficient professional skepticism and is not unduly influenced by the former employee of the firm (see Table 19–4 for details). In fact, Interpretation 101-2 indicates that if a member of the attest engagement team or an individual in a position to influence the attest engagement has a job offer from or even *develops the intention* to seek or discuss potential employment with an attest client, independence is impaired with respect to the client unless the person promptly reports the situation to an appropriate person in the firm and removes himself or herself from the engagement until the offer is rejected or employment is no longer being sought. If another employee of the CPA firm becomes aware that a member of the attest engagement team (or an individual in a position to influence the attest engagement) is considering employment with a client, the employee should notify an appropriate person in the firm so the firm can take steps to prevent the impairment of its independence.

Practice INSIGHT

Despite the SEC's restrictions on auditors accepting key positions for former audit clients, auditors continue to be highly sought to fill high-level financial management positions. The breadth and depth of the business knowledge and expertise auditors develop by working with various clients over time makes them highly valuable to companies as prospective employees, especially once the auditor has reached the manager or partner level. Thus, companies continue to find various ways to hire former auditors while allowing the auditors and their former firms to comply with professional standards.

Another type of business relationship can arise when a CPA is asked to serve as an *honorary* director or trustee for a not-for-profit client. It is not unusual for members of a CPA firm to be asked to lend the prestige of their names to a charitable, religious, civic, or similar organization and for their firm to provide accounting and auditing services to the not-for-profit organization. Interpretation 101-4 allows a member to serve as a director or trustee for a not-for-profit client "so long as his or her position is clearly honorary, and he or she cannot vote or otherwise participate in board or management functions." Any of the organization's documents that contain the member's name must identify the member's position as honorary.

Effect of Family Relationships
The issues related to a CPA's financial or business interest in a client may extend to members of the CPA's family. Certain relationships between members of a CPA's family and a client are considered to affect the CPA's independence. This is an area where the AICPA's independence rules have been modified to recognize changing social factors such as dual-career families. A distinction is made in Interpretation 101-1 between a covered member's immediate family (spouse, spousal equivalent, or dependent) and close relatives (parent, sibling, or nondependent child). A covered member's immediate family is subject to Rule 101 and its interpretations and rulings. Table 19–3

contains two exceptions, the first of which is that a covered member's spouse employed by a client would not impair independence if he or she were not employed in a *key position.*

Financial or business interests by close relatives that are not members of the auditor's immediate family, such as nondependent children, brothers, sisters, parents, grandparents, parents-in-law, and their respective spouses, do not normally impair independence. Interpretation 101-1 (Table 19–3) lists the situations where independence would be impaired by a close relative. The two major situations that can impair independence are:

- A close relative has a financial interest in the client that is material to the close relative, and the CPA participating in the engagement is aware of the interest.

- An individual participating in the engagement has a close relative who could exercise significant influence over the financial or accounting policies of the client (i.e., a key position).

For example, suppose a staff auditor's brother works as the controller for a client of the CPA firm. Because the staff auditor's brother exercises influence over significant accounting functions for the client, the staff auditor would not be allowed to participate in the audit of this client.

Practice
INSIGHT

The PCAOB sanctioned a regional accounting firm and its partners for, among other things, violating PCAOB independence standards. At the time of the firm's audit of a client, the mother of one of the partners owned stock in the client along with warrants to purchase additional stock. The partner knew of his mother's investments and their material nature to her. He also helped purchase the shares of stock before the audit commenced and then actually sold the shares for his mother after the issuance of the audit report. The partner and the firm also failed to conduct basic audit procedures during the course of this audit and other audits and, as a result, the firm was permanently revoked of its registration and the partner in question was permanently banned from association with a registered public accounting firm. (PCAOB Release 105-2007-009.)

Effect of Actual or Threatened Litigation   Sometimes threatened or actual litigation between the client and the auditor can impair the auditor's independence. Such situations affect the CPA's independence when a possible adversarial relationship exists between the client and the CPA. Interpretation 101-6 cites three categories of litigation: (1) litigation between the client and the CPA; (2) litigation by security holders; and (3) other third-party litigation where the CPA's independence may be impaired.

In order for a CPA to provide an opinion on a client's financial statements, the relationship between the client's management and the CPA must be one of "complete candor and full disclosure regarding all aspects of the client's business operations." When actual or threatened litigation exists between management and the CPA, complete candor may not be possible. The following criteria are offered as guidelines for assessing independence when actual or threatened litigation exists between the client and the CPA:

- The commencement of litigation by the present management alleging deficiencies in audit work for the client would be considered to impair independence.

- An expressed intention by the present management to commence litigation against the CPA alleging deficiencies in audit work would also impair independence if the auditor concluded that it is probable that such a claim will be filed.

- The commencement of litigation by the CPA against the present management alleging management fraud or deceit would be considered to impair independence.

Litigation by client security holders or other third parties also may impair the auditor's independence under certain circumstances. For example, litigation may arise from a class action lawsuit by stockholders alleging that the client's management, officers, directors, underwriters, and auditors were involved in the issuance of "false or misleading financial statements." Generally, such lawsuits do not alter the fundamental relationship between the CPA and the client. However, independence may be impaired if material client-auditor cross-claims are filed. For example, suppose that a class action suit is filed and the current client management intends to testify against the CPA, alleging that an improper audit was conducted. In such a situation, an adversarial relationship would exist and the CPA would no longer be independent. When this occurs, the CPA should either (1) withdraw from the engagement; or (2) disclaim an opinion because of a lack of independence.

Provision of Nonaudit Services The AICPA Code of Professional Conduct restricts the types of nonaudit services that can be provided to attest clients. Interpretation 101-3 outlines these requirements and also binds member CPAs to follow the relevant requirements of other regulatory bodies where applicable. The Code permits CPAs to provide bookkeeping, systems implementation, internal audit outsourcing, and other services to non-public attest clients subject to certain conditions and limits. For example, a CPA may assist an audit client in implementing a computer software package but may not "design" the financial information system by creating or changing the computer source code underlying the system. If the auditor makes any such modifications, the changes cannot be "more than insignificant." In addition, the Code indicates that CPAs may not perform appraisal, valuation, or actuarial services if the results of those services will have a material effect on the client's financial statements *and* the service involves considerable subjectivity.

Interpretation 101-3 of the Code outlines general requirements for performing other professional services for attest clients:

1. The CPA should not perform management functions or make management decisions for the attest client. However, the CPA may provide advice, research materials, and recommendations to assist the client's management in performing its functions and making decisions.
2. The client must agree to make all management decisions and perform all management functions with respect to the nonattest services. The client must also designate a competent employee (preferably within senior management) to oversee the services and must evaluate the adequacy and results of the services performed. Finally, the client must accept responsibility for the results of the services.
3. Before performing nonattest services, the CPA should establish with the client and document in writing the objectives of the engagement, the services to be performed, the client's acceptance of its responsibilities, the CPA's responsibilities, and any anticipated limitations of the engagement.

Some examples offered in interpretation 101-3 of general activities that would be considered to impair a CPA's independence include:

- Authorizing, executing, or consummating a transaction or otherwise exercising authority on behalf of a client.

- Preparing source documents, in electronic or other form, evidencing the occurrence of a transaction.
- Having custody of client assets.
- Supervising the client's employees in the performance of their normal recurring activities.
- Determining which recommendations of the member should be implemented.
- Establishing or maintaining internal controls, including performing ongoing monitoring activities for a client.

So long as the CPA stays within the general guidelines listed above, the AICPA does not strictly prohibit the provision of most types of professional services to nonpublic attest clients. For example, Interpretation 101-3 allows a CPA firm to provide outsourced internal audit services for a client for which the member also performs a professional service that requires independence (i.e., an audit or other attest service). Performing these extended audit services would not be considered to impair independence provided the member or his or her firm does not act or appear to act as either employee or management of the client.

While the AICPA Code of Professional Ethics permits internal audit outsourcing for nonpublic attest clients, the SEC prohibits providing this and several other types of nonaudit professional services to public company audit clients. The ways in which SEC and PCAOB independence rules for the audits of public companies differ from AICPA standards are discussed next.

Practice **INSIGHT**	The PCAOB sanctioned a regional accounting firm and its partners for, among other things, providing prohibited services to a client. During the course of the audit, the audit firm actually made journal entries, generated the trial balances for the financial statements, made accounting decisions for the issuer, and generated the financial statements and footnotes. As a result of this and other violations, the firm was permanently revoked of its registration and the partner in charge was permanently banned from association with a registered public accounting firm. (PCAOB Release 105-2007-009)

⁊ [LO 9]   SEC and PCAOB Independence Requirements for Audits of Public Companies   The SEC's mission is to protect investors and maintain the integrity of the capital markets in which the securities of publicly traded companies are bought and sold. As part of its mission, the SEC has authority to establish standards relating to financial accounting, auditing, and the professional conduct of public accountants in the context of public company accounting and auditing. The SEC delegates its authority to set standards for audits of public companies to the PCAOB but the SEC must review and approve those standards before they become effective.

In this section we discuss the primary areas in which the SEC and PCAOB independence rules differ from those of the AICPA Code of Professional Conduct. Until the past few years, the SEC's independence rules for auditors of public companies closely followed those of the AICPA. However, in November 2000 the SEC implemented more stringent rules, which were further revised in January 2003, after Title II of the Sarbanes-Oxley Act required additional independence restrictions. You will better understand the reasoning behind the SEC's new auditor independence (and other) requirements if you keep in mind that they were in response to specific circumstances that came to light in the frauds of the early 2000s. For example, Arthur Andersen was earning more in consulting than in auditing fees at Enron, and David Duncan, Andersen's lead partner on the Enron engagement, was compensated in part based on the amount of nonaudit services he sold to the company. Further, several of Enron's employees in important accounting and finance positions were former Andersen auditors who had worked on the Enron audit engagement.

While most of the SEC's independence rules are very similar to the AICPA's, the recent changes resulted in some important differences relating to (1) provision of other professional services; (2) handling of human resource and compensation-related issues; and (3) certain required communications.[12] The major differences in these three areas are discussed next.

Provision of Other Professional Services. The SEC's rules with respect to services provided by auditors are predicated on three basic principles of auditor objectivity and independence: (1) an auditor should not audit his or her own work; (2) an auditor should not function in the role of management; and (3) an auditor should not serve in an advocacy role for his or her client. Consistent with these principles, the SEC prohibits several types of professional services by accounting firms for public company audit and review clients, sometimes with the qualifier "unless it is reasonable to conclude that the results of these services will not be subject to audit procedures during an audit of the client's financial statements." Note that the rules do not limit the scope of nonaudit services provided by accounting firms to nonpublic companies or to public companies that are not audit clients. Additionally, accounting firms are expressly allowed to provide certain types of tax services to their audit clients.

The SEC specifies nine categories of nonaudit services that, with few exceptions, are considered to impair independence if provided to a public company audit client:

- Bookkeeping or other services related to the accounting records or financial statements of the audit client.
- Financial information systems design and implementation.
- Appraisal or valuation services, fairness opinions, or contribution-in-kind reports.
- Actuarial services.
- Internal audit outsourcing services.
- Management functions or human resources.
- Broker or dealer, investment adviser, or investment banking services.
- Legal services.
- Expert services.

While the first eight categories of services listed above were prohibited under pre-Sarbanes SEC independence rules ("expert services" is a newly added category), a number of exceptions to these prohibitions were eliminated under the Act.

Consistent with the Sarbanes-Oxley Act, SEC regulations also prohibit any other service that the PCAOB determines impermissible. The PCAOB adopted several new independence-related rules, which were approved by the SEC in April 2006. While the rules do not prohibit the provision of tax services, they do identify circumstances in which the provision of tax services impairs an auditor's independence, including services that involve aggressive interpretations of applicable tax laws and regulations. The rules also treat registered public accounting firms as not independent of their audit clients if they enter into contingent

---

[12]A number of other minor differences exist between AICPA and SEC independence rules, but this text focuses on only the major areas of divergence. For a thorough and detailed comparison of AICPA and SEC independence rules, see the document titled "AICPA and SEC Independence Rule Comparison" under the "Professional Ethics" link at www.aicpa.org.

fee arrangements with those clients for any professional services or if the firms provide tax services to members of management who serve in financial reporting oversight roles at an audit client or to their immediate family members.

The SEC and PCAOB rulings require that all audit and nonaudit services provided by a public company's auditor must be considered and approved by the company's audit committee. This requirement is intended to facilitate the proper oversight by the audit committee on the external audit by requiring the audit committee to consider the potential effects of nonaudit services on the auditor's objectivity and on investors' perceptions of the auditor's independence from the company.

Practice
INSIGHT

While SEC rules prohibit many types of consulting for public company audit clients, many public accounting firms are still heavily engaged in providing consulting services for nonaudit clients.

Human Resource and Compensation-Related Issues.   SEC rules in this area are primarily concerned with the potential for audit partners to become "too close" to an engagement or a client over time and with potential threats to an auditor's objectivity resulting from employment and compensation arrangements that can create conflicts of interest. These rules can be summarized in three areas.

First, the lead and engagement quality review partners on the engagement team for a public company audit are prohibited from providing audit services to the company for more than five consecutive years.[13] Once the partners "roll off" a client, a five-year "time-out" period is required before they can return to their former duties with that client. Audit partners other than the lead and quality review partners are prohibited from performing audit services for a particular client for more than seven consecutive years, with a two-year time-out period.

Second, unless a one-year "cooling-off" period has passed, an accounting firm is prohibited from auditing a public company's financial statements where a former member of the audit team is now employed by the client in a "financial reporting oversight role."[14]

Finally, the SEC does not consider an accounting firm to be independent from a public company audit client if an audit partner receives compensation based on selling engagements to that client for services other than audit, review, and attest services. This applies not only to audits of domestic issuers but also to audits of foreign subsidiaries and affiliates of U.S. issuers.

Practice
INSIGHT

While there are benefits associated with mandatory partner rotation, it comes with considerable cost. The first general auditing standard requires that the audit be performed by a person who has adequate technical training and proficiency as an auditor. While the 5-year "time-out" requirement for the engagement partner provides for a new set of eyes and a fresh look at the engagement, it can also lead to a sharp drop-off in client-specific experience on the engagement every five years.

---

[13]The *lead* partner is the partner primarily responsible for the decisions made on an audit engagement. The engagement quality review partner is not directly involved with the decisions made during the engagement, but instead is charged with reviewing significant evidence and conclusions to determine whether or not the engagement was conducted properly and conclusions appropriately made.

[14]The *cooling-off period* is defined as the one-year period preceding the commencement of audit procedures for the period that included the date the engagement team member was first employed by the client company.

Required Communication.   SEC rules also differ from those of the AICPA in requiring additional communication between auditors and their clients' audit committees and in requiring public company audit clients to reveal information regarding the fees paid to their auditors for any type of service.

The auditor of a public company must report to the company's audit committee all "critical accounting policies" used by the company, all alternative treatments within GAAP for policies and procedures related to material items discussed with management, and other material written communications between the auditor and the company's management. In addition, the audit committee must be responsible for the appointment, compensation, and oversight of the external auditor's work. This requirement is important, because it establishes the audit committee as the entity to which the auditor reports, rather than management itself. Remember that management is ultimately responsible for a company's financial statements. Because the audit committee of a public company must be independent of management, establishing the audit committee as the point of contact for the auditor creates a healthier environment in which the auditor does not answer directly to or receive compensation from management.

Proxy statements and annual reports issued by public companies must contain disclosures regarding (1) audit fees, (2) audit-related fees, (3) tax fees, and (4) all other fees billed during the prior two fiscal years by the principal auditor of the company's financial statements. Details must also be provided on the nature of services provided in earning "other fees." The preapproval policies of the company's audit committee must also be disclosed. A purpose of this requirement is to make companies more sensitive to public perceptions of auditor independence and objectivity.

Integrity and Objectivity

Rule 102: In the performance of any professional service, a member shall maintain objectivity and integrity, shall be free of conflicts of interest, and shall not knowingly misrepresent facts or subordinate his or her judgment to others.

This rule expands slightly on the principle from which it was developed and requires that a member maintain integrity and objectivity. There are a number of important interpretations of this rule. Interpretation 102-1 indicates that a member who knowingly makes or permits false and misleading entries in financial statements or records violates Rule 102. Interpretation 102-2 states that a conflict of interest may occur if a CPA performs a professional service for a client or employer and the CPA or the CPA's firm has a relationship with another person, entity, product, or service that could be viewed as impairing the CPA's objectivity. For example, a CPA might be hired to provide recommendations to a client on which commercially available software package the client should select for managing inventory. A conflict of interest would exist if the CPA had a substantial business or financial interest in one of the potential software providers.

Two other interpretations relate mainly to members employed in industry. Interpretation 102-3 states that, in dealing with his or her employer's external accountants, a member must be candid and not knowingly misrepresent facts or knowingly fail to disclose material facts. Interpretation 102-4 indicates that, if a CPA working in industry (e.g., as an accountant in a company) has a disagreement or dispute with his or her supervisor relating to the preparation of financial statements or the recording of transactions, the member must take steps to ensure that the situation does not result in a subordination of judgment. If the member concludes that the financial statements or records could be materially misstated, he or she should communicate those concerns to a higher level of management within the organization. If appropriate action is not taken, the member should consider whether to continue the relationship with the employer. The member should also consider whether any responsibility exists to communicate the problem to third parties, such as regulatory agencies or the employer's external accountants.

Educational services are professional services and therefore are subject to Rule 102 (Interpretation 102-5). Thus a member must maintain objectivity and integrity when performing such services. Finally, a member may be asked by a client to act as an advocate in performing tax or consulting services or in support of a nonaudit client's position on an accounting or auditing issue (Interpretation 102-6). While a member may accept such an engagement for nonattest clients, he or she must be sure that the requested service does not go beyond the bounds of sound professional practice and thereby impair the member's integrity and objectivity.

General Standards and Accounting Principles

✂ [LO 10]　This section of the Rules of Conduct contains two rules related to general standards and one rule related to accounting principles.

General Standards and Compliance with Standards

Rule 201: A member shall comply with the following standards and with any interpretations thereof by bodies designated by Council.

A. *Professional Competence.* Undertake only those professional services that the member or the member's firm can reasonably expect to be completed with professional competence.

B. *Due Professional Care.* Exercise due professional care in the performance of professional services.

C. *Planning and Supervision.* Adequately plan and supervise the performance of professional services.

D. *Sufficient Relevant Data.* Obtain sufficient relevant data to afford a reasonable basis for conclusions or recommendations in relation to any professional services performed.

Rule 201 essentially captures much of what is contained in the 10 generally accepted auditing standards pertaining to auditor conduct and makes it part of the code. Interpretation 201-1 provides some additional clarification of "professional competence." In particular, when a CPA agrees to perform professional services, he or she is expected to have the necessary competence to complete those services according to professional standards. However, it is not necessary for the CPA to have all the technical knowledge required to perform the engagement at the time the engagement commences. The CPA may conduct additional research or consult with other professionals during the conduct of the engagement. This need for additional information does not indicate a lack of competence on the part of the CPA unless he or she fails to acquire the needed information. The technical, legal definition of "due care" is covered in Chapter 20.

Rule 202: A member who performs auditing, review, compilation, management consulting, tax, or other professional services shall comply with standards promulgated by bodies designated by Council.

This rule is straightforward yet important because it requires that members of the AICPA comply with professional standards when performing professional services, whether or not they are practicing in public accounting.

Accounting Principles

While Rule 202 addresses compliance with standards for professional services, Rule 203 requires CPAs to report in compliance with appropriate accounting principles.

Rule 203: A member shall not (1) express an opinion or state affirmatively that the financial statements or other financial data of any entity are presented in conformity with generally accepted accounting principles or (2) state that he or she is not aware of any material modifications that should be made to such statements or data in order for them to be in conformity with generally accepted accounting principles, if such statements or data contain any departure from an accounting principle promulgated by bodies designated by Council to establish such principles that has a material effect on the statements or data taken as a whole. . . .

Interpretation 203-2 reiterates that the AICPA Council has designated the Financial Accounting Standards Board (FASB), the Governmental Accounting Standards Board (GASB), and the Federal Accounting Standards Advisory Board (FASAB) as the bodies authorized to establish accounting principles.

Interpretation 203-4, which relates mainly to members in industry, states that any representation regarding conformity with GAAP in a letter or other communication from a client to its auditor or others related to that entity's financial statements is subject to Rule 203. Thus, for example, if a member knowingly signs a representation letter indicating that the financial statements were in conformity with GAAP when in fact they were not, he or she has violated Rule 203.

Responsibilities to Clients

[LO 11]   This section of the Rules of Conduct contains two rules related to a CPA's responsibilities to his or her clients.

Confidential Client Information

Rule 301 (excerpted): A member in public practice shall not disclose any confidential client information without the specific consent of the client.

Rule 301 and its interpretations generally prohibit the auditor from disclosing confidential client information but specify five situations in which a CPA can disclose confidential information without the client's consent: (1) to meet disclosure and performance requirements under GAAP and GAAS; (2) to comply with a valid subpoena; (3) to allow a review of a member's professional practice under the authority of the AICPA, a state CPA society, or a state board of accountancy; (4) to comply with an investigative or disciplinary proceeding; and (5) to allow a review of a CPA's professional practice in conjunction with the purchase, sale, or merger of the practice. In the last case, the CPA should take precautions that the prospective buyer does not disclose any confidential client information to outside parties, usually through a confidentiality agreement. The prospective buyer should not use information they obtain to their advantage or disclose confidential information to outside parties.

Contingent Fees

Rule 302 (excerpted): A member in public practice shall not

(1) Perform for a contingent fee any professional services for, or receive such a fee from, a client for whom the member or the member's firm performs

    (a) an audit or review of a financial statement; or

    (b) a compilation of a financial statement when the member expects, or reasonably might expect, that a third party will use the financial statement and the member's compilation report does not disclose a lack of independence; or

    (c) an examination of prospective financial information; or

(2) Prepare an original or amended tax return or claim for a tax refund for a contingent fee for any client.

Rule 302 goes on to explain that the prohibition of contingent fees applies during the period in which the member or member's firm is engaged to perform any of the services listed and the period covered by any historical financial statements involved in any such services. A contingent fee is a fee that depends on the finding or result attained as a result of the member's work. With respect to this rule, fees are not regarded as being contingent if fixed by courts or other public authorities, or, in tax matters, if determined based on the results of judicial proceedings or the findings of governmental agencies. It is permissible for a member's fees to vary depending on other factors, for example, on the complexity of the services rendered.

If contingent fees were allowed for attestation-related services, users of those services might question the CPA's independence. As mentioned previously, PCAOB independence rules do not allow auditors to provide any services to public company audit clients for a contingent fee, including tax services.

Other Responsibilities and Practices

❧ [LO 12]   This section contains four rules of conduct that relate to other aspects of the profession.

Acts Discreditable   **Rule 501:** A member shall not commit an act discreditable to the profession.

This rule allows the AICPA to remove a member for committing acts that may affect the profession's reputation. For example, a CPA who is convicted of a serious crime could lose his or her membership in the AICPA. Eight interpretations have been issued that identify acts considered discreditable under Rule 501:

- Inappropriate response to requests by clients and former clients for certain records (501-1).
- Discrimination and harassment in employment practices (501-2).
- Failure to follow standards and/or procedures or other requirements in government audits (501-3).
- Negligence in the preparation of financial statements or records (501-4).
- Failure to follow the requirements of government bodies, commissions, or other regulatory agencies in performing attest or similar services (501-5).
- Solicitation or disclosure of CPA examination questions and answers (501-6).
- Failure to file tax return or pay tax liability (501-7).
- Including certain types of indemnification and limitation of liability provisions in agreements for the performance of audit or other attest services in jurisdictions where such provisions are prohibited (501-8).

For example, under Interpretation 501-1, records provided by the client in the member's custody or control should be returned to the client even if there are fees still unpaid. If the CPA retains certain client records such as journals or ledgers, the client may be unable to continue operations. If a CPA does not appropriately respond to a client's request to return the client's accounting records within 45 days (absent extenuating circumstances), that member commits a discreditable act under Rule 501. The CPA may decline to provide client records and other supporting records *prepared by the CPA* if there are fees due for the preparation of those records. The CPA's *working papers,* by contrast, are the property of the CPA, and need not be provided to the client unless required by state or federal statutes or regulations, or contractual agreements.

A CPA also commits a discreditable act if he or she discriminates in hiring, promotion, or salary practices on the basis of race, color, religion, sex, age, or national origin. Similarly, a CPA commits a discreditable act when, by virtue of his or her negligence, makes, permits, or directs another to make false or misleading entries in the financial statements or records of an entity. Another example of a discreditable act is the failure to file a tax return or pay the related tax liability.

Advertising and Other Forms of Solicitation

Rule 502: A member in public practice shall not seek to obtain clients by advertising or other forms of solicitation in a manner that is false, misleading, or deceptive. Solicitation by the use of coercion, over-reaching, or harassing conduct is prohibited.

Interpretation 502-2 provides specific examples of activities that are prohibited by this rule. These include:

- Creating false or unjustifiable expectations of favorable results.
- Implying an ability to influence any court, tribunal, regulatory agency, or similar body or official.
- Claiming that specific professional services in current or future periods will be performed for a stated fee, estimated fee, or fee range when it is likely at the time of representation that such fees will be substantially increased and the prospective client is not advised of that likelihood.
- Making any other representations that would be likely to cause a reasonable person to misunderstand or be deceived.

CPAs are often asked to provide professional services to clients or customers of third parties when those clients or customers have been obtained through advertising and/or solicitation. Interpretation 502-5 allows CPAs to render such services to clients or customers of third parties as long as all promotional efforts used to obtain such clients were conducted within the Code.

Commissions and Referral Fees

Rule 503: A. *Prohibited commissions*

A member in public practice shall not for a commission recommend or refer to a client any product or service, or for a commission recommend or refer any product or service to be supplied by a client, or receive a commission, when a member or the member's firm also performs for that client:

- an audit or review of financial statements; or
- a compilation of a financial statement when the member expects, or reasonably might expect, that a third party will use the financial statement and the member's compilation report does not disclose a lack of independence; or
- an examination of prospective financial information.

This prohibition applies during the period in which the member is engaged to perform any of the services listed above and the period covered by any historical financial statements involved in the listed services.

B. *Disclosure of permitted commissions*
A member in public practice who is not prohibited by this rule from performing services for or receiving a commission and who is paid or expects to be paid a commission shall disclose that fact to any person or entity to whom the member recommends or refers a product or service to which the commission relates.

C. *Referral fees*
Any member who accepts a referral fee for recommending or referring any service of a CPA to any person or entity or who pays a referral fee to obtain a client shall disclose such acceptance or payment to the client.

Many professions, including doctors and lawyers, have been permitted to use referral fees. However, commissions and referral fees are prohibited for CPAs in situations where the CPA's independence and objectivity are a focal point of attestation-related services.

Form of Organization and Name

Rule 505: A member may practice public accounting only in a form of organization permitted by law or regulation whose characteristics conform to resolutions of Council.

A member shall not practice public accounting under a firm name that is misleading. Names of one or more past partners may be included in the firm name of a successor organization.

A firm may not designate itself as "Members of the American Institute of Certified Public Accountants" unless all of its CPA owners are members of the Institute.

This rule requires that the form of a CPA's public accounting practice conform to law or regulations whose characteristics conform to AICPA resolutions. In recent years, virtually all states have passed laws that allow CPAs to practice as limited liability partnerships. Rule 505 also prohibits firms from operating under names that may mislead the public.

A resolution by the AICPA Council requires, among other things, that a majority of the financial interests in a firm engaged in attest services be owned by CPAs. In recent years, alternative practice structures have evolved under which, for example, CPA firms were purchased by other entities, and (1) the majority of the financial interests in the attest firm was owned by CPAs; and (2) all or substantially all of the revenues were paid to another entity in return for services and the lease of employees, equipment, and office space. If the CPAs who own the firm remain financially responsible, under applicable state law or regulation the member is considered to be in compliance with the financial interests provision of the resolution.

Disciplinary Actions

The AICPA has a number of avenues by which members can be disciplined for violating the Code of Professional Conduct. For violations that are not sufficient to warrant formal action, the PEEC can direct a member to take remedial or corrective actions. If the member rejects the committee's recommendation, the committee can refer the case to a hearing panel of the Trial Board. Membership in the AICPA can be suspended or terminated without a hearing if the member has been convicted of certain criminal offenses (such as a crime punishable by imprisonment for more than one year or filing a false income tax return on a client's behalf) or if the member's CPA certificate is suspended or revoked by a government agency. A member may also be expelled or suspended from the AICPA for up to two years for violating any rule of the Code of Professional Conduct. For more information on the AICPA's disciplinary processes, see the bylaws of the AICPA on the AICPA's Web site. In addition, because the Code of Professional Conduct has been adopted by most State Boards of Accountancy, which have authority to grant or revoke professional licenses, violations of the Code can result in suspension or revocation of a practitioner's CPA license. Of course, the SEC and the PCAOB also have several options for pursuing disciplinary actions against auditors. These are briefly discussed in Chapter 20 in the context of auditor legal liability.

Don't Lose Sight of the Forest for the Trees

As you can see from the preceding discussion, auditor independence and professional conduct are complicated subjects, involving a great deal of technical detail. A sense for the depth of detail involved is essential. However, we encourage you not to lose sight of the big picture. The primary purpose of professional ethics rules is to establish a minimum level of professionalism to help auditors remain independent of their clients and to be objective and honest in their judgments. The essence of even the mind-numbingly detailed independence requirements is that independence in fact and appearance is critical to the CPA's reputation and the value she or he provides to society. Unfortunately, even practicing auditors can get so lost in the detail of the specific requirements that they sometimes lose sight of the fundamental principles on which the rules are based. If you pursue a career in accounting, you should at least occasionally step back and review the fundamental principles of the Code of Professional Conduct, which involve appropriate professional and moral judgments in all you do, an obligation to honor the public trust, and a commitment to perform professional responsibilities with the highest sense of integrity.

Quality Control Standards

✂ [LO 13]   CPA firms are required to implement policies and procedures to monitor the firms' practices and ensure that professional standards are being followed. In 1977 the AICPA started a voluntary peer review program, and by January 1988 had approved mandatory quality peer reviews. The program is structured in two tiers: one for firms that have public company audit clients and one for (usually smaller) firms that audit only private companies. The purpose of the quality review program is to ensure that firms comply with relevant quality control standards.

CPA firms are required to implement policies and procedures to monitor the firms' practices and ensure that professional standards are being followed. In 1977 the AICPA started a voluntary peer review program, and by January 1988 had approved mandatory quality peer reviews. The purpose of the quality review program is to ensure that firms comply with relevant quality control standards.

In 2004, the PCAOB assumed the AICPA's oversight responsibilities relating to the parts of firms' practices relating to the audits of public companies and instituted a mandatory quality inspection program for those firms. The PCAOB also took responsibility for the issuance of new quality control standards pertaining to firms that audit public company clients. The AICPA, however, maintains a Peer Review Program (PRP) designed to review and evaluate those portions of firms' accounting and auditing practices that are not subject to inspection by the PCAOB. The goal of the PRP is to promote quality in the accounting and audit services provided by individual members of the AICPA and their firms. Reviews are performed by firms and individuals approved by the Peer Review Board. The AICPA's National Peer Review Committee (PRC) oversees and approves reviews for firms that also require PCAOB inspection (and for firms that perform audits of non-SEC issuers pursuant to the standards of the PCAOB). All other firms may have their reviews approved by the National PRC or by another administrative entity approved by the Peer Review Board.

The AICPA's PRP consists of two types of reviews: system reviews and engagement reviews. CPA firms that perform audits and related accounting work undergo *system reviews,* which focus on a firm's system of quality control. The peer reviewer's objective in a system review is to determine if the firm's policies and procedures for quality control conform to professional standards and if the firm is complying with its quality control system. The peer reviewer gains an understanding of the company's system of quality control and then tests the system by reviewing a sample of the firm's engagements. CPA firms that don't perform audits or similar engagements, but perform other accounting work such as reviews and compilations, undergo *engagement reviews,* which focus on work performed on particular selected engagements rather than the quality control system as a whole. Neither system nor engagement reviews include a review of a firm's tax or consulting practice.

While the PCAOB adopted the AICPA's quality control standards in April 2003, the AICPA has since released Statement on Quality Control Standards (SQCS) No. 7, "A Firm's System of Quality Control," which supersedes all previous SQCS. While the PCAOB has not yet adopted this standard, many auditing firms have already integrated its concepts into their systems of quality control, since it represents the state of the art in quality control for accounting firms. Thus, the remainder of this section discusses only the requirements of the newest standard, SQCS No. 7. SQCS No. 7 applies only to auditing and accounting practice (audit, attest, compilation, review, and any other services for which standards have been established by the AICPA). While not required, it is recommended that the guidance in this statement be applied to other services such as tax and consulting services.

System of Quality Control

A firm's system of quality control should be designed to provide the firm with reasonable assurance that the firm and its personnel comply with professional, legal, and regulatory requirements and that the partners issue appropriate reports (QC 10.03). A firm's system of quality control, however, has to be tailored to the firm's size, the nature of its practice, its organization, and cost-benefit considerations. For a sole practitioner or small firm, a system of quality control is likely to be much less formal than for a national or international firm. For example, a sole practitioner with three professional staff members may use a simple checklist and conduct periodic informal discussions to monitor his or her firm's compliance with professional standards. On the other had, a large international CPA firm may develop involved in-house procedures and assign full- or part-time staff to oversee and ensure compliance with the firm's quality control system.

Elements of Quality Control

✎ **[LO 15]**

SQCS No.7 identifies the following six elements of quality control:

1. Leadership responsibilities for quality in the firm ("tone at the top")
2. Relevant ethical requirements
3. Acceptance and continuance of client relationships and specific engagements
4. Human resources
5. Engagement performance
6. Monitoring

Table 19–5 defines each of the elements. It should be apparent from the definitions that these elements are interrelated. For example, the human resources element encompasses criteria for professional development, hiring, advancement, and assignment of the firm's personnel to engagements, which affect policies and procedures developed to meet quality control objectives. It is important for a firm to develop a system of quality control that takes each of these elements into account and to ensure that members of the firm understand the firm's quality control policies and procedures. While not required, communication of the firm's quality control system normally should be in writing, with the extent of documentation varying with the size of the firm. A firm's quality control policies and the Code of Professional Ethics should be covered in the firm's training programs.

Table 19–6 provides some selected examples of the types of policies or procedures a firm might implement to comply with a sound system of quality control. The standards require that the firms continually monitor the appropriateness of the design and the effectiveness of the operation of their quality control system (QC 10.100). Firms should implement monitoring procedures to identify and communicate circumstances that may necessitate changes and improvements to the firm's system of quality control. Procedures for monitoring include:

- Review of records pertaining to the quality control elements.
- Review of engagement working papers, reports, and clients' financial statements.

TABLE 19–5	**Elements of Quality Control**

1. *Leadership responsibilities for quality in the firm (the "tone at the top"):* The firm's leadership should promote an internal culture based on performing high quality work that complies with professional standards and regulatory and legal requirements. Policies and procedures should be established to support that culture; management is held responsible for the firm's system of quality control (SQCS 7.15-16).
2. *Relevant ethical requirements:* Policies and procedures should be established to provide reasonable assurance that the firm and its personnel perform their work in an ethical manner and according to the relevant ethics requirements (SQCS 7.19).
3. *Acceptance and continuance of client relationships and specific engagements:* Policies and procedures should be established for deciding whether to accept or continue a client relationship and whether to perform a specific engagement for that client. Such procedures should provide the firm with reasonable assurance that the likelihood of association with a client whose management lacks integrity is minimized, the firm has sufficient competent personnel to perform the engagement, and the firm can comply with legal and ethical requirements (SQCS 7.27).
4. *Human resources:* Policies and procedures should be established to provide reasonable assurance that the firm's personnel are able to comply with regulatory and legal requirements and perform engagements according to professional standards. Such procedures should cover (SQCS 7.37-38):
   a. Recruitment and hiring.
   b. Determining capabilities and competencies.
   c. Assigning personnel to engagements.
   d. Professional development.
   e. Performance evaluation, compensation, and advancement.
5. *Engagement performance:* Policies and procedures should be established to provide the firm with reasonable assurance that engagements performed meet applicable standards, regulatory requirements, and the firm's standards of quality. The procedures should also ensure that the partner issues the proper audit report given the circumstances. These procedures should cover (SQCS 7.57):
   a. Engagement performance.
   b. Supervision responsibilities.
   c. Review responsibilities.
6. *Monitoring:* Policies and procedures should be established to provide reasonable assurance that the policies and procedures over each of the other elements of quality control are suitably designed and are being applied effectively (SQCS 7.100).

TABLE 19–6	**Selected Quality Control Policies and Procedures**

Leadership responsibilities for quality in the firm (the "tone at the top"):

- Establish management responsibilities to avoid letting commercial objectives override the quality of the work performed (SQCS 7.17a).
- Devote the needed resources to support quality control policies and procedures (SQCS 7.17c).

Relevant ethical requirements:

- Communicate the firm's independence requirements to all parties who are subject to them (SQCS 7.21a).
- Require personnel to promptly notify the engagement partner and the firm whenever a situation arises that may create a threat to independence so that appropriate actions can be taken (SQCS 7.22b).

Acceptance and continuance of client relationships and specific engagements:

- Establish procedures for evaluating the integrity of a client. Factors that should be considered include the nature of the client's operations and information about the attitude of owners, key management, and those charged with governance toward matters such as internal control and aggressive accounting stances (SQCS 7.30).
- Establish policies ensuring that firm personnel have sufficient knowledge, experience, and capabilities to service the client appropriately (SQCS 7.31).

Human resources:

- Establish hiring practices to seek only individuals who meet academic requirements and exhibit attributes such as integrity, maturity, and competence (SQCS 7.39).
- Ensure that personnel who advance in the firm are capable and qualified to fulfill their new responsibilities (SQCS 7.55).

Engagement performance:

- Provide adequate supervision at all organizational levels, considering the training, ability, and experience of the personnel assigned (SQCS 7.58-59).
- Develop guidelines for the documentation of the engagement quality control review (SQCS 7.99).

Monitoring:

- Provide an ongoing evaluation of the firm's system of quality control to ensure the system is designed appropriately and operating effectively (SQCS 7.100).
- Establish procedures for dealing with complaints about the failure of the firm to comply with professional standards, legal requirements, and the firm's own quality control procedures (SQCS 7.120).

- Interviews with the firm's personnel.
- Review of summarized reports, at least annually, on the findings of the monitoring procedures and the investigation of their causes so that improvements can be made.
- Determination of any corrective actions to be taken or improvements to be made.
- Communication of findings to appropriate firm management.
- Follow-up on a timely basis by appropriate firm management and determination of what actions are necessary, including modifications to the quality control system (QC 10.102).

The AICPA requires member firms to have their practices reviewed by peer firms every three-and-a-half years.

PCAOB Inspections of Registered Public Accounting Firms

✂ [LO 15]

In addition to the AICPA peer review programs discussed above, the PCAOB conducts regular inspections of public accounting firms that are required to register with the Board. These inspections focus on selected audit and quarterly review engagements and evaluate the sufficiency of the quality control system of registered firms. The purpose of these inspections is to ensure that registered firms, in connection with their audits of public companies, comply with the Sarbanes-Oxley Act, PCAOB rules, SEC rules, and professional standards.

The PCAOB conducts special inspections on an ad hoc basis when it has specific cause, but the frequency with which regular inspections are conducted is established by law. Registered firms that issue more than 100 audit reports for public companies per year are subject to an annual inspection, while those firms that regularly issue more than 1 but less than 100 audit reports in a year must be inspected at least once every three years.

Should a PCAOB inspection find that a firm, or anyone associated with it, may be in violation of legislation, accounting regulations, any professional standard, or even the firm's own quality control policies, then the PCAOB can conduct a special investigation into the possible violation. Following an investigation, the board issues a draft report, at which time the firm has 30 days to respond to any allegations. At the end of this period, the Board then issues a final report outlining the violations; however, assuming such violations do not involve fraud, the firm is granted a 12-month period in which to take necessary corrective action. If sufficient action is taken, the PCAOB does not publicly reveal the specifics of the firm's violations—otherwise, public disciplinary action ensues against responsible parties.

Mandatory inspections apply to all firms that audit public U.S. companies. However, if the accounting firm is not based in the United States, there may be some exceptions to the inspection requirements. For instance, at the PCAOB's discretion, the Board may rely (at least in part) on foreign authorities to conduct inspections.

KEY TERMS

Attest engagement. An engagement that requires independence as defined in AICPA Professional Standards. Attest engagements include financial statement audits, reviews, and examinations of prospective financial information.

Close relative. A parent, sibling, or nondependent child.

Covered member. A member that is:

a. An individual on the attest engagement team.

b. An individual in a position to influence the attest engagement.

c. A partner or manager who provides nonattest services to the attest client beginning once he or she provides 10 hours of nonattest services to the client within any fiscal year and ending on the later of the date (i) the firm signs the report on the financial statements for the fiscal year during which those services were provided; or (ii) he or she no longer expects to provide 10 or more hours of nonattest services to the attest client on a recurring basis.

   d. A partner in the office in which the lead attest engagement partner primarily practices in connection with the attest engagement.

   e. The firm, including the firm's employee benefit plans.

   f. An entity whose operating, financial, or accounting policies can be controlled (as defined by generally accepted accounting principles for consolidation purposes) by any of the individuals or entities described in parts (a) through (e), or by two or more such individuals or entities if they act together.

Ethics. A system or code of conduct based on moral duties and obligations that indicates how an individual should behave.

Financial interest. An ownership interest in an equity or a debt security issued by an entity, including rights and obligations to acquire such an interest and derivatives directly related to such interest. A *direct financial* interest is a financial interest that is owned directly by an individual or entity, or is under the control of an individual or entity. An *indirect financial* interest is a financial interest that is beneficially owned through an investment vehicle, estate, trust, or other intermediary when the beneficiary does not control the intermediary or have authority to supervise or participate in the intermediary's investment decisions.

Generally accepted auditing standards. Measures of the quality of the auditor's performance.

Holding out. In general, any action initiated by a member that informs others of his or her status as a CPA or AICPA-accredited specialist constitutes holding out as a CPA. This would include, for example, use of the CPA designation on business cards or letterhead, or listing as a CPA in local telephone directories.

Immediate family. A spouse, spousal equivalent, or dependent (whether or not related).

Key position. A position in which an individual:

   a. Has primary responsibility for significant accounting functions that support material components of the financial statements.

   b. Has primary responsibility for the preparation of the financial statements.

   c. Has the ability to exercise influence over the contents of the financial statements, including when the individual is a member of the board of directors or similar governing body, chief executive officer, president, chief financial officer, chief operating officer, general counsel, chief accounting officer, controller, director of internal audit, director of financial reporting, treasurer, or any equivalent position.

For purposes of attest engagements not involving a client's financial statements, a key position is one in which an individual is primarily responsible for, or able to influence, the subject matter of the attest engagement, as described above.

Period of the professional engagement. The period for which a member either signs an initial engagement letter or other agreement to perform attest services or begins to perform an attest engagement for a client, whichever is earlier. The period lasts for the entire duration of the professional relationship and ends with the formal or informal notification, either by the member or the client, of the termination of the professional relationship or by the issuance of a report, whichever is later. Accordingly, the period does not end with the issuance of a report and recommence with the beginning of the following year's attest engagement.

Practice of public accounting. The performance for a client, by a member or a member's firm, while holding out as CPA(s), of the professional services of accounting, tax, personal financial planning, litigation support services, and those professional services for which standards are promulgated by bodies designated by Council.

Professionalism. The conduct, aims, or qualities that characterize or mark a profession or professional person.

www.mhhe.com/ messier7e	Visit the book's Online Learning Center for a multiple-choice quiz that will allow you to assess your understanding of chapter concepts.

REVIEW QUESTIONS

[LO 2]   19-1   Briefly describe the three theories of ethical behavior that can be used to analyze ethical issues in accounting.

[4]   19-2   Why are companies like Kmart able to continue in business after experiencing federal indictments, convictions of top executives, and bankruptcy, while accounting firms, like the once highly respected, financially strong Arthur Andersen, can be destroyed by a single federal indictment?

[4]   19-3   What entities are involved in establishing standards and rules for the professional conduct of public accountants? Who establishes such standards for auditors of public versus private companies?

[5]   19-4   What are the two major sections of the Code of Professional Conduct? What additional guidance is provided for applying the Rules of Conduct?

[6]   19-5   Describe the six Principles of Professional Conduct.

[7]   19-6   What are the five major sections of the Rules of Conduct?

[8]   19-7   What types of personal loans from a financial institution are allowed by the Rules of Conduct? What is meant by *normal lending procedures, terms, and requirements* within this context?

[9]   19-8   Summarize the major differences between the AICPA's Code of Professional Ethics independence rules and the SEC's independence rules for auditors of public companies. Briefly describe why the SEC's requirements diverged from those of the AICPA in the early 2000s.

[11]   19-9   Generally a CPA is not allowed to disclose confidential client information without the consent of the client. Identify four circumstances in which confidential client information can be disclosed under the Rules of Conduct without the client's permission.

[12]   19-10   Give three examples of acts that are considered discreditable under the Rules of Conduct.

[12]   19-11   A CPA is allowed to advertise as long as the advertising is not false, misleading, or deceptive. Provide three examples of advertising that might be considered false, misleading, or deceptive. Why are such acts of concern to the profession?

[13,14]   19-12   What is the purpose of a CPA firm's establishing a system of quality control? List the six elements of quality control and provide one example of a policy or procedure that can be used to fulfill each element.

[13,15]   19-13   How are the roles of the PCAOB inspection program and the AICPA peer review program similar, and how are they different?

MULTIPLE-CHOICE QUESTIONS

[1,2,4]   19-14   Which of the following statements best explains why public accounting, as a profession, promulgates ethical standards and establishes means for ensuring their observance?
  a. Vigorous enforcement of an established code of ethics is the best way to prevent unscrupulous acts.

    b. Ethical standards that emphasize excellence in performance over material rewards establish individual reputations for competence and character.

    c. Ethical standards are established so that users of accounting services know what to expect and accounting professionals know what behaviors are acceptable, and so that discipline can be applied when necessary.

    d. A requirement for a profession is to establish ethical standards that primarily stress responsibility to clients and colleagues.

[9]   19-15   All of the following nonaudit services are identified by the SEC as generally impairing an auditor's independence except

    a. Information systems design and implementation.

    b. Human resource services.

    c. Management functions.

    d. Some specific tax services.

    e. All of the above are seen by the SEC as impairing independence.

[9]   19-16   Under the SEC's rules regarding independence, which of the following must a client disclose?

    a. Only fees for the external audit.

    b. Only fees for internal and external audit services provided by the audit firm.

    c. Fees for the external audit, audit-related fees, tax fees, and fees for other nonaudit services performed by the audit firm.

    d. Only fees for systems implementation and design, and nonaudit services performed by the audit firm.

[5]   19-17   The AICPA Code of Professional Conduct contains both general ethical principles that are aspirational in character and also a

    a. List of violations that would cause the automatic suspension of a CPA's license.

    b. Set of specific, mandatory rules describing minimum levels of conduct a CPA must maintain.

    c. Description of a CPA's procedures for responding to an inquiry from a trial board.

    d. List of specific crimes that would be considered as acts discreditable to the profession.

[8]   19-18   In which of the following situations would a CPA's independence be considered impaired according to the Code of Professional Conduct?

    1. The CPA has a car loan from a bank that is an audit client. The loan was made under the same terms available to all customers.

    2. The CPA has a direct financial interest in an audit client, but the interest is maintained in a blind trust.

    3. The CPA owns a commercial building and leases it to an audit client. The rental income is material to the CPA.

        a. 1 and 2.

        b. 2 and 3.

        c. 1 and 3.

        d. 1, 2, and 3.

[8]   19-19   A client company has not paid its 2009 audit fees. According to the AICPA Code of Professional Conduct, for the auditor to be considered independent with respect to the 2010 audit, the 2009 audit fees must be paid before the

    a. 2009 report is issued.

    b. 2010 fieldwork is started.

    c. 2010 report is issued.

    d. 2011 fieldwork is started.

[8]   19-20 Which of the following legal situations would be considered to impair the auditor's independence?

a. An expressed intention by the present management to commence litigation against the auditor, alleging deficiencies in audit work for the client, although the auditor considers that there is only a remote possibility that such a claim will be filed.

b. Actual litigation by the auditor against the client for an amount not material to the auditor or to the financial statements of the client arising out of disputes as to billings for management advisory services.

c. Actual litigation by the auditor against the present management, alleging management fraud or deceit.

d. Actual litigation by the client against the auditor for an amount not material to the auditor or to the financial statements of the client arising out of a dispute as to billings for tax services.

[8,10,11,12]   19-21 A violation of the profession's ethical standards is least likely to occur when a CPA

a. Purchases another CPA's accounting practice and bases the price on a percentage of the fees accruing from clients over a three-year period.

b. Receives a percentage of the amounts invested by the CPA's audit clients in a tax shelter with the clients' knowledge and approval.

c. Has a public accounting practice and also is president and sole stockholder of a corporation that engages in data processing services for the public. The CPA often refers his clients to the data processing company.

d. Forms an association—not a legally binding partnership—with two other sole practitioners and calls the association "Adams, Betts & Associates."

[3]   19-22 Rick, an independent CPA, must make an ethical judgment related to the audit of a client. If he primarily focuses on whether his decision might yield advantages for some at the expense of others, he is using:

a. A utilitarian perspective.

b. A rights-based approach.

c. A justice-based perspective.

d. Rule-based AICPA guidelines.

[3]   19-23 During the audit of Moon Co., the auditor disagrees with management's estimation of collectible accounts receivable. The possible misstatement amount is material. Which of the statements below should weigh more heavily for the auditor in this instance?

a. Moon management has the right to make company estimates.

b. Requiring an adjustment to the allowance for doubtful accounts would give stockholders access to fair and adequate information.

c. Accounts Receivable as stated by Moon Co., might turn out to be fully collectible.

d. The interests of Moon Co., the auditor, and the public should be weighed equally in the decision.

[11]   19-24 Without the consent of the client, a CPA should not disclose confidential client information contained in working papers to a(n)

a. Authorized quality control review board.

b. CPA firm that has been engaged to audit a former client.

c. Federal court that has issued a valid subpoena.

d. Disciplinary body created under state statute.

[13]   19-25 One of a CPA firm's basic objectives is to provide professional services that conform with professional standards. Reasonable assurance of achieving this basic objective is provided through

a. A system of quality control.

b. A system of peer review.

    c. Continuing professional education.

    d. Compliance with generally accepted reporting standards.

[14] 19-26 In connection with the element of engagement performance, a CPA firm's system of quality control should ordinarily include procedures covering all of the following except:

    a. Performance evaluation.

    b. Engagement performance.

    c. Supervision responsibilities.

    d. Review responsibilities.

PROBLEMS

[9] 19-27 Dean Wareham, an audit manager, is preparing a proposal for a publicly held company in the manufacturing industry. The potential client is growing rapidly and introducing many new products, yet still has a manual accounting system. The company also has never undertaken any tax planning activities and feels that it pays a higher percentage of its income in taxes than its competitors. Additionally, it is concerned that its monitoring activities are inadequate because it does not have an internal audit department. Dean knows that the SEC recently passed new rules regarding auditor independence.

Required:

1. Prepare a summary of nonaudit services that Dean can include in his proposal that do not violate the SEC's independence rules.
2. How would your answer to part 1 differ if the potential client were not publicly held? In other words, what additional nonaudit services could Dean include in his proposal? What conditions would have to be met in order for the firm to provide the additional services?

[8] 19-28 Each of the following situations involves a possible violation of the AICPA's Code of Professional Conduct, rule 101. Indicate whether each situation violates the Code. If it violates the Code, explain why.

    a. Julia Roberto, a sole practitioner, has provided extensive advisory services for her audit client, Leather Ltd. She has interpreted financial statements, provided forecasts and other analyses, counseled on potential expansion plans, and counseled on banking relationships but has not made any management decisions. Leather is a privately held entity.

    b. Steve Rackwill, CPA, has been asked by his audit client, Petry Plumbing Supply, to help implement a new control system. Rackwill will arrange interviews for Petry's hiring of new personnel and instruct and oversee the training of current client personnel. Petry Plumbing is a privately held company. Petry will make all hiring decisions and supervise employees once they are trained.

    c. Kraemeer & Kraemeer recently won the audit of Garvin Clothiers, a large manufacturer of women's clothing. Jock Kraemeer had a substantial investment in Garvin prior to bidding on the engagement. In anticipation of winning the engagement, Kraemeer placed his shares of Garvin stock in a blind trust.

    d. Zeker & Associates audits a condominium association in which the parents of a member of the firm own a unit and reside. The unit is material to the parents' net worth, and the member participates in the engagement.

    e. Jimmy Saad, a sole practitioner, audited Dallas Conduit, Inc.'s, financial statements for the year ended June 30, 2009, and was issued stock by the client as payment of the audit fee. Saad disposed of the stock before commencing fieldwork planning for the audit of the June 30, 2010, financial statements.

f. Dip-It Paint Corporation requires an audit for the current year. However, Dip-It has not paid Allen & Allen the fees due for tax-related services performed two years ago. Dip-It issued Allen & Allen a note for the unpaid fees, and Allen & Allen proceeded with the audit services.

[8]   19-29   The questions that follow are based on Rule 101 of the AICPA Code of Professional Conduct as it relates to independence and family relationships. Check yes if the situation violates the rule, no if it does not.

Situation	Yes	No
a. A partner's dependent parent is a 5% limited partner in a firm client. Does the parent's direct financial interest in the client impair the firm's independence?		
b. A partner assigned to a firm's New York office is married to the president of a client for which the firm's Connecticut office performs audit services. If the partner does not perform services out of or for the Connecticut office, cannot exercise significant influence over the engagement, and has no involvement with the engagement, such as consulting on accounting or auditing issues, is the firm's independence impaired?		
c. A CPA's father acquired a 10% interest in his son's audit client. The investment is material to the father's net worth. If the son is aware of his father's investment and the CPA participates in the audit engagement, is the firm's independence impaired?		
d. An audit partner has a brother who owns a 60% interest in an audit client, which is material to the brother's net worth. If the partner participates in the audit engagement, but does not know about his brother's investment, is the firm's independence impaired?		

[8,10,11,12]   19-30   Each of the following situations involves a possible violation by a member in industry of the AICPA's Code of Professional Conduct. For each situation, indicate whether it violates the Code. If it violates the Code, indicate which rule is violated and explain why.

a. Jack Jackson is a CPA and controller of Acme Trucking Company. Acme's external auditors have asked Jackson to sign the management representation letter. Jackson has signed the management representation letter, even though he knows that full disclosures have not been made to Acme's external auditors.

b. Mary McDermott, CPA, is employed in the internal audit department of the United Fund of America. The United Fund raises money from individuals and distributes it to other organizations. McDermott has audited Children's Charities, an organization that receives funds from United Fund.

c. Janet Jett, CPA, formerly worked for Delta Disk Drive, Inc. She is currently interviewing for a new position with Maxiscribe, Inc., another manufacturer of disk drives. Jett has agreed to provide confidential information about Delta's trade secrets if she is hired by Maxiscribe.

d. Brian Thorough, CPA, is currently employed as controller of TransLouisiana Oil Company. He has discovered that TransLouisiana has been illegally paying state environmental employees so that they will not charge TransLouisiana with dumping highly toxic chemicals into the bayous. Thorough discloses this information to the state attorney general.

e. Jill Burnett, CPA, was hired by Cooper Corporation to supervise its accounting department in preparing financial statements and presenting them to senior management. Due to considerable time incurred on other financial activities, Burnett was unable to supervise the accounting staff adequately. It is later discovered that Cooper's financial statements contain false and misleading information.

[8,10] 19-31 Perez, CPA, has been asked by a nonpublic company audit client to perform a nonrecurring engagement involving implementing an IT information and control system. The client requests that, in setting up the new system and during the period prior to conversion to the new system, Perez
- Counsel on potential expansion of business activity plans.
- Search for and interview new personnel.
- Hire new personnel.
- Train personnel.

In addition, the client requests that, during the three months subsequent to the conversion, Perez
- Supervise the operation of the new system.
- Monitor client-prepared source documents and make changes in basic IT-generated data as Perez may deem necessary without the concurrence of the client.

Perez responds that he may perform some of the services requested but not all of them.

Required:
a. Which of these services may Perez perform, and which of them may Perez not perform?
b. Before undertaking this engagement, Perez should inform the client of all significant matters related to the engagement. What are these significant matters that should be included in the engagement letter?

(AICPA, adapted)

DISCUSSION CASES

[3,10,11,12] 19-32 Refer back to the hypothetical Sun City Savings and Loan case presented in this chapter, and consider each of the following independent situations:
a. Suppose that Pina, Johnson & Associates also audited one of the entities who had received one of the large loans that are in dispute. Sam Johnson is not involved with auditing that entity. Is it ethical for Johnson to seek information on the financial condition of that entity from the auditors in his firm? What are the rights of the affected parties in this instance, and what are the costs and benefits of using such information?
b. Suppose that Johnson has determined that one of the entities that owes a disputed loan is being investigated for violating environmental laws and may be sued to the point of bankruptcy by the Environmental Protection Agency. Can Johnson use this information in deciding on the proper loan-loss reserve? What are the ethical considerations?

[8,12] 19-33 Schoeck, CPA, is considering leaving a position at a major public accounting firm to join the staff of a local financial institution that does write-up work, tax preparation and planning, and financial planning.

Required:
a. Are the Rules of Conduct applied differently to CPAs that work for a local financial institution that is not CPA-owned, as compared to a major public accounting firm?
b. Do you think the rules should be applied differently to CPAs depending on the type of entity they work for?

[9] 19-34 For each of the following scenarios, please indicate whether or not independence-related SEC rules are being violated, assuming that the audit client is a public company. Briefly explain why or why not.

a. Adrian Reynolds now works as a junior member of the accounting team at Swiss Precision Tooling, a publicly traded manufacturing company. Three months ago, he worked as a staff auditor for Crowther & Sutherland, a local accounting firm, where he worked on the Swiss Precision Tooling audit team. Crowther & Sutherland is still the auditor for Swiss Precision Tooling.

b. Susana Millar finished working for Bircham, Dyson & Bell in August 2006. During that time, she was a concurring partner on the Unigate Dairies assignment (the engagement period on this audit ended in April 2007). In February 2008, Susana took up a position as controller of Unigate Dairies. Bircham, Dyson & Bell is still the dairy's auditor and plans to finish its current audit assignment in March 2008 (19 months after Susana left the firm).

c. Janay Butler, a senior auditor, is aware that under SEC rules her accounting firm should not conduct appraisal or valuation services for a public company audit client. However, her manager has requested that she appraise some specific large inventory items to verify a public client's estimates, which are relied upon by others.

d. Heath & Associates, CPAs, is the auditor of Halifax Investments, Inc., a public company. Heath makes most of its money by selling nonaudit services to its audit clients, but it ensures every service it provides for Halifax is in accordance with SEC rules and is preapproved by the company's audit committee. Last year, it billed the following to Halifax: audit fees $0.8 million, tax fees $2.3 million, and other fees $5.2 million. No services prohibited by the SEC were provided by Heath to Halifax, and the fee figures are appropriately disclosed in Halifax's financial statements.

[2,3] 19-35 Your supervisor tells you that for the next month you will be working on an audit client with a controller who loves to talk. She explains that the client will want you to spend an hour or so talking about politics, sports, and life's mysteries and you need to keep him happy. She also wants you to follow the time budget, which was based on prior years when those in your position would take work home each night to stay on budget. The prior auditors didn't record the "social" time at the client. Will you record all of your time, including "social" time, or only the time associated with the technical work of the audit?

Required:
1. Analyze this situation with its possible outcomes using
   a. The utilitarian theory.
   b. The rights-based approach.
   c. The justice-based approach.
2. Which approach do you feel is most appropriate in this situation, and why?

[2,3] 19-36 While completing a test of controls, you appropriately cleared two minor exceptions by examining related documents. The client will need to do some serious digging to find the documents to resolve a third, similar, exception and wants to know if you really need the documents. You ask the in-charge senior, and he decides it was probably not a serious potential problem and tells you to sign off to clear the third exception without examining the underlying documents.

Required:
1. Analyze this situation with its possible outcomes using
   a. The utilitarian theory.
   b. The rights-based approach.
   c. The justice-based approach.
2. Which approach do you feel is most appropriate in this situation, and why?

INTERNET ASSIGNMENT

[5,6,7]   19-37   Visit the AICPA's Web site (www.aicpa.org), under Professional Resources→Accounting and Auditing→Authoritative Standards. Toward the bottom of the page click "Go to Code of Professional Conduct." Find Section 100 of the Code of Professional Conduct. Research the relevant rules, interpretations, and ethics rulings to answer the following questions:

a. Would independence be considered impaired if a member joined a trade association that is a client of the firm?

b. A member provides extensive advisory services for a client. In that connection, the member attends board meetings; interprets financial statements, forecasts, and other analyses; and counsels on potential expansion plans and on banking relationships. Would independence be considered impaired under these circumstances?

c. If a member signs or cosigns checks issued by a debtor corporation for a creditors' committee in control of the debtor corporation, which will continue to operate under its existing management, would independence be impaired with respect to the debtor corporation?

d. A member has been designated to serve as an executor or trustee of the estate of an individual who owns the majority of a client's stock. Would independence be considered impaired with respect to the client?

e. A member serves as a director or officer of a United Way or similar fund-raising organization. Certain local charities receive funds from the organization. Would independence be considered impaired with respect to such charities?

f. A client of the member's firm has not paid fees for previously rendered professional services. Would independence be considered impaired for the current year?

 **HANDS-ON CASES**

EarthWear Online	**Ethics**
	Review ethical challenges facing a Willis & Adams staff auditor and indicate what you would do in a similar situation.
	Visit the book's Online Learning Center at www.mhhe.com/messier7e to find a detailed description of the case and to download required materials.

ACL

www.mhhe.com/ messier7e	Visit the book's Online Learning Center for problem material to be completed using the ACL software packaged with your new text.

CHAPTER 20

LEARNING OBJECTIVES

Upon completion of this chapter you will

[1] Understand the four general stages in an audit-related legal dispute.

[2] Know the definitions of key legal terms.

[3] Know the auditor's liability to clients under common law.

[4] Understand the auditor's liability to third parties under common law.

[5] Understand the auditor's legal liability under the Securities Act of 1933.

[6] Understand the auditor's legal liability under the Securities Exchange Act of 1934.

[7] Be able to explain how the Private Securities Litigation Reform Act of 1995 and the Securities Litigation Uniform Standards Act of 1998 relieve some of the auditor's legal liability.

[8] Understand the auditor's legal liability under the Sarbanes-Oxley Act of 2002.

[9] Know how the SEC and PCAOB can sanction an auditor or audit firm.

[10] Understand how the Foreign Corrupt Practices Act can result in legal liability for auditors.

[11] Understand how the Racketeer Influenced and Corrupt Organizations Act can affect the auditor's legal liability.

[12] Be able to explain how an auditor can be held criminally liable under various federal and state laws.

RELEVANT ACCOUNTING AND AUDITING PRONOUNCEMENTS

AICPA, Code of Professional Conduct (ET 50-500)
AU 316, Consideration of Fraud in a Financial Statement Audit
AU 317, Illegal Acts by Clients

AU 325, Communicating Internal Control-Related Matters Identified in an Audit
AU 380, The Auditor's Communication with Those Charged with Governance

Legal Liability

I n Chapter 1 we presented an economic view of auditing, and we provided a house inspector analogy to illustrate the concepts. The auditor (or inspector) adds value to the principal–agent relationship by providing an objective, independent opinion on the quality of the information reported. However, what prevents the auditor from "looking the other way" or even from cooperating with management and issuing an unqualified report on financial statements that are materially misstated? The main deterrent, other than the individual's ethical principles, is the threat of legal liability. If a client or third party suffers a loss from such fraudulent behavior, the auditor's personal wealth and professional reputation will be affected by litigation.

This chapter discusses auditors' legal liability. The chapter starts by presenting an overview of legal liability that includes the stages of the auditor dispute process and briefly discusses the types of legal liability an auditor may encounter. Auditors' liability under common law to clients and third parties is discussed first, followed by a discussion of statutory liability for both civil and criminal complaints.

| www.mhhe.com/ messier7e | A number of legal cases discussed in this chapter are described in detail on the book's Web site including an in-depth look at the Phar-Mor trial, an actual auditor-liability case, with coverage of courtroom strategies and quotes based on trial transcripts. |

Introduction

Auditors can be held legally liable for actions that represent failure to perform professional services adequately. In this chapter we discuss the types of claims that can be brought against auditors, the types of plaintiffs that typically sue auditors, what must be proved to sue auditors successfully, and the defenses available to the auditor. Before discussing the details of the various legal theories, we provide a brief historical perspective and broad overview.

Historical Perspective

Although auditors have always been liable to clients and certain third parties, claims against auditors were relatively uncommon before the 1970s. In fact, the number of claims against auditors in the last 15 years is nearly double the number of all claims previously brought.[1] Not only has the number of claims risen, their severity has also risen dramatically. After the U.S. economy slumped in the early 1970s, numerous business failures led to a dramatic increase in the number of lawsuits filed against auditors under federal law. After the economic recession in the early 1980s it became more common for banks to sue auditors to recover loan losses. The recession of 1990–1992 led to another upsurge in litigation culminating with a settlement related to savings and loan audits against Ernst & Young in excess of $400 million.

While some of the lawsuits brought against auditors were certainly legitimate, the 1980s and 1990s also found the profession expending enormous time and effort defending against weak claims. During this time, it took large firms an average of three years and over $3 million to defend against a single weak claim under federal securities laws. "Practice protection costs" (e.g., litigation costs and the cost of professional liability insurance) soared and quickly became the second largest cost to public accounting firms behind the cost of human resources. The profession pushed for reform, and in the 1990s Congress passed litigation reform acts that provided some limits to auditor liability and made it more difficult to sue auditors successfully. However, the Sarbanes-Oxley Act of 2002 refocused attention on auditor performance, duties, and legal liability after the capital markets were shaken by the massive high-profile accounting frauds at Enron and WorldCom.

The monetary size of the legal claims against auditors combined with a small number of large audit firms has made it difficult or impossible for the largest audit

Practice INSIGHT

The Costs of Litigation

The following list provides the settlement amounts of recent audit-related lawsuits for the Big 4:

Audit Firm	Client	Settlement Amount
Ernst & Young	Cendant	$335 million
PricewaterhouseCoopers	Tyco	225 million
Deloitte	Adelphia	210 million
Deloitte	Parmalat	149 million
KMPG	Rite Aid	125 million

Audit-related litigation can be very expensive, but auditors do not have a monopoly on expensive litigation. Tax-related litigation is actually more frequent, and while many tax claims are for relatively small amounts, tax-related settlements can be very large. For example, in 2005, KPMG LLP settled a lawsuit with the U.S. Justice Department for $456 million for selling aggressive and improper tax shelters that helped wealthy Americans avoid taxes. In a related case with purchasers of the tax shelters, KPMG also agreed to pay $123 million, and there are many cases still pending related to the sale of the tax shelters.

---

[1] Approximately 4,000 claims are currently being asserted against accounting firms in the United States each year, whereas in the late 1960s the number of such claims did not exceed a few hundred per year. See Goldwasser, Arnold, and Eickemeyer, *Accountants' Liability* (Practising Law Institute, 2008), for additional information on the magnitude and severity of claims.

firms to obtain sufficient liability insurance. The largest audit firms are basically self-insured for small and large claims (e.g., less than $10 million and more than $100 million). It is generally believed that the single greatest threat to large firms and the audit profession is catastrophic legal liability. The collapse of Arthur Anderson illustrated how severe the lack of available audit services would be if another big firm collapsed. For this reason, some European countries have established caps that limit auditor liability. While such caps have been discussed in the U.S., it seems unlikely that legislation capping liability will be forthcoming in the near future.

Overview of Auditor Legal Liability

[LO 1]

There are four general stages in the initiation and disposition of audit-related disputes: (1) the occurrence of events that result in losses for users of the financial statements; (2) the investigation by plaintiff attorneys before filing suit to link the user losses with allegations of material omissions or misstatements of financial statements; (3) the legal process that commences with the filing of the suit; and (4) the final resolution of the dispute.[2] The first stage includes events that result in losses, such as client bankruptcy, financial distress, fraudulent financial reporting, and misappropriation of assets. The second stage pre-suit investigation, may involve investigation activities by plaintiffs and their attorneys before initiating legal proceedings. For example, a board of directors may hire a public accounting firm other than their external auditors to investigate potential fraud. The legal process makes up the third stage. The stage involves activities such as filing of complaints, discovery, trial preparation, and the trial. The last stage involves the resolution of the dispute, which may include a summary judgment, a settlement to avoid or discontinue litigation, or a court decision on appeal after a trial.

[LO 2]

Auditors can be sued by clients, investors, creditors, and the government for failure to perform professional services with due professional care. Auditors can be held liable under two broad categories of law:

1. ***Common law.*** Case law developed over time by judges who issue legal opinions when deciding a case (the legal principles announced in these cases become precedent for judges deciding similar cases in the future).

2. ***Statutory law.*** Written law enacted by the legislative branch of federal and state governments.

It is important to understand the differences between these two legal categories. Table 20–1 defines key legal terms, and Table 20–2 summarizes the auditor's liability by category of law and actions resulting in liability.

TABLE 20–1	**Definitions of Key Legal Terms**
Breach of contract	Occurs when the client or auditor fails to meet the terms and obligations established in the contract (either expressly or implied), which is normally finalized in the engagement letter. Third parties may have privity or near privity of contract.
Civil law	All law that does not relate to criminal matters.
Class action	Lawsuit filed by one or more individuals on behalf of all persons who may have invested on the basis of the same false and misleading information.
Criminal law	Statutory law that defines the duties citizens owe to society and prescribes penalties for violations.
Fraud	Actions taken with the knowledge and intent to deceive.
Gross negligence	An extreme, flagrant, or reckless departure from professional standards of due care. This is also referred to as *constructive fraud.*
Ordinary negligence	An absence of reasonable or due care in the conduct of an engagement. Due care is evaluated in terms of what other professional accountants would have done under similar circumstances.
Privity	A contract or specific agreement exists between two parties. Absent a contractual or fiduciary relationship, the accountant does not owe a duty of care to an injured party.
Scienter	Acting with intent to deceive, defraud or with knowledge of a false representation.
Tort	A wrongful act, other than a breach of contract, for which civil action may be taken.

---

[2]See Chapter 2 in Z. Palmrose, *Empirical Research in Auditor Litigation: Considerations and Data*, Studies in Accounting Research #33 (Sarasota, FL: American Accounting Association, 1999), for a detailed discussion of the four stages of the process.

TABLE 20–2	Summary of Types of Liability and Auditors' Actions Resulting in Liability
Type of Liability	*Auditors' Actions Resulting in Liability*
Common law—liability to clients	Breach of contract Negligence Gross negligence/constructive fraud Fraud
Common law—liability to third parties	Negligence Gross negligence/constructive fraud Fraud
Federal statutory law—civil liability*	Negligence Gross negligence/constructive fraud Fraud
Federal statutory law—criminal liability*	Willful violation of federal statutes

*Auditors may also be civilly and criminally liable under state statutes. Coverage of liability under specific state statutes is beyond the scope of this book.

Under common law, auditors can be held civilly, but not criminally, liable. Typical civil actions under common law allege that the auditor did not properly perform the audit. For example, under common law, an auditor can be held liable to clients for breach of contract, negligence, gross negligence, and fraud. The auditor's liability to third parties (e.g., investors and creditors) under common law is complicated by the fact that legal precedent differs by jurisdiction. In other words, the law applicable to a common-law case depends on the location where the case is tried (i.e., state by state). Some jurisdictions follow a common-law doctrine that provides a very narrow interpretation of auditors' liability to third parties, while others follow a more liberal interpretation. Most common-law cases are decided in state courts, but there are circumstances where common-law cases can be decided in federal court (for example, a negligence claim may be brought in federal court where parties are from different states and the amount of damages being sought exceeds $75,000).

Under statutory law an auditor can be held civilly or criminally liable. A civil claim can result in fines and sanctions but not incarceration. While there are federal and state statutes, in this text we focus only on federal statutes. Federal statutes such as the Securities Act of 1933, the Securities Exchange Act of 1934, and the Sarbanes-Oxley Act of 2002 (and related SEC rulings) provide the legal basis for action against auditors. Auditors are liable mainly for gross negligence and fraud under these statutes; however, some parts of the acts have been used to hold auditors liable for ordinary negligence. While under certain circumstances an auditor can be held criminally liable under statutory law, there have been relatively few instances of major criminal actions against auditors.

The remainder of the chapter is organized according to the four categories of liability faced by auditors outlined in Table 20–2:

- Common law—liability to clients.
- Common law—liability to third parties.
- Federal statutory law—civil liability (clients and third parties).
- Federal statutory law—criminal liability (government).

Common Law—Clients

[LO 3] Common law does not require that the public accountant guarantee his or her work product. It does, however, require that the auditor perform professional services with *due care*. Due care or due professional care requires that the auditor perform his or her professional services with the same degree of skill, knowledge, and judgment possessed by other members of the profession. This includes, but is not limited to, an expectation that auditors will perform an audit in conformance with GAAS or standards of the PCAOB, and that the audited financial statements will comply with GAAP. When an auditor fails to carry out contractual arrangements with the client, he or she may be held liable for breach of contract or negligence. Under common law, the auditor can be held liable to the client for gross negligence and fraud.

Breach of Contract—Client Claims

A breach of contract occurs when the client fails to complete its obligation or when the auditor fails to complete the services agreed to in the contract. As discussed in Chapter 5, an engagement letter should establish the responsibilities for both the auditor and the client. In performing an audit, the auditor's obligation is to examine the client's financial statements and issue the appropriate opinion in accordance with professional standards. The contract between the client and the auditor stipulates the amount of fees to be charged for the designated professional services, and deadlines for completing the services are normally indicated or implied in the contract. If the client breaches its obligations under the engagement letter, the auditor is excused from his or her contractual obligations. If the auditor discontinues an audit without adequate cause, he or she may be liable for economic injury suffered by the client (see Exhibit 20–1). Similarly, other issues (such as timely delivery of the audit report or failure to detect a material defalcation) can lead to litigation by the client against the auditor. When the auditor is found to have breached the contract, the auditor is only liable for damages caused by the breach.

Negligence—Client Claims

A *tort* is a wrongful act, other than a breach of contract, for which civil action may be taken. If an engagement is performed without due care, the public accountant may be held liable for an actionable tort in negligence. The auditor typically faces

EXHIBIT 20–1	Deloitte & Touche's Withdrawal from Medtrans Audit Upheld

Medtrans, an ambulance service provider, retained Deloitte & Touche to audit its financial statements. Medtrans needed capital and sought $10 million in financing from an outside investor. Medtrans gave the potential investor *unaudited* financial statements showing profits of $1.9 million. Deloitte & Touche was in the process of completing its audit during Medtrans's negotiations with the outside investor. Deloitte & Touche proposed adjustments that resulted in Medtrans's financial statements showing a $500,000 loss. Prior to Deloitte & Touche proposing the adjustments, the company's CFO resigned after indicating that he could not sign the management representation letter. When presented with the proposed adjustments, Medtrans's CEO threatened to get a court order forcing Deloitte & Touche to complete the audit. Deloitte withdrew from the engagement. Medtrans retained two other CPA firms, both of which were either discharged or withdrew. A third firm issued an unqualified audit report that contained the adjustments proposed by Deloitte & Touche.

Medtrans alleged that Deloitte & Touche's wrongful withdrawal resulted in the company's failure to complete the financing, and that the subsequent sale of the company was for significantly less than its true value. At trial Medtrans asserted that, under California law, a CPA firm could not, under any circumstances, withdraw from an engagement if it unduly jeopardized the interest of the client. The jury in this case ruled in favor of Medtrans and awarded the company nearly $10 million. Deloitte & Touche argued that the approved California jury instructions on the duration of a professional's duty were contrary to professional standards, which authorize the auditor to resign.

In 1998 the California Court of Appeals reversed the decision, holding that judges should instruct juries about the profession's standards. The court held that an auditor, by auditing financial statements, assumes a public responsibility that transcends any employment relationship with the client. This decision is significant because it held that an accountant's duty of care can be based on professional standards rather than rules of law that are contrary to professional standards.

Source: National Medical Transportation Network v. Deloitte & Touche, 98 D.A.R., 2850, 1998, and "Court Rules on Importance of GAAP and GAAS," *Journal of Accountancy* (June 1998), p. 24.

larger legal damage assessments for a tort than for a breach of contract. Liability for negligence represents a deviation from a standard of behavior that is consistent with that of a "reasonable person." When an individual such as a public accountant possesses special skills and knowledge, ordinary reasonable care is not sufficient. An oft-cited quote from Cooley's *Torts*[3] indicates the responsibility of those offering special skills:

> In all those employments where particular skill is requisite, if one offers his services, he is understood as holding himself out to the public as possessing the degree of skill commonly possessed by others in the same employment, and if his pretensions are unfounded, he commits a species of fraud upon every man who employs him in reliance on his public profession. But no man, whether skilled or unskilled, undertakes that the task he assumes shall be performed successfully, and without fault or error; he undertakes for good faith and integrity, but not for infallibility, and he is liable to his employer for negligence, bad faith, or dishonesty, but not for losses consequent upon mere errors of judgment.

Thus, a CPA has the duty to conduct an engagement using the same degree of care that would be used by an ordinary, prudent member of the public accounting profession.

To recover against an auditor in a negligence case, the client must prove the following:

1. The auditor had a *duty* to the client to conform to a required standard of care.
2. The auditor *breached* that duty by failing to act with due professional care.
3. There was a direct *causal connection* between the auditor's negligence and the client's damage.
4. The client suffered actual *losses* or damages as a result.

Negligence suits by clients against auditors often allege that the auditor was negligent in not detecting a misstatement or fraud. Auditors' defenses against client negligence claims include the following:

1. No duty was owed.
2. The client was negligent (contributory negligence, comparative negligence, or management fraud).
3. The auditor's work was performed in accordance with professional standards.
4. The client suffered no loss.
5. Any loss was caused by other events.
6. The claim is invalid because the statute of limitations has expired.[4]

The client can typically prove the existence of a duty of care based on the engagement contract. However, the auditor may be able to argue successfully that the client's loss was due to the client's negligence. Some states permit a defense of *contributory negligence* or *in pari delicto* (in equal fault) as a complete bar to recovery by a client. A recent case where the auditor successfully used the *in pari delicto* defense, *Official Comm. of Unsecured Creditors of Allegheny Health, Educ. & Research Foundation v. PricewaterhouseCoopers,* is discussed on the book's

---

[3]D. Haggard, *Cooley on Torts*, 4th ed., p. 472.

[4]Statute limitations for negligence claims vary from jurisdiction to jurisdiction with a range of 1 to 6 years. The statute in most jurisdictions is 3 years or less. The statutes do not restrict auditor liability for fraud.

EXHIBIT 20-2	*Cenco, Inc. v. Seidman & Seidman*

Between 1970 and 1975, managerial employees of Cenco, Inc., engaged in a massive fraud. The fraud began in the company's Medical/Health Division and eventually spread to Cenco's top management. By the time the fraud was made public, the chairman and president, plus a number of other top managers, were involved in the fraud. A number of the board of directors were not involved in the fraud, but there was evidence that they had been negligent in allowing the fraud to continue. Seidman & Seidman was Cenco's auditor throughout the period of the fraud.

The fraud involved primarily the inflating of inventories in the Medical/Health Division above their fair market value to increase its stock price. Thus, the fraud did not involve stealing from the company. Rather, the fraudsters had devised ways to steal from outsiders (e.g., creditors and insurers) to the benefit of existing shareholders.

Cenco's new management filed breach-of-contract, negligence, and fraud claims against Seidman & Seidman, and a trial date was set. One day before the start of the trial, Seidman & Seidman offered to pay $3.5 million to settle the class action suit, but Cenco turned the offer down. Prior to submitting the case to the jury, the trial judge granted a directed verdict in favor of Seidman & Seidman on the claim that the CPA firm had aided and abetted the fraud. The case went to the jury on the three remaining counts of breach of contract, negligence, and fraud. The jury found that Seidman & Seidman was innocent on all counts. The verdict was appealed by Cenco. The U.S. Court of Appeals upheld the lower court and found that Seidman & Seidman had not been responsible for any liability for breach of contract, negligence, or fraud. The court held that the auditors of a corporation could use the fraud of corporate managers as a defense to claims against the auditor by the corporation.

Web site (www.mhhe.com/messier7e). However, most states follow the view of comparative negligence because it is not as harsh as an all-or-nothing approach. Under the comparative negligence view, the jury is permitted to assess the relative fault of the parties. For example, if a client's system of internal control is deficient because the client failed to provide adequate training or personnel, any recovery by the client against the auditor is reduced in proportion to the fault of the client. When top management of the client has engaged in fraud, the auditor may be able to attribute the fraud to the client and prevent recovery for a negligently performed audit. This defense has been used successfully by auditors, including in the well-known *Cenco, Inc. v. Seidman & Seidman* case involving such circumstances. Exhibit 20–2 presents a summary of the case. In this instance, the client (new management) alleged that Seidman & Seidman was negligent for not having uncovered the prior management's fraudulent actions. The court ruled that, considering management's involvement in the fraud, the CPA firm had not been negligent.

Another well-known case that alleged negligence by an accountant is the *1136 Tenants' Corp. v. Max Rothenberg & Co.*, which relates to unaudited financial statements and the CPA's failure to communicate suspicious circumstances to the client. Exhibit 20–3 presents a summary of the case. The *1136 Tenants'* case established a duty on the part of a CPA doing work on unaudited financial statements to communicate to the client any circumstances that give reason to believe that fraud may exist. One outcome of this case was the establishment of Statements on Standards for Accounting and Review Services, which prescribe procedures that CPAs should follow when performing engagements such as compilations and reviews (discussed in Chapter 21).

Fraud—Client Claims

An auditor can be held liable to clients for fraud when he or she acted with knowledge and intent to deceive. Generally, however, actions alleging fraud on the part of the auditor result from lawsuits by third parties and thus are discussed in more detail in the next section.

EXHIBIT 20–3	*1136 Tenants' Corp. v. Max Rothenberg & Co.*

Jerome Riker was a powerful New York City businessman with extensive business interests in the real estate industry. During the early 1960s, Riker diverted money from a number of trust funds of cooperatives that he managed for use in a personal real estate investment.

One of the cooperatives that was involved in the embezzlement was the 1136 Tenants' Corporation. Riker had misappropriated approximately $130,000 of the cooperative's funds. When the cooperative was unable to recover the funds from Riker, it filed a civil suit against the public accounting firm, Max Rothenberg & Company, which had prepared the annual financial statements and tax return. The plaintiffs alleged that the accounting firm should have discovered the embezzlement of funds by Riker.

One issue that arose during the trial was the contractual agreement between the public accounting firm and the 1136 Tenants' Corporation. There was no written engagement letter, only an oral agreement between one of the firm's partners and Riker. The cooperative alleged that the firm had been retained to do an audit, while the firm alleged that it had been retained only to prepare the tax return and perform "write-up" services. Another issue was the fact that the firm had identified some missing invoices and had not investigated these items further. The workpapers detailed $44,000 of expenses for which no supporting documentation could be located. These were fictitious expenses used by Riker to extract funds from the cooperative.

The court ruled that even if the firm had agreed to provide only write-up services, it had an obligation to notify the tenants about the suspicious nature of the missing invoices. Damaging to the firm's defense was the admission by one of its partners that the engagement had been more extensive than that called for by a normal write-up engagement. The income statement also included an expense labeled "audit." The court ruled in favor of the tenants and awarded them damages of more than $230,000. The decision was upheld upon appeal by the New York appellate court. The size of the judgment was far in excess of the fee of $600 paid to the firm.

This court decision resulted in two significant changes in the profession:

- It reinforced the need by firms to have *written* engagement letters.
- It led to the issuance by the AICPA of Statements on Standards for Accounting and Review Services.

Common Law—Third Parties

[LO 4] Under common law, auditors can be held liable to third parties for negligence, gross negligence, and fraud. This area of liability is very complex, and court rulings are not always consistent across state and federal judicial jurisdictions. As mentioned earlier, most common law claims are decided in state courts.

Ordinary
Negligence—
Third-Party
Claims

When an auditor fails to conduct an engagement with due care, he or she can, in some situations, be held liable for *ordinary negligence* to third parties (plaintiffs) under common law. To prevail in a suit alleging negligence, the third party must prove all of the following:

1. The auditor had a *duty* to the plaintiff to exercise due care.
2. The auditor *breached* that duty by failing to act with due professional care.
3. There was a direct *causal connection* between the auditor's negligence and the third party's injury (e.g., the financial statements were misleading and the third party relied on the financial statements).
4. The third party suffered an actual *loss* as a result.

The main difficulty faced by third parties in proving negligence against an auditor is showing that the auditor's duty to exercise due care extended to them. Over time, four common-law standards have evolved for determining the types of third parties that can successfully sue auditors for ordinary negligence. The four legal standards are *privity, near privity, foreseen third parties (or Restatement Standard),* and *reasonably foreseeable third parties.* The doctrine that will be applied in deciding a case depends on the precedents established in the state where the case is decided.

EXHIBIT 20–4	*Ultramares v. Touche et al.*

Fred Stern & Company imported and sold rubber during the 1920s. This industry required extensive working capital, and the company used borrowings from banks for its financing activities. In 1924 Stern requested a $100,000 loan from Ultramares Corporation. Before deciding to make the loan, Ultramares requested that Stern provide an audited balance sheet. Touche, Niven & Company had just issued an unqualified audit report on the December 31, 1923, balance sheet.

Stern's management asked Touche to provide 32 serially numbered copies of the audit report. Touche had audited Stern for three years and knew that the audit reports were being used by Stern to obtain external debt financing. Touche, however, did not know which specific banks or finance companies would be given the reports. The balance sheet showed assets of $2.5 million. Ultramares provided the $100,000 loan and two additional loans totaling $65,000. In addition, Stern obtained bank loans of approximately $300,000 by providing the December 31, 1923, balance sheet audited by Touche.

In 1925 the company declared bankruptcy. It came to light during the trial that Stern had already been bankrupt in 1923 and that false accounting record entries had concealed the company's problems. Ultramares alleged that Touche had been both negligent and fraudulent in its audit of Stern.

The jury in the case dismissed the fraud charges against Touche but ruled that Touche had been negligent and awarded approximately $186,000 in damages. The trial judge overturned the jury's verdict on the grounds that Ultramares had not been in privity with Touche. The appellate division of the New York Supreme Court voted 3 to 2 in favor of Ultramares, ruling that the judge had inappropriately overruled the jury verdict. Touche's attorneys appealed the decision to the court of appeals, which ruled unanimously in favor of Touche, therefore upholding the privity doctrine. The quote included in the text by Judge Cardozo, the chief justice of the court of appeals, summarizes the decision.

Privity   The most restrictive view under common law is that auditors have no liability for ordinary negligence to third parties who do not have a *privity* relationship with the auditor. Privity means that a contract or specific agreement exists between two parties. Third parties to a contract between an auditor and a client, such as investors or creditors of the client, typically lack privity because they were not directly involved in the agreement between the auditor and the client and thus cannot successfully sue the auditor, even if the auditor was negligent. The landmark decision in this area, *Ultramares v. Touche et al.*, held that the auditor was not liable to third parties who relied on a negligently prepared audit report. Exhibit 20–4 provides a summary of the *Ultramares* case. The rationale for this finding by the New York Court of Appeals is summarized in a famous quote by Judge Benjamin Cardozo:

> If a liability for negligence exists, a thoughtless slip or blunder, the failure to detect a theft or forgery beneath the cover of deceptive entries, may expose accountants to a liability in an indeterminate amount for an indeterminate time to an indeterminate class. The hazards of a business on these terms are so extreme as to enkindle doubt whether a flaw may not exist in the implication of a duty that exposes to these circumstances.

The privity requirement under the *Ultramares doctrine* does not apply when the auditor is charged with *fraud*. Furthermore, while Judge Cardozo followed a strict privity doctrine in the *Ultramares* case, he opened the door for third parties without privity to sue if the negligence was so great as to constitute gross negligence, also known as constructive fraud. In other words, in a jurisdiction that follows the *Utramares doctrine*, plaintiffs can successfully sue auditors even if they do not have privity so long as the plaintiff can prove the auditors were guilty of gross negligence or fraud.

States that have followed the strict privity or *Ultramares doctrine* include Pennsylvania and Nevada.

Near Privity   While the *Ultramares* decision established a strict privity standard, a number of subsequent court decisions in other states have moved away from this standard over time. In 1985 the New York Court of Appeals expanded the privity standard in the case of *Credit Alliance v. Arthur Andersen & Co.* to include third parties whose relationship with the accountant *approaches* privity. In this lawsuit, Credit Alliance alleged that the auditor had known that the plaintiff was the client's principal lender and had frequently communicated with the plaintiff regarding the audited financial statements. The court upheld the lender's claim that Arthur Andersen had known that Credit Alliance was relying on the financial statements prior to extending credit. The court also ruled that there had been direct communication between the lender and the auditor regarding the client. The *Credit Alliance* case lists the following tests that must be satisfied for holding auditors liable for ordinary negligence to third parties: (1) the accountant must be aware that the financial statements are to be used for a particular purpose or purposes, (2) in the furtherance of which a known party or parties was intended to rely; and (3) there must have been some conduct on the part of the accountants linking them to that party or parties, which provides evidence of the accountants' understanding of intended reliance.

In a 1992 case, *Security Pacific Business Credit, Inc. v. Peat Marwick Main & Co.*, the New York Court of Appeals ruled in favor of Peat Marwick because the plaintiff's reliance was based on one telephone call to the firm's audit partner. In 2005, a court ruled that payment of some of the accountant's fees by a third party for services provided to the client was not sufficient to establish near privity because there was no communication between the third party and the accountant *(Carter v. Carlis)*. Based on these cases, it appears that a critical test is the third test, the requirement that the third party be known to the auditor and that the auditor has directly conveyed the audit report or acted to induce reliance on the audit report. Most third parties who are not in actual privity of contract with the auditors will not likely meet the demanding near privity standard, since the auditor will usually not have communicated directly with the plaintiff. States that have followed the near privity doctrine include Idaho, Illinois, Indiana, Montana, and New York.

It is important to remember that third-party plaintiffs in all jurisdictions are able to successfully sue auditors for gross negligence or fraud, regardless of their privity status.

Foreseen Third Party or Restatement Standard   The "middle ground" approach followed by the vast majority of states (and federal courts located within those states) expands the class of third parties that can successfully sue an auditor for negligence beyond near privity to a person or limited group of persons whose reliance is actually *foreseen*, even if the specific person or group is unknown to the auditor. In essence, the courts in these jurisdictions have reexamined the notion of *caveat emptor* ("buyer beware") and substituted the concept of public responsibility. Among the reasons that have been advanced by the courts for expanding the scope beyond near privity are (1) the increased liability of other professionals to nonprivity users of their services; (2) the lack of fairness of imposing the burden of economic loss on innocent financial statement users; (3) the assumption that expanded liability will cause auditors to improve their auditing procedures; (4) the ability of auditors to obtain insurance against the increased risks; and (5) the ability of the auditors to pass the increased audit costs and insurance premiums on to their clients. However, as discussed earlier, large firms may not be able to obtain adequate liability insurance.

In 1968 a federal district court decision, *Rusch Factors, Inc. v. Levin*, applied Section 552 of the Restatement (Second) of the Law of Torts to an accountant's third-party liability suit. The case is described in Exhibit 20–5. Basically, a company engaged Levin to audit the financial statements for the purpose of obtaining financing from Rusch Factors. The statements portrayed the company as solvent. The plaintiff made a large loan to the company, which subsequently went

EXHIBIT 20–5	*Rusch Factors, Inc. v. Levin*

In this case, the plaintiff, Rusch Factors, Inc., had requested audited financial statements as a prerequisite for providing a loan to a Rhode Island corporation. Levin issued a clean audit opinion on the financial statements, indicating the company to be solvent when it was actually insolvent. Rusch Factors loaned the corporation $337,000 based on the audited financial statements. When the company went into receivership, Rusch Factors sued Levin for a loss of $121,000.

The federal district court, sitting in Rhode Island, denied Levin's motion to dismiss for a lack of privity. In finding Levin liable for negligence, the court concluded that the *Ultramares doctrine* was inappropriate and relied heavily on the Restatement (Second) of the Law of Torts. The court stated that the auditor had known that his certification was to be used and relied upon by Rusch Factors, and therefore he could be held liable for financial misrepresentations relied upon by *foreseen and limited classes of persons*.

bankrupt. The federal district court found the public accounting firm negligent, relying on Section 552 of the Restatement in reaching its decision.

The Restatement is a compendium of common law prepared by legal scholars and presents an alternative view to the traditional privity doctrine. Section 552 states the following:

> One who, in the course of his business, profession, or employment . . . supplies false information for the guidance of others in their business transactions, is subject to liability for pecuniary loss caused to them by their justifiable reliance upon the information, if he fails to exercise reasonable care or competence in obtaining or communicating the information.

> The liability . . . is limited to loss suffered (a) by the person or one of the persons for whose benefit and guidance he intends to supply the information, or knows that the recipient intends to supply it; and (b) through reliance upon it in a transaction which he intends the information to influence, or knows that the recipient so intends. . . .

> The liability of one who is under a public duty to give the information extends to loss suffered by any of the class of persons for whose benefit the duty is created, in any of the transactions in which it is intended to protect them.

The Restatement broadens the auditor's liability beyond those with near privity to a small group of persons and classes who are or should be foreseen by the auditor as relying on the financial information. However, because the language of the Restatement is general, it is subject to different interpretations. The following examples abstracted from the Restatement help illustrate the possibilities for auditor liability.

Example 1

Cornelius Manufacturing Co. is negotiating for a $1,000,000 loan from the First National Bank of Sun City. The bank requires that Cornelius Manufacturing provide audited financial statements. Cornelius engages the public accounting firm of Cantbe & Mustbe (C&M) to conduct the audit, informing them that the audit is for the express purpose of obtaining credit from the First National Bank of Sun City. C&M accepts the engagement with the understanding that the financial statements are for the bank's use. The First National Bank of Sun City goes into bankruptcy, and Cornelius submits the audited financial statements to Waldo National Bank without communicating with C&M. Waldo National Bank lends Cornelius the $1,000,000. The financial statements materially overstate the financial resources of Cornelius, and Waldo National Bank suffers a loss on the loan. In this example, the Restatement indicates that C&M is not liable to Waldo National Bank because Waldo was *not* a foreseen third party.

> **Example 2**
>
> The same facts apply as in Example 1, except that Cornelius says nothing to C&M about supplying the financial statements to the First National Bank of Sun City; Cornelius merely tells C&M that the company expects to negotiate a bank loan and is considering going to the First National Bank of Sun City. In this instance, the Restatement indicates that C&M would be liable to Waldo National Bank because Waldo was a foreseen third party.

> **Example 3**
>
> The same facts apply as in Example 2, except that Cornelius informs C&M that the company is planning on negotiating a bank loan without mentioning a specific bank. Again, under the Restatement, C&M would be liable to Waldo National Bank because Waldo was a foreseen third party.

Subsequent to the *Rusch Factors* case, a number of state and federal courts have followed the approach outlined in the Restatement Standard to determine third parties eligible to sue auditors for ordinary negligence (you can think of this as the *"Rusch Factors doctrine"*).

Several cases (e.g., *Loop Corp. v. McIlroy,* 2004; *Tocchet v. Cater,* 2003) have dealt with the issue of whether purchasers of a company's stock on the open market should be foreseen users and can hold auditors liable under Restatement Section 552. Plaintiffs argue that federal securities laws impose public duties upon auditors that should extend to Section 552. If courts agree with the plaintiffs' arguments, then auditors would owe a duty under Section 552 to every shareholder and perhaps to all potential investors in a publicly held corporation. Essentially, this would mean that all shareholders and potential shareholders could sue auditors for ordinary negligence under common law. Thus far, courts have ruled that Section 552 does not impose a public duty.

Reasonably Foreseeable Third Parties   The courts of three jurisdictions (Mississippi, New Jersey, and Wisconsin) have used a more expansive view of auditors' liability to third parties: *reasonably foreseeable third parties*. In the precedent-setting case in this area, *H. Rosenblum, Inc. v. Adler,* the New Jersey Supreme Court ruled that Touche Ross & Co. was responsible for damages incurred by all reasonably foreseeable third parties who had relied on the financial statements. Exhibit 20–6 provides more details on this case.[5]

Another important case that followed this approach was *Citizens State Bank v. Timm, Schmidt & Company* (1983). In this case, the bank sued the public accounting firm after relying on financial statements for one of its debtors that had been audited by Timm, Schmidt & Company. The Wisconsin court extended the scope of third parties to include all reasonably foreseeable users. The court used a number of the reasons just cited for extending auditors' liability beyond privity. The following quote from this case demonstrates the court's thoughts.

---

[5]While the precedent set by the *Rosenblum* case in New Jersey has been followed by other states, subsequent legislation in New Jersey (1995) overturned *Rosenblum* and restricts auditor liability to the near privity standard. Recent court cases in New Jersey have upheld the near privity standard (e.g., *E. Dickerson & Sons, Inc. v. Ernst & Young,* 2003).

EXHIBIT 20–6	*H. Rosenblum, Inc. v. Adler*

The Rosenblum family agreed to sell its retail catalog showroom business, H. Rosenblum, Inc., to Giant Stores in exchange for Giant common stock. The Rosenblums relied on Giant's 1971 and 1972 financial statements, which had been audited by Touche Ross & Co. A year later, it was revealed that Giant Stores' financial statements contained material misstatements. Giant Stores filed for bankruptcy, and the company's stock became worthless. The Rosenblums sued Touche, alleging negligence. Touche did not know the Rosenblums and had not known that the financial statements would be relied on during merger negotiations.

The lower courts in this case did not allow the Rosenblums' claims against Touche, on the grounds that the Rosenblums did not meet either the *Ultramares* privity test or the Restatement (Second) of the Law of Torts' "foreseen third parties" test. The New Jersey Supreme Court overturned the lower courts' decisions. The court held that the auditor had "a duty to all those whom the auditor should reasonably foresee as recipient from the company of the statements for its proper business purposes, provided that the recipients rely on the statements." Thus the court concluded that auditors should be liable to all reasonably foreseeable third parties who rely on the financial statements. The court indicated that the auditor's function had expanded from one of a watchdog for management to that of an independent evaluator of the adequacy and fairness of the financial statements presented by management to third parties. The court also cited the accountant's ability to obtain insurance against third-party claims.

If relying third parties, such as creditors, are not allowed to recover, the cost of credit to the general public will increase because creditors will either have to absorb the cost of bad loans made in reliance on faulty information or hire independent accountants to verify the information received. Accountants may spread the risk through the use of liability insurance.

A weakness in this argument is that the larger public accounting firms may not be able to secure sufficient liability insurance, or the cost of such insurance may be exorbitant.

Since 1987 no state high court has adopted the foreseeability approach to accountant liability, while a large number have approved or adopted one of the narrower standards.[6] For example, in *Bily v. Arthur Young & Co.* (1992) the California Supreme Court expressly rejected the foreseeability approach in favor of the *Rusch Factors* or Restatement Standard. The court gave a number of reasons for rejecting the *Rosenblum* foreseeablity approach, including that the foreseeability rule exposes auditors to potential liability in excess of their proportionate share and that sophisticated plaintiffs have other ways to protect themselves from the risk of inaccurate financial statements (e.g., they can negotiate improved terms or hire their own auditor).

However, in *Murphy v. BDO Seidman, LLP*, (2003), the California Court of Appeals ruled that "grapevine plaintiffs," who alleged indirect reliance based on what others (e.g., stockholders and stockbrokers) told them about the financial statements, had legal claims for ordinary negligence against the auditors so long as the auditor would have reasonably foreseen that stockholders or stockbrokers would tell other people of the content of the financial statements and that the other people would rely upon the misrepresentations in purchasing the corporate stock. The court ruled that nothing in the *Bily* decision precludes indirect reliance.

Figure 20–1 illustrates the four legal doctrines just covered and how moving from left to right there is a broader class of third parties eligible to sue auditors for ordinary negligence under common law. Students interested in reading an actual court case that considers these legal doctrines can find the *Anjoorian vs. Pascarella & Trench* case at the book's Online Learning Center (www.mhhe.com/messier7e).

---

[6]See Chapter 4 in Goldwasser, Arnold, and Eickemeyer, *Accountants' Liability* (Practising Law Institute, 2008).

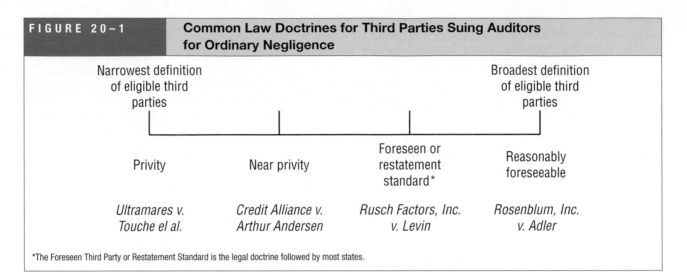

FIGURE 20-1	Common Law Doctrines for Third Parties Suing Auditors for Ordinary Negligence

Narrowest definition of eligible third parties — Broadest definition of eligible third parties

Privity	Near privity	Foreseen or restatement standard*	Reasonably foreseeable
Ultramares v. Touche el al.	*Credit Alliance v. Arthur Andersen*	*Rusch Factors, Inc. v. Levin*	*Rosenblum, Inc. v. Adler*

*The Foreseen Third Party or Restatement Standard is the legal doctrine followed by most states.

Auditor Defenses   The defenses presented earlier in this chapter under liability to clients above are also available to auditors sued by third parties for ordinary negligence under common law. In addition, depending on the jurisdiction, the auditor can argue that the third party does not qualify as a foreseen party or does not have near privity.

Practice INSIGHT	While the large international audit firms market themselves as global firms with uniform practices and quality control standards in offices worldwide, these entities are legally formed as a network of affiliated firms (e.g., U.S. affiliate, Canadian affiliate, Japanese affiliate). To date, the courts have declined to find that a global accounting firm is legally responsible for the misconduct of one of the affiliates in the network (obviously, the affiliate involved can be, and often is, held responsible). Investors and creditors who suffered losses as a result of the massive 2009 fraud at Satyam Computer Services, headquartered in New Delhi, India, will ask the courts to reconsider this precedence as they file claims against the PricewaterhouseCoopers global firm as well as the Indian and U.S. affiliates.

Fraud and Gross Negligence— Third-Party Claims

If an auditor has acted with knowledge and intent to deceive a third party, he or she can be held liable for fraud. As noted earlier, common-law liability for fraud is available to any third parties in any jurisdiction. The plaintiff (third party) must prove:

1. A *false representation* by the accountant.
2. *Knowledge or belief* by the accountant that the representation was false.
3. That the accountant *intended* to induce the third party to rely on false representation.
4. That the third party *relied* on the false representation.
5. That the third party suffered *damages*.

Courts have held that fraudulent intent or *scienter* may be established by proof that the accountant acted with knowledge of the false representation.

However, liability for fraud is not limited only to cases where the auditor was *knowingly* deceitful. Some courts have interpreted gross negligence as an instance of fraud (also referred to as *constructive fraud*). Gross negligence is defined to be an extreme, flagrant, or reckless deviation from professional standards of due care. An important case in this area is *State Street Trust Co. v. Ernst*. In this case, the auditors issued an unqualified opinion on their client's financial statements, knowing that State Street Trust Company was making a loan based on those financial statements. A month later, the auditors sent a letter to the client indicating that receivables had been overstated. The auditors, however, did not communicate this information to State Street Trust Company, and the client subsequently went bankrupt. The New York court ruled that the auditor's actions appeared to be grossly negligent and that "reckless disregard of consequences may take the place of deliberate intention." In such cases, while fraudulent intent or scienter may not be present, the court "constructs" fraud due to the grossness of the negligence.

The *Phar-Mor v. Coopers & Lybrand* case is another example of how auditors were found guilty of fraud under both common and statutory law, even though the plaintiffs acknowledged that the auditors had no intent to deceive. Instead, the plaintiff successfully argued reckless disregard for the truth (i.e., gross negligence or constructive fraud) which gives rise to an inference of fraud. Thus, plaintiffs that are barred from suing for ordinary negligence in a particular jurisdiction, because they are not in privity or not foreseen users, can opt to sue the auditor for fraud because for the auditor to be found guilty under a fraud charge, the plaintiffs need only prove gross negligence. The Phar-Mor case write-up and excerpts from the actual trial are available on the book's Online Learning Center (www.mhhe.com/messier7e).

In recent cases (e.g., *Houbigant, Inc. v. Deloitte & Touche LLP*, 2003, and *Reisman v. KPMG Peat Marwick LLP*, 2003) courts ruled that for an auditor to be found guilty of fraud, the plaintiffs must only prove that the auditor was aware that its misrepresentations might reasonably be relied upon by the plaintiff, not that the auditor *intended* to induce the detrimental reliance. In the *Houbigant* decision the court referred to the recent audit failures in its decision:

> It should be sufficient that the complaint contains some rational basis for inferring that the alleged misrepresentation was knowingly made. Indeed, to require anything beyond that would be particularly undesirable at this time, when it has been widely acknowledged that our society is experiencing a proliferation of frauds perpetrated by officers of large corporations . . . unchecked by the "impartial" auditors they hired.

Auditor Defenses   The defenses presented earlier in this chapter are also available to auditors sued for fraud or gross negligence. If the auditor has been only negligent, he or she can claim that his or her negligence did not rise to the level of gross negligence or fraud. The auditor can also raise the statute of limitations as a defense. Finally, the auditor can claim that the plaintiff's lack of due diligence led unjustifiably to reliance on a false representation.

Damages under Common Law

Plaintiffs who are awarded damages for an ordinary or gross negligence claim against an auditor are eligible for compensatory damages, which means they are awarded damages to return them to a position equivalent to where they would have been in the absence of the auditor's negligence. Punitive damages are awarded to punish outrageous conduct and may be awarded when the auditor is found guilty of fraud or constructive fraud under common law. Punitive damages are not permitted under federal statutory law, which provides plaintiffs incentive to file fraud charges under common law (often in addition to statutory fraud charges). However, the Securities Litigation Uniform Standards Act of 1998 (discussed below) forces certain fraud charges to be brought in federal court under statutory law.

Where the damages to the plaintiff can be apportioned between contributing parties, the auditor is only liable for his or her share of the total damages. If apportionment is not possible, some states follow the principle of *joint and several liability.* Joint and several liability means that the auditor can be responsible for the entire loss even if other parties contributed to the loss. Some courts have ruled that joint and several liability is inconsistent with the comparative fault concept, and some state legislatures have abolished joint and several liability in favor of a proportionate fault approach (i.e., if the auditor is found to be 30 percent at fault, he or she is only liable for 30 percent of the damages awarded).

Statutory Law—Civil Liability

Various statutes have been passed at both the federal and state levels that are intended to protect the public from malfeasance in the marketplace. While not aimed directly at auditors, these statutes do raise the potential for auditor legal liability. The discussion in this chapter is limited to the major federal statutes.

The Securities Act of 1933, the Securities Exchange Act of 1934, and the Sarbanes-Oxley Act of 2002 are the three major federal statutes that provide the basis of legal liability for auditors. On the other hand, the Private Securities Litigation Reform Act of 1995 and the Securities Litigation Uniform Standards Act of 1998 provide some protection for auditors, and others, from securities litigation. The Foreign Corrupt Practices Act and the Racketeer Influenced and Corrupt Organizations Act (RICO) are two other federal statutes that have the potential of imposing liability on auditors. The reader should also note that most states also have securities laws and RICO statutes.

Securities Act of 1933

≫ [LO 5]

The Securities Act of 1933 generally regulates the disclosure of information in a registration statement for a new public offering of securities (i.e., new securities sold from the company to the public), whereas the Securities Exchange Act of 1934 regulates documents filed with the SEC and thus addresses new offerings as well as trading of securities *after* they are issued (i.e., traded from one investor to another).[7] The SEC's "S-forms" (e.g., S-1, S-2) are filed in connection with registration of securities under the 1933 Act. Common forms filed under the 1934 Act include the 10K (annual report), 10Q (quarterly reports), and the 8K (material events report). While a number of sections of the Securities Act of 1933 may subject auditors to liability, Section 11 imposes a liability on issuers and others, including auditors, for losses suffered by third parties when false or misleading information is included in a registration statement. Section 11 states:

> (a) *Persons possessing cause of action; persons liable.* In case any part of the registration statement, when such part became effective, contained an untrue statement of a material fact or omitted to state a material fact required to be stated therein or necessary to make the statements therein not misleading, any person acquiring such security (unless it is proved that at the time of such acquisition he knew of such untruth or omission) may, either at law or in equity, in any court of competent jurisdiction, sue—
>
> (4) every accountant . . . who has with his consent been named as having prepared or certified any part of the registration statement. . . .

In contrast to the situation under common law, under the 1933 Act the plaintiff does not have to prove negligence or fraud, reliance on the auditor's opinion, a causal relationship, or a contractual relationship. The plaintiff need only prove that:

1. A *loss* was suffered by investing in the registered security;
2. The audited financial statements contained a *material omission or misstatement*.

---

[7]The term "security" means any instrument commonly known as a "security" (e.g., note, stock, bond, debenture, investment contract, certificate of deposit).

The misstatement can be the result of mere ordinary negligence. Section 11 of the 1933 Act is more favorable for plaintiffs than is common law because the burden of proof is shifted to the *auditor* to prove that he or she was not negligent. In other words, the auditor is presumed to have been negligent unless he or she can prove otherwise. The extremely plaintiff-friendly legal standards under the 1933 Act reflect the fact that audited financial statements are typically more crucial for purchase decisions for new public offerings because few other credible sources of information are typically available for new issues.

Practice **INSIGHT**	Forms 10KSB and 10QSB are the annual and quarterly reports for "small business issuers" (revenues less than $25 million). A small business issuer is entitled to use abbreviated forms for reporting.

One defense available to the auditor sued under Section 11 is that of "due diligence." That is, the auditor must have made a reasonable investigation of the facts supporting or contradicting the information included in the registration statement. Such an investigation should be similar to one that a prudent person would make under similar circumstances. A leading case under Section 11 is *Escott v. BarChris Construction Corp.*, in which the court held that the auditor's actions for events subsequent to the audited balance sheet date had not been conducted with due diligence. In this instance, the senior auditor reviewing subsequent events had not spent sufficient time on this important task and had accepted glib answers to key questions. The court determined that there had been sufficient danger signals that further investigation was necessary. The *Escott v. BarChris Construction Corp.* case is also of interest because of the court's ruling on certain accounting matters and its determination of materiality. A detailed summary of the *BarChris* case is provided on the book's Web site (www.mhhe.com/messier7e).

A more recent and significant case under Section 11 and other sections of the 1933 Act was *Bernstein v. Crazy Eddie, Inc.* Crazy Eddie, Inc., made a number of new public offerings of securities. Then the founder and president of the company resigned, and the successor management team discovered that the financial statements issued by the company during the public offering were fraudulent. The company's financial statements had been misstated through inflated inventory and improper transactions by the founder and his family. The court ruled against the auditors, indicating that the plaintiffs did not have to prove fraud or gross negligence. They had to prove only that the misstated information was material and that they suffered a loss. Exhibit 20–7 describes the case.

Other important cases tried under the Securities Act of 1933 are Continental Vending (*United States v. Simon*) and National Student Marketing (*United States v. Natelli*). Both cases resulted in criminal proceedings against the auditor, and are described on the book's Web site (www.mhhe.com/messier7e).

Damages for a violation of Section 11 of the 1933 Act are generally equal to the difference between the amount paid for the security and the value of the security at the time the lawsuit was brought. Punitive damages are not permitted under federal statutory law, but, as noted earlier, may be recovered in a concurrent common-law fraud action.

Securities Exchange Act of 1934

✄ **[LO 6]**

This statute regulates documents filed with the SEC and is concerned primarily with ongoing reporting by companies whose securities are listed and traded on a stock exchange or that meet certain other statutory requirements. Typical reporting requirements under the 1934 Act include the quarterly filing of a 10Q form, the annual filing of a 10K form, and the periodic filing of an 8K form whenever

EXHIBIT 20–7	*Bernstein v. Crazy Eddie, Inc.*

Eddie Antar was the founder of and major shareholder in Crazy Eddie. The company made several public offerings of securities, including the sale of shares held by Eddie Antar and his family. The prospectuses and financial statements from 1984 through 1987 erroneously gave the impression that Crazy Eddie was a rapidly growing firm. When Antar resigned his position as president, the successor management discovered that the financial statements issued prior to and included in the public offerings had been materially misstated. In particular, there was an estimated inventory shortage of $65 million, and the company's net worth was really only $7 million.

The financial statements had been misstated by a number of schemes. Net income and inventory had been inflated through improper financial reporting practices. First, inventory marked for return to manufacturers had been included as inventory merchandise. Second, certain consignments had been treated as sales. Last, there had been related inventory sales to the founder and members of his family that were later resold to others. The company had also overstated per-store sales figures. All of these actions appear to have been taken to support the price of Crazy Eddie stock and to directly benefit Antar and his family. The discovery of the extent of the problems was complicated by the fact that certain documents had been altered or destroyed prior to the new management's assuming control.

The plaintiffs in this case were purchasers of the company's stock prior to the disclosure of the fraudulent financial statements. They sued the public accounting firm, the board of directors, and others, alleging that the accounting firm had violated GAAS and GAAP by failing to uncover the company's fraudulent and fictitious activities. The plaintiffs were able to show that they suffered a loss and that the certified financial statements in the registration statements and prospectuses had been false and misleading in violation of Sections 11 and 12 of the Securities Act of 1933.

The court ruled against the public accounting firm and upheld the plaintiffs' Section 11 and 12 claims. The court held that the plaintiffs did not have to prove fraud or gross negligence, only that any material misstatement in the registration statements was misleading and that they had suffered a loss. In this case, the auditor was unable to prove that they had exercised appropriate due professional care.

a significant event takes place affecting the entity. While a number of sections of this statute may have liability consequences for the auditor, two sections are particularly important: Section 18 and Section 10(b), including Rule 10b-5.

Section 18 imposes liability on any person who makes a material false or misleading statement in documents filed with the Securities and Exchange Commission (SEC). The auditor's liability can be limited if the auditor can show that he or she "acted in good faith and had no knowledge that such statement was false or misleading." However, a number of cases have limited the auditor's good-faith defense when the auditor's action has been judged to be grossly negligent.

A common source of liability for auditors under the 1934 Act is Section 10(b) and Rule 10b-5. Section 10(b) provides for a wide scope of liability. Rule 10b-5 amplifies Section 10(b) and states that it is

> unlawful for any person, directly or indirectly, by the use of any means or instrumentality of interstate commerce, or of the mails, or of any facility of any national securities exchange,
>
>   a. To employ any device, scheme, or artifice to defraud,
>
>   b. To make any untrue statement of a material fact or to omit to state a material fact necessary in order to make the statement made, in the light of the circumstances under which they were made, not misleading, or
>
>   c. To engage in any act, practice, or course of business which operates or would operate as a fraud or deceit upon any person, in connection with the purchase or sale of any security.

Once a plaintiff has established that he or she can sue under Rule 10b-5, the plaintiff must prove the following elements:

1. A material, factual *misrepresentation or omission*.
2. *Reliance* by the plaintiff on the financial statements.

3. *Damages* suffered as a result of reliance on the financial statements.
4. *Scienter*.

The first element can include materially misleading information or the omission of material information. The fourth element, *scienter*, is defined as intent to deceive, manipulate, or defraud. However, some courts have ruled that gross negligence or reckless behavior is sufficient to satisfy the fourth element.

Practice **INSIGHT**	*Scienter Pleading in the WorldCom Case:* In the WorldCom pleading (*re WorldCom, Inc. Sec. Litig.*, 2003), a court determined that the plaintiff adequately established scienter against the auditor based on the fact that subsequent to the release of clean audit opinions the financial statements required enormous restatements and the company's underlying books and records contained no support or documentation related to items that were highly materially misstated in accounting areas such as merger reserves.

A number of important cases have used Section 10(b) as a basis for actions against auditors. In *Herzfeld v. Laventhol, Krekstein, Horwath & Horwath*, the U.S. district court allowed recovery by an investor. The investor had purchased securities from the client prior to an audit conducted by Laventhol. After the audit, the client offered to refund all investments made prior to the audit. The plaintiff declined the refund based on the audited financial statements and lost his investment when the company went bankrupt a year later. The plaintiff sued, claiming that the financial statements had been false and misleading because profits from the sale of properties were reported in the income statement even though there was some uncertainty about the collectibility of the related receivables. Laventhol's opinion was qualified "subject to" the collectibility of the receivables. The court held that the disclosure of the qualification footnote had been inadequate and that Laventhol was liable "because of their active participation in the preparation and issuance of false and materially misleading accounting reports upon which Herzfeld relied to his damage."

In *Ernst & Ernst v. Hochfelder*, which is described in more detail at the book's Web site (www.mhhe.com/messier7e), the president of a brokerage firm, Leston Nay, induced brokerage customers to invest in high-yield accounts that he personally managed. The accounts were fictitious, and he used the funds for his own purposes. The defrauded customers sued Ernst & Ernst, arguing that the firm, as the auditor, should have been aware of Nay's inappropriate control over the mail and that such knowledge would have led to discovery of the fraud. Ernst & Ernst argued that Rule 10b-5 did not encompass negligent behavior. The U.S. Supreme Court ruled that an action under Rule 10b-5 may not be maintained by showing that the defendant was negligent; the rule requires that *scienter*, or intent to deceive, be present. Unfortunately, the Supreme Court did not decide whether gross negligence or reckless behavior was sufficient for liability under Section 10(b). However, a number of subsequent decisions by lower courts have recognized that reckless behavior or gross negligence by the auditor satisfies the scienter requirement of Rule 10b-5. For example, in two high-profile fraud cases, WorldCom, Inc. and Tyco, Int'l Ltd., judges found that the complaints against the auditors met the initial pleading requirements of scienter, even though no intent on behalf of the auditors (Andersen and PricewaterhouseCoopers, respectively) was claimed. Reckless conduct is behavior that represents an extreme departure from standards of ordinary care, that is, failure to see the obvious or a disregard for the truth.

Prior to 1994, courts frequently held that an auditor who was not liable as a primary violator of Section 10(b) and Rule 10b-5 could still be held liable for *aiding and abetting* if the auditor had knowledge and had substantially assisted in the primary violation. In fact, prior to 1994, the aiding and abetting approach was the primary strategy followed by attorneys seeking damages against auditors under Section 10(b). However, in 1994 the Supreme Court held in *Central Bank v. First Interstate Bank* that there is no aiding and abetting liability under Section 10(b).

After the *Central Bank* case, the strategy for holding auditors liable under Section 10(b) shifted to an attempt to broaden the definition of a primary violator, whereby an accountant does not have to be the initiator or issuer of a misrepresentation in order to be considered a primary violator. The auditor only would have to be a party to a "fraudulent scheme." However, the question of whether an auditor who has made no public statement and has not violated a duty to disclose important matters may be held liable as a primary violator for "participating" in a fraud scheme may have been settled in the 2008 Supreme Court ruling in the *Stoneridge Investment Partners, LLC v. Scientific-Atlanta, Inc.* case. In this case, the defendant, a supplier, schemed with a cable television provider to inflate the cable provider's reported advertising revenue (offset by overcharging for supplies). The Supreme Court ruled that although the defendant knowingly participated in the fraud scheme on investors, it was not a primary violator of Section 10(b) because it had made no misleading statement that was relied upon by plaintiff investors. Based on the *Central Bank* and *Stoneridge* rulings, an accountant who assists in the preparation and issuance of fraudulent financial statements cannot be held liable under Section 10(b) if the accountant does not make false and misleading statements that are relied upon by investors. A description of the *Stoneridge* case is found on the book's Web site (www.mhhe.com/messier7e).

The issue of what is necessary to establish primary liability under Section 10(b) can be significant in determining when an individual accountant may be held liable. This is an issue in the litigation arising out of the Enron-Andersen collapse. While Andersen as a firm clearly made statements that permit Section 10(b) claims, stating primary liability claims against most of the individual Andersen defendants has proved difficult for plaintiffs. See Exhibit 20–8 for more information on the Enron–Andersen litigation.

The proper measure of damages in most Section 10(b) cases is the out-of-pocket loss suffered by the plaintiff. The out-of-pocket loss is the difference between what the plaintiff paid or received for the securities and what he or she would have paid or received had there been no wrongful conduct by the auditor. Punitive damages are not permitted under federal statutory law, although, as noted earlier, such damages can sometimes be recovered in a concurrent common-law fraud action.

In the wake of the Enron and WorldCom accounting frauds, the Sarbanes-Oxley Act lengthened the statute of limitations for actions under Section 10(b) based on claims of "fraud, deceit, manipulation, or contrivance in contravention of a regulatory requirement concerning the securities laws." The Sarbanes-Oxley Act provides that any action shall be brought no later than two years from discovery and within five years from when the fraudulent conduct occurred. This provision was the only portion of Sarbanes-Oxley that specifically affected private securities fraud actions. The prior statute of limitations were one and three years, respectively.

The book's Web site (www.mhhe.com/messier7e) describes three other recent cases tried under the 1934 Act: *Continental Vending, Mini-Scribe,* and *Phar-Mor.*

EXHIBIT 20-8	Enron Corp. and Arthur Andersen LLP

Enron Corporation, based in Houston, Texas, was formed as a result of the 1985 merger of Houston Natural Gas and InterNorth Inc. In its early years, Enron was a traditional natural gas pipeline company, delivering natural gas to businesses and utilities. However, changes in the government regulations of electrical power markets opened the door for change. Enron transformed itself into a market maker for numerous different energy-related commodities. Enron's stock price surged during the late 1990s, moving Enron into the spotlight of U.S. business. It became the seventh largest company in the United States and was praised for being one of America's most innovative companies.

In 2001, after showing profits for the previous several years, Enron reported a third quarter loss of $618 million and a $1.2 billion reduction in owner's equity related to off-balance sheet partnerships. The news resulted in a sharp drop in Enron's stock price and a formal SEC inquiry. On November 8, 2001, Enron announced that it had overstated profits by $586 million, erasing almost all its profits from the past five years, collapsing the stock price, and diminishing the confidence of its clients. Within a month of this announcement, Enron filed for Chapter 11 bankruptcy. At the time, Enron's was the one of the largest corporate bankruptcies in history.

The Enron collapse involved many players, including company executives, investment bankers, financial analysts, and accountants. Enron's auditor Arthur Andersen, one of the largest national accounting firms at the time, quickly became the target of public scrutiny.

The government's investigation of Enron's accounting practices revealed a number of accounting improprieties, including misuse of special-purpose entities (SPE) to sell off underperforming assets at a profit. Because of undisclosed Enron guarantees related to the transactions, most of these "sales" were really schemes to overstate "paper" gains and understate liabilities.

Fueled by a public uproar, the government began criminal proceedings. The Justice Department accused top Andersen officials of directing employees to alter and/or shred Enron-related documents after it knew about the SEC investigation. In June 2002, Andersen was found guilty of one count of obstruction of justice, fined $500,000, and sentenced to five years' probation. However, the criminal indictment in itself so severely harmed Andersen's reputation that clients fled and the firm essentially liquidated within months.

In 2004 Andrew Fastow, Enron's former CFO and principal player in the company's accounting schemes, pleaded guilty to two counts of conspiracy, and was sentenced to serve the maximum 10-year sentence.

In 2006 former Enron chairman Kenneth Lay and former president Jeffery Skilling were convicted on numerous federal fraud and conspiracy charges. Shortly after the conviction, Lay died of a massive heart attack and his conviction was vacated. Skilling was sentenced to 24 years in prison.

Private Securities Litigation Reform Act of 1995, the Securities Litigation Uniform Standards Act of 1998, and The Class Action Fairness Act of 2005

✘ **[LO 7]**

Prior to the passage of the Private Securities Litigation Reform Act of 1995, auditors who were sued under federal statutory law were held to the legal doctrine of *joint and several liability,* which holds each defendant fully liable for all assessed damages, regardless of the extent to which he or she contributed to the injury. The 1995 Act amends the Securities Exchange Act of 1934 to provide, in general, for *proportionate liability,* where each defendant is liable solely for the portion of the damages that corresponds to the percentage of responsibility of that defendant. To encourage more forward-looking disclosures, the 1995 Act also reduced auditor liability by creating a legal "safe harbor" related to forward-looking financial statements (see a discussion of financial forecasts and projections in Chapter 21). The 1995 Act also amends the 1934 Act to include in federal law the auditor's responsibility to detect fraud and requires auditors to promptly notify the audit committee and the board of directors of illegal acts. The Act further requires the auditor to notify the SEC within one business day when a client's management fails to take appropriate action in response to reports of material fraud.

The 1995 Act allows class members with the greatest financial interests to control the class action litigation, rather than "professional" plaintiffs who defer to attorneys initiating the litigation. Finally, the 1995 Act raises the pleading requirement at the beginning of a case. For example, no longer can plaintiffs plead a general claim of fraud and then use discovery proceedings to conduct a "fishing expedition" in the auditors' workpapers and files in search of actionable conduct. Rather, the 1995 Act requires that misrepresentation claims state the time, place, and contents of the allegedly false representations; the identity of the person making them; facts providing strong inference that the auditor acted with intent to deceive; and what he or she obtained as a result of the fraud. In the 2007 case of *Tellabs, Inc. v. Makor Issues & Rights, Ltd*, the Supreme Court held that in determining whether the plaintiff's complaint provides evidence of scienter, a court must consider both sides of the story and the plaintiff "must demonstrate that it is more likely than not that the defendant acted with scienter." Allegations of GAAP and GAAS violations alone are not adequate evidence of scienter. The increased pleading requirements may discourage baseless "deep-pockets" lawsuits where plaintiffs hope to pressure defendants to settle out of court because the legal costs to fight the lawsuit may be greater than the costs to settle. Another case connected to the 1995 Act, *Xerion Partners I LLC v. Resurgence Asset Mgmt. LLC*, where the judge ruled that "fraud by hindsight" is not a recognized pleading, is discussed on the book's Web site (www.mhhe.com/messier7e).

In response to concerns that plaintiff lawyers were circumventing the Private Securities Litigation Reform Act of 1995 by bringing class action suits involving nationally traded securities to state court, Congress passed the Securities Litigation Uniform Standards Act of 1998. The purpose of the Uniform Standards Act was to "prevent plaintiffs from seeking to evade the protections that Federal law provides against abusive litigation by filing suit in State, rather than Federal Court." The primary federal protections to which the 1998 Act refers are proportionate liability, disallowed punitive damages, and higher filing standards. As a result of the 1998 Act, most large class actions against auditors alleging securities fraud must now be brought in federal court. The 1998 Act defines a "covered class action" to include any lawsuit or group of lawsuits where damages are sought on behalf of more than 50 persons. Thus, smaller class actions lawsuits can still be pursued in state court. In an attempt to circumvent the Uniform Standards Act, attorneys brought a number of Enron-related lawsuits in Texas state court with each suit filed on behalf of fewer than 50 persons (e.g., see *Newby v. Enron Corp.*, 2002).

The Class Action Fairness Act of 2005 ("CAFA") was passed in response to perceived abuses in nationwide class action lawsuits filed in various state courts. CAFA expands the federal jurisdiction to include most multistate class actions where there is more than $5 million in dispute. It is believed that federal judges are more likely than state judges to dismiss dubious claims. CAFA also imposes increased judicial and regulatory scrutiny over the propriety of class action settlements because in some past settlements the only parties that actually benefited were the attorneys.

Sarbanes-Oxley Act of 2002

✂ [LO 8]

The Sarbanes-Oxley Act of 2002 is considered the most sweeping securities law since the 1933 and 1934 Acts. Its main objectives are to restore investor confidence in the securities markets and to deter future corporate frauds. The Act does include sections directly addressing legal liability, but the other aspects of the Act (e.g., the creation of the PCAOB, stricter independence rules, audits of internal controls, and increased reporting responsibilities) are more important to auditors' performance and create new federal laws with which the auditor must comply. The creation of the PCAOB is the single most significant aspect of the legislation, ending decades of self-regulation by the accounting profession. While the Sarbanes-Oxley Act and PCAOB standards and enforcement actions only relate to public company auditors, state boards of accountancy may very well adopt or refer to the PCAOB rules in carrying out their regulatory functions for all public accountants.

Although Congress created and passed the Sarbanes-Oxley Act, as is customary with similar legislation, Congress did not develop the detailed accounting and securities rules and regulations needed to execute the Act's provisions. Instead, the Act delegates substantial authority and responsibility to the SEC to create the detailed rules and regulations. For example, Section 302 of the Sarbanes-Oxley Act directed the SEC to create rules requiring CEO and CFO certification of periodic financial reports within 30 days of the legislation's signing, which the SEC did.[8]

The Act does not prohibit the SEC from extending the rules beyond what is required by the Act. For instance, Section 802 stipulates that audit firms must retain their audit documentation for a period of five years, while the SEC's final ruling extends the period to seven years. Failure to retain audit documentation can result in fines and imprisonment for up to 10 years.

Some of the most important provisions of the Sarbanes-Oxley Act are aimed at increasing the responsibility of corporate officers and directors for the reliability of their company's financial statements. Congress understands that the primary culprits in corporate fraud are dishonest officers and directors. Sections 302 and 906 of the act require the chief executive and chief financial officers of each public company to certify personally, among other things, the fairness of the financial information and the company's compliance with the 1934 Act in each quarterly and annual report filed with the SEC. Regarding executive certifications, the courts have ruled that merely signing documents governed by Section 302 that ultimately are shown to contain material misstatements does not automatically make the signatories liable for fraud.

Rather than address the various legal liability aspects of the act in this section, we discuss them in the pertinent sections which follow because most of the legal liability legislation in the Sarbanes-Oxley Act represents enhancements or revisions to existing laws.

Practice **INSIGHT**	*Personal Liability:* After learning about auditor liability, students may wonder if legal liability extends to junior-level accountants or auditors. The answer is no, because staff should be supervised and their work should be reviewed by more experienced accountants. Thus, the firm, and potentially senior executives responsible for planning, reviewing, and overseeing the audit, ultimately face legal liability. However, liability and potential criminal action do extend to accountants and auditors of all levels if they commit fraudulent acts.

SEC and PCAOB Sanctions

✄ **[LO 9]**

SEC Rule 102(e) empowers the SEC to suspend for any person the privilege of appearing and practicing before it if that person is found:

1. To not possess the necessary qualifications to represent others before the SEC; including, but not limited to persons whose license to practice as an accountant has been revoked or suspended by any state, territory, district, etc.;
2. To be lacking in character or integrity;
3. To have engaged in unethical or improper professional conduct; including, but not limited to felony conviction or misdemeanor conviction involving moral turpitude; or
4. To have willfully violated or willfully aided and abetted any violations of the federal securities laws or any rules or regulations promulgated pursuant to those laws.

This sanction can be applied not only to an individual auditor but also to an entire accounting firm. If a firm is suspended or barred from practice before the SEC, the impact on the firm's clients can be severe. For example, if a firm is suspended, its clients may not be able to file their reports with the SEC on a timely basis. Typically, if a firm is faced with suspension, it will work out some type of consent

---

[8]U.S. Securities Exchange Commission, "Final Rule: Certification of Disclosure in Companies' Quarterly and Annual Reports" (Release No. 33-8124, August 2002).

agreement in which the firm does not admit guilt but agrees to lesser sanctions. These sanctions may include not taking on new SEC clients for a specified period and subjecting the firm to special reviews to ensure that the alleged problems have been corrected. For example, in 2004 Ernst & Young was sanctioned by the SEC for violating independence standards during the audit of PeopleSoft for the years 1994–1999. The sanctions included fines and a six-month suspension from accepting new SEC registrant audit clients.

The SEC can also impose fines, such as the $7 million fine imposed in 2001 on Arthur Andersen in connection with audits of Waste Management. The Waste Management case was particularly egregious because Andersen agreed to a plan to cover up Waste Management's financial misstatements by reversing them over a period of years rather than correcting them immediately. It also followed on the heels of other Andersen audit failures at Sunbeam Corporation and the Arizona Baptist Foundation, and was a foreshadowing of the Enron and WorldCom failures disclosed within a year of the $7 million fine.

A study of SEC sanctions imposed on auditors for their association with fraudulently misstated financial statements found that the most common problems cited were the auditor's failure to gather sufficient audit evidence, properly apply GAAP, exercise due professional care, apply an appropriate level of professional skepticism, and properly tailor audit procedures to address inherent risk.[9]

The Sarbanes-Oxley Act grants the PCAOB broad investigative and disciplinary authority over registered public accounting firms and persons associated with such firms. As directed by the Act, the board adopted rules relating to investigations and adjudications in September 2003. Under the rules, the PCAOB may conduct investigations concerning any Acts or practices involving auditors of publicly traded firms that may "violate any provision of the Act, the rules of the Board, the provisions of the securities laws relating to the preparation and issuance of audit reports and the obligations and liabilities of accountants with respect thereto, including the rules of the SEC issued under the Act, or professional standards."

When violations are detected, the board has the authority to impose sanctions. The sanctions can include revoking a firm's registration, barring a person from participating in audits of public companies, monetary penalties (up to $750,000 per individual or $15 million per firm), and requirements for remedial measures, such as training, new quality control procedures, and the appointment of an independent monitor. In 2007, the PCAOB censured and penalized Deloitte & Touche $1 million for not following auditing standards on the audit of Ligand Pharmaceuticals (PCAOB Releases 105-2007-05). The PCAOB was particularly critical of the audit partner's performance on the Ligand audits. The PCAOB barred the partner from public accounting for two years. The PCOAB's rules, disciplinary decisions, and sanctions are subject to the approval of the SEC.

Foreign Corrupt Practices Act
✎ [LO 10]

The Foreign Corrupt Practices Act (FCPA) was passed by Congress in 1977 in response to the discovery of bribery and other misconduct on the part of more than 300 American companies. The Act was codified in 1988 as an amendment to the Securities Exchange Act of 1934. As a result, an auditor may be subject to administrative proceedings, civil liability, and civil penalties under the FCPA. The FCPA prohibits corporate officers from knowingly participating in bribing foreign officials to obtain or retain business. The FCPA also imposes record-keeping and internal control requirements on public companies. Basically, corporations must keep their books, records, and accounts in sufficient detail to accurately reflect transactions. Companies are also required to develop and maintain adequate systems of internal control. To comply with the provisions of the FCPA, many

---

[9]M. Beasley, J. Carcello, and D. Hermanson, "Lessons from Fraud-Related SEC Cases: Top 10 Audit Deficiencies," *Journal of Accountancy* (April 2001).

corporations have established codes of conduct that prohibit bribery. Compliance with corporate codes of conduct should be checked by the audit committee and the internal auditors. The external auditor may detect activities that violate the FCPA; such violations should be communicated to management immediately. Guidance for such reporting can be found in AU 325, Communicating Internal Control Related Matters Identified in an Audit, and AU 380, The Auditor's Communication with Those Charged with Governance. These standards were covered in Chapters 6 and 17, respectively.

Practice **INSIGHT**	In 2008, the U.S. Justice Department brought a landmark enforcement action under the Foreign Corrupt Practices Act against Siemens AG based in Germany. Siemens pleaded guilty to violating U.S. anti-bribery statutes and agreed to pay $1.6 billion in fines and restitution. News reports indicate the external auditor, KPMG, provided warnings to Siemens regarding corruption. It remains to be seen whether KPMG will face litigation related to their audits of Siemens.

Source: "How KPMG's warning on Siemens was ignored," *Punch*, www.punchng.com, January 15, 2009.

Racketeer Influenced and Corrupt Organizations Act

✂ [LO 11]

Although the Racketeer Influenced and Corrupt Organizations Act (RICO) was enacted by Congress in 1970 to combat the infiltration of legitimate businesses by organized crime, it has been used against auditors. RICO provides civil and criminal sanctions for certain types of illegal acts. A major factor in bringing an action under RICO is that the law provides for treble damages (i.e., three times the actual loss) in civil RICO cases. Racketeering activity includes a long list of federal and state crimes, with mail fraud and wire fraud the most common allegations against auditors.

Generally, a single instance of racketeering activity is not sufficient to establish a pattern of racketeering. In the case of *Reves v. Ernst & Young* (1993), the Supreme Court established an "operations and management test" for auditors that requires that the plaintiff prove that the accounting firm participated in the operation or management of the client's business. A description of this case is presented on the book's Web site (www.mhhe.com/messier7e).

Prior to the Private Securities Litigation Reform Act of 1995, securities fraud was an offense under RICO. The reform Act eliminated securities fraud as an offense in civil suits under RICO unless the auditor is criminally convicted of the fraud. Thus, experts believe that after the reform Act, Section 10(b) and Rule 10b-5 violations will almost never be grounds for a civil damage claim against an auditor under RICO.[10]

Statutory Law—Criminal Liability

✂ [LO 8,12]

Auditors can be held criminally liable under the statutory laws discussed in the previous sections if they commit illegal acts. In addition, auditors can be held criminally liable for various other federal and state laws, such as banking and insurance regulations. Criminal prosecutions require that some form of criminal intent be present. However, many of the laws described in this chapter contain provisions for criminal penalties to be levied if an auditor's actions reflect gross negligence. In a famous quote from *United States v. Benjamin*, the Court stated that an auditor would be held criminally liable if he "deliberately closed his eyes to facts he had a duty to see . . . or recklessly stated as facts things of which he was ignorant."

---

[10]See Chapter 5 in Goldwasser, Arnold, and Eickemeyer, *Accountants' Liability* (Practising Law Institute, 2008).

A number of significant cases against auditors have resulted in criminal prosecution, with auditors being assessed large fines and serving time in prison. Included among these cases are Continental Vending (*United States v. Simon*), National Student Marketing (*United States v. Natelli*), Equity Funding (*United States v. Weiner*), ESM Government Securities, Inc. (*in re Alexander Grant & Co. Litigation*) and HealthSouth Corporation *(SEC v. William T. Owens)*. Note that in addition to criminal prosecution of the auditors, the auditors' firms were civilly liable for violating various statutes and paid large sums to settle the cases. These cases are described on the book's Web site (www.mhhe.com/messier7e).

Of course, the most damaging criminal conviction against an audit firm to date came in June 2002, when Arthur Andersen was found guilty of one count of obstruction of justice in the Enron investigation (see Exhibit 20–8). Ironically, in 2006 the U.S. Supreme Court unanimously reversed the conviction due to vague instructions provided to the jury for determining whether Andersen obstructed justice. However, the Supreme Court's decision did little to help Andersen because the 2002 conviction had already killed the firm.

Numerous sections of the Sarbanes-Oxley Act include criminal provisions. The Act enhances prosecutorial tools available in major fraud cases by expanding statutory prohibitions against fraud and obstruction of justice, increasing criminal penalties for traditional fraud and cover-up crimes, and strengthening sentencing guidelines applicable to large-scale financial frauds. The Act adds a new securities fraud offense and increases authorized penalties for securities and financial reporting fraud (e.g., up to 25 years in prison). It is expected that the Act's increased penalties will result in longer prison terms because of the corresponding changes in the federal sentencing guidelines.

The Sarbanes-Oxley Act increases penalties for impeding official investigations. Because most frauds are discovered by employees rather than external auditors, the Act also strengthens the legal protections accorded whistleblowers. It is common for employers to retaliate against informants by demoting or firing them. The Act makes it a felony punishable by 10-year imprisonment to retaliate against anyone who voluntarily comes forward to report suspected violations of any federal laws.

As we noted in Chapter 19, individual ethics and integrity cannot be legislated. As such, the Sarbanes-Oxley Act will not be a cure-all for corporate reform. Greed, mismanagement, conflicts of interest, and professional failures will never completely disappear. However, most observers in the legal and accounting professions generally believe that the reforms imposed by the Sarbanes-Oxley Act were needed, will contribute to improved governance, and will send a signal that society does not tolerate widespread deceit in financial reporting.

Practice
INSIGHT

Minimizing Litigation Costs: The threat of legal liability serves to prevent or limit inappropriate behavior on the part of auditors. However, auditors cannot be expected to ensure the accuracy of either financial statements or the financial health of a business entity. Thus, everyone involved with the public accounting profession has an interest in minimizing auditors' exposure to legal liability. Lawsuits against public accountants not only result in direct financial effects such as large settlement costs but also impact the profession and society in other ways. The accounting profession and its insurers are increasingly exploring the possibility of utilizing alternative dispute resolution procedures (i.e., arbitration and mediation) as a means of reducing litigation costs. Using arbitration and mediation to settle disputes does not remove legal liability (except perhaps punitive damages), but it may significantly reduce the administrative and legal support costs of litigation.*

*In 2005 Sun Microsystems Inc. disclosed in its proxy statement that the company's engagement agreement with Ernst & Young LLP was "subject to alternative dispute resolution procedures and an exclusion of punitive damages." See David Reilly, "More Companies Disclose Pacts That Prevent Suits, Limit Awards If Accounting Problems Arise," *The Wall Street Journal,* March 6, 2006.

KEY TERMS

Due professional care. A legal standard requiring that the auditor perform his or her professional services with the same degree of skill, knowledge, and judgment possessed by other members of the profession.

Engagement letter. A letter that formalizes the contract between the auditor and the client and outlines the responsibilities of both parties.

Generally accepted auditing standards. Measures of the quality of the auditor's performance.

Gross negligence. An extreme, flagrant, or reckless departure from professional standards of due care.

Joint and several liability. The auditor can be responsible for the entire loss even if other parties contributed to the loss.

Ordinary negligence. An absence of reasonable or due care in the conduct of an engagement.

Privity. A party's contractual or fiduciary relationship with the accountant.

Professional skepticism. An attitude that includes a questioning mind and a critical assessment of audit evidence. The auditor should not assume that management is either honest or dishonest.

Reasonable assurance. A term that implies some risk that a material misstatement could be present in the financial statements without the auditor detecting it.

Scienter. Acting with intent to deceive, defraud or with knowledge of a false representation.

Tort. A wrongful act other than a breach of contract for which civil action may be taken.

www.mhhe.com/ messier7e	Visit the book's Online Learning Center for a multiple-choice quiz that will allow you to assess your understanding of chapter concepts.

REVIEW QUESTIONS

[LO1] 20-1 Briefly describe the four stages of the auditor dispute process.

[2,3,4] 20-2 What is meant by *proportionate liability*? Contrast this legal doctrine with the doctrine of *joint and several liability*.

[3] 20-3 For what types of actions are auditors liable to a client under common law? Why would the client prefer to sue the auditor for a tort action rather than for a breach of contract?

[3] 20-4 What elements must a client prove to maintain an action against an auditor for negligence?

[4] 20-5 Distinguish among the four standards that have evolved for defining auditors' liability for ordinary negligence to third parties under common law. Why is this area of auditors' liability so complex?

[5,6] 20-6 Distinguish between the Securities Act of 1933 and the Securities Exchange Act of 1934. Why is it easier for a plaintiff to sue an auditor under the Securities Act of 1933?

[6] 20-7 What elements must a plaintiff prove in order to win action under Rule 10b-5 of the Securities Exchange Act of 1934? What was the significance of the outcome of the *Ernst & Ernst v. Hochfelder* case for auditors' liability?

[7] 20-8 What were the most significant components of the Private Securities Litigation Reform Act of 1995 and the Securities Litigation Uniform Standards Act of 1998?

[8,12] 20-9 In what ways does the Sarbanes-Oxley Act of 2002 change criminal liability for auditors of public companies?

[9] 20-10 What types of sanctions can the SEC and the PCAOB impose on auditors?

[10] 20-11 What types of activities should the auditor be alert to that may violate the Foreign Corrupt Practices Act?

[11] 20-12 Briefly describe the Racketeer Influenced and Corrupt Organizations Act and why plaintiffs seek to sue auditors under this statute.

[12] 20-13 What actions can result in an auditor being held criminally liable under statutes and regulations?

MULTIPLE-CHOICE QUESTIONS

[2,3,4] 20-14 Cable Corporation orally engaged Drake & Company, CPAs, to audit its financial statements. Though the financial statements Drake audited included a materially overstated accounts receivable balance, Drake issued an unqualified opinion. Cable used the financial statements to obtain a loan to expand its operations. Cable defaulted on the loan and incurred a substantial loss.

If Cable sues Drake for negligence in failing to discover the overstatement, Drake's best defense would be that Drake did not

a. Have privity of contract with Cable.

b. Sign an engagement letter.

c. Perform the audit recklessly or with an intent to deceive.

d. Violate generally accepted auditing standards in performing the audit.

[3] 20-15 Which of the following best describes whether a CPA has met the required standard of care in auditing a client's financial statements?

a. Whether the client's expectations are met with regard to the accuracy of audited financial statements.

b. Whether the statements conform to generally accepted accounting principles.

c. Whether the CPA conducted the audit with the same skill and care expected of an ordinarily prudent CPA under the circumstances.

d. Whether the audit was conducted to investigate and discover all acts of fraud.

[3,4] 20-16 Jenna Corporation approved a merger plan with Cord Corporation. One of the determining factors in approving the merger was the financial statements of Cord, which had been audited by Frank & Company, CPAs. Jenna had engaged Frank to audit Cord's financial statements. While performing the audit, Frank failed to discover fraud that later caused Jenna to suffer substantial losses. For Frank to be liable under common-law negligence, Jenna at a minimum must prove that Frank

a. Knew of the fraud.

b. Failed to exercise due care.

c. Was grossly negligent.

d. Acted with scienter.

[4] 20-17 Brown & Company, CPAs, issued an unqualified opinion on the financial statements of its client King Corporation. Based on the strength of King's financial statements, Safe Bank loaned King $500,000. King Corporation and Safe Bank are both located in a state that follows the *Ultramares doctrine*. Brown was unaware that Safe would receive a copy of the financial statements or that they would be used by King in obtaining a loan. King defaulted on the loan.

If Safe commences an action for ordinary negligence against Brown, and Brown believes it will be able to prove that it conducted the audit in conformity with GAAS, Brown will

a. Be liable to Safe, because Safe relied on the financial statements.

b. Be liable to Safe, because the statute of frauds has been satisfied.

c. Not be liable to Safe, because there is a conclusive legal presumption that following GAAS is the equivalent of acting reasonably and with due care.

d. Not be liable to Safe, because there was a lack of privity of contract.

[5]   20-18   How does the Securities Act of 1933, which imposes civil liability on auditors for misrepresentations or omissions of material facts in a registration statement, expand auditors' liability to purchasers of securities beyond that of common law?

a. Purchasers have to prove only that a loss was caused by reliance on audited financial statements.

b. Privity with purchasers is not a necessary element of proof.

c. Purchasers have to prove either fraud or gross negligence as a basis for recovery.

d. Auditors are held to a standard of care described as "professional skepticism."

[5]   20-19   To be successful in a civil action under Section 11 of the Securities Act of 1933 concerning liability for a misleading registration statement, the plaintiff must prove

	Defendant's Intent to Deceive	Plaintiff's Reliance on the Registration Statement
a.	Yes	Yes
b.	Yes	No
c.	No	Yes
d.	No	No

Questions 20-20 and 20-21 are based on the following information:

Dart Corporation engaged Jay Associates, CPAs, to assist in a public stock offering. Jay audited Dart's financial statements and gave an unqualified opinion, despite knowing that the financial statements contained misstatements. Jay's opinion was included in Dart's registration statement. Hansen purchased shares in the offering and suffered a loss when the stock declined in value after the misstatements became known.

[5]   20-20   In a suit against Jay and Dart under the Section 11 liability provisions of the Securities Act of 1933, Hansen must prove that

a. Jay knew of the misstatements.

b. Jay was negligent.

c. The misstatements contained in Dart's financial statements were material.

d. The unqualified opinion contained in the registration statement was relied on by Hansen.

[5]   20-21   If Hansen succeeds in the Section 11 suit against Dart, Hansen will be entitled to

a. Damages of three times the original public offering price.

b. Rescind the transaction.

c. Monetary damages comparable to the loss suffered.

d. Damages, but only if the shares were resold before the suit was started.

[6]   20-22   Fritz Corporation, whose shares are publicly traded, engaged Hay Associates, CPAs, to audit its financial statements. Hay gave an unqualified opinion, despite knowing that the financial statements contained misstatements. Hay's opinion was included in Fritz's form 10-K filed with the Securities and Exchange Commission. Samson purchased shares and suffered a loss when the stock declined in value after the misstatements became known.

In a suit against Hay under the antifraud provisions of Section 10(b) and Rule 10b-5 of the Securities Exchange Act of 1934, Samson must prove all of the following *except* that

a. Samson was a foreseen user of the financial statements.

b. Samson suffered a loss as a result of reliance on the financial statements.

    c. The stock purchase involved a national securities exchange.

    d. Hay acted with intent to deceive.

[7]   **20-23**   Under the Private Securities Litigation Reform Act of 1995, Baker, CPA, reported certain uncorrected illegal acts to Supermart's board of directors. Baker believed that failure to take remedial action would warrant a qualified audit opinion because the illegal acts had a material effect on Supermart's financial statements. Supermart failed to take appropriate remedial action, and the board of directors refused to inform the SEC that it had received such notification from Baker. Under these circumstances, Baker is required to

    a. Resign from the audit engagement within 10 business days.

    b. Deliver a report concerning the illegal acts to the SEC within one business day.

    c. Notify the stockholders that the financial statements are materially misstated.

    d. Withhold an audit opinion until Supermart takes appropriate remedial action.

[8,9,12]   **20-24**   Which of the following is not a provision of the Sarbanes-Oxley Act of 2002?

    a. A requirement to retain audit workpapers for at least five years.

    b. It is a criminal offense to take any harmful action in retaliation against anyone who voluntarily comes forward to report a suspected accounting or securities fraud.

    c. Broad investigative and disciplinary authority over registered public accounting firms is granted to the Public Company Accounting Oversight Board.

    d. The statute of limitations for actions under Section 10(b) and Rule 10b-5 was reduced to one year from the discovery of fraud and five years after the fraud occurred.

[10]   **20-25**   Which of the following is a provision of the Foreign Corrupt Practices Act?

    a. It is a criminal offense for an auditor to fail to detect and report a bribe paid by an American business entity to a foreign official for the purpose of obtaining business.

    b. The auditor's detection of illegal acts committed by officials of the auditor's publicly held client in conjunction with foreign officials should be reported to the Enforcement Division of the Securities and Exchange Commission.

    c. If the auditor of a publicly held company concludes that the effects on the financial statements of a bribe given to a foreign official are not reasonably estimated, the auditor's report should be modified.

    d. Every publicly held company must devise, document, and maintain a system of internal accounting controls sufficient to provide reasonable assurance that internal control objectives are met.

PROBLEMS

[2,3,4]   **20-26**   Becker, Inc., purchased the assets of Bell Corporation. A condition of the purchase agreement was that Bell retain a CPA to audit its financial statements. The purpose of the audit was to determine whether the unaudited financial statements furnished to Becker fairly presented Bell's financial position. Bell retained Salam & Company, CPAs, to perform the audit.

    While performing the audit, Salam discovered that Bell's bookkeeper had embezzled $500. Salam had some evidence of other embezzlements by the bookkeeper. However, Salam decided that the $500 was immaterial and that the other suspected embezzlements did not require further investigation. Salam did not discuss the matter with Bell's management.

Unknown to Salam, the bookkeeper had, in fact, embezzled large sums of cash from Bell. In addition, the accounts receivable were significantly overstated. Salam did not detect the overstatement because of Salam's failure to follow its audit program.

Despite the foregoing, Salam issued an unqualified opinion on Bell's financial statements and furnished a copy of the audited financial statements to Becker. Unknown to Salam, Becker required financing to purchase Bell's assets and furnished a copy of Bell's audited financial statements to City Bank to obtain approval of the loan. Based on Bell's audited financial statements, City loaned Becker $600,000.

Becker paid Bell $750,000 to purchase Bell's assets. Within six months, Becker began experiencing financial difficulties resulting from the undiscovered embezzlements and overstated accounts receivable. Becker later defaulted on the City loan.

City has commenced a lawsuit against Salam based on the following causes of action:
- Ordinary negligence
- Constructive fraud (gross negligence)

Required:
In separate paragraphs, discuss whether City is likely to prevail on the causes of action it has raised. Set forth reasons for each conclusion.

(AICPA, adapted)

[3,4,5,6]   20-27   Astor Electronics, Inc., markets a wide variety of computer-related products throughout the United States. Astor's officers decided to raise $1 million by selling shares of Astor's common stock in an exempt offering under Regulation D of the Securities Act of 1933. In connection with the offering, Astor engaged Apple & Company, CPAs, to audit Astor's financial statements. The audited financial statements, including Apple's unqualified opinion, were included in the offering memorandum given to prospective purchasers of Astor's stock. Apple was aware that Astor intended to include the statements in the offering materials.

Astor's financial statements reported certain inventory items at a cost of $930,000 when in fact they had a fair market value of less than $100,000 because of technological obsolescence. Apple accepted the assurances of Astor's controller that cost was the appropriate valuation, despite the fact that Apple was aware of ongoing sales of the products at prices substantially less than cost. All of this was thoroughly documented in Apple's workpapers.

Musk purchased 10,000 shares of Astor's common stock in the Regulation D offering at a total price of $300,000. In deciding to make the purchase, Musk had reviewed the audited financial statements of Astor that accompanied the other offering materials and had been impressed by Astor's apparent financial strength.

Shortly after the stock offering was completed, Astor's management discovered that the audited financial statements reflected the materially overstated valuation of the company's inventory. Astor advised its shareholders of the problem.

Upon receiving notice from Astor of the overstated inventory amount, Musk became very upset because the stock value was now substantially less than what it would have been had the financial statements been accurate. In fact, the stock was worth only about $200,000.

Musk has commenced an action against Apple, alleging that Apple is liable to Musk based on the following causes of action:
- Common-law fraud.
- Negligence.

- A violation of Section 10(b) and Rule 10b-5 of the Securities Exchange Act of 1934.

The state law applicable to this action follows the *Ultramares* decision with respect to accountants' liability to third parties for negligence or fraud. Apple has also asserted that the actions should be dismissed because of the absence of any contractual relationship between Apple and Musk, that is, a lack of privity.

Required:
Answer the following, setting forth your reasons for any conclusions stated.
a. What elements must be established by Musk to support a cause of action based on negligence?
b. What elements must be established by Musk to support a cause of action based on a Rule 10b-5 violation?
c. Is Apple's assertion regarding lack of privity correct with regard to Musk's causes of action for negligence and fraud?

(AICPA, adapted)

[5,6]   20-28   Butler Manufacturing Corporation planned to raise capital for a plant expansion by borrowing from banks and making several stock offerings. Butler engaged Meng, CPA, to audit its December 31, 2009, financial statements. Butler told Meng that the financial statements would be given to certain named banks and included in the prospectuses for the stock offerings.

In performing the audit, Meng did not confirm accounts receivable and, as a result, failed to discover a material overstatement of accounts receivable. Also, Meng was aware of a pending class action product liability lawsuit that was not disclosed in Butler's financial statements. Despite being advised by Butler's legal counsel that Butler's potential liability under the lawsuit would result in material losses, Meng issued an unqualified opinion on Butler's financial statements.

In May 2010, Union Bank, one of the named banks, relied on the financial statements and Meng's opinion in giving Butler a $500,000 loan.

A couple of months after obtaining the Bank loan, Butler also raised $16,450,000 through stock offerings.

Shortly after obtaining the Union loan, Butler began experiencing financial problems but was able to stay in business because of the money raised by the offerings. Then Butler was found liable in the product liability suit. This resulted in a judgment Butler could not pay. Butler also defaulted on the Union loan and was involuntarily petitioned into bankruptcy. This caused Union to sustain a loss and Butler's stockholders to lose their investments. As a result,

- Union sued Meng for negligence and common-law fraud.
- The stockholders who purchased Butler's stock through the offerings, as well as stockholders who purchased shares subsequently traded on a national securities exchange, sued Meng, alleging fraud under Section 10(b) and Rule 10b-5 of the Securities Exchange Act of 1934.

These transactions took place in a jurisdiction providing for accountants' liability for negligence to known and intended users of financial statements.

Required:
Answer the following questions and give the reasons for your conclusions:

    a. Will Union be successful in its suit against Meng for

      1. Negligence?

      2. Common-law fraud?

    b. Will the stockholders who purchased Butler's stock succeed against Meng under the antifraud provisions of Section 10(b) and Rule 10b-5 of the Securities Exchange Act of 1934?

(AICPA, adapted)

[5,6] **20-29** Sleek Corporation is a public corporation whose stock is traded on a national securities exchange. Sleek hired Garson Associates, CPAs, to audit Sleek's financial statements. Sleek needed the audit to obtain bank loans and to offer public stock so that it could expand.

Before the engagement, Fred Hedge, Sleek's president, told Garson's managing partner that the audited financial statements would be submitted to Sleek's banks to obtain the necessary loans.

During the course of the audit, Garson's managing partner found that Hedge and other Sleek officers had embezzled substantial amounts of money from the corporation. These embezzlements threatened Sleek's financial stability. When these findings were brought to Hedge's attention, Hedge promised that the money would be repaid and begged that the audit not disclose the embezzlements.

Hedge also told Garson's managing partner that several friends and relatives of Sleek's officers had been advised about the projected business expansion and proposed stock offering and had purchased significant amounts of Sleek's stock based on this information.

Garson submitted an unqualified opinion on Sleek's financial statements, which did not include adjustments for or disclosures about the embezzlements and insider stock transactions. The financial statements and audit report were submitted to Sleek's regular banks, including Knox Bank. Knox, relying on the financial statements and Garson's report, gave Sleek a $2 million loan.

Sleek's audited financial statements were also incorporated into a registration statement prepared under the provisions of the Securities Act of 1933. The registration statement was filed with the SEC in conjunction with Sleek's public offering of 100,000 shares of its common stock at $100 per share.

An SEC investigation of Sleek disclosed the embezzlements and the insider trading. Trading in Sleek's stock was suspended, and Sleek defaulted on the Knox loan.

As a result, the following legal actions were taken:

• Knox sued Garson.

• The general-public purchasers of Sleek's stock offering sued Garson.

Required:

Answer the following questions and give the reasons for your conclusions.

a. Would Knox recover from Garson for fraud?

b. Would the general-public purchasers of Sleek's stock offerings recover from Garson

    1. Under the liability provisions of Section 11 of the Securities Act of 1933?

    2. Under the antifraud provisions of Rule 10b-5 of the Securities Exchange Act of 1934?

(AICPA, adapted)

DISCUSSION CASES

[4,5,6]   20-30   Conan Doyle & Associates (CD&A), CPAs, served as the auditors for Lestrad Corporation and Watson Corporation, publicly held companies traded on NASDAQ. Watson recently acquired Lestrad Corporation in a merger that involved swapping 1.75 shares of Watson for 1 share of Lestrad. In connection with that merger, CD&A issued an unqualified report on the financial statements and participated in the preparation of the pro forma unaudited financial statements contained in the combined prospectus and proxy statement circulated to obtain shareholder approval of the merger and to register the shares to be issued in connection with the merger. Watson prepared a Form 8K and Form 10K in connection with the merger. Shortly thereafter, financial disaster beset the merged company, resulting in large losses to the shareholders and creditors. A class action suit on behalf of shareholders and creditors has been filed against Watson and its management. In addition, it names CD&A as a codefendant, challenging the fairness, accuracy, and truthfulness of the financial statements.

Required:
Discuss the various bases of CD&A's potential civil liability to the shareholders and creditors of Watson as a result of issuing an unqualified report on the audited financial statements of Watson and Lestrad and having participated in preparing the unaudited financial statements required in connection with the merger under
a. State common law.
b. The federal securities acts.

(AICPA, adapted)

[8]   20-31   Critics of the Sarbanes-Oxley Act of 2002 do not believe the Act will be effective at deterring accounting frauds because it primarily relies on specifying new crimes and higher penalties (i.e., increasing the maximum fine and prison terms). Critics argue that if corporate executives are not deterred by the prospect of 5 or 10 years in prison (pre-Sarbanes penalties), the threat of imprisonment will have little or no practical effect no matter what the maximum is raised to. Thus, critics conclude that the Act was more of an expression of political outrage than good policy.

   Proponents of the Act believe the new crimes, increased penalties, and the other provisions in the Act will be effective at significantly reducing corporate accounting frauds.

Required:
Provide arguments for both sides of the debate and formulate your own opinion.

HANDS-ON CASES

ACL

www.mhhe.com/ messier7e	Visit the book's Online Learning Center for problem material to be completed using the ACL software packaged with your new text.

Part 8

ASSURANCE, ATTESTATION, AND INTERNAL AUDITING SERVICES

21

Assurance, Attestation, and Internal Auditing Services

CHAPTER 21

LEARNING OBJECTIVES

Upon completion of this chapter you will

[1] Know the definition of assurance services.

[2] Be familiar with the types of assurance services offered by CPAs.

[3] Know the definition of an attestation engagement.

[4] Know the types of attestation engagements.

[5] Be familiar with the 11 attestation standards and how they compare to the 10 generally accepted auditing standards.

[6] Understand the type of attestation engagement that involves reporting on an entity's internal control over financial reporting.

[7] Understand the type of attestation engagement that involves reporting on an entity's financial forecasts and projections.

[8] Be familiar with accounting and review services.

[9] Understand the role of standards pertaining to and services provided by internal auditors.

[10] Be familiar with two specific types of assurance services that have been offered by CPAs—CPA Trust Services and CPA PrimePlus.

RELEVANT ACCOUNTING AND AUDITING PRONOUNCEMENTS

Committee of Sponsoring Organizations of the Treadway Commission, *Internal Control–Integrated Framework* (New York: AICPA, 1992)
AU 314, Understanding the Entity and Its Environment and Assessing the Risks of Material Misstatement
AU 325, Communicating Internal Control Related Matters Identified in an Audit

Attestation Standards: Revision and Recodification (SSAE No. 10, Chapters 1–7)
Codification of Statements on Standards for Accounting and Review Services (AR 100–600)
Professional Practices Framework of the Institute of Internal Auditors

Assurance, Attestation, and Internal Auditing Services

Because of their reputation for competence and objectivity, CPAs for many years have been asked to perform a variety of services beyond the audit of historical financial statements. However, prior to the development of standards specifically relating to nonaudit attestation services, auditors found it difficult to provide such services within the bounds of auditing standards. To accommodate the demand for services by CPAs, the AICPA developed attestation standards in 1986. The attestation standards are broader in scope than auditing standards so that they can be applied to the array of services being requested of the accounting profession. In 2001, the Auditing Standards Board completed a substantial revision and recodification of the attestation standards. The PCAOB adopted the AICPA attestation standards on an interim basis in April 2003.

In addition to accommodating society's increasing demand for CPA-provided attestation services, the profession aggressively sought to expand the opportunities for assurance-related services in the late 1990s. The AICPA Special Committee on Assurance Services ("the Elliott Committee") issued a report in 1996 that led to the AICPA establishing a program to promote various nontraditional assurance services. While the profession's emphasis on nontraditional assurance services has cooled in the wake of Sarbanes-Oxley and the subsequent "back-to-basics" trend, some accounting firms continue to provide such services.

This chapter begins with an overview of assurance services. An *Advanced Module* offers a brief overview of three specific types of such services. Attest services and standards are presented next. The reader should note that many of the so-called assurance services actually are conducted as attestation engagements. The chapter also covers other types of accounting services offered by CPAs. The last part of the chapter discusses the services and standards relating to internal auditing, an important area that has seen significantly increased emphasis over the past few years.

Assurance Services

[LO 1]   Figure 21–1 expands on Figure 1–2 and presents the relationship of assurance services to attest and auditing. As discussed in Chapter 1, the broad umbrella of assurance services includes attestation and auditing services, among others. The AICPA Special Committee on Assurance Services defined assurance services as follows:

> **Assurance services** are independent professional services that improve the quality of information, or its context, for decision makers.

This definition captures a number of important concepts. First, the definition focuses on decision making. Making good decisions requires quality information, which can be financial or nonfinancial in nature. Figure 21–2, adapted from the AICPA Special Committee on Assurance Services' ("the Elliott Committee") report, presents a model for decision making and the role of information in decision-making activities. You will note that information is critical in this decision model. For example, the Elliott Committee points out that three types of information enter into the problem definition stage of the model: (1) environmental information; (2) process monitoring and diagnostic information; and (3) outcome feedback information. An assurance service engagement can help the decision maker search through this information in order to identify which pieces of information are relevant for the required decision.

The second concept relates to improving the quality of information or its context. In the decision model shown in Figure 21–2, an assurance service engagement can improve quality by increasing confidence in the information's reliability, relevance, and timeliness. Context can be improved via the format in which information is presented or through the provision of other relevant benchmarking information.

The third important concept in the definition of assurance services is independence. As we indicated in our earlier discussions of financial statement auditing, independence is the hallmark of the accounting profession. The last concept is professional services, which encompasses the application of professional judgment to the information that is the subject of the assurance service. In summary, assurance

---

FIGURE 21–1   **The Relationship between Assurance Services, Attest, and Auditing**

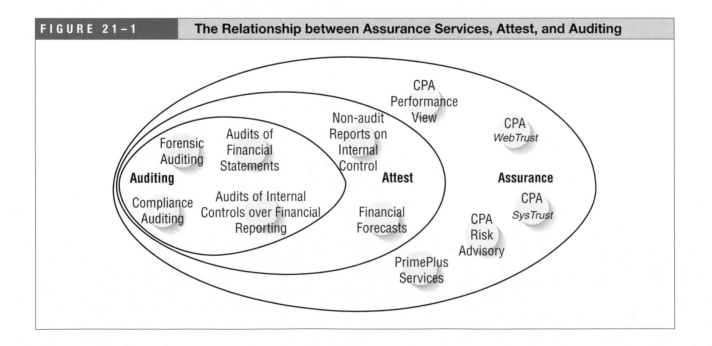

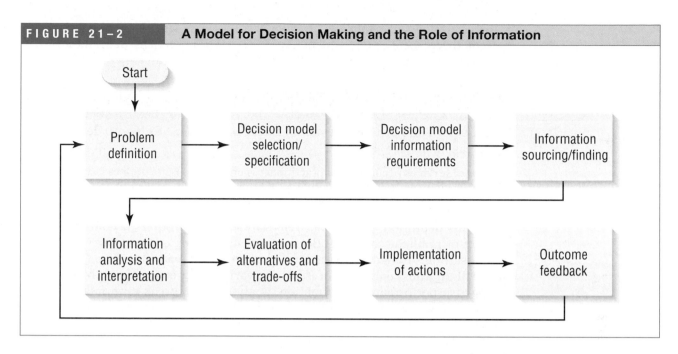

FIGURE 21-2 — A Model for Decision Making and the Role of Information

services can capture information, improve its quality, and enhance its usefulness for decision makers in a way that is free from conflict of interest or bias.

Types of Assurance Services

 [LO 2]

The AICPA, through its Assurance Services Executive Committee, initially identified and developed six general categories of assurance services.

- *Risk assessment*—assurance that an entity's profile of business risks is comprehensive and evaluation of whether the entity has appropriate systems in place to effectively manage those risks.
- *Business performance measurement*—assurance that an entity's performance measurement system contains relevant and reliable measures for assessing the degree to which the entity's goals and objectives are achieved or how its performance compares to that of competitors.
- *Information system reliability*—assurance that an entity's internal information systems provide reliable information for operating and financial decisions.
- *Electronic commerce*—assurance that systems and tools used in electronic commerce provide appropriate data integrity, security, privacy, and reliability.
- *Health care performance measurement*—assurance about the effectiveness of health care services provided by HMOs, hospitals, doctors, and other providers.
- *PrimePlus*—assurance that specified goals regarding the elderly are being met by various caregivers.

The committee also identified seven other areas where assurance services might be in demand: corporate policy compliance, outsourced internal auditing, trading partner accountability, mergers and acquisitions, ISO 9000 certification, investment managers' compliance with relevant professional standards, and World Wide Web assertions. These proposed service areas should give the reader a sense of the wide variety of opportunities that exist for practitioners to provide assurance services to their existing and new clients. To give you a better understanding of the nature of such services, this chapter's *Advanced Module* offers a brief overview of three specific types of nonaudit attestation services developed by the AICPA over the last several years (WebTrust, SysTrust, and PrimePlus services).

Attest Engagements[1]

[LO 3]   Chapter 1 of Standard for Attestation Engagements (SSAE) No. 10 defines an attest engagement as follows:

> **Attest services** occur when a practitioner is engaged to issue or does issue an examination, a review, or an agreed-upon procedures report on subject matter, or an assertion about subject matter, that is the responsibility of another party.

In this definition, *practitioner* refers to a certified public accountant in the practice of public accounting. Because attestation engagements are not audits, the attestation standards use the term *practitioner* instead of *auditor*. The *subject matter* of an attest engagement may take various forms, including historical or prospective performance information, analyses (e.g., break-even analysis), systems and processes (e.g., internal control), physical characteristics (e.g., square footage of facilities), historical events (e.g., the price of market goods on a certain date), and behavior (e.g., compliance with laws and regulations). The term *assertion* here refers to any declaration, or set of related declarations, about whether the subject matter is based on or in conformity with the criteria selected. Examples of an assertion by management are "Gregorio's Restaurants maintains effective internal control over financial reporting," and "Ticaboo Marine complies with all applicable maritime regulations."

Typically, an attestation engagement involves three parties: a user or users; a party responsible for the subject matter or the assertion, such as management; and a CPA. Figure 21–3 depicts the relationship among the three parties to an attestation engagement. Note the direction of the arrows in this figure. The responsible party is responsible for the subject matter or assertion to the user and acknowledges that responsibility to the CPA. The CPA expresses a conclusion to the user on the subject matter or assertion. In some cases, the engagement may involve only two parties because the user and the responsible party are the same.

FIGURE 21–3	The Three-Party Relationship in an Attest Engagement

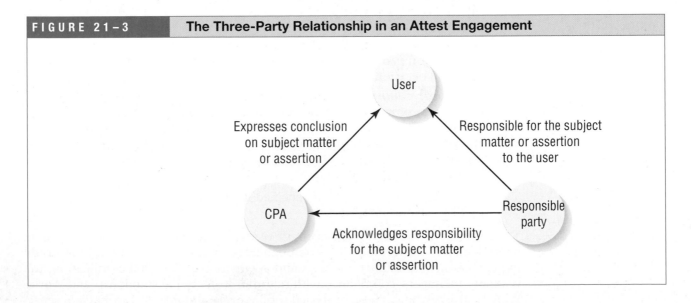

---

[1]See J. M. Marino and C. E. Landes, "A New Look at the Attestation Standards," *Journal of Accountancy* (July 2001), pp. 41–45, for a discussion of the revisions made to the SSAEs in 2001.

The practitioner should use an attestation risk model to meet the standards of fieldwork in an attestation engagement. Attestation risk is defined in a manner similar to audit risk and is composed of the same basic components (inherent risk, control risk, and detection risk) as the audit risk model discussed in Chapter 3. The attestation risk should be set consistent with the type of engagement being performed.

Types of Attest Engagements

✂ [LO 4]

Attestation standards generally provide for three types of engagements: *examination, review,* and *agreed-upon procedures.* The AICPA's Statements on Standards for Attestation Engagements (SSAEs) provide additional guidance on these types of engagements. The PCAOB adopted the SSAEs along with the rest of the AICPA's professional standards on an interim basis in April 2003.

Examination   In an examination, the practitioner expresses an opinion that (a) the subject matter is based on (or in conformity with) the criteria in all material respects; or (b) the assertion is presented (or fairly stated), in all material respects, based on the criteria. Such an opinion may be for general or limited distribution. If distribution is limited, the opinion must state the limitations on the use of the report. For example, a limited distribution report might indicate: "This report is intended for use only by Offshore Bank." Because an examination engagement provides the highest level of assurance on an assertion, the practitioner must gather sufficient evidence to limit the attestation risk to a low level, and express positive assurance.

Review   In a review engagement, the practitioner does not express an affirmative opinion but rather expresses negative assurance. That is, the accountant indicates that no information came to his or her attention indicating that (a) the subject matter is not based on (or in conformity with) the criteria in all material respects or (b) the assertion is not presented (or fairly stated), in all material respects, based on the criteria. Distribution of a review report can also be either general or limited. A review engagement should provide sufficient evidence to limit the attestation risk to a moderate level.

Agreed-Upon Procedures   An agreed-upon procedures engagement is one in which a practitioner is engaged by a client to issue a report of findings based on specific procedures performed on the subject matter. The level of assurance provided by such an engagement depends on the nature and scope of the procedures agreed upon with the specified parties. Thus, attestation risk is a function of the intended level of assurance. Distribution of the report based on such an engagement is always limited to the specified users. The report on an agreed-upon procedures engagement simply summarizes findings from the application of the agreed-upon procedures; it does not include an opinion.

Table 21–1 provides an overview of the types of attestation engagements.

TABLE 21–1	Overview of Attestation Engagements			
Type of Engagement	*Level of Assurance*	*Attestation Risk*	*Type of Report*	*Report Distribution*
Examination	High	Low	Opinion	General or limited
Review	Moderate	Moderate	Negative assurance	General or limited
Agreed-upon procedures	Variable	Variable	Summary of findings	Limited

Attestation Standards

ꕯ [LO 5]   Table 21–2 lists the 11 attestation standards and the 10 generally accepted auditing standards for comparative purposes.

General Standards

There are five general standards for attestation engagements. All but the second and third general standards have counterparts in generally accepted auditing standards. The second standard requires that the practitioner have adequate

TABLE 21–2	Attestation Standards Compared with Generally Accepted Auditing Standards
Attestation Standards	*Generally Accepted Auditing Standards*
General Standards	
1. The practitioner must have adequate technical training and proficiency to perform the attestation engagement. 2. The practitioner must have adequate knowledge of the subject matter. 3. The practitioner must have reason to believe that the subject matter is capable of evaluation against criteria that are suitable and available to users. 4. The practitioner must maintain independence in mental attitude in all matters relating to the engagement. 5. The practitioner must exercise due professional care in the planning and performance of the engagement and the preparation of the report.	1. The auditor must have adequate technical training and proficiency to perform the audit. 2. The auditor must maintain independence in mental attitude in all matters relating to the audit. 3. The auditor must exercise due professional care in the performance of the audit and the preparation of the report.
Standards of Fieldwork	
1. The practitioner must adequately plan the work and must properly supervise any assistants. 2. The practitioner must obtain sufficient evidence to provide a reasonable basis for the conclusion that is expressed in the report.	1. The auditor must adequately plan the work and must properly supervise any assistants. 2. The auditor must obtain a sufficient understanding of the entity and its environment, including its internal control, to assess the risk of material misstatement of the financial statements whether due to error or fraud, and to design the nature, timing, and extent of further audit procedures. 3. The auditor must obtain sufficient appropriate audit evidence by performing audit procedures to afford a reasonable basis for an opinion regarding the financial statements under audit.
Standards of Reporting	
1. The practitioner must identify the subject matter or the assertion being reported on and state the character of the engagement in the report. 2. The practitioner must state the practitioner's conclusion about the subject matter or the assertion in relation to the criteria against which the subject matter was evaluated in the report. 3. The practitioner must state all of the practitioner's significant reservations about the engagement, the subject matter, and, if applicable, the assertion related thereto in the report. 4. The practitioner must state in the report that the report is intended solely for the information and use of the specified parties under the following circumstances: • When the criteria used to evaluate the subject matter are determined by the practitioner to be appropriate only for a limited number of parties who either participated in their establishment or can be presumed to have an adequate understanding of the criteria. • When the criteria used to evaluate the subject matter are available only to specified parties. • When reporting on subject matter and a written assertion has not been provided by the responsible party. • When the report is on an attestation engagement to apply agreed-upon procedures to the subject matter.	1. The auditor must state in the auditor's report whether the financial statements are presented in accordance with generally accepted accounting principles (GAAP). 2. The auditor must identify in the auditor's report those circumstances in which such principles have not been consistently observed in the current period in relation to the preceding period. 3. When the auditor determines that informative disclosures are not reasonably adequate, the auditor must so state in the auditor's report. 4. The auditor must either express an opinion regarding the financial statements, taken as a whole, or state that an opinion cannot be expressed, in the auditor's report. When the auditor cannot express an overall opinion, the auditor should state the reasons therefor in the auditor's report. In all cases where an auditor's name is associated with financial statements, the auditor should clearly indicate the character of the auditor's work, if any, and the degree of responsibility the auditor is taking, in the auditor's report.

knowledge of the subject matter. Such a requirement can be met by the CPA through education and practical experience. The CPA may also use a specialist to help meet this knowledge requirement.

The third standard is particularly important because it stipulates that the practitioner should perform the engagement only if he or she has reason to believe that the subject matter is capable of evaluation against criteria that are suitable and available to users. *Criteria* are standards or benchmarks used to measure and present the subject matter and against which the practitioner evaluates the subject matter. Criteria can be established or developed by the client, the responsible party, industry associations, or other groups, including those that do not follow due process procedures. For example, criteria can be issued by bodies designated under the AICPA's Code of Professional Conduct. With respect to attestation engagements for reporting on internal control for privately held companies (see discussion below), the practitioner can use criteria from the Committee of Sponsoring Organizations of the Treadway Commission's document *Internal Control—Integrated Framework* (the COSO Report). Criteria can be made available to users publicly, by inclusion in the presentation of the subject matter or assertion, or by inclusion in the practitioner's report. The criteria can also be such that they are available only to specified parties.

Standards of Field work

The primary difference in the standards of field work between the attestation standards and generally accepted auditing standards is that the attestation standards do not require an understanding of the entity's environment, including its internal control. Given the varied nature of services that can be performed under the attestation standards, such a requirement would be prohibitively restrictive. The approach to fieldwork for an attestation engagement should involve proper planning and supervision, and sufficient evidence must be gathered to provide a reasonable basis for the practitioner's conclusion about the subject matter or assertion.

Standards of Reporting

As you can see in Table 21–2, reporting standards for attestation engagements differ in a number of respects from those of generally accepted auditing standards. First, in view of the wide variety of possible services, the attestation standards do not make reference to consistent application of GAAP or informative disclosures. However, they do require that the report identify the subject matter or assertion and the type of engagement being performed. The reporting standards also require that the practitioner state any significant reservation about the engagement or presentation of the assertion. The fourth standard of reporting lists four situations where the use of the report is restricted to specified parties, for example, when the attest engagement involves the application of agreed-upon procedures.

Reporting on an Entity's Internal Control over Financial Reporting

[LO 6] In recent years, accountants have increasingly been asked to provide attest services on the effectiveness of an entity's internal control. Impetus was given for such reporting when Congress passed the Federal Deposit Insurance Corporation Improvement Act of 1991 (FDICIA), which requires that the management of large financial institutions issue a report on the effectiveness of the institution's internal control. The Act also requires that these institutions engage accountants to attest to management's report. As discussed in Chapter 7, the Sarbanes-Oxley Act of 2002 imposed similar requirements on all publicly held companies. While an audit of internal control is not required of privately held companies by law (except private financial institutions subject to FDICIA requirements), these companies sometimes engage an accounting firm to provide attestation services relating to internal control.

In such cases, the practitioner should obtain from the responsible party a written assertion about the effectiveness of internal control. The responsible party may present the written assertion in either (1) a separate report that will accompany the practitioner's report; or (2) a representation letter to the practitioner. When management's assertion does not accompany the practitioner's report, the first paragraph of the report should also contain a statement of management's assertion.

Practice **INSIGHT**	The banking crisis of 2007–2009 is a salient and painful reminder that an organization can get a clean opinion on "internal controls" at a transactional or detail level and still essentially be "out of control" from a broader risk management perspective. Both management and auditors should take care not to focus so much on the details of internal control that they miss more critical strategic and operational risk management issues.

Conditions for Conducting an Engagement

In order for the practitioner to examine management's assertions about the effectiveness of internal control in an attestation engagement, the following conditions must be met:

- Management of the entity accepts responsibility for the effectiveness of the entity's internal control.
- The responsible party evaluates the effectiveness of the entity's internal control using suitable criteria (referred to as *control criteria*).
- Sufficient appropriate evidence exists or could be developed to support the responsible party's evaluation.

Criteria issued by the AICPA, regulatory agencies, and other bodies of experts that follow due process qualify as control criteria. For example, management may use the criteria provided by COSO's *Internal Control—Integrated Framework*, or COSO's more recent and more comprehensive *Enterprise Risk Management— Integrated Framework*.

A practitioner is allowed to perform either of two types of attestation engagements for reporting on internal control: (1) examination (i.e., similar in scope and detail to an audit); or (2) agreed-upon procedures. The standard specifically prohibits the practitioner from accepting an engagement to perform a review on management's assertion relating to internal control.

Examination Engagement

The practitioner's objective in an engagement to examine an entity's internal control is to express an opinion on the effectiveness of the entity's internal control, in all material respects, based on the control criteria. An examination engagement is conducted similarly to the audit of internal control required of public companies, as described in Chapter 7.

While examining the entity's internal control, the practitioner may encounter control deficiencies. Attestation standards rely on auditing standards (AU 325—Communicating Internal Control Related Matters Identified in an Audit) to distinguish between significant deficiencies and material weaknesses.[2] The presence of a material weakness will preclude the practitioner from concluding that the entity has effective internal control. If the practitioner identifies significant deficiencies, they should be communicated to management and to those charged with governance.

---

[2]The PCAOB adopted the terms *significant deficiency* and *material weakness* in connection with the audit of internal control over financial reporting for public companies (see Chapter 7 for definitions of these terms, which were revised by AS5). The AICPA has since issued SSAE No. 15, *An Examination of an Entity's Internal Control Over Financial Reporting That Is Integrated With an Audit of Its Financial Statements* and SAS No. 115, *Communicating Internal Control Related Matters Noted in an Audit,* which now include terminology consistent with PCAOB standards. Thus, we use the updated attestation terminology in this chapter, consistent with current PCAOB definitions.

Finally, the practitioner should obtain written representations from management, similar to those listed in Table 7–8 in Chapter 7. If management refuses to provide written representations, a scope limitation exists.

Reporting on Management's Assertion about Internal Control

The practitioner's report should include:

- A title that includes the word *independent*.
- An identification of the subject matter (internal control over financial reporting) and the responsible party.
- A statement that the responsible party is responsible for maintaining effective internal control over financial reporting.
- A statement that the practitioner's responsibility is to express an opinion on the effectiveness of an entity's internal control based on his or her examination.
- A statement that the examination was conducted in accordance with attestation standards established by the AICPA.
- A statement that the practitioner believes the examination provides a reasonable basis for his or her opinion.
- A paragraph stating that, because of the inherent limitations of any internal control, misstatements due to errors or fraud may occur and not be detected.
- The practitioner's opinion on whether the entity has maintained, in all material respects, effective internal control over financial reporting as of the specified date, based on control criteria.
- A statement restricting the use of the report to the specified parties (if the report's distribution is to be limited).

Again, these reporting requirements are similar to those for reporting on the audit of internal control over financial reporting as part of an integrated audit (see Chapter 7).

Financial Forecasts and Projections

[LO 7]

Auditors have been asked to provide assurance with respect to prospective financial statements. Attestation standards (Chapter 3, SSAE No. 10) provide guidance for practitioners providing such services. The practitioner's involvement may include (1) assembling or assisting the client in assembling prospective financial statements; or (2) reporting on prospective financial statements. In either of these situations, the practitioner can enter into an engagement to *examine*, apply *agreed-upon procedures*, or *compile* the prospective financial statements.

Types of Prospective Financial Statements

Prospective financial statements contain financial information made up of either financial forecasts or financial projections. *Financial forecasts* are prospective financial statements that present an entity's *expected* financial position, results of operations, and cash flows. They are based on assumptions reflecting conditions the responsible party *expects to exist* and the course of action it *expects to take*. *Financial projections* are prospective financial statements that present, given one or more *hypothetical assumptions*, an entity's expected financial position, results of operations, and cash flows. These assumptions may not reflect the most likely or expected conditions. The primary difference between the two is that the financial projection is based on hypothetical assumptions rather than what is actually expected and is intended to respond to a specific question, such as "What would happen if the company were to outsource its customer support operations to India?" A financial projection is sometimes prepared to present one or more possible courses of action for evaluation.

Prospective financial statements are for either general use or limited use. *General use* of prospective financial statements refers to the use of the statements by persons with whom the responsible party is not negotiating directly. An example would be an offering statement containing prospective financial statements for an entity's debt or equity securities. Because the intended users may not be able to question the responsible party to clarify any hypothetical assumptions made, the only appropriate basis of presentation for general-use prospective financial statements is the *expected results*. Therefore, only a financial forecast can be made available for general use; financial projections are not to be made available for general use if an accountant's report is involved.

Limited use of prospective financial statements refers to use of the statements by the responsible party alone or by the responsible party and third parties with whom the responsible party is directly negotiating. Examples of limited use include negotiations for a bank loan, submission to a regulatory agency, or use solely within the entity. In such cases, the third party can question the responsible party about the prospective financial information and can question, understand, or even negotiate concerning the assumed conditions on which it is based. Thus, any type of prospective financial statement can be issued for limited use.

While the responsible party is responsible for presentation of prospective financial statements, other parties, such as accountants, may assist in meeting the presentation guidelines specified in the attestation standards. Prospective financial statements should preferably be in the same format as the historical financial statements; however, they may be limited to the items shown in Table 21–3. A presentation that omits any item in Table 21–3 is referred to as a *partial* presentation.

Examination of Prospective Financial Statements

An *examination* of prospective financial statements involves four steps: (1) evaluating the preparation of the prospective financial statements; (2) evaluating the support underlying the assumptions; (3) evaluating the presentation of the prospective financial statements for conformity with AICPA presentation guidelines; and (4) issuing an examination report. The accountant should be independent, have adequate technical training and proficiency to examine prospective financial statements, and obtain sufficient evidence to issue an examination report. Exhibits 21–1 and 21–2 present examples of the standard examination report for a forecast and a projection, respectively. The only major difference between the two reports, aside from the description of the nature of the prospective information involved, is the paragraph limiting distribution of the projection to specified users.

TABLE 21–3	Minimum Presentation Guidelines for Prospective Financial Information

Sales or gross revenues.
Gross profit or cost of sales.
Unusual or infrequently occurring items.
Provision for income taxes.
Discontinued operations or extraordinary items.
Income from continuing operations.
Net income.
Basic and fully diluted earnings per share.
Significant changes in financial position.
A description of what the responsible party intends the prospective financial statements to present, a statement that the assumptions are based on information about circumstances and conditions existing at the time the prospective information was prepared, and a caveat that the prospective results may not be achieved.
Summary of significant assumptions.
Summary of significant accounting policies.

EXHIBIT 21–1	**Example of a Standard Examination Report on a Forecast**

Independent Accountant's Report

We have examined the accompanying forecasted balance sheet, statements of income, retained earnings, and cash flows of Panatta Company as of December 31, 2009, and for the year then ending. Panatta Company's management is responsible for the forecast. Our responsibility is to express an opinion on the forecast based on our examination.

Our examination was made in accordance with attestation standards established by the American Institute of Certified Public Accountants and, accordingly, included such procedures as we considered necessary to evaluate both the assumptions used by management and the preparation and presentation of the forecast. We believe that our examination provides a reasonable basis for our opinion.

In our opinion, the accompanying forecast is presented in conformity with guidelines for presentation of a forecast established by the American Institute of Certified Public Accountants, and the underlying assumptions provide a reasonable basis for management's forecast. However, there will usually be differences between the forecasted and actual results, because events and circumstances frequently do not occur as expected, and those differences may be material. We have no responsibility to update this report for events and circumstances occurring after the date of this report.

EXHIBIT 21–2	**Example of a Standard Examination Report on a Projection**

Independent Accountant's Report

We have examined the accompanying projected balance sheet, statements of income, retained earnings, and cash flows of Hansen Company as of December 31, 2009, and for the year then ending. Hansen Company's management is responsible for the projection, which was prepared for the Panama City National Bank for the purpose of negotiating a loan to expand Hansen Company's plant. Our responsibility is to express an opinion on the projection based on our examination.

Our examination was made in accordance with attestation standards established by the American Institute of Certified Public Accountants and, accordingly, included such procedures as we considered necessary to evaluate both the assumptions used by management and the preparation and presentation of the projection. We believe that our examination provides a reasonable basis for our opinion.

In our opinion, the accompanying projection is presented in conformity with guidelines for presentation of a projection established by the American Institute of Certified Public Accountants, and the underlying assumptions provide a reasonable basis for management's projection, assuming the granting of the requested loan for the purpose of expanding Hansen Company's plant as described in the summary of significant assumptions. However, even if the loan is granted and the plant is expanded, there will likely be differences between the projected and actual results, because events and circumstances frequently do not occur as expected, and those differences may be material. We have no responsibility to update this report for events and circumstances occurring after the date of this report.

The accompanying projection and this report are intended solely for the information and use of Hansen Company and Panama City National Bank and are not intended to be and should not be used by anyone other than these parties.

The following circumstances may require a departure from the standard examination report:

- Departure from AICPA presentation guidelines.
- Unreasonable assumptions.
- Scope limitation.

The presence of such events can result in a report that is either qualified or adverse. A disclaimer may also be issued.

Agreed-Upon Procedures for Prospective Financial Statements

An *agreed-upon procedures* engagement is significantly more limited in scope than is an examination. An accountant may perform an agreed-upon procedures attestation engagement for prospective financial statements provided attestation standards are complied with and each of the following applies:

1. The practitioner is independent.
2. The practitioner and the specified users agree upon the procedures performed or to be performed by the practitioner.
3. The specified users take responsibility for the sufficiency of the agreed-upon procedures for their purposes.
4. The prospective financial statements include a summary of significant assumptions.
5. The prospective financial statements to which the procedures are to be applied are subject to reasonably consistent evaluation against criteria that are suitable and available to the specified parties.
6. Criteria to be used to determine findings are agreed upon between the practitioner and the specified users.
7. The procedures to be applied to the prospective financial statements are expected to result in reasonably consistent findings using the criteria.
8. Relevant evidence is expected to exist to provide a reasonable basis for the practitioner's report.
9. The practitioner and the specified users agree on materiality limits for reporting purposes, where applicable.
10. Use of the report is restricted to the parties who have agreed with the practitioner on the procedures to be performed.

The accountant must satisfy the requirement that the specified users take full responsibility for the sufficiency of the procedures to be performed by comparing the procedures to be applied to the written requirements of the specified users, discussing the procedures to be applied with an appropriate representative of the specified users, or reviewing relevant contracts with or correspondence from the specified users.

Exhibit 21–3 presents an example of a report on the use of agreed-upon procedures. Use of an agreed-upon procedures report is always explicitly restricted to the users specified in the report.

Compilation of Prospective Financial Statements

A practitioner can perform a *compilation* of prospective financial information for a client. A compilation of prospective financial statements involves:

- Assembling, to the extent necessary, the prospective financial statements based on the responsible party's assumptions.
- Performing the required compilation procedures, which include reading the prospective financial statements with their summaries of significant assumptions and accounting policies and considering whether they appear to be (1) presented in conformity with the attestation standards; and (2) not obviously inappropriate.
- Issuing a compilation report.

A practitioner should not issue a compilation report on prospective financial statements that exclude disclosure of the *summary of significant assumptions*. Exhibit 21–4 provides an example of a compilation report for a forecast. Note that the report explicitly indicates that the accountant does not offer assurance when providing a compilation service.

EXHIBIT 21-3	Example of an Agreed-Upon Procedures Report for a Forecast

Independent Accountant's Report on Applying Agreed-Upon Procedures

Board of Directors—Donnay Corporation
Board of Directors—Clinkton Company

At your request, we have performed certain agreed-upon procedures, as enumerated below, with respect to the forecasted balance sheet, and the related forecasted statements of income, retained earnings, and cash flows of Matlin Company, a subsidiary of Clinkton Company, as of December 31, 2009, and for the year then ending. These procedures, which were agreed to by the boards of directors of Donnay Corporation and Clinkton Company, were performed solely to assist you in evaluating the forecast in connection with the sale of Matlin Company to Clinkton Company.

This agreed-upon procedures engagement was conducted in accordance with attestation standards established by the American Institute of Certified Public Accountants. The sufficiency of these procedures is solely the responsibility of the specified users of the report. Consequently, we make no representation regarding the sufficiency of the procedures described below either for the purpose for which this report has been requested or for any other purpose.

The procedures and associated findings are as follows:

a. With respect to forecasted rental income, we compared the assumptions about expected demand for rental of the housing units to demand for similar housing units at similar rental prices in the city area in which Matlin Company's housing units are located.

No exceptions were found as a result of this comparison.

b. We tested the forecast for mathematical accuracy.

The forecast was mathematically accurate.

We were not engaged to and did not conduct an examination, the objective of which would be the expression of an opinion on the accompanying prospective financial statements. Accordingly, we do not express an opinion on whether the prospective financial statements are presented in conformity with AICPA presentation guidelines or on whether the underlying assumptions provide a reasonable basis for the presentation. Had we performed additional procedures, other matters might have come to our attention that would have been reported to you. Furthermore, there will usually be differences between the forecasted and actual results, because events and circumstances frequently do not occur as expected, and those differences may be material. We have no responsibility to update this report for events and circumstances occurring after the date of this report.

This report is intended solely for the use of the boards of directors of Donnay Corporation and Clinkton Company and is not intended to be nor should be used by anyone other than these parties.

EXHIBIT 21-4	Example of Standard Compilation Report for a Forecast

Independent Accountant's Report

We have compiled the accompanying forecasted balance sheet, statements of income, retained earnings, and cash flows of Lumatta Company as of December 31, 2009, and for the year then ending, in accordance with attestation standards established by the American Institute of Certified Public Accountants.

A compilation is limited to presenting, in the form of a forecast, information that is the representation of management and does not include evaluation of the support for the assumptions underlying the forecast. We have not examined the forecast and, accordingly, do not express an opinion or any other form of assurance on the accompanying statements or assumptions. Furthermore, there will usually be differences between the forecasted and actual results, because events and circumstances frequently do not occur as expected, and those differences may be material. We have no responsibility to update this report for events and circumstances occurring after the date of this report.

Accounting and Review Services

[LO 8] Many nonpublic businesses do not choose to contract for an audit of their financial statements. This typically occurs because the entity is small, the owner is involved in the day-to-day operations, and there are no loan covenants or regulations requiring an audit. However, these same entities often employ a CPA to assist with preparing their financial statements, tax returns, or other financial documents.

FIGURE 21–4	Assurance Levels for a Compilation, a Review, and an Audit

No assurance	Limited assurance	Reasonable assurance	Absolute assurance
Compilation	Review	Audit	

Until 1977 there was relatively little guidance on how to perform or report on engagements involving *unaudited* financial statements. As discussed in Chapter 20, the *1136 Tenants'* case involved auditors' liability for unaudited financial statements. One outcome of this case was the establishment of the Accounting and Review Services Committee by the AICPA. This committee was designated by the AICPA to issue Statements on Standards for Accounting and Review Services (SSARS) in connection with unaudited financial statements.

SSARS provide guidance for two types of services: *compilation* of financial statements and *review* of financial statements. A compilation differs significantly from a review. The work done on a compilation provides no assurance about the fair presentation of the financial statements. A review, on the other hand, provides the accountant with a reasonable basis for expressing limited assurance that no material modifications should be made to the financial statements. This can be compared to an audit, in which the auditor provides an explicit opinion about whether the financial statements present fairly the financial position and results of operations of the entity. Figure 21–4 compares the assurance provided by an audit with the assurance provided by a review and by a compilation.

Compilation and review engagements performed under SSARS specifically apply to engagements for which the output of the service is a set of historical financial statements. An accountant may provide other types of services, such as preparing a working trial balance; assisting in adjusting the account books; consulting on accounting, tax, and similar matters; preparing tax returns; and providing various manual or automated bookkeeping or data processing services, without having to comply with the standards for compilations and reviews.

Compilation of Financial Statements

A *compilation* is defined as presenting, in the form of financial statements, information that is the representation of management or owners without undertaking to express any assurance on the statements. In conducting a compilation, the accountant must have the following knowledge about the entity:

- The accounting principles and practices of the industry in which the entity operates.
- A general understanding of the nature of the entity's business transactions, the form of its accounting records, and the stated qualifications of its accounting personnel.
- The accounting basis on which the financial statements are to be presented and the form and content of the financial statements.

Note that the accountant is not required to conduct any inquiries or to perform any procedures to verify or corroborate any information supplied by the client. Neither is the practitioner required to obtain a management representation letter. However, the accountant should read the compiled financial statements to determine whether they are in appropriate form and free from obvious errors, such as mathematical or clerical mistakes or mistakes in the application of accounting principles. Because this service is usually provided to small companies that have few accounting personnel, the accountant is normally heavily involved with preparing the financial statements.

There are three forms of compilation reports:

- Compilation with full disclosure.
- Compilation that omits substantially all disclosures.
- Compilation when the accountant is not independent.

The report should be dated as of the completion of the compilation. Additionally, each page of the financial statements should be marked with a notation such as "See Accountant's Compilation Report."

Compilation with Full Disclosure

When the entity presents a set of financial statements that contain all necessary financial disclosures required by generally accepted accounting principles or another comprehensive basis of accounting, the accountant can issue what might be referred to as a standard compilation report. Exhibit 21–5 is an example of such a report.

Compilation That Omits Substantially All Disclosures

Sometimes an entity may request that the accountant compile financial statements without adding all the necessary disclosures (footnotes, etc.). Many times this request is made to minimize the cost of the engagement. The accountant can compile such financial statements so long as the omission is clearly indicated in the report and the client does not intend to mislead the user. Exhibit 21–6 is an example of a compilation report in which financial disclosures have been omitted.

Compilation When the Accountant Is Not Independent

The Code of Professional Conduct allows an accountant to perform a compilation engagement even though he or she is not independent of the entity. The lack of independence must be disclosed in the report. However, the reasons for the lack of independence should not be described. This requirement prevents the accountant from trying to minimize the lack of independence by "explaining away"

EXHIBIT 21–5	Example of a Compilation Report with Full Disclosure

We have compiled the accompanying balance sheet of Learn Medical Services as of December 31, 2009, and the related statements of income, retained earnings, and cash flows for the year then ended, in accordance with Statements on Standards for Accounting and Review Services issued by the American Institute of Certified Public Accountants.

A compilation is limited to presenting in the form of financial statements information that is the representation of management. We have not audited or reviewed the accompanying financial statements and accordingly do not express an opinion or any other form of assurance on them.

EXHIBIT 21–6	Example of a Compilation Report That Omits Substantially All Disclosures

We have compiled the accompanying balance sheet of Loisel Company as of December 31, 2009, and the related statements of income, retained earnings, and cash flows for the year then ended, in accordance with Statements on Standards for Accounting and Review Services issued by the American Institute of Certified Public Accountants.

A compilation is limited to presenting, in the form of financial statements, information that is the representation of management. We have not audited or reviewed the accompanying financial statements and accordingly do not express an opinion or any other form of assurance on them.

Management has elected to omit substantially all of the disclosures required by generally accepted accounting principles. If the omitted disclosures were included in the financial statements, they might influence the user's conclusions about the company's financial position, results of operations, and cash flows. Accordingly, these financial statements are not designed for those who are not informed about such matters.

the circumstances. The following sentence is added as the last paragraph of the report when the accountant is not independent: "We are not independent with respect to Wahweap Medical Services."

Review of Financial Statements

A *review* is defined as the performance of inquiry and analytical procedures to provide the accountant with a reasonable basis for expressing *limited assurance* that *no material modifications* should be made to the statements in order for them to conform to generally accepted accounting principles or another comprehensive basis of accounting. In conducting a review, the accountant's work involves the following:

- Obtaining knowledge of the accounting principles and practices of the industry in which the entity operates and an understanding of the entity's business.
- Obtaining a general understanding of the entity's organization, its operating characteristics, and the nature of its assets, liabilities, revenues, and expenses (this would include general knowledge of the entity's production, distribution, and compensation methods, types of products and services, operating locations, and material transactions with related parties).
- Asking the entity's personnel about important matters, some examples of which are noted in Table 21–4.
- Performing analytical procedures to identify relationships and individual items that appear to be unusual (the process followed for conducting analytical procedures is similar to the one described for audits in Chapter 5).
- Reading the financial statements to determine if they conform to GAAP.
- Obtaining reports from other accountants, if any, who have audited or reviewed the financial statements or significant components thereof.
- Obtaining a representation letter from management (generally signed by the chief executive officer and chief financial officer).

Note that a review engagement does not require the accountant to obtain an understanding of internal control, test accounting records by performing detailed tests, or corroborate inquiries, as would normally be done on an audit. However, if while conducting the review the accountant becomes aware of information that is incorrect, incomplete, or misleading, he or she should perform any additional procedures necessary to provide limited assurance that no material modifications to the financial statements are required.

Practice INSIGHT

Because a review costs substantially less than an audit engagement, smaller privately held companies often choose to have an annual review to satisfy requirements associated with their lines of credit or commercial loans if such an approach is acceptable to the company's creditors.

TABLE 21–4   **Examples of Inquiries Made during a Review Engagement**

1. Inquiries concerning the client's accounting principles and practices.
2. Inquiries concerning the client's procedures for recording, classifying, and summarizing accounting transactions.
3. Inquiries concerning actions taken at stockholders', board of directors', and other committee meetings.
4. Inquiries of persons responsible for the financial statements concerning:
   - Whether the statements are in accordance with GAAP.
   - Changes in the client's business activities or accounting principles.
   - Any exceptions concerning other analytical procedures.
   - Subsequent events having a material effect on the statements.

| EXHIBIT 21–7 | **Example of a Standard Review Report** |

We have reviewed the accompanying balance sheet of Sierra Company as of December 31, 2009, and the related statements of income, retained earnings, and cash flows for the year then ended, in accordance with Statements on Standards for Accounting and Review Services issued by the American Institute of Certified Public Accountants. All information included in these financial statements is the representation of the management of Sierra Company.

A review consists principally of inquiries of company personnel and analytical procedures applied to financial data. It is substantially less in scope than an audit in accordance with generally accepted auditing standards, the objective of which is the expression of an opinion regarding the financial statements taken as a whole. Accordingly, we do not express such an opinion.

Based on our review, we are not aware of any material modifications that should be made to the accompanying financial statements in order for them to be in conformity with generally accepted accounting principles.

| EXHIBIT 21–8 | **Example of a Modified Review Report for a Departure from GAAP** |

[*Same wording as in the first and second paragraphs of the standard review report*]

Based on our review, *with the exception of the matter described in the following paragraph,* we are not aware of any material modifications that should be made to the accompanying financial statements in order for them to be in conformity with generally accepted accounting principles.

As disclosed in Note 4 to the financial statements, generally accepted accounting principles require that inventory cost consist of material, labor, and overhead. Management has informed us that the inventory of finished goods and work in process is stated in the accompanying financial statements at material and labor cost only, and that the effects of this departure from generally accepted accounting principles on financial position, results of operations, and cash flows have not been determined.

Review Report A standard review report assumes that the financial statements are in accordance with generally accepted accounting principles or another comprehensive basis of accounting. This includes all necessary disclosures. The review report should be dated as of the completion of the accountant's inquiry and analytical procedures. Additionally, each page of the financial statements should contain a notation such as "See Accountant's Review Report." Exhibit 21–7 is an example of the standard review report.

Conditions That May Result in Modification of a Compilation or Review Report
When the accountant conducts a compilation or review, he or she may become aware of situations that require modification to the standard report. Two particular situations are (1) a departure from generally accepted accounting principles; and (2) a going concern uncertainty. If there is a departure from GAAP, the departure should be disclosed in a separate paragraph of the report. Exhibit 21–8 is an example of a review report modified for a departure from GAAP.

If the accountant believes that there are questions concerning the continuing viability of the entity, the accountant should add wording similar to the following after the standard three paragraphs:

The accompanying financial statements have been prepared assuming that the company will continue as a going concern. As discussed in Note *x* to the financial statements, the company has suffered recurring losses from operations and has a net capital deficiency that raises substantial doubt about its ability to continue as a going concern. Management's plans in regard to these matters are also described in Note *x*. The financial statements do not include any adjustments that might result from the outcome of this uncertainty.

The process the accountant follows in determining whether the entity is a going concern is similar to the process used for assessing going concern issues during an audit, discussed in Chapter 17.

Internal Auditing

✕ [LO 9] Up to this point in the chapter, we have focused on nonaudit assurance and attestation services that are provided by public accountants. The remainder of the chapter focuses on the role of, standards pertaining to, and services provided by internal auditors.

The largest financial statement fraud in the history of the United States may not have been discovered were it not for the persistent investigative efforts of Cynthia Cooper and her internal audit team (see Exhibit 14–2). Cynthia Cooper, the whistle-blower of the $9 billion WorldCom fraud, was head of internal audit at the communications giant at the time. According to the 2003 *Report of Investigation by the Special Investigative Committee of the Board of Directors of World-Com, Inc.*, despite being ordered by the company's management to discontinue investigations in the areas where the fraud had been committed, Cooper's team aggressively pushed ahead and eventually uncovered the massive fraud.

After the Enron and WorldCom frauds, the Sarbanes-Oxley Act of 2002 placed increased emphasis on the importance of public companies' internal audit functions, and in August 2002 the New York Stock Exchange (NYSE) required all companies wishing to trade on the exchange to have a viable internal audit function. The role of the internal auditor has become increasingly crucial to effective corporate governance and to the success of large organizations.[3]

Internal auditing can be a challenging and rewarding career path. Many public accountants who work as external auditors eventually become internal auditors, and many internal auditors eventually become executives within their organizations. These opportunities arise because internal auditors are in a unique position to understand the organization from a perspective that is both broad and deep.

Internal Auditing Defined

The Institute of Internal Auditors (IIA), which oversees and sets standards for internal auditing internationally, defines *internal auditing* as follows:

> Internal auditing is an independent, objective assurance and consulting activity designed to add value and improve an organization's operations. It helps an organization accomplish its objectives by bringing a systematic, disciplined approach to evaluate and improve the effectiveness of risk management, control, and governance processes.

This definition outlines the main goals of the profession and broadly states the methods whereby these goals may be achieved. The IIA has issued detailed and rigorous standards for the practice of internal auditing; however, there are several important differences between the internal and external auditing professions. Now that you know what internal auditing is, consider what attributes a good internal auditor should possess. How would these attributes be similar to or different from those a good external auditor would possess? How might the incentives and perspectives of internal and external auditors differ?

The Institute for Internal Auditors

Established in 1941, the IIA is an international professional association with world headquarters in Altamonte Springs, Florida. The IIA has over 160,000 members in 165 countries, specializing in internal auditing, risk management, governance, internal control, IT audit, education, and security. The Institute is the recognized authority, principal educator, and acknowledged leader in certification, research, and technological guidance for the internal auditing profession worldwide. The IIA offers not only the general Certified Internal Auditor (CIA) certification but also specialty certifications in areas including government accounting and financial services.

---

[3]Academic research confirms the importance of internal auditing. For example, a recent study indicates that high quality internal auditing leads to more reliable externally reported earnings. (See D. Prawitt, J. Smith, and D. Wood, "Internal Audit Quality and Earnings Management," *The Accounting Review*, July 2009).

IIA Standards

The IIA's professional guidance is organized into an *International Professional Practices Framework*. This framework consists of two categories of authoritative guidance:

Mandatory guidance

- Definition of internal auditing.
- Code of ethics.
- *Standards.*

Strongly recommended guidance

- Position papers.
- Practice advisories.
- Practice guides.

Practice INSIGHT

CIA candidates who have already earned the CPA designation are eligible to receive credit for Part IV of the CIA exam. Proof of certification along with an application and the payment of an administrative fee is required before credit is granted to the CIA candidate.

The first of these areas provides mandatory guidance for IIA members and consists of the *Definition of Internal Auditing* (stated previously), the *Code of Ethics*, and the *International Standards for the Professional Practice of Internal Auditing*. The International Standards for the Professional Practice of Internal Auditing are in turn divided into three main areas: attribute standards, performance standards, and implementation standards.

Attribute standards address the characteristics of organizations and parties performing internal audit activities, and *performance standards* describe the nature of internal audit activities and provide criteria against which the performance of these services can be evaluated. The standards in these two areas are similar in scope to the 10 generally accepted auditing standards applicable to external auditors. Table 21–5 presents the IIA's attribute and performance standards. Given the substantial variation in internal audit environments across the world, attribute and performance standards are necessarily general; however, the third category of IIA standards, known as *implementation standards*, are more detailed, providing guidance applicable to specific types of engagements.

Practice INSIGHT

The IIA's Internal Auditing Standards Board (IASB) approved a revision to Standard 1312 on external quality assessments that was implemented in January 2007. A "quality assessment" is used to evaluate compliance with IIA standards, the internal audit activity and audit committee charters, the organization's risk and control assessment, and the use of successful practices. It is mandatory that every internal audit function have an external quality assessment at least once every five years to be in compliance with IIA standards. The potential need for more frequent external assessments should be assessed based on the size, complexity, and industry of the organization in relation to the experience of the reviewer or review team (IIA Standard 1312).

Code of Ethics

As with most reputable professions, internal auditors must follow guidelines promoting ethical conduct (see Chapter 19 for a discussion of the AICPA/PCAOB Code of Professional Conduct, which applies to external auditors). The IIA Code of Ethics is important for internal auditors because the reliability of their work

TABLE 21–5	International Standards for the Professional Practice of Internal Auditing
Standard	*Definition*
Attribute Standards	
1000—Purpose, authority, and responsibility	The purpose, authority, and responsibility of the internal audit activity must be formally defined in an internal audit charter, consistent with the Definition of Internal Auditing, the Code of Ethics, and the *Standards*. The chief audit executive must periodically review the internal audit charter and present it to senior management and the board for approval.
1100—Independence and objectivity	The internal audit activity must be independent, and internal auditors must be objective in performing their work.
1200—Proficiency and due professional care	Engagements must be performed with proficiency and due professional care.
1300—Quality assurance and improvement program	The chief audit executive must develop and maintain a quality assurance and improvement program that covers all aspects of the internal audit activity.
Performance Standards	
2000—Managing the internal audit activity	The chief audit executive must effectively manage the internal audit activity to ensure it adds value to the organization.
2100—Nature of work	The internal audit activity must evaluate and contribute to the improvement of governance, risk management, and control processes using a systematic and disciplined approach.
2200—Engagement planning	Internal auditors must develop and document a plan for each engagement, including the engagement's objectives, scope, timing, and resource allocations.
2300—Performing the engagement	Internal auditors must identify, analyze, evaluate, and document sufficient information to achieve the engagement's objectives.
2400—Communicating results	Internal auditors must communicate the engagement results.
2500—Monitoring progress	The chief audit executive must establish and maintain a system to monitor the disposition of results communicated to management.
2600—Management's acceptance of risks	When the chief audit executive believes that senior management has accepted a level of residual risk that may be unacceptable to the organization, the chief audit executive must discuss the matter with senior management. If the decision regarding residual risk is not resolved, the chief audit executive must report the matter to the board for resolution.

depends on a reputation for high levels of objectivity and personal integrity. The Code of Ethics specifies four main principles of ethical conduct and some associated rules that underpin the expected conduct of IIA members: integrity, objectivity, confidentiality, and competency (see Tables 21–6 and 21–7).

Internal Auditors' Roles

Internal auditors are called "internal" because they work within an individual entity and report the results of their work to management or (ideally) to the entity's audit committee or board of directors. They are not typically expected to report to the public or to parties outside the entity. However, internal audit

TABLE 21–6	IIA Code of Ethics Principles	
	Principles	*Definition*
	Integrity	The integrity of internal auditors establishes trust and thus provides the basis for reliance on their judgment.
	Objectivity	Internal auditors exhibit the highest level of professional objectivity in gathering, evaluating, and communicating information about the activity or process being examined. Internal auditors make a balanced assessment of all the relevant circumstances and are not unduly influenced by their own interests or by others in forming judgments.
	Confidentiality	Internal auditors respect the value and ownership of information they receive and do not disclose information without appropriate authority unless there is a legal or professional obligation to do so.
	Competency	Internal auditors apply the knowledge, skills, and experience needed in the performance of internal auditing services.

TABLE 21-7	IIA Rules of Conduct

Principles	Expectations
Integrity	Internal auditors:
	1.1. Shall perform their work with honesty, diligence, and responsibility.
	1.2. Shall observe the law and make disclosures expected by the law and the profession.
	1.3. Shall not knowingly be a party to any illegal activity, or engage in acts that are discreditable to the profession of internal auditing or to the organization.
	1.4. Shall respect and contribute to the legitimate and ethical objectives of the organization.
Objectivity	Internal auditors:
	2.1. Shall not participate in any activity or relationship that may impair or be presumed to impair their unbiased assessment. This participation includes those activities or relationships that may be in conflict with the interests of the organization.
	2.2. Shall not accept anything that may impair or be presumed to impair their professional judgment.
	2.3. Shall disclose all material facts known to them that, if not disclosed, may distort the reporting of activities under review.
Confidentiality	Internal auditors:
	3.1. Shall be prudent in the use and protection of information acquired in the course of their duties.
	3.2. Shall not use information for any personal gain or in any manner that would be contrary to the law or detrimental to the legitimate and ethical objectives of the organization.
Competency	Internal auditors:
	4.1. Shall engage only in those services for which they have the necessary knowledge, skills, and experience.
	4.2. Shall perform internal auditing services in accordance with the *International Standards for the Professional Practice of Internal Auditing.*
	4.3. Shall continually improve their proficiency and the effectiveness and quality of their services.

functions differ widely in how they are managed and staffed. Some entities have internal audit functions that are staffed entirely "in-house," while others are "co-sourced." When an organization co-sources its internal audit function, the entity typically hires a public accounting firm to provide internal audit services in conjunction with the entity's own internal auditors. This has become a significant source of revenue for many large accounting firms. Ideally an entity will have a chief audit executive (CAE), whose role is to oversee the internal audit function (whether in-house or co-sourced) and to help coordinate the work of the internal and external auditors. You will recall from Chapter 19, however, that SEC rules prohibit a public accounting firm from providing internal audit services to a public company that is also the firm's external audit client.

The roles played by internal auditors fall into two primary categories—*assurance services* and *consulting services.*

Assurance services involve the internal auditor's objective assessment of evidence to provide an independent opinion or conclusions regarding a process, system or other subject matter. The nature and scope of the assurance engagement are determined by the internal auditor. There are generally three parties involved in assurance services: (1) the person or group directly involved with the process, system or other subject matter—the process owner; (2) the person or group making the assessment—the internal auditor; and (3) the person or group using the assessment—the user.

Consulting services are advisory in nature, and are generally performed at the specific request of an engagement client. The nature and scope of the consulting engagement are subject to agreement with the engagement client. Consulting services generally involve two parties: (1) the person or group offering the advice—the internal auditor; and (2) the person or group seeking and receiving the advice—the engagement client. When performing consulting services the internal auditor should maintain objectivity and not assume management responsibility.[4]

In general, an organization's internal audit function is most often deployed by management and the board of directors in the broad areas of evaluating risks, evaluating compliance, and performing financial and operational auditing. Through these activities, internal auditors contribute to effective *corporate governance* within an organization, which includes all management-administered policies and procedures to control risk and oversee operations within a company. Indeed, the IIA and other influential organizations, such as the NYSE, identify the internal audit function as one of the cornerstones of effective corporate governance.

Evaluating Risks and Controls

As outlined by IIA Standard 2110, internal auditors should be involved in an entity's risk management process. In fact, IIA standards require internal auditors to conduct an evaluation of the organization's risk management process. Although the internal auditor's industry expertise allows him or her to stay abreast of general industry risks, it is his or her specific experience within the organization that enables him or her to accurately gauge risks relating to the integrity of financial and operational information, the safeguarding of assets, and compliance with laws and regulations. Internal auditors are often asked to determine the sources of these risks, and may sometimes be called on to recommend approaches to manage identified risks.

As we discussed in Chapter 7, Section 404 of the Sarbanes-Oxley Act requires public companies to implement and annually assess internal control over financial reporting. Internal auditors have long been involved in evaluating and enhancing their organizations' system of internal control over financial reporting and over other areas of the organization, and internal auditors often play a substantial role in ensuring compliance with these new requirements. By testing and assessing internal control, internal auditors also facilitate senior management's ability to provide the certifications required by Section 302 of the Sarbanes-Oxley Act—*Corporate Responsibility for Financial Reports.*

Practice **INSIGHT**	The IIA offers a Certification in Control Self-Assessment (CSA) designed for practitioners of control assessment. Professionals who hold the CSA designation include individuals from a variety of backgrounds. They use their knowledge about risk and controls to help their clients implement and maintain effective controls to achieve their objectives.

Reviewing Compliance

In many industries, compliance with relevant laws and regulations is a complicated and important endeavor. For example, if a company fails to comply with the many requirements of the Occupational Safety and Health Act of 1970 (OSHA), the government can levy significant fines and penalties. Many other governmental agencies have also issued rules and regulations that must be followed by businesses and other organizations. Such agencies include the Environmental Protection Agency (EPA) and the Food & Drug Administration (FDA), among many others. Internal auditors play an important role in helping management ensure that the organization complies with the laws,

---

[4]*Introduction to the International Standards for the Professional Practice of Internal Auditing* (www.theiia.org).

EXHIBIT 21–9	**Internal Financial Audit Uncovers Employee Fraud**

At a major research university, the internal audit team was called in to facilitate required budget cuts in the accounting department. The accounting department was understaffed and had only one staff member assigned to review procurement card transactions through the accounting office for staff and faculty. The internal auditor quickly identified some suspicious receipts that totaled $1,200. The investigation led to a single employee, and eventually over four vanloads of suspected unauthorized purchases were removed from the employee's home and personal vehicle. The fraud amounted to approximately $60,000 and led to the criminal prosecution of the suspect. The internal audit function saved the accounting department money immediately, but by identifying several weaknesses in the department's internal control system, it no doubt improved the efficiency and effectiveness of internal control for the entire university.

Source: Internal Auditor (June 2004), pp. 97–99.

rules, and regulations that apply to the entity, as well as in ensuring that employees comply with organizational guidelines and rules.

Financial Auditing   Although the financial auditing performed by internal auditors involves many of the same concepts you have already studied in this text, it differs from the audits conducted by external auditors in several ways. For example, internal auditors do not generally audit periodic financial statements, but tend to focus on specific financial issues as directed by management. The nature of their reporting is also different. Because the focus of the audit may relate to either general or specific factors, it is impossible to require a standardized internal audit report. Consequently, internal audit reports are normally uniquely composed to fulfill the requirements of the particular assignment, as opposed to external audit reports which are quite standardized. Exhibit 21–9 describes a real-life situation where an organization's internal auditor uncovered a fraud while evaluating a specific financial area at the request of the organization's management.

Operational Auditing   Due to their unique position in an organization, internal auditors typically achieve a thorough understanding of how the organization operates, and internal auditors are thus able to provide various types of services to improve the entities in which they work. Operational audits serve a wide variety of purposes. They are primarily conducted to identify the causes of problems or to enhance the efficiency or effectiveness of operations. In many organizations, internal auditors spend most of their time performing operational audits. In fact, because they often spend relatively little of their time performing financial audits, the term *internal auditing* is often (incorrectly) used interchangeably with *operational auditing*.

Internal Audit Product Offerings   In order to illustrate the diversity of services offered by internal auditors, refer to Figure 21–5, which shows how DuPont decided to deploy its internal audit resources. The figure illustrates two important points. First, the management of risk is the central focus of internal audit at DuPont. Risk management is important because a successful company must be able to not only deal with current problems but also anticipate and prepare for other potential obstacles. Second, the wheel in Figure 21–5 is not static, but contains several ongoing and interdependent processes. A modern internal audit function must be adaptable and able to keep up with the changing demands of the modern business environment in

FIGURE 21–5	DuPont's Uses of the Internal Audit Function

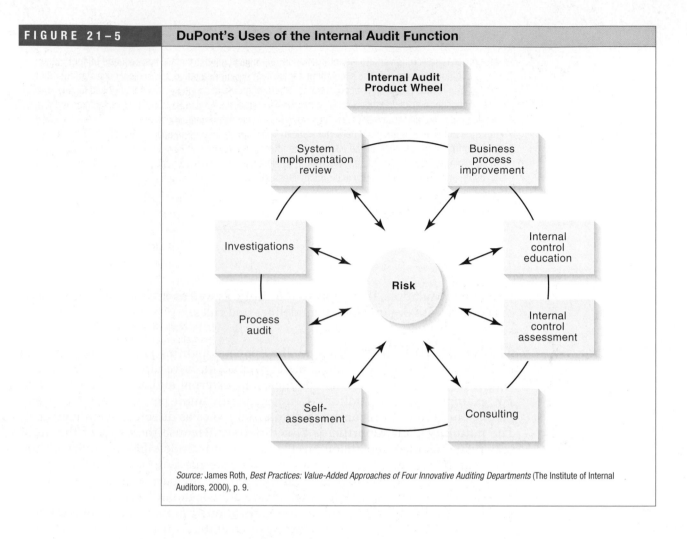

Source: James Roth, *Best Practices: Value-Added Approaches of Four Innovative Auditing Departments* (The Institute of Internal Auditors, 2000), p. 9.

large and complex organizations like DuPont. Exhibit 21–10 offers a more detailed description of each of the product categories outlined in DuPont's "internal audit product wheel."

Interactions between Internal and External Auditors

The objectives and types of work performed by internal and external auditors are often quite different, but there is considerable overlap as you might imagine. External auditors do their work with the purpose of expressing an opinion as to whether the entity's financial statements are free of material misstatements. Because external auditors rely on the concept of materiality, they typically are not concerned with auditing a particular area in a great deal of depth—they gather evidence until they obtain reasonable assurance that no misstatements are present that would be considered material in the context of the financial statements taken as a whole. They then report externally—outside of the organization being audited.

Internal auditors, on the other hand, assist management and the board of directors in evaluating and managing risk, assessing compliance with laws and regulations, assessing operational efficiency, and performing detailed financial audits of areas requiring particular attention. Because their objectives are often different from those of external auditors, the concept of materiality is usually quite different as well. For example, in auditing for employee fraud, the amounts involved are usually far from material in terms of the financial statements taken as a whole. However, internal auditors can reduce the incidence of employee fraud, saving money and improving controls in the process.

| EXHIBIT 21–10 | Definitions of the Services Provided by DuPont's Internal Auditors |

Process Audits   Internal auditing undertakes comprehensive analyses and appraisals of all phases of business activities and provides management with appropriate recommendations concerning the activities reviewed. This product includes business process audits, which appraise the adequacy and efficiency of accounting, financial, and operating controls; information systems audits, which focus on technical IS audit activities, system implementation and application reviews; reviews of emerging technology; and new site reviews which occur in the early stages of start-up operations, joint ventures, or acquisitions to ensure that cost-effective internal control is in place.

Special Investigation   This service provides the client with an independent review of facts and circumstances surrounding an event or series of events and presents recommendations to management for appropriate resolution/action. Investigations are often associated with known or suspected wrongdoing, waste, fraud, abuse of company assets, other business ethics violations, and/or serious mismanagement.

System Implementation Review   System implementation reviews are conducted as part of the prevention quadrant of internal auditing's products. The System Implementation Review promotes the inclusion of cost-effective controls into systems prior to implementation and assures that the controls will operate as intended when implemented.

Business Process Improvement   In limited circumstances, internal auditing may initiate or participate in internal control-related business process improvement activities. This product is used to identify and minimize control deficiencies in business processes and is designed to assist organizations in making process changes that result in strengthened internal control and optimal performance.

Internal Control Education   This offering assists the client organization to reduce risk through an enhanced understanding of the business value of internal control and business ethics. Instructional sessions may be conducted by internal auditing or by the client with internal auditing support.

Internal Control Assessment   This product provides the client with an overall opinion or assessment of the current state of internal control and future risks. Internal control assessments are conducted periodically on a corporate, regional, SBU, and functional basis. The COSO model serves as the methodology for conducting these assessments.

Consulting   This is an internal auditing activity normally provided in response to a request from management. It is designed to provide expertise in the resolution of internal control issues. Consulting may involve answering questions, developing solutions to problems, recommending courses of action, and/or formulating an opinion. Consulting may also involve the review of proposed procedures for internal control content.

Self-Assessment   Self-assessments are performed by the client based upon a framework and facilitation provided by internal auditing. Internal auditing will be an active participant in self-assessment activities, which involve an assessment of risk and control activities within the business and/or function under review.

Source: James Roth, *Best Practices: Value-Added Approaches of Four Innovative Auditing Departments* (The Institute of Internal Auditors, 2000), pp. 9–10.

Some of the work performed by internal auditors is directly relevant to the work of the independent auditor. For example, as discussed in Chapter 7, the external auditor can sometimes make use of controls-testing work performed by the internal auditor. Similarly, Chapter 5 briefly discusses the external auditor's use of work performed by the internal audit function in the context of the financial statement audit. Before relying on the work of internal auditors, the external auditor must evaluate the internal auditor's objectivity and competence. If the external auditor decides that some reliance is justified, the cost savings in terms of the reduction in the external audit fee can be significant.[5]

---

[5]William L. Felix, Audrey Gramling, and Mario Maletta, "Determinants of External Audit Fees: The Importance of a Client's Internal Audit Department," *The Journal of Accounting Research*, Vol. 39, No. 3 (December 2001).

℀ [LO 10] Advanced Module: Examples of Assurance Services—Trust Services and PrimePlus Services

Trust Services

Electronic commerce involves individuals and organizations conducting business transactions without paper documents, using computer and telecommunications networks. This includes transactions under electronic data interchange (EDI), where formal contracts exist between the parties, and business over the Internet, where the parties do not have a preexisting contractual relationship. Electronic commerce over the Internet has grown tremendously, as have the system requirements necessary to support this technology.

This growth in technology also led to some new concerns by businesses and individuals. Businesses are concerned with maintaining reliable, effective systems, while individuals worry about such things as the confidentiality of their information (such as credit card numbers). To respond to these concerns, the AICPA and the Canadian Institute of Chartered Accountants (CICA) developed *SysTrust* and *WebTrust*—two unique sets of principles by which CPAs could evaluate business systems and controls. In 2003, the AICPA and CICA combined the underlying principles of these two services into one common set of principles called *Trust Services*. These formerly separate services are now based on a common set of principles and criteria.

As seen in Table 21–8, Trust Services are built on five principles: security, availability, processing integrity, online privacy, and confidentiality. These are broad principles that are nontechnical and easy to understand. Using these principles, CPAs can offer a wide variety of advisory and assurance services to their clients.

CPA WebTrust

Three broad risks are associated with electronic commerce: business practices, transaction integrity, and information protection. Because commerce over the Internet may involve transactions between parties who do not know each other, how can a consumer know that the entity behind the Web page is "real"? How can the consumer be sure that the entity follows good business practices and that consumers will not be defrauded? Similarly, how can the consumer have assurance that electronic transactions will not be changed, lost, duplicated, or processed incorrectly? And how can the consumer be sure that private information will be protected? While setting up a Web page on the Internet is relatively easy, establishing strong security controls can be complex and costly. As a result of these risks, consumers have legitimate concerns about transaction integrity and confidentiality. An objective third party, such as a CPA, can provide assurance

---

TABLE 21–8	**Trust Services Principles**

Security
The system is protected against unauthorized access (both physical and logical).

Availability
The system is available for operation and use as committed or agreed.

Processing Integrity
System processing is complete, accurate, timely, and authorized.

Confidentiality
Information designated as confidential is protected as committed or agreed.

Privacy
Personal information is collected, used, retained, and disclosed in conformity with the commitments in the entity's privacy notice and with criteria set forth in Generally Accepted Privacy Principles issued by the AICPA/CICA.

Complete Trust Services Principles and Criteria may be found online at www.aicpa.org.

TABLE 21–9	Selected WebTrust Criteria for EarthWear Clothiers

Processing Integrity

Criterion	Controls
1. The entity maintains controls to provide reasonable assurance that: • Each order is checked for accuracy and completeness. • Positive acknowledgment is received from the customer before the order is processed.	• EarthWear's order entry system automatically checks each order for accuracy and completeness. • All customer order information is stored in a "shopping basket." When the customer has finished shopping, the contents of the shopping basket are displayed. The customer clicks "yes" to accept the order.

Confidentiality

Criterion	Controls
1. The entity maintains controls to protect transmissions of private customer information over the Internet from unintended recipients.	• Private customer information is protected during transmission by encryption technology. • EarthWear has registered its domain name and Internet IP address. The address is unique. • The company's Web page has a digital certificate that can be checked using features in a standard Web browser. • EarthWear's Webmaster updates and reviews the site daily to ensure that no improper content or links have been added.

to customers about these risks. The WebTrust seal of assurance symbolizes to potential customers that a CPA has evaluated the Web site's business practices and controls to determine that it conforms to the principles and criteria. Table 21–9 presents a WebTrust criterion and related disclosures for each of two principles for EarthWear Clothiers.

In order to obtain the WebTrust seal of assurance, an entity must meet all the Trust Services principles as measured by the Trust Services criteria and engage a CPA who is licensed by the AICPA to provide WebTrust service. Generally, this service will cover a period of three months or more. Once the seal is obtained, the entity can display it on its Web site provided the assurance examination is updated regularly and the entity informs the practitioner of any significant changes in its business policies, practices, processes, or controls. The entity's WebTrust seal will be managed by a trusted third-party service organization (the "seal manager"). If the entity receives an unqualified report, the practitioner notifies the seal manager that the seal can be displayed on the entity's Web site and provides an expiration date. Unless update notification is received, the authorization to display the seal expires on the expiration date, and the seal manager will remove the seal's display authorization. The seal displayed at the Web site can be verified by clicking on the seal, which displays a special WebTrust digital certificate.

A WebTrust assurance engagement is performed as an examination under the attestation standards described in this chapter. In examining an entity's Web site, the practitioner would use guidance provided in SSAE No. 10 and COSO's *Internal Control—Integrated Framework*. In such an examination, the practitioner expresses a positive opinion as to whether the presentation of assertions conforms to the AICPA's Trust Services principles and criteria. Exhibit 21–11 presents EarthWear's management's assertions about its Web site. The report of management's assertions is signed by the president and CEO and the chief financial officer. Exhibit 21–12 contains a public accounting firm's unqualified report on those assertions. Note that because EarthWear is a publicly traded company and a WebTrust attestation service involves reporting on internal control, independence considerations prohibit the company's financial statement auditor, Willis & Adams, from providing a WebTrust attestation service to the company (see Chapter 19). Thus, EarthWear engaged another accounting firm, Felix & Waller, CPAs, to provide the service.

EXHIBIT 21–11	**Management's Assertions for EarthWear's Web site**

EarthWear Clothiers, on its Web site for electronic commerce (at www.mhhe.com/earthwear), asserts the following:

- We have maintained effective controls to provide reasonable assurance that customers' orders placed using e-commerce were completed and billed as agreed; and
- We have maintained effective controls to provide reasonable assurance that private customer information obtained as a result of e-commerce was protected from uses not related to our business during the period from December 16, 2009, through March 15, 2010, in conformity with the AICPA *WebTrust* Principles and Criteria.

Calvin J. Rogers   James C. Watts
President & CEO   Chief Financial Officer

The first paragraph of the Felix & Waller report states that the assertions have been examined. The second paragraph states that management is responsible for the assertions while the accountant's responsibility is to express an opinion based on the examination. The third paragraph states the four steps that were undertaken to complete the examination of management's assertions. In particular, Felix & Waller (1) obtained an understanding of EarthWear's e-commerce business and information privacy practices and its controls over the processing of e-commerce transactions and the protection of related private customer information; (2) selectively tested transactions executed in accordance with the disclosed business and information privacy practices; (3) tested and evaluated the operating effectiveness of the controls; and (4) performed other procedures that it considered necessary. The opinion paragraph provides an unqualified opinion on EarthWear's management's assertions.

SysTrust

As more organizations become dependent on information technology to run their businesses and to interact with customers, suppliers, and business partners, it is critical that an entity's information systems operate effectively. The AICPA and CICA have identified this as an opportunity for CPAs and CAs to provide assurance on the information system by offering a service called *SysTrust*. The system components include its infrastructure, software, personnel, procedures, and data. SysTrust follows the Trust Services principles and criteria.

A SysTrust engagement is conducted under attestation standards. The CPA evaluates a system against the Trust Services principles and criteria and determines whether controls over the system exist. The CPA then performs tests to determine whether those controls were operating effectively during the specified period. In order for the entity to receive an unqualified opinion, the system must meet all of the Trust Services principles and criteria. The accountant's report would look similar to the WebTrust report shown in Exhibit 21–12, except that it would include management's assertions about the effectiveness of the controls over the system.

CPA PrimePlus[6] Services

The population in the United States and Canada is aging, and individuals are often living to ages at which they require some form of assisted living. The U.S. Census Bureau estimates that as of 2000, 16.6 million people in the United States were 75 years of age or older; and they controlled between $11 and $13 trillion in wealth. At the same time, younger generations are increasingly mobile. In many of these younger families, both spouses work outside the home, and they do not have adequate time to care for elderly relatives. The CPA can bring a level

---

[6]Until recently, PrimePlus Services were known as ElderCare Services. Upon discussions with clients and CPAs, the AICPA found that the term "ElderCare" was not appealing. The AICPA and the CICA therefore decided to change the name from ElderCare to PrimePlus.

EXHIBIT 21–12	**Accountant's WebTrust Attestation Report for EarthWear's Web site**

To the Management of EarthWear Clothiers:

We have examined the assertion by the management of EarthWear Clothiers regarding the effectiveness of its controls over transaction integrity and information protection for e-commerce (at www.mhhe.com/earthwear) based on the AICPA/CICA WebTrust Criteria during the period from December 16, 2009, through March 15, 2010.

These e-commerce disclosures and controls are the responsibility of EarthWear Clothiers management. Our responsibility is to express an opinion based on our examination.

Our examination was conducted in accordance with attestation standards established by the American Institute of Certified Public Accountants, and, accordingly, included: (1) obtaining an understanding of the EarthWear Clothier's e-commerce business and information privacy practices and its controls over the processing of e-commerce transactions and the protection of related private customer information; (2) selectively testing transactions executed in accordance with disclosed business and information privacy practices; (3) testing and evaluating the operating effectiveness of the controls; and (4) performing other such procedures as we considered necessary in the circumstances. We believe that our examination provides a reasonable basis for our opinion.

Because of inherent limitations in controls, errors or fraud may occur and not be detected. Furthermore, the projection of any conclusions, based on our findings, to future periods is subject to the risk that: (1) changes made to the system or controls, (2) changes in processing requirements, or (3) changes required because of the passage of time, such as to accommodate dates in the year 2008, or (4) the degree of compliance with the policies or procedures may alter the validity of such conclusions.

In our opinion, during the period from December 16, 2009, to March 15, 2010, EarthWear Clothiers, in all material respects

- maintained effective controls to provide reasonable assurance that customers' orders placed using e-commerce were completed and billed as agreed, and
- maintained effective controls to provide reasonable assurance that private customer information obtained as a result of e-commerce was protected from uses not related to the company's business based on the AICPA/CICA WebTrust Criteria.

The CPA *WebTrust* Seal of assurance on EarthWear Clothiers' Web site for e-commerce constitutes a symbolic representation of the contents of this report and it is not intended, nor should it be construed, to update this report or provide any additional assurance.

This report does not include any representation as to the quality of the EarthWear Clothiers' goods or services nor their suitability for any customer's intended purpose.

Felix & Waller
Tucson, Arizona
April 3, 2010

of assurance or comfort to the elderly person and his or her family members through PrimePlus services.

PrimePlus services are defined as

> a unique, customizable package of services offered by Certified Public Accountants to assist the elderly in maintaining—for as long as possible—their lifestyle and financial independence. Practitioners who provide PrimePlus Services draw upon their strengths and competencies in a variety of areas, including cash flow planning and budgeting, pre- and post-retirement planning, insurance reviews and tax planning . . . the services included in each individual PrimePlus engagement will be based upon the needs and wants of each PrimePlus client as well as the skill set of the PrimePlus practitioner. (www.aicpa.org)

The practitioner acts in the place of the absent family members and relies on qualified specialists, employed by the client or the responsible family member, to provide the services outside the scope of the practitioner's expertise. The practitioner observes and reports on whether those service providers are meeting the needs of the client and the criteria for care established by the family members. This service is often combined with traditional financial services, and the practitioner often establishes strategic alliances with other professionals (such as elder law attorneys, geriatric care managers, and social workers or medical personnel).

Practitioners can offer three types of PrimePlus services. The first is *consulting/facilitating* services, which involve the practitioner consulting with the client or third party (the responsible individual) to establish the standards of care expected. Consulting services might also include assisting the client or third party in selecting the care provider and level of care for each type of care required. The second category of PrimePlus service is known as *direct* services. For example, the practitioner might receive, deposit, and account for the individual's income; pay bills and conduct routine financial transactions for the client; and supervise investments and accounting for the estate. The third category of PrimePlus service is *assurance* services. In this type of service, the practitioner issues periodic reports about the quality of care provided to the elderly person. PrimePlus assurance services are conducted as agreed-upon procedures in attestation engagements as described in this chapter. This type of assurance service may involve the practitioner visiting the elderly person and inspecting documentation such as logs, diaries, or other evidence to support that the contracted services have been provided at the appropriate level of care.

KEY TERMS

Agreed-upon procedures. Specific procedures performed on the subject matter of an assertion while a practitioner is engaged by a client to issue a report of findings.

Assurance services. Independent professional services that improve the quality of information, or its context, for decision makers.

Attest services. A service when a practitioner is engaged to issue or does issue a report on subject matter, or an assertion about subject matter, that is the responsibility of another party.

Compilation of financial statements. The presentation, in the form of financial statements, of information that is the representation of management or owners without undertaking to express any assurance on the statements.

Electronic (Internet) commerce. Business transactions between individuals and organizations that occur without paper documents, using computers and telecommunications networks.

Electronic data interchange. The transmission of business transactions over telecommunications networks.

Financial forecasts. Prospective financial statements that present an entity's expected financial position, results of operations, and cash flows.

Financial projections. Prospective financial statements that present, given one or more hypothetical assumptions, an entity's expected financial position, results of operations, and cash flows.

Internal auditing. An independent, objective assurance and consulting activity designed to add value and improve an organization's operations. It helps an organization accomplish its objectives by bringing a systematic, disciplined approach to evaluate and improve the effectiveness of risk management, control, and governance processes.

Reasonable assurance. A term that implies some risk that a material misstatement could be present in the financial statements without the auditor detecting it.

Review of financial statements. The performance of inquiry and analytical procedures that give the accountant a reasonable basis for expressing limited assurance that no material modifications should be made to the statements in order for them to conform to GAAP.

Risk assessment process. The process through which management of an entity identifies, plans for, and controls the possible threats to achieving the entity's objectives.

www.mhhe.com/ messier7e	Visit the book's Online Learning Center for a multiple-choice quiz that will allow you to assess your understanding of chapter concepts.

REVIEW QUESTIONS

[LO 1] 21-1 Define *assurance services*. Discuss why the definition focuses on decision making and information.

[5] 21-2 Define an attest engagement. List the two conditions that are necessary, according to the third general standard for attestation engagements, in order to perform an attest engagement.

[3,4] 21-3 What types of engagements can be provided under the attestation standards? Give two examples of attestation engagements.

[7] 21-4 How can the practitioner satisfy the requirement that specified users take responsibility for the adequacy of procedures performed on an agreed-upon procedures engagement?

[6] 21-5 What kind of entity might request an attestation report on internal control, and why?

[7] 21-6 What are the two types of prospective financial statements? How do they differ from each other?

[8] 21-7 What types of services can be performed under Statements on Standards for Accounting and Review Services?

[8] 21-8 What type of knowledge must an accountant possess about the entity in order to perform a compilation engagement? A review engagement?

[9] 21-9 Define *corporate governance*. Why do you think an effective internal audit function is referred to as one of the cornerstones of corporate governance?

[9] 21-10 Explain how internal auditors play a role in helping management comply with the requirements of the Sarbanes-Oxley Act of 2002.

[2] 21-11 The Elliott Committee developed six assurance services with significant market potential for CPA firms. What are these six services?

[10] 21-12 What are the risks of electronic commerce? What are the Trust Services Principles?

[10] 21-13 What is the main difference between WebTrust and SysTrust Services?

[10] 21-14 Why is PrimePlus potentially a major service for CPA firms? What types of PrimePlus services can a practitioner offer?

MULTIPLE-CHOICE QUESTIONS

[1,2] 21-15 An assurance report on information can provide assurance about the information's
a. Reliability.
b. Relevance.
c. Timeliness.
d. All of the above.

[3,4] 21-16 Which of the following professional services would be considered an attest engagement?

    a. A management consulting engagement to provide IT advice to a client.

    b. An engagement to report on compliance with statutory requirements.

    c. An income tax engagement to prepare federal and state tax returns.

    d. Compilation of financial statements from a client's accounting records.

[4] 21-17 An accountant may accept an engagement to apply agreed-upon procedures to prospective financial statements, provided that

    a. The prospective financial statements are also examined.

    b. Responsibility for the adequacy of the procedures performed is taken by the accountant.

    c. Negative assurance is expressed on the prospective financial statements taken as a whole.

    d. Distribution of the report is restricted to the specified users.

[7] 21-18 Which of the following statements concerning prospective financial statements is correct?

    a. Only a financial forecast would normally be appropriate for limited use.

    b. Only a financial projection would normally be appropriate for general use.

    c. Any type of prospective financial statement would normally be appropriate for limited use.

    d. Any type of prospective financial statement would normally be appropriate for general use.

[8] 21-19 When compiling the financial statements of a nonpublic entity, an accountant should

    a. Review agreements with financial institutions for restrictions on cash balances.

    b. Understand the accounting principles and practices of the entity's industry.

    c. Inquire of key personnel concerning related parties and subsequent events.

    d. Perform ratio analyses of the financial data of comparable prior periods.

[8] 21-20 Which of the following statements is correct concerning both an engagement to compile and an engagement to review a nonpublic entity's financial statements?

    a. The accountant is not required to obtain an understanding of internal control.

    b. The accountant must be independent in fact and appearance.

    c. The accountant expresses *no* assurance on the financial statements.

    d. The accountant should obtain a written management representation letter.

[8] 21-21 The standard report issued by an accountant after reviewing the financial statements of a nonpublic entity states that

    a. A review includes assessing the accounting principles used and significant estimates made by management.

    b. A review includes examining, on a test basis, evidence supporting the amounts and disclosures in the financial statements.

    c. The accountant is not aware of any material modifications that should be made to the financial statements.

    d. The accountant does not express an opinion or any other form of assurance on the financial statements.

[8] 21-22 Financial statements of a nonpublic entity that have been reviewed by an accountant should be accompanied by a report stating that

    a. The scope of the inquiry and the analytical procedures performed by the accountant have not been restricted.

b. All information included in the financial statements is the representation of the management of the entity.

c. A review includes examining, on a test basis, evidence supporting the amounts and disclosures in the financial statements.

d. A review is greater in scope than a compilation, the objective of which is to present financial statements that are free of material misstatements.

[9] 21-23 The general accreditation granted by the Institute of Internal Auditors is known as the

a. CFE.

b. CGAP.

c. CFSA.

d. CIA.

[9] 21-24 Which of the following is not one of the general areas of the IIA's International Standards for the Professional Practice of Internal Auditing?

a. Performance standards.

b. Implementation standards.

c. Ethical standards.

d. Attribute standards.

[9] 21-25 The four principles of the IIA Code of Ethics are

a. Confidentiality, competency, objectivity, and integrity.

b. Objectivity, independence, compliance, and due diligence.

c. Honesty, integrity, independence, and competency.

d. Integrity, confidentiality, independence, and compliance.

[10] 21-26 Which of the following is not a Trust Services principle?

a. Processing integrity.

b. Online privacy.

c. Digital certificate authorization.

d. Availability.

[10] 21-27 Which of the following assurances is not provided by an unqualified opinion on a SysTrust report?

a. There are procedures to protect the system against unauthorized physical access.

b. The financial statements created by the system are free of material misstatements.

c. The documented system availability objectives, policies, and standards have been communicated to authorized users and controls are functioning as documented.

d. Documented system processing integrity objectives, policies, and standards have been communicated to authorized users and controls are functioning as documented.

[10] 21-28 PrimePlus engagements are mainly designed to

a. Provide guidance to assisted-living care facilities to enhance quality of life for the elderly.

b. Provide guidance to health care providers in giving high-quality health care.

c. Assist the elderly to maintain their financial independence and desired lifestyle as they age.

d. Assist the elderly in perfecting their shuffleboard techniques.

[10] 21-29 Which of the following is not a type of PrimePlus service?

a. Assurance services.

b. Consulting/facilitating services.

c. Direct services.

d. Systems design services.

PROBLEMS

[6] 21-30 Orange Grove Farms has approached your CPA firm with some questions. Orange Grove's management has spoken with a bank about obtaining a loan to expand its operations. The bank has informed Orange Grove that the bank will not make the requested loan unless the company submits financial statements. Further, the interest rate on the loan will depend on whether Orange Grove's financial statements are compiled, reviewed, or audited by an independent auditor. Orange Grove's management is not familiar with the differences between these three services and wonders why the interest rate charged on the loan would depend on the type of service they obtain from your CPA firm.

Required:
Describe for Orange Grove the differences between compilation, review, and audit engagements. Be sure to include the level of assurance provided by each one as part of your explanation.

[7] 21-31 Your client, Cheaney Rental Properties, has engaged you to perform a compilation of its forecasted financial statements for a loan with the National Bank of Rockwood.

Required:
a. Describe the steps an accountant should complete when conducting a compilation of prospective financial statements.
b. Prepare a standard compilation report for Cheaney Rental Properties.

[7] 21-32 You are the manager of the examination engagement of the financial projection of Honey's Health Foods as of December 31, 2009, and for the year then ended. The audit senior, Currie, has prepared the following draft of the examination report:

> To the Board of Directors of Honey's Health Foods:
>
> We have examined the accompanying projected balance sheet and statements of income, retained earnings, and cash flows of Honey's Health Foods as of December 31, 2009, and for the year then ending. Our examination was made in accordance with standards for an examination of a projection and accordingly included such procedures as we considered necessary to evaluate the assumptions used by management.
>
> In our opinion, the accompanying forecast is presented in conformity with guidelines for presentation of a forecast established by the American Institute of Certified Public Accountants, and the underlying assumptions provide a reasonable basis for management's projection. However, there will usually be differences between the projected and actual results because events and circumstances frequently do not occur as expected, and those differences may be material.
>
> Libby & Nelson, CPAs

Required:
Identify the deficiencies in Currie's draft of the examination report. Group the deficiencies by paragraph.

[8] 21-33 The following report was drafted on October 25, 2009, by Major, CPA, at the completion of an engagement to compile the financial statements of Ajax Company for the year ended September 30, 2009. Ajax is a nonpublic entity in which Major's child has a material direct financial interest. Ajax decided to omit substantially all of the disclosures required by generally accepted accounting principles because the financial statements will be for management's use only. The statement of cash flows was also omitted because management does not believe it to be a useful financial statement.

> To the Board of Directors of Ajax Company:
>
> I have compiled the accompanying financial statements of Ajax Company as of September 30, 2009, and for the year then ended. I planned and performed the compilation to obtain limited assurance about whether the financial statements are free of material misstatements.
>
> A compilation is limited to presenting information in the form of financial statements. It is substantially less in scope than an audit in accordance with generally accepted auditing standards, the objective of which is the expression of an opinion regarding the financial statements taken as a whole. I have not audited the accompanying financial statements and accordingly do not express any opinion on them.
>
> Management has elected to omit substantially all of the disclosures required by generally accepted accounting principles. If the omitted disclosures were included in the financial statements, they might influence the user's conclusions about the company's financial position, results of operations, and changes in financial position.
>
> I am not independent with respect to Ajax Company. This lack of independence is due to my daughter's ownership of a material direct financial interest in Ajax Company.
>
> This report is intended solely for the information and use of the board of directors and management of Ajax Company and should not be used for any other purpose.
>
> Major, CPA

Required:
Identify the deficiencies contained in Major's report on the compiled financial statements. Group the deficiencies by paragraph where applicable. Do not redraft the report.

(AICPA, adapted)

[8]   21-34   This question consists of 13 items pertaining to possible deficiencies in an accountant's review report. Select the best answer for each item. Indicate your answers in the space provided.

Jordan & Stone, CPAs, audited the financial statements of Tech Company, a nonpublic entity, for the year ended December 31, 2008, and expressed an unqualified opinion. For the year ended December 31, 2009, Tech issued comparative financial statements. Jordan & Stone reviewed Tech's 2009 financial statements, and Kent, an assistant on the engagement, drafted the following accountant's review report. Land, the engagement supervisor, decided not to reissue the prior year's auditor's report but instructed Kent to include a separate paragraph in the current year's review report describing the responsibility assumed for the prior year's audited financial statements. This is an appropriate reporting procedure.

Land reviewed Kent's draft and indicated in the supervisor's review notes (shown following the accountant's review report) that there were several deficiencies in Kent's draft.

Accountant's Review Report

We have reviewed and audited the accompanying balance sheets of Tech Company as of December 31, 2009 and 2008, and the related statements of income, retained earnings, and cash flows for the years then ended, in accordance with Statements on Standards for Accounting and Review Services issued by the

American Institute of Certified Public Accountants and generally accepted auditing standards. All information included in these financial statements is the representation of the management of Tech Company.

A review consists principally of inquiries of company personnel and analytical procedures applied to financial data. It is substantially less in scope than an audit in accordance with generally accepted auditing standards, the objective of which is the expression of an opinion regarding the financial statements taken as a whole.

Based on our review, we are not aware of any material modifications that should be made to the accompanying financial statements. Because of the inherent limitations of a review engagement, this report is intended for the information of management and should not be used for any other purpose.

The financial statements for the year ended December 31, 2008 were audited by us, and our report was dated March 2, 2009. We have no responsibility for updating that report for events and circumstances occurring after that date.

Jordan and Stone, CPAs

March 1, 2010

Required:

Items 1 through 13 represent deficiencies noted by Land. For each deficiency, indicate whether Land is correct (C) or incorrect (I) in the criticism of Kent's draft.

(AICPA, adapted)

Supervisor's Review Notes	C or I
1. There should be *no* reference to the prior year's audited financial statements in the first (introductory) paragraph.	
2. All the current-year basic financial statements are *not* properly identified in the first (introductory) paragraph.	
3. There should be *no* reference to the American Institute of Certified Public Accountants in the first (introductory) paragraph.	
4. The accountant's review and audit responsibilities should follow management's responsibilities in the first (introductory) paragraph.	
5. There should be *no* comparison of the scope of a review to an audit in the second (scope) paragraph.	
6. Negative assurance should be expressed on the current year's reviewed financial statements in the second (scope) paragraph.	
7. There should be a statement that *no* opinion is expressed on the current year's financial statements in the second (scope) paragraph.	
8. There should be a reference to "conformity with generally accepted accounting principles" in the third paragraph.	
9. There should be *no* restriction on the distribution of the accountant's review report in the third paragraph.	
10. There should be *no* reference to "material modifications" in the third paragraph.	
11. There should be an indication of the type of opinion expressed on the prior year's audited financial statements in the fourth (separate) paragraph.	
12. There should be an indication that *no* auditing procedures were performed after the date of the report on the prior year's financial statements in the fourth (separate) paragraph.	
13. There should be *no* reference to "updating the prior year's auditor's report for events and circumstances occurring after that date" in the fourth (separate) paragraph.	

[10] 21-35 Rhett Corporation, a local sporting goods company, has asked your firm for assistance in setting up its Web site. Eric Rhett, the CEO, is concerned that potential customers will be reluctant to place orders over the Internet to a relatively unknown entity. He recently heard about companies finding ways to provide assurance to customers about secure Web sites, and Rhett has asked to meet with you about this issue.

Required:
Prepare answers to each of the following questions that may be asked by Rhett.
a. Why are customers reluctant to engage in e-commerce?
b. What type of assurance can your firm provide to his customers concerning the company's Web site?
c. What process will your firm follow in providing a WebTrust assurance service for Rhett's Web site?

[10]   21-36   Beachwood Sparks Company, a nonpublic company that supplies apparel to retail stores, recently has implemented a new information system. However, during system development and implementation, the company experienced a great deal of turnover in personnel involved with designing and implementing the system. Consequently, the company's board of directors is concerned about whether the system is reliable. It has heard of an assurance service called SysTrust, but would like to know more about it before discussing it with its CPA firm.

Required:
a. What types of assurances does a SysTrust examination provide? What are the main principles underlying a reliable system that a SysTrust examination considers?
b. What special skills does a CPA undertaking a SysTrust examination require?
c. Beachwood's board of directors is wondering whether any of its constituents would be interested in the SysTrust report. For example, the company is interested in renewing its business interruption insurance, winning business from new retailers, and making itself attractive as a takeover target. Describe how an unqualified SysTrust report would benefit Beachwood from the point of view of the insurance company, potential customers, and potential buyers of the company. (*Hint:* Examine the SysTrust principles and underlying criteria perhaps by obtaining SysTrust documentation available on the AICPA Web site, www.aicpa.org, specifically considering which principles and criteria would be of interest to each of the three constituents.)

[10]   21-37   Mr. and Mrs. Greg Jun called your firm, Hillison & Reimer, in response to a brochure they received from Greg's elderly mother. The Juns reside in Ann Arbor, Michigan, while Greg's mother has retired to Tallahassee, Florida. In recent months, the Juns have become very concerned about Greg's mother and her ability to care for herself. On a number of occasions, Greg has received calls from his mother's friends expressing concern that she has not been eating properly and is not regularly taking her medicine for a heart condition.

Required:
a. Describe the PrimePlus service to the Juns, including the types of services that can be offered.
b. Because the Juns' concerns do not relate to areas of your expertise as a CPA, explain to them how you will be able to provide assurance on the care providers.

DISCUSSION CASE

[3,4,5,6]   21-38   The accounting profession is concerned about whether companies are in compliance with various federal and state environmental laws and regulations and whether they have reported environmental liabilities in their financial statements. *Environmental auditing* typically refers to the process of assessing compliance with environmental laws and regulations, as well as compliance with company policies and procedures. SSAE No. 10, Chapter 6, "Compliance Attestation," allows a practitioner to perform agreed-upon procedures to assist users in evaluating management's written assertions about (1) the entity's compliance with specified requirements; (2) the effectiveness of the entity's internal control over compliance; or (3) both.

Required:
a. Discuss how a practitioner would conduct an agreed-upon procedures engagement to evaluate an entity's written assertion that it was in compliance with its state's environmental laws and regulations.
b. Assume that this same entity maintained an internal control system that monitored the entity's compliance with its state's environmental laws and regulations. Discuss how a practitioner would evaluate the effectiveness of the entity's internal control over compliance.

INTERNET ASSIGNMENTS

[9]   21-39   The IIA maintains its own Web site containing useful information about the Institute and the internal auditing profession in general. Visit the IIA's home page (www.theiia.org).

Required:
a. Follow the link to the official magazine of the IIA (*Internal Auditor*). What is the mission of this respected publication?
b. Although the IIA does not require that its members obtain CIA certification, it is becoming popular worldwide. What advantages are afforded to those who certify, according to the IIA's Web site? Who might benefit from the CIA designation?

[10]   21-40   The AICPA has developed an assurance service related to electronic commerce called *WebTrust*. Visit the WebTrust home page (www.webtrust.org) and examine the WebTrust seal.

Required:
a. Under the overview of Trust Services section, find and list the four broad areas that the Trust Service principles are organized into.
b. On that same page, there is a heading: "Need for Trust." List two reasons given in that section for why trust in online transactions is an issue today.

[10]   21-41   EarthWear has a number of competitors that sell goods over the Internet. Visit the home page for any two of EarthWear's competitors. For example, visit the home page for Timberland (www.timberland.com), L.L. Bean (www.llbean.com), or Lands' End (www.landsend.com).

Required:
a. Determine if any of the sites selected provides any type of assurance on its electronic commerce. Note that you may have to prepare to order a product before any assurances are presented on the site. (You may need to go into tools, properties, or page info in your browser to look for the certificates).

b. If any of the sites provides assurance on electronic commerce, compare the assurances provided with the Trust Services principles and criteria.

[10]   21-42   Using an Internet search engine, find the Web page on PrimePlus services created by the AICPA. On the Web site, find the PrimePlus/ElderCare glossary (under the "CPA's Role" page).

Required:
Describe the "funeral rule" defined in the glossary.

 HANDS-ON CASES

ACL

www.mhhe.com/ messier7e	Visit the book's Online Learning Center for problem material to be completed using the ACL software packaged with your new text.

CPA Review

www.mhhe.com/ messier7e	**Riley & Associates** This simulation will test understanding of audits, reviews, and compilations, as well as the responsibilities of a CPA in performing each service. *To begin this simulation, visit the book's Online Learning Center.*

Index

Note: Page numbers followed by *n* refer to material in footnotes.